PEARSON
mymanagementlab™

mymanagementlab is an online assessment solution for courses in Principles of Management, Human Resources, Strategy, and Organizational Behavior that helps you hold your students accountable for class preparation. Built-in pretests and posttests inform an online study plan, focusing students on the areas where they need it most.

Visit www.mymanagementlab.com to learn more.

KEY CHANGES TO THE FOURTEENTH EDITION

- A new chapter – Managing Diversity – presents cutting-edge research on this important topic.

- New in-depth cases for each section provide a more holistic, integrative, and evidence-based perspective. Fully half of the end-of-chapter cases have been updated for this edition.

- A new feature to each chapter – OB Poll – offers timely and interesting survey results.

- Another new addition to each chapter – Ethical Choice – provides advice for ethical situations that occur in organizations.

- A new opening vignette in each chapter captures current business and economic conditions.

- Examples throughout the book are based on the current state of the global economy.

- A consolidated leadership chapter presents material on the latest research.

- More than half of the photos have been updated.

- Ten new or updated Point/Counterpoint boxes are offered.

- Ten new or updated International OB boxes are presented.

- 30 percent of the research citations have been updated, with half of those citations occurring in 2008-2009.

Organizational Behavior

Organizational Behavior

edition

14

STEPHEN P. ROBBINS
San Diego State University

TIMOTHY A. JUDGE
University of Florida

Prentice Hall

Boston   Columbus   Indianapolis   New York   San Francisco   Upper Saddle River
Amsterdam   Cape Town   Dubai   London   Madrid   Milan   Munich   Paris   Montreal   Toronto
Delhi   Mexico City   Sao Paulo   Sydney   Hong Kong   Seoul   Singapore   Taipei   Tokyo

Editorial Director: Sally Yagan
Editor in Chief: Eric Svendsen
Acquisitions Editor: Jennifer M. Collins
Assistant Editor: Susan Abraham
Editorial Assistant: Meg O'Rourke
Director of Marketing: Patrice Lumumba Jones
Marketing Manager: Nikki Ayana Jones
Marketing Assistant: Ian Gold
Senior Managing Editor: Judy Leale
Project Manager: Becca Richter
Senior Operations Supervisor: Arnold Vila
Creative Director: Christy Mahon
Senior Art Director: Kenny Beck
Interior Designer: Wanda Espana
Cover Designer: Ray Cruz
OB Poll Graphics: Electra Graphics
Manager, Visual Research: Beth Brenzel
Manager, Rights and Permissions: Zina Arabia
Manager, Cover Visual Research & Permissions: Karen Sanatar
Image Interior Permission Coordinator: Cynthia Vincenti
Cover Art: Peas in pea pod/Comstock Images/Getty Images, Inc.—Comstock Images RF
Permissions Project Manager: Shannon Barbe
Media Project Manager, Editorial: Denise Vaughn
Media Project Manager, Production: Lisa Rinaldi
Full-Service Project Management: S4Carlisle Publishing Services
Composition: S4Carlisle Publishing Services
Printer/Binder: Courier/Kendalville
Cover Printer: Lehigh-Phoenix Color/Hagerstown
Text Font: 10.5/12 New Baskerville

Credits and acknowledgments borrowed from other sources and reproduced, with permission, in this textbook appear on appropriate page within text (or on page 650).

Copyright © 2011, 2009, 2007, 2005, 2003 Pearson Education, Inc., publishing as Prentice Hall, One Lake Street, Upper Saddle River, New Jersey 07458. All rights reserved. Manufactured in the United States of America. This publication is protected by Copyright, and permission should be obtained from the publisher prior to any prohibited reproduction, storage in a retrieval system, or transmission in any form or by any means, electronic, mechanical, photocopying, recording, or likewise. To obtain permission(s) to use material from this work, please submit a written request to Pearson Education, Inc., Permissions Department, One Lake Street, Upper Saddle River, New Jersey 07458.

Many of the designations by manufacturers and seller to distinguish their products are claimed as trademarks. Where those designations appear in this book, and the publisher was aware of a trademark claim, the designations have been printed in initial caps or all caps.

Library of Congress Cataloging-in-Publication Data

Robbins, Stephen P.
  Organizational behavior / Stephen P. Robbins, Timothy A. Judge. —
14th ed.
    p. cm.
Includes bibliographical references and index.
ISBN 978-0-13-612401-6 (alk. paper)
1. Organizational behavior. I. Judge, Tim. II. Title.
HD58.7.R62 2011
658.3—dc22   2009047331

Prentice Hall
is an imprint of

www.pearsonhighered.com

10 9 8 7 6 5 4 3 2 1
ISBN 10: 0-13-612401-1
ISBN 13: 978-0-13-612401-6

Brief Contents

v

4 The Organization System

Contents

2 The Individual

2 *Diversity in Organizations* 38

3 *Attitudes and Job Satisfaction* 70

4 *Emotions and Moods* 98

5 *Personality and Values* 132

6 *Perception and Individual Decision Making* 166

7 *Motivation Concepts* 202

3 The Group

9 *Foundations of Group Behavior* 274

10   *Understanding Work Teams* 312

11 *Communication* 340

Functions of Communication 342

The Communication Process 343

Direction of Communication 344

Downward Communication 344 • Upward Communication 345 • Lateral Communication 346

Interpersonal Communication 346

Oral Communication 346 • Written Communication 347 • Nonverbal Communication 348

Organizational Communication 349

Formal Small-Group Networks 349 • The Grapevine 350 • Electronic Communications 351 • Managing Information 355

Choice of Communication Channel 357

Barriers to Effective Communication 359

Filtering 359 • Selective Perception 359 • Information Overload 359 • Emotions 359 • Language 360 • Silence 360 • Communication Apprehension 361 • Gender Differences 361 • "Politically Correct" Communication 361

Global Implications 362

Summary and Implications for Managers 365

14 *Conflict and Negotiation*

4 The Organization System

15 *Foundations of Organization Structure* 486

18 *Organizational Change and Stress Management* 588

About the Authors

Stephen P. Robbins

Education
Ph.D. University of Arizona

Professional Experience

Academic Positions: Professor, San Diego State University, Southern Illinois University at Edwardsville, University of Baltimore, Concordia University in Montreal, and University of Nebraska at Omaha.

Research: Research interests have focused on conflict, power, and politics in organizations, behavioral decision making, and the development of effective interpersonal skills.

Books Published: World's best-selling author of textbooks in both management and organizational behavior. His books have sold more than five million copies, have been translated into 20 languages, and editions have been adapted for Canada, Australia, South Africa, and India, such as these:

- *Essentials of Organizational Behavior*, 10th ed. (Prentice Hall, 2010)
- *Management*, 10th ed. with Mary Coulter (Prentice Hall, 2009)
- *Human Resource Management*, 10th ed., with David DeCenzo (Wiley, 2010)
- *Prentice Hall's Self-Assessment Library 3.4* (Prentice Hall, 2010)
- *Fundamentals of Management*, 7th ed., with David DeCenzo and Mary Coulter (Prentice Hall, 2011)
- *Supervision Today!* 6th ed., with David DeCenzo (Prentice Hall, 2010)
- *Training in Interpersonal Skills*, 5th ed., with Phillip Hunsaker (Prentice Hall, 2009)
- *Managing Today!* 2nd ed. (Prentice Hall, 2000)
- *Organization Theory*, 3rd ed. (Prentice Hall, 1990)
- *The Truth About Managing People*, 2nd ed. (Financial Times/Prentice Hall, 2008)
- *Decide and Conquer: Make Winning Decisions and Take Control of Your Life* (Financial Times/Prentice Hall, 2004).

Other Interests

In his "other life," Dr. Robbins actively participates in masters' track competition. Since turning 50 in 1993, he has won 18 national championships and 12 world titles. He is the current world record holder at 100 meters (12.37 seconds) and 200 meters (25.20 seconds) for men 65 and over.

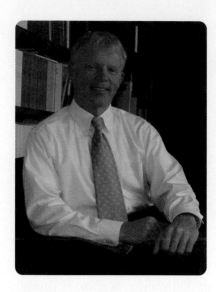

Timothy A. Judge

Education

Ph.D., University of Illinois at Urbana-Champaign

Professional Experience

Academic Positions: Matherly-McKethan Eminent Scholar in Management, Warrington College of Business Administration, University of Florida; Stanley M. Howe Professor in Leadership, Henry B. Tippie College of Business, University of Iowa; Associate Professor (with tenure), Department of Human Resource Studies, School of Industrial and Labor Relations, Cornell University; Lecturer, Charles University, Czech Republic, and Comenius University, Slovakia; Instructor, Industrial/Organizational Psychology, Department of Psychology, University of Illinois at Urbana-Champaign.

Research: Dr. Judge's primary research interests are in (1) personality, moods, and emotions, (2) job attitudes, (3) leadership and influence behaviors, and (4) careers (person-organization fit, career success). Dr. Judge has published more than 120 articles in these and other major topics in journals such as *Journal of Organizational Behavior, Personnel Psychology, Academy of Management Journal, Journal of Applied Psychology, European Journal of Personality,* and *European Journal of Work and Organizational Psychology.*

Fellowship: Dr. Judge is a fellow of the American Psychological Association, the Academy of Management, the Society for Industrial and Organizational Psychology, and the American Psychological Society.

Awards: In 1995, Dr. Judge received the Ernest J. McCormick Award for Distinguished Early Career Contributions from the Society for Industrial and Organizational Psychology. In 2001, he received the Larry L. Cummings Award for mid-career contributions from the Organizational Behavior Division of the Academy of Management. In 2007, he received the Professional Practice Award from the Institute of Industrial and Labor Relations, University of Illinois.

Books Published: H. G. Heneman III and T. A. Judge, *Staffing Organizations,* 6th ed. (Madison, WI: Mendota House/Irwin, 2009).

Other Interests

Although he cannot keep up (literally!) with Dr. Robbin's accomplishments on the track, Dr. Judge enjoys golf, cooking and baking, literature (he's a particular fan of Thomas Hardy, and is a member of the Thomas Hardy Society), and keeping up with his three children, who range in age from 20 to 6.

Welcome to the fourteenth edition of *Organizational Behavior!* Long considered the standard for all organizational behavior textbooks, this edition continues its tradition of making current, relevant research come alive for students. While maintaining its hallmark features—clear writing style, cutting-edge content, and compelling pedagogy—the fourteenth edition has been updated to reflect the most recent research within the field of organizational behavior. This is one of the most comprehensive and thorough revisions of *Organizational Behavior* we've undertaken, and while we've preserved the core material, we're confident that this edition reflects cutting edge research and topical issues facing organizations, managers, and employees.

Key Changes to the Fourteenth Edition

- New chapter—*Managing Diversity*—that reflects cutting-edge research on this important topic
- New in-depth cases for each section that provide a more holistic, integrative, and evidence-based perspective, plus 50 percent of end-of-chapter cases updated for this edition
- New addition—*OB Poll*—in each chapter that reflects timely and interesting poll results relevant to each chapter
- New addition—*An Ethical Choice*—in each chapter, that provides prescriptive advice for ethical situations that occur in organizations
- New *Opening Vignette* in each chapter, many of which reflect current business and economic conditions
- In each chapter, more examples reflecting the current state of the global economy
- Consolidated leadership chapter, which presents more material on the latest research and practical examples
- Extensive updates throughout the book, including updated examples, research findings, photographs, and end-of-chapter material
- More than 50 percent of the photos are updated
- 10 new or updated *Point/Counterpoint* boxes
- 10 new or updated *International OB* boxes
- 30% of the research citations have been updated, with half of those citations occurring in 2008–2009
- **Mymanagementlab**—a powerful online tool that combines assessment, reporting, personalized study, and a complete Robbins/Judge ebook to help both students and instructors succeed.
- NEW videos—up-to-date videos showing management topics in action, access to the complete management video library, as well as instructional materials for integrating clips from popular movies into your class, will be available at www.managementlab.com. Visit there to gain access and learn more.

*This *new* chapter focuses on the latest thinking on diversity, diversity management, and diversity training, as well as such individual differences as cognitive ability and such demographic characteristics as age, sex, race, and other biographical characteristics.

Chapter-by-Chapter Changes

Chapter 1
- New *Opening Vignette* (The Psychic Is In)
- New *An Ethical Choice* (Statistics Can Lie!)
- New *OB Poll* (Employee Concerns During Recession)
- Updated *Point/Counterpoint*
- New *Case Incident 2* (The Global Recession and Workplace Malfeasance)
- Updated material on evidence-based management
- New section, "Responding to Economic Pressures," to lead off *Challenges to OB* section
- Revised and updated material on *Challenges to OB: Responding to Globalization*
- Revised and updated material on *Challenges to OB: Improving Customer Service*
- Revised and updated material on *Challenges to OB: Improving Ethical Behavior*

Chapter 2
- New *Opening Vignette* (Reaching New Resources)
- New *An Ethical Choice* (Are You More Biased Than You Think?)
- New *OB Poll* (Room at the Top)
- New *Case Incident 2* (What Does Diversity Training Teach?)
- New *Point/Counterpoint* (The Time Has Come to Move Past Race and Ethnicity)
- Updated *Ethical Dilemma*
- Updated *Case Incident 1*
- Describes how organizations can capitalize on the opportunities created by a diverse workforce
- Describes how different forms of diversity might have different effects on employee attitudes and behavior
- Reviews some of the major forms of discriminatory behavior that hamper organizational effectiveness
- Reviews research on age, gender, race and ethnicity, disability, and other biographical characteristics
- Discusses the role of abilities in job performance
- Summarizes the research on effective diversity management practices
- Discusses how diversity efforts work across cultures

Chapter 3
- New *Opening Vignette* (Employees First, Customers Second)
- New *An Ethical Choice* ("I Don't Hate My Job . . . I Hate You")
- New *OB Poll* (What Do Employees Love—and Hate—About Their Jobs?)
- Updated *International OB*
- New material in *Point/Counterpoint*
- Update for *Case Incident 2*
- Describes how the social relationships one has at work contribute to job satisfaction
- Updated material on the relationship between satisfaction and performance
- Includes new research on satisfaction and citizenship

Chapter 4
- New *Opening Vignette* (Fear and Hope in Finance)
- New *Ethical Dilemma* (Is There An Emotional Double-Standard for Men and Women at Work?)
- New *An Ethical Choice* (Workplace Romance)
- New *OB Poll* (Would You Date a Co-Worker?)

- New *Case Incident 2* (Becoming a Facial Decoder)
- Revised and updated *International OB*
- Updated information on emotional labor
- Updated coverage on emotional intelligence
- Description of new research on creativity and performance
- Review of the latest research on emotions and leadership, negotiation, and deviance
- New section on safety and emotions at work

Chapter 5

- New *Opening Vignette* (Do You Live in a Neurotic [or Nice] State?)
- New Exhibit 5-1 (Traits That Matter Most to Business Success at Buyout Companies)
- New *An Ethical Choice* ("What If I Have the 'Wrong' Personality?")
- New material in *Point/Counterpoint*
- Updated *Case Incident 1*
- New *OB Poll* (How Do Millennials Prefer to Dress for Work?)
- Updated information on faking in personality tests
- New research on how personality changes with age
- Includes new research on satisfaction and citizenship
- Includes new research on personality and leadership
- Includes new information on cross-cultural research designs
- Includes updated material in Generational Values section
- Updated Exhibit 5-5

Chapter 6

- New *Opening Vignette* (Google's Innovation Machine)
- New *An Ethical Choice* (Is It Wrong to Rationalize?)
- New *Case Incident 2* (Predictions)
- New *OB Poll* (Inflated Self-Views)
- New *Myth or Science?* ("Is There Really a Black Swan?")
- New *International OB* (East-West Differences: It's Perceptual)
- New section: Risk Aversion (and its implications for organizations)
- New coverage of the role of mental ability in decision-making errors
- Updated example on anchoring bias
- Updated example on availability bias
- Updated material and examples on hindsight bias
- New example on overconfidence bias
- Expanded discussion of the limits of the rational decision-making model
- Updated discussion of the relationships among moods and creativity
- Updated discussion of cross-cultural differences in attributions
- Updated material on intuition

Chapter 7

- New *Opening Vignette* (The Big Broker Exodus)
- New *An Ethical Choice* (Putting Off Work)
- New *Case Incident 2* (Bullying Bosses)
- New *OB Poll* (Thriving at Work)
- New *Point/Counterpoint* (Failure Motivates!)
- New section: Self-Determination Theory
- Review of new research on culture and motivation
- Discussion of the potential dangers in goal-setting research
- Integration of more material regarding reinforcement theory

Chapter 8

- New *Opening Vignette* (Bye-Bye Bonus—and Base Pay)
- New *An Ethical Choice* (You Might Work Less Than You Think)
- New *Ethical Dilemma* (Did Executives' Pay Cause the Recession?)
- New *OB Poll* (Do Most of Us Feel Underpaid?)
- New *Case Incident 1* (Multitasking: A Good Use of Your Time?)
- New, updated job enrichment example (University of New Mexico)
- Updated *Point/Counterpoint*
- Updated material on bonuses
- New section about social context as an important job characteristic
- Description of ergonomic factors in job design
- Updates on how to provide effective feedback at work
- Outlines new findings on how the meaningfulness of work can be enhanced
- New information about flextime and alternative work arrangements
- Updates to information on wages, profit sharing, gainsharing, and ESOP

Chapter 9

- New *Opening Vignette* (Brainstorming: A Lousy Idea for Ideas?)
- Major new section—(Why Do People Form Groups?)—that presents research on social identities and their implications for group membership
- New *An Ethical Choice* (How Groups Infect Your Deviant Behavior—and How to Immunize Yourself)
- New *Case Incident 2* (Herd Behavior and the Housing Bubble [and Collapse])
- Revised *International OB*
- New *OB Poll* (Do We Like Working in Groups?)
- Updated research on role conflict
- Update on a major replication of Zimbardo's famous prison experiment
- Updated research on workplace deviance in groups
- Updated material on groupshift or group polarization
- Expanded discussion on cohesiveness in cross-cultural settings

Chapter 10

- New *Opening Vignette* (Everyone Here's Going To Die)
- New *An Ethical Choice* (Preventing Team Mistakes)
- New *Case Incident 1* (Toyota's Team Culture)
- New *Case Incident 2* (IBM'S Multicultural Teams)
- Revised *International OB*
- Updated *Myth or Science?* (Old Teams Can't Learn New Tricks)
- Updated *Point/Counterpoint*
- New *OB Poll* (Relative Importance of Teamwork Skills)
- Update to research on demographic diversity and team performance
- Expanded description of how to effectively manage teams with diverse knowledge
- Increased attention to the importance of assigning members to roles in teams
- Discussion of the latest research on team processes

Chapter 11

- New *Opening Vignette* (Will E-mail Send These Traders to Jail?)
- Updated *Myth or Science?* (People Are Good at Catching Liars at Work)
- Updated *International OB*
- Updated *Point/Counterpoint*
- Extensive updating of e-mail communication and video conferencing
- New *An Ethical Choice* (Managing Your Tweeting and Twittering)
- New *Case Incident 2* (Should Companies That Fire Shoot First?)

- New *OB Poll* (How Long Do Employees Go Without Checking E-mail?)
- New section on how to minimize intrusion of e-mails
- New section: "Managing Information"
- Updated information on potentially divisive issues in cross-cultural communication
- Discussion of the role of communication technology in employee burnout and work–life conflict
- New sections on noncommunication and silence in organizations
- Discussion of emotion in electronic communications

Chapter 12

- New merged chapter
- New *Opening Vignette* (Private Equity's Poster Boy)
- New *An Ethical Choice* (Working for a Toxic Boss)
- Updated *Ethical Dilemma*
- New *Case Incident 1* (The Making of a Great President)
- New *Case Incident 2* (Leadership Factories)
- Updated *International OB*
- New *OB Poll* (Confidence in Business Leaders Falling)
- Updated discussion of the functions and processes underlying transformational and charismatic leadership
- Major revision of the discussion of trust and leadership
- Major revision to "Mentoring" section: expanded discussion of the role of mentoring as a means of preserving organizational knowledge
- Discussion of the role of follower prototypes and preferences in the leadership process
- New example on attributional approach to leadership: Stan O'Neal, former CEO of Merrill Lynch

Chapter 13

- New *Opening Vignette* (Does Power Corrupt?)
- New *An Ethical Choice* (Making Excuses)
- New *Ethical Dilemma* (Does "Aping" Others Work? Is It Ethical?)
- New *Case Incident 2* (The Persuasion Imperative)
- New *OB Poll* (How Do You Deal with Office Politics?)
- Update on résumé fraud in *Point/Counterpoint*
- Updated research on legitimate power
- Several updates to material on influence tactics
- Revised introduction to "The Reality of Politics"
- Extensive updates to "Impression Management" section
- Revision of Exhibit 13-7 (Impression Management [IM] Techniques)

Chapter 14

- New *Opening Vignette* (Kidnapping the Boss)
- New *International OB* (Negotiating Emotions Across Cultures)
- New *An Ethical Choice* (Sharing Your Salary)
- New *Case Incident 2* (Mediation: Master Solution to Employment Disputes?)
- Updated *Ethical Dilemma*
- New *OB Poll* (When to Mention Salary?)
- Update to *Myth or Science?* on sealed bid auctions and bid jumping
- Extensive updates to "Functional View of Conflict" section
- Updates to personality and negotiation and moods/emotions and negotiation sections
- Extensive updates to "Dysfunctional View of Conflict" section
- Updates to "Transitions in Conflict Thought" section

- New material on managing functional conflict
- Extensive updates to "Global Implications" section
- Revision to definition of negotiation and accompanying material
- New material in "Negotiation: Preparation and Planning" section
- New section, "Resolution Focused View of Conflict," which focuses on latest research on this emerging topic

Chapter 15

- New *Opening Vignette* (Restructuring Chrysler)
- New *An Ethical Choice* ("I Fell Into a Big Black Hole")
- New *International OB* (Structuring Organizations Across National Borders)
- New *Case Incident 2* (Siemens Simple Structure—Not)
- New *Point/Counterpoint* (Mergers Are an Excellent Way to Screw Employees)
- Substantially updated *Ethical Dilemma* (How Much Should Directors Direct?)
- New *OB Poll* (Are You Currently Downsizing?)
- Major new section: "The Leaner Organization: Downsizing"

Chapter 16

- New *Opening Vignette* (Is a 5S Culture for You?)
- New *An Ethical Choice* (Working in a Spiritual Culture)
- New *Case Incident 2* (Google and P&G Swap Employees)
- New *OB Poll* (Is Your Organization's Culture Religious?)
- New example of effect of top management on culture formation (Wegman's)
- New example on dark side of socialization (Siemens)

Chapter 17

- New *Opening Vignette* (Smarts in the NFL?)
- New *An Ethical Choice* (Is Honesty the Best Policy in Getting a Job?)
- New *Case Incident 1* (Peering into Your Past)
- Revised *Ethical Dilemma* (Is It Unethical to "Shape" Your Résumé?)
- Revised *Point/Counterpoint* (Telecommuting)
- New *OB Poll* (Employer Concern over Résumé Gaps)
- New *International OB* (Does Personality Testing Work Outside the United States?)
- New Exhibit 17-3 (Grade Inflation at Four Universities)

Chapter 18

- New *Opening Vignette* (Change or Die, or Change *and* Die?)
- New *An Ethical Choice* (Your Responsibility to Your Stress)
- New *Case Incident 1* (Innovation—and Continuity—at Toyota)
- New *OB Poll* (Stress Gap)
- New *Myth or Science?* ("Job Stress Can Kill You")
- New *International OB* (Coping with Stress: East and West)
- Revised Exhibit 18-1 (Forces for Change)
- Updated material in "Forces for Change" section

Teaching and Learning Support

PEARSON mymanagementlab

Mymanagementlab (www.mymanagementlab.com) is an easy-to-use online tool that personalizes course content and provides robust assessment and reporting to measure student and class performance. All the resources you need for course success are in one place—flexible and easily adapted for your course experience. Some of the resources include an eBook version of all chapters, quizzes, personalized study plan, video clips, and PowerPoint presentations that engage students while helping them to study independently.

In particular, mymanagementlab supports more active learning styles, involving students as they study management and prepare for test and quizzes. mymanagementlab also contains key video, testing, and other support resources that offer instructors many ways to enliven their classroom and save time—all in one convenient place.

Instructor's Resource Center

At www.pearsonhighered.com/irc, instructors can access a variety of print, digital, and presentation resources available with this text in downloadable format. Registration is simple and gives you immediate access to new titles and new editions. As a registered faculty member, you can download resource files and receive immediate access and instructions for installing course management content on your campus server.

If you need assistance, our dedicated technical support team is ready to help with the media supplements that accompany this text. Visit 247pearsoned .custhelp.com for answers to frequently asked questions and toll-free user support phone numbers.

The following supplements are available to adopting instructors (for detailed descriptions, please visit www.pearsonhighered.com/irc):

- Instructor's Manual—updated and revised to provide ideas and resources in the classroom.
- Test Item File—Over 500 new questions. Revised and updated to include questions that require students to apply the knowledge that they've read about in the text. Questions are also tagged to reflect the AACSB Learning Standards.
- TestGen Test Generating Software—Test management software containing all the material from the Test Item File. This software is completely user friendly and allows instructors to view, edit, and add test questions with just a few mouse clicks.
- PowerPoint Presentation—A ready-to-use PowerPoint slideshow designed for classroom presentation. Use it as is, or edit content to fit your individual classroom needs.
- Library of Images—includes all the charts, tables, and graphs that are found in the text.

CourseSmart eTextbooks Online

Developed for students looking to save money on required or recommended textbooks, CourseSmart eTextbooks online save students money compared with the suggested list price of the print text. Students simply select their eText by title or author and purchase immediate access to the content for the duration of the course using any major credit card. With CourseSmart eText, students can search for specific keywords or page numbers, make notes online, print reading assignments that incorporate lecture notes, and bookmark important passages for later review. For more information, or to purchase a CourseSmart eTextbook, visit www.coursesmart.com.

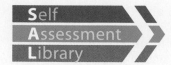

Prentice Hall's Self-Assessment Library (S.A.L.)

A hallmark of the Robbins series, S.A.L. is a unique learning tool that allows you to assess your knowledge, beliefs, feelings, and actions in regard to a wide range of personal skills, abilities, and interests. Self-Assessments have been integrated into each chapter, including a self-assessment at the beginning of each chapter. S.A.L. helps students better understand their interpersonal and behavioral skills as they relate to the theoretical concepts presented in each chapter.

Highlights

- **68 research-based self-assessments**—All 68 instruments of our collection are from sources such as *Journal of Social Behavior and Personality, Harvard Business Review, Organizational Behavior: Experiences and Cases, Journal of Experimental Education, Journal of Applied Measurement,* and more.
- **Work–life and career focused**—All self-assessments are focused to help individuals better manage their work lives or careers. Organized in four parts, these instruments offer you one source from which to learn more about yourself.
- **Choice of formats**—The Prentice Hall Self-Assessment Library is available in either CD-ROM, online, or print format.
- **Save feature**—Students can take the self-assessments an unlimited number of times, and they can save and print their scores for class discussion.
- **Scoring key**—The key to the self-assessments has been edited by Steve Robbins to allow students to quickly make sense of the results of their score.
- **Instructor's manual**—An *Instructor's Manual* guides instructors in interpreting self-assessments and helps facilitate better classroom discussion.

Acknowledgments

Getting this book into your hands was a team effort. It took faculty reviewers and a talented group of designers and production specialists, editorial personnel, and marketing and sales staff.

More than a hundred instructors reviewed parts or all of *Organizational Behavior*, Thirteenth Edition. Their comments, compliments, and suggestions have significantly improved the final product. The authors would like to extend their sincerest thank you to the following instructors:

Mihran Aroian, The University of Texas at Austin

Carl Blencke, University of Central Florida

Bryan Bonner, University of Utah

Michael Hadani, Long Island University

David Jalajas, Long Island University

Andrew Johnson, Santa Clara University

Catherine Marsh, Northpark University

Cynthia Ozeki, California State University, Dominguez Hills

Herbert Ricardo, Indian River Community College

Mary Ellen Zuckerman, State University of New York at Geneseo

Over the last editions this text has grown stronger with the contribution and feedback of the following instructors:

David Abramis, California State University

Chris Adalikwu, Concordia College

Basil Adams, Notre Dame de Namur University

Janet Adams, Kennesaw State University

Cheryl Adkins, Longwood College

Vicky Aitken, St. Louis Community College

David Albritton, Northern Arizona University

Bradley Alge, Purdue University

Lois Antonen, CSUS

Lucy Arendt, University of Wisconsin, Green Bay

Anke Arnaud, University of Central Florida

Mihran Aroian, University of Texas, Austin

Gary Ballinger, Purdue University

Deborah Balser, University of Missouri at St. Louis

Christopher Barlow, DePaul University

Joy Benson, University of Wisconsin at Green Bay

Lehman Benson III, University of Arizona

Jacqui Bergman, Appalachian State University

Anne Berthelot, University of Texas at El Paso

David Bess, Shidler College of Business at the University of Hawaii

Bruce Bikle, California State University, Sacramento

Richard Blackburn, University of North Carolina–Chapel Hill

Weldon Blake, Bethune-Cookman College

Michael Bochenek, Elmhurst College

Alicia Boisnier, State University of New York

William H. Bommer, Cleveland State University

Bryan Bonner, University of Utah

Jessica Bradley, Clemson University

Dr. Jerry Bream, Empire State College/Niagara Frontier Center

Jim Breaugh, University of Missouri

Peggy Brewer, Eastern Kentucky University

Deborah Brown, North Carolina State University

Reginald Bruce, University of Louisville

Jeff Bruns, Bacone College

Pamela Buckle, Adelphi University

Patricia Buhler, Goldey-Beacom College

Allen Bures, Radford University

Edith Busija, University of Richmond

Holly Buttner, University of North Carolina at Greensboro

Michael Cafferky, Southern Adventist University

Scott Campbell, Francis Marion University

Elena Capella, University of San Francisco

Don Capener, Monmouth University

Dan Caprar, University of Iowa

David Carmichael, Oklahoma City University

Carol Carnevale, SUNY Empire State College

Donald W. Caudill, Bluefield College

Suzanne Chan, Tulane University

Anthony Chelte, Midwestern State University

Bongsoon Cho, State University of New York–Buffalo

Savannah Clay, Central Piedmont Community College

David Connelly, Western Illinois State University

Jeffrey Conte, San Diego State University

Jane Crabtree, Benedictine University

Suzanne Crampton, Grand Valley State University

Douglas Crawford, Wilson College

Michael Cruz, San Jose State University

Robert Cyr, Northwestern University

Evelyn Dadzie, Clark Atlanta University

Joseph Daly, Appalachian State University

Denise Daniels, Seattle Pacific University

Marie Dasborough, Oklahoma State University

Nancy Da Silva, San Jose State University

Christine Day, Eastern Michigan University

Emmeline de Pillis, University of Hawaii, Hilo

Kathy Lund Dean, Idaho State University

Roger Dean, Washington & Lee University

Robert DelCampo, University of New Mexico

Kristen Detienne, Brigham Young University

Doug Dierking, University of Texas at Austin

Cynthia Doil, Southern Illinois University

Jennifer Dose, Messiah College

Ceasar Douglas, Florida State University

David Duby, Liberty University

Ken Dunegan, Cleveland State University

Michael Dutch, Greensboro College

Kathleen Edwards, University of Texas at Austin

Berrin Erdogan, Portland State University

Ellen Fagenson Eland, George Mason University

Lenny Favara, Central Christian College

Claudia Ferrante, U.S. Air Force Academy

Andy Fitorre, Nyack College

Kathleen Fleming, Averett University

Erin Fluegge, University of Florida

Edward Fox, Wilkes University

Alison Fragale, University of North Carolina at Chapel Hill

Lucy Franks, Bellevue University

Dean Frear, Wilkes University

Jann Freed, Central College

Crissie Frye, Eastern Michigan University

Diane Galbraith, Slippery Rock University

Carolyn Gardner, Radford University

Janice Gates, Western Illinois University

Ellen Kaye Gehrke, Alliant International University

James Gelatt, University of Maryland University College

Joe Gerard, University of Wisconsin at Milwaukee

Matthew Giblin, Southern Illinois University

Donald Gibson, Fairfield University

Cindi Gilliland, The University of Arizona

Mary Giovannini, Truman State University

David Glew, University of North Carolina at Wilmington

Leonard Glick, Northeastern University

Reginald Goodfellow, California State University

Jeffrey Goldstein, Adelphi University

Jodi Goodman, University of Connecticut

Claude Graeff, Illinois State University

Richard Grover, University of Southern Maine

W. Lee Grubb III, East Carolina University

John Guarino, Averett University

Rebecca Guidice, University of Nevada at Las Vegas

Andra Gumbus, Sacred Heart University

Linda Hackleman, Concordia University Austin

Deniz Hackner, Tidewater Community College

Jonathon Halbesleben, University of Missouri-Columbia

Dan Hallock, University of North Alabama

Tracey Rockett Hanft, University of Texas at Dallas

Edward Hampton, University of Central Florida

Vernard Harrington, Radford University

Nell Hartley, Robert Morris University

Barbara Hassell, Indiana University, Kelley School of Business

Erin Hayes, George Washington University

Tom Head, Roosevelt University

Douglas Heeter, Ferris State University

David Henderson, University of Illinois at Chicago

Scott Henley, Oklahoma City University

Ted Herbert, Rollins College

Susan Herman, University of Alaska Fairbanks

James Hess, Ivy Tech Community College

Ronald Hester, Marymount University

Patricia Hewlin, Georgetown University

Chad Higgins, University of Washington

Kim Hinrichs, Minnesota State University Mankato

Kathie Holland, University of Central Florida

Elaine Hollensbe, University of Cincinnati

Kristin Holmberg-Wright, University of Wisconsin at Parkside

Brooks Holtom, Georgetown University

Lisa Houts, California State University Fullerton

Abigail Hubbard, University of Houston

Paul Hudec, Milwaukee School of Engineering

Stephen Humphrey, Florida State University

Charlice Hurst, University of Florida

Warren Imada, Leeward Community College

Gazi Islam, Tulane University

Alan Jackson, Peru State College

Christine Jackson, Purdue University

Marsha Jackson, Bowie State University

Kathryn Jacobson, Arizona State University

Paul Jacques, Western Carolina University

Elizabeth Jamison, Radford University

Stephen Jenner, California State University, Dominguez Hills

John Jermier, University of South Florida

Jack Johnson, Consumnes River College

Michael Johnson, University of Washington

David Jones, South University

Ray Jones, University of Pittsburgh

Anthony Jost, University of Delaware

Louis Jourdan, Clayton College

Rusty Juban, Southeastern Illinois University

Carole L. Jurkiewicz, Louisiana State University

John Kammeyer-Mueller, University of Florida

Edward Kass, Saint Joseph's University

Marsha Katz, Governors State College

James Katzenstein, California State University

John Keiser, SUNY College at Brockport

Mark Kendrick, Methodist University

Mary Kern, Baruch College

Robert Key, University of Phoenix

Sigrid Khorram, University of Texas at El Paso

Hal Kingsley, Erie Community College

Jeffrey Kobles, California State University San Marcos

Jack Kondrasuk, University of Portland

Leslie A. Korb, University of Nebraska at Kearney

Glen Kreiner, University of Cincinnati

James Kroeger, Cleveland State University

Frederick Lane, Baruch College

Rebecca Lau, Virginia Polytechnic Institute and State University

David Leuser, Plymouth State College

Julia Levashina, Indiana State University Kokomo

Benyamin Lichtenstein, University of Massachusetts at Boston

Robert Liden, University of Illinois at Chicago

Don Lifton, Ithaca College

Ginamarie Ligon, Villanova University

Beth Livingston, University of Florida

Barbara Low, Dominican University

Doyle Lucas, Anderson University

Alexandra Luong, University of Minnesota

Rick Maclin, Missouri Baptist University

Peter Madsen, Brigham Young University

Lou Marino, University of Alabama

Timothy A. Matherly, Florida State University

J. David Martin, Midwestern State University

John Mattoon, State University of New York

Paul Maxwell, Saint Thomas University

Brenda McAleer, University of Maine at Augusta

Christina McCale, Regis Colllege

Don McCormick, California State University Northridge

James McElroy, Iowa State University

Bonnie McNeely, Murray State University

Melony Mead, University of Phoenix

Steven Meisel, La Salle University

Nancy Meyer-Emerick, Cleveland State University

Catherine Michael, St. Edwards University

Sandy Miles, Murray State University

Janice Miller, University of Wisconsin at Milwaukee

Leann Mischel, Susquehanna University

Atul Mitra, University of Northern Iowa

Linda Morable, Richland College

Paula Morrow, Iowa State University

Mark Mortensen, Massachusetts Institute of Technology

Lori Muse, Western Michigan University

Padmakumar Nair, University of Texas at Dallas

Judy Nixon, University of Tennessee at Chattanooga

Jeffrey Nystrom, University of Colorado at Denver

Alison O'Brien, George Mason University

Heather Odle-Dusseau, Clemson University

Miguel Olivas-Lujan, Lujan Clarion University

Kelly Ottman, University of Wisconsin at Milwaukee

Peg Padgett, Butler University

Jennifer Palthe, Western Michigan University

Dennis Passovoy, University of Texas at Austin

Karen Paul, Florida International University

Laura Finnerty Paul, Skidmore College

Anette Pendergrass, Arkansas State University at Mountain Home

Bryan Pesta, Cleveland State University

Jeff Peterson, University of Washington

Nanette Philibert, Missouri Southern State University

Larry Phillips, Indiana University South Bend

William Pinchuk, Rutgers University at Camden

Eric Popkoff, Brooklyn College

Paul Preston, University of Montevallo

Scott Quatro, Grand Canyon University

Aarti Ramaswami, Indiana University Bloomington

Jere Ramsey, Cal Poly at San Luis Obispo

Amy Randel, San Diego State University

Anne Reilly, Loyola University Chicago

Clint Relyea, Arkansas State University

David Ritchey, University of Texas at Dallas

Chris Roberts, University of Massachusetts Amherst

Sherry Robinson, Pennsylvania State University Hazleton

Christopher Ann Robinson-Easley, Governors State University

Joe Rode, Miami University

Bob Roller, LeTourneau University

Andrea Roofe, Florida International University

Philip Roth, Clemson University

Craig Russell, University of Oklahoma at Norman

Manjula Salimath, University of North Texas

Mary Saunders, Georgia Gwinnett College

Andy Schaffer, North Georgia College and State University

Holly Schroth, University of California at Berkeley

Elizabeth Scott, Elizabeth City University

Mark Seabright, Western Oregon University

Joseph Seltzer, LaSalle University

John Shaw, Mississippi State University

John Sherlock, Western Carolina University

Daniel Sherman, University of Alabama, Huntsville

Heather Shields, Texas Tech University

Ted Shore, California State University at Long Beach

Stuart Sidle, University of New Haven

Bret Simmons, University of Nevada Reno

Randy Sleeth, Virginia Commonwealth University

William Smith, Emporia State University

Kenneth Solano, Northeastern University

Shane Spiller, Morehead State University

Lynda St. Clair, Bryant University

John B. Stark, California State University, Bakersfield

Merwyn Strate, Purdue University

Joo-Seng Tan, Cornell University

Karen Thompson, Sonoma State University

Linda Tibbetts, Antioch University McGregor

Ed Tomlinson, John Carroll University

Bob Trodella, Webster University

Tom Tudor, University of Arkansas at Little Rock

William D. Tudor, Ohio State University

Daniel Turban, University of Missouri

Albert Turner, Webster University

Jim Turner, Morehead State University

Leslie Tworoger, Nova Southeastern University

M. A. Viets, University of Vermont

Roger Volkema, American University

William Walker, University of Houston

Ian Walsh, Boston College

Charles F. Warren, Salem State College

Christa Washington, Saint Augustine's College

Jim Westerman, Appalachian State University

William J. White, Northwestern University

David Whitlock, Southwest Baptist University

Dan Wiljanen, Grand Valley State University

Dean Williamson, Brewton-Parker College

Hilda Williamson, Hampton University

Alice Wilson, Cedar Crest College

Barry Wisdom, Southeast Missouri State University

Craig Wishart, Fayetteville State University

Laura Wolfe, Louisiana State University

Melody Wollan, Eastern Illinois University

Evan Wood, Taylor University Fort Wayne

Chun-Sheng Yu, University of Houston-Victoria

Jun Zhao, Governors State University

Lori Ziegler, University of Texas at Dallas

Gail Zwart, Riverside Community College

We owe a debt of gratitude to all those at Prentice Hall who have supported this text over the last 30 years and who have worked so hard on the development of this latest edition. On the development and editorial side, we want to thank Elisa Adams, Development Editor; Steve Deitmer, Director of Development; Meg O'Rourke, Editorial Assistant; Susie Abraham, Editorial Project Manager; Jennifer M. Collins, Acquisitions Editor; Eric Svendsen, Editor in Chief; and Sally Yagan, Editorial Director. On the design and production side, Judy Leale, Senior Managing Editor, did an outstanding job, as did Becca Richter, Production Project Manager, and Nancy Moundry, Photo Development Editor. Last but not least, we would like to thank Nikki Ayana Jones, Marketing Manager; Patrice Lumumba Jones, Director of Marketing; and their sales staff, who have been selling this book over its many editions. Thank you for the attention you've given this book.

LEARNING OBJECTIVES

After studying this chapter, you should be able to:

1 Demonstrate the importance of interpersonal skills in the workplace.

2 Describe the manager's functions, roles, and skills.

3 Define *organizational behavior (OB)*.

4 Show the value to OB of systematic study.

5 Identify the major behavioral science disciplines that contribute to OB.

6 Demonstrate why few absolutes apply to OB.

7 Identify the challenges and opportunities managers have in applying OB concepts.

8 Compare the three levels of analysis in this book's OB model.

What Is Organizational Behavior?

The stellar universe is not so difficult of comprehension as the real actions of other people. —Marcel Proust

THE PSYCHIC IS IN

You are right to wonder why the first chapter of your new book has an advertisement for a psychic on the first page. Allow us to explain.

The psychic business is booming, and it has a lot to do with organizational behavior.

Psychics say their business is thriving, as do astrologists, spirit channelers, healers, shamans, and palm readers. Most give credit to the global recession. "We started seeing more around the time it was announced that Britain was in a recession," reported Vicky of the Psychic Sisters, who schedules appointments. Psychics are finding more people are turning to them for job and career advice than for relationships or any other issue.

Tori Hartman, a Los Angeles psychic, saw her Internet traffic grow sixfold, from 30 daily visitors to more than 200. She charges $150 for a 30-minute telephone reading, $500 for 90 minutes of "intuitive counseling." Like other psychics, Hartman has seen her business growing from those seeking work advice, and men now constitute half her clientele.

Thomas Taccetta is a case in point. As a stock trader in better days, Taccetta checked his financial charts before plotting the day's investments. During the worst of the recession, he was more likely to check with his psychic. "I'll play the broadest index, the S&P 500," he said, "and if she tells me she is getting a negative view, I will sell."

It's not just the psychic business that's booming. *The Secret,* Rhonda Byrne's paean to self-help and positive thinking, has chalked up more than $300 million in sales since 2007. Another popular guru, James Arthur Ray, offers this promise: "Let me assist you in building the millionaire lifestyle you deserve. I can show you how to create a comprehensive state of fulfillment, joy and prosperity that everyone wants, but few ever achieve." His book, *Harmonic Wealth,* premiered on the *New York Times* bestseller list the week it was published.

Not all users of psychics and self-help gurus are sold on their effectiveness. Says Stuart McFaul, who runs a marketing and public relations firm in San Francisco and consults a psychic when stumped about where his business, or the competition, is headed, "It pays to cover all your bets."[1]

Y ou might think this story merely reveals the desperate acts of desperate people in desperate times. Perhaps, but the growth in psychics and other self-help gurus illustrates a deeper truth, relevant in good times and bad. Those who work in and with organizations are often not the purely rational actors we assume, but neither is most behavior wholly unpredictable. In fact, there is a lot to learn about how people act in organizations, why they act as they do, and what we can do to predict and manage their behavior.

This is where organizational behavior comes into play. And, as we'll learn, it is much more than common sense, intuition, and soothsaying.

To see how far common sense gets you, try the following from the Self-Assessment Library.

Self Assessment Library

HOW MUCH DO I KNOW ABOUT ORGANIZATIONAL BEHAVIOR?

In the Self-Assessment Library (available on CD and online), take assessment IV.G.1 (How Much Do I Know About OB?) and answer the following questions:

1. *How did you score? Are you surprised by your score?*
2. *How much of effective management do you think is common sense? Did your score on the test change your answer to this question?*

The Importance of Interpersonal Skills

1 Demonstrate the importance of interpersonal skills in the workplace.

Until the late 1980s, business school curricula emphasized the technical aspects of management, focusing on economics, accounting, finance, and quantitative techniques. Course work in human behavior and people skills received relatively less attention. Over the past three decades, however, business faculty have come to realize the role that understanding human behavior plays in determining a manager's effectiveness, and required courses on people skills have been added to many curricula. As the director of leadership at MIT's Sloan School of Management put it, "M.B.A. students may get by on their technical and quantitative skills the first couple of years out of school. But soon, leadership and communication skills come to the fore in distinguishing the managers whose careers really take off."[2]

Developing managers' interpersonal skills also helps organizations attract and keep high-performing employees. Regardless of labor market conditions, outstanding employees are always in short supply.[3] Companies known as good places to work—such as Starbucks, Adobe Systems, Cisco, Whole Foods, Google, American Express, Amgen, Pfizer, and Marriott—have a big advantage. A recent survey of hundreds of workplaces, and over 200,000 respondents, showed the social relationships among co-workers and supervisors were strongly related to overall job satisfaction. Positive social relationships also were associated with lower stress at work and lower intentions to quit.[4] So having managers with good interpersonal skills is likely to make the workplace more pleasant, which in turn makes it easier to hire and keep qualified people. Creating a pleasant workplace also appears to make good economic sense. Companies with reputations as good places to work (such as the "100 Best Companies to Work for in America") have been found to generate superior financial performance.[5]

Succeeding in management today requires good people skills. Communication and leadership skills distinguish managers such as John Chambers, who rise to the top of their profession. Chambers is CEO of Cisco Systems, the world's largest maker of networking equipment. He is recognized worldwide as a visionary leader and innovator who has the ability to drive an entrepreneurial culture. As an effective communicator, he is described as warmhearted and straight talking. In this photo, Chambers delivers a speech during the launch ceremony of a green technology partnership Cisco formed with a university in China.

We have come to understand that in today's competitive and demanding workplace, managers can't succeed on their technical skills alone. They also have to have good people skills. This book has been written to help both managers and potential managers develop those people skills.

What Managers Do

2 Describe the manager's functions, roles, and skills.

Let's begin by briefly defining the terms *manager* and *organization*—the place where managers work. Then let's look at the manager's job; specifically, what do managers do?

Managers get things done through other people. They make decisions, allocate resources, and direct the activities of others to attain goals. Managers do their work in an **organization**, which is a consciously coordinated social unit, composed of two or more people, that functions on a relatively continuous basis to achieve a common goal or set of goals. By this definition, manufacturing and service firms are organizations, and so are schools, hospitals, churches, military units, retail stores, police departments, and local, state, and federal government agencies. The people who oversee the activities of others and who are responsible for attaining goals in these organizations are managers (sometimes called *administrators*, especially in not-for-profit organizations).

Management Functions

In the early part of the twentieth century, French industrialist Henri Fayol wrote that all managers perform five management functions: planning, organizing,

manager *An individual who achieves goals through other people.*

organization *A consciously coordinated social unit, composed of two or more people, that functions on a relatively continuous basis to achieve a common goal or set of goals.*

commanding, coordinating, and controlling.[6] Today, we have condensed these to four: planning, organizing, leading, and controlling.

Because organizations exist to achieve goals, someone has to define those goals and the means for achieving them; management is that someone. The **planning** function encompasses defining an organization's goals, establishing an overall strategy for achieving those goals, and developing a comprehensive set of plans to integrate and coordinate activities. Evidence indicates this function increases the most as managers move from lower-level to mid-level management.[7]

Managers are also responsible for designing an organization's structure. We call this function **organizing**. It includes determining what tasks are to be done, who is to do them, how the tasks are to be grouped, who reports to whom, and where decisions are to be made.

Every organization contains people, and it is management's job to direct and coordinate those people. This is the **leading** function. When managers motivate employees, direct their activities, select the most effective communication channels, or resolve conflicts among members, they're engaging in leading.

To ensure things are going as they should, management must monitor the organization's performance and compare it with previously set goals. If there are any significant deviations, it is management's job to get the organization back on track. This monitoring, comparing, and potential correcting is the **controlling** function.

So, using the functional approach, the answer to the question "What do managers do?" is that they plan, organize, lead, and control.

Management Roles

In the late 1960s, Henry Mintzberg, then a graduate student at MIT, undertook a careful study of five executives to determine what they did on their jobs. On the basis of his observations, Mintzberg concluded that managers perform ten different, highly interrelated roles—or sets of behaviors.[8] As shown in Exhibit 1-1, these ten roles are primarily (1) interpersonal, (2) informational, or (3) decisional.

Interpersonal Roles   All managers are required to perform duties that are ceremonial and symbolic in nature. For instance, when the president of a college hands out diplomas at commencement or a factory supervisor gives a group of high school students a tour of the plant, he or she is acting in a *figurehead* role. All managers also have a *leadership* role. This role includes hiring, training, motivating, and disciplining employees. The third role within the interpersonal grouping is the *liaison* role, or contacting others who provide the manager with information. The sales manager who obtains information from the quality-control manager in his or her own company has an internal liaison relationship. When that sales manager has contacts with other sales executives through a marketing trade association, he or she has an outside liaison relationship.

Informational Roles   All managers, to some degree, collect information from outside organizations and institutions, typically by scanning the news media (including the Internet) and talking with other people to learn of changes in the public's tastes, what competitors may be planning, and the like. Mintzberg called this the *monitor* role. Managers also act as a conduit to transmit information to organizational members. This is the *disseminator* role. In addition, managers perform a *spokesperson* role when they represent the organization to outsiders.

Decisional Roles   Mintzberg identified four roles that require making choices. In the *entrepreneur* role, managers initiate and oversee new projects that will improve their organization's performance. As *disturbance handlers,* managers

Exhibit 1-1	Mintzberg's Managerial Roles
Role	**Description**
Interpersonal	
Figurehead	Symbolic head; required to perform a number of routine duties of a legal or social nature
Leader	Responsible for the motivation and direction of employees
Liaison	Maintains a network of outside contacts who provide favors and information
Informational	
Monitor	Receives a wide variety of information; serves as nerve center of internal and external information of the organization
Disseminator	Transmits information received from outsiders or from other employees to members of the organization
Spokesperson	Transmits information to outsiders on organization's plans, policies, actions, and results; serves as expert on organization's industry
Decisional	
Entrepreneur	Searches organization and its environment for opportunities and initiates projects to bring about change
Disturbance handler	Responsible for corrective action when organization faces important, unexpected disturbances
Resource allocator	Makes or approves significant organizational decisions
Negotiator	Responsible for representing the organization at major negotiations

Source: Adapted from *The Nature of Managerial Work* by H. Mintzberg. Copyright © 1973 by H. Mintzberg. MINTZBERG, HENRY, THE NATURE OF MANAGERIAL WORK, 1st Edition, © 1980, pp. 92–93. Reprinted with permission of Pearson Education, Inc., Upper Saddle River, NJ.

take corrective action in response to unforeseen problems. As *resource allocators*, managers are responsible for allocating human, physical, and monetary resources. Finally, managers perform a *negotiator* role, in which they discuss issues and bargain with other units to gain advantages for their own unit.

Management Skills

Still another way of considering what managers do is to look at the skills or competencies they need to achieve their goals. Researchers have identified a number of skills that differentiate effective from ineffective managers.[9]

Technical Skills   **Technical skills** encompass the ability to apply specialized knowledge or expertise. When you think of the skills of professionals such as civil engineers or oral surgeons, you typically focus on the technical skills they have

planning   *A process that includes defining goals, establishing strategy, and developing plans to coordinate activities.*

organizing   *Determining what tasks are to be done, who is to do them, how the tasks are to be grouped, who reports to whom, and where decisions are to be made.*

leading   *A function that includes motivating employees, directing others, selecting the most effective communication channels, and resolving conflicts.*

controlling   *Monitoring activities to ensure they are being accomplished as planned and correcting any significant deviations.*

technical skills   *The ability to apply specialized knowledge or expertise.*

learned through extensive formal education. Of course, professionals don't have a monopoly on technical skills, and not all technical skills have to be learned in schools or other formal training programs. All jobs require some specialized expertise, and many people develop their technical skills on the job.

Human Skills   The ability to understand, communicate with, motivate, and support other people, both individually and in groups, defines **human skills**. Many people are technically proficient but poor listeners, unable to understand the needs of others, or weak at managing conflicts. Because managers get things done through other people, they must have good human skills.

Conceptual Skills   Managers must have the mental ability to analyze and diagnose complex situations. These tasks require **conceptual skills**. Decision making, for instance, requires managers to identify problems, develop alternative solutions to correct those problems, evaluate those alternative solutions, and select the best one. After they have selected a course of action, managers must be able to organize a plan of action and then execute it. The ability to integrate new ideas with existing processes and innovate on the job are also crucial conceptual skills for today's managers.

Effective versus Successful Managerial Activities

Fred Luthans and his associates looked at what managers do from a somewhat different perspective.[10] They asked, "Do managers who move up the quickest in an organization do the same activities and with the same emphasis as managers who do the best job?" You might think the answer is yes, but that's not always the case.

Luthans and his associates studied more than 450 managers. All engaged in four managerial activities:

1. **Traditional management:**   Decision making, planning, and controlling
2. **Communication:**   Exchanging routine information and processing paperwork
3. **Human resource management:**   Motivating, disciplining, managing conflict, staffing, and training
4. **Networking:**   Socializing, politicking, and interacting with outsiders

The "average" manager spent 32 percent of his or her time in traditional management activities, 29 percent communicating, 20 percent in human resource management activities, and 19 percent networking. However, the time and effort different *individual* managers spent on those activities varied a great deal. As shown in Exhibit 1-2, among managers who were *successful* (defined in terms of speed of promotion within their organization), networking made the largest relative contribution to success, and human resource management activities made the least relative contribution. Among *effective* managers (defined in terms of quantity and quality of their performance and the satisfaction and commitment of employees), communication made the largest relative contribution and networking the least. More recent studies in Australia, Israel, Italy, Japan, and the United States confirm the link between networking and social relationships and success within an organization.[11] And the connection between communication and effective managers is also clear. A study of 410 U.S. managers indicates those who seek information from colleagues and employees—even if it's negative—and who explain their decisions are the most effective.[12]

This research offers important insights. Successful managers give almost the opposite emphases to traditional management, communication, human resource management, and networking as do effective managers. This finding

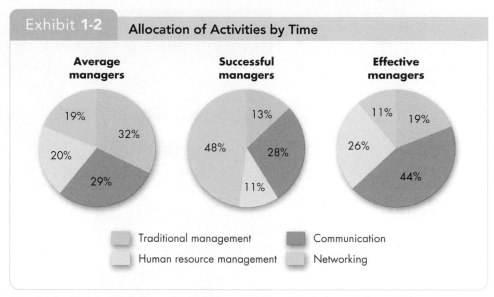

Exhibit **1-2**   Allocation of Activities by Time

Average managers

Successful managers

Effective managers

Traditional management   Communication

Human resource management   Networking

Source: Based on F. Luthans, R. M. Hodgetts, and S. A. Rosenkrantz, *Real Managers* (Cambridge, MA: Ballinger, 1988).

challenges the historical assumption that promotions are based on performance, and it illustrates the importance of networking and political skills in getting ahead in organizations.

A Review of the Manager's Job

One common thread runs through the functions, roles, skills, activities, and approaches to management: Each recognizes the paramount importance of managing people, whether it is called "the leading function," "interpersonal roles," "human skills," or "human resource management, communication, and networking activities." It's clear managers must develop their people skills to be effective and successful.

Enter Organizational Behavior

3   Define *organizational behavior (OB)*.

We've made the case for the importance of people skills. But neither this book nor the discipline on which it is based is called "people skills." The term that is widely used to describe the discipline is *organizational behavior*.

Organizational behavior (often abbreviated OB) is a field of study that investigates the impact that individuals, groups, and structure have on behavior within organizations, for the purpose of applying such knowledge toward improving an organization's effectiveness. That's a mouthful, so let's break it down.

human skills   *The ability to work with, understand, and motivate other people, both individually and in groups.*

conceptual skills   *The mental ability to analyze and diagnose complex situations.*

organizational behavior (OB)   *A field of study that investigates the impact that individuals, groups, and structure have on behavior within organizations, for the purpose of applying such knowledge toward improving an organization's effectiveness.*

Microsoft understands how organizational behavior affects an organization's performance. The company maintains good employee relationships by providing a great work environment, generous benefits, and challenging jobs. The two-story wall painting shown here is one of 4,500 pieces of contemporary art displayed at Microsoft's corporate campus for employees' enjoyment. At Microsoft, employee loyalty and productivity are high, contributing to the company's growth into the largest software company in the world.

Organizational behavior is a field of study, meaning that it is a distinct area of expertise with a common body of knowledge. What does it study? It studies three determinants of behavior in organizations: individuals, groups, and structure. In addition, OB applies the knowledge gained about individuals, groups, and the effect of structure on behavior in order to make organizations work more effectively.

To sum up our definition, OB is the study of what people do in an organization and how their behavior affects the organization's performance. And because OB is concerned specifically with employment-related situations, you should not be surprised that it emphasizes behavior as related to concerns such as jobs, work, absenteeism, employment turnover, productivity, human performance, and management.

Although debate exists about the relative importance of each, OB includes the core topics of motivation, leader behavior and power, interpersonal communication, group structure and processes, learning, attitude development and perception, change processes, conflict, work design, and work stress.[13]

Complementing Intuition with Systematic Study

4 Show the value to OB of systematic study.

Each of us is a student of behavior. Whether you've explicitly thought about it before, you've been "reading" people almost all your life, watching their actions and trying to interpret what you see or predict what people might do under different conditions. Unfortunately, the casual or common sense approach to reading others can often lead to erroneous predictions. However, you can improve your predictive ability by supplementing intuition with a more systematic approach.

The systematic approach in this book will uncover important facts and relationships and provide a base from which to make more accurate predictions of behavior. Underlying this systematic approach is the belief that behavior is not random. Rather, we can identify fundamental consistencies underlying the behavior of all individuals and modify them to reflect individual differences.

Myth or Science?

"Preconceived Notions versus Substantive Evidence"

Assume you signed up to take an introductory college course in finance. On the first day of class, your instructor asks you to answer this question: "What is the net present value at a discount rate of 12 percent per year of an investment made by spending $1,000,000 this year on a portfolio of stocks, with an initial dividend next year of $100,000 and an expected rate of dividend growth thereafter of 4 percent per year?" It's unlikely you'd be able to answer without some instruction in finance.

Now, change the scenario. You're in an introductory course in organizational behavior. On the first day of class, your instructor asks you the following: "What's the most effective way to motivate employees at work?" After a little thought you'd likely have no problem coming up with suggestions on motivation.

That's one of the main challenges of teaching, or taking, a course in OB. We enter with a lot of *preconceived notions* we accept as *facts.*[14] In contrast to many other disciplines, OB not only introduces a comprehensive set of concepts and theories; it also has to deal with commonly accepted "facts" about human behavior and organizations we've all acquired over the years, like "You can't teach an old dog new tricks," "Leaders are born, not made," and "Two heads are better than one." But these "facts" aren't necessarily true. So one of the objectives of a course in organizational behavior is to *replace* them with science-based conclusions.

As you'll see in this book, the field of OB is built on decades of research. In boxes titled "Myth or Science?" we call your attention to some of the most popular notions or myths about organizational behavior and show how OB research has disproved or, in some cases, proved them. They'll help remind you that the study of human behavior at work is a science and that you need to be vigilant about "seat-of-the-pants" explanations of work-related behaviors.

These fundamental consistencies are very important. Why? Because they allow predictability. Behavior is generally predictable, and the *systematic study* of behavior is a means to making reasonably accurate predictions. When we use the term **systematic study**, we mean looking at relationships, attempting to attribute causes and effects, and basing our conclusions on scientific evidence—that is, on data gathered under controlled conditions and measured and interpreted in a reasonably rigorous manner. (See Appendix A for a basic review of research methods used in studies of organizational behavior.)

Evidence-based management (EBM) complements systematic study by basing managerial decisions on the best available scientific evidence. For example, we want doctors to make decisions about patient care based on the latest available evidence, and EBM argues that managers should do the same, becoming more scientific in how they think about management problems. For example, a manager might pose a managerial question, search for the best available evidence, and apply the relevant information to the question or case at hand. You might think it difficult to argue against this (what manager would say decisions shouldn't be based on evidence?), but the vast majority of management decisions are still made "on the fly," with little or systematic study of available evidence.[15]

Systematic study and EBM add to **intuition**, or those "gut feelings" about what makes others (and ourselves) "tick." Of course, the things you have come to believe

---

systematic study   *Looking at relationships, attempting to attribute causes and effects, and drawing conclusions based on scientific evidence.*

evidence-based management (EBM)   *The basing of managerial decisions on the best available scientific evidence.*

intuition   *A gut feeling not necessarily supported by research.*

in an unsystematic way are not necessarily incorrect. Jack Welch (former CEO of GE) noted, "The trick, of course, is to know when to go with your gut." But if we make *all* decisions with intuition or gut instinct, we're likely working with incomplete information—like making an investment decision with only half the data.

Relying on intuition is made worse because we tend to overestimate the accuracy of what we think we know. In a recent survey, 86 percent of managers thought their organization was treating their employees well, but only 55 percent of the employees thought so. Surveys of human resource managers have also shown many managers hold "common sense" opinions regarding effective management that have been flatly refuted by empirical evidence.

We find a similar problem in chasing the business and popular media for management wisdom. The business press tends to be dominated by fads. As a writer for *The New Yorker* put it, "Every few years, new companies succeed, and they are scrutinized for the underlying truths they might reveal. But often there is no underlying truth; the companies just happened to be in the right place at the right time."[16] Although we try to avoid it, we might also fall into this trap. It's not that the business press stories are all wrong; it's that without a systematic approach, it's hard to separate the wheat from the chaff.

We're not advising that you throw your intuition, or all the business press, out the window. Nor are we arguing that research is always right. Researchers make mistakes, too. What we are advising is to use evidence as much as possible to inform your intuition and experience. That is the promise of OB.

Disciplines That Contribute to the OB Field

5 Identify the major behavioral science disciplines that contribute to OB.

Organizational behavior is an applied behavioral science built on contributions from a number of behavioral disciplines, mainly psychology and social psychology, sociology, and anthropology. Psychology's contributions have been mainly at the individual or micro level of analysis, while the other disciplines have contributed to our understanding of macro concepts such as group processes and organization. Exhibit 1-3 is an overview of the major contributions to the study of organizational behavior.

Psychology

Psychology seeks to measure, explain, and sometimes change the behavior of humans and other animals. Those who have contributed and continue to add to the knowledge of OB are learning theorists, personality theorists, counseling psychologists, and, most important, industrial and organizational psychologists.

Early industrial/organizational psychologists studied the problems of fatigue, boredom, and other working conditions that could impede efficient work performance. More recently, their contributions have expanded to include learning, perception, personality, emotions, training, leadership effectiveness, needs and motivational forces, job satisfaction, decision-making processes, performance appraisals, attitude measurement, employee-selection techniques, work design, and job stress.

Social Psychology

Social psychology, generally considered a branch of psychology, blends concepts from both psychology and sociology to focus on peoples' influence on one another. One major study area is *change*—how to implement it and how to reduce barriers to its acceptance. Social psychologists also contribute to measuring, un-

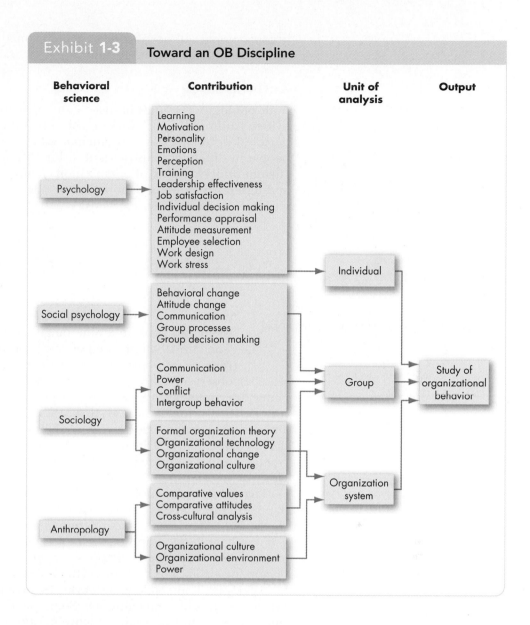

Exhibit 1-3   **Toward an OB Discipline**

Behavioral science	Contribution	Unit of analysis	Output
Psychology	Learning Motivation Personality Emotions Perception Training Leadership effectiveness Job satisfaction Individual decision making Performance appraisal Attitude measurement Employee selection Work design Work stress	Individual	Study of organizational behavior
Social psychology	Behavioral change Attitude change Communication Group processes Group decision making	Group	
Sociology	Communication Power Conflict Intergroup behavior	Group	
	Formal organization theory Organizational technology Organizational change Organizational culture	Organization system	
Anthropology	Comparative values Comparative attitudes Cross-cultural analysis	Organization system	
	Organizational culture Organizational environment Power		

derstanding, and changing attitudes; identifying communication patterns; and building trust. Finally, they have made important contributions to our study of group behavior, power, and conflict.

Sociology

While psychology focuses on the individual, **sociology** studies people in relation to their social environment or culture. Sociologists have contributed to OB through their study of group behavior in organizations, particularly formal and complex organizations. Perhaps most important, sociologists have studied

psychology *The science that seeks to measure, explain, and sometimes change the behavior of humans and other animals.*

social psychology *An area of psychology that blends concepts from psychology and sociology and that focuses on the influence of people on one another.*

sociology *The study of people in relation to their social environment or culture.*

organizational culture, formal organization theory and structure, organizational technology, communications, power, and conflict.

Anthropology

Anthropology is the study of societies to learn about human beings and their activities. Anthropologists' work on cultures and environments has helped us understand differences in fundamental values, attitudes, and behavior between people in different countries and within different organizations. Much of our current understanding of organizational culture, organizational environments, and differences among national cultures is a result of the work of anthropologists or those using their methods.

There Are Few Absolutes in OB

6 Demonstrate why few absolutes apply to OB.

Laws in the physical sciences—chemistry, astronomy, physics—are consistent and apply in a wide range of situations. They allow scientists to generalize about the pull of gravity or to be confident about sending astronauts into space to repair satellites. But as a noted behavioral researcher observed, "God gave all the easy problems to the physicists." Human beings are complex, and few, if any, simple and universal principles explain organizational behavior. Because we are not alike, our ability to make simple, accurate, and sweeping generalizations is limited. Two people often act very differently in the same situation, and the same person's behavior changes in different situations. Not everyone is motivated by money, and people may behave differently at a religious service than they do at a party.

That doesn't mean, of course, that we can't offer reasonably accurate explanations of human behavior or make valid predictions. It does mean that OB concepts must reflect situational, or contingency, conditions. We can say *x* leads to *y*, but only under conditions specified in *z*—the **contingency variables**. The science of OB was developed by applying general concepts to a particular situation, person, or group. For example, OB scholars would avoid stating that everyone likes complex and challenging work (the general concept). Why? Because not everyone wants a challenging job. Some people prefer routine over varied, or simple over complex. A job attractive to one person may not be to another; its appeal is contingent on the person who holds it.

As you proceed through this book, you'll encounter a wealth of research-based theories about how people behave in organizations. But don't expect to find a lot of straightforward cause-and-effect relationships. There aren't many! Organizational behavior theories mirror the subject matter with which they deal, and people are complex and complicated.

Challenges and Opportunities for OB

7 Identify the challenges and opportunities managers have in applying OB concepts.

Understanding organizational behavior has never been more important for managers. Take a quick look at the dramatic changes in organizations. The typical employee is getting older; more women and people of color are in the workplace; corporate downsizing and the heavy use of temporary workers are severing the bonds of loyalty that

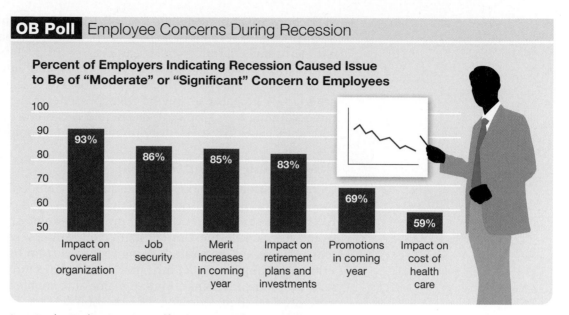

Source: Based on "Employee Concerns," *Workforce Management* (February 16, 2009), p. 17.

tied many employees to their employers; and global competition requires employees to become more flexible and cope with rapid change. The global recession has brought to the forefront the challenges of working with and managing people during uncertain times.

In short, today's challenges bring opportunities for managers to use OB concepts. In this section, we review some of the most critical issues confronting managers for which OB offers solutions—or at least meaningful insights toward solutions.

Responding to Economic Pressures

When the U.S. economy plunged into a deep and prolonged recession in 2008, virtually all other large economies around the world followed suit. Layoffs and job losses were widespread, and those who survived the ax were often asked to accept pay cuts.

During difficult economic times, effective management is often at a premium. Anybody can run a company when business is booming because the difference between good and bad management reflects the difference between making a lot of money and making a lot more money. When times are bad, though, managers are on the front lines with employees who must be fired, who are asked to make due with less, and who worry about their futures. The difference between good and bad management can be the difference between profit and loss or, ultimately, between survival and failure.

Consider Enterprise Rent-A-Car. The company prided itself on never having laid off a U.S. employee in its 51-year history. Even in the 2001–2002 recession after the 9/11 terrorist attacks, Enterprise kept hiring. In 2008–2009, however, Enterprise was forced to lay off more than a thousand employees. "These types

anthropology   *The study of societies to learn about human beings and their activities.*

contingency variables   *Situational factors: variables that moderate the relationship between two or more variables.*

of declines are unprecedented," said Patrick Farrell, Enterprise's vice president of corporate responsibility. Gentex Corp, a Michigan-based auto parts supplier, had never had a layoff in its 34-year history—until 2008–2009. "We didn't even have a layoff policy," said Gentex's vice-president of human resources.[17]

Managing employees well when times are tough is just as hard as when times are good—if not more so. But the OB approaches sometimes differ. In good times, understanding how to reward, satisfy, and retain employees is at a premium. In bad times, issues like stress, decision making, and coping come to the fore.

Responding to Globalization

Organizations are no longer constrained by national borders. Burger King is owned by a British firm, and McDonald's sells hamburgers in Moscow. ExxonMobil, a so-called U.S. company, receives almost 75 percent of its revenues from sales outside the United States. New employees at Finland-based phone maker Nokia are increasingly being recruited from India, China, and other developing countries—non-Finns now outnumber Finns at Nokia's renowned research center in Helsinki. And all major automobile makers now manufacture cars outside their borders; Honda builds cars in Ohio, Ford in Brazil, Volkswagen in Mexico, and both Mercedes and BMW in South Africa.

The world has become a global village. In the process, the manager's job has changed.

Increased Foreign Assignments   If you're a manager, you are increasingly likely to find yourself in a foreign assignment—transferred to your employer's operating division or subsidiary in another country. Once there, you'll have to manage a workforce very different in needs, aspirations, and attitudes from those you are used to back home.

Working with People from Different Cultures   Even in your own country, you'll find yourself working with bosses, peers, and other employees born and raised in different cultures. What motivates you may not motivate them. Or your

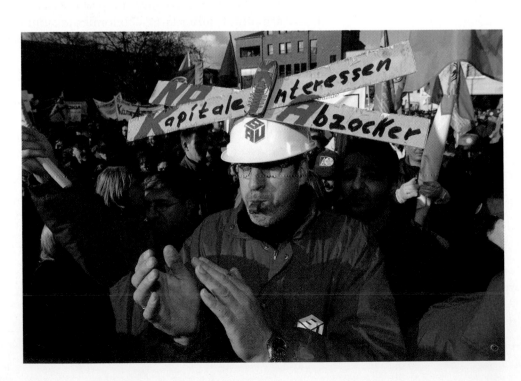

In the global economy, jobs tend to shift from developed nations to countries where lower labor costs provide firms with a comparative advantage. In this photo, an employee wearing a sign on his head reading "Capital Interests" joins fellow workers at a Nokia factory in Germany to protest the company's management decision to terminate production of mobile phones at the plant, resulting in the loss of 2,300 jobs. Nokia announced plans to shift production from Germany to a factory in Romania, where labor costs are lower.

communication style may be straightforward and open, which others may find uncomfortable and threatening. To work effectively with people from different cultures, you need to understand how their culture, geography, and religion have shaped them and how to adapt your management style to their differences.

Managers at global companies such as McDonald's, Disney, and Coca-Cola have come to realize that economic values are not universally transferable. Management practices need to be modified to reflect the values of the different countries in which an organization operates.

Overseeing Movement of Jobs to Countries with Low-Cost Labor It's increasingly difficult for managers in advanced nations, where minimum wages are typically $6 or more an hour, to compete against firms that rely on workers from China and other developing nations where labor is available for 30 cents an hour. It's not by chance that many in the United States wear clothes made in China, work on computers whose microchips came from Taiwan, and watch movies filmed in Canada. In a global economy, jobs tend to flow where lower costs give businesses a comparative advantage, though labor groups, politicians, and local community leaders see the exporting of jobs as undermining the job market at home. Managers face the difficult task of balancing the interests of their organization with their responsibilities to the communities in which they operate.

Managing Workforce Diversity

One of the most important challenges for organizations is adapting to people who are different. We describe this challenge as *workforce diversity*. Whereas globalization focuses on differences among people *from* different countries, workforce diversity addresses differences among people *within* given countries.

Workforce diversity acknowledges a workforce of women and men; many racial and ethnic groups; individuals with a variety of physical or psychological abilities; and people who differ in age and sexual orientation. Managing this diversity is a global concern. Most European countries have experienced dramatic growth in immigration from the Middle East; Argentina and Venezuela host a significant number of migrants from other South American countries; and nations from India to Iraq to Indonesia find great cultural diversity within their borders.

The most significant change in the U.S. labor force during the last half of the twentieth century was the rapid increase in the number of female workers. In 1950, for instance, only 29.6 percent of the workforce was female. By 2008, it was 46.5 percent. The first half of the twenty-first century will be notable for changes in racial and ethnic composition and an aging baby boom generation. By 2050, Hispanics will grow from today's 11 percent of the workforce to 24 percent, blacks will increase from 12 to 14 percent, and Asians will increase from 5 to 11 percent. Meanwhile, in the near term the labor force will be aging. The 55-and-older age group, currently 13 percent of the labor force, will increase to 20 percent by 2014.

Though we have more to say about workforce diversity in the next chapter, suffice it to say here that it presents great opportunities and poses challenging

workforce diversity *The concept that organizations are becoming more heterogeneous in terms of gender, age, race, ethnicity, sexual orientation, and inclusion of other diverse groups.*

questions for managers and employees in all countries. How can we leverage differences within groups for competitive advantage? Should we treat all employees alike? Should we recognize individual and cultural differences? How can we foster cultural awareness in employees without lapsing into political correctness? What are the legal requirements in each country? Does diversity even matter?

Improving Customer Service

American Express recently turned Joan Weinbel's worst nightmare into a non-event. It was 10:00 P.M. Joan was home in New Jersey, packing for a weeklong trip, when she suddenly realized she had left her AmEx Gold card at a restaurant in New York City earlier in the evening. The restaurant was 30 miles away. She had a flight to catch at 7:30 the next morning, and she wanted her card for the trip. She called American Express. The phone was quickly answered by a courteous and helpful AmEx customer service representative who told Ms. Weinbel not to worry. He asked her a few questions and told her "Help is on the way." To say Joan was flabbergasted when her doorbell rang at 11:45 P.M. is an understatement—it was less than 2 hours after her call. At the door was a courier with a new card. How the company was able to produce the card and get it to her so quickly still puzzles Joan, but she said the experience made her a customer for life.

Today, the majority of employees in developed countries work in service jobs, including 80 percent in the United States. In Australia, 73 percent work in service industries. In the United Kingdom, Germany, and Japan, the percentages are 69, 68, and 65, respectively. Service jobs include technical support representatives, fast-food counter workers, sales clerks, waiters and waitresses, nurses, automobile repair technicians, consultants, credit representatives, financial planners, and flight attendants. The common characteristic of these jobs is substantial interaction with an organization's customers. And because an organization can't exist without customers—whether it is American Express, L.L. Bean, a law firm, a museum, a school, or a government agency—management needs to ensure employees do what it takes to please customers.[18] At Patagonia—a retail outfitter for climbers, mountain bikers, skiers and boarders, and other outdoor fanatics—customer service is the store manager's most important general responsibility: "Instill in your employees the meaning and importance of customer service as outlined in the retail philosophy, 'Our store is a place where the word "no" does not exist'; empower staff to 'use their best judgment' in all customer service matters."[19] OB can help managers at Patagonia achieve this goal and, more generally, can contribute to improving an organization's performance by showing managers how employee attitudes and behavior are associated with customer satisfaction.

Many an organization has failed because its employees failed to please customers. Management needs to create a customer-responsive culture. OB can provide considerable guidance in helping managers create such cultures—in which employees are friendly and courteous, accessible, knowledgeable, prompt in responding to customer needs, and willing to do what's necessary to please the customer.[20]

Improving People Skills

As you proceed through the chapters of this book, we'll present relevant concepts and theories that can help you explain and predict the behavior of people at work. In addition, you'll gain insights into specific people skills that you can use on the job. For instance, you'll learn ways to design motivating jobs, techniques for improving your listening skills, and how to create more effective teams.

The Ritz Carlton Hotel Company is recognized worldwide as the gold standard of the hospitality industry. Its motto—"We are ladies and gentlemen serving ladies and gentlemen"—is exemplified by the employee shown here serving a guest on the summer terrace at the Ritz-Carlton Moscow. The Ritz-Carlton's customer-responsive culture, which is articulated in the company's motto, credo, and service values, is designed to build strong relationships that create guests for life.

Stimulating Innovation and Change

Whatever happened to Montgomery Ward, Woolworth, Smith Corona, TWA, Bethlehem Steel, and WorldCom? All these giants went bust. Why have other giants, such as General Motors, Sears, Boeing, and Lucent Technologies, implemented huge cost-cutting programs and eliminated thousands of jobs? The answer is to avoid going broke.

Today's successful organizations must foster innovation and master the art of change, or they'll become candidates for extinction. Victory will go to the organizations that maintain their flexibility, continually improve their quality, and beat their competition to the marketplace with a constant stream of innovative products and services. Domino's single-handedly brought on the demise of small pizza parlors whose managers thought they could continue doing what they had been doing for years. Amazon.com is putting a lot of independent bookstores out of business as it proves you can successfully sell books (and most anything else) from a Web site. After years of lackluster performance, Boeing realized it needed to change its business model. The result was its 787 Dreamliner and a return to being the world's largest airplane manufacturer.

An organization's employees can be the impetus for innovation and change, or they can be a major stumbling block. The challenge for managers is to stimulate their employees' creativity and tolerance for change. The field of OB provides a wealth of ideas and techniques to aid in realizing these goals.

Coping with "Temporariness"

Globalization, expanded capacity, and advances in technology have required organizations to be fast and flexible if they are to survive. The result is that most managers and employees today work in a climate best characterized as "temporary."

Workers must continually update their knowledge and skills to perform new job requirements. Production employees at companies such as Caterpillar, Ford, and Alcoa now need to operate computerized production equipment. That was not part of their job descriptions 20 years ago. In the past, employees were assigned to a specific work group, gaining a considerable amount of security working with the same people day in and day out. That predictability has been replaced by temporary work groups, with members from different departments, and the increased use of employee rotation to fill constantly changing work assignments. Finally, organizations themselves are in a state of flux. They continually reorganize their various divisions, sell off poorly performing businesses, downsize operations, subcontract noncritical services and operations to other organizations, and replace permanent employees with temporary workers.

Today's managers and employees must learn to cope with temporariness, flexibility, spontaneity, and unpredictability. The study of OB can help you better understand a work world of continual change, overcome resistance to change, and create an organizational culture that thrives on change.

Working in Networked Organizations

Networked organizations allow people to communicate and work together even though they may be thousands of miles apart. Independent contractors can telecommute via computer to workplaces around the globe and change employers as the demand for their services changes. Software programmers, graphic designers, systems analysts, technical writers, photo researchers, book and media editors, and medical transcribers are just a few examples of people who can work from home or other non-office locations.

The manager's job is different in a networked organization. Motivating and leading people and making collaborative decisions online requires different techniques than when individuals are physically present in a single location. As more employees do their jobs by linking to others through networks, managers must develop new skills. OB can provide valuable insights to help with honing those skills.

Helping Employees Balance Work–Life Conflicts

The typical employee in the 1960s or 1970s showed up at a specified workplace Monday through Friday and worked for clearly defined 8- or 9-hour chunks of time. That's no longer true for a large segment of today's workforce. Employees are increasingly complaining that the line between work and nonwork time has become blurred, creating personal conflicts and stress.[21] At the same time, today's workplace presents opportunities for workers to create and structure their roles.

How do work–life conflicts come about? First, the creation of global organizations means the world never sleeps. At any time on any day, thousands of General Electric employees are working somewhere. The need to consult with colleagues or customers eight or ten time zones away means many employees of global firms are "on call" 24 hours a day. Second, communication technology allows many technical and professional employees to do their work at home, in their cars, or on the beach in Tahiti—but it also means many feel like they never really get away from the office. Third, organizations are asking employees to put in longer hours. Over a recent 10-year period, the average U.S. workweek increased from 43 to 47 hours; and the number of people working 50 or more hours a week jumped from 24 to 37 percent. Finally, the rise of the dual-career couple makes it difficult for married employees to find time to fulfill commitments to home, spouse, children, parents, and friends. Millions of single-parent households and employees with dependent parents have even more significant challenges in balancing work and family responsibilities.

Employees increasingly recognize that work infringes on their personal lives, and they're not happy about it. Recent studies suggest employees want jobs that give them flexibility in their work schedules so they can better manage work–life

In response to the increasing prevalence of adoption in the United States, more and more organizations are offering adoption benefits to employees. At Bank of America–Merrill Lynch, adoption assistance is part of an extensive program of work/life benefits. Merrill Lynch employee Keli Tuschman and her husband are shown here with their adopted daughter from China. Creating a family-friendly workplace helps Bank of America–Merrill Lynch attract and retain a motivated workforce.

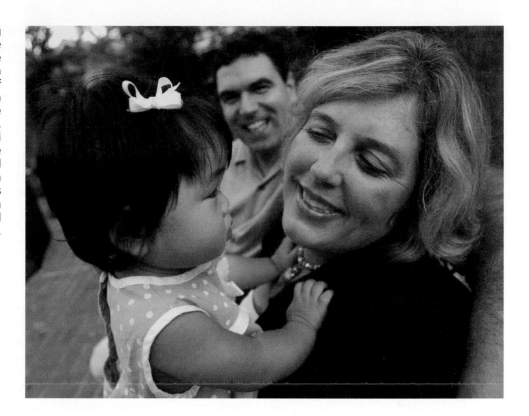

conflicts.[22] In fact, balancing work and life demands now surpasses job security as an employee priority.[23] The next generation of employees is likely to show similar concerns.[24] Most college and university students say attaining a balance between personal life and work is a primary career goal; they want "a life" as well as a job. Organizations that don't help their people achieve work–life balance will find it increasingly difficult to attract and retain the most capable and motivated employees.

As you'll see in later chapters, the field of OB offers a number of suggestions to guide managers in designing workplaces and jobs that can help employees deal with work–life conflicts.

Creating a Positive Work Environment

Although competitive pressures on most organizations are stronger than ever, some organizations are trying to realize a competitive advantage by fostering a positive work environment. Jeff Immelt and Jim McNerney, both disciples of Jack Welch, have tried to maintain high-performance expectations (a characteristic of GE's culture) while fostering a positive work environment in their organizations (GE and Boeing). "In this time of turmoil and cynicism about business, you need to be passionate, positive leaders," Mr. Immelt recently told his top managers.

A real growth area in OB research is **positive organizational scholarship** (also called *positive organizational behavior*), which studies how organizations develop

positive organizational scholarship   *An area of OB research that concerns how organizations develop human strength, foster vitality and resilience, and unlock potential.*

human strengths, foster vitality and resilience, and unlock potential. Researchers in this area say too much of OB research and management practice has been targeted toward identifying what's wrong with organizations and their employees. In response, they try to study what's *good* about them.[25] Some key independent variables in positive OB research are engagement, hope, optimism, and resilience in the face of strain.

Positive organizational scholars have studied a concept called "reflected best-self"—asking employees to think about when they were at their "personal best" in order to understand how to exploit their strengths. The idea is that we all have things at which we are unusually good, yet too often we focus on addressing our limitations and too rarely think about how to exploit our strengths.[26]

Although positive organizational scholarship does not deny the value of the negative (such as critical feedback), it does challenge researchers to look at OB through a new lens and pushes organizations to exploit employees' strengths rather than dwell on their limitations.

Improving Ethical Behavior

In an organizational world characterized by cutbacks, expectations of increasing productivity, and tough competition, it's not surprising many employees feel pressured to cut corners, break rules, and engage in other questionable practices.

Increasingly they face **ethical dilemmas** and **ethical choices**, in which they are required to identify right and wrong conduct. Should they "blow the whistle" if they uncover illegal activities in their company? Do they follow orders with which they don't personally agree? Should they give an inflated performance evaluation to an employee they like, knowing it could save that employee's job? Do they "play politics" to advance their career?

What constitutes good ethical behavior has never been clearly defined, and, in recent years, the line differentiating right from wrong has blurred. Employees see people all around them engaging in unethical practices—elected officials pad expense accounts or take bribes; corporate executives inflate profits so they can cash in lucrative stock options; and university administrators look the other way when winning coaches encourage scholarship athletes to take easy courses. When caught, these people give excuses such as "Everyone does it" or "You have to seize every advantage nowadays." Determining the ethically correct way to behave is especially difficult in a global economy because different cultures have different perspectives on certain ethical issues.[27] Fair treatment of employees in an economic downturn varies considerably across cultures, for instance. As we'll see in Chapter 2, perceptions of religious, ethnic, and gender diversity differ across countries. Is it any wonder employees are expressing decreased confidence in management and increasing uncertainty about what is appropriate ethical behavior in their organizations?[28]

Managers and their organizations are responding to the problem of unethical behavior in a number of ways.[29] They're writing and distributing codes of ethics to guide employees through ethical dilemmas. They're offering seminars, workshops, and other training programs to try to improve ethical behaviors. They're providing in-house advisors who can be contacted, in many cases anonymously, for assistance in dealing with ethical issues, and they're creating protection mechanisms for employees who reveal internal unethical practices.

Today's manager must create an ethically healthy climate for his or her employees, where they can do their work productively with minimal ambiguity about what right and wrong behaviors are. Companies that promote a strong ethical mission, encourage employees to behave with integrity, and provide strong ethical leadership can influence employee decisions to behave ethically.[30] In upcoming chapters, we'll discuss the actions managers can take to create an ethically healthy climate and help employees sort through ethically ambiguous situations.

An Ethical Choice

Statistics Can Lie!

Although a major theme of this chapter—and this book—is that evidence can help you be a better manager, evidence is not perfect. For example, people can manipulate numbers to suit their purpose or confirm their bias.

Sometimes statistics lie because the information is purposely manipulated or distorted. We might show that Republicans report more satisfaction with their sex lives than Democrats, or that a majority of white collar criminals come from New York and California. While both statistics are true, they are misleading because the real cause of the difference is not what is implied (men are more likely to report high satisfaction with sex and are also more likely to be Republican).

Sometimes the problem is interpretation. One report tells us workplace crime is up; another says it's down. A close look reveals that while incidents of workplace violence like murder and assault are down, theft is up.

So what *should* you do?

1. **Use evidence, but be an active consumer.** Evidence is crucial to making effective management decisions. But realize that evidence is created, and it often is not independent of its creator. Ask questions not only about the data but also about how it was gathered. Consider other sources. The questioning mind has a way of getting to the bottom of things.
2. **Be fair and balanced yourself.** You will often be in the position of compiling and producing evidence yourself. Try your best to be fair and unbiased. If there are two sides to an argument, present evidence for both. For example, people in favor of tax increases on the wealthy point out that income inequality (the gap between the rich and the poor) is rising. Those on the side of tax cuts like to counter that the richest 1 percent to 5 percent pay a higher percentage of the total federal income taxes collected than they ever have. Both are right.
3. **Don't give up.** Because numbers can lie (or mislead), we are often tempted to throw in the towel and go back to wholesale reliance on intuition and experience. Remember, evidence is very valuable, which is also the reason it's so often manipulated.

Source: Based on B. Gewen, "What Are the Odds a Handy, Quotable Statistic Is Lying? Better Than Even," *New York Times* (February 3, 2009), p. C6.

We'll also present ethical-dilemma exercises at the end of each chapter that allow you to think through ethical issues and assess how you would handle them.

Coming Attractions: Developing an OB Model

8   Compare the three levels of analysis in this book's OB model.

We conclude this chapter by presenting a general model that defines the field of OB, stakes out its parameters, and identifies its primary dependent and independent variables. The result will be "coming attractions" of the topics in the remainder of this book.

An Overview

A **model** is an abstraction of reality, a simplified representation of some real-world phenomenon. Exhibit 1-4 presents the skeleton on which we will construct our OB

ethical dilemmas and ethical choices   *Situations in which individuals are required to define right and wrong conduct.*

model   *An abstraction of reality. A simplified representation of some real-world phenomenon.*

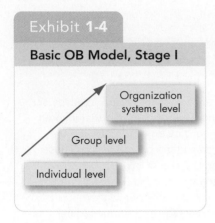

Exhibit 1-4

Basic OB Model, Stage I

model. It proposes three levels of analysis, each constructed on the preceding like building blocks. As we move from the individual level to the organization systems level, we systematically add to our understanding of behavior in organizations. Group concepts grow out of the foundation laid in the individual section; we overlay structural constraints on the individual and group to arrive at organizational behavior.

The Dependent Variables

A **dependent variable** is the key factor that you want to explain or predict and that is affected by some other factor. What are the primary dependent variables in OB? Scholars have emphasized productivity, absenteeism, turnover, and job satisfaction. More recently, deviant workplace behavior and organizational citizenship behavior have been added. We'll briefly discuss each.

Productivity   An organization is productive if it achieves its goals by transforming inputs into outputs at the lowest cost. Thus **productivity** requires both **effectiveness** and **efficiency**.

A hospital is *effective* when it successfully meets the needs of its clientele. It is *efficient* when it can do so at a low cost. If a hospital manages to achieve higher output from its present staff by reducing the average number of days a patient is confined to bed or increasing the number of staff–patient contacts per day, we say the hospital has gained productive efficiency. A business firm is effective when it attains its sales or market share goals, but its productivity also depends on achieving those goals efficiently. Popular measures of organizational efficiency include return on investment, profit per dollar of sales, and output per hour of labor.

We also can look at productivity from the perspective of the individual employee. Mike and Al are both long-distance truckers. If Mike is supposed to haul his fully loaded rig from New York to Los Angeles in 75 hours or less, he is effective if he makes the 3,000-mile trip within that time period. But measures of productivity must take into account the costs incurred in reaching the goal. That's where efficiency comes in. Let's assume that, with identical rigs and loads, Mike made the New York to Los Angeles run in 68 hours and averaged 7 miles per gallon. Al, however, made it in 68 hours also but averaged 9 miles per gallon. Both Mike and Al were effective—they accomplished their goal—but Al was more efficient than Mike because his rig consumed less gas, and therefore he achieved his goal at lower cost.

Service organizations must include customer needs and requirements in assessing their effectiveness. Why? Because a clear chain of cause and effect runs from employee attitudes and behavior to customer attitudes and behavior to a service organization's productivity. Sears has carefully documented this chain.[31] The company's management found that a 5 percent improvement in employee attitudes leads to a 1.3 percent increase in customer satisfaction, which in turn translates into a 0.5 percent improvement in revenue growth. By training employees to improve the employee–customer interaction, Sears was able to improve customer satisfaction by 4 percent over a 12-month period, generating an estimated $200 million in additional revenues.

In summary, one of OB's major concerns is productivity. We want to know what factors influence the effectiveness and efficiency of individuals, of groups, and of the overall organization.

Absenteeism   **Absenteeism**, the failure to report to work, is a huge cost and disruption to employers. For instance, a recent survey found the average direct cost to U.S. employers of unscheduled absences is $789 per year per employee— and this doesn't include lost productivity or overtime pay or the cost of hiring

Employees of Worthington Industries take part in a lunchtime kickboxing class at the company's fitness center. The class is part of Worthington's employee health and wellness initiative, which helps reduce absenteeism and increase productivity. Worthington also operates an on-site medical center staffed with doctors and nurses. The center helps decrease the time employees spend on doctors' visits and minimizes absenteeism through preventive screenings and wellness programs.

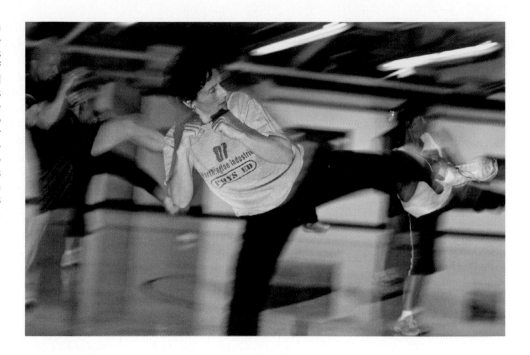

temporary employees to cover for absent workers.[32] Comparable costs in the United Kingdom are also high—approximately $694 per year per employee.[33] In Sweden, an average of 10 percent of the country's workforce is on sick leave at any given time.[34]

It's obviously difficult for an organization to operate smoothly and attain its objectives if employees fail to report to their jobs. The work flow is disrupted, and important decisions may be delayed. In organizations that rely heavily on assembly-line production, absenteeism can be considerably more than a disruption; it can drastically reduce the quality of output or even shut down the facility. Levels of absenteeism beyond the normal range have a direct impact on any organization's effectiveness and efficiency.

Are *all* absences bad? Probably not. In jobs in which an employee must remain alert—surgeons and airline pilots, for example—it may be better for the organization if an ill or fatigued employee does *not* report to work. An accident could be disastrous. But these examples are clearly atypical. For the most part, we can assume organizations benefit when employee absenteeism is low.

Turnover   **Turnover** is voluntary or involuntary permanent withdrawal from an organization. A high turnover rate increases recruiting, selection, and training costs. What are those costs? They're higher than you might think. The price for a typical information technology company in the United States to replace a programmer or systems analyst is about $34,100; to replace a lost sales clerk costs a retail store about $10,445.[35] A high rate of turnover can also disrupt the efficient running of an organization when knowledgeable and experienced personnel leave and replacements must be found to assume positions of responsibility.

dependent variable   *A response that is affected by an independent variable.*

productivity   *A performance measure that includes effectiveness and efficiency.*

effectiveness   *Achievement of goals.*

efficiency   *The ratio of effective output to the input required to achieve it.*

absenteeism   *The failure to report to work.*

turnover   *Voluntary and involuntary permanent withdrawal from an organization.*

All organizations, of course, have some turnover. The U.S. national turnover rate averages about 3 percent per month, about a 36 percent turnover per year. This average varies a lot by occupation, of course; the monthly turnover rate for government jobs is less than 1 percent versus 5 to 7 percent in the construction industry.[36] If the "right" people are leaving the organization—the marginal and submarginal employees—turnover can actually be positive. It can create an opportunity to replace an underperforming individual with someone who has higher skills or motivation, open up increased opportunities for promotions, and bring new and fresh ideas to the organization.[37] In today's changing world of work, reasonable levels of employee-initiated turnover improve organizational flexibility and employee independence, and they can lessen the need for management-initiated layoffs.

But turnover often costs the organization people it doesn't want to lose. One study covering 900 employees who resigned from their jobs found 92 percent had earned performance ratings of "satisfactory" or better from their superiors.[38] So when turnover is excessive, or when it involves valuable performers, it can be a disruptive factor that hinders the organization's effectiveness.

Deviant Workplace Behavior   Given the cost of absenteeism and turnover to employers, more OB researchers are studying these behaviors as indicators or markers of deviant behavior. Deviance can range from playing music too loudly to violence. Managers need to understand this wide range of behaviors to address any form of employee dissatisfaction. If they don't understand *why* an employee is acting up, the problem will never be solved.

We can define **deviant workplace behavior** (also called *antisocial behavior* or *workplace incivility*) as voluntary behavior that violates significant organizational norms and, in doing so, threatens the well-being of the organization or its members. What are organizational norms in this context? They can be company policies that prohibit certain behaviors such as stealing. They also can be unspoken rules that are widely shared, such as not playing loud music in the workspace. Consider an employee who plays the latest heavy metal album at work with the speakers amped up. Yes, he is showing up at work, but he may not be getting his work done, and he could be irritating coworkers or customers (unless they are hard rock fans themselves), but deviant workplace behaviors can be serious. An employee who insults a colleague, steals, gossips excessively, or engages in sabotage can wreak havoc on an organization.

Managers want to understand the source of workplace deviance so they can avoid a chaotic work environment, and workplace deviance can also have a considerable financial impact. Although the annual costs are hard to quantify, estimates are that deviant behavior costs employers dearly, from $4.2 billion for violence to $7.1 billion for corporate security against cyberattacks to $200 billion for theft.[39]

Deviant workplace behavior is a response to dissatisfaction, and employees express dissatisfaction in many ways. Controlling one behavior may be ineffective unless we get to the root cause.

Organizational Citizenship Behavior   Organizational citizenship behavior (OCB) is discretionary behavior that is not part of an employee's formal job requirements but nevertheless promotes the effective functioning of the organization.[40]

Successful organizations need employees who will do more than their usual job duties—who will provide performance *beyond* expectations. In today's dynamic workplace, where tasks are increasingly performed by teams and flexibility is critical, employees who engage in "good citizenship" behaviors help others on their team, volunteer for extra work, avoid unnecessary conflicts, respect the spirit as well as the letter of rules and regulations, and gracefully tolerate occasional work-related impositions and nuisances.

International OB

Transfer Pricing and International Corporate Deviance

Workplace deviance isn't limited to the harmful behaviors of employees within one location. It can extend across country borders. Consider transfer pricing, which governs the price one part of a company charges another for a product or service. What happens if parts of the company are in different countries?

Tax rates on company profits differ—sometimes greatly—from country to country. Transfer pricing, when used to shift income from high-tax to low-tax countries, can be a deviant corporate policy if abused. One way to increase overall profit—that is, the combined profit of the multinational's headquarters and its subsidiaries—is to take profits in the country with the lower taxes.

Consider a multinational firm whose headquarters sold toothbrushes to a subsidiary for $5,000—each. The subsidiary, with the higher tax of the two, claimed a loss (after all, it paid $5,000 per toothbrush). The multinational firm, with the lower tax, took the profit and paid the tax on it. Because the two firms were part of the same organization, they combined the results of the transaction, and the company made a staggering profit.

Transfer pricing, according to a survey by the international auditing firm Ernst & Young, has become a heated issue among multinational companies. Why? The U.S. Multistate Tax Commission estimated that states were losing almost one-third of their corporate tax income because of the tax-sheltering practices of multinational companies—transfer pricing among them. The U.S. Internal Revenue Service is keeping a watchful eye on international transactions.

Source: Based on "Case of the U.S. $5000 Toothbrush," *Finance Week,* April 27, 2005, pp. 45–46.

Organizations want and need employees who will do things that aren't in any job description. Evidence indicates organizations that have such employees outperform those that don't.[41] As a result, OB is concerned with OCB as a dependent variable.

Job Satisfaction   The final dependent variable we look at is **job satisfaction**, a positive feeling about your job resulting from an evaluation of its characteristics. Unlike the other five variables, job satisfaction represents an attitude rather than a behavior. Why, then, has it become a primary dependent variable? For two reasons: its demonstrated relationship to performance factors and the value preferences held by many OB researchers.

The belief that satisfied employees are more productive than dissatisfied employees has been a basic tenet among managers for years, though only now has research begun to support it.[42] Ample evidence shows employees who are more satisfied and treated fairly are more willing to engage in the above-and-beyond organizational citizenship behavior we've said is so vital in the contemporary business environment.[43] A study of more than 2,500 business units also found those scoring in the top 25 percent on the employee opinion survey were, on average, 4.6 percent *above* their sales budget for the year, while those scoring in the bottom 25 percent were 0.8 percent *below* budget. In real numbers, this was a difference of $104 million in sales per year between the two groups.[44]

We can also argue that advanced societies should be concerned not only with the quantity of life—that is, with higher productivity and material acquisitions—but also with its quality. Researchers with strong humanistic values argue that

---

deviant workplace behavior   *Voluntary behavior that violates significant organizational norms and, in so doing, threatens the well-being of the organization or its members.*

organizational citizenship behavior (OCB)   *Discretionary behavior that is not part of an employee's formal job requirements but that nevertheless promotes the effective functioning of the organization.*

job satisfaction   *A positive feeling about one's job resulting from an evaluation of its characteristics.*

satisfaction is a legitimate objective of an organization. Not only is it negatively related to absenteeism and turnover, but, they say, organizations have a responsibility to provide employees with jobs that are challenging and intrinsically rewarding. Therefore, although job satisfaction is an attitude rather than a behavior, OB researchers typically consider it an important dependent variable.

The Independent Variables

What are the major determinants of productivity, absenteeism, turnover, deviant workplace behavior, OCB, and job satisfaction? Our answer brings us to the **independent variable**, the presumed cause of some change in a dependent variable.

The first level of our model of organizational behavior is individual behavior, so we look at individual-level independent variables first.

Individual-Level Variables   "Managers, unlike parents, must work with used, not new, human beings—human beings whom others have gotten to first."[45] When individuals enter an organization, they are a bit like used cars. Each is different. Some are "low mileage"—they have been treated carefully and have had only limited exposure to the realities of the elements. Others are "well worn," having been driven over some rough roads. This metaphor reflects that people enter organizations with characteristics that influence their behavior at work. The most obvious are personal or biographical characteristics such as age, gender, and marital status; personality characteristics; an inherent emotional framework; values and attitudes; and basic ability levels. There is little management can do to alter these. Yet they have a very real impact on employee behavior. We discuss each of these factors—biographical characteristics, ability, values, attitudes, personality, and emotions—as independent variables in Chapters 2 through 4 and 8.

Four other individual-level variables affect employee behavior: perception, individual decision making, learning, and motivation. We discuss these in Chapters 2, 6, 7, and 8.

Group-Level Variables   The complexity of our model increases when we acknowledge that the behavior of people in groups is more than the sum of all the individuals acting in their own way. Therefore, the next step in understanding OB is the study of group behavior.

Chapter 9 lays the foundation for understanding the dynamics of group behavior and how individuals in groups are influenced by the patterns of behavior they are expected to exhibit, what the group considers acceptable, and the degree to which group members are attracted to each other. Chapter 10 translates our understanding of groups to the design of effective work teams. Chapters 11 through 14 demonstrate how communication patterns, leadership, power and politics, and levels of conflict affect group behavior.

Organization System-Level Variables   Organizational behavior reaches its highest level of sophistication when we add formal structure to our knowledge of individual and group behavior. Just as groups are more than the sum of their individual members, so are organizations more than the sum of their member groups. The design of the formal organization, the organization's internal culture, its human resource policies and practices, and change and stress all have an impact on the dependent variables. We discuss these in detail in Chapters 15 through 18.

Toward a Contingency OB Model

Our final model is shown in Exhibit 1-5. It shows the six key dependent variables and relevant independent variables, organized by level of analysis. This model

Exhibit **1-5**   **Basic OB Model, Stage II**

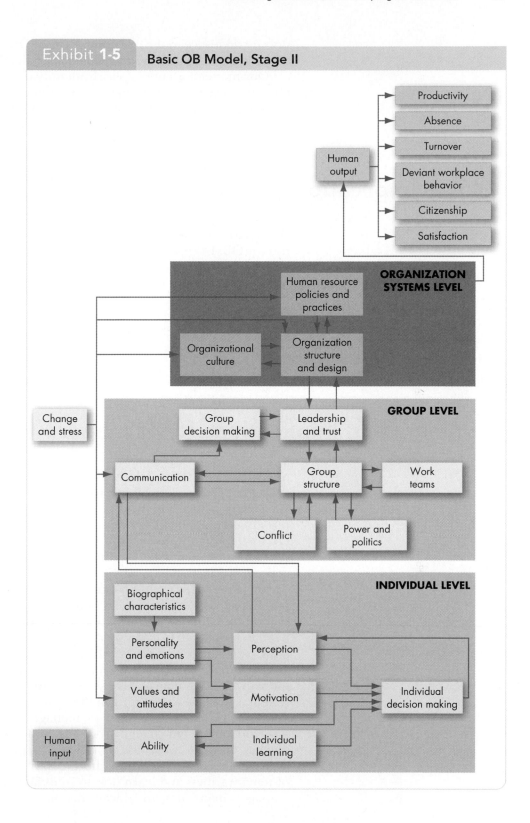

doesn't do justice to the real complexity of OB, but it should guide you through this book and help you to explain and predict the behavior of people at work.

Our model does not explicitly identify the vast number of contingency variables because they would make it too complex to read. Rather, throughout the book we'll introduce the important contingency variables that strengthen the links between the independent and dependent variables.

Global Implications

We've already discussed how globalization presents challenges and opportunities for OB. In every chapter that follows, a section titled "Global Implications" discusses how some of the things we know about OB are affected by cultural differences within and between countries. Most OB research has been conducted in Western cultures (especially the United States). That's changing, however, and compared to even a few years ago, we're now in a much better position to answer the question "How does what we know about OB vary based on culture?" You'll find that some OB principles don't vary much across cultures, and others vary a great deal.

Summary and Implications for Managers

Managers need to develop their interpersonal, or people, skills to be effective in their jobs. Organizational behavior (OB) investigates the impact that individuals, groups, and structure have on behavior within an organization, and it applies that knowledge to make organizations work more effectively. Specifically, OB focuses on how to improve productivity; reduce absenteeism, turnover, and deviant workplace behavior; and increase organizational citizenship behavior and job satisfaction.

Some generalizations provide valid insights into human behavior, but many are erroneous. Organizational behavior uses systematic study to improve predictions of behavior over intuition alone. But because people are different, we need to look at OB in a contingency framework, using situational variables to explain cause-and-effect relationships.

Organizational behavior offers specific insights to improve a manager's people skills. It helps managers to see the value of workforce diversity and practices that may need to be changed in different countries. It can improve quality and employee productivity by showing managers how to empower their people, design and implement change programs, improve customer service, and help employees balance work–life conflicts. It provides suggestions for helping managers meet chronic labor shortages. It can help managers cope in a world of temporariness and learn how to stimulate innovation. Finally, OB can guide managers in creating an ethically healthy work climate.

POINT ⬅➡ COUNTERPOINT

In Search of the Quick Fix

Walk into your nearest major bookstore. You'll undoubtedly find a large section of books devoted to management and managing human behavior. A close look at the titles will reveal there is no shortage of popular books on topics related to organizational behavior. Consider the following popular books on the topic of leadership:

- *The Verbal Judo Way of Leadership* (Looseleaf, 2007)
- *If Harry Potter Ran General Electric: Leadership Wisdom from the World of Wizards* (Currency/Doubleday, 2006)
- *High Altitude Leadership: What the World's Most Forbidding Peaks Teach Us About Success* (Jossey-Bass, 2008)
- *Killing Cockroaches: And Other Scattered Musings on Leadership* (B&H Publishing, 2009)
- *The Leadership Secrets of Santa Claus* (Performance Systems, 2004)
- *Leadership Lessons from a Chef: Finding Time to Be Great* (Wiley, 2008)
- *Leadership Wisdom from the Monk Who Sold His Ferrari* (Hay House, 2003)
- *Leadership 101 for White Men: How to Work Successfully with Black Colleagues and Customers* (Morgan James, 2008)
- *A Pirate Captain's Guide to Leadership* (Lighthouse, 2008)

Organizations are always looking for leaders; and managers and manager-wannabes are continually looking for ways to hone their leadership skills. Publishers respond to this demand by offering hundreds of titles that promise insights into the subject of leadership. Books like these can provide people with the secrets to leadership that others know about. Moreover, isn't it better to learn about management and leadership from people in the trenches, as opposed to the latest esoteric musings from the "Ivory Tower"? Many of the most important insights we gain from life aren't necessarily the product of careful empirical research studies.

Beware the quick fix! We all want to find quick and simple solutions to our complex problems. But here's the bad news: For problems related to organizational behavior, quick and simple solutions are often wrong because they fail to consider the diversity among organizations, situations, and individuals. As Einstein said, "Everything should be made as simple as possible, but not simpler."

When it comes to understanding people at work, there are plenty of simplistic ideas and books and consultants to promote them. And these books aren't just about leadership. Consider three recent bestsellers. *Who Moved My Cheese?* is a metaphor about two mice that is meant to convey the benefits of accepting change. *Fish!* tells how a fish market in Seattle made its jobs more motivating. And *Whale Done!* proposes that managers can learn a lot about motivating people from techniques used by whale trainers at SeaWorld in San Diego. Are the "insights" from these books generalizable to people working in hundreds of different countries, in a thousand different organizations, and doing a million different jobs? It's very unlikely.

Popular books on organizational behavior often have cute titles and are fun to read, but they make the job of managing people seem much simpler than it is. Some are based on the author's opinions rather than substantive research.

Organizational behavior is a complex subject. Few, if any, simple statements about human behavior are generalizable to all people in all situations. Should you really try to apply leadership insights you got from a book about Geronimo or Tony Soprano to managing software engineers in the twenty-first century?

Questions for Review

1 What is the importance of interpersonal skills?

2 What do managers do in terms of functions, roles, and skills?

3 What is organizational behavior (OB)?

4 Why is it important to complement intuition with systematic study?

5 What are the major behavioral science disciplines that contribute to OB?

6 Why are there few absolutes in OB?

7 What are the challenges and opportunities for managers in using OB concepts?

8 What are the three levels of analysis in this book's OB model?

Experiential Exercise

WORKFORCE DIVERSITY

Purpose
To learn about the different needs of a diverse workforce.

Time Required
Approximately 40 minutes.

Participants and Roles
Divide the class into six groups of approximately equal size. Assign each group one of the following roles:

Nancy is 28 years old. The divorced mother of three children ages 3, 5, and 7, she is the department head. She earns $40,000 per year on her job and receives another $3,600 per year in child support from her ex-husband.

Ethel is a 72-year-old widow. She works 25 hours per week at an hourly wage of $8.50 to supplement her $8,000 annual pension and earns a total of $19,000 per year.

John is a 34-year-old born in Trinidad who is now a U.S. resident. He is married and the father of two small children. John attends college at night and is within a year of earning his bachelor's degree. His salary is $27,000 per year. His wife is an attorney and earns approximately $50,000 per year.

Lu is 26 years old and single with a master's degree in education. He is paralyzed and confined to a wheelchair as a result of an auto accident. He earns $32,000 per year.

Maria is a single, 22-year-old woman born and raised in Mexico. She came to the United States only 3 months ago, and her English needs considerable improvement. She earns $20,000 per year.

Mike is a 16-year-old high school sophomore who works 15 hours per week after school and during vacations. He earns $7.20 per hour, or approximately $5,600 per year.

The members of each group are to assume the character consistent with their assigned role.

Background
The six participants work for a company that has recently installed a flexible benefits program. Instead of the traditional "one benefit package fits all," the company is allocating an additional 25 percent of each employee's annual pay to be used for discretionary benefits. Those benefits and their annual cost are as follows:

- Supplementary health care for employee:
  Plan A (no deductible and pays 90 percent) = $3,000
  Plan B ($200 deductible and pays 80 percent) = $2,000
  Plan C ($1,000 deductible and pays 70 percent) = $500
- Supplementary health care for dependents (same deductibles and percentages as above):
  Plan A = $2,000
  Plan B = $1,500
  Plan C = $500
- Supplementary dental plan = $500
- Life insurance:
  Plan A ($25,000 coverage) = $500
  Plan B ($50,000 coverage) = $1,000
  Plan C ($100,000 coverage) = $2,000
  Plan D ($250,000 coverage) = $3,000
- Mental health plan = $500
- Prepaid legal assistance = $300
- Vacation = 2 percent of annual pay for each week, up to 6 weeks a year
- Pension at retirement equal to approximately 50 percent of final annual earnings = $1,500
- 4-day workweek during the 3 summer months (available only to full-time employees) = 4 percent of annual pay

MSN Money, under the headline "Businesses See Rise in Employee Theft," reported the poll results as follows: "When asked if they had noticed a recent rise in monetary theft among employees, such as fraudulent transactions or missing cash, 18% said yes, 41% were unsure and the rest said they hadn't." You'll notice that, put another way, 18 percent agree that theft is up, and 82 percent either disagree or are unsure. But that makes for a less sexy headline.

Another mischief factor is companies that exist to provide services, software, and technology to deter workplace theft. While they might provide a valuable service to the organizations they serve, it is in their interest for employers and the general public to believe incidences of workplace violence and theft are increasing. These companies often produce press releases, which then work their way into the media and presumably generate potential clients for the organizations. One such company, for example, publicizes a study of workplace theft, reporting it has increased each and every year since 2003.

We are not arguing that all business press articles—or all studies done by organizations—are inaccurate. But these examples do illustrate one of the benefits of learning OB:

Put on your investigator hat, ask questions, analyze the situation, and consider the source!

Questions

1. Does this case prove economic downturns and company layoffs *fail* to lead to workplace malfeasance? Why or why not?

2. Does the case prove we can learn nothing from the business press?

3. Does this chapter provide any clues for how you can be an informed consumer of business news on OB issues?

4. Some companies install surveillance equipment (cameras, computer software) to monitor their employees. Valenti Management, which owns and runs 117 Wendy's and 17 Chili's restaurants, has installed fingerprint scanners on all its cash registers. Do you think these measures infringe too much on individual privacy? Can a company take prevention too far? How do you strike a balance between prevention and intrusion?

Sources: Based on J. Bone, "Gunman Kills 13 and Takes 40 Hostage in Upstate New York Town," *The Times* (April 4, 2009), http://www.timesonline.co.uk/tol/news/world/us_and_americas/article6031421.ece; S. E. Needleman, "Businesses Say Theft by Their Workers Is Up," *Wall Street Journal* (December 11, 2008), p. B8; M. Conlin, "To Catch a Corporate Thief," *Business Week* (February 16, 2009), p. 52; P. McGeehan, "Well Educated, and Now Collecting Unemployment," *New York Times* (April 5, 2009), p. Y23; and "Businesses See Rise in Employee Theft," *MSN Money* (December 12, 2008), articles.moneycentral.msn.com/Investing/Extra/businesses-see-rise-in-emplloyee-theft.aspx.

Endnotes

1. E. Saner, "The Future Is Looking Up for Psychics," *The Guardian* (May 5, 2009), p. 2; S. Salerno, "If I Don't See It, It's Not There," *Wall Street Journal* (May 1, 2009), p. W13; R. La Ferla, "Love, Jobs & 401(k)s," *New York Times* (November 21, 2008), pp. ST1, 8–9; and S. Parke, "Cashing in on the Crunch: The Self-Help Gurus Helping Themselves to Your Money," *Mail Online* (April 23, 2009).
2. Cited in R. Alsop, "Playing Well with Others," *Wall Street Journal,* September 9, 2002.
3. See, for instance, C. Penttila, "Hiring Hardships," *Entrepreneur,* October 2002, pp. 34–35.
4. S. E. Humphrey, J. D. Nahrgang, and F. P. Morgeson, "Integrating Motivational, Social, and Contextual Work Design Features: A Meta-Analytic Summary and Theoretical Extension of the Work Design Literature," *Journal of Applied Psychology* 92, no. 5 (2007), pp. 1332–1356.
5. I. S. Fulmer, B. Gerhart, and K. S. Scott, "Are the 100 Best Better? An Empirical Investigation of the Relationship Between Being a 'Great Place to Work' and Firm Performance," *Personnel Psychology,* Winter 2003, pp. 965–993.
6. H. Fayol, *Industrial and General Administration* (Paris: Dunod, 1916).
7. A. I. Kraut, P. R. Pedigo, D. D. McKenna, and M. D. Dunnette, "The Role of the Manager: What's Really Important in Different Management Jobs," *Academy of Management Executive* 19, no. 4 (2005), pp. 122–129.
8. H. Mintzberg, *The Nature of Managerial Work* (Upper Saddle River, NJ: Prentice Hall, 1973).
9. R. L. Katz, "Skills of an Effective Administrator," *Harvard Business Review,* September–October 1974, pp. 90–102; D. Bartram, "The Great Eight Competencies: A Criterion-Centric Approach to Validation," *Journal of Applied Psychology* 90, no. 6 (2005), pp. 1185–1203; and S. E. Scullen, M. K. Mount, and T. A. Judge, "Evidence of the Construct Validity of Developmental Ratings of Managerial Performance," *Journal of Applied Psychology* 88, no. 1 (2003), pp. 50–66.
10. F. Luthans, "Successful vs. Effective Real Managers," *Academy of Management Executive,* May 1988, pp. 127–132; and F. Luthans, R. M. Hodgetts, and S. A. Rosenkrantz, *Real Managers* (Cambridge, MA: Ballinger, 1988). See also F. Shipper and J. Davy, "A Model and Investigation of Managerial Skills, Employees' Attitudes, and Managerial Performance," *Leadership Quarterly* 13 (2002), pp. 95–120.
11. P. Wu, M. Foo, and D. B. Turban, "The Role of Personality in Relationship Closeness, Developer Assistance, and Career Success," *Journal of Vocational Behavior* 73, no. 3 (2008), pp. 440–448; and A. M. Konrad, R. Kashlak, I. Yoshioka, R. Waryszak, and N. Toren, "What Do Managers Like to Do?

A Five-Country Study," *Group & Organization Management*, December 2001, pp. 401–433.

12. A. S. Tsui, S. J. Ashford, L. St. Clair, and K. R. Xin, "Dealing with Discrepant Expectations: Response Strategies and Managerial Effectiveness," *Academy of Management Journal*, December 1995, pp. 1515–1543.

13. See, for instance, C. Heath and S. B. Sitkin, "Big-B Versus Big-O: What Is *Organizational* about Organizational Behavior?" *Journal of Organizational Behavior*, February 2001, pp. 43–58. For a review of what one eminent researcher believes *should* be included in organizational behavior, based on survey data, see J. B. Miner, "The Rated Importance, Scientific Validity, and Practical Usefulness of Organizational Behavior Theories: A Quantitative Review," *Academy of Management Learning & Education*, September 2003, pp. 250–268.

14. See L. A. Burke and J. E. Moore, "A Perennial Dilemma in OB Education: Engaging the Traditional Student," *Academy of Management Learning & Education*, March 2003, pp. 37–52.

15. D. M. Rousseau and S. McCarthy, "Educating Managers from an Evidence-Based Perspective," *Academy of Management Learning & Education* 6, no. 1 (2007), pp. 84–101; and S. L. Rynes, T. L. Giluk, and K. G. Brown, "The Very Separate Worlds of Academic and Practitioner Periodicals in Human Resource Management: Implications for Evidence-Based Management," *Academy of Management Journal* 50, no. 5 (2007), pp. 987–1008.

16. J. Surowiecki, "The Fatal-Flaw Myth," *The New Yorker*, July 31, 2006, p. 25.

17. C. Tuna, "No-Layoff Policies Crumble," *Wall Street Journal* (December 29, 2008), p. B2.

18. See, for instance, S. D. Pugh, J. Dietz, J. W. Wiley, and S. M. Brooks, "Driving Service Effectiveness Through Employee-Customer Linkages," *Academy of Management Executive*, November 2002, pp. 73–84; and H. Liao and A. Chuang, "A Multilevel Investigation of Factors Influencing Employee Service Performance and Customer Outcomes," *Academy of Management Journal*, February 2004, pp. 41–58.

19. See www.patagonia.com/jobs/retail_asst_mgr.shtml; and "Patagonia Sets the Pace for Green Business," *Grist Magazine*, October 22, 2004, www.grist.org.

20. See, for instance, M. Workman and W. Bommer, "Redesigning Computer Call Center Work: A Longitudinal Field Experiment," *Journal of Organizational Behavior*, May 2004, pp. 317–337.

21. See, for instance, V. S. Major, K. J. Klein, and M. G. Ehrhart, "Work Time, Work Interference with Family, and Psychological Distress," *Journal of Applied Psychology*, June 2002, pp. 427–436; D. Brady, "Rethinking the Rat Race," *BusinessWeek*, August 26, 2002, pp. 142–143; J. M. Brett and L. K. Stroh, "Working 61 Plus Hours a Week: Why Do Managers Do It?" *Journal of Applied Psychology*, February 2003, pp. 67–78.

22. See, for instance, *The 2002 National Study of the Changing Workforce* (New York: Families and Work Institute, 2002); and W. J. Casper and L. C. Buffardi, "Work-Life Benefits and Job Pursuit Intentions: The Role of Anticipated Organizational Support," *Journal of Vocational Behavior* 65, no. 3 (2004), pp. 391–410.

23. Cited in S. Armour, "Workers Put Family First Despite Slow Economy, Jobless Fears."

24. S. Shellenbarger, "What Job Candidates Really Want to Know: Will I Have a Life?" *Wall Street Journal*, November 17, 1999, p. B1; and "U.S. Employers Polish Image to Woo a Demanding New Generation," *Manpower Argus*, February 2000, p. 2.

25. F. Luthans and C. M. Youssef, "Emerging Positive Organizational Behavior," *Journal of Management*, June 2007, pp. 321–349; C. M. Youssef and F. Luthans, "Positive Organizational Behavior in the Workplace: The Impact of Hope, Optimism, and Resilience," *Journal of Management* 33, no. 5 (2007), pp. 774–800; and J. E. Dutton and S. Sonenshein, "Positive Organizational Scholarship," in C. Cooper and J. Barling (eds.), *Encyclopedia of Positive Psychology* (Thousand Oaks, CA: Sage, 2007).

26. L. M. Roberts, G. Spreitzer, J. Dutton, R. Quinn, E. Heaphy, and B. Barker, "How to Play to Your Strengths," *Harvard Business Review*, January 2005, pp. 1–6; and L. M. Roberts, J. E. Dutton, G. M. Spreitzer, E. D. Heaphy, and R. E. Quinn, "Composing the Reflected Best-Self Portrait: Becoming Extraordinary in Work Organizations," *Academy of Management Review* 30, no. 4 (2005), pp. 712–736.

27. W. Bailey and A. Spicer, "When Does National Identity Matter? Convergence and Divergence in International Business Ethics," *Academy of Management Journal* 50, no. 6, pp. 1462–1480; and A. B. Oumlil and J. L. Balloun, "Ethical Decision-Making Differences Between American and Moroccan Managers," *Journal of Business Ethics* 84, no. 4 (2009), pp. 457–478.

28. J. Merritt, "For MBAs, Soul-Searching 101," *BusinessWeek*, September 16, 2002, pp. 64–66; and S. Greenhouse, "The Mood at Work: Anger and Anxiety," *New York Times*, October 29, 2002, p. E1.

29. See, for instance, G. R. Weaver, L. K. Trevino, and P. L. Cochran, "Corporate Ethics Practices in the Mid-1990's: An Empirical Study of the Fortune 1000," *Journal of Business Ethics*, February 1999, pp. 283–294; and C. De Mesa Graziano, "Promoting Ethical Conduct: A Review of Corporate Practices," *Strategic Investor Relations*, Fall 2002, pp. 29–35.

30. D. M. Mayer, M. Kuenzi, R. Greenbaum, M. Bardes, and R. Salvador, "How Low Does Ethical Leadership Flow? Test of a Trickle-Down Model," *Organizational Behavior and Human Decision Processes* 108, no. 1 (2009), pp. 1–13; and A. Ardichvili, J. A. Mitchell, and D. Jondle, "Characteristics of Ethical Business Cultures," *Journal of Business Ethics* 85, no. 4 (2009), pp. 445–451.

31. A. J. Rucci, S. P. Kirn, and R. T. Quinn, "The Employee-Customer-Profit Chain at Sears," *Harvard Business Review*, January–February 1998, pp. 83–97.

32. J. Britt, "Workplace No-Shows' Cost to Employers Rise Again," *HRMagazine*, December 2002, pp. 26–29.

33. "Absence-Minded Workers Cost Business Dearly," *Works Management*, June 2001, pp. 10–14.

34. W. Hoge, "Sweden's Cradle-to-Grave Welfare Starts to Get Ill," *International Herald Tribune*, September 25, 2002, p. 8.

35. "Employee Turnover Costs in the U.S.," *Manpower Argus*, January 2001, p. 5.

36. See www.bls.gov/data (May 11, 2005).

37. See, for example, M. C. Sturman and C. O. Trevor, "The Implications of Linking the Dynamic Performance and Turnover Literatures," *Journal of Applied Psychology*, August 2001, pp. 684–696.

38. Cited in "You Often Lose the Ones You Love," *IndustryWeek*, November 21, 1988, p. 5.

39. R. J. Bennett and S. L. Robinson, "Development of a Measure of Workplace Deviance," *Journal of Applied Psychology* 85, no. 3 (2000), pp. 349–360; A. M. O'Leary-Kelly, M. K. Duffy, and R.W. Griffin, "Construct Confusion in the Study of Antisocial Work Behavior," *Research in Personnel and Human Resources Management* 18 (2000), pp. 275–303; and C. Porath, C. Pearson, and D. L. Shapiro, "Turning the Other Cheek or an Eye for an Eye: Targets' Responses to Incivility," paper interactively presented at the annual meeting of the National Academy of Management, August 1999.

40. D. W. Organ, *Organizational Citizenship Behavior: The Good Soldier Syndrome* (Lexington, MA: Lexington Books, 1988), p. 4; and J. A. LePine, A. Erez, and D. E. Johnson, "The Nature and Dimensionality of Organizational Citizenship Behavior: A Critical Review and Meta-Analysis," *Journal of Applied Psychology*, February 2002, pp. 52–65.

41. P. M. Podsakoff, S. B. MacKenzie, J. B. Paine, and D. G. Bachrach, "Organizational Citizenship Behaviors: A Critical Review of the Theoretical and Empirical Literature and Suggestions for Future Research," *Journal of Management* 26, no. 3 (2000), pp. 543–548; and S. W. Whiting, P. M. Podsakoff, and J. R. Pierce, "Effects of Task Performance, Helping, Voice, and Organizational Loyalty on Performance Appraisal Ratings." *Journal of Applied Psychology* 93, no. 1 (2008), pp. 125–139.

42. T. A. Judge, C. J. Thoresen, J. E. Bono, and G. R. Patton, "The Job Satisfaction–Job Performance Relationship: A Qualitative and Quantitative Review," *Psychological Bulletin* 127 (2001), pp. 376–407; and M. Riketta, "The Causal Relation Between Job Attitudes and Performance: A Meta-Analysis of Panel Studies," *Journal of Applied Psychology* 93, no. 2 (2008), pp. 472–481.

43. S. C. Payne and S. S. Webber, "Effects of Service Provider Attitudes and Employment Status on Citizenship Behaviors and Customers' Attitudes and Loyalty Behavior," *Journal of Applied Psychology*, 91, no. 2 (2006), pp. 365–378; and H. Liao and D. E. Rupp, "The Impact of Justice Climate and Justice Orientation on Work Outcomes: A Cross-Level Multifoci Framework," *Journal of Applied Psychology* 90, no. 2 (2005), pp. 242–256.

44. M. Buckingham and C. Coffman, *First, Break All the Rules: What the World's Greatest Managers Do Differently* (New York: Simon & Schuster, 1999).

45. H. J. Leavitt, *Managerial Psychology*, rev. ed. (Chicago: University of Chicago Press, 1964), p. 3.

LEARNING OBJECTIVES

After studying this chapter, you should be able to:

1 Describe the two major forms of workforce diversity.

2 Identify the key biographical characteristics and describe how they are relevant to OB.

3 Define *intellectual ability* and demonstrate its relevance to OB.

4 Contrast intellectual from physical ability.

5 Describe how organizations manage diversity effectively.

6 Show how culture affects our understanding of biographical characteristics and intellectual abilities.

Diversity in Organizations

2

I think that God in creating Man somewhat overestimated his ability. —Oscar Wilde

REACHING NEW RESOURCES

Consider this—a 70 year-old, continually profitable company, known for its resilience in the face of adversity, finds itself scrambling to retain enough high-quality employees to meet growing demands in a tight labor market. The company is Nebraska Furniture Mart (NFM), and its solution to the problem exemplifies how diversity in the workplace can be a win-win situation for employees as well as employers.

Rather than trying the same approaches used in the past to find new hires, Ed Lipsett, the company's director of human resources, targeted recruitment efforts directly at the Hispanic community. Hispanics represent not only the largest minority group in the United States but also the fastest growing. It is estimated that by the year 2050, Hispanics will constitute over 30 percent of the workforce. Other data project that over the coming decade, 25 percent of new entrants to the workforce will consist of legal immigrants from Latin America.

NFM's plan to attract Hispanic workers was multifaceted. The firm reexamined where and how it recruited new employees and tailored new efforts to reach more people in Hispanic communities. It also recognized the need for translation services during the application and interview processes, as well as orientation and training. An interpreter joined the HR staff to meet these needs and to assist managers during coaching and performance appraisals.

The company didn't stop there. NFM has a mission to improve people's lifestyles, which also applies to its employees. In that tradition, while working with Kansas City Community College, the firm was able to provide English language and U.S. culture classes to its new employees. All costs were covered and employees were kept on the clock during classes, which were held at the work site.

NFM is not the only organization taking steps to make the most of the growing Hispanic workforce. Florida Power and Light has fostered ties with Miami Dade College to provide training and development that better serves the large Hispanic community in their area.

For NFM, cultivating a larger Hispanic workforce was a risk. Hispanic community organizations were initially wary of the company's outreach efforts, and some employees were concerned about having coworkers and subordinates who didn't speak English. In the end, the risk paid off. NFM managed to attract and retain Hispanic employees, who then introduced their families and friends to the company, both as employees and as customers. The plan was so successful, the firm implemented it at another location because, as Lipsett said, it provided "an excellent source for quality staff," as well as creating a more diverse workforce.[1]

Ethnicity is but one characteristic people bring with them when they join an organization. In this chapter, we look at how organizations work to maximize the potential contributions of a diverse workforce. We also show how demographic characteristics such as ethnicity and individual differences in the form of ability affect employee performance and satisfaction.

But first check out the following Self-Assessment Library, where you can assess your views on one of the characteristics we'll discuss in this chapter: age.

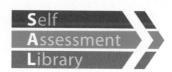

WHAT'S MY ATTITUDE TOWARD OLDER PEOPLE?

In the Self-Assessment Library (available on CD or online), take assessment IV.C.1 (What's My Attitude Toward Older People?) and answer the following questions:

1. *Are you surprised by your results?*
2. *How do your results compare to those of others?*

Diversity

1 Describe the two major forms of workforce diversity.

We aren't all the same. This is obvious enough, but managers sometimes forget that they need to recognize and capitalize on these differences to get the most out of their employees. Effective diversity management increases an organization's access to the widest possible pool of skills, abilities, and ideas. Managers also need to recognize that differences among people can lead to miscommunication, misunderstanding, and conflict. In this chapter, we'll learn about how individual characteristics like age, gender, race, ethnicity, and abilities can influence employee performance. We'll also see how managers can develop awareness about these characteristics and manage a diverse workforce effectively.

Demographic Characteristics of the U.S. Workforce

In the past, OB textbooks noted that rapid change was about to occur as the predominantly white, male managerial workforce gave way to a gender-balanced, multiethnic workforce. Today, that change is no longer happening: It has happened, and it is increasingly reflected in the makeup of managerial and professional jobs. Compared to 1976, in 2000 women were much more likely to be employed full time, have more education, and earn wages comparable to those of men.[2] In addition, over the past 50 years the earnings gap between Whites and other racial and ethnic groups has decreased significantly; past differences between Whites and Asians have disappeared or reversed.[3] Workers over the age of 55 are an increasingly large portion of the workforce as well. This permanent shift toward a diverse workforce means organizations need to make diversity management a central component of their policies and practices. At the same time, however, differences in wages across genders and racial and ethnic groups persist, and executive positions in *Fortune 500* corporations continue to be held by white males far beyond their representation in the workforce in general.

A survey by the Society for Human Resources Management shows some major employer concerns and opportunities resulting from the demographic makeup of the U.S. workforce.[4] The aging of the workforce was consistently the

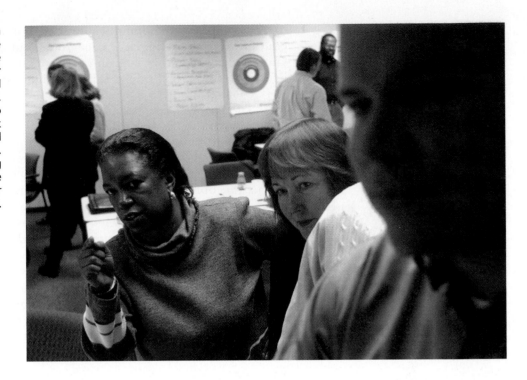

Progress Energy, headquartered in Raleigh, North Carolina, reflects the demographic characteristics of the U.S. workforce today. It is gender balanced, multiethnic, and engaged in learning about diversity issues. Progress encourages employees to participate in various network groups, diversity councils, and training workshops, as shown here. The company believes recognizing and embracing diversity maximize employee potential, customer satisfaction, and business success.

most significant concern of HR managers. The loss of skills resulting from the retirement of many baby boomers, increased medical costs due to an aging workforce, and many employees' needs to care for elderly relatives topped the list of issues. Other issues include developing multilingual training materials and providing work–life benefits for dual-career couples.

Levels of Diversity

Although much has been said about diversity in age, race, gender, ethnicity, religion, and disability status, experts now recognize that these demographic characteristics are just the tip of the iceberg.[5] Demographics mostly reflect **surface-level diversity**, not thoughts and feelings, and can lead employees to perceive one another through stereotypes and assumptions. However, evidence has shown that as people get to know one another, they become less concerned about demographic differences if they see themselves as sharing more important characteristics, such as personality and values, that represent **deep-level diversity**.[6]

To understand this difference between surface and deep-level diversity, consider a few examples. Luis and Lisa are co-workers who seem to have little in common at first glance. Luis is a young, recently hired male college graduate with a business degree, raised in a Spanish-speaking neighborhood in Miami. Lisa is an older, long-tenured woman raised in rural Kansas, who achieved her current level in the organization by starting as a high school graduate and working her way up through the hierarchy. At first, these co-workers may experience

surface-level diversity *Differences in easily perceived characteristics, such as gender, race, ethnicity, age, or disability, that do not necessarily reflect the ways people think or feel but that may activate certain stereotypes.*

deep-level diversity *Differences in values, personality, and work preferences that become progressively more important for determining similarity as people get to know one another better.*

some differences in communication based on their surface-level differences in education, ethnicity, regional background, and gender. However, as they get to know one another, they may find they are both deeply committed to their families, share a common way of thinking about important work problems, like to work collaboratively, and are interested in international assignments in the future. These deep-level similarities will overshadow the more superficial differences between them, and research suggests they will work well together.

On the other hand, Steve and Dave are two unmarried white male college graduates from Oregon who recently started working together. Superficially they seem well matched. But Steve is highly introverted, prefers to avoid risks, solicits the opinions of others before making decisions, and likes the office quiet, and Dave is extroverted, risk seeking, and assertive and likes a busy, active, and energetic work environment. Their surface-level similarity will not necessarily lead to positive interactions because they have such fundamental, deep-level differences. It will be a challenge for them to collaborate regularly at work, and they'll have to make some compromises to get things done together.

Throughout this book, we will encounter differences between deep and surface-level diversity in various contexts. Individual differences in personality and culture shape preferences for rewards, communication styles, reactions to leaders, negotiation styles, and many other aspects of behavior in organizations.

Discrimination

Although diversity does present many opportunities for organizations, effective diversity management also means working to eliminate unfair **discrimination**. To discriminate is to note a difference between things, which in itself isn't necessarily bad. Noticing one employee is more qualified is necessary for making hiring decisions; noticing another is taking on leadership responsibilities exceptionally well is necessary for making promotion decisions. Usually when we talk about discrimination, though, we mean allowing our behavior to be influenced by stereotypes about *groups* of people. Rather than looking at individual characteristics, unfair discrimination assumes everyone in a group is the same. This discrimination is often very harmful to organizations and employees.

Exhibit 2-1 provides definitions and examples of some forms of discrimination in organizations. Although many of these actions are prohibited by law, and therefore aren't part of almost any organization's official policies, thousands of cases of employment discrimination are documented every year, and many more go unreported. As discrimination has increasingly come under both legal scrutiny and social disapproval, most overt forms have faded, which may have resulted in an increase in more covert forms like incivility or exclusion.[7]

As you can see, discrimination can occur in many ways, and its effects can be just as varied. The form it takes is likely to be contingent on the organizational context and the personal biases of its members. Some forms, like exclusion or incivility, are especially hard to root out because they are impossible to observe and may occur simply because the actor isn't aware of the effects of his or her actions. Whether intentional or not, discrimination can lead to serious negative consequences for employers, including reduced productivity and citizenship behavior, negative conflicts, and increased turnover. Unfair discrimination also means leaving qualified job candidates out of initial hiring and promotions. Even if an employment discrimination lawsuit is never filed, a strong business case can be made for aggressively working to eliminate unfair discrimination.

Diversity is a broad term, and the phrase *workplace diversity* can refer to any characteristic that makes people different from one another. The following section covers some important surface-level characteristics that differentiate members of the workforce.

Exhibit 2-1	Forms of Discrimination	
Type of Discrimination	**Definition**	**Examples from Organizations**
Discriminatory policies or practices	Actions taken by representatives of the organization that deny equal opportunity to perform or unequal rewards for performance	Older workers may be targeted for layoffs because they are highly paid and have lucrative benefits.[8]
Sexual harassment	Unwanted sexual advances and other verbal or physical conduct of a sexual nature that create a hostile or offensive work environment	Salespeople at one company went on company-paid visits to strip clubs, brought strippers into the office to celebrate promotions, and fostered pervasive sexual rumors.[9]
Intimidation	Overt threats or bullying directed at members of specific groups of employees	African-American employees at some companies have found nooses hanging over their work stations.[10]
Mockery and insults	Jokes or negative stereotypes; sometimes the result of jokes taken too far	Arab-Americans have been asked at work whether they were carrying bombs or were members of terrorist organizations.[11]
Exclusion	Exclusion of certain people from job opportunities, social events, discussions, or informal mentoring; can occur unintentionally	Many women in finance claim they are assigned to marginal job roles or are given light workloads that don't lead to promotion.[12]
Incivility	Disrespectful treatment, including behaving in an aggressive manner, interrupting the person, or ignoring his or her opinions	Female lawyers note that male attorneys frequently cut them off or do not adequately address their comments.[13]

Biographical Characteristics

2 Identify the key biographical characteristics and describe how they are relevant to OB.

Biographical characteristics such as age, gender, race, disability, and length of service are some of the most obvious ways employees differ. As discussed in Chapter 1, this textbook is essentially concerned with finding and analyzing the variables that affect employee productivity, absence, turnover, deviance, citizenship, and satisfaction (refer back to Exhibit 1–5). Many organizational concepts—motivation, say, or power and politics or organizational culture—are hard to assess. Let's begin, then, by looking at factors that are easily definable and readily available—data that can be obtained, for the most part, from an employee's human resources (HR) file. Variations in these surface-level characteristics may be the basis for discrimination against classes of employees, so it is worth knowing how closely related they actually are to important work outcomes. Many are not as important as people believe, and far more variation occurs *within* groups sharing biographical characteristics than between them.

discrimination *Noting of a difference between things; often we refer to unfair discrimination, which means making judgments about individuals based on stereotypes regarding their demographic group.*

biographical characteristics *Personal characteristics—such as age, gender, race, and length of tenure—that are objective and easily obtained from personnel records. These characteristics are representative of surface-level diversity.*

Age

The relationship between age and job performance is likely to be an issue of increasing importance during the next decade for at least three reasons. First, belief is widespread that job performance declines with increasing age. Regardless of whether this is true, a lot of people believe it and act on it. Second, as noted in Chapter 1, the workforce is aging. Many employers recognize that older workers represent a huge potential pool of quality applicants. Companies such as Borders and the Vanguard Group have sought to increase their attractiveness to older workers by providing targeted training that meets their needs and offering flexible work schedules and part-time work to draw in those who are semi-retired.[14] The third reason is U.S. legislation that, for all intents and purposes, outlaws mandatory retirement. Most U.S. workers today no longer have to retire at age 70.

What is the perception of older workers? Employers hold mixed feelings.[15] They see a number of positive qualities older workers bring to their jobs, such as experience, judgment, a strong work ethic, and commitment to quality. But older workers are also perceived as lacking flexibility and resisting new technology. And when organizations are actively seeking individuals who are adaptable and open to change, the negatives associated with age clearly hinder the initial hiring of older workers and increase the likelihood they will be let go during cutbacks.

Now let's take a look at the evidence. What effect does age actually have on turnover, absenteeism, productivity, and satisfaction? The older you get, the less likely you are to quit your job. That conclusion is based on studies of the age–turnover relationship.[16] Of course, this shouldn't be too surprising. As workers get older, they have fewer alternative job opportunities. Their long tenure also tends to provide them with higher wage rates, longer paid vacations, and more attractive pension benefits.

It's tempting to assume that age is also inversely related to absenteeism. After all, if older workers are less likely to quit, won't they also demonstrate higher stability by coming to work more regularly? Not necessarily. Most studies do show an inverse relationship, but close examination finds it is partially a function of whether the absence is avoidable or unavoidable.[17] In general, older employees have lower rates of avoidable absence than do younger employees. However, they have higher rates of unavoidable absence, probably due to the poorer health associated with aging and the longer recovery period they need when injured.

How does age affect productivity? Many believe productivity declines with age. It is often assumed that skills like speed, agility, strength, and coordination decay over time and that prolonged job boredom and lack of intellectual stimulation contribute to reduced productivity. The evidence, however, contradicts those assumptions. During a 3-year period, a large hardware chain staffed one of its stores solely with employees over age 50 and compared its results with those of five stores with younger employees. The store staffed by the over-50 employees was significantly more productive (in terms of sales generated against labor costs) than two of the stores and held its own against the other three.[18] Other reviews of the research find that age and job performance are unrelated.[19]

Our final concern is the relationship between age and job satisfaction, where the evidence is mixed. Most studies indicate a positive association between age and satisfaction, at least up to age 60.[20] Other studies, however, have found a U-shaped relationship.[21] Several explanations could clear up these results, the most plausible being that these studies are intermixing professional and nonprofessional employees. When we separate the two types, satisfaction tends to continually increase among professionals as they age, whereas it falls among nonprofessionals during middle age and then rises again in the later years.

Home Depot values the work ethic of older employees, such as assistant manager Ellen Van Valen, shown here, who is in her late sixties. Home Depot is one of a growing number of firms that are recruiting older workers because, compared with younger workers, they have lower turnover rates and training costs and, in many cases, better work performance. Van Valen believes that age has little to do with the desire to work but says that "older folks seem to catch on a lot quicker."

Gender

Few issues initiate more debates, misconceptions, and unsupported opinions than whether women perform as well on jobs as men do.

The best place to begin to consider this is with the recognition that few, if any, important differences between men and women affect job performance. There are no consistent male–female differences in problem-solving ability, analytical skills, competitive drive, motivation, sociability, or learning ability.[22] Psychological studies have found women are more agreeable and willing to conform to authority, whereas men are more aggressive and more likely to have expectations of success, but those differences are minor. Given the significantly increased female participation in the workforce over the last 40 years and the rethinking of what constitutes male and female roles, we can assume no significant difference in job productivity between men and women.[23] Unfortunately, gender still affects our perceptions. For example, women who succeed in traditionally male domains are perceived as less likable, more hostile, and less desirable as supervisors.[24]

One issue that does seem to differ between genders, especially when the employee has preschool-age children, is preference for work schedules.[25] Working mothers are more likely to prefer part-time work, flexible work schedules, and telecommuting in order to accommodate their family responsibilities. Women also prefer jobs that encourage work–life balance, which has the effect of limiting their options for career advancement.

What about absence and turnover rates? Are women less stable employees than men? First, evidence from a study of nearly 500,000 professional employees indicates significant differences, with women more likely to turn over than men.[26] Women also have higher rates of absenteeism than men do.[27] The most logical explanation is that the research was conducted in North America, and North American culture has historically placed home and family responsibilities on women. When a child is ill or someone needs to stay home to wait for a plumber, the woman has traditionally taken time from work. However, this

Myth or Science?

"Men Are Better at Science and Math Than Women"

This statement is partially false but partially true. The answer is not entirely straightforward because being "good at science" taps into several types of abilities.[28] The consistent difference between the numbers of men and women obtaining graduate degrees in some math, science, and engineering fields cannot be denied. The National Science Foundation has focused much attention on this issue, noting that women make up only about a quarter of physical scientists and engineers but nearly half the U.S. workforce.[29] A number of possible explanations have been offered. Many focus on sociological factors, like the lack of female faculty and other role models in these fields, and a tendency for teachers to have higher expectations for boys in math and science areas. The possibility that underlying gender differences in ability contribute to gender differences in scientific careers is a major social and political flash point. When Larry Summers (president of Harvard University before

becoming one of President Barack Obama's senior advisors) proposed that men are genetically more likely to have exceptional abilities in math and science, he received intense criticism that contributed to his decision to resign.

Did Summers have a point? As we've noted, men and women generally do equally well on tests of general mental ability. However, men's scores on standardized math ability tests show more variability than women's—men are more likely to be exceptionally low or exceptionally high in math abilities. While there is not much difference between men and women in general mental ability, that doesn't mean men and women do equally well in all aspects—men tend to score significantly higher on mathematical ability whereas women score higher on verbal ability. These differences appear early—even in kindergarten-age children. Boys score higher on mathematics and science tests, whereas girls score significantly higher in tests of reading and writing ability. Girls do as

well as or better than boys in elementary school when math courses require computational knowledge and algebra, but males show higher scores when visual-spatial abilities are important, as in geometry, physics, and calculus.

Bear in mind that scientific careers do require a substantial amount of writing, one of the areas where women consistently perform better than men. A second point is the fairly dramatic change in the upper reaches of ability test scores. In the 1970s in the SAT math test, 13 boys scored over 700 for every girl who did. By 2005 the ratio was 2.8 boys for every girl. Third, specialized education programs to improve visual-spatial abilities can reduce the gap in test scores. Finally, women who are high achievers in math and science subjects are more likely to major in scientific disciplines such as biology and medicine than high-achieving men, so just because women are not represented in physics and engineering does not mean they are consistently opting out of scientific careers.

research is also undoubtedly time-bound.[30] The role of women has definitely changed over the past generation. Men are increasingly sharing responsibility for child care, and an increasing number report feeling a conflict between their home responsibilities and their work lives.[31] One interesting result of this research was that parents, regardless of gender, were rated lower in job commitment, achievement striving, and dependability than individuals without children, but mothers were rated especially low in competence.[32]

Race and Ethnicity

Race is a controversial issue. Most people in the United States identify themselves according to racial group. The U.S. Bureau of the Census classifies individuals according to seven broad racial categories: American Indian and Alaska Native, Asian, Black or African American, Native Hawaiian and Other Pacific Islander, Some Other Race, White, and Two or More Races. An ethnicity distinction is also made between native English speakers and Hispanics: Hispanics can be of any race. We define race in this book as the biological heritage people use to identify themselves; ethnicity is the additional set of cultural characteristics that often overlaps with race. This definition allows each individual to define his or her race or ethnicity. Tiger Woods, for example, refuses to place himself into a single racial category, emphasizing his multiethnic roots.

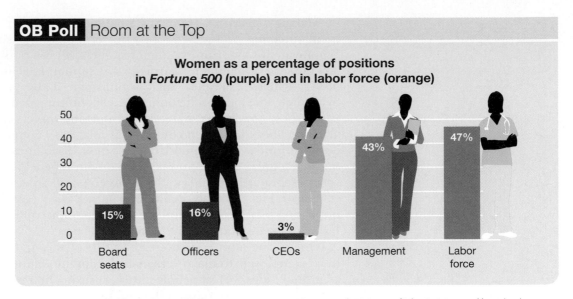

OB Poll Room at the Top

Women as a percentage of positions in *Fortune 500* (purple) and in labor force (orange)

- Board seats: 15%
- Officers: 16%
- CEOs: 3%
- Management: 43%
- Labor force: 47%

Source: Based on "A Dead End for Women," *Workforce Management* (June 22, 2009), p. 16; and *U.S. Bureau of Labor Statistics*, www.bls.gov/cps/cpsaat9.pdf.

Race and ethnicity have been studied as they relate to employment outcomes such as hiring decisions, performance evaluations, pay, and workplace discrimination. Most research has concentrated on the differences in outcomes and attitudes between Whites and African Americans, with little study of issues relevant to Asian, Native American, and Hispanic populations. Doing justice to all this research isn't possible here, so let's summarize a few points.

First, in employment settings, individuals tend to favor colleagues of their own race in performance evaluations, promotion decisions, and pay raises.[33] These preference effects are consistent but small. Second, substantial racial differences exist in attitudes toward affirmative action, with African Americans approving of such programs to a greater degree than Whites.[34] Third, African Americans generally fare worse than Whites in employment decisions. They receive lower ratings in employment interviews, receive lower job performance ratings, are paid less, and are promoted less frequently.[35] Yet there are no statistically significant differences between African Americans and Whites in observed absence rates, applied social skills at work, or accident rates. African Americans and Hispanics also have higher turnover rates than Whites.

Employers' major concern about using mental ability tests for selection, promotion, training, and similar personnel decisions is that they may have a negative impact on racial and ethnic groups.[36] However, evidence suggests that "despite group differences in mean test performance, there is little convincing evidence that well-constructed tests are more predictive of educational, training, or occupational performance for members of the majority group than for members of minority groups."[37] The observed difference in IQ test scores by racial or ethnic group is smaller in more recent samples.[38] The issue of racial differences in general mental ability tests continues to be hotly debated.[39]

Disability

With the passage of the Americans with Disabilities Act (ADA) in 1990, the representation of individuals with disabilities in the U.S. workforce rapidly increased.[40] According to the ADA, employers are required to make reasonable accommodations so their workplaces will be accessible to individuals with physical or mental disabilities.

Making inferences about the relationship between disability and employment outcomes is difficult because the term *disability* is so broad. The U.S. Equal Employment Opportunity Commission classifies a person as disabled who has any physical or mental impairment that substantially limits one or more major life activities. Examples include missing limbs, seizure disorder, Down Syndrome, deafness, schizophrenia, alcoholism, diabetes, and chronic back pain. These conditions share almost no common features, so there's no generalization about how each condition is related to employment. Some jobs obviously cannot be accommodated to some disabilities—the law and common sense recognize that a blind person could not be a bus driver, a person with severe cerebral palsy could not be a surgeon, and a person with profound mobility constraints probably could not be a police patrol officer. However, the increasing presence of computer technology and other adaptive devices is shattering many traditional barriers to employment.

One of the most controversial aspects of the ADA is the provision that requires employers to make reasonable accommodations for people with psychiatric disabilities.[41] Most people have very strong biases against those with mental illnesses, who are therefore reluctant to disclose this information to employers. Many who do, report negative consequences.

The impact of disabilities on employment outcomes has been explored from a variety of perspectives. On the one hand, a review of the evidence suggests workers with disabilities receive higher performance evaluations. However, this same review found that despite their higher performance, individuals with disabilities tend to encounter lower performance expectations and are less likely to be hired.[42] These negative effects are much stronger for individuals with mental disabilities, and there is some evidence to suggest mental disabilities may impair performance more than physical disabilities: Individuals with such common mental health issues as depression and anxiety are significantly more likely to be absent from work.[43]

Several studies have examined participants who received résumés that were identical, except that some mentioned a disability. The résumés that mentioned mental illness or a physical disability were associated with much lower ratings for

Microsoft views employees with disabilities as valuable assets because they help ensure that its products meet all customer needs. At the Microsoft Accessibility Lab, employees can experience assistive technologies and ergonomic hardware designs that enable them to be more productive, comfortable, and injury-free at work. Kelly Ford, who has been blind since birth, is shown here in the lab testing accessibility features of the Windows operating system. Ford also manages a team that is working on improving Web page browsing for all users, not just those with disabilities.

perceived employability, especially in jobs requiring a great deal of personal contact with the public.[44] Employability ratings for individuals with mental illnesses were especially low. Similarly, when given randomly manipulated academic portfolios, students preferred not to work with individuals who had a learning disability even though there were no effects of disability on performance ratings or expectations.[45]

Contrast these selection-oriented results with studies showing the accomplishments of those with disabilities are often rated as more impressive than the same accomplishments in people without disabilities. Participants watched three individuals completing a carpentry task, and one was described as having recently been hospitalized for a debilitating mental illness.[46] The raters consistently gave that person higher performance ratings. In this case, it may be that disabled individuals were being treated as an outgroup in need of special help. Similarly, when disability status is randomly manipulated among hypothetical candidates, disabled individuals are rated as having superior personal qualities like dependability and potency.[47]

Other Biographical Characteristics: Tenure, Religion, Sexual Orientation, and Gender Identity

The last set of biographical characteristic we'll look at are tenure, religion, sexual orientation, and gender identity.

Tenure   Except for gender and racial differences, few issues are more subject to misconceptions and speculations than the impact of seniority on job performance.

Extensive reviews have been conducted of the seniority–productivity relationship.[48] If we define *seniority* as time on a particular job, the most recent evidence demonstrates a positive relationship between seniority and job productivity. So tenure, expressed as work experience, appears to be a good predictor of employee productivity.

The research relating tenure to absence is quite straightforward. Studies consistently demonstrate seniority to be negatively related to absenteeism.[49] In fact, in terms of both frequency of absence and total days lost at work, tenure is the single most important explanatory variable.[50]

Tenure is also a potent variable in explaining turnover. The longer a person is in a job, the less likely he or she is to quit.[51] Moreover, consistent with research suggesting past behavior is the best predictor of future behavior,[52] evidence indicates tenure on an employee's previous job is a powerful predictor of that employee's future turnover.[53]

Evidence indicates tenure and job satisfaction are positively related.[54] In fact, when age and tenure are treated separately, tenure appears a more consistent and stable predictor of job satisfaction than age.

Religion   Not only do religious and nonreligious people question each other's belief systems; often people of different religious faiths conflict. As the war in Iraq and the past conflict in Northern Ireland demonstrate, violent differences can erupt among sects of the same religion. U.S. federal law prohibits employers from discriminating against employees based on their religion, with very few exceptions. However, that doesn't mean religion is a nonissue in OB.

Perhaps the greatest religious diversity issue in the United States today revolves around Islam. There are nearly two million Muslims in the United States, and across the world Islam is one of the most popular religions. There are a wide variety of perspectives on Islam. As one Islamic scholar has noted, "There is no such thing as a single American Muslim community, much as there is no single

An Ethical Choice

Are You More Biased Than You Think?

Late one Wednesday afternoon, a 34-year-old white woman sat down in her Washington, D.C., office to take a test. She prided herself on being a civil rights advocate, and her office décor gave ample testament to her liberal beliefs.

The woman accessed a test on a Web site run by a research team at Harvard. The test was relatively simple: it asked her to distinguish between a series of black and white faces. When she saw a black face, she was to press a key on the left, and when she saw a white face, she was to press a key on the right. Next, she was asked to distinguish between a series of positive and negative words. Words such as *wonderful* required pressing the "i" key, words such as *terrible* required pressing the "e" key. The test remained simple when two categories were combined: The person pressed "e" if she saw either a white face or a positive word, and she pressed "i" if she saw either a black face or a negative word.

Then the groupings were reversed. The test now required the woman to group black faces with positive words

and white faces with negative words. Her index fingers hovered over her keyboard. She leaned forward intently. She made no mistakes, but it took her longer to correctly sort the words and images.

Her result appeared on the screen, and the activist became very silent. The test found she had a bias for Whites over Blacks.

"It surprises me I have any preferences at all," she said. "By the work I do, by my education, my background, I'm progressive, and I think I have no bias. Being a minority myself, I don't feel I should or would have biases."

As it turns out, evidence is starting to accumulate—more than 60 studies so far—showing most people have these sorts of implicit biases. They're implicit because we don't consciously realize they're there. But they are. We may have implicit biases against minorities or women, or people of a certain religion or sexual orientation. Some people do not have an implicit bias in one area (say, toward race) but do in another area (say, toward Republicans).

So how can organizations deal with these latent biases? The very fact that they are unconscious is part of the reason they may be hard to confront or change. "Mind bugs operate without us being conscious of them," says one of the Harvard researchers. "They are not special things that happen in our heart because we are evil." Using objective criteria for evaluating performance appears to help minimize the influence of these biases, as we will see in our discussion of diversity management strategies. It also is likely that making yourself aware of your potential unconscious biases will make it easier for you to take conscious steps to offset these biases.

Sources: Based on L. S. Son Hing, G. A. Chung-Yan, L. K. Hamilton, and M. P. Zanna, "A Two-Dimensional Model that Employs Explicit and Implicit Attitudes to Characterize Prejudice," *Journal of Personality and Social Psychology* 94, no. 6 (2008), pp. 971–987; A. S. Baron and M. R. Banaji, "The Development of Implicit Attitudes: Evidence of Race Evaluations from Ages 6 and 10 and Adulthood," *Psychological Science,* January 2006, pp. 53–58; and S. Vedantam, "See No Bias," *Washington Post,* January 23, 2005, p. W12.

Christian community. Muslims vary hugely by ethnicity, faith, tradition, education, income, and degree of religious observance."[55] For the most part, U.S. Muslims have attitudes similar to those of other U.S. citizens (though the differences tend to be greater for younger U.S. Muslims). Still, there are both perceived and real differences. Nearly 4 in 10 U.S. adults admit they harbor negative feelings or prejudices toward U.S. Muslims, and 52 percent believe U.S. Muslims are not respectful of women. Some take these general biases a step further. Motaz Elshafi, a 28-year-old software engineer for Cisco Systems, born and raised in New Jersey, received an e-mail from a co-worker addressed "Dear Terrorist." Although such acts are relatively isolated, they do occur.

Faith can be an employment issue when religious beliefs prohibit or encourage certain behaviors. Based on their religious beliefs, some pharmacists refuse to hand out RU-486, the "morning after" abortion pill. Many Christians do not believe they should work on Sundays, and many conservative Jews believe they should not work on Saturdays. Religious individuals may also believe they have an obligation to express their beliefs in the workplace, and those who do not share those beliefs may object. Perhaps as a result of different perceptions of religion's role in the workplace, religious discrimination claims have been a growing source of discrimination claims in the United States.

Sexual Orientation and Gender Identity Employers differ widely in their treatment of sexual orientation. Federal law does not prohibit discrimination against employees based on sexual orientation, though many states and municipalities do. Many employers practice some version of the "Don't ask, don't tell" military policy, some do not hire gays, but an increasing number are implementing policies and practices to protect the rights of gays in the workplace. Raytheon, builder of Tomahawk cruise missiles and other defense systems, offers domestic-partner benefits, supports a wide array of gay rights groups, and wants to be an employer of choice for gays. The firm believes these policies give it an advantage in the ever-competitive market for engineers and scientists.

Raytheon is not alone. More than half the Fortune 500 companies offer domestic-partner benefits for gay couples, including American Express, IBM, Intel, Morgan Stanley, Motorola, and Wal-Mart. Some companies are against domestic partner benefits or nondiscrimination clauses for gay employees. Among these are Alltel, ADM, ExxonMobil, H. J. Heinz, Nissan, Nestle, and Rubbermaid.[56]

As for gender identity, companies are increasingly putting in place policies to govern how their organization treats employees who change genders (often called *transgender employees*). In 2001, only eight companies in the Fortune 500 had policies on gender identity. By 2006, that number had swelled to 124. IBM is one of them. Brad Salavich, a diversity manager for IBM, says, "We believe that having strong transgender and gender identification policies is a natural extension of IBM's corporate culture." Dealing with transgender employees requires some special considerations, such as for bathrooms, employee names, and so on.[57]

Ability

We've so far covered surface characteristics unlikely, on their own, to directly relate to job performance. Now we turn to deep-level abilities that *are* closely related to job performance. Contrary to what we were taught in grade school, we weren't all created equal in our abilities. Most people are to the left or to the right of the median on some normally distributed ability curve. For example, regardless of how motivated you are, it's unlikely you can act as well as Scarlett Johansson, play basketball as well as LeBron James, write as well as J. K. Rowling, or play the guitar as well as Pat Metheny. Of course, just because we aren't all equal in abilities does not imply that some individuals are inherently inferior. Everyone has strengths and weaknesses that make him or her relatively superior or inferior to others in performing certain tasks or activities. From management's standpoint, the issue is not whether people differ in terms of their abilities. They clearly do. The issue is using the knowledge that people differ to increase the likelihood an employee will perform his or her job well.

What does *ability* mean? As we use the term, **ability** is an individual's current capacity to perform the various tasks in a job. Overall abilities are essentially made up of two sets of factors: intellectual and physical.

ability *An individual's capacity to perform the various tasks in a job.*

Intellectual Abilities

3 Define *intellectual ability* and demonstrate its relevance to OB.

Intellectual abilities are abilities needed to perform mental activities—thinking, reasoning, and problem solving. Most societies place a high value on intelligence, and for good reason. Smart people generally earn more money and attain higher levels of education. They are also more likely to emerge as leaders of groups. Intelligence quotient (IQ) tests, for example, are designed to ascertain a person's general intellectual abilities. So, too, are popular college admission tests, such as the SAT and ACT and graduate admission tests in business (GMAT), law (LSAT), and medicine (MCAT).

Testing firms don't claim their tests assess intelligence, but experts know they do.[58] The seven most frequently cited dimensions making up intellectual abilities are number aptitude, verbal comprehension, perceptual speed, inductive reasoning, deductive reasoning, spatial visualization, and memory.[59] Exhibit 2-2 describes these dimensions.

Intelligence dimensions are positively related, so if you score high on verbal comprehension, for example, you're more likely to also score high on spatial visualization. The correlations aren't perfect, meaning people do have specific abilities. However, they are high enough that researchers also recognize a general factor of intelligence, **general mental ability (GMA)**.

Jobs differ in the demands they place on intellectual abilities. The more complex a job in terms of information-processing demands, the more general intelligence and verbal abilities will be necessary to perform successfully.[60] Where employee behavior is highly routine and there are few or no opportunities to exercise discretion, a high IQ is not as important to performing well. However, that does not mean people with high IQs cannot have an impact on traditionally less complex jobs.

It might surprise you that the most widely used intelligence test in hiring decisions takes only 12 minutes. It's the Wonderlic Personnel Test. There are different forms, and each has 50 questions. Here are a few examples:

- When rope is selling at $.10 a foot, how many feet can you buy for $.60?
- Assume the first two statements are true. Is the final one:
    1. true,
    2. false,

Exhibit 2-2   Dimensions of Intellectual Ability

Dimension	Description	Job Example
Number aptitude	Ability to do speedy and accurate arithmetic	Accountant: Computing the sales tax on a set of items
Verbal comprehension	Ability to understand what is read or heard and the relationship of words to each other	Plant manager: Following corporate policies on hiring
Perceptual speed	Ability to identify visual similarities and differences quickly and accurately	Fire investigator: Identifying clues to support a charge of arson
Inductive reasoning	Ability to identify a logical sequence in a problem and then solve the problem	Market researcher: Forecasting demand for a product in the next time period
Deductive reasoning	Ability to use logic and assess the implications of an argument	Supervisor: Choosing between two different suggestions offered by employees
Spatial visualization	Ability to imagine how an object would look if its position in space were changed	Interior decorator: Redecorating an office
Memory	Ability to retain and recall past experiences	Salesperson: Remembering the names of customers

International OB

The Benefits of Cultural Intelligence

Have you ever noticed that some individuals seem to have a knack for relating well to people from different cultures? Some researchers have labeled this skill *cultural intelligence,* an outsider's natural ability to correctly interpret an individual's unfamiliar gestures and behaviors. Cultural intelligence is valuable when conducting business with people from different cultures, because when misunderstandings occur, cooperation and productivity may suffer.

Consider this: A U.S. manager was meeting with his fellow design team engineers, two of whom were German. As ideas floated around the table, the Germans quickly rejected them. The American thought the feedback was harsh and concluded his German colleagues were rude. However, they were merely critiquing the ideas, not

the individual—a distinction the U.S. manager was unable to make, perhaps due to a lack of cultural intelligence. As a result, he became wary of contributing potentially good ideas. Had he been more culturally intelligent, the U.S. executive likely would have recognized the true motives behind his colleagues' remarks and thus might have been able to use them to improve his ideas.

It is unclear whether cultural intelligence is separate from other forms of intelligence, such as emotional intelligence, and even whether it is different from general mental ability. Researchers propose that people who are both able and willing to simultaneously recognize their own culture and the culture of others will be higher in cultural intelligence. Being able to recognize, adjust, and correct your typical way of thinking and recognize alternative cultural

points of view does require cognitive resources, so some aspect of general mental ability likely affects cultural intelligence. Whether it is distinct from general mental ability or not, the ability to interact well with individuals from different cultures is a key asset in today's global business environment.

Sources: Based on C. Earley and E. Mosakowski, "Cultural Intelligence," *Harvard Business Review,* October 2004, pp. 139–146; S. Ang, L. Van Dyne, C. Koh, K. Y. Ng, K. J. Templar, and C. Tay, "Cultural Intelligence: Its Measurement and Effects on Cultural Judgment and Decision Making, Cultural Adaptation and Task Performance," *Management and Organization Review* 3, no. 3 (2007), pp. 335–371; and D. C. Thomas, E. Elron, G. Stahl, B. Z. Ekelund, E. C. Ravlin, J. Cerdin, et al., "Cultural Intelligence: Domain and Assessment," *International Journal of Cross-Cultural Management* 8, no. 2 (2008), pp. 123–143.

3. not certain?
     a. The boy plays baseball.
     b. All baseball players wear hats.
     c. The boy wears a hat.

The Wonderlic measures both speed (almost nobody has time to answer every question) and power (questions get harder as you go along), so the average score is pretty low—about 21/50. And because it is able to provide valid information cheaply ($5–$10/applicant), more companies are using the Wonderlic in hiring decisions. The Factory Card & Party Outlet, with 182 stores nationwide, uses the Wonderlic. So do Subway, Peoples Flowers, Security Alarm, Workforce Employment Solutions, and many others. Most companies that use the Wonderlic don't give up other hiring tools, such as application forms or interviews. Rather, they add the Wonderlic for its ability to provide valid data on applicants' intelligence levels.

Interestingly, while intelligence is a big help in performing a job well, it doesn't make people happier or more satisfied with their jobs. The correlation between intelligence and job satisfaction is about zero. Why? Research suggests that although intelligent people perform better and tend to have more interesting jobs, they are

---

intellectual abilities   *The capacity to do mental activities—thinking, reasoning, and problem solving.*

general mental ability (GMA)   *An overall factor of intelligence, as suggested by the positive correlations among specific intellectual ability dimensions.*

Exhibit 2-3	Nine Basic Physical Abilities
Strength Factors	
1. Dynamic strength	Ability to exert muscular force repeatedly or continuously over time
2. Trunk strength	Ability to exert muscular strength using the trunk (particularly abdominal) muscles
3. Static strength	Ability to exert force against external objects
4. Explosive strength	Ability to expend a maximum of energy in one or a series of explosive acts
Flexibility Factors	
5. Extent flexibility	Ability to move the trunk and back muscles as far as possible
6. Dynamic flexibility	Ability to make rapid, repeated flexing movements
Other Factors	
7. Body coordination	Ability to coordinate the simultaneous actions of different parts of the body
8. Balance	Ability to maintain equilibrium despite forces pulling off balance
9. Stamina	Ability to continue maximum effort requiring prolonged effort over time

also more critical in evaluating their job conditions. Thus, smart people have it better, but they also expect more.[61]

Physical Abilities

4 Contrast intellectual from physical ability.

Though the changing nature of work suggests intellectual abilities are increasingly important for many jobs, **physical abilities** have been and will remain valuable. Research on hundreds of jobs has identified nine basic abilities needed in the performance of physical tasks.[62] These are described in Exhibit 2-3. Individuals differ in the extent to which they have each of these abilities. Not surprisingly, there is also little relationship among them: a high score on one is no assurance of a high score on others. High employee performance is likely to be achieved when management has ascertained the extent to which a job requires each of the nine abilities and then ensures that employees in that job have those abilities.

The Role of Disabilities

The importance of ability at work obviously creates problems when attempting to formulate workplace policies that recognize diversity in terms of disability status. As we have noted, recognizing that individuals have different abilities that can be taken into account when making hiring decisions is not problematic. However, it is discriminatory to make blanket assumptions about people on the basis of a disability. It is also possible to make accommodations for disabilities.

Implementing Diversity Management Strategies

Having discussed a variety of ways in which people differ, we now look at how a manager can and should manage these differences. **Diversity management** makes everyone more aware of and sensitive to the needs and differences of others. This definition highlights the fact that diversity programs include and are meant for everyone. When seen as everyone's business, diversity is much more likely to be successful than if we believe it helps only certain groups of employees.

Attracting, Selecting, Developing, and Retaining Diverse Employees

One method of enhancing workforce diversity is to target recruiting messages to specific demographic groups underrepresented in the workforce. This means placing advertisements in publications geared toward specific demographic groups; recruiting at colleges, universities, and other institutions with significant numbers of underrepresented minorities; and forming partnerships with associations like the Society for Women Engineers or the Graduate Minority Business Association. These efforts can be successful, as research has shown that women and minorities do have greater interest in employers that make special efforts to highlight a commitment to diversity in their recruiting materials. Advertisements depicting groups of diverse employees are seen as more attractive to women and racioethnic minorities, which is probably why most organizations depict workforce diversity prominently in their recruiting materials. Diversity advertisements that fail to show women and minorities in positions of organizational leadership send a negative message about the diversity climate at an organization.[63]

The selection process is one of the most important places for diversity efforts. Managers who hire need to value fairness and objectivity in selecting employees and focus on the productive potential of new recruits. Fortunately, ensuring that hiring is bias free does appear to work. Where managers use a well-defined protocol for assessing applicant talent and the organization clearly prioritizes nondiscrimination policies, qualifications are far more important in determining who gets hired than demographic characteristics.[64] These results show up in workplaces with a pro-diversity climate, however; organizations that do not discourage discriminatory behavior are more likely to see problems.

Similarity in personality does appear to affect career advancement. Those whose personality traits are similar to those of their co-workers are more likely to be promoted than those whose personalities are different.[65] There's an important qualifier to these results: in collectivistic cultures, similarity to supervisors is more important for predicting advancement, whereas in individualistic cultures, similarity to peers is more important. Once again, deep-level diversity factors appear to be more important in shaping people's reactions to one another than surface-level characteristics.

Evidence from a study of over six thousand workers in a major retail organization indicated that in stores with a less supportive diversity climate, African Americans or Hispanics made significantly fewer sales than White employees, but when diversity climate was positive, Hispanics and Whites sold about the same amount and African Americans made more sales than Whites.[66] Whites sold about the same amount whether there was a positive diversity climate or not, but African Americans and Hispanics sold far more when there was. There are obvious bottom-line implications of this research: stores that fostered a positive diversity climate were able to capitalize on their diverse workforce and make more money.

physical abilities *The capacity to do tasks that demand stamina, dexterity, strength, and similar characteristics.*

diversity management *The process and programs by which managers make everyone more aware of and sensitive to the needs and differences of others.*

Some data suggest individuals who are demographically different from their co-workers are more likely to feel low commitment and to turn over: women are more likely to turn over from predominantly male work groups and men from predominantly female work groups; non-Whites are more likely to turn over from predominantly White work groups and Whites from predominantly non-White work groups.[67] However, this behavior is more prominent among new hires. After people become better acquainted with one another, demographic differences are less consistently related to turnover. One very large-scale study showed a positive diversity climate was related to higher organizational commitment and lower turnover intentions among African-American, Hispanic, *and* White managers.[68] In other words, all workers appeared to prefer an organization that values diversity.

Diversity in Groups

Most contemporary workplaces require extensive work in group settings. When people work in groups they need to establish a common way of looking at and accomplishing the major tasks, and they need to communicate with one another often. If they feel little sense of membership and cohesion in their groups, all these group attributes are likely to suffer.

Does diversity help or hurt group performance? The answer is "yes." In some cases, diversity in traits can hurt team performance, whereas in others it can facilitate it.[69] Whether diverse or homogeneous teams are more effective depends on the characteristic of interest. Demographic diversity (in gender, race, and ethnicity) does not appear to either help or hurt team performance in general. On the other hand, teams of individuals who are highly intelligent, conscientious, and interested in working in team settings are more effective. Thus diversity on these variables is likely to be a bad thing—it makes little sense to try to form teams that mix in members who are lower in intelligence, conscientiousness, and uninterested in teamwork. In other cases, differences can be a strength. Groups of individuals with different types of expertise and education are more effective than homogeneous groups. Similarly, a group made entirely of assertive people who want to be in charge, or a group whose members all prefer to follow the lead of others, will be less effective than a group that mixes leaders and followers.

Regardless of the composition of the group, differences can be leveraged to achieve superior performance. The most important way is to emphasize the higher-level similarities among members.[70] In other words, groups of diverse individuals will be much more effective if leaders can show how members have a common interest in the group's success. Evidence also shows transformational leaders (who emphasize higher-order goals and values in their leadership style) are more effective in managing diverse teams.[71]

Effective Diversity Programs

5 Describe how organizations manage diversity effectively.

Organizations use a variety of efforts to capitalize on diversity, including the recruiting and selection policies we have already discussed, as well as training and development practices. Effective, comprehensive workforce programs encouraging diversity have three distinct components. First, they teach managers about the legal framework for equal employment opportunity and encourage fair treatment of all people regardless of their demographic characteristics. Second, they teach managers how a diverse workforce will be better able to serve a diverse market of customers and clients. Third, they foster personal development practices that bring out the skills and abilities of all workers, acknowledging how differences in perspective can be a valuable way to improve performance for everyone.[72]

Nissan Motor Company's Diversity Development Office in Japan is helping female employees develop their careers. Nissan provides women, such as its assembly-line employees shown here, with the one-on-one counseling services of career advisors and training programs to develop skills. Women also can visit Nissan's corporate intranet to read interviews with "role models," women who have made huge contributions to the company. Nissan believes that hiring more women and supporting their careers will contribute to the company's competitive advantage.

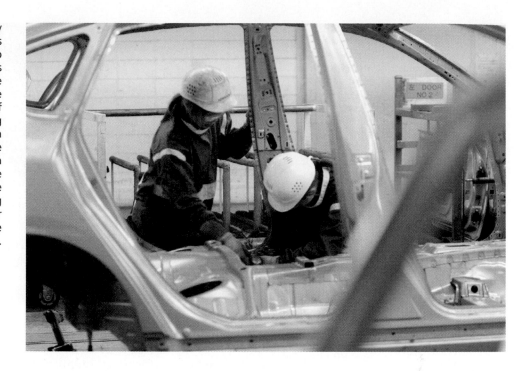

Much concern about diversity has to do with fair treatment.[73] Most negative reactions to employment discrimination are based on the idea that discriminatory treatment is unfair. Regardless of race or gender, people are generally in favor of diversity-oriented programs, including affirmative action, if they believe the policies ensure everyone a fair opportunity to show their skills and abilities.

A major study of the consequences of diversity programs came to what might seem a surprising conclusion.[74] Organizations that provided diversity training were not consistently more likely to have women and minorities in upper management positions than organizations that did not. On closer examination though, these results are not surprising. Experts have long known that one-shot training sessions without strategies to encourage effective diversity management back on the job are not likely to be very effective. Some diversity programs are truly effective in improving representation in management. They include strategies to measure the representation of women and minorities in managerial positions, and they hold managers accountable for achieving more demographically diverse management teams.

Organizational leaders should examine their workforce to determine whether target groups have been underutilized. If groups of employees are not proportionally represented in top management, managers should look for any hidden barriers to advancement. They can often improve recruiting practices, make selection systems more transparent, and provide training for those employees who have not had adequate exposure to certain material in the past. The organization should also clearly communicate its policies to employees so they can understand how and why certain practices are followed. Communications should focus as much as possible on qualifications and job performance; emphasizing certain groups as needing more assistance could well backfire.

To ensure the top-level management team represents the diversity of its workforce and client base, Safeway implemented the Retail Leadership Development (RLD) Program, a formal career development program. This program is open to all employees, so it is inclusive, but women and underrepresented racial or ethnic groups are particularly encouraged to participate. Interested individuals

NASCAR, an American sport with a worldwide following, promotes diversity within its organization and throughout the motorsports industry. Through its Drive for Diversity program, NASCAR ensures that everyone is given a fair opportunity to show and develop his or her skills and abilities. The program seeks to develop minority and female drivers and crew members as shown in this photo. Drivers participate in a scouting combine and earn the chance to compete with an established NASCAR team for a full season. Crew member trainees can compete with a racing team upon completion of their training.

take a series of examinations to determine whether they have management potential. Those who perform well on the tests are provided with work in roles that expose them to managerial opportunities. The program's comprehensive nature is underscored by its additional support activities: All managers attend workshops that help them bring diversity concerns front and center in their staff meetings. They are also charged with providing promising RLD participants with additional training and development opportunities to ensure they have the skills needed for advancement. The program incorporates the type of accountability we have said is crucial to the success of diversity efforts; performance bonuses are provided to managers who meet concrete diversity goals. This program has shown real success: the number of White women store managers has increased by 31 percent since its inception, and the number of women-of-color store managers has increased by 92 percent.[75]

Global Implications

As you will see, there may be no global or cross-cultural research on some of the topics we discuss in a given chapter, and this chapter is no exception. We therefore confine our comments here to areas where there has been the most cross-cultural research: (1) How does research on intellectual abilities generalize across cultures? (2) Do biographical characteristics such as gender and age operate similarly across cultures? and (3) How is diversity managed in different cultures?

Biographical Characteristics

Obviously, some biographical characteristics vary across cultures. Some cultures are more racially homogeneous than others, and the average age of citizens varies across countries (for example, in Italy and Japan, a far greater percentage of the population is over age 65 than in India or China). That doesn't mean, however, that the relationships we've described between age and performance, or between gender and turnover, are different across cultures.

6   Show how culture affects our understanding of biographical characteristics and intellectual abilities.

In contrast to the U.S. tendency to make strong differentiations on the basis of race, in some countries, such as Brazil, people are less likely to define themselves according to distinct racial categories. One Accenture survey of U.S. managers in eight countries revealed some surprising differences. Compared with British managers, female managers in the Philippines believed their country was more supportive of women's advancement into leadership positions.[76] Another interview study showed many of the work–life issues found in U.S. business contexts are also common in France despite government subsidies for childcare.[77] More research on cross-cultural differences in the perceptions of biographical characteristics would be very useful for managers.

Intellectual Abilities

Evidence strongly supports the idea that the structures and measures of intellectual abilities generalize across cultures. Thus, someone in Venezuela or Sudan does not have a different set of mental abilities than a U.S. or Czech worker. Moreover, data from across many cultures support the finding that specific mental abilities indicate a higher-order factor we call general mental ability (GMA). There is some evidence that IQ scores vary to some degree across cultures, but those differences are much smaller when we consider educational and economic differences.[78]

Diversity Management

Besides the mere presence of diversity in international work settings, there are international differences in how diversity is managed. Each country has its own legal framework for dealing with diversity, and these are a powerful reflection of the diversity-related concerns of each country. Many countries require specific targets and quotas for achieving affirmative action goals, whereas the legal framework in the United States specifically forbids their use. Some countries have strong prohibitions on sexual harassment, whereas in other countries behavior unacceptable in U.S. workplaces is common. The types of demographic differences considered important for diversity management also vary across countries. For example, in India the nondiscrimination framework includes quotas and set-aside programs for individuals from lower castes.[79] A case study of the multinational Finnish company TRANSCO found it was possible to develop a consistent global philosophy for diversity management. However, differences in legal and cultural factors across nations forced TRANSCO to develop unique policies to match the cultural and legal frameworks of each country in which it operated.[80]

Summary and Implications for Managers

This chapter looked at diversity from many perspectives. We paid particular attention to three variables—ability, biographical characteristics, and learning. Let's summarize what we found and consider its importance for a manager trying to understand organizational behavior.

Ability   Ability directly influences an employee's level of performance. Given the desire to get high-performing employees, what can a manager do about ability?

First, an effective selection process will improve the fit between employees and job requirements. A job analysis will provide information about jobs currently being done and the abilities individuals need to perform the jobs adequately. Applicants can then be tested, interviewed, and evaluated on the degree to which they possess the necessary abilities.

Second, promotion and transfer decisions affecting individuals already in the organization's employ should reflect candidates' abilities. As with new employees, care should be taken to assess critical abilities incumbents will need in the job and match those with the organization's human resources.

Third, managers can improve the fit by fine-tuning the job to better match an incumbent's abilities. Often, modifications with no significant impact on the job's basic activities, such as changing equipment or reorganizing tasks within a group, can better adapt work to the specific talents of a given employee.

Biographical Characteristics   We can readily observe biographical characteristics, but that doesn't mean we should explicitly use them in management decisions. We also need to be aware of implicit biases we or other managers may have.

Diversity Management   Diversity management must be an ongoing commitment that crosses all levels of the organization. Group management, recruiting, hiring, retention, and development practices can all be designed to leverage diversity for the organization's competitive advantage. Policies to improve the climate for diversity can be effective, so long as they are designed to acknowledge all employees' perspectives. One-shot diversity training sessions are less likely to be effective than comprehensive programs that address the climate for diversity at multiple levels.

The Time Has Come to Move Past Race and Ethnicity

There can be no disputing the tragic divisions that have arisen as a result of racial and ethnic discrimination in the world.[81] Within the U.S. context, we can look to issues like slavery, Jim Crow Laws, and continuing evidence of discrimination in employment. The problem, in all these cases, is people treating one another as members of a group rather than as individuals. The time has come for us to move past identifying ourselves with race and ethnic background so we can truly achieve a society in which each person is judged by his or her own individual characteristics. A number of factors suggest racial and ethnic categories should become less relevant in today's United States:

Ingroup bias. Hundreds of social psychology studies show people tend to develop negative stereotypes about people from other groups. It is practically inevitable that once someone starts to see someone else as being from a different category, there will be tension and prejudice.

Questions about race in biology and upbringing. Geneticists have shown many different genetic strains make up human beings, such that the old categories of Asian, African, and European ancestry are scientifically dubious. There is also more genetic variation within groups than between groups. Many populations do not fit into the standard racial categories at all. And a growing number of children are being raised in multicultural households, presenting a real challenge to those who wish to pigeonhole people into a small number of distinct groups.

Focus on deeper characteristics. Some have argued that the increased prominence of highly successful members of ethnic and racial minority groups means income, rather than race or gender, is the real limiting factor in today's economy. Programs to enhance diversity should be targeted at those with fewer opportunities, whether they are African American, Hispanic, White, Asian, or any other race or ethnicity.

The fact is, racial and ethnic divisions represent a very hurtful part of human history, and we have reached a point where we can move beyond these broad categories and see ourselves primarily as part of the human race.

It may be tempting to try to sweep racial and ethnic differences under the rug as if they no longer existed, but people do differ based on group memberships. When we pretend we are all the same, we are bypassing many of the unique cultural differences that make us interesting. Group memberships can serve a number of valuable functions, including making our differences at the group level meaningful and worthwhile:

A sense of identity. People get a sense of who they are and how they fit into their world by understanding their unique cultural histories. Learning about your ancestors and the struggles your group endured can help to foster a sense of personal pride.

Denying differences doesn't make them go away. Although there is difficulty in defining race genetically, there is a surprisingly strong concordance between people's self-identified racial categories and certain genes. These genetic groupings do also generally correspond to geographic differences in indigenous populations. Although most people would also like to see discrimination go away, there is no denying it still exists. When we do not assess differences in work outcomes across racial and ethnic categories, we cannot confront this discrimination.

Colorblind usually means conforming. Minority groups are often pressured to lose their unique way of dressing, speaking, relating to one another, and even their religion so they can conform to the way mainstream U.S. citizens act. The result is not really a colorblind society but, rather, a monochromatic society in which everyone adopts the dominant culture.

An opportunity for support. Acknowledging group differences helps us to identify other people who have similar cultural experiences. There is a feeling of kinship and bonding that people of Irish ancestry experience on St. Patrick's Day, or that Mexican Americans experience on Cinco de Mayo. Celebrating these cultural holidays gives us a chance to see that we are part of a larger cultural milieu.

The old metaphor of America as a melting pot has been replaced by the idea of a salad bar, made up of many distinct identities that do not need to blend into one homogeneous soup.

Questions for Review

1 Describe forms of workforce diversity.

2 Identify the key biographical characteristics and describe how they are relevant to OB.

3 Define *intellectual ability* and demonstrate its relevance to OB.

4 Contrast intellectual from physical ability.

5 Describe how organizations manage diversity effectively.

6 Show how culture affects our understanding of biographical characteristics and intellectual abilities.

Experiential Exercise

FEELING EXCLUDED

This 6-step exercise takes approximately 20 minutes.

Individual Work (Steps 1–2)

1. All participants are asked to recall a time when they have felt uncomfortable or targeted because of their demographic status. Ideally, situations at work should be used, but if no work situations come to mind, any situation will work. Encourage students to use any demographic characteristic they think is most appropriate, so they can write about feeling excluded on the basis of race, ethnicity, gender, age, disability status, religion, or any other characteristic. They should briefly describe the situation, what precipitated the event, how they felt at the time, how they reacted, and how they believe the other party could have made the situation better.

2. The instructor asks the students to then think about a time when they might have either deliberately or accidentally done something that made someone else feel excluded or targeted because of their demographic status. Once again, they should briefly describe the situation, what precipitated the event, how they felt at the time, how the other person reacted, and how they could have made the situation better.

Small Groups (Steps 3 and 4)

3. Once everyone has written their descriptions, divide the class into small groups of not more than four people. If

at all possible, try to compose groups that are somewhat demographically diverse, to avoid intergroup conflicts in the class review discussion. Students should be encouraged to discuss their situations and consider how their experiences were similar or different.

4. After reading through everyone's reactions, each group should develop a short list of principles for how they personally can work to avoid excluding or targeting people in the future. Encourage them to be as specific as possible, and also ask each group to find solutions that work for everyone. Solutions should focus on both avoiding getting into these situations in the first place and also on resolving these situations when they do occur.

Class Review (Steps 5 and 6)

5. Members of each group are invited to provide a very brief summary of the major principles of how they've felt excluded or targeted, and then to describe their groups' collective decisions regarding how these situations can be minimized in the future.

6. The instructor should lead a discussion on how companies might be able to develop comprehensive policies that will encourage people to be sensitive in their interactions with one another.

Ethical Dilemma

YOU MUST HAVE SEX

Recently, The University of Florida changed its policy to provide health benefits for cohabiting partners. The change ignited some dissent. For example, Larry Cretul, a member of the state legislature whose district includes the university, introduced a bill to make it illegal to use taxpayer dollars to fund a domestic-partner benefit program.

In explaining his bill, Cretul said, "I just happen to be one who supports the idea that marriage should continue to be held in the elevated position."

Another part of the policy sparked as much controversy—to qualify for benefits, cohabiting partners must sign an agreement indicating they're having sex with each other.

The policy stipulates that enrollees "must have been in a non-platonic relationship for the preceding 12 months." One employee of the university said she was offended by the policy and wondered how the university was going to enforce it.

In response, the university's director of human resources, Kyle Cavanaugh, said that the "non-platonic" clause was increasingly common in domestic-partner benefit plans, to rule out qualification for people who happen to be living together but aren't in a romantic relationship. Cavanaugh promises that responses to the question are confidential, but some still wonder. "That's a personal question," said one employee.

In the meantime, a 2008 survey revealed 39 percent of all employers offer domestic partner benefits. Among large employers, the percentage is higher—57 percent among the Fortune 500. Benefit policies continue to operate in a sea of public policy controversy. President Obama extended domestic partner benefits to federal workers only in 2009, earning jeers from conservative leaders on one side and from many gay activists (for not pushing for more comprehensive legislation) on the other. Voters in some states and municipalities—notably California—have rejected statutes that would provide domestic partner benefits. This may be one case where change in practice is occurring faster than change in law.

Questions

1. What do you think about same-sex domestic partner benefits? To what extent are your views affected by your religious or political views?

2. What do you think about the policy that requires employees to stipulate they have sexual relations with their domestic partner? If you think it's a bad policy, what (if anything) would you propose in its place?

3. Do you perceive age differences in how people view this issue?

Sources: Based on "Domestic Partner Benefits: Prevalence Among Private Employers," *Human Rights Campaign* (February 12, 2009), www.hrc.org; J. Stripling, "UF Requirement for Partner Benefits: You Must Have Sex," *Gainesville (Florida) Sun,* January 20, 2006, pp. 1A, 7A; M. Winter, "Obama Gives Some Benefits to Gay Partners of U.S. Workers," *USA Today* (June 17, 2009), blogs.usatoday.com/ondeadline/2009/06/obama-gives-some-benefits-to-gay-partners-of-us-workers.html.

Case Incident 1

THE FLYNN EFFECT

Given that a substantial amount of intellectual ability (up to 80 percent) is inherited, it might surprise you to learn that intelligence test scores are rising. In fact, scores have risen so dramatically that today's great-grandparents seem mentally deficient by comparison.

First, let's review the evidence for rising test scores. Then, we'll review explanations for the results.

On an IQ scale where 100 is the average, scores have been rising about 3 points per decade, meaning if your grandparent scored 100, the average score for your generation would be around 115. That's a pretty big difference—about a standard deviation, meaning someone from your grandparent's generation whose score was at the 84th percentile would be only average (50th percentile) by today's norms.

James Flynn is a New Zealand researcher credited with first documenting the rising scores. He reported the results in 1984, when he found that almost everyone who took a well-validated IQ test in the 1970s did better than those who took one in the 1940s. The results appear to hold up across cultures. Test scores are rising not only in the United States but in most other countries in which the effect has been tested, too.

What explains the Flynn Effect? Researchers are not entirely sure, but some of the explanations offered are these:

1. **Education.** Students today are better educated than their ancestors, and education leads to higher test scores.

2. **Smaller families.** In 1900, the average couple had four children; today the number is less than two. We know firstborns tend to have higher IQs than other children, probably because they receive more attention than their later-born siblings.

3. **Test-taking savvy.** Today's children have been tested so often that they are test savvy: they know how to take tests and how to do well on them.

4. **Genes.** Although smart couples tend to have fewer, not more, children (which might lead us to expect intelligence in the population to drop over time), it's possible that due to better education, tracking, and testing, those who do have the right genes are better able to exploit those advantages. Some genetics researchers also have argued that if genes for intelligence carried by both parents are dominant, they win

out, meaning the child's IQ will be as high as or higher than those of the parents.

Questions

1. Do you believe people are really getting smarter? Why or why not?

2. Which of the factors explaining the Flynn Effect do you accept?

3. Are there any societal advantages or disadvantages to the Flynn Effect?

Sources: Based on S. Begley, "Sex, Race, and IQ: Off Limits?" *Newsweek* (April 20, 2009), www.newsweek.com; and M. A. Mingroni, "Resolving the IQ Paradox: Heterosis as a Cause of the Flynn Effect and Other Trends," *Psychological Review,* July 2007, pp. 806–829; W. Johnson, "What Is Intelligence? Beyond the Flynn Effect," *Times Higher Education* (January 10, 2008), www.timeshighereducation.co.uk.

Case Incident 2

WHAT DOES DIVERSITY TRAINING TEACH?

We noted in the chapter that some researchers have provided evidence that diversity training programs may not be delivering the expected outcomes. The authors interpret this evidence as a sign that corporate efforts to improve diversity are more effective when the focus is on concrete measurable goals with accountability. It may be that entrenched attitudes related to race, ethnicity, and gender are just too hard to change in short-term classroom settings.

Others argue that diversity training isn't really designed to increase the number of women and minorities in top management positions but rather to improve relationships among workers.

Reviews of the historical development of diversity programs demonstrate some significant changes in the ways diversity trainers conceptualize their role. Early diversity training efforts focused primarily on legal compliance and the regulatory framework. This may have created an attitude that diversity was a problem to be solved and avoided when possible, rather than an opportunity. Demographic diversity was also the only focus of these programs, meaning other forms of workforce diversity, like differences in abilities or attitudes, were ignored.

There were also features that led to unintended consequences. Some diversity programs encouraged participants to describe stereotypical language regarding different groups in an effort to expose the content of people's assumptions. Unfortunately, follow-up discussions with participants showed the discussions may have reinforced the very stereotypes the programs were supposed to undermine. These practices also could be very embarrassing for participants. Because the training focused primarily on portraying historically underrepresented minorities and women in White male-dominated environments, White males (who make up a significant portion of the workforce) felt excluded and stigmatized.

Contemporary diversity management programs have changed their focus considerably in response to these concerns. Diversity training sessions are now designed to minimize public shame or embarrassment. Legal compliance is still a major part of diversity training, but the business case for effective diversity management is a much more central component of training sessions.

Questions

1. Do you think representation in top management is a fair indicator of the effects of diversity training programs? Why or why not?

2. Why might one-shot diversity training programs be ineffective?

3. What significant obstacles must be overcome to make diversity programs effective?

4. How could you design more effective diversity programs?

Sources: Based on A. Kalev, F. Dobbin, and E. Kelly, "Best Practices or Best Guesses? Assessing the Efficacy of Corporate Affirmative Action and Diversity Policies," *American Sociological Review* 71, no. 4 (2006), pp. 589–617; R. Anand and M. Winters, "A Retrospective View of Corporate Diversity Training from 1964 to the Present," *Academy of Management Learning and Education* 7, no. 3 (2008), pp. 356–372.

Endnotes

1. Based on T. F. Shea, "Dismantling Language Barriers," *HRMagazine,* November 2008, pp. 48–52; C. Huff, "Special Report on Training & Development: Powering Up a Hispanic Workforce," *Workforce Management,* May 18, 2009, pp. 25–29; and S. J. Wells, "Say ¡Hola! to the Majority Minority," *HRMagazine,* September 2008, pp. 38–50.

2. M. DiNatale and S. Boraas, "The Labor Force Experience of Women from Generation X," *Monthy Labor Review,* March 2002, pp. 1–15.

3. See, for example, F. Welch, "Catching Up: Wages of Black Men," *The American Economic Review* 93, no. 2 (2003), pp. 320–325; and A. Sakamoto, H. Wu, and J. M. Tzeng, "The Declining Significance of Race Among American Men During the Latter Half of the Twentieth Century," *Demography* 37, January 2000, pp. 41–51.

4. J. Schram, *SHRM Workplace Forecast* (Alexandria, VA: Society for Human Resource Management, 2006).

5. D. A. Harrison, K. H. Price, J. H. Gavin, and A. T. Florey, "Time, Teams, and Task Performance: Changing Effects of Surface- and Deep-Level Diversity on Group Functioning," *Academy of Management Journal* 45, no. 5 (2002), pp. 1029–1045; and D. A. Harrison, K. H. Price, and M. P. Bell, "Beyond Relational Demography: Time and the Effects of Surface- and Deep-Level Diversity on Work Group Cohesion," *Academy of Management Journal* 41, no. 1 (1998), pp. 96–107.

6. P. Chattopadhyay, M. Tluchowska, and E. George, "Identifying the Ingroup: A Closer Look at the Influence of Demographic Dissimilarity on Employee Social Identity," *Academy of Management Review* 29, no. 2 (2004), pp. 180–202; and P. Chattopadhyay, "Beyond Direct and Symmetrical Effects: The Influence of Demographic Dissimilarity on Organizational Citizenship Behavior," *Academy of Management Journal* 42, no. 3 (1999), pp. 273–287.

7. L. M. Cortina, "Unseen Injustice: Incivility as Modern Discrimination in Organizations," *Academy of Management Review* 33, no. 1 (2008), pp. 55–75.

8. J. Levitz and P. Shishkin, "More Workers Cite Age Bias After Layoffs," *Wall Street Journal,* March 11, 2009, pp. D1–D2.

9. W. M. Bulkeley, "A Data-Storage Titan Confronts Bias Claims," *Wall Street Journal,* September 12, 2007, pp. A1, A16.

10. D. Walker, "Incident with Noose Stirs Old Memories," *McClatchy-Tribune Business News,* June 29, 2008; and D. Solis, "Racial Horror Stories Keep EEOC Busy," *Knight-Ridder Tribune Business News,* July 30, 2005, p. 1.

11. H. Ibish and A. Stewart, *Report on Hate Crimes and Discrimination Against Arab Americans: The Post-September 11 Backlash, September 11, 2001—October 11, 2001* (Washington, DC: American-Arab Anti-Discrimination Committee, 2003).

12. A. Raghavan, "Wall Street's Disappearing Women," *Forbes,* March 16, 2009, pp. 72–78.

13. L. M. Cortina, "Unseen Injustice: Incivility as Modern Discrimination in Organizations."

14. R. J. Grossman, "Keep Pace with Older Workers," *HR Magazine,* May 2008, pp. 39–46.

15. K. Greene, "Older Workers Can Get a Raw Deal—Some Employers Admit to Promoting, Challenging Their Workers Less," *Wall Street Journal,* April 10, 2003, p. D2; and K. A. Wrenn and T. J. Maurer, "Beliefs About Older Workers' Learning and Development Behavior in Relation to Beliefs About Malleability of Skills, Age-Related Decline, and Control," *Journal of Applied Social Psychology* 34, no. 2 (2004), pp. 223–242.

16. D. R. Davies, G. Matthews, and C. S. K. Wong, "Ageing and Work," in C. L. Cooper and I. T. Robertson (eds.), *International Review of Industrial and Organizational Psychology,* vol. 6 (Chichester, UK: Wiley, 1991), pp. 183–187.

17. R. D. Hackett, "Age, Tenure, and Employee Absenteeism," *Human Relations,* July 1990, pp. 601–619.

18. Cited in K. Labich, "The New Unemployed," *Fortune,* March 8, 1993, p. 43.

19. See G. M. McEvoy and W. F. Cascio, "Cumulative Evidence of the Relationship Between Employee Age and Job Performance," *Journal of Applied Psychology,* February 1989, pp. 11–17; and F. L. Schmidt and J. E. Hunter, "The Validity and Utility of Selection Methods in Personnel Psychology: Practical and Theoretical Implications of 85 Years of Research Findings," *Psychological Bulletin* 124 (1998), pp. 262–274.

20. R. Lee and E. R. Wilbur, "Age, Education, Job Tenure, Salary, Job Characteristics, and Job Satisfaction: A Multivariate Analysis," *Human Relations,* August 1985, pp. 781–791.

21. K. M. Kacmar and G. R. Ferris, "Theoretical and Methodological Considerations in the Age–Job Satisfaction Relationship," *Journal of Applied Psychology,* April 1989, pp. 201–207; and W. A. Hochwarter, G. R. Ferris, P. L. Perrewe, L. A. Witt, and C. Kiewitz, "A Note on the Nonlinearity of the Age–Job Satisfaction Relationship," *Journal of Applied Social Psychology,* June 2001, pp. 1223–1237.

22. See E. M. Weiss, G. Kemmler, E. A. Deisenhammer, W. W. Fleischhacker, and M. Delazer, "Sex Differences in Cognitive Functions," *Personality and Individual Differences,* September 2003, pp. 863–875; and A. F. Jorm, K. J. Anstey, H. Christensen, and B. Rodgers, "Gender Differences in Cognitive Abilities: The Mediating Role of Health State and Health Habits," *Intelligence,* January 2004, pp. 7–23.

23. See M. M. Black and E. W. Holden, "The Impact of Gender on Productivity and Satisfaction Among Medical School Psychologists," *Journal of Clinical Psychology in Medical Settings,* March 1998, pp. 117–131.

24. M. E. Heilman and T. G. Okimoto, "Why Are Women Penalized for Success at Male Tasks? The Implied Communality Deficit," *Journal of Applied Psychology* 92, no. 1 (2007), pp. 81–92.

25. C. Kirchmeyer, "The Different Effects of Family on Objective Career Success Across Gender: A Test of Alternative Explanations," *Journal of Vocational Behavior* 68, no. 2 (2006), pp. 323–346; and C. Guillaume and S. Pochic, "What Would You Sacrifice? Access to Top Management and the Work-Life Balance," *Gender, Work & Organization* 16, no. 1 (2009), pp. 14–36.

26. P. W. Hom, L. Roberson, and A. D. Ellis, "Challenging Conventional Wisdom About Who Quits: Revelations from Corporate America," *Journal of Applied Psychology* 93, no. 1 (2008), pp. 1–34.

27. See, for instance, K. D. Scott and E. L. McClellan, "Gender Differences in Absenteeism," *Public Personnel Management,* Summer 1990, pp. 229–253; and A. VandenHeuvel and M. Wooden, "Do Explanations of Absenteeism Differ for

Men and Women?" *Human Relations,* November 1995, pp. 1309–1329.

28. This discussion is largely based on D. F. Halpern, C. P. Benbow, D. C. Geary, R. C. Gur, J. Shibley Hyde, and M. A. Gernsbacher, "The Science of Sex Differences in Science and Mathematics," *Psychological Science in the Public Interest* 8, no. 1 (2007), pp. 1–51.

29. National Science Foundation, *Gender Differences in the Careers of Academic Scientists and Engineers* (NSF 04-323) (Arlington VA: Division of Science Resources Statistics, 2002).

30. See, for instance, M. Tait, M. Y. Padgett, and T. T. Baldwin, "Job and Life Satisfaction: A Reevaluation of the Strength of the Relationship and Gender Effects as a Function of the Date of the Study," *Journal of Applied Psychology,* June 1989, pp. 502–507; and M. B. Grover, "Daddy Stress," *Forbes,* September 6, 1999, pp. 202–208.

31. S. Halrynjo, "Men's Work-Life Conflict: Career, Care and Self-Realization: Patterns of Privileges and Dilemmas," *Gender, Work & Organization* 16, no. 1 (2009), pp. 98–125; and S. Jayson, "Gender Roles See a 'Conflict' Shift," *USA Today,* March 26, 2009, p. 1A.

32. M. E. Heilman and T. G. Okimoto, "Motherhood: A Potential Source of Bias in Employment Decisions," *Journal of Applied Psychology* 93, no. 1 (2008), pp. 189–198.

33. J. M. Sacco, C. R. Scheu, A. M. Ryan, and N. Schmitt, "An Investigation of Race and Sex Similarity Effects in Interviews: A Multilevel Approach to Relational Demography," *Journal of Applied Psychology* 88, no. 5 (2003), pp. 852–865; and G. N. Powell and D. A. Butterfield, "Exploring the Influence of Decision Makers' Race and Gender on Actual Promotions to Top Management," *Personnel Psychology* 55, no. 2 (2002), pp. 397–428.

34. D. A. Kravitz, D. M. Mayer, L. M. Leslie, and D. Lev-Arey, "Understanding Attitudes Toward Affirmative Action Programs in Employment: Summary and Meta-Analysis of 35 Years of Research," *Journal of Applied Psychology* 91 (2006), pp. 1013–1036.

35. J. M. Sacco, C. R. Scheu, A. M. Ryan, and N. Schmitt, "An Investigation of Race and Sex Similarity Effects in Interviews: A Multilevel Approach to Relational Demography," *Journal of Applied Psychology* 88, no. 5 (2003), pp. 852–865; P. F. McKay and M. A. McDaniel, "A Reexamination of Black-White Mean Differences in Work Performance: More Data, More Moderators," *Journal of Applied Psychology* 91, no. 3 (2006), pp. 538–554.

36. P. Bobko, P. L. Roth, and D. Potosky, "Derivation and Implications of a Meta-Analytic Matrix Incorporating Cognitive Ability, Alternative Predictors, and Job Performance," *Personnel Psychology,* Autumn 1999, pp. 561–589.

37. M. J. Ree, T. R. Carretta, and J. R. Steindl, "Cognitive Ability," in N. Anderson, D. S. Ones, H. K. Sinangil, and C. Viswesvaran (eds.), *Handbook of Industrial, Work, and Organizational Psychology,* vol. 1 (London: Sage Publications, 2001), pp. 219–232.

38. W. T. Dickens and J. R. Flynn, "Black Americans Reduce the Racial IQ Gap: Evidence from Standardization Samples," *Psychological Science* 17 (2006), pp. 913–920; and C. Murray, "The Magnitude and Components of Change in the Black-White IQ Difference from 1920 to 1991: A Birth Cohort Analysis of the Woodcock-Johnson Standardizations," *Intelligence* 35, no. 44 (2007), pp. 305–318.

39. See J. P. Rushton and A. R. Jenson, "Thirty Years of Research on Race Differences in Cognitive Ability," *Psychology, Public Policy, and the Law* 11, no. 2 (2005), pp. 235–295; and R. E. Nisbett, "Heredity, Environment, and Race Differences in IQ: A Commentary on Rushton and Jensen (2005)," *Psychology, Public Policy, and the Law* 11, no. 2 (2005), pp. 302–310.

40. *Americans with Disabilities Act,* 42 U.S.C. § 12101, et seq. (1990).

41. S. G. Goldberg, M. B. Killeen, and B. O'Day, "The Disclosure Conundrum: How People with Psychiatric Disabilities Navigate Employment," *Psychology, Public Policy, and Law* 11, no. 3 (2005), pp. 463–500; M. L. Ellison, Z. Russinova, K. L. MacDonald-Wilson, and A. Lyass, "Patterns and Correlates of Workplace Disclosure Among Professionals and Managers with Psychiatric Conditions," *Journal of Vocational Rehabilitation* 18, no. 1 (2003), pp. 3–13.

42. L. R. Ren, R. L. Paetzold, and A. Colella, "A Meta-Analysis of Experimental Studies on the Effects of Disability on Human Resource Judgments," *Human Resource Management Review* 18, no. 3 (2008), pp. 191–203.

43. S. Almond and A. Healey, "Mental Health and Absence from Work: New Evidence from the UK Quarterly Labour Force Survey," *Work, Employment, and Society* 17, no. 4 (2003), pp. 731–742.

44. E. Louvet, "Social Judgment Toward Job Applicants with Disabilities: Perception of Personal Qualities and Competences," *Rehabilitation Psychology* 52, no. 3 (2007), pp. 297–303; and W. D. Gouvier, S. Sytsma-Jordan, and S. Mayville, "Patterns of Discrimination in Hiring Job Applicants with Disabilities: The Role of Disability Type, Job Complexity, and Public Contact," *Rehabilitation Psychology* 48, no. 3 (2003), pp. 175–181.

45. A. Colella, A. S. DeNisi, and A. Varma, "The Impact of Ratee's Disability on Performance Judgments and Choice as Partner: The Role of Disability-Job Fit Stereotypes and Interdependence of Rewards," *Journal of Applied Psychology* 83, no. 1 (1998), pp. 102–111.

46. J. M. Czajka and A. S. DeNisi, "Effects of Emotional Disability and Clear Performance Standards on Performance Ratings," *Academy of Management Journal* 31, no. 2 (1988), pp. 394–404.

47. B. S. Bell and K. J. Klein, "Effect of Disability, Gender, and Job Level on Ratings of Job Applicants," *Rehabilitation Psychology* 46, no. 3 (2001), pp. 229–246; E. Louvet, "Social Judgment Toward Job Applicants with Disabilities: Perception of Personal Qualities and Competences."

48. M. A. Quinones, J. K. Ford, and M. S. Teachout, "The Relationship Between Work Experience and Job Performance: A Conceptual and Meta-analytic Review," *Personnel Psychology,* Winter 1995, pp. 887–910.

49. I. R. Gellatly, "Individual and Group Determinants of Employee Absenteeism: Test of a Causal Model," *Journal of Organizational Behavior,* September 1995, pp. 469–485.

50. P. O. Popp and J. A. Belohlav, "Absenteeism in a Low Status Work Environment," *Academy of Management Journal,* September 1982, p. 681.

51. Griffeth, Hom, and Gaertner, "A Meta-analysis of Antecedents," pp. 463–488.

52. R. D. Gatewood and H. S. Field, *Human Resource Selection* (Chicago: Dryden Press, 1987).

53. J. A. Breaugh and D. L. Dossett, "The Effectiveness of Biodata for Predicting Turnover," paper presented at the National Academy of Management Conference, New Orleans, August 1987.

54. W. van Breukelen, R. van der Vlist, and H. Steensma, "Voluntary Employee Turnover: Combining Variables from the 'Traditional' Turnover Literature with the Theory of Planned Behavior," *Journal of Organizational Behavior* 25, no. 7 (2004), pp. 893–914.

55. M. Elias, "USA's Muslims Under a Cloud," *USA Today,* August 10, 2006, pp. 1D, 2D; and R. R. Hastings, "Muslims Seek Acknowledgement of Mainstream Americans," *HRWeek,* May 11, 2007, p. 1.

56. *HRC Corporate Equality Index,* 2006, http://www.hrc.org/ documents/ HRCCorporateEqualityIndex2006.pdf; and R. R. Hastings, "Necessity Breeds Inclusion: Reconsidering 'Don't Ask, Don't Tell,'" *HRWeek,* January 2007, pp. 1–2.

57. B. Leonard, "Transgender Issues Test Diversity Limits," *HRMagazine,* June 2007, pp. 32–34.

58. L. S. Gottfredson, "The Challenge and Promise of Cognitive Career Assessment," *Journal of Career Assessment* 11, no. 2 (2003), pp. 115–135.

59. M. D. Dunnette, "Aptitudes, Abilities, and Skills," in M. D. Dunnette (ed.), *Handbook of Industrial and Organizational Psychology* (Chicago: Rand McNally, 1976), pp. 478–483.

60. J. F. Salgado, N. Anderson, S. Moscoso, C. Bertua, F. de Fruyt, and J. P. Rolland, "A Meta-analytic Study of General Mental Ability Validity for Different Occupations in the European Community," *Journal of Applied Psychology,* December 2003, pp. 1068–1081; and F. L. Schmidt and J. E. Hunter, "Select on Intelligence," in E. A. Locke (ed.), *Handbook of Principles of Organizational Behavior* (Malden, MA: Blackwell, 2004).

61. Y. Ganzach, "Intelligence and Job Satisfaction," *Academy of Management Journal* 41, no. 5 (1998), pp. 526–539; and Y. Ganzach, "Intelligence, Education, and Facets of Job Satisfaction," *Work and Occupations* 30, no. 1 (2003), pp. 97–122.

62. E. A. Fleishman, "Evaluating Physical Abilities Required by Jobs," *Personnel Administrator,* June 1979, pp. 82–92.

63. D. R. Avery, "Reactions to diversity in recruitment advertising: Are the differences black and white?" *Journal of Applied Psychology* 88, no. 4 (2003), pp. 672–679; P. F. McKay and D. R. Avery, "What Has Race Got to Do with It? Unraveling the Role of Racioethnicity in Job Seekers' Reactions to Site Visits," *Personnel Psychology* 59, no. 2 (2006), pp. 395–429; and D. R. Avery and P. F. McKay, "Target Practice: An Organizational Impression Management Approach to Attracting Minority and Female Job Applicants," *Personnel Psychology* 59, no. 1 (2006), pp. 157–187.

64. M. R. Buckley, K. A. Jackson, M. C. Bolino, J. G. Veres, and H. S. Field, "The Influence of Relational Demography on Panel Interview Ratings: A Field Experiment," *Personnel Psychology* 60 (2007), pp. 627–646; J. M. Sacco, C. R. Scheu, A. M. Ryan, and N. Schmitt, "An Investigation of Race and Sex Similarity Effects in Interviews: A Multilevel Approach to Relational Demography," *Journal of Applied Psychology* 88, (2003), pp. 852–865; and J. C. Ziegert and P. J. Hanges, "Employment Discrimination: The Role of Implicit Attitudes, Motivation, and a Climate for Racial Bias," *Journal of Applied Psychology* 90 (2005), pp. 553–562.

65. J. Schaubroeck and S. S. K. Lam, "How Similarity to Peers and Supervisor Influences Organizational Advancement in Different Cultures," *Academy of Management Journal* 45 (2002), pp. 1120–1136.

66. P. F. McKay, D. R. Avery, and M. A. Morris, "Mean Racial-Ethnic Differences in Employee Sales Performance: The Moderating Role of Diversity Climate," *Personnel Psychology* 61, no. 2 (2008), pp. 349–374.

67. A. S. Tsui, T. D. Egan, and C. A. O'Reilly, "Being different: Relational demography and organizational attachment," *Administrative Science Quarterly* 37 (1992), pp. 547–579; and J. M. Sacco and N. Schmitt, "A Dynamic Multilevel Model of Demographic Diversity and Misfit Effects," *Journal of Applied Psychology* 90 (2005), pp. 203–231.

68. P. F. McKay, D. R. Avery, S. Tonidandel, M. A. Morris, M. Hernandez, and M. R. Hebl, "Racial Differences in Employee Retention: Are Diversity Climate Perceptions the Key?" *Personnel Psychology* 60, no. 1 (2007), pp. 35–62.

69. S. T. Bell, "Deep-Level Composition Variables as Predictors of Team Performance: A Meta–Analysis," *Journal of Applied Psychology* 92, no. 3 (2007), pp. 595–615; S. K. Horwitz and I. B. Horwitz, "The Effects of Team Diversity on Team Outcomes: A Meta-Analytic Review of Team Demography," *Journal of Management* 33, no. 6 (2007), pp. 987–1015; G. L. Stewart, "A Meta-Analytic Review of Relationships Between Team Design Features and Team Performance," *Journal of Management* 32, no. 1 (2006), pp. 29–54; and A. Joshi and H. Roh, "The Role of Context in Work Team Diversity Research: A Meta-Analytic Review," *Academy of Management Journal* 52, no. 3 (2009), pp. 599–627.

70. A. C. Homan, J. R. Hollenbeck, S. E. Humphrey, D. Van Knippenberg, D. R. Ilgen, and G. A. Van Kleef, "Facing Differences with an Open Mind: Openness to Experience, Salience of Intragroup Differences, and Performance of Diverse Work Groups," *Academy of Management Journal* 51, no. 6 (2008), pp. 1204–1222.

71. E. Kearney and D. Gebert, "Managing Diversity and Enhancing Team Outcomes: The Promise of Transformational Leadership," *Journal of Applied Psychology* 94, no. 1 (2009), pp. 77–89.

72. D. A. Thomas and R. J. Ely, "Making Differences Matter: A New Paradigm for Managing Diversity," *Harvard Business Review* 74, no. 5 (1996), pp. 79–90; C. L. Holladay and M. A. Quiñones, "The Influence of Training Focus and Trainer Characteristics on Diversity Training Effectiveness," *Academy of Management Learning and Education* 7, no. 3 (2008), pp. 343–354; and R. Anand and M. Winters, "A Retrospective View of Corporate Diversity Training from 1964 to the Present," *Academy of Management Learning and Education* 7, no. 3 (2008), pp. 356–372.

73. Q. M. Roberson and C. K. Stevens, "Making Sense of Diversity in the Workplace: Organizational Justice and Language Abstraction in Employees' Accounts of Diversity-Related Incidents," *Journal of Applied Psychology* 91 (2006), pp. 379–391; and D. A. Harrison, D. A. Kravitz, D. M. Mayer, L. M. Leslie, and D. Lev-Arey, "Understanding Attitudes Toward Affirmative Action Programs in Employment: Summary and Meta-Analysis of 35 Years of Research," *Journal of Applied Psychology* 91 (2006), pp. 1013–1036.

74. A. Kalev, F. Dobbin, and E. Kelly, "Best Practices or Best Guesses? Assessing the Efficacy of Corporate Affirmative Action and Diversity Policies," *American Sociological Review* 71, no. 4 (2006), pp. 589–617.

75. A. Pomeroy, "Cultivating Female Leaders," *HR Magazine,* February 2007, pp. 44–50.

76. S. Falk, "The Anatomy of the Glass Ceiling," *Accenture* (2006), www.accenture.com.

77. C. Guillaume and S. Pochic, "What Would You Sacrifice? Access to Top Management and the Work-Life Balance," *Gender, Work & Organization* 16, no. 1 (2009), pp. 14–36.

78. N. Barber, "Educational and Ecological Correlates of IQ: A Cross-National Investigation," *Intelligence* (May–June 2005), pp. 273–284.

79. E. Bellman, "Reversal of Fortune Isolates India's Brahmins," *Wall Street Journal,* December 29, 2007, p. A4.

80. A. Sippola and A. Smale, "The Global Integration of Diversity Management: A Longitudinal Case Study," *International Journal of Human Resource Management* 18, no. 11 (2007), pp. 1895–1916.

81. Points in this argument are based in part on J. Lee, and F. D. Bean, "America's Changing Color Lines: Immigration, Race/Ethnicity, and Multiracial Identification," *Annual Review of Sociology* 30 (2004), pp. 221–242; J. E. Helms, M. Jernigan, and J. Mascher, "The Meaning of Race in Psychology and How to Change It," *American Psychologist* 60, no. 1 (2005), pp. 27–36; and E. Bazar and P. Overberg, "Census Projects More Diversity in Workforce," *USA Today,* August 14 (2008), p. 4A.

LEARNING OBJECTIVES

After studying this chapter, you should be able to:

1 Contrast the three components of an attitude.

2 Summarize the relationship between attitudes and behavior.

3 Compare and contrast the major job attitudes.

4 Define *job satisfaction* and show how we can measure it.

5 Summarize the main causes of job satisfaction.

6 Identify four employee responses to dissatisfaction.

7 Show whether job satisfaction is a relevant concept in countries other than the United States.

Attitudes and Job Satisfaction

3

Attitude isn't everything, but it's close.

—*New York Times* headline, August 6, 2006

EMPLOYEES FIRST, CUSTOMERS SECOND

India-based HCL Technologies recently decided on a radical change in its mission. HCL sells various information technology product services, such as laptop, custom software development, and technology consulting. With nearly 50,000 employees—making it one of the largest companies in India—HCL is hardly a small start-up that can afford to be quirky. However, because luring and keeping top talent comprise one of its greatest business challenges, HCL felt it had little choice.

The new mission, called Employee First, explicitly informed HCL's constituents—including its customers—that employee satisfaction was its top priority. Of course, that is easier to say than to do. How did HCL attempt to fulfill this mission?

Part of the initiative was structural—HCL inverted its organizational structure to place more power in the hands of front-line employees, especially those in direct contact with customers and clients. It increased its investment in employee development and improved communication through greater transparency. Employees were encouraged to communicate directly with HCL's CEO, Vineet Nayar; through a forum called U&I, Nayar fielded more than a hundred questions from employees every week. "I threw open the door and invited criticism," he said.

Perhaps the signature piece of the mission was what HCL called "trust pay." In contrast to the industry standard—in which the average employee's pay is 30 percent variable—HCL decided to pay higher fixed salaries and reduce the variable component.

These moves not only made sense from a human resource perspective, but by making it easier to attract and retain valued technology employees they also supported HCL's marketing strategy to pursue more complex, high-value contracts with global giants IBM and Accenture.

How well has Employee First worked? Evaluating such programs is difficult. HCL appears to have fielded the global recession—which hit high-tech companies in India particularly hard—in better shape than many of its competitors. Even skeptics of the program, such as Shami Khorana, president of HCL's U.S. unit, were won over. "My first thought was 'How will the customers react when they hear employee first, customer second?'" Khorana said. "In the end, it's very easy for them to understand and even appreciate."[1]

Though most will not go as far as HCL Technologies to promote employee satisfaction, many organizations are very concerned with the attitudes of their employees. In this chapter, we look at attitudes, their link to behavior, and how employees' satisfaction or dissatisfaction with their jobs affects the workplace.

What are your attitudes toward your job? Use the following Self-Assessment Library to determine your level of satisfaction with your current or past jobs.

Self Assessment Library

HOW SATISFIED AM I WITH MY JOB?

In the Self-Assessment Library (available on CD or online), take assessment I.B.3 (How Satisfied Am I with My Job?) and then answer the following questions. If you currently do not have a job, answer the questions for your most recent job.

1. *How does your job satisfaction compare to that of others in your class who have taken the assessment?*
2. *Why do you think your satisfaction is higher or lower than average?*

Attitudes

1 Contrast the three components of an attitude.

Attitudes are evaluative statements—either favorable or unfavorable—about objects, people, or events. They reflect how we feel about something. When I say "I like my job," I am expressing my attitude about work.

Attitudes are complex. If you ask people about their attitude toward religion, Paris Hilton, or the organization they work for, you may get a simple response, but the reasons underlying the response are probably complex. In order to fully understand attitudes, we must consider their fundamental properties or components.

What Are the Main Components of Attitudes?

Typically, researchers have assumed that attitudes have three components: cognition, affect, and behavior.[2] Let's look at each.

The statement "My pay is low" is the **cognitive component** of an attitude—a description of or belief in the way things are. It sets the stage for the more critical part of an attitude—its **affective component**. Affect is the emotional or feeling segment of an attitude and is reflected in the statement "I am angry over how little I'm paid." Finally, affect can lead to behavioral outcomes. The **behavioral component** of an attitude describes an intention to behave in a certain way toward someone or something—to continue the example, "I'm going to look for another job that pays better."

Viewing attitudes as having three components—cognition, affect, and behavior—is helpful in understanding their complexity and the potential relationship between attitudes and behavior. Keep in mind that these components are closely related, and cognition and affect in particular are inseparable in many ways. For example, imagine you concluded that someone had just treated you unfairly. Aren't you likely to have feelings about that, occurring virtually instantaneously with the thought? Thus, cognition and affect are intertwined.

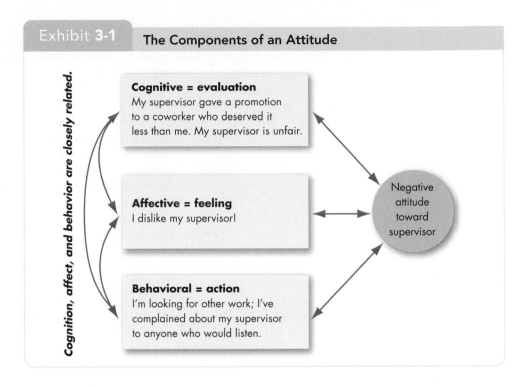

Exhibit 3-1   The Components of an Attitude

Cognition, affect, and behavior are closely related.

Cognitive = evaluation
My supervisor gave a promotion to a coworker who deserved it less than me. My supervisor is unfair.

Affective = feeling
I dislike my supervisor!

Behavioral = action
I'm looking for other work; I've complained about my supervisor to anyone who would listen.

Negative attitude toward supervisor

Exhibit 3-1 illustrates how the three components of an attitude are related. In this example, an employee didn't get a promotion he thought he deserved; a co-worker got it instead. The employee's attitude toward his supervisor is illustrated as follows: The employee thought he deserved the promotion (cognition), he strongly dislikes his supervisor (affect), and he is looking for another job (behavior). As we've noted, although we often think cognition causes affect, which then causes behavior, in reality these components are often difficult to separate.

2   Summarize the relationship between attitudes and behavior.

In organizations, attitudes are important for their behavioral component. If workers believe, for example, that supervisors, auditors, bosses, and time-and-motion engineers are all in conspiracy to make employees work harder for the same or less money, it makes sense to try to understand how these attitudes formed, their relationship to actual job behavior, and how they might be changed.

Does Behavior Always Follow from Attitudes?

Early research on attitudes assumed they were causally related to behavior—that is, the attitudes people hold determine what they do. Common sense, too, suggests a relationship. Isn't it logical that people watch television programs they like, or that employees try to avoid assignments they find distasteful?

However, in the late 1960s, a review of the research challenged this assumed effect of attitudes on behavior.[3] One researcher—Leon Festinger—argued that attitudes *follow* behavior. Did you ever notice how people change what they say

---

attitudes   *Evaluative statements or judgments concerning objects, people, or events.*

cognitive component   *The opinion or belief segment of an attitude.*

affective component   *The emotional or feeling segment of an attitude.*

behavioral component   *An intention to behave in a certain way toward someone or something.*

so it doesn't contradict what they do? Perhaps a friend of yours has consistently argued that the quality of U.S. cars isn't up to that of imports and that he'd never own anything but a Japanese or German car. But his dad gives him a late-model Ford Mustang, and suddenly he says U.S. cars aren't so bad. Festinger proposed that cases of attitude following behavior illustrate the effects of **cognitive dissonance**,[4] any incompatibility an individual might perceive between two or more attitudes or between behavior and attitudes. Festinger argued that any form of inconsistency is uncomfortable and that individuals will therefore attempt to reduce it. They will seek a stable state, which is a minimum of dissonance.

Research has generally concluded that people do seek consistency among their attitudes and between their attitudes and their behavior.[5] They either alter the attitudes or the behavior, or they develop a rationalization for the discrepancy. Tobacco executives provide an example.[6] How, you might wonder, do these people cope with the continuing revelations about the health dangers of smoking? They can deny any clear causation between smoking and cancer. They can brainwash themselves by continually articulating the benefits of tobacco. They can acknowledge the negative consequences of smoking but rationalize that people are going to smoke and that tobacco companies merely promote freedom of choice. They can accept the evidence and make cigarettes less dangerous or reduce their availability to more vulnerable groups, such as teenagers. Or they can quit their job because the dissonance is too great.

No individual, of course, can completely avoid dissonance. You know cheating on your income tax is wrong, but you fudge the numbers a bit every year and hope you're not audited. Or you tell your children to floss their teeth, but you don't do it yourself. Festinger proposed that the desire to reduce dissonance depends on moderating factors, including the *importance* of the elements creating it and the degree of *influence* we believe we have over them. Individuals will be more motivated to reduce dissonance when the attitudes or behavior are important or when they believe the dissonance is due to something they can control. A third factor is the *rewards* of dissonance; high rewards accompanying high dissonance tend to reduce the tension inherent in the dissonance.

Marriott International strives for consistency between employee attitudes and behavior through its motto "Spirit to Serve." CEO and Chairman J. W. Marriott, Jr., models the behavior of service by visiting hotel employees throughout the year. "I want our associates to know that there really is a guy named Marriott who cares about them," he says. The company honors employees with job excellence awards for behavior that exemplifies an attitude of service to customers and fellow employees.

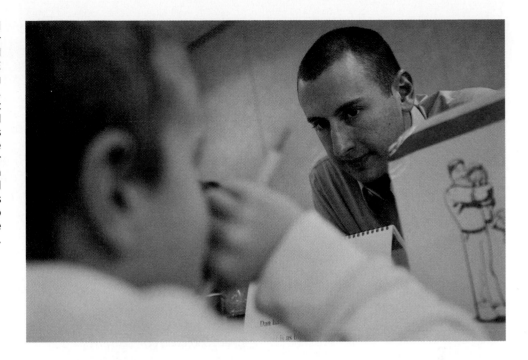

General Electric invites all employees to build stronger communities where they live and work. This photo shows GE employees volunteering as reading coaches for second grade students. GE gives its employees direct experience with helping others and improving their lives through its online Volunteer Portal, where employees find volunteer opportunities in their own neighborhoods. During its Global Community Days, GE coordinates employee efforts companywide to address projects throughout the world.

While Festinger argued that attitudes follow behavior, other researchers asked whether there was any relationship at all. More recent research shows that attitudes predict future behavior and confirmed Festinger's idea that "moderating variables" can strengthen the link.[7]

Moderating Variables   The most powerful moderators of the attitudes relationship are the *importance* of the attitude, its *correspondence to behavior*, its *accessibility*, the presence of *social pressures*, and whether a person has *direct experience* with the attitude.[8]

Important attitudes reflect our fundamental values, self-interest, or identification with individuals or groups we value. These attitudes tend to show a strong relationship to our behavior.

Specific attitudes tend to predict specific behaviors, whereas general attitudes tend to best predict general behaviors. For instance, asking someone about her intention to stay with an organization for the next 6 months is likely to better predict turnover for that person than asking her how satisfied she is with her job overall. On the other hand, overall job satisfaction would better predict a general behavior, such as whether the individual was engaged in her work or motivated to contribute to her organization.[9]

Attitudes that our memories can easily access are more likely to predict our behavior. Interestingly, you're more likely to remember attitudes you frequently express. So the more you talk about your attitude on a subject, the more likely you are to remember it, and the more likely it is to shape your behavior.

Discrepancies between attitudes and behavior tend to occur when social pressures to behave in certain ways hold exceptional power, as in most organizations. This may explain why an employee who holds strong anti-union attitudes attends pro-union organizing meetings, or why tobacco executives, who are not smokers

cognitive dissonance   *Any incompatibility between two or more attitudes or between behavior and attitudes.*

Though most employees find co-workers among the most satisfying aspects of their job, if a co-worker is dissatisfying, he or she is often *very* dissatisfying. Consider the case of "Jane," executive assistant at a large consumer products company. At one time, Jane and a co-worker were close work friends. They had lunch together, went on Starbucks runs for one another, and routinely helped each other with work. However, when both Jane and the co-worker wanted the same vacation slot and Jane won because of greater seniority, the relationship quickly turned sour. The co-worker would deposit smelly items in Jane's wastebasket, toss tissues in it that "just missed," and engage in other passive-aggressive unpleasantries. Despite mining plenty of revenge ideas from *The Office* (like putting the co-worker's stapler in JELL-O), Jane says, "So far I haven't had the guts. But I'm working up to it."

Here are a few steps for handling a dissatisfying co-worker in an effective and ethical way:

- *First, try a direct but conciliatory approach.* Invite the co-worker to coffee, and be forward but even-handed (try to see the situation from his or her point of view). A direct approach can clarify misunderstandings, alert co-workers to unintentional irritations (or, conversely, let them know you see their actions for what they are), and allow you to take some responsibility for the problem (few conflicts are totally one sided).

- *Resist the urge to play tit for tat.* Though tempting, such games often escalate and may only make you appear as petty as your co-worker.

- *If you can't solve the problem, ignore it.* This is easier said than done, but sometimes the best way to extinguish petty, childish behavior is to ignore it. Involve management only when you have a proactive, positive solution in mind (to avoid appearing to be a whiner or, worse, a backstabber) or when you feel your safety or career is threatened.[10]

themselves and who tend to believe the research linking smoking and cancer, don't actively discourage others from smoking in their offices.

Finally, the attitude–behavior relationship is likely to be much stronger if an attitude refers to something with which we have direct personal experience. Asking college students with no significant work experience how they would respond to working for an authoritarian supervisor is far less likely to predict actual behavior than asking that same question of employees who have actually worked for such an individual.

What Are the Major Job Attitudes?

3 Compare and contrast the major job attitudes.

We each have thousands of attitudes, but OB focuses our attention on a very limited number of work-related attitudes. These tap positive or negative evaluations that employees hold about aspects of their work environment. Most of the research in OB has looked at three attitudes: job satisfaction, job involvement, and organizational commitment.[11] A few other important attitudes are perceived organizational support and employee engagement; we'll also briefly discuss these.

Job Satisfaction   When people speak of employee attitudes, they usually mean **job satisfaction**, which describes a positive feeling about a job, resulting from an evaluation of its characteristics. A person with a high level of job satisfaction holds positive feelings about his or her job, while a person with a low level holds negative feelings. Because OB researchers give job satisfaction high importance, we'll review this attitude in detail later in the chapter.

Job Involvement   Related to job satisfaction is **job involvement**,[12] which measures the degree to which people identify psychologically with their job and consider their perceived performance level important to self-worth.[13] Employees with a high level of job involvement strongly identify with and really care about the kind of work they do. Another closely related concept is **psychological empowerment**, employees' beliefs in the degree to which they influence their work environment, their competence, the meaningfulness of their job, and their perceived autonomy.[14] One study of nursing managers in Singapore found that good leaders empower their employees by involving them in decisions, making them feel their work is important, and giving them discretion to "do their own thing."[15]

High levels of both job involvement and psychological empowerment are positively related to organizational citizenship and job performance.[16] High job involvement is also related to reduced absences and lower resignation rates.[17]

Organizational Commitment   In **organizational commitment**, an employee identifies with a particular organization and its goals and wishes to remain a member.

There are three separate dimensions to organizational commitment:[18]

1. **Affective commitment** is an emotional attachment to the organization and a belief in its values. For example, a Petco employee may be affectively committed to the company because of its involvement with animals.
2. **Continuance commitment** is the perceived economic value of remaining with an organization. An employee may be committed to an employer because she is paid well and feels it would hurt her family to quit.
3. **Normative commitment** is an obligation to remain with the organization for moral or ethical reasons. An employee spearheading a new initiative may remain with an employer because he feels he would "leave the employer in the lurch" if he left.

A positive relationship appears to exist between organizational commitment and job productivity, but it is a modest one.[19] A review of 27 studies suggested the relationship between commitment and performance is strongest for new employees, and considerably weaker for more experienced employees.[20] And, as with job involvement, the research evidence demonstrates negative relationships between organizational commitment and both absenteeism and turnover.[21]

Different forms of commitment have different effects on behavior. One study found managerial affective commitment more strongly related to organizational performance than was continuance commitment.[22] Another study showed that continuance commitment was related to a lower intention to quit but an increased tendency to be absent and lower job performance. These results make sense in that continuance commitment really isn't a commitment at all. Rather

---

job satisfaction   *A positive feeling about one's job resulting from an evaluation of its characteristics.*

job involvement   *The degree to which a person identifies with a job, actively participates in it, and considers performance important to self-worth.*

psychological empowerment   *Employees' belief in the degree to which they affect their work environment, their competence, the meaningfulness of their job, and their perceived autonomy in their work.*

organizational commitment   *The degree to which an employee identifies with a particular organization and its goals and wishes to maintain membership in the organization.*

affective commitment   *An emotional attachment to an organization and a belief in its values.*

continuance commitment   *The perceived economic value of remaining with an organization compared with leaving it.*

normative commitment   *An obligation to remain with an organization for moral or ethical reasons.*

International OB

Chinese Employees and Organizational Commitment

Are employees from different cultures committed to their organizations in similar ways? Several studies—most recently of Chinese and British employees in 2008—have compared the organizational commitment of employees from China, Britain, Canada, and South Korea.

They found all three types of commitment—normative, continuance, and affective—in all four cultures. When employees in different cultures think of commitment to their employers, they do so in fairly similar ways.

Another finding is that normative commitment, an obligation to remain with an organization for moral or ethical reasons, appears higher among Chinese employees. This may reflect a stronger collective mind-set, such that quitting a job is seen as harming one's organization or co-workers. Or it may reflect the greater degree of govern-

ment control over employees' work decisions (employees express greater normative commitment because they have little choice but to remain).

Affective commitment, an emotional attachment to the organization and belief in its values, appears higher among Chinese employees. According to the authors of one study, Chinese culture explains why. The Chinese emphasize loyalty to one's group, in this case the employer, so employees may feel a certain loyalty from the start and become more emotionally attached as their time with the organization grows.

The results for continuance commitment, the perceived economic value of remaining with an organization, also have been fairly consistent, showing it as *lower* among Chinese employees than among Canadian, British, and South Korean workers. This, too, may reflect Chinese employ-

ment practices; pay variability may be lower, and there may be more economic barriers to switching employers.

So, although Chinese and employees in other nations similarly experience all three types of organizational commitment (normative, continuance, and affective), Chinese employees appear to have higher levels of normative and affective commitment and lower levels of continuance.

Source: Based on E. Snape, C. Lo, and T. Redman, "The Three-Component Model of Occupational Commitment: A Comparative Study of Chinese and British Accountants." *Journal of Cross-Cultural Psychology,* November 2008, pp. 765–781; and Y. Cheng and M. S. Stockdale, "The Validity of the Three-Component Model of Organizational Commitment in a Chinese Context," *Journal of Vocational Behavior,* June 2003, pp. 465–489.

than an allegiance (affective commitment) or an obligation (normative commitment) to an employer, a continuance commitment describes an employee "tethered" to an employer simply because there isn't anything better available.[23]

Perceived Organizational Support **Perceived organizational support (POS)** is the degree to which employees believe the organization values their contribution and cares about their well-being (for example, an employee believes his organization would accommodate him if he had a child-care problem or would forgive an honest mistake on his part). Research shows that people perceive their organization as supportive when rewards are deemed fair, when employees have a voice in decisions, and when they see their supervisors as supportive.[24] Research suggests employees with strong POS perceptions are more likely to have higher levels of organizational citizenship behaviors, lower levels of tardiness, and better customer service.[25] Though little cross-cultural research has been done, one study found POS predicted only the job performance and citizenship behaviors of untraditional or low power-distance Chinese employees—in short, those more likely to think of work as an exchange rather than a moral obligation.[26]

Employee Engagement A new concept is **employee engagement,** an individual's involvement with, satisfaction with, and enthusiasm for, the work she does. We might ask employees about the availability of resources and the opportunities to learn new skills, whether they feel their work is important and

Employee engagement is high at Genentech, a biotechnology firm where employees share a serious commitment to science and patients and are passionate about the work they do. Genentech employees discover, develop, manufacture, and commercialize medicines that treat patients with serious or life-threatening medical conditions. Feeling that their contributions are important and meaningful, employees cite the chance to make a difference in the lives of patients as the number one reason they enjoy working at Genentech.

meaningful, and whether their interactions with co-workers and supervisors are rewarding.[27] Highly engaged employees have a passion for their work and feel a deep connection to their company; disengaged employees have essentially checked out—putting time but not energy or attention into their work. A study of nearly 8,000 business units in 36 companies found that those whose employees had high-average levels of engagement had higher levels of customer satisfaction, were more productive, had higher profits, and had lower levels of turnover and accidents than at other companies.[28] Molson Coors found engaged employees were five times less likely to have safety incidents, and when one did occur it was much less serious and less costly for the engaged employee than for a disengaged one ($63 per incident versus $392). Engagement becomes a real concern for most organizations because surveys indicate that few employees—between 17 percent and 29 percent—are highly engaged by their work. Caterpillar set out to increase employee engagement and recorded a resulting 80 percent drop in grievances and a 34 percent increase in highly satisfied customers.[29]

Such promising findings have earned employee engagement a following in many business organizations and management consulting firms. However, the concept is relatively new and still generates active debate about its usefulness. One review of the literature concluded, "The meaning of employee engagement is ambiguous among both academic researchers and among practitioners who use it in conversations with clients." Another reviewer called engagement "an umbrella term for whatever one wants it to be."[30]

Organizations will likely continue using employee engagement, and it will remain a subject of research. The ambiguity surrounding it arises from its newness

perceived organizational support (POS) *The degree to which employees believe an organization values their contribution and cares about their well-being.*

employee engagement *An individual's involvement with, satisfaction with, and enthusiasm for the work he or she does.*

and may also, ironically, reflect its popularity: Engagement is a very general concept, perhaps broad enough to capture the intersection of the other variables we've discussed. In other words, it may be what these attitudes have in common.

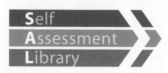

AM I ENGAGED?

In the Self-Assessment Library (available on CD or online), take assessment IV.B.1 (Am I Engaged?). (Note: If you do not currently have a job, answer the questions for your most recent job.)

Are These Job Attitudes Really All That Distinct? You might wonder whether these job attitudes are really distinct. If people feel deeply engaged by their job (high job involvement), isn't it probable they like it (high job satisfaction)? Won't people who think their organization is supportive (high perceived organizational support) also feel committed to it (strong organizational commitment)?

Evidence suggests these attitudes *are* highly related, perhaps to a troubling degree. For example, the correlation between perceived organizational support and affective commitment is very strong.[31] That means the variables may be redundant—if you know someone's affective commitment, you know her perceived organizational support. Why is redundancy troubling? Because it is inefficient and confusing. Why have two steering wheels on a car when you need only one? Why have two concepts—going by different labels—when you need only one?

Although we OB researchers like proposing new attitudes, often we haven't been good at showing how they compare and contrast with each other. There is some distinctiveness among them, but they overlap greatly, for various reasons including the employee's personality. Some people are predisposed to be positive or negative about almost everything. If someone tells you she loves her company, it may not mean a lot if she is positive about everything else in her life. Or the overlap may mean some organizations are just all-around better places to work than others. Then if you as a manager know someone's level of job satisfaction, you know most of what you need to know about how that person sees the organization.

Job Satisfaction

4 Define *job satisfaction* and show how we can measure it.

We have already discussed job satisfaction briefly. Now let's dissect the concept more carefully. How do we measure job satisfaction? What causes an employee to have a high level of job satisfaction? How do dissatisfied and satisfied employees affect an organization?

Measuring Job Satisfaction

Our definition of job satisfaction—a positive feeling about a job resulting from an evaluation of its characteristics—is clearly broad.[32] Yet that breadth is appropriate. A job is more than just shuffling papers, writing programming code, waiting on customers, or driving a truck. Jobs require interacting with co-workers and bosses, following organizational rules and policies, meeting performance standards, living with less than ideal working conditions, and the like.[33] An employee's assessment of his satisfaction with the job is thus a complex summation of many discrete elements. How, then, do we measure it?

Two approaches are popular. The single global rating is a response to one question, such as "All things considered, how satisfied are you with your job?" Respondents circle a number between 1 and 5 on a scale from "highly satisfied" to "highly dissatisfied." The second method, the summation of job facets, is more sophisticated. It identifies key elements in a job such as the nature of the work, supervision, present pay, promotion opportunities, and relations with co-workers.[34] Respondents rate these on a standardized scale, and researchers add the ratings to create an overall job satisfaction score.

Is one of these approaches superior? Intuitively, summing up responses to a number of job factors seems likely to achieve a more accurate evaluation of job satisfaction. Research, however, doesn't support the intuition.[35] This is one of those rare instances in which simplicity seems to work as well as complexity, making one method essentially as valid as the other. The best explanation is that the concept of job satisfaction is so broad a single question captures its essence. The summation of job facets may also leave out some important data. Both methods are helpful. The single global rating method isn't very time consuming, thus freeing time for other tasks, and the summation of job facets helps managers zero in on problems and deal with them faster and more accurately.

How Satisfied Are People in Their Jobs?

Are most people satisfied with their jobs? The answer seems to be a qualified "yes" in the United States and most other developed countries. Independent studies conducted among U.S. workers over the past 30 years generally indicate more workers are satisfied with their jobs than not.[36] But a caution is in order.

Research shows satisfaction levels vary a lot, depending on which facet of job satisfaction you're talking about. As shown in the OB Poll box and Exhibit 3-2, people are, on average, satisfied with their jobs overall, with the work itself, and with their supervisors and co-workers. However, they tend to be less satisfied with their pay and with promotion opportunities. It's not really clear why people dislike their pay and promotion possibilities more than other aspects of their jobs.[37]

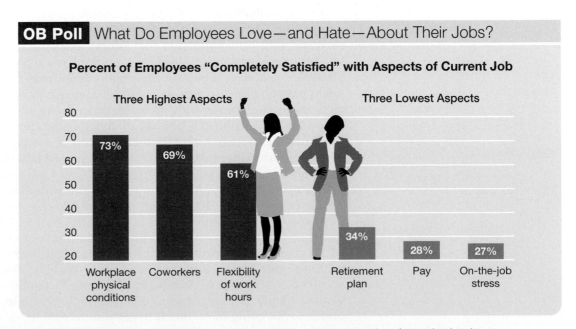

OB Poll What Do Employees Love—and Hate—About Their Jobs?

Percent of Employees "Completely Satisfied" with Aspects of Current Job

Three Highest Aspects — Three Lowest Aspects

- Workplace physical conditions: 73%
- Coworkers: 69%
- Flexibility of work hours: 61%
- Retirement plan: 34%
- Pay: 28%
- On-the-job stress: 27%

Source: Based on Gallup Poll, August 7–10, 2008 (http://www.gallup.com/poll/109738/US-Workers-Job-Satisfaction-Relatively-High.aspx).

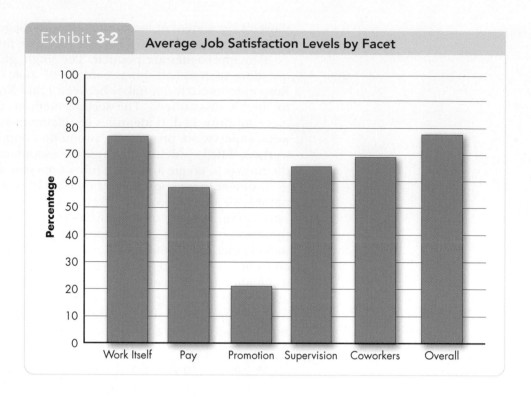

Exhibit **3-2** Average Job Satisfaction Levels by Facet

What Causes Job Satisfaction?

5 Summarize the main causes of job satisfaction.

Think about the best job you've ever had. What made it so? Chances are you liked the work you did and the people with whom you worked. Interesting jobs that provide training, variety, independence, and control satisfy most employees.[38] There is also a strong correspondence between how well people enjoy the social context of their workplace and how satisfied they are overall. Interdependence, feedback, social support, and interaction with co-workers outside the workplace are strongly related to job satisfaction even after accounting for characteristics of the work itself.[39]

You've probably noticed that pay comes up often when people discuss job satisfaction. For people who are poor or who live in poor countries, pay does correlate with job satisfaction and overall happiness. But once an individual reaches a level of comfortable living (in the United States, that occurs at about $40,000 a year, depending on the region and family size), the relationship between pay and job satisfaction virtually disappears. People who earn $80,000 are, on average, no happier with their jobs than those who earn closer to $40,000. Take a look at Exhibit 3-3. It shows the relationship between the average pay for a job and the average level of job satisfaction. As you can see, there isn't much of a relationship there. Handsomely compensated jobs have average satisfaction levels no higher than those that pay much less. One researcher even found no significant difference when he compared the overall well-being of the richest people on the Forbes 400 list with that of Maasai herders in East Africa.[40]

Money does motivate people, as we will discover in Chapter 6. But what motivates us is not necessarily the same as what makes us happy. A recent poll by UCLA and the American Council on Education found that entering college freshmen rated becoming "very well off financially" first on a list of 19 goals, ahead of choices such as helping others, raising a family, or becoming proficient in an academic pursuit. Maybe your goal isn't to be happy. But if it is, money's probably not going to do much to get you there.[41]

Job satisfaction is not just about job conditions. Personality also plays a role. Research has shown that people who have positive **core self-evaluations**—who

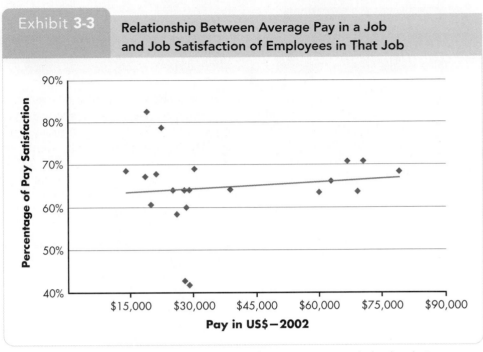

Exhibit **3-3**   **Relationship Between Average Pay in a Job and Job Satisfaction of Employees in That Job**

Source: T. A. Judge, R. F. Piccolo, N. P. Podsakoff, J. C. Shaw, and B. L. Rich, "Can Happiness Be 'Earned'? The Relationship Between Pay and Job Satisfaction," working paper, University of Florida, 2009.

believe in their inner worth and basic competence—are more satisfied with their jobs than those with negative core self-evaluations. Not only do they see their work as more fulfilling and challenging, they are more likely to gravitate toward challenging jobs in the first place. Those with negative core self-evaluations set less ambitious goals and are more likely to give up when confronting difficulties. Thus, they're more likely to be stuck in boring, repetitive jobs than those with positive core self-evaluations.[42]

The Impact of Satisfied and Dissatisfied Employees on the Workplace

6 Identify four employee responses to dissatisfaction.

What happens when employees like their jobs, and when they dislike their jobs? One theoretical model—the exit–voice–loyalty–neglect framework—is helpful in understanding the consequences of dissatisfaction. Exhibit 3-4 illustrates the framework's four responses, which differ along two dimensions: constructive/destructive and active/passive. The responses are as follows:[43]

- *Exit.* The **exit** response directs behavior toward leaving the organization, including looking for a new position as well as resigning.
- *Voice.* The **voice** response includes actively and constructively attempting to improve conditions, including suggesting improvements, discussing problems with superiors, and undertaking some forms of union activity.

---

core self-evaluations *Bottom-line conclusions individuals have about their capabilities, competence, and worth as a person.*

exit *Dissatisfaction expressed through behavior directed toward leaving the organization.*

voice *Dissatisfaction expressed through active and constructive attempts to improve conditions.*

Myth or Science?

"Happy Workers Are Productive Workers"

This statement is generally true. The idea that "happy workers are productive workers" developed in the 1930s and 1940s, largely as a result of findings from the Hawthorne studies at Western Electric. Based on those conclusions, managers focused on working conditions and the work environment to make employees happier. Then, in the 1980s, an influential review of the research suggested the relationship between job satisfaction and job performance was not particularly high. The authors of that review even labeled it "illusory."[44]

More recently, a review of more than three hundred studies corrected some errors in that earlier review and found the correlation between job satisfaction and job performance to be moderately strong, even across international contexts. The correlation is higher for complex jobs that provide employees with more discretion to act on their attitudes.[45] A review of 16 studies that assessed job performance and satisfaction over time also linked job satisfaction to job performance[46] and suggested the relationship mostly works one way: Satisfaction was a likely cause of better performance, but higher performance was not a cause of higher job satisfaction.

- *Loyalty.* The **loyalty** response means passively but optimistically waiting for conditions to improve, including speaking up for the organization in the face of external criticism and trusting the organization and its management to "do the right thing."
- *Neglect.* The **neglect** response passively allows conditions to worsen and includes chronic absenteeism or lateness, reduced effort, and increased error rate.

Exit and neglect behaviors encompass our performance variables—productivity, absenteeism, and turnover. But this model expands employee response to include voice and loyalty—constructive behaviors that allow

Exhibit 3-4   Responses to Job Dissatisfaction

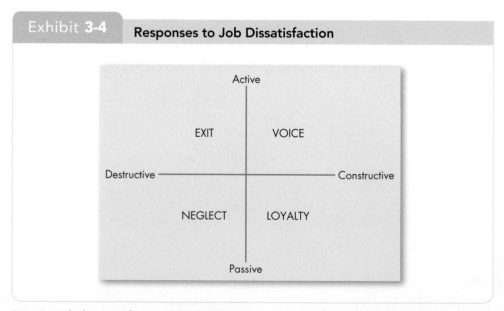

individuals to tolerate unpleasant situations or revive satisfactory working conditions. It helps us understand situations, such as we sometimes find among unionized workers, for whom low job satisfaction is coupled with low turnover.[47] Union members often express dissatisfaction through the grievance procedure or formal contract negotiations. These voice mechanisms allow them to continue in their jobs while convincing themselves they are acting to improve the situation.

As helpful as this framework is, it's quite general. We now discuss more specific outcomes of job satisfaction and dissatisfaction in the workplace.

Job Satisfaction and Job Performance As the "Myth or Science?" box concludes, happy workers are more likely to be productive workers. Some researchers used to believe the relationship between job satisfaction and job performance was a myth. But a review of three hundred studies suggested the correlation is pretty strong.[48] As we move from the individual to the organizational level, we also find support for the satisfaction–performance relationship.[49] When we gather satisfaction and productivity data for the organization as a whole, we find organizations with more satisfied employees tend to be more effective than organizations with fewer.

Job Satisfaction and OCB It seems logical to assume job satisfaction should be a major determinant of an employee's organizational citizenship behavior (OCB).[50] Satisfied employees would seem more likely to talk positively about the organization, help others, and go beyond the normal expectations in their job. They might go beyond the call of duty because they want to reciprocate their positive experiences. Consistent with this thinking, evidence suggests job satisfaction is moderately correlated with OCBs; people who are more satisfied with their jobs are more likely to engage in OCBs.[51] Why? Fairness perceptions help explain the relationship.[52] Those who feel their co-workers support them are more likely to engage in helpful behaviors, whereas those who have antagonistic relationships with co-workers are less likely to do so.[53]

Job Satisfaction and Customer Satisfaction As we noted in Chapter 1, employees in service jobs often interact with customers. Since service organization managers should be concerned with pleasing those customers, it is reasonable to ask, Is employee satisfaction related to positive customer outcomes? For frontline employees who have regular customer contact, the answer is "yes." Satisfied employees increase customer satisfaction and loyalty.[54]

A number of companies are acting on this evidence. The first core value of shoe retailer Zappos, "Deliver WOW through service," seems fairly obvious, but the way in which it does it is not. Employees are encouraged to "create fun and a little weirdness" and are given unusual discretion in making customers satisfied; they are encouraged to use their imaginations, including sending flowers to disgruntled customers, and Zappos even offers a $2,000 bribe to quit the company after training (to weed out the half-hearted).[55] Other organizations seem to work the other end of the spectrum. Two independent reports—one on the Transportation Security Administration (TSA) and the other on airline passenger complaints—argue that low employee morale was a major factor undermining

loyalty *Dissatisfaction expressed by passively waiting for conditions to improve.*

neglect *Dissatisfaction expressed through allowing conditions to worsen.*

Passengers of Singapore Airlines appreciate the outstanding customer service provided by the airline's satisfied frontline employees who have earned a reputation as friendly, upbeat, and responsive. In recruiting flight attendants, Singapore Airlines carefully selects people who are warm, hospitable, and happy to serve others. Then, through extensive training, the airline instills in them its "putting people first" philosophy, which focuses on complete customer satisfaction.

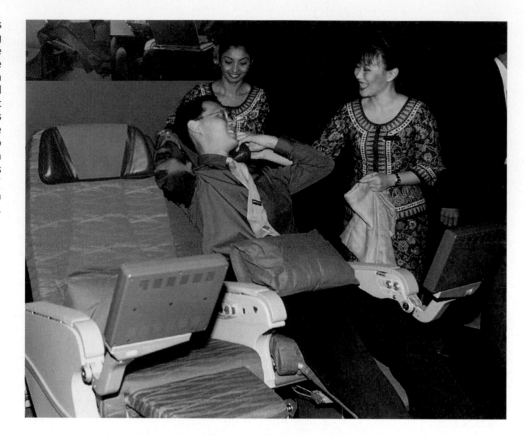

passenger satisfaction. At US Airways, employees have posted comments on blogs such as "Our plans (sic) smell filthy" and, from another, "How can I take pride in this product?"[56]

Job Satisfaction and Absenteeism We find a consistent negative relationship between satisfaction and absenteeism, but it is moderate to weak.[57] While it certainly makes sense that dissatisfied employees are more likely to miss work, other factors affect the relationship. Organizations that provide liberal sick leave benefits are encouraging all their employees—including those who are highly satisfied—to take days off. You can find work satisfying yet still want to enjoy a 3-day weekend if those days come free with no penalties. When numerous alternative jobs are available, dissatisfied employees have high absence rates, but when there are few they have the same (low) rate of absence as satisfied employees.[58]

Job Satisfaction and Turnover The relationship between job satisfaction and turnover is stronger than between satisfaction and absenteeism.[59] The satisfaction–turnover relationship also is affected by alternative job prospects. If an employee is presented with an unsolicited job offer, job dissatisfaction is less predictive of turnover because the employee is more likely leaving because of "pull" (the lure of the other job) than "push" (the unattractiveness of the current job). Similarly, job dissatisfaction is more likely to translate into turnover when employment opportunities are plentiful because employees perceive it is easy to move. Finally, when employees have high "human capital" (high education, high ability), job dissatisfaction is more likely to translate into turnover because they have, or perceive, many available alternatives.[60]

When employees do not like their work environment, they will respond in some way. An attempt to form a union is one specific behavior that may stem from job dissatisfaction. At several different Wal-Mart locations throughout the United States, dissatisfied employees have tried, unsuccessfully, to organize a union as a way to receive better pay and more affordable health insurance. Joined by supporters, the employees shown here work at a Wal-Mart warehouse and distribution center in California and are protesting low wages and no health care or other benefits.

Job Satisfaction and Workplace Deviance Job dissatisfaction and antagonistic relationships with co-workers predict a variety of behaviors organizations find undesirable, including unionization attempts, substance abuse, stealing at work, undue socializing, and tardiness. Researchers argue these behaviors are indicators of a broader syndrome called *deviant behavior in the workplace* (or *counterproductive behavior* or *employee withdrawal*).[61] If employees don't like their work environment, they'll respond somehow, though it is not always easy to forecast exactly *how*. One worker might quit. Another might use work time to surf the Internet or take work supplies home for personal use. In short, workers who don't like their jobs "get even" in various ways—and because those ways can be quite creative, controlling only one behavior, such as with an absence control policy, leaves the root cause untouched. To effectively control the undesirable consequences of job dissatisfaction, employers should attack the source of the problem—the dissatisfaction—rather than try to control the different responses.

Managers Often "Don't Get It"   Given the evidence we've just reviewed, it should come as no surprise that job satisfaction can affect the bottom line. One study by a management consulting firm separated large organizations into high morale (more than 70 percent of employees expressed overall job satisfaction) and medium or low morale (fewer than 70 percent). The stock prices of companies in the high morale group grew 19.4 percent, compared with 10 percent for the medium or low morale group. Despite these results, many managers are unconcerned about employee job satisfaction. Still others overestimate how satisfied employees are with their jobs, so they don't think there's a problem when there is. In one study of 262 large employers, 86 percent of senior managers believed their organization treated its employees well, but only 55 percent of employees agreed. Another study found 55 percent of managers thought morale was good in their organization, compared to only 38 percent of employees.[62]

Regular surveys can reduce gaps between what managers *think* employees feel and what they *really* feel. Jonathan McDaniel, manager of a KFC restaurant in Houston, surveys his employees every 3 months. Some results led him to make changes, such as giving employees greater say about which workdays they have off. However, McDaniel believes the process itself is valuable. "They really love giving their opinions," he says. "That's the most important part of it—that they have a voice and that they're heard." Surveys are no panacea, but if job attitudes are as important as we believe, organizations need to find out where they can be improved.[63]

Global Implications

Is Job Satisfaction a U.S. Concept?

Most of the research on job satisfaction has been conducted in the United States. Is job satisfaction a U.S. concept? The evidence strongly suggests it is *not;* people in other cultures can and do form judgments of job satisfaction. Moreover, similar factors seem to cause, and result from, job satisfaction across cultures: We noted earlier that pay is positively, but relatively weakly, related to job satisfaction. This relationship appears to hold in other industrialized nations as well as in the United States.

7 Show whether job satisfaction is a relevant concept in countries other than the United States.

Are Employees in Western Cultures More Satisfied with Their Jobs?

Although job satisfaction appears relevant across cultures, that doesn't mean there are no cultural differences in job satisfaction. Evidence suggests employees in Western cultures have higher levels of job satisfaction than those in Eastern cultures.[64] Exhibit 3-5 provides the results of a global study of job satis-

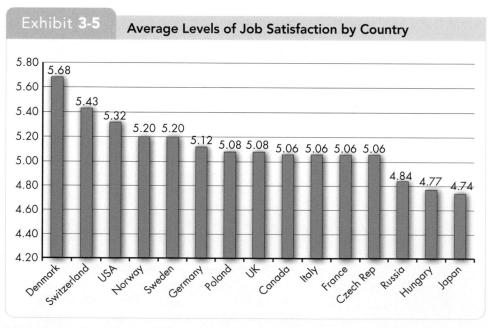

Exhibit 3-5 **Average Levels of Job Satisfaction by Country**

Note: Scores represent average job-satisfaction levels in each country as rated on a 1 = very dissatisfied to 10 = very satisfied scale.

Source: M. Benz and B. S. Frey, "The Value of Autonomy: Evidence from the Self-Employed in 23 Countries," working paper 173, Institute for Empirical Research in Economics, University of Zurich, November 2003 (ssrn.com/abstract=475140).

faction levels of workers in 15 countries. (This study included 23 countries, but for presentation purposes we report the results for only the largest.) As the exhibit shows, the highest levels appear in the United States and western Europe. Do employees in Western cultures have better jobs? Or are they simply more positive (and less self critical)? Although both factors are probably at play, evidence suggests that individuals in Eastern cultures find negative emotions less aversive more than do individuals in Western cultures, who tend to emphasize positive emotions and individual happiness.[65] That may be why employees in Western cultures such as the United States and Scandinavia are more likely to have higher levels of satisfaction.

Summary and Implications for Managers

Managers should be interested in their employees' attitudes because attitudes give warnings of potential problems and influence behavior. Satisfied and committed employees, for instance, have lower rates of turnover, absenteeism, and withdrawal behaviors. They also perform better on the job. Given that managers want to keep resignations and absences down—especially among their most productive employees—they'll want to do things that generate positive job attitudes. As one review put it, "A sound measurement of overall job attitude is one of the most useful pieces of information an organization can have about its employees."[66]

The most important thing managers can do to raise employee satisfaction is focus on the intrinsic parts of the job, such as making the work challenging and interesting. Although paying employees poorly will likely not attract high-quality employees to the organization, or keep high performers, managers should realize that high pay alone is unlikely to create a satisfying work environment. Creating a satisfied workforce is hardly a guarantee of successful organizational performance, but evidence strongly suggests that whatever managers can do to improve employee attitudes will likely result in heightened organizational effectiveness.

POINT ⟷ COUNTERPOINT

Managers Can Create Satisfied Employees

A review of the evidence has identified four factors conducive to high levels of employee job satisfaction: mentally challenging work, equitable rewards, supportive working conditions, and supportive colleagues.[67] Management is able to control each of these:

Mentally challenging work. Generally, people prefer jobs that give them opportunities to use their skills and abilities and offer a variety of tasks, freedom, and feedback on how well they're doing. These characteristics make work mentally challenging.

Equitable rewards. Employees want pay systems they perceive as just, unambiguous, and in line with their expectations. When they see pay as fair—based on job demands, individual skill level, and community pay standards—satisfaction is likely to result.

Supportive working conditions. Employees want their work environment both to be safe and personally comfortable and to facilitate their doing a good job. Most prefer working relatively close to home, in clean and up-to-date facilities with adequate tools and equipment.

Supportive colleagues. People get more out of work than merely money and other tangible achievements. Work also fulfills the need for social interaction. Not surprisingly, therefore, friendly and supportive co-workers lead to increased job satisfaction. The boss's behavior is also a major factor; employee satisfaction is increased when the immediate supervisor is understanding and friendly, offers praise for good performance, listens to employees' opinions, and shows a personal interest in employees.

The notion that managers and organizations can control the level of employee job satisfaction is inherently attractive. It fits nicely with the view that managers directly influence organizational processes and outcomes. Unfortunately, a growing body of evidence challenges this idea. The most recent findings indicate job satisfaction is largely genetically determined.[68]

Whether a person is happy is essentially determined by gene structure. Approximately 50 to 80 percent of people's differences in happiness, or subjective well-being, has been found to be attributable to their genes. Identical twins, for example, tend to have very similar careers, report similar levels of job satisfaction, and change jobs at similar rates.

Analysis of satisfaction data for a selected sample of individuals over a 50-year period found that individual results were stable over time, even when subjects changed employers and occupations. This and other research suggests an individual's disposition toward life—positive or negative—is established by genetic makeup, holds over time, and influences disposition toward work.

Given these findings, most managers can probably do little to influence employee satisfaction. Despite their manipulating job characteristics, working conditions, and rewards, people will inevitably return to their own "set point." A bonus may temporarily increase the satisfaction level of a negatively disposed worker, but it is unlikely to sustain it. Sooner or later, a dissatisfied worker will find new fault with the job.

The only place managers will have any significant influence is in the selection process. If managers want satisfied workers, they need to screen out negative people who derive little satisfaction from their jobs, irrespective of work conditions.

Questions for Review

1 What are the main components of attitudes? Are these components related or unrelated?

2 Does behavior always follow from attitudes? Why or why not? Discuss the factors that affect whether behavior follows from attitudes.

3 What are the major job attitudes? In what ways are these attitudes alike? What is unique about each?

4 How do we measure job satisfaction?

5 What causes job satisfaction? For most people, is pay or the work itself more important?

6 What outcomes does job satisfaction influence? What implications does this have for management?

7 Is job satisfaction a uniquely U.S. concept? Does job satisfaction appear to vary by country?

Experiential Exercise

WHAT FACTORS ARE MOST IMPORTANT TO YOUR JOB SATISFACTION?

Most of us probably want a job we think will satisfy us. But because no job is perfect, we often have to trade off job attributes. One job may pay well but provide limited opportunities for advancement or skill development. Another may offer work we enjoy but have poor benefits. The following is a list of 21 job factors or attributes:

- Autonomy and independence
- Benefits
- Career advancement opportunities
- Career development opportunities
- Compensation/pay
- Communication between employees and management
- Contribution of work to organization's business goals
- Feeling safe in the work environment
- Flexibility to balance life and work issues
- Job security
- Job-specific training
- Management recognition of employee job performance
- Meaningfulness of job
- Networking
- Opportunities to use skills/abilities
- Organization's commitment to professional development
- Overall corporate culture
- Relationship with co-workers
- Relationship with immediate supervisor
- The work itself
- The variety of work

On a sheet of paper, rank-order these job factors from top to bottom so number 1 is the job factor you think is most important to your job satisfaction, number 2 is the second most important factor to your job satisfaction, and so on.

Next, gather in teams of three or four people and try the following:

1. Appoint a spokesperson who will take notes and report the answers to the following questions, on behalf of your group, back to the class.

2. Averaging across all members in your group, generate a list of the top five job factors.

3. Did most people in your group seem to value the same job factors? Why or why not?

4. Your instructor will provide you the results of a study of a random sample of 600 employees conducted by the Society for Human Resource Management (SHRM). How do your group's rankings compare with the SHRM results?

5. The chapter says pay doesn't correlate all that well with job satisfaction, but in the SHRM survey, people say it is relatively important. Can your group suggest a reason for the apparent discrepancy?

6. Now examine your own list again. Does your list agree with the group list? Does your list agree with the SHRM study?

Ethical Dilemma

ARE U.S. WORKERS OVERWORKED?

Europeans pride themselves on their quality of life, and rightly so. A recent worldwide analysis of quality of life considered material well-being, health, political stability, divorce rates, job security, political freedom, and gender equality. The United States ranked 13th. The 12 nations that finished ahead were all in Europe.

Many Europeans would credit their high quality of life to their nations' free health care, generous unemployment benefits, and greater emphasis on leisure as opposed to work. Most European nations mandate restricted workweek hours and a month or more of vacation time, but U.S. workers have among the fewest vacation days and longest average workweeks in the world. Juliet Schor, a Harvard economist, argues the United States "is the world's standout workaholic nation" and that U.S. workers are trapped in a "squirrel cage" of overwork. Some argue that mandated leisure time would force companies to compete within their industry by raising productivity and product quality, rather than by requiring workers to put in more hours.

Many European nations limit the work hours employers can require. France, Germany, and other nations have set the workweek at 35 hours. Recently, after much debate, the French parliament voted to do away with the rule, to allow French companies to compete more effectively by paying employees for longer hours if required. Opponents say letting the individual decide how much to work will inevitably detract from quality of life and give employers power to exploit workers. A French union leader said, "They say it's the worker who will choose how much to work, but they're lying because it's always the employer who decides."

Questions

1. Why do you think quality of life is lower in the United States than in many European nations? Do you think U.S. quality of life would improve if the government required a minimum number of vacation days or limited workweek hours?

2. Do you think the French parliament was right to eliminate the 35-hour workweek limit? Do you think the quality of French life will suffer? Why or why not?

3. Do you think employers have an obligation to consider the quality of life of their employees? Could such an obligation mean protecting employees from being overworked?

4. Do you think it makes a difference in the research results that the unemployment rate in Europe is roughly double that of the United States and that Europe's gross domestic product (GDP) is about half that of the United States?

Source: Based on Juliet Schor, *The Overworked American: The Unexpected Decline of Leisure* (New York: Basic Books, 1992); C. S. Smith, "Effort to Extend Workweek Advances in France," *New York Times,* February 10, 2005, p. A9; "The World in 2005: The Economist Intelligence Unit's Quality-of-Life Index," *The Economist,* www.economist.com/media/pdf/QUALITY_OF_LIFE.pdf; and E. Olsen, "The Vacation Deficit," *Budget Travel,* October 29, 2004, www.msnbc.msn.com/id/6345416.

Case Incident 1

THINKING YOUR WAY TO A BETTER JOB

You have probably been dissatisfied with a job at one time or another in your life. When faced with a dissatisfying job, researchers and job holders alike usually think in terms of job: Ask for more pay, take control over your work, change your schedule, minimize contact with a toxic co-worker, or even change jobs. While each of these remedies may be appropriate in certain situations, increasingly researchers are uncovering an interesting truth about job satisfaction: it is as much a state of mind as a function of job conditions.

Here, we're not talking about the dispositional source of job satisfaction. It's true that some people have trouble finding any job satisfying, whereas others can't be brought down by even the most onerous of jobs. However, by state of mind, we mean changeable, easily implemented ways of thinking that can affect your job satisfaction. Lest you think we've gone the way of self-help gurus Deepak Chopra and Wayne Dyer, think again. There is some solid, albeit fairly preliminary, evidence supporting the view that our views of our job and life can be significantly impacted by changing the way we think.

One main area where this "state of mind" research might help you change the way you think about your job (or life) is in gratitude. Researchers have found that when people are asked to make short lists of things for which they are grateful, they report being happier, and the increased happiness seems to last well beyond the moments when people made the list.

Indeed, gratitude may explain why, when the economy is in bad shape, people actually become more satisfied with their jobs. One survey revealed that, from 2007 to 2008, when the economy slid into recession, the percentage of people reporting that they were "very satisfied" with their jobs increased a whopping 38 percent (from 28 percent to 38 percent). When we see other people suffering, particularly those we see as similar to ourselves, it often leads us to realize that, as bad as things may seem, they can always be worse. As *Wall Street Journal* columnist Jeffrey Zaslow wrote,

"People who still have jobs are finding reasons to be appreciative."

Questions

1. So, right now, make a short list of things about your job and life for which you are grateful. Now, after having done that, do you feel more positively about your job and your life?

2. Now try doing this every day for a week. Do you think this exercise might make a difference in how you feel about your job and your life?

Source: J. Zaslow, "From Attitude to Gratitude: This Is No Time for Complaints," *Wall Street Journal* (March 4, 2009), p. D1; A. M. Wood, S. Joseph, and J. Maltby, "Gratitude Uniquely Predicts Satisfaction with Life: Incremental Validity Above the Domains and Facets of the Five Factor Model," *Personality and Individual Differences* 45, no. 1 (2008), pp. 49–54; R. A. Emmons, "Gratitude, Subjective Well-Being, and the Brain," In M. Eid and R. J. Larsen, *The Science of Subjective Well-Being*, New York: Guilford Press, 2008, pp. 469–489.

Case Incident 2

LONG HOURS, HUNDREDS OF E-MAILS, AND NO SLEEP: DOES THIS SOUND LIKE A SATISFYING JOB?

Although the 40-hour workweek is now the exception rather than the norm, some individuals are taking things to the extreme:

- John Bishop, 31, is an investment banker who works for Citigroup's global energy team in New York. A recent workday for Bishop consisted of heading to the office for a conference call at 6:00 P.M. He left the office at 1:30 A.M. and had to be on a plane that same morning for a 9:00 A.M. presentation in Houston. Following the presentation, Bishop returned to New York the same day, and by 7:00 P.M. he was back in his office to work an additional 3 hours. Says Bishop, "I might be a little skewed to the workaholic, but realistically, expecting 90 to 100 hours a week is not at all unusual."

- Irene Tse, 34, heads the government bond-trading division at Goldman Sachs. For 10 years, she has seen the stock market go from all-time highs to recession levels. Such fluctuations can mean millions of dollars in either profits or losses. "There are days when you can make a lot, and other days where you lose so much you're just stunned by what you've done," says Tse. She also states that she hasn't slept completely through the night in years and frequently wakes up several times during the night to check the global market status. Her average workweek? Eighty hours. "I've done this for 10 years, and I can count on the fingers of one hand the number

of days in my career when I didn't want to come to work. Every day I wake up and I can't wait to get here."

- Tony Kurz, 33, is a managing director at Capital Alliance Partners, and he raises funds for real estate investments. However, these are not your average properties. He often travels to exotic locations such as Costa Rica and Hawaii to woo prospective clients. He travels more than 300,000 miles per year, often sleeping on planes and dealing with jet lag. Kurz is not the only one he knows with such a hectic work schedule. His girlfriend, Avery Baker, logs around 400,000 miles a year, working as the senior vice president of marketing for Tommy Hilfiger. "It's not easy to maintain a relationship like this," says Kurz. But do Kurz and Baker like their jobs? You bet.

- David Clark, 35, is the vice president of global marketing for MTV. His job often consists of traveling around the globe to promote the channel as well as to keep up with the global music scene. If he is not traveling (Clark typically logs 200,000 miles a year), a typical day consists of waking at 6:30 A.M. and immediately responding to numerous messages that have accumulated over the course of the night. He then goes to his office, where throughout the day he responds to another 500 or so messages from clients around the world. If he's lucky, he gets to spend an hour a day with his son, but then it's back to work until he finally goes to bed around midnight. Says Clark, "There are plenty of people who would love to have this job. They're knocking on the door all the time. So that's motivating."

Many individuals would balk at the prospect of a 60-hour or more workweek with constant traveling and little time for anything else. However, some individuals are exhilarated by such professions. According to the U.S. Bureau of Labor Statistics, in 2004 about 17 percent of managers worked more than 60 hours per week. But the demands of such jobs are clearly not for everyone. Many quit, with turnover levels at 55 percent for consultants and 30 percent for investment bankers, according to Vault.com. However, it is clear that such jobs, which arc time-consuming and often stressful, can be satisfying to some individuals.

Questions

1. Do you think only certain individuals are attracted to these types of jobs, or is it the characteristics of the jobs themselves that are satisfying?

2. What characteristics of these jobs might contribute to increased levels of job satisfaction?

3. Given that the four individuals we just read about tend to be satisfied with their jobs, how might this satisfaction relate to their job performance, citizenship behavior, and turnover?

4. Recall David Clark's statement that "There are plenty of people who would love to have this job. They're knocking on the door all the time." How might Clark's perceptions that he has a job many others desire contribute to his job satisfaction?

Source: Based on L. Tischler, "Extreme Jobs (And the People Who Love Them)," *Fast Company,* April 2005, pp. 55–60, www.glo-jobs.com/article.php?article_no=87.

Endnotes

1. E. Frauenheim, "2008 Winner Innovation: HCL Technologies," *Workforce Management,* October 20, 2008, p. 25.

2. S. J. Breckler, "Empirical Validation of Affect, Behavior, and Cognition as Distinct Components of Attitude," *Journal of Personality and Social Psychology,* May 1984, pp. 1191–1205.

3. A. W. Wicker, "Attitude Versus Action: The Relationship of Verbal and Overt Behavioral Responses to Attitude Objects," *Journal of Social Issues,* Autumn 1969, pp. 41–78.

4. L. Festinger, *A Theory of Cognitive Dissonance* (Stanford, CA: Stanford University Press, 1957).

5. See, for instance, L. R. Fabrigar, R. E. Petty, S. M. Smith, and S. L. Crites, "Understanding Knowledge Effects on Attitude-Behavior Consistency: The Role of Relevance, Complexity, and Amount of Knowledge," *Journal of Personality and Social Psychology* 90, no. 4 (2006), pp. 556–577; and D. J. Schleicher, J. D. Watt, and G. J. Greguras, "Reexamining the Job Satisfaction-Performance Relationship: The Complexity of Attitudes," *Journal of Applied Psychology* 89, no. 1 (2004), pp. 165–177.

6. See, for instance, J. Nocera, "If It's Good for Philip Morris, Can It Also Be Good for Public Health?" *New York Times,* June 18, 2006.

7. See L. R. Glasman and D. Albarracín, "Forming Attitudes That Predict Future Behavior: A Meta-analysis of the Attitude–Behavior Relation," *Psychological Bulletin,* September 2006, pp. 778–822; I. Ajzen, "Nature and Operation of Attitudes," in S. T. Fiske, D. L. Schacter, and C. Zahn-Waxler (eds.), *Annual Review of Psychology,* vol. 52 (Palo Alto, CA: Annual Reviews, Inc., 2001), pp. 27–58; and M. Riketta, "The Causal Relation Between Job Attitudes and Performance: A Meta-Analysis of Panel Studies," *Journal of Applied Psychology,* 93, no. 2 (2008), pp. 472–481.

8. Ibid.

9. D. A. Harrison, D. A. Newman, and P. L. Roth, "How Important Are Job Attitudes? Meta-analytic Comparisons of Integrative Behavioral Outcomes and Time Sequences," *Academy of Management Journal* 49, no. 2 (2006), pp. 305–325.

10. L. Belkin, "It's Not the Job I Despise, It's You," *New York Times* (February 7, 2008), p. B5.

11. D. P. Moynihan and S. K. Pandey, "Finding Workable Levers Over Work Motivation: Comparing Job Satisfaction, Job Involvement, and Organizational Commitment," *Administration & Society* 39, no. 7 (2007), pp. 803–832.

12. See, for example, J. M. Diefendorff, D. J. Brown, and A. M. Kamin, "Examining the Roles of Job Involvement and Work Centrality in Predicting Organizational Citizenship Behaviors and Job Performance," *Journal of Organizational Behavior,* February 2002, pp. 93–108.

13. Based on G. J. Blau and K. R. Boal, "Conceptualizing How Job Involvement and Organizational Commitment Affect Turnover and Absenteeism," *Academy of Management Review,* April 1987, p. 290.

14. G. Chen and R. J. Klimoski, "The Impact of Expectations on Newcomer Performance in Teams as Mediated by Work Characteristics, Social Exchanges, and Empowerment," *Academy of Management Journal* 46, no. 5 (2003), pp. 591–607; A. Ergeneli, G. Saglam, and S. Metin, "Psychological Empowerment and Its Relationship to Trust in Immediate Managers," *Journal of Business Research,* January 2007, pp. 41–49; and S. E. Seibert, S. R. Silver, and W. A. Randolph, "Taking Empowerment to the Next Level: A Multiple-Level Model of Empowerment, Performance, and Satisfaction," *Academy of Management Journal* 47, no. 3 (2004), pp. 332–349.

15. B. J. Avolio, W. Zhu, W. Koh, and P. Bhatia, "Transformational Leadership and Organizational Commitment: Mediating Role of Psychological Empowerment and Moderating Role of Structural Distance," *Journal of Organizational Behavior* 25, no. 8, 2004, pp. 951–968.

16. J. M. Diefendorff, D. J. Brown, A. M. Kamin, and R. G. Lord, "Examining the Roles of Job Involvement and Work Centrality in Predicting Organizational Citizenship Behaviors and Job Performance," *Journal of Organizational Behavior,* February 2002, pp. 93–108.

17. M. R. Barrick, M. K. Mount, and J. P. Strauss, "Antecedents of Involuntary Turnover Due to a Reduction in Force," *Personnel Psychology* 47, no. 3 (1994), pp. 515–535.

18. J. P. Meyer, N. J. Allen, and C. A. Smith, "Commitment to Organizations and Occupations: Extension and Test of a Three-Component Conceptualization," *Journal of Applied Psychology* 78, no. 4 (1993), pp. 538–551.

19. B. J. Hoffman, C. A. Blair, J. P. Meriac, and D. J. Woehr. "Expanding the Criterion Domain? A Quantitative Review of the OCB Literature," *Journal of Applied Psychology* 92, no. 2 (2007), pp. 555–566.

20. T. A. Wright and D. G. Bonett, "The Moderating Effects of Employee Tenure on the Relation Between Organizational Commitment and Job Performance: A Meta-analysis," *Journal of Applied Psychology,* December 2002, pp. 1183–1190.

21. See, for instance, T. Simons and Q. Roberson, "Why Managers Should Care About Fairness: The Effects of Aggregate Justice Perceptions on Organizational Outcomes," *Journal of Applied Psychology* 88, no. 3 (2003), pp. 432–443.

22. Y. Gong, K. S. Law, S. Chang, and K. R. Xin, "Human Resources Management and Firm Performance: The Differential Role of Managerial Affective and Continuance Commitment," *Journal of Applied Psychology* 94, no. 1 (2009), pp. 263–275.

23. A. A. Luchak and I. R. Gellatly, "A Comparison of Linear and Nonlinear Relations Between Organizational Commitment and Work Outcomes," *Journal of Applied Psychology* 92, no. 3 (2007), pp. 786–793.

24. L. Rhoades, R. Eisenberger, and S. Armeli, "Affective Commitment to the Organization: The Contribution of Perceived Organizational Support," *Journal of Applied Psychology* 86, no. 5 (2001), pp. 825–836.

25. C. Vandenberghe, K. Bentein, R. Michon, J. Chebat, M. Tremblay, and J. Fils, "An Examination of the Role of Perceived Support and Employee Commitment in Employee–Customer Encounters," *Journal of Applied Psychology* 92, no. 4 (2007), pp. 1177–1187; P. Eder and R. Eisenberger, "Perceived Organizational Support: Reducing the Negative Influence of Coworker Withdrawal Behavior," *Journal of Management* 34, no. 1 (2008), pp. 55–68.

26. J. Farh, R. D. Hackett, and J. Liang, "Individual-Level Cultural Values as Moderators of Perceived Organizational Support—Employee Outcome Relationships in China: Comparing the Effects of Power Distance and Traditionality," *Academy of Management Journal* 50, no. 3 (2007), pp. 715–729.

27. D. R. May, R. L. Gilson, and L. M. Harter, "The Psychological Conditions of Meaningfulness, Safety and Availability and the Engagement of the Human Spirit at Work," *Journal of Occupational and Organizational Psychology* 77, no. 1 (2004), pp. 11–37.

28. J. K. Harter, F. L. Schmidt, and T. L. Hayes, "Business-Unit-Level Relationship Between Employee Satisfaction, Employee Engagement, and Business Outcomes: A Meta-analysis," *Journal of Applied Psychology* 87, no. 2 (2002), pp. 268–279.

29. N. R. Lockwood, *Leveraging Employee Engagement for Competitive Advantage* (Alexandria, VA: Society for Human Resource Management, 2007); and R. J. Vance, *Employee Engagement and Commitment* (Alexandria, VA: Society for Human Resource Management, 2006).

30. W. H. Macey and B. Schneider, "The Meaning of Employee Engagement," *Industrial and Organizational Psychology* 1 (2008), pp. 3–30; A. Saks, "The Meaning and Bleeding of Employee Engagement: How Muddy Is the Water?" *Industrial and Organizational Psychology* 1 (2008), pp. 40–43.

31. L. Rhoades and R. Eisenberger, "Perceived Organizational Support: A Review of the Literature," *Journal of Applied Psychology* 87, no. 4 (2002), pp. 698–714; and R. L. Payne and D. Morrison, "The Differential Effects of Negative Affectivity on Measures of Well-Being Versus Job Satisfaction and Organizational Commitment," *Anxiety, Stress & Coping: An International Journal* 15, no. 3 (2002), pp. 231–244.

32. For problems with the concept of job satisfaction, see R. Hodson, "Workplace Behaviors," *Work and Occupations,* August 1991, pp. 271–290; and H. M. Weiss and R. Cropanzano, "Affective Events Theory: A Theoretical Discussion of the Structure, Causes and Consequences of Affective Experiences at Work," in B. M. Staw and L. L. Cummings (eds.), *Research in Organizational Behavior,* vol. 18 (Greenwich, CT: JAI Press, 1996), pp. 1–3.

33. The Wyatt Company's 1989 national WorkAmerica study identified 12 dimensions of satisfaction: work organization, working conditions, communications, job performance and performance review, coworkers, supervision, company management, pay, benefits, career development and training, job content and satisfaction, and company image and change.

34. See E. Spector, *Job Satisfaction: Application, Assessment, Causes, and Consequences* (Thousand Oaks, CA: Sage, 1997), p. 3.

35. J. Wanous, A. E. Reichers, and M. J. Hudy, "Overall Job Satisfaction: How Good Are Single-Item Measures?" *Journal of Applied Psychology,* April 1997, pp. 247–252.

36. A. F. Chelte, J. Wright, and C. Tausky, "Did Job Satisfaction Really Drop During the 1970s?" *Monthly Labor Review,* November 1982, pp. 33–36; "Job Satisfaction High in America, Says Conference Board Study," *Monthly Labor Review,* February 1985, p. 52; E. Graham, "Work May Be a Rat Race, but It's Not a Daily Grind," *Wall Street Journal,* September 19, 1997, p. R1; and K. Bowman, "Attitudes About Work, Chores, and Leisure in America," *AEI Opinion Studies,* August 25, 2003.

37. W. K. Balzer, J. A. Kihm, P. C. Smith, J. L. Irwin, P. D. Bachiochi, C. Robie, E. F. Sinar, and L. F. Parra, *Users' Manual for the Job Descriptive Index (JDI; 1997 Revision) and the Job in General Scales* (Bowling Green, OH: Bowling Green State University, 1997).

38. J. Barling, E. K. Kelloway, and R. D. Iverson, "High-Quality Work, Job Satisfaction, and Occupational Injuries," *Journal of Applied Psychology* 88, no. 2 (2003), pp. 276–283; and F. W. Bond and D. Bunce, "The Role of Acceptance and Job Control in Mental Health, Job Satisfaction, and Work Performance," *Journal of Applied Psychology* 88, no. 6 (2003), pp. 1057–1067.

39. S. E. Humphrey, J. D. Nahrgang, and F. P. Morgeson, "Integrating Motivational, Social, and Contextual Work Design Features: A Meta-Analytic Summary and Theoretical Extension of the Work Design Literature," *Journal of Applied Psychology* 92, no. 5 (2007), pp. 1332–1356; and D. S. Chiaburu and D. A. Harrison, "Do Peers Make the Place? Conceptual Synthesis and Meta-analysis of Coworker Effect

on Perceptions, Attitudes, OCBs, and Performance," *Journal of Applied Psychology* 93, no. 5 (2008), pp. 1082–1103.

40. E. Diener, E. Sandvik, L. Seidlitz, and M. Diener, "The Relationship Between Income and Subjective Well-Being: Relative or Absolute?" *Social Indicators Research* 28 (1993), pp. 195–223.

41. E. Diener and M. E. P. Seligman, "Beyond Money: Toward an Economy of Well-Being," *Psychological Science in the Public Interest* 5, no. 1 (2004), pp. 1–31; and A. Grant, "Money = Happiness? That's Rich: Here's the Science Behind the Axiom," *The (South Mississippi) Sun Herald*, January 8, 2005.

42. T. A. Judge and C. Hurst, "The Benefits and Possible Costs of Positive Core Self-Evaluations: A Review and Agenda for Future Research," in D. Nelson and C. L. Cooper (eds.), *Positive Organizational Behavior* (London, UK: Sage Publications, 2007), pp. 159–174.

43. See D. Farrell, "Exit, Voice, Loyalty, and Neglect as Responses to Job Dissatisfaction: A Multidimensional Scaling Study," *Academy of Management Journal*, December 1983, pp. 596–606; C. E. Rusbult, D. Farrell, G. Rogers, and A. G. Mainous III, "Impact of Exchange Variables on Exit, Voice, Loyalty, and Neglect: An Integrative Model of Responses to Declining Job Satisfaction," *Academy of Management Journal*, September 1988, pp. 599–627; M. J. Withey and W. H. Cooper, "Predicting Exit, Voice, Loyalty, and Neglect," *Administrative Science Quarterly*, December 1989, pp. 521–539; J. Zhou and J. M. George, "When Job Dissatisfaction Leads to Creativity: Encouraging the Expression of Voice," *Academy of Management Journal*, August 2001, pp. 682–696; J. B. Olson-Buchanan and W. R. Boswell, "The Role of Employee Loyalty and Formality in Voicing Discontent," *Journal of Applied Psychology*, December 2002, pp. 1167–1174; and A. Davis-Blake, J. P. Broschak, and E. George, "Happy Together? How Using Nonstandard Workers Affects Exit, Voice, and Loyalty Among Standard Employees," *Academy of Management Journal* 46, no. 4 (2003), pp. 475–485.

44. M. T. Iaffaldano and M. Muchinsky, "Job Satisfaction and Job Performance: A Meta-analysis," *Psychological Bulletin*, March 1985, pp. 251–273.

45. T. A. Judge, C. J. Thoresen, J. E. Bono, and G. K. Patton, "The Job Satisfaction–Job Performance Relationship: A Qualitative and Quantitative Review," *Psychological Bulletin*, May 2001, pp. 376–407; T. Judge, S. Parker, A. E. Colbert, D. Heller, and R. Ilies, "Job Satisfaction: A Cross-Cultural Review," in N. Anderson, D. S. Ones, H. K. Sinangil, and C. Viswesvaran (eds.), *Handbook of Industrial, Work, & Organizational Psychology*, vol. 2 (Thousand Oaks, CA: Sage, 2001), p. 41.

46. M. Riketta, "The Causal Relation Between Job Attitudes and Performance: A Meta-Analysis of Panel Studies," *Journal of Applied Psychology* 93, no. 2 (2008), pp. 472–481.

47. R. B. Freeman, "Job Satisfaction as an Economic Variable," *American Economic Review*, January 1978, pp. 135–141.

48. T. A. Judge, C. J. Thoresen, J. E. Bono, and G. K. Patton, "The Job Satisfaction–Job Performance Relationship: A Qualitative and Quantitative Review," *Psychological Bulletin*, May 2001, pp. 376–407.

49. C. Ostroff, "The Relationship Between Satisfaction, Attitudes, and Performance: An Organizational Level Analysis," *Journal of Applied Psychology*, December 1992, pp. 963–974; A. M. Ryan, M. J. Schmit, and R. Johnson, "Attitudes and Effectiveness: Examining Relations at an Organizational Level," *Personnel Psychology*, Winter 1996, pp. 853–882; and J. K. Harter, F. L. Schmidt, and T. L. Hayes, "Business-Unit Level Relationship Between Employee Satisfaction, Employee Engagement, and Business Outcomes: A Meta-analysis," *Journal of Applied Psychology*, April 2002, pp. 268–279.

50. See P. Podsakoff, S. B. MacKenzie, J. B. Paine, and D. G. Bachrach, "Organizational Citizenship Behaviors: A Critical Review of the Theoretical and Empirical Literature and Suggestions for Future Research," *Journal of Management* 26, no. 3 (2000), pp. 513–563.

51. B. J. Hoffman, C. A. Blair, J. P. Maeriac, and D. J. Woehr, "Expanding the Criterion Domain? A Quantitative Review of the OCB Literature," *Journal of Applied Psychology* 92, no. 2 (2007), pp. 555–566; and J. A. LePine, A. Erez, and D. E. Johnson, "The Nature and Dimensionality of Organizational Citizenship Behavior: A Critical Review and Meta-analysis," *Journal of Applied Psychology*, February 2002, pp. 52–65.

52. S. L. Blader and T. R. Tyler, "Testing and Extending the Group Engagement Model: Linkages Between Social Identity, Procedural Justice, Economic Outcomes, and Extrarole Behavior," *Journal of Applied Psychology* 94, no. 2 (2009), pp. 445–464; J. Fahr, P. M. Podsakoff, and D. W. Organ, "Accounting for Organizational Citizenship Behavior: Leader Fairness and Task Scope Versus Satisfaction," *Journal of Management*, December 1990, pp. 705–722; and M. A. Konovsky and D. W. Organ, "Dispositional and Contextual Determinants of Organizational Citizenship Behavior," *Journal of Organizational Behavior*, May 1996, pp. 253–266.

53. D. S. Chiaburu and D. A. Harrison, "Do Peers Make the Place? Conceptual Synthesis and Meta-Analysis of Coworker Effect on Perceptions, Attitudes, OCBs, and Performance," *Journal of Applied Psychology* 93, no. 5 (2008), pp. 1082–1103.

54. See, for instance, D. J. Koys, "The Effects of Employee Satisfaction, Organizational Citizenship Behavior, and Turnover on Organizational Effectiveness: A Unit-Level, Longitudinal Study," *Personnel Psychology*, Spring 2001, pp. 101–114; J. Griffith, "Do Satisfied Employees Satisfy Customers? Support-Services Staff Morale and Satisfaction Among Public School Administrators, Students, and Parents," *Journal of Applied Social Psychology*, August 2001, pp. 1627–1658; and C. Vandenberghe, K. Bentein, R. Michon, J. Chebat, M. Tremblay, and J. Fils, "An Examination of the Role of Perceived Support and Employee Commitment in Employee-Customer Encounters," *Journal of Applied Psychology* 92, no. 4, pp. 1177–1187.

55. J. M. O'Brien, "Zappos Knows How to Kick It," *Fortune* (February 2, 2009), pp. 55–60.

56. T. Frank, "Report: Low Morale May Hurt Airport Security," *USA Today* (June 25, 2008), p. 3A; and J. Bailey, "Fliers Fed Up? The Employees Feel the Same," *New York Times* (December 22, 2007), pp. A1, A18.

57. E. A. Locke, "The Nature and Causes of Job Satisfaction," in M. D. Dunnette (ed.), *Handbook of Industrial and Organizational Psychology* (Chicago: Rand McNally, 1976), p. 1331; K. D. Scott and G. S. Taylor, "An Examination of Conflicting Findings on the Relationship Between Job Satisfaction and Absenteeism: A Meta-analysis," *Academy of Management Journal*, September 1985, pp. 599–612; and R. Steel and J. R. Rentsch, "Influence of Cumulation Strategies

on the Long-Range Prediction of Absenteeism," *Academy of Management Journal* December 1995, pp. 1616–1634.

58. J. P. Hausknecht, N. J. Hiller, and R. J. Vance, "Work-Unit Absenteeism: Effects of Satisfaction, Commitment, Labor Market Conditions, and Time," *Academy of Management Journal* 51, no. 6 (2008), pp. 1123–1245.

59. W. Hom and R. W. Griffeth, *Employee Turnover* (Cincinnati, OH: South-Western Publishing, 1995); R. W. Griffeth, P. W. Hom, and S. Gaertner, "A Meta-analysis of Antecedents and Correlates of Employee Turnover: Update, Moderator Tests, and Research Implications for the Next Millennium," *Journal of Management* 26, no. 3 (2000), p. 479.

60. T. H. Lee, B. Gerhart, I. Weller, and C. O. Trevor, "Understanding Voluntary Turnover: Path-Specific Job Satisfaction Effects and the Importance of Unsolicited Job Offers," *Academy of Management Journal* 51, no. 4 (2008), pp. 651–671.

61. P. E. Spector, S. Fox, L. M. Penney, K. Bruursema, A. Goh, and S. Kessler, "The Dimensionality of Counterproductivity: Are All Counterproductive Behaviors Created Equal?" *Journal of Vocational Behavior* 68, no. 3 (2006), pp. 446–460; and D. S. Chiaburu and D. A. Harrison, "Do Peers Make the Place? Conceptual Synthesis and Meta-analysis of Coworker Effect on Perceptions, Attitudes, OCBs, and Performance," *Journal of Applied Psychology* 93, no. 5 (2008), pp. 1082–1103.

62. K. Holland, "Inside the Minds of Your Employees," *New York Times* (January 28, 2007), p. B1; "Study Sees Link Between Morale and Stock Price," *Workforce Management* (February 27, 2006), p. 15; and "The Workplace as a Solar System," *New York Times* (October 28, 2006), p. B5.

63. E. White, "How Surveying Workers Can Pay Off," *Wall Street Journal* (June 18, 2007), p. B3.

64. M. J. Gelfand, M. Erez, and Z. Aycan, "Cross-Cultural Organizational Behavior," *Annual Review of Psychology* 58 (2007), pp. 479–514; A. S. Tsui, S. S. Nifadkar, and A. Y. Ou, "Cross-National, Cross-Cultural Organizational Behavior Research: Advances, Gaps, and Recommendations," *Journal of Management*, June 2007, pp. 426–478.

65. M. Benz and B. S. Frey, "The Value of Autonomy: Evidence from the Self-Employed in 23 Countries," working paper 173, Institute for Empirical Research in Economics, University of Zurich, November 2003 (ssrn.com/abstract=475140); and P. Warr, *Work, Happiness, and Unhappiness* (Mahwah, NJ: Laurence Erlbaum, 2007).

66. Harrison, Newman, and Roth, "How Important Are Job Attitudes?" pp. 320–321.

67. L. Saari and T. A. Judge, "Employee Attitudes and Job Satisfaction," *Human Resource Management* 43, no. 4 (2004), pp. 395–407.

68. See R. Ilies and T. A. Judge, "On the Heritability of Job Satisfaction: The Mediating Role of Personality," *Journal of Applied Psychology* 88, no. 4 (2003), pp. 750–759.

LEARNING OBJECTIVES

After studying this chapter, you should be able to:

1 Differentiate emotions from moods and list the basic emotions and moods.

2 Discuss whether emotions are rational and what functions they serve.

3 Identify the sources of emotions and moods.

4 Show the impact emotional labor has on employees.

5 Describe affective events theory and identify its applications.

6 Contrast the evidence for and against the existence of emotional intelligence.

7 Apply concepts about emotions and moods to specific OB issues.

8 Contrast the experience, interpretation, and expression of emotions across cultures.

Emotions and Moods

Time cools, time clarifies; no mood can be maintained quite unaltered through the course of hours. —Mark Twain

FEAR AND HOPE IN FINANCE

In the halcyon days of a few years ago, jobs in finance were plentiful and amply rewarded.

How times have changed. To be clear, most of those graduating with degrees in finance do find gainful employment and, gradually, people's expectations have adjusted. However, those who entered undergraduate or graduate business schools at the peak of the market, with high hopes for six-figure salaries, were particularly ill prepared for the recession. Anxiety, fear, resentment, and depression were common emotional reactions. A recent poll by the Rockefeller Foundation found that people ages 18–29 were more pessimistic about the economy than any other age group.

Jian Yang (pictured on opposite page) is in his second year at the University of Chicago's graduate business school. "It's definitely impacting the mood of the student body," he said. While Yang expects to graduate with $200,000 in debt, he's still optimistic about the future. "It's a good way to spend three years of downturn," Yang said.

It's been harder for Jon Cifuentes. After graduating, Cifuentes landed a job in investment banking at Smith Barney. By now, he expected to be making more than $100,000 a year. Instead, he lost his job, lost another in investment banking, and now has a temporary job and is living with his sister. Still, Cifuentes refuses to lick his wounds. Some people are "in a much worse spot," he said.[1]

As the examples of Jian Yang and Jon Cifuentes show, life deals us unexpected hands, often generating complex emotional reactions. Before we delve further into emotions and moods, get an evaluation of your mood state right now. Take the self-assessment noted on the following page to find out what sort of mood you're in.

Given the obvious role emotions play in our lives, it might surprise you that, until recently, the field of OB has given the topic of emotions little attention.[2] Why? We offer two possible explanations.

First is the *myth of rationality*.[3] Until very recently, the protocol of the work world kept a damper on emotions. A well-run organization didn't allow employees to express frustration, fear, anger, love, hate, joy, grief, or similar feelings thought to be the antithesis of rationality. Though researchers and managers knew emotions were an inseparable part of everyday life, they tried to create organizations that were emotion free. Of course, that wasn't possible.

The second explanation is that many believed emotions of any kind were disruptive.[4] Researchers looked at strong negative emotions—especially anger—that interfered with an employee's ability to work effectively. They rarely viewed emotions as constructive or contributing to enhanced performance.

Certainly some emotions, particularly exhibited at the wrong time, can hinder performance. But employees do bring their emotions to work every day, and no study of OB would be comprehensive without considering their role in workplace behavior.

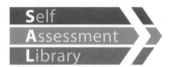

HOW ARE YOU FEELING RIGHT NOW?

In the Self-Assessment Library (available on CD or online), take assessment IV.D.1 (How Are You Feeling Right Now?) and answer the following questions.

1. *What was higher—your positive mood score or negative mood score? How do these scores compare with those of your classmates?*
2. *Did your score surprise you? Why or why not?*
3. *What sorts of things influence your positive moods, your negative moods?*

What Are Emotions and Moods?

1 Differentiate emotions from moods and list the basic emotions and moods.

In our analysis, we'll need three terms that are closely intertwined: *affect, emotions,* and *moods.*

Affect is a generic term that covers a broad range of feelings people experience, including both emotions and moods.[5] **Emotions** are intense feelings directed at someone or something.[6] **Moods** are less intense feelings than emotions and often (though not always) lack a contextual stimulus.[7]

Most experts believe emotions are more fleeting than moods.[8] For example, if someone is rude to you, you'll feel angry. That intense feeling probably comes and goes fairly quickly, maybe even in a matter of seconds. When you're in a bad mood, though, you can feel bad for several hours.

Emotions are reactions to a person (seeing a friend at work may make you feel glad) or an event (dealing with a rude client may make you feel angry). You show your emotions when you're "happy about something, angry at someone, afraid of something."[9] Moods, in contrast, aren't usually directed at a person or an event. But emotions can turn into moods when you lose focus on the event or object that started the feeling. And, by the same token, good or bad moods can make you more emotional in response to an event. So when a colleague criticizes how you

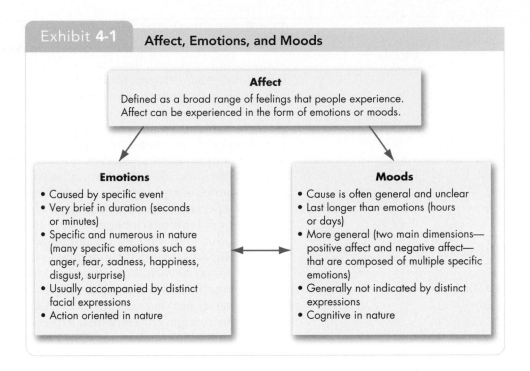

Exhibit 4-1 Affect, Emotions, and Moods

Affect

Defined as a broad range of feelings that people experience. Affect can be experienced in the form of emotions or moods.

Emotions

- Caused by specific event
- Very brief in duration (seconds or minutes)
- Specific and numerous in nature (many specific emotions such as anger, fear, sadness, happiness, disgust, surprise)
- Usually accompanied by distinct facial expressions
- Action oriented in nature

Moods

- Cause is often general and unclear
- Last longer than emotions (hours or days)
- More general (two main dimensions— positive affect and negative affect— that are composed of multiple specific emotions)
- Generally not indicated by distinct expressions
- Cognitive in nature

spoke to a client, you might show emotion (anger) toward a specific object (your colleague). But as the specific emotion dissipates, you might just feel generally dispirited. You can't attribute this feeling to any single event; you're just not your normal self. You might then overreact to other events. This affect state describes a mood. Exhibit 4-1 shows the relationships among affect, emotions, and mood.

First, as the exhibit shows, affect is a broad term that encompasses emotions and moods. Second, there are differences between emotions and moods. Some of these differences—that emotions are more likely to be caused by a specific event, and emotions are more fleeting than moods—we just discussed. Other differences are subtler. For example, unlike moods, emotions like anger and disgust tend to be more clearly revealed by facial expressions. Also, some researchers speculate that emotions may be more action oriented—they may lead us to some immediate action—while moods may be more cognitive, meaning they may cause us to think or brood for a while.[10]

Finally, the exhibit shows that emotions and moods are closely connected and can influence each other. Getting your dream job may generate the emotion of joy, which can put you in a good mood for several days. Similarly, if you're in a good or bad mood, it might make you experience a more intense positive or negative emotion than otherwise. In a bad mood, you might blow up in response to a co-worker's comment that would normally have generated only a mild reaction.

Affect, emotions, and moods are separable in theory; in practice the distinction isn't always crystal clear. In some areas, researchers have studied mostly moods, in other areas mainly emotions. So, when we review the OB topics on emotions and moods, you may see more information on emotions in one area and on moods in another. This is simply the state of the research.

---

affect *A broad range of feelings that people experience.*

emotions *Intense feelings that are directed at someone or something.*

moods *Feelings that tend to be less intense than emotions and that lack a contextual stimulus.*

The Basic Emotions

How many emotions are there? There are dozens, including anger, contempt, enthusiasm, envy, fear, frustration, disappointment, embarrassment, disgust, happiness, hate, hope, jealousy, joy, love, pride, surprise, and sadness. Numerous researchers have tried to limit them to a fundamental set.[11] But some argue that it makes no sense to think in terms of "basic" emotions because even emotions we rarely experience, such as shock, can have a powerful effect on us.[12] Other researchers, even philosophers, say there are universal emotions common to all of us. René Descartes, often called the founder of modern philosophy, identified six "simple and primitive passions"—wonder, love, hatred, desire, joy, and sadness—and argued that "all the others are composed of some of these six or are species of them."[13] Although other philosophers like Hume, Hobbes, and Spinoza identified categories of emotions, proof of the existence of a basic set of emotions still waits for contemporary researchers.

Psychologists have tried to identify basic emotions by studying facial expressions.[14] One problem is that some emotions are too complex to be easily represented on our faces. Many think of love as the most universal of all emotions,[15] for example, yet it's not easy to express it through only a facial expression. Cultures also have norms that govern emotional expression, so how we *experience* an emotion isn't always the same as how we *show* it. And many companies today offer anger-management programs to teach people to contain or even hide their inner feelings.[16]

It's unlikely psychologists or philosophers will ever completely agree on a set of basic emotions, or even on whether there is such a thing. Still, many researchers have agreed on six essentially universal emotions—anger, fear, sadness, happiness, disgust, and surprise.[17] Some even plot them along a continuum: happiness—surprise—fear—sadness—anger—disgust.[18] The closer two emotions are to each other on this continuum, the more likely people will confuse them. We sometimes mistake happiness for surprise, but rarely do we confuse happiness and disgust. In addition, as we'll see later on, cultural factors can also influence interpretations.

The Basic Moods: Positive and Negative Affect

One way to classify emotions is by whether they are positive or negative.[19] Positive emotions—such as joy and gratitude—express a favorable evaluation or feeling. Negative emotions—such as anger or guilt—express the opposite. Keep in mind that emotions can't be neutral. Being neutral is being nonemotional.[20]

When we group emotions into positive and negative categories, they become mood states because we are now looking at them more generally instead of isolating one particular emotion. In Exhibit 4-2, excited is a pure marker of high positive affect, while boredom is a pure marker of low positive affect. Nervous is a pure marker of high negative affect; relaxed is a pure marker of low negative affect. Finally, some emotions—such as contentment (a mixture of high positive affect and low negative affect) and sadness (a mixture of low positive affect and high negative affect)—are in between. You'll notice this model does not include all emotions. Some, such as surprise, don't fit well because they're not as clearly positive or negative.

So, we can think of **positive affect** as a mood dimension consisting of positive emotions such as excitement, self-assurance, and cheerfulness at the high end and boredom, sluggishness, and tiredness at the low end. **Negative affect** is a mood dimension consisting of nervousness, stress, and anxiety at the high end and relaxation, tranquility, and poise at the low end. (*Note:* Positive and negative affect *are* moods. We're using these labels, rather than *positive mood* and *negative mood* because that's how researchers label them.)

Positive affect and negative affect play out at work and beyond in that they color our perceptions, and these perceptions can become their own reality. One

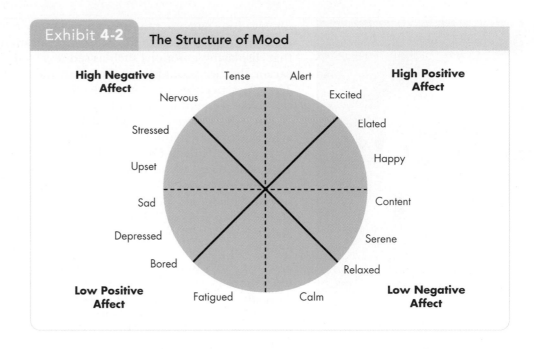

Exhibit 4-2 The Structure of Mood

flight attendant posted an anonymous blog on the Web that said, "I work in a pressurized aluminum tube and the environment outside my 'office' cannot sustain human life. That being said, the human life inside is not worth sustaining sometimes . . . in fact, the passengers can be jerks, and idiots. I am often treated with no respect, nobody listens to me . . . until I threaten to kick them off the plane."[21] Clearly, if a flight attendant is in a bad mood, it's going to influence his perceptions of passengers, which will, in turn, influence his behavior.

Negative emotions are likely to translate into negative moods. People think about events that created strong negative emotions five times as long as they do about events that created strong positive ones.[22] So, we should expect people to recall negative experiences more readily than positive ones. Perhaps one reason is that, for most of us, they're also more unusual. Indeed, research finds a **positivity offset**, meaning that at zero input (when nothing in particular is going on), most individuals experience a mildly positive mood.[23] So, for most people, positive moods are somewhat more common than negative moods. The positivity offset also appears to operate at work. One study of customer-service representatives in a British call center (a job where it's probably pretty difficult to feel positive) revealed people reported experiencing positive moods 58 percent of the time.[24]

The Function of Emotions

2 Discuss whether emotions are rational and what functions they serve.

Do Emotions Make Us Irrational? How often have you heard someone say "Oh, you're just being emotional"? You might have been offended. The famous astronomer Carl Sagan once wrote, "Where we have strong emotions, we're liable to fool ourselves." These

positive affect *A mood dimension that consists of specific positive emotions such as excitement, self-assurance, and cheerfulness at the high end and boredom, sluggishness, and tiredness at the low end.*

negative affect *A mood dimension that consists of emotions such as nervousness, stress, and anxiety at the high end and relaxation, tranquility, and poise at the low end.*

positivity offset *The tendency of most individuals to experience a mildly positive mood at zero input (when nothing in particular is going on).*

By studying brain injuries, such as the one experienced by Phineas Gage, whose skull is shown here, researchers discovered an important link between emotions and rational thinking. They found that losing the ability to emote led to loss of the ability to reason. From this discovery, researchers learned that our emotions provide us with valuable information that helps our thinking process.

observations suggest rationality and emotion are in conflict, and that if you exhibit emotion you are likely to act irrationally. One team of authors argues that displaying emotions such as sadness to the point of crying is so toxic to a career that we should leave the room rather than allow others to witness it.[25] These perspectives suggest the demonstration or even experience of emotions can make us seem weak, brittle, or irrational. However, research is increasingly showing that emotions are actually critical to rational thinking.[26] There has been evidence of such a link for a long time.

Consider Phineas Gage, a railroad worker in Vermont. One September day in 1848, while Gage was setting an explosive charge at work, a 3-foot 7-inch iron bar flew into his lower-left jaw and out through the top of his skull. Remarkably, Gage survived his injury. He was still able to read and speak, and he performed well above average on cognitive ability tests. However, it became clear he had lost his ability to experience emotion; he was emotionless at even the saddest misfortunes or the happiest occasions. Gage's inability to express emotion eventually took away his ability to reason. He started making irrational choices about his life, often behaving erratically and against his self-interests. Despite being an intelligent man whose intellectual abilities were unharmed by the accident, Gage drifted from job to job, eventually taking up with a circus. In commenting on Gage's condition, one expert noted, "Reason may not be as pure as most of us think it is or wish it were . . . emotions and feelings may not be intruders in the bastion of reason at all: they may be enmeshed in its networks, for worse *and* for better."[27]

The example of Phineas Gage and many other brain injury studies show emotions are critical to rational thinking. We must have the ability to experience emotions to be rational. Why? Because our emotions provide important information about how we understand the world around us. Would we really want a manager to make a decision about firing an employee without regarding either his or the employee's emotions? The key to good decision making is to employ both thinking *and* feeling in our decisions.

Sources of Emotions and Moods

3 Identify the sources of emotions and moods.

Have you ever said "I got up on the wrong side of the bed today"? Have you ever snapped at a co-worker or family member for no particular reason? If you have, it probably makes you wonder where emotions and moods come from. Here we discuss some of the primary influences.

Personality   Moods and emotions have a trait component: most people have built-in tendencies to experience certain moods and emotions more frequently than others do. People also experience the same emotions with different intensities. Contrast Texas Tech basketball coach Bobby Knight to Microsoft CEO Bill Gates. One is easily moved to anger, while the other is relatively distant and unemotional. Knight and Gates probably differ in **affect intensity**, or how strongly they experience their emotions.[28] Affectively intense people experience both positive and negative emotions more deeply: when they're sad, they're really sad, and when they're happy, they're really happy.

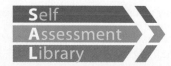

WHAT'S MY AFFECT INTENSITY?

In the Self-Assessment Library (available on CD or online), take assessment IV.D.2 (What's My Affect Intensity?).

| Exhibit 4-3 | Our Moods Are Affected by the Day of the Week |

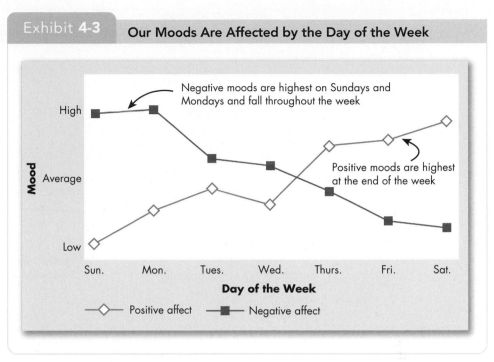

Source: "Our Moods Are Affected by the Day of the Week" from *Mood and Temperament*, by D. Watson. Reprinted by permission of Guilford Publications, Inc.

Day of the Week and Time of the Day   Are people in their best moods on the weekends? As Exhibit 4-3 shows, people tend to be in their worst moods (highest negative affect and lowest positive affect) early in the week, and in their best moods (highest positive affect and lowest negative affect) late in the week.[29]

What about time of the day? (See Exhibit 4-4.) We often think we are either "morning" or "evening" people. However, most of us actually follow the same pattern. Regardless of what time we go to bed at night or get up in the morning, levels of positive affect tend to peak at around the halfway point between waking and sleeping. Negative affect, however, shows little fluctuation throughout the day.

What does this mean for organizational behavior? Monday morning is probably not the best time to ask someone for a favor or convey bad news. Our workplace interactions will probably be more positive from midmorning onward and also later in the week.

Weather   When do you think you would be in a better mood—when it's 70 degrees and sunny or on a gloomy, cold, rainy day? Many people believe their mood is tied to the weather. However, a fairly large and detailed body of evidence conducted by multiple researchers suggests weather has little effect on mood.[30] One expert concluded, "Contrary to the prevailing cultural view, these data indicate that people do not report a better mood on bright and sunny days (or, conversely, a worse mood on dark and rainy days)."[31] **Illusory correlation** explains why people tend to *think* nice weather improves their mood. It occurs when people associate two events that in reality have no connection.

affect intensity   *Individual differences in the strength with which individuals experience their emotions.*

illusory correlation   *The tendency of people to associate two events when in reality there is no connection.*

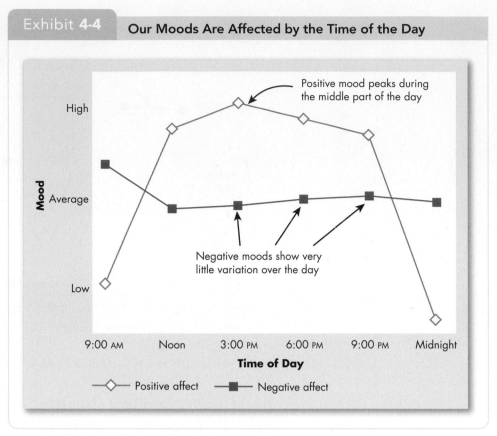

Exhibit 4-4 — **Our Moods Are Affected by the Time of the Day**

Source: "Our Moods Are Affected by the Day of the Week" from Mood and Temperament, by D. Watson. Reprinted by permission of Guilford Publications, Inc.

Stress   As you might imagine, stressful daily events at work (a nasty e-mail, an impending deadline, the loss of a big sale, a reprimand from the boss) negatively affect moods. The effects of stress also build over time. As the authors of one study note, "a constant diet of even low-level stressful events has the potential to cause workers to experience gradually increasing levels of strain over time."[32] Mounting levels of stress can worsen our moods, and we experience more negative emotions. Consider the following entry from a worker's blog: "I'm in a bit of a blah mood today . . . physically, I feel funky, though and the weather out combined with the amount of personal and work I need to get done are getting to me." Although sometimes we thrive on stress, most of us, like this blogger, find stress takes a toll on our mood.[33]

Social Activities   Do you tend to be happiest when out with friends? For most people, social activities increase positive mood and have little effect on negative mood. But do people in positive moods seek out social interactions, or do social interactions cause people to be in good moods? It seems both are true.[34] Does the *type* of social activity matter? Indeed it does. Research suggests activities that are physical (skiing or hiking with friends), informal (going to a party), or epicurean (eating with others) are more strongly associated with increases in positive mood than events that are formal (attending a meeting) or sedentary (watching TV with friends).[35]

Sleep   U.S. adults report sleeping less than adults a generation ago.[36] Does lack of sleep make people grumpier? Sleep quality does affect mood. Undergraduates and adult workers who are sleep deprived report greater feelings of fatigue, anger,

"People Can't Accurately Forecast Their Own Emotions"

This statement is essentially true. People tend to do a pretty bad job of predicting how they're going to feel when something happens. The research on this topic—called *affective forecasting*—reveals our poor job takes two forms.

First, we tend to overestimate the pleasure we'll receive from a future positive event. We think we'll be happier with a new car than is actually the case, that owning our own home will feel better than it does once we buy it, and even that marriage will make us happier than it will. We overestimate both the intensity of future positive

events (how happy we'll feel) and their duration (how long we'll feel happy). When Joakim Noah was contemplating being a first-round basketball draft pick, a reporter asked him what he'd most look forward to. Noah said he couldn't wait to have "the best bathroom in the NBA." Chances are Noah got his world-class bathroom as a Chicago Bull, but it likely didn't make him as happy as he thought it would.

A second area we forecast poorly is negative events. Just as positive events tend not to make us feel as good as we think they will, negative events don't make us feel as bad as we anticipate.

Many different studies have supported our poor affective forecasting abilities: College students overestimate how happy or unhappy they'll be after being assigned to a good or bad dormitory, people overestimate how unhappy they'll be 2 months after a breakup, untenured college professors overestimate how happy they will be with tenure, and women overestimate the emotional impact of unwanted results for a pregnancy test.[37]

So, there is good news and bad news in this story: It's true the highs aren't as high as we think, but the lows aren't as low as we fear.

and hostility.[38] One reason is that poor or reduced sleep impairs decision making and makes it difficult to control emotions.[39] A recent study suggests poor sleep also impairs job satisfaction because people feel fatigued, irritable, and less alert.[40]

Exercise   You often hear people should exercise to improve their mood. Does "sweat therapy" really work? It appears so. Research consistently shows exercise enhances peoples' positive mood.[41] While not terribly strong overall, the effects

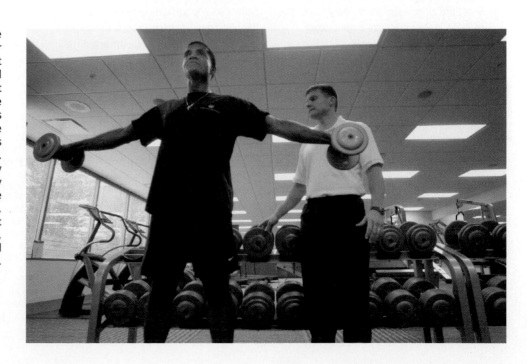

"Sweat therapy" enhances the mood of Mark Saunders, senior marketing manager at GlaxoSmithKline, a pharmaceutical firm. Saunders regularly works out with the help of a trainer at the company's fitness center. Saunders says exercise makes him more energetic and sharp and boosts his creativity and productivity. "Especially in winter, this keeps my engine going," he says. Like many other companies that provide fitness centers for employees, GlaxoSmithKline believes that exercise increases positive moods, resulting in happier, healthier, and more productive employees.

are strongest for those who are depressed. So, exercise may help put you in a better mood, but don't expect miracles.

Age Do young people experience more extreme positive emotions (so-called youthful exuberance) than older people? If you answered "yes," you were wrong. One study of people ages 18 to 94 revealed that negative emotions seem to occur less as people get older. Periods of highly positive moods lasted longer for older individuals, and bad moods faded more quickly.[42] The study implies emotional experience improves with age; as we get older, we experience fewer negative emotions.

Gender Many believe women are more emotional than men. Is there any truth to this? Evidence does confirm women are more emotionally expressive than men;[43] they experience emotions more intensely, they tend to "hold onto" emotions longer than men, and they display more frequent expressions of both positive and negative emotions, except anger.[44] Thus, there are some gender differences in the experience and expression of emotions. Does the same emotional expression by men and women generate different reactions from *others?* We take up this issue in the Ethical Dilemma.

International OB

Emotional Recognition: Universal or Culture Specific?

Early researchers studying how we understand emotions based on others' expressions believed all individuals could recognize the same emotion regardless of culture: a frown would indicate sadness no matter where you were from. However, recent research suggests some emotions are more widely recognized than others.

One study found that people from more collectivistic cultures, such as Japan, were more likely to interpret the emotions in a target person's facial expressions by examining the social context—the faces of other individuals in the picture. Subjects from individualistic cultures, such as the United States, interpreted an individual's emotion by focusing on the person.

One study examined how quickly and accurately we can read the facial expressions of people of different cultural backgrounds. Although individuals were at first faster at recognizing the emotional expression of others from their own culture, when living in a different culture they increased their speed and

accuracy as they became more familiar with the culture. As Chinese residing in the United States adapted to their surroundings, they were able to recognize the emotions of people native to the United States more quickly.

In fact, foreigners are sometimes better at recognizing emotions among the citizens in their adopted country than its citizens are. Interestingly, these effects begin to occur relatively quickly. Chinese students living in the United States for an average of 2.4 years were better at recognizing the facial expressions of U.S. citizens than the facial expressions of Chinese citizens. Why? The authors of the study suggest that limited language skills force foreigners to rely more on nonverbal communication.

Finally, another study revealed that recognition of some emotions does appear to generalize across cultures. Specifically, prideful facial expressions were accurately recognized in the United States, Italy, and West Africa. Other research provides support for

the cross-cultural recognition of additional emotions, including anger, disgust, and surprise.

Taken together, these findings suggest both generality to the recognition of facial expressions but also some cultural differences. A U.S. worker and a Tanzanian in the same organization would likely be able to interpret many emotions similarly, but they might do so in somewhat different ways, and they would probably agree less often than two Americans or two Tanzanians.

Source: Based on J. L. Tracy and R. W. Robins, "The Nonverbal Expression of Pride: Evidence for Cross-cultural Recognition," *Journal of Personality and Social Psychology* 94, no. 3 (2008), pp. 516–530; T. Masuda, P. Ellsworth, B. Mesquita, J. Leu, S. Tanida, and E. Van de Veerdonk, "Placing the Face in Context: Cultural Differences in the Perception of Facial Emotion," *Journal of Personality and Social Psychology* 94, no. 3 (2008), pp. 365–381; and H. A. Elfenbein and N. Ambady, "When Familiarity Breeds Accuracy: Cultural Exposure and Facial Emotion Recognition," *Journal of Personality and Social Psychology,* August 2003, pp. 276–290.

Emotional Labor

4 Show the impact emotional labor has on employees.

If you've ever had a job in retail sales or waited on tables in a restaurant, you know the importance of projecting a friendly demeanor and smiling. Even though there were days when you didn't feel cheerful, you knew management expected you to be upbeat when dealing with customers. So you faked it. Every employee expends physical and mental labor by putting body and mind, respectively, into the job. But jobs also require **emotional labor** an employee's expression of organizationally desired emotions during interpersonal transactions at work.

The concept of emotional labor emerged from studies of service jobs. Airlines expect their flight attendants to be cheerful; we expect funeral directors to be sad and doctors emotionally neutral. But emotional labor is relevant to almost every job. At the least your managers expect you to be courteous, not hostile, in interactions with co-workers. The true challenge arises when employees have to project one emotion while feeling another.[45] This disparity is **emotional dissonance**, and it can take a heavy toll. Bottled-up feelings of frustration, anger, and resentment can eventually lead to emotional exhaustion and burnout.[46] It's from the increasing importance of emotional labor as a key component of effective job performance that we have come to understand the relevance of emotion within the field of OB.

Emotional labor creates dilemmas for employees. There are people with whom you have to work that you just plain don't like. Maybe you consider their personality abrasive. Maybe you know they've said negative things about you behind your back. Regardless, your job requires you to interact with these people on a regular basis. So you're forced to feign friendliness.

Employees of this new Apple store in Scottsdale, Arizona, enthusiastically greeted shoppers standing in line and waiting to get into the store. Giving customers this warm reception with smiling faces and high fives is an example of the displayed emotions an organization requires employees to show and considers appropriate in a given job.

emotional labor *A situation in which an employee expresses organizationally desired emotions during interpersonal transactions at work.*

emotional dissonance *Inconsistencies between the emotions people feel and the emotions they project.*

It can help you, on the job especially, if you separate emotions into *felt* or *displayed emotions*.[47] **Felt emotions** are an individual's actual emotions. In contrast, **displayed emotions** are those that the organization requires workers to show and considers appropriate in a given job. They're not innate; they're learned. "The ritual look of delight on the face of the first runner-up as the new Miss America is announced is a product of the display rule that losers should mask their sadness with an expression of joy for the winner."[48] Similarly, most of us know we're expected to act sad at funerals, regardless of whether we consider the person's death a loss, and to appear happy at weddings even if we don't feel like celebrating.[49]

Effective managers have learned to be serious when giving an employee a negative performance evaluation and to hide their anger when they've been passed over for promotion. A salesperson who hasn't learned to smile and appear friendly, despite his or her true feelings at the moment, typically won't last long in the job. How we *experience* an emotion isn't always the same as how we *show* it.[50]

Displaying fake emotions requires us to suppress real ones. **Surface acting** is hiding inner feelings and forgoing emotional expressions in response to display rules. A worker who smiles at a customer even when he doesn't feel like it is surface acting. **Deep acting** is trying to modify our true inner feelings based on display rules. A health care provider trying to genuinely feel more empathy for her patients is deep acting.[51] Surface acting deals with *displayed* emotions, and deep acting deals with *felt* emotions. Research shows surface acting is more stressful to employees because it entails feigning their true emotions.[52] Displaying emotions we don't really feel is exhausting, so it is important to give employees who engage in surface displays a chance to relax and recharge. A study that looked at how cheerleading instructors spent their breaks from teaching found those who used their breaks to rest and relax were more effective instructors after their

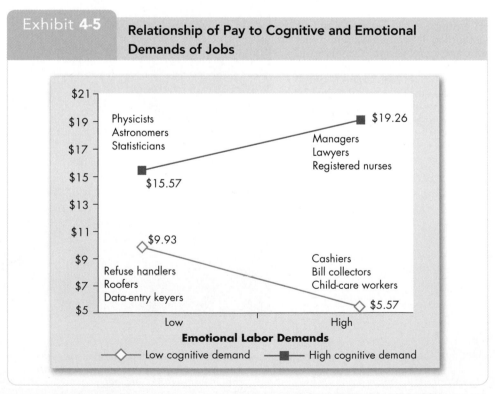

Exhibit 4-5   **Relationship of Pay to Cognitive and Emotional Demands of Jobs**

Source: Based on: T. M. Glomb, J. D. Kammeyer-Mueller, and M. Rotundo, "Emotional Labor Demands and Compensating Wage Differentials," *Journal of Applied Psychology* 89, no. 4 (August 2004), pp. 700–714.

breaks.[53] Instructors who did chores during their breaks were only about as effective after their break as they were before.

Interestingly, as important as managing emotions is to many jobs, the market does not necessarily financially reward emotional labor. A 2004 study found emotional demands of a job matter in setting compensation levels, but only when jobs are already cognitively demanding—such as in law and nursing. But child-care workers and waiters—holders of jobs with high emotional demands but relatively low cognitive demands—receive little compensation for the emotional demands of their work.[54] Exhibit 4-5 shows the relationship between cognitive and emotional demands and pay. The model doesn't seem to depict a fair state of affairs. After all, why should emotional demands be rewarded in only cognitively complex jobs? One explanation may be that it's hard to find qualified people who are willing and able to work in such jobs.

Affective Events Theory

5 Describe affective events theory and identify its applications.

We've seen that emotions and moods are an important part of our lives and our work lives. But how do they influence our job performance and satisfaction? A model called **affective events theory (AET)** demonstrates that employees react emotionally to things that happen to them at work, and this reaction influences their job performance and satisfaction.[55]

Exhibit 4-6 summarizes AET. The theory begins by recognizing that emotions are a response to an event in the work environment. The work environment includes everything surrounding the job—the variety of tasks and degree of autonomy, job demands, and requirements for expressing emotional labor. This environment creates work events that can be hassles, uplifting events, or both. Examples of hassles are colleagues who refuse to carry their share of work, conflicting directions from different managers, and excessive time pressures. Uplifting events include meeting a goal, getting support from a colleague, and receiving recognition for an accomplishment.[56]

These work events trigger positive or negative emotional reactions, to which employees' personalities and moods predispose them to respond with greater or lesser intensity. People who score low on emotional stability are more likely to react strongly to negative events. And our emotional response to a given event can change, depending on mood. Finally, emotions influence a number of performance and satisfaction variables, such as organizational citizenship behavior, organizational commitment, level of effort, intention to quit, and workplace deviance.

felt emotions *An individual's actual emotions.*

displayed emotions *Emotions that are organizationally required and considered appropriate in a given job.*

surface acting *Hiding one's inner feelings and forgoing emotional expressions in response to display rules.*

deep acting *Trying to modify one's true inner feelings based on display rules.*

affective events theory (AET) *A model that suggests that workplace events cause emotional reactions on the part of employees, which then influence workplace attitudes and behaviors.*

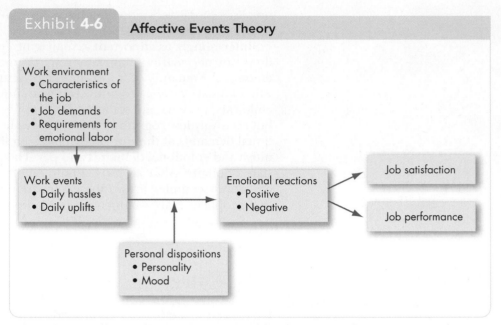

Source: Based on N. M. Ashkanasy and C. S. Daus, "Emotion in the Workplace: The New Challenge for Managers," *Academy of Management Executive*, February 2002, p. 77.

Tests of affective events theory suggest the following:

1. An emotional episode is actually a series of emotional experiences, precipitated by a single event and containing elements of both emotions and mood cycles.
2. Current emotions influence job satisfaction at any given time, along with the history of emotions surrounding the event.
3. Because moods and emotions fluctuate over time, their effect on performance also fluctuates.
4. Emotion-driven behaviors are typically short in duration and of high variability.
5. Because emotions, even positive ones, tend to be incompatible with behaviors required to do a job, they typically have a negative influence on job performance.[57]

Consider an example.[58] Say you work as an aeronautical engineer for Boeing. Because of the downturn in demand for commercial jets, you've just learned the company is considering laying off 10,000 employees, possibly including you. This event is likely to make you feel negative emotions, especially fear that you might lose your primary source of income. And because you're prone to worry a lot and obsess about problems, this event increases your feelings of insecurity. The layoff also sets in motion a series of smaller events that create an episode: You talk with your boss, and he assures you your job is safe; you hear rumors your department is high on the list to be eliminated; and you run into a former colleague who was laid off 6 months ago and still hasn't found work. These events, in turn, create emotional ups and downs. One day, you're feeling upbeat that you'll survive the cuts. The next, you might be depressed and anxious. These emotional swings take your attention away from your work and lower your job performance and satisfaction. Finally, your response is magnified because this is the fourth-largest layoff Boeing has initiated in the past 3 years.

In summary, AET offers two important messages.[59] First, emotions provide valuable insights into how workplace hassles and uplifting events influence employee performance and satisfaction. Second, employees and managers shouldn't ignore emotions or the events that cause them, even when they appear minor, because they accumulate.

Emotional Intelligence

6 Contrast the evidence for and against the existence of emotional intelligence.

Diane Marshall is an office manager. Her awareness of her own and others' emotions is almost nil. She's moody and unable to generate much enthusiasm or interest in her employees. She doesn't understand why employees get upset with her. She often overreacts to problems and chooses the most ineffectual responses to emotional situations.[60] Diane has low emotional intelligence. **Emotional intelligence (EI)** is a person's ability to (1) be self-aware (to recognize her own emotions when she experiences them), (2) detect emotions in others, and (3) manage emotional cues and information. People who know their own emotions and are good at reading emotion cues—for instance, knowing why they're angry and how to express themselves without violating norms—are most likely to be effective.[61] One simulation study showed that students who were good at identifying and distinguishing among their feelings were able to make more profitable investment decisions.[62]

Several studies suggest EI plays an important role in job performance. One study looked at the characteristics of engineers at Lucent Technologies who were rated stars by their peers and concluded stars were better at relating to others. That is, EI, not IQ, characterized high performers. Another study looked at the successes and failures of 11 U.S. presidents—from Franklin Roosevelt to Bill Clinton—and evaluated them on six qualities: communication, organization, political skill, vision, cognitive style, and emotional intelligence. The key quality that differentiated the successful (such as Roosevelt, Kennedy, and Reagan) from the unsuccessful (such as Johnson, Carter, and Nixon) was emotional intelligence.[63]

EI has been a controversial concept in OB, with supporters and detractors. In the following sections, we review the arguments for and against its viability.

The Case for EI

The arguments in favor of EI include its intuitive appeal, the fact that it predicts criteria that matter, and the idea that it is biologically based.

Intuitive Appeal   Almost everyone would agree it is good to possess street smarts and social intelligence. Intuition suggests people who can detect emotions in others, control their own emotions, and handle social interactions well have a powerful leg up in the business world. Partners in a multinational consulting firm who scored above the median on an EI measure delivered $1.2 million more in business than did the other partners.[64]

EI Predicts Criteria That Matter   Evidence suggests a high level of EI means a person will perform well on the job. One study found EI predicted the performance of employees in a cigarette factory in China.[65] Another study

emotional intelligence (EI)   *The ability to detect and to manage emotional cues and information.*

Diane Hoskins, a top leader at Gensler, a global architectural firm, has high emotional intelligence. She is one of three executive directors who operate the firm along with the management committee. Hoskins is a star performer in a job that demands interacting with employees and customers throughout the world. She brings confidence and cultural sensitivity to her work in recruiting employees and developing their careers to ensure that Gensler has the talent it needs to serve clients. Hoskins is shown here discussing a new internship program that could help Gensler build its global business.

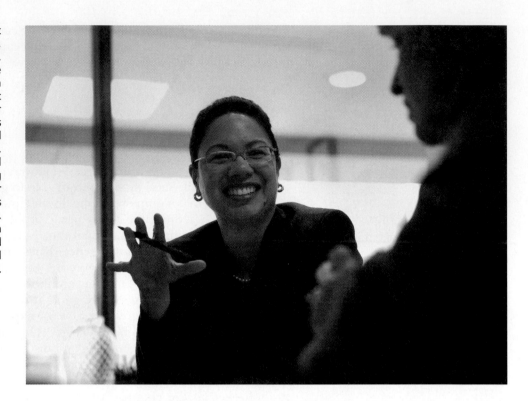

found the ability to recognize emotions in others' facial expressions and to emotionally "eavesdrop" (pick up subtle signals about peoples' emotions) predicted peer ratings of how valuable people were to their organization.[66] Finally, a review of 59 studies indicated that, overall, EI correlated moderately with job performance.[67]

EI Is Biologically Based   In one study, people with damage to the brain area that governs emotional processing (part of the prefrontal cortex) scored no lower on standard measures of intelligence than people without similar damage. But they scored significantly lower on EI tests and were impaired in normal decision making, as demonstrated by their poor performance in a card game with monetary rewards. This study suggests EI is neurologically based in a way that's unrelated to standard measures of intelligence.[68] There is also evidence EI is genetically influenced, further supporting the idea that it measures a real underlying biological factor.[69]

The Case Against EI

For all its supporters, EI has just as many critics who say it is vague and impossible to measure, and they question its validity.

EI Is Too Vague a Concept   To many researchers, it's not clear what EI is. Is it a form of intelligence? Most of us wouldn't think being self-aware or self-motivated or having empathy is a matter of intellect. Is EI a misnomer? Moreover, different researchers often focus on different skills, making it difficult to define EI. One researcher may study self-discipline, another empathy, another self-awareness. As one reviewer noted, "The concept of EI has now become so broad and the components so variegated that . . . it is no longer even an intelligible concept."[70]

EI Can't Be Measured   Many critics have raised questions about measuring EI. Because EI is a form of intelligence, they argue, there must be right and wrong answers for it on tests. Some tests do have right and wrong answers, although the validity of some questions is doubtful. One measure asks you to associate feelings with colors, as if purple always makes us feel cool and not warm. Other measures are self reported, such as "I'm good at 'reading' other people," and have no right or wrong answers. The measures of EI are diverse, and researchers have not subjected them to as much rigorous study as they have measures of personality and general intelligence.[71]

The Validity of EI Is Suspect   Some critics argue that because EI is so closely related to intelligence and personality, once you control for these factors, it has nothing unique to offer. There is some foundation to this argument. EI appears to be highly correlated with measures of personality, especially emotional stability.[72] If this is true, then the evidence for a biological component to EI is spurious, and biological markers like brain activity and heritability are attributable to other well known and much more researched psychological constructs. But there hasn't been enough research on whether EI adds insight beyond measures of personality and general intelligence in predicting job performance. Still, EI is wildly popular among consulting firms and in the popular press. One company's promotional materials for an EI measure claimed, "EI accounts for more than 85 percent of star performance in top leaders."[73] To say the least, it's difficult to validate this statement with the research literature.

Weighing the arguments for and against EI, it's still too early to tell whether the concept is useful. It *is* clear, though, that it's here to stay.

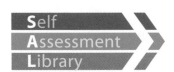

WHAT'S MY EMOTIONAL INTELLIGENCE SCORE?

In the Self-Assessment Library (available on CD or online), take assessment I.E.1 (What's My Emotional Intelligence Score?).

OB Applications of Emotions and Moods

7 Apply concepts about emotions and moods to specific OB issues.

In this section, we assess how an understanding of emotions and moods can improve our ability to explain and predict the selection process in organizations, decision making, creativity, motivation, leadership, interpersonal conflict, negotiation, customer service, job attitudes, and deviant workplace behaviors. We also look at how managers can influence our moods.

Selection

One implication from the evidence on EI to date is that employers should consider it a factor in hiring employees, especially in jobs that demand a high degree of social interaction. In fact, more employers *are* starting to use EI measures to hire people. A study of U.S. Air Force recruiters showed that top-performing recruiters exhibited high levels of EI. Using these findings, the Air Force revamped its selection criteria. A follow-up investigation found future hires who had high EI scores were 2.6 times more successful than those who didn't. At L'Oreal, salespersons selected on EI scores outsold those hired using the company's old selection procedure. On an annual basis, salespeople selected for

Hiring employees with high emotional intelligence is important for companies such as Starbucks, whose baristas have a high degree of social interaction with customers. In keeping with Starbucks mission "to inspire and nurture the human spirit," baristas are selected who relate well to customers, connect with them, and uplift their lives. At Starbucks, emotional intelligence plays an important role in job performance, as the company enjoys a loyal customer base and a reputation as one of the most admired companies in America.

their emotional competence sold $91,370 more than other salespeople did, for a net revenue increase of $2,558,360.[74]

Decision Making

As you will see in Chapter 6, traditional approaches to the study of decision making in organizations have emphasized rationality. But OB researchers are increasingly finding that moods and emotions have important effects on decision making.

Positive moods and emotions seem to help. People in good moods or experiencing positive emotions are more likely than others to use heuristics, or rules of thumb,[75] to help make good decisions quickly. Positive emotions also enhance problem-solving skills, so positive people find better solutions to problems.[76]

OB researchers continue to debate the role of negative emotions and moods in decision making. Although one often-cited study suggested depressed people reach more accurate judgments,[77] more recent evidence hints they make poorer decisions. Why? Because depressed people are slower at processing information and tend to weigh all possible options rather than the most likely ones.[78] They search for the perfect solution, when there rarely is one.

Creativity

People in good moods tend to be more creative than people in bad moods.[79] They produce more ideas and more options, and others think their ideas are original.[80] It seems people experiencing positive moods or emotions are more flexible and open in their thinking, which may explain why they're more creative.[81] Supervisors should actively try to keep employees happy because doing so creates more good moods (employees like their leaders to encourage them and provide positive feedback on a job well done), which in turn leads people to be more creative.[82]

Some researchers, however, do not believe a positive mood makes people more creative. They argue that when people are in positive moods, they may relax ("If I'm in a good mood, things must be going okay, and I must not need to think of new ideas") and not engage in the critical thinking necessary for some forms of creativity.[83] The answer may lie in thinking of moods somewhat differently. Rather than looking at positive or negative affect, it's possible to conceptualize moods as active feelings like anger, fear, or elation and contrast these with deactivating moods like sorrow, depression, or serenity. All the activating moods, whether positive *or* negative, seem to lead to more creativity, whereas deactivating moods lead to less.[84]

Motivation

Several studies have highlighted the importance of moods and emotions on motivation. One study set two groups of people to solving word puzzles. The first group saw a funny video clip, intended to put the subjects in a good mood first. The other group was not shown the clip and started working on the puzzles right away. The results? The positive-mood group reported higher expectations of being able to solve the puzzles, worked harder at them, and solved more puzzles as a result.[85]

The second study found that giving people performance feedback—whether real or fake—influenced their mood, which then influenced their motivation.[86] So a cycle can exist in which positive moods cause people to be more creative, which leads to positive feedback from those observing their work. This positive feedback further reinforces their positive mood, which may make them perform even better, and so on.

Another study looked at the moods of insurance sales agents in Taiwan.[87] Agents in a good mood were more helpful toward their co-workers and also felt better about themselves. These factors in turn led to superior performance in the form of higher sales and better supervisor reports of performance.

Leadership

Effective leaders rely on emotional appeals to help convey their messages.[88] In fact, the expression of emotions in speeches is often the critical element that makes us accept or reject a leader's message. "When leaders feel excited, enthusiastic, and active, they may be more likely to energize their subordinates and convey a sense of efficacy, competence, optimism, and enjoyment."[89] Politicians, as a case in point, have learned to show enthusiasm when talking about their chances of winning an election, even when polls suggest otherwise.

The general manager of a professional sports team is the organizational leader responsible for developing a winning team. As general manager of the Los Angeles Dodgers, Ned Colletti is shown here delivering an inspirational talk to employees right before a game between the Dodgers and the San Diego Padres. Colletti relies on emotional appeals to employees of all the individual divisions of the team, from administrative affairs to public relations, to work well together in achieving a victorious season.

Corporate executives know emotional content is critical if employees are to buy into their vision of the company's future and accept change. When higher-ups offer new visions, especially with vague or distant goals, it is often difficult for employees to accept the changes they'll bring. By arousing emotions and linking them to an appealing vision, leaders increase the likelihood that managers and employees alike will accept change.[90] Leaders who focus on inspirational goals also generate greater optimism and enthusiasm in employees, leading to more positive social interactions with co-workers and customers.[91]

Negotiation

Negotiation is an emotional process; however, we often say a skilled negotiator has a "poker face." The founder of Britain's Poker Channel, Crispin Nieboer, stated, "It is a game of bluff and there is fantastic human emotion and tension, seeing who can bluff the longest."[92] Several studies have shown that a negotiator who feigns anger has an advantage over the opponent. Why? Because when a negotiator shows anger, the opponent concludes the negotiator has conceded all she can and so gives in.[93] Anger should be used selectively in negotiation: angry negotiators who have less information or less power than their opponents have significantly worse outcomes.[94] It appears that a powerful, better-informed individual will be less willing to share information or meet an angry opponent halfway.

Displaying a negative emotion (such as anger) can be effective, but feeling bad about your performance appears to impair future negotiations. Individuals who do poorly in a negotiation experience negative emotions, develop negative perceptions of their counterpart, and are less willing to share information or be cooperative in future negotiations.[95] Interestingly, then, while moods and emotions have benefits at work, in negotiation—unless we're putting up a false front like feigning anger—emotions may impair negotiator performance. A 2005 study found people who suffered damage to the emotional centers of their brains (the same part that was injured in Phineas Gage) may be the *best* negotiators, because they're not likely to overcorrect when faced with negative outcomes.[96]

Customer Service

A worker's emotional state influences customer service, which influences levels of repeat business and of customer satisfaction.[97] Providing quality customer service makes demands on employees because it often puts them in a state of emotional dissonance. Over time, this state can lead to job burnout, declines in job performance, and lower job satisfaction.[98]

Employees' emotions can transfer to the customer. Studies indicate a matching effect between employee and customer emotions called **emotional contagion**—the "catching" of emotions from others.[99] How does it work? The primary explanation is that when someone experiences positive emotions and laughs and smiles at you, you tend to respond positively. Emotional contagion is important because customers who catch the positive moods or emotions of employees shop longer. But are negative emotions and moods contagious, too? Absolutely. When an employee feels unfairly treated by a customer, for example, it's harder for him to display the positive emotions his organization expects of him.[100]

Job Attitudes

Ever hear the advice "Never take your work home with you," meaning you should forget about work once you go home? That's easier said than done. Several studies have shown people who had a good day at work tend to be in a better mood at home that evening, and vice versa.[101] People who have a stressful day at work also have trouble relaxing after they get off work.[102] One study had married couples describing their moods when responding to timed cell-phone surveys through the course of the day. As most married readers might suspect, if one member of the couple was in a negative mood during the workday, that mood spilled over to the spouse at night.[103] In other words, if you've had a bad day at work, your spouse is likely to have an unpleasant evening. Even though people do emotionally take their work home with them, however, by the next day the effect is usually gone.[104]

Deviant Workplace Behaviors

Anyone who has spent much time in an organization realizes people often behave in ways that violate established norms and threaten the organization, its members, or both. As we saw in Chapter 1, these actions are called *workplace deviant behaviors*.[105] Many can be traced to negative emotions.

For instance, envy is an emotion that occurs when you resent someone for having something you don't have but strongly desire—such as a better work assignment, larger office, or higher salary.[106] It can lead to malicious deviant behaviors. An envious employee could backstab another employee, negatively distort others' successes, and positively distort his own accomplishments.[107] Angry people look for

An Ethical Choice

Workplace Romance

A large percentage of married couples first met in the workplace. A 2006 survey showed 40 percent of all employees have been in an office romance. Given the amount of time people spend at work, this isn't terribly surprising. Yet office romances pose sensitive ethical issues for organizations and employees and, as the OB Poll shows, most of us hesitate to initiate one. Perhaps we realize that many romances fade, and the aftermath can be particularly difficult if the other party remains a co-worker.

Take the case of Julie Roehm, senior VP of marketing at Wal-Mart, who began dating Sean Womack, VP of communications architecture. When Wal-Mart learned of the relationship, it fired both executives, arguing the undisclosed relationship violated its policy against workplace romances. Roehm sued Wal-Mart, claiming the company breached her contract and damaged her reputation. Wal-Mart countersued, alleging Roehm showed favoritism on Womack's behalf. Eventually, Roehm dropped her lawsuit in exchange for Wal-Mart's dropping its countersuit.

This story shows that while workplace romances are personal matters, it's hard to keep them out of the political complexities of organizational life. Here are some recommendations to follow if you're considering a workplace romance:

1. Nearly three-quarters of organizations have no policies governing workplace romances. Before initiating or accepting any romantic contact with a co-worker or supervisor, make sure you know the rules. Your career could depend on it.

2. Be particularly cautious about "dating up" (dating your supervisor) and "dating down" (dating your direct report). These relationships are particularly prone to misunderstandings, resentments, and even lawsuits.

3. If you and your romantic partner work in the same area, avoid the temptation to hide the relationship from your boss. Sooner or later, he or she will find out. It is better to be proactive.

4. If you're single, it may not be wise to rule out office romances altogether. Many individuals report meeting their spouse or significant other at work. Just remember to keep organizational policies in mind.

Sources: K. Gurchiek, "Be Prepared for Cupid's Arrows Among the Cubicles," SHRM Online (March 3, 2008); J. Greenwald, "Employers Are the Losers in the Dating Game," *Workforce Week,* June 3, 2007, pp. 1–2; and "My Year at Wal-Mart," *Businessweek,* February 12, 2007.

emotional contagion   *The process by which peoples' emotions are caused by the emotions of others.*

other people to blame for their bad mood, interpret other people's behavior as hostile, and have trouble considering others' point of view.[108] It's not hard to see how these thought processes, too, can lead directly to verbal or physical aggression.

Evidence suggests people who feel negative emotions, particularly anger or hostility, are more likely than others to engage in deviant behavior at work.[109] Once aggression starts, it's likely that other people will become angry and aggressive, so the stage is set for a serious escalation of negative behavior.

Safety and Injury at Work

Research relating negative affectivity to increased injuries at work suggests employers might improve health and safety (and reduce costs) by ensuring workers aren't engaged in potentially dangerous activities when they're in a bad mood. Bad moods can contribute to injury at work in several ways.[110] Individuals in negative moods tend to be more anxious, which can make them less able to cope effectively with hazards. A person who is always scared will be more pessimistic about the effectiveness of safety precautions because she feels she'll just get hurt anyway, or she might panic or freeze up when confronted with a threatening situation. Negative moods also make people more distractable, and distractions can obviously lead to careless behaviors.

How Managers Can Influence Moods

You can usually improve a friend's mood by sharing a funny video clip, giving the person a small bag of candy, or even offering a pleasant beverage.[111] But what can companies do to improve employees' moods? Managers can use humor and give their employees small tokens of appreciation for work well done. Also, when leaders are in good moods, group members are more positive, and as a result they cooperate more.[112]

Finally, selecting positive team members can have a contagion effect as positive moods transmit from team member to team member. One study of professional cricket teams found players' happy moods affected the moods of their team members and positively influenced their performance.[113] It makes sense, then, for managers to select team members predisposed to experience positive moods.

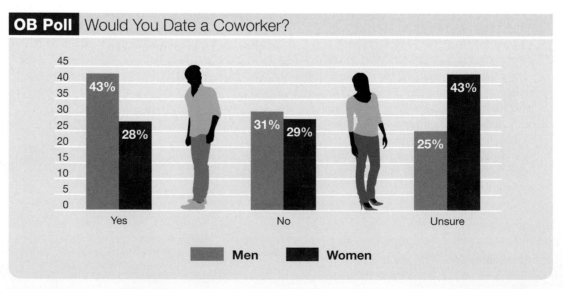

Source: Based on Spherion Workplace survey of 1,391 employees, USA Today, February 14, 2008, p. 1B.

Global Issues

8   Contrast the experience, interpretation, and expression of emotions across cultures.

Does the degree to which people *experience* emotions vary across cultures? Do peoples' *interpretations* of emotions vary across cultures? Finally, do the norms for the *expression* of emotions differ across cultures? Let's tackle each question.

Does the Degree to Which People Experience Emotions Vary Across Cultures? Yes. In China, people report experiencing fewer positive and negative emotions than people in other cultures, and the emotions they experience are less intense. Compared with Mainland Chinese, Taiwanese are more like U.S. workers in their experience of emotions: on average, they report more positive and fewer negative emotions than their Chinese counterparts.[114] People in most cultures appear to experience certain positive and negative emotions, but the frequency and intensity varies to some degree.[115]

Do Peoples' Interpretations of Emotions Vary Across Cultures? People from all over the world interpret negative and positive emotions in much the same way. We all view negative emotions, such as hate, terror, and rage, as dangerous and destructive, and we desire positive emotions, such as joy, love, and happiness. However, some cultures value certain emotions more than others. U.S. culture values enthusiasm, while the Chinese consider negative emotions more useful and constructive than do people in the United States. Pride is generally a positive emotion in Western individualistic cultures such as the United States, but Eastern cultures such as China and Japan view pride as undesirable.[116]

Do the Norms for the Expression of Emotions Differ Across Cultures? Absolutely. People in the United States and the Middle East recognize a smile as indicating happiness, but in the Middle East a smile is more likely to be seen as a sign of sexual attraction, so women have learned not to smile at men.[117] In collectivist countries people are more likely to believe another's emotional displays have something to do with the relationship between them, while people in individualistic cultures don't think others' emotional expressions are directed at them. In the United States there's a bias against expressing emotions, especially intense negative ones. French retail clerks, in contrast, are infamous for being surly toward customers (as a report from the French government itself confirmed). Serious German shoppers have reportedly been turned off by Wal-Mart's friendly greeters and helpful staff.[118]

In general, and not surprisingly, it's easier for people to accurately recognize emotions within their own culture than in others. A Chinese businessperson is more likely to accurately label the emotions underlying the facial expressions of a Chinese colleague than those of a U.S. colleague.[119]

Some cultures lack words for standard U.S. emotional terms such as *anxiety, depression,* and *guilt.* Tahitians don't have a word directly equivalent to *sadness;* when they are sad, their peers attribute their state to a physical illness.[120]

Our discussion illustrates that cultural factors influence what managers think is emotionally appropriate.[121] What's acceptable in one culture may seem unusual or even dysfunctional in another. Managers need to know the emotional norms in each culture they do business in or with so they don't send unintended signals or misread the reactions of others. A U.S. manager in Japan, for instance, should know that while U.S. culture tends to view smiling positively, the Japanese attribute frequent smiling to a lack of intelligence.[122]

Summary and Implications for Managers

Emotions and moods are similar in that both are affective in nature. But they're also different—moods are more general and less contextual than emotions. And events do matter. The time of day and day of the week, stressful events, social activities, and sleep patterns are some of the factors that influence emotions and moods.

Emotions and moods have proven relevant for virtually every OB topic we study. Increasingly, organizations are selecting employees they believe have high levels of emotional intelligence. Emotions and positive moods appear to facilitate effective decision making and creativity. Recent research suggests mood is linked to motivation, especially through feedback, and that leaders rely on emotions to increase their effectiveness. The display of emotions is important to negotiation and customer service, and the experience of emotions is closely linked to job attitudes and behaviors that follow from attitudes, such as deviant workplace behavior.

Can managers control colleagues' and employees' emotions and moods? Certainly there are limits, practical and ethical. Emotions and moods are a natural part of an individual's makeup. Where managers err is in ignoring co-workers' and employees' emotions and assessing others' behavior as if it were completely rational. As one consultant aptly put it, "You can't divorce emotions from the workplace because you can't divorce emotions from people."[123] Managers who understand the role of emotions and moods will significantly improve their ability to explain and predict their co-workers' and employees' behavior.

The Costs and Benefits of Organizational Display Rules

Organizations today realize that good customer service means good business. After all, who wants to end a shopping trip at the grocery store with a surly checker? Research clearly shows organizations that provide good customer service have higher profits than those with poor customer service.[124] An integral part of customer-service training is to set forth display rules to teach employees to interact with customers in a friendly, helpful, professional way—and evidence indicates such rules work: having display rules increases the odds employees will display the emotions expected of them.[125]

As one Starbucks manager says, "What makes Starbucks different is our passion for what we do. We're trying to provide a great experience for people, with a great product. That's what we all care about."[126] Cashiers are friendly and will get to know you by name if you are a repeat customer. Starbucks may have good coffee, but a big part of the company's growth has been due to the customer experience.

Asking employees to act friendly is good for them, too. Employees of organizations that require them to display positive emotions actually feel better as a result.[127] Someone who feels being asked to smile is bad for him doesn't belong in the service industry in the first place.

Companies should not be "thought police" and force employees to feel and act in ways that serve only organizational needs. Service employees should be professional and courteous, yes, but many companies expect them to take abuse and refrain from defending themselves. That's wrong. As the philosopher Jean Paul Sartre proposed, we have a responsibility to be authentic—true to ourselves—and within reasonable limits organizations have no right to ask us to be otherwise.

Customers might even prefer that employees be themselves rather than smiling punching bags. Employees shouldn't be openly nasty or hostile, of course, but who appreciates a fake smile? Think about trying on an outfit in a store where the clerk automatically says it looks "wonderful" when you know it doesn't and you sense the clerk is lying. Furthermore, if an employee doesn't feel like slapping on an artificial smile, then it's only going to create dissonance between her and her employer.[128]

Finally, forcing display rules on employees takes a heavy emotional toll.[129] It's unnatural to smile all the time or passively take abuse from customers, clients, or fellow employees. Organizations can improve employees' psychological health by encouraging them to be themselves, within reasonable limits.

Questions for Review

1 What are the similarities and differences between emotions and moods? What are the basic emotions and the basic mood dimensions?

2 Are emotions and moods rational? What functions do they serve?

3 What are the primary sources of emotions and moods?

4 What is emotional labor, and why is it important to understanding OB?

5 What is affective events theory? What insight does it contribute to understanding emotions?

6 What is emotional intelligence, and what are the arguments for and against its importance?

7 What effect do emotions and moods have on different OB issues? As a manager, what steps would you take to improve your employees' moods?

8 Does the degree to which people *experience* emotions vary across cultures? Do peoples' *interpretations* of emotions vary across cultures, and do different norms across cultures govern the expression of emotions?

Experiential Exercise

WHO CAN CATCH A LIAR?

Research has studied whether people can tell someone is lying based on facial expression. Let's see who is good at catching liars.

Split up into teams and follow these instructions.

1. Randomly choose someone to be the team organizer. Have this person write down on a piece of paper "T" for truth and "L" for lie. If there are, say, six people in the group (other than the organizer), then three people will get a slip with a "T" and three a slip with an "L." It's important that all team members keep what's on their paper a secret.

2. Each team member who holds a T slip needs to come up with a true statement, and each team member who holds an L slip needs to come up with a false state-

ment. Try not to make the statement so outrageous that no one would believe it (for example, "I have flown to the moon").

3. The organizer will have each member make his or her statement. Group members should then examine the person making the statement closely to try to determine whether he or she is telling the truth or lying. Once each person has made his or her statement, the organizer will ask for a vote and record the tallies.

4. Each person should now indicate whether the statement was the truth or a lie.

5. How good was your group at catching the liars? Were some people good liars? What did you look for to determine if someone was lying?

Ethical Dilemma

IS THERE AN EMOTIONAL DOUBLE-STANDARD FOR MEN AND WOMEN AT WORK?

Although we all have emotions, norms moderate the display of emotions at work. You might wonder whether this informal rule applies more to one gender than another. Are there norms against men displaying "feminine" emotions such as compassion or tearfulness, and are women discouraged from displaying "masculine" emotions such as angry hostility or bravado?

Although evidence continues to accumulate, there is some support for existence of this double standard—at least for the few emotions that have been studied. Research consistently shows that displays of anger raise men's status and

lower women's. One study found female managers who displayed anger were viewed as having an angry personality ("She's a witch," "She's out of control"), whereas men's anger was attributed to external circumstances ("He was under pressure," "His colleague's behavior caused his anger").

What about crying at work? Stereotype theory would suggest that crying hurts men more than women, but that does not appear to be the case. A Penn State study found that crying on the job was more damaging to a woman's career than a man's.

These studies suggest that, to some degree, women are in a no-win situation. They are expected to be more emotional than men, but when they show those emotions they are punished for it.

Questions

1. Nancy Albertini, chairwoman of an executive search firm, said flatly: "Tears don't work in the workplace." On the other hand, Tory Johnson, CEO of a New York recruitment services firm, thinks crying at work is natural and people should be themselves. She says: "You have to let people know you can react naturally to a situation." Whose advice do you think is right?

2. If one of your co-workers cried at work, would it influence your opinion of him or her? What factors might be relevant to your appraisal?

3. If you were concerned about a possible no-win situation for women displaying emotions at work, what specific things might you do to change the culture if you were in charge?

Source: V. L. Brescoll and E. L. Uhlmann, "Can an Angry Woman Get Ahead?" *Psychological Science* 19, no. 3 (2008), pp. 268–275; S. Armour, "Tears at Work Not Recommended," *USA Today* (January 18, 2008), p. 9B; and L. R. Warner and S. A. Shields, "The Perception of Crying in Women and Men: Angry Tears, Sad Tears, and the 'Right Way' to Cry," in U. Hess and P. Philippot, Pierre (eds.), *Group Dynamics and Emotional Expression* (pp. 92–117), New York: Cambridge University Press, 2007.

Case Incident 1

THE UPSIDE OF ANGER?

A researcher doing a case study on emotions in organizations interviewed Laura, a 22-year-old customer-service representative in Australia. The following is a summary of the interview (with some paraphrasing of the interviewer questions):

Interviewer: How would you describe your workplace?

Laura: *Very cold, unproductive, [a] very, umm, cold environment, atmosphere.*

Interviewer: What kinds of emotions are prevalent in your organization?

Laura: *Anger, hatred toward other people, other staff members.*

Interviewer: So it seems that managers keep employees in line using fear tactics?

Laura: *Yeah. [The General Manager's] favorite saying is, "Nobody's indispensable." So, it's like, "I can't do that because I'll get sacked!"*

Interviewer: How do you survive in this situation?

Laura: *You have to cater your emotions to the sort of situation, the specific situation . . . because it's just such a hostile environment, this is sort of the only way you can survive.*

Interviewer: Are there emotions you have to hide?

Laura: *Managers don't like you to show your emotions . . . They don't like to show that there is anything wrong or anything emotional in the working environment.*

Interviewer: Why do you go along?

Laura: *I feel I have to put on an act because . . . to show your true emotions, especially toward my managers*

[Laura names two of her senior managers], it would be hatred sometimes. So, you just can't afford to do that because it's your job and you need the money.

Interviewer: Do you ever rebel against this system?

Laura: *You sort of put on a happy face just so you can annoy [the managers]. I find that they don't like people being happy, so you just annoy them by being happy. So, yeah. It just makes you laugh. You just "put it on" just because you know it annoys [management]. It's pretty vindictive and manipulative but you just need to do that.*

Interviewer: Do you ever find that this gets to you?

Laura: *I did care in the beginning, and I think it just got me into more trouble. So now I just tell myself, "I don't care." If you tell yourself something for long enough, eventually you believe it. Yeah, so now I just go "Oh well."*

Interviewer: Do you intend to keep working here?

Laura: *It's a means to an end now. So every time I go [to work] and every week I just go, "Well, one week down, one week less until I go away." But if I knew that I didn't have this goal, I don't know if I could handle it, or if I would even be there now.*

Interviewer: Is there an upside to working here?

Laura: *I'm so much better at telling people off now than I ever used to be. I can put people in place in about three sentences. Like, instead of, before I would walk away from it. But now I just stand there and fight. . . . I don't know if that's a good thing or a bad thing.*

Questions

1. Do you think Laura is justified in her responses to her organization's culture? Why or why not?

2. Do you think Laura's strategic use and display of emotions serve to protect her?

3. Assuming that Laura's description is accurate, how would *you* react to the organization's culture?

4. Research shows that acts of co-workers (37 percent) and management (22 percent) cause more negative emotions for employees than do acts of customers (7 percent).[130] What can Laura's company do to change its emotional climate?

Source: J. Perrone and M. H. Vickers, "Emotions as Strategic Game in a Hostile Workplace: An Exemplar Case," *Employee Responsibilities and Rights Journal* 16, no. 3 (2004), pp. 167–178.

Case Incident 2

BECOMING A FACIAL DECODER

We mentioned previously that some researchers—the psychologist Paul Ekman is the best known—have studied whether facial expressions reveal true emotions. These researchers have distinguished real smiles (so-called Duchenne smiles, named after French physician Guillaume Duchenne) from "fake" smiles. Duchenne found genuine smiles raised not only the corners of the mouth (easily faked) but also cheek and eye muscles (much more difficult to fake). So, one way to determine whether someone is genuinely happy or amused is to look at the muscles around the upper cheeks and eyes—if the person's eyes are smiling or twinkling, the smile is genuine. Ekman and his associates have developed similar methods to detect other emotions, such as anger, disgust, and distress. They call their method Facial Action Coding System (FACS). According to Ekman, the key to identifying real emotions is to focus on micro-expressions, or those facial muscles we cannot easily manipulate.

Dan Hill has used FACS to study the facial expressions of CEOs and found they vary dramatically not only in their Duchenne smiles but also in the degree to which they display positive versus negative facial expressions. Below is Hill's analysis of the facial expressions of some prominent executives:

Jeff Bezos, Amazon	51% positive
Warren Buffet, Berkshire Hathaway	69% positive
Michael Dell, Dell Computers	47% positive
Larry Ellison, Oracle	0% positive
Bill Gates, Microsoft	73% positive
Steve Jobs, Apple	48% positive
Phil Knight, Nike	67% positive
Donald Trump, The Trump Organization	16% positive

Questions

1. Most research suggests we are not very good at detecting lying, and we think we're much better than we are. Do you believe FACS would improve your ability to detect lying in others?

2. Do you think the information in this case could help you tell whether someone's smile is genuine?

3. Is your impression of the facial expressions of the eight business leaders consistent with what the researcher found? If not, why do you think your views might be at odds with his?

4. One research study found people's ratings of the positive affect displayed in CEO's faces had very little correlation to their company's profits. Does that suggest to you that Hill's analysis is immaterial?

5. Assuming you could become better at detecting the real emotions in facial expressions, do you think it would help your career? Why or why not?

Source: Based on P. Ekman, *Telling Lies: Clues to Deceit in the Marketplace, Politics, and Marriage* (New York: W.W. Norton & Co., 2009); D. Jones, "It's Written All Over Their Faces," *USA Today* (February 25, 2008), pp. 1B-2B; and N. O. Rule and N. Ambady, "The Face of Success," *Psychological Science* 19, no. 2 (2008), pp. 109–111.

Endnotes

1. Based on J. LeLand, "Finance Students Keep Their Job Hopes Alive," *New York Times* (October 12, 2008), p. Y16.

2. See, for instance, C. D. Fisher and N. M. Ashkanasy, "The Emerging Role of Emotions in Work Life: An Introduction," *Journal of Organizational Behavior*, Special Issue 2000, pp. 123–129; N. M. Ashkanasy, C. E. J. Hartel, and W. J. Zerbe (eds.), *Emotions in the Workplace: Research, Theory, and Practice* (Westport, CT: Quorum Books, 2000); N. M. Ashkanasy and C. S. Daus, "Emotion in the Workplace: The New Challenge for Managers," *Academy of Management Executive*, February 2002, pp. 76–86; and N. M. Ashkanasy, C. E. J. Hartel, and C. S. Daus, "Diversity and Emotion: The New Frontiers in Organizational Behavior Research," *Journal of Management* 28, no. 3 (2002), pp. 307–338.

3. See, for example, L. L. Putnam and D. K. Mumby, "Organizations, Emotion and the Myth of Rationality," in S. Fineman (ed.), *Emotion in Organizations* (Thousand Oaks, CA: Sage, 1993), pp. 36–57; and J. Martin, K. Knopoff, and C. Beckman, "An Alternative to Bureaucratic Impersonality and Emotional Labor: Bounded Emotionality at the Body Shop," *Administrative Science Quarterly*, June 1998, pp. 429–469.

4. B. E. Ashforth and R. H. Humphrey, "Emotion in the Workplace: A Reappraisal," *Human Relations*, February 1995, pp. 97–125.

5. S. G. Barsade and D. E. Gibson, "Why Does Affect Matter in Organizations?" *Academy of Management Perspectives*, February 2007, pp. 36–59.

6. See N. H. Frijda, "Moods, Emotion Episodes and Emotions," in M. Lewis and J. M. Haviland (eds.), *Handbook of Emotions* (New York: Guilford Press, 1993), pp. 381–403.

7. H. M. Weiss and R. Cropanzano, "Affective Events Theory: A Theoretical Discussion of the Structure, Causes and Consequences of Affective Experiences at Work," in B. M. Staw and L. L. Cummings (eds.), *Research in Organizational Behavior*, vol. 18 (Greenwich, CT: JAI Press, 1996), pp. 17–19.

8. See P. Ekman and R. J. Davidson (eds.), *The Nature of Emotions: Fundamental Questions* (Oxford, UK: Oxford University Press, 1994).

9. Frijda, "Moods, Emotion Episodes and Emotions," p. 381.

10. See Ekman and Davidson (eds.), *The Nature of Emotions*.

11. See, for example, P. Ekman, "An Argument for Basic Emotions," *Cognition and Emotion*, May/July 1992, pp. 169–200; C. E. Izard, "Basic Emotions, Relations Among Emotions, and Emotion–Cognition Relations," *Psychological Bulletin*, November 1992, pp. 561–565; and J. L. Tracy and R. W. Robins, "Emerging Insights into the Nature and Function of Pride," *Current Directions in Psychological Science* 16, no. 3 (2007), pp. 147–150.

12. R. C. Solomon, "Back to Basics: On the Very Idea of 'Basic Emotions,'" *Journal for the Theory of Social Behaviour* 32, no. 2 (June 2002), pp. 115–144.

13. R. Descartes, *The Passions of the Soul* (Indianapolis: Hackett, 1989).

14. P. Ekman, *Emotions Revealed: Recognizing Faces and Feelings to Improve Communication and Emotional Life* (New York: Times Books/Henry Holt and Co., 2003).

15. P. R. Shaver, H. J. Morgan, and S. J. Wu, "Is Love a 'Basic' Emotion?" *Personal Relationships* 3, no. 1 (March 1996), pp. 81–96.

16. Solomon, "Back to Basics."

17. Weiss and Cropanzano, "Affective Events Theory," pp. 20–22.

18. Cited in R. D. Woodworth, *Experimental Psychology* (New York: Holt, 1938).

19. D. Watson, L. A. Clark, and A. Tellegen, "Development and Validation of Brief Measures of Positive and Negative Affect: The PANAS Scales," *Journal of Personality and Social Psychology*, 1988, pp. 1063–1070.

20. A. Ben-Ze'ev, *The Subtlety of Emotions* (Cambridge, MA: MIT Press, 2000), p. 94.

21. "Flight Attendant War Stories . . . Stewardess," AboutMyJob .com, http://www.aboutmyjob.com/?p=2111.

22. Ibid., cited on p. 99.

23. J. T. Cacioppo and W. L. Gardner, "Emotion," in *Annual Review of Psychology*, vol. 50 (Palo Alto, CA: Annual Reviews, 1999), pp. 191–214.

24. D. Holman, "Call Centres," in D. Holman, T. D. Wall, C. Clegg, P. Sparrow, and A. Howard (eds.), *The Essentials of the New Work Place: A Guide to the Human Impact of Modern Working Practices* (Chichester, UK: Wiley, 2005), pp. 111–132.

25. L. M. Poverny and S. Picascia, "There Is No Crying in Business," *Womensmedia.com*, www.womensmedia.com/ncw/ Crying-at-Work.shtml.

26. A. R. Damasio, *Descartes' Error: Emotion, Reason, and the Human Brain* (New York: Quill, 1994).

27. Ibid.

28. R. J. Larsen and E. Diener, "Affect Intensity as an Individual Difference Characteristic: A Review," *Journal of Research in Personality* 21 (1987), pp. 1–39.

29. D. Watson, *Mood and Temperament* (New York: Guilford Press, 2000).

30. J. J. A. Denissen, L. Butalid, L. Penke, and M. A. G. van Aken, "The Effects of Weather on Daily Mood: A Multilevel Approach," *Emotion* 8, no. 5, pp. 662–667; M. C. Keller, B. L. Fredrickson, O. Ybarra, S. Côté, K. Johnson, J. Mikels, A. Conway, and T. Wagner (2005), "A Warm Heart and a Clear Head: The Contingent Effects of Weather on Mood and Cognition," *Psychological Science* 16, (2005) pp. 724–731; and Watson, *Mood and Temperament*.

31. Watson, *Mood and Temperament*, p. 100.

32. J. A. Fuller, J. M. Stanton, G. G. Fisher, C. Spitzmüller, S. S. Russell, and P. C. Smith, "A Lengthy Look at the Daily Grind: Time Series Analysis of Events, Mood, Stress, and Satisfaction," *Journal of Applied Psychology* 88, no. 6 (December 2003), pp. 1019–1033.

33. See "Monday Blahs," May 16, 2005, www.ashidome.com/ blogger/housearrest.asp?c=809&m=5&y=2005.

34. A. M. Isen, "Positive Affect as a Source of Human Strength," in L. G. Aspinwall and U. Staudinger (eds.), *The Psychology of Human Strengths* (Washington, DC: American Psychological Association, 2003), pp. 179–195.

35. Watson, *Mood and Temperament*.

36. *Sleep in America Poll* (Washington, DC: National Sleep Foundation, 2005), http://www.kintera.org/atf/cf/ %7Bf6bf2668-a1b4-4fe8-8d1a-a5d39340d9cb%7D/ 2005_summary_of_findings.pdf.

37. T. D. Wilson and D. T. Gilbert, "Affective Forecasting: Knowing What to Want," *Current Directions in Psychological Science,* June 2005, pp. 131–134.

38. M. Lavidor, A. Weller, and H. Babkoff, "How Sleep Is Related to Fatigue," *British Journal of Health Psychology* 8 (2003), pp. 95–105; and J. J. Pilcher and E. Ott, "The Relationships Between Sleep and Measures of Health and Well-Being in College Students: A Repeated Measures Approach," *Behavioral Medicine* 23 (1998), pp. 170–178.

39. E. K. Miller and J. D. Cohen, "An Integrative Theory of Prefrontal Cortex Function," *Annual Review of Neuroscience* 24 (2001), pp. 167–202.

40. B. A. Scott and T. A. Judge, "Insomnia, Emotions, and Job Satisfaction: A Multilevel Study," *Journal of Management* 32, no. 5 (2006), pp. 622–645.

41. P. R. Giacobbi, H. A. Hausenblas, and N. Frye, "A Naturalistic Assessment of the Relationship Between Personality, Daily Life Events, Leisure-Time Exercise, and Mood," *Psychology of Sport & Exercise* 6, no. 1 (January 2005), pp. 67–81.

42. L. L. Carstensen, M. Pasupathi, M. Ulrich, and J. R. Nesselroade, "Emotional Experience in Everyday Life Across the Adult Life Span," *Journal of Personality and Social Psychology* 79, no. 4 (2000), pp. 644–655.

43. K. Deaux, "Sex Differences," in M. R. Rosenzweig and L. W. Porter (eds.), *Annual Review of Psychology,* vol. 26 (Palo Alto, CA: Annual Reviews, 1985), pp. 48–82; M. LaFrance and M. Banaji, "Toward a Reconsideration of the Gender–Emotion Relationship," in M. Clark (ed.), *Review of Personality and Social Psychology,* vol. 14 (Newbury Park, CA: Sage, 1992), pp. 178–197; and A. M. Kring and A. H. Gordon, "Sex Differences in Emotion: Expression, Experience, and Physiology," *Journal of Personality and Social Psychology,* March 1998, pp. 686–703.

44. L. R. Brody and J. A. Hall, "Gender and Emotion," in M. Lewis and J. M. Haviland (eds.), *Handbook of Emotions* (New York: Guilford Press, 1993), pp. 447–460; M. G. Gard and A. M. Kring, "Sex Differences in the Time Course of Emotion," *Emotion* 7, no. 2 (2007), pp. 429–437; and M. Grossman and W. Wood, "Sex Differences in Intensity of Emotional Experience: A Social Role Interpretation," *Journal of Personality and Social Psychology,* November 1992, pp. 1010–1022.

45. P. Ekman, W. V. Friesen, and M. O'Sullivan, "Smiles When Lying," in P. Ekman and E. L. Rosenberg (eds.), *What the Face Reveals: Basic and Applied Studies of Spontaneous Expression Using the Facial Action Coding System (FACS)* (London: Oxford University Press, 1997), pp. 201–216.

46. A. Grandey, "Emotion Regulation in the Workplace: A New Way to Conceptualize Emotional Labor," *Journal of Occupational Health Psychology* 5, no. 1 (2000), pp. 95–110; and R. Cropanzano, D. E. Rupp, and Z. S. Byrne, "The Relationship of Emotional Exhaustion to Work Attitudes, Job Performance, and Organizational Citizenship Behavior," *Journal of Applied Psychology,* February 2003, pp. 160–169.

47. A. R. Hochschild, "Emotion Work, Feeling Rules, and Social Structure," *American Journal of Sociology,* November 1979, pp. 551–575; W.-C. Tsai, "Determinants and Consequences of Employee Displayed Positive Emotions," *Journal of Management* 27, no. 4 (2001), pp. 497–512; M. W. Kramer and J. A. Hess, "Communication Rules for the Display of Emotions in Organizational Settings," *Management Communication Quarterly,* August 2002, pp. 66–80; and J. M. Diefendorff and E. M. Richard, "Antecedents and Consequences of Emotional Display Rule Perceptions," *Journal of Applied Psychology,* April 2003, pp. 284–294.

48. B. M. DePaulo, "Nonverbal Behavior and Self-Presentation," *Psychological Bulletin,* March 1992, pp. 203–243.

49. C. S. Hunt, "Although I Might Be Laughing Loud and Hearty, Deep Inside I'm Blue: Individual Perceptions Regarding Feeling and Displaying Emotions at Work," paper presented at the Academy of Management Conference, Cincinnati, August 1996.

50. Solomon, "Back to Basics."

51. C. M. Brotheridge and R. T. Lee, "Development and Validation of the Emotional Labour Scale," *Journal of Occupational & Organizational Psychology* 76, no. 3 (September 2003), pp. 365–379.

52. A. A. Grandey, "When 'The Show Must Go On': Surface Acting and Deep Acting as Determinants of Emotional Exhaustion and Peer-Rated Service Delivery," *Academy of Management Journal,* February 2003, pp. 86–96; and A. A. Grandey, D. N. Dickter, and H. Sin, "The Customer Is Not Always Right: Customer Aggression and Emotion Regulation of Service Employees," *Journal of Organizational Behavior* 25, no. 3 (May 2004), pp. 397–418.

53. J. P. Trougakos, D. J. Beal, S. G. Green, and H. M. Weiss, "Making the Break Count: An Episodic Examination of Recovery Activities, Emotional Experiences, and Positive Affective Displays," *Academy of Management Journal* 51, no. 1 (2008), pp. 131–146.

54. T. M. Glomb, J. D. Kammeyer-Mueller, and M. Rotundo, "Emotional Labor Demands and Compensating Wage Differentials," *Journal of Applied Psychology* 89, no. 4 (August 2004), pp. 700–714.

55. H. M. Weiss and R. Cropanzano, "An Affective Events Approach to Job Satisfaction," *Research in Organizational Behavior* 18 (1996), pp. 1–74.

56. J. Basch and C. D. Fisher, "Affective Events–Emotions Matrix: A Classification of Work Events and Associated Emotions," in N. M. Ashkanasy, C. E. J. Hartel, and W. J. Zerbe (eds.), *Emotions in the Workplace* (Westport, CT: Quorum Books, 2000), pp. 36–48.

57. See, for example, H. M. Weiss and R. Cropanzano, "Affective Events Theory"; and C. D. Fisher, "Antecedents and Consequences of Real-Time Affective Reactions at Work," *Motivation and Emotion,* March 2002, pp. 3–30.

58. Based on Weiss and Cropanzano, "Affective Events Theory," p. 42.

59. N. M. Ashkanasy, C. E. J. Hartel, and C. S. Daus, "Diversity and Emotion: The New Frontiers in Organizational Behavior Research," *Journal of Management* 28, no. 3 (2002), p. 324.

60. Based on D. R. Caruso, J. D. Mayer, and P. Salovey, "Emotional Intelligence and Emotional Leadership," in R. E. Riggio, S. E. Murphy, and F. J. Pirozzolo (eds.), *Multiple Intelligences and Leadership* (Mahwah, NJ: Lawrence Erlbaum, 2002), p. 70.

61. This section is based on Daniel Goleman, *Emotional Intelligence* (New York: Bantam, 1995); P. Salovey and D. Grewal, "The Science of Emotional Intelligence," *Current Directions in Psychological Science* 14, no. 6 (2005), pp. 281–285; M. Davies, L. Stankov, and R. D. Roberts, "Emotional Intelligence: In Search of an Elusive Construct," *Journal of Personality and*

Social Psychology, October 1998, pp. 989–1015; D. Geddes and R. R. Callister, "Crossing the Line(s): A Dual Threshold Model of Anger in Organizations," *Academy of Management Review* 32, no. 3 (2007), pp. 721–746; and J. Ciarrochi, J. P. Forgas, and J. D. Mayer (eds.), *Emotional Intelligence in Everyday Life* (Philadelphia: Psychology Press, 2001).

62. M. Seo and L. F. Barrett, "Being Emotional During Decision Making—Good or Bad? An Empirical Investigation," *Academy of Management Journal* 50, no. 4 (2007), pp. 923–940.

63. F. I. Greenstein, *The Presidential Difference: Leadership Style from FDR to Clinton* (Princeton, NJ: Princeton University Press, 2001).

64. C. Cherniss, "The Business Case for Emotional Intelligence," *Consortium for Research on Emotional Intelligence in Organizations,* 1999, www.eiconsortium.org/reports/business_case_for_ei.html.

65. K. S. Law, C. Wong, and L. J. Song, "The Construct and Criterion Validity of Emotional Intelligence and Its Potential Utility for Management Studies," *Journal of Applied Psychology* 89, no. 3 (2004), pp. 483–496.

66. H. A. Elfenbein and N. Ambady, "Predicting Workplace Outcomes from the Ability to Eavesdrop on Feelings," *Journal of Applied Psychology* 87, no. 5 (October 2002), pp. 963–971.

67. D. L. Van Rooy and C. Viswesvaran, "Emotional Intelligence: A Meta-analytic Investigation of Predictive Validity and Nomological Net," *Journal of Vocational Behavior* 65, no. 1 (August 2004), pp. 71–95.

68. R. Bar-On, D. Tranel, N. L. Denburg, and A. Bechara, "Exploring the Neurological Substrate of Emotional and Social Intelligence," *Brain* 126, no. 8 (August 2003), pp. 1790–1800.

69. P. A. Vernon, K. V. Petrides, D. Bratko, J. A. Schermer, "A Behavioral Genetic Study of Trait Emotional Intelligence," *Emotion* 8, no. 5 (2008), pp. 635–642.

70. E. A. Locke, "Why Emotional Intelligence Is an Invalid Concept," *Journal of Organizational Behavior* 26, no. 4 (June 2005), pp. 425–431.

71. J. M. Conte, "A Review and Critique of Emotional Intelligence Measures," *Journal of Organizational Behavior* 26, no. 4 (June 2005), pp. 433–440; and M. Davies, L. Stankov, and R. D. Roberts, "Emotional Intelligence," pp. 989–1015.

72. T. Decker, "Is Emotional Intelligence a Viable Concept?" *Academy of Management Review* 28, no. 2 (April 2003), pp. 433–440; and Davies, Stankov, and Roberts, "Emotional Intelligence."

73. F. J. Landy, "Some Historical and Scientific Issues Related to Research on Emotional Intelligence," *Journal of Organizational Behavior* 26, no. 4 (June 2005), pp. 411–424.

74. L. M. J. Spencer, D. C. McClelland, and S. Kelner, *Competency Assessment Methods: History and State of the Art* (Boston: Hay/McBer, 1997).

75. J. Park and M. R. Banaji, "Mood and Heuristics: The Influence of Happy and Sad States on Sensitivity and Bias in Stereotyping," *Journal of Personality and Social Psychology* 78, no. 6 (2000), pp. 1005–1023.

76. See A. M. Isen, "Positive Affect and Decision Making," in M. Lewis and J. M. Haviland-Jones (eds.), *Handbook of Emotions,* 2nd ed. (New York: Guilford, 2000), pp. 261–277.

77. L. B. Alloy and L. Y. Abramson, "Judgement of Contingency in Depressed and Nondepressed Students: Sadder but Wiser?" *Journal of Experimental Psychology: General* 108 (1979), pp. 441–485.

78. N. Ambady and H. M. Gray, "On Being Sad and Mistaken: Mood Effects on the Accuracy of Thin-Slice Judgments," *Journal of Personality and Social Psychology* 83, no. 4 (2002), pp. 947–961.

79. A. M. Isen, "On the Relationship Between Affect and Creative Problem Solving," in S. W. Russ (ed.), *Affect, Creative Experience and Psychological Adjustment* (Philadelphia, PA: Brunner/Mazel, 1999), pp. 3–17; and S. Lyubomirsky, L. King, and E. Diener, "The Benefits of Frequent Positive Affect: Does Happiness Lead to Success?" *Psychological Bulletin* 131, no. 6 (2005), pp. 803–855.

80. M. J. Grawitch, D. C. Munz, and E. K. Elliott, "Promoting Creativity in Temporary Problem-Solving Groups: The Effects of Positive Mood and Autonomy in Problem Definition on Idea-Generating Performance," *Group Dynamics* 7, no. 3 (September 2003), pp. 200–213.

81. S. Lyubomirsky, L. King, and E. Diener, "The Benefits of Frequent Positive Affect: Does Happiness Lead to Success?" *Psychological Bulletin* 131, no. 6 (2005), pp. 803–855.

82. N. Madjar, G. R. Oldham, and M. G. Pratt, "There's No Place Like Home? The Contributions of Work and Nonwork Creativity Support to Employees' Creative Performance," *Academy of Management Journal* 45, no. 4 (2002), pp. 757–767.

83. J. M. George and J. Zhou, "Understanding When Bad Moods Foster Creativity and Good Ones Don't: The Role of Context and Clarity of Feelings," *Journal of Applied Psychology* 87, no. 4 (August 2002), pp. 687–697; and J. P. Forgas and J. M. George, "Affective Influences on Judgments and Behavior in Organizations: An Information Processing Perspective," *Organizational Behavior and Human Decision Processes* 86, no. 1 (2001), pp. 3–34.

84. C. K. W. De Dreu, M. Baas, and B. A. Nijstad, "Hedonic Tone and Activation Level in the Mood-Creativity Link: Toward a Dual Pathway to Creativity Model," *Journal of Personality and Social Psychology* 94, no. 5 (2008), pp. 739–756; J. M. George and J. Zhou, "Dual Tuning in a Supportive Context: Joint Contributions of Positive Mood, Negative Mood, and Supervisory Behaviors to Employee Creativity," *Academy of Management Journal* 50, no. 3 (2007), pp. 605–622.

85. A. Erez and A. M. Isen, "The Influence of Positive Affect on the Components of Expectancy Motivation," *Journal of Applied Psychology* 87, no. 6 (2002), pp. 1055–1067.

86. R. Ilies and T. A. Judge, "Goal Regulation Across Time: The Effect of Feedback and Affect," *Journal of Applied Psychology* 90, no. 3 (May 2005), pp. 453–467.

87. W. Tsai, C. Chen, and H. Liu, "Test of a Model Linking Employee Positive Moods and Task Performance," *Journal of Applied Psychology* 92, no. 6 (2007), pp. 1570–1583.

88. K. M. Lewis, "When Leaders Display Emotion: How Followers Respond to Negative Emotional Expression of Male and Female Leaders," *Journal of Organizational Behavior,* March 2000, pp. 221–234; and J. M. George, "Emotions and Leadership: The Role of Emotional Intelligence," *Human Relations,* August 2000, pp. 1027–1055.

89. J. M. George, "Trait and State Affect," In K. Murphy (ed.), *Individual Differences and Behavior in Organizations,* 1996, pp. 145–171. San Francisco: Jossey Bass.

90. Ashforth and Humphrey, "Emotion in the Workplace," p. 116.

91. J. E. Bono, H. J. Foldes, G. Vinson, and J. P. Muros, "Workplace Emotions: The Role of Supervision and Leadership," *Journal of Applied Psychology* 92, no. 5 (2007), pp. 1357–1367.

92. N. Reynolds, "Whiz-Kids Gamble on TV Channel for Poker," *telegraph.co.uk*, April 16, 2005, www.telegraph.co.uk/news/uknews/1487949/Whiz-kids-gamble-on-TV-channel-for-poker.html.

93. G. A. Van Kleef, C. K. W. De Dreu, and A. S. R. Manstead, "The Interpersonal Effects of Emotions in Negotiations: A Motivated Information Processing Approach," *Journal of Personality and Social Psychology* 87, no. 4 (2004), pp. 510–528; and G. A. Van Kleef, C. K. W. De Dreu, and A. S. R. Manstead, "The Interpersonal Effects of Anger and Happiness in Negotiations," *Journal of Personality and Social Psychology* 86, no. 1 (2004), pp. 57–76.

94. E. van Dijk, G. A. van Kleef, W. Steinel, and I. van Beest, "A Social Functional Approach to Emotions in Bargaining: When Communicating Anger Pays and When It Backfires," *Journal of Personality and Social Psychology* 94, no. 4 (2008), pp. 600–614.

95. K. M. O'Connor and J. A. Arnold, "Distributive Spirals: Negotiation Impasses and the Moderating Role of Disputant Self-Efficacy," *Organizational Behavior and Human Decision Processes* 84, no. 1 (2001), pp. 148–176.

96. B. Shiv, G. Loewenstein, A. Bechara, H. Damasio, and A. R. Damasio, "Investment Behavior and the Negative Side of Emotion," *Psychological Science* 16, no. 6 (2005), pp. 435–439.

97. W.-C. Tsai and Y.-M. Huang, "Mechanisms Linking Employee Affective Delivery and Customer Behavioral Intentions," *Journal of Applied Psychology*, October 2002, pp. 1001–1008.

98. Grandey, "When 'The Show Must Go On.'"

99. See P. B. Barker and A. A. Grandey, "Service with a Smile and Encounter Satisfaction: Emotional Contagion and Appraisal Mechanisms," *Academy of Management Journal* 49, no. 6 (2006), pp. 1229–1238; and S. D. Pugh, "Service with a Smile: Emotional Contagion in the Service Encounter," *Academy of Management Journal*, October 2001, pp. 1018–1027.

100. D. E. Rupp and S. Spencer, "When Customers Lash Out: The Effects of Customer Interactional Injustice on Emotional Labor and the Mediating Role of Emotions," *Journal of Applied Psychology* 91, no. 4 (2006), pp. 971–978; and Tsai and Huang, "Mechanisms Linking Employee Affective Delivery and Customer Behavioral Intentions."

101. R. Ilies and T. A. Judge, "Understanding the Dynamic Relationships Among Personality, Mood, and Job Satisfaction: A Field Experience Sampling Study," *Organizational Behavior and Human Decision Processes* 89 (2002), pp. 1119–1139.

102. R. Rau, "Job Strain or Healthy Work: A Question of Task Design," *Journal of Occupational Health Psychology* 9, no. 4 (October 2004), pp. 322–338; and R. Rau and A. Triemer, "Overtime in Relation to Blood Pressure and Mood During Work, Leisure, and Night Time," *Social Indicators Research* 67, no. 1–2 (June 2004), pp. 51–73.

103. Z. Song, M. Foo, and M. A. Uy, "Mood Spillover and Crossover Among Dual-Earner Couples: A Cell Phone Event Sampling Study," *Journal of Applied Psychology* 93, no. 2 (2008), pp. 443–452.

104. T. A. Judge and R. Ilies, "Affect and Job Satisfaction: A Study of Their Relationship at Work and at Home," *Journal of Applied Psychology* 89 (2004), pp. 661–673.

105. See R. J. Bennett and S. L. Robinson, "Development of a Measure of Workplace Deviance," *Journal of Applied Psychology*, June 2000, pp. 349–360; see also P. R. Sackett and C. J. DeVore, "Counterproductive Behaviors at Work," in N. Anderson, D. S. Ones, H. K. Sinangil, and C. Viswesvaran (eds.), *Handbook of Industrial, Work & Organizational Psychology*, vol. 1 (Thousand Oaks, CA: Sage, 2001), pp. 145–164.

106. A. G. Bedeian, "Workplace Envy," *Organizational Dynamics*, Spring 1995, p. 50; and Ben-Ze'ev, *The Subtlety of Emotions*, pp. 281–326.

107. Bedeian, "Workplace Envy," p. 54.

108. S. C. Douglas, C. Kiewitz, M. Martinko, P. Harvey, Y. Kim, and J. U. Chun, "Cognitions, Emotions, and Evaluations: An Elaboration Likelihood Model for Workplace Aggression," *Academy of Management Review* 33, no. 2 (2008), pp. 425–451.

109. K. Lee and N. J. Allen, "Organizational Citizenship Behavior and Workplace Deviance: The Role of Affect and Cognition," *Journal of Applied Psychology* 87, no. 1 (2002), pp. 131–142; T. A. Judge, B. A. Scott, and R. Ilies, "Hostility, Job Attitudes, and Workplace Deviance: Test of a Multilevel Model," *Journal of Applied Psychology* 91, no. 1 (2006), 126–138; and S. Kaplan, J. C. Bradley, J. N. Luchman, and D. Haynes, "On the Role of Positive and Negative Affectivity in Job Performance: A Meta-analytic Investigation," *Journal of Applied Psychology* 94, no. 1 (2009), pp. 162–176.

110. R. D. Iverson and P. J. Erwin, "Predicting Occupational Injury: The Role of Affectivity," *Journal of Occupational and Organizational Psychology* 70, no. 2 (1997), pp. 113–128; and S. Kaplan, J. C. Bradley, J. N. Luchman, and D. Haynes, "On the Role of Positive and Negative Affectivity in Job Performance: A Meta-Analytic Investigation."

111. A. M. Isen, A. A. Labroo, and P. Durlach, "An Influence of Product and Brand Name on Positive Affect: Implicit and Explicit Measures," *Motivation & Emotion* 28, no. 1 (March 2004), pp. 43–63.

112. T. Sy, S. Côté, and R. Saavedra, "The Contagious Leader: Impact of the Leader's Mood on the Mood of Group Members, Group Affective Tone, and Group Processes," *Journal of Applied Psychology* 90, no. 2 (2005), pp. 295–305.

113. P. Totterdell, "Catching Moods and Hitting Runs: Mood Linkage and Subjective Performance in Professional Sports Teams," *Journal of Applied Psychology* 85, no. 6 (2000), pp. 848–859.

114. M. Eid and E. Diener, "Norms for Experiencing Emotions in Different Cultures: Inter- and International Differences," *Journal of Personality & Social Psychology* 81, no. 5 (2001), pp. 869–885.

115. S. Oishi, E. Diener, and C. Napa Scollon, "Cross-Situational Consistency of Affective Experiences Across Cultures," *Journal of Personality & Social Psychology* 86, no. 3 (2004), pp. 460–472.

116. Eid and Diener, "Norms for Experiencing Emotions in Different Cultures."

117. Ibid.

118. Ashforth and Humphrey, "Emotion in the Workplace," p. 104; B. Plasait, "Accueil des Touristes Dans les Grands Centres de Transit Paris," *Rapport du Bernard Plasait*, October 4, 2004, www

.tourisme.gouv.fr/fr/navd/presse/dossiers/att00005767/dp_plasait.pdf; B. Mesquita, "Emotions in Collectivist and Individualist Contexts," *Journal of Personality and Social Psychology* 80, no. 1 (2001), pp. 68–74; and D. Rubin, "Grumpy German Shoppers Distrust the Wal-Mart Style," *Seattle Times,* December 30, 2001, p. A15.

119. H. A. Elfenbein and N. Ambady, "When Familiarity Breeds Accuracy: Cultural Exposure and Facial Emotional Recognition," *Journal of Personality and Social Psychology* 85, no. 2 (2003), pp. 276–290.

120. R. I. Levy, *Tahitians: Mind and Experience in the Society Islands* (Chicago: University of Chicago Press, 1973).

121. B. Mesquita and N. H. Frijda, "Cultural Variations in Emotions: A Review," *Psychological Bulletin,* September 1992, pp. 179–204; and B. Mesquita, "Emotions in Collectivist and Individualist Contexts," *Journal of Personality and Social Psychology,* January 2001, pp. 68–74.

122. D. Matsumoto, "Cross-Cultural Psychology in the 21st Century," http://teachpsych.org/resources/e-books/faces/script/Ch05.htm.

123. S. Nelton, "Emotions in the Workplace," *Nation's Business,* February 1996, p. 25.

124. H. Liao and A. Chuang, "A Multilevel Investigation of Factors Influencing Employee Service Performance and Customer Outcomes," *Academy of Management Journal* 47, no. 1 (2004), pp. 41–58.

125. D. J. Beal, J. P. Trougakos, H. M. Weiss, and S. G. Green, "Episodic Processes in Emotional Labor: Perceptions of Affective Delivery and Regulation Strategies," *Journal of Applied Psychology* 91, no. 5 (2006), pp. 1057–1065.

126. *Starbucks.com,* May 16, 2005, www.starbucks.com.

127. D. Zapf and M. Holz, "On the Positive and Negative Effects of Emotion Work in Organizations," *European Journal of Work and Organizational Psychology* 15, no. 1 (2006), pp. 1–28.

128. D. Zapf, "Emotion Work and Psychological Well-Being: A Review of the Literature and Some Conceptual Considerations," *Human Resource Management Review* 12, no. 2 (2002), pp. 237–268.

129. J. E. Bono and M. A. Vey, "Toward Understanding Emotional Management at Work: A Quantitative Review of Emotional Labor Research," in C. E. Härtel and W. J. Zerbe (eds.), *Emotions in Organizational Behavior* (Mahwah, NJ: Lawrence Erlbaum, 2005), pp. 213–233.

130. Kruml and Geddes, "Catching Fire Without Burning Out."

LEARNING OBJECTIVES

After studying this chapter, you should be able to:

1 Define *personality*, describe how it is measured, and explain the factors that determine an individual's personality.

2 Describe the Myers-Briggs Type Indicator personality framework and assess its strengths and weaknesses.

3 Identify the key traits in the Big Five personality model.

4 Demonstrate how the Big Five traits predict behavior at work.

5 Identify other personality traits relevant to OB.

6 Define *values*, demonstrate the importance of values, and contrast terminal and instrumental values.

7 Compare generational differences in values and identify the dominant values in today's workforce.

8 Identify Hofstede's five value dimensions of national culture.

Personality and Values

I am driven by fear of failure. It is a strong motivator for me. —Dennis Manning, CEO of Guardian Life Insurance Co.

DO YOU LIVE IN A NEUROTIC (OR NICE) STATE?

One of the most exciting—and important—findings from personality research is how each of us can be described in terms of five basic personality factors, or the Big Five. What may surprise you is that these same factors can describe the personalities of U.S. states.

A recent study of survey responses from over a half million U.S. residents revealed fairly marked differences in each of the Big Five traits across the 50 states (and District of Columbia [D.C.]). The rankings for each of the five traits (highest and lowest) appear below:

Five most conscientious states:	New Mexico, North Carolina, Georgia, Utah, Kansas
Five least conscientious states:	Alaska, Maine, Hawaii, Rhode Island, Wyoming
Five most agreeable states:	North Dakota, Minnesota, Mississippi, Utah, Wisconsin
Five least agreeable states:	Alaska, District of Columbia, Wyoming, Nevada, New York
Five most extroverted states:	North Dakota, Wisconsin, District of Columbia, Nebraska, Minnesota
Five most introverted states:	Maryland, New Hampshire, Alaska, Washington, Vermont
Five most neurotic states:	West Virginia, Rhode Island, New York, Mississippi, New Jersey
Five least neurotic states:	Utah, Colorado, South Dakota, Oregon, Alaska
Five most open states:	District of Columbia, New York, Oregon, Massachusetts, Washington
Five least open states:	North Dakota, Wyoming, Alaska, Alabama, Wisconsin

To show the results for each state, the above lists show the top and bottom five states according to five personality traits: neuroticism (tendency to be negative, pessimistic, and anxious) and agreeableness (tendency to be cooperative, kind, and compliant). Some regional trends are apparent. For example, Midwesterners (such as the farmer pictured here during harvest) and Southerners tend to be more agreeable and Northeasterners more disagreeable. As for neuroticism, there appears to be what the researchers

called a "stress belt"—neuroticism appears highest in the east, from Maine to Louisiana.

Even though there are differences by state, differences between people are greater. In other words, there are plenty of extraverts in Maryland, and not everyone in New Mexico is conscientious. We also

Source: Based on P. J. Rentfrow, S. D. Gosling, and J. Potter, "A Theory of the Emergence, Persistence, and Expression of Geographic Variation in Psychological Characteristics," *Perspectives on Psychological Science* 5, no. 3 (2008), pp. 339–369; and S. Simon, "The United States of Mind," *Wall Street Journal* (September 23, 2008), p. A26.

don't really know why the state differences exist. It's possible that personality is part of the reason people are attracted to different states. Or the culture or environment of a state may shape the personality of its residents.

Whether you accept these findings may depend, ironically, on your own personality, as well as how favorably your favorite state came out. Then again, favorable is in the eye of the beholder. When Ted Ownby saw his home state of Mississippi listed as high neurotic, he thought his fellow residents would be proud. "Here in the home of William Faulkner," Ownby said, "we take intense, almost perverse neuroticism as a sign of emotional depth."

Although it's always interesting to speculate about how personality differs across people or, as in the preceding example, across states, are personality differences important? Indeed they are. Personalities shape our behaviors. So if we want to better understand the behavior of someone in an organization, it helps if we know something about his or her personality. In the first half of this chapter, we review the research on personality and its relationship to behavior. In the latter half, we look at how values shape many of our work-related behaviors.

Although we focus much of our discussion on the Big Five personality traits, they are not the only traits that describe people. One of the other traits we'll discuss is narcissism. Check out the Self-Assessment Library to see how you score on narcissism (remember: be honest!).

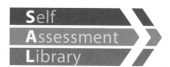

AM I A NARCISSIST?

In the Self-Assessment Library (available on CD or online), take assessment IV.A.1 (Am I a Narcissist?) and answer the following questions.

1. *How did you score? Did your scores surprise you? Why or why not?*
2. *On which facet of narcissism did you score highest? lowest?*
3. *Do you think this measure is accurate? Why or why not?*

Personality

1 Define *personality,* describe how it is measured, and explain the factors that determine an individual's personality.

Why are some people quiet and passive, while others are loud and aggressive? Are certain personality types better adapted than others for certain job types? Before we can answer these questions, we need to address a more basic one: What is personality?

What Is Personality?

When we talk of personality, we don't mean a person has charm, a positive attitude toward life, a smiling face, or a place as a finalist for "Happiest and Friendliest" in this year's Miss America contest. When psychologists talk of personality, they mean a dynamic concept describing the growth and development of a person's whole psychological system.

Defining Personality   The definition of *personality* we most frequently use was produced by Gordon Allport nearly 70 years ago. He said personality is "the dynamic organization within the individual of those psychophysical systems that determine his unique adjustments to his environment."[1] For our purposes, you should think of **personality** as the sum total of ways in which an individual reacts to and interacts with others. We most often describe it in terms of the measurable traits a person exhibits.

Measuring Personality   The most important reason managers need to know how to measure personality is that research has shown personality tests are useful in hiring decisions and help managers forecast who is best for a job.[2] Some managers use personality test scores to better understand and more effectively manage the people who work for them. The most common means of measuring personality is through self-report surveys, with which individuals evaluate themselves on a series of factors, such as "I worry a lot about the future." Though self-report measures work well when well constructed, one weakness is that the respondent might lie or practice impression management—that is, "fake good" on the test to create a good impression. Evidence shows that when people know that their personality scores are going to be used for hiring decisions, they rate themselves as about half a standard deviation more conscientious and emotionally stable than if they are taking the test just to learn more about themselves.[3] Another problem is accuracy. A perfectly good candidate could have just been in a bad mood when the survey was taken and that will make the test scores less accurate.

Observer-ratings surveys provide an independent assessment of personality. Here a co-worker or another observer does the rating (sometimes with the subject's knowledge and sometimes not). Though the results of self-report surveys and observer-ratings surveys are strongly correlated, research suggests observer-ratings surveys are a better predictor of success on the job.[4] However, each can tell us something unique about an individual's behavior in the workplace.

Personality Determinants   An early debate in personality research centered on whether an individual's personality was the result of heredity or of environment. Clearly, there's no simple black-and-white answer. Personality appears to be a result of both hereditary and environmental factors. However, it might surprise you that research has tended to support the importance of heredity over the environment.

Heredity refers to factors determined at conception. Physical stature, facial attractiveness, gender, temperament, muscle composition and reflexes, energy level, and biological rhythms are generally considered to be either completely or substantially influenced by who your parents are—that is, by their biological, physiological, and inherent psychological makeup. The heredity approach argues that the ultimate explanation of an individual's personality is the molecular structure of the genes, located in the chromosomes.

Researchers in many different countries have studied thousands of sets of identical twins who were separated at birth and raised separately.[5] If heredity played little or no part in determining personality, you would expect to find few similarities between the separated twins. But twins raised apart have much in

personality   The sum total of ways in which an individual reacts to and interacts with others.

heredity   Factors determined at conception; one's biological, physiological, and inherent psychological makeup.

A study of identical twins reared apart concluded that heredity plays an important role in determining personality. Dr. Nancy Segal, co-director of the University of Minnesota research project, is shown here with twins separated at birth, reared in different family environments, and reunited after 31 years. Segal and her team of researchers discovered that the sets of twins they studied shared more personality characteristics than did siblings brought up in the same family.

common. For almost every behavioral trait, a significant part of the similarity between them turns out to be associated with genetic factors. One set of twins separated for 39 years and raised 45 miles apart were found to drive the same model and color car. They chain-smoked the same brand of cigarette, owned dogs with the same name, and regularly vacationed within three blocks of each other in a beach community 1,500 miles away. Researchers have found that genetics accounts for about 50 percent of the personality similarities between twins and more than 30 percent of the similarities in occupational and leisure interests.

Interestingly, twin studies have suggested parents don't add much to our personality development. The personalities of identical twins raised in different households are more similar to each other than to the personalities of siblings with whom the twins were raised. Ironically, the most important contribution our parents may make to our personalities is giving us their genes!

This is not to suggest that personality never changes. People's scores on measures of dependability tend to increase over time, as when young adults take on roles like starting a family and establishing a career that require great responsibility. However, despite this increase, strong individual differences in dependability remain; everyone tends to change by about the same amount, so their rank order stays roughly the same.[6] An analogy to intelligence may make this clearer. Children become smarter as they age, so nearly everyone is smarter at age 20 than at age 10. Still, if Madison is smarter than Blake at age 10, she is likely to be so at age 20, too. Consistent with the notion that the teenage years are periods of great exploration and change, research has shown that personality is more changeable in adolescence and more stable among adults.[7]

Early work on the structure of personality tried to identify and label enduring characteristics that describe an individual's behavior, including shy, aggressive, submissive, lazy, ambitious, loyal, and timid. When someone exhibits these characteristics in a large number of situations, we call them **personality traits** of that person.[8] The more consistent the characteristic over time, and the more frequently it occurs in diverse situations, the more important that trait is in describing the individual.

Early efforts to identify the primary traits that govern behavior[9] often resulted in long lists that were difficult to generalize from and provided little practical guidance to organizational decision makers. Two exceptions are the Myers-Briggs Type Indicator and the Big Five Model, now the dominant frameworks for identifying and classifying traits.

The Myers-Briggs Type Indicator

2 Describe the Myers-Briggs Type Indicator personality framework and assess its strengths and weaknesses.

The **Myers-Briggs Type Indicator (MBTI)** is the most widely used personality-assessment instrument in the world.[10] It is a 100-question personality test that asks people how they usually feel or act in particular situations. On the basis of their answers, individuals are classified as extraverted or introverted (E or I), sensing or intuitive (S or N), thinking or feeling (T or F), and judging or perceiving (J or P). These terms are defined as follows:

- *Extraverted (E) versus Introverted (I).* Extraverted individuals are outgoing, sociable, and assertive. Introverts are quiet and shy.
- *Sensing (S) versus Intuitive (N).* Sensing types are practical and prefer routine and order. They focus on details. Intuitives rely on unconscious processes and look at the "big picture."
- *Thinking (T) versus Feeling (F).* Thinking types use reason and logic to handle problems. Feeling types rely on their personal values and emotions.
- *Judging (J) versus Perceiving (P).* Judging types want control and prefer their world to be ordered and structured. Perceiving types are flexible and spontaneous.

These classifications together describe 16 personality types, with every person identified with one of the items in each of the four pairs. Let's explore several examples. Introverted/Intuitive/Thinking/Judging people (INTJs) are visionaries. They usually have original minds and great drive for their own ideas and purposes. They are skeptical, critical, independent, determined, and often stubborn. ESTJs are organizers. They are realistic, logical, analytical, and decisive and have a natural head for business or mechanics. They like to organize and run activities. The ENTP type is a conceptualizer, innovative, individualistic, versatile, and attracted to entrepreneurial ideas. This person tends to be resourceful in solving challenging problems but may neglect routine assignments. A book profiling 13 contemporary businesspeople who created super-successful firms, including Apple Computer, FedEx, Honda Motors, Microsoft, and Sony, found that all were intuitive thinkers (NTs).[11] This result is particularly interesting because intuitive thinkers represent only about 5 percent of the population.

The MBTI is widely used by organizations including Apple Computer, AT&T, Citigroup, GE, 3M Co., many hospitals and educational institutions, and even the U.S. Armed Forces. In spite of its popularity, evidence is mixed about the MBTI's validity as a measure of personality—with most of the evidence suggesting it isn't.[12] One problem is that it forces a person into either one type or another (that is, you're either introverted or extraverted). There is no in-between, though people can be both extraverted and introverted to some degree. The best we can say is that the MBTI can be a valuable tool for increasing self-awareness and providing career guidance. But because results tend to be unrelated to job performance, managers probably shouldn't use it as a selection test for job candidates.

personality traits *Enduring characteristics that describe an individual's behavior.*

Myers-Briggs Type Indicator (MBTI) *A personality test that taps four characteristics and classifies people into 1 of 16 personality types.*

The Big Five Personality Model

3 Identify the key traits in the Big Five personality model.

The MBTI may lack strong supporting evidence, but the same can't be said for the **Big Five Model**. An impressive body of research supports its thesis that five basic dimensions underlie all others and encompass most of the significant variation in human personality.[13] The following are the Big Five factors:

- *Extraversion.* The **extraversion** dimension captures our comfort level with relationships. Extraverts tend to be gregarious, assertive, and sociable. Introverts tend to be reserved, timid, and quiet.
- *Agreeableness.* The **agreeableness** dimension refers to an individual's propensity to defer to others. Highly agreeable people are cooperative, warm, and trusting. People who score low on agreeableness are cold, disagreeable, and antagonistic.
- *Conscientiousness.* The **conscientiousness** dimension is a measure of reliability. A highly conscientious person is responsible, organized, dependable, and persistent. Those who score low on this dimension are easily distracted, disorganized, and unreliable.
- *Emotional stability.* The **emotional stability** dimension—often labeled by its converse, neuroticism—taps a person's ability to withstand stress. People with positive emotional stability tend to be calm, self-confident, and secure. Those with high negative scores tend to be nervous, anxious, depressed, and insecure.
- *Openness to experience.* The **openness to experience** dimension addresses range of interests and fascination with novelty. Extremely open people are creative, curious, and artistically sensitive. Those at the other end of the openness category are conventional and find comfort in the familiar.

How Do the Big Five Traits Predict Behavior at Work?   Research on the Big Five has found relationships between these personality dimensions and job performance.[14] As the authors of the most-cited review put it, "The preponderance of evidence shows that individuals who are dependable, reliable, careful, thorough, able to plan, organized, hardworking, persistent, and achievement-oriented tend to have higher job performance in most if not all occupations."[15] In addition, employees who score higher in conscientiousness develop higher levels of job knowledge, probably because highly conscientious people learn more (a review of 138 studies revealed conscientiousness was rather strongly related to GPA).[16] Higher levels of job knowledge then contribute to higher levels of job performance.

Conscientiousness is as important for managers as for front-line employees. As Exhibit 5-1 shows, a study of the personality scores of 313 CEO candidates in private equity companies (of whom 225 were hired, and their company's performance

PepsiCo chief executive officer Indra Nooyi scores high on all personality dimensions of the Big Five model. She is described as sociable, agreeable, conscientious, emotionally stable, and open to experiences. These personality traits have contributed to Nooyi's high job performance and career success. Nooyi joined PepsiCo in 1994 as senior vice president of strategy and development and was promoted to president and chief financial officer before moving into the firm's top management position.

Exhibit 5-1	Traits that Matter Most to Business Success at Buyout Companies
Most Important	**Less Important**
Persistence	Strong oral communication
Attention to detail	Teamwork
Efficiency	Flexibility/adaptability
Analytical skills	Enthusiasm
Setting high standards	Listening skills

4 Demonstrate how the Big Five traits predict behavior at work.

later correlated with their personality scores) found conscientiousness—in the form of persistence, attention to detail, and setting of high standards—was more important than other traits. The results might surprise you, but they attest to the importance of conscientiousness to organizational success.

Although conscientiousness is the Big Five trait most consistently related to job performance, the other traits are related to aspects of performance in some situations. All five traits also have other implications for work and for life. Let's look at these one at a time. Exhibit 5-2 summarizes the discussion.

People who score high on emotional stability are happier than those who score low. Of the Big Five traits, emotional stability is most strongly related to life satisfaction, job satisfaction, and low stress levels. This is probably true because

---

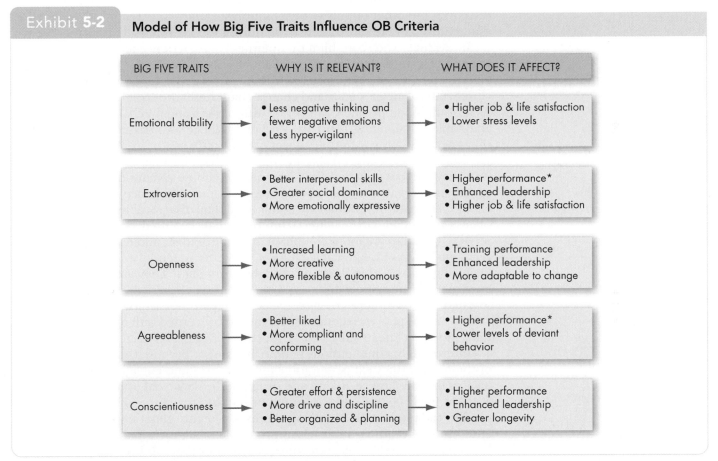

Exhibit 5-2   Model of How Big Five Traits Influence OB Criteria

BIG FIVE TRAITS	WHY IS IT RELEVANT?	WHAT DOES IT AFFECT?
Emotional stability	• Less negative thinking and fewer negative emotions • Less hyper-vigilant	• Higher job & life satisfaction • Lower stress levels
Extroversion	• Better interpersonal skills • Greater social dominance • More emotionally expressive	• Higher performance* • Enhanced leadership • Higher job & life satisfaction
Openness	• Increased learning • More creative • More flexible & autonomous	• Training performance • Enhanced leadership • More adaptable to change
Agreeableness	• Better liked • More compliant and conforming	• Higher performance* • Lower levels of deviant behavior
Conscientiousness	• Greater effort & persistence • More drive and discipline • Better organized & planning	• Higher performance • Enhanced leadership • Greater longevity

* In jobs requiring significant teamwork or frequent interpersonal interactions.

Big Five Model *A personality assessment model that taps five basic dimensions.*

extraversion *A personality dimension describing someone who is sociable, gregarious, and assertive.*

agreeableness *A personality dimension that describes someone who is good natured, cooperative, and trusting.*

conscientiousness *A personality dimension that describes someone who is responsible, dependable, persistent, and organized.*

emotional stability *A personality dimension that characterizes someone as calm, self-confident, secure (positive) versus nervous, depressed, and insecure (negative).*

openness to experience *A personality dimension that characterizes someone in terms of imagination, sensitivity, and curiosity.*

high scorers are more likely to be positive and optimistic in their thinking and experience fewer negative emotions. People low on emotional stability are hypervigilant (looking for problems or impending signs of danger) and are especially vulnerable to the physical and psychological effects of stress. Extraverts tend to be happier in their jobs and in their lives as a whole. They experience more positive emotions than do introverts, and they more freely express these feelings. They also tend to perform better in jobs that require significant interpersonal interaction, perhaps because they have more social skills—they usually have more friends and spend more time in social situations than introverts. Finally, extraversion is a relatively strong predictor of leadership emergence in groups; extraverts are more socially dominant, "take charge" sorts of people, and they are generally more assertive than introverts.[17] One downside of extraversion is that extraverts are more impulsive than introverts; they are more likely to be absent from work and engage in risky behavior such as unprotected sex, drinking, and other impulsive or sensation-seeking acts.[18] One study also found that extraverts were more likely to lie during job interviews than introverts.[19]

Individuals who score high on openness to experience are more creative in science and art than those who score low. Because creativity is important to leadership, open people are more likely to be effective leaders. They also are more comfortable with ambiguity and change than those who score lower on this trait. As a result, open people cope better with organizational change and are more adaptable in changing contexts. Recent evidence also suggests, however, that they are especially susceptible to workplace accidents.[20]

You might expect agreeable people to be happier than disagreeable people. And they are, but only slightly. When people choose romantic partners, friends, or organizational team members, agreeable individuals are usually their first choice. Agreeable individuals are better liked than disagreeable people, which explains why they tend to do better in interpersonally oriented jobs such as customer service. They also are more compliant and rule abiding and less likely to get into accidents as a result. Agreeable children do better in school and as adults are less likely to get involved in drugs or excessive drinking.[21] They are also less likely to engage in organizational deviance. One downside of agreeableness is that it is associated with lower levels of career success (especially earnings). Agreeable individuals may be poorer negotiators; they are so concerned with pleasing others that they often don't negotiate as much for themselves as they might.[22]

Interestingly, conscientious people live longer because they take better care of themselves (they eat better and exercise more) and engage in fewer risky behaviors like smoking, drinking and drugs, and risky sexual or driving behavior.[23] Still, probably because they're so organized and structured, conscientious people don't adapt as well to changing contexts. They are generally performance oriented and have more trouble learning complex skills early in the training process because their focus is on performing well rather than on learning. Finally, they are often less creative than less conscientious people, especially artistically.[24]

Other Personality Traits Relevant to OB

Although the Big Five traits have proven highly relevant to OB, they don't exhaust the range of traits that can describe someone's personality. Now we'll look at other, more specific, attributes that are powerful predictors of behavior in organizations. The first relates to our core self-evaluation. The others are Machiavellianism, narcissism, self-monitoring, propensity for risk taking, and the Type A and proactive personalities.

5   Identify other personality traits relevant to OB.

Core Self-Evaluation   People who have positive **core self-evaluations** like themselves and see themselves as effective, capable, and in control of their

The personality trait of positive core self-evaluation helps Satoru Iwata meet the challenges and complexity of his job as CEO of Nintendo. Confident and capable, Iwata has applied his years of experience and innovation as a game developer to introducing new products, such as Wii and the Nintendo DS portable game device. Iwata views his job as an opportunity to cultivate new customers by widening the appeal of video games to new market segments in developed nations and introducing products to developing countries.

environment. Those with negative core self-evaluations tend to dislike themselves, question their capabilities, and view themselves as powerless over their environment.[25] We discussed in Chapter 3 that core self-evaluations relate to job satisfaction because people positive on this trait see more challenge in their job and actually attain more complex jobs.

But what about job performance? People with positive core self-evaluations perform better than others because they set more ambitious goals, are more committed to their goals, and persist longer in attempting to reach these goals. One study of life insurance agents found core self-evaluations were critical predictors of performance. Ninety percent of life insurance sales calls end in rejection, so an agent has to believe in him- or herself to persist. In fact, this study showed the majority of successful salespersons did have positive core self-evaluations.[26] Such people also provide better customer service, are more popular co-workers, and have careers that both begin on better footing and ascend more rapidly over time.[27]

You might wonder whether someone can be *too* positive. What happens when someone thinks he is capable, but he is actually incompetent? One study of Fortune 500 CEOs, for example, showed that many are overconfident, and their perceived infallibility often causes them to make bad decisions.[28] Teddy Forstmann, chairman of the sports marketing giant IMG, said of himself, "I know God gave me an unusual brain. I can't deny that. I have a God-given talent for seeing potential."[29] One might say people like Forstmann are overconfident, but very often we humans sell ourselves short and are less happy and effective than we could be because of it. If we decide we can't do something, for example, we won't try, and not doing it only reinforces our self-doubts.

Machiavellianism   Kuzi is a young bank manager in Taiwan. He's had three promotions in the past 4 years and makes no apologies for the aggressive tactics he's used to propel his career upward. "I'm prepared to do whatever I have to do to get ahead," he says. Kuzi would properly be called Machiavellian. Shawna led her St. Louis–based company last year in sales performance. She's assertive and persuasive, and she's effective at manipulating customers to buy her product line. Many of her colleagues, including her boss, consider Shawna Machiavellian.

The personality characteristic of **Machiavellianism** (often abbreviated *Mach*) is named after Niccolo Machiavelli, who wrote in the sixteenth century on how to gain and use power. An individual high in Machiavellianism is pragmatic, maintains emotional distance, and believes ends can justify means. "If it works, use it" is consistent with a high-Mach perspective. A considerable amount of research has related high- and low-Mach personalities to behavioral outcomes. High Machs manipulate more, win more, are persuaded less, and persuade others more than do low Machs.[30] They like their jobs less, are more stressed by their work, and engage in more deviant work behaviors.[31] Yet high-Mach outcomes are moderated by situational factors. High Machs flourish (1) when they interact face to face with others rather than indirectly; (2) when the situation has a minimal number of rules and regulations, allowing latitude for improvisation; and

core self-evaluation   *The degree to which an individual likes or dislikes himself or herself, whether the person sees himself or herself as capable and effective, and whether the person feels in control of his or her environment or powerless over the environment.*

Machiavellianism   *The degree to which an individual is pragmatic, maintains emotional distance, and believes that ends can justify means.*

(3) when emotional involvement with details irrelevant to winning distracts low Machs.[32] Thus, whether high Machs make good employees depends on the type of job. In jobs that require bargaining skills (such as labor negotiation) or that offer substantial rewards for winning (such as commissioned sales), high Machs will be productive. But if ends can't justify the means, there are absolute standards of behavior, or the three situational factors we noted are not in evidence, our ability to predict a high Mach's performance will be severely curtailed.

Narcissism   Hans likes to be the center of attention. He looks at himself in the mirror a lot, has extravagant dreams, and considers himself a person of many talents. Hans is a narcissist. The term is from the Greek myth of Narcissus, a man so vain and proud he fell in love with his own image. In psychology, **narcissism** describes a person who has a grandiose sense of self-importance, requires excessive admiration, has a sense of entitlement, and is arrogant. Are the youth of today narcissistic? Despite claims to that effect, the evidence is unclear. High school seniors in 2006 were more likely than in 1975 to agree they would be "very good" spouses (56 percent of 2006 seniors, compared to 37 percent in 1975), parents (54 percent of 2006 seniors, 36 percent in 1975), and workers (65 percent of 2006 seniors, 49 percent in 1975). On the other hand, scores on the Narcissistic Personality Inventory—the most common measure of narcissism—have not increased since 1982.[33]

Whether it is increasing or not, narcissism can have pretty toxic consequences. A study found that while narcissists thought they were *better* leaders than their colleagues, their supervisors actually rated them as *worse*. For example, an Oracle executive described that company's CEO Larry Ellison as follows: "The difference between God and Larry is that God does not believe he is Larry."[34] Because narcissists often want to gain the admiration of others and receive affirmation of their superiority, they tend to "talk down" to those who threaten them, treating others as if they were inferior. Narcissists also tend to be selfish and exploitive and believe others exist for their benefit.[35] Their bosses rate them as less effective at their jobs than others, particularly when it comes to helping other people.[36]

Self-Monitoring   Joyce McIntyre is always in trouble at work. Though she's competent, hardworking, and productive, in performance reviews she is rated no better than average, and she seems to have made a career of irritating bosses. Joyce's problem is that she's politically inept. She's unable to adjust her behavior to fit changing situations. As she puts it, "I'm true to myself. I don't remake myself to please others." We would describe Joyce as a low self-monitor.

Self-monitoring refers to an individual's ability to adjust his or her behavior to external, situational factors.[37] Individuals high in self-monitoring show considerable adaptability in adjusting their behavior to external situational factors. They are highly sensitive to external cues and can behave differently in different situations. High self-monitors are capable of presenting striking contradictions between their public persona and their private self. Low self-monitors, like Joyce, can't disguise themselves in that way. They tend to display their true dispositions and attitudes in every situation; hence, there is high behavioral consistency between who they are and what they do.

Evidence indicates high self-monitors pay closer attention to the behavior of others and are more capable of conforming than are low self-monitors.[38] They also receive better performance ratings, are more likely to emerge as leaders, and show less commitment to their organizations.[39] In addition, high self-monitoring managers tend to be more mobile in their careers, receive more promotions (both internal and cross-organizational), and are more likely to occupy central positions in an organization.[40]

Risk Taking   Donald Trump stands out for his willingness to take risks. He started with almost nothing in the 1960s. By the mid-1980s, he had made a fortune by betting on a resurgent New York City real estate market. Then, trying to capitalize on his successes, Trump overextended himself. By 1994, he had a *negative* net worth of $850 million. Never fearful of taking chances, "The Donald" leveraged the few assets he had left on several New York, New Jersey, and Caribbean real estate ventures. He hit it big again. In 2007, *Forbes* estimated his net worth at $2.9 billion.

People differ in their willingness to take chances, a quality that affects how much time and information managers need to make a decision. For instance, 79 managers worked on simulated personnel exercises that required them to make hiring decisions.[41] High risk-taking managers made more rapid decisions and used less information than did the low risk-taking managers. Interestingly, decision accuracy was the same for both groups.

Although previous studies have shown managers in large organizations to be more risk averse than growth-oriented entrepreneurs who actively manage small businesses, recent findings suggest managers in large organizations may actually be more willing to take risks than entrepreneurs.[42] The work population as a whole also differs in risk propensity.[43] It makes sense to recognize these differences and even consider aligning them with specific job demands. A high risk-taking propensity may lead to more effective performance for a stock trader in a brokerage firm because that type of job demands rapid decision making. On the other hand, a willingness to take risks might prove a major obstacle to an accountant who performs auditing activities. The latter job might be better filled by someone with a low risk-taking propensity.

Type A Personality   Do you know people who are excessively competitive and always seem to be experiencing a sense of time urgency? If you do, it's a good bet those people have Type A personalities. A person with a **Type A personality** is "aggressively involved in a chronic, incessant struggle to achieve more and more in less and less time, and, if required to do so, against the opposing efforts of other things or other persons."[44] In the North American culture, such characteristics tend to be highly prized and positively associated with ambition and the successful acquisition of material goods. Type A's exhibit the following characteristics:

- Are always moving, walking, and eating rapidly
- Feel impatient with the rate at which most events take place
- Strive to think or do two or more things at once
- Cannot cope with leisure time
- Are obsessed with numbers, measuring their success in terms of how many or how much of everything they acquire

The Type B is exactly the opposite, "rarely harried by the desire to obtain a wildly increasing number of things or participate in an endless growing series of events in an ever-decreasing amount of time."[45] Type B's never suffer from a sense of time urgency with its accompanying impatience, can relax without guilt, and so on.

---

narcissism   *The tendency to be arrogant, have a grandiose sense of self-importance, require excessive admiration, and have a sense of entitlement.*

self-monitoring   *A personality trait that measures an individual's ability to adjust his or her behavior to external, situational factors.*

Type A personality   *Aggressive involvement in a chronic, incessant struggle to achieve more and more in less and less time and, if necessary, against the opposing efforts of other things or other people.*

Myth or Science?

"Entrepreneurs Are a Breed Apart"

This statement is true. A review of 23 studies on the personality of entrepreneurs revealed significant differences between entrepreneurs and managers on four of the Big Five: entrepreneurs scored significantly higher on conscientiousness, emotional stability, and openness to experience, and significantly lower on agreeableness. Though, of course, not every entrepreneur achieves these scores, the results clearly suggest entrepreneurs are different from managers in key ways.

A fascinating study provides one explanation. It found male MBA students with prior entrepreneurial experience had significantly higher levels of testosterone (measured by a saliva sample) and also scored higher on risk propensity than those with no such experience. The study authors concluded that testosterone, because it is associated with social dominance and aggressiveness, energizes individuals to take entrepreneurial risks. Individual differences in testosterone are 80 percent inherited, so this study also adds more weight to the conclusion that entrepreneurs are different from others.

What's the upshot of all this? An individual considering a career as an entrepreneur or business owner might look at how she scores on the Big Five. To the extent she is high in conscientiousness, emotional stability, and openness and low in agreeableness, such a career might be for her.[46]

Type A's operate under moderate to high levels of stress. They subject themselves to more or less continuous time pressure, creating a life of deadlines. These characteristics result in some rather specific behavioral outcomes. Type A's are fast workers because they emphasize quantity over quality. In managerial positions, they demonstrate their competitiveness by working long hours and, not infrequently, making poor decisions to new problems. They rarely vary in their responses to specific challenges in their milieu; hence, their behavior is easier to predict than that of Type B's.

Do Type A's differ from Type B's in their ability to get hired? The answer appears to be "yes."[47] Type A's do better than Type B's in job interviews because they are more likely to be judged as having desirable traits such as high drive, competence, aggressiveness, and success motivation.

Proactive Personality   Did you ever notice that some people actively take the initiative to improve their current circumstances or create new ones? These are proactive personalities.[48] Those with a **proactive personality** identify opportunities, show initiative, take action, and persevere until meaningful change occurs, compared to others who passively react to situations. Proactives create positive change in their environment, regardless of, or even in spite of, constraints or obstacles.[49] Not surprisingly, they have many desirable behaviors that organizations covet. They are more likely than others to be seen as leaders and to act as change agents within an organization.[50]

Other actions of proactives can be positive or negative, depending on the organization and the situation. Proactives are more likely to challenge the status quo or voice their displeasure when situations aren't to their liking.[51] If an organization requires people with entrepreneurial initiative, proactives make good candidates; however, they're also more likely to leave an organization to start their own business.[52] As individuals, proactives are more likely than others to achieve career success.[53] They select, create, and influence work situations in their favor. They seek out job and organizational information, develop contacts in high places, engage in career planning, and demonstrate persistence in the face of career obstacles.

A Global Personality

Determining which employees will succeed on overseas business assignments is often difficult because the same qualities that predict success in one culture may not in another. However, researchers are naming personality traits that can help managers zero in on which employees would be suited for foreign assignments.

You might suspect that, of the Big Five traits, openness to experience would be most important to effectiveness in international assignments. Open people are more likely to be cul-

turally flexible—to "go with the flow" when things are different in another country. Research is not fully consistent on the issue, but most does suggest that managers who score high on openness perform better than others in international assignments.

James Eyring, Dell's director of learning and development for Asia, agrees personality is important for success in overseas assignments. "I've seen people fail the openness test—they worked exactly as they would in the U.S. They just weren't open to understanding how things

work in a different culture," says Eyring.

What does the research mean for organizations? When it comes to choosing employees for global assignments, personality can make a difference.

_____

Source: Based on M. A. Shaffer, D. A. Harrison, and H. Gregersen, "You Can Take It with You: Individual Differences and Expatriate Effectiveness," *Journal of Applied Psychology,* January 2006, pp. 109–125; and E. Silverman, "The Global Test," *Human Resource Executive Online,* June 16, 2006, www.hreonline.com/hre/story.jsp?storyid=5669803.

Having discussed personality traits—the enduring characteristics that describe a person's behavior—we now turn to values. Although personality and values are related, values are often very specific and describe belief systems rather than behavioral tendencies. Some beliefs or values don't say much about a person's personality, and we don't always act consistently with our values.

Values

6   Define *values,* demonstrate the importance of values, and contrast terminal and instrumental values.

Is capital punishment right or wrong? If a person likes power, is that good or bad? The answers to these questions are value laden. Some might argue capital punishment is right because it is an appropriate retribution for crimes such as murder and treason. Others might argue, just as strongly, that no government has the right to take anyone's life.

Values represent basic convictions that "a specific mode of conduct or end-state of existence is personally or socially preferable to an opposite or converse mode of conduct or end-state of existence."[54] They contain a judgmental element in that they carry an individual's ideas as to what is right, good, or desirable. Values have both content and intensity attributes. The content attribute says a mode of conduct or end-state of existence is *important.* The intensity attribute specifies *how important* it is. When we rank an individual's values in terms of their intensity, we obtain that person's **value system**. All of us have a hierarchy

proactive personality *People who identify opportunities, show initiative, take action, and persevere until meaningful change occurs.*

values *Basic convictions that a specific mode of conduct or end-state of existence is personally or socially preferable to an opposite or converse mode of conduct or end-state of existence.*

value system *A hierarchy based on a ranking of an individual's values in terms of their intensity.*

of values that forms our value system. We find it in the relative importance we assign to values such as freedom, pleasure, self-respect, honesty, obedience, and equality.

Are values fluid and flexible? Generally speaking, no. They tend to be relatively stable and enduring.[55] A significant portion of the values we hold is established in our early years—by parents, teachers, friends, and others. As children, we are told certain behaviors or outcomes are *always* desirable or *always* undesirable, with few gray areas. You were never taught to be just a little bit honest or a little bit responsible, for example. It is this absolute, or "black-or-white," learning of values that ensures their stability and endurance. If we question our values, of course, they may change, but more often it reinforces them. There is also evidence linking personality to values, implying our values may be partly determined by our genetically transmitted traits.[56]

The Importance of Values

Values lay the foundation for our understanding of people's attitudes and motivation and influence our perceptions. We enter an organization with preconceived notions of what "ought" and "ought not" to be. These notions are not value free; on the contrary, they contain our interpretations of right and wrong. Furthermore, they imply we prefer certain behaviors or outcomes over others. As a result, values cloud objectivity and rationality; they influence attitudes and behavior.[57]

Suppose you enter an organization with the view that allocating pay on the basis of performance is right, while allocating pay on the basis of seniority is wrong. How will you react if you find the organization you've just joined rewards seniority and not performance? You're likely to be disappointed—and this can lead to job dissatisfaction and a decision not to exert a high level of effort because "It's probably not going to lead to more money anyway." Would your attitudes and behavior be different if your values aligned with the organization's pay policies? Most likely.

Terminal versus Instrumental Values

Can we classify values? Yes. In this section, we review two approaches to developing value typologies.

Rokeach Value Survey   Milton Rokeach created the Rokeach Value Survey (RVS).[58] It consists of two sets of values, each containing 18 individual value items. One set, called **terminal values**, refers to desirable end-states. These are the goals a person would like to achieve during his or her lifetime. The other set, called **instrumental values**, refers to preferable modes of behavior, or means of achieving the terminal values. Exhibit 5-3 gives common examples for each of these sets.

Several studies confirm that RVS values vary among groups.[59] People in the same occupations or categories (corporate managers, union members, parents, students) tend to hold similar values. One study compared corporate executives, members of the steelworkers' union, and members of a community activist group. Although there was a good deal of overlap among them,[60] there were also significant differences (see Exhibit 5-4). The activists ranked "equality" as their most important terminal value; executives and union members ranked this value 12 and 13, respectively. Activists ranked "helpful" as their second-highest instrumental value. The other two groups both ranked it 14. Because executives, union members, and activists all have a vested interest in what corporations do, these differences can create serious conflicts when groups contend with each other over an organization's economic and social policies.[61]

Exhibit 5-3   Terminal and Instrumental Values in the Rokeach Value Survey

Terminal Values	Instrumental Values
A comfortable life (a prosperous life)	Ambitious (hardworking, aspiring)
An exciting life (a stimulating, active life)	Broad-minded (open-minded)
A sense of accomplishment (lasting contribution)	Capable (competent, efficient)
A world at peace (free of war and conflict)	Cheerful (lighthearted, joyful)
A world of beauty (beauty of nature and the arts)	Clean (neat, tidy)
Equality (brotherhood, equal opportunity for all)	Courageous (standing up for your beliefs)
Family security (taking care of loved ones)	Forgiving (willing to pardon others)
Freedom (independence, free choice)	Helpful (working for the welfare of others)
Happiness (contentedness)	Honest (sincere, truthful)
Inner harmony (freedom from inner conflict)	Imaginative (daring, creative)
Mature love (sexual and spiritual intimacy)	Independent (self-reliant, self-sufficient)
National security (protection from attack)	Intellectual (intelligent, reflective)
Pleasure (an enjoyable, leisurely life)	Logical (consistent, rational)
Salvation (saved, eternal life)	Loving (affectionate, tender)
Self-respect (self-esteem)	Obedient (dutiful, respectful)
Social recognition (respect, admiration)	Polite (courteous, well-mannered)
True friendship (close companionship)	Responsible (dependable, reliable)
Wisdom (a mature understanding of life)	Self-controlled (restrained, self-disciplined)

Source: Reprinted with the permission of The Free Press, a Division of Simon & Schuster Adult Publishing Group, from *The Nature of Human Values* by Milton Rokeach. Copyright © 1973 by The Free Press. Copyright renewed © 2001 by Sandra J. Ball-Rokeach. All rights reserved.

Exhibit 5-4   Mean Value Ranking of Executives, Union Members, and Activists (Top Five Only)

EXECUTIVES		UNION MEMBERS		ACTIVISTS	
Terminal	Instrumental	Terminal	Instrumental	Terminal	Instrumental
1. Self-respect	1. Honest	1. Family security	1. Responsible	1. Equality	1. Honest
2. Family security	2. Responsible	2. Freedom	2. Honest	2. A world of peace	2. Helpful
3. Freedom	3. Capable	3. Happiness	3. Courageous	3. Family security	3. Courageous
4. A sense of accomplishment	4. Ambitious	4. Self-respect	4. Independent	4. Self-respect	4. Responsible
5. Happiness	5. Independent	5. Mature love	5. Capable	5. Freedom	5. Capable

Source: Based on W. C. Frederick and J. Weber, "The Values of Corporate Managers and Their Critics: An Empirical Description and Normative Implications," in W. C. Frederick and L. E. Preston (eds.), *Business Ethics: Research Issues and Empirical Studies* (Greenwich, CT: JAI Press, 1990), pp. 123–144.

terminal values *Desirable end-states of existence; the goals a person would like to achieve during his or her lifetime.*

instrumental values *Preferable modes of behavior or means of achieving one's terminal values.*

Generational Values

7 Compare generational differences in values and identify the dominant values in today's workforce.

Contemporary Work Cohorts   Researchers have integrated several recent analyses of work values into four groups that attempt to capture the unique values of different cohorts or generations in the U.S. workforce.[62] Exhibit 5-5 segments employees by the era during which they entered the workforce. Because most people start work between the ages of 18 and 23, the eras also correlate closely with employee age.

Let's start with some limitations of this analysis. First, we make no assumption that the framework would apply universally across all cultures. Second, despite a steady stream of press coverage, there is very little rigorous research on generational values, so we have to rely on an intuitive framework. Finally, these are imprecise categories. There is no law that someone born in 1985 can't have values similar to those of someone born in 1955. You may see your values better reflected in other generations than in your own. Despite these limitations, values do change over generations,[63] and we can gain some useful insights from analyzing values this way.

Workers who grew up influenced by the Great Depression and World War II are called *Veterans* (or *Traditionalists*). Once hired, Veterans are thought to be loyal to their employer and respectful of authority, hardworking, and practical. More than other generations, they like their work and their jobs. These are the people Tom Brokaw wrote about in his book *The Greatest Generation*. In terms of terminal values on the RVS, these employees are likely to place the greatest importance on a comfortable life and family security.

Boomers (*Baby Boomers*) are a large cohort born after World War II when veterans returned to their families and times were good. Boomers entered the workforce from the mid-1960s through the mid-1980s. They brought with them a large measure of the "hippie ethic" and distrust of authority. But they place a great deal of emphasis on achievement and material success. They work hard and want to enjoy the fruits of their labors. They're pragmatists who believe ends can justify means. Boomers see the organizations that employ them merely as vehicles for their careers. Terminal values such as a sense of accomplishment and social recognition rank high with them.

The lives of *Xers* (*Generation Xers*) have been shaped by globalization, two-career parents, MTV, AIDS, and computers. Xers value flexibility, life options, and the achievement of job satisfaction. Family and relationships are very important to this cohort. Unlike Veterans, Xers are skeptical, particularly of authority. They also en-

Exhibit 5-5	Dominant Work Values in Today's Workforce		
Cohort	Entered the Workforce	Approximate Current Age	Dominant Work Values
Veterans	1950s or early 1960s	65+	Hardworking, conservative, conforming; loyalty to the organization
Boomers	1965–1985	Mid-40s to mid-60s	Success, achievement, ambition, dislike of authority; loyalty to career
Xers	1985–2000	Late 20s to early 40s	Work/life balance, team-oriented, dislike of rules; loyalty to relationships
Nexters	2000 to present	Under 30	Confident, financial success, self-reliant but team-oriented; loyalty to both self and relationships

Patagonia, Inc., understands the dominant work values of young people in the workforce (Generation Xers) who place great importance on flexibility, work–life balance, and relationships. A marketer of outdoor clothing and equipment, Patagonia was one of the first U.S. companies to offer employees flexible working hours, maternity and paternity leave, and on-site day care. Through an internship program, employees can leave their jobs for up to 2 months to work full time for the environmental group of their choice while Patagonia continues to pay their salaries and benefits.

joy team-oriented work. In search of balance in their lives, Xers are less willing to make personal sacrifices for the sake of their employer than previous generations were. On the RVS, they rate high on true friendship, happiness, and pleasure.

The most recent entrants to the workforce, the *Millennials* (also called *Netters, Nexters, Generation Yers,* and *Generation Nexters*) grew up during prosperous times. They have high expectations and seek meaning in their work. Millennials have life goals more oriented toward becoming rich (81 percent) and famous (51 percent) than do Generation Xers (62 percent and 29 percent, respectively), but they also see themselves as socially responsible. Millennials are at ease with diversity and are the first generation to take technology for granted. More than other generations,

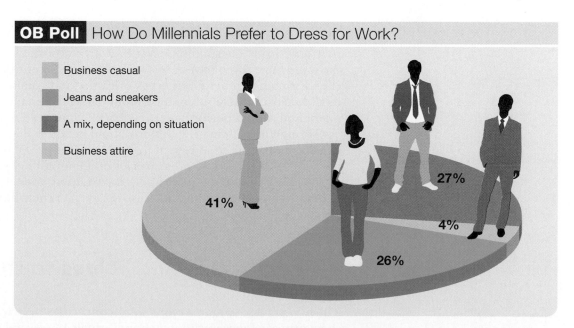

OB Poll How Do Millennials Prefer to Dress for Work?

- Business casual
- Jeans and sneakers
- A mix, depending on situation
- Business attire

41%

27%

4%

26%

Source: Based on *What Millennial Workers Want: How to Attract and Retain Gen Y Employees,* Robert Half International web interviews of 1,007 individuals age 21–28, 2008.

An Ethical Choice

What If I Have the "Wrong" Personality?

You might think personality presents no ethical choice. After all, you are who you are. Yet organizations tend to want you to behave a certain way, and that does present ethical choices. Indeed, most personality traits are clearly what researchers call "socially desirable." That is, most people, if given the choice, would prefer to be highly conscientious, agreeable, open, emotionally stable, and extraverted. It's also clear that employers value socially desirable traits in employees—especially conscientiousness, emotional stability, and agreeableness. So what can—or *should*—you do if you score low on these traits?

1. *Put your best foot forward.* We all vary in how conscientious we are, depending on the situation (we may keep our offices fairly neat but leave our bedroom a mess) and the time (we all go through periods in which we are more reliable or disciplined than others). Remember, as important as personality is, it is not synony-

mous with behavior. If your employer is big on conscientiousness, make an extra effort to be that way. In the workplace, your "true" level of conscientiousness is less important than how conscientious you act.

2. *Find an organization that suits you.* Not all organizational cultures are for everyone. The right job for you is not just one that fits your skills or pays well but also one where your personality matches the culture of the organization and the nature of the work. Big corporations tend to be "tilted" toward extraverts, so a highly introverted person may constantly struggle to keep up. But that tilt depends on the specific company—you need to find the organization that works best for you.

3. *Remember: Time is on your side.* As people age, their scores on conscientiousness and agreeableness increase rather dramatically, and neuroticism decreases

substantially (the results for openness and extraversion are more complex). It may be comforting to realize your personality is likely to become more socially desirable over time.

4. *Realize that all traits have upsides—and downsides.* Extraverted people are more impulsive and more likely to be absent. Conscientious individuals adjust less well to change. Agreeable individuals are less successful in their careers. Open people are more likely to have accidents. So, even if you think you don't have the "right stuff" for a particular job, remember every dog has his day, and even seemingly undesirable scores can produce benefits.

Source: Based on B. W. Roberts and D. Mroczek, "Personality Trait Change in Adulthood," *Current Directions in Psychological Science,* no. 1 (2008), pp. 31–35; J. Welch and S. Welch, "Release Your Inner Extrovert," *Business Week* (December 8, 2008), p. 92.

they tend to be questioning, electronically networked, and entrepreneurial. At the same time, some have described Millennials as entitled and needy. They may clash with other generations over work attire and communication. They also like feedback. An Ernst & Young survey found that 85 percent of Millennials want "frequent and candid performance feedback," compared to only half of Boomers.[64]

Though it is fascinating to think about generational values, remember these classifications lack solid research support. Over two years of collecting information, we found scores of press articles on generational values, and *zero* research articles. Generational classifications may help us understand our own and other generations better, but we must also appreciate their limits.

Linking an Individual's Personality and Values to the Workplace

Thirty years ago, organizations were concerned only with personality because their primary focus was to match individuals to specific jobs. That concern still exists, but it has expanded to include how well the individual's personality *and*

Exhibit 5-6 Holland's Typology of Personality and Congruent Occupations

Type	Personality Characteristics	Congruent Occupations
Realistic: Prefers physical activities that require skill, strength, and coordination	Shy, genuine, persistent, stable, conforming, practical	Mechanic, drill press operator, assembly-line worker, farmer
Investigative: Prefers activities that involve thinking, organizing, and understanding	Analytical, original, curious, independent	Biologist, economist, mathematician, news reporter
Social: Prefers activities that involve helping and developing others	Sociable, friendly, cooperative, understanding	Social worker, teacher, counselor, clinical psychologist
Conventional: Prefers rule-regulated, orderly, and unambiguous activities	Conforming, efficient, practical, unimaginative, inflexible	Accountant, corporate manager, bank teller, file clerk
Enterprising: Prefers verbal activities in which there are opportunities to influence others and attain power	Self-confident, ambitious, energetic, domineering	Lawyer, real estate agent, public relations specialist, small business manager
Artistic: Prefers ambiguous and unsystematic activities that allow creative expression	Imaginative, disorderly, idealistic, emotional, impractical	Painter, musician, writer, interior decorator

values match the organization. Why? Because managers today are less interested in an applicant's ability to perform a *specific* job than with his or her *flexibility* to meet changing situations and commitment to the organization.

We'll now discuss person–job fit and person–organization fit in more detail.

Person–Job Fit

The effort to match job requirements with personality characteristics is best articulated in John Holland's **personality–job fit theory**.[65] Holland presents six personality types and proposes that satisfaction and the propensity to leave a position depend on how well individuals match their personalities to a job. Exhibit 5-6 describes the six types, their personality characteristics, and examples of the congruent occupations for each.

Holland developed the Vocational Preference Inventory questionnaire, which contains 160 occupational titles. Respondents indicate which they like or dislike, and their answers form personality profiles. Research strongly supports the resulting hexagonal diagram shown in Exhibit 5-7.[66] The closer two fields or orientations are in the hexagon, the more compatible they are. Adjacent categories are quite similar, whereas diagonally opposite ones are highly dissimilar.

What does all this mean? The theory argues that satisfaction is highest and turnover lowest when personality and occupation are in agreement. A realistic person in a realistic job is in a more congruent situation than a realistic person in an investigative job. A realistic person in a social job is in the most incongruent situation possible. The key points of this model are that (1) there do appear to be intrinsic differences in personality among individuals, (2) there are different types of jobs, and (3) people in jobs congruent with their personality

personality–job fit theory *A theory that identifies six personality types and proposes that the fit between personality type and occupational environment determines satisfaction and turnover.*

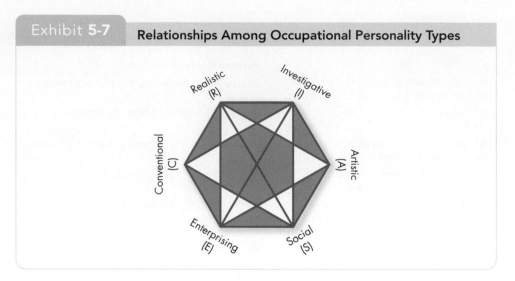

should be more satisfied and less likely to voluntarily resign than people in incongruent jobs.

Person–Organization Fit

We've noted that researchers in recent years have looked at matching people to organizations as well as to jobs. If an organization faces a dynamic and changing environment and requires employees able to readily change tasks and move easily between teams, it's more important that employees' personalities fit with the overall organization's culture than with the characteristics of any specific job.

The person–organization fit essentially argues that people are attracted to and selected by organizations that match their values, and they leave organizations that are not compatible with their personalities.[67] Using the Big Five terminology, for instance, we could expect that people high on extraversion fit well with aggressive and team-oriented cultures, that people high on agreeableness match up better with a supportive organizational climate than one focused on aggressiveness, and that people high on openness to experience fit better in organizations that emphasize innovation rather than standardization.[68] Following these guidelines at the time of hiring should identify new employees who fit better with the organization's culture, which should, in turn, result in higher employee satisfaction and reduced turnover. Research on person–organization fit has also looked at whether people's values match the organization's culture. This match predicts job satisfaction, commitment to the organization, and low turnover.[69]

Global Implications

8   Identify Hofstede's five value dimensions of national culture.

Personality

Do personality frameworks, such as the Big Five model, transfer across cultures? Are dimensions such as the Type A personality relevant in all cultures? Let's try to answer these questions.

The five personality factors identified in the Big Five model appear in almost all cross-cultural studies.[70] These studies have included a wide variety of diverse cultures—such as China, Israel, Germany, Japan, Spain, Nigeria, Norway,

Pakistan, and the United States. Differences tend to be in the emphasis on dimensions and whether countries are predominantly individualistic or collectivistic. Chinese managers use the category of conscientiousness more often and agreeableness less often than do U.S. managers. And the Big Five appear to predict a bit better in individualistic than in collectivist cultures.[71] But there is a surprisingly high amount of agreement, especially among individuals from developed countries. A comprehensive review of studies covering people from what was then the 15-nation European Community found conscientiousness a valid predictor of performance across jobs and occupational groups.[72] This is exactly what U.S. studies have found.

Values

An understanding of how values differ across cultures should help explain and predict behavior of employees from different countries.

Hofstede's Framework for Assessing Cultures One of the most widely referenced approaches for analyzing variations among cultures was done in the late 1970s by Geert Hofstede.[73] He surveyed more than 116,000 IBM employees in 40 countries about their work-related values and found that managers and employees vary on five value dimensions of national culture:

- *Power distance.* **Power distance** describes the degree to which people in a country accept that power in institutions and organizations is distributed unequally. A high rating on power distance means that large inequalities of power and wealth exist and are tolerated in the culture, as in a class or caste system that discourages upward mobility. A low power distance rating characterizes societies that stress equality and opportunity.
- *Individualism versus collectivism.* **Individualism** is the degree to which people prefer to act as individuals rather than as members of groups and believe in individual rights above all else. **Collectivism** emphasizes a tight social framework in which people expect others in groups of which they are a part to look after them and protect them.
- *Masculinity versus femininity.* Hofstede's construct of **masculinity** is the degree to which the culture favors traditional masculine roles such as achievement, power, and control, as opposed to viewing men and women as equals. A high masculinity rating indicates the culture has separate roles for men and women, with men dominating the society. A high **femininity** rating means the culture sees little differentiation between male and female roles and treats women as the equals of men in all respects.
- *Uncertainty avoidance.* The degree to which people in a country prefer structured over unstructured situations defines their **uncertainty avoidance**. In cultures that score high on uncertainty avoidance, people have an increased level

power distance *A national culture attribute that describes the extent to which a society accepts that power in institutions and organizations is distributed unequally.*

individualism *A national culture attribute that describes the degree to which people prefer to act as individuals rather than as members of groups.*

collectivism *A national culture attribute that describes a tight social framework in which people expect others in groups of which they are a part to look after them and protect them.*

masculinity *A national culture attribute that describes the extent to which the culture favors traditional masculine work roles of achievement, power, and control. Societal values are characterized by assertiveness and materialism.*

femininity *A national culture attribute that indicates little differentiation between male and female roles; a high rating indicates that women are treated as the equals of men in all aspects of the society.*

uncertainty avoidance *A national culture attribute that describes the extent to which a society feels threatened by uncertain and ambiguous situations and tries to avoid them.*

Exhibit 5-8   **Hofstede's Cultural Values by Nation**

Country	Power Distance		Individualism versus Collectivism		Masculinity versus Femininity		Uncertainty Avoidance		Long- versus Short-Term Orientation	
	Index	Rank	Index	Rank	Index	Rank	Index	Rank	Index	Rank
Argentina	49	35–36	46	22–23	56	20–21	86	10–15		
Australia	36	41	90	2	61	16	51	37	31	22–24
Austria	11	53	55	18	79	2	70	24–25	31	22–24
Belgium	65	20	75	8	54	22	94	5–6	38	18
Brazil	69	14	38	26–27	49	27	76	21–22	65	6
Canada	39	39	80	4–5	52	24	48	41–42	23	30
Chile	63	24–25	23	38	28	46	86	10–15		
Colombia	67	17	13	49	64	11–12	80	20		
Costa Rica	35	42–44	15	46	21	48–49	86	10–15		
Denmark	18	51	74	9	16	50	23	51	46	10
Ecuador	78	8–9	8	52	63	13–14	67	28		
El Salvador	66	18–19	19	42	40	40	94	5–6		
Finland	33	46	63	17	26	47	59	31–32	41	14
France	68	15–16	71	10–11	43	35–36	86	10–15	39	17
Germany	35	42–44	67	15	66	9–10	65	29	31	22–24
Great Britain	35	42–44	89	3	66	9–10	35	47–48	25	28–29
Greece	60	27–28	35	30	57	18–19	112	1		
Guatemala	95	2–3	6	53	37	43	101	3		
Hong Kong	68	15–16	25	37	57	18–19	29	49–50	96	2
India	77	10–11	48	21	56	20–21	40	45	61	7
Indonesia	78	8–9	14	47–48	46	30–31	48	41–42		
Iran	58	29–30	41	24	43	35–36	59	31–32		
Ireland	28	49	70	12	68	7–8	35	47–48	43	13
Israel	13	52	54	19	47	29	81	19		
Italy	50	34	76	7	70	4–5	75	23	34	19
Jamaica	45	37	39	25	68	7–8	13	52		
Japan	54	33	46	22–23	95	1	92	7	80	4
Korea (South)	60	27–28	18	43	39	41	85	16–17	75	5
Malaysia	104	1	26	36	50	25–26	36	46		
Mexico	81	5–6	30	32	69	6	82	18		
The Netherlands	38	40	80	4–5	14	51	53	35	44	11–12
New Zealand	22	50	79	6	58	17	49	39–40	30	25–26
Norway	31	47–48	69	13	8	52	50	38	44	11–12
Pakistan	55	32	14	47–48	50	25–26	70	24–25	0	34
Panama	95	2–3	11	51	44	34	86	10–15		
Peru	64	21–23	16	45	42	37–38	87	9		
Philippines	94	4	32	31	64	11–12	44	44	19	31–32
Portugal	63	24–25	27	33–35	31	45	104	2	30	25–26
Singapore	74	13	20	39–41	48	28	8	53	48	9
South Africa	49	35–36	65	16	63	13–14	49	39–40		
Spain	57	31	51	20	42	37–38	86	10–15	19	31–32
Sweden	31	47–48	71	10–11	5	53	29	49–50	33	20
Switzerland	34	45	68	14	70	4–5	58	33	40	15–16
Taiwan	58	29–30	17	44	45	32–33	69	26	87	3
Thailand	64	21–23	20	39–41	34	44	64	30	56	8
Turkey	66	18–19	37	28	45	32–33	85	16–17		
United States	40	38	91	1	62	15	46	43	29	27
Uruguay	61	26	36	29	38	42	100	4		
Venezuela	81	5–6	12	50	73	3	76	21–22		
Yugoslavia	76	12	27	33–35	21	48–49	88	8		
Regions:										
Arab countries	80	7	38	26–27	53	23	68	27		
East Africa	64	21–23	27	33–35	41	39	52	36	25	28–29
West Africa	77	10–11	20	39–41	46	30–31	54	34	16	33

Scores range from 0 = extremely low on dimension to 100 = extremely high.

Note: 1 = highest rank. LTO ranks: 1 = China; 15–16 = Bangladesh; 21 = Poland; 34 = lowest.

Source: Copyright Geert Hofstede BV, hofstede@bart.nl. Reprinted with permission.

of anxiety about uncertainty and ambiguity and use laws and controls to reduce uncertainty. Cultures low on uncertainty avoidance are more accepting of ambiguity, are less rule oriented, take more risks, and more readily accept change.

- *Long-term versus short-term orientation.* This newest addition to Hofstede's typology measures a society's devotion to traditional values. People in a culture with **long-term orientation** look to the future and value thrift, persistence, and tradition. In a **short-term orientation**, people value the here and now; they accept change more readily and don't see commitments as impediments to change.

How do different countries score on Hofstede's dimensions? Exhibit 5-8 shows the ratings for the countries for which data are available. For example, power distance is higher in Malaysia than in any other country. The United States is very individualistic; in fact, it's the most individualistic nation of all (closely followed by Australia and Great Britain). The United States also tends to be short term in orientation and low in power distance (people in the United States tend not to accept built-in class differences between people). It is also relatively low on uncertainty avoidance, meaning most adults are relatively tolerant of uncertainty and ambiguity. The United States scores relatively high on masculinity; most people emphasize traditional gender roles (at least relative to countries such as Denmark, Finland, Norway, and Sweden).

Understanding differences in values across cultures helps explain the behavior of employees from different countries. According to Hofstede's framework for assessing cultures, China ranks high in long-term orientation and power distance, low in individualism, and average in masculinity and uncertainty avoidance. Using these ratings, companies considering doing business in China can predict the behavior of the managers and factory workers shown here painting glassware.

long-term orientation *A national culture attribute that emphasizes the future, thrift, and persistence.*

short-term orientation *A national culture attribute that emphasizes the past and present, respect for tradition, and fulfillment of social obligations.*

You'll notice regional differences. Western and northern nations such as Canada and the Netherlands tend to be more individualistic. Poorer countries such as Mexico and the Philippines tend to be higher on power distance. South American nations tend to be higher than other countries on uncertainty avoidance, and Asian countries tend to have a long-term orientation.

Hofstede's culture dimensions have been enormously influential on OB researchers and managers. Nevertheless, his research has been criticized. First, although the data have since been updated, the original work is more than 30 years old and was based on a single company (IBM). A lot has happened on the world scene since then. Some of the most obvious changes include the fall of the Soviet Union, the transformation of central and eastern Europe, the end of apartheid in South Africa, the spread of Islam throughout the world, and the rise of China as a global power. Second, few researchers have read the details of Hofstede's methodology closely and are therefore unaware of the many decisions and judgment calls he had to make (for example, reducing the number of cultural values to just five). Some results are unexpected. Japan, which is often considered a highly collectivist nation, is considered only average on collectivism under Hofstede's dimensions.[74] Despite these concerns, Hofstede has been one of the most widely cited social scientists ever, and his framework has left a lasting mark on OB.

The GLOBE Framework for Assessing Cultures   Begun in 1993, the Global Leadership and Organizational Behavior Effectiveness (GLOBE) research program is an ongoing cross-cultural investigation of leadership and national culture. Using data from 825 organizations in 62 countries, the GLOBE team identified nine dimensions on which national cultures differ.[75] Some—such as power distance, individualism/collectivism, uncertainty avoidance, gender differentiation (similar to masculinity versus femininity), and future orientation (similar to long-term versus short-term orientation)—resemble the Hofstede dimensions. The main difference is that the GLOBE framework added dimensions, such as humane orientation (the degree to which a society rewards individuals for being altruistic, generous, and kind to others) and performance orientation (the degree to which a society encourages and rewards group members for performance improvement and excellence).

Which framework is better? That's hard to say, and each has its adherents. We give more emphasis to Hofstede's dimensions here because they have stood the test of time and the GLOBE study confirmed them. However, researchers continue to debate the differences between these frameworks, and future studies may, in time, favor the more nuanced perspective of the GLOBE study.[76]

Summary and Implications for Managers

Personality   What value, if any, does the Big Five model provide to managers? From the early 1900s through the mid-1980s, researchers sought a link between personality and job performance. "The outcome of those 80-plus years of research was that personality and job performance were not meaningfully related across traits or situations."[77] However, the past 20 years have been more promising, largely due to the findings about the Big Five.

Screening job candidates for high conscientiousness—as well as the other Big Five traits, depending on the criteria an organization finds most important—should pay dividends. Of course, managers still need to take situational factors into consideration.[78] Factors such as job demands, the degree of required interaction with others, and the organization's culture are examples of situational variables that moderate the personality–job performance relationship. You need to evaluate the job, the work group, and the organization to determine the optimal personality fit. Other traits, such as core self-evaluation or narcissism, may be relevant in certain situations, too.

Although the MBTI has been widely criticized, it may have a place in organizations. In training and development, it can help employees to better understand themselves, and it can help team members to better understand each other. And it can open up communication in work groups and possibly reduce conflicts.

Values   Why is it important to know an individual's values? Values often underlie and explain attitudes, behaviors, and perceptions. So knowledge of an individual's value system can provide insight into what makes the person "tick."

Employees' performance and satisfaction are likely to be higher if their values fit well with the organization. The person who places great importance on imagination, independence, and freedom is likely to be poorly matched with an organization that seeks conformity from its employees. Managers are more likely to appreciate, evaluate positively, and allocate rewards to employees who fit in, and employees are more likely to be satisfied if they perceive they do fit in. This argues for management to seek job candidates who have not only the ability, experience, and motivation to perform but also a value system compatible with the organization's.

Traits are Powerful Predictors of Behavior

The essence of trait approaches in OB is that employees possess stable personality characteristics that significantly influence their attitudes toward, and behavioral reactions to, organizational settings.[79] People with particular traits tend to be relatively consistent in their attitudes and behavior over time and across situations.

Of course, trait theorists recognize that all traits are not equally powerful. They tend to put them into one of three categories. *Cardinal traits* are those so strong and generalized that they influence every act a person performs. *Primary traits* are generally consistent influences on behavior, but they may not show up in all situations. Finally, *secondary traits* are attributes that do not form a vital part of the personality but come into play only in particular situations. For the most part, trait theories have focused on the power of primary traits to predict employee behavior.

The Big Five traits are primary traits, and they predict virtually all aspects of life success (job and career success, divorce, and even mortality). A recent review found that personality had stronger effects on these outcomes than socioeconomic background and, in some cases, intelligence.[80]

Managers seem to have a strong belief in the power of traits to predict behavior. If managers believed that situations determined behavior, they would hire people almost at random and structure the situation properly. But the employee selection process in most organizations places a great deal of emphasis on how applicants perform in interviews and on tests. Assume that you're an interviewer; ask yourself "What am I looking for in job candidates?" If you answered with terms such as *conscientious, hardworking, persistent, confident,* and *dependable,* you're a trait theorist.

Few people would dispute that some stable individual attributes affect reactions to the workplace. But trait theorists go beyond that and argue that individual behavior consistencies are widespread and account for much of the differences in behavior among people.

Two problems with using traits to explain a large proportion of behavior in organizations are that the evidence isn't all that impressive, and individuals are highly adaptive so that personality traits change in response to organizational situations.

First, though personality does influence workplace attitudes and behaviors, the effects aren't all that strong; traits explain a minority of the variance in attitudes and behavior.[81] Why is this so? The effects of traits are likely to be strongest in relatively weak situations and weakest in relatively strong situations. Organizational settings tend to be strong situations because they have rules and other formal regulations that define acceptable behavior and punish deviant behavior; and they have informal norms that dictate appropriate behaviors. These formal and informal constraints minimize the effects of personality traits.

By arguing that employees possess stable traits that lead to cross-situational consistencies in behaviors, trait theorists imply that individuals don't really adapt to different situations. But a growing body of evidence suggests that an individual's traits are changed by the organizations in which the individual participates. If the individual's personality changes as a result of exposure to organizational settings, in what sense can that individual be said to have traits that persistently and consistently affect his or her reactions to those very settings?

Questions for Review

1 What is personality? How do we typically measure it? What factors determine personality?

2 What is the Myers-Briggs Type Indicator (MBTI), and what does it measure?

3 What are the Big Five personality traits?

4 How do the Big Five traits predict work behavior?

5 Besides the Big Five, what other personality traits are relevant to OB?

6 What are values, why are they important, and what is the difference between terminal and instrumental values?

7 Do values differ across generations? How so?

8 Do values differ across cultures? How so?

Experiential Exercise

WHAT ORGANIZATIONAL CULTURE DO YOU PREFER?

The Organizational Culture Profile (OCP) can help assess whether an individual's values match the organization's.[82] The OCP helps individuals sort their characteristics in terms of importance, which indicates what a person values.

1. Working on your own, complete the following OCP.

2. Your instructor may ask you the following questions individually or as a group of three or four students (with a spokesperson appointed to speak to the class for each group):

   a. What were your most preferred and least preferred values? Do you think your most preferred and least preferred values are similar to those of other class or group members?

   b. Do you think there are generational differences in the most preferred and least preferred values?

   c. Research has shown that individuals tend to be happier, and perform better, when their OCP values match those of their employer. How important do you think a "values match" is when you're deciding where you want to work?

Ethical Dilemma

HIRING BASED ON BODY ART

Leonardo's Pizza in Gainesville, Florida, regularly employs heavily tattooed workers. Tina Taladge and Meghan Dean, for example, are covered from their shoulders to their ankles in colorful tattoos. So many of the employees at Leonardo's sport tattoos that body art could almost be a qualification for the job. Many employers, however, are not that open to tattoos. Consider Russell Parrish, 29, who lives near Orlando, Florida, and has dozens of tattoos on his arms, hands, torso, and neck. In searching for a job, Parrish walked into 100 businesses, and in 60 cases he was refused an application. "I want a career," Parrish says, "I want the same shot as everybody else."

Parrish isn't alone. Many employers, including Walt Disney World, GEICO, SeaWorld, the U.S. Postal Service, and Walmart, have policies against visible tattoos. A survey of employers revealed that 58 percent indicated they would be less likely to hire someone with visible tattoos or body piercings. "Perception is everything when it comes to getting a job," says Elaine Stover, associate director of career services at Arizona State University. "Some employers and clients could perceive body art negatively."

However, other employers—such as Bank of America, Allstate, and IBM—allow tattoos. Bank of America goes so far as to have a policy against using tattoos as a factor in hiring decisions.

Policies toward tattoos vary because, legally, employers can do as they wish. As long as the rule is applied equally to everyone (it would not be permissible to allow tattoos on men but not on women, for example), policies against tattoos are perfectly legal. Though not hiring people with tattoos is discrimination, "it's legal discrimination," said Gary Wilson, a Florida employment lawyer.

Thirty-six percent of those ages 18 to 25, and 40 percent of those ages 26 to 40, have at least one tattoo, whereas only 15 percent of those over 40 do, according to a fall 2006 survey by the Pew Research Center. One study in *American Demographics* suggested that 57 percent of senior citizens viewed visible tattoos as "freakish."

Clint Womack, like most other people with multiple tattoos, realizes there's a line that is dangerous to cross. While the 33-year-old hospital worker's arms, legs, and much of his torso are covered with tattoos, his hands, neck, and face are clear. "Tattoos are a choice you make," he says, "and you have to live with your choices."

Questions

1. Why do some employers ban tattoos while others don't mind them?

2. Is it fair for employers to reject applicants who have tattoos? Is it fair to require employees, if hired, to conceal their tattoos?

3. Should it be illegal to allow tattoos to be a factor at all in the hiring process?

Sources: Based on R. R. Hastings, "Survey: The Demographics of Tattoos and Piercings," *HRWeek,* February 2007, www.shrm.org; and H. Wessel, "Taboo of Tattoos in the Workplace," *Orlando (Florida) Sentinel,* May 28, 2007, www.tmcnet.com/usubmit/2007/05/28/2666555.htm.

Case Incident 1

THE NICE TRAP?

In these pages we've already noted that one downside of agreeableness is that agreeable people tend to have lower levels of career success. Though agreeableness doesn't appear to be related to job performance, agreeable people do earn less money. Though we're not sure why this is so, it may be that agreeable individuals are less aggressive in negotiating starting salaries and pay raises for themselves.

Yet there is clear evidence that agreeableness is something employers value. Several recent books argue in favor of the "power of nice" (Thaler & Koval, 2006) and "the kindness revolution" (Horrell, 2006). Other articles in the business press have argued that the sensitive, agreeable CEO—as manifested in CEOs such as GE's Jeffrey Immelt and Boeing's James McNerney—signals a shift in business culture (Brady, 2007). In many circles, individuals desiring success in their careers are exhorted to be "complimentary," "kind," and "good" (for example, Schillinger, 2007).

Take the example of 500-employee Lindblad Expeditions. It emphasizes agreeableness in its hiring decisions. The VP of HR commented, "You can teach people any technical skill, but you can't teach them how to be a kindhearted, generous-minded person with an open spirit."

So, while employers want agreeable employees, agreeable employees are not better job performers, and they are *less* successful in their careers. One might explain this apparent contradiction by noting that employers value agreeable employees for other reasons: They are more pleasant to be around, and they may help others in ways that aren't reflected in their job performance. While the former point seems fair enough—agreeable people are better liked—it's not clear that agreeable individuals actually help people more. A review of the "organizational citizenship" literature revealed a pretty weak correlation between an employee's agreeableness and how much he or she helped others.

Moreover, a 2008 study of CEO and CEO candidates revealed that this contradiction applies to organizational leaders as well. Using ratings made of candidates from an executive search firm, these researchers studied the personalities and abilities of 316 CEO candidates for companies involved in buyout and venture capital transactions. They found that what gets a CEO candidate hired is not what makes him or her effective. Specifically, CEO candidates who were rated high on "nice" traits such as respecting others, developing others, and teamwork were more likely to be hired. However, these same characteristics—especially teamwork and respecting others for venture capital CEOs—made the organizations that the CEOs led less successful.

Questions

1. Do you think there is a contradiction between what employers want in employees (agreeable employees) and what employees actually do best (disagreeable employees)? Why or why not?

2. Often, the effects of personality depend on the situation. Can you think of some job situations in which agreeableness is an important virtue? And in which it is harmful?

3. In some research we've conducted, we've found that the negative effects of agreeableness on earnings is stronger for men than for women (that is, being agreeable hurt men's earnings more than women's). Why do you think this might be the case?

Source: T. A. Judge, B. A. Livingston, and C. Hurst, "Do Nice Guys—and Gals—Really Finish Last? The Joint Effects of Sex and Agreeableness on Earnings," working paper, University of Florida, 2009; S. N. Kaplan, M. M. Klebanov, and M. Sorensen, "Which CEO Characteristics and Abilities Matter?" working paper, University of Chicago Graduate School of Business, 2008, faculty.chicagobooth.edu/steven.kaplan/research/kks.pdf; L. K. Thaler and R. Koval, *The Power of Nice: How to Conquer the Business World with Kindness.* New York: Doubleday/Currency, 2006; E. Horrell, *The Kindness Revolution,* New York: AMACOM, 2006; D. Brady, "Being Mean Is So Last Millennium," *Business Week* (January 15, 2007), p. 61; L. Schillinger, "Nice and Ambitious: Either, Neither, or Both?" *New York Times* (January 14, 2007), p. 1; "Congeniality Factor: Employers Become Pickier About Personality," *Gainesville (Florida) Sun* (November 6, 2007), p. 6B.

Case Incident 2

REACHING OUT, LITERALLY

"Why are people at work always touching me?" asked Elizabeth Bernstein. It's a problem not everyone has, but it makes you wonder why people like Bernstein are touched a lot at work. It also makes you wonder who does the touching.

Though there is no literature on this, the part of the "toucher" is perhaps easier to analyze. We know that extraverts are more expressive, demonstrative, and physically affectionate than are introverts. So one might well conjecture that extraverted people are doing more of the touching at work.

As for the "touchee," that's harder to figure. Some evidence suggests that women are more likely recipients of touches than are men. One study of Japanese women suggested that agreeable women are more likely to be touched than less agreeable women.

Elizabeth Bernstein is not sure what causes her to be the target of so many touches. "I get bear hugs from men and unsolicited kisses on the cheek from women," Bernstein wrote. "Co-workers of both sexes grip my elbows, tap my knees, and pat my back. . . . One friend hugs me every time she sees me in the elevator."

There also may be personality differences in the degree to which someone likes to be touched.

Greg Farrall, a 39-year-old financial advisor, has the worst of both worlds: he receives touches all the time and hates getting them. He has repeatedly asked people not to touch him, to no avail. "If you're looking over me at my computer screen, you don't need to put your hand on my shoulder. You can easily put it somewhere else."

Farrall is not alone in his dislike of workplace touching. One employee commented, "Few things are more annoying than employees who put their creepy-crawlies on co-workers."

As for when touching is inappropriate, obviously, touching someone in an inappropriate place, or continuing to touch someone when the recipient lets you know it's unwelcome, constitutes sexual harassment. But many touches fall into neither of these categories. "There aren't standards about what touching is nonsexual other than handshakes," said Larry Stybel, a Boston-area management consultant.

Of course, some people like being touched at work. Todd Adler, a Florida equities trader, recently started working from home. He says, "I work with myself and can only touch myself . . . which has its pluses and minuses."

Questions

1. What causes others to want to touch others at work?

2. How would you feel if a teacher in one of your classes put his or her arm on your shoulder? Can you imagine a situation in which that would be acceptable? Do you think your answers say something about your personality?

3. Some experts advise that employees should avoid all physical contact with co-workers at all times. Do you think that's a wise policy? Why or why not?

4. Do you think the social mores against are distinctly American? If so, why?

Source: E. Bernstein, "Touching Me, Touching You—At Work," *Wall Street Journal* (June 30, 2009), p. D6; N. Hunter, "Hands off, Mister!" *The Gleaner* (January 3, 2009), www.jamaica-gleaner.com; and K. Sakaguchi and T. Hasegawa, "Personality Correlates with Frequency of Being Targeted for Unexpected Advances by Strangers," *Journal of Applied Social Psychology* 37, no. 5 (2007), pp. 948–968.

Endnotes

1. G. W. Allport, *Personality: A Psychological Interpretation* (New York: Holt, Rinehart & Winston, 1937), p. 48. For a brief critique of current views on the meaning of personality, see R. T. Hogan and B. W. Roberts, "Introduction: Personality and Industrial and Organizational Psychology," in B. W. Roberts and R. Hogan (eds.), *Personality Psychology in the Workplace* (Washington, DC: American Psychological Association, 2001), pp. 11–12.

2. K. I. van der Zee, J. N. Zaal, and J. Piekstra, "Validation of the Multicultural Personality Questionnaire in the Context of Personnel Selection," *European Journal of Personality* 17 (2003), pp. S77–S100.

3. S. A. Birkeland, T. M. Manson, J. L. Kisamore, M. T. Brannick, and M. A. Smith, "A Meta-analytic Investigation of Job Applicant Faking on Personality Measures," *International Journal of Selection and Assessment* 14, no. 14 (2006), pp. 317–335.

4. T. A. Judge, C. A. Higgins, C. J. Thoresen, and M. R. Barrick, "The Big Five Personality Traits, General Mental Ability, and Career Success Across the Life Span," *Personnel Psychology* 52, no. 3 (1999), pp. 621–652.

5. See R. Illies, R. D. Arvey, and T. J. Bouchard, "Darwinism, Behavioral Genetics, and Organizational Behavior: A Review and Agenda for Future Research," *Journal of Organizational Behavior* 27, no. 2 (2006), pp. 121–141; W. Wright, *Born That Way: Genes, Behavior, Personality* (New York: Knopf, 1998); and T. J. Bouchard, Jr., and J. C. Loehlin, "Genes, Evolution, and Personality," *Behavior Genetics*, May 2001, pp. 243–273.

6. S. Srivastava, O. P. John, and S. D. Gosling, "Development of Personality in Early and Middle Adulthood: Set Like Plaster or Persistent Change?" *Journal of Personality and Social Psychology*, May 2003, pp. 1041–1053; and B. W. Roberts, K. E. Walton, and W. Viechtbauer, "Patterns of Mean-Level Change in Personality Traits Across the Life Course: A Meta-analysis of Longitudinal Studies," *Psychological Bulletin* 132, no. 1 (2006), pp. 1–25.

7. S. E. Hampson and L. R. Goldberg, "A First Large Cohort Study of Personality Trait Stability Over the 40 Years Between Elementary School and Midlife," *Journal of Personality and Social Psychology* 91, no. 4 (2006), pp. 763–779.

8. See A. H. Buss, "Personality as Traits," *American Psychologist*, November 1989, pp. 1378–1388; R. R. McCrae, "Trait Psychology and the Revival of Personality and Culture Studies," *American Behavioral Scientist*, September 2000, pp. 10–31; and L. R. James and M. D. Mazerolle, *Personality in Work Organizations* (Thousand Oaks, CA: Sage, 2002).

9. See, for instance, G. W. Allport and H. S. Odbert, "Trait Names, A Psycholexical Study," *Psychological Monographs*, no. 47 (1936); and R. B. Cattell, "Personality Pinned Down," *Psychology Today*, July 1973, pp. 40–46.

10. R. B. Kennedy and D. A. Kennedy, "Using the Myers-Briggs Type Indicator in Career Counseling," *Journal of Employment Counseling*, March 2004, pp. 38–44.

11. G. N. Landrum, *Profiles of Genius* (New York: Prometheus, 1993).

12. See, for instance, D. J. Pittenger, "Cautionary Comments Regarding the Myers-Briggs Type Indicator," *Consulting Psychology Journal: Practice and Research*, Summer 2005, pp. 10–221; L. Bess and R. J. Harvey, "Bimodal Score Distributions and the Myers-Briggs Type Indicator: Fact or Artifact?" *Journal of Personality Assessment*, February 2002, pp. 176–186; R. M. Capraro and M. M. Capraro, "Myers-Briggs Type Indicator Score Reliability Across Studies: A Meta-analytic Reliability Generalization Study," *Educational & Psychological Measurement*, August 2002, pp. 590–602; and R. C. Arnau, B. A. Green, D. H. Rosen, D. H. Gleaves, and J. G. Melancon, "Are Jungian Preferences Really Categorical? An Empirical Investigation Using Taxometric Analysis," *Personality & Individual Differences*, January 2003, pp. 233–251.

13. See, for example, J. M. Digman, "Personality Structure: Emergence of the Five-Factor Model," in M. R. Rosenzweig and L. W. Porter (eds.), *Annual Review of Psychology*, vol. 41 (Palo Alto, CA: Annual Reviews, 1990), pp. 417–440; D. B. Smith, P. J. Hanges, and M. W. Dickson, "Personnel Selection and the Five-Factor Model: Reexamining the Effects of Applicant's Frame of Reference," *Journal of Applied Psychology*, April 2001, pp. 304–315; and M. R. Barrick and M. K. Mount, "Yes, Personality Matters: Moving On to More Important Matters," *Human Performance* 18, no. 4 (2005), pp. 359–372.

14. See, for instance, M. R. Barrick and M. K. Mount, "The Big Five Personality Dimensions and Job Performance: A Meta-analysis," *Personnel Psychology*, Spring 1991, pp. 1–26; G. M. Hurtz and J. J. Donovan, "Personality and Job Performance: The Big Five Revisited," *Journal of Applied Psychology*, December 2000, pp. 869–879; J. Hogan and B. Holland, "Using Theory to Evaluate Personality and Job-Performance Relations: A Socioanalytic Perspective," *Journal of Applied Psychology*, February 2003, pp. 100–112; and M. R. Barrick and M. K. Mount, "Select on Conscientiousness and Emotional Stability," in E. A. Locke (ed.), *Handbook of Principles of Organizational Behavior* (Malden, MA: Blackwell, 2004), pp. 15–28.

15. M. K. Mount, M. R. Barrick, and J. P. Strauss, "Validity of Observer Ratings of the Big Five Personality Factors," *Journal of Applied Psychology*, April 1994, p. 272. Additionally confirmed by G. M. Hurtz and J. J. Donovan, "Personality and Job Performance: The Big Five Revisited"; and M. R. Barrick, M. K. Mount, and T. A. Judge, "The FFM Personality Dimensions and Job Performance: Meta-analysis of Meta-analyses," *International Journal of Selection and Assessment* 9 (2001), pp. 9–30.

16. A. E. Poropat, "A Meta-Analysis of the Five-Factor Model of Personality and Academic Performance," *Psychological Bulletin* 135, no. 2 (2009), pp. 322–338.

17. R. J. Foti and M. A. Hauenstein, "Pattern and Variable Approaches in Leadership Emergence and Effectiveness," *Journal of Applied Psychology*, March 2007, pp. 347–355.

18. L. I. Spirling and R. Persaud, "Extraversion as a Risk Factor," *Journal of the American Academy of Child & Adolescent Psychiatry* 42, no. 2 (2003), p. 130.

19. B. Weiss, and R. S. Feldman, "Looking Good and Lying to Do It: Deception as an Impression Management Strategy in Job Interviews," *Journal of Applied Social Psychology* 36, no. 4 (2006), pp. 1070–1086.

20. J. A. LePine, J. A. Colquitt, and A. Erez, "Adaptability to Changing Task Contexts: Effects of General Cognitive Ability, Conscientiousness, and Openness to Experience," *Personnel Psychology* 53 (2000), pp. 563–595; S. Clarke and I. Robertson,

"An Examination of the Role of Personality in Accidents Using Meta-analysis," *Applied Psychology: An International Review* 57, no. 1 (2008), pp. 94–108.

21. B. Laursen, L. Pulkkinen, and R. Adams, "The Antecedents and Correlates of Agreeableness in Adulthood," *Developmental Psychology* 38, no. 4 (2002), pp. 591–603.

22. B. Barry and R. A. Friedman, "Bargainer Characteristics in Distributive and Integrative Negotiation," *Journal of Personality and Social Psychology,* February 1998, pp. 345–359.

23. T. Bogg and B. W. Roberts, "Conscientiousness and Health-Related Behaviors: A Meta-analysis of the Leading Behavioral Contributors to Mortality," *Psychological Bulletin* 130, no. 6 (2004), pp. 887–919.

24. S. Lee and H. J. Klein, "Relationships Between Conscientiousness, Self-Efficacy, Self-Deception, and Learning over Time," *Journal of Applied Psychology* 87, no. 6 (2002), pp. 1175–1182; and G. J. Feist, "A Meta-analysis of Personality in Scientific and Artistic Creativity," *Personality and Social Psychology Review* 2, no. 4 (1998), pp. 290–309.

25. T. A. Judge and J. E. Bono, "A Rose by Any Other Name . . . Are Self-Esteem, Generalized Self-Efficacy, Neuroticism, and Locus of Control Indicators of a Common Construct?" in B. W. Roberts and R. Hogan (eds.), *Personality Psychology in the Workplace* (Washington, DC: American Psychological Association), pp. 93–118.

26. A. Erez and T. A. Judge, "Relationship of Core Self-Evaluations to Goal Setting, Motivation, and Performance," *Journal of Applied Psychology* 86, no. 6 (2001), pp. 1270–1279.

27. A. N. Salvaggio, B. Schneider, L. H. Nishi, D. M. Mayer, A. Ramesh, and J. S. Lyon, "Manager Personality, Manager Service Quality Orientation, and Service Climate: Test of a Model," *Journal of Applied Psychology* 92, no. 6 (2007), pp. 1741–1750; B. A. Scott and T. A. Judge, "The Popularity Contest at Work: Who Wins, Why, and What Do They Receive?" *Journal of Applied Psychology* 94, no. 1 (2009), pp. 20–33; and T. A. Judge and C. Hurst, "How the Rich (and Happy) Get Richer (and Happier): Relationship of Core Self-Evaluations to Trajectories in Attaining Work Success," *Journal of Applied Psychology* 93, no. 4 (2008), pp. 849–863.

28. U. Malmendier and G. Tate, "CEO Overconfidence and Corporate Investment," *Journal of Finance* 60, no. 6 (December 2005), pp. 2661–2700.

29. R. Sandomir, "Star Struck," *New York Times,* January 12, 2007, pp. C10, C14.

30. R. Christie and F. L. Geis, *Studies in Machiavellianism* (New York: Academic Press, 1970), p. 312; and N. V. Ramanaiah, A. Byravan, and F. R. J. Detwiler, "Revised Neo Personality Inventory Profiles of Machiavellian and Non-Machiavellian People," *Psychological Reports,* October 1994, pp. 937–938.

31. J. J. Dahling, B. G. Whitaker, and P. E. Levy, "The Development and Validation of a New Machiavellianism Scale," *Journal of Management* 35, no. 2 (2009), pp. 219–257.

32. Christie and Geis, *Studies in Machiavellianism.*

33. M. Elias, "Study: Today's Youth Think Quite Highly of Themselves," *USA Today* (November 19, 2008), p. 7D; and K. H. Trzesniewski, M. B. Donnellan, and R. W. Robins, "Do Today's Young People Really Think They Are So Extraordinary?" *Psychological Science* 19, no. 2 (2008), pp. 181–188.

34. M. Maccoby, "Narcissistic Leaders: The Incredible Pros, the Inevitable Cons," *The Harvard Business Review,* January–February 2000, pp. 69–77, www.maccoby.com/Articles/NarLeaders.shtml.

35. W. K. Campbell and C. A. Foster, "Narcissism and Commitment in Romantic Relationships: An Investment Model Analysis," *Personality and Social Psychology Bulletin* 28, no. 4 (2002), pp. 484–495.

36. T. A. Judge, J. A. LePine, and B. L. Rich, "The Narcissistic Personality: Relationship with Inflated Self-Ratings of Leadership and with Task and Contextual Performance," *Journal of Applied Psychology* 91, no. 4 (2006), pp. 762–776.

37. See M. Snyder, *Public Appearances/Private Realities: The Psychology of Self-Monitoring* (New York: W. H. Freeman, 1987); and S. W. Gangestad and M. Snyder, "Self-Monitoring: Appraisal and Reappraisal," *Psychological Bulletin,* July 2000, pp. 530–555.

38. F. J. Flynn and D. R. Ames, "What's Good for the Goose May Not Be as Good for the Gander: The Benefits of Self-Monitoring for Men and Women in Task Groups and Dyadic Conflicts," *Journal of Applied Psychology* 91, no. 2 (2006), pp. 272–281; and Snyder, *Public Appearances/Private Realities.*

39. D. V. Day, D. J. Shleicher, A. L. Unckless, and N. J. Hiller, "Self-Monitoring Personality at Work: A Meta-analytic Investigation of Construct Validity," *Journal of Applied Psychology,* April 2002, pp. 390–401.

40. H. Oh and M. Kilduff, "The Ripple Effect of Personality on Social Structure: Self-monitoring Origins of Network Brokerage," *Journal of Applied Psychology* 93, no. 5 (2008), pp. 1155–1164; and A. Mehra, M. Kilduff, and D. J. Brass, "The Social Networks of High and Low Self-Monitors: Implications for Workplace Performance," *Administrative Science Quarterly,* March 2001, pp. 121–146.

41. R. N. Taylor and M. D. Dunnette, "Influence of Dogmatism, Risk-Taking Propensity, and Intelligence on Decision-Making Strategies for a Sample of Industrial Managers," *Journal of Applied Psychology,* August 1974, pp. 420–423.

42. I. L. Janis and L. Mann, *Decision Making: A Psychological Analysis of Conflict, Choice, and Commitment* (New York: The Free Press, 1977); W. H. Stewart, Jr., and L. Roth, "Risk Propensity Differences Between Entrepreneurs and Managers: A Meta-analytic Review," *Journal of Applied Psychology,* February 2001, pp. 145–153; J. B. Miner and N. S. Raju, "Risk Propensity Differences Between Managers and Entrepreneurs and Between Low- and High-Growth Entrepreneurs: A Reply in a More Conservative Vein," *Journal of Applied Psychology* 89, no. 1 (2004), pp. 3–13; and W. H. Stewart, Jr., and P. L. Roth, "Data Quality Affects Meta-analytic Conclusions: A Response to Miner and Raju (2004) Concerning Entrepreneurial Risk Propensity," *Journal of Applied Psychology* 89, no. 1 (2004), pp. 14–21.

43. J. K. Maner, J. A. Richey, K. Cromer, M. Mallott, C. W. Lejuez, T. E. Joiner, and N. B. Schmidt, "Dispositional Anxiety and Risk-Avoidant Decision Making," *Personality and Individual Differences* 42, no. 4 (2007), pp. 665–675.

44. M. Friedman and R. H. Rosenman, *Type A Behavior and Your Heart* (New York: Alfred A. Knopf, 1974), p. 84.

45. Ibid., pp. 84–85.

46. R. E. White, S. Thornhill, and E. Hampson, "Entrepreneurs and Evolutionary Biology: The Relationship Between Testosterone and New Venture Creation," *Organizational Behavior and Human Decision Processes* 100 (2006), pp. 21–34;

and H. Zhao and S. E. Seibert, "The Big Five Personality Dimensions and Entrepreneurial State: A Meta-analytical Review," *Journal of Applied Psychology* 91, no. 2 (2006), pp. 259–271.

47. K. W. Cook, C. A. Vance, and E. Spector, "The Relation of Candidate Personality with Selection-Interview Outcomes," *Journal of Applied Social Psychology* 30 (2000), pp. 867–885.

48. J. M. Crant, "Proactive Behavior in Organizations," *Journal of Management* 26, no. 3 (2000), p. 436.

49. S. E. Seibert, M. L. Kraimer, and J. M. Crant, "What Do Proactive People Do? A Longitudinal Model Linking Proactive Personality and Career Success," *Personnel Psychology,* Winter 2001, p. 850.

50. T. S. Bateman and J. M. Crant, "The Proactive Component of Organizational Behavior: A Measure and Correlates," *Journal of Organizational Behavior,* March 1993, pp. 103–118; and J. M. Crant and T. S. Bateman, "Charismatic Leadership Viewed from Above: The Impact of Proactive Personality," *Journal of Organizational Behavior,* February 2000, pp. 63–75.

51. Crant, "Proactive Behavior in Organizations," p. 436.

52. See, for instance, R. C. Becherer and J. G. Maurer, "The Proactive Personality Disposition and Entrepreneurial Behavior Among Small Company Presidents," *Journal of Small Business Management,* January 1999, pp. 28–36.

53. S. E. Seibert, J. M. Crant, and M. L. Kraimer, "Proactive Personality and Career Success," *Journal of Applied Psychology,* June 1999, pp. 416–427; Seibert, Kraimer, and Crant, "What Do Proactive People Do?" p. 850; D. J. Brown, R. T. Cober, K. Kane, P. E. Levy, and J. Shalhoop, "Proactive Personality and the Successful Job Search: A Field Investigation with College Graduates," *Journal of Applied Psychology* 91, no. 3 (2006), pp. 717–726; and J. D. Kammeyer-Mueller and C. R. Wanberg, "Unwrapping the Organizational Entry Process: Disentangling Multiple Antecedents and Their Pathways to Adjustment," *Journal of Applied Psychology* 88, no. 5 (2003), pp. 779–794.

54. M. Rokeach, *The Nature of Human Values* (New York: The Free Press, 1973), p. 5.

55. M. Rokeach and S. J. Ball-Rokeach, "Stability and Change in American Value Priorities, 1968–1981," *American Psychologist* 44, no. 5 (1989), pp. 775–784; and B. M. Meglino and E. C. Ravlin, "Individual Values in Organizations: Concepts, Controversies, and Research," *Journal of Management* 24, no. 3 (1998), p. 355.

56. S. Roccas, L. Sagiv, S. H. Schwartz, and A. Knafo, "The Big Five Personality Factors and Personal Values," *Personality and Social Psychology Bulletin* 28, no. 6 (2002), pp. 789–801.

57. See, for instance, Meglino and Ravlin, "Individual Values in Organizations," pp. 351–389.

58. Rokeach, *The Nature of Human Values,* p. 6.

59. J. M. Munson and B. Z. Posner, "The Factorial Validity of a Modified Rokeach Value Survey for Four Diverse Samples," *Educational and Psychological Measurement,* Winter 1980, pp. 1073–1079; and W. C. Frederick and J. Weber, "The Values of Corporate Managers and Their Critics: An Empirical Description and Normative Implications," in W. C. Frederick and L. E. Preston (eds.), *Business Ethics: Research Issues and Empirical Studies* (Greenwich, CT: JAI Press, 1990), pp. 123–144.

60. Frederick and Weber, "The Values of Corporate Managers and Their Critics," pp. 123–144.

61. Ibid., p. 132.

62. See, for example, *The Multigenerational Workforce,* Alexandria, VA: Society for Human Resource Management, 2009.

63. K. W. Smola and C. D. Sutton, "Generational Differences: Revisiting Generational Work Values for the New Millennium," *Journal of Organizational Behavior* 23 (2002), pp. 363–382; and K. Mellahi and C. Guermat, "Does Age Matter? An Empirical Examination of the Effect of Age on Managerial Values and Practices in India," *Journal of World Business* 39, no. 2 (2004), pp. 199–215.

64. B. Hite, "Employers Rethink How They Give Feedback," *Wall Street Journal* (October 13, 2008), p. B5.

65. J. L. Holland, *Making Vocational Choices: A Theory of Vocational Personalities and Work Environments* (Odessa, FL: Psychological Assessment Resources, 1997).

66. See, for example, J. L. Holland and G. D. Gottfredson, "Studies of the Hexagonal Model: An Evaluation (or, The Perils of Stalking the Perfect Hexagon)," *Journal of Vocational Behavior,* April 1992, pp. 158–170; T. J. Tracey and J. Rounds, "Evaluating Holland's and Gati's Vocational-Interest Models: A Structural Meta-analysis," *Psychological Bulletin,* March 1993, pp. 229–246; J. L. Holland, "Exploring Careers with a Typology: What We Have Learned and Some New Directions," *American Psychologist,* April 1996, pp. 397–406; and S. X. Day and J. Rounds, "Universality of Vocational Interest Structure Among Racial and Ethnic Minorities," *American Psychologist,* July 1998, pp. 728–736.

67. See B. Schneider, "The People Make the Place," *Personnel Psychology,* Autumn 1987, pp. 437–453; B. Schneider, H. W. Goldstein, and D. B. Smith, "The ASA Framework: An Update," *Personnel Psychology,* Winter 1995, pp. 747–773; A. L. Kristof, "Person–Organization Fit: An Integrative Review of Its Conceptualizations, Measurement, and Implications," *Personnel Psychology,* Spring 1996, pp. 1–49; B. Schneider, D. B. Smith, S. Taylor, and J. Fleenor, "Personality and Organizations: A Test of the Homogeneity of Personality Hypothesis," *Journal of Applied Psychology,* June 1998, pp. 462–470; W. Arthur, Jr., S. T. Bell, A. J. Villado, and D. Doverspike, "The Use of Person-Organization Fit in Employment Decision-Making: An Assessment of Its Criterion-Related Validity," *Journal of Applied Psychology* 91, no. 4 (2006), pp. 786–801; and J. R. Edwards, D. M. Cable, I. O. Williamson, L. S. Lambert, and A. J. Shipp, "The Phenomenology of Fit: Linking the Person and Environment to the Subjective Experience of Person–Environment Fit," *Journal of Applied Psychology* 91, no. 4 (2006), pp. 802–827.

68. Based on T. A. Judge and D. M. Cable, "Applicant Personality, Organizational Culture, and Organization Attraction," *Personnel Psychology,* Summer 1997, pp. 359–394.

69. M. L. Verquer, T. A. Beehr, and S. E. Wagner, "A Meta-analysis of Relations Between Person–Organization Fit and Work Attitudes," *Journal of Vocational Behavior* 63, no. 3 (2003), pp. 473–489; and J. C. Carr, A. W. Pearson, M. J. Vest, and S. L. Boyar, "Prior Occupational Experience, Anticipatory Socialization, and Employee Retention, *Journal of Management* 32, no. 32 (2006), pp. 343–359.

70. See, for instance, R. R. McCrae and P. T. Costa, Jr., "Personality Trait Structure as a Human Universal," *American Psychologist,* May 1997, pp. 509–516; S. Yamagata, A. Suzuki, J. Ando, Y. Ono, K. Yutaka, N. Kijima, et al., "Is the Genetic

Structure of Human Personality Universal? A Cross-Cultural Twin Study from North America, Europe, and Asia," *Journal of Personality and Social Psychology* 90, no. 6 (2006), pp. 987–998; H. C. Triandis and E. M. Suh, "Cultural Influences on Personality," in S. T. Fiske, D. L. Schacter, and C. Zahn-Waxler (eds.), *Annual Review of Psychology,* vol. 53 (Palo Alto, CA: Annual Reviews, 2002), pp. 133–160; R. R. McCrae and J. Allik, *The Five-Factor Model of Personality Across Cultures* (New York: Kluwer Academic/Plenum, 2002); and R. R. McCrae, P. T. Costa, Jr., T. A. Martin, V. E. Oryol, A. A. Rukavishnikov, I. G. Senin, et al., "Consensual Validation of Personality Traits Across Cultures," *Journal of Research in Personality* 38, no. 2 (2004), pp. 179–201.

71. A. T. Church and M. S. Katigbak, "Trait Psychology in the Philippines," *American Behavioral Scientist,* September 2000, pp. 73–94.

72. J. F. Salgado, "The Five Factor Model of Personality and Job Performance in the European Community," *Journal of Applied Psychology,* February 1997, pp. 30–43.

73. G. Hofstede, *Culture's Consequences: International Differences in Work-Related Values* (Beverly Hills, CA: Sage, 1980); G. Hofstede, *Cultures and Organizations: Software of the Mind* (London: McGraw-Hill, 1991); G. Hofstede, "Cultural Constraints in Management Theories," *Academy of Management Executive* 7, no. 1 (1993), pp. 81–94; G. Hofstede and M. F. Peterson, "National Values and Organizational Practices," in N. M. Ashkanasy, C. M. Wilderom, and M. F. Peterson (eds.), *Handbook of Organizational Culture and Climate* (Thousand Oaks, CA: Sage, 2000), pp. 401–416; and G. Hofstede, *Culture's Consequences: Comparing Values, Behaviors, Institutions, and Organizations Across Nations,* 2nd ed. (Thousand Oaks, CA: Sage, 2001). For criticism of this research, see B. McSweeney, "Hofstede's Model of National Cultural Differences and Their Consequences: A Triumph of Faith—A Failure of Analysis," *Human Relations* 55, no. 1 (2002), pp. 89–118.

74. G. Ailon, "Mirror, Mirror on the Wall: *Culture's Consequences* in a Value Test of Its Own Design," *Academy of Management Review* 33, no. 4 (2008), pp. 885–904; M. H. Bond, "Reclaiming the Individual from Hofstede's Ecological Analysis—A 20-Year Odyssey: Comment on Oyserman et al. (2002), *Psychological Bulletin* 128, no. 1 (2002), pp. 73–77; and G. Hofstede, "The Pitfalls of Cross-National Survey Research: A Reply to the Article by Spector et al. on the Psychometric Properties of the Hofstede Values Survey Module 1994," *Applied Psychology: An International Review* 51, no. 1 (2002), pp. 170–178.

75. M. Javidan and R. J. House, "Cultural Acumen for the Global Manager: Lessons from Project GLOBE," *Organizational Dynamics* 29, no. 4 (2001), pp. 289–305; and R. J. House, P. J. Hanges, M. Javidan, and P. W. Dorfman (eds.), *Leadership, Culture, and Organizations: The GLOBE Study of 62 Societies* (Thousand Oaks, CA: Sage, 2004).

76. P. C. Early, "Leading Cultural Research in the Future: A Matter of Paradigms and Taste," *Journal of International Business Studies,* September 2006, pp. 922–931; G. Hofstede, "What Did GLOBE Really Measure? Researchers' Minds Versus Respondents' Minds," *Journal of International Business Studies,* September 2006, pp. 882–896; and M. Javidan, R. J. House, P. W. Dorfman, P. J. Hanges, and M. S. de Luque, "Conceptualizing and Measuring Cultures and Their Consequences: A Comparative Review of GLOBE's and Hofstede's Approaches," *Journal of International Business Studies,* September 2006, pp. 897–914.

77. L. A. Witt, "The Interactive Effects of Extraversion and Conscientiousness on Performance," *Journal of Management* 28, no. 6 (2002), p. 836.

78. R. P. Tett and D. D. Burnett, "A Personality Trait–Based Interactionist Model of Job Performance," *Journal of Applied Psychology,* June 2003, pp. 500–517.

79. R. Hogan, "In Defense of Personality Measurement: New Wine for Old Whiners," *Human Performance* 18, no. 4 (2005), pp. 331–341; and N. Schmitt, "Beyond the Big Five: Increases in Understanding and Practical Utility," *Human Performance* 17, no. 3 (2004), pp. 347–357.

80. B. W. Roberts, N. R. Kuncel, R. Shiner, A. Caspi, and L. R. Goldberg, "The Power of Personality," *Perspectives on Psychological Science* 2, no. 4 (2007), pp. 313–344.

81. F. P. Morgeson, M. A. Campion, R. L. Dipboye, J. R. Hollenbeck, K. Murphy, and N. Schmitt, "Are We Getting Fooled Again? Coming to Terms with Limitations in the Use of Personality Tests in Personnel Selection," *Personnel Psychology* 60, no. 4 (2007), pp. 1029–1049.

82. B. Adkins and D. Caldwell, "Firm or Subgroup Culture: Where Does Fitting in Matter Most?" *Journal of Organizational Behavior* 25, no. 8 (2004), pp. 969–978; H. D. Cooper-Thomas, A. van Vianen, and N. Anderson, "Changes in Person–Organization Fit: The Impact of Socialization Tactics on Perceived and Actual P–O Fit," *European Journal of Work & Organizational Psychology* 13, no. 1 (2004), pp. 52–78; and C. A. O'Reilly, J. Chatman, and D. F. Caldwell, "People and Organizational Culture: A Profile Comparison Approach to Assessing Person–Organization Fit," *Academy of Management Journal* 34, no. 3 (1991), pp. 487–516.

LEARNING OBJECTIVES

After studying this chapter, you should be able to:

1 Define *perception* and explain the factors that influence it.

2 Explain attribution theory and list the three determinants of attribution.

3 Identify the shortcuts individuals use in making judgments about others.

4 Explain the link between perception and decision making.

5 Apply the rational model of decision making and contrast it with bounded rationality and intuition.

6 List and explain the common decision biases or errors.

7 Explain how individual differences and organizational constraints affect decision making.

8 Contrast the three ethical decision criteria.

9 Define *creativity* and discuss the three-component model of creativity.

Perception and Individual Decision Making

6

Indecision may or may not be my problem.

—Jimmy Buffett

GOOGLE'S INNOVATION MACHINE

When you think about the roots of creativity and innovation, you might imagine pure inspiration, that singular *Eureka!* moment that's more artistic (right brain) than analytical (left brain). In reality, though, the division between art and analysis is mostly false, as Google's process for making creative and effective decisions illustrates.

Nicholas Fox, director of business product management, is a critical member of Google's creative culture. However, like many at Google, he is an extraordinarily analytical thinker.

A key part of Google's profitability is advertising revenues: it earns about $2 million in ad revenues *per hour*. Google sells ads through a complex auction system. For every aspect of an ad's placement and order, Fox runs an analysis to determine how each variable affects user behavior, advertisers, and Google's revenue.

Fox, a soft-spoken 30-year-old with a degree in economics and past experience at management consulting powerhouse McKinsey & Company, has been at Google since 2003. He believes the secret to Google's success—it not only sells many more ads than its main rivals Yahoo and Microsoft but it also earns 60 to 70 percent more ad revenue on every search—rests on its ability to make intricate and fast adjustments, which in turn are based on the fact that Google "measures just about everything."

Fox and Google don't rest on their laurels, either. At the height of the company's growth in number of users, Fox and others thought revenue-per-click was too low. So Fox, along with chief economist Hal Varian and principle engineer Diane Tang, devised complex ad-pricing schemes whereby they charge advertisers rates based on a "quality score"—an algorithm of the ad's ability to generate positive reactions among Google's users. Google will even advise advertisers about how to increase their quality score (without, of course, giving away the secrets of its algorithm).

Google's culture is unique, but its successes suggest that if more organizations decided to blend creativity and analysis, they too would be more effective at innovation.

How has Google's unusual approach to innovation fared during the recession? CEO Eric Schmidt remarked, "Innovation has nothing to do with downturns."[1]

As the Google example shows, decision making and creativity—the subjects of this chapter—are often linked. Decision making is often intuitive, and creativity is often the product of analysis. We begin with a factor that feeds into both: perception.

In the following Self-Assessment Library, consider one perception, that of appropriate gender roles.

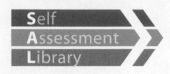

WHAT ARE MY GENDER ROLE PERCEPTIONS?

In the Self-Assessment Library (available on CD or online), take assessment IV.C.2 (What Are My Gender Role Perceptions?) and answer the following questions.

1. *Did you score as high as you thought you would?*
2. *Do you think a problem with measures like this is that people aren't honest in responding?*
3. *If others, such as friends, classmates, and family members, rated you, would they rate you differently? Why or why not?*
4. *Research has shown that people's gender role perceptions are becoming less traditional over time. Why do you suppose this is so?*

What Is Perception?

1 Define *perception* and explain the factors that influence it.

Perception is a process by which individuals organize and interpret their sensory impressions in order to give meaning to their environment. However, what we perceive can be substantially different from objective reality. For example, all employees in a firm may view it as a great place to work—favorable working conditions, interesting job assignments, good pay, excellent benefits, understanding and responsible management—but, as most of us know, it's very unusual to find such agreement.

Why is perception important in the study of OB? Simply because people's behavior is based on their perception of what reality is, not on reality itself. *The world as it is perceived is the world that is behaviorally important.*

Factors That Influence Perception

How do we explain the fact that individuals may look at the same thing yet perceive it differently? A number of factors operate to shape and sometimes distort perception. These factors can reside in the *perceiver;* in the object, or *target,* being perceived; or in the context of the *situation* in which the perception is made (see Exhibit 6-1).

When you look at a target and attempt to interpret what you see, your interpretation is heavily influenced by your personal characteristics. Characteristics that affect perception include your attitudes, personality, motives, interests, past experiences, and expectations. For instance, if you expect police officers to be authoritative, young people to be lazy, or individuals holding public office to be unscrupulous, you may perceive them as such, regardless of their actual traits.

Characteristics of the target we observe can affect what we perceive. Loud people are more likely to be noticed in a group than quiet ones. So, too, are extremely attractive or unattractive individuals. Because we don't look at targets in isolation, the relationship of a target to its background also influences perception, as does our tendency to group close things and similar things together. For instance, we often perceive women, men, Whites, African Americans, Asians, or members of any other group that has clearly distinguishable characteristics as alike in other, unrelated ways as well.

Context is also important. The time at which we see an object or event can influence our attention, as can location, light, heat, or any number of situational factors. At a nightclub on Saturday night, you may not notice a young guest

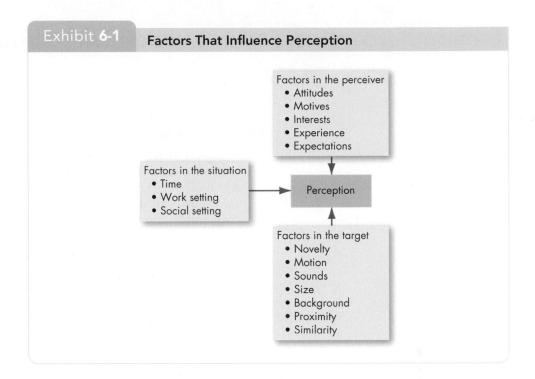

Exhibit 6-1 **Factors That Influence Perception**

"dressed to the nines." Yet that same person so attired for your Monday morning management class would certainly catch your attention (and that of the rest of the class). Neither the perceiver nor the target has changed between Saturday night and Monday morning, but the situation is different.

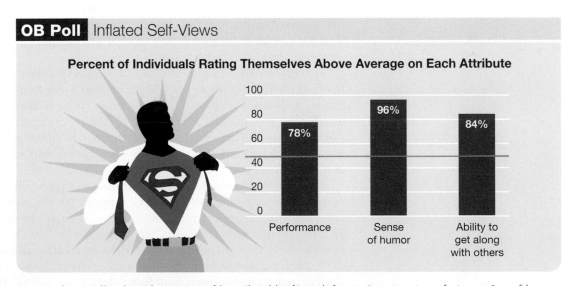

OB Poll Inflated Self-Views

Percent of Individuals Rating Themselves Above Average on Each Attribute

Source: Based on C. Merkle and M. Weber, *True Overconfidence—The Inability of Rational Information Processing to Account for Apparent Overconfidence* (March 2009). Available at SSRN: http://ssrn.com/abstract=1373675

perception *A process by which individuals organize and interpret their sensory impressions in order to give meaning to their environment.*

Person Perception: Making Judgments About Others

Now we turn to the application of perception concepts most relevant to OB—*person perception,* or the perceptions people form about each other.

Attribution Theory

Nonliving objects such as desks, machines, and buildings are subject to the laws of nature, but they have no beliefs, motives, or intentions. People do. That's why when we observe people, we attempt to explain why they behave in certain ways. Our perception and judgment of a person's actions, therefore, will be significantly influenced by the assumptions we make about that person's internal state.

2 Explain attribution theory and list the three determinants of attribution.

Attribution theory tries to explain the ways in which we judge people differently, depending on the meaning we attribute to a given behavior.[2] It suggests that when we observe an individual's behavior, we attempt to determine whether it was internally or externally caused. That determination, however, depends largely on three factors: (1) distinctiveness, (2) consensus, and (3) consistency. First, let's clarify the differences between internal and external causation, and then we'll elaborate on each of the three determining factors.

Internally caused behaviors are those we believe to be under the personal control of the individual. *Externally* caused behavior is what we imagine the situation forced the individual to do. If one of your employees is late for work, you might attribute that to his partying into the wee hours and then oversleeping. This is an internal attribution. But if you attribute his arriving late to an automobile accident that tied up traffic, then you are making an external attribution.

Now let's discuss each of the three determining factors. *Distinctiveness* refers to whether an individual displays different behaviors in different situations. Is the employee who arrives late today also the one co-workers say regularly "blows off" commitments? What we want to know is whether this behavior is unusual. If it is, we are likely to give it an external attribution. If it's not, we will probably judge the behavior to be internal.

If everyone who faces a similar situation responds in the same way, we can say the behavior shows *consensus.* The behavior of our tardy employee meets this criterion if all employees who took the same route to work were also late. From an attribution perspective, if consensus is high, you would probably give an external attribution to the employee's tardiness, whereas if other employees who took the same route made it to work on time, you would attribute his lateness to an internal cause.

Finally, an observer looks for *consistency* in a person's actions. Does the person respond the same way over time? Coming in 10 minutes late for work is not perceived in the same way for an employee who hasn't been late for several months as it is for an employee who is late two or three times a week. The more consistent the behavior, the more we are inclined to attribute it to internal causes.

Exhibit 6-2 summarizes the key elements in attribution theory. It tells us, for instance, that if an employee, Kim Randolph, generally performs at about the same level on other related tasks as she does on her current task (low distinctiveness), other employees frequently perform differently—better or worse—than Kim does on that current task (low consensus), and Kim's performance on this current task is consistent over time (high consistency), anyone judging Kim's work will likely hold her primarily responsible for her task performance (internal attribution).

One of the most interesting findings from attribution theory research is that errors or biases distort attributions. When we make judgments about the behavior of other people, we tend to underestimate the influence of external factors and overestimate the influence of internal or personal factors.[3] This **fundamental attri-**

Exhibit 6-2   Attribution Theory

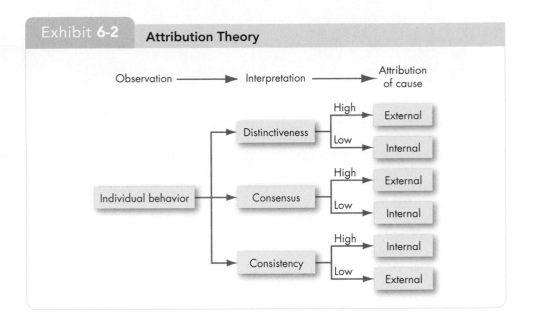

bution error can explain why a sales manager is prone to attribute the poor performance of her sales agents to laziness rather than to the innovative product line introduced by a competitor. Individuals and organizations also tend to attribute their own successes to internal factors such as ability or effort, while putting the blame for failure on external factors such as bad luck or unproductive co-workers. This is the **self-serving bias**.[4] A *U.S. News & World Report* study showed the power of the self-serving bias. Researchers asked one group of people "If someone sues you and you win the case, should he pay your legal costs?" Eighty-five percent responded "yes." Another group was asked "If you sue someone and lose the case, should you pay his costs?" Only 44 percent answered "yes."[5]

Common Shortcuts in Judging Others

3 Identify the shortcuts individuals use in making judgments about others.

We use a number of shortcuts when we judge others. These techniques are frequently valuable: they allow us to make accurate perceptions rapidly and provide valid data for making predictions. However, they are not foolproof. They can and do get us into trouble. Understanding these shortcuts can help you recognize when they can result in significant distortions.

Selective Perception   Any characteristic that makes a person, an object, or an event stand out will increase the probability that we will perceive it. Why? Because it is impossible for us to assimilate everything we see; we can take in only certain stimuli. This tendency explains why you're more likely to notice cars like your own or why a boss may reprimand some people and not others who are doing the same thing. Because we can't observe everything going on about us,

---

attribution theory   *An attempt to determine whether an individual's behavior is internally or externally caused.*

fundamental attribution error   *The tendency to underestimate the influence of external factors and overestimate the influence of internal factors when making judgments about the behavior of others.*

self-serving bias   *The tendency for individuals to attribute their own successes to internal factors and put the blame for failures on external factors.*

International OB

East–West Differences: It's Perceptual

As you read this book, you'll find we often compare how organizational behavior concepts and theories work in the East (particularly Asia) and the West (particularly the United States). Given the size, economic power, and value differences between them, the comparison makes sense.

Nowhere are their OB differences clearer than in perception. First, Asians are less likely to commit the fundamental attribution error. Specifically, Japanese are less likely to show a bias in attributing a person's behavior to internal factors rather than external or situational forces.

Second, and related, Asians appear to focus more on the context or environment than on the person. When researchers showed Chinese and U.S. participants a photo with a focal object (like a train) with a busy background, using eye-tracking devices they found U.S. subjects were more likely to focus

on the focal object, whereas Chinese were more likely to look at the background. As one researcher, University of Michigan's Richard Nisbett, concluded, "If people are seeing different things, it may be because they are looking differently at the world."

These differences may even be rooted in our brain architecture. Using brain scanning devices (fMRI), Denise Park of the University of Illinois found that when Singaporeans were shown pictures where either the foreground or background was varied, their brains were less attuned to new foreground images and more attuned to new background images that those of U.S. subjects. This suggests that the tendency to focus on the person or the context is rooted deep in the "hard wiring" of our brains.

Finally, Cornell's Qi Wang has found that culture affects what we remember as well. When asked to remember

events, U.S. subjects recall more personal detail and their own personal characteristics, whereas Asians recall more about personal relationships and group activities.

As a set, these studies provide striking evidence that Eastern and Western cultures differ in one of the deepest aspects of organizational behavior: how we see the world around us.

Source: Based on T. Masuda, R. Gonzalez, L. Kwan, and R. E. Nisbett, "Culture and Aesthetic Preference: Comparing the Attention to Context of East Asians and Americans," *Personality and Social Psychology Bulletin* 34, no. 9 (2008), pp. 1260–1275; Q. Wang, "On the Cultural Constitution of Collective Memory," *Memory* 16, no. 3 (2008), pp. 305–317; D. C. Park, "Developing a Cultural Cognitive Neuroscience of Aging," in S. M. Hofer and D. F. Alwin (Eds.), *Handbook of Cognitive Aging* (Thousand Oaks, CA: Sage Publications, 2008), pp. 352-367; and C. West, "How Culture Affects the Way We Think," *APS Observer* 20, no. 7 (2007), pp. 25–26.

we engage in **selective perception**. A classic example shows how vested interests can significantly influence which problems we see.

Dearborn and Simon asked 23 business executives (6 in sales, 5 in production, 4 in accounting, and 8 in miscellaneous functions) to read a comprehensive case describing the organization and activities of a steel company.[6] Each manager was asked to write down the most important problem in the case. Eighty-three percent of the sales executives rated sales important; only 29 percent of the others did so. The researchers concluded that participants perceived as important the aspects of a situation specifically related to their own unit's activities and goals. A group's perception of organizational activities is selectively altered to align with the vested interests the group represents.

Because we cannot assimilate all that we observe, we take in bits and pieces. But we don't choose randomly; rather, we select according to our interests, background, experience, and attitudes. Selective perception allows us to speed-read others, but not without the risk of drawing an inaccurate picture. Seeing what we want to see, we can draw unwarranted conclusions from an ambiguous situation.

We find another example of selective perception in financial analysis. From 2007 to 2009, the U.S. stock market lost roughly half its value. Yet during that time, sell ratings (typically, analysts rate a company's stock with three recommendations: buy, sell, or hold) from analysts actually *decreased* slightly. Although there are several reasons why analysts are reluctant to put sell ratings on stocks,

characterized more by the absence of unfavorable characteristics than by the presence of favorable ones.

Performance Expectations   People attempt to validate their perceptions of reality even when they are faulty.[16] The terms **self-fulfilling prophecy** and *Pygmalion effect* describe how an individual's behavior is determined by others' expectations. If a manager expects big things from her people, they're not likely to let her down. Similarly, if she expects only minimal performance, they'll likely meet those low expectations. Expectations become reality. The self-fulfilling prophecy has been found to affect the performance of students, soldiers, and even accountants.[17]

Performance Evaluation   We'll discuss performance evaluations more fully in Chapter 17, but note for now that they very much depend on the perceptual process.[18] An employee's future is closely tied to the appraisal—promotion, pay raises, and continuation of employment are among the most obvious outcomes. Although the appraisal can be objective (for example, a salesperson is appraised on how many dollars of sales he generates in his territory), many jobs are evaluated in subjective terms. Subjective evaluations, though often necessary, are problematic because all the errors we've discussed thus far—selective perception, contrast effects, halo effects, and so on—affect them. Ironically, sometimes performance ratings say as much about the evaluator as they do about the employee!

The Link Between Perception and Individual Decision Making

4 Explain the link between perception and decision making.

Individuals in organizations make **decisions**, choices from among two or more alternatives. Top managers determine their organization's goals, what products or services to offer, how best to finance operations, or where to locate a new manufacturing plant. Middle- and lower-level managers set production schedules, select new employees, and decide how to allocate pay raises. Nonmanagerial employees decide how much effort to put forth at work and whether to comply with a request by the boss. In recent years, organizations have been empowering their nonmanagerial employees with decision making authority historically reserved for managers alone. Individual decision making is thus an important part of organizational behavior. But how individuals make decisions and the quality of their choices are largely influenced by their perceptions.

Decision making occurs as a reaction to a **problem**.[19] That is, a discrepancy exists between the current state of affairs and some desired state, requiring us to consider alternative courses of action. If your car breaks down and you rely on it to get to work, you have a problem that requires a decision on your part. Unfortunately, most problems don't come neatly labeled "problem." One person's *problem* is

self-fulfilling prophecy   *A situation in which a person inaccurately perceives a second person, and the resulting expectations cause the second person to behave in ways consistent with the original perception.*

decisions   *Choices made from among two or more alternatives.*

problem   *A discrepancy between the current state of affairs and some desired state.*

Delta Airlines management made a decision in reaction to the problem of negative publicity resulting from a growing number of customer complaints about poor service. To improve service, Delta reinstated the personal assistance of its elite Red Coat airport agents that it started in the 1960s but eliminated in 2005 due to budget cuts. The primary mission of the Red Coats, such as Charmaine Gordon shown here helping customers at Kennedy International Airport in New York, is to fix customer problems. The agents help customers on the spot with everything from printing boarding passes to directing them to the right concourse.

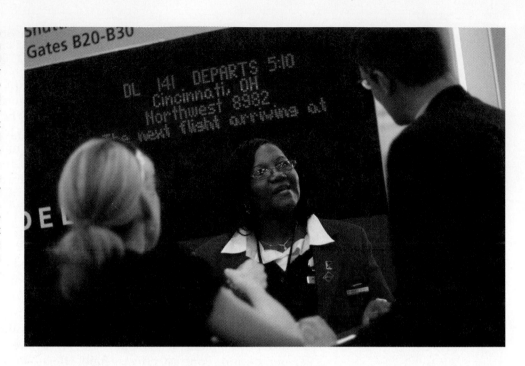

another person's *satisfactory state of affairs*. One manager may view her division's 2 percent decline in quarterly sales to be a serious problem requiring immediate action on her part. In contrast, her counterpart in another division, who also had a 2 percent sales decrease, might consider that quite acceptable. So awareness that a problem exists and that a decision might or might not be needed is a perceptual issue.

Every decision requires us to interpret and evaluate information. We typically receive data from multiple sources and need to screen, process, and interpret it. Which data are relevant to the decision, and which are not? The decision maker's perceptions will answer that question. We also need to develop alternatives and evaluate their strengths and weaknesses. Again, the individual's perceptual process will affect the final outcome. Finally, throughout the entire decision-making process, perceptual distortions often surface that can bias analysis and conclusions.

Decision Making in Organizations

Business schools generally train students to follow rational decision-making models. While these models have considerable merit, they don't always describe how people actually make decisions. This is where OB enters the picture: to improve how we make decisions in organizations, we must understand the decision-making errors people commit (in addition to the perception errors we've discussed). Next we describe these errors, beginning with a brief overview of the rational decision-making model.

The Rational Model, Bounded Rationality, and Intuition

5 Apply the rational model of decision making and contrast it with bounded rationality and intuition.

Rational Decision Making   We often think the best decision maker is **rational** and makes consistent, value-maximizing choices within specified constraints.[20] These decisions follow a six-step **rational decision-making model**.[21] The six steps are listed in Exhibit 6-3.

Exhibit **6-3**	Steps in the Rational Decision-Making Model

1. Define the problem.
2. Identify the decision criteria.
3. Allocate weights to the criteria.
4. Develop the alternatives.
5. Evaluate the alternatives.
6. Select the best alternative.

The rational decision-making model relies on a number of assumptions, including that the decision maker has complete information, is able to identify all the relevant options in an unbiased manner, and chooses the option with the highest utility.[22] As you might imagine, most decisions in the real world don't follow the rational model. People are usually content to find an acceptable or reasonable solution to a problem rather than an optimal one. Choices tend to be limited to the neighborhood of the problem symptom and the current alternative. As one expert in decision making put it, "Most significant decisions are made by judgment, rather than by a defined prescriptive model."[23] What's more, people are remarkably unaware of making suboptimal decisions.[24]

Bounded Rationality   The limited information-processing capability of human beings makes it impossible to assimilate and understand all the information necessary to optimize.[25] So most people respond to a complex problem by reducing it to a level at which they can readily understand it. Also many problems likely don't have an optimal solution because they are too complicated to be broken down into the parameters of the rational decision-making model. So people *satisfice;* that is, they seek solutions that are satisfactory and sufficient.

When you considered which college to attend, did you look at every viable alternative? Did you carefully identify all the criteria that were important in your decision? Did you evaluate each alternative against the criteria in order to find the optimal college? The answers are probably "no." Well, don't feel bad. Few people made their college choice this way. Instead of optimizing, you probably satisficed.

Because the human mind cannot formulate and solve complex problems with full rationality, we operate within the confines of **bounded rationality**. We construct simplified models that extract the essential features from problems without capturing all their complexity.[26] We can then behave rationally within the limits of the simple model.

How does bounded rationality work for the typical individual? Once we've identified a problem, we begin to search for criteria and alternatives. But the list of criteria is likely to be far from exhaustive. We identify a limited list of the most conspicuous choices, both easy to find and highly visible, that usually represent familiar criteria and tried-and-true solutions. Next, we begin reviewing them, but our review will not be comprehensive. Instead, we focus on alternatives that differ only in a relatively small degree from the choice currently in effect. Following

rational   *Characterized by making consistent, value-maximizing choices within specified constraints.*

rational decision-making model   *A decision-making model that describes how individuals should behave in order to maximize some outcome.*

bounded rationality   *A process of making decisions by constructing simplified models that extract the essential features from problems without capturing all their complexity.*

Top managers of Nike, Inc., operated within the confines of bounded rationality in making a decision about its operations in China. To reinforce its future development and rapid growth in China, Nike decided to invest $99 million to build a new distribution center in Jiangsu for the company's footwear, apparel, and equipment products. With China overtaking Japan as Nike's second-largest market after the United States, the new distribution center is expected to reduce product delivery times by up to 14 percent to the more than 3,000 Nike retail stores in China.

familiar and well-worn paths, we review alternatives only until we identify one that is "good enough"—that meets an acceptable level of performance. That ends our search. So the solution represents a satisficing choice—the first *acceptable* one we encounter—rather than an optimal one.

This process of satisficing is not always a bad idea—using a simple process may frequently be more sensible than the traditional rational decision-making model.[27] To use the rational model in the real world, you need to gather a great deal of information about all the options, compute applicable weights, and then calculate values across a huge number of criteria. All these processes can cost you time, energy, and money. And if there are a great number of unknowns when it comes to weights and preferences, the fully rational model may not be any more accurate than a best guess. Sometimes a fast-and-frugal process of solving problems might be your best option. Returning to your college choice, would it really be smarter to fly around the country to visit dozens of potential campuses, paying application fees for all these options? Can you really even know what type of college is "best" for you when you're just graduating from high school, or is there a lot of unknown information about how your interests are going to develop over time? Maybe you won't major in the same subject you started with. It might be much smarter to find a few colleges that match most of your preferences and then focus your attention on differentiating between those.

Intuition   Perhaps the least rational way of making decisions is to rely on intuition. **Intuitive decision making** is an unconscious process created from distilled experience.[28] Its defining qualities are that it occurs outside conscious thought; it relies on holistic associations, or links between disparate pieces of information; it's fast; and it's *affectively charged*, meaning it usually engages the emotions.[29]

While intuition isn't rational, it isn't necessarily wrong. Nor does it always operate in opposition to rational analysis; rather, the two can complement each other. But intuition is not superstition, or the product of some magical or paranormal sixth sense. As one recent review noted, "Intuition is a highly complex and highly developed form of reasoning that is based on years of experience and learning."[30]

For most of the twentieth century, experts believed decision makers' use of intuition was irrational or ineffective. That's no longer the case.[31] We now recognize that rational analysis has been overemphasized and, in certain instances, relying on intuition can improve decision making.[32] But we can't rely on it too much. Because it is so unquantifiable, it's hard to know when our hunches are right or wrong. The key is neither to abandon nor rely solely on intuition but to supplement it with evidence and good judgment.

Common Biases and Errors in Decision Making

6 List and explain the common decision biases or errors.

Decision makers engage in bounded rationality, but they also allow systematic biases and errors to creep into their judgments.[33] To minimize effort and avoid difficult trade-offs, people tend to rely too heavily on experience, impulses, gut feelings, and convenient rules of thumb. In many instances, these shortcuts are helpful. However, they can lead to severe distortions of rationality. Following are the most common biases in decision making.

Overconfidence Bias   It's been said that "no problem in judgment and decision making is more prevalent and more potentially catastrophic than overconfidence."[34] When we're given factual questions and asked to judge the probability that our answers are correct, we tend to be far too optimistic. When people say they're 65 to 70 percent confident they're right, they are actually correct only about 50 percent of the time.[35] When they say they're 100 percent sure, they tend to be 70 to 85 percent correct.[36] Here's another interesting example. In one random-sample national poll, 90 percent of U.S. adults said they expected to go to heaven. But in another random-sample national poll, only 86 percent thought Mother Teresa was in heaven. Talk about an overconfidence bias!

Individuals whose intellectual and interpersonal abilities are *weakest* are most likely to overestimate their performance and ability.[37] So as managers and employees become more knowledgeable about an issue, they become less likely to display overconfidence.[38] There's also a negative relationship between entrepreneurs' optimism and the performance of their new ventures: the more optimistic, the less successful.[39] The tendency for some entrepreneurs to be too confident about their ideas might keep them from planning how to avoid problems that arise.

Though overconfidence is most likely to surface when organizational members are working outside their area of expertise, that doesn't mean so-called experts are immune: *Fortune* investment strategist Ken Fisher proclaimed in April 2008, "The year will end in the plus column," and noted market losses "reassure me that my bet . . . was a wise one." Well, it didn't, and it wasn't! Fisher then confidently recommended buying four stocks: Toyota (then $107, trading a year later at $77), BP ($62, a year later $40), JPMorgan Chase ($46, later $33), and Abbott Labs ($55, later $43). If you split a $10,000 investment in these four stocks, you'd have had $7,162 left. At least you have to admire the triumph of confidence over merit![40]

intuitive decision making   *An unconscious process created out of distilled experience.*

Anchoring Bias   The **anchoring bias** is a tendency to fixate on initial information and fail to adequately adjust for subsequent information.[41] It occurs because our mind appears to give a disproportionate amount of emphasis to the first information it receives.[42] Anchors are widely used by people in professions in which persuasion skills are important—such as advertising, management, politics, real estate, and law. Assume two pilots—Jason and Glenda—have been laid off their current jobs, and after an extensive search their best offers are from Northwest Airlines (now merged with Delta). Each would earn the average annual pay of Northwest's narrow-body jet pilots: $126,000. Jason was a pilot for Pinnacle, a regional airline where the average annual salary is $82,000. Glenda was a pilot for FedEx, where the average annual salary is $200,000. Which pilot is most likely to accept, or be happiest with, Northwest's offer? Obviously Jason, because he is anchored by the lower salary.[43]

Any time a negotiation takes place, so does anchoring. As soon as someone states a number, it compromises your ability to ignore that number. When a prospective employer asks how much you made in your prior job, your answer typically anchors the employer's offer. (Remember this when you negotiate your salary, but set the anchor only as high as you realistically can.) Finally, the more precise your anchor, the smaller the adjustment. Some research suggests people think of adjustment after an anchor is set as rounding off a number. If you suggest an initial target salary of $55,000, your boss will consider $50,000 to $60,000 a reasonable range for negotiation, but if you mention $55,650, your boss is more likely to consider $55,000 to $56,000 the range of likely values for negotiation.[44]

Confirmation Bias   The rational decision-making process assumes that we objectively gather information. But we don't. We *selectively* gather it. The **confirmation bias** represents a specific case of selective perception: we seek out information that reaffirms our past choices, and we discount information that contradicts them.[45] We also tend to accept at face value information that confirms our preconceived views, while we are critical and skeptical of information that challenges these views. Therefore, the information we gather is typically biased toward supporting views we already hold. We even tend to seek out sources most likely to tell us what we want to hear, and we give too much weight to supporting information and too little to contradictory.

Availability Bias   More people fear flying than fear driving in a car. But if flying on a commercial airline really were as dangerous as driving, the equivalent of two 747s filled to capacity would crash every week, killing all aboard. Yet the media give much more attention to air accidents, so we tend to overstate the risk of flying and understate the risk of driving.

The **availability bias** is our tendency to base judgments on information readily available.[46] Events that evoke emotions, are particularly vivid, or are more recent tend to be more available in our memory, leading us to overestimate the chances of unlikely events such as an airplane crash. The availability bias can also explain why managers doing performance appraisals give more weight to recent employee behaviors than to behaviors of 6 or 9 months earlier or why credit-rating agencies such as Moody's or Standard & Poor's may issue overly positive ratings by relying on information presented by debt issuers, who have an incentive to offer data favorable to their case.[47]

Escalation of Commitment   Another distortion that creeps into decisions is a tendency to escalate commitment.[48] **Escalation of commitment** refers to staying with a decision even when there is clear evidence it's wrong. Consider a friend who has been dating someone for several years. Although he admits things

Myth or Science?

"Is There Really a Black Swan?"

Wall Street trader and NYU professor Nassim Nicholas Taleb is famous for his best-selling book *The Black Swan*. The title comes from John Stuart Mill's philosophical position that just because all swans we have seen are white doesn't prove there is no such thing as a black swan (there *are* black swans, though Europeans had not seen one until they were discovered in Australia in 1697). Taleb uses the term *black swan* to denote rare but highly consequential events we often fail to appreciate and argues that the subprime meltdown, the financial sector collapse, and global recession all represent such occurrences.

Taleb is correct, of course, that there are black swans. Outlier events often define the course of organizations. Yet they are generally hard to predict and difficult to manage because they are rare. Long-Term Capital Management, the hedge fund founded by Nobel laureates, did quite well until, like many investment firms, it found itself surprised by "shocks" its complex models had not considered. Once its returns went negative, like many funds, it experienced a flight-to-liquidity crisis and is no more.

How is Taleb's black swan useful? Taleb argues we are too focused on, and too confident about, future predictions. "What is surprising is not the magnitude of our forecast errors," he writes, "but our absence of awareness of it." Danger is especially great when times are good and volatility is low because, like the turkey fed every day until Thanksgiving, we discount the possibility of calamitous shocks.

According to Taleb, we should recognize the importance of what we don't know—the "unknown unknowns"—rely less on our financial models, weigh risk more, and resist the temptation to rationalize past black swan events as predictable. "Trying to model something that escapes modelization is the heart of the problem," he says.

Source: Based on N. N. Taleb, *The Black Swan: The Impact of the Highly Improbable* (New York: Random House, 2007); "Fear of the Black Swan," *Fortune* (April 14, 2008), pp. 90–91; and R. Langreth, "Black Swan Bets," *Forbes* (January 15, 2009), www.forbes.com.

aren't going too well, he says he is still going to marry her. His justification: "I have a lot invested in the relationship!"

Individuals escalate commitment to a failing course of action when they view themselves as responsible for the failure.[49] They "throw good money after bad" to demonstrate their initial decision wasn't wrong and to avoid admitting they made a mistake.[50] In fact, people who carefully gather and consider information consistent with the rational decision-making model are *more* likely to engage in escalation of commitment than those who spend less time thinking about their choices.[51] Perhaps they have invested so much time and energy into making their decisions that they have convinced themselves they're taking the right course of action and don't update their knowledge in the face of new information. Many an organization has suffered because a manager was determined to prove his or her original decision right by continuing to commit resources to a lost cause.

anchoring bias *A tendency to fixate on initial information, from which one then fails to adequately adjust for subsequent information.*

confirmation bias *The tendency to seek out information that reaffirms past choices and to discount information that contradicts past judgments.*

availability bias *The tendency for people to base their judgments on information that is readily available to them.*

escalation of commitment *An increased commitment to a previous decision in spite of negative information.*

Randomness Error   Human beings have difficulty dealing with chance. Most of us like to believe we have some control over our world and our destiny. Our tendency to believe we can predict the outcome of random events is the **randomness error**.

Decision making suffers when we try to create meaning in random events, particularly when we turn imaginary patterns into superstitions.[52] These can be completely contrived ("I never make important decisions on Friday the 13th") or evolve from a reinforced past pattern of behavior (Tiger Woods often wears a red shirt during a golf tournament's final round because he won many junior tournaments wearing red shirts). Superstitious behavior can be debilitating when it affects daily judgments or biases major decisions.

Risk Aversion   Mathematically, we should find a 50–50 flip of the coin for $100 to be worth as much as a sure promise of $50. After all, the expected value of the gamble over a number of trials is $50. However, most people don't consider these options equally valuable. Rather, nearly everyone but committed gamblers would rather have the sure thing than a risky prospect.[53] For many people, a 50–50 flip of a coin even for $200 might not be worth as much as a sure promise of $50, even though the gamble is mathematically worth twice as much as the sure thing! This tendency to prefer a sure thing over a risky outcome is **risk aversion**.

Risk aversion has important implications. To offset the risks inherent in a commission-based wage, companies pay commissioned employees considerably more than they do those on straight salaries. Risk-averse employees will stick with the established way of doing their jobs, rather than taking a chance on innovative or creative methods. Sticking with a strategy that has worked in the past does minimize risk, but in the long run it will lead to stagnation. Ambitious people with power that can be taken away (most managers) appear to be especially risk averse, perhaps because they don't want to lose on a gamble everything they've worked so hard to achieve.[54] CEOs at risk of being terminated are also exceptionally risk averse, even when a riskier investment strategy is in their firms' best interests.[55]

Because people are less likely to escalate commitment where there is a great deal of uncertainty, the implications of risk aversion aren't all bad.[56] When a risky investment isn't paying off, most people would rather play it safe and cut their losses, but if they think the outcome is a sure thing, they'll keep escalating.

Risk preference is sometimes reversed: people prefer to take their chances when trying to prevent a negative outcome.[57] They would rather take a 50–50 gamble on losing $100 than accept the certain loss of $50. Thus they will risk losing a lot of money at trial rather than settle out of court. Trying to cover up wrongdoing instead of admitting a mistake, despite the risk of truly catastrophic press coverage or even jail time, is another example. Stressful situations can make these risk preferences stronger. People will more likely engage in risk-seeking behavior for negative outcomes, and risk-averse behavior for positive outcomes, when under stress.[58]

Hindsight Bias   The **hindsight bias** is the tendency to believe falsely, after the outcome is known, that we'd have accurately predicted it.[59] When we have accurate feedback on the outcome, we seem pretty good at concluding it was obvious.

In late 2007, when former Citigroup CEO Charles O. Prince III asked Thomas Maheras, who oversaw lending at the bank, whether everything was okay, Maheras reportedly told his boss that no big losses were looming. Maheras continued to calm concerns over the bank's risks and vulnerabilities, and Prince and other Citigroup executives relied on his word. Everything was not okay, of course, and it now seems all too clear Prince should not have taken Maheras at his word. Citigroup lost billions in its mortgage-related holdings, and Prince's job went with it.

Experts faulted Prince for relying on Maheras, Maheras for relying on credit-rating agencies, and credit-rating agencies for trusting debt issuers. Former Merrill Lynch CEO John Thain—and many other Wall Street executives—took similar blame for supposedly failing to see what now seems obvious (that housing prices were inflated, too many risk loans were made, and the values of many "securities" were based on fragile assumptions). Though the criticisms may have merit, things are often all too clear in hindsight. As Malcolm Gladwell, author of *Blink* and *The Tipping Point,* writes, "What is clear in hindsight is rarely clear before the fact."[60]

The hindsight bias reduces our ability to learn from the past. It lets us think we're better predictors than we are and can make us falsely confident. If your actual predictive accuracy is only 40 percent, but you think it's 90, you're likely to be less skeptical about your predictive skills.

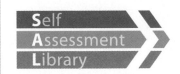

AM I A DELIBERATE DECISION MAKER?

In the Self-Assessment Library (available on CD or online), take assessment IV.A.2 (Am I a Deliberate Decision Maker?). Would it be better to be a more deliberate decision maker? Why or why not?

Influences on Decision Making: Individual Differences and Organizational Constraints

We turn here to factors that influence how people make decisions and the degree to which they are susceptible to errors and biases. We discuss individual differences and organizational constraints.

Individual Differences

7 Explain how individual differences and organizational constraints affect decision making.

Decision making in practice is characterized by bounded rationality, common biases and errors, and the use of intuition. In addition, individual differences create deviations from the rational model. In this section, we look at two such differences: personality and gender.

Personality   The little research so far conducted on personality and decision making suggests personality does influence our decisions. Let's look at conscientiousness and self-esteem (both discussed in Chapter 4).

---

randomness error   *The tendency of individuals to believe that they can predict the outcome of random events.*

risk aversion   *The tendency to prefer a sure gain of a moderate amount over a riskier outcome, even if the riskier outcome might have a higher expected payoff.*

hindsight bias   *The tendency to believe falsely, after an outcome of an event is actually known, that one would have accurately predicted that outcome.*

An Ethical Choice

Is It Wrong to Rationalize?

The self-serving bias lets us claim credit for our successes but avoid responsibility for our failures. A related concept, *rationalization,* lets us construct explanations for our behaviors that may be inaccurate or self-serving.

When are rationalizations right and wrong? The easy answer is that rationalizations are right when they're factually correct—we should explain our behavior accurately, acknowledging that luck or others' help may explain our success and that some failures are our own fault.

But even our perceptions of fact may be self serving. In one experiment, individuals rated the desirability of owning various objects and were told they could take home one of two objects they rated the same. After the subjects had made their choice, the researchers found they perceived the ob-

ject they chose as much more desirable than the one they didn't—even though minutes before they had rated them equally desirable.

How can you avoid rationalizing? Here are some guidelines:

1. **First, admit you have a problem (as do we all).** Several studies of physicians reveal that while they deny the influence on their prescribing behavior of gifts and meals from pharmaceutical representatives, such contacts do influence them. It's hard to analyze the ethicality of our behavior if we don't start by being honest with ourselves.
2. **Don't rely on public disclosure and accountability to shame people out of rationalizing.** They may only exacerbate self-serving biases because they make people more defensive. We may only succeed

in burying the rationalization so it's harder for everyone to see.
3. **Let yourself off the hook.** Everyone rationalizes at one time or another. Our tendency to rationalize may be biological—even monkeys show evidence of self-serving attributions. As one review concluded, "Bias is not a crime, is not necessarily intentional, and is not a sign of lack of integrity; rather, it is a natural human phenomenon."

Source: Based on J. Shepperd, W. Malone, and K. Sweeny, "Exploring Causes of the Self-Serving Bias," *Social and Personality Psychology Compass* 2, no. 2 (2008), pp. 895–908; D. M. Cain and A. S. Little, "Everyone's a Little Bit Biased (even Physicians)," *JAMA: Journal of the American Medical Association* 299, no. 24 (2008), pp. 2893–2895; and J. Tierney, "Go Ahead, Rationalize. Monkeys Do It, Too," *New York Times* (November 6, 2007), pp. S1–S2.

Specific facets of conscientiousness—rather than the broad trait itself—may affect escalation of commitment (see preceding "Escalation of Commitment").[61] Two such facets—achievement striving and dutifulness—actually had opposite effects. Achievement-striving people were more likely to escalate their commitment, whereas dutiful people were less likely. Why? Generally, achievement-oriented people hate to fail, so they escalate their commitment, hoping to forestall failure. Dutiful people, however, are more inclined to do what they see as best for the organization. Second, achievement-striving individuals appear to be more susceptible to the hindsight bias, perhaps because they have a greater need to justify their actions.[62] Unfortunately, we don't have evidence on whether dutiful people are immune to this bias.

Finally, people with high self-esteem are strongly motivated to maintain it, so they use the self-serving bias to preserve it. They blame others for their failures while taking credit for successes.[63]

Gender Research on rumination offers insights into gender differences in decision making.[64]

Rumination refers to reflecting at length. In terms of decision making, it means overthinking problems. Twenty years of study find women spend much more time than men analyzing the past, present, and future. They're more likely to overanalyze problems before making a decision and to rehash a decision once made. This can lead to more careful consideration of problems and choices. However, it can make problems harder to solve, increase regret over past decisions, and increase depression. Women are nearly twice as likely as men to develop depression.[65]

Why women ruminate more than men is not clear. One view is that parents encourage and reinforce the expression of sadness and anxiety more in girls than in boys. Another theory is that women, more than men, base their self-esteem and well-being on what others think of them. A third idea is that women are more empathetic and more affected by events in others' lives, so they have more to ruminate about.

By age 11, girls are ruminating more than boys. But this gender difference seems to lessen with age. Differences are largest during young adulthood and smallest after age 65, when both men and women ruminate the least.[66]

Mental Ability   We know people with higher levels of mental ability are able to process information more quickly, solve problems more accurately, and learn faster, so you might expect them also to be less susceptible to common decision errors. However, mental ability appears to help people avoid only some of these.[67] Smart people are just as likely to fall prey to anchoring, overconfidence, and escalation of commitment, probably because just being smart doesn't alert you to the possibility you're too confident or emotionally defensive. That doesn't mean intelligence never matters. Once warned about decision-making errors, more intelligent people learn more quickly to avoid them. They are also better able to avoid logical errors like false syllogisms or incorrect interpretation of data.

Organizational Constraints

Organizations can constrain decision makers, creating deviations from the rational model. For instance, managers shape their decisions to reflect the organization's performance evaluation and reward system, to comply with its formal regulations, and to meet organizationally imposed time constraints. Precedent can also limit decisions.

Performance Evaluation   Managers are strongly influenced by the criteria on which they are evaluated. If a division manager believes the manufacturing plants under his responsibility are operating best when he hears nothing negative, we shouldn't be surprised to find his plant managers spending a good part of their time ensuring that negative information doesn't reach him.

Reward Systems   The organization's reward system influences decision makers by suggesting what choices have better personal payoffs. If the organization rewards risk aversion, managers are more likely to make conservative decisions. From the 1930s through the mid-1980s, General Motors consistently gave promotions and bonuses to managers who kept a low profile and avoided controversy. They became very adept at dodging tough issues and passing controversial decisions on to committees.

Formal Regulations   David Gonzalez, a shift manager at a Taco Bell restaurant in San Antonio, Texas, describes constraints he faces on his job: "I've got rules and regulations covering almost every decision I make—from how to make a burrito to how often I need to clean the restrooms. My job doesn't come with much freedom of choice." David's situation is not unique. All but the smallest organizations create rules and policies to program decisions and get individuals to act in the intended manner. And of course, in so doing, they limit decision choices.

System-Imposed Time Constraints   Almost all important decisions come with explicit deadlines. A report on new-product development may have to be ready for executive committee review by the first of the month. Such conditions often make it difficult, if not impossible, for managers to gather all the information they might like before making a final choice.

Formal regulations shape employee decisions at McDonald's restaurants throughout the world. McDonald's standardizes the behavior of restaurant crew members such as the employee shown here preparing the company's specialty coffee, McCafé Mocha. McDonald's requires employees to follow rules and regulations for food preparation and service to meet its high standards of food quality and safety and reliable and friendly service. For example, McDonald's requires 72 safety protocols to be conducted every day in each restaurant as part of a daily monitoring routine for restaurant managers.

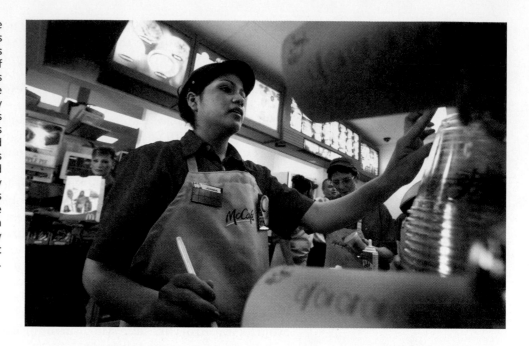

Historical Precedents Decisions aren't made in a vacuum; they have a context. In fact, individual decisions are points in a stream of choice. Those made in the past are like ghosts that haunt and constrain current choices. It's common knowledge that the largest determinant of the size of any given year's budget is last year's budget.[68] Choices made today are largely a result of choices made over the years.

What About Ethics in Decision Making?

8 Contrast the three ethical decision criteria.

Ethical considerations should be an important criterion in all organizational decision making. In this section, we present three ways to frame decisions ethically.[69]

Three Ethical Decision Criteria

The first ethical yardstick is **utilitarianism**, in which decisions are made solely on the basis of their *outcomes*, ideally to provide the greatest good for the greatest number. This view dominates business decision making. It is consistent with goals such as efficiency, productivity, and high profits.

Another ethical criterion is to make decisions consistent with fundamental liberties and privileges, as set forth in documents such as the Bill of Rights. An emphasis on *rights* in decision making means respecting and protecting the basic rights of individuals, such as the right to privacy, free speech, and due process. This criterion protects **whistle-blowers** when they reveal an organization's unethical practices to the press or government agencies, using their right to free speech.

A third criterion is to impose and enforce rules fairly and impartially to ensure *justice* or an equitable distribution of benefits and costs. Union members typically favor this view. It justifies paying people the same wage for a given job regardless of performance differences and using seniority as the primary determination in layoff decisions.

Each criterion has advantages and liabilities. A focus on utilitarianism promotes efficiency and productivity, but it can sideline the rights of some individuals, particularly those with minority representation. The use of rights protects individuals from injury and is consistent with freedom and privacy, but it can create a legalistic environment that hinders productivity and efficiency. A focus on justice protects the interests of the underrepresented and less powerful, but it can encourage a sense of entitlement that reduces risk taking, innovation, and productivity.

Decision makers, particularly in for-profit organizations, feel comfortable with utilitarianism. The "best interests" of the organization and its stockholders can justify a lot of questionable actions, such as large layoffs. But many critics feel this perspective needs to change.[70] Public concern about individual rights and social justice suggests managers should develop ethical standards based on nonutilitarian criteria. This presents a challenge because satisfying individual rights and social justice creates far more ambiguities than utilitarian effects on efficiency and profits. This helps explain why managers are increasingly criticized for their actions. Raising prices, selling products with questionable effects on consumer health, closing down inefficient plants, laying off large numbers of employees, moving production overseas to cut costs, and similar decisions can be justified in utilitarian terms. But that may no longer be the single measure by which good decisions are judged.

Improving Creativity in Decision Making

9 Define *creativity* and discuss the three-component model of creativity.

Although the rational decision-making model will often improve decisions, a rational decision maker also needs **creativity**, the ability to produce novel and useful ideas.[71] These are different from what's been done before but appropriate to the problem presented.

Why is creativity valuable in decision making? It allows the decision maker to more fully appraise and understand the problem, including seeing problems others can't see. L'Oréal puts its managers through creative exercises such as cooking or making music, and the University of Chicago requires MBA students to make short movies about their experiences.

Creative Potential   Most people have useful creative potential. But to unleash it, they have to escape the psychological ruts many of us fall into and to learn how to think about a problem in divergent ways.

Exceptional creativity is scarce. We all know of creative geniuses in science (Albert Einstein), art (Pablo Picasso), and business (Steve Jobs). But what about the typical individual? Intelligent people and those who score high on openness to experience (see Chapter 4) are more likely to be creative.[72] Other traits of creative people are independence, self-confidence, risk taking, an internal locus of control, tolerance for ambiguity, a low need for structure, and perseverance.[73] Exposure to a variety of cultures can also improve creativity.[74] Those who spend extensive periods of time in other cultures generate more innovative solutions to problems. It may be that taking an international assignment, or even an international vacation, could jump-start your creative process.

A study of the lifetime creativity of 461 men and women found fewer than 1 percent were exceptionally creative.[75] But 10 percent were highly creative and about 60 percent were somewhat creative. This reinforces that most of us have creative potential; we just need to learn to unleash it.

---

utilitarianism   *A system in which decisions are made to provide the greatest good for the greatest number.*

whistle-blowers   *Individuals who report unethical practices by their employer to outsiders.*

creativity   *The ability to produce novel and useful ideas.*

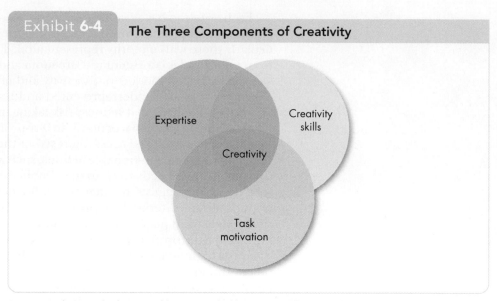

Exhibit 6-4   The Three Components of Creativity

Expertise

Creativity skills

Creativity

Task motivation

Source: Copyright © 1997, by The Regents of the University of California. Reprinted from *The California Management Review* 40, no. 1. By permission of The Regents.

Three-Component Model of Creativity   What can individuals and organizations do to stimulate employee creativity? The best answer lies in the **three-component model of creativity**,[76] which proposes that individual creativity essentially requires expertise, creative thinking skills, and intrinsic task motivation (see Exhibit 6-4). Studies confirm that the higher the level of each, the higher the creativity.

Expertise is the foundation for all creative work. The film writer, producer, and director Quentin Tarantino spent his youth working in a video rental store, where he built up an encyclopedic knowledge of movies. The potential for creativity is enhanced when individuals have abilities, knowledge, proficiencies, and similar expertise in their field of endeavor. You wouldn't expect someone with minimal knowledge of programming to be very creative as a software engineer.

The second component is *creative-thinking skills*. This encompasses personality characteristics associated with creativity, the ability to use analogies, and the talent to see the familiar in a different light.

A meta-analysis of 102 studies found positive moods increase creativity, but it depends on what sort of positive mood was considered.[77] Moods such as happiness that encourage interaction with the world are more conducive to creativity than passive moods such as calm. This means the common advice to relax and clear your mind to develop creative ideas may be misplaced. It would be better to get in an upbeat mood and then frame your work as an opportunity to have fun and experiment. Negative moods also don't always have the same effects on creativity. Passive negative moods such as sadness doesn't seem to have much effect, but avoidance-oriented negative moods such as fear and anxiety decrease creativity. Feeling threatened reduces your desire to try new activities; risk aversion increases when you're scared. Active negative moods, such as anger, however, do appear to enhance creativity, especially if you are taking your task seriously.

Being around creative others can make us more inspired, especially if we're creatively "stuck."[78] One study found that having "weak ties" to creative people— knowing them but not well—facilitates creativity because the people are there as a resource if we need them but not so close as to stunt our own independent thinking.[79]

Analogies allow decision makers to apply an idea from one context to another. One of the most famous examples was Alexander Graham Bell's observation that it might be possible to apply the way the ear operates to his "talking box." Bell noticed the bones in the ear are operated by a delicate, thin membrane. He wondered why, then, a thicker and stronger piece of membrane shouldn't be able to move a piece of steel. From that analogy, the telephone was conceived. Thinking in terms of analogies is a complex intellectual skill, which helps explain why cognitive ability is related to creativity. Demonstrating this effect, one study found children who got high scores on cognitive ability tests at age 13 were significantly more likely to have made creative achievements in their professional lives 25 years later.[80]

Some people develop creative skills because they see problems in a new way. They're able to make the strange familiar and the familiar strange.[81] For instance, most of us think of hens laying eggs. But how many of us have considered that a hen is only an egg's way of making another egg?

Creative people often love their work, to the point of seeming obsession. The final component in the three-component model of creativity is *intrinsic task motivation*. This is the desire to work on something because it's interesting, involving, exciting, satisfying, or personally challenging. It's what turns creativity *potential* into *actual* creative ideas. Environmental stimulants that foster creativity include a culture that encourages the flow of ideas; fair and constructive judgment of ideas; rewards and recognition for creative work; sufficient financial, material, and information resources; freedom to decide what work is to be done and how to do it; a supervisor who communicates effectively, shows confidence in others, and supports the work group; and work group members who support and trust each other.[82]

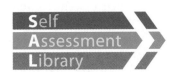

HOW CREATIVE AM I?

In the Self-Assessment Library (available on CD or online), take assessment I.A.5 (How Creative Am I?).

Global Implications

In considering potential global differences in this chapter's concepts, let's consider the three areas that have attracted the most research: (1) attributions, (2) decision making, and (3) ethics.

Attributions   The evidence on cultural differences in perception is mixed, but most suggest there *are* differences across cultures in the attributions people make.[83] We noted earlier the tendency for Asians (Japanese) to be less susceptible to the fundamental attribution error. Another study found Korean managers less likely to use the self-serving bias—they tended to accept responsibility for group failure "because I was not a capable leader" instead of attributing failure to group members.[84] On the other hand, Asian managers are

---

three-component model of creativity   *The proposition that individual creativity requires expertise, creative thinking skills, and intrinsic task motivation.*

more likely to lay blame on institutions or whole organizations, whereas Western observers are more likely to believe individual managers should be the focus of blame or praise.[85] That probably explains why U.S. newspapers prominently report the names of individual executives when firms do poorly, whereas Asian media provide more coverage of how the firm as a whole has failed. This tendency to make group-based attributions also explains why individuals from Asian cultures are more likely to make group-based stereotypes.[86] Attribution theory was developed largely based on experiments with U.S. and western European workers. But these studies suggest caution in making attribution theory predictions in non-Western societies, especially in countries with strong collectivist traditions.

These differences in attribution tendencies don't mean the basic concepts of attribution and blame completely differ across cultures, though. Recent studies suggest Chinese managers assess blame for mistakes using the same distinctiveness, consensus, and consistency cues Western managers use.[87] Chinese managers also become angry and punish those who are deemed responsible for failure, a reaction shown in many studies of Western managers. This means the basic process of attribution applies across cultures but that it takes more evidence for Asian managers to conclude someone else should be blamed.

Decision Making   The rational model makes no acknowledgment of cultural differences, nor does the bulk of OB research literature on decision making. A 2007 review of cross-cultural OB research covered 25 areas, but cultural influence on decision making was not among them. Another 2007 review identified 15 topics, but the result was the same: no research on culture and decision making.[88]

But Indonesians, for instance, don't necessarily make decisions the same way Australians do. Therefore, we need to recognize that the cultural background of a decision maker can have a significant influence on the selection of problems, the depth of analysis, the importance placed on logic and rationality, and whether organizational decisions should be made autocratically by an individual manager or collectively in groups.[89]

Cultures differ in their time orientation, the importance of rationality, their belief in the ability of people to solve problems, and their preference for col-

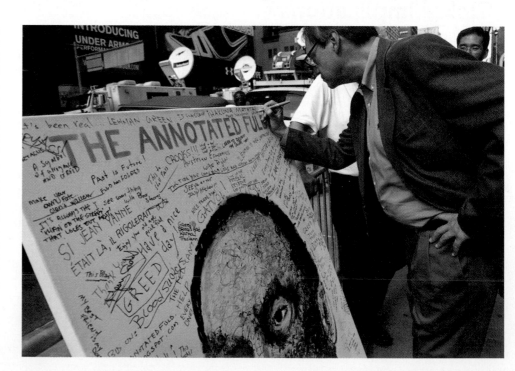

Research points to some differences across cultures in the attributions people make. For example, Asians tend to make group-based attributions about organizations, while Westerners tend to believe that individual managers should be the focus of blame or praise. When the U.S.-based financial services firm Lehman Brothers failed, many people blamed Richard Fuld, the company's chief executive, accusing him of overconfidence and anchoring biases and a lack of knowledge about complicated financial investment instruments. Comments by former employees and passersby blaming Fuld were recorded on an artist's rendering of him placed in front of Lehman's offices in New York City,

lective decision making. Differences in time orientation help us understand why managers in Egypt make decisions at a much slower and more deliberate pace than their U.S. counterparts. While rationality is valued in North America, that's not true elsewhere in the world. A North American manager might make an important decision intuitively but know it's important to appear to proceed in a rational fashion because rationality is highly valued in the West. In countries such as Iran, where rationality is not as paramount as other factors, efforts to appear rational are not necessary.

Some cultures emphasize solving problems, while others focus on accepting situations as they are. The United States falls in the first category; Thailand and Indonesia are examples of the second. Because problem-solving managers believe they can and should change situations to their benefit, U.S. managers might identify a problem long before their Thai or Indonesian counterparts would choose to recognize it as such. Decision making by Japanese managers is much more group-oriented than in the United States. The Japanese value conformity and cooperation. So before Japanese CEOs make an important decision, they collect a large amount of information, which they use in consensus-forming group decisions.

In short, there are probably important cultural differences in decision making, but unfortunately not yet much research to identify them.

Ethics   There are no global ethical standards,[90] as contrasts between Asia and the West illustrate.[91] Because bribery is commonplace in countries such as China, a Canadian working in China might face a dilemma: Should I pay a bribe to secure business if it is an accepted part of that country's culture? A manager of a large U.S. company operating in China caught an employee stealing. Following company policy, she fired him and turned him over to the local authorities. Later, she was horrified to learn the employee had been summarily executed.[92]

Although ethical standards may seem ambiguous in the West, criteria defining right and wrong are actually much clearer there than in Asia, where few issues are black and white and most are gray. Global organizations must establish ethical principles for decision makers in countries such as India and China and modify them to reflect cultural norms if they want to uphold high standards and consistent practices.

Summary and Implications for Managers

Perception   Individuals base their behavior not on the way their external environment actually is but rather on what they see or believe it to be. Whether a manager successfully plans and organizes the work of employees and actually helps them to structure their work more efficiently and effectively is far less important than how employees perceive the manager's efforts. Similarly, employees judge issues such as fair pay, performance appraisals, and working conditions in very individual ways; we cannot be assured they will interpret conditions about their jobs in a favorable light. To influence productivity, we need to assess how workers perceive their jobs.

Absenteeism, turnover, and job satisfaction are also reactions to an individual's perceptions. Dissatisfaction with working conditions and the belief that an organization lacks promotion opportunities are judgments based on attempts to create meaning in the job. The employee's conclusion that a job is good or bad is an interpretation. Managers must spend time understanding how each individual interprets reality and, when there is a significant difference between what someone sees and what exists, try to eliminate the distortions.

Individual Decision Making   Individuals think and reason before they act. This is why an understanding of how people make decisions can be helpful for explaining and predicting their behavior.

In some decision situations, people follow the rational decision-making model. But few important decisions are simple or unambiguous enough for the rational model's assumptions to apply. So we find individuals looking for solutions that satisfice rather than optimize, injecting biases and prejudices into the decision process, and relying on intuition.

What can managers do to improve their decision making? We offer four suggestions.

First, analyze the situation. Adjust your decision-making approach to the national culture you're operating in and to the criteria your organization evaluates and rewards. If you're in a country that doesn't value rationality, don't feel compelled to follow the rational decision-making model or to try to make your decisions appear rational. Similarly, organizations differ in terms of the importance they place on risk, the use of groups, and the like. Adjust your decision approach to ensure it's compatible with the organization's culture.

Second, be aware of biases. Then try to minimize their impact. Exhibit 6-5 offers some suggestions.

Third, combine rational analysis with intuition. These are not conflicting approaches to decision making. By using both, you can actually improve your decision-making effectiveness. As you gain managerial experience, you should feel increasingly confident in imposing your intuitive processes on top of your rational analysis.

Finally, try to enhance your creativity. Actively look for novel solutions to problems, attempt to see problems in new ways, and use analogies. Try to remove work and organizational barriers that might impede your creativity.

Exhibit 6-5   Reducing Biases and Errors

Focus on Goals. Without goals, you can't be rational, you don't know what information you need, you don't know which information is relevant and which is irrelevant, you'll find it difficult to choose between alternatives, and you're far more likely to experience regret over the choices you make. Clear goals make decision making easier and help you eliminate options that are inconsistent with your interests.

Look for Information That Disconfirms Your Beliefs. One of the most effective means for counteracting overconfidence and the confirmation and hindsight biases is to actively look for information that contradicts your beliefs and assumptions. When we overtly consider various ways we could be wrong, we challenge our tendencies to think we're smarter than we actually are.

Don't Try to Create Meaning out of Random Events. The educated mind has been trained to look for cause-and-effect relationships. When something happens, we ask why. And when we can't find reasons, we often invent them. You have to accept that there are events in life that are outside your control. Ask yourself if patterns can be meaningfully explained or whether they are merely coincidence. Don't attempt to create meaning out of coincidence.

Increase Your Options. No matter how many options you've identified, your final choice can be no better than the best of the option set you've selected. This argues for increasing your decision alternatives and for using creativity in developing a wide range of diverse choices. The more alternatives you can generate, and the more diverse those alternatives, the greater your chance of finding an outstanding one.

Source: S. P. Robbins, *Decide & Conquer: Making Winning Decisions and Taking Control of Your Life* (Upper Saddle River, NJ: Financial Times/Prentice Hall, 2004), pp. 164–168.

POINT  COUNTERPOINT

When in Doubt, Do!

Life is full of decisions and choices. The real question is not "To be, or not to be" but rather "To do, or not to do?" For example, "Should I confront my professor about my midterm grade?" "Should I buy a new car?" "Should I accept a new job?" "Should I choose this major?" Very often, we are unsure of our decision. In such cases, it is almost always better to choose action over inaction. In life, people more often regret inaction than action. Take the following simple example:

Say you carry an umbrella and it doesn't rain, or you don't carry an umbrella and it does rain. In which situation are you worse off? Would you rather experience the mild inconvenience of the extra weight of the umbrella or get drenched? Chances are you'll regret inaction more than action. Research shows that after we make a decision, we indeed regret inaction more than action. Although we often regret actions in their immediate aftermath, over time these regrets decline markedly, whereas regrets over missed opportunities increase. Suppose you finally decide to take a trip to Europe. You have an amazing time, but a few weeks after you get back, your credit card bill arrives—and it isn't pretty. Unfortunately, you have to work overtime and miss a few dinners out with friends to pay off the bills. A few months down the road, however, you decide to reminisce by looking through your photos from the trip, and you can't imagine not having gone. So, when in doubt, just do!

It's just silly to think that, when in doubt, you should always act. People will undoubtedly make mistakes following such simple advice. For example, you're out of work, but you still decide to purchase your dream car—a BMW, fully loaded. Not the smartest idea. So why is the motto "Just do it" dangerous? Because there are two types of regrets: hot regret, in which an individual kicks herself for having caused something bad, and wistful regret, in which she fantasizes about how else things might have turned out. The danger is that actions are more likely to lead to anguish or hot regret, and inaction is more likely to lead to wistful regret. So the bottom line is that we can't apply simple rules such as "just do it" to important decisions.[93]

Act	State	
	Rain	Shine
Carry umbrella	Dry (except your feet!)	Inconvenience
Don't carry umbrella	Miserable drenching	Unqualified bliss

Questions for Review

1 What is perception, and what factors influence our perception?

2 What is attribution theory? What are the three determinants of attribution? What are its implications for explaining organizational behavior?

3 What shortcuts do people frequently use in making judgments about others?

4 What is the link between perception and decision making? How does one affect the other?

5 What is the rational model of decision making? How is it different from bounded rationality and intuition?

6 What are some of the common decision biases or errors that people make?

7 What are the influences of individual differences, organizational constraints, and culture on decision making?

8 Are unethical decisions more a function of an individual decision maker or the decision maker's work environment? Explain.

9 What is creativity, and what is the three-component model of creativity?

Experiential Exercise

BIASES IN DECISION MAKING

Step 1
Answer each of the following problems.

1. *Fortune* magazine ranked the following 10 corporations as being among the 500 largest United States–based firms according to sales volume for 2008:

   Group A: Apple Computer, Hershey Foods, Kellogg, McDonald's, U.S. Airways

   Group B: Altria Group, AmerisourceBergen, Cardinal Health, McKesson, Valero Energy

   Which group would you say (A or B) had the larger total sales volume? By what percentage (10 percent, 50 percent, 100 percent)?

2. The best student in your introductory MBA class this past semester writes poetry and is rather shy and small in stature. What was the student's undergraduate major: Chinese studies or psychology?

3. Which of the following causes more deaths in the United States each year?

   a. Stomach cancer

   b. Motor vehicle accidents

4. Which would you choose?

   a. A sure gain of $240

   b. A 25 percent chance of winning $1,000 and a 75 percent chance of winning nothing

5. Which would you choose?

   a. A sure loss of $750

   b. A 75 percent chance of losing $1,000 and a 25 percent chance of losing nothing

6. Which would you choose?

   a. A sure loss of $3,000

   b. An 80 percent chance of losing $4,000 and a 20 percent chance of losing nothing

Step 2
Break into groups of three to five students. Compare your answers. Explain why you chose the answers you did.

Step 3
Your instructor will give you the correct answers to each problem. Now discuss the accuracy of your decisions, the biases evident in the decisions you reached, and how you might improve your decision making to make it more accurate.

Source: These problems are based on examples provided in M. H. Bazerman, *Judgment in Managerial Decision Making*, 3rd ed. (New York: Wiley, 1994).

Ethical Dilemma

FIVE ETHICAL DECISIONS: WHAT WOULD YOU DO?

How would you respond to each of the following situations?

1. You're a middle manager in a company with about a thousand employees. You're negotiating a contract with a very large potential customer whose representative has hinted you could almost certainly be assured of getting his business if you gave him and his wife an all-expenses-paid cruise to the Caribbean. You know the representative's employer wouldn't approve of such a "payoff," but you have the discretion to authorize it. What would you do?

2. You have an autographed CD by Sean Combs (signed "PuffD") and put it up for sale on eBay. So far, the highest bid is $74.50. A friend has offered you $100 for the CD, commenting that he could get $150 for it on eBay in a year. You know this is highly unlikely. Should you sell your friend the CD for what he offered ($100)? Do you have an obligation to tell your friend you have listed your CD on eBay?

3. Your company's policy on reimbursement for meals while traveling on business is that you will be repaid for out-of-pocket costs, not to exceed $80 per day. You don't need receipts for these expenses—the company will take your word. When traveling, you tend to eat at fast-food places and rarely spend in excess of $20 a day. Most of your colleagues put in reimbursement requests in the range of $55 to $60 per day, regardless of what their actual expenses are. How much would you request for your meal reimbursements?

4. You work for a company that manufactures, markets, and distributes various products, including nutritional supplements, to health food and nutrition stores. One of the company's best-selling products is Rosalife, an herbal supplement. The company advertises that Rosalife "achieves all the gains of estrogen hormone replacement therapy without any of the side effects." One day, a research assistant stops by your office with some troubling information. While researching another product, she came across a recent study that suggests Rosalife does not offer the benefits the company claims it does. You show this study to your supervisor, who says, "We're not responsible for validating non-FDA-controlled products, and nobody's hurt anyway." Indeed, you know this is not the case. What is your ethical responsibility?

5. You're the manager at a gaming company, and you're responsible for outsourcing the production of a highly anticipated new game. Because your company is a giant in the industry, numerous companies are trying to get the bid. One of them offers you some kickbacks if you give that firm the bid, but ultimately, it is up to your bosses to decide on the company. You don't mention the incentive, but you push upper management to give the bid to the company that offered you the kickback. Is withholding the truth as bad as lying? Why or why not?

Case Incident 1

NATURAL DISASTERS AND THE DECISIONS THAT FOLLOW

Jeff Rommel's introduction to Florida could be described as trial by hurricane. Rommel took over Florida operations for Nationwide Insurance in 2004. Over a 2-month period that year, Florida experienced its worst hurricane season in history—four major hurricanes (Charley, Frances, Ivan, and Jeanne) slammed the state, causing an estimated $40 billion in damage. In the hurricanes' wake, Nationwide received more than 119,000 claims, collectively worth $850 million.

Although dealing with those claims was difficult, even more difficult was Rommel's later decision to cancel approximately 40,000 homeowners' policies. Nationwide received a huge amount of media attention as a result, almost all negative. In reflecting on the decision, Rommel said,

"Pulling out was a sound business decision. Was it good for the individual customer? No, I can't say it was. But the rationale was sound."

Hurricanes aren't the only weapons in nature's arsenal, and the insurance industry is hardly the only industry affected by nature. Consider the airline industry. American Airlines has 80,000 employees, 4 of whom make decisions to cancel flights. One of them is Danny Burgin. When a weather system approaches, Burgin needs to consider a host of factors in deciding which flights to cancel and how to reroute affected passengers. He argues that of two major weather factors, winter snowstorms and summer thunderstorms, snowstorms are easier to handle because they are more predictable.

Don't tell that to JetBlue, however. On February 14, 2007, JetBlue was unprepared for a snowstorm that hit the East Coast. Due to the lack of planning, JetBlue held hundreds of passengers on its planes at JFK, in some cases for as long as 10 hours (with bathrooms closed!). To the stranded travelers, JetBlue's tepid offer of a refund was just as outrageous. For a carrier that prided itself on customer service and had regularly been rated the top U.S. airline in customer satisfaction, it was a public relations disaster. Linda Hirneise, an analyst at J.D. Power, said, "It did not appear JetBlue had a plan." In defending the airline, JetBlue's founder and then-CEO, David Neeleman, said, "Is our good will gone? No, it isn't. We fly 30 million people a year. Ten thousand were affected by this." In responding to another interviewer, he said, "You're overdoing it. Delta screwed people for two days, and we did it for three and a half, okay? So go ask Delta what they did about it. Why don't you grill them?" Eventually, though, Neeleman himself was affected by it, and he stepped down.

Questions

1. Insurance companies in the state of Florida earned record profits in 2006, suggesting in light of the calm hurricane seasons (in Florida) in 2005–2007 that Nationwide's decision to cancel policies may have cost the company potential revenue and customer goodwill. Do you think Rommel's quote about making a "sound business decision" reveals any perceptual or decision-making biases? Why or why not?

2. Review the section on common biases and errors in decision making. For companies such as Nationwide, American Airlines, and JetBlue that must respond to natural events, which biases and errors are relevant and why?

3. In each of the three cases discussed here, which organizational constraints were factors in the decisions made?

4. How do you think people like Rommel, Burgin, and Neeleman factor ethics into their decisions? Do you think the welfare of policy owners and passengers enter into their decisions?

Source: Based on M. Blomberg, "Insuring the Nation," *Gainesville (Florida) Sun* (February 27, 2006), pp. 1D, 8D; M. Trottman, "Choices in Stormy Weather," *Wall Street Journal* (February 14, 2006), pp. B1, B2; C. Salter, "Lessons from the Tarmac," *Fast Company,* May 2007, pp. 31–32; and D. Q. Wilber, "Tale of Marooned Passengers Galvanizes Airline Opponents," *Washington Post* (February 16, 2007), p. D1.

Case Incident 2

PREDICTIONS

Consider the following:

- **Prediction:** "A very powerful and durable rally is in the works."—Richard Band, editor, *Profitable Investing Letter* (March 27, 2008)

  Status: At that time, the Dow average was trading at 12,300; one year later, it was at 6,626.

- **Prediction:** AIG "could have huge gains in the second quarter."—Bijan Moazami, analyst, Friedman, Billings, Ramsey (May 9, 2008)

  Status: AIG lost $5 billion that quarter, $25 billion the next, and $62 billion the quarter after that, before being given a $90 billion credit by the U.S. government in 2008–2009.

- **Prediction:** "Freddie Mac and Fannie Mae are fundamentally sound . . . in good shape moving forward."—Barnie Frank, House Financial Services Chairman (July 14, 2008)

  Status: By August 2008, Fannie Mae and Freddie Mac were downgraded to the lowest credit ratings; on September 7, 2008, they were placed in conservatorship in "one of the most sweeping government interventions in private financial markets" in history.

- **Prediction:** "I think Bob Steel's the one guy I trust to turn this bank around, which is why I've told you . . . buy Wachovia."—Jim Cramer, CNBC (September 15, 2008)

  Status: Wachovia shares lost half their value from September 15 to December 29, and Wachovia was taken over by Wells Fargo.

- **Prediction:** "I think you'll see $150 a barrel [oil] by the end of the year."—T. Boone Pickens, investor (June 20, 2008)

  Status: By December of 2008, oil was trading at $40 per barrel.

- **Prediction:** "In today's regulatory environment, it's virtually impossible to violate rules . . . your money is safe with me."—Bernie Madoff (October 20, 2007)

  Status: In 2009 Judge Denny Chin handed Madoff a 150-year sentence for his "extraordinarily evil" Ponzi scheme, defrauding investors in the biggest financial swindle in history.

• **Prediction:** "Smart investors should buy [Merrill Lynch] stock before everyone else comes to their senses."—Jon Birger, senior writer, *Fortune's Investors Guide 2008*

Status: Merrill agreed to be acquired by Bank of America to avoid insolvency; the takeover nearly cost Bank of America its own solvency.

Questions

1. Do you think these examples paint a misleading or unfair picture of financial market predictions? Why or why not?

2. What perceptual or decision-making errors can you identify in these predictions?

3. Why do we like making predictions so much?

4. Why do you think predictions seem so hard to make?

Source: Based on P. Coy, "Worst Predictions about 2008," *Business Week* (January 12, 2009), pp. 15–16; D. Ng, "How Wrong They Were!" *The World I Know* (January 4, 2009), danielngsh.blogspot.com; and R. Frank and A. Efrati, "'Evil' Madoff Gets 150 Years in Epic Fraud," *Wall Street Journal* (June 30, 2009), pp. A1, A12.

Endnotes

1. M. Helft, "The Human Hands Behind the Google Money Machine," *New York Times* (June 2, 2008), pp. B1, B7; "How Google Fuels Its Idea Factor," *Business Week* (May 12, 2008), pp. 54–55; C. Danulotf, "Is The Hype Over Google AdWords Quality Score Justified?," *Search Engine Land* (April 27, 2009), searchengineland.com.

2. H. H. Kelley, "Attribution in Social Interaction," in E. Jones et al. (eds.), *Attribution: Perceiving the Causes of Behavior* (Morristown, NJ: General Learning Press, 1972).

3. See L. Ross, "The Intuitive Psychologist and His Shortcomings," in L. Berkowitz (ed.), *Advances in Experimental Social Psychology*, vol. 10 (Orlando, FL: Academic Press, 1977), pp. 174–220; and A. G. Miller and T. Lawson, "The Effect of an Informational Option on the Fundamental Attribution Error," *Personality and Social Psychology Bulletin*, June 1989, pp. 194–204.

4. See, for instance, G. Johns, "A Multi-Level Theory of Self-Serving Behavior in and by Organizations," in R. I. Sutton and B. M. Staw (eds.), *Research in Organizational Behavior*, vol. 21 (Stamford, CT: JAI Press, 1999), pp. 1–38; N. Epley and D. Dunning, "Feeling 'Holier Than Thou': Are Self-Serving Assessments Produced by Errors in Self- or Social Prediction?" *Journal of Personality and Social Psychology*, December 2000, pp. 861–875; and M. Goerke, J. Moller, S. Schulz-Hardt, U. Napiersky, and D. Frey, "'It's Not My Fault—But Only I Can Change It': Counterfactual and Prefactual Thoughts of Managers," *Journal of Applied Psychology*, April 2004, pp. 279–292.

5. See D. M. Cain and A. S. Little, "Everyone's a Little Bit Biased (even Physicians)," *JAMA: Journal of the American Medical Association* 299, no. 24 (2008), pp. 2893–2895.

6. D. C. Dearborn and H. A. Simon, "Selective Perception: A Note on the Departmental Identification of Executives," *Sociometry*, June 1958, pp. 140–144. Some of the conclusions in this classic study have recently been challenged in J. Walsh, "Selectivity and Selective Perception: An Investigation of Managers' Belief Structures and Information Processing," *Academy of Management Journal*, December 1988, pp. 873–896; M. J. Waller, G. Huber, and W. H. Glick, "Functional Background as a Determinant of Executives' Selective Perception," *Academy of Management Journal*, August 1995, pp. 943–974; and J. M. Beyer, P. Chattopadhyay, E. George, W. H. Glick, D. T. Ogilvie, and D. Pugliese, "The Selective Perception of Managers Revisited," *Academy of Management Journal*, June 1997, pp. 716–737.

7. J. Healy and M. M. Grynbaum, "Why Analysts Keep Telling Investors to Buy," *New York Times* (February 9, 2009), pp. B1, B7.

8. See K. R. Murphy, R. A. Jako, and R. L. Anhalt, "Nature and Consequences of Halo Error: A Critical Analysis," *Journal of Applied Psychology*, April 1993, pp. 218–225; P. Rosenzweig, *The Halo Effect* (New York: The Free Press, 2007); I. Dennis, "Halo Effects in Grading Student Projects," *Journal of Applied Psychology* 92, no. 4 (2007), pp. 1169–1176; and C. E. Naquin and R. O. Tynan, "The Team Halo Effect: Why Teams Are Not Blamed for Their Failures," *Journal of Applied Psychology*, April 2003, pp. 332–340.

9. S. E. Asch, "Forming Impressions of Personality," *Journal of Abnormal and Social Psychology*, July 1946, pp. 258–290.

10. J. L. Hilton and W. von Hippel, "Stereotypes," in J. T. Spence, J. M. Darley, and D. J. Foss (eds.), *Annual Review of Psychology*, vol. 47 (Palo Alto, CA: Annual Reviews, 1996), pp. 237–271.

11. See, for example, G. N. Powell, "The Good Manager: Business Students' Stereotypes of Japanese Managers Versus Stereotypes of American Managers," *Group & Organizational Management*, March 1992, pp. 44–56; C. Ostroff and L. E. Atwater, "Does Whom You Work with Matter? Effects of Referent Group Gender and Age Composition on Managers' Compensation," *Journal of Applied Psychology*, August 2003, pp. 725–740; M. E. Heilman, A. S. Wallen, D. Fuchs, and M. M. Tamkins, "Penalties for Success: Reactions to Women Who Succeed at Male Gender-Typed Tasks," *Journal of Applied Psychology*, June 2004, pp. 416–427; and R. A. Posthuma and M. A. Campion, "Age Stereotypes in the Workplace: Common Stereotypes, Moderators, and Future Research Directions," *Journal of Management* 35, no. 1 (2009), pp. 158–188.

12. J. L. Eberhardt, P. G. Davies, V. J. Purdic-Vaughns, and S. L. Johnson, "Looking Deathworthy: Perceived Stereotypicality of Black Defendants Predicts Capital-Sentencing Outcomes," *Psychological Science* 17, no. 5 (2006), pp. 383–386.

13. H. G. Heneman III and T. A. Judge, *Staffing Organizations* (Middleton, WI: Mendota House, 2006).

14. J. Willis and A. Todorov, "First Impressions: Making Up Your Mind After a 100ms Exposure to a Face," *Psychological Science,* July 2006, pp. 592–598.

15. See, for example, E. C. Webster, *Decision Making in the Employment Interview* (Montreal: McGill University, Industrial Relations Center, 1964).

16. See, for example, D. B. McNatt, "Ancient Pygmalion Joins Contemporary Management: A Meta-analysis of the Result," *Journal of Applied Psychology,* April 2000, pp. 314–322; O. B. Davidson and D. Eden, "Remedial Self-Fulfilling Prophecy: Two Field Experiments to Prevent Golem Effects Among Disadvantaged Women," *Journal of Applied Psychology,* June 2000, pp. 386–398; D. Eden, "Self-Fulfilling Prophecies in Organizations," in J. Greenberg (ed.), *Organizational Behavior: The State of the Science,* 2nd ed. (Mahwah, NJ: Lawrence Erlbaum, 2003), pp. 91–122; and G. Natanovich and D. Eden, "Pygmalion Effects Among Outreach Supervisors and Tutors: Extending Sex Generalizability," *Journal of Applied Psychology* 93, no. 6 (2008), pp. 1382–1389.

17. D. Eden and A. B. Shani, "Pygmalion Goes to Boot Camp: Expectancy, Leadership, and Trainee Performance," *Journal of Applied Psychology,* April 1982, pp. 194–199; and D. B. McNatt and T. A. Judge, "Boundary Conditions of the Galatea Effect: A Field Experiment and Constructive Replication," *Academy of Management Journal,* August 2004, pp. 550–565.

18. See, for example, K. F. E. Wong and J. Y. Y. Kwong, "Effects of Rater Goals on Rating Patterns: Evidence from an Experimental Field Study," *Journal of Applied Psychology* 92, no. 2 (2007), pp. 577–585; and S. E. DeVoe and S. S. Iyengar, "Managers' Theories of Subordinates: A Cross-Cultural Examination of Manager Perceptions of Motivation and Appraisal of Performance," *Organizational Behavior and Human Decision Processes,* January 2004, pp. 47–61.

19. R. Sanders, *The Executive Decisionmaking Process: Identifying Problems and Assessing Outcomes* (Westport, CT: Quorum, 1999).

20. See H. A. Simon, "Rationality in Psychology and Economics," *Journal of Business,* October 1986, pp. 209–224; and E. Shafir and R. A. LeBoeuf, "Rationality," in S. T. Fiske, D. L. Schacter, and C. Zahn-Waxler, eds., *Annual Review of Psychology,* vol. 53 (Palo Alto, CA: Annual Reviews, 2002), pp. 491–517.

21. For a review of the rational decision-making model, see E. F. Harrison, *The Managerial Decision-Making Process,* 5th ed. (Boston: Houghton Mifflin, 1999), pp. 75–102.

22. J. G. March, *A Primer on Decision Making* (New York: The Free Press, 1994), pp. 2–7; and D. Hardman and C. Harries, "How Rational Are We?" *Psychologist,* February 2002, pp. 76–79.

23. M. Bazerman, *Judgment in Managerial Decision Making,* 3rd ed. (New York: Wiley, 1994), p. 5.

24. J. E. Russo, K. A. Carlson, and M. G. Meloy, "Choosing an Inferior Alternative," *Psychological Science* 17, no. 10 (2006), pp. 899–904.

25. D. Kahneman, "Maps of Bounded Rationality: Psychology for Behavioral Economics," *The American Economic Review* 93, no. 5 (2003), pp. 1449–1475; and J. Zhang, C. K. Hsee, and Z. Xiao, "The Majority Rule in Individual Decision Making," *Organizational Behavior and Human Decision Processes* 99 (2006), pp. 102–111.

26. See H. A. Simon, *Administrative Behavior,* 4th ed. (New York: The Free Press, 1997); and M. Augier, "Simon Says: Bounded Rationality Matters," *Journal of Management Inquiry,* September 2001, pp. 268–275.

27. G. Gigerenzer, "Why Heuristics Work," *Perspectives on Psychological Science* 3, no. 1 (2008), pp. 20–29; and A. K. Shah and D. M. Oppenheimer, "Heuristics Made Easy: An Effort-Reduction Framework," *Psychological Bulletin* 134, no. 2 (2008), pp. 207–222.

28. See T. Gilovich, D. Griffin, and D. Kahneman, *Heuristics and Biases: The Psychology of Intuitive Judgment* (New York: Cambridge University Press, 2002).

29. E. Dane and M. G. Pratt, "Exploring Intuition and Its Role in Managerial Decision Making," *Academy of Management Review* 32, no. 1 (2007), pp. 33–54.

30. P. D. Brown, "Some Hunches About Intuition," *New York Times* (November 17, 2007), p. B5.

31. See, for instance, L. A. Burke and M. K. Miller, "Taking the Mystery Out of Intuitive Decision Making," *Academy of Management Executive,* November 1999, pp. 91–99; N. Khatri and H. A. Ng, "The Role of Intuition in Strategic Decision Making," *Human Relations,* January 2000, pp. 57–86; J. A. Andersen, "Intuition in Managers: Are Intuitive Managers More Effective?" *Journal of Managerial Psychology* 15, no. 1–2 (2000), pp. 46–63; D. Myers, *Intuition: Its Powers and Perils* (New Haven, CT: Yale University Press, 2002); and L. Simpson, "Basic Instincts," *Training,* January 2003, pp. 56–59.

32. See, for instance, Burke and Miller, "Taking the Mystery Out of Intuitive Decision Making," pp. 91–99.

33. S. P. Robbins, *Decide & Conquer: Making Winning Decisions and Taking Control of Your Life* (Upper Saddle River, NJ: Financial Times/Prentice Hall, 2004), p. 13.

34. S. Plous, *The Psychology of Judgment and Decision Making* (New York: McGraw-Hill, 1993), p. 217.

35. S. Lichtenstein and B. Fischhoff, "Do Those Who Know More Also Know More About How Much They Know?" *Organizational Behavior and Human Performance,* December 1977, pp. 159–183.

36. B. Fischhoff, P. Slovic, and S. Lichtenstein, "Knowing with Certainty: The Appropriateness of Extreme Confidence," *Journal of Experimental Psychology: Human Perception and Performance,* November 1977, pp. 552–564.

37. J. Kruger and D. Dunning, "Unskilled and Unaware of It: How Difficulties in Recognizing One's Own Incompetence Lead to Inflated Self-Assessments," *Journal of Personality and Social Psychology,* November 1999, pp. 1121–1134.

38. B. Fischhoff, P. Slovic, and S. Lichtenstein, "Knowing with Certainty: The Appropriateness of Extreme Confidence," *Journal of Experimental Psychology* 3 (1977), pp. 552–564.

39. K. M. Hmieleski and R. A. Baron, "Entrepreneurs' Optimism and New Venture Performance: A Social Cognitive Perspective," *Academy of Management Journal* 52, no. 3 (2009), pp. 473–488.

40. K. Fisher, "Dear Abby," *Fortune* (April 21, 2008), p. 242; Kruger and Dunning, "Unskilled and Unaware of It."

41. See, for instance, A. Tversky and D. Kahneman, "Judgment Under Uncertainty: Heuristics and Biases," *Science,* September 1974, pp. 1124–1131.

42. J. S. Hammond, R. L. Keeney, and H. Raiffa, *Smart Choices* (Boston: HBS Press, 1999), p. 191.

43. J. Bailey, "Dreams Fly Into Reality," *New York Times* (April 10, 2008), pp. B1, B4.

44. C. Janiszewski and D. Uy, "Precision of the Anchor Influences the Amount of Adjustment," *Psychological Science* 19, no. 2 (2008), pp. 121–127.

45. See R. S. Nickerson, "Confirmation Bias: A Ubiquitous Phenomenon in Many Guises," *Review of General Psychology,* June 1998, pp. 175–220; and E. Jonas, S. Schultz-Hardt, D. Frey, and N. Thelen, "Confirmation Bias in Sequential Information Search After Preliminary Decisions," *Journal of Personality and Social Psychology,* April 2001, pp. 557–571.

46. See A. Tversky and D. Kahneman, "Availability: A Heuristic for Judging Frequency and Probability," in D. Kahneman, P. Slovic, and A. Tversky (eds.), *Judgment Under Uncertainty: Heuristics and Biases* (Cambridge, UK: Cambridge University Press, 1982), pp. 163–178; and B. J. Bushman and G. L. Wells, "Narrative Impressions of Literature: The Availability Bias and the Corrective Properties of Meta-analytic Approaches," *Personality and Social Psychology Bulletin,* September 2001, pp. 1123–1130.

47. G. Morgenson, "Debt Watchdogs: Tamed or Caught Napping?" *New York Times* (December 7, 2009), pp. 1, 32.

48. See B. M. Staw, "The Escalation of Commitment to a Course of Action," *Academy of Management Review,* October 1981, pp. 577–587; K. Fai, E. Wong, M. Yik, and J. Y. Y. Kwong, "Understanding the Emotional Aspects of Escalation of Commitment: The Role of Negative Affect," *Journal of Applied Psychology* 91, no. 2 (2006), pp. 282–297; H. Moon, "Looking Forward and Looking Back: Integrating Completion and Sunk-Cost Effects Within an Escalation-of-Commitment Progress Decision," *Journal of Applied Psychology,* February 2001, pp. 104–113; and A. Zardkoohi, "Do Real Options Lead to Escalation of Commitment? Comment," *Academy of Management Review,* January 2004, pp. 111–119.

49. B. M. Staw, "Knee-Deep in the Big Muddy: A Study of Escalating Commitment to a Chosen Course of Action," *Organizational Behavior and Human Performance* 16 (1976), pp. 27–44; and B. M. Staw, "The Escalation of Commitment: An Update and Appraisal," in Z. Shapira (ed.), *Organizational Decision Making* (New York; Cambridge University Press, 1997), pp. 121–215.

50. K. F. E. Wong and J. Y. Y. Kwong, "The Role of Anticipated Regret in Escalation of Commitment," *Journal of Applied Psychology* 92, no. 2 (2007), pp. 545–554.

51. K. F. E. Wong, J. Y. Y. Kwong, and C. K. Ng, "When Thinking Rationally Increases Biases: The Role of Rational Thinking Style in Escalation of Commitment," *Applied Psychology: An International Review* 57, no. 2 (2008), pp. 246–271.

52. See, for instance, A. James and A. Wells, "Death Beliefs, Superstitious Beliefs and Health Anxiety," *British Journal of Clinical Psychology,* March 2002, pp. 43–53.

53. See, for example, D. J. Keys and B. Schwartz, "Leaky Rationality: How Research on Behavioral Decision Making Challenges Normative Standards of Rationality," *Psychological Science* 2, no. 2 (2007), pp. 162–180; and U. Simonsohn, "Direct Risk Aversion: Evidence from Risky Prospects Valued Below Their Worst Outcome," *Psychological Science* 20, no. 6 (2009), pp. 686–692.

54. J. K. Maner, M. T. Gailliot, D. A. Butz, and B. M. Peruche, "Power, Risk, and the Status Quo: Does Power Promote Riskier or More Conservative Decision Making," *Personality and Social Psychology Bulletin* 33, no. 4 (2007), pp. 451–462.

55. A. Chakraborty, S. Sheikh, and N. Subramanian, "Termination Risk and Managerial Risk Taking," *Journal of Corporate Finance* 13, (2007), pp. 170–188.

56. X. He and V. Mittal, "The Effect of Decision Risk and Project Stage on Escalation of Commitment," *Organizational Behavior and Human Decision Processes* 103, no. 2 (2007), pp. 225–237.

57. D. Kahneman and A. Tversky, "Prospect Theory: An Analysis of Decisions Under Risk," *Econometrica* 47, no. 2 (1979), pp. 263–291; P. Bryant and R. Dunford, "The Influence of Regulatory Focus on Risky Decision-Making," *Applied Psychology: An International Review* 57, no. 2 (2008), pp. 335–359.

58. A. J. Porcelli and M. R. Delgado, "Acute Stress Modulates Risk Taking in Financial Decision Making," *Psychological Science* 20, no. 3 (2009), pp. 278–283.

59. R. L. Guilbault, F. B. Bryant, J. H. Brockway, and E. J. Posavac, "A Meta-analysis of Research on Hindsight Bias," *Basic and Applied Social Psychology,* September 2004, pp. 103–117; and L. Werth, F. Strack, and J. Foerster, "Certainty and Uncertainty: The Two Faces of the Hindsight Bias," *Organizational Behavior and Human Decision Processes,* March 2002, pp. 323–341.

60. E. Dash and J. Creswell, "Citigroup Pays for a Rush to Risk," *New York Times* (November 20, 2008), pp. 1, 28; S. Pulliam, S. Ng, and R. Smith, "Merrill Upped Ante as Boom in Mortgage Bonds Fizzled," *Wall Street Journal* (April 16, 2008), pp. A1, A14; and M. Gladwell, "Connecting the Dots," *The New Yorker,* March 10, 2003.

61. H. Moon, J. R. Hollenbeck, S. E. Humphrey, and B. Maue, "The Tripartite Model of Neuroticism and the Suppression of Depression and Anxiety within an Escalation of Commitment Dilemma," *Journal of Personality* 71 (2003), pp. 347–368; and H. Moon, "The Two Faces of Conscientiousness: Duty and Achievement Striving in Escalation of Commitment Dilemmas," *Journal of Applied Psychology* 86 (2001), pp. 535–540.

62. J. Musch, "Personality Differences in Hindsight Bias," *Memory* 11 (2003), pp. 473–489.

63. W. K. Campbell and C. Sedikides, "Self-Threat Magnifies the Self-Serving Bias: A Meta-analytic Integration," *Review of General Psychology* 3 (1999), pp. 23–43.

64. This section is based on S. Nolen-Hoeksema, J. Larson, and C. Grayson, "Explaining the Gender Difference in Depressive Symptoms," *Journal of Personality & Social Psychology,* November 1999, pp. 1061–1072; J. S. Hyde, A. H. Mezulis, and L. Y. Abramson, "The ABCs of Depression: Integrating Affective, Biological, and Cognitive Models to Explain the Emergence of the Gender Difference in Depression," *Psychological Review* 115, no. 2 (2008), pp. 291–313; and S. Nolen-Hoeksema, *Women Who Think Too Much* (New York: Henry Holt, 2003).

65. H. Connery and K. M. Davidson, "A Survey of Attitudes to Depression in the General Public: A Comparison of Age and Gender Differences," *Journal of Mental Health* 15, no. 2 (April 2006), pp. 179–189.

66. M. Elias, "Thinking It Over, and Over, and Over," *USA Today,* February 6, 2003, p. 10D.

67. K. E. Stanovich and R. F. West, "On the Relative Independence of Thinking Biases and Cognitive Ability," *Journal of Personality and Social Psychology* 94, no. 4 (2008), pp. 672–695.

68. A. Wildavsky, *The Politics of the Budgetary Process* (Boston: Little, Brown, 1964).

69. G. F. Cavanagh, D. J. Moberg, and M. Valasquez, "The Ethics of Organizational Politics," *Academy of Management Journal,* June 1981, pp. 363–374.

70. See, for example, T. Machan, ed., *Commerce and Morality* (Totowa, NJ: Rowman and Littlefield, 1988).

71. T. M. Amabile, "A Model of Creativity and Innovation in Organizations," in B. M. Staw and L. L. Cummings (eds.), *Research in Organizational Behavior,* vol. 10 (Greenwich, CT: JAI Press, 1988), p. 126; and J. E. Perry-Smith and C. E. Shalley, "The Social Side of Creativity: A Static and Dynamic Social Network Perspective," *Academy of Management Review,* January 2003, pp. 89–106.

72. G. J. Feist and F. X. Barron, "Predicting Creativity from Early to Late Adulthood: Intellect, Potential, and Personality," *Journal of Research in Personality,* April 2003, pp. 62–88.

73. R. W. Woodman, J. E. Sawyer, and R. W. Griffin, "Toward a Theory of Organizational Creativity," *Academy of Management Review,* April 1993, p. 298; J. M. George and J. Zhou, "When Openness to Experience and Conscientiousness Are Related to Creative Behavior: An Interactional Approach," *Journal of Applied Psychology,* June 2001, pp. 513–524; and E. F. Rietzschel, C. K. W. de Dreu, and B. A. Nijstad, "Personal Need for Structure and Creative Performance: The Moderating Influence of Fear of Invalidity," *Personality and Social Psychology Bulletin,* June 2007, pp. 855–866.

74. A. K. Leung, W. W. Maddux, A. D. Galinsky, and C. Chiu, "Multicultural Experience Enhances Creativity," *American Psychologist* 63, no. 3 (2008), pp. 169–180.

75. Cited in C. G. Morris, *Psychology: An Introduction,* 9th ed. (Upper Saddle River, NJ: Prentice Hall, 1996), p. 344.

76. This section is based on T. M. Amabile, "Motivating Creativity in Organizations: On Doing What You Love and Loving What You Do," *California Management Review* 40, no. 1 (Fall 1997), pp. 39–58.

77. M. Baas, C. K. W. De Dreu, and B. A. Nijstad, "A Meta-analysis of 25 Years of Mood-Creativity Research: Hedonic Tone, Activation, or Regulatory Focus?" *Psychological Bulletin* 134, no. 6 (2008), pp. 779–806.

78. J. Zhou, "When the Presence of Creative Coworkers Is Related to Creativity: Role of Supervisor Close Monitoring, Developmental Feedback, and Creative Personality," *Journal of Applied Psychology* 88, no. 3 (June 2003), pp. 413–422.

79. J. E. Perry-Smith, "Social yet Creative: The Role of Social Relationships in Facilitating Individual Creativity," *Academy of Management Journal* 49, no. 1 (2006), pp. 85–101.

80. G. Park, D. Lubinski, and C. P. Benbow, "Contrasting Intellectual Patterns Predict Creativity in the Arts and Sciences," *Psychological Science* 18, no. 11 (2007), pp. 948–952.

81. W. J. J. Gordon, *Synectics* (New York: Harper & Row, 1961).

82. See C. E. Shalley, J. Zhou, and G. R. Oldham, "The Effects of Personal and Contextual Characteristics on Creativity: Where Should We Go from Here?" *Journal of Management,* November 2004, pp. 933–958; G. Hirst, D. Van Knippenberg, and J. Zhou, "A Cross-Level Perspective on Employee Creativity: Goal Orientation, Team Learning Behavior, and Individual Creativity," *Academy of Management Journal* 52, no. 2 (2009), pp. 280–293; and C. E. Shalley, L. L. Gilson, and T. C. Blum, "Interactive Effects of Growth Need Strength, Work Context, and Job Complexity on Self-Reported Creative Performance," *Academy of Management Journal* 52, no. 3 (2009), pp. 489–505.

83. See, for instance, D. S. Krull, M. H.-M. Loy, J. Lin, C.-F. Wang, S. Chen, and X. Zhao, "The Fundamental Attribution Error: Correspondence Bias in Individualistic and Collectivist Cultures," *Personality & Social Psychology Bulletin,* October 1999, pp. 1208–1219; and F. F. T. Chiang and T. A. Birch, "Examining the Perceived Causes of Successful Employee Performance: An East-West Comparison," *International Journal of Human Resource Management* 18, no. 2 (2007), pp. 232–248.

84. S. Nam, "Cultural and Managerial Attributions for Group Performance," unpublished doctoral dissertation, University of Oregon. Cited in R. M. Steers, S. J. Bischoff, and L. H. Higgins, "Cross-Cultural Management Research," *Journal of Management Inquiry,* December 1992, pp. 325–326.

85. T. Menon, M. W. Morris, C. Y. Chiu, and Y. Y. Hong, "Culture and the Construal of Agency: Attribution to Individual Versus Group Dispositions," *Journal of Personality and Social Psychology* 76, (1999), pp. 701–717; and R. Friedman, W. Liu, C. C. Chen, and S. S. Chi, "Causal Attribution for Interfirm Contract Violation: A Comparative Study of Chinese and American Commercial Arbitrators," *Journal of Applied Psychology* 92, no. 3 (2007), pp. 856–864.

86. J. Spencer-Rodgers, M. J. Williams, D. L. Hamilton, K. Peng, and L. Wang, "Culture and Group Perception: Dispositional and Stereotypic Inferences About Novel and National Groups," *Journal of Personality and Social Psychology* 93, no. 4 (2007), pp. 525–543.

87. A. Zhang, C. Reyna, Z. Qian, and G. Yu, "Interpersonal Attributions of Responsibility in the Chinese Workplace: A Test of Western Models in a Collectivistic Context," *Journal of Applied Social Psychology* 38, no. 9 (2008), pp. 2361–2377; and A. Zhang, F. Xia, and C. Li, "The Antecedents of Help Giving in Chinese Culture: Attribution, Judgment of Responsibility, Expectation Change and the Reaction of Affect," *Social Behavior and Personality* 35, no. 1 (2007), pp. 135–142.

88. M. J. Gelfand, M. Erez, and Z. Aycan, "Cross-Cultural Organizational Behavior," *Annual Review of Psychology,* January 2007, pp. 479–514; and A. S. Tsui, S. S. Nifadkar, and A. Y. Ou, "Cross-National, Cross-Cultural Organizational Behavior Research: Advances, Gaps, and Recommendations," *Journal of Management,* June 2007, pp. 426–478.

89. N. J. Adler, *International Dimensions of Organizational Behavior,* 4th ed. (Cincinnati, OH: South-Western Publishing, 2002), pp. 182–189.

90. T. Jackson, "Cultural Values and Management Ethics: A 10-Nation Study," *Human Relations,* October 2001, pp. 1267–1302; see also J. B. Cullen, K. P. Parboteeah, and M. Hoegl, "Cross-National Differences in Managers' Willingness to Justify Ethically Suspect Behaviors: A Test of

Institutional Anomie Theory," *Academy of Management Journal,* June 2004, pp. 411–421.

91. W. Chow Hou, "To Bribe or Not to Bribe?" *Asia, Inc.,* October 1996, p. 104.

92. P. Digh, "Shades of Gray in the Global Marketplace," *HRMagazine,* April 1997, p. 91.

93. Based on T. Gilovich, V. H. Medvec, and D. Kahneman, "Varieties of Regret: A Debate and Partial Resolution," *Psychological Review* 105 (1998), pp. 602–605; see also M. Tsiros and V. Mittal, "Regret: A Model of Its Antecedents and Consequences in Consumer Decision Making," *Journal of Consumer Research,* March 2000, pp. 401–417.

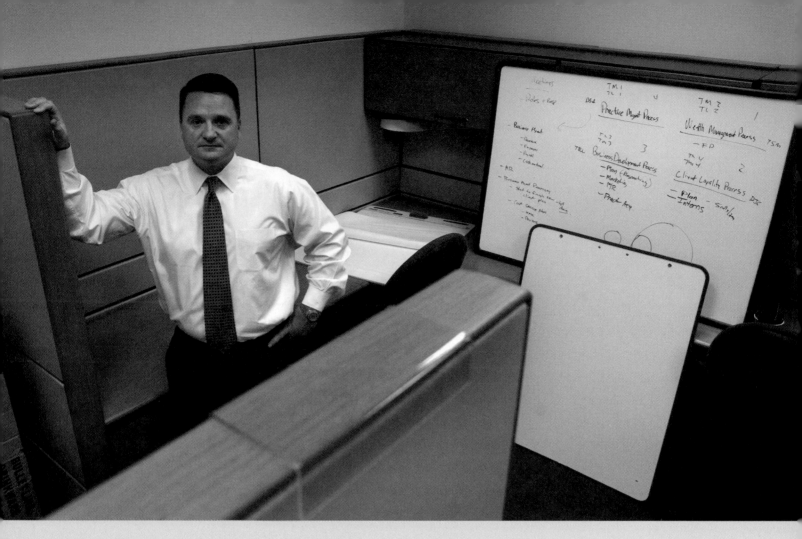

LEARNING OBJECTIVES

After studying this chapter, you should be able to:

1 Describe the three key elements of motivation.

2 Identify early theories of motivation and evaluate their applicability today.

3 Apply the predictions of self-determination theory to intrinsic and extrinsic rewards.

4 Compare and contrast goal-setting theory and management by objectives.

5 Contrast reinforcement theory and goal-setting theory.

6 Demonstrate how organizational justice is a refinement of equity theory.

7 Apply the key tenets of expectancy theory to motivating employees.

8 Compare contemporary theories of motivation.

9 Show how motivation theories are culture bound.

Motivation Concepts

Luke: "I don't believe it." Yoda: "That is why you fail." —The Empire Strikes Back

THE BIG BROKER EXODUS

The global recession has upended the status quo in many areas of business, and nowhere is that more evident than in the financial sector. Former Wall Street icons—Lehman Brothers, Merrill Lynch, Bear Stearns—have been absorbed by other companies or vanished altogether. Other stalwart companies, such as Citigroup, JPMorgan Chase, American International Group (AIG), and Morgan Stanley, were forced to become wards of the state. Said one business writer, "It's been a ghastly two years."

Much has been written about the leaders in charge, and the shareholders whose investments were wiped out. You might wonder, however, about the fates of the hundreds of thousands of employees who worked at these companies. Many have suffered greatly and were forced to accept jobs with dramatically lower paychecks. The less fortunate ones remain unemployed. Others, however, seem to have landed on their feet. And in general the Wall Street job losses—while significant—have not been as catastrophic as most predicted. "A lot of people thought the cumulative job loss would be worse by now," said Barbara Byrne Denham, an economist who has tracked the layoffs.

What explains this?

In many cases, employees were retained by the acquiring organization. When Barclays Capital purchased Lehman Brothers at a fire-sale price, it kept about 80 percent of the workers. When Bank of America acquired Merrill Lynch, it retained most Merrill employees.

Another reason unemployment claims on Wall Street have not spiked as much as anticipated, though, is the employees themselves. Many saw trouble coming and simply jumped ship before it sank. As companies fortunes fell, too, the incentives to stay in the form of stock options became less valuable. As one analyst put it: "The golden handcuffs which have tied them to these companies because of deferred compensation are now essentially gone."

David B. Armstrong (pictured on opposite page) left Merrill in May 2008 to form his own investment firm. He said, "I will never have to worry about another person in my firm making bad business decisions that can put the entire business in jeopardy."[1]

As the example of David Armstrong shows, motivation is as much about where you direct your efforts as it is about the level of effort itself. Motivation is not simply working hard—it also reflects your view of your own abilities. Try a self-assessment of your confidence in your ability to succeed.

Motivation is one of the most frequently researched topics in OB.[2] A recent Gallup poll revealed one reason for its popularity—a majority of U.S. employees (55 percent) have no enthusiasm for their work.[3] Another study suggested that, by their own reports, workers waste roughly 2 hours per day, not counting lunch and scheduled breaks (the biggest time wasters were Internet surfing and talking with co-workers).[4] Clearly, motivation is an issue. The good news is that all this research provides us with considerable insights into how to improve motivation.

In this chapter, we'll review the basics of motivation, assess a number of motivation theories, and provide an integrative model that shows how the best of these theories fit together.

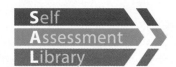

HOW CONFIDENT AM I IN MY ABILITIES TO SUCCEED?

In the Self-Assessment Library (available on CD or online), take assessment IV.A.3 (How Confident Am I in My Abilities to Succeed?) and answer the following questions.

1. *How did you score relative to other class members? Does that surprise you?*
2. *Do you think self-confidence is critical to success? Can a person be too confident?*

Defining Motivation

1 Describe the three key elements of motivation.

Some individuals, such as David Armstrong, seem driven to succeed. But the same student who finds it difficult to read a textbook for more than 20 minutes may devour a *Harry Potter* book in a day. For this student, the difference in motivation is the situation. So as we analyze the concept of motivation, keep in mind that the level of motivation varies both between individuals and within individuals at different times.

We define **motivation** as the processes that account for an individual's intensity, direction, and persistence of effort toward attaining a goal.[5] While general motivation is concerned with effort toward *any* goal, we'll narrow the focus to *organizational* goals in order to reflect our singular interest in work-related behavior.

The three key elements in our definition are intensity, direction, and persistence. *Intensity* describes how hard a person tries. This is the element most of us focus on when we talk about motivation. However, high intensity is unlikely to lead to favorable job-performance outcomes unless the effort is channeled in a *direction* that benefits the organization. Therefore, we consider the quality of effort as well as its intensity. Effort directed toward, and consistent with, the organization's goals is the kind of effort we should be seeking. Finally, motivation has a *persistence* dimension. This measures how long a person can maintain effort. Motivated individuals stay with a task long enough to achieve their goal.

Early Theories of Motivation

2   Identify early theories of motivation and evaluate their applicability today.

The 1950s were a fruitful period in the development of motivation concepts. Four specific theories formulated during this period, although heavily attacked and now questionable in terms of validity, are probably still the best-known explanations for employee motivation. As you'll see later in this chapter, we have since developed more valid explanations of motivation, but you should know these early theories for at least two reasons: (1) They represent a foundation from which contemporary theories have grown, and (2) practicing managers still regularly use them and their terminology in explaining employee motivation.

Hierarchy of Needs Theory

It's probably safe to say the best-known theory of motivation is Abraham Maslow's **hierarchy of needs**.[6] Maslow hypothesized that within every human being, there exists a hierarchy of five needs:

1. **Physiological.**   Includes hunger, thirst, shelter, sex, and other bodily needs.
2. **Safety.**   Security and protection from physical and emotional harm.
3. **Social.**   Affection, belongingness, acceptance, and friendship.
4. **Esteem.**   Internal factors such as self-respect, autonomy, and achievement, and external factors such as status, recognition, and attention.
5. **Self-actualization.**   Drive to become what we are capable of becoming; includes growth, achieving our potential, and self-fulfillment.

Although no need is ever fully gratified, a substantially satisfied need no longer motivates. Thus as each of these needs becomes substantially satisfied, the next one becomes dominant. In terms of Exhibit 7-1, we move up the steps

Exhibit 7-1   Maslow's Hierarchy of Needs

Self-actualization
Esteem
Social
Safety
Physiological

Source: A. H. Maslow, *Motivation and Personality,* 3rd ed., R. D. Frager and J. Fadiman (eds.). © 1997. Adapted by permission of Pearson Education, Inc., Upper Saddle River, New Jersey.

motivation   *The processes that account for an individual's intensity, direction, and persistence of effort toward attaining a goal.*

hierarchy of needs   *Abraham Maslow's hierarchy of five needs—physiological, safety, social, esteem, and self-actualization—in which, as each need is substantially satisfied, the next need becomes dominant.*

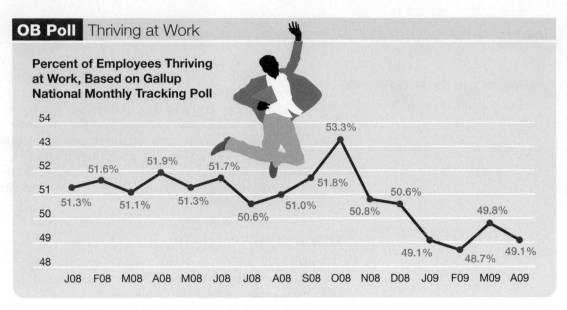

OB Poll Thriving at Work

Percent of Employees Thriving at Work, Based on Gallup National Monthly Tracking Poll

51.3% 51.6% 51.1% 51.9% 51.3% 51.7% 50.6% 51.0% 51.8% 53.3% 50.8% 50.6% 49.1% 48.7% 49.8% 49.1%

J08 F08 M08 A08 M08 J08 J08 A08 S08 O08 N08 D08 J09 F09 M09 A09

Source: Based on "Employee Concerns," *Workforce Management* (February 16, 2009), p. 17.

of the hierarchy. So if you want to motivate someone, according to Maslow, you need to understand what level of the hierarchy that person is currently on and focus on satisfying the needs at or above that level.

Maslow separated the five needs into higher and lower orders. Physiological and safety needs were **lower-order needs** and social, esteem, and **self-actualization** were **higher-order needs**. The difference is that higher-order needs are satisfied internally (within the person), whereas lower-order needs are predominantly satisfied externally (by things such as pay, union contracts, and tenure).

Maslow's needs theory has received wide recognition, particularly among practicing managers. It is intuitively logical and easy to understand. Unfortunately, however, research does not validate it. Maslow provided no empirical substantiation, and several studies that sought to validate the theory found no support for it.[7] There is little evidence that need structures are organized along the dimensions proposed by Maslow, that unsatisfied needs motivate, or that a satisfied need activates movement to a new need level.[8] But old theories, especially intuitively logical ones, apparently die hard.

Theory X and Theory Y

Douglas McGregor proposed two distinct views of human beings: one basically negative, labeled Theory X, and the other basically positive, labeled Theory Y.[9] After viewing the way in which managers dealt with employees, McGregor concluded that managers' views of the nature of human beings are based on a certain grouping of assumptions, and that managers tend to mold their behavior toward employees according to these assumptions.

Under **Theory X**, managers believe employees inherently dislike work and must therefore be directed or even coerced into performing it. Under **Theory Y**, in contrast, managers assume employees can view work as being as natural as rest or play, and therefore the average person can learn to accept, and even seek, responsibility.

To understand Theory X and Theory Y more fully, think in terms of Maslow's hierarchy. Theory Y assumes higher-order needs dominate individuals. McGregor himself held to the belief that Theory Y assumptions were more valid than Theory X. Therefore, he proposed such ideas as participative decision

Myth or Science?

"Women Are More Motivated to Get Along, and Men Are More Motivated to Get Ahead"

This statement is generally true. Compared with women, men are relatively more motivated to excel at tasks and jobs. Women are more motivated to maintain relationships.

Note these gender differences do *not* mean every man is more motivated by his career than every woman. Consider gender and longevity. Women, on average, live longer than men, but in a significant percentage of couples (roughly 45 percent), a husband will outlive his wife. In the same way, there are disparities in motivation between women and men, but we need to resist the human tendency to turn a group difference into a universal generalization or stereotype.

Research indicates we are more likely to describe men by "agentic traits," such as *active, decisive,* and *competitive.* Women are often described by "communal" traits, such as *caring, emotional,* and *considerate.* This evidence, however, might reflect gender stereotypes of the traits of men and women, not proof that men and women are motivated by different things.

A study of 1,398 working Germans, however, revealed that men *were* more motivated by agentic strivings and women by communal strivings, and these gender differences did not change over the 17-month course of the study. As a result of these differences, men had higher levels of "objective" career success (income, occupational status) than women. Women, however, were more involved in their families than were men.

We don't know whether these differences are ingrained or socialized. If they are socialized, though, evidence suggests the process begins early. A study of the stories that children ages 4 through 9 told about their lives revealed that girls were more likely to emphasize communion (friendships, helping others, affectionate contact) than were boys.[10]

making, responsible and challenging jobs, and good group relations as approaches to maximize an employee's job motivation.

Unfortunately, there is no evidence to confirm that *either* set of assumptions is valid, or that accepting Theory Y assumptions and altering our actions accordingly will lead to more motivated workers. OB theories need empirical support before we can accept them. Theory X and Theory Y lack such support as much as the hierarchy of needs theories.

Two-Factor Theory

Psychologist Frederick Herzberg proposed the **two-factor theory**—also called *motivation-hygiene theory.*[11] Believing an individual's relationship to work is basic and that attitude toward work can very well determine success or failure, Herzberg investigated the question "What do people want from their jobs?" He asked people to describe, in detail, situations in which they felt exceptionally *good* or *bad* about their jobs. He then tabulated and categorized the responses.

lower-order needs *Needs that are satisfied externally, such as physiological and safety needs.*

self-actualization *The drive to become what a person is capable of becoming.*

higher-order needs *Needs that are satisfied internally, such as social, esteem, and self-actualization needs.*

Theory X *The assumption that employees dislike work, are lazy, dislike responsibility, and must be coerced to perform.*

Theory Y *The assumption that employees like work, are creative, seek responsibility, and can exercise self-direction.*

two-factor theory *A theory that relates intrinsic factors to job satisfaction and associates extrinsic factors with dissatisfaction. Also called motivation-hygiene theory.*

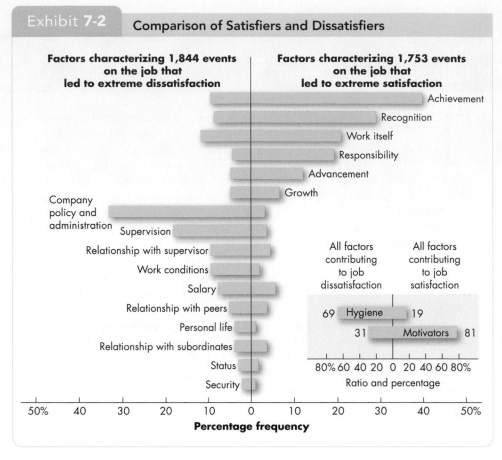

Exhibit 7-2   Comparison of Satisfiers and Dissatisfiers

Factors characterizing 1,844 events on the job that led to extreme dissatisfaction

Factors characterizing 1,753 events on the job that led to extreme satisfaction

Achievement
Recognition
Work itself
Responsibility
Advancement
Growth
Company policy and administration
Supervision
Relationship with supervisor
Work conditions
Salary
Relationship with peers
Personal life
Relationship with subordinates
Status
Security

All factors contributing to job dissatisfaction

All factors contributing to job satisfaction

69 Hygiene 19
31 Motivators 81

80% 60 40 20 0 20 40 60 80%
Ratio and percentage

50% 40 30 20 10 0 10 20 30 40 50%
Percentage frequency

Herzberg concluded that the replies people gave when they felt good about their jobs differed significantly from the replies given when they felt bad. As shown in Exhibit 7-2, intrinsic factors such as advancement, recognition, responsibility, and achievement seem related to job satisfaction. Respondents who felt good about their work tended to attribute these factors to themselves. On the other hand, dissatisfied respondents tended to cite extrinsic factors, such as supervision, pay, company policies, and working conditions.

The data suggest, said Herzberg, that the opposite of satisfaction is not dissatisfaction, as was traditionally believed. Removing dissatisfying characteristics from a job does not necessarily make the job satisfying. As illustrated in Exhibit 7-3, Herzberg proposed that his findings indicated the existence of a dual continuum: The opposite of "satisfaction" is "no satisfaction," and the opposite of "dissatisfaction" is "no dissatisfaction."

According to Herzberg, the factors that lead to job satisfaction are separate and distinct from those that lead to job dissatisfaction. Therefore, managers who seek to eliminate factors that can create job dissatisfaction may bring about peace but not necessarily motivation. They will be placating rather than motivating their workers. As a result, Herzberg characterized conditions such as quality of supervision, pay, company policies, physical working conditions, relationships with others, and job security as **hygiene factors.** When they're adequate, people will not be dissatisfied; neither will they be satisfied. If we want to motivate people on their jobs, Herzberg suggested emphasizing factors associated with the

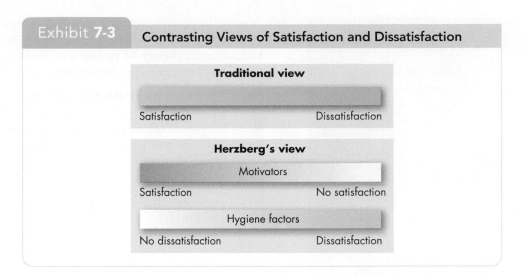

Exhibit **7-3**   **Contrasting Views of Satisfaction and Dissatisfaction**

Traditional view

Satisfaction   Dissatisfaction

Herzberg's view

Motivators

Satisfaction   No satisfaction

Hygiene factors

No dissatisfaction   Dissatisfaction

work itself or with outcomes directly derived from it, such as promotional opportunities, personal growth opportunities, recognition, responsibility, and achievement. These are the characteristics people find intrinsically rewarding.

The two-factor theory has not been well supported in the literature, and it has many detractors.[12] Criticisms include the following:

1. The procedure Herzberg used is limited by its methodology. When things are going well, people tend to take credit themselves. Contrarily, they blame failure on the extrinsic environment.
2. The reliability of Herzberg's methodology is questionable. Raters have to make interpretations, so they may contaminate the findings by interpreting one response in one manner while treating a similar response differently.
3. No overall measure of satisfaction was utilized. A person may dislike part of a job yet still think the job is acceptable overall.
4. Herzberg assumed a relationship between satisfaction and productivity, but the research methodology he used looked only at satisfaction and not at productivity. To make such research relevant, we must assume a strong relationship between satisfaction and productivity.

Regardless of the criticisms, Herzberg's theory has been widely read, and few managers are unfamiliar with its recommendations.

McClelland's Theory of Needs

You have one beanbag, and five targets are set up in front of you. Each target is farther away than the last and thus more difficult to hit. Target A is a cinch. It sits almost within arm's reach. If you hit it, you get $2. Target B is a bit farther out, but about 80 percent of the people who try can hit it. It pays $4. Target C pays $8, and about half the people who try can hit it. Very few people can hit Target D, but the payoff is $16 for those who do. Finally, Target E pays $32, but

hygiene factors *Factors—such as company policy and administration, supervision, and salary—that, when adequate in a job, placate workers. When these factors are adequate, people will not be dissatisfied.*

As a high achiever, Patricia Woertz is motivated by work that demands a high degree of personal responsibility. Today she is the CEO, president, and chair of the board of Archer Daniels Midland, an agricultural food processing firm. She started her career as a certified public accountant but was attracted to the complexity and opportunity of global energy. For the next 30 years she worked for Gulf Oil and Chevron in refining, marketing, strategic planning, and finance positions. Since joining ADM, Woertz continues to shift company resources toward fuel production in a drive to accelerate ADM's global leadership in bioenergy.

it's almost impossible to achieve. Which target would you try for? If you selected C, you're likely to be a high achiever. Why? Read on.

McClelland's theory of needs was developed by David McClelland and his associates.[13] The theory focuses on three needs, defined as follows:

- **Need for achievement (nAch)** is the drive to excel, to achieve in relation to a set of standards, to strive to succeed.
- **Need for power (nPow)** is the need to make others behave in a way in which they would not have behaved otherwise.
- **Need for affiliation (nAff)** is the desire for friendly and close interpersonal relationships.

Of the three needs, McClelland and subsequent researchers focused most of their attention on nAch. High achievers perform best when they perceive their probability of success as 0.5—that is, a 50–50 chance of success. They dislike gambling with high odds because they get no achievement satisfaction from success that comes by pure chance. Similarly, they dislike low odds (high probability of success) because then there is no challenge to their skills. They like to set goals that require stretching themselves a little.

Relying on an extensive amount of research, we can make some reasonably well-supported predictions of the relationship between achievement need and job performance. Although less research has been done on power and affiliation needs, findings are consistent there, too. First, when jobs have a high degree of personal responsibility and feedback and an intermediate degree of risk, high achievers are strongly motivated. They are successful in entrepreneurial activities such as running their own businesses, for example, and managing self-contained units within large organizations.[14] Second, a high need to achieve does not necessarily make someone a good manager, especially in large organizations. People with a high achievement need are interested in how well they do personally and not in influencing others to do well. High-nAch salespeople do not necessarily make good sales managers, and the good general manager in a large organization does not typically have a high need to achieve.[15] Third, needs for affiliation and power tend to be closely related to managerial success. The best managers are high in their need for power and low in their need for affiliation.[16] In fact, a high power motive may be a requirement for managerial effectiveness.[17]

As you might have gathered, among the early theories of motivation McClelland's has had the best research support. Unfortunately, it has less practical effect than the others. Because McClelland argued that the three needs are subconscious—meaning we may be high on them but not know it—measuring them is not easy. In the most common approach, a trained expert presents pictures to individuals, asks them to tell a story about each, and then scores their responses in terms of the three needs. However, the process is time consuming and expensive, and few organizations have been willing to invest time and resources in measuring McClelland's concept.

Contemporary Theories of Motivation

Early theories of motivation either have not held up under close examination or have fallen out of favor. In contrast, contemporary theories have one thing in common: Each has a reasonable degree of valid supporting documentation. This doesn't mean they are unquestionably right. We call them "contemporary theories" because they represent the current state of thinking in explaining employee motivation.

An Ethical Choice

Putting Off Work

Dana Moylan Wright found herself in a vicious cycle. The more her work piled up, the more she procrastinated. "At that point, I had many deadlines and was having trouble making myself do anything," she said.

You've probably found yourself in a similar situation. We all procrastinate from time to time, especially with work that doesn't interest us. Still, uninteresting is not necessarily the same as unimportant.

So, how can we avoid procrastination?

1. Though as occasional or habitual procrastinators we may rationalize our behavior—telling ourselves that waiting until the last minute is efficient—realize that procrastination is usually counterproductive. Says one researcher who has studied procrastinators: "My research showed that they do not perform better. They just think they do." So, be honest with yourself—in the long run, we pay for our procrastination, both in terms of getting less done and in feeling guilty.

2. One way to eliminate procrastination is to set intermediate deadlines for yourself. Researchers studied MIT undergraduates who had three assignments due over a 12-week course. Of three groups of students—those who had a separate deadline for each assignment after 4, 8, and 12 weeks; those who had no intermediate deadlines; and those who were asked to impose their own deadlines—the first group had the best grades for the course. So, one way you can avoid procrastination is to cluster your projects into concrete goals so that each one is attainable and less overwhelming.

3. Some evidence suggests that making commitments public—such as telling others about your goals—may discipline ourselves against the temptations of distraction.

4. Give yourself sufficient time when you are disconnected from your cell phone, e-mail, the Internet, and so on. One expert commented, "How often have we said, 'We'll check e-mail, it'll only take a minute,' and three hours later we're still on it?"

Source: Based on A. Tugend, "The Popular Practice of Putting Stuff Off," *New York Times* (January 30, 2009), p. B6; and C. Tuna, "How to Put Off Work—Constructively," *Wall Street Journal* (September 30, 2008), p. B14.

Self-Determination Theory

3 Apply the predictions of self-determination theory to intrinsic and extrinsic rewards.

"It's strange," said Marcia. "I started work at the Humane Society as a volunteer. I put in fifteen hours a week helping people adopt pets. And I loved coming to work. Then, three months ago, they hired me full-time at eleven dollars an hour. I'm doing the same work I did before. But I'm not finding it near as much fun."

Does Marcia's reaction seem counterintuitive? There's an explanation for it. It's called **self-determination theory**, which proposes that people prefer to feel they have control over their actions, so anything that makes a previously enjoyed task feel more like an obligation than a freely chosen activity will undermine motivation.[18] Much research on self-determination theory in OB has focused on **cognitive evaluation theory**, which hypothesizes that extrinsic rewards will reduce intrinsic interest in a task. When people are paid for work, it feels less like something they *want* to do and more like something they *have* to do. Self-determination

---

McClelland's theory of needs   *A theory that states achievement, power, and affiliation are three important needs that help explain motivation.*

need for achievement (nAch)   *The drive to excel, to achieve in relationship to a set of standards, and to strive to succeed.*

need for power (nPow)   *The need to make others behave in a way in which they would not have behaved otherwise.*

need for affiliation (nAff)   *The desire for friendly and close interpersonal relationships.*

self-determination theory   *A theory of motivation that is concerned with the beneficial effects of intrinsic*

motivation and the harmful effects of extrinsic motivation.

cognitive evaluation theory   *A version of self-determination theory which holds that allocating extrinsic rewards for behavior that had been previously intrinsically rewarding tends to decrease the overall level of motivation if the rewards are seen as controlling.*

theory also proposes that in addition to being driven by a need for autonomy, people seek ways to achieve competence and positive connections to others. A large number of studies support self-determination theory.[19] As we'll show, its major implications relate to work rewards.

When organizations use extrinsic rewards as payoffs for superior performance, employees feel less like they are doing a good job because of their own intrinsic desire to excel and more like they are doing a good job because that's what the organization wants. Eliminating extrinsic rewards can also shift from an external to an internal explanation of an individual's perception of why she works on a task. If you're reading a novel a week because your English literature instructor requires you to, you can attribute your reading behavior to an external source. However, if you find yourself continuing to read a novel a week after the course is over, your natural inclination is to say "I must enjoy reading novels because I'm still reading one a week."

Recent studies examining how extrinsic rewards increased motivation for some creative tasks suggests we might need to place cognitive evaluation theory's predictions in a broader context.[20] Goal setting is more effective in improving motivation, for instance, when we provide rewards for achieving the goals. The original authors of self-determination theory acknowledge that extrinsic rewards such as verbal praise and feedback about competence can improve even intrinsic motivation under specific circumstances. Deadlines and specific work standards do, too, if people believe they are in control of their behavior.[21] This is consistent with the central theme of self-determination theory: rewards and deadlines diminish motivation if people see them as coercive.

What does self-determination theory suggest for providing rewards? Consider two situations. If a senior sales representative really enjoys selling and making the

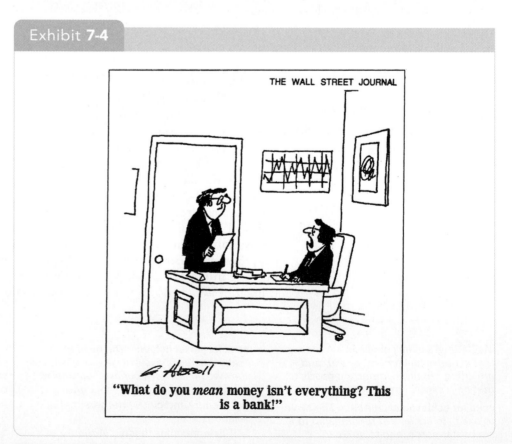

Exhibit 7-4

"What do you *mean* money isn't everything? This is a bank!"

Source: From the *Wall Street Journal*, February 8, 1995. Reprinted with permission of Cartoon Features Syndicate.

International OB

How Managers Evaluate Their Employees Depends on Culture

A recent study of managers from North America, Asia, and Latin America found interesting differences in their perceptions of employee motivation. North American managers perceive their employees as motivated more by extrinsic factors (for example, pay) than by intrinsic factors (for example, doing meaningful work). Asian managers perceive their employees as being motivated by both extrinsic and intrinsic factors, while Latin American managers perceive their employees as motivated by intrinsic factors.

Even more interesting, these differences affected evaluations of employee performance. As you might expect, Asian managers focused on both types of motivation when evaluating their employees' performance, and Latin American managers focused on intrinsic motivation. North American managers, though believing employees are motivated primarily by extrinsic factors, actually focused more on *intrinsic* factors when evaluating employee performance. Why the paradox? One explanation is that North Americans value uniqueness, so any deviation from the norm—such as being perceived as unusually high in intrinsic motivation—is rewarded.

Latin American managers' focus on intrinsic motivation may be related to a cultural norm termed *simpatía,* a tradition that compels employees to display their internal feelings. Consequently, Latin American managers are more sensitized to these displays and can more easily notice their employees' intrinsic motivation.

So, from an employee perspective, the cultural background of your manager can play an important role in how you are evaluated.

Source: Based on S. E. DeVoe and S. S. Iyengar, "Managers' Theories of Subordinates: A Cross-Cultural Examination of Manager Perceptions of Motivation and Appraisal of Performance," *Organizational Behavior and Human Decision Processes,* January 2004, pp. 47–61.

deal, a commission indicates she's been doing a good job at this valued task. The reward will increase her sense of competence by providing feedback that could improve intrinsic motivation. On the other hand, if a computer programmer values writing code because she likes to solve problems, a reward for working to an externally imposed standard she does not accept could feel coercive, and her intrinsic motivation would suffer. She would be less interested in the task and might reduce her effort.

A recent outgrowth of self-determination theory is **self-concordance**, which considers how strongly peoples' reasons for pursuing goals are consistent with their interests and core values. If individuals pursue goals because of an intrinsic interest, they are more likely to attain their goals and are happy even if they do not. Why? Because the process of striving toward them is fun. In contrast, people who pursue goals for extrinsic reasons (money, status, or other benefits) are less likely to attain their goals and less happy even when they do achieve them. Why? Because the goals are less meaningful to them.[22] OB research suggests that people who pursue work goals for intrinsic reasons are more satisfied with their jobs, feel like they fit into their organizations better, and may perform better.[23]

What does all this mean? It means choose your job for reasons other than extrinsic rewards. For organizations, it means managers should provide intrinsic as well as extrinsic incentives. They need to make the work interesting, provide recognition, and support employee growth and development. Employees who feel what they do is within their control and a result of free choice are likely to be more motivated by their work and committed to their employers.[24]

self-concordance   *The degree to which peoples' reasons for pursuing goals are consistent with their interests and core values.*

Goal-Setting Theory

4 Compare and contrast goal-setting theory and management by objectives.

Gene Broadwater, coach of the Hamilton High School cross-country team, gave his squad these last words before they approached the starting line for the league championship race: "Each one of you is physically ready. Now, get out there and do your best. No one can ever ask more of you than that."

You've heard the sentiment a number of times yourself: "Just do your best. That's all anyone can ask for." But what does "do your best" mean? Do we ever know if we've achieved that vague goal? Would the cross-country runners have recorded faster times if Coach Broadwater had given each a specific goal? Might you have done better in your high school English class if your parents had said, "You should strive for 85 percent or higher on all your work in English" rather than telling you to "do your best"? The research on **goal-setting theory** addresses these issues, and the findings, as you'll see, are impressive in terms of the effect that goal specificity, challenge, and feedback have on performance.

In the late 1960s, Edwin Locke proposed that intentions to work toward a goal are a major source of work motivation.[25] That is, goals tell an employee what needs to be done and how much effort will need to be expended.[26] The evidence strongly supports the value of goals. More to the point, we can say that specific goals increase performance; that difficult goals, when accepted, result in higher performance than do easy goals; and that feedback leads to higher performance than does nonfeedback.[27]

Specific goals produce a higher level of output than does the generalized goal of "do your best." Why? The specificity of the goal itself seems to act as an internal stimulus. For instance, when a trucker commits to making 12 round-trip hauls between Toronto and Buffalo, New York, each week, this intention gives him a specific objective to try to attain. All things being equal, the trucker with a specific goal will outperform a counterpart with no goals or the generalized goal of "do your best."

If factors such as acceptance of the goals are held constant, the more difficult the goal, the higher the level of performance. Of course, it's logical to assume easier goals are more likely to be accepted. But once a hard task is accepted, we can expect the employee to exert a high level of effort to try to achieve it.

But why are people motivated by difficult goals?[28] First, challenging goals get our attention and thus tend to help us focus. Second, difficult goals energize us because we have to work harder to attain them. Do you study as hard for an easy

Chung Mong-koo, chairman of Hyundai Motor Company, is well known for articulating difficult and specific goals as a potent motivating force for employees. For example, although Hyundai is a latecomer in the development of a hybrid vehicle, the South Korean automaker plans to launch its first U.S. hybrid in 2010, with annual sales set at 50,000 units. By 2018, the company expects hybrid sales to balloon to 500,000 units worldwide. Challenging employees to reach high goals has helped Hyundai experience tremendous growth in recent years.

exam as you do for a difficult one? Probably not. Third, when goals are difficult, people persist in trying to attain them. Finally, difficult goals lead us to discover strategies that help us perform the job or task more effectively. If we have to struggle to solve a difficult problem, we often think of a better way to go about it.

People do better when they get feedback on how well they are progressing toward their goals, because feedback helps to identify discrepancies between what they have done and what they want to do—that is, feedback acts to guide behavior. But all feedback is not equally potent. Self-generated feedback—with which employees are able to monitor their own progress—has been shown to be a more powerful motivator than externally generated feedback.[29]

If employees can participate in the setting of their own goals, will they try harder? The evidence is mixed.[30] In some cases, participatively set goals yielded superior performance; in others, individuals performed best when assigned goals by their boss. But a major advantage of participation may be that it increases acceptance of the goal as a desirable one toward which to work.[31] Commitment is important. If participation isn't used, then the individual assigning the goal needs to clearly explain its purpose and importance.[32]

Are there any contingencies in goal-setting theory, or will difficult and specific goals *always* lead to higher performance? In addition to feedback, three other factors have been found to influence the goals–performance relationship: goal commitment, task characteristics, and national culture.

Goal-setting theory assumes an individual is committed to the goal and is determined not to lower or abandon it. In terms of behavior the individual (1) believes he or she can achieve the goal and (2) wants to achieve it.[33] Goal commitment is most likely to occur when goals are made public, when the individual has an internal locus of control (see Chapter 4), and when the goals are self-set rather than assigned.[34] Goal-setting theory doesn't work equally well on all tasks. The evidence suggests goals seem to have a more substantial effect on performance when tasks are simple rather than complex, well learned rather than novel, and independent rather than interdependent.[35] On interdependent tasks, group goals are preferable.

Finally, setting specific, difficult, individual goals may have different effects in different cultures. Most goal-setting research has been done in the United States and Canada, where individual achievement and performance are most highly valued. To date, research has not shown that group-based goals are more effective in collectivists than in individualist cultures. There is evidence that in collectivistic and high-power-distance cultures, achievable moderate goals can be more highly motivating than difficult ones.[36] Finally, assigned goals appear to generate greater goal commitment in high rather than low power-distance cultures.[37] Much more research is needed to assess how goal constructs might differ across cultures.

Although goal setting has positive outcomes, some goals may be *too* effective.[38] When learning something is important, goals related to performance undermine adaptation and creativity because people become too focused on outcomes and ignore changing conditions. In this case, a goal to learn and generate alternative solutions will be more effective than a goal to perform. Some authors have also argued that goals can lead employees to be too focused on a single standard to the exclusion of all others. Consider the narrow focus on short-term stock prices in many businesses—so much attention to this one standard for performance may have led organizations to ignore long-term success,

goal-setting theory *A theory that says that specific and difficult goals, with feedback, lead to higher performance.*

and even to engage in such unethical behavior as accounting fraud or excessively risky investments. Of course it is possible for organizations to establish goals for ethical performance. Despite differences of opinion, most researchers do agree that goals are powerful in shaping behavior. Managers should make sure they are actually aligned with the company's objectives.

Research has demonstrated the motivating power of goal-setting theory in more than 100 tasks with more than 40,000 participants in many different kinds of industries—from lumber to insurance to automobiles. Setting specific, challenging goals for employees is the best thing managers can do to improve performance.

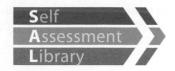

WHAT ARE MY COURSE PERFORMANCE GOALS?

In the Self-Assessment Library (available on CD or online), take assessment I.C.5 (What Are My Course Performance Goals?).

Implementing Goal-Setting   Goal-setting theory has an impressive base of research support. But as a manager, how do you make it operational? That's often left up to the individual manager or leader. Some managers set aggressive performance targets—what General Electric called "stretch goals." Some CEOs, such as Procter & Gamble's A. G. Lafley and SAP AG's Hasso Plattner, are known for the demanding performance goals they set. The problem with leaving it up to the individual manager is that many managers don't set goals. A recent survey revealed that when asked whether their job had clearly defined goals, only a minority of employees said yes.[39]

A more systematic way to utilize goal setting is with a management by objectives program. **Management by objectives (MBO)** emphasizes participatively set goals that are tangible, verifiable, and measurable. As depicted in Exhibit 7-5, the organization's overall objectives are translated into specific objectives for each succeeding level in the organization (divisional, departmental, individual). But because lower-unit managers jointly participate in setting their own goals,

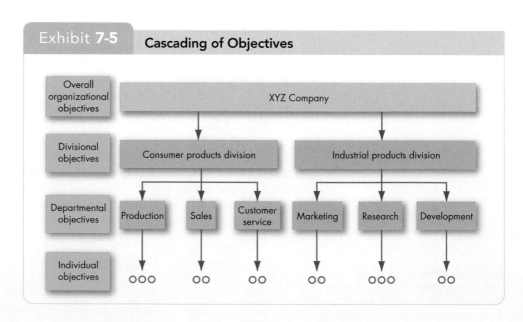

Exhibit **7-5**   **Cascading of Objectives**

MBO works from the bottom up as well as from the top down. The result is a hierarchy that links objectives at one level to those at the next. And for the individual employee, MBO provides specific personal performance objectives.

Four ingredients are common to MBO programs: goal specificity, participation in decision making (including participation in the setting of goals or objectives), an explicit time period, and performance feedback.[40] Many elements in MBO programs match propositions of goal-setting theory. For example, having an explicit time period to accomplish objectives matches goal-setting theory's emphasis on goal specificity. Similarly, we noted earlier that feedback about goal progress is a critical element of goal-setting theory. The only area of possible disagreement between MBO and goal-setting theory is participation: MBO strongly advocates it, whereas goal-setting theory demonstrates that managers assigning goals is usually just as effective.

You'll find MBO programs in many business, health care, educational, government, and nonprofit organizations.[41] Its popularity does not mean it always works. In a number of documented cases MBO has been implemented but failed to meet management's expectations.[42] The culprits tend to be unrealistic expectations, lack of commitment by top management, and an inability or unwillingness of management to allocate rewards based on goal accomplishment. Failures can also arise out of cultural incompatibilities. For instance, Fujitsu recently scrapped its MBO-type program because management found it didn't fit well with the Japanese culture's emphasis on minimizing risk and emphasizing long-term goals.

Self-Efficacy Theory

Self-efficacy (also known as *social cognitive theory* or *social learning theory*) refers to an individual's belief that he or she is capable of performing a task.[43] The higher your self-efficacy, the more confidence you have in your ability to succeed. So, in difficult situations, people with low self-efficacy are more likely to lessen their effort or give up altogether, while those with high self-efficacy will try harder to master the challenge.[44] In addition, individuals high in self-efficacy seem to respond to negative feedback with increased effort and motivation, while those low in self-efficacy are likely to lessen their effort when given negative feedback.[45] How can managers help their employees achieve high levels of self-efficacy? By bringing together goal-setting theory and self-efficacy theory.

Goal-setting theory and self-efficacy theory don't compete with one another; rather, they complement each other. As Exhibit 7-6 shows, when a manager sets difficult goals for employees, they will have a higher level of self-efficacy and set higher goals for their own performance. Why? Research shows setting difficult goals for people communicates your confidence in them. Imagine you learn your boss sets a higher goal for you than for your co-workers. How would you interpret this? As long as you didn't feel you were being picked on, you would probably think, "Well, I guess my boss thinks I'm capable of performing better than others." This sets in motion a psychological process in which you're more confident in yourself (higher self-efficacy) and you set higher personal goals, causing you to perform better both inside and outside the workplace.

management by objectives (MBO) *A program that encompasses specific goals, participatively set, for an explicit time period, with feedback on goal progress.*

self-efficacy *An individual's belief that he or she is capable of performing a task.*

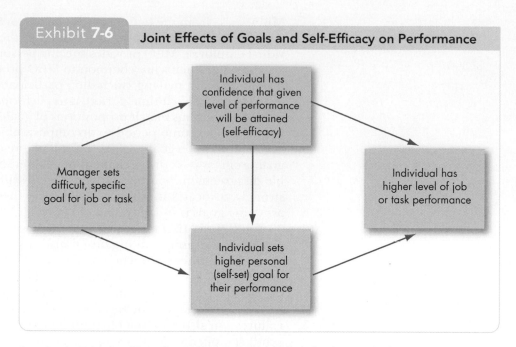

Exhibit 7-6   Joint Effects of Goals and Self-Efficacy on Performance

Source: Based on E. A. Locke and G. P. Latham, "Building a Practically Useful Theory of Goal Setting and Task Motivation: A 35-Year Odyssey," *American Psychologist*, September 2002, pp. 705–717.

The researcher who developed self-efficacy theory, Albert Bandura, proposes four ways self-efficacy can be increased:[46]

1. Enactive mastery
2. Vicarious modeling
3. Verbal persuasion
4. Arousal

According to Bandura, the most important source of increasing self-efficacy is *enactive mastery*—that is, gaining relevant experience with the task or job. If you've been able to do the job successfully in the past, then you're more confident you'll be able to do it in the future.

The second source is *vicarious modeling*—or becoming more confident because you see someone else doing the task. For example, if your friend slims down, it increases your confidence that you can lose weight, too. Vicarious modeling is most effective when you see yourself as similar to the person you are observing. Watching Tiger Woods play a difficult golf shot might not increase your confidence in being able to play the shot yourself, but if you watch a golfer with a handicap similar to yours, it's persuasive.

The third source is *verbal persuasion:* becoming more confident because someone convinces you that you have the skills necessary to be successful. Motivational speakers use this tactic a lot.

Finally, Bandura argues that *arousal* increases self-efficacy. Arousal leads to an energized state, which drives a person to complete a task. The person gets "psyched up" and performs better. But if the task requires a steady, lower-key perspective (say, carefully editing a manuscript), arousal may in fact hurt performance.

What are the OB implications of self-efficacy theory? Well, it's a matter of applying Bandura's sources of self-efficacy to the work setting. Training programs often make use of enactive mastery by having people practice and build their skills. In fact, one of the reasons training works is that it increases self-efficacy.[47]

The best way for a manager to use verbal persuasion is through the *Pygmalion effect* or the *Galatea effect*. As discussed in Chapter 5, the Pygmalion effect is a form of self-fulfilling prophecy in which believing something can make it true. The

The U.S. Coast Guard illustrates the importance of enactive mastery in increasing self-efficacy. Since the September 11 terrorist attacks, the duties of the Coast Guard in protecting U.S. ports, ships, and waterways have expanded. The Coast Guard men and women shown here participate in a tactical law enforcement training program by playing out a hostage scenario. Practicing and building their skills in boarding ships help the Coast Guard personnel increase their confidence to succeed at their task.

Pygmalion effect increases self-efficacy when we communicate to an individual's teacher or supervisor that the person is of high ability. In some studies, teachers were told their students had very high IQ scores when in fact they spanned a range—some high, some low, some in between. Consistent with the Pygmalion effect, the teachers spent more time with the students they *thought* were smart, gave them more challenging assignments, and expected more of them—all of which led to higher student self-efficacy and better student grades.[48] This strategy also has been used in the workplace.[49] The Galatea effect occurs when high performance expectations are communicated directly to an employee. Sailors who were told convincingly that they would not get seasick in fact were much less likely to do so.[50]

Note that intelligence and personality are absent from Bandura's list. Much research shows that intelligence and personality (especially conscientiousness and emotional stability) can increase self-efficacy.[51] Those individual traits are so strongly related to self-efficacy (people who are intelligent, conscientiousness, and emotionally stable are much more likely to have high self-efficacy than those who score low on these characteristics) that some researchers would argue self-efficacy does not exist.[52] They believe it is simply a by-product in a smart person with a confident personality. Although Bandura strongly disagrees with this conclusion, more research is needed.

Reinforcement Theory

5 Contrast reinforcement theory and goal-setting theory.

A counterpoint to goal-setting theory is **reinforcement theory**. Goal-setting is a cognitive approach, proposing that an individual's purposes direct his action. Reinforcement theory takes a behavioristic approach,

reinforcement theory *A theory that says that behavior is a function of its consequences.*

arguing that reinforcement conditions behavior. The two theories are clearly at odds philosophically. Reinforcement theorists see behavior as environmentally caused. You need not be concerned, they would argue, with internal cognitive events; what controls behavior is reinforcers—any consequences that, when immediately following responses, increase the probability that the behavior will be repeated.

Reinforcement theory ignores the inner state of the individual and concentrates solely on what happens when he or she takes some action. Because it does not concern itself with what initiates behavior, it is not, strictly speaking, a theory of motivation. But it does provide a powerful means of analyzing what controls behavior, and this is why we typically consider it in discussions of motivation.[53]

Operant conditioning theory, probably the most relevant component of reinforcement theory for management, argues that people learn to behave to get something they want or to avoid something they don't want. Unlike reflexive or unlearned behavior, operant behavior is influenced by the reinforcement or lack of reinforcement brought about by its consequences. Therefore, reinforcement strengthens a behavior and increases the likelihood it will be repeated.[54] B. F. Skinner, one of the most prominent advocates of operant conditioning, argued that creating pleasing consequences to follow specific forms of behavior would increase the frequency of that behavior. He demonstrated that people will most likely engage in desired behaviors if they are positively reinforced for doing so; that rewards are most effective if they immediately follow the desired response; and that behavior that is not rewarded, or is punished, is less likely to be repeated. We know a professor who places a mark by a student's name each time the student makes a contribution to class discussions. Operant conditioning would argue this practice is motivating because it conditions a student to expect a reward (earning class credit) each time she demonstrates a specific behavior (speaking up in class). The concept of operant conditioning was part of Skinner's broader concept of **behaviorism**, which argues that behavior follows stimuli in a relatively unthinking manner. Skinner's form of radical behaviorism rejects feelings, thoughts, and other states of mind as causes of behavior. In short, people learn to associate stimulus and response, but their conscious awareness of this association is irrelevant.[55]

You can see illustrations of operant conditioning everywhere that reinforcements are contingent on some action on your part. Your instructor says if you want a high grade in the course, you must supply correct answers on the test. A commissioned salesperson wanting to earn a sizable income finds doing so is contingent on generating high sales in her territory. Of course, the linkage can also teach individuals to engage in behaviors that work against the best interests of the organization. Assume your boss says if you work overtime during the next 3-week busy season you'll be compensated for it at your next performance appraisal. However, when performance-appraisal time comes, you are given no positive reinforcement for your overtime work. The next time your boss asks you to work overtime, what will you do? You'll probably decline! Your behavior can be explained by operant conditioning: if a behavior fails to be positively reinforced, the probability the behavior will be repeated declines.

Although reinforcers such as pay can motivate people, it's just as clear that the process is much more complicated than stimulus–response. In its pure form, reinforcement theory ignores feelings, attitudes, expectations, and other cognitive variables known to affect behavior. In fact, some researchers look at the same experiments reinforcement theorists use to support their position and interpret the findings in a *cognitive* framework.[56]

Reinforcement is undoubtedly an important influence on behavior, but few scholars are prepared to argue it is the only one. The behaviors you engage in at work and the amount of effort you allocate to each task are affected by the consequences that follow. If you're consistently reprimanded for outproducing your colleagues, you'll likely reduce your productivity. But we might also explain your lower productivity in terms of goals, inequity, or expectancies.

Individuals can learn by being told or by observing what happens to other people, as well as through direct experiences. Much of what we have learned comes from watching models—parents, teachers, peers, film and television performers, bosses, and so forth. This view that we can learn through both observation and direct experience is called **social-learning theory**.[57]

Although social-learning theory is an extension of operant conditioning—that is, it assumes behavior is a function of consequences—it also acknowledges the effects of observational learning and perception. People respond to the way they perceive and define consequences, not to the objective consequences themselves.

Models are central to the social-learning viewpoint. Four processes determine their influence on an individual:

1. **Attentional processes.**   People learn from a model only when they recognize and pay attention to its critical features. We tend to be most influenced by models that are attractive, repeatedly available, important to us, or similar to us in our estimation.
2. **Retention processes.**   A model's influence depends on how well the individual remembers the model's action after the model is no longer readily available.
3. **Motor reproduction processes.**   After a person has seen a new behavior by observing the model, watching must be converted to doing. This process demonstrates that the individual can perform the modeled activities.
4. **Reinforcement processes.**   Individuals are motivated to exhibit the modeled behavior if positive incentives or rewards are provided. Behaviors that are positively reinforced are given more attention, learned better, and performed more often.

Equity Theory/Organizational Justice

6   Demonstrate how organizational justice is a refinement of equity theory.

Jane Pearson graduated last year from State University with a degree in accounting. After interviews with a number of organizations on campus, she accepted a position with a top public accounting firm and was assigned to the firm's Boston office. Jane was very pleased with the offer she received: challenging work with a prestigious firm, an excellent opportunity to gain valuable experience, and the highest salary any accounting major at State was offered last year—$4,550 per month—but Jane was the top student in her class; she was articulate and mature, and she fully expected to receive a commensurate salary.

Twelve months have passed since Jane joined her employer. The work has proved to be as challenging and satisfying as she had hoped. Her employer is extremely pleased with her performance; in fact, Jane recently received a $200-per-month raise. However, Jane's motivational level has dropped dramatically in the past few weeks. Why? Her employer has just hired a fresh graduate out of State University who lacks the year of experience Jane has gained, for $4,800 per month—$50 more than Jane now makes! Jane is irate. She is even talking about looking for another job.

behaviorism   *A theory that argues that behavior follows stimuli in a relatively unthinking manner.*

social-learning theory   *The view that we can learn through both observation and direct experience.*

| Exhibit 7-7 | Equity Theory |

Ratio Comparisons*	Perception
$\dfrac{O}{I_A} < \dfrac{O}{I_B}$	Inequity due to being underrewarded
$\dfrac{O}{I_A} = \dfrac{O}{I_B}$	Equity
$\dfrac{O}{I_A} > \dfrac{O}{I_B}$	Inequity due to being overrewarded

*Where $\dfrac{O}{I_A}$ represents the employee; and $\dfrac{O}{I_B}$ represents relevant others

Jane's situation illustrates the role equity plays in motivation. Employees perceive what they get from a job situation (salary levels, raises, recognition) in relationship to what they put into it (effort, experience, education, competence) and then compare their outcome–input ratio with that of relevant others. This is shown in Exhibit 7-7. If we perceive our ratio to be equal to that of the relevant others with whom we compare ourselves, a state of equity exists; we perceive that our situation is fair and justice prevails. When we see the ratio as unequal, we experience equity tension. When we see ourselves as underrewarded, the tension creates anger; when we see ourselves as overrewarded, it creates guilt. J. Stacy Adams has proposed that this negative state of tension provides the motivation to do something to correct it.[58]

The referent an employee selects adds to the complexity of **equity theory**.[59] There are four referent comparisons:

1. **Self–inside.**   An employee's experiences in a different position inside the employee's current organization.
2. **Self–outside.**   An employee's experiences in a situation or position outside the employee's current organization.
3. **Other–inside.**   Another individual or group of individuals inside the employee's organization.
4. **Other–outside.**   Another individual or group of individuals outside the employee's organization.

Employees might compare themselves to friends, neighbors, co-workers, or colleagues in other organizations or compare their present job with past jobs they themselves have had. Which referent an employee chooses will be influenced by the information the employee holds about referents as well as by the attractiveness of the referent. Four moderating variables are gender, length of tenure, level in the organization, and amount of education or professionalism.[60]

Research shows both men and women prefer same-sex comparisons. Women are typically paid less than men in comparable jobs and have lower pay expectations than men for the same work.[61] So a woman who uses another woman as a referent tends to calculate a lower comparative standard. This leads us to conclude that employees in jobs that are not sex segregated will make more cross-sex comparisons than those in jobs that are either male or female dominated. This also suggests that if women are tolerant of lower pay, it may be due to the comparative standard they use. Of course, employers' stereotypes about women (for example, the belief that women are less committed to the organization or that "women's work" is less valuable) also may contribute to the pay gap.[62]

Employees with short tenure in their current organizations tend to have little information about others inside the organization, so they rely on their

comes to decision makers. *Explanations* are clear reasons management gives for the outcome. Thus, for employees to see a process as fair, they need to feel they have some control over the outcome and that they were given an adequate explanation about why the outcome occurred. It's also important that a manager is *consistent* (across people and over time), is *unbiased*, makes decisions based on *accurate information*, and is *open to appeals*.[70]

The effects of procedural justice become more important when distributive justice is lacking. This makes sense. If we don't get what we want, we tend to focus on *why*. If your supervisor gives a cushy office to a co-worker instead of to you, you're much more focused on your supervisor's treatment of you than if you had gotten the office. Explanations are beneficial when they take the form of post hoc excuses ("I know this is bad, and I wanted to give you the office, but it wasn't my decision") rather than justifications ("I decided to give the office to Sam, but having it isn't a big deal.").[71]

A recent addition to research on organizational justice is **interactional justice**, an individual's perception of the degree to which she is treated with dignity, concern, and respect. When people are treated in an unjust manner (at least in their own eyes), they retaliate (for example, badmouthing a supervisor).[72] Because people intimately connect interactional justice or injustice to the conveyer of the information, we would expect perceptions of injustice to be more closely related to the supervisor. Generally, that's what the evidence suggests.[73]

Of these three forms of justice, distributive justice is most strongly related to organizational commitment and satisfaction with outcomes such as pay. Procedural justice relates most strongly to job satisfaction, employee trust, withdrawal from the organization, job performance, and citizenship behaviors. There is less evidence about interactional justice.[74]

Managers can help foster employees' perceptions of fairness. First, they should realize that employees are especially sensitive to unfairness in procedures when bad news has to be communicated (that is, when distributive justice is low). Thus, it's especially important to openly share information about how allocation decisions are made, follow consistent and unbiased procedures, and engage in similar practices to increase the perception of procedural justice. Second, when addressing perceived injustices, managers need to focus their actions on the source of the problem. In one weekend in June 2007, Northwest Airlines was forced to cancel 352 flights because many pilots and flight attendants called in sick to protest their pay. Northwest should have realized it needed to offer a tangible remedy rather than apologies or changes in procedures.[75]

Expectancy Theory

7 Apply the key tenets of expectancy theory to motivating employees.

Currently, one of the most widely accepted explanations of motivation is Victor Vroom's **expectancy theory**.[76] Although it has its critics, most of the evidence supports the theory.[77]

Expectancy theory argues that the strength of a tendency to act in a certain way depends on the strength of our expectation of a given outcome and its attractiveness. In more practical terms, employees will be motivated to exert

---

distributive justice *Perceived fairness of the amount and allocation of rewards among individuals.*

organizational justice *An overall perception of what is fair in the workplace, composed of distributive, procedural, and interactional justice.*

procedural justice *The perceived fairness of the process used to determine the distribution of rewards.*

interactional justice *The perceived degree to which an individual is treated with dignity, concern, and respect.*

expectancy theory *A theory that says that the strength of a tendency to act in a certain way depends on the strength of an expectation that the act will be followed by a given outcome and on the attractiveness of that outcome to the individual.*

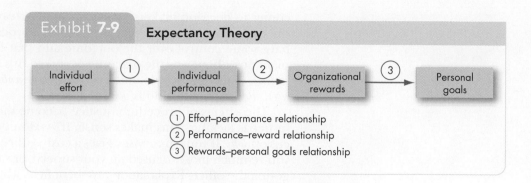

Exhibit 7-9   Expectancy Theory

1. Effort–performance relationship
2. Performance–reward relationship
3. Rewards–personal goals relationship

a high level of effort when they believe it will lead to a good performance appraisal; that a good appraisal will lead to organizational rewards such as bonuses, salary increases, or promotions; and that the rewards will satisfy the employees' personal goals. The theory, therefore, focuses on three relationships (see Exhibit 7-9):

1. **Effort–performance relationship.**   The probability perceived by the individual that exerting a given amount of effort will lead to performance.
2. **Performance–reward relationship.**   The degree to which the individual believes performing at a particular level will lead to the attainment of a desired outcome.
3. **Rewards–personal goals relationship.**   The degree to which organizational rewards satisfy an individual's personal goals or needs and the attractiveness of those potential rewards for the individual.[78]

Expectancy theory helps explain why a lot of workers aren't motivated on their jobs and do only the minimum necessary to get by. Let's frame the theory's three relationships as questions employees need to answer in the affirmative if their motivation is to be maximized.

First, *if I give a maximum effort, will it be recognized in my performance appraisal?* For many employees, the answer is "no." Why? Their skill level may be deficient, which means that no matter how hard they try, they're not likely to be high performers. The organization's performance appraisal system may be designed to assess nonperformance factors such as loyalty, initiative, or courage, which means more effort won't necessarily result in a higher evaluation. Another possibility is that employees, rightly or wrongly, perceive the boss doesn't like them. As a result, they expect to get a poor appraisal, regardless of level of effort. These examples suggest one possible source of low motivation is employees' belief that, no matter how hard they work, the likelihood of getting a good performance appraisal is low.

Second, *if I get a good performance appraisal, will it lead to organizational rewards?* Many organizations reward a lot of things besides performance. When pay is based on factors such as having seniority, being cooperative, or "kissing up" to the boss, employees are likely to see the performance–reward relationship as weak and demotivating.

Finally, *if I'm rewarded, are the rewards attractive to me?* The employee works hard in the hope of getting a promotion but gets a pay raise instead. Or the employee wants a more interesting and challenging job but receives only a few words of praise. Or the employee puts in extra effort to be relocated to the Paris office but instead is transferred to Singapore. It's important to tailor rewards to individual employee needs. Unfortunately, many managers are limited in the rewards they can distribute, which makes this difficult. Some incorrectly assume all employees want the same thing, thus overlooking the motivational effects of differentiating rewards. In either case, employee motivation is submaximized.

At Mary Kay Cosmetics, the performance-reward relationship is strong. The company offers a generous rewards and recognition program based on the achievement of personal goals set by each employee. Mary Kay also understands the motivational effects of differentiating rewards. For some employees, the best reward is the opportunity to work from home while others are motivated by the opportunity to win a luxury trip. In this photo, a Mary Kay sales director explains career opportunities at a job fair to women interested in joining the company.

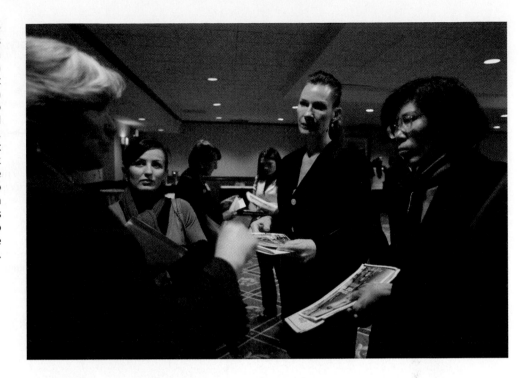

As a vivid example of how expectancy theory can work, consider stock analysts. They make their living by trying to forecast the future of a stock's price; the accuracy of their buy, sell, or hold recommendations is what keeps them in work or gets them fired. But it's not quite that simple. Analysts place few sell ratings on stocks, although in a steady market, by definition, as many stocks are falling as are rising. Expectancy theory provides an explanation: analysts who place a sell rating on a company's stock have to balance the benefits they receive by being accurate against the risks they run by drawing the company's ire. What are these risks? They include public rebuke, professional blackballing, and exclusion from information. When analysts place a buy rating on a stock, they face no such trade-off because, obviously, companies love that they are recommending that investors buy their stock. So, the incentive structure suggests the expected outcome of buy ratings is higher than the expected outcome of sell ratings, and that's why buy ratings vastly outnumber sell ratings.[79]

Does expectancy theory work? Some critics suggest it has only limited use and is more valid where individuals clearly perceive effort–performance and performance–reward linkages.[80] Because few individuals do perceive these links, the theory tends to be idealistic. If organizations actually rewarded individuals for performance rather than according to criteria such as seniority, effort, skill level, and job difficulty, expectancy theory might be much more valid. However, rather than invalidating it, this criticism can explain why a significant segment of the workforce exerts low levels of effort on the job.

Integrating Contemporary Theories of Motivation

8 Compare contemporary theories of motivation.

Things might be simpler if, after presenting a half dozen theories, we could say only one was found valid. But the theories we've presented are not all in competition with one another. That one is valid doesn't invalidate the others. In fact, many of the theories in this chapter are complementary. We now tie them together to help you understand their interrelationships.[81]

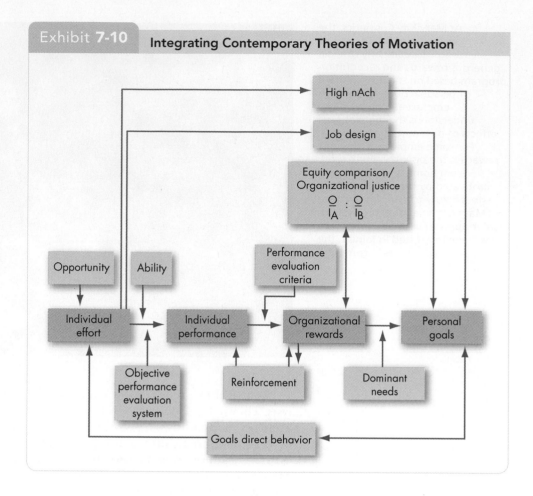

Exhibit **7-10**   **Integrating Contemporary Theories of Motivation**

Exhibit 7-10 presents a model that integrates much of what we know about motivation. Its basic foundation is the expectancy model shown in Exhibit 7-9. Let's work through Exhibit 7-10. (We will look at job design closely in Chapter 8.)

We begin by explicitly recognizing that opportunities can either aid or hinder individual effort. The individual effort box on the left also has another arrow leading into it, from the person's goals. Consistent with goal-setting theory, the goals–effort loop is meant to remind us that goals direct behavior.

Expectancy theory predicts employees will exert a high level of effort if they perceive a strong relationship between effort and performance, performance and rewards, and rewards and satisfaction of personal goals. Each of these relationships is, in turn, influenced by other factors. For effort to lead to good performance, the individual must have the ability to perform, and the performance appraisal system must be perceived as fair and objective. The performance–reward relationship will be strong if the individual perceives that performance (rather than seniority, personal favorites, or other criteria) is rewarded. If cognitive evaluation theory were fully valid in the actual workplace, we would predict here that basing rewards on performance should decrease the individual's intrinsic motivation. The final link in expectancy theory is the rewards–goals relationship. Motivation is high if the rewards an individual received for high performance satisfied the dominant needs consistent with individual goals.

A closer look at Exhibit 7-10 also reveals that the model considers achievement motivation, job design, reinforcement, and equity theories/organizational justice. A high achiever is not motivated by an organization's assessment of performance or organizational rewards, hence the jump from effort to personal goals for those with a high nAch. Remember, high achievers are internally driven as long as their jobs provide them with personal responsibility, feedback, and moderate risks. They are not concerned with the effort–performance, performance–rewards, or rewards–goal linkages.

Reinforcement theory enters the model by recognizing that the organization's rewards reinforce the individual's performance. If employees see a reward system as "paying off" for good performance, the rewards will reinforce and encourage continued good performance. Rewards also play the key part in organizational justice research. Individuals will judge the favorability of their outcomes (for example, their pay) relative to what others receive but also with respect to how they are treated: when people are disappointed in their rewards, they are likely to be sensitive to the perceived fairness of the procedures used and the consideration given to them by their supervisor.

Global Implications

9 Show how motivation theories are culture bound.

Most current motivation theories were developed in the United States by and about U.S. adults.[82] Goal-setting and expectancy theories emphasize goal accomplishment as well as rational and individual thought—characteristics consistent with U.S. culture. Let's look at several motivation theories and consider their cross cultural transferability.

Maslow's needs hierarchy says people start at the physiological level and progress up the hierarchy to safety, social, esteem, and self-actualization needs. This hierarchy, if it applies at all, aligns with U.S. culture. In Japan, Greece, and Mexico, where uncertainty-avoidance characteristics are strong, security needs would be on top of the hierarchy. Countries that score high on nurturing characteristics—Denmark, Sweden, Norway, the Netherlands, and Finland—would have social needs on top.[83] Group work will motivate employees more when the country's culture scores high on the nurturing criterion.

The view that a high achievement need acts as an internal motivator presupposes two U.S. cultural characteristics—willingness to accept a moderate degree of risk (which excludes countries with strong uncertainty avoidance characteristics) and concern with performance (which applies to countries with strong achievement characteristics). This combination is found in Anglo-American countries such as the United States, Canada, and Great Britain[84] and much less so in Chile and Portugal.

Equity theory has gained a strong following in the United States because U.S.-style reward systems assume workers are highly sensitive to equity in reward allocations. And in the United States equity is meant to closely tie pay to performance. However, in collectivist cultures, especially the former socialist countries of Central and Eastern Europe, employees expect rewards to reflect their individual needs as well as their performance.[85] Consistent with a legacy of communism and centrally planned economies, employees exhibited an entitlement attitude—that is, they expected outcomes to be *greater* than their inputs.[86] These findings suggest that U.S.-style pay practices may need modification, especially in Russia and former communist countries, to be perceived as fair by employees.

But don't assume there are *no* cross-cultural consistencies. The desire for interesting work seems important to almost all workers, regardless of their national culture. In a study of seven countries, employees in Belgium, Britain, Israel, and the United States ranked work number 1 among 11 work goals, and workers in Japan, the Netherlands, and Germany ranked it either second or third.[87] In a study comparing job-preference outcomes among graduate students in the United States, Canada, Australia, and Singapore, growth, achievement, and responsibility had identical rankings as the top three.[88] Meta-analytic evidence shows individuals in both individualistic and collectivistic cultures prefer an equitable distribution of rewards (the most effective workers get paid the most) over an equal division (everyone gets paid the same regardless of performance).[89] Across nations, the same basic principles of procedural justice are respected, and workers around the world prefer rewards based on performance and skills over rewards based on seniority.[90]

Summary and Implications for Managers

Some theories in this chapter address turnover, while others emphasize productivity. They also differ in their predictive strength. In this section, we (1) review the most established motivation theories to determine their relevance in explaining the dependent variables and (2) assess the predictive power of each.[91]

Need Theories   Maslow's hierarchy, McClelland's needs, and the two-factor theory focus on needs. None has found widespread support, although McClelland's is the strongest, particularly regarding the relationship between achievement and productivity. In general, need theories are not very valid explanations of motivation.

Self-Determination Theory and **Cognitive Evaluation Theory**   As research on the motivational effects of rewards has accumulated, it increasingly appears extrinsic rewards can undermine motivation if they are seen as coercive. They can increase motivation if they provide information about competence and relatedness.

Goal-Setting Theory   Clear and difficult goals lead to higher levels of employee productivity, supporting goal-setting theory's explanation of this dependent variable. The theory does not address absenteeism, turnover, or satisfaction, however.

Reinforcement Theory   This theory has an impressive record for predicting quality and quantity of work, persistence of effort, absenteeism, tardiness, and accident rates. It does not offer much insight into employee satisfaction or the decision to quit.

Equity Theory/Organizational Justice   Equity theory deals with productivity, satisfaction, absence, and turnover variables. However, its strongest legacy is that it provided the spark for research on organizational justice, which has more support in the literature.

Expectancy Theory   Expectancy theory offers a powerful explanation of performance variables such as employee productivity, absenteeism, and turnover. But it assumes employees have few constraints on decision making, such as bias or incomplete information, and this limits its applicability. Expectancy theory has some validity because for many behaviors people consider expected outcomes. However, it goes only so far in explaining behavior.

Failure Motivates!

POINT

Many of the best lessons we learn in life come from our failures. Consider Chris Gardner. In 1982, Gardner was homeless, raising a 20-month-old son in San Francisco, and peddling medical devices few wanted to buy. Unable to afford both housing and child care, Gardner boarded himself and his son where he could—even in the bathroom at the Bay Area Rapid Transit office. A happy ending was nowhere in sight.

After seeing a stockbroker drive a red Ferrari, Gardner resolved he'd be a stockbroker, too. He looked up the offices of Dean Witter, then one of the largest U.S. investment banking firms (it later merged with Morgan Stanley). Gardner was able to line up an interview for a spot in the firm's internship program.

The night before his interview, Gardner was taken to jail for a backlog of parking tickets he couldn't afford to pay. Unshaven and disheveled, in yesterday's clothes, he explained his situation in the interview, and Dean Witter took a chance on him. Gardner remembered advice his mother had given him: "You can only depend on yourself. The cavalry ain't coming."

At Dean Witter, Gardner made two hundred calls a day. "Every time I picked up the phone," he said, "I knew I was getting closer to digging myself out of the hole." Gardner made it at Dean Witter, became a top earner at Bear Stearns, and now runs his own brokerage firm in Chicago. His story became a best-selling book and a major motion picture (*The Pursuit of Happyness*) starring Will Smith, which Gardner helped produce. A table in his office is piled high with letters from people inspired by his story. On occasion, he'll call one of the letter writers. He says, "I find myself saying over and over 'Baby steps count.'"

Not only does failure bring perspective to people such as Gardner, it provides important feedback on how to improve. The important thing is to learn from failure and to persist. As Gardner told students in his commencement address at the University of California in 2009, "You can draw inspiration from others, but what happens when there ain't nobody else there? You have to be there for yourself."[92]

COUNTERPOINT

Do people learn from failure? One of the decision-making errors people make is escalation of commitment: they persist in a failed venture because they think persistence is a virtue or because their ego is involved, even when logic suggests they should move on. One research study found managers often illogically persist in launching new products, even when it's clear the product is going nowhere. As the authors note, "It sometimes takes more courage to kill a product that's going nowhere than to sustain it." Learning from failure is a nice ideal, but most people are too defensive to do that. Failure is helpful only if the person benefits from it, and that's a big assumption. Many times people don't recover, or they would have been more successful if not for the failure.

Evidence shows that when people fail they often rationalize their failures to preserve their self-esteem and thus don't learn at all. Although the example of Chris Gardner is interesting, it doesn't prove his success comes from learning from his failures. When we fail or experience painful episodes, we often wish to explain the past—by rationalizing that the failure and painful experiences were key to our success. These rationalizations may not be correct, but we engage in them to preserve our often fragile self-esteem and to make sense of what is often simply bad luck. We need to believe in ourselves to motivate ourselves, and because failing undermines that self-belief, we do what we can to recover our self-confidence.[93]

Although it makes a nice story that failure is actually good, as one songwriter wrote, "The world is not a song." Failure hurts, and to either protect ourselves or recover from the pain, we often do *not* learn from failure—we rationalize it away.

Questions for Review

1 Define *motivation*. What are the key elements of motivation?

2 What are the early theories of motivation? How well have they been supported by research?

3 What is cognitive evaluation theory? What does it assume about the effects of intrinsic and extrinsic rewards on behavior?

4 What are the major predictions of goal-setting theory? Have these predictions been supported by research?

5 What is reinforcement theory? How is it related to goal-setting theory? Has research supported reinforcement theory?

6 What is equity theory? Why has it been supplanted by organizational justice?

7 What are the key tenets of expectancy theory? What has research had to say about this theory?

8 How do the contemporary theories of work motivation complement one another?

9 Do you think motivation theories are often culture bound? Why or why not?

Experiential Exercise

GOAL-SETTING TASK

Purpose

This exercise will help you learn how to write tangible, verifiable, measurable, and relevant goals that might evolve from an MBO program.

Time

Approximately 20 to 30 minutes.

Instructions

1. Break into groups of three to five.
2. Spend a few minutes discussing your class instructor's job. What does he or she do? What defines good performance? What behaviors lead to good performance?
3. Each group is to develop a list of five goals that, although not established participatively with your instructor, you believe might be developed in an MBO program at your college. Try to select goals that seem most critical to the effective performance of your instructor's job.
4. Each group will select a leader who will share the group's goals with the entire class. For each group's goals, class discussion should focus on the goals' (a) specificity, (b) ease of measurement, (c) importance, and (d) motivational properties.

Ethical Dilemma

IS GOAL-SETTING MANIPULATION?

Managers are interested in the subject of motivation because they want to learn how to get the most effort from their employees. Is this ethical? When managers set hard, specific goals for employees, aren't they manipulating them?

Manipulate is defined as "(1) to handle, manage, or use, especially with skill, in some process of treatment or performance; (2) to manage or influence by artful skill; (3) to adapt or change to suit one's purpose or advantage."

Aren't these definitions compatible with the notion of managers skillfully seeking to influence employee productivity for the benefit of the manager and the organization?

Do managers have the right to seek control over their employees? Does anyone, for that matter, have the right to control others? Does control imply manipulation? And if so, is there anything wrong with managers manipulating employees through goal setting or other motivational techniques?

Case Incident 1

DO U.S. WORKERS "LIVE TO WORK"?

Many people around the world believe U.S. adults live only to work. Do we really work that much harder than people in other countries? To answer this question, we turn to data collected by OECD, an organization that researches economic development issues. The following figures represent the average hours worked per week (total number of hours an average employee works per year, divided by 52), averaged over the most recent 5 years available, for member countries of the OECD:

1.	South Korea	46.7
2.	Greece	39.9
3.	Hungary	38.6
4.	Czech Republic	38.2
5.	Poland	38.1
6.	Mexico	36.0
7.	Italy	35.2
8.	Iceland	34.9
9.	New Zealand	34.9
10.	Japan	34.5
11.	Canada	33.6
12.	Slovak Republic	33.5
13.	Australia	33.4
14.	Finland	33.2
15.	United States	33.0
16.	Spain	32.7
17.	Portugal	32.5
18.	United Kingdom	32.4
19.	Ireland	31.8
20.	Switzerland	31.7
21.	Austria	31.6
22.	Luxembourg	30.5
23.	Sweden	30.4
24.	Denmark	29.8
25.	France	29.8
26.	Belgium	29.6
27.	Germany	27.8
28.	Netherlands	26.1
29.	Norway	26.0

Questions

1. Do these results surprise you? Why or why not?
2. Why do you think U.S. employees have a reputation for "living to work"?
3. Do these results prove that Koreans, for example, are more motivated to work than their U.S. counterparts? Why or why not?
4. A research study has suggested that changes in hours worked over time are due, in part, to changes in tax rates. "If taxes and [government expenditures] are high, that may lead to less work," said one of the researchers. Supporting this theory, since 2001, workers in the United States have increased their hours worked while tax rates have dropped. What theory or theories of motivation might explain such a change?

Source: L. Ohanian, A. Raffo, and R. Rogerson, *Long-Term Changes in Labor Supply and Taxes: Evidence from OECD Countries, 1956–2004,* NBER working paper 12786, December 2006; and J. J. Smith, "Taxes Likely Causing Some Countries' Workers to Labor Fewer Hours," *SHRM Online,* May 2007, www.shrm.org.

Case Incident 2

BULLYING BOSSES

After a long weekend, Kara stared at her computer with a sick feeling in her stomach: Her boss had added her as a friend on Facebook. Kara did not feel particularly close to her boss, nor did she like the idea of mixing her social life with her work. Still, it was her boss. Kara reluctantly accepted her boss as a Facebook friend. Little did she know her troubles were only beginning.

Kara's boss soon began using her online information to manipulate her work life. It began with inappropriate innuendos regarding Facebook photos. Eventually, Kara's boss manipulated her work hours, confronted her both on and off Facebook, and repeatedly called Kara's cell phone questioning her whereabouts. "My boss was a gossiping, domineering, contriving megalomaniac, and her behavior dramatically intensified when she used Facebook to pry," Kara said. Eventually, Kara was forced to quit. "I feel like I got my freedom back and can breathe again," she said.

Although many individuals recall bullies from elementary school days, some are realizing bullies can exist in the workplace, too. In a recent poll, 37 percent of employees report being victims of a bullying boss. And these bullies don't pick on just the weakest in the group; any subordinate may fall prey. As Kara found, bullying is not limited to male bosses: 40 percent of bullies are women, and women are their targets 70 percent of the time.

How does bullying affect employee motivation and behavior? Surprisingly, though victims may feel less motivated to go to work every day, they continue performing their required job duties. However, some are less motivated to perform extra-role or citizenship behaviors. Helping others, speaking positively about the organization, and going beyond the call of duty are reduced as a result of bullying. According to Dr. Bennett Tepper of the University of North Carolina, fear may be the reason many workers continue to perform. And not all individuals reduce their citizenship behaviors. Some continue to engage in extra-role behaviors to make themselves look better than their colleagues.

What should you do if your boss is bullying you? Don't necessarily expect help from co-workers. As Emelise Aleandri, an actress and producer from New York who left her job after being bullied, stated, "Some people were afraid to do anything. But others didn't mind what was happening at all, because they wanted my job." Moreover, according to Dr. Michelle Duffy of the University of

Kentucky, co-workers often blame victims of bullying in order to resolve their own guilt. "They do this by wondering whether maybe the person deserved the treatment, that he or she has been annoying, or lazy, [or] did something to earn it," she says.

Questions

1. Workplace bullying demonstrates a lack of which one of the three types of organizational justice?

2. What aspects of motivation might workplace bullying reduce? For example, are there likely to be effects on an employee's self-efficacy? If so, what might those effects be?

3. If you were a victim of workplace bullying, what steps would you take to try to reduce its occurrence? What strategies would be most effective? Least effective? What would you do if one of your colleagues were a victim?

4. What factors do you believe contribute to workplace bullying? Are bullies a product of the situation, or do they have flawed personalities? What situations and what personality factors might contribute to the presence of bullies?

Sources: Based on M. Wilding, "Is Your Boss Your Friend or Foe?" *Sydney Morning Herald* (May 19, 2009), pp. 1–3; and C. Benedict, "The Bullying Boss," *New York Times,* June 22, 2004, p. F1.

Endnotes

1. A. Sloan, "An Unhappy Anniversary for the Financial Crisis," *Washington Post* (May 26, 2009), www.washingtonpost.com; and L. Story, "The Broker Rebellion," *New York Times* (October 25, 2008), pp. B1, B6. H. Potkewitz, "Wall Street Job Losses Not Quite Adding Up," *Workforce Management* (May 26, 2009), www.workforce.com/.

2. C. A. O'Reilly III, "Organizational Behavior: Where We've Been, Where We're Going," in M. R. Rosenzweig and L. W. Porter (eds.), *Annual Review of Psychology,* vol. 42 (Palo Alto, CA: Annual Reviews, 1991), p. 431; see also M. L. Ambrose and C. T. Kulik, "Old Friends, New Faces: Motivation Research in the 1990s," *Journal of Management* 25, no. 3 (1999), pp. 231–292.

3. Cited in D. Jones, "Firms Spend Billions to Fire Up Workers—With Little Luck," *USA Today,* May 10, 2001, p. 1A.

4. "Wasted Time at Work Costs Employers Billions," *IPMA-HR Bulletin,* August 11, 2006, pp. 1–7.

5. See, for instance, T. R. Mitchell, "Matching Motivational Strategies with Organizational Contexts," in L. L. Cummings and B. M. Staw (eds.), *Research in Organizational Behavior,* vol. 19 (Greenwich, CT: JAI Press, 1997), pp. 60–62.

6. A. Maslow, *Motivation and Personality* (New York: Harper & Row, 1954).

7. See, for example, E. E. Lawler III and J. L. Suttle, "A Causal Correlation Test of the Need Hierarchy Concept," *Organizational Behavior and Human Performance,* April 1972, pp. 265–287; D. T. Hall and K. E. Nougaim, "An Examination of Maslow's Need Hierarchy in an Organizational Setting," *Organizational Behavior and Human Performance,* February 1968, pp. 12–35; A. K. Korman, J. H. Greenhaus, and I. J. Badin, "Personnel Attitudes and Motivation," in M. R. Rosenzweig and L. W. Porter (eds.), *Annual Review of Psychology* (Palo Alto, CA: Annual Reviews, 1977), pp. 178–179; and J. Rauschenberger, N. Schmitt, and J. E. Hunter, "A Test of the Need Hierarchy Concept by a Markov Model of Change in Need Strength," *Administrative Science Quarterly,* December 1980, pp. 654–670.

8. M. A. Wahba and L. G. Bridwell, "Maslow Reconsidered: A Review of Research on the Need Hierarchy Theory," *Organizational Behavior and Human Performance,* April 1976, pp. 212–240.

9. D. McGregor, *The Human Side of Enterprise* (New York: McGraw-Hill, 1960). For an updated analysis of Theory X and Theory Y constructs, see R. J. Summers and S. F. Cronshaw, "A Study of McGregor's Theory X, Theory Y and the Influence of Theory X, Theory Y Assumptions on Causal Attributions for Instances of Worker Poor Performance," in S. L. McShane (ed.), *Organizational Behavior, ASAC 1988 Conference Proceedings,* vol. 9, part 5. Halifax, Nova Scotia, 1988, pp. 115–123.

10. A. E. Abele, "The Dynamics of Masculine-Agentic and Feminine-Communal Traits: Findings from a Prospective Study," *Journal of Personality and Social Psychology*, October 2003, pp. 768–776; and R. Ely, G. Melzi, and L. Hadge, "Being Brave, Being Nice: Themes of Agency and Communion in Children's Narratives," *Journal of Personality*, April 1998, pp. 257–284.

11. F. Herzberg, B. Mausner, and B. Snyderman, *The Motivation to Work* (New York: Wiley, 1959).

12. R. J. House and L. A. Wigdor, "Herzberg's Dual-Factor Theory of Job Satisfaction and Motivations: A Review of the Evidence and Criticism," *Personnel Psychology*, Winter 1967, pp. 369–389; D. P. Schwab and L. L. Cummings, "Theories of Performance and Satisfaction: A Review," *Industrial Relations*, October 1970, pp. 403–430; and J. Phillipchuk and J. Whittaker, "An Inquiry into the Continuing Relevance of Herzberg's Motivation Theory," *Engineering Management Journal* 8 (1996), pp. 15–20.

13. D. C. McClelland, *The Achieving Society* (New York: Van Nostrand Reinhold, 1961); J. W. Atkinson and J. O. Raynor, *Motivation and Achievement* (Washington, DC: Winston, 1974); D. C. McClelland, *Power: The Inner Experience* (New York: Irvington, 1975); and M. J. Stahl, *Managerial and Technical Motivation: Assessing Needs for Achievement, Power, and Affiliation* (New York: Praeger, 1986).

14. D. C. McClelland and D. G. Winter, *Motivating Economic Achievement* (New York: The Free Press, 1969); and J. B. Miner, N. R. Smith, and J. S. Bracker, "Role of Entrepreneurial Task Motivation in the Growth of Technologically Innovative Firms: Interpretations from Follow-up Data," *Journal of Applied Psychology*, October 1994, pp. 627–630.

15. D. C. McClelland, *Power;* D. C. McClelland and D. H. Burnham, "Power Is the Great Motivator," *Harvard Business Review*, March–April 1976, pp. 100–110; and R. E. Boyatzis, "The Need for Close Relationships and the Manager's Job," in D. A. Kolb, I. M. Rubin, and J. M. McIntyre, *Organizational Psychology: Readings on Human Behavior in Organizations*, 4th ed. (Upper Saddle River, NJ: Prentice Hall, 1984), pp. 81–86.

16. D. G. Winter, "The Motivational Dimensions of Leadership: Power, Achievement, and Affiliation," in R. E. Riggio, S. E. Murphy, and F. J. Pirozzolo (eds.), *Multiple Intelligences and Leadership* (Mahwah, NJ: Lawrence Erlbaum, 2002), pp. 119–138.

17. J. B. Miner, *Studies in Management Education* (New York: Springer, 1965).

18. E. Deci and R. Ryan (eds.), *Handbook of self-determination research* (Rochester, NY: University of Rochester Press, 2002); R. Ryan, and E. Deci, "Self-Determination Theory and the Facilitation of Intrinsic Motivation, Social Development, and Well-Being," *American Psychologist* 55, no. 1 (2000), pp. 68–78; and M. Gagné and E. L. Deci, "Self-Determination Theory and Work Motivation," *Journal of Organizational Behavior* 26, no. 4 (2005), pp. 331–362.

19. E. L. Deci, R. Koestner, and R. M. Ryan, "A Meta-analytic Review of Experiments Examining the Effects of Extrinsic Rewards on Intrinsic Motivation," *Psychological Bulletin* 125, no. 6 (1999), pp. 627–668; N. Houlfort, R. Koestner, M. Joussemet, A. Nantel-Vivier, and N. Lekes, "The Impact of Performance-Contingent Rewards on Perceived Autonomy and Competence," *Motivation & Emotion* 26, no. 4 (2002),

pp. 279–295; and G. J. Greguras and J. M. Diefendorff, "Different Fits Satisfy Different Needs: Linking Person-Environment Fit to Employee Commitment and Performance Using Self-Determination Theory," *Journal of Applied Psychology* 94, no. 2 (2009), pp. 465–477.

20. R. Eisenberger and L. Rhoades, "Incremental Effects of Reward on Creativity," *Journal of Personality and Social Psychology* 81, no. 4 (2001), 728–741; and R. Eisenberger, W. D. Pierce, and J. Cameron, "Effects of Reward on Intrinsic Motivation—Negative, Neutral, and Positive: Comment on Deci, Koestner, and Ryan (1999)," *Psychological Bulletin* 125, no. 6 (1999), pp. 677–691.

21. M. Burgess, M. E. Enzle, and R. Schmaltz, "Defeating the Potentially Deleterious Effects of Externally Imposed Deadlines: Practitioners' Rules-of-Thumb," *Personality and Social Psychology Bulletin* 30, no. 7 (2004), pp. 868–877.

22. K. M. Sheldon, A. J. Elliot, and R. M. Ryan, "Self-Concordance and Subjective Well-being in Four Cultures," *Journal of Cross-Cultural Psychology* 35, no. 2 (2004), pp. 209–223.

23. J. E. Bono and T. A. Judge, "Self-Concordance at Work: Toward Understanding the Motivational Effects of Transformational Leaders," *Academy of Management Journal* 46, no. 5 (2003), pp. 554–571.

24. J. P. Meyer, T. E. Becker, and C. Vandenberghe, "Employee Commitment and Motivation: A Conceptual Analysis and Integrative Model," *Journal of Applied Psychology* 89, no. 6 (2004), pp. 991–1007.

25. E. A. Locke, "Toward a Theory of Task Motivation and Incentives," *Organizational Behavior and Human Performance*, May 1968, pp. 157–189.

26. P. C. Earley, P. Wojnaroski, and W. Prest, "Task Planning and Energy Expended: Exploration of How Goals Influence Performance," *Journal of Applied Psychology*, February 1987, pp. 107–114.

27. See M. E. Tubbs "Goal Setting: A Meta-analytic Examination of the Empirical Evidence," *Journal of Applied Psychology*, August 1986, pp. 474–483; E. A. Locke and G. P. Latham, "Building a Practically Useful Theory of Goal Setting and Task Motivation," *American Psychologist*, September 2002, pp. 705–717; and E. A. Locke and G. P. Latham, "New Directions in Goal-Setting Theory," *Current Directions in Psychological Science* 15, no. 5 (2006), pp. 265–268.

28. Locke and Latham, "Building a Practically Useful Theory of Goal Setting and Task Motivation," pp. 705–717.

29. J. M. Ivancevich and J. T. McMahon, "The Effects of Goal Setting, External Feedback, and Self-Generated Feedback on Outcome Variables: A Field Experiment," *Academy of Management Journal*, June 1982, pp. 359–372; and E. A. Locke, "Motivation Through Conscious Goal Setting," *Applied and Preventive Psychology* 5 (1996), pp. 117–124.

30. See, for example, G. P. Latham, M. Erez, and E. A. Locke, "Resolving Scientific Disputes by the Joint Design of Crucial Experiments by the Antagonists: Application to the Erez-Latham Dispute Regarding Participation in Goal Setting," *Journal of Applied Psychology*, November 1988, pp. 753–772; T. D. Ludwig and E. S. Geller, "Assigned Versus Participative Goal Setting and Response Generalization: Managing Injury Control among Professional Pizza Deliverers," *Journal of Applied Psychology*, April 1997, pp. 253–261; and S. G. Harkins

and M. D. Lowe, "The Effects of Self-Set Goals on Task Performance," *Journal of Applied Social Psychology,* January 2000, pp. 1–40.

31. M. Erez, P. C. Earley, and C. L. Hulin, "The Impact of Participation on Goal Acceptance and Performance: A Two-Step Model," *Academy of Management Journal,* March 1985, pp. 50–66.

32. E. A. Locke, "The Motivation to Work: What We Know," *Advances in Motivation and Achievement* 10 (1997), pp. 375–412; and Latham, Erez, and Locke, "Resolving Scientific Disputes by the Joint Design of Crucial Experiments by the Antagonists," pp. 753–772.

33. H. J. Klein, M. J. Wesson, J. R. Hollenbeck, P. M. Wright, and R. D. DeShon, "The Assessment of Goal Commitment: A Measurement Model Meta-analysis," *Organizational Behavior and Human Decision Processes* 85, no. 1 (2001), pp. 32–55.

34. J. R. Hollenbeck, C. R. Williams, and H. J. Klein, "An Empirical Examination of the Antecedents of Commitment to Difficult Goals," *Journal of Applied Psychology,* February 1989, pp. 18–23. See also J. C. Wofford, V. L. Goodwin, and S. Premack, "Meta-analysis of the Antecedents of Personal Goal Level and of the Antecedents and Consequences of Goal Commitment," *Journal of Management,* September 1992, pp. 595–615; M. E. Tubbs, "Commitment as a Moderator of the Goal-Performance Relation: A Case for Clearer Construct Definition," *Journal of Applied Psychology,* February 1993, pp. 86–97; and J. E. Bono and A. E. Colbert, "Understanding Responses to Multi-Source Feedback: The Role of Core Self-evaluations," *Personnel Psychology,* Spring 2005, pp. 171–203.

35. See R. E. Wood, A. J. Mento, and E. A. Locke, "Task Complexity as a Moderator of Goal Effects: A Meta-analysis," *Journal of Applied Psychology,* August 1987, pp. 416–425; R. Kanfer and P. L. Ackerman, "Motivation and Cognitive Abilities: An Integrative/Aptitude-Treatment Interaction Approach to Skill Acquisition," *Journal of Applied Psychology (monograph),* vol. 74, 1989, pp. 657–690; T. R. Mitchell and W. S. Silver, "Individual and Group Goals When Workers Are Interdependent: Effects on Task Strategies and Performance," *Journal of Applied Psychology,* April 1990, pp. 185–193; and A. M. O'Leary-Kelly, J. J. Martocchio, and D. D. Frink, "A Review of the Influence of Group Goals on Group Performance," *Academy of Management Journal,* October 1994, pp. 1285–1301.

36. D. F. Crown, "The Use of Group and Groupcentric Individual Goals for Culturally Heterogeneous and Homogeneous Task Groups: An Assessment of European Work Teams," *Small Group Research* 38, no. 4 (2007), pp. 489–508; J. Kurman, "Self-Regulation Strategies in Achievement Settings: Culture and Gender Differences," *Journal of Cross-Cultural Psychology* 32, no. 4 (2001), pp. 491–503; and M. Erez and P. C. Earley, "Comparative Analysis of Goal-Setting Strategies Across Cultures," *Journal of Applied Psychology* 72, no. 4 (1987), pp. 658–665.

37. C. Sue-Chan and M. Ong, "Goal Assignment and Performance: Assessing the Mediating Roles of Goal Commitment and Self-Efficacy and the Moderating Role of Power Distance," *Organizational Behavior and Human Decision Processes* 89, no. 2 (2002), pp. 1140–1161.

38. G. P. Latham and E. A. Locke, "Enhancing the Benefits and Overcoming the Pitfalls of Goal Setting," *Organizational Dynamics* 35, no. 6, pp. 332–340; L. D. Ordóñez, M. E. Schweitzer, A. D. Galinsky, and M. Bazerman, "Goals Gone Wild: The Systematic Side Effects of Overprescribing Goal Setting," *Academy of Management Perspectives* 23, no. 1 (2009), pp. 6–16; and E. A. Locke and G. P. Latham, "Has Goal Setting Gone Wild, or Have Its Attackers Abandoned Good Scholarship?" *Academy of Management Perspectives* 23, no. 1 (2009), pp. 17–23.

39. "KEYGroup Survey Finds Nearly Half of All Employees Have No Set Performance Goals," *IPMA-HR Bulletin,* March 10, 2006, p. 1; S. Hamm, "SAP Dangles a Big, Fat Carrot," *BusinessWeek,* May 22, 2006, pp. 67–68; and "P&G CEO Wields High Expectations but No Whip," *USA Today,* February 19, 2007, p. 3B.

40. See, for instance, S. J. Carroll and H. L. Tosi, *Management by Objectives: Applications and Research* (New York: Macmillan, 1973); and R. Rodgers and J. E. Hunter, "Impact of Management by Objectives on Organizational Productivity," *Journal of Applied Psychology,* April 1991, pp. 322–336.

41. See, for instance, R. C. Ford, F. S. MacLaughlin, and J. Nixdorf, "Ten Questions About MBO," *California Management Review,* Winter 1980, p. 89; T. J. Collamore, "Making MBO Work in the Public Sector," *Bureaucrat,* Fall 1989, pp. 37–40; G. Dabbs, "Nonprofit Businesses in the 1990s: Models for Success," *Business Horizons,* September–October 1991, pp. 68–71; R. Rodgers and J. E. Hunter, "A Foundation of Good Management Practice in Government: Management by Objectives," *Public Administration Review,* January–February 1992, pp. 27–39; T. H. Poister and G. Streib, "MBO in Municipal Government: Variations on a Traditional Management Tool," *Public Administration Review,* January/February 1995, pp. 48–56; and C. Garvey, "Goalsharing Scores," *HRMagazine,* April 2000, pp. 99–106.

42. See, for instance, C. H. Ford, "MBO: An Idea Whose Time Has Gone?" *Business Horizons,* December 1979, p. 49; R. Rodgers and J. E. Hunter, "Impact of Management by Objectives on Organizational Productivity," *Journal of Applied Psychology,* April 1991, pp. 322–336; R. Rodgers, J. E. Hunter, and D. L. Rogers, "Influence of Top Management Commitment on Management Program Success," *Journal of Applied Psychology,* February 1993, pp. 151–155; and M. Tanikawa, "Fujitsu Decides to Backtrack on Performance-Based Pay," *New York Times,* March 22, 2001, p. W1.

43. A. Bandura, *Self-Efficacy: The Exercise of Control* (New York: Freeman, 1997).

44. A. D. Stajkovic and F. Luthans, "Self-Efficacy and Work-Related Performance: A Meta-analysis," *Psychological Bulletin,* September 1998, pp. 240–261; and A. Bandura, "Cultivate Self-Efficacy for Personal and Organizational Effectiveness," in E. Locke (ed.), *Handbook of Principles of Organizational Behavior* (Malden, MA: Blackwell, 2004), pp. 120–136.

45. A. Bandura and D. Cervone, "Differential Engagement in Self-Reactive Influences in Cognitively-Based Motivation," *Organizational Behavior and Human Decision Processes,* August 1986, pp. 92–113.

46. Bandura, *Self-Efficacy.*

47. C. L. Holladay and M. A. Quiñones, "Practice Variability and Transfer of Training: The Role of Self-Efficacy Generality," *Journal of Applied Psychology* 88, no. 6 (2003), pp. 1094–1103.

48. R. C. Rist, "Student Social Class and Teacher Expectations: The Self-Fulfilling Prophecy in Ghetto Education," *Harvard Educational Review* 70, no. 3 (2000), pp. 266–301.

49. D. Eden, "Self-Fulfilling Prophecies in Organizations," in J. Greenberg (ed.), *Organizational Behavior: The State of the Science*, 2nd ed. (Mahwah, NJ: Lawrence Erlbaum, 2003), pp. 91–122.

50. Ibid.

51. T. A. Judge, C. L. Jackson, J. C. Shaw, B. Scott, and B. L. Rich, "Self-Efficacy and Work-Related Performance: The Integral Role of Individual Differences," *Journal of Applied Psychology* 92, no. 1 (2007), pp. 107–127.

52. Ibid.

53. J. L. Komaki, T. Coombs, and S. Schepman, "Motivational Implications of Reinforcement Theory," in R. M. Steers, L. W. Porter, and G. Bigley (eds.), *Motivation and Work Behavior*, 6th ed. (New York: McGraw-Hill, 1996), pp. 87–107.

54. B. F. Skinner, *Contingencies of Reinforcement* (East Norwalk, CT: Appleton-Century-Crofts, 1971).

55. J. A. Mills, *Control: A History of Behavioral Psychology* (New York: New York University Press, 2000).

56. E. A. Locke, "Latham vs. Komaki: A Tale of Two Paradigms," *Journal of Applied Psychology*, February 1980, pp. 16–23.

57. A. Bandura, *Social Learning Theory* (Upper Saddle River, NJ: Prentice Hall, 1977).

58. J. S. Adams, "Inequity in Social Exchanges," in L. Berkowitz (ed.), *Advances in Experimental Social Psychology* (New York: Academic Press, 1965), pp. 267–300.

59. P. S. Goodman, "An Examination of Referents Used in the Evaluation of Pay," *Organizational Behavior and Human Performance*, October 1974, pp. 170–195; S. Ronen, "Equity Perception in Multiple Comparisons: A Field Study," *Human Relations*, April 1986, pp. 333–346; R. W. Scholl, E. A. Cooper, and J. F. McKenna, "Referent Selection in Determining Equity Perception: Differential Effects on Behavioral and Attitudinal Outcomes," *Personnel Psychology*, Spring 1987, pp. 113–127; and T. P. Summers and A. S. DeNisi, "In Search of Adams' Other: Reexamination of Referents Used in the Evaluation of Pay," *Human Relations*, June 1990, pp. 497–511.

60. C. T. Kulik and M. L. Ambrose, "Personal and Situational Determinants of Referent Choice," *Academy of Management Review*, April 1992, pp. 212–237.

61. C. Ostroff and L. E. Atwater, "Does Whom You Work with Matter? Effects of Referent Group Gender and Age Composition on Managers' Compensation," *Journal of Applied Psychology* 88, no. 4 (2003), pp. 725–740.

62. Ibid.

63. See, for example, E. Walster, G. W. Walster, and W. G. Scott, *Equity: Theory and Research* (Boston: Allyn & Bacon, 1978); and J. Greenberg, "Cognitive Reevaluation of Outcomes in Response to Underpayment Inequity," *Academy of Management Journal*, March 1989, pp. 174–184.

64. P. S. Goodman and A. Friedman, "An Examination of Adams' Theory of Inequity," *Administrative Science Quarterly*, September 1971, pp. 271–288; R. P. Vecchio, "An Individual-Differences Interpretation of the Conflicting Predictions Generated by Equity Theory and Expectancy Theory," *Journal of Applied Psychology*, August 1981, pp. 470–481; R. T. Mowday, "Equity Theory Predictions of Behavior in Organizations," in R. Steers, L. W. Porter, and G. Bigley (eds.), *Motivation and Work Behavior*, 6th ed. (New York: McGraw-Hill, 1996), pp. 111–131; R. W.

Griffeth and S. Gaertner, "A Role for Equity Theory in the Turnover Process: An Empirical Test," *Journal of Applied Social Psychology*, May 2001, pp. 1017–1037; and L. K. Scheer, N. Kumar, and J.-B. E. M. Steenkamp, "Reactions to Perceived Inequity in U.S. and Dutch Interorganizational Relationships," *Academy of Management* 46, no. 3 (2003), pp. 303–316.

65. See, for example, R. C. Huseman, J. D. Hatfield, and E. W. Miles, "A New Perspective on Equity Theory: The Equity Sensitivity Construct," *Academy of Management Journal*, April 1987, pp. 222–234; K. S. Sauley and A. G. Bedeian, "Equity Sensitivity: Construction of a Measure and Examination of Its Psychometric Properties," *Journal of Management* 26, no. 5 (2000), pp. 885–910; and J. A. Colquitt, "Does the Justice of One Interact with the Justice of Many? Reactions to Procedural Justice in Teams," *Journal of Applied Psychology* 89, no. 4 (2004), pp. 633–646.

66. J. Greenberg and S. Ornstein, "High Status Job Title as Compensation for Underpayment: A Test of Equity Theory," *Journal of Applied Psychology*, May 1983, pp. 285–297; and J. Greenberg, "Equity and Workplace Status: A Field Experiment," *Journal of Applied Psychology*, November 1988, pp. 606–613.

67. See, for instance, J. Greenberg, *The Quest for Justice on the Job* (Thousand Oaks, CA: Sage, 1996); R. Cropanzano and J. Greenberg, "Progress in Organizational Justice: Tunneling Through the Maze," in C. L. Cooper and I. T. Robertson (eds.), *International Review of Industrial and Organizational Psychology*, vol. 12 (New York: Wiley, 1997); J. A. Colquitt, D. E. Conlon, M. J. Wesson, C. O. L. H. Porter, and K. Y. Ng, "Justice at the Millennium: A Meta-analytic Review of the 25 Years of Organizational Justice Research," *Journal of Applied Psychology*, June 2001, pp. 425–445; T. Simons and Q. Roberson, "Why Managers Should Care About Fairness: The Effects of Aggregate Justice Perceptions on Organizational Outcomes," *Journal of Applied Psychology*, June 2003, pp. 432–443; and G. P. Latham and C. C. Pinder, "Work Motivation Theory and Research at the Dawn of the Twenty-First Century," *Annual Review of Psychology* 56 (2005), pp. 485–516.

68. K. Leung, K. Tong, and S. S. Ho, "Effects of Interactional Justice on Egocentric Bias in Resource Allocation Decisions," *Journal of Applied Psychology* 89, no. 3 (2004), pp. 405–415.

69. "Americans Feel They Pay Fair Share of Taxes, Says Poll," *NaturalNews.com*, May 2, 2005, http://www.naturalnews.com/007297.html.

70. G. S. Leventhal, "What Should Be Done with Equity Theory? New Approaches to the Study of Fairness in Social Relationships," in K. Gergen, M. Greenberg, and R. Willis (eds.), *Social Exchange: Advances in Theory and Research* (New York: Plenum, 1980), pp. 27–55.

71. J. C. Shaw, E. Wild, and J. A. Colquitt, "To Justify or Excuse? A Meta-analytic Review of the Effects of Explanations," *Journal of Applied Psychology* 88, no. 3 (2003), pp. 444–458.

72. D. P. Skarlicki and R. Folger, "Retaliation in the Workplace: The Roles of Distributive, Procedural, and Interactional Justice," *Journal of Applied Psychology* 82, no. 3 (1997), pp. 434–443.

73. R. Cropanzano, C. A. Prehar, and P. Y. Chen, "Using Social Exchange Theory to Distinguish Procedural from

Interactional Justice," *Group & Organization Management* 27, no. 3 (2002), pp. 324–351; and S. G. Roch and L. R. Shanock, "Organizational Justice in an Exchange Framework: Clarifying Organizational Justice Dimensions," *Journal of Management*, April 2006, pp. 299–322.

74. Colquitt, Conlon, Wesson, Porter, and Ng, "Justice at the Millennium," pp. 425–445.

75. J. Reb, B. M. Goldman, L. J. Kray, and R. Cropanzano, "Different Wrongs, Different Remedies? Reactions to Organizational Remedies After Procedural and Interactional Injustice," *Personnel Psychology* 59 (2006), pp. 31–64; and "Northwest Airlines Flight Cancellations Mount as Labor Woes Continue," *Aero-News.net*, June 26, 2007, www.aero-news.net.

76. V. H. Vroom, *Work and Motivation* (New York: Wiley, 1964).

77. For criticism, see H. G. Heneman III and D. P. Schwab, "Evaluation of Research on Expectancy Theory Prediction of Employee Performance," *Psychological Bulletin*, July 1972, pp. 1–9; T. R. Mitchell, "Expectancy Models of Job Satisfaction, Occupational Preference and Effort: A Theoretical, Methodological and Empirical Appraisal," *Psychological Bulletin*, November 1974, pp. 1053–1077; and W. Van Eerde and H. Thierry, "Vroom's Expectancy Models and Work-Related Criteria: A Meta-analysis," *Journal of Applied Psychology*, October 1996, pp. 575–586. For support, see L. W. Porter and E. E. Lawler III, *Managerial Attitudes and Performance* (Homewood, IL: Irwin, 1968); and J. J. Donovan, "Work Motivation," in N. Anderson et al (eds.), *Handbook of Industrial, Work & Organizational Psychology*, vol. 2 (Thousand Oaks, CA: Sage, 2001), pp. 56–59.

78. Vroom refers to these three variables as expectancy, instrumentality, and valence, respectively.

79. J. Nocera, "The Anguish of Being an Analyst," *New York Times*, March 4, 2006, pp. B1, B12.

80. R. J. House, H. J. Shapiro, and M. A. Wahba, "Expectancy Theory as a Predictor of Work Behavior and Attitudes: A Re-evaluation of Empirical Evidence," *Decision Sciences*, January 1974, pp. 481–506.

81. For other examples of models that seek to integrate motivation theories, see H. J. Klein, "An Integrated Control Theory Model of Work Motivation," *Academy of Management Review*, April 1989, pp. 150–172; E. A. Locke, "The Motivation Sequence, the Motivation Hub, and the Motivation Core," *Organizational Behavior and Human Decision Processes*, December 1991, pp. 288–299; and T. R. Mitchell, "Matching Motivational Strategies with Organizational Contexts," pp. 60–62.

82. N. J. Adler, *International Dimensions of Organizational Behavior*, 4th ed. (Cincinnati, OH: South-Western Publishing, 2002), p. 174.

83. G. Hofstede, "Motivation, Leadership, and Organization: Do American Theories Apply Abroad?" *Organizational Dynamics*, Summer 1980, p. 55.

84. Ibid.

85. J. K. Giacobbe-Miller, D. J. Miller, and V. I. Victorov, "A Comparison of Russian and U.S. Pay Allocation Decisions, Distributive Justice Judgments, and Productivity Under Different Payment Conditions," *Personnel Psychology*, Spring 1998, pp. 137–163.

86. S. L. Mueller and L. D. Clarke, "Political-Economic Context and Sensitivity to Equity: Differences Between the United States and the Transition Economies of Central and Eastern Europe," *Academy of Management Journal*, June 1998, pp. 319–329.

87. I. Harpaz, "The Importance of Work Goals: An International Perspective," *Journal of International Business Studies*, First Quarter 1990, pp. 75–93.

88. G. E. Popp, H. J. Davis, and T. T. Herbert, "An International Study of Intrinsic Motivation Composition," *Management International Review*, January 1986, pp. 28–35.

89. R. Fischer and P. B. Smith, "Reward Allocation and Culture: A Meta-analysis," *Journal of Cross-Cultural Psychology* 34, no. 3 (2003), pp. 251–268.

90. F. F. T. Chiang and T. Birtch, "The Transferability of Management Practices: Examining Cross-National Differences in Reward Preferences," *Human Relations* 60, no. 9 (2007), pp. 1293–1330; A. E. Lind, T. R. Tyler, and Y. J. Huo, "Procedural Context and Culture: Variation in the Antecedents of Procedural Justice Judgments," *Journal of Personality and Social Psychology* 73, no. 4 (1997), pp. 767–780; M. J. Gelfand, M. Erez, and Z. Aycan, "Cross-Cultural Organizational Behavior," *Annual Review of Psychology* 58, (2007), pp. 479–514.

91. This section is based on F. J. Landy and W. S. Becker, "Motivation Theory Reconsidered," in L. L. Cummings and B. M. Staw (eds.), *Research in Organizational Behavior*, vol. 9 (Greenwich, CT: JAI Press, 1987), pp. 24–35.

92. R. Freedman, "'Happyness' Author Gardner Hopes We're Each Our Own Champ," *Marin Independent Journal* (May 13, 2009), www.marinij.com.

93. E. Biyalogorsky, W. Boulding, and R. Staelin, "Stuck in the Past: Why Managers Persist with New Product Failures," *Journal of Marketing*, April 2006, pp. 108–121.

LEARNING OBJECTIVES

After studying this chapter, you should be able to:

1 Describe the job characteristics model and evaluate the way it motivates by changing the work environment.

2 Compare and contrast the main ways jobs can be redesigned.

3 Identify three alternative work arrangements and show how they might motivate employees.

4 Give examples of employee involvement measures and show how they can motivate employees.

5 Demonstrate how the different types of variable-pay programs can increase employee motivation.

6 Show how flexible benefits turn benefits into motivators.

7 Identify the motivational benefits of intrinsic rewards.

Motivation: From Concepts to Applications

Money is better than poverty, if only for financial reasons. —Woody Allen

BYE-BYE BONUS—AND BASE PAY

In the past, when companies faced a drop-off in business, they usually resorted to layoffs to cut costs. Though layoffs have recently been significant in most industries—manufacturing, financial services, and banking have been hit particularly hard—many companies have taken another approach: reduce or eliminate employee bonuses and pay raises, or cut base pay in general.

To cut labor costs—which are the single biggest expense for most companies—United Technologies tried hiring freezes, deferred pay increases, and furloughs (unpaid leave). In 2009 alone, the company eliminated more than 11,000 jobs. One area where company president Ari Bousbib refused to cut costs was base salaries. Once such cuts are made, Bousbib said, "It is very difficult to rebuild motivation." One compensation consultant agrees, noting that a base pay cut "creates very deep emotional scars" that are long lasting.

For these reasons, nearly any company will cut pay increases before cutting base pay. However, even those cuts can be painful. Anthony Abraham, age 33, a Chicago-based management consultant, has seen his annual bonus cut in half. Already he has cancelled travel plans and a new car purchase and is paying back less than he planned on his student loans. Although

bonuses appear, by definition, to be an extra, in many jobs they represent a substantial portion of take-home pay. In 2007, Jan Klincewicz received a huge bonus—$143,000—relative to his base salary of $87,000. Klincewicz used his bonus to buy a house, a plasma TV, and a saxophone. His most recent bonus was $24,000. How did he adjust? "I shop for bargains," he said.

As painful as cuts in bonuses and pay raises can be, they pale in comparison to cuts in base pay. After all, few employees expect their salary or wage rate to decline. Major companies like AMD, Black & Decker, FedEx, Seagate, American Express, *The New York Times,* and Hewlett-Packard have all cut base pay. According to a Hewitt Associates survey, 16 percent of large U.S. employers have made base salary reductions, and a further 21 percent are considering one. In the 2001–2002 recession, comparable figures were so low Hewitt did not even publish them.

In a crisis, is it better to lay off some people or force everyone to absorb equal cuts? Though some compensation experts think pay cuts make sense, most believe across-the-board cuts to base pay are a bad idea. One concern is that they lead to a permanent reduction in motivation. "People have long memories," says the individual who ran GE's human resources department for 14 years. Another worry is that these cuts will cause those with the most options—the top performers—to leave. One California employee who intended to start a job search after a pay cut said, "While layoffs are hard for everyone to see, especially at a small company, you can see the downside to cutting everyone: The best people start to look for better-paying work elsewhere."[1]

As these examples show, companies vary widely in their approaches to motivating employees. Though pay is one central means of motivation we consider in this chapter—what we call extrinsic motivation—it's not the only one. The other is intrinsic. The following self-assessment will provide some information about how intrinsically motivating *your* job might be.

In Chapter 7, we focused on motivation theories. In this chapter, we start applying motivation concepts. We link motivation theories to practices such as employee involvement and skill-based pay. Why? Because it's one thing to be able to know specific motivation theories; it's quite another to see how, as a manager, you can use them.

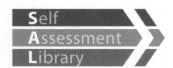

WHAT'S MY JOB'S MOTIVATING POTENTIAL?

In the Self-Assessment Library (available on CD or online), take assessment I.C.9 (What's My Job's Motivating Potential?) and answer the following questions. If you currently do not have a job, answer the questions for your most recent job.

1. *How did you score relative to your classmates?*
2. *Did your score surprise you? Why or why not?*
3. *How might your results affect your career path?*

Motivating by Job Design: The Job Characteristics Model

Increasingly, research on motivation is focused on approaches that link motivational concepts to changes in the way work is structured.

Research in **job design** suggests the way the elements in a job are organized can act to increase or decrease effort and also suggests what those elements are. We'll first review the job characteristics model and then discuss some ways jobs can be redesigned. Finally, we'll explore some alternative work arrangements.

1 Describe the job characteristics model and evaluate the way it motivates by changing the work environment.

The Job Characteristics Model

Developed by J. Richard Hackman and Greg Oldham, the **job characteristics model (JCM)** says we can describe any job in terms of five core job dimensions:[2]

1. **Skill variety.**   **Skill variety** is the degree to which a job requires a variety of different activities so the worker can use a number of different skills and talent. For instance, the work of a garage owner-operator who does electrical repairs, rebuilds engines, does bodywork, and interacts with customers scores high on skill variety. The job of a bodyshop worker who sprays paint 8 hours a day scores low on this dimension.

2. **Task identity.**   **Task identity** is the degree to which a job requires completion of a whole and identifiable piece of work. A cabinetmaker who designs a piece of furniture, selects the wood, builds the object, and finishes it to perfection has a job that scores high on task identity. A job scoring low on this dimension is operating a factory lathe solely to make table legs.
3. **Task significance.**   **Task significance** is the degree to which a job has an impact on the lives or work of other people. The job of a nurse handling the diverse needs of patients in a hospital intensive care unit scores high on task significance; sweeping floors in a hospital scores low.
4. **Autonomy.**   **Autonomy** is the degree to which a job provides the worker freedom, independence, and discretion in scheduling the work and determining the procedures in carrying it out. A salesperson who schedules his or her own work each day and decides on the most effective sales approach for each customer without supervision has a highly autonomous job. A salesperson who is given a set of leads each day and is required to follow a standardized sales script with each potential customer has a job low on autonomy.
5. **Feedback.**   **Feedback** is the degree to which carrying out work activities generates direct and clear information about your own performance. A job with high feedback is assembling iPods and testing them to see whether they operate properly. A factory worker who assembles iPods but then routes them to a quality-control inspector for testing and adjustments receives low feedback from his or her activities.

Exhibit 8-1 presents the job characteristics model. Note how the first three dimensions—skill variety, task identity, and task significance—combine to create meaningful work the incumbent will view as important, valuable, and worthwhile. Note, too, that jobs with high autonomy give incumbents a feeling of personal responsibility for the results and that, if a job provides feedback, employees will know how effectively they are performing. From a motivational standpoint, the JCM proposes that individuals obtain internal rewards when they learn (knowledge of results) that they personally (experienced responsibility) have performed well on a task they care about (experienced meaningfulness).[3] The more these three psychological states are present, the greater will be employees' motivation, performance, and satisfaction, and the lower their absenteeism and likelihood of leaving. As Exhibit 8-1 shows, individuals with a high growth need are more likely to experience the critical psychological states when their jobs are enriched—and respond to them more positively—than are their counterparts with low growth need.

job design   *The way the elements in a job are organized.*

job characteristics model (JCM)   *A model that proposes that any job can be described in terms of five core job dimensions: skill variety, task identity, task significance, autonomy, and feedback.*

skill variety   *The degree to which a job requires a variety of different activities.*

task identity   *The degree to which a job requires completion of a whole and identifiable piece of work.*

task significance   *The degree to which a job has a substantial impact on the lives or work of other people.*

autonomy   *The degree to which a job provides substantial freedom and discretion to the individual in scheduling the work and in determining the procedures to be used in carrying it out.*

feedback   *The degree to which carrying out the work activities required by a job results in the individual obtaining direct and clear information about the effectiveness of his or her performance.*

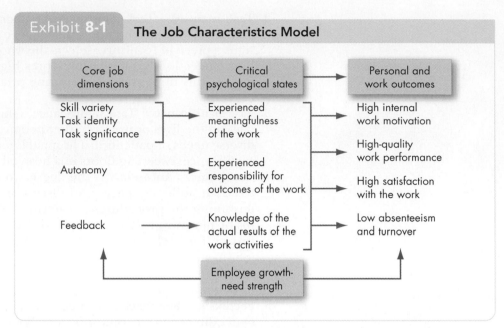

Exhibit 8-1   The Job Characteristics Model

Source: J. R. Hackman and G. R. Oldham, *Work Redesign* © 1980; pp. 78–80. Adapted by permission of Pearson Education, Inc., Upper Saddle River, New Jersey.

We can combine the core dimensions into a single predictive index, called the **motivating potential score (MPS)**, and calculated as follows:

$$\text{MPS} = \frac{\text{Skill variety} + \text{Task identity} + \text{Task significance}}{3} \times \text{Autonomy} \times \text{Feedback}$$

To be high on motivating potential, jobs must be high on at least one of the three factors that lead to experienced meaningfulness and high on both autonomy and feedback. If jobs score high on motivating potential, the model predicts motivation, performance, and satisfaction will improve and absence and turnover will be reduced.

Much evidence supports the JCM concept that the presence of a set of job characteristics—variety, identity, significance, autonomy, and feedback—does generate higher and more satisfying job performance.[4] But apparently we can better calculate motivating potential by simply adding the characteristics rather than using the formula.[5] Take some time to think about your job. Do you have the opportunity to work on different tasks, or is your day pretty routine? Are you able to work independently, or do you constantly have a supervisor or co-worker looking over your shoulder? What do you think your answers to these questions say about your job's motivating potential? Revisit your answers to the self-assessment at the beginning of this chapter and then calculate your MPS from the job characteristics model. You might try computing your MPS score two ways: Using the traditional MPS formula, and simply adding the dimensions. Then compare.

How Can Jobs Be Redesigned?

"Every day was the same thing," Frank Greer said. "Stand on that assembly line. Wait for an instrument panel to be moved into place. Unlock the mechanism and drop the panel into the Jeep Liberty as it moved by on the line. Then I plugged in the harnessing wires. I repeated that for eight hours a day. I don't care that they were paying me

2   Compare and contrast the main ways jobs can be redesigned.

Myth or Science?

"Everyone Wants a Challenging Job"

This statement is false. Many employees do want challenging, interesting, complex work. But despite all the attention the media, academicians, and social scientists focus on human potential and the needs of individuals, some people prosper in simple, routinized work.[6]

The variable that seems to best explain who prefers a challenging job is the strength of an individual's higher-order needs.[7] Individuals with high growth needs are more responsive to challenging work. But what percentage of rank-and-file workers actually desire higher-order need satisfaction and will respond positively to challenging jobs? No current data are available, but a study from the 1970s estimated the figure at about 15 percent.[8] Even after adjusting for technological and economic changes in the nature of work, it seems unlikely the number today exceeds 40 percent.

Many employees relish challenging work. But this desire has been overgeneralized to all workers. Organizations increasingly have pushed extra responsibilities onto workers, often without knowing whether they want or can handle the increased responsibilities.

Many workers meet their higher-order needs *off* the job. There are 168 hours in a week, and work rarely consumes more than 30 percent of them. That leaves considerable opportunity, even for individuals with strong growth needs, to find higher-order need satisfaction outside the workplace.

---

twenty-four dollars an hour. I was going crazy. I did it for almost a year and a half. Finally, I just said to my wife that this isn't going to be the way I'm going to spend the rest of my life. My brain was turning to JELL-O on that Jeep assembly line. So I quit. Now I work in a print shop and I make less than fifteen dollars an hour. But let me tell you, the work I do is really interesting. The job changes all the time, I'm continually learning new things, and the work really challenges me! I look forward every morning to going to work again."

The repetitive tasks in Frank Greer's job at the Jeep plant provided little variety, autonomy, or motivation. In contrast, his job in the print shop is challenging and stimulating. Let's look at some of the ways to put JCM into practice to make jobs more motivating.

Job Rotation   If employees suffer from overroutinization of their work, one alternative is **job rotation**, or the periodic shifting of an employee from one task to another with similar skill requirements at the same organizational level (also called *cross-training*). At Singapore Airlines, a ticket agent may take on the duties of a baggage handler. Extensive job rotation is one of the reasons Singapore Airlines is rated one of the best airlines in the world and a highly desirable place to work. Many manufacturing firms have adopted job rotation as a means of increasing flexibility and avoiding layoffs.[9] Managers at Apex Precision Technologies, a custom-machine shop in Indiana, train workers on all the company's equipment so they can move around as needed in response to incoming orders. During the 2001 recession, Cleveland-based Lincoln Electric moved some salaried workers to hourly clerical jobs and rotated production workers among various machines. This manufacturer of welding and cutting

---

motivating potential score (MPS)   *A predictive index that suggests the motivating potential in a job.*

job rotation   *The periodic shifting of an employee from one task to another.*

parts was able to minimize layoffs because of its commitment to continually cross-training and moving workers wherever they're needed.

The strengths of job rotation are that it reduces boredom, increases motivation, and helps employees better understand how their work contributes to the organization. An indirect benefit is that employees with a wider range of skills give management more flexibility in scheduling work, adapting to changes, and filling vacancies.[10] However, job rotation is not without drawbacks. Training costs increase, and productivity is reduced by moving a worker into a new position just when efficiency at the prior job is creating organizational economies. Job rotation also creates disruptions when members of the work group have to adjust to the new employee. And supervisors may also have to spend more time answering questions and monitoring the work of recently rotated employees.

Job Enrichment   **Job enrichment** expands jobs by increasing the degree to which the worker controls the planning, execution, and evaluation of the work. An enriched job organizes tasks to allow the worker to do a complete activity, increases the employee's freedom and independence, increases responsibility, and provides feedback so individuals can assess and correct their own performance.[11]

How does management enrich an employee's job? Exhibit 8-2 offers suggested guidelines based on the job characteristics model. *Combining tasks* puts fractionalized tasks back together to form a new and larger module of work. *Forming natural work units* makes an employee's tasks create an identifiable and meaningful whole. *Establishing client relationships* increases the direct relationships between workers and their clients (clients can be internal as well as outside the organization). *Expanding jobs vertically* gives employees responsibilities and control formerly reserved for management. *Opening feedback channels* lets employees know how well they are doing and whether their performance is improving, deteriorating, or remaining constant.

Some newer versions of job enrichment concentrate more specifically on improving the meaningfulness of work. One significant method is to relate employee experiences to customer outcomes, simply by providing employees with stories from customers who benefitted from the company's products or services. The medical device manufacturer Medtronic invites people to describe how Medtronic products have improved, or even saved, their lives and shares these

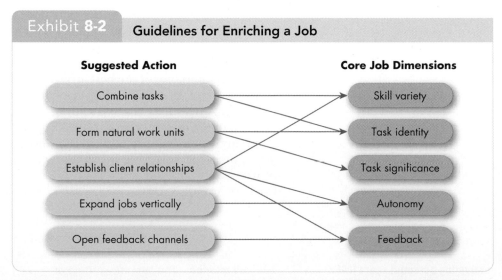

Exhibit 8-2   Guidelines for Enriching a Job

Suggested Action

- Combine tasks
- Form natural work units
- Establish client relationships
- Expand jobs vertically
- Open feedback channels

Core Job Dimensions

- Skill variety
- Task identity
- Task significance
- Autonomy
- Feedback

Source: J. R. Hackman and J. L. Suttle (eds.), *Improving Life at Work* (Glenview, IL: Scott Foresman, 1977), p. 138. Reprinted by permission of Richard Hackman and J. Lloyd Suttle.

stories with employees during annual meetings, providing a powerful reminder of the impact of their work. Researchers recently found that when university fund-raisers briefly interacted with the undergraduates who would receive the scholarships they raised, they persisted 42 percent longer, and raised nearly twice as much money, as those who didn't interact with potential recipients.[12]

Another method for improving the meaningfulness of work is providing employees with mutual assistance programs.[13] Employees who can help each other directly through their work come to see themselves, and the organizations for which they work, in more positive, pro-social terms. This, in turn, can increase employee affective commitment.

The University of New Mexico provides job enrichment through cross-training to learn new skills and job rotation to perform new tasks in another position. To participate, employees work with their manager to set a job enrichment goal, identify desired competencies, and find an appropriate placement. Participation typically lasts 90 days, after which employees either return to their former position or obtain a new position that leverages their newfound skills.

Two university employees held administrative positions in the same academic department. One specialized in handling student records, and the other processed tuition payments. Through the enrichment program, the student-records assistant received cross-training in HR classes to learn about purchasing and the accounting system. The accounting assistant worked with the student records assistant 2 hours per week learning about that job. The two then proposed rotating their jobs for a summer. As a result, both expanded their repertoire of skills and experiences to enable them to cover for or help the other employee, and to better prepare for future promotions.[14]

The evidence on job enrichment shows it reduces absenteeism and turnover costs and increases satisfaction, but not all job enrichment programs are equally effective.[15] A review of 83 organizational interventions designed to improve performance management showed that frequent, specific feedback related to solving problems was linked to consistently higher performance, but infrequent feedback that focused more on past problems than future solutions was much less effective.[16] Some recent evidence suggests job enrichment works best when it compensates for poor feedback and reward systems.[17] Work design may also not affect everyone in the same way, as noted in this chapter's "Myth or Science" feature. One recent study showed employees with a higher preference for challenging work experienced larger reductions in stress following job redesign than individuals who did not prefer challenging work.[18]

Alternative Work Arrangements

3 Identify three alternative work arrangements and show how they might motivate employees.

Beyond redesigning work itself and including employees in decisions, another approach to motivation is to alter work arrangements with flextime, job sharing, or telecommuting. These arrangements are likely to be especially important for a diverse workforce of dual-earner couples, single parents, and employees caring for a sick or aging relative.

Flextime   Susan Ross is the classic "morning person." She rises each day at 5:00 A.M. sharp and full of energy. However, as she puts it, "I'm usually ready for bed right after the 7:00 P.M. news."

job enrichment   *The vertical expansion of jobs, which increases the degree to which the worker controls the planning, execution, and evaluation of the work.*

Susan's work schedule as a claims processor at The Hartford Financial Services Group is flexible. Her office opens at 6:00 A.M. and closes at 7:00 P.M. It's up to her how she schedules her 8-hour day within this 13-hour period. Because Susan is a morning person and also has a 7-year-old son who gets out of school at 3:00 P.M. every day, she opts to work from 6:00 A.M. to 3:00 P.M. "My work hours are perfect. I'm at the job when I'm mentally most alert, and I can be home to take care of my son after he gets out of school."

Susan's schedule is an example of **flextime**, short for "flexible work time." Employees must work a specific number of hours per week but are free to vary their hours of work within certain limits. As in Exhibit 8-3, each day consists of a common core, usually 6 hours, with a flexibility band surrounding it. The core may be 9:00 A.M. to 3:00 P.M., with the office actually opening at 6:00 A.M. and closing at 6:00 P.M. All employees are required to be at their jobs during the common core period, but they may accumulate their other 2 hours before, after, or before and after that. Some flextime programs allow employees to accumulate extra hours and turn them into a free day off each month.

Flextime has become extremely popular; the proportion of full-time U.S. employees on flextime more than doubled between the late 1980s and 2005, and

---

Exhibit 8-3   Possible Flextime Staff Schedules

Schedule 1

Percent Time:	100% = 40 hours per week
Core Hours:	9:00 A.M.–5:00 P.M., Monday through Friday (1 hour lunch)
Work Start Time:	Between 8:00 A.M. and 9:00 A.M.
Work End Time:	Between 5:00 P.M. and 6:00 P.M.

Schedule 2

Percent Time:	100% = 40 hours per week
Work Hours:	8:00 A.M.–6:30 P.M., Monday through Thursday (1/2 hour lunch)
	Friday off
Work Start Time:	8:00 A.M.
Work End Time:	6:30 P.M.

Schedule 3

Percent Time:	90% = 36 hours per week
Work Hours:	8:30 A.M.–5:00 P.M., Monday through Thursday (1/2 hour lunch)
	8:00 A.M.–Noon Friday (no lunch)
Work Start Time:	8:30 A.M. (Monday–Thursday); 8:00 A.M. (Friday)
Work End Time:	5:00 P.M. (Monday–Thursday); Noon (Friday)

Schedule 4

Percent Time:	80% = 32 hours per week
	8:00 A.M.–6:00 P.M., Monday through Wednesday (1/2 hour lunch)
Work Hours:	8:00 A.M.–11:30 A.M. Thursday (no lunch)
	Friday off
Work Start Time:	Between 8:00 A.M. and 9:00 A.M.
Work End Time:	Between 5:00 P.M. and 6:00 P.M.

Eli Lilly and Company, a pharmaceutical firm, offers flexible work options to research scientists and other employees with the approval of their managers. The company's daily flextime option allows full-time employees to arrive at work between 6:00 A.M. and 9:00 A.M. and to leave work between 3:00 P.M. and 6:00 P.M. Lilly also offers employees a flexweek option that includes four 10-hour days or four 9-hour days followed by one half-day.

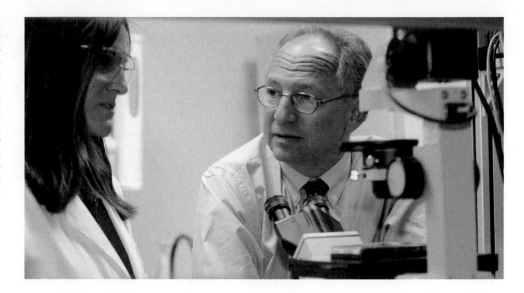

approximately 43 percent of the U.S. full-time workforce now have flexible daily arrival and departure times.[19] And this is not just a U.S. phenomenon. In Germany, for instance, 29 percent of businesses offer flextime.[20]

The claimed benefits are numerous. They include reduced absenteeism, increased productivity, reduced overtime expenses, reduced hostility toward management, reduced traffic congestion around work sites, elimination of tardiness, and increased autonomy and responsibility for employees, any of which may increase employee job satisfaction.[21] But what's flextime's actual record?

Most of the performance evidence stacks up favorably. Flextime tends to reduce absenteeism and frequently improves worker productivity,[22] probably for several reasons. Employees can schedule their work hours to align with personal demands, reducing tardiness and absences, and they can work when they are most productive. Flextime can also help employees balance work and family lives; it is a popular criterion for judging how "family friendly" a workplace is.

Flextime's major drawback is that it's not applicable to every job. It works well with clerical tasks for which an employee's interaction with people outside his or her department is limited. It is not a viable option for receptionists, sales personnel in retail stores, or similar jobs for which comprehensive service demands that people be at their workstations at predetermined times.

Job Sharing Job sharing allows two or more individuals to split a traditional 40-hour-a-week job. One might perform the job from 8:00 A.M. to noon and the other from 1:00 P.M. to 5:00 P.M., or the two could work full, but alternate, days. Sue Manix and Charlotte Schutzman share the title of vice president of employee communications in the Philadelphia office of Verizon.[23] Schutzman works Monday and Tuesday, Manix Thursday and Friday, and they alternate Wednesdays. The two women have job-shared for 10 years, acquiring promotions, numerous bonuses, and a 20-person staff and better balancing their work and family responsibilities.

Approximately 19 percent of large organizations now offer job sharing.[24] Reasons it is not more widely adopted are likely the difficulty of finding

---

flextime *Flexible work hours.*

job sharing *An arrangement that allows two or more individuals to split a traditional 40-hour-a-week job.*

compatible partners to share a job and the historically negative perceptions of individuals not completely committed to their job and employer.

Job sharing allows an organization to draw on the talents of more than one individual in a given job. A bank manager who oversees two job sharers describes it as an opportunity to get two heads but "pay for one."[25] It also opens up the opportunity to acquire skilled workers—for instance, women with young children and retirees—who might not be available on a full-time basis.[26] Many Japanese firms are increasingly considering job sharing—but for a very different reason.[27] Because Japanese executives are extremely reluctant to fire people, job sharing is seen as a potentially humanitarian means of avoiding layoffs due to overstaffing.

From the employee's perspective, job sharing increases flexibility and can increase motivation and satisfaction when a 40-hour-a-week job is just not practical. But the major drawback from management's perspective is finding compatible pairs of employees who can successfully coordinate the intricacies of one job.[28]

Telecommuting It might be close to the ideal job for many people. No commuting, flexible hours, freedom to dress as you please, and few or no interruptions from colleagues. It's called **telecommuting**, and it refers to working at home at least 2 days a week on a computer linked to the employer's office.[29] (A closely related term—the *virtual office*—describes working from home on a relatively permanent basis.)

The U.S. Department of the Census estimated that in 2002 approximately 15 percent of the workforce worked from home at least one day a week.[30] One recent survey of over 5,000 HR professionals found that 35 percent of organizations allowed employees to telecommute at least part of the time, and 21 percent allowed employees to telecommute full-time.[31] Well-known organizations that actively encourage telecommuting include AT&T, IBM, American Express, Sun Microsystems, and a number of U.S. government agencies.[32] In Finland, Sweden, Britain, and Germany, telecommuters represent 17, 15, 8, and 6 percent of the workforce, respectively.[33]

What kinds of jobs lend themselves to telecommuting? There are three categories: routine information-handling tasks, mobile activities, and professional and other knowledge-related tasks.[34] Writers, attorneys, analysts, and employees who spend the majority of their time on computers or the telephone—such as telemarketers, customer-service representatives, reservation agents, and product-support specialists—are natural candidates. As telecommuters, they can access information on their computers at home as easily as in the company's office.

There are numerous stories of telecommuting's success.[35] Putnam Investments, in Boston, has made telecommuting an attractive recruitment tool that increased the number of applicants 20-fold. Putnam's management calculates that the 12 percent of its employees who telecommute have substantially higher productivity than in-office staff and about one-tenth the attrition rate.

The potential pluses of telecommuting for management include a larger labor pool from which to select, higher productivity, less turnover, improved morale, and reduced office-space costs. A positive relationship exists between telecommuting and supervisor performance ratings, but the relationship between telecommuting and turnover intentions has not been substantiated in research to date.[36] The major downside for management is less direct supervision of employees. In addition, in today's team-focused workplace, telecommuting may make it more difficult for management to coordinate teamwork.[37] From the employee's standpoint, telecommuting offers a considerable increase in flexibility—but not without costs. For employees with a high social need, telecommuting can increase feelings of isolation and reduce job satisfaction. And all telecommuters are vulnerable to the "out of sight, out of mind" effect.[38] Employees who aren't

Telecommuting is appropriate for the information-handling and knowledge-related tasks of Brent Cranfield, who works for Glenn Richardson, the speaker of the Georgia House of Representatives. Richardson allows his staffers to work from their homes one day a week. Although miles apart from each other, the staffers stay connected with each other through videoconferencing, instant messaging, and other communications technology.

at their desks, who miss meetings, and who don't share in day-to-day informal workplace interactions may be at a disadvantage when it comes to raises and promotions.

The Social and Physical Context of Work

Robin and Chris both graduated from college a couple years ago with degrees in elementary education. They took jobs as first-grade teachers in different school districts. Robin immediately confronted a number of obstacles on the job: a large class (42 students), a small and dingy classroom, and inadequate supplies. Chris's situation couldn't have been more different. He had only 15 students in his class, plus a teaching aide 15 hours each week, a modern and well-lighted room, a well-stocked supply cabinet, an iMac for every student, and a highly supportive principal. Not surprisingly, at the end of the first year, Chris had been a considerably more effective teacher than Robin.

The job characteristics model shows most employees are more motivated and satisfied when their intrinsic work tasks are engaging. However, having the most interesting workplace characteristics in the world may not always lead to satisfaction if you feel isolated from your co-workers, and having good social relationships can make even the most boring and onerous tasks more fulfilling. Research demonstrates that social aspects and work context are as important as other job design features.[39] Policies such as job rotation, worker empowerment, and employee participation have positive effects on productivity, at least partially because they encourage more communication and a positive social environment.

Some social characteristics that improve job performance include interdependence, social support, and interactions with other people outside work. Social interactions are strongly related to positive moods and give employees more opportunities to clarify their work role and how well they are performing.

telecommuting   *Working from home at least two days a week on a computer that is linked to the employer's office.*

Social support gives employees greater opportunities to obtain assistance with their work. Constructive social relationships can bring about a positive feedback loop as employees assist one another in a "virtuous circle."

The work context is also likely to affect employee satisfaction. Work that is hot, loud, and dangerous is less satisfying than work conducted in climate-controlled, relatively quiet, and safe environments. This is probably why most people would rather work in a coffee shop than a metalworking foundry. Physical demands make people physically uncomfortable, which is likely to show up in lower levels of job satisfaction.

To assess why an employee is not performing to her best level, look at the work environment to see whether it's supportive. Does the employee have adequate tools, equipment, materials, and supplies? Does the employee have favorable working conditions, helpful co-workers, supportive work rules and procedures, sufficient information to make job-related decisions, adequate time to do a good job, and the like? If not, performance will suffer.

Employee Involvement

Wegmans grocery stores involve their employees in making decisions that affect their work and please their customers. For example, Wegmans bakery employee Maria Benjamin, shown here, persuaded the company president to sell her chocolate meatball cookies that she makes using a recipe passed down from her Italian ancestors. Wegmans empowers employees to make on-the-spot decisions without consulting their immediate supervisors.

What is **employee involvement**? It's a participative process that uses employees' input to increase their commitment to the organization's success. The logic is that if we engage workers in decisions that affect them and increase their autonomy and control over their work lives, they will become more motivated, more committed to the organization, more productive, and more satisfied with their jobs.[40]

Examples of Employee Involvement Programs

Let's look at two major forms of employee involvement—participative management and representative participation—in more detail.

Participative Management The distinct characteristic common to all **participative management** programs is joint decision making, in which subordinates share a significant degree of decision-making power with their immediate superiors. Participative management has, at times, been promoted as a panacea for poor morale and low productivity. But for it to work, the issues in which employees are engaged must be relevant to their interests so they'll be motivated, employees must have the competence and knowledge to make a useful contribution, and trust and confidence must exist among all parties.[41]

Dozens of studies have been conducted on the participation–performance relationship. The findings, however, are mixed.[42] Organizations that institute participative management do have higher stock returns, lower turnover rates, and higher estimated labor productivity, although these effects are typically not large.[43] A careful review of the research at the individual level shows participation typically has only a modest influence on variables such as employee productivity, motivation, and job satisfaction. Of course, this doesn't mean participative management can't be beneficial under the right conditions. What it says, however, is that it is not a sure means for improving employee performance.

Representative Participation Almost every country in western Europe requires companies to practice **representative participation**, called "the most widely legislated form of employee involvement around the world."[44] Its goal is to redistribute power within an organization, putting labor on a more equal footing with the interests of management and stockholders by letting workers be represented by a small group of employees who actually participate.

4 Give examples of employee involvement measures and show how they can motivate employees.

The two most common forms are works councils and board representatives.[45] Works councils are groups of nominated or elected employees who must be consulted when management makes decisions about employees. Board representatives are employees who sit on a company's board of directors and represent the interests of the firm's employees.

The influence of representative participation on working employees seems to be minimal.[46] Works councils are dominated by management and have little impact on employees or the organization. While participation might increase the motivation and satisfaction of employee representatives, there is little evidence this trickles down to the operating employees they represent. Overall, "the greatest value of representative participation is symbolic. If one is interested in changing employee attitudes or in improving organizational performance, representative participation would be a poor choice."[47]

Linking Employee Involvement Programs and Motivation Theories

Employee involvement draws on a number of the motivation theories we discussed in Chapter 7. Theory Y is consistent with participative management and Theory X with the more traditional autocratic style of managing people. In terms of two-factor theory, employee involvement programs could provide intrinsic motivation by increasing opportunities for growth, responsibility, and involvement in the work itself. The opportunity to make and implement decisions—and then see them work out—can help satisfy an employee's needs for responsibility, achievement, recognition, growth, and enhanced self-esteem. And extensive employee involvement programs clearly have the potential to increase employee intrinsic motivation in work tasks.

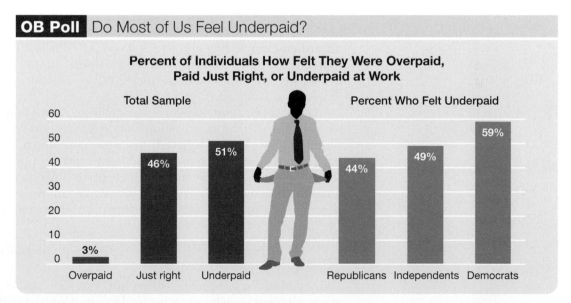

OB Poll Do Most of Us Feel Underpaid?

Source: Based on D. Jacobe, "Half of Americans Say They Are Underpaid," *Gallup Poll* (August 18, 2008), http://www.gallup.com/poll/109618/half-americans-say-they-underpaid.aspx.

---

employee involvement *A participative process that uses the input of employees and is intended to increase employee commitment to an organization's success.*

participative management *A process in which subordinates share a significant degree of decision-making power with their immediate superiors.*

representative participation *A system in which workers participate in organizational decision making through a small group of representative employees.*

Using Rewards to Motivate Employees

5 Demonstrate how the different types of variable-pay programs can increase employee motivation.

As we saw in Chapter 3, pay is not a primary factor driving job satisfaction. However, it does motivate people, and companies often underestimate its importance in keeping top talent. A 2006 study found that while 45 percent of employers thought pay was a key factor in losing top talent, 71 percent of top performers indicated it was a top reason.[48]

Given that pay is so important, management must make some strategic decisions. Will the organization lead, match, or lag the market in pay? How will individual contributions be recognized? In this section, we consider (1) what to pay employees (decided by establishing a pay structure), (2) how to pay individual employees (decided through variable pay plans and skill-based pay plans), (3) what benefits and choices to offer (such as flexible benefits), and (4) how to construct employee recognition programs.

What to Pay: Establishing a Pay Structure

There are many ways to pay employees. The process of initially setting pay levels can be complex and entails balancing *internal equity*—the worth of the job to the organization (usually established through a technical process called job evaluation)—and *external equity*—the external competitiveness of an organization's pay relative to pay elsewhere in its industry (usually established through pay surveys). Obviously, the best pay system pays what the job is worth (internal equity) while also paying competitively relative to the labor market.

Some organizations prefer to be pay leaders by paying above the market, while some may lag the market because they can't afford to pay market rates, or they are willing to bear the costs of paying below market (namely, higher turnover as people are lured to better-paying jobs). Walmart, for example, pays less than its competitors and often outsources jobs overseas. Chinese workers in Shenzhen earn $120 a month (that's $1,440 per year) to make stereos for Walmart. Of the 6,000 factories that are worldwide suppliers to Walmart, 80 percent are located in China. In fact, one-eighth of all Chinese exports to the United States go to Walmart.[49]

Pay more, and you may get better-qualified, more highly motivated employees who will stay with the organization longer. A study covering 126 large organizations found employees who believed they were receiving a competitive pay level had higher morale and were more productive, and customers were more satisfied as well.[50] But pay is often the highest single operating cost for an organization, which means paying too much can make the organization's products or services too expensive. It's a strategic decision an organization must make, with clear trade-offs.

How to Pay: Rewarding Individual Employees Through Variable-Pay Programs

"Why should I put any extra effort into this job?" asked Anne Garcia, a fourth-grade elementary schoolteacher in Denver, Colorado. "I can excel or I can do the bare minimum. It makes no difference. I get paid the same. Why do anything above the minimum to get by?"

Comments like Anne's have been voiced by schoolteachers for decades because pay increases were tied to seniority. Recently, however, a number of states have revamped their compensation systems to motivate people like Anne to strive for excellence in their jobs. Arizona, Florida, Iowa, and Kentucky tie teacher pay to the performance of the students in their classrooms.[51] In California, some teachers can earn performance bonuses as high as $25,000 per year.[52]

Science teacher John Roper-Batker at Seward Montessori School in Minneapolis supports the variable-pay initiative being adopted by many school districts in Minnesota. The new pay plan motivates teachers by basing their pay on their performance in raising student achievement rather than on seniority or degrees. The move toward rewarding teachers with bonuses for their individual performance follows the widespread adoption of variable-pay plans in many businesses and government agencies.

A number of organizations—business firms as well as school districts and other government agencies—are moving away from paying solely on credentials or length of service. Piece-rate plans, merit-based pay, bonuses, profit sharing, gainsharing, and employee stock ownership plans are all a form of a **variable-pay program**, which bases a portion of an employee's pay on some individual and/or organizational measure of performance. Earnings therefore fluctuate up and down.[53]

Variable-pay plans have long been used to compensate salespeople and executives. IBM, Wal-Mart, Pizza Hut, Cigna Corp., and John Deere are just a few companies now using variable pay with rank-and-file employees.[54] Today, more than 70 percent of U.S. companies have some form of variable-pay plan, up from only about 5 percent in 1970.[55] Unfortunately, recent survey data indicate most employees still don't see a strong connection between pay and performance. Only 29 percent say that their performance is rewarded when they do a good job.[56]

The fluctuation in variable pay is what makes these programs attractive to management. It turns part of an organization's fixed labor costs into a variable cost, thus reducing expenses when performance declines. When the U.S. economy encountered a recession in 2001 and 2008, companies with variable pay were able to reduce their labor costs much faster than others.[57] When pay is tied to performance, the employee's earnings also recognize contribution rather than being a form of entitlement. Over time, low performers' pay stagnates, while high performers enjoy pay increases commensurate with their contributions.

Let's examine the different types of variable-pay programs in more detail.

Piece-Rate Pay   The **piece-rate pay plan** has long been popular as a means of compensating production workers by paying a fixed sum for each unit of production completed. A pure piece-rate plan provides no base salary and pays the employee only for what he or she produces. Ballpark workers selling peanuts and soda are frequently paid this way. If they sell 40 bags of peanuts at $1 each, their take is $40. The harder they work and the more peanuts they sell, the more they earn. The limitation of these plans is that they're not feasible for many jobs.

variable-pay program   *A pay plan that bases a portion of an employee's pay on some individual and/or organizational measure of performance.*

piece-rate pay plan   *A pay plan in which workers are paid a fixed sum for each unit of production completed.*

Alabama college football coach Nick Saban earns $4 million per year regardless of how many games he wins. Would it be better to pay him $400,000 for each win? It seems unlikely he would accept such a deal, and it may cause unanticipated consequences as well (such as cheating). So, although incentives are motivating and relevant for some jobs, it is unrealistic to think they can constitute the only piece of some employees' pay.

Merit-Based Pay   A **merit-based pay plan** pays for individual performance based on performance appraisal ratings. A main advantage is that people thought to be high performers can be given bigger raises. If they are designed correctly, merit-based plans let individuals perceive a strong relationship between their performance and the rewards they receive.[58]

Most large organizations have merit pay plans, especially for salaried employees. IBM's merit pay plan increases employees' base salary based on their annual performance evaluation. Since the 1990s, when the economy stumbled badly, an increasing number of Japanese companies have abandoned seniority-based pay in favor of merit-based pay. Koichi Yanashita of Takeda Chemical Industries, commented, "The merit-based salary system is an important means to achieve goals set by the company's top management, not just a way to change wages."[59]

To motivate and retain the best, more companies are increasing the differential between top and bottom performers. The consulting firm Hewitt Associates found that, in 2006, employers gave their best performers roughly 10 percent raises, compared to 3.6 percent for average performers and 1.3 percent for below-average performers. These differences have increased over time. Martyn Fisher of Imperial Chemical in the United Kingdom said his company has widened the merit pay gap between top and average performers because "as much as we would regret our average performers leaving, we regret more an above-target performer leaving."[60]

Despite the intuitive appeal of paying for performance, merit pay plans have several limitations. One is that they are typically based on an annual performance appraisal and thus are only as valid as the performance ratings. Another limitation is that the pay-raise pool fluctuates on economic or other conditions that have little to do with individual performance. One year, a colleague at a top university who performed very well in teaching and research was given a pay raise of $300. Why? Because the pay-raise pool was very small. Yet that is hardly pay-for-performance. Finally, unions typically resist merit pay plans. Relatively few teachers are covered by merit pay for this reason. Instead, seniority-based pay, where all employees get the same raises, predominates.

Bonuses   An annual **bonus** is a significant component of total compensation for many jobs. Among Fortune 100 CEOs, the bonus (mean of $1.01 million) generally exceeds the base salary (mean of $863,000). But bonus plans increasingly include lower-ranking employees; many companies now routinely reward production employees with bonuses in the thousands of dollars when company profits improve. The incentive effects of performance bonuses should be higher than those of merit pay because, rather than paying for performance years ago (that was rolled into base pay), bonuses reward recent performance. Moreover, when times are bad, firms can cut bonuses to reduce compensation costs. Steel company Nucor, for example, guarantees its employees only about $10 per hour, but bonuses can be substantial. In 2006, the average Nucor worker made roughly $91,000. When the recession hit, bonuses were cut dramatically: in 2009, total pay had dropped 40 percent.[61]

This example also highlights the downside of bonuses: employees' pay is more vulnerable to cuts. This is particularly problematic when bonuses are a

Like other organizations, Walmart includes hourly workers in the company's bonus plans. In this photo, a Walmart manager distributes bonus checks to store employees. In a recent year, 80 million hourly employees split more than $500 million dollars for bonuses. The bonus amount for employees depends on their full- or part-time status and on the amount of profit individual stores earn each year. Walmart also offers customer satisfaction bonuses for employees who go above and beyond helping customers. Bonuses give Walmart employees an incentive to increase sales and improve customer service.

large percentage of total pay or when employees come to take bonuses for granted. "People have begun to live as if bonuses were not bonuses at all but part of their expected annual income," said Jay Lorsch, a Harvard Business School professor. KeySpan Corp., a 9,700-employee utility company in New York, tried to combine yearly bonuses with a smaller merit-pay raise. Elaine Weinstein, KeySpan's senior vice president of HR, credits the plan with changing the culture from "entitlement to meritocracy."[62]

Skill-Based Pay   **Skill-based pay** (also called *competency-based* or *knowledge-based pay*) is an alternative to job-based pay that bases pay levels on how many skills employees have or how many jobs they can do.[63] Employees at American Steel & Wire can boost their annual salaries by up to $12,480 by acquiring as many as ten new skills. Frito-Lay Corporation ties its compensation for frontline operations managers to their developing skills in leadership, workforce development, and functional excellence. For employers, the lure of skill-based pay plans is that they increase the flexibility of the workforce: filling staffing needs is easier when employee skills are interchangeable. Skill-based pay also facilitates communication across the organization because people gain a better understanding of each others' jobs.

What about the downsides? People can "top out"—that is, they can learn all the skills the program calls for them to learn. This can frustrate employees after they've been challenged by an environment of learning, growth, and continual pay raises. IDS Financial Services[64] found itself paying people more even though there was little immediate use for their new skills. IDS eventually dropped its skill-based pay plan for one that equally balances individual contribution and

---

merit-based pay plan   *A pay plan based on performance appraisal ratings.*

bonus   *A pay plan that rewards employees for recent performance rather than historical performance.*

skill-based pay   *A pay plan that sets pay levels on the basis of how many skills employees have or how many jobs they can do.*

gains in work-team productivity. Finally, skill-based plans don't address level of performance. They deal only with whether someone can perform the skill.

Profit-Sharing Plans   A **profit-sharing plan** is an organizationwide program that distributes compensation based on some established formula designed around a company's profitability. Compensation can be direct cash outlays or, particularly for top managers, allocations of stock options. When you read about executives like Oracle's Larry Ellison earning $75.33 million in pay, it almost all (88.8 percent in Ellison's case) comes from cashing in stock options previously granted based on company profit performance. Not all profit-sharing plans need be so grand in scale. Jacob Luke, age 13, started his own lawn-mowing business after getting a mower from his uncle. Jacob employs his brother, Isaiah, and friend, Marcel Monroe, and pays them each 25 percent of the profits he makes on each yard. Profit-sharing plans at the organizational level appear to have positive impacts on employee attitudes; employees working under profit-sharing plans have a greater feeling of psychological ownership.[65]

Gainsharing   **Gainsharing**[66] is a formula-based group incentive plan that uses improvements in group productivity from one period to another determine the total amount of money allocated. Approximately 45 percent of Fortune 1000 firms have implemented gainsharing plans;[67] its popularity seems narrowly focused among large manufacturing companies such as Champion Spark Plug and Mead Paper. Gainsharing is different from profit sharing in that it ties rewards to productivity gains rather than profits. Employees in a gainsharing plan can receive incentive awards even when the organization isn't profitable. Because the benefits accrue to groups of workers, high-performing workers pressure weaker performers to work harder, improving performance for the group as a whole.[68]

Employee Stock Ownership Plans   An **employee stock ownership plan** (ESOP) is a company-established benefit plan in which employees acquire stock, often at below-market prices, as part of their benefits. Companies as varied as Publix Supermarkets and W.L. Gore & Associates are now over 50 percent employee-owned.[69] But most of the 10,000 or so ESOPs in the United States are in small, privately held companies.[70]

Research on ESOPs indicates they increase employee satisfaction.[71] But their impact on performance is less clear. ESOPs have the potential to increase employee job satisfaction and work motivation. But for this potential to be realized, employees need to psychologically experience ownership.[72] That is, in addition to their financial stake in the company, they need to be kept regularly informed of the status of the business and have the opportunity to exercise influence over it to achieve significant improvements in the organization's performance.[73]

ESOP plans for top management can reduce unethical behavior. CEOs are more likely to manipulate firm earnings reports to make themselves look good in the short run when they don't have an ownership share, even though this manipulation will eventually lead to lower stock prices. However, when CEOs own a large value of stock they report earnings accurately because they don't want the negative consequences of declining stock prices.[74]

Evaluation of Variable Pay   Do variable-pay programs increase motivation and productivity? The answer is a qualified "yes." Studies generally support the idea that organizations with profit-sharing plans have higher levels of profitability than those without them.[75] Similarly, gainsharing has been found to

An Ethical Choice

You Might Work Less Than You Think

Traditionally, full-time meant at least 40 hours of work per week. Many jobs today, however, while full-time, require more than 40 hours per week. So how many hours does a job require? Of course answers vary, depending on the culture of the organization and individuals' own expectations. It may surprise you to learn most people dramatically overestimate their work hours.

Most studies of work motivation simply asked workers and managers to self-report their weekly work hours. However, starting in the 1980s, researchers began studying work (and nonwork) hours more carefully, with "time diaries" that track time use minute by minute. In 1985, time diary studies revealed that the average worker claimed to work 40 to 44 hours per week and actually worked 36.2.

As estimated hours rise, the discrepancy between estimated and ac-

tual work hours rises, too. Those who claim to work 60 to 64 hours a week in fact average only 44.2 hours. Individuals who estimate they work 65 to 74 hours really work 52.9. Those who claim to work 75 hours or more work only 54.9 hours on average.

The overestimations do not appear to be changing much over time. We overestimate our work hours now about as much as workers did in the 1980s.

Why does any of this matter? People may wrongly think their job is unrewarding (or underrewarding) because they overestimate the hours they work. They may also think they work harder than their co-workers, which might make them less likely to help them. So, when evaluating what you earn relative to how much you think you work, keep the following in mind:

1. Be honest with yourself. Realize we tend to overestimate the time we spend working (and underesti-

mate the time we spend sleeping). You'll make better decisions about how to spend your time if your current "time inventory" is accurate and realistic.

2. If you're prone to overestimating—those in white-collar jobs and those who work the most hours are most likely to overestimate their actual work hours—take particular care to be honest and accurate.

3. Also realize blending work and play can cause overestimating. If you're "working" on your laptop while watching *American Idol* or *House,* how much are you really working?

Source: L. Vanderkam, "Overestimating Our Overworking," *Wall Street Journal* (May 29, 2009), p. W13.

---

improve productivity in a majority of cases and often has a positive impact on employee attitudes.[76] Another study found that whereas piece-rate pay-for-performance plans stimulated higher levels of productivity, this positive affect was not observed for risk-averse employees. Thus economist Ed Lazear seems generally right when he says, "Workers respond to prices just as economic theory predicts. Claims by sociologists and others that monetizing incentives may actually reduce output are unambiguously refuted by the data." But that doesn't mean everyone responds positively to variable-pay plans.[77]

Flexible Benefits: Developing a Benefits Package

6 Show how flexible benefits turn benefits into motivators.

Todd Evans and Allison Murphy both work for Citigroup, but they need very different employee benefits. Todd is married and has three young children; his wife is at home full time. Allison, too, is married, but her husband has a high-paying job with the federal government, and they have no children. Todd is concerned about having a good medical plan and

---

profit-sharing plan *An organizationwide program that distributes compensation based on some established formula designed around a company's profitability.*

gainsharing *A formula-based group incentive plan.*

employee stock ownership plan (ESOP) *A company-established benefits plan in which employees acquire stock, often at below-market prices, as part of their benefits.*

Employees of software developer Oracle Corporation, shown here in the company's cafeteria, receive a basic benefits package and may also choose coverage levels and additional benefits that meet their individual needs and those of their dependents. Such flexible benefits are consistent with the expectancy theory thesis that links rewards to individual employee goals. The OracleFlex plan gives employees flex credits they can use to purchase benefits so they can control the amount they spend for each benefit option. Employees with remaining credits may direct them toward taxable income or to their 401(k) savings, health care reimbursement, or dependent care reimbursement accounts.

7   Identify the motivational benefits of intrinsic rewards.

enough life insurance to support his family in case it's needed. In contrast, Allison's husband already has her medical needs covered on his plan, and life insurance is a low priority. Allison is more interested in extra vacation time and long-term financial benefits such as a tax-deferred savings plan.

A standardized benefits package would be unlikely to meet the needs of Todd and Allison well. Citigroup could, however, cover both sets of needs with flexible benefits.

Consistent with expectancy theory's thesis that organizational rewards should be linked to each individual employee's goals, **flexible benefits** individualize rewards by allowing each employee to choose the compensation package that best satisfies his or her current needs and situation. These plans replace the "one-benefit-plan-fits-all" programs designed for a male with a wife and two children at home that dominated organizations for more than 50 years.[78] Fewer than 10 percent of employees now fit this image: About 25 percent are single, and one-third are part of two-income families with no children. Flexible benefits can accommodate differences in employee needs based on age, marital status, spouses' benefit status, number and age of dependents, and the like.

The three most popular types of benefits plans are modular plans, core-plus options, and flexible spending accounts.[79] *Modular plans* are predesigned packages or modules of benefits, each of which meets the needs of a specific group of employees. A module designed for single employees with no dependents might include only essential benefits. Another, designed for single parents, might have additional life insurance, disability insurance, and expanded health coverage. *Core-plus plans* consist of a core of essential benefits and a menulike selection of others from which employees can select. Typically, each employee is given "benefit credits," which allow the "purchase" of additional benefits that uniquely meet his or her needs. *Flexible spending plans* allow employees to set aside pretax dollars up to the dollar amount offered in the plan to pay for particular benefits, such as health care and dental premiums. Flexible spending accounts can increase take-home pay because employees don't pay taxes on the dollars they spend out of these accounts.

Intrinsic Rewards: Employee Recognition Programs

Laura Schendell makes only $8.50 per hour working at her fast-food job in Pensacola, Florida, and the job isn't very challenging or interesting. Yet Laura talks enthusiastically about the job, her boss, and the company that employs her. "What I like is the fact that Guy [her supervisor] appreciates the effort I make. He compliments me regularly in front of the other people on my shift, and I've been chosen Employee of the Month twice in the past six months. Did you see my picture on that plaque on the wall?"

Organizations are increasingly recognizing what Laura Schendell knows: Important work rewards can be both intrinsic and extrinsic. Rewards are intrinsic in the form of employee recognition programs and extrinsic in the form of compensation systems. In this section, we deal with ways in which managers can reward and motivate employee performance.

Employee recognition programs range from a spontaneous and private thank-you to widely publicized formal programs in which specific types of behavior are encouraged and the procedures for attaining recognition are clearly identified. Some research suggests financial incentives may be more motivating in the short term, but in the long run it's nonfinancial incentives.[80]

Nichols Foods Ltd., a British bottler of soft drinks and syrups, has a comprehensive recognition program.[81] The central hallway in its production area is lined with "bragging boards," where the accomplishments of various individuals and teams are regularly updated. Monthly awards are presented to people nominated by peers for extraordinary effort on the job. And monthly award winners are eligible for further recognition at an annual off-site meeting for all employ-

Exhibit **8-4**

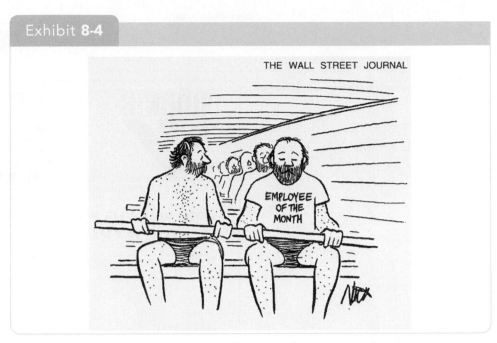

Source: From the *Wall Street Journal*, October 21, 1997. Reprinted by permission of Cartoon Features Syndicate.

ees. In contrast, most managers use a far more informal approach. Julia Stewart, president of Applebee's restaurants, frequently leaves sealed notes on the chairs of employees after everyone has gone home.[82] These notes explain how critical Stewart thinks the person's work is or how much she appreciates the completion of a recent project. Stewart also relies heavily on voice-mail messages left after office hours to tell employees how appreciative she is of a job well done.

A few years ago, 1,500 employees were surveyed in a variety of work settings to find out what they considered the most powerful workplace motivator. Their response? Recognition, recognition, and more recognition. As illustrated in Exhibit 8-5, Phoenix Inn, a West Coast chain of small hotels, encourages employees to smile by letting customers identify this desirable behavior and then recognizing employees who are identified smiling most often by giving them rewards and publicity.

An obvious advantage of recognition programs is that they are inexpensive since praise is free![83] It shouldn't be surprising then that they've grown in popularity. A 2002 survey of 391 companies found 84 percent had some program to recognize worker achievements, and 4 in 10 said they were doing more to foster employee recognition than they had just a year earlier.[84]

Despite the increased popularity of employee recognition programs, critics argue they are highly susceptible to political manipulation by management.[85] When applied to jobs for which performance factors are relatively objective, such as sales, recognition programs are likely to be perceived by employees as fair. However, in most jobs, the criteria for good performance aren't self evident, which allows managers to manipulate the system and recognize their favorites. Abuse can undermine the value of recognition programs and demoralize employees.

flexible benefits *A benefits plan that allows each employee to put together a benefits package individually tailored to his or her own needs and situation.*

Global Implications

Do the motivational approaches we've discussed vary by culture? Because we've covered some very different approaches in this chapter, let's break down our analysis by approach. Not every approach has been studied by cross-cultural researchers, so we consider cross-cultural differences in (1) job characteristics and job enrichment, (2) telecommuting, (3) variable pay, (4) flexible benefits, and (5) employee involvement.

Job Characteristics and Job Enrichment

A few studies have tested the job characteristics model in different cultures, but the results aren't very consistent. One study suggested that when employees are "other oriented" (concerned with the welfare of others at work), the relationship between intrinsic job characteristics and job satisfaction was weaker. The fact that the job characteristics model is relatively individualistic (considering the relationship between the employee and his or her work) suggests job enrichment strategies may not have the same effects in collectivistic cultures as in individualistic cultures (such as the United States).[86] However, another study suggested the degree to which jobs had intrinsic job characteristics predicted job satisfaction and job involvement equally well for U.S., Japanese, and Hungarian employees.[87]

Telecommuting

Does the degree to which employees telecommute vary by nation? Does its effectiveness depend on culture? First, one study suggests that telecommuting is more common in the United States than in all the European Union (EU) nations except the Netherlands. In the study, 24.6 percent of U.S. employees

International OB

Cultural Differences in Job Characteristics and Job Satisfaction

How do various factors of a job contribute to satisfaction in different cultures? A recent study that surveyed about 50 countries distinguished between intrinsic job characteristics (for example, having a job that allows one to use one's skills, frequently receiving recognition from one's supervisor) and extrinsic job characteristics (for example, receiving pay competitive within a given industry, working in comfortable physical conditions) and assessed differences between the two in predicting employee job satisfaction.

Across all countries, extrinsic job characteristics were consistently and positively related to job satisfaction. However, countries differed in the extent to which intrinsic job characteristics predicted job satisfaction. Wealthier countries, countries with stronger social security, countries that stress individualism rather than collectivism, and countries with a smaller power distance (those that value a more equal distribution of power in organizations and institutions) showed a stronger relationship between the presence of intrinsic job characteristics and job satisfaction.

What explains these findings? One rationale is that in countries with greater wealth and social security, people take survival for granted, and employees are free to place greater importance on intrinsic aspects of the job. Another is that cultures that emphasize the individual and have less power asymmetry socialize individuals to focus on the intrinsic aspects of the job. In other words, such norms tell individuals it is okay to want jobs that are intrinsically rewarding.

Source: Based on X. Huang and E. Van De Vliert, "Where Intrinsic Job Satisfaction Fails to Work: National Moderators of Intrinsic Motivation," *Journal of Organizational Behavior* 24, no. 2 (2003), pp. 159–179.

engaged in telecommuting, compared to only 13.0 percent of EU employees. Of the EU countries, the Netherlands had the highest rate of telecommuting (26.4 percent); the lowest rates were in Spain (4.9 percent) and Portugal (3.4 percent). What about the rest of the world? Unfortunately, there are few data comparing telecommuting rates in other parts of the world. Similarly, we don't really know whether telecommuting works better in the United States than in other countries. However, the same study that compared telework rates between the United States and the EU determined that employees in Europe appeared to have the same level of interest in telework: regardless of country, interest is higher among employees than among employers.[88]

Variable Pay

You'd probably think individual pay systems (such as merit pay or pay-for-performance) work better in individualistic cultures such as the United States than in collectivistic cultures such as China or Venezuela. Similarly, you'd probably hypothesize that group-based rewards such as gainsharing or profit sharing work better in collectivistic cultures than in individualistic cultures. Unfortunately, there isn't much research on the issue. One recent study did suggest, though, that beliefs about the fairness of a group incentive plan were more predictive of pay satisfaction for employees in the United States than for employees in Hong Kong. One interpretation of these findings is that U.S. employees are more critical in appraising a group pay plan, and therefore it's more critical that the plan be communicated clearly and administered fairly.[89]

Flexible Benefits

Today, almost all major corporations in the United States offer flexible benefits. And they're becoming the norm in other countries, too. A recent survey of 136 Canadian organizations found that 93 percent have adopted or will adopt flexible benefits in the near term.[90] And a similar survey of 307 firms in the

United Kingdom found that while only 16 percent have flexible benefits programs in place, another 60 percent are either in the process of implementing them or are seriously considering it.[91]

Employee Involvement

Employee involvement programs differ among countries.[92] A study comparing the acceptance of employee involvement programs in four countries, including the United States and India, confirmed the importance of modifying practices to reflect national culture.[93] Specifically, while U.S. employees readily accepted these programs, managers in India who tried to empower their employees through employee involvement programs were rated low by those employees. These reactions are consistent with India's high power–distance culture, which accepts and expects differences in authority. Similarly, Chinese workers who were very accepting of traditional Chinese values showed few benefits from participative decision making, but workers who were less traditional were more satisfied and had higher performance ratings under participative management.[94] This study illustrates the substantial differences in how management practices are perceived by individuals within as well as between countries.

Summary and Implications for Managers

We've presented a number of motivation theories and applications in Chapter 7 and in this chapter. Although it's always dangerous to synthesize a large number of complex ideas, the following suggestions summarize what we know about motivating employees in organizations.

Recognize Individual Differences Managers should be sensitive to individual differences. For example, employees from Asian cultures prefer not to be singled out as special because it makes them uncomfortable. Spend the time necessary to understand what's important to each employee. This allows you to individualize goals, level of involvement, and rewards to align with individual needs. Design jobs to align with individual needs and maximize their motivation potential.

Use Goals and Feedback Employees should have firm, specific goals, and they should get feedback on how well they are faring in pursuit of those goals.

Allow Employees to Participate in Decisions That Affect Them Employees can contribute to setting work goals, choosing their own benefits packages, and solving productivity and quality problems. Participation can increase employee productivity, commitment to work goals, motivation, and job satisfaction.

Link Rewards to Performance Rewards should be contingent on performance, and employees must perceive the link between the two. Regardless of how strong the relationship is, if individuals perceive it to be weak, the results will be low performance, a decrease in job satisfaction, and an increase in turnover and absenteeism.

Check the System for Equity Employees should perceive that experience, skills, abilities, effort, and other obvious inputs explain differences in performance and hence in pay, job assignments, and other obvious rewards.

Praise Motivates

Some of the most memorable, and meaningful, words we've ever heard have probably been words of praise. Genuine compliments mean a lot to people—and can go a long way toward inspiring the best performance. Numerous research studies show that students who receive praise from their teachers are more motivated, and often this motivation lasts well after the praise is given. Too often we assume simple words mean little, but most of us yearn for genuine praise from people in a position to evaluate us.

Companies are starting to learn this lesson. Walt Disney, Lands' End, and Hallmark have worked to use praise as a work reward to motivate employees. The 1,000-employee Scooter Store has a "celebrations assistant" whose job is to celebrate employee successes. The Container Store estimates 1 of its 4,000 employees receives praise every 20 seconds. A recent research study of two retail stores suggested managers who praise their employees get higher performance out of them.

Praise is important even to long-term relationships. The Gottman Institute, a relationship research and training firm in Seattle, says its research suggests the happiest marriages are those in which couples make five times as many positive statements to and about each other as negative ones.

Finally, a recent neuropsychology study found that praise activated the same part of the human brain as material rewards, which points to another benefit to praise: It may be just as motivating as money and, best of all, it's free.

Praise is highly overrated. Sure, in theory it's nice to receive compliments, but in practice praise has some real pitfalls. First, a lot of praise isn't genuine, and false praise breeds narcissism. Researcher Jean Twenge says scores on narcissism have risen steadily since 1982, and lavishing praise may be the culprit. If told we're wonderful time after time, we start to believe it even when we aren't.

Second, praise is paradoxical—if we tell everyone they're special, soon it means nothing to those who do achieve something terrific. In the animated film *The Incredibles,* a superhero's mom tells her son "Everyone's special!" His reply: "Which is another way of saying no one is."

Third, praise can be manipulative. A study of hairdressers found those who complimented their customers earned significantly higher tips. So praise often means the "praiser" wants something from the "praisee."

Fourth, some of the most motivating people are difficult to please. Think of Jack Welch, former CEO of GE, or A. G. Lafley, ex-CEO of Procter & Gamble. They are known for being difficult to please, which means most people will work harder to meet their expectations. When you dish out kudos for an employee who merely shows up, you've sent a message that simply showing up is enough.

Often what people really need is a gentle kick in the pants. As Steve Smolinsky of the Wharton School at the University of Pennsylvania says, "You have to tell students, 'It's not as good as you can do. . . . You can do better.'"

One management consultant says, "People want to know how they're doing. Don't sugarcoat it. Just give them the damn data."[95]

Questions for Review

1 What is the job characteristics model? How does it motivate employees?

2 What are the three major ways that jobs can be redesigned? In your view, in what situations would one of the methods be favored over the others?

3 What are the three alternative work arrangements of flextime, job sharing, and telecommuting? What are the advantages and disadvantages of each?

4 What are employee involvement programs? How might they increase employee motivation?

5 What is variable pay? What are the variable-pay programs that are used to motivate employees? What are their advantages and disadvantages?

6 How can flexible benefits motivate employees?

7 What are the motivational benefits of intrinsic rewards?

Experiential Exercise

ASSESSING EMPLOYEE MOTIVATION AND SATISFACTION USING THE JOB CHARACTERISTICS MODEL

Purpose

This exercise will help you examine outcomes of the job characteristics model for different professions.

Time

Approximately 30 to 45 minutes.

Background

Data were collected on 6,930 employees in 56 different organizations in the United States, using the Job Diagnostic Survey. The following table contains data on the five core job dimensions of the job characteristics model for several professions. Also included are growth-needs strength, internal motivation, and pay satisfaction for each profession. The values are averages based on a 7-point scale.

Instructions

1. Break into groups of three to five.

2. Calculate the MPS score for each of the professions and compare them. Discuss whether you think these scores accurately reflect your perceptions of the motivating potential of these professions.

3. Graph the relationship between each profession's core job dimensions and its corresponding value for internal motivation and for pay satisfaction, using the core job dimensions as independent variables. What conclusions can you draw about motivation and satisfaction of employees in these professions?

Job Characteristics Averages for Six Professions

Variable	Professional/ Technical	Managerial	Sales	Service	Clerical	Machine Trades
Skill variety	5.4	5.6	4.8	5.0	4.0	5.1
Task identity	5.1	4.7	4.4	4.7	4.7	4.9
Task significance	5.6	5.8	5.5	5.7	5.3	5.6
Autonomy	5.4	5.4	4.8	5.0	4.5	4.9
Feedback	5.1	5.2	5.4	5.1	4.6	4.9
Growth-needs strength	5.6	5.3	5.7	5.4	5.0	4.8
Internal motivation	5.8	5.8	5.7	5.7	5.4	5.6
Pay satisfaction	4.4	4.6	4.2	4.1	4.0	4.2

Source: J. R. Hackman and G. R. Oldham, *Work Redesign* (Reading, MA: Addison-Wesley, 1980).

Ethical Dilemma

DID EXECUTIVES' PAY CAUSE THE RECESSION?

Long the prestige and power center of organizations and industries, banking and finance are now widely blamed for the global recession. President Obama has argued that executive compensation wreaked "havoc in our financial system" and called the pay practices "shameful." In banking haven Switzerland, bankers have been booed out of restaurants, and some maître d's refuse to seat them.

To some, the source of the problem is the industry's culture of greed. One business reporter alleged executives rigged the compensation system so it "would reward them no matter what." Others feel executives' incentive structure caused the problem. Specifically, these critics argue executives' pay is boosted more under rosy scenarios than it is penalized under bleak scenarios. Say you're contemplating a series of risky investments that could generate a bonus equal to triple your annual salary. Should they fail, you receive no bonus, but you would still have your salary. Such

pay plans encourage excessive risk taking, the argument goes. One labor economist opined, "Give smart people go-for-broke incentives and they will go for broke. Duh."

Do you agree pay incentives are to blame for the financial crisis and, by extension, the global recession? Why or why not? If you agree, how might executive/manager compensation plans be modified? One suggestion is a "bonus bank" where managers' bonuses are held for a period of time and against which subsequent losses are charged. What is an advantage, and a possible downside, of such a plan? Because boards of directors don't want to restrict executive compensation, should the federal government modify pay plans, as the Obama administration has done? Putting your own political preferences aside for the moment, consider the advantages and disadvantages of a system that would, say, limit executives' salaries to $500,000 annually, and their bonuses to 50 percent of their base salary.

Sources: A. S. Blinder, "Crazy Compensation and the Crisis," *Wall Street Journal* (May 28, 2009), p. A15; M. Mandel, "CEO Pay: Obama's Reagan Moment," *BusinessWeek* (February 16, 2009), pp. 28–29; and D. Leonhardt, "A.I.G.'s Bailout Priorities Are in Critics' Cross Hairs," *New York Times* (March 18, 2009), pp. B1, B4.

Case Incident 1

MULTITASKING: A GOOD USE OF YOUR TIME?

Multitasking—doing two or more things at once, or rapidly switching from one task to another—is a characteristic of the Millennial generation. One recent study revealed that during a typical week, 81 percent of young people report "media multitasking" at least some of the time.

Multitasking nicely illustrates our point that motivation is not just effort but also how you direct your efforts. However, is the direction of efforts in multitasking efficient or inefficient?

Many people who multitask say it makes them more efficient: "Why not do two things at once if I can accomplish about as much as if I only did one thing?" they ask. Research, however, suggests multitasking is inefficient, that it actually takes longer to do two things at once than to do one thing first and then turn to the other. David Meyer, a University of Michigan psychologist who has studied multitasking, argues, "You wind up needing to use the same sorts of mental and physical resources for performing each of the tasks. You're having to switch back and forth between the two tasks as opposed to really doing them simultaneously."

Multitasking appears to result in adverse outcomes beyond inefficiency. Another study found multitaskers absorb material more superficially; they notice more things in

their environment but are able to learn material less deeply. "It's not that they can't focus," says one researcher. "It's that they focus on everything. They hear everything—even things they would normally be able to block out—because they are now so used to attending to many things at once." Other research suggests that while multitaskers have more friends, these friends are more likely to be superficial contacts who quickly fade away. One researcher says, "There's a danger that having few long-term relationships is giving way to many superficial, fleeting relationships."

Questions

1. One expert who has studied multitasking calls it "a big illusion," arguing that multitaskers think they are more motivated and productive even when they aren't. Do you consider yourself a multitasker? If so, does this case make you reconsider whether multitasking makes you more motivated or productive?

2. The effects of multitasking have been found to be more negative when the tasks are complex. Why do you think this is the case?

3. You might think multitasking makes you happy. While there is less research on this topic, some evidence suggests multitaskers feel more stress in their work. Multitaskers "feel a constant low-level panic." Do you agree? Why or why not?

4. One expert recommends we "recreate boundaries" by training ourselves, while doing something, not to look at other devices like cell phone or television for increasing periods of time. Do you think you could do that? For how long?

Sources: R. A. Clay, "Mini-Multitaskers," *Monitor on Psychology* 40, no. 2 (2009), pp. 38–40; and A. Tugend, "Multitasking Can Make You Lose . . . Um . . . Focus," *New York Times* (October 25, 2008), p. B7.

Case Incident 2

THANKS FOR NOTHING

Although it may seem fairly obvious that receiving praise and recognition from one's company is a motivating experience, it is sad that many companies are failing miserably when it comes to saying thanks to their employees. According to Curt Coffman, global practice leader at Gallup, 71 percent of U.S. workers are "disengaged," essentially meaning that they couldn't care less about their organization. Coffman states, "We're operating at one-quarter of the capacity in terms of managing human capital. It's alarming." Employee recognition programs, which became more popular as the U.S. economy shifted from industrial to knowledge based, can be an effective way to motivate employees and make them feel valued. In many cases, however, recognition programs are doing "more harm than good," according to Coffman.

Consider Ko, a 50-year-old former employee of a dot-com in California. Her company proudly instituted a rewards program designed to motivate employees. What were the rewards for a job well done? Employees would receive a badge that read "U Done Good" and, each year, would receive a T-shirt as a means of annual recognition. Once an employee received 10 "U Done Good" badges, he or she could trade them in for something bigger and better—a paperweight. Ko states that she would have preferred a raise. "It was patronizing. There wasn't any deep thought involved in any of this." To make matters worse, she says, the badges were handed out arbitrarily and were not tied to performance. And what about those T-shirts? Ko states that the company instilled a strict dress code, so employees couldn't even wear the shirts if they wanted to do so. Needless to say, the employee recognition program seemed like an empty gesture rather than a motivator.

Even programs that provide employees with more expensive rewards can backfire, especially if the rewards are given insincerely. Eric Lange, an employee of a trucking company, recalls a time when one of the company's vice presidents achieved a major financial goal for the company. The vice president, who worked in an office next to Lange, received a Cadillac Seville as his company car and a new Rolex wristwatch that cost the company $10,000. Both were lavish gifts, but the way they were distributed left a sour taste in the vice president's mouth. He entered his office to find the Rolex in a cheap cardboard box sitting on his desk, along with a brief letter explaining that he would be receiving a 1099 tax form so he could pay taxes on the watch. Lange states of the vice president, "He came into my office, which was right next door, and said, 'Can you believe this?'" A mere 2 months later, the vice president pawned the watch. Lange explains, "It had absolutely no meaning for him."

Such experiences resonate with employees who may find more value in a sincere pat on the back than in gifts from management that either are meaningless or aren't conveyed with respect or sincerity. However, sincere pats on the back may be hard to come by. A Gallup poll found that 61 percent of employees stated that they hadn't received a sincere thank-you from management in the past year. Findings such as these are troubling, as verbal rewards are not only inexpensive for companies to hand out but also quick and easy to distribute. Of course, verbal rewards do need to be paired sometimes with tangible benefits that employees value—after all, money talks. In addition, when praising employees for a job well done, managers need to ensure that the praise is given in conjunction with the specific accomplishment. In this way, employees may not only feel valued by their organization but will also know what actions to take to be rewarded in the future.

Questions

1. If praising employees for doing a good job seems to be a fairly easy and obvious motivational tool, why do you think companies and managers don't often do it?

2. As a manager, what steps would you take to motivate your employees after observing them perform well?

3. Are there any downsides to giving employees too much verbal praise? What might these downsides be, and as a manager how could you alleviate them?

4. As a manager, how would you ensure that recognition given to employees is distributed fairly and justly?

Source: Based on J. Sandberg, "Been Here 25 Years and All I Got Was This Lousy T-Shirt," *Wall Street Journal* (January 28, 2004), p. B1.

Endnotes

1. M. Richtel, "Who Moved My Bonus?" *New York Times* (February 19, 2009), pp. B1, B4; J. McGregor, "Cutting Salaries Instead of Jobs," *BusinessWeek* (June 8, 2009), pp. 46–48; D. Robinson, "What to Do When Pay Cuts Are Too Deep," *San Francisco Chronicle* (June 7, 2009), www.sfgate.com.

2. J. R. Hackman and G. R. Oldham, "Motivation Through the Design of Work: Test of a Theory," *Organizational Behavior and Human Performance*, August 1976, pp. 250–279; and J. R. Hackman and G. R. Oldham, *Work Redesign* (Reading, MA: Addison-Wesley, 1980).

3. J. R. Hackman, "Work Design," in J. R. Hackman and J. L. Suttle (eds.), *Improving Life at Work* (Santa Monica, CA: Goodyear, 1977), p. 129.

4. See "Job Characteristics Theory of Work Redesign," in J. B. Miner, *Theories of Organizational Behavior* (Hinsdale, IL: Dryden Press, 1980), pp. 231–266; B. T. Loher, R. A. Noe, N. L. Moeller, and M. P. Fitzgerald, "A Meta-analysis of the Relation of Job Characteristics to Job Satisfaction," *Journal of Applied Psychology*, May 1985, pp. 280–289; S. J. Zaccaro and E. F. Stone, "Incremental Validity of an Empirically Based Measure of Job Characteristics," *Journal of Applied Psychology*, May 1988, pp. 245–252; J. R. Rentsch and R. P. Steel, "Testing the Durability of Job Characteristics as Predictors of Absenteeism over a Six-Year Period," *Personnel Psychology*, Spring 1998, pp. 165–190; S. J. Behson, E. R. Eddy, and S. J. Lorenzet, "The Importance of the Critical Psychological States in the Job Characteristics Model: A Meta-analytic and Structural Equations Modeling Examination," *Current Research in Social Psychology*, May 2000, pp. 170–189; T. A. Judge, "Promote Job Satisfaction Through Mental Challenge," in E. A. Locke (ed.), *Handbook of Principles of Organizational Behavior*, pp. 75–89 (Hoboken, NJ: Wiley-Blackwell, 2003); and S. E. Humphrey, J. D. Nahrgang, and F. P. Morgeson, "Integrating Motivational, Social, and Contextual Work Design Features: A Meta-analytic Summary and Theoretical Extension of the Work Design Literature," *Journal of Applied Psychology* 92, no. 5 (2007), pp.1332–1356.

5. T. A. Judge, S. K. Parker, A. E. Colbert, D. Heller, and R. Ilies, "Job Satisfaction: A Cross-Cultural Review," in N. Anderson, D. S. Ones (eds.), *Handbook of Industrial, Work and Organizational Psychology*, vol. 2 (Thousand Oaks, CA: Sage Publications, 2002), pp. 25–52.

6. Hackman, "Work Design," pp. 115–120.

7. J. P. Wanous, "Individual Differences and Reactions to Job Characteristics," *Journal of Applied Psychology*, October 1974, pp. 616–622; and H. P. Sims and A. D. Szilagyi, "Job Characteristic Relationships: Individual and Structural Moderators," *Organizational Behavior and Human Performance*, June 1976, pp. 211–230.

8. M. Fein, "The Real Needs and Goals of Blue-Collar Workers," *The Conference Board Record*, February 1972, pp. 26–33.

9. C. Ansberry, "In the New Workplace, Jobs Morph to Suit Rapid Pace of Change," *Wall Street Journal* (March 22, 2002), p. A1.

10. J. Ortega, "Job Rotation as a Learning Mechanism," *Management Science*, October 2001, pp. 1361–1370.

11. Hackman and Oldham, *Work Redesign*.

12. A. M. Grant, E. M. Campbell, G. Chen, K. Cottone, D. Lapedis, and K. Lee, "Impact and the Art of Motivation Maintenance: The Effects of Contact with Beneficiaries on Persistence Behavior," *Organizational Behavior and Human Decision Processes* 103 (2007), pp. 53–67.

13. A. M. Grant, J. E. Dutton, and B. D. Rosso, "Giving Commitment: Employee Support Programs and the Prosocial Sensemaking Process," *Academy of Management Journal* 51, no. 5 (2008), pp. 898–918.

14. "Career Development—Job Enrichment," University of New Mexico Department of Human Resources (hr.unm.edu/compensation/jobenrichment.php).

15. See, for example, Hackman and Oldham, *Work Redesign;* Miner, *Theories of Organizational Behavior*, pp. 231–266; R. W. Griffin, "Effects of Work Redesign on Employee Perceptions, Attitudes, and Behaviors: A Long-Term Investigation," *Academy of Management Journal* 34, no. 2 (1991), pp. 425–435; and J. L. Cotton, *Employee Involvement* (Newbury Park, CA: Sage, 1993), pp. 141–172.

16. R. D. Pritchard, M. M. Harrell, D. DiazGrandos, and M. J. Guzman, "The Productivity Measurement and Enhancement System: A Meta-analysis," *Journal of Applied Psychology* 93, no. 3 (2008), pp. 540–567.

17. F. P. Morgeson, M. D. Johnson, M. A. Campion, G. J. Medsker, and T. V. Mumford, "Understanding Reactions to Job Redesign: A Quasi-Experimental Investigation of the Moderating Effects of Organizational Contact on Perceptions of Performance Behavior," *Personnel Psychology* 39 (2006), pp. 333–363.

18. F. W. Bond, P. E. Flaxman, and D. Bunce, "The Influence of Psychological Flexibility on Work Redesign: Mediated Moderation of a Work Reorganization Intervention," *Journal of Applied Psychology* 93, no. 3 (2008), pp. 645–654.

19. From the National Study of the Changing Workforce, cited in S. Shellenbarger, "Number of Women Managers Rise," *Wall Street Journal* (September 30, 2003), p. D2.

20. Cited in "Flextime Gains in Popularity in Germany," *Manpower Argus*, September 2000, p. 4.

21. D. R. Dalton and D. J. Mesch, "The Impact of Flexible Scheduling on Employee Attendance and Turnover," *Administrative Science Quarterly,* June 1990, pp. 370–387; K. S. Kush and L. K. Stroh, "Flextime: Myth or Reality," *Business Horizons,* September–October 1994, p. 53; and L. Golden, "Flexible Work Schedules: What Are We Trading Off to Get Them?" *Monthly Labor Review,* March 2001, pp. 50–55.

22. See, for example, D. A. Ralston and M. F. Flanagan, "The Effect of Flextime on Absenteeism and Turnover for Male and Female Employees," *Journal of Vocational Behavior,* April 1985, pp. 206–217; D. A. Ralston, W. P. Anthony, and D. J. Gustafson, "Employees May Love Flextime, but What Does It Do to the Organization's Productivity?" *Journal of Applied Psychology,* May 1985, pp. 272–279; Dalton and Mesch, "The Impact of Flexible Scheduling on Employee Attendance and Turnover," pp. 370–387; B. B. Baltes, T. E. Briggs, J. W. Huff, J. A. Wright, and G. A. Neuman, "Flexible and Compressed Workweek Schedules: A Meta-analysis of Their Effects on Work-Related Criteria," *Journal of Applied Psychology* 84, no. 4 (1999), pp. 496–513; K. M. Shockley, and T. D. Allen, "When Flexibility Helps: Another Look at the Availability of Flexible Work Arrangements and Work-Family Conflict," *Journal of Vocational Behavior* 71, no. 3 (2007), pp. 479–493; and J. G. Grzywacz, D. S. Carlson, and S. Shulkin, "Schedule Flexibility and Stress: Linking Formal Flexible Arrangements and Perceived Flexibility to Employee Health." *Community, Work, and Family* 11, no. 2 (2008), pp. 199–214.

23. Cited in S. Caminiti, "Fair Shares," *Working Woman,* November 1999, pp. 52–54.

24. Society for Human Resource Management, *2008 Employee Benefits* (Alexandria, VA: Author, 2008).

25. S. Shellenbarger, "Two People, One Job: It Can Really Work," *Wall Street Journal* (December 7, 1994), p. B1.

26. "Job-Sharing: Widely Offered, Little Used," *Training,* November 1994, p. 12.

27. C. Dawson, "Japan: Work-Sharing Will Prolong the Pain," *BusinessWeek* (December 24, 2001), p. 46.

28. Shellenbarger, "Two People, One Job," p. B1.

29. See, for example, K. E. Pearlson and C. S. Saunders, "There's No Place Like Home: Managing Telecommuting Paradoxes," *Academy of Management Executive,* May 2001, pp. 117–128; S. J. Wells, "Making Telecommuting Work," *HRMagazine,* October 2001, pp. 34–45; E. J. Hill, M. Ferris, and V. Martinson, "Does It Matter Where You Work? A Comparison of How Three Work Venues (Traditional Office, Virtual Office, and Home Office) Influence Aspects of Work and Personal/Family Life," *Journal of Vocational Behavior* 63, no. 2 (2003), pp. 220–241; and Anonymous, "Labour Movement," *The Economist,* April 12, 2008, p. 5.

30. U.S. Census Bureau, *Statistical Abstract of the United States: 2002, The National Data Book, Section 12, Labor Force, Employment, and Earnings.* (Washington, DC: Author, 2002).

31. Society for Human Resource Management, *2008 Employee Benefits.*

32. See, for instance, M. Conlin, "The Easiest Commute of All," *BusinessWeek,* (December 12, 2005), p. 78; and S. Shellenbarger, "Telework Is on the Rise, but It Isn't Just Done from Home Anymore," *Wall Street Journal* (January 23, 2001), p. B1.

33. U. Huws, "Wired in the Country," *People Management,* November 1999, pp. 46–47.

34. Conlin, "The Easiest Commute of All."

35. Cited in Wells, "Making Telecommuting Work," pp. 34–45.

36. E. E. Kossek, B. A. Lautsch, S. C. Eaton, "Telecommuting, Control, and Boundary Management: Correlates of Policy Use and Practice, Job Control, and Work-Family Effectiveness," *Journal of Vocational Behavior* 68, no. 2 (2006), pp. 347–367.

37. J. M. Stanton and J. L. Barnes-Farrell, "Effects of Electronic Performance Monitoring on Personal Control, Task Satisfaction, and Task Performance," *Journal of Applied Psychology,* December 1996, pp. 738–745; B. Pappas, "They Spy," *Forbes,* February 8, 1999, p. 47; S. Armour, "More Bosses Keep Tabs on Telecommuters," *USA Today,* July 24, 2001, p. 1B; and D. Buss, "Spies Like Us," *Training,* December 2001, pp. 44–48.

38. J. Welch and S. Welch, "The Importance of Being There," *BusinessWeek* (April 16, 2007), p. 92; Z. I. Barsness, K. A. Diekmann, and M. L. Seidel, "Motivation and Opportunity: The Role of Remote Work, Demographic Dissimilarity, and Social Network Centrality in Impression Management," *Academy of Management Journal* 48, no. 3 (2005), pp. 401–419.

39. F. P. Morgeson and S. E. Humphrey, "The Work Design Questionnaire (WDQ): Developing and Validating a Comprehensive Measure for Assessing Job Design and the Nature of Work," *Journal of Applied Psychology* 91, no. 6 (2006), pp. 1321–1339; S. E. Humphrey, J. D. Nahrgang, and F. P. Morgeson, "Integrating Motivational, Social, and Contextual Work Design Features: A Meta-analytic Summary and Theoretical Extension of the Work Design Literature," *Journal of Applied Psychology* 92, no. 5 (2007), pp. 1332–1356; and R. Takeuchi, D. P. Lepak, H. Wang, and K. Takeuchi, "An Empirical Examination of the Mechanisms Mediating Between High-Performance Work Systems and the Performance of Japanese Organizations," *Journal of Applied Psychology* 92, no. 4 (2007), pp. 1069–1083.

40. See, for example, the increasing body of literature on empowerment, such as W. A. Randolph, "Re-Thinking Empowerment: Why Is It So Hard to Achieve?" *Organizational Dynamics,* 29, no. 2 (2000), pp. 94–107; K. Blanchard, J. P. Carlos, and W. A. Randolph, *Empowerment Takes More Than a Minute,* 2nd ed. (San Francisco: Berrett-Koehler, 2001); D. P. Ashmos, D. Duchon, R. R. McDaniel, Jr., and J. W. Huonker, "What a Mess! Participation as a Simple Managerial Rule to 'Complexify' Organizations," *Journal of Management Studies,* March 2002, pp. 189–206; and S. E. Seibert, S. R. Silver, and W. A. Randolph, "Taking Empowerment to the Next Level: A Multiple-Level Model of Empowerment, Performance, and Satisfaction" *Academy of Management Journal* 47, no. 3 (2004), pp. 332–349.

41. F. Heller, E. Pusic, G. Strauss, and B. Wilpert, *Organizational Participation: Myth and Reality* (Oxford, UK: Oxford University Press, 1998).

42. See, for instance, K. L. Miller and P. R. Monge, "Participation, Satisfaction, and Productivity: A Meta-analytic Review," *Academy of Management Journal,* December 1986, pp. 727–753; J. A. Wagner III, "Participation's Effects on Performance and Satisfaction: A Reconsideration of Research Evidence," *Academy of Management Review,* April 1994, pp. 312–330; C. Doucouliagos, "Worker Participation and Productivity in Labor-Managed and Participatory Capitalist Firms: A Meta-analysis," *Industrial and Labor*

Relations Review, October 1995, pp. 58–77; J. A. Wagner III, C. R. Leana, E. A. Locke, and D. M. Schweiger, "Cognitive and Motivational Frameworks in U.S. Research on Participation: A Meta-analysis of Primary Effects," *Journal of Organizational Behavior* 18 (1997), pp. 49–65; E. A. Locke, M. Alavi, and J. A. Wagner III, "Participation in Decision Making: An Information Exchange Perspective," in G. R. Ferris (ed.), *Research in Personnel and Human Resource Management,* vol. 15 (Greenwich, CT: JAI Press, 1997), pp. 293–331; and J. A. Wagner III and J. A. LePine, "Effects of Participation on Performance and Satisfaction: Additional Meta-analytic Evidence," *Psychological Reports,* June 1999, pp. 719–725.

43. D. K. Datta, J. P. Guthrie, and P. M. Wright, "Human Resource Management and Labor Productivity: Does Industry Matter? *Academy of Management Journal* 48, no. 1 (2005), pp. 135–145; C. M. Riordan, R. J. Vandenberg, and H. A. Richardson,. "Employee Involvement Climate and Organizational Effectiveness." *Human Resource Management* 44, no. 4 (2005), pp. 471–488.

44. Cotton, *Employee Involvement,* p. 114.

45. See, for example, M. Gilman and P. Marginson, "Negotiating European Works Council: Contours of Constrained Choice," *Industrial Relations Journal,* March 2002, pp. 36–51; J. T. Addison and C. R. Belfield, "What Do We Know About the New European Works Council? Some Preliminary Evidence from Britain," *Scottish Journal of Political Economy,* September 2002, pp. 418–444; and B. Keller, "The European Company Statute: Employee Involvement—and Beyond," *Industrial Relations Journal,* December 2002, pp. 424–445.

46. Cotton, *Employee Involvement,* pp. 129–130, 139–140.

47. Ibid., p. 140.

48. E. White, "Opportunity Knocks, and It Pays a Lot Better," *Wall Street Journal* (November 13, 2006), p. B3.

49. P. S. Goodman and P. P. Pan, "Chinese Workers Pay for Wal-Mart's Low Prices," *The Washington Post* (February 8, 2004), p. A1.

50. M. Sabramony, N. Krause, J. Norton, and G. N. Burns "The Relationship Between Human Resource Investments and Organizational Performance: A Firm-Level Examination of Equilibrium Theory," *Journal of Applied Psychology* 93, no. 4 (2008), pp. 778–788.

51. See T. Henry, "States to Tie Teacher Pay to Results," *USA Today* (September 30, 1999), p. 1A.

52. D. Kollars, "Some Educators Win $25,000 Bonus as Test Scores Rise," *Sacramento (California) Bee* (January 8, 2001), p. 1.

53. Based on J. R. Schuster and P. K. Zingheim, "The New Variable Pay: Key Design Issues," *Compensation & Benefits Review,* March–April 1993, p. 28; K. S. Abosch, "Variable Pay: Do We Have the Basics in Place?" *Compensation & Benefits Review,* July–August 1998, pp. 12–22; and K. M. Kuhn and M. D. Yockey, "Variable Pay as a Risky Choice: Determinants of the Relative Attractiveness of Incentive Plans," *Organizational Behavior and Human Decision Processes,* March 2003, pp. 323–341.

54. W. Zellner, "Trickle-Down Is Trickling Down at Work," *BusinessWeek* (March 18, 1996), p. 34; and "Linking Pay to Performance Is Becoming a Norm in the Workplace," *Wall Street Journal* (April 6, 1999), p. A1.

55. L. Wiener, "Paycheck Plus," *U.S. News & World Report,* February 24/March 3, 2003, p. 58.

56. Cited in "Pay Programs: Few Employees See the Pay-for-Performance Connection," *Compensation & Benefits Report,* June 2003, p. 1.

57. B. Wysocki, Jr., "Chilling Reality Awaits Even the Employed," *Wall Street Journal* (November 5, 2001), p. A1.

58. M. Fein, "Work Measurement and Wage Incentives," *Industrial Engineering,* September 1973, pp. 49–51. For updated reviews of the effect of pay on performance, see G. D. Jenkins, Jr., N. Gupta, A. Mitra, and J. D. Shaw, "Are Financial Incentives Related to Performance? A Meta-analytic Review of Empirical Research," *Journal of Applied Psychology,* October 1998, pp. 777–787; and S. L. Rynes, B. Gerhart, and L. Parks, "Personnel Psychology: Performance Evaluation and Pay for Performance," *Annual Review of Psychology* 56, no. 1 (2005), pp. 571–600.

59. E. Arita, "Teething Troubles Aside, Merit-Based Pay Catching On," *Japan Times* (April 23, 2004), search.japantimes.co.jp/cgi-bin/nb20040423a3.html.

60. E. White, "The Best vs. the Rest," *Wall Street Journal* (January 30, 2006), pp. B1, B3.

61. N. Byrnes, "Pain, But No Layoffs at Nucor," *Business Week* (March 26, 2009), www.businessweek.com.

62. E. White, "Employers Increasingly Favor Bonuses to Raises," *Wall Street Journal* (August 28, 2006), p. B3; and J. S. Lublin, "Boards Tie CEO Pay More Tightly to Performance," *Wall Street Journal* (February 21, 2006), pp. A1, A14.

63. G. E. Ledford, Jr., "Paying for the Skills, Knowledge, and Competencies of Knowledge Workers," *Compensation & Benefits Review,* July–August 1995, pp. 55–62; B. Murray and B. Gerhart, "An Empirical Analysis of a Skill-Based Pay Program and Plant Performance Outcomes," *Academy of Management Journal,* February 1998, pp. 68–78; J. R. Thompson and C. W. LeHew, "Skill-Based Pay as an Organizational Innovation," *Review of Public Personnel Administration,* Winter 2000, pp. 20–40; and J. D. Shaw, N. Gupta, A. Mitra, and G. E. Ledford, Jr., "Success and Survival of Skill-Based Pay Plans," *Journal of Management,* February 2005, pp. 28–49.

64. "Tensions of a New Pay Plan," *New York Times* (May 17, 1992), p. F5.

65. N. Chi and T. Han, "Exploring the Linkages Between Formal Ownership and Psychological Ownership for the Organization: The Mediating Role of Organizational Justice," *Journal of Occupational and Organizational Psychology* 81, no. 4 (2008), pp. 691–711.

66. See, for instance, D.-O. Kim, "Determinants of the Survival of Gainsharing Programs," *Industrial & Labor Relations Review,* October 1999, pp. 21–42; "Why Gainsharing Works Even Better Today Than in the Past," *HR Focus,* April 2000, pp. 3–5; L. R. Gomez-Mejia, T. M. Welbourne, and R. M. Wiseman, "The Role of Risk Sharing and Risk Taking Under Gainsharing," *Academy of Management Review,* July 2000, pp. 492–507; W. Atkinson, "Incentive Pay Programs That Work in Textile," *Textile World,* February 2001, pp. 55–57; M. Reynolds, "A Cost-Reduction Strategy That May Be Back," *Healthcare Financial Management,* January 2002, pp. 58–64; and M. R. Dixon, L. J. Hayes, and J. Stack, "Changing Conceptions of Employee Compensation," *Journal of Organizational Behavior Management* 23, no. 2–3 (2003), pp. 95–116.

67. Employment Policy Foundation, *U.S. Wage and Productivity Growth Attainable Through Gainsharing,* May 10, 2000.

68. T. M. Welbourne and C. J. Ferrante, "To Monitor or Not to Monitor: A Study of Individual Outcomes from Monitoring One's Peers under Gainsharing and Merit Pay," *Group & Organization Management* 33, no. 2 (2008), pp. 139–162.

69. "The Employee Ownership 100," *National Center for Employee Ownership,* July 2003, www.nceo.org.

70. Cited in K. Frieswick, "ESOPs: Split Personality," *CFO,* July 7, 2003, p. 1.

71. A. A. Buchko, "The Effects of Employee Ownership on Employee Attitudes: A Test of Three Theoretical Perspectives," *Work and Occupations* 19, no. 1 (1992), 59–78.

72. J. L. Pierce and C. A. Furo, "Employee Ownership: Implications for Management," *Organizational Dynamics* 18 no. 3 (1990), pp. 32–43.

73. See data in D. Stamps, "A Piece of the Action," *Training,* March 1996, p. 66.

74. X. Zhang, K. M. Bartol, K. G. Smith, M. D. Pfarrer, and D. M. Khanin, "CEOs on the Edge: Earnings Manipulation and Stock-Based Incentive Misalignment," *Academy of Management Journal* 51, no. 2 (2008), pp. 241–258.

75. C. G. Hanson and W. D. Bell, *Profit Sharing and Profitability: How Profit Sharing Promotes Business Success* (London: Kogan Page, 1987); M. Magnan and S. St-Onge, "Profit-Sharing and Firm Performance: A Comparative and Longitudinal Analysis," paper presented at the 58th annual meeting of the Academy of Management, San Diego, August 1998; and D. D'Art and T. Turner, "Profit Sharing, Firm Performance, and Union Influence in Selected European Countries," *Personnel Review* 33, no. 3 (2004), pp. 335–350.

76. T. M. Welbourne and L. R. Gomez-Mejia, "Gainsharing: A Critical Review and a Future Research Agenda," *Journal of Management* 21, no. 3 (1995), pp. 559–609.

77. C. B. Cadsby, F. Song, and F. Tapon, "Sorting and Incentive Effects of Pay for Performance: An Experimental Investigation," *Academy of Management Journal* 50, no. 2 (2007), pp. 387–405.

78. See, for instance, M. W. Barringer and G. T. Milkovich, "A Theoretical Exploration of the Adoption and Design of Flexible Benefit Plans: A Case of Human Resource Innovation," *Academy of Management Review,* April 1998, pp. 305–324; D. Brown, "Everybody Loves Flex," *Canadian HRReporter,* November 18, 2002, p. 1; J. Taggart, "Putting Flex Benefits Through Their Paces," *Canadian HR Reporter,* December 2, 2002, p. G3; and N. D. Cole and D. H. Flint, "Perceptions of Distributive and Procedural Justice in Employee Benefits: Flexible Versus Traditional Benefit Plans," *Journal of Managerial Psychology* 19, no. 1 (2004), pp. 19–40.

79. D. A. DeCenzo and S. P. Robbins, *Human Resource Management,* 7th ed. (New York: Wiley, 2002), pp. 346–348.

80. S. E. Markham, K. D. Scott, and G. H. McKee, "Recognizing Good Attendance: A Longitudinal, Quasi-Experimental Field Study," *Personnel Psychology,* Autumn 2002, p. 641; and S. J. Peterson and F. Luthans, "The Impact of Financial and Nonfinancial Incentives on Business Unit Outcomes over Time," *Journal of Applied Psychology* 91, no. 1 (2006), pp. 156–165.

81. D. Drickhamer, "Best Plant Winners: Nichols Foods Ltd.," *IndustryWeek,* October 1, 2001, pp. 17–19.

82. M. Littman, "Best Bosses Tell All," *Working Woman,* October 2000, p. 54.

83. A. D. Stajkovic and F. Luthans, "Differential Effects of Incentive Motivators on Work Performance," *Academy of Management Journal,* June 2001, p. 587. See also F. Luthans and A. D. Stajkovic, "Provide Recognition for Performance Improvement," in E. A. Locke (ed.), *Handbook of Principles of Organizational Behavior* (Malden, MA: Blackwell, 2004), pp. 166–180.

84. Cited in K. J. Dunham, "Amid Shrinking Workplace Morale, Employers Turn to Recognition," *Wall Street Journal* (November 19, 2002), p. B8.

85. Ibid.

86. B. M. Meglino and A. M. Korsgaard, "The Role of Other Orientation in Reactions to Job Characteristics," *Journal of Management,* February 2007, pp. 57–83.

87. M. F. Peterson and S. A. Ruiz-Quintanilla, "Cultural Socialization as a Source of Intrinsic Work Motivation," *Group & Organization Management,* June 2003, pp. 188–216.

88. P. Peters and L. den Dulk, "Cross Cultural Differences in Managers' Support for Home-Based Telework: A Theoretical Elaboration," *International Journal of Cross Cultural Management,* December 2003, pp. 329–346.

89. S. C. L. Fong and M. A. Shaffer, "The Dimensionality and Determinants of Pay Satisfaction: A Cross-Cultural Investigation of a Group Incentive Plan," *International Journal of Human Resource Management,* June 2003, pp. 559–580.

90. Brown, "Everybody Loves Flex," p. 1.

91. E. Unsworth, "U.K. Employers Find Flex Benefits Helpful: Survey," *Business Insurance,* May 21, 2001, pp. 19–20.

92. See, for instance, A. Sagie and Z. Aycan, "A Cross-Cultural Analysis of Participative Decision-Making in Organizations," *Human Relations,* April 2003, pp. 453–473; and J. Brockner, "Unpacking Country Effects: On the Need to Operationalize the Psychological Determinants of Cross-National Differences," in R. M. Kramer and B. M. Staw (eds.), *Research in Organizational Behavior,* vol. 25 (Oxford, UK: Elsevier, 2003), pp. 336–340.

93. C. Robert, T. M. Probst, J. J. Martocchio, R. Drasgow, and J. J. Lawler, "Empowerment and Continuous Improvement in the United States, Mexico, Poland, and India: Predicting Fit on the Basis of the Dimensions of Power Distance and Individualism," *Journal of Applied Psychology,* October 2000, pp. 643–658.

94. Z. X. Chen and S. Aryee, "Delegation and Employee Work Outcomes: An Examination of the Cultural Context of Mediating Processes in China," *Academy of Management Journal* 50, no. 1 (2007), pp. 226–238.

95. K. Izuma, D. N. Saito, and N. Sadato, "Processing of Social and Monetary Rewards in the Human Striatum," *Neuron* 58, no. 2 (2008), pp. 284–294; "The Most Praised Generation Goes to Work," *Gainesville (Florida) Sun* (April 29, 2007), pp. 5G, 6G; J. Zaslow, "In Praise of Less Praise," *Wall Street Journal* (May 3, 2007), p. D1; S. Loewy and J. Bailey, "The Effects of Graphic Feedback, Goal-Setting, and Manager Praise on Customer Service Behaviors," *Journal of Organizational Behavior Management* 27, no. 3 (2007), pp. 15–26; and J. S. Seiter and E. Dutson, "The Effect of Compliments on Tipping Behavior in Hairstyling Salons," *Journal of Applied Social Psychology* 37, no. 9 (2007), pp. 1999–2007.

LEARNING OBJECTIVES

After studying this chapter, you should be able to:

1 Define *group* and distinguish the different types of groups.

2 Identify the five stages of group development.

3 Show how role requirements change in different situations.

4 Demonstrate how norms and status exert influence on an individual's behavior.

5 Show how group size affects group performance.

6 Contrast the benefits and disadvantages of cohesive groups.

7 Contrast the strengths and weaknesses of group decision making.

8 Compare the effectiveness of interacting, brainstorming, nominal, and electronic meeting groups.

9 Evaluate evidence for cultural differences in group status and social loafing as well as the effects of diversity in groups.

Foundations of Group Behavior

Madness is the exception in individuals but the rule in groups. —Friedrich Nietzsche

BRAINSTORMING: A LOUSY IDEA FOR IDEAS?

You know the drill. Gather a small group of people together, and appoint someone to write the ideas on an easel with paper (or type them on a laptop). It's called brainstorming, and it's been around for a long time.

Some brainstorming sessions flounder because group members are afraid of saying something stupid. Joe Polidoro, a manager who has worked at several banks, says, "We sit there looking embarrassed like we're all new to a nudist colony." Participation is particularly difficult for introverts. As one manager noted, "I'm having trouble getting all of my team members to contribute during brainstorming sessions. I realize some of the quietest people have some of the best ideas, but I'm struggling to get them to step up and contribute."

Others dislike the scheduled nature of such sessions. Some feel as if they're put in a room and told, "Okay, be creative now." "I'm more mercurial than that," says Kate Lee, a former manager at GE.

Others think the whole idea of brainstorming is fatally flawed, that such sessions rarely produce the creative ideas they are meant to produce. Martha McGuire, senior VP of a bank, argues that most recommendations from brainstorming sessions are obvious. "You end up with a more pedestrian solution than you would have had, had you not held the session," she says.

Despite these criticisms, some feel brainstorming works wonders. Health care provider Kaiser Permanente uses brainstorming groups consisting of nurses, doctors, patients, and vendors to make treatment safer, more effective, and efficient. Other fans of brainstorming include P&G and Silicon Valley's IDEO.

Others say the real purpose of brainstorming is not to produce the best idea but to get buy-in for decisions that have already been made. Christopher Holland, a policy analyst for the Australian government, said, "These things are usually designed to give people the idea that they have input into decisions when the decisions have already been decided."

One researcher says the problems of brainstorming demonstrate the problems of groups. "If you leave groups to their own devices," he says, "they're going to do a very miserable job."[1]

From what you've just read, you might think groups are hopeless, but that's not the case. Groups have their place—and their pitfalls. Before we discuss them, examine your own attitude toward working in groups. Take the following self-assessment and answer the accompanying questions.

The objectives of this chapter and Chapter 10 are to introduce you to basic group concepts, provide you with a foundation for understanding how groups work, and show you how to create effective teams. Let's begin by defining *group* and explaining why people join groups.

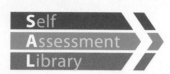

DO I HAVE A NEGATIVE ATTITUDE TOWARD WORKING IN GROUPS?

In the Self-Assessment Library (available on CD or online), take assessment IV.E.1 (Do I Have a Negative Attitude Toward Working in Groups?) and answer the following questions.

1. Are you surprised by your results? If yes, why? If not, why not?
2. Do you think it is important to always have a positive attitude toward working in groups? Why or why not?

Defining and Classifying Groups

1 Define *group* and distinguish the different types of groups.

We define a **group** as two or more individuals, interacting and interdependent, who have come together to achieve particular objectives. Groups can be either formal or informal. By a **formal group**, we mean one defined by the organization's structure, with designated work assignments establishing tasks. In formal groups, the behaviors team members should engage in are stipulated by and directed toward organizational goals. The six members of an airline flight crew are a formal group. In contrast, an **informal group** is neither formally structured nor organizationally determined. Informal groups are natural formations in the work environment that appear in response to the need for social contact. Three employees from different departments who regularly have lunch or coffee together are an informal group. These types of interactions among individuals, though informal, deeply affect their behavior and performance.

It's possible to further subclassify groups as command, task, interest, or friendship groups.[2] Command and task groups are dictated by formal organization, whereas interest and friendship groups are informal alliances.

A **command group** is determined by the organization chart. It is composed of the individuals who report directly to a given manager. An elementary school principal and her 18 teachers form a command group, as do a director of postal audits and his five inspectors.

A **task group**, also organizationally determined, represents individuals working together to complete a job task. However, a task group's boundaries are not limited to its immediate hierarchical superior; the group can cross command relationships. If a college student is accused of a campus crime, dealing with the problem might require coordination among the dean of academic affairs, the dean of students, the registrar, the director of security, and the student's advisor. Such a formation constitutes a task group. All command groups are also task

The employees of the Swedish transportation company Scania shown here exercising at a sports complex comprise an informal group. At different company locations, Scania offers employees free access to sports facilities during working hours. The company puts a high priority on employee health and offers employees many opportunities to reinforce an active lifestyle. The informal groups that participate in sports and exercise activities are neither formally structured nor organizationally determined. However, informal groups like these can fulfill employee desires for social interaction at work.

groups. But because task groups can cut across the organization, they are not always command groups.

Whether they are in command or task groups together or not, people may affiliate to attain a specific objective with which each individual is concerned. This creates an **interest group**. Employees who band together to have their vacation schedules altered, to support a peer who has been fired, or to seek improved working conditions have formed a united body to further their common interest.

Groups often develop because individual members have one or more common characteristics. We call these formations **friendship groups**. Social alliances, which frequently extend outside the work situation, can be based on common age or ethnic heritage, support for Notre Dame football, interest in the same alternative rock band, or similar political views, to name just a few such characteristics.

Why Do People Form Groups?

Why do people form groups, and why do they feel so strongly about them? Consider the celebrations that follow a football, basketball, or baseball team's winning a national championship. Fans have staked their own self-image on the performance of someone else. Supporters of the winning team are elated, and sales of team-related shirts, jackets, and hats declaring support for the team skyrocket. Fans of the losing team feel dejected, even embarrassed. If you're not into sports, perhaps you can relate to the feeling of emotional attachment by

group *Two or more individuals, interacting and interdependent, who have come together to achieve particular objectives.*

formal group *A designated work group defined by an organization's structure.*

informal group *A group that is neither formally structured nor organizationally determined; such a group appears in response to the need for social contact.*

command group *A group composed of the individuals who report directly to a given manager.*

task group *People working together to complete a job task.*

interest group *People working together to attain a specific objective with which each is concerned.*

friendship group *People brought together because they share one or more common characteristics.*

Social identities help Bal Seal Engineering employees interact with co-workers. At Bal Seal, Spanish-speaking employees gather at the home of a co-worker to participate in an English-as-a-second-language program. Bal Seal, which supports the program by buying the training materials, reports that it has improved the company's communications, cooperation among fellow workers, and customer service. As social identity theory proposes, graduates of the program identify with the high performance of a winning team. As a result, many graduates who previously ruled out the option of going back to school are motivated to continue the pursuit of their education outside the workplace by enrolling in GED programs, community college courses, and citizenship classes.

thinking about the rush of pride some people feel when they see a flag, the shame when their company receives negative press attention, or the anger and defensiveness that arise if someone criticizes your profession. Our tendency to take personal pride or offense for the accomplishments of a group is the territory of **social identity theory**. This perspective has come to occupy a major role in describing behavior in organizations.

Social identity theory proposes that people have emotional reactions to the failure or success of their group because their self-esteem gets tied into the performance of the group.[3] When your group does well, you bask in reflected glory, and your own self-esteem rises because you're affiliated with the winning team. When your group does poorly, you might feel bad about yourself, or you might even go so far as to reject that part of your identity, like "fair weather fans." Social identities also help people reduce uncertainty about who they are and what they should do.[4]

People develop a lot of identities through the course of their lives. You might define yourself in terms of the organization you work for, the city you live in, your profession, your religious background, your ethnicity, or your gender. We "switch on" different identities in different situations. A U.S. expatriate working in Rome might be very aware of being from the United States but won't give this national identity a second thought when transferring from Tulsa to Tucson. An accountant will probably not think about the identity of her profession in discussions with other accountants, but she will be very aware of what it means to be an accountant when having a discussion with someone in sales.[5]

Social identities help us understand who we are and where we fit in with other people, but they can have a negative side as well. Probably the biggest downside is that social identities encourage **ingroup favoritism**. This means we see members of our ingroup as better than other people, and people not in our group as all the same. This obviously paves the way for stereotyping.

When do people develop a social identity? Several characteristics make a social identity important to a person:

- *Similarity.* Not surprisingly, people who have the same values or characteristics as other members of their organization have higher levels of group identification.[6] Demographic similarity can also lead to stronger identification for new hires, while those who are demographically different may have a hard time identifying with the group as a whole.[7]

- *Distinctiveness.* People are more likely to notice identities that show how they are different from other groups. Respondents in one study identified more strongly with those in their work group with whom they shared uncommon or rare demographic characteristics.[8] For example, two women in an otherwise all-male work group might bond over their shared distinctive identity. Another study found that veterinarians who work in veterinary medicine (where everyone is a veterinarian) identify with their organization, and veterinarians in non-veterinary medicine fields such as animal research or food inspection (where being a veterinarian is a more distinctive characteristic) identify with their profession.[9]
- *Status.* Because people use identities to define themselves and increase self-esteem, it makes sense that they are most interested in linking themselves to high-status groups. Graduates of prestigious universities will go out of their way to emphasize their links to their alma maters and are also more likely to make donations.[10] Members of prestigious law firms similarly advertise their high-status positions. People are likely to not identify with a low-status organization and will be more likely to turn over in order to leave that identity behind.[11]
- *Uncertainty reduction.* Membership in a group also helps some people understand who they are and how they fit into the world.[12] One study showed how the creation of a spin-off company created questions about whether employees should identify with the old parent organization or develop a unique identity that corresponded more closely to what the division was becoming.[13] Managers at this restructuring organization worked to define and communicate an idealized identity for the new organization when it became clear employees were confused.

Stages of Group Development

2 Identify the five stages of group development.

Groups generally pass through a predictable sequence in their evolution, which we call the five-stage model of group development. Although not all groups follow this pattern,[14] it is a useful framework for understanding group development. In this section, we describe the five-stage general model and an alternative model for temporary groups with deadlines.

The Five-Stage Model

As shown in Exhibit 9-1, the **five-stage group-development model** characterizes groups as proceeding through the distinct stages of forming, storming, norming, performing, and adjourning.[15]

The first stage, **forming**, is characterized by a great deal of uncertainty about the group's purpose, structure, and leadership. Members "test the waters" to

---

social identity theory   *Perspective that considers when and why individuals consider themselves members of groups.*

ingroup favoritism   *Perspective in which we see members of our ingroup as better than other people, and people not in our group as all the same.*

five-stage group-development model   *The five distinct stages groups go through: forming, storming, norming, performing, and adjourning.*

forming stage   *The first stage in group development, characterized by much uncertainty.*

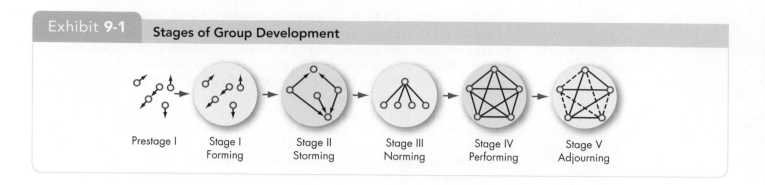

Exhibit 9-1   **Stages of Group Development**

Prestage I → Stage I Forming → Stage II Storming → Stage III Norming → Stage IV Performing → Stage V Adjourning

determine what types of behaviors are acceptable. This stage is complete when members have begun to think of themselves as part of a group.

The **storming stage** is one of intragroup conflict. Members accept the existence of the group but resist the constraints it imposes on individuality. Furthermore, there is conflict over who will control the group. When this stage is complete, there will be a relatively clear hierarchy of leadership within the group.

In the third stage, close relationships develop and the group demonstrates cohesiveness. There is now a strong sense of group identity and camaraderie. This **norming stage** is complete when the group structure solidifies and the group has assimilated a common set of expectations of what defines correct member behavior.

The fourth stage is **performing**. The structure at this point is fully functional and accepted. Group energy has moved from getting to know and understand each other to performing the task at hand.

For permanent work groups, performing is the last stage in development. However, for temporary committees, teams, task forces, and similar groups that have a limited task to perform, the **adjourning stage** is a preparation for disbanding. Wrapping up activities is the focus rather than high task performance. Some group members are upbeat, basking in the group's accomplishments. Others may be depressed over the loss of camaraderie and friendships gained during the work group's life.

Many interpreters of the five-stage model have assumed a group becomes more effective as it progresses through the first four stages. Although this may be generally

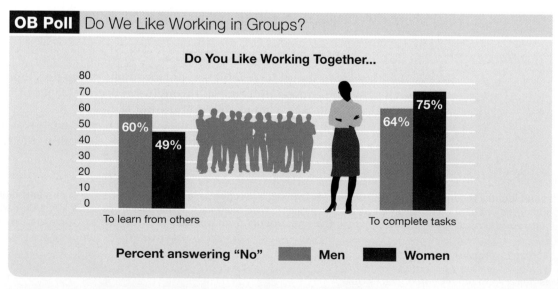

OB Poll   Do We Like Working in Groups?

Do You Like Working Together...

To learn from others: Men 60%, Women 49%
To complete tasks: Men 64%, Women 75%

Percent answering "No"   ■ Men   ■ Women

Source: Based on "White Collar Workers Shoulder Together—Like It or Not," *Business Week* (April 28, 2008), p. 58.

true, what makes a group effective is actually more complex.[16] Under some conditions, high levels of conflict may be conducive to high group performance. So we might expect to find situations in which groups in Stage II outperform those in Stage III or IV. Nor do groups always proceed clearly from one stage to the next. Sometimes, in fact, several stages go on simultaneously, as when groups are storming and performing at the same time. Groups even occasionally regress to previous stages. Therefore, even the strongest proponents of this model do not assume all groups follow its five-stage process precisely or that Stage IV is always preferable.

Another problem with the five-stage model is that it ignores organizational context.[17] A study of the cockpit crew in an airliner found that within 10 minutes three strangers assigned to fly together for the first time had become a high-performing group. What allowed for this speedy group development was the strong organizational context surrounding the group's tasks, which provided the rules, task definitions, information, and resources the group needed to perform. The group members didn't need to develop plans, assign roles, determine and allocate resources, resolve conflicts, and set norms the way the five-stage model predicts.

An Alternative Model for Temporary Groups with Deadlines

Temporary groups with deadlines don't seem to follow the usual five-stage model. Studies indicate they have their own unique sequencing of actions (or inaction): (1) Their first meeting sets the group's direction; (2) this first phase of group activity is one of inertia; (3) a transition takes place at the end of this phase, which occurs exactly when the group has used up half its allotted time; (4) a transition initiates major changes; (5) a second phase of inertia follows the transition; and (6) the group's last meeting is characterized by markedly accelerated activity.[18] This pattern, called the **punctuated-equilibrium model**, is shown in Exhibit 9-2.

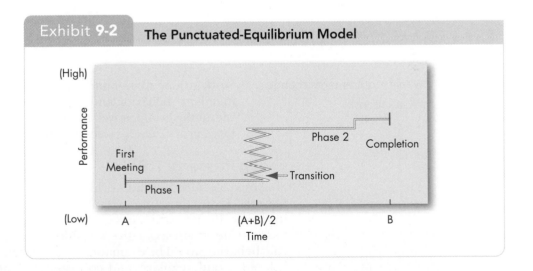

Exhibit 9-2   The Punctuated-Equilibrium Model

storming stage   *The second stage in group development, characterized by intragroup conflict.*

norming stage   *The third stage in group development, characterized by close relationships and cohesiveness.*

performing stage   *The fourth stage in group development, during which the group is fully functional.*

adjourning stage   *The final stage in group development for temporary groups, characterized by concern with wrapping up activities rather than task performance.*

punctuated-equilibrium model   *A set of phases that temporary groups go through that involves transitions between inertia and activity.*

The first meeting sets the group's direction, and then a framework of behavioral patterns and assumptions through which the group will approach its project emerges. These lasting patterns can appear as early as the first few seconds of the group's existence. Once set, the group's direction is solidified and is unlikely to be reexamined throughout the first half of its life. This is a period of inertia—the group tends to stand still or become locked into a fixed course of action. Even if it gains new insights that challenge initial patterns and assumptions, the group is incapable of acting on these in Phase 1.

One of the most interesting discoveries made in studies of groups[19] was that each group experienced its transition at the same point in its calendar—precisely halfway between its first meeting and its official deadline—despite the fact that some groups spent as little as an hour on their project while others spent 6 months. It was as if the groups universally experienced a midlife crisis at this point. The midpoint appears to work like an alarm clock, heightening members' awareness that their time is limited and they need to get moving. This transition ends Phase 1 and is characterized by a concentrated burst of changes, dropping of old patterns, and adoption of new perspectives. The transition sets a revised direction for Phase 2, a new equilibrium or period of inertia in which the group executes plans created during the transition period.

The group's last meeting is characterized by a final burst of activity to finish its work. In summary, the punctuated-equilibrium model characterizes groups as exhibiting long periods of inertia interspersed with brief revolutionary changes triggered primarily by members' awareness of time and deadlines. Keep in mind, however, that this model doesn't apply to all groups. It's essentially limited to temporary task groups working under a time-constrained completion deadline.[20]

Group Properties: Roles, Norms, Status, Size, and Cohesiveness

3 Show how role requirements change in different situations.

Work groups are not unorganized mobs; they have properties that shape members' behavior and help explain and predict individual behavior within the group as well as the performance of the group itself. Some of these properties are roles, norms, status, size, and cohesiveness.

Group Property 1: Roles

Shakespeare said, "All the world's a stage, and all the men and women merely players." Using the same metaphor, all group members are actors, each playing a **role**. By this term, we mean a set of expected behavior patterns attributed to someone occupying a given position in a social unit. Our understanding of role behavior would be dramatically simplified if each of us chose one role and "played it out" regularly and consistently. Unfortunately, we are required to play a number of diverse roles, both on and off our jobs. As we'll see, one of the tasks in understanding behavior is grasping the role a person is currently playing.

Bill Patterson is a plant manager with EMM Industries, a large electrical equipment manufacturer in Phoenix. He fulfills a number of roles—EMM employee, member of middle management, electrical engineer, and primary company spokesperson in the community. Off the job, Bill Patterson finds himself in still more roles: husband, father, Catholic, Rotarian, tennis player, member of

Trumpeter Wynton Marsalis plays a variety of roles. As artistic director of Jazz at Lincoln Center, Marsalis serves on the senior management team in leading the world's largest not-for-profit arts organization dedicated to jazz. He is also a composer, performer, music teacher, and fundraiser. Each of these positions imposes different role requirements on Marsalis. This photo shows him joining chef Emeril Lagasse at a free educational event for schoolchildren in New Orleans that explored two aspects of the city's culture: jazz and food.

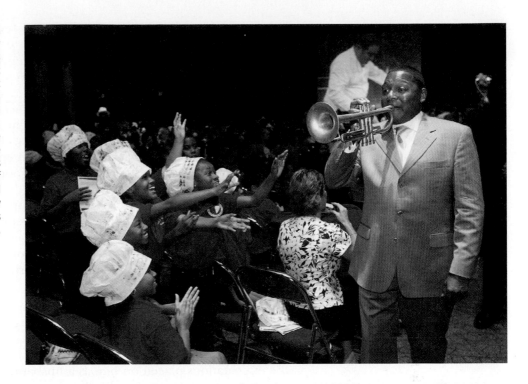

the Thunderbird Country Club, and president of his homeowners' association. Many of these roles are compatible; some create conflicts. How does Bill's religious commitment influence his managerial decisions regarding layoffs, expense account padding, and provision of accurate information to government agencies? A recent offer of promotion requires Bill to relocate, yet his family wants to stay in Phoenix. Can the role demands of his job be reconciled with the demands of his husband and father roles?

Like Bill Patterson, we are all required to play a number of roles, and our behavior varies with each. Bill's behavior when he attends church on Sunday morning is different from his behavior on the golf course later that same day. So different groups impose different role requirements on individuals.

Role Perception   Our view of how we're supposed to act in a given situation is a **role perception**. We engage in certain types of behavior based on how we believe we are supposed to behave. We get these perceptions from stimuli all around us—for example, friends, books, films, television, as when we form an impression of the work of doctors from watching *Grey's Anatomy*. Of course, the primary reason apprenticeship programs exist in many trades and professions is to allow beginners to watch an expert so they can learn to act as they should.

Role Expectations   **Role expectations** are the way others believe you should act in a given context. The role of a U.S. federal judge is viewed as having

---

role   *A set of expected behavior patterns attributed to someone occupying a given position in a social unit.*

role perception   *An individual's view of how he or she is supposed to act in a given situation.*

role expectations   *How others believe a person should act in a given situation.*

propriety and dignity, while a football coach is seen as aggressive, dynamic, and inspiring to his players.

In the workplace, we look at role expectations through the perspective of the **psychological contract**: an unwritten agreement that exists between employees and employer. This agreement sets out mutual expectations: what management expects from workers and vice versa.[21] In effect, it defines the behavioral expectations that go with every role. Management is expected to treat employees justly, provide acceptable working conditions, clearly communicate what is a fair day's work, and give feedback on how well an employee is doing. Employees are expected to respond by demonstrating a good attitude, following directions, and showing loyalty to the organization.

What happens when role expectations implied in the psychological contract are not met? If management is derelict in keeping its part of the bargain, we can expect negative repercussions on employee performance and satisfaction. When employees fail to live up to expectations, the result is usually some form of disciplinary action up to and including firing.

Role Conflict   When compliance with one role requirement may make it difficult to comply with another, the result is **role conflict**.[22] At the extreme, two or more role expectations are mutually contradictory.

Bill Patterson had to deal with role conflicts, such as his attempt to reconcile the expectations placed on him as a husband and father with those placed on him as an executive with EMM Industries. Bill's wife and children want to remain in Phoenix, while EMM expects its employees to be responsive to the company's needs and requirements. Although it might be in Bill's financial and career interests to accept a relocation, the conflict comes down to choosing between family and career role expectations. Most employees are simultaneously in occupations, work groups, divisions, and demographic groups, and these different identities can come into conflict when the expectations of one identity conflict with the expectations of another.[23] During mergers and acquisitions, employees can be torn between their identities as members of their original organization and of the new parent company.[24] Organizations structured around multinational operations also have been shown to lead to dual identification, with employees distinguishing between the local division of the organization and the overarching international organization.[25]

Zimbardo's Prison Experiment   One of the most illuminating role and identity experiments was done a number of years ago by Stanford University psychologist Philip Zimbardo and his associates.[26] They created a "prison" in the basement of the Stanford psychology building; hired at $15 a day two dozen emotionally stable, physically healthy, law-abiding students who scored "normal average" on extensive personality tests; randomly assigned them the role of either "guard" or "prisoner"; and established some basic rules.

It took the "prisoners" little time to accept the authority positions of the "guards" or for the mock guards to adjust to their new authority roles. Consistent with social identity theory, the guards came to see the prisoners as a negative outgroup, and their comments to researchers showed they had developed stereotypes about the "typical" prisoner personality type. After the guards crushed a rebellion attempt on the second day, the prisoners became increasingly passive. Whatever the guards "dished out," the prisoners took. The prisoners actually began to believe and act as if they were inferior and powerless, as the guards constantly reminded them. And every guard, at some time during the simulation, engaged in abusive, authoritative behavior. One said, "I was surprised at myself. . . . I made them call each other names and clean the toilets out with their bare hands. I practically considered the prisoners cattle, and I kept thinking: 'I have to watch out for them in case they try something.'" Another guard added, "I was tired of seeing the prisoners in their rags and smelling the strong odors of their bodies that filled the cells. I watched them tear at each other on orders given by us. They didn't see it as an experiment. It was real, and they were fighting to keep their identity. But we were always there to show them who was boss." Surprisingly, during the entire experiment—even after days of abuse—not one prisoner said, "Stop this. I'm a student like you. This is just an experiment!"

The simulation actually proved *too successful* in demonstrating how quickly individuals learn new roles. The researchers had to stop it after only 6 days because of the participants' pathological reactions. And remember, these were individuals chosen precisely for their normalcy and emotional stability.

What can we conclude from this prison simulation? Like the rest of us, the participants had learned stereotyped conceptions of guard and prisoner roles from the mass media and their own personal experiences in power and power-lessness relationships gained at home (parent–child), in school (teacher–student), and in other situations. This, then, allowed them easily and rapidly to assume roles very different from their inherent personalities. People with no prior personality pathology or training in their roles could execute extreme forms of behavior consistent with the roles they were playing.

A follow-up reality television show conducted by the BBC that used a lower-fidelity simulated prison setting provides some insights into these results.[27] The results were dramatically different from those of the Stanford experiment. The "guards" were far more careful in their behavior and limited the aggressive treatment of "prisoners." They often described their concerns about how their actions might be perceived. In short, they did not fully take on their roles, possibly because they knew their behavior was being observed by millions of viewers. As shared identity increased among "prisoners," they provided higher levels of social support to one another, and an egalitarian system developed between them and the guards. Philip Zimbardo has contended that the BBC study is not a replication of his study for several reasons, but he acknowledges the results demonstrate how both guards and prisoners act differently when closely monitored. These results suggest abuse of roles can be limited when people are made conscious of their behavior.

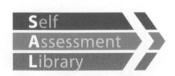

DO I TRUST OTHERS?

In the Self-Assessment Library (available on CD or online), take assessment II.B.3 (Do I Trust Others?). You can also check out assessment II.B.4 (Do Others See Me as Trusting?).

Group Property 2 : Norms

4 Demonstrate how norms and status exert influence on an individual's behavior.

Did you ever notice that golfers don't speak while their partners are putting on the green or that employees don't criticize their bosses in public? Why not? The answer is norms.

All groups have established **norms**—acceptable standards of behavior shared by their members that express what they ought and ought not to do under certain circumstances. When agreed to and accepted by the

---

psychological contract   *An unwritten agreement that sets out what management expects from an employee and vice versa.*

role conflict   *A situation in which an individual is confronted by divergent role expectations.*

norms   *Acceptable standards of behavior within a group that are shared by the group's members.*

group, norms influence members' behavior with a minimum of external controls. Different groups, communities, and societies have different norms, but they all have them.[28]

Norms can cover virtually any aspect of group behavior.[29] Probably the most common is a *performance norm,* providing explicit cues about how hard members should work, what the level of output should be, how to get the job done, what level of tardiness is appropriate, and the like. These norms are extremely powerful in affecting an individual's performance—they are capable of significantly modifying a performance prediction based solely on ability and level of personal motivation. Although arguably the most important, performance norms aren't the only kind. Other types include *appearance norms* (dress codes, unspoken rules about when to look busy), *social arrangement norms* (with whom to eat lunch, whether to form friendships on and off the job), and *resource allocation norms* (assignment of difficult jobs, distribution of resources like pay or equipment).

The Hawthorne Studies   Full-scale appreciation of the influence of norms on worker behavior did not occur until the early 1930s, following studies undertaken between 1924 and 1932 at the Western Electric Company's Hawthorne Works in Chicago.[30] Originally initiated by Western Electric officials and later overseen by Harvard professor Elton Mayo, the Hawthorne studies concluded that a worker's behavior and sentiments were closely related, that group influences were significant in affecting individual behavior, that group standards were highly effective in establishing individual worker output, and that money was less a factor in determining worker output than were group standards, sentiments, and security.

The Hawthorne researchers began by examining the relationship between the physical environment and productivity. Illumination and other working conditions were selected to represent this physical environment. The researchers' initial findings contradicted their anticipated results.

From the Hawthorne studies, observers gained valuable insights into how individual behavior is influenced by group norms. The group of workers determined the level of fair output and established norms for individual work rates that conformed to the output. To enforce the group norms, workers used sarcasm, ridicule, and even physical force to influence individual behaviors that were not acceptable to the group.

Otsuka Yuriko has high status at the Canon manufacturing plant in Ami, Japan. As an employee in a cell-manufacturing unit, she wears a badge on the sleeve of her work uniform labeled Eiji Meister. Yuriko earned the badge by completing an apprenticeship program and becoming proficient in all the tasks required to assemble a machine. Because she has mastered all the tasks, Yuriko can train other employees in her work unit, and her contributions are critical to her group's success.

thought NBA star Kobe Bryant had more say over player decisions than his coaches (though not as much as Bryant wanted!).

3. **An individual's personal characteristics.**   Someone whose personal characteristics are positively valued by the group (good looks, intelligence, money, or a friendly personality) typically has higher status than someone with fewer valued attributes.

Status and Norms   Status has some interesting effects on the power of norms and pressures to conform. High-status individuals are often given more freedom to deviate from norms than are other group members.[43] People in high-status jobs (such as physicians, lawyers, or executives) have especially negative reactions to social pressure exerted by people in low-status jobs. Physicians actively resist administrative decisions made by lower-ranking insurance company employees.[44] High-status people are also better able to resist conformity pressures than their lower-status peers. An individual who is highly valued by a group but doesn't need or care about the group's social rewards is particularly able to disregard conformity norms.[45]

These findings explain why many star athletes, celebrities, top-performing salespeople, and outstanding academics seem oblivious to appearance and social norms that constrain their peers. As high-status individuals, they're given a wider range of discretion as long as their activities aren't severely detrimental to group goal achievement.[46]

Status and Group Interaction   High-status people tend to be more assertive group members.[47] They speak out more often, criticize more, state more

status   *A socially defined position or rank given to groups or group members by others.*

status characteristics theory   *A theory that states that differences in status characteristics create status hierarchies within groups.*

commands, and interrupt others more often. But status differences actually inhibit diversity of ideas and creativity in groups, because lower-status members tend to participate less actively in group discussions. When lower-status members possess expertise and insights that could aid the group, they are not likely to be fully utilized, thus reducing the group's overall performance.

Status Inequity   It is important for group members to believe the status hierarchy is equitable. Perceived inequity creates disequilibrium, which inspires various types of corrective behavior.[48]

The concept of equity we presented in Chapter 6 applies to status. People expect rewards to be proportionate to costs incurred. If Dana and Anne are the two finalists for the head nurse position in a hospital, and Dana clearly has more seniority and better preparation, Anne will view the selection of Dana as equitable. However, if Anne is chosen because she is the daughter-in-law of the hospital director, Dana will believe an injustice has been committed.

Groups generally agree within themselves on status criteria and, hence, there is usually high concurrence in group rankings of individuals. However, individuals can find themselves in conflicts when they move between groups whose status criteria are different, or when they join groups whose members have heterogeneous backgrounds. Business executives may use personal income or the growth rate of their companies as determinants of status. Government bureaucrats may use the size of their budgets, and blue-collar workers years of seniority. When groups are heterogeneous or when heterogeneous groups must be interdependent, status differences may initiate conflict as the group attempts to reconcile the differing hierarchies. As we'll see in Chapter 10, this can be a problem when management creates teams of employees from varied functions.

Group Property 4: Size

Does the size of a group affect the group's overall behavior? The answer is a definite "yes," but the effect depends on what dependent variables you look at.[49] The evidence indicates smaller groups are faster at completing tasks than larger ones and that individuals perform better in smaller groups than in larger ones.[50] However, in problem solving, large groups consistently get better marks than their smaller counterparts.[51] Translating these results into specific numbers is a bit more hazardous, but large groups—those with a dozen or more members—are good for gaining diverse input. So if the goal of the group is fact-finding, larger groups should be more effective. Smaller groups are better at doing something productive with that input. Groups of approximately seven members tend to be more effective for taking action.

5   Show how group size affects group performance.

One of the most important findings about the size of a group concerns **social loafing**, the tendency for individuals to expend less effort when working collectively than alone.[52] It directly challenges the logic that the productivity of the group as a whole should at least equal the sum of the productivity of the individuals in that group.

A common stereotype about groups is that team spirit spurs individual effort and enhances the group's overall productivity. But that stereotype may be wrong. In the late 1920s, German psychologist Max Ringelmann compared the results of individual and group performance on a rope-pulling task.[53] He expected that three people pulling together should exert three times as much pull on the rope as one person, and eight people eight times as much. Ringelmann's results, however, didn't confirm his expectations. One person pulling on a rope alone exerted an average of 63 kilograms of force. In groups of three, the per-person force dropped to 53 kilograms. And in groups of eight, it fell to only 31 kilograms per person.

Replications of Ringelmann's research with similar tasks have generally supported his findings.[54] Group performance increases with group size, but the addition of new members has diminishing returns on productivity. So more may be better in that total productivity of a group of four is greater than that of three, but the individual productivity of each member declines.

What causes social loafing? It may be a belief that others in the group are not carrying their fair share. If you see others as lazy or inept, you can reestablish equity by reducing your effort. Another explanation is the dispersion of responsibility. Because group results cannot be attributed to any single person, the relationship between an individual's input and the group's output is clouded. Individuals may then be tempted to become free riders and coast on the group's efforts. The implications for OB are significant. When managers use collective work situations to enhance morale and teamwork, they must also be able to identify individual efforts. Otherwise they must weigh the potential losses in productivity from using groups against possible gains in worker satisfaction.[55]

There are several ways to prevent social loafing: (1) Set group goals, so the group has a common purpose to strive toward; (2) increase intergroup competition, which again focuses on the shared outcome; (3) engage in peer evaluation so each person evaluates each other person's contribution; (4) select members who have high motivation and prefer to work in groups, and (5) if possible, base group rewards in part on each member's unique contributions.[56] Although none of these is a magic bullet that will prevent social loafing in all cases, they should help minimize its effect.

Group Property 5: Cohesiveness

6 Contrast the benefits and disadvantages of cohesive groups.

Groups differ in their **cohesiveness**—the degree to which members are attracted to each other and motivated to stay in the group. Some work groups are cohesive because the members have spent a great deal of time together, or the group's small size facilitates high interaction, or external threats have brought members close together. Cohesiveness is important because it affects group productivity.[57]

Studies consistently show that relationship between cohesiveness and productivity depends on the group's performance-related norms.[58] If performance-related norms for quality, output, and cooperation with outsiders, for instance, are high, a cohesive group will be more productive than will a less cohesive group. But if cohesiveness is high and performance norms are low, productivity will be low. If cohesiveness is low and performance norms are high, productivity increases, but less than in the high-cohesiveness/high-norms situation. When cohesiveness and performance-related norms are both low, productivity tends to fall into the low-to-moderate range. These conclusions are summarized in Exhibit 9-6.

What can you do to encourage group cohesiveness? (1) Make the group smaller, (2) encourage agreement with group goals, (3) increase the time members spend together, (4) increase the group's status and the perceived difficulty of attaining membership, (5) stimulate competition with other groups, (6) give rewards to the group rather than to individual members, and (7) physically isolate the group.[59]

social loafing *The tendency for individuals to expend less effort when working collectively than when working individually.*

cohesiveness *The degree to which group members are attracted to each other and are motivated to stay in the group.*

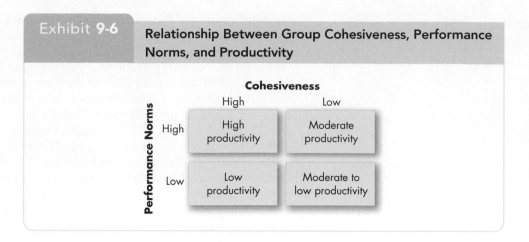

Exhibit 9-6   **Relationship Between Group Cohesiveness, Performance Norms, and Productivity**

Group Decision Making

7 Contrast the strengths and weaknesses of group decision making.

The belief—characterized by juries—that two heads are better than one has long been accepted as a basic component of the U.S. legal system and those of many other countries. Today, many decisions in organizations are made by groups, teams, or committees.[60] In this section, we discuss group decision making.

International OB

Group Cohesiveness Across Cultures

A recent study attempted to determine whether motivating work groups by giving them more complex tasks and greater autonomy resulted in increased group cohesiveness. Researchers studied bank teams in the United States, an individualist culture, and a collectivist culture in Hong Kong. Regardless of their culture, teams with difficult tasks and more freedom to accomplish them were more tight knit and their performance was enhanced.

However, the teams in individualist cultures responded more strongly to increases in task complexity and autonomy, became more united and committed, and, as a result, received higher performance ratings from their supervisors than teams from collectivist cultures. Collectivists appear more sensitive to the moods of their co-workers, so the motivation and positive mood of one group member is likely to spill over to increase motivation and positive moods in others. Why do these cultural differences exist? One explanation is that collectivist teams already have a strong predisposition to work together as a group, so there's less need for increased teamwork. This conclusion is supported by other research showing collectivists are less likely to engage in social loafing when working in groups than are individualists.

What's the lesson? Managers in individualist cultures may need to work harder to increase team cohesiveness. One way to do this is to give teams more challenging assignments and provide them with more independence.

Sources: Based on R. Ilies, D. T. Wagner, and F. P. Morgeson, "Explaining Affective Linkages in Teams: Individual Differences in Susceptibility to Contagion and Individualism-Collectivism," *Journal of Applied Psychology* 92, no. 4 (2007), pp. 1140–1148; E. M. Stark, J. D. Shaw, and M. K. Duffy, "Preference for Group Work, Winning Orientation, and Social Loafing Behavior in Groups," *Group and Organization Management* 32, no. 6 (2007), pp. 699–723; and D. Man and S. S. K. Lam, "The Effects of Job Complexity and Autonomy on Cohesiveness in Collectivist and Individualistic Work Groups: A Cross-Cultural Analysis," *Journal of Organizational Behavior*, December 2003, pp. 979–1001.

Groups versus the Individual

Decision-making groups may be widely used in organizations, but are group decisions preferable to those made by an individual alone? The answer depends on a number of factors. Let's begin by looking at the strengths and weaknesses of group decision making.[61]

Strengths of Group Decision Making Groups generate *more complete information and knowledge*. By aggregating the resources of several individuals, groups bring more input as well as heterogeneity into the decision process. They offer *increased diversity of views*. This opens up the opportunity to consider more approaches and alternatives. Finally, groups lead to increased *acceptance of a solution*. Many decisions fail because people don't accept the solution. Group members who participated in making a decision are more likely to enthusiastically support the decision and encourage others to accept it.

Weaknesses of Group Decision Making Group decisions have their drawbacks. They're time consuming because groups typically take more time to reach a solution. There are *conformity pressures*. The desire by group members to be accepted and considered an asset to the group can squash any overt disagreement. Group discussion can be *dominated by one or a few members*. If they're low- and medium-ability members, the group's overall effectiveness will suffer. Finally, group decisions suffer from *ambiguous responsibility*. In an individual decision, it's clear who is accountable for the final outcome. In a group decision, the responsibility of any single member is diluted.

Effectiveness and Efficiency Whether groups are more effective than individuals depends on how you define effectiveness. Group decisions are generally more *accurate* than the decisions of the average individual in a group but less accurate than the judgments of the most accurate.[62] In terms of *speed*, individuals are superior. If *creativity* is important, groups tend to be more effective. And if effectiveness means the degree of *acceptance* the final solution achieves, the nod again goes to the group.[63]

But we cannot consider effectiveness without also assessing efficiency. Groups almost always stack up a poor second to the individual decision maker. With few exceptions, group decision making consumes more work hours than if an individual were to tackle the same problem alone. The exceptions tend to be the instances in which, to achieve comparable quantities of diverse input, the single decision maker must spend a great deal of time reviewing files and talking to people. Because groups can include members from diverse areas, the time spent searching for information can be reduced. However, as we noted, these advantages in efficiency tend to be the exception. Groups are generally less efficient than individuals. In deciding whether to use groups, then, managers must assess whether increases in effectiveness are more than enough to offset the reductions in efficiency.

Summary In summary, groups are an excellent vehicle for performing many of the steps in the decision-making process and offer both breadth and depth of input for information gathering. If group members have diverse backgrounds, the alternatives generated should be more extensive and the analysis more critical. When the final solution is agreed on, there are more people in a group decision to support and implement it. These pluses, however, can be more than offset by the time consumed by group decisions, the internal conflicts they create, and the pressures they generate toward conformity. In some cases, therefore, individuals can be expected to make better decisions than groups.

"Are Two Heads Better Than One?"

Two heads are not necessarily always better than one. In fact, evidence generally confirms the superiority of individuals over groups when brainstorming. The best individual in a group also makes better decisions than groups as a whole, though groups do tend to do better than the average group member.[64]

Research also indicates groups are superior only when they meet certain criteria:[65]

1. **The group must have diversity among members.** To get benefits from "two heads," the heads must differ in relevant skills and abilities.
2. **Group members must be able to communicate their ideas freely and** openly. This requires an absence of hostility and intimidation.
3. **The task being undertaken must be complex.** Relative to individuals, groups do better on complex rather than simple tasks.

Groupthink and Groupshift

Two by-products of group decision making have the potential to affect a group's ability to appraise alternatives objectively and arrive at high-quality solutions.

The first phenomenon, called **groupthink**, relates to norms. It describes situations in which group pressures for conformity deter the group from critically appraising unusual, minority, or unpopular views. Groupthink is a disease that attacks many groups and can dramatically hinder their performance. The second phenomenon is **groupshift**, which describes the way, in discussing a given set of alternatives and arriving at a solution, group members tend to exaggerate the initial positions they hold. In some situations, caution dominates and there is a conservative shift. More often, however, groups tend toward a risky shift. Let's look at each of these phenomena in more detail.

Groupthink Have you ever felt like speaking up in a meeting, a classroom, or an informal group but decided against it? One reason may have been shyness. Or you may have been a victim of groupthink, which occurs when the norm for consensus overrides the realistic appraisal of alternative courses and the full expression of deviant, minority, or unpopular views. The individual's mental efficiency, reality testing, and moral judgment deteriorate as a result of group pressures.[66]

We have all seen the symptoms of the groupthink phenomenon:

1. Group members rationalize any resistance to the assumptions they have made. No matter how strongly the evidence may contradict their basic assumptions, members behave so as to reinforce them.
2. Members apply direct pressures on those who momentarily express doubts about any of the group's shared views, or who question the validity of arguments supporting the alternative favored by the majority.
3. Members who have doubts or differing points of view seek to avoid deviating from what appears to be group consensus by keeping silent about misgivings and even minimizing to themselves the importance of their doubts.
4. There is an illusion of unanimity. If someone doesn't speak, it's assumed he or she is in full accord. In other words, abstention becomes a "yes" vote.[67]

Groupthink appears closely aligned with the conclusions Asch drew in his experiments with a lone dissenter. Individuals who hold a position different from

An Ethical Choice

How Groups Infect Your Deviant Behavior—and How to Immunize Yourself

Most organizations face scores of ethical decisions every day. When ethics and self-interest align, the choice is easy. Very often, however, the two choices aren't perfectly aligned and we must choose between what is expedient and what is ethical. What drives such choices?

Given the topic of this chapter, it won't be surprising to learn that one factor appears to be groups. Earlier we discussed how individuals tend to engage in more deviant behavior when working in groups than when they're working alone. Here we're interested in a related group effect: how individuals respond to dishonesty they perceive in the group.

A recent research study suggested some surprising group dynamics, and some implications for our own ethical behavior. First, whereas observing cheating on the part of "in-group" members (people who are similar to us and we like and identify with) increased an individual's propensity to cheat,

cheating on the part of "out-group" members decreased it.

Second, other research suggests that cheating in groups is reduced by making moral standards explicit. This fits with research showing that drawing attention to moral standards can reduce dishonesty in a group. In one condition, participants were asked to read the Ten Commandments and were then given an opportunity to cheat. In the other condition, participants were given the same chance to cheat, but without the moral reminder. Participants in the first group didn't cheat at all, whereas those in the second group cheated a lot.

As the authors of one of the studies notes, "Dishonest behavior can be contagious."

1. Given the findings of this study, it's important to make sure our "in-group" is honest. Should they be dishonest, we may be influenced by their behavior more than we realize.

2. The findings on saliency also suggest actions we might take: Reminding ourselves or other group members of ethical standards can have an effect on our own or on our group's ethical behavior.

3. It is dangerous to assume we're not capable of unethical behavior. All of us are. If we assume we're above such behavior, we may be particularly likely to be naïve about group factors that affect unethical behavior and to deny the unethical nature of our own actions. The point: We'll be better able to resist group pressures toward unethical behavior if we're open and honest with ourselves about the pressures and temptations.

Sources: Based on: F. Gino, S. Ayal, and D. Ariely, "Contagion and Differentiation in Unethical Behavior," *Psychological Science* 20, no. 3 (2009), pp. 393–398; and N. Mazar, O. Amir, and D. Ariely, "The Dishonesty of Honest People: A Theory of Self-Concept Maintenance," *Journal of Marketing Research* 45, no. 6 (2008), pp. 633–644.

that of the dominant majority are under pressure to suppress, withhold, or modify their true feelings and beliefs. As members of a group, we find it more pleasant to be in agreement—to be a positive part of the group—than to be a disruptive force, even if disruption is necessary to improve the effectiveness of the group's decisions.

Does groupthink attack all groups? No. It seems to occur most often when there is a clear group identity, when members hold a positive image of their group that they want to protect, and when the group perceives a collective threat to this positive image.[68] So groupthink is not a dissenter-suppression mechanism as much as it's a means for a group to protect its positive image. For NASA, groupthink's problems stem from its attempt to confirm its identity as "the elite organization that could do no wrong."[69]

groupthink *A phenomenon in which the norm for consensus overrides the realistic appraisal of alternative courses of action.*

groupshift *A change in decision risk between a group's decision and an individual decision that a member within the group would make; the shift can be toward either conservatism or greater risk.*

What can managers do to minimize groupthink?[70] First, they can monitor group size. People grow more intimidated and hesitant as group size increases, and, although there is no magic number that will eliminate groupthink, individuals are likely to feel less personal responsibility when groups get larger than about 10 members. Managers should also encourage group leaders to play an impartial role. Leaders should actively seek input from all members and avoid expressing their own opinions, especially in the early stages of deliberation. In addition, managers should appoint one group member to play the role of devil's advocate; this member's role is to overtly challenge the majority position and offer divergent perspectives. Still another suggestion is to use exercises that stimulate active discussion of diverse alternatives without threatening the group and intensifying identity protection. One such exercise is to have group members delay discussion of possible gains so they can first talk about the dangers or risks inherent in a decision. Requiring members to first focus on the negatives of an alternative makes the group less likely to stifle dissenting views and more likely to gain an objective evaluation.

Group Shift or Group Polarization   There are differences between group decisions and the individual decisions of group members.[71] Sometimes group decisions are more conservative. More often, they lean toward greater risk.[72]

What appears to happen in groups is that the discussion leads members toward a more extreme view of the position they already held. Conservatives become more cautious, and more aggressive types take on more risk. The group discussion tends to exaggerate the initial position of the group.

We can view group polarization as a special case of groupthink. The group's decision reflects the dominant decision-making norm that develops during discussion. Whether the shift in the group's decision is toward greater caution or more risk depends on the dominant pre-discussion norm.

The shift toward risk has generated several explanations.[73] It's been argued, for instance, that discussion makes the members more comfortable with each other and, thus, more bold and daring. Another argument is that the group diffuses responsibility. Group decisions free any single member from accountability for the group's final choice, so greater risks can be taken. It's also likely that people take on extreme positions because they want to demonstrate how different they are from the outgroup.[74] People on the fringes of political or social movements take on more and more extreme positions just to prove they are really committed to the cause.

So how should you use the findings on groupshift? Recognize that group decisions exaggerate the initial position of the individual members, that the shift has been shown more often to be toward greater risk, and that which way a group will shift is a function of the members' pre-discussion inclinations.

We now turn to the techniques by which groups make decisions. These reduce some of the dysfunctional aspects of group decision making.

Group Decision-Making Techniques

8 Compare the effectiveness of interacting, brainstorming, nominal, and electronic meeting groups.

The most common form of group decision making takes place in **interacting groups**. Members meet face to face and rely on both verbal and nonverbal interaction to communicate. But as our discussion of groupthink demonstrated, interacting groups often censor themselves and pressure individual members toward conformity of opinion. Brainstorming, the nominal group technique, and electronic meetings have been proposed as ways to reduce problems inherent in the traditional interacting group.

Brainstorming can overcome the pressures for conformity that dampen creativity[75] by encouraging any and all alternatives while withholding criticism.

In a typical brainstorming session, a half dozen to a dozen people sit around a table. The group leader states the problem in a clear manner so all participants understand. Members then freewheel as many alternatives as they can in a given length of time. No criticism is allowed, and all alternatives are recorded for later discussion and analysis. One idea stimulates others, and judgments of even the most bizarre suggestions are withheld until later to encourage group members to "think the unusual."

Brainstorming may indeed generate ideas—but not in a very efficient manner. Research consistently shows individuals working alone generate more ideas than a group in a brainstorming session. One reason for this is "production blocking." When people are generating ideas in a group, many are talking at once, which blocks the thought process and eventually impedes the sharing of ideas.[76] The following two techniques go further than brainstorming by helping groups arrive at a preferred solution.[77]

The **nominal group technique** restricts discussion or interpersonal communication during the decision-making process, hence the term *nominal*. Group members are all physically present, as in a traditional committee meeting, but they operate independently. Specifically, a problem is presented and then the group takes the following steps:

1. Members meet as a group, but before any discussion takes place, each independently writes down ideas on the problem.
2. After this silent period, each member presents one idea to the group. No discussion takes place until all ideas have been presented and recorded.
3. The group discusses the ideas for clarity and evaluates them.
4. Each group member silently and independently rank-orders the ideas. The idea with the highest aggregate ranking determines the final decision.

The chief advantage of the nominal group technique is that it permits a group to meet formally but does not restrict independent thinking, as does an interacting group. Research generally shows nominal groups outperform brainstorming groups.[78]

The most recent approach to group decision making blends the nominal group technique with sophisticated computer technology.[79] It's called a computer-assisted group, or an **electronic meeting**. Once the required technology is in place, the concept is simple. Up to 50 people sit around a horseshoe-shaped table, empty except for a series of networked laptops. Issues are presented to them, and they type their responses into their computers. These individual but anonymous comments, as well as aggregate votes, are displayed on a projection screen. This technique also allows people to be brutally honest without penalty. And it's fast because chitchat is eliminated, discussions don't digress, and many participants can "talk" at once without stepping on one another's toes. Early evidence, however, suggests electronic meetings don't achieve most of their proposed benefits. They actually lead to *decreased* group effectiveness, require *more* time to complete tasks, and result in *reduced* member satisfaction compared with

interacting groups *Typical groups in which members interact with each other face to face.*

brainstorming *An idea-generation process that specifically encourages any and all alternatives while withholding any criticism of those alternatives.*

nominal group technique *A group decision-making method in which individual members meet face to face to pool their judgments in a systematic but independent fashion.*

electronic meeting *A meeting in which members interact on computers, allowing for anonymity of comments and aggregation of votes.*

Exhibit 9-7   **Evaluating Group Effectiveness**

Effectiveness Criteria	Type of Group			
	Interacting	Brainstorming	Nominal	Electronic
Number and quality of ideas	Low	Moderate	High	High
Social pressure	High	Low	Moderate	Low
Money costs	Low	Low	Low	High
Speed	Moderate	Moderate	Moderate	Moderate
Task orientation	Low	High	High	High
Potential for interpersonal conflict	High	Low	Moderate	Low
Commitment to solution	High	Not applicable	Moderate	Moderate
Development of group cohesiveness	High	High	Moderate	Low

face-to-face groups.[80] Nevertheless, current enthusiasm for computer-mediated communications suggests this technology is here to stay and is likely to increase in popularity in the future.

Each of the four group-decision techniques has its own set of strengths and weaknesses. The choice depends on what criteria you want to emphasize and the cost–benefit trade-off. As Exhibit 9-7 indicates, an interacting group is good for achieving commitment to a solution, brainstorming develops group cohesiveness, the nominal group technique is an inexpensive means for generating a large number of ideas, and electronic meetings minimize social pressures and conflicts.

Global Implications

9 Evaluate evidence for cultural differences in group status and social loafing as well as the effects of diversity in groups.

Most research on groups has been conducted in North America, but that situation is changing quickly. Cross-cultural issues are particularly important in three areas.

Status and Culture   Do cultural differences affect status? The answer is a resounding "yes."[81]

The importance of status does vary among cultures. The French are highly status conscious. Countries also differ on the criteria that create status. Latin Americans and Asians derive status from family position and formal roles in organizations. In the United States and Australia, in contrast, status is more often conferred for accomplishments than for titles or family trees.[82]

Thus it is important to understand who and what holds status when interacting with people from a culture different from one's own. A U.S. manager who doesn't know that office size is not a measure of a Japanese executive's position is likely to unintentionally offend his overseas counterparts and lessen his interpersonal effectiveness, as is someone who fails to grasp the importance the British place on family genealogy and social class.

Social Loafing   Social loafing appears to have a Western bias. It's consistent with individualistic cultures, such as the United States and Canada, that are dominated by self-interest. It is *not* consistent with collective societies, in which individuals are motivated by in-group goals. In studies comparing U.S. employees with employees from the People's Republic of China and Israel (both

Studies indicate that the employees shown here producing "Spice" handsets at a semi-high-tech factory in China show no propensity to engage in social loafing. In collectivist societies such as China, employees actually prefer working in a group and are motivated by in-group goals. However, in individualistic societies such as the United States that are dominated by self-interest, social loafing is more likely.

collectivist societies), the Chinese and Israelis showed no propensity to engage in social loafing and actually performed better in a group than alone.

Group Diversity   More research is being done on how diversity influences group performance. Some looks at cultural diversity and some at racial, gender, and other differences. Overall, studies identify both benefits and costs from group diversity.

Diversity appears to increase group conflict, especially in the early stages of a group's tenure, which often lowers group morale and raises dropout rates. One study compared groups that were culturally diverse (composed of people from different countries) and homogeneous (composed of people from the same country). On a wilderness survival exercise (not unlike the Experiential Exercise at the end of this chapter), the groups performed equally well, but the diverse groups were less satisfied with their groups, were less cohesive, and had more conflict.[83]

However, evidence is accumulating that, over time, culturally and demographically diverse groups may perform better, if they can get over their initial conflicts. Why might this be so?

Surface-level diversity—observable characteristics such as national origin, race, and gender—alerts people to possible differences in deep-level diversity—underlying attitudes, values, and opinions. One researcher argues, "The mere presence of diversity you can see, such as a person's race or gender, actually cues a team that there's likely to be differences of opinion." Although those differences can lead to conflict, they also provide an opportunity to solve problems in unique ways.

One study of jury behavior found diverse juries more likely to deliberate longer, share more information, and make fewer factual errors when discussing evidence. Two studies of MBA student groups found surface-level diversity led to greater openness even when there was no deep-level diversity. In such cases, the surface-level diversity of a group may subconsciously cue team members to be more open minded in their views.[84]

In summary, the impact of cultural diversity on groups is mixed. It is difficult to be in a diverse group in the short term. However, if members can weather their differences, over time diversity may help them be more open minded and creative, allowing them to do better in the long run. But even positive effects are unlikely to be especially strong. As one review stated, "The business case (in terms of demonstrable financial results) for diversity remains hard to support based on the extant research."[85]

Summary and Implications for Managers

Performance   Among the most prominent properties related to group performance are role perception, norms, status differences, size of the group, and cohesiveness.

Role perception and an employee's performance evaluation are positively related.[86] The degree of congruence between the employee's and the boss's perception of the employee's job influences the degree to which the boss will judge that employee effective. An employee whose role perception fulfills the boss's role expectations will receive a higher performance evaluation.

Norms control behavior by establishing standards of right and wrong. The norms of a given group can help explain members' behaviors for managers. When norms support high output, managers can expect markedly higher individual performance than when they aim to restrict output. Norms that support antisocial behavior increase the likelihood that individuals will engage in deviant workplace activities.

Status inequities create frustration and can adversely influence productivity and willingness to remain with an organization. Incongruence is likely to reduce motivation and motivate a search for ways to bring about fairness (say, by taking another job). Because lower-status people tend to participate less in group discussions, groups with high status differences are likely to inhibit input from lower-status members and reduce their potential.

The impact of size on a group's performance depends on the type of task. Larger groups are more effective at fact-finding activities, smaller groups at action-taking tasks. Our knowledge of social loafing suggests that managers using larger groups should also provide measures of individual performance.

Cohesiveness can influence a group's level of productivity or not, depending on the group's performance-related norms.

Satisfaction   High congruence between a boss's and an employee's perception of the employee's job correlates strongly with high employee satisfaction.[87] Role conflict is associated with job-induced tension and job dissatisfaction.[88]

Most people prefer to communicate with others at their own status level or a higher one rather than with those below them.[89] As a result, we should expect satisfaction to be greater among employees whose job minimizes interaction with individuals lower in status than themselves.

The group size–satisfaction relationship is what we would intuitively expect: Larger groups are associated with lower satisfaction.[90] As size increases, opportunities for participation and social interaction decrease, as does the ability of members to identify with the group's accomplishments. At the same time, having more members also prompts dissension, conflict, and the formation of subgroups, which all act to make the group a less pleasant entity of which to be a part.

All Jobs Should Be Designed Around Groups

Groups, not individuals, are the ideal building blocks for an organization. There are several reasons for designing all jobs around groups.

First, in general, groups make better decisions than the average individual acting alone.

Second, with the growth in technology, society is becoming more intertwined. Look at the growth of social networking media such as Twitter, Facebook, and LinkedIn. People are connected anyway, so why not design work in the same way?

Third, small groups are good for people. They can satisfy social needs and provide support for employees in times of stress and crisis. Evidence indicates that social support—both when they provide it and when they receive it—makes people happier and even allows them to live longer.

Fourth, groups are very effective tools for implementation for decisions. Groups gain commitment from their members so that group decisions are likely to be willingly and more successfully carried out.

Fifth, groups can control and discipline individual members in ways that are often extremely difficult through impersonal quasi-legal disciplinary systems. Group norms are powerful control devices.

Sixth, groups are a means by which large organizations can fend off many of the negative effects of increased size. Groups help prevent communication lines from growing too long, the hierarchy from growing too steep, and individuals from getting lost in the crowd.

The rapid growth of team-based organizations in recent years suggests that we may well be on our way toward a day when almost all jobs are designed around groups.

Capitalistic countries such as the United States, Canada, Australia, and the United Kingdom value the individual. Designing jobs around groups is inconsistent with the economic values of these countries. Moreover, as capitalism and entrepreneurship have spread throughout eastern Europe, Asia, and other more collective societies, we should expect to see *less* emphasis on groups and *more* on the individual in workplaces throughout the world. Let's look at the United States to see how cultural and economic values shape employee attitudes toward groups.

The United States was built on the ethic of the individual. Its culture strongly values individual achievement and encourages competition. Even in team sports, people want to identify individuals for recognition. U.S. adults enjoy being part of a group in which they can maintain a strong individual identity. They don't enjoy sublimating their identity to that of the group. When they are assigned to groups, all sorts of bad things happen, including conflict, groupthink, social loafing, and deviant behavior.

The U.S. worker likes a clear link between individual effort and a visible outcome. It's not by chance that the United States, as a nation, has a considerably larger proportion of high achievers than exists in most of the rest of the world. It breeds achievers, and achievers seek personal responsibility. They would be frustrated in job situations in which their contribution was commingled and homogenized with the contributions of others.

U.S. workers want to be hired, evaluated, and rewarded on their individual achievements. They are not likely to accept a group's decision on such issues as their job assignments and wage increases, nor are they comfortable in a system in which the sole basis for their promotion or termination is the performance of their group.

Though teams have grown in popularity as a device for employers to organize people and tasks, we should expect resistance to any effort to treat individuals solely as members of a group—especially among workers raised in capitalistic economies.

Questions for Review

1 Define *group*? What are the different types of groups?

2 What are the five stages of group development?

3 Do role requirements change in different situations? If so, how?

4 How do group norms and status influence an individual's behavior?

5 How does group size affect group performance?

6 What are the advantages and limitations of cohesive groups?

7 What are the strengths and weaknesses of group (versus individual) decision making?

8 How effective are interacting, brainstorming, nominal, and electronic meeting groups?

9 What is the evidence for the effect of culture on group status and social loafing? How does diversity affect groups and their effectiveness over time?

Experiential Exercise

WILDERNESS SURVIVAL

You are a member of a hiking party. After reaching base camp on the first day, you decide to take a quick sunset hike by yourself. After a few exhilarating miles, you decide to return to camp. On your way back, you realize that you are lost. You have shouted for help, to no avail. It is now dark. And getting cold.

Your Task

Without communicating with anyone else in your group, read the following scenarios and choose the best answer. Keep track of your answers on a sheet of paper. You have 10 minutes to answer the 10 questions.

1. The first thing you decide to do is to build a fire. However, you have no matches, so you use the bow-and-drill method. What is the bow-and-drill method?

   a. A dry, soft stick is rubbed between one's hands against a board of supple green wood.

   b. A soft green stick is rubbed between one's hands against a hardwood board.

   c. A straight stick of wood is quickly rubbed back and forth against a dead tree.

   d. Two sticks (one being the bow, the other the drill) are struck to create a spark.

2. It occurs to you that you can also use the fire as a distress signal. When signaling with fire, how do you form the international distress signal?

   a. 2 fires

   b. 4 fires in a square

   c. 4 fires in a cross

   d. 3 fires in a line

3. You are very thirsty. You go to a nearby stream and collect some water in the small metal cup you have in your backpack. How long should you boil the water?

   a. 15 minutes

   b. A few seconds

   c. 1 hour

   d. It depends on the altitude.

4. You are very hungry, so you decide to eat what appear to be edible berries. When performing the universal edibility test, what should you do?

   a. Do not eat for 2 hours before the test.

   b. If the plant stings your lip, confirm the sting by holding it under your tongue for 15 minutes.

   c. If nothing bad has happened 2 hours after digestion, eat half a cup of the plant and wait again.

   d. Separate the plant into its basic components and eat each component, one at a time.

5. Next, you decide to build a shelter for the evening. In selecting a site, what do you *not* have to consider?

   a. It must contain material to make the type of shelter you need.

   b. It must be free of insects, reptiles, and poisonous plants.

   c. It must be large enough and level enough for you to lie down comfortably.

   d. It must be on a hill so you can signal rescuers and keep an eye on your surroundings.

6. In the shelter that you built, you notice a spider. You heard from a fellow hiker that black widow spiders populate the area. How do you identify a black widow spider?

a. Its head and abdomen are black; its thorax is red.

b. It is attracted to light.

c. It runs away from light.

d. It is a dark spider with a red or orange marking on the female's abdomen.

7. After getting some sleep, you notice that the night sky has cleared, so you decide to try to find your way back to base camp. You believe you should travel north and can use the North Star for navigation. How do you locate the North Star?

a. Hold your right hand up as far as you can and look between your index and middle fingers.

b. Find Sirius and look 60 degrees above it and to the right.

c. Look for the Big Dipper and follow the line created by its cup end.

d. Follow the line of Orion's belt.

8. You come across a fast-moving stream. What is the best way to cross it?

a. Find a spot downstream from a sandbar, where the water will be calmer.

b. Build a bridge.

c. Find a rocky area, as the water will be shallow and you will have hand- and footholds.

d. Find a level stretch where it breaks into a few channels.

9. After walking for about an hour, you feel several spiders in your clothes. You don't feel any pain, but you know some spider bites are painless. Which of these spider bites is painless?

a. Black widow

b. Brown recluse

c. Wolf spider

d. Harvestman (daddy longlegs)

10. You decide to eat some insects. Which insects should you avoid?

a. Adults that sting or bite

b. Caterpillars and insects that have a pungent odor

c. Hairy or brightly colored ones

d. All of the above

Group Task

Break into groups of five or six people. Now imagine that your whole group is lost. Answer each question as a group, employing a consensus approach to reach each decision. Once the group comes to an agreement, write down the decision on the same sheet of paper that you used for your individual answers. You will have approximately 20 minutes for the group task.

Scoring Your Answers

Your instructor will provide you with the correct answers, which are based on expert judgments in these situations. Once you have received the answers, calculate (A) your individual score; (B) your group's score; (C) the average individual score in the group; and (D) the best individual score in the group. Write these down and consult with your group to ensure that these scores are accurate.

A. Your individual score _____

B. Your group's score _____

C. Average individual score in group _____

D. Best individual score in group _____

Discussion Questions

1. How did your group (B) perform relative to yourself (A)?

2. How did your group (B) perform relative to the average individual score in the group (C)?

3. How did your group (B) perform relative to the best individual score in the group (D)?

4. Compare your results with those of other groups. Did some groups do a better job of outperforming individuals than others?

5. What do these results tell you about the effectiveness of group decision making?

6. What can groups do to make group decision making more effective?

Ethical Dilemma

DEALING WITH SHIRKERS

We've noted that one of the most common problems in groups is social loafing, which means group members contribute less than if they were working on their own. We might call such individuals "shirkers"—those who are contributing far less than other group members.

Most of us have experienced social loafing, or shirking, in groups. And we may even admit to times when we shirked ourselves. We discussed earlier in this chapter some ways of discouraging social loafing, such as limiting group size, holding individuals responsible for their contributions, and setting group goals. While these tactics may be effective, in our experience many students simply work around shirkers. "We just did it ourselves—it was easier that way," says one group member.

Consider the following questions for dealing with shirking in groups:

1. If group members end up "working around" shirkers, do you think this information should be communi-

cated to the instructor so that each individual's contribution to the project is judged more fairly? If so, does the group have an ethical responsibility to communicate this to the shirking group member? If not, isn't the shirking group member unfairly reaping the rewards of a free ride?

2. Do you think confronting the shirking group member is justified? Does this depend on the skills of the shirker (whether he or she is capable of doing good-quality work)?

3. Social loafing has been found to be higher in Western, more individualist, nations than in other countries. Do you think this means we should tolerate shirking on the part of U.S. workers to a greater degree than if it occurred with someone from Asia?

Case Incident 1

"IF TWO HEADS ARE BETTER THAN ONE, ARE FOUR EVEN BETTER?"

Maggie Becker, age 24, is a marketing manager for Kavu, a small chain of coffee shops in eastern Ohio. Recently, Maggie's wealthy uncle passed away and left her, his only niece, $100,000. Maggie considers her current salary adequate to meet her current living expenses, so she'd like to invest the money so that when she buys a house she'll have a nice nest egg on which to draw.

One of Maggie's neighbors, Brian, is a financial advisor. Brian told Maggie that the array of investment options is virtually endless. She asked him to present her with two of the best options, and this is what he offered her:

1. **A very low-risk AAA municipal bond fund.** With this option, based on the information Brian provided, Maggie estimates that after 5 years she stands virtually zero chance of losing money, with an expected gain of approximately $7,000.

2. **A moderate-risk mutual fund.** Based on the information Brian provided her, Maggie estimates that with this option she stands a 50 percent chance of making $40,000 but also a 50 percent chance of losing $20,000.

Maggie prides herself on being rational and objective in her thinking. However, she's unsure of what to do in this

case. Brian refuses to help her, telling her that she's already limited herself by asking for only two options. While driving to her parents' house for the weekend, Maggie finds herself vacillating between the two options. Her older brother is also visiting the folks this weekend, so Maggie decides to gather her family around the table after dinner, lay out the two options, and go with their decision. "You know the old saying—two heads are better than one," she says to herself, "so four heads should be even better."

Questions

1. Has Maggie made a good decision about the way she is going to make the decision?

2. Which investment would you choose? Why?

3. Which investment do you think most people would choose?

4. Based on what you have learned about groupshift, which investment do you think Maggie's family will choose?

Case Incident 2

HERD BEHAVIOR AND THE HOUSING BUBBLE (AND COLLAPSE)

It is sometimes easy to forget that, in many ways, humans are not unlike other animals. Economist John Maynard Keynes recognized this when he commented, "Most, probably, of our decisions to do something positive, the full consequences of which will be drawn out over many days to come, can only be taken as the result of animal spirits—a spontaneous urge to action rather than inaction, and not as the outcome of a weighted average of quantitative benefits multiplied by quantitative probabilities."

When such "animal spirits" are particularly dangerous is at the collective level. One animal's decision to charge over a cliff is a tragedy for the animal, but it may also lead the entire herd over the cliff.

You may be wondering how this is applicable to organizational behavior. Consider the recent housing bubble and its subsequent collapse. As housing prices rose ever higher, people discounted risk, seemingly based only on observing what others were doing. Homeowners and investors rushed to buy properties because everyone else was doing it. Banks rushed to provide loans with little due diligence because, well, everyone else was doing it. "Banks didn't want to get left behind. Everybody lowered their underwriting standards, no matter who they are," said Regions Bank executive Michael Menk. "As bankers that's who we are; we follow the herd."

Yale Economist Robert Shiller called this "herd behavior" and cited research showing people often rely heavily on the behavior of groups in formulating decisions about what they should do. A recent study in behavioral finance confirmed herd behavior in investment decisions and showed that analysts were especially likely to follow other analysts' behavior when they had private information that was less accurate or reliable.

Questions

1. Some research suggests herd behavior increases as the size of the group increases. Why do you think this might be the case?

2. One researcher argues that "pack behavior" comes about because it has benefits. What is the upside of such behavior?

3. Shiller argues that herd behavior can go both ways: It explains the housing bubble, but it also explains the bust. As he notes, "Rational individuals become excessively pessimistic as they see others bidding down home prices to abnormally low levels." Do you agree with Shiller?

4. How might organizations combat the problems resulting from herd behavior?

Sources: Based on R. J. Shiller, "How a Bubble Stayed Under the Radar," *New York Times* (March 2, 2008), p. BU6; W. Hobson, "Reversal of Fortune," *Panama City News Herald* (March 22, 2009), www.newsherald.com; P. Leoni, "Pack Behavior," *Journal of Mathematical Psychology* 52, no. 6 (2008), pp. 348–351; and J. Reiczigel, Z. Lang, L. Rózsa, and B. Tóthmérész, "Measures of Sociality: Two Different Views of Group Size," *Animal Behaviour* 75, no. 2 (2008), pp. 715–721.

Endnotes

1. J. Scanlon, "Brainstorming for Better Business," *BusinessWeek* (June 4, 2009), www.businessweek.com; M. Crom, "Success Coach: Build Trust to Encourage Brainstorming," *Shreveport Times* (June 15, 2009), www.shreveporttimes.com; and J. Sandberg, "Brainstorming Works Best if People Scramble for Ideas on Their Own," *Wall Street Journal* (June 13, 2006), p. B1.

2. L. R. Sayles, "Work Group Behavior and the Larger Organization," in C. Arensburg, et al. (eds.), *Research in Industrial Relations* (New York: Harper & Row, 1957), pp. 131–145.

3. B. E. Ashforth and F. Mael, "Social Identity Theory and the Organization," *Academy of Management Review* 14, no. 1 (1989), pp. 20–39; and M. A. Hogg and D. J. Terry, "Social Identity and Self-Categorization Processes in Organizational Contexts," *Academy of Management Review* 25, no. 1 (2000), pp. 121–140.

4. M. A. Hogg and B. A. Mullin, "Joining Groups to Reduce Uncertainty: Subjective Uncertainty Reduction and Group Identification," in D. Abrams and M. A. Hogg (eds.), *Social Identity and Social Cognition* (Maiden MA: Blackwell, 1999), pp. 249–279.

5. Hogg and Terry, "Social Identity and Self-Categorization Processes in Organizational Contexts."; J. C. Turner et al., *Rediscovering the Social Group: A Self-Categorization Theory* (Cambridge, MA: Basil Blackwell), 1987.

6. D. M. Cable and D. S. DeRue, "The Convergent and Discriminant Validity of Subjective Fit Perceptions," *Journal of Applied Psychology* 87, no. 5 (2002), pp. 875–884; E. George and P. Chattopadhyay, "One Foot in Each Camp: The Dual Identification of Contract Workers," *Administrative Science Quarterly* 50, no. 1 (2005), pp. 68–99; and D. M. Cable and J. R. Edwards, "Complementary and Supplementary Fit: A Theoretical and Empirical Integration," *Journal of Applied Psychology* 89, no. 5 (2004), pp. 822–834.

7. P. F. McKay and D. R. Avery, "What Has Race Got to Do with It? Unraveling the Role of Racioethnicity in Job Seekers' Reactions to Site Visits," *Personnel Psychology* 59, no. 2 (2006), pp. 395–429.

8. A. Mehra, M. Kilduff, and D. J. Brass, "At the Margins: A Distinctiveness Approach to the Social Identity and Social Networks of Underrepresented Groups," *Academy of Management Journal* 41, no. 4 (1998), pp. 441–452.

9. M. D. Johnson, F. P. Morgeson, D. R. Ilgen, C. J. Meyer, and J. W. Lloyd, "Multiple Professional Identities: Examining Differences in Identification Across Work-Related Targets," *Journal of Applied Psychology* 91, no. 2 (2006), pp. 498–506.

10. F. Mael and B. E. Ashforth, "Alumni and Their Alma Mater: A Partial Test of the Reformulated Model of Organizational Identification," *Journal of Organizational Behavior* 13, no. 2 (1992), pp. 103–123.

11. K. Mignonac, O. Herrbach, and S. Guerrero, "The Interactive Effects of Perceived External Prestige and Need for Organizational Identification on Turnover Intentions," *Journal of Vocational Behavior* 69, no. 3 (2006), pp. 477–493.

12. M. Hogg and D. Abrams, "Towards a Single-Process Uncertainty-Reduction Model of Social Motivation in Groups," in M. Hogg and D. Abrams (eds.), *Group Motivation: Social Psychological Perspectives* (New York: Harvester-Wheatsheaf, 1993), pp. 173–190.

13. K. G. Corley and D. A. Gioia, "Identity Ambiguity and Change in the Wake of a Corporate Spin-off," *Administrative Science Quarterly* 49, no. 2 (2004), pp. 173–208.

14. J. F. McGrew, J. G. Bilotta, and J. M. Deeney, "Software Team Formation and Decay: Extending the Standard Model for Small Groups," *Small Group Research* 30, no. 2, (1999), pp. 209–234.

15. B. W. Tuckman, "Developmental Sequences in Small Groups," *Psychological Bulletin,* June 1965, pp. 384–399; B. W. Tuckman and M. C. Jensen, "Stages of Small-Group Development Revisited," *Group and Organizational Studies,* December 1977, pp. 419–427; M. F. Maples, "Group Development: Extending Tuckman's Theory," *Journal for Specialists in Group Work,* Fall 1988, pp. 17–23; and K. Vroman and J. Kovacich, "Computer-Mediated Interdisciplinary Teams: Theory and Reality," *Journal of Interprofessional Care* 16, no. 2 (2002), pp. 159–170.

16. J. F. George and L. M. Jessup, "Groups Over Time: What Are We Really Studying?" *International Journal of Human-Computer Studies* 47, no. 3 (1997), pp. 497–511.

17. R. C. Ginnett, "The Airline Cockpit Crew," in J. R. Hackman (ed.), *Groups That Work (and Those That Don't)* (San Francisco: Jossey-Bass, 1990).

18. C. J. G. Gersick, "Time and Transition in Work Teams: Toward a New Model of Group Development," *Academy of Management Journal,* March 1988, pp. 9–41; C. J. G. Gersick, "Marking Time: Predictable Transitions in Task Groups," *Academy of Management Journal,* June 1989, pp. 274–309; M. J. Waller, J. M. Conte, C. B. Gibson, and M. A. Carpenter, "The Effect of Individual Perceptions of Deadlines on Team Performance," *Academy of Management Review,* October 2001, pp. 586–600; and A. Chang, P. Bordia, and J. Duck, "Punctuated Equilibrium and Linear Progression: Toward a New Understanding of Group Development," *Academy of Management Journal,* February 2003, pp. 106–117. See also H. Arrow, M. S. Poole, K. B. Henry, S. Wheelan, and

R. Moreland, "Time, Change, and Development: The Temporal Perspective on Groups," *Small Group Research,* February 2004, pp. 73–105.

19. Gersick, "Time and Transition in Work Teams;" and Gersick, "Marking Time."

20. A. Seers and S. Woodruff, "Temporal Pacing in Task Forces: Group Development or Deadline Pressure?" *Journal of Management* 23, no. 2 (1997), pp. 169–187.

21. See D. M. Rousseau, *Psychological Contracts in Organizations: Understanding Written and Unwritten Agreements* (Thousand Oaks, CA: Sage, 1995); E. W. Morrison and S. L. Robinson, "When Employees Feel Betrayed: A Model of How Psychological Contract Violation Develops," *Academy of Management Review,* April 1997, pp. 226–256; D. Rousseau and R. Schalk (eds.), *Psychological Contracts in Employment: Cross-Cultural Perspectives* (San Francisco: Jossey-Bass, 2000); L. Sels, M. Janssens, and I. Van den Brande, "Assessing the Nature of Psychological Contracts: A Validation of Six Dimensions," *Journal of Organizational Behavior,* June 2004, pp. 461–488; and C. Hui, C. Lee, and D. M. Rousseau, "Psychological Contract and Organizational Citizenship Behavior in China: Investigating Generalizability and Instrumentality," *Journal of Applied Psychology,* April 2004, pp. 311–321.

22. See M. F. Peterson et al., "Role Conflict, Ambiguity, and Overload: A 21-Nation Study," *Academy of Management Journal,* April 1995, pp. 429–452; and I. H. Settles, R. M. Sellers, and A. Damas, Jr., "One Role or Two? The Function of Psychological Separation in Role Conflict," *Journal of Applied Psychology,* June 2002, pp. 574–582.

23. M. A. Hogg and D. J. Terry, "Social Identity and Self-Categorization Processes in Organizational Contexts," *Academy of Management Review* 25, no. 1 (2000), pp. 121–140.

24. D. Vora and T. Kostova. "A Model of Dual Organizational Identification in the Context of the Multinational Enterprise," *Journal of Organizational Behavior* 28, (2007), pp. 327–350.

25. C. Reade, "Dual Identification in Multinational Corporations: Local Managers and Their Psychological Attachment to the Subsidiary Versus the Global Organization," *International Journal of Human Resource Management,* 12, no. 3 (2001), pp. 405–424.

26. P. G. Zimbardo, C. Haney, W. C. Banks, and D. Jaffe, "The Mind Is a Formidable Jailer: A Pirandellian Prison," *New York Times* (April 8, 1973), pp. 38–60; and C. Haney and P. G. Zimbardo, "Social Roles and Role-Playing: Observations from the Stanford Prison Study," *Behavioral and Social Science Teacher,* January 1973, pp. 25–45.

27. S. A. Haslam and S. Reicher, "Stressing the Group: Social Identity and the Unfolding Dynamics of Responses to Stress," *Journal of Applied Psychology* 91, no. 5 (2006), pp. 1037–1052; S. Reicher and S. A. Haslam, "Rethinking the Psychology of Tyranny: The BBC Prison Study," *British Journal of Social Psychology* 45, no. 1 (2006), pp. 1–40; and P. G. Zimbardo, "On Rethinking the Psychology of Tyranny: The BBC Prison Study," *British Journal of Social Psychology* 45, no. 1 (2006), pp. 47–53.

28. For a review of the research on group norms, see J. R. Hackman, "Group Influences on Individuals in Organizations," in M. D. Dunnette and L. M. Hough (eds.), *Handbook of Industrial & Organizational Psychology,* 2nd ed., vol. 3 (Palo Alto, CA: Consulting Psychologists Press, 1992),

pp. 235–250. For a more recent discussion, see M. G. Ehrhart and S. E. Naumann, "Organizational Citizenship Behavior in Work Groups: A Group Norms Approach," *Journal of Applied Psychology,* December 2004, pp. 960–974.

29. Adapted from P. S. Goodman, E. Ravlin, and M. Schminke, "Understanding Groups in Organizations," in L. L. Cummings and B. M. Staw (eds.), *Research in Organizational Behavior,* vol. 9 (Greenwich, CT: JAI Press, 1987), p. 159.

30. E. Mayo, *The Human Problems of an Industrial Civilization* (New York: Macmillan, 1933); and F. J. Roethlisberger and W. J. Dickson, *Management and the Worker* (Cambridge, MA: Harvard University Press, 1939).

31. C. A. Kiesler and S. B. Kiesler, *Conformity* (Reading, MA: Addison-Wesley, 1969).

32. Ibid., p. 27.

33. S. E. Asch, "Effects of Group Pressure upon the Modification and Distortion of Judgments," in H. Guetzkow (ed.), *Groups, Leadership and Men* (Pittsburgh: Carnegie Press, 1951), pp. 177–190; and S. E. Asch, "Studies of Independence and Conformity: A Minority of One Against a Unanimous Majority," *Psychological Monographs: General and Applied* 70, no. 9 (1956), pp. 1–70.

34. R. Bond and P. B. Smith, "Culture and Conformity: A Meta-analysis of Studies Using Asch's (1952, 1956) Line Judgment Task," *Psychological Bulletin,* January 1996, pp. 111–137.

35. See S. L. Robinson and A. M. O'Leary-Kelly, "Monkey See, Monkey Do: The Influence of Work Groups on the Antisocial Behavior of Employees," *Academy of Management Journal,* December 1998, pp. 658–672; R. J. Bennett and S. L. Robinson, "The Past, Present, and Future of Workplace Deviance," in J. Greenberg (ed.), *Organizational Behavior: The State of the Science,* 2nd ed. (Mahwah, NJ: Erlbaum, 2003), pp. 237–271; and C. M. Berry, D. S. Ones, and P. R. Sackett, "Interpersonal Deviance, Organizational Deviance, and Their Common Correlates: A Review and Meta-Analysis," *Journal of Applied Psychology* 92, no. 2 (2007), pp. 410–424.

36. C. M. Pearson, L. M. Andersson, and C. L. Porath, "Assessing and Attacking Workplace Civility," *Organizational Dynamics* 29, no. 2 (2000), p. 130; see also C. Pearson, L. M. Andersson, and C. L. Porath, "Workplace Incivility," in S. Fox and P. E. Spector (eds.), *Counterproductive Work Behavior: Investigations of Actors and Targets* (Washington, DC: American Psychological Association, 2005), pp. 177–200.

37. S. Lim, L. M. Cortina, V. J. Magley, "Personal and Workgroup Incivility: Impact on Work and Health Outcomes," *Journal of Applied Psychology* 93, no. 1 (2008), pp. 95–107.

38. Robinson and O'Leary-Kelly, "Monkey See, Monkey Do"; and T. M. Glomb and H. Liao, "Interpersonal Aggression in Workgroups: Social Influence, Reciprocal, and Individual Effects," *Academy of Management Journal* 46 (2003), pp. 486–496.

39. P. Bamberger and M. Biron, "Group Norms and Excessive Absenteeism: The Role of Peer Referent Others," *Organizational Behavior and Human Decision Processes* 103, no. 2 (2007), pp. 179–196; and A. Väänänen, N. Tordera, M. Kivimäki, A. Kouvonen, J. Pentti, A. Linna, and J. Vahtera, "The Role of Work Group in Individual Sickness Absence Behavior," *Journal of Health & Human Behavior* 49, no. 4 (2008), pp. 452–467.

40. A. Erez, H. Elms, and E. Fong, "Lying, Cheating, Stealing: It Happens More in Groups," paper presented at the European Business Ethics Network Annual Conference, Budapest, Hungary, August 30, 2003.

41. S. L. Robinson and M. S. Kraatz, "Constructing the Reality of Normative Behavior: The Use of Neutralization Strategies by Organizational Deviants," in R. W. Griffin and A. O'Leary-Kelly (eds.), *Dysfunctional Behavior in Organizations: Violent and Deviant Behavior* (Greenwich, CT: JAI Press, 1998), pp. 203–220.

42. See R. S. Feldman, *Social Psychology,* 3rd ed. (Upper Saddle River, NJ: Prentice Hall, 2001), pp. 464–465.

43. Cited in Hackman, "Group Influences on Individuals in Organizations," p. 236.

44. R. R. Callister and J. A. Wall Jr., "Conflict Across Organizational Boundaries: Managed Care Organizations Versus Health Care Providers," *Journal of Applied Psychology* 86, no. 4 (2001), pp. 754–763; and P. Chattopadhyay, W. H. Glick, and G. P. Huber, "Organizational Actions in Response to Threats and Opportunities," *Academy of Management Journal* 44, no. 5 (2001), pp. 937–955.

45. O. J. Harvey and C. Consalvi, "Status and Conformity to Pressures in Informal Groups," *Journal of Abnormal and Social Psychology,* Spring 1960, pp. 182–187.

46. J. A. Wiggins, F. Dill, and R. D. Schwartz, "On 'Status-Liability,'" *Sociometry,* April–May 1965, pp. 197–209.

47. See J. M. Levine and R. L. Moreland, "Progress in Small Group Research," in J. T. Spence, J. M. Darley, and D. J. Foss (eds.), *Annual Review of Psychology,* vol. 41 (Palo Alto, CA: Annual Reviews, 1990), pp. 585–634; S. D. Silver, B. P. Cohen, and J. H. Crutchfield, "Status Differentiation and Information Exchange in Face-to-Face and Computer-Mediated Idea Generation," *Social Psychology Quarterly,* 1994, pp. 108–123; and J. M. Twenge, "Changes in Women's Assertiveness in Response to Status and Roles: A Cross-Temporal Meta-analysis, 1931–1993," *Journal of Personality and Social Psychology,* July 2001, pp. 133–145.

48. J. Greenberg, "Equity and Workplace Status: A Field Experiment," *Journal of Applied Psychology,* November 1988, pp. 606–613.

49. E. J. Thomas and C. F. Fink, "Effects of Group Size," *Psychological Bulletin,* July 1963, pp. 371–384; A. P. Hare, *Handbook of Small Group Research* (New York: The Free Press, 1976); and M. E. Shaw, *Group Dynamics: The Psychology of Small Group Behavior,* 3rd ed. (New York: McGraw-Hill, 1981).

50. G. H. Seijts and G. P. Latham, "The Effects of Goal Setting and Group Size on Performance in a Social Dilemma," *Canadian Journal of Behavioural Science* 32, no. 2 (2000), pp. 104–116.

51. Shaw, *Group Dynamics.*

52. See, for instance, D. R. Comer, "A Model of Social Loafing in Real Work Groups," *Human Relations,* June 1995, pp. 647–667; S. M. Murphy, S. J. Wayne, R. C. Liden, and B. Erdogan, "Understanding Social Loafing: The Role of Justice Perceptions and Exchange Relationships," *Human Relations,* January 2003, pp. 61–84; and R. C. Liden, S. J. Wayne, R. A. Jaworski, and N. Bennett, "Social Loafing: A Field Investigation," *Journal of Management,* April 2004, pp. 285–304.

53. W. Moede, "Die Richtlinien der Leistungs-Psychologie," *Industrielle Psychotechnik* 4 (1927), pp. 193–207. See also D. A. Kravitz and B. Martin, "Ringelmann Rediscovered: The Original Article," *Journal of Personality and Social Psychology,* May 1986, pp. 936–941.

54. See, for example, J. A. Shepperd, "Productivity Loss in Performance Groups: A Motivation Analysis," *Psychological Bulletin*, January 1993, pp. 67–81; and S. J. Karau and K. D. Williams, "Social Loafing: A Meta-analytic Review and Theoretical Integration," *Journal of Personality and Social Psychology*, October 1993, pp. 681–706.

55. S. G. Harkins and K. Szymanski, "Social Loafing and Group Evaluation," *Journal of Personality and Social Psychology*, December 1989, pp. 934–941.

56. A. Gunnthorsdottir and A. Rapoport, "Embedding Social Dilemmas in Intergroup Competition Reduces Free-Riding," *Organizational Behavior and Human Decision Processes* 101 (2006), pp. 184–199; E. M. Stark, J. D. Shaw, and M. K. Duffy, "Preference for Group Work, Winning Orientation, and Social Loafing Behavior in Groups," *Group and Organization Management* 32, no. 6 (2007), pp. 699–723.

57. B. Mullen and C. Cooper, "The Relation Between Group Cohesiveness and Performance: An Integration," *Psychological Bulletin*, March 1994, pp. 210–227; P. M. Podsakoff, S. B. MacKenzie, and M. Ahearne, "Moderating Effects of Goal Acceptance on the Relationship Between Group Cohesiveness and Productivity," *Journal of Applied Psychology*, December 1997, pp. 974–983; and D. J. Beal, R. R. Cohen, M. J. Burke, and C. L. McLendon, "Cohesion and Performance in Groups: A Meta-analytic Clarification of Construct Relations," *Journal of Applied Psychology*, December 2003, pp. 989–1004.

58. Ibid.

59. Based on J. L. Gibson, J. M. Ivancevich, and J. H. Donnelly, Jr., *Organizations*, 8th ed. (Burr Ridge, IL: Irwin, 1994), p. 323.

60. N. Foote, E. Matson, L. Weiss, and E. Wenger, "Leveraging Group Knowledge for High-Performance Decision-Making," *Organizational Dynamics* 31, no. 2 (2002), pp. 280–295.

61. See N. R. F. Maier, "Assets and Liabilities in Group Problem Solving: The Need for an Integrative Function," *Psychological Review*, April 1967, pp. 239–249; G. W. Hill, "Group Versus Individual Performance: Are N+1 Heads Better Than One?" *Psychological Bulletin*, May 1982, pp. 517–539; M. D. Johnson and J. R. Hollenbeck, "Collective Wisdom as an Oxymoron: Team-Based Structures as Impediments to Learning," in J. Langan-Fox, C. L. Cooper, and R. J. Klimoski (eds), *Research Companion to the Dysfunctional Workplace: Management Challenges and Symptoms* (Northampton, MA: Edward Elgar Publishing, 2007), pp. 319–331; and R. F. Martell and M. R. Borg, "A Comparison of the Behavioral Rating Accuracy of Groups and Individuals," *Journal of Applied Psychology*, February 1993, pp. 43–50.

62. D. Gigone and R. Hastie, "Proper Analysis of the Accuracy of Group Judgments," *Psychological Bulletin*, January 1997, pp. 149–167; and B. L. Bonner, S. D. Sillito, and M. R. Baumann, "Collective Estimation: Accuracy, Expertise, and Extroversion as Sources of Intra-Group Influence," *Organizational Behavior and Human Decision Processes* 103 (2007), pp. 121–133.

63. See, for example, W. C. Swap and Associates, *Group Decision Making* (Newbury Park, CA: Sage, 1984).

64. D. D. Henningsen, M. G. Cruz, and M. L. Miller, "Role of Social Loafing in Predeliberation Decision Making," *Group Dynamics: Theory, Research, and Practice* 4, no. 2 (June 2000), pp. 168–175.

65. J. H. Davis, *Group Performance* (Reading, MA: Addison-Wesley, 1969); J. P. Wanous and M. A. Youtz, "Solution Diversity and the Quality of Group Decisions," *Academy of Management Journal*, March 1986, pp. 149–159; and R. Libby, K. T. Trotman, and I. Zimmer, "Member Variation, Recognition of Expertise, and Group Performance," *Journal of Applied Psychology*, February 1987, pp. 81–87.

66. I. L. Janis, *Groupthink* (Boston: Houghton Mifflin, 1982); W. Park, "A Review of Research on Groupthink," *Journal of Behavioral Decision Making*, July 1990, pp. 229–245; J. N. Choi and M. U. Kim, "The Organizational Application of Groupthink and Its Limits in Organizations," *Journal of Applied Psychology*, April 1999, pp. 297–306; and W. W. Park, "A Comprehensive Empirical Investigation of the Relationships Among Variables of the Groupthink Model," *Journal of Organizational Behavior*, December 2000, pp. 873–887.

67. Janis, *Groupthink*.

68. M. E. Turner and A. R. Pratkanis, "Mitigating Groupthink by Stimulating Constructive Conflict," in C. De Dreu and E. Van de Vliert (eds.), *Using Conflict in Organizations* (London: Sage, 1997), pp. 53–71.

69. Ibid., p. 68.

70. See N. R. F. Maier, *Principles of Human Relations* (New York: Wiley, 1952); I. L. Janis, *Groupthink: Psychological Studies of Policy Decisions and Fiascoes*, 2nd ed. (Boston: Houghton Mifflin, 1982); N. Richardson Ahlfinger and J. K. Esser, "Testing the Groupthink Model: Effects of Promotional Leadership and Conformity Predisposition," *Social Behavior & Personality* 29, no. 1 (2001), pp. 31–41; and S. Schultz-Hardt, F. C. Brodbeck, A. Mojzisch, R. Kerschreiter, and D. Frey, "Group Decision Making in Hidden Profile Situations: Dissent as a Facilitator for Decision Quality," *Journal of Personality and Social Psychology* 91, no. 6 (2006), pp. 1080–1093.

71. See D. J. Isenberg, "Group Polarization: A Critical Review and Meta-analysis," *Journal of Personality and Social Psychology*, December 1986, pp. 1141–1151; J. L. Hale and F. J. Boster, "Comparing Effect Coded Models of Choice Shifts," *Communication Research Reports*, April 1988, pp. 180–186; and P. W. Paese, M. Bieser, and M. E. Tubbs, "Framing Effects and Choice Shifts in Group Decision Making," *Organizational Behavior and Human Decision Processes*, October 1993, pp. 149–165.

72. See, for example, N. Kogan and M. A. Wallach, "Risk Taking as a Function of the Situation, the Person, and the Group," in *New Directions in Psychology*, vol. 3 (New York: Holt, Rinehart and Winston, 1967); and M. A. Wallach, N. Kogan, and D. J. Bem, "Group Influence on Individual Risk Taking," *Journal of Abnormal and Social Psychology* 65 (1962), pp. 75–86.

73. R. D. Clark III, "Group-Induced Shift Toward Risk: A Critical Appraisal," *Psychological Bulletin*, October 1971, pp. 251–270.

74. Z. Krizan and R. S. Baron, "Group Polarization and Choice-Dilemmas: How Important is Self-Categorization?" *European Journal of Social Psychology* 37, no. 1 (2007), pp. 191–201.

75. A. F. Osborn, *Applied Imagination: Principles and Procedures of Creative Thinking*, 3rd ed. (New York: Scribner, 1963). See also R. P. McGlynn, D. McGurk, V. S. Effland, N. L. Johll, and D. J. Harding, "Brainstorming and Task Performance in Groups Constrained by Evidence," *Organizational Behavior and*

Human Decision Processes, January 2004, pp. 75–87; and R. C. Litchfield, "Brainstorming Reconsidered: A Goal-Based View," *Academy of Management Review* 33, no. 3 (2008), pp. 649–668.

76. N. L. Kerr and R. S. Tindale, "Group Performance and Decision-Making," *Annual Review of Psychology* 55 (2004), pp. 623–655.

77. See A. L. Delbecq, A. H. Van deVen, and D. H. Gustafson, *Group Techniques for Program Planning: A Guide to Nominal and Delphi Processes* (Glenview, IL: Scott Foresman, 1975); and P. B. Paulus and H.-C. Yang, "Idea Generation in Groups: A Basis for Creativity in Organizations," *Organizational Behavior and Human Decision Processing,* May 2000, pp. 76–87.

78. C. Faure, "Beyond Brainstorming: Effects of Different Group Procedures on Selection of Ideas and Satisfaction with the Process," *Journal of Creative Behavior* 38 (2004), pp. 13–34.

79. See, for instance, A. B. Hollingshead and J. E. McGrath, "Computer-Assisted Groups: A Critical Review of the Empirical Research," in R. A. Guzzo and E. Salas (eds.), *Team Effectiveness and Decision Making in Organizations* (San Francisco: Jossey-Bass, 1995), pp. 46–78.

80. B. B. Baltes, M. W. Dickson, M. P. Sherman, C. C. Bauer, and J. LaGanke, "Computer-Mediated Communication and Group Decision Making: A Meta-analysis," *Organizational Behavior and Human Decision Processes,* January 2002, pp. 156–179.

81. See G. Hofstede, *Cultures and Organizations: Software of the Mind* (New York, McGraw-Hill, 1991).

82. This section is based on P. R. Harris and R. T. Moran, *Managing Cultural Differences,* 5th ed. (Houston: Gulf Publishing, 1999).

83. D. S. Staples and L. Zhao, "The Effects of Cultural Diversity in Virtual Teams Versus Face-to-Face Teams," *Group Decision and Negotiation,* July 2006, pp. 389–406.

84. K. W. Phillips and D. L. Loyd, "When Surface and Deep-Level Diversity Collide: The Effects on Dissenting Group Members," *Organizational Behavior and Human Decision Processes* 99 (2006), pp. 143–160; and S. R. Sommers, "On Racial Diversity and Group Decision Making: Identifying Multiple Effects of Racial Composition on Jury Deliberations," *Journal of Personality and Social Psychology,* April 2006, pp. 597–612.

85. E. Mannix and M. A. Neale, "What Differences Make a Difference? The Promise and Reality of Diverse Teams in Organizations," *Psychological Science in the Public Interest,* October 2005, pp. 31–55.

86. T. P. Verney, "Role Perception Congruence, Performance, and Satisfaction," in D. J. Vredenburgh and R. S. Schuler (eds.), *Effective Management: Research and Application,* Proceedings of the 20th Annual Eastern Academy of Management, Pittsburgh, PA, May 1983, pp. 24–27.

87. Ibid.

88. A. G. Bedeian and A. A. Armenakis, "A Path-Analytic Study of the Consequences of Role Conflict and Ambiguity," *Academy of Management Journal,* June 1981, pp. 417–424; and P. L. Perrewe, K. L. Zellars, G. R. Ferris, A. M. Rossi, C. J. Kacmar, and D. A. Ralston, "Neutralizing Job Stressors: Political Skill as an Antidote to the Dysfunctional Consequences of Role Conflict," *Academy of Management Journal,* February 2004, pp. 141–152.

89. Shaw, *Group Dynamics.*

90. B. Mullen, C. Symons, L. Hu, and E. Salas, "Group Size, Leadership Behavior, and Subordinate Satisfaction," *Journal of General Psychology,* April 1989, pp. 155–170.

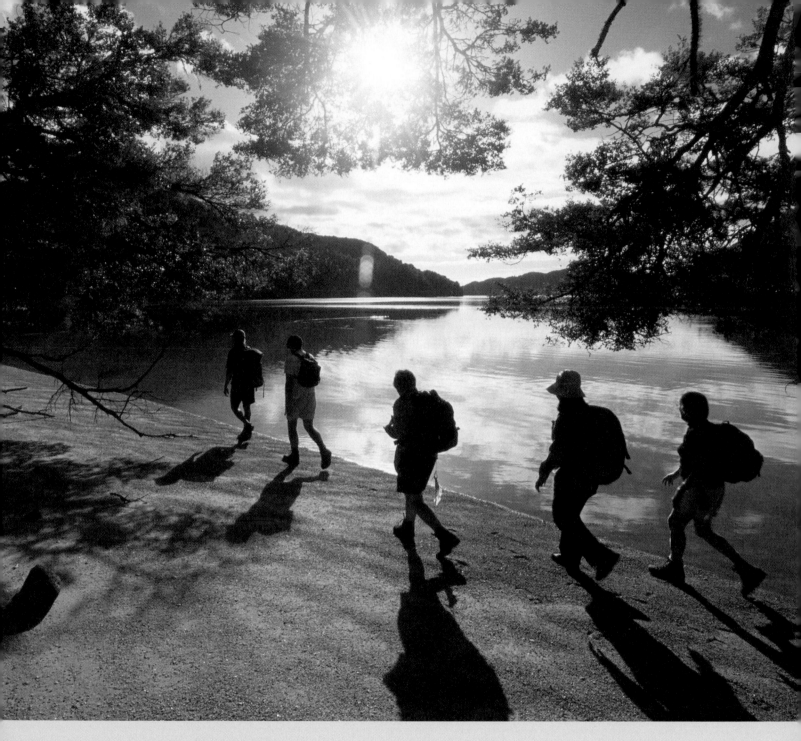

LEARNING OBJECTIVES

After studying this chapter, you should be able to:

1 Analyze the growing popularity of teams in organizations.

2 Contrast groups and teams.

3 Compare and contrast four types of teams.

4 Identify the characteristics of effective teams.

5 Show how organizations can create team players.

6 Decide when to use individuals instead of teams.

7 Show how our understanding of teams differs in a global context.

Understanding Work Teams

We're going to turn this team around 360 degrees.
—Jason Kidd

"EVERYONE HERE'S GOING TO DIE"

In these times, spending over $2 million for a team-building exercise for 200 employees seems extravagant. But don't tell that to Seagate Technology. Every year, the world's leading manufacturer of hard disk drives has sent 200 employees from its Silicon Valley home to far-flung corners of the globe for a week of team building. Employees have biked the streets of Malaysia and Thailand and hiked mountain locations near (Colorado and California) and far (China and the Alps).

This past year, Seagate's team-building retreat took place in the mountains of New Zealand. This is *Lord of the Rings* territory; New Zealand is one of the most mountainous countries on Earth, and more than 75 percent of the country's surface consists of mountains and hills. So, even though Seagate's engineers, managers, and developers are an educated, smart, and confident lot, when their team leader, CEO Bill Watkins, told them they were going to die, some were a bit nervous.

Why has Seagate put its best and brightest through this stressful—and extraordinarily expensive—exercise every year? Even though 2,000 employees always apply for the 200 spots, Watkins denies it's merely a perk. "I'm challenging your life," he says. Another organizer says, "This is about behavior modification." The week in New Zealand includes a 40-kilometer race through the mountains that stood for Middle-earth in the film series, a 17-kilometer hike through a bog, and an 18-kilometer bike ride over mountain terrain. Despite the rigors of the exercises, Watkins' comment about dying has less to do with these challenges than with asking participants to think about their life's choices. "Are you doing what you want to do in your life?" he asks.

Watkins and Seagate justify their team-building adventures on the premise that teamwork, and therefore team building, are crucial to the success of their business. "What's so fascinating, and sometimes so frustrating, about drives is that no single person knows how to make one," Watkins says. "It takes people from a lot of different disciplines coming together—from a lot of different cultures, too." According to Watkins, by being forced to depend on others in an environment in which most have little experience, the 40 five-person teams learn lifelong lessons outside work that they are particularly likely to bring to the office.

Though the business press has been enthusiastic about the exercises—*Business Week* and *Fortune* reporters have been asked to participate over the years—the return on the team-building investment was difficult to quantify. Then in 2009, following several years of lackluster performance, Seagate laid off more than 4,000 employees in two waves. Watkins was one of the casualties, and so, perhaps, was Seagate's interesting but expensive foray into team-building.[1]

313

T eams are increasingly the primary means for organizing work in contemporary business firms. As the Seagate example shows, organizations are often willing to invest millions in building team skills. In fact, there are few more damaging insults than "not a team player." Do you think you're a team player? Take the following self-assessment to find out.

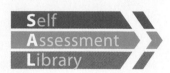

HOW GOOD AM I AT BUILDING AND LEADING A TEAM?

In the Self-Assessment Library (available on CD or online), take assessment II.B.6 (How Good Am I at Building and Leading a Team?) and answer the following questions.

1. *Did you score as high as you thought you would? Why or why not?*
2. *Do you think you can improve your score? If so, how? If not, why not?*
3. *Do you think there is such a thing as team players? If yes, what are their behaviors?*

Why Have Teams Become So Popular?

Decades ago, when companies such as W. L. Gore, Volvo, and General Foods introduced teams into their production processes, it made news because no one else was doing it. Today, it's just the opposite. The organization that *doesn't* use teams has become newsworthy. Teams are everywhere.

How do we explain the current popularity of teams? As organizations have restructured themselves to compete more effectively and efficiently, they have turned to teams as a better way to use employee talents. Teams

1 Analyze the growing popularity of teams in organizations.

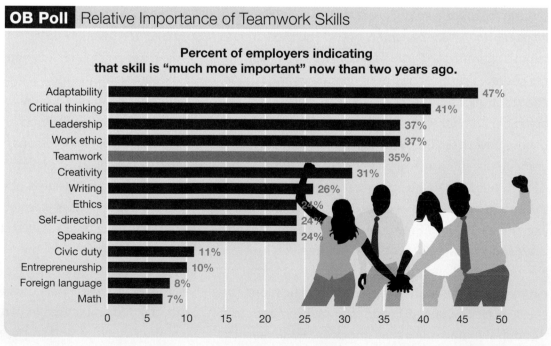

OB Poll Relative Importance of Teamwork Skills

Percent of employers indicating that skill is "much more important" now than two years ago.

Skill	Percent
Adaptability	47%
Critical thinking	41%
Leadership	37%
Work ethic	37%
Teamwork	35%
Creativity	31%
Writing	26%
Ethics	24%
Self-direction	24%
Speaking	24%
Civic duty	11%
Entrepreneurship	10%
Foreign language	8%
Math	7%

Source: Based on Critical Skills Needs and Resources for the Changing Workforce (Alexandria, VA: Society for Human Resource Management), 2008.

are more flexible and responsive to changing events than traditional departments or other forms of permanent groupings. They can quickly assemble, deploy, refocus, and disband. But don't overlook the motivational properties of teams. Consistent with our discussion in Chapter 7 of employee involvement as a motivator, teams facilitate employee participation in operating decisions. So another explanation for their popularity is that they are an effective means for management to democratize organizations and increase employee motivation.

The fact that organizations have turned to teams doesn't necessarily mean they're always effective. Decision makers, as humans, can be swayed by fads and herd mentality. Are teams truly effective? What conditions affect their potential? How do members work together? These are some of the questions we'll answer in this chapter.

Differences Between Groups and Teams

2 Contrast groups and teams.

Groups and teams are not the same thing. In this section, we define and clarify the difference between work groups and work teams.[2]

In Chapter 9, we defined a *group* as two or more individuals, interacting and interdependent, who have come together to achieve particular objectives. A **work group** is a group that interacts primarily to share information and make decisions to help each member perform within his or her area of responsibility.

Work groups have no need or opportunity to engage in collective work that requires joint effort. So their performance is merely the summation of each group member's individual contribution. There is no positive synergy that would create an overall level of performance greater than the sum of the inputs.

A **work team**, on the other hand, generates positive synergy through coordinated effort. The individual efforts result in a level of performance greater than the sum of those individual inputs. Exhibit 10-1 highlights the differences between work groups and work teams.

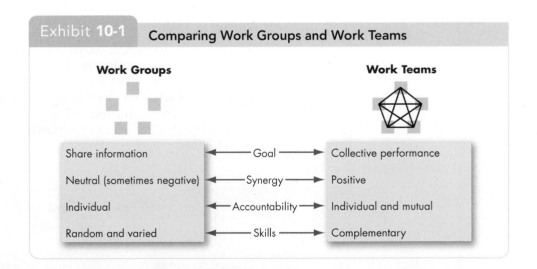

Exhibit 10-1   Comparing Work Groups and Work Teams

Work Groups		Work Teams
Share information	←— Goal —→	Collective performance
Neutral (sometimes negative)	←— Synergy —→	Positive
Individual	←— Accountability —→	Individual and mutual
Random and varied	←— Skills —→	Complementary

work group   *A group that interacts primarily to share information and to make decisions to help each group member perform within his or her area of responsibility.*

work team   *A group whose individual efforts result in performance that is greater than the sum of the individual inputs.*

These definitions help clarify why so many organizations have recently restructured work processes around teams. Management is looking for positive synergy that will allow the organizations to increase performance. The extensive use of teams creates the *potential* for an organization to generate greater outputs with no increase in inputs. Notice, however, that we said *potential*. There is nothing inherently magical that ensures the achievement of positive synergy in the creation of teams. Merely calling a *group* a *team* doesn't automatically improve its performance. As we show later in this chapter, effective teams have certain common characteristics. If management hopes to gain increases in organizational performance through the use of teams, its teams must possess these.

Types of Teams

3 Compare and contrast four types of teams.

Teams can make products, provide services, negotiate deals, coordinate projects, offer advice, and make decisions.[3] In this section, we describe the four most common types of teams in an organization: *problem-solving teams, self-managed work teams, cross-functional teams*, and *virtual teams* (see Exhibit 10-2).

Problem-Solving Teams

In the past, teams were typically composed of 5 to 12 hourly employees from the same department who met for a few hours each week to discuss ways of improving quality, efficiency, and the work environment.[4] In these **problem-solving teams**, members share ideas or suggest how work processes and methods can be improved; they rarely have the authority to unilaterally implement any of their suggestions. Merrill Lynch created a problem-solving team to figure out ways to reduce the number of days it took to open a new cash management account.[5] By suggesting cutting the number of steps from 46 to 36, the team reduced the average number of days from 15 to 8.

Self-Managed Work Teams

Problem-solving teams only make recommendations. Some organizations have gone further and created teams that not only solve problems but implement solutions and take responsibility for outcomes.

Self-managed work teams are groups of employees (typically 10 to 15 in number) who perform highly related or interdependent jobs and take on many of the responsibilities of their former supervisors.[6] Typically, these tasks are planning and scheduling work, assigning tasks to members, making operating deci-

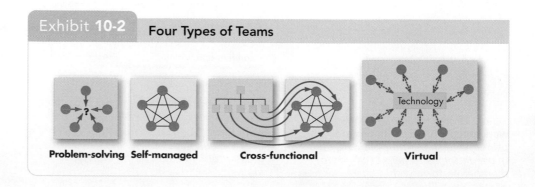

Exhibit **10-2**   Four Types of Teams

Problem-solving   Self-managed   Cross-functional   Virtual

All employees at the Louis Vuitton factory in Ducey, France, work in problem-solving teams, with each team member focusing on one product at a time. Team members are encouraged to suggest improvements in manufacturing work methods and processes as well as product quality. When a team was asked to make a test run on a prototype of a new handbag, team members discovered that decorative studs were causing the bag's zipper to bunch up. The team alerted managers, who had technicians move the studs away from the zipper, which solved the problem.

sions, taking action on problems, and working with suppliers and customers. Fully self-managed work teams even select their own members and evaluate each other's performance. Supervisory positions take on decreased importance and are sometimes even eliminated.

But research on the effectiveness of self-managed work teams has not been uniformly positive.[7] Self-managed teams do not typically manage conflicts well. When disputes arise, members stop cooperating and power struggles ensue, which leads to lower group performance.[8] Moreover, although individuals on these teams report higher levels of job satisfaction than other individuals, they also sometimes have higher absenteeism and turnover rates.

Cross-Functional Teams

The Boeing Company created a team made up of employees from production, planning, quality control, tooling, design engineering, and information systems to automate shims on the company's C-17 program. The team's suggestions resulted in drastically reduced cycle time and cost as well as improved quality.[9] This example illustrates the use of **cross-functional teams**, made up of employees from about the same hierarchical level but different work areas, who come together to accomplish a task.

Many organizations have used horizontal, boundary-spanning groups for decades. In the 1960s IBM created a large task force of employees from across departments to develop its highly successful System 360. Today cross-functional teams are so widely used it is hard to imagine a major organizational undertaking without one. All the major automobile manufacturers—Toyota, Honda,

---

problem-solving teams *Groups of 5 to 12 employees from the same department who meet for a few hours each week to discuss ways of improving quality, efficiency, and the work environment.*

self-managed work teams *Groups of 10 to 15 people who take on responsibilities of their former supervisors.*

cross-functional teams *Employees from about the same hierarchical level, but from different work areas, who come together to accomplish a task.*

Nissan, BMW, GM, Ford, and Chrysler—currently use this form of team to co-ordinate complex projects. Harley-Davidson relies on specific cross-functional teams to manage each line of its motorcycles. The teams include employees from design, manufacturing, and purchasing as well as representatives from key outside suppliers.[10]

Cross-functional teams are an effective means of allowing people from diverse areas within or even between organizations to exchange information, develop new ideas, solve problems, and coordinate complex projects. Of course, cross-functional teams are no picnic to manage. Their early stages of development are often long, as members learn to work with diversity and complexity. It takes time to build trust and teamwork, especially among people from different backgrounds with different experiences and perspectives.

Virtual Teams

The teams described in the preceding section do their work face to face. **Virtual teams** use computer technology to unite physically dispersed members and achieve a common goal.[11] They allow people to collaborate online—using communication links such as wide-area networks, video conferencing, or e-mail—whether they're a room away or continents apart. Virtual teams are so pervasive, and technology has advanced so far, that it's probably a bit of a misnomer to call them "virtual." Nearly all teams today do at least some of their work remotely.

Despite their ubiquity, virtual teams face special challenges. They may suffer because there is less social rapport and direct interaction among members. They aren't able to duplicate the normal give-and-take of face-to-face discussion. Especially when members haven't personally met, virtual teams tend to be more task oriented and exchange less social–emotional information than face-to-face teams do. Not surprisingly, their members report less satisfaction with the group interaction process than do face-to-face teams. For virtual teams to be effective, management should ensure that (1) trust is established among members (one inflammatory remark in a team member e-mail can severely undermine team trust); (2) team progress is monitored closely (so the team doesn't lose sight of its goals and no team member "disappears"); and (3) the efforts and products of the team are publicized throughout the organization (so the team does not become invisible).[12]

Creating Effective Teams

4 Identify the characteristics of effective teams.

Many have tried to identify factors related to team effectiveness.[13] However, some studies have organized what was once a "veritable laundry list of characteristics"[14] into a relatively focused model.[15] Exhibit 10-3 summarizes what we currently know about what makes teams effective. As you'll see, it builds on many of the group concepts introduced in Chapter 9.

The following discussion is based on the model in Exhibit 10-3. Keep in mind two points. First, teams differ in form and structure. Because the model attempts to generalize across all varieties of teams, avoid rigidly applying its predictions to all teams.[16] Use it as a guide. Second, the model assumes teamwork is preferable to individual work. Creating "effective" teams when individuals can do the job better is like solving the wrong problem perfectly.

We can organize the key components of effective teams into three general categories. First are the resources and other *contextual* influences that make teams effective. The second relates to the team's *composition*. Finally, *process* variables are events within the team that influence effectiveness. What does *team ef-*

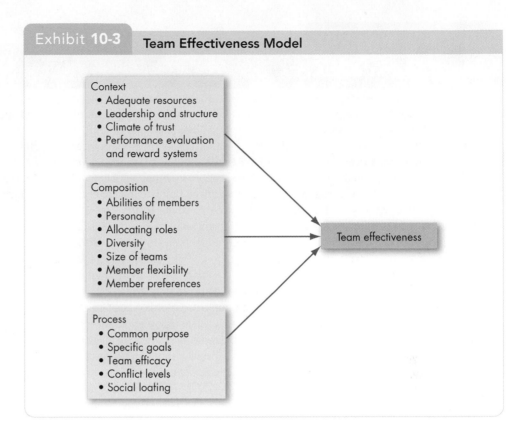

Exhibit 10-3   Team Effectiveness Model

fectiveness mean in this model? Typically, it has included objective measures of the team's productivity, managers' ratings of the team's performance, and aggregate measures of member satisfaction.

Context: What Factors Determine Whether Teams Are Successful

The four contextual factors most significantly related to team performance are adequate resources, effective leadership, a climate of trust, and a performance evaluation and reward system that reflects team contributions.

Adequate Resources   Teams are part of a larger organization system; every work team relies on resources outside the group to sustain it. A scarcity of resources directly reduces the ability of a team to perform its job effectively and achieve its goals. As one study concluded, after looking at 13 factors related to group performance, "perhaps one of the most important characteristics of an effective work group is the support the group receives from the organization."[17] This support includes timely information, proper equipment, adequate staffing, encouragement, and administrative assistance.

Leadership and Structure   Teams can't function if they can't agree on who is to do what and ensure all members share the workload. Agreeing on the

International OB

Global Virtual Teams

Years ago, before e-mail, instant messaging, or live video conferencing were ever dreamed of, work team members used to gather in one location, possibly with one or two members a train or plane ride away. Today, however, the reach of corporations spans many countries, so teams must work together across international lines. Multinationals use global virtual teams to gain a competitive advantage.

Global virtual teams have pros and cons. On the positive side, because team members come from different countries with different knowledge and points of view, they may develop creative ideas and solutions to problems that work for multiple cultures. On the negative side, such teams face more challenges than traditional teams. Members who do not accept individuals from different cultures may

hesitate to share information openly, which can create problems of trust.

Another challenge is that global virtual team members may have different ideas about how they should interact. One study of Belgian, Indian, and U.S. work teams revealed that the Belgian and Indian teams were more likely to value respectfulness in their virtual interactions. This makes sense since Belgium and India score higher on power distance (see Chapter 4), meaning people are more attuned to status, hierarchical, and power differences.

To create and implement effective global virtual teams, managers must carefully select employees they believe will thrive in such an environment. Employees must be comfortable with communicating electronically and be open to different ideas. Speaking multiple languages may also be necessary. In

addition, team members must realize the values they hold may be vastly different from those of their teammates.

Although global virtual teams face many challenges, companies that implement them effectively can realize tremendous rewards through the diverse knowledge they gain.

Sources: Based on D. M. Dekker, C. G. Rutte, and P. T. Van den Berg, "Cultural Differences in the Perception of Critical Interaction Behaviors in Global Virtual Teams," *International Journal of Intercultural Relations* 32, no. 5 (2008), pp. 441–452; N. Zakaria, A. Amelinckx, and D. Wilemon, "Working Together Apart? Building a Knowledge-Sharing Culture for Global Virtual Teams," *Creativity and Innovation Management* 13, no. 1 (March 2004), pp. 15–29; C. J. Friday, "Global Virtual Teams: Challenges of Technology and Culture," in E. Biech (ed.), *The 2008 Pfeiffer Annual: Consulting* (pp. 205–213), San Francisco, CA: Pfeiffer/Wiley.

specifics of work and how they fit together to integrate individual skills requires leadership and structure, either from management or from the team members themselves. It's true in self-managed teams that team members absorb many of the duties typically assumed by managers. However, a manager's job then becomes managing *outside* (rather than inside) the team.

Leadership is especially important in **multi-team systems**, in which different teams coordinate their efforts to produce a desired outcome. Here, leaders need to empower teams by delegating responsibility to them, and they play the role of facilitator, making sure the teams work together rather than against one another.[18] Teams that establish shared leadership by effectively delegating it are more effective than teams with a traditional single-leader structure.[19]

Climate of Trust   Members of effective teams trust each other. They also exhibit trust in their leaders.[20] Interpersonal trust among team members facilitates cooperation, reduces the need to monitor each others' behavior, and bonds members around the belief that others on the team won't take advantage of them. Team members are more likely to take risks and expose vulnerabilities when they believe they can trust others on their team. And, as we will discuss in Chapter 12, trust is the foundation of leadership. It allows a team to accept and commit to its leader's goals and decisions.

Performance Evaluation and Reward Systems   How do you get team members to be both individually and jointly accountable? Individual performance

An Ethical Choice

Preventing Team Mistakes

Surgery is almost always performed by a team, but in many cases it's a team in name only. So says a new study of more than 2,100 surgeons, anesthesiologists, and nurses.

Researchers asked the respondents to "describe the quality of communication and collaboration you have experienced" with other members of the surgical unit. Perhaps not surprisingly, surgeons were given the lowest ratings for teamwork and nurses the highest. "The study is somewhat humbling to me," said Martin Makary, the lead author on the study and a surgeon at Johns Hopkins. "There's a lot of pride in the surgical community. We need to balance out the captain-of-the-ship doctrine."

The researchers attribute many operating room errors, such as sponges left in patients and operations performed on the wrong part of the body, to poor teamwork. But improving the system is easier said than done. One recent study in Pennsylvania found that, over an 18-month period, there were 174 cases of surgeons operating on the wrong limb or body part. Johns Hopkins is modeling surgical team training after airline crew training.

"Teamwork is an important component of patient safety," says Makary.

Tell that to a patient at Rhode Island Hospital. In 2009, a surgeon operated on the wrong side of a child's mouth. No one on the surgical team bothered to check the surgeon's mark. What's especially discouraging about the case is that it appears the surgical team followed existing protocols, including a time-out in which all members agreed the surgery should take place on the right side of the mouth (when in fact it should have been the left). The error was the fourth wrong-site surgery at Rhode Island Hospital since 2007.

These cases are hardly unusual. One study of British surgical teams revealed errors in 40 percent of cases. In 2009, a surgical team at Atlanta's Northside Hospital performed a double mastectomy when only one breast was to be removed. At Atlanta Medical Center, a surgical team mistakenly drilled into the wrong side of a patient's head.

Assuming you aren't headed for a career as a surgical team member, what can this research tell you about your individual ethical responsibilities as a team member?

1. Recognize that the pressure to be a good team player and the diffusion of responsibility often lead us to question too little and assume someone else will catch any error. Yes, by questioning, you run the risk of being labeled as "not a team player," but if you accept errors or marginal performance the outcomes may reflect negatively on your career.

2. Realize all members of teams are not created equal. A surgeon in the operating room and a pilot in the cockpit tend to dominate teams. That makes it all the more important that you question their decision making, taking care to be respectful and civil in so doing.

3. If you have a say in the composition of the team, aim for diversity. As we noted in Chapter 2, some evidence suggests diverse teams are less prone to groupthink.

Sources: A. Young, "Medical Mistakes Unhappy Reality," *The Atlanta Journal-Constitution* (May 03, 2009), www.ajc.com; F. J. Freyer, "R.I. Hospital Says Marking Wasn't Verified in Wrong-Site Surgery," *The Providence Journal* (June 13, 2009), www.projo.com; E. Nagourney, "Surgical Teams Found Lacking, in Teamwork," *New York Times* (May 9, 2006), p. D6; and "Nurses Give Surgeons Poor Grades on Teamwork in OR," *Forbes* (May 5, 2006), www.forbes.com.

---

evaluations and incentives may interfere with the development of high-performance teams. So in addition to evaluating and rewarding employees for their individual contributions, management should modify the traditional, individually oriented evaluation and reward system to reflect team performance.[21] Group-based appraisals, profit sharing, gainsharing, small-group incentives, and other system modifications can reinforce team effort and commitment.

multi-team systems   *Systems in which different teams need to coordinate their efforts to produce a desired outcome.*

Team Composition

The team composition category includes variables that relate to how teams should be staffed—the ability and personality of team members, allocation of roles and diversity, size of the team, and members' preference for teamwork.

Abilities of Members   Part of a team's performance depends on the knowledge, skills, and abilities of its individual members.[22] It's true we occasionally read about an athletic team of mediocre players who, because of excellent coaching, determination, and precision teamwork, beat a far more talented group. But such cases make the news precisely because they are unusual. A team's performance is not merely the summation of its individual members' abilities. However, these abilities set limits on what members can do and how effectively they will perform on a team.

A team requires three different types of skills. First, it needs people who have *technical expertise*. Second, it needs people who have the *problem-solving and decision-making skills* to identify problems, generate and evaluate alternatives, and make competent choices. Finally, teams need people with good listening, feedback, conflict resolution, and other *interpersonal skills*.[23] The right mix of these skills is crucial, but they don't all have to be in place at the beginning. It's not uncommon for one or more members to take responsibility for learning the skills in which the group is deficient, thus allowing the team to reach its full potential.

Research reveals some insights into team composition and performance. First, when the task entails considerable thought (solving a complex problem such as reengineering an assembly line), high-ability teams (composed of mostly intelligent members) do better than lower-ability teams, especially when the workload is distributed evenly. That way, team performance does not depend on the weakest link. High-ability teams are also more adaptable to changing situations; they can more effectively apply existing knowledge to new problems.

Second, when tasks are simple, high-ability teams do not perform as well, perhaps because members become bored and turn their attention to other activi-

Senior product scientists Syed Abbas and Albert Post and technology team manager Laurie Coyle functioned as a high-ability team in developing Unilever's Dove Nutrium bar soap. In solving the complex problems involved in product innovation, the intelligent members of Unilever's research and development teams have advanced science degrees, the ability to think creatively, and the interpersonal skills needed to perform effectively with other team members.

ties that are more stimulating, whereas low-ability teams stay on task. High-ability teams should be reserved for tackling the tough problems. So matching team ability to the task is important.

Finally, the ability of the team's leader also matters. Smart team leaders help less-intelligent team members when they struggle with a task. But a less-intelligent leader can neutralize the effect of a high-ability team.[24]

Personality of Members   We demonstrated in Chapter 5 that personality significantly influences individual employee behavior. Many of the dimensions identified in the Big Five personality model are also relevant to team effectiveness; a recent review of the literature identified three.[25] Specifically, teams that rate higher on mean levels of conscientiousness and openness to experience tend to perform better, and the minimum level of team member agreeableness also matters: teams did worse when they had one or more highly disagreeable members. Perhaps one bad apple *can* spoil the whole bunch!

Research has also provided us with a good idea about why these personality traits are important to teams. Conscientious people are valuable in teams because they're good at backing up other team members, and they're also good at sensing when that support is truly needed. Open team members communicate better with one another and throw out more ideas, which makes teams composed of open people more creative and innovative.[26]

Suppose an organization needs to create 20 teams of 4 people each and has 40 highly conscientious people and 40 who score low on conscientiousness. Would the organization be better off (a) forming 10 teams of highly conscientious people and 10 teams of members low on conscientiousness, or (b) "seeding" each team with 2 people who scored high and 2 who scored low on conscientiousness?

Perhaps surprisingly, evidence suggests option (a) is the best choice; performance across the teams will be higher if the organization forms 10 highly conscientious teams and 10 teams low in conscientiousness. "This may be because, in such teams, members who are highly conscientious not only must perform their own tasks but also must perform or re-do the tasks of low-conscientious members. It may also be because such diversity leads to feelings of contribution inequity."[27]

Allocation of Roles   Teams have different needs, and members should be selected to ensure all the various roles are filled. A study of 778 major league baseball teams over a 21-year period highlights the importance of assigning roles appropriately.[28] As you might expect, teams with more experienced and skilled members performed better. However, the experience and skill of those in core roles who handle more of the workflow of the team, and who are central to all work processes (in this case, pitchers and catchers), were especially vital. In other words, put your most able, experienced, and conscientious workers in the most central roles in a team.

We can identify nine potential team roles (see Exhibit 10-4). Successful work teams have selected people to play all these roles based on their skills and preferences.[29] (On many teams, individuals will play multiple roles.) To increase the likelihood the team members will work well together, managers need to understand the individual strengths each person can bring to a team, select members with their strengths in mind, and allocate work assignments that fit with members' preferred styles.

Diversity of Members   In Chapter 9, we discussed research on the effect of diversity on groups. How does *team* diversity affect *team* performance?

Many of us hold the optimistic view that diversity should be a good thing— diverse teams should benefit from differing perspectives and do better. Two

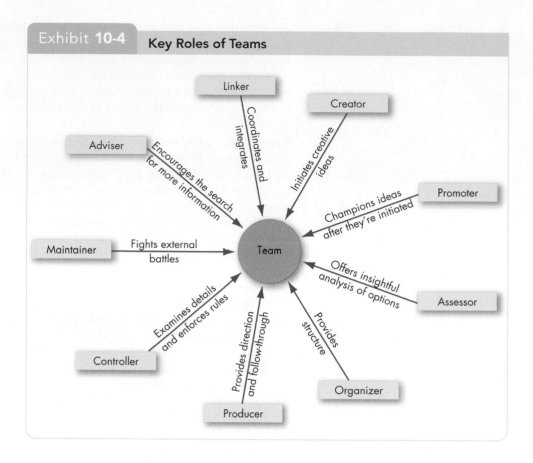

Exhibit 10-4   **Key Roles of Teams**

meta-analytic reviews of the research literature show, however, that demographic diversity is essentially unrelated to team performance overall.[30] One qualifier is that gender and ethnic diversity have more negative effects in occupations dominated by white or male employees, but in more demographically balanced occupations diversity is less of a problem. Diversity in function and expertise are positively related to group performance, but these effects are quite small and depend on the situation.

One of the pervasive challenges with teams is that while diversity may have real potential benefits, a team is deeply focused on commonly held information. But to realize their creative potential, diverse teams need to focus not on their similarities but on their differences. Some evidence suggests when team members believe others have more expertise, they will work to support those members, leading to higher levels of effectiveness.[31] The key is for members of diverse teams to communicate what they uniquely know and also what they don't know. Proper leadership can also improve the performance of diverse teams.[32] When leaders provide an inspirational common goal for members with varying types of education and knowledge, teams are very creative. When leaders don't provide such goals, diverse teams fail to take advantage of their unique skills and are actually *less* creative than teams with homogeneous skills.

The degree to which members of a work unit (group, team, or department) share a common demographic attribute, such as age, sex, race, educational level, or length of service in the organization, is the subject of **organizational demography**. Organizational demography suggests that attributes such as age or the date of joining should help us predict turnover. The logic goes like this: Turnover will be greater among those with dissimilar experiences because communication is more difficult. Conflict and power struggles are more likely and are more severe when they occur. Increased conflict makes membership less at-

Members of Wells Fargo's ethnography teams are diversified in function and expertise. Working in the bank's strategic account-management group, team members possess a variety of banking experience and skills in treasury management, investments, credit cards, and relationship management. The team visits clients to interview their key managers and observe how employees perform various financial workflows such as payroll and accounts payable. From these studies, the teams help clients improve their work processes and use of technology. Wells Fargo benefits by gaining a deeper understanding of customer needs and improving its customer responsiveness.

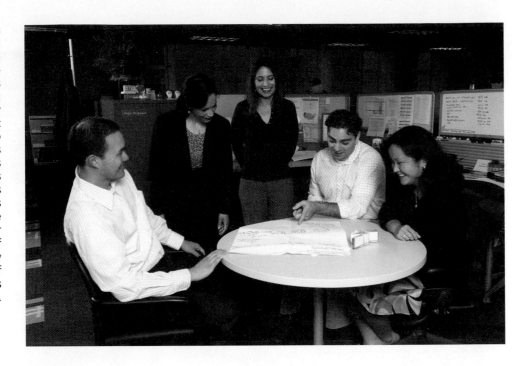

tractive, so employees are more likely to quit. Similarly, the losers in a power struggle are more apt to leave voluntarily or be forced out.[33]

Size of Teams   The president of AOL Technologies says the secret to a great team is to "think small. Ideally, your team should have seven to nine people."[34] His advice is supported by evidence.[35] Generally speaking, the most effective teams have five to nine members. And experts suggest using the smallest number of people who can do the task. Unfortunately, managers often err by making teams too large. It may require only four or five members to develop diversity of views and skills, while coordination problems can increase exponentially as team members are added. When teams have excess members, cohesiveness and mutual accountability decline, social loafing increases, and more people communicate less. Members of large teams have trouble coordinating with one another, especially under time pressure. Keep teams at nine or fewer members. If a natural working unit is larger and you want a team effort, consider breaking the group into subteams.[36]

Member Preferences   Not every employee is a team player. Given the option, many employees will select themselves *out* of team participation. When people who would prefer to work alone are required to team up, there is a direct threat to the team's morale and to individual member satisfaction.[37] This suggests that, when selecting team members, managers should consider individual preferences along with abilities, personalities, and skills. High-performing teams are likely to be composed of people who prefer working as part of a group.

organizational demography   *The degree to which members of a work unit share a common demographic attribute, such as age, sex, race, educational level, or length of service in an organization, and the impact of this attribute on turnover.*

Myth or Science?

"Old Teams Can't Learn New Tricks"

This statement is true for some types of teams and false for others. Let's look at why.

Researchers at Michigan State University composed 80 four-person teams from undergraduate business students. In a command-and-control computer simulation developed for the Department of Defense, each team's mission was to monitor a geographic area, keep unfriendly forces from moving in, and support friendly forces. Team members played on networked computers, and performance was measured by both speed (how quickly they identified targets and friendly forces) and accuracy (the number of friendly fire errors and missed opportunities).

Teams were rewarded either cooperatively (in which case team members shared rewards equally) or competitively (in which case team members were rewarded based on their individual contributions). After playing a few rounds, the reward structures were switched so that the cooperatively rewarded teams were given competitive rewards and the competitively rewarded teams were now cooperatively rewarded.

The researchers found the initially cooperatively rewarded teams easily adapted to the competitive reward conditions and learned to excel. However, the formerly competitively rewarded teams could not adapt to cooperative rewards. It seems teams that "cut their teeth" being cooperative can learn to be competitive, but competitive teams find it much harder to learn to cooperate. As the authors note, their results may shed light on the intelligence failures of the CIA and FBI; when these formerly separate organizations were asked to cooperate, they found it very difficult to do so.

In a follow-up study, this research team found the same results: cooperative teams more easily adapted to competitive conditions than competitive teams did to cooperative conditions.

However, they also found competitive teams could adapt to cooperative conditions when given freedom to allocate their roles (as opposed to having the roles assigned). That freedom may lead to intrateam cooperation, and thus the process of structuring team roles helps the formerly competitive team learn to be cooperative.

The lesson of these studies is that it is hard for old teams to learn new tricks. However, if competitive teams can restructure themselves, they can learn to be cooperative.

Sources: B. Beersma, J. R. Hollenbeck, D. E. Conlon, S. E. Humphrey, H. Moon, and D. R. Ilgen, "Cutthroat Cooperation: The Effects of Team Role Decisions on Adaptation to Alternative Reward Structures," *Organizational Behavior and Human Decision Processes* 108, no. 1 (2009), pp. 131–142; and M. D. Johnson, S. E. Humphrey, D. R. Ilgen, D. Jundt, and C. J. Meyer, "Cutthroat Cooperation: Asymmetrical Adaptation to Changes in Team Reward Structures," *Academy of Management Journal* 49, no. 1 (2006), pp. 103–119.

Team Processes

The final category related to team effectiveness is process variables such as member commitment to a common purpose, establishment of specific team goals, team efficacy, a managed level of conflict, and minimized social loafing. These will be especially important in larger teams, and in teams that are highly interdependent.[38]

Why are processes important to team effectiveness? Let's return to the topic of social loafing. We found that $1 + 1 + 1$ doesn't necessarily add up to 3. When each member's contribution is not clearly visible, individuals tend to decrease their effort. Social loafing, in other words, illustrates a process loss from using teams. But teams should create outputs greater than the sum of their inputs, as when a diverse group develops creative alternatives. Exhibit 10-5 illustrates how

Exhibit **10-5**   **Effects of Group Processes**

| Potential group effectiveness | + | Process gains | − | Process losses | = | Actual group effectiveness |

Employee teams at New Balance Athletic Shoe, Inc., share the common purpose of continuously improving their work processes. In the company's stitching department, shown here, sharing the purpose of quality improvement motivated members of team CS-39 to develop a cross-training program so all members could learn and perform each other's job skills.

group processes can have an impact on a group's actual effectiveness.[39] Teams are often used in research laboratories because they can draw on the diverse skills of various individuals to produce more meaningful research than could be generated by all the researchers working independently—that is, they produce positive synergy, and their process gains exceed their process losses.

Common Plan and Purpose   Effective teams begin by analyzing the team's mission, developing goals to achieve that mission, and creating strategies for achieving the goals. Teams that establish a clear sense of what needs to be done and how consistently perform better.[40]

Members of successful teams put a tremendous amount of time and effort into discussing, shaping, and agreeing on a purpose that belongs to them both collectively and individually. This common purpose, when accepted by the team, becomes what celestial navigation is to a ship captain: It provides direction and guidance under any and all conditions. Like a ship following the wrong course, teams that don't have good planning skills are doomed; perfectly executing the wrong plan is a lost cause.[41] Effective teams also show **reflexivity**, meaning they reflect on and adjust their master plan when necessary. A team has to have a good plan, but it also has to be willing and able to adapt when conditions call for it.[42]

Specific Goals   Successful teams translate their common purpose into specific, measurable, and realistic performance goals. Specific goals facilitate clear communication. They also help teams maintain their focus on getting results.

Consistent with the research on individual goals, team goals should also be challenging. Difficult goals raise team performance on those criteria for which they're set. So, for instance, goals for quantity tend to raise quantity, goals for accuracy raise accuracy, and so on.[43]

reflexivity   *A team characteristic of reflecting on and adjusting the master plan when necessary.*

Team Efficacy   Effective teams have confidence in themselves; they believe they can succeed. We call this *team efficacy*.[44] Teams that have been successful raise their beliefs about future success, which, in turn, motivates them to work harder. What can management do to increase team efficacy? Two options are helping the team achieve small successes that build confidence and providing training to improve members' technical and interpersonal skills. The greater the abilities of team members, the more likely the team will develop confidence and the ability to deliver on that confidence.

Mental Models   Effective teams share accurate **mental models**—knowledge and beliefs (a "psychological map") about how the work gets done. If team members have the wrong mental models, which is particularly likely with teams under acute stress, their performance suffers.[45] In the Iraq War, many military leaders said they underestimated the power of the insurgency and the infighting among Iraqi religious sects. The similarity of team members' mental models matters, too. If team members have different ideas about how to do things, the team will fight over how to do things rather than focus on what needs to be done.[46]

Conflict Levels   Conflict on a team isn't necessarily bad. As we discuss in Chapter 15, teams completely devoid of conflict are likely to become apathetic and stagnant. Thus, conflict—but not all types—can actually improve team effectiveness.[47] Relationship conflicts—those based on interpersonal incompatibilities, tension, and animosity toward others—are almost always dysfunctional. However, on teams performing nonroutine activities, disagreements among members about task content (called *task conflicts*) stimulate discussion, promote critical assessment of problems and options, and can lead to better team decisions. The way conflicts are resolved can also make the difference between effective and ineffective teams. A study of ongoing comments made by 37 autonomous work groups showed that effective teams resolved conflicts by explicitly discussing the issues, whereas ineffective teams had conflicts focused more on personalities and the way things were said.[48]

Social Loafing   Individuals can engage in social loafing and coast on the group's effort because their particular contributions can't be identified. Effective teams undermine this tendency by making members individually and jointly accountable for the team's purpose, goals, and approach.[49] Therefore, members should be clear on what they are individually responsible for and what they are jointly responsible for on the team.

WHAT IS MY TEAM EFFICACY?

In the Self-Assessment Library (available on CD or online), take assessment IV.E.2 (What Is My Team Efficacy?).

Turning Individuals into Team Players

5   Show how organizations can create team players.

We've made a strong case for the value and growing popularity of teams. But many people are not inherently team players, and many organizations have historically nurtured individual accomplishments. Finally, teams fit well in countries that score high on collectivism. But what if an organization wants to introduce teams into a work population of individuals born and raised in an individualistic society? A veteran employee of a large company, who had done well working in an individualistic company in an individualist country, described the experience of joining a team: "I'm learning my lesson. I just had my first negative performance appraisal in 20 years."[50]

So what can organizations do to enhance team effectiveness—to turn individual contributors into team members? Here are options for managers trying to turn individuals into team players.

Selecting: Hiring Team Players

Some people already possess the interpersonal skills to be effective team players. When hiring team members, be sure candidates can fulfill their team roles as well as technical requirements.[51]

When faced with candidates who lack team skills, managers have three options. The candidates can undergo training to make them into team players. If this isn't possible or doesn't work, the other two options are to transfer them to another unit that does not have teams (if possible) or not to hire them. In established organizations that decide to redesign jobs around teams, some employees will resist being team players and may be untrainable. Unfortunately, they typically become casualties of the team approach. Creating teams often means resisting the urge to hire the best talent no matter what. The Los Angeles Galaxy professional soccer team paid enormously for British star David Beckham's talents, seemingly without considering whether he was a team player.[52]

Training: Creating Team Players

Training specialists conduct exercises that allow employees to experience the satisfaction teamwork can provide. Workshops help employees improve their problem-solving, communication, negotiation, conflict-management, and coaching skills. L'Oréal, for example, found that successful sales teams required much more than being staffed with high-ability salespeople: management had to focus much of its efforts on team building. "What we didn't account for was that many members of our top team in sales had been promoted because they had excellent technical and executional skills," said L'Oréal's senior VP of sales, David Waldock. As a result of the focus on team training, Waldock says, "We are no longer a team just on paper, working independently. We have a real group dynamic now, and it's a good one."[53] Employees also learn the five-stage group development model described in Chapter 9. Developing an effective team doesn't happen overnight—it takes time.

Rewarding: Providing Incentives to Be a Good Team Player

An organization's reward system must be reworked to encourage cooperative efforts rather than competitive ones.[54] Hallmark Cards, Inc., added to its basic individual-incentive system an annual bonus based on achievement of team goals. Whole Foods directs most of its performance-based rewards toward team performance. As a result, teams select new members carefully so they will contribute to team effectiveness (and thus team bonuses).[55] It is usually best to set a cooperative tone as soon as possible in the life of a team. As we already noted, teams that switch from a competitive to a cooperative system do not share information and make rushed, poor-quality decisions.[56] Apparently, the low trust

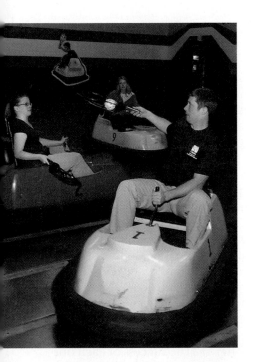

Employees of Cigna, a global health services corporation, learn how to become team players by participating in WhirlyBall competitions. Organizations like Cigna use the team sport as a team-building exercise in which two teams maneuver WhirlyBugs on a court while using scoops to toss a ball back and forth among team members in trying to score a goal. WhirlyBall is one of many team-building activities organizations use to help employees build teamwork skills and experience the satisfaction that teamwork can provide.

mental models   *Team members' knowledge and beliefs about how the work gets done by the team.*

typical of the competitive group will not be readily replaced by high trust with a quick change in reward systems. These problems are not seen in teams that have consistently cooperative systems.

Promotions, pay raises, and other forms of recognition should be given to individuals who work effectively as team members by training new colleagues, sharing information, helping resolve team conflicts, and mastering needed new skills. This doesn't mean individual contributions should be ignored; rather, they should be balanced with selfless contributions to the team.

Finally, don't forget the intrinsic rewards, such as camaraderie, that employees can receive from teamwork. It's exciting and satisfying to be part of a successful team. The opportunity for personal development of self and teammates can be a very satisfying and rewarding experience.

Beware! Teams Aren't Always the Answer

6 Decide when to use individuals instead of teams.

Teamwork takes more time and often more resources than individual work. Teams have increased communication demands, conflicts to manage, and meetings to run. So the benefits of using teams have to exceed the costs, and that's not always the case.[57] Before you rush to implement teams, carefully assess whether the work requires or will benefit from a collective effort.

How do you know whether the work of your group would be better done in teams? You can apply three tests to see whether a team fits your situation.[58] First, can the work be done better by more than one person? A good indicator is the complexity of the work and the need for different perspectives. Simple tasks that don't require diverse input are probably better left to individuals. Second, does the work create a common purpose or set of goals for the people in the group that is more than the aggregate of individual goals? Many service departments of new-vehicle dealers have introduced teams that link customer-service people, mechanics, parts specialists, and sales representatives. Such teams can better manage collective responsibility for ensuring customer needs are properly met. The final test is to determine whether the members of the group are interdependent. Using teams makes sense when there is interdependence between tasks—the success of the whole depends on the success of each one, *and* the success of each one depends on the success of the others. Soccer, for instance, is an obvious *team* sport. Success requires a great deal of coordination between interdependent players. Conversely, except possibly for relays, swim teams are not really teams. They're groups of individuals performing individually, whose total performance is merely the aggregate summation of their individual performances.

Global Implications

7 Show how our understanding of teams differs in a global context.

Research on global considerations in the use of teams is just beginning, but three areas are particularly worth mentioning: the extent of teamwork, self-managed teams, and team cultural diversity.

Extent of Teamwork

Although work teams are pervasive in the United States, some evidence suggests the degree to which teams affect the way work is done is not as significant in the United States as in other countries. One study comparing U.S. workers to Canadian and Asian workers revealed that 51 percent of workers in Asian-Pacific countries and 48 percent of Canadian employees report high levels of teamwork. But only 32 percent of U.S. employees say their organization has a high level of teamwork.[59] Thus, there still is a heavy role for individual contributions in the United States. Given that U.S. culture is highly individualistic, that may continue to be true for quite some time.

Self-Managed Teams

Evidence suggests self-managed teams have not fared well in Mexico, largely due to that culture's low tolerance of ambiguity and uncertainty and employees' strong respect for hierarchical authority.[60] Thus, in countries relatively high in power distance—where roles of leaders and followers are clearly delineated—a team may need to be structured so leadership roles are spelled out and power relationships identified.

Team Cultural Diversity and Team Performance

We have discussed research on team diversity in race or gender. But what about diversity created by national differences? Like the earlier research, evidence here indicates these elements of diversity interfere with team processes, at least in the short term.[61] Cultural diversity does seem to be an asset for tasks that call for a variety of viewpoints. But culturally heterogeneous teams have more difficulty learning to work with each other and solving problems. The good news is that these difficulties seem to dissipate with time. Although newly formed culturally diverse teams underperform newly formed culturally homogeneous teams, the differences disappear after about 3 months.[62] Fortunately, some team performance–enhancing strategies seem to work well in many cultures. One study found that teams in the European Union made up of members from collectivist and individualist countries benefitted equally from group goals.[63]

Summary and Implications for Managers

Few trends have influenced jobs as much as the massive movement to introduce teams into the workplace. The shift from working alone to working on teams requires employees to cooperate with others, share information, confront differences, and sublimate personal interests for the greater good of the team.

Effective teams have common characteristics. They have adequate resources, effective leadership, a climate of trust, and a performance evaluation and reward system that reflects team contributions. These teams have individuals with technical expertise as well as problem-solving, decision-making, and interpersonal skills and the right traits, especially conscientiousness and openness. Effective teams also tend to be small—with fewer than 10 people, preferably of diverse backgrounds. They have members who fill role demands and who prefer to be part of a group. And the work that members do provides freedom and autonomy, the opportunity to use different skills and talents, the ability to complete a whole and identifiable task or product, and work that has a substantial impact on others. Finally, effective teams have members who believe in the team's capabilities and are committed to a common plan and purpose, an accurate shared mental model of what is to be accomplished, specific team goals, a manageable level of conflict, and a minimal degree of social loafing.

Because individualistic organizations and societies attract and reward individual accomplishments, it can be difficult to create team players in these environments. To make the conversion, management should try to select individuals who have the interpersonal skills to be effective team players, provide training to develop teamwork skills, and reward individuals for cooperative efforts.

Sports Teams Are Good Models for Workplace Teams

Studies from football, soccer, basketball, hockey, and baseball have found a number of elements of successful sports teams that can be extrapolated to successful work teams.

Goals foster team cohesion. A study of basketball teams found that while those that set team goals and those that did not had similar levels of cohesion when the season began, those with goals were more cohesive at the end of the season.

Successful teams score early wins. Early successes build teammates' faith in themselves and their capacity as a team. Research on hockey teams of relatively equal ability found that 72 percent of the time, the team leading at the end of the first period went on to win. So managers should provide teams with early tasks that are simple and provide "easy wins."

Successful teams avoid losing streaks. A couple of failures can lead to a downward spiral if a team becomes demoralized. Managers need to instill the confidence in team members that they can turn things around when they encounter setbacks.

Practice makes perfect. Successful sport teams execute on game day but learn from their mistakes in practice. Practice should be used to try new things and fail. A wise manager encourages work teams to experiment and learn.

Successful teams use halftime breaks. The best coaches in basketball and football use halftime during a game to reassess what is working and what isn't. Managers of work teams should similarly build in assessments at the approximate halfway point in a team project to evaluate what it can do to improve.

Being slightly behind can be motivating. A recent study of 6,572 NCAA basketball games revealed that the team slightly behind at halftime won more games than it lost. Teams that are slightly ahead may suffer from "victory disease" by relaxing and trying not to lose, whereas those slightly behind may be more motivated.

Winning teams have stable membership. Stability improves performance. Studies of professional basketball teams found that when teammates have more time together they can better anticipate one another's moves, and they are clearer about one another's roles.

There are flaws in using sports as a model for developing effective work teams. Here are five caveats.

All sport teams aren't alike. In baseball, for instance, there is little interaction among teammates. Rarely are more than two or three players directly involved in a play. The performance of the team is largely the sum of the performance of its individual players. In contrast, basketball has much more interdependence among players: team members are densely clustered and must switch from offense to defense at a moment's notice. The performance of this team is more than the sum of its individual players. So when using sports teams as a model for work teams, you have to make sure you're making the correct comparison. As one expert noted, "The problem with sports metaphors is that the meaning you extract from a sports metaphor is entirely dependent on the sport you pick."

Work teams are more varied and complex than sports teams. In an athletic league, the design of the task, the design of the team, and the team's context vary relatively little from team to team. But these variables can vary tremendously between work teams. As a result, coaching plays a much more significant part in a sports team's performance than in that of a work team. Performance of work teams is a function of getting the team's structural and design variables right. Managers of work teams should focus more on getting the team set up for success than on coaching.

A lot of employees can't relate to sports metaphors. Not everyone on work teams is interested in sports or savvy about sports terminology. And team members from different cultures may not know the sports metaphors you're using. Most U.S. workers, for instance, are unfamiliar with the rules and terminology of Australian Rules football.

Work team outcomes aren't easily defined in terms of wins and losses. Sports teams typically measure success in terms of wins and losses. Success is rarely as clear or black and white for work teams.

Sports team metaphors oversimplify. Sports team metaphors simplify a complicated world. While such shortcuts hold an intuitive appeal, we also have to recognize they serve as "mind funnels"—rather than expanding our minds to the full range of possibilities, sports metaphors reduce and simplify—not something to recommend to the enlightened manager.

Sources: J. Berger and D. Pope, "When Losing Leads to Winning," working paper, Wharton School of Business, University of Pennsylvania (2009); J. Senécal, T. M. Loughead, and G. A. Bloom, "A Season-Long Team-Building Intervention: Examining the Effect of Team Goal Setting on Cohesion," *Journal of Sport & Exercise Psychology* 30, no. 2 (2008), pp. 186–199; N. Katz, "Sports Teams as a Model for Workplace Teams: Lessons and Liabilities," *Academy of Management Executive,* August 2001, pp. 56–67; and "Talent Inc.," The New Yorker Online Only, July 22, 2002, www.newyorker.com/online.

Questions for Review

1 How do you explain the growing popularity of teams in organizations?

2 What is the difference between a group and a team?

3 What are the four types of teams?

4 What conditions or context factors determine whether teams are effective?

5 How can organizations create team players?

6 When is work performed by individuals preferred over work performed by teams?

7 What are three ways in which our understanding of teams differs in a global context?

Experiential Exercise

FIXED VERSUS VARIABLE FLIGHT CREWS

Break into teams of five. Assume that you've been hired by AJet, a start-up airline based in St. Louis. Your team has been formed to consider the pros and cons of using variable flight crews and to arrive at a recommendation on whether to follow this industry practice at AJet.

Variable flight crews are crews formed when pilots, copilots, and flight attendants typically bid for schedules on specific planes (for instance, Boeing 737s, 757s, or 767s) based on seniority. Then they're given a monthly schedule made up of 1- to 4-day trips. So any given flight crew on a plane is rarely together for more than a few days at a time. A complicated system is required to complete the schedules. Because of this system, it's not unusual for a senior pilot at a large airline to fly with a different copilot on every trip during any given month. And a pilot and copilot who work together for 3 days in

January may never work together again the rest of the year. (In contrast, a fixed flight crew consists of the same group of pilots and attendants who fly together for a period of time.)

In considering whether to use variable flight crews, your team is to answer the following questions:

1. What are the primary advantages of variable flight crews?
2. If you were to recommend some version of fixed flight crews, drawing from the material in this chapter, on what criteria would you assign AJet crews?

When your team has considered the advantages and disadvantages of variable flight crews and answered these questions, be prepared to present to the class your recommendations and justification.

Ethical Dilemma

PRESSURE TO BE A TEAM PLAYER

"Okay, I admit it. I'm not a team player. I work best when I work alone and am left alone," says Zachery Sanders.

Zach's employer, Broad's Furniture, an office furniture manufacturer, recently reorganized around teams. All production in the company's Michigan factory is now done in teams. And Zach's design department has been divided into three design teams. To Zach's dismay, he was assigned to the modular-office design (MOD) team, which does work Zach finds less interesting and challenging than other work he's done. What's worse, Zach believes some low-performing individuals have been put on the team. Maddie Saunders, MOD's new team leader, seems to agree with Zach. She told him, "Zach, listen, I know you're not wild about the work MOD is doing, and it's true some weaker individual contributors have been assigned to the

team. But that's why we formed the team. We really think that when we work together, the strengths of the team will be magnified and the weaknesses limited."

Although Zach respects Maggie, he's not convinced. "I've worked here for four years. I'm very good at what I do. And my performance reviews confirm that. I've been rated in the highest performance category every year I've been here. But now everything is changing. My evaluations and pay raises are going to depend on how well the team does. And, get this, fifty percent of my evaluation will depend on how well the team does—and this isn't a great team. I'm really frustrated and demoralized. They hired me for my design skills. They knew I wasn't a social type. Now they're forcing me to be a team player. This doesn't play to my strengths at all."

Is it unethical for Zach's employer to force him to be a team leader? Is his firm breaking an implied contract that it made with him at the time he was hired? Does this employer have any responsibility to provide Zach with an alternative that would allow him to continue to work independently? If you were Zach, how would you respond?

Case Incident 1

TOYOTA'S TEAM CULTURE

Many companies proudly promote their team culture. At Toyota, the promotion seems sincere.

Teamwork is one of Toyota's core values, along with trust, continuous improvement, long-term thinking, standardization, innovation, and problem solving. The firm's value statement says the following: "To ensure the success of our company, each team member has the responsibility to work together, and communicate honestly, share ideas, and ensure team member understanding."

So how does Toyota's culture reflect its emphasis on teamwork?

First, although individualism is a prominent value in Western culture, it is deemphasized at Toyota. In its place is an emphasis on systems, in which people and products are seen as intertwined value streams and people are trained to be problem solvers so as to make the product system leaner and better.

Second, before hiring, Toyota tests candidates to ensure they are not only competent and technically skilled but also oriented toward teamwork—able to trust their team, be comfortable solving problems collaboratively, and motivated to achieve collective outcomes.

Third, and not surprisingly, Toyota structures its work around teams. Every Toyota employee knows the adage "All of us are smarter than any of us." Teams are used not only in the production process but also at every level and in every function: in sales and marketing, in finance, in engineering, in design, and at the executive level.

Fourth, Toyota considers the team to be the power center of the organization. The leader serves the team, not the other way around. When asked whether he would feature himself in advertisements the way other automakers had (most famously, "Dr. Z," Daimler's CEO Dieter Zetsche), Toyota USA's CEO, Yuki Funo, said, "No. We want to show everybody in the company. The heroes. Not one single person."

Questions

1. Do you think Toyota has succeeded because of its team-oriented culture, or do you think it would have succeeded without it?

2. Do you think you would be comfortable working in Toyota's culture? Why or why not?

3. In response to the recession and the firm's first-ever quarterly loss, Toyota's managers accepted a 10 percent pay cut in 2009 to avoid employee layoffs. Do you think such a response is a good means of promoting camaraderie? What are the risks in such a plan?

4. Recently, DCH Group, a company comprised of 33 auto dealerships, decided to adapt Toyota's culture to its own, particularly its emphasis on teamwork. DCH's CEO, Susan Scarola, said, "Trying to bring it down to day-to-day operations is tough. It was not something that everybody immediately embraced, even at the senior level." Do you think the culture will work in what is typically the dog-eat-dog world of auto dealerships? Why or why not?

Sources: Based on A. Webb, "The Trials and Tribulations of Teamwork," *Automotive News* (March 2, 2009), www.autonews.com; J. K. Liker and M. Hoseus, "Toyota's Powerful HR," *Human Resource Executive* (November 1, 2008), www.hreonline.com; J. K. Liker and M. Hoseus, *Toyota Culture: The Heart and Soul of the Toyota Way,* New York: McGraw-Hill, 2008; and D. Kiley, "The Toyota Way to No. 1," *Business Week* (April 26, 2007), www.businessweek.com.

Case Incident 2

IBM'S MULTICULTURAL MULTINATIONAL TEAMS

Historically, IBM was one of the most tradition-bound companies on the planet. It was famous for its written and unwritten rules—such as its no-layoff policy, its focus on individual promotions and achievement, the expectation of lifetime service at the company, and its requirement of suits and white shirts at work.

How times have changed.

IBM has clients in 170 countries and now does two-thirds of its business outside the United States. As a result, it has overturned virtually all aspects of its old culture. One relatively new focus is in the teamwork area. While IBM, like almost all large organizations, uses work teams extensively, the way it does so is unique.

To instill in its managers an appreciation of local culture, and as a means of opening up emerging markets, IBM sends hundreds of its employees to month-long volunteer project teams in regions of the world where most big companies don't do business. Al Chakra, a software development manager located in Raleigh, North Carolina, was sent to join GreenForest, a furniture manufacturing team in Timisoara, Romania. With Chakra were IBM employees from five other countries. Together, the team helped GreenForest become more computer savvy to help its business. In return for the IBM team's assistance, GreenForest was charged . . . well . . . nothing.

This is hardly pure altruism at work. IBM calculates these multicultural, multinational teams are good investments for several reasons. First, they help lay the groundwork for opening up business in emerging economies, many of which might be expected to enjoy greater future growth than mature markets. Stanley Litow, the IBM VP who oversees the program, also thinks it helps IBMers de-

velop multicultural team skills and an appreciation of local markets. He notes, "We want to build a leadership cadre that learns about these places and also learns to exchange their diverse backgrounds and skills." Among the countries where IBM has sent its multicultural teams are Turkey, Tanzania, Vietnam, Ghana, and the Philippines.

As for Chakra, he was thrilled to be selected for the team. "I felt like I won the lottery," he said. He advised GreenForest on how to become a paperless company in 3 years and recommended computer systems to boost productivity and increase exports to western Europe.

Another team member, Bronwyn Grantham, an Australian who works at IBM in London, advised GreenForest about sales strategies. Describing her team experience, Grantham said, "I've never worked so closely with a team of IBMers from such a wide range of competencies."

Questions

1. If you calculate the person-hours devoted to IBM's team projects, they amount to more than 180,000 hours of management time each year. Do you think this is a wise investment of IBM's human resources? Why or why not?

2. Why do you think IBM's culture changed from formal, stable, and individualistic to informal, impermanent, and team oriented?

3. Would you like to work on one of IBM's multicultural, multinational project teams? Why or why not?

4. Multicultural project teams often face problems with communication, expectations, and values. How do you think some of these challenges can be overcome?

Sources: Based on C. Hymowitz, "IBM Combines Volunteer Service, Teamwork to Cultivate Emerging Markets," *Wall Street Journal* (August 4, 2008), p. B6; S. Gupta, "Mine the Potential of Multicultural Teams," *HR Magazine* (October, 2008), pp. 79–84; and H. Aguinis and K. Kraiger, "Benefits of Training and Development for Individuals and Teams, Organizations, and Society," *Annual Review of Psychology* 60, no. 1 (2009), pp. 451–474.

Endnotes

1. J. M. O'Brien, "Team-Building in Paradise," *Fortune* (May 26, 2008), pp. 113–122; J. Paczkowski, "Latest Seagate Layoffs Offer Improved Capacity, Performance," *Digital Daily* (May 13, 2009), digitaldaily.allthingsd.com; "Times Were Good: Seagate Spent US$9000 per Employee for Teambuilding Challenge," *Singapore Retrenchment Blog* (January 28, 2009), retrenchment-blog.breaking.sg/2009.

2. This section is based on J. R. Katzenbach and D. K. Smith, *The Wisdom of Teams* (Cambridge, MA: Harvard University Press, 1993), pp. 21, 45, 85; and D. C. Kinlaw, *Developing Superior Work Teams* (Lexington, MA: Lexington Books, 1991), pp. 3–21.

3. See, for instance, E. Sunstrom, K. DeMeuse, and D. Futrell, "Work Teams: Applications and Effectiveness," *American Psychologist*, February 1990, pp. 120–133.

4. J. H. Shonk, *Team-Based Organizations* (Homewood, IL: Business One Irwin, 1992); and M. A. Verespej, "When Workers Get New Roles," *IndustryWeek*, February 3, 1992, p. 11.

5. G. Bodinson and R. Bunch, "AQP's National Team Excellence Award: Its Purpose, Value and Process," *The Journal for Quality and Participation*, Spring 2003, pp. 37–42.

6. See, for example, A. Erez, J. A. LePine, and H. Elms, "Effects of Rotated Leadership and Peer Evaluation on the Functioning and Effectiveness of Self-Managed Teams: A Quasi-experiment," *Personnel Psychology*, Winter 2002, pp. 929–948.

7. See, for instance, R. A. Cook and J. L. Goff, "Coming of Age with Self-Managed Teams: Dealing with a Problem Employee," *Journal of Business and Psychology*, Spring 2002, pp. 485–496; and C. W. Langfred, "Too Much of a Good Thing? Negative Effects of High Trust and Individual Autonomy in Self-Managing Teams," *Academy of Management Journal*, June 2004, pp. 385–399.

8. C. W. Langfred, "The Downside of Self-Management: A Longitudinal Study of the Effects of Conflict on Trust, Autonomy, and Task Interdependence in Self-Managing Teams," *Academy of Management Journal* 50, no. 4 (2007), pp. 885–900.

9. Bodinson and Bunch, "AQP's National Team Excellence Award."

10. M. Brunelli, "How Harley-Davidson Uses Cross-Functional Teams," *Purchasing Online*, November 4, 1999, www.purchasing.com/article/CA147865.html.

11. See, for example, J. Lipnack and J. Stamps, *Virtual Teams: People Working Across Boundaries and Technology*, 2nd ed. (New York: Wiley, 2000); C. B. Gibson and S. G. Cohen (eds.), *Virtual Teams That Work* (San Francisco: Jossey-Bass, 2003); and L. L. Martins, L. L. Gilson, and M. T. Maynard, "Virtual Teams: What Do We Know and Where Do We Go from Here?" *Journal of Management*, November 2004, pp. 805–835.

12. A. Malhotra, A. Majchrzak, and B. Rosen, "Leading Virtual Teams," *Academy of Management Perspectives*, February 2007, pp. 60–70; and J. M. Wilson, S. S. Straus, and B. McEvily, "All in Due Time: The Development of Trust in Computer-Mediated and Face-to-Face Teams," *Organizational Behavior and Human Decision Processes* 19 (2006), pp. 16–33.

13. See, for instance, J. R. Hackman, "The Design of Work Teams," in J. W. Lorsch (ed.), *Handbook of Organizational Behavior* (Upper Saddle River, NJ: Prentice Hall, 1987), pp. 315–342; and M. A. Campion, G. J. Medsker, and C. A. Higgs, "Relations Between Work Group Characteristics and Effectiveness: Implications for Designing Effective Work Groups," *Personnel Psychology*, Winter 1993, pp. 823–850.

14. D. E. Hyatt and T. M. Ruddy, "An Examination of the Relationship Between Work Group Characteristics and Performance: Once More into the Breech," *Personnel Psychology*, Autumn 1997, p. 555.

15. This model is based on M. A. Campion, E. M. Papper, and G. J. Medsker, "Relations Between Work Team Characteristics and Effectiveness: A Replication and Extension," *Personnel Psychology*, Summer 1996, pp. 429–452; D. E. Hyatt and T. M. Ruddy, "An Examination of the Relationship Between Work Group Characteristics and Performance," pp. 553–585; S. G. Cohen and D. E. Bailey, "What Makes Teams Work: Group Effectiveness Research from the Shop Floor to the Executive Suite," *Journal of Management* 23, no. 3 (1997), pp. 239–290; L. Thompson, *Making the Team* (Upper Saddle River, NJ: Prentice Hall, 2000), pp. 18–33; and J. R. Hackman, *Leading Teams: Setting the Stage for Great Performance* (Boston: Harvard Business School Press, 2002).

16. See G. L. Stewart and M. R. Barrick, "Team Structure and Performance: Assessing the Mediating Role of Intrateam Process and the Moderating Role of Task Type," *Academy of Management Journal*, April 2000, pp. 135–148.

17. Hyatt and Ruddy, "An Examination of the Relationship Between Work Group Characteristics and Performance," p. 577.

18. P. Balkundi and D. A. Harrison, "Ties, Leaders, and Time in Teams: Strong Inference About Network Structure's Effects on Team Viability and Performance," *Academy of Management Journal* 49, no. 1 (2006), pp. 49–68; G. Chen, B. L. Kirkman, R. Kanfer, D. Allen, and B. Rosen, "A Multilevel Study of Leadership, Empowerment, and Performance in Teams," *Journal of Applied Psychology* 92, no. 2 (2007), pp. 331–346; L. A. DeChurch and M. A. Marks, "Leadership in Multiteam Systems," *Journal of Applied Psychology* 91, no. 2 (2006), pp. 311–329; A. Srivastava, K. M. Bartol, and E. A. Locke, "Empowering Leadership in Management Teams: Effects on Knowledge Sharing, Efficacy, and Performance," *Academy of Management Journal* 49, no. 6 (2006), pp. 1239–1251; and J. E. Mathieu, K. K. Gilson, and T. M. Ruddy, "Empowerment and Team Effectiveness: An Empirical Test of an Integrated Model," *Journal of Applied Psychology* 91, no. 1 (2006), pp. 97–108.

19. J. B. Carson, P. E. Tesluk, and J. A. Marrone, "Shared Leadership in Teams: An Investigation of Antecedent Conditions and Performance," *Academy of Management Journal* 50, no. 5 (2007), pp. 1217–1234.

20. K. T. Dirks, "Trust in Leadership and Team Performance: Evidence from NCAA Basketball," *Journal of Applied Psychology*, December 2000, pp. 1004–1012; and M. Williams, "In Whom We Trust: Group Membership as an Affective Context for Trust Development," *Academy of Management Review*, July 2001, pp. 377–396.

21. See S. T. Johnson, "Work Teams: What's Ahead in Work Design and Rewards Management," *Compensation & Benefits Review*, March–April 1993, pp. 35–41; and L. N. McClurg, "Team Rewards: How Far Have We Come?" *Human Resource Management*, Spring 2001, pp. 73–86.

22. R. R. Hirschfeld, M. H. Jordan, H. S. Feild, W. F. Giles, and A. A. Armenakis, "Becoming Team Players: Team Members' Mastery of Teamwork Knowledge as a Predictor of Team Task Proficiency and Observed Teamwork Effectiveness," *Journal of Applied Psychology* 91, no. 2 (2006), pp. 467–474.

23. For a more detailed breakdown of team skills, see M. J. Stevens and M. A. Campion, "The Knowledge, Skill, and Ability Requirements for Teamwork: Implications for Human Resource Management," *Journal of Management*, Summer 1994, pp. 503–530.

24. H. Moon, J. R. Hollenbeck, and S. E. Humphrey, "Asymmetric Adaptability: Dynamic Team Structures as One-Way Streets," *Academy of Management Journal* 47, no. 5 (October 2004), pp. 681–695; A. P. J. Ellis, J. R. Hollenbeck, and D. R. Ilgen, "Team Learning: Collectively Connecting the Dots," *Journal of Applied Psychology* 88, no. 5 (October 2003), pp. 821–835; C. L. Jackson and J. A. LePine, "Peer Responses to a Team's Weakest Link: A Test and Extension of LePine and Van Dyne's Model," *Journal of Applied Psychology* 88, no. 3 (June 2003), pp. 459–475; and J. A. LePine, "Team Adaptation and Postchange Performance: Effects of Team Composition in Terms of Members' Cognitive Ability and Personality," *Journal of Applied Psychology* 88, no. 1 (February 2003), pp. 27–39.

25. S. T. Bell, "Deep-Level Composition Variables as Predictors of Team Performance: A Meta-analysis," *Journal of Applied Psychology* 92, no. 3 (2007), pp. 595–615; and M. R. Barrick, G. L. Stewart, M. J. Neubert, and M. K. Mount, "Relating Member Ability and Personality to Work-Team Processes and Team Effectiveness," *Journal of Applied Psychology*, June 1998, pp. 377–391.

26. Ellis, Hollenbeck, and Ilgen, "Team Learning"; C. O. L. H. Porter, J. R. Hollenbeck, and D. R. Ilgen, "Backing Up Behaviors in Teams: The Role of Personality and Legitimacy of Need," *Journal of Applied Psychology* 88, no. 3 (June 2003), pp. 391–403; A. Colquitt, J. R. Hollenbeck, and D. R. Ilgen, "Computer-Assisted Communication and Team Decision-Making Performance: The Moderating Effect of Openness to Experience," *Journal of Applied Psychology* 87, no. 2 (April 2002), pp. 402–410; J. A. LePine, J. R. Hollenbeck, D. R. Ilgen, and J. Hedlund, "The Effects of Individual Differences on the Performance of Hierarchical Decision Making Teams: Much More Than G," *Journal of Applied Psychology* 82 (1997), pp. 803–811; Jackson and LePine, "Peer Responses to a Team's Weakest Link"; and LePine, "Team Adaptation and Postchange Performance."

27. Barrick, Stewart, Neubert, and Mount, "Relating Member Ability and Personality to Work-Team Processes and Team Effectiveness," p. 388; and S. E. Humphrey, J. R. Hollenbeck, C. J. Meyer, and D. R. Ilgen, "Trait Configurations in Self-Managed Teams: A Conceptual Examination of the Use of Seeding for Maximizing and Minimizing Trait Variance in Teams," *Journal of Applied Psychology* 92, no. 3 (2007), pp. 885–892.

28. S. E. Humphrey, F. P. Morgeson, and M. J. Mannor, "Developing a Theory of the Strategic Core of Teams: A Role Composition Model of Team Performance," *Journal of Applied Psychology* 94, no. 1 (2009), pp. 48–61.

29. C. Margerison and D. McCann, *Team Management: Practical New Approaches* (London: Mercury Books, 1990).

30. A. Joshi and H. Roh, "The Role of Context in Work Team Diversity Research: A Meta-analytic Review," *Academy of Management Journal* 52, no. 3 (2009), pp. 599–627; and S. K. Horwitz and I. B. Horwitz, "The Effects of Team Diversity on Team Outcomes: A Meta-analytic Review of Team Demography," *Journal of Management* 33, no. 6 (2007), pp. 987–1015.

31. G. S. Van Der Vegt, J. S. Bunderson, and A. Oosterhof, "Expertness Diversity and Interpersonal Helping in Teams: Why Those Who Need the Most Help End Up Getting the Least," *Academy of Management Journal* 49, no. 5 (2006), pp. 877–893.

32. S. J. Shin and J. Zhou, "When Is Educational Specialization Heterogeneity Related to Creativity in Research and Development Teams? Transformational Leadership as a Moderator," *Journal of Applied Psychology* 92, no. 6 (2007), pp. 1709–1721.

33. K. Y. Williams and C. A. O'Reilly III, "Demography and Diversity in Organizations: A Review of 40 Years of Research," in B. M. Staw and L. L. Cummings (eds.), *Research in Organizational Behavior*, vol. 20, pp. 77–140; and A. Joshi, "The Influence of Organizational Demography on the External Networking Behavior of Teams," *Academy of Management Review*, July 2006, pp. 583–595.

34. J. Katzenbach, "What Makes Teams Work?" *Fast Company*, November 2000, p. 110.

35. The evidence in this section is described in Thompson, *Making the Team*, pp. 65–67. See also L. A. Curral, R. H. Forrester, and J. F. Dawson, "It's What You Do and the Way That You Do It: Team Task, Team Size, and Innovation-Related Group Processes," *European Journal of Work & Organizational Psychology* 10, no. 2 (June 2001), pp. 187–204; R. C. Liden, S. J. Wayne, and R. A. Jaworski, "Social Loafing: A Field Investigation," *Journal of Management* 30, no. 2 (2004), pp. 285–304; and J. A. Wagner, "Studies of Individualism–Collectivism: Effects on Cooperation in Groups," *Academy of Management Journal* 38, no. 1 (February 1995), pp. 152–172.

36. "Is Your Team Too Big? Too Small? What's the Right Number? *Knowledge@Wharton*, June 14, 2006, pp. 1–5.

37. Hyatt and Ruddy, "An Examination of the Relationship Between Work Group Characteristics and Performance"; J. D. Shaw, M. K. Duffy, and E. M. Stark, "Interdependence and Preference for Group Work: Main and Congruence Effects on the Satisfaction and Performance of Group Members," *Journal of Management* 26, no. 2 (2000), pp. 259–279; and S. A. Kiffin-Peterson and J. L. Cordery, "Trust, Individualism, and Job Characteristics of Employee Preference for Teamwork," *International Journal of Human Resource Management*, February 2003, pp. 93–116.

38. J. A. LePine, R. F. Piccolo, C. L. Jackson, J. E. Mathieu, and J. R. Saul, "A Meta-analysis of Teamwork Processes: Tests of a Multidimensional Model and Relationships with Team Effectiveness Criteria," *Personnel Psychology* 61 (2008), pp. 273–307.

39. I. D. Steiner, *Group Processes and Productivity* (New York: Academic Press, 1972).

40. J. A. LePine, R. F. Piccolo, C. L. Jackson, J. E. Mathieu, and J. R. Saul, "A Meta-analysis of Teamwork Processes: Tests of a Multidimensional Model and Relationships with Team

Effectiveness Criteria"; and J. E. Mathieu and T. L. Rapp, "Laying the Foundation for Successful Team Performance Trajectories: The Roles of Team Charters and Performance Strategies," *Journal of Applied Psychology* 94, no. 1 (2009), pp. 90–103.

41. J. E. Mathieu and W. Schulze, "The Influence of Team Knowledge and Formal Plans on Episodic Team Process—Performance Relationships," *Academy of Management Journal* 49, no. 3 (2006), pp. 605–619.

42. A. Gurtner, F. Tschan, N. K. Semmer, and C. Nagele, "Getting Groups to Develop Good Strategies: Effects of Reflexivity Interventions on Team Process, Team Performance, and Shared Mental Models," *Organizational Behavior and Human Decision Processes* 102 (2007), pp. 127–142; M. C. Schippers, D. N. Den Hartog, and P. L. Koopman, "Reflexivity in Teams: A Measure and Correlates," *Applied Psychology: An International Review* 56, no. 2 (2007), pp. 189–211; and C. S. Burke, K. C. Stagl, E. Salas, L. Pierce, and D. Kendall, "Understanding Team Adaptation: A Conceptual Analysis and Model," *Journal of Applied Psychology* 91, no. 6 (2006), pp. 1189–1207.

43. E. Weldon and L. R. Weingart, "Group Goals and Group Performance," *British Journal of Social Psychology*, Spring 1993, pp. 307–334. See also R. P. DeShon, S. W. J. Kozlowski, A. M. Schmidt, K. R. Milner, and D. Wiechmann, "A Multiple-Goal, Multilevel Model of Feedback Effects on the Regulation of Individual and Team Performance," *Journal of Applied Psychology*, December 2004, pp. 1035–1056.

44. K. Tasa, S. Taggar, and G. H. Seijts, "The Development of Collective Efficacy in Teams: A Multilevel and Longitudinal Perspective," *Journal of Applied Psychology* 92, no. 1 (2007), pp. 17–27; D. I. Jung and J. J. Sosik, "Group Potency and Collective Efficacy: Examining Their Predictive Validity, Level of Analysis, and Effects of Performance Feedback on Future Group Performance," *Group & Organization Management*, September 2003, pp. 366–391; and R. R. Hirschfeld and J. B. Bernerth, "Mental Efficacy and Physical Efficacy at the Team Level: Inputs and Outcomes Among Newly Formed Action Teams," *Journal of Applied Psychology* 93, no. 6 (2008), pp. 1429–1437.

45. A. P. J. Ellis, "System Breakdown: The Role of Mental Models and Transactive Memory on the Relationships Between Acute Stress and Team Performance," *Academy of Management Journal* 49, no. 3 (2006), pp. 576–589.

46. S. W. J. Kozlowski and D. R. Ilgen, "Enhancing the Effectiveness of Work Groups and Teams," *Psychological Science in the Public Interest*, December 2006, pp. 77–124; and B. D. Edwards, E. A. Day, W. Arthur, Jr., and S. T. Bell, "Relationships Among Team Ability Composition, Team Mental Models, and Team Performance," *Journal of Applied Psychology* 91, no. 3 (2006), pp. 727–736.

47. K. A. Jehn, "A Qualitative Analysis of Conflict Types and Dimensions in Organizational Groups," *Administrative Science Quarterly*, September 1997, pp. 530–557. See also R. S. Peterson and K. J. Behfar, "The Dynamic Relationship Between Performance Feedback, Trust, and Conflict in Groups: A Longitudinal Study," *Organizational Behavior and Human Decision Processes*, September–November 2003, pp. 102–112.

48. K. J. Behfar, R. S. Peterson, E. A. Mannix, and W. M. K. Trochim, "The Critical Role of Conflict Resolution in Teams: A Close Look at the Links Between Conflict Type, Conflict Management Strategies, and Team Outcomes," *Journal of Applied Psychology* 93, no. 1 (2008), pp. 170–188.

49. K. H. Price, D. A. Harrison, and J. H. Gavin, "Withholding Inputs in Team Contexts: Member Composition, Interaction Processes, Evaluation Structure, and Social Loafing," *Journal of Applied Psychology* 91, no. 6 (2006), pp. 1375–1384.

50. See, for instance, B. L. Kirkman and D. L. Shapiro, "The Impact of Cultural Values on Employee Resistance to Teams: Toward a Model of Globalized Self-Managing Work Team Effectiveness," *Academy of Management Review*, July 1997, pp. 730–757; and B. L. Kirkman, C. B. Gibson, and D. L. Shapiro, "'Exporting' Teams: Enhancing the Implementation and Effectiveness of Work Teams in Global Affiliates," *Organizational Dynamics* 30, no. 1 (2001), pp. 12–29.

51. G. Hertel, U. Konradt, and K. Voss, "Competencies for Virtual Teamwork: Development and Validation of a Web-Based Selection Tool for Members of Distributed Teams," *European Journal of Work and Organizational Psychology* 15, no. 4 (2006), pp. 477–504.

52. I. Galarcep, "Beckham Loan Makes No Sense for the Galaxy," *ESPNsoccernet* (October 24, 2008), soccernet.espn .go.com.

53. H. M. Guttman, "The New High-Performance Player," *The Hollywood Reporter* (October 27, 2008), www.hollywoodreporter .com.

54. J. S. DeMatteo, L. T. Eby, and E. Sundstrom, "Team-Based Rewards: Current Empirical Evidence and Directions for Future Research," in B. M. Staw and L. L. Cummings (eds.), *Research in Organizational Behavior*, vol. 20, pp. 141–183.

55. T. Erickson and L. Gratton, "What It Means to Work Here," *Business Week* (January 10, 2008), www.businessweek.com.

56. M. D. Johnson, J. R. Hollenbeck, S. E. Humphrey, D. R. Ilgen, D. Jundt, and C. J. Meyer, "Cutthroat Cooperation: Asymmetrical Adaptation to Changes in Team Reward Structures," *Academy of Management Journal* 49, no. 1 (2006), pp. 103–119.

57. C. E. Naquin and R. O. Tynan, "The Team Halo Effect: Why Teams Are Not Blamed for Their Failures," *Journal of Applied Psychology*, April 2003, pp. 332–340.

58. A. B. Drexler and R. Forrester, "Teamwork—Not Necessarily the Answer," *HRMagazine*, January 1998, pp. 55–58. See also R. Saavedra, P. C. Earley, and L. Van Dyne, "Complex Interdependence in Task-Performing Groups," *Journal of Applied Psychology*, February 1993, pp. 61–72; and K. A. Jehn, G. B. Northcraft, and M. A. Neale, "Why Differences Make a Difference: A Field Study of Diversity, Conflict, and Performance in Workgroups," *Administrative Science Quarterly*, December 1999, pp. 741–763.

59. "Watson Wyatt's Global Work Studies," www.watsonwyatt .com/research/featured/workstudy.asp.

60. Nicholls, Lane, and Brehm Brechu, "Taking Self-Managed Teams to Mexico."

61. W. E. Watson, K. Kumar, and L. K. Michaelsen, "Cultural Diversity's Impact on Interaction Process and Performance: Comparing Homogeneous and Diverse Task Groups,"

Academy of Management Journal, June 1993, pp. 590–602; P. C. Earley and E. Mosakowski, "Creating Hybrid Team Cultures: An Empirical Test of Transnational Team Functioning," *Academy of Management Journal,* February 2000, pp. 26–49; and S. Mohammed and L. C. Angell, "Surface- and Deep-Level Diversity in Workgroups: Examining the Moderating Effects of Team Orientation and Team Process on Relationship Conflict," *Journal of Organizational Behavior,* December 2004, pp. 1015–1039.

62. Watson, Kumar, and Michaelsen, "Cultural Diversity's Impact on Interaction Process and Performance."
63. D. F. Crown, "The use of Group and Groupcentric Individual Goals for Culturally Heterogeneous and Homogeneous Task Groups: An Assessment of European Work Teams," *Small Group Research* 38, no. 4 (2007), pp. 489–508.

LEARNING OBJECTIVES

After studying this chapter, you should be able to:

1 Identify the main functions of communication.

2 Describe the communication process and distinguish between formal and informal communication.

3 Contrast downward, upward, and lateral communication, and provide examples of each.

4 Contrast oral, written, and nonverbal communication.

5 Contrast formal communication networks and the grapevine.

6 Analyze the advantages and challenges of electronic communication.

7 Show how channel richness underlies the choice of communication channel.

8 Identify common barriers to effective communication.

9 Show how to overcome the potential problems in cross-cultural communication.

Communication

Constantly talking isn't necessarily communicating. —Joel in *Eternal Sunshine of the Spotless Mind*

DID E-MAIL (ALMOST) SEND THESE TRADERS TO JAIL?

Matthew M. Tannin and Ralph R. Cioffi had what most finance majors would consider dream careers: they were senior executives at Bear Stearns—one of the most successful and longest-standing Wall Street investment banks. At the peak of the market, the two were sitting on top of the financial world: responsible for two multibillion-dollar hedge funds and drawing eight-figure salaries. Cioffi owned homes in four states, one worth nearly $20 million. His net worth was estimated to be $100 million.

Like most Bear Stearns employees, Tannin and Cioffi found themselves out of work when the company collapsed in early 2008. But their lost jobs are the least of their problems. In mid-2008 the two were indicted on charges of fraud.

Mark Mershon, head of the New York FBI office that brought the charges, alleges, "This is not about mismanagement of a hedge fund investment strategy. It is about premeditated lies to investors and lenders." Mershon alleges that the two men, desperate to keep investors' assets attached to the funds, deceived investors by not telling them how poorly the funds were doing. Though the funds were highly leveraged—they borrowed as much as $20 for each dollar invested—through 2006 they performed well. When their fortunes turned, the alleged lying began.

To prove its case, the government is relying on e-mails from Tannin and Cioffi as key pieces of evidence. To their investors, Tannin and Cioffi were enthusiastic: "We have an awesome opportunity," Cioffi wrote

to a broker. Privately, though, Cioffi expressed deep worry over the funds' results. "I'm sick to my stomach over our performance," he wrote in an e-mail to a colleague. He warned another colleague, "Don't talk about [the funds' February results] to anyone or I'll shoot you." Meanwhile, unknown to investors, Cioffi moved money out of the poor-performing funds into safer funds, all the while persuading investors to up their investments. "Believe it or not, I've been able to convince people to add more money," he e-mailed a colleague.

Tannin e-mailed Cioffi his own worries, commenting in one e-mail that "there is simply no way for us to make money" and that the fund looked "pretty damn ugly" and they should consider closing it down. Two days later, though, the two presented a happy face about the fund's performance, arguing it was in good shape. "We are seeing opportunities now and are excited about what is possible. I am adding capital to the Fund. If you guys are in a position to do the same I think this is a good opportunity," wrote Tannin.

Just before the total collapse of the fund, Cioffi wrote in an e-mail, "I've effectively washed a 30-year career down the drain." If only he had known the very medium he used to express his fears would make his future prospects far, far worse.[1]

…jurors decided that there was not enough evidence for conviction in this case, and the accused were found not guilty of securities fraud.

This example illustrates the profound consequences of communication. In this chapter, we'll analyze the power of communication and ways in which it can be made more effective. One of the topics we'll discuss is gossip. Consider the following self-assessment and how you score on your attitudes toward gossip at work.

Poor communication is probably the most frequently cited source of interpersonal conflict.[2] Because individuals spend nearly 70 percent of their waking hours communicating—writing, reading, speaking, listening—it seems reasonable to conclude that one of the biggest inhibitors of group performance is lack of effective communication. Good communication skills are critical to career success. Polls of recruiters nearly always show communication skills near the top of the list of desired characteristics.[3]

No individual, group, or organization can exist without sharing meaning among its members. It is only thus that we can convey information and ideas. Communicating, however, is more than merely imparting meaning; that meaning must also be understood. If one group member speaks only German and the others do not know the language, the German speaker will not be fully understood. Therefore, **communication** must include both the *transfer and the understanding of meaning*.

No idea, no matter how great, is useful until transmitted and understood by others. Perfect communication, if it existed, would occur when a thought or idea was transmitted so the receiver perceived exactly the same mental picture as the sender. Though it sounds elementary, perfect communication is never achieved in practice, for reasons we shall see later in this chapter.

First let's briefly review the functions communication performs and describe the communication process.

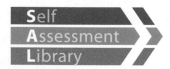

AM I A GOSSIP?

In the Self-Assessment Library (available on CD or online), take assessment IV.E.3 (Am I a Gossip?) and answer the following questions.

1. *How did you score relative to your classmates?*
2. *Do you think gossiping is morally wrong? Why or why not?*

Functions of Communication

1   Identify the main functions of communication.

Communication serves four major functions within a group or organization: control, motivation, emotional expression, and information.[4]

Communication acts to *control* member behavior in several ways. Organizations have authority hierarchies and formal guidelines employees are required to follow. When employees are required to communicate any job-related grievance to their immediate boss, to follow their job description, or to comply with company policies, communication is performing a control function. But informal communication also controls behavior. When work groups tease or harass a member who produces too much (and makes the rest of the group look bad), they are informally communicating with, and controlling, the member's behavior.

Globalization has changed the way Toyota Motor Corporation provides employees with the information they need for decision making. In the past, Toyota transferred employee knowledge on the job from generation to generation through "tacit understanding," a common communication method used in the conformist and subdued Japanese culture. Today, however, as a global organization, Toyota transfers knowledge of its production methods to overseas employees by bringing them to its training center in Japan, shown here, to teach them production methods by using how-to manuals, practice drills, and lectures.

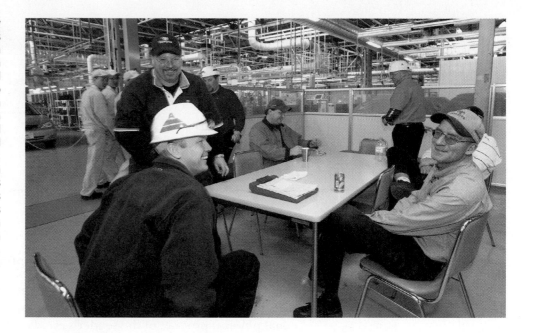

Communication fosters *motivation* by clarifying to employees what they must do, how well they are doing, and how to improve performance if it's subpar. We saw this operating in our review of goal-setting theory in Chapter 7. The formation of specific goals, feedback on progress toward the goals, and reward of desired behavior all stimulate motivation and require communication.

Their work group is a primary source of social interaction for many employees. The communication within the group is a fundamental mechanism by which members show their satisfaction and frustrations. Communication, therefore, provides for the *emotional expression* of feelings and fulfillment of social needs.

The final function of communication is to facilitate decision making. Communication provides the *information* individuals and groups need to make decisions by transmitting the data to identify and evaluate alternative choices.

None of these four functions is more important than the others. To perform effectively, groups need to maintain some form of control over members, stimulate members to perform, allow emotional expression, and make decision choices. Almost every communication interaction that takes place in a group or organization performs one or more of these functions.

The Communication Process

2 Describe the communication process and distinguish between formal and informal communication.

Before communication can take place it needs a purpose, a message to be conveyed between a sender and a receiver. The sender encodes the message (converts it to a symbolic form) and passes it through a medium (channel) to the receiver, who decodes it. The result is transfer of meaning from one person to another.[5]

communication   *The transfer and understanding of meaning.*

Exhibit 11-1   The Communication Process

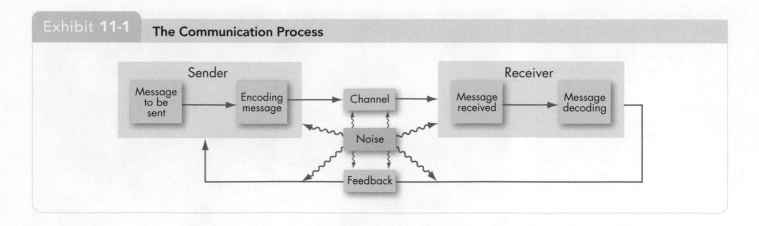

Exhibit 11-1 depicts this **communication process**. The key parts of this model are (1) the sender, (2) encoding, (3) the message, (4) the channel, (5) decoding, (6) the receiver, (7) noise, and (8) feedback.

The *sender* initiates a message by encoding a thought. The *message* is the actual physical product of the sender's *encoding*. When we speak, the speech is the message. When we write, the writing is the message. When we gesture, the movements of our arms and the expressions on our faces are the message. The *channel* is the medium through which the message travels. The sender selects it, determining whether to use a formal or informal channel. **Formal channels** are established by the organization and transmit messages related to the professional activities of members. They traditionally follow the authority chain within the organization. Other forms of messages, such as personal or social, follow **informal channels**, which are spontaneous and emerge as a response to individual choices.[6] The *receiver* is the person(s) to whom the message is directed, who must first translate the symbols into understandable form. This step is the *decoding* of the message. *Noise* represents communication barriers that distort the clarity of the message, such as perceptual problems, information overload, semantic difficulties, or cultural differences. The final link in the communication process is a feedback loop. *Feedback* is the check on how successful we have been in transferring our messages as originally intended. It determines whether understanding has been achieved.

Direction of Communication

3 Contrast downward, upward, and lateral communication, and provide examples of each.

Communication can flow vertically or laterally. We further subdivide the vertical dimension into downward and upward directions.[7]

Downward Communication

Communication that flows from one level of a group or organization to a lower level is *downward communication*. It's used by group leaders and managers communicating with employees to assign goals, provide job instructions, explain policies and procedures, point out problems that need attention, and offer feedback about performance. But downward communication doesn't have to be oral or face to face. When management sends letters to employees' homes to advise them of the organization's new sick-leave policy, it's using downward communication. A team leader e-mailing members of her team about an upcoming deadline uses downward communication.

As president of Home Depot's southern division, Ann-Marie Campbell demonstrates downward communication (our term, not hers) when speaking with the manager and employees of a store in St. Petersburg, Florida. Serving as a member of Home Depot's senior leadership team, Campbell oversees 100,000 workers at 640 stores in 15 states, Puerto Rico, and the Virgin Islands. On her store visits, Campbell communicates the retailer's goals of focusing on clean warehouses, stocked shelves, and top customer service. Her personal, face-to-face meetings with employees give her the opportunity to solicit upward communication from them.

When engaging in downward communication, managers must explain the reasons *why* a decision was made. One study found employees were twice as likely to be committed to changes when the reasons behind them were fully explained. Although this may seem like common sense, many managers feel they are too busy to explain things or that explanations will "open up a big can of worms." Evidence clearly indicates, though, that explanations increase employee commitment and support of decisions.[8]

Another problem in downward communication is its one-way nature; generally, managers inform employees but rarely solicit their advice or opinions. A 2006 study revealed that nearly two-thirds of employees say their boss rarely or never asks their advice. The study noted, "Organizations are always striving for higher employee engagement, but evidence indicates they unnecessarily create fundamental mistakes. People need to be respected and listened to." Companies like cell phone maker Nokia actively listen to employee's suggestions, a practice the company thinks is especially important to innovation.[9]

The best communicators explain the reasons behind their downward communications but also solicit communication from the employees they supervise. That leads us to the next direction: upward communication.

Upward Communication

Upward communication flows to a higher level in the group or organization. It's used to provide feedback to higher-ups, inform them of progress toward goals, and relay current problems. Upward communication keeps managers aware of

communication process *The steps between a source and a receiver that result in the transfer and understanding of meaning.*

formal channels *Communication channels established by an organization to transmit messages related to the professional activities of members.*

informal channels *Communication channels that are created spontaneously and that emerge as responses to individual choices.*

how employees feel about their jobs, co-workers, and the organization in general. Managers also rely on upward communication for ideas on how conditions can be improved.

Given that most managers' job responsibilities have expanded, upward communication is increasingly difficult because managers are overwhelmed and easily distracted. To engage in effective upward communication, try to reduce distractions (meet in a conference room if you can, rather than your boss's office or cubicle), communicate in headlines not paragraphs (your goal is to get your boss's attention, not to engage in a meandering discussion), support your headlines with actionable items (what you believe should happen), and prepare an agenda to make sure you use your boss's attention well.[10]

Lateral Communication

When communication takes place among members of the same work group, members of work groups at the same level, managers at the same level, or any other horizontally equivalent workers, we describe it as *lateral communication*.

Why are horizontal communications needed if a group or an organization's vertical communications are effective? Horizontal communication saves time and facilitates coordination. Some lateral relationships are formally sanctioned. More often, they are informally created to short-circuit the vertical hierarchy and expedite action. So from management's viewpoint, lateral communications can be good or bad. Because strictly adhering to the formal vertical structure for all communications can be inefficient, lateral communication occurring with management's knowledge and support can be beneficial. But it can create dysfunctional conflicts when the formal vertical channels are breached, when members go above or around their superiors to get things done, or when bosses find actions have been taken or decisions made without their knowledge.

Interpersonal Communication

4 Contrast oral, written, and nonverbal communication.

How do group members transfer meaning between and among each other? They essentially rely on oral, written, and nonverbal communication.

Oral Communication

The chief means of conveying messages is oral communication. Speeches, formal one-on-one and group discussions, and the informal rumor mill or grapevine are popular forms of oral communication.

The advantages of oral communication are speed and feedback. We can convey a verbal message and receive a response in minimal time. If the receiver is unsure of the message, rapid feedback allows the sender to quickly detect and correct it. As one professional put it, "Face-to-face communication on a consistent basis is still the best way to get information to and from employees."[11]

The major disadvantage of oral communication surfaces whenever a message has to pass through a number of people: the more people, the greater the potential distortion. If you've ever played the game "Telephone," you know the problem. Each person interprets the message in his or her own way. The message's content, when it reaches its destination, is often very different from the original. In an organization, where decisions and other communiqués are verbally passed up and down the authority hierarchy, considerable opportunities arise for messages to become distorted.

Based on C. F. Bond, Jr., and B. M. DePaulo, "Individual Differences in Judging Deception: Accuracy and Bias," *Psychological Bulletin* 134, no. 4 (2008), pp. 477–492; M. G. Aamodt and H. Custer, "Who Can Best Catch a Liar? A Meta-analysis of Individual Differences in Detecting Deception," *The Forensic Examiner*, Spring 2006, pp. 6–11; and A. Vrij, "Nonverbal Dominance Versus Verbal Accuracy in Lie Detection: A Plea to Change Police Practice," *Criminal Justice and Behavior* 35, no. 10 (2008), pp. 1323–1336.

Myth or Science?

"People Are Good at Catching Liars at Work"

This statement is essentially false. The core purpose of communication in the workplace may be to convey business-related information. However, we also communicate to manage the impressions others form of us. Some impression management is unintentional and harmless (for example, complimenting your boss on his clothing). However, sometimes people manage impressions through outright lies, such as making up excuses for missing work or failing to make a deadline.

One of the reasons people lie—in the workplace and elsewhere—is that it works. Although most of us think we're good at detecting a lie, research shows otherwise. A recent review of 247 studies revealed that people detect lies, on average, only 4.05 percent more accurately than chance. What's even more discouraging is that so-called experts—police officers, parole officers, detectives, judges, and psychologists—perform no better than other people.

And detecting lying in one situation has no correlation to detecting lying in another. Another review found people's confidence in their judgments of whether someone was lying bore almost no relationship to their actual accuracy; we think we're a lot better at catching people lying than we really are. As the authors of this review conclude, "People are not good detectors of deception regardless of their age, sex, confidence, and experience."

One of the reasons people are so bad at detecting lying is that they overattend to cues such as eye movement, voice tone, and nervous movement and underattend to what is said. Verbal content matters more: truth-tellers are more likely to tell stories that contain significant detail (including irrelevant detail), less likely to tell them in a chronological sequence, and more likely to apply their own interpretations to events they report. They also are more likely to convey information that seems contrary to the stereotype of truth telling: they make corrections to their story ("She wore a blue dress, uh, no, sorry, black"), admit forgetfulness ("I think . . .", "I'm not sure . . ."), raise doubts about the truth of their own prior reports ("I know this sounds really strange. . . ."), and mention something unfavorable ("I know I shouldn't have been looking at his e-mail . . .").

The point? Don't believe everything you hear, and don't place too much weight on your ability to catch a liar based on your intuition. When someone makes a claim that it's reasonable to doubt, ask her or him to back it up with evidence, and pay more attention to *what* is communicated than *how*.

Written Communication

Written communications include memos, letters, fax transmissions, e-mail, instant messaging, organizational periodicals, notices placed on bulletin boards (including electronic ones), and any other device that transmits via written words or symbols.

Why would a sender choose written communication? It's often tangible and verifiable. When it's printed, both the sender and receiver have a record of the communication; and the message can be stored for an indefinite period. If there are questions about its content, the message is physically available for later reference. This feature is particularly important for complex and lengthy communications. The marketing plan for a new product, for instance, is likely to contain a number of tasks spread out over several months. By putting it in writing, those who have to initiate the plan can readily refer to it over its lifespan. A final benefit of all written communication comes from the process itself. People are usually forced to think more thoroughly about what they want to convey in a written message than in a spoken one. Thus, written communications are more likely to be well thought out, logical, and clear.

Of course, written messages have drawbacks. They're time consuming. You could convey far more information to a college instructor in a 1-hour oral exam than in a 1-hour written exam. In fact, what you can say in 10 to 15 minutes might take you an hour to write. The other major disadvantage is lack of a built-in feedback mechanism. Oral communication allows the receiver to respond rapidly to what he thinks he hears. But mailing a memo provides no assurance it has been received or that the recipient will interpret it as the sender intended.

Nonverbal Communication

Every time we deliver a verbal message, we also impart a nonverbal message.[12] Sometimes the nonverbal component may stand alone. In a singles bar, a glance, a stare, a smile, a frown, and a provocative body movement all convey meaning. No discussion of communication would thus be complete without consideration of *nonverbal communication*—which includes body movements, the intonations or emphasis we give to words, facial expressions, and the physical distance between the sender and receiver.

We could argue that every *body movement* has a meaning, and no movement is accidental (though some are unconscious). Through body language, we say, "Help me, I'm lonely"; "Take me, I'm available"; and "Leave me alone, I'm depressed." We act out our state of being with nonverbal body language. We lift one eyebrow for disbelief. We rub our noses for puzzlement. We clasp our arms to isolate ourselves or to protect ourselves. We shrug our shoulders for indifference, wink for intimacy, tap our fingers for impatience, slap our forehead for forgetfulness.[13]

The two most important messages body language conveys are (1) the extent to which we like another and are interested in his or her views and (2) the perceived status between a sender and receiver.[14] We're more likely to position ourselves closer to people we like and touch them more often. Similarly, if you feel you're of higher status than another, you're more likely to display body movements—such as crossed legs or a slouched seated position—that reflect a casual and relaxed manner.[15]

Body language adds to, and often complicates, verbal communication. A body position or movement does not by itself have a precise or universal meaning, but when it is linked with spoken language, it gives fuller meaning to a sender's message.

If you read the verbatim minutes of a meeting, you wouldn't grasp the impact of what was said the same way as if you had been there or saw the meeting on video. Why? There is no record of nonverbal communication. The emphasis given to words or phrases is missing. Exhibit 11-2 illustrates how *intonations* can change the meaning of a message. *Facial expressions* also convey meaning. A snarling face says something different from a smile. Facial expressions, along with intonations, can show arrogance, aggressiveness, fear, shyness, and other characteristics.

Physical distance also has meaning. What is considered proper spacing between people largely depends on cultural norms. A businesslike distance in some European countries feels intimate in many parts of North America. If someone stands closer to you than is considered appropriate, it may indicate aggressiveness or sexual interest; if farther away than usual, it may mean disinterest or displeasure with what is being said.

It's important to be alert to these nonverbal aspects of communication and look for nonverbal cues as well as the literal meaning of a sender's words. You should particularly be aware of contradictions between the messages. Someone who frequently glances at her wristwatch is giving the message that she would prefer to terminate the conversation no matter what she actually says. We misinform others when we express one message verbally, such as trust, but nonverbally communicate a contradictory message that reads, "I don't have confidence in you."

Change your tone and you change your meaning:

Placement of the emphasis	What it means
Why don't I take **you** to dinner tonight?	I was going to take someone else.
Why don't **I** take you to dinner tonight?	Instead of the guy you were going with.
Why **don't** I take you to dinner tonight?	I'm trying to find a reason why I **shouldn't** take you.
Why don't I take you to dinner tonight?	Do you have a problem with me?
Why don't I **take** you to dinner tonight?	Instead of going on your own.
Why don't I take you to **dinner** tonight?	Instead of lunch tomorrow.
Why don't I take you to dinner **tonight**?	Not tomorrow night.

Source: Based on M. Kiely, "When 'No' Means 'Yes,'" *Marketing,* October 1993, pp. 7–9. Reproduced in A. Huczynski and D. Buchanan, *Organizational Behavior,* 4th ed. (Essex, UK: Pearson Education, 2001), p. 194.

Organizational Communication

5 Contrast formal communication networks and the grapevine.

In this section, we move from interpersonal communication to organizational communication. Our first focus will be to describe and distinguish formal networks and the grapevine. Then we discuss technological innovations in communication.

Formal Small-Group Networks

Formal organizational networks can be very complicated, including hundreds of people and a half-dozen or more hierarchical levels. To simplify our discussion, we've condensed these networks into three common small groups of five people each (see Exhibit 11-3): chain, wheel, and all channel.

The *chain* rigidly follows the formal chain of command; this network approximates the communication channels you might find in a rigid three-level organization. The *wheel* relies on a central figure to act as the conduit for all the

Exhibit **11-3**	Three Common Small-Group Networks

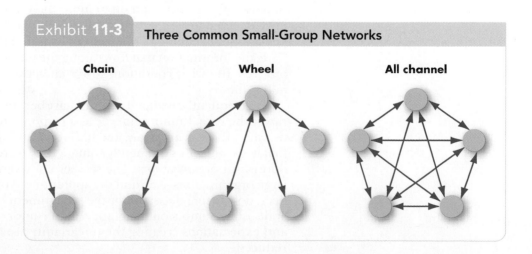

Chain   **Wheel**   **All channel**

Exhibit 11-4	Small-Group Networks and Effective Criteria		

| | Networks | | |
Criteria	Chain	Wheel	All Channel
Speed	Moderate	Fast	Fast
Accuracy	High	High	Moderate
Emergence of a leader	Moderate	High	None
Member satisfaction	Moderate	Low	High

group's communication; it simulates the communication network you would find on a team with a strong leader. The *all-channel* network permits all group members to actively communicate with each other; it's most often characterized in practice by self-managed teams, in which all group members are free to contribute and no one person takes on a leadership role.

As Exhibit 11-4 demonstrates, the effectiveness of each network depends on the dependent variable that concerns you. The structure of the wheel facilitates the emergence of a leader, the all-channel network is best if you desire high member satisfaction, and the chain is best if accuracy is most important. Exhibit 11-4 leads us to the conclusion that no single network will be best for all occasions.

The Grapevine

The informal communication network in a group or organization is called the **grapevine**.[16] Although the grapevine may be informal, it's still an important source of information. A survey found it's where 75 percent of employees hear about matters first.[17] A recent study shows that grapevine or word-of-mouth information from peers about a company has important effects on whether job applicants join an organization.[18]

The grapevine has three main characteristics.[19] First, it is not controlled by management. Second, most employees perceive it as more believable and reliable than formal communiqués issued by top management. Finally, it is largely used to serve the interests of the people within it.

One of the most famous studies of the grapevine investigated communication patterns among 67 managers in a small manufacturing firm.[20] The study asked each communication recipient how he or she first received a given piece of information and then traced it back to its source. While the grapevine was an important source, only 10 percent of the executives acted as liaison individuals (that is, passed the information on to more than one other person). When one executive decided to resign to enter the insurance business, 81 percent of the others knew about it, but only 11 percent transmitted this information to someone else.

Is the information that flows along the grapevine accurate? About 75 percent of it is.[21] But what conditions foster an active grapevine? What gets the rumor mill rolling?

It's frequently assumed rumors start because they make good gossip. This is rarely the case. Rumors emerge as a response to situations that are *important* to us, when there is *ambiguity*, and under conditions that arouse *anxiety*.[22] The fact that work situations frequently contain these three elements explains why rumors flourish in organizations. The secrecy and competition that typically prevail in large organizations—around the appointment of new bosses, the relocation of offices, downsizing decisions, or the realignment of work assignments—encourage and sustain rumors on the grapevine. A rumor will persist either until the wants and expectations creating the uncertainty are fulfilled or the anxiety has been reduced.

Exhibit 11-5	Suggestions for Reducing the Negative Consequences of Rumors

1. **Provide** information—in the long run, the best defense against rumors is a good offense (in other words, rumors tend to thrive in the absence of formal communication).
2. **Explain** actions and decisions that may appear inconsistent, unfair, or secretive.
3. **Refrain** from shooting the messenger—rumors are a natural fact of organizational life, so respond to them calmly, rationally, and respectfully.
4. **Maintain** open communication channels—constantly encourage employees to come to you with concerns, suggestions, and ideas.

Source: Based on L. Hirschhorn, "Managing Rumors," in L. Hirschhorn (ed.), *Cutting Back* (San Francisco: Jossey-Bass, 1983), pp. 54–56.

What can we conclude about the grapevine? Certainly it's an important part of any group or organization communication network and is well worth understanding. It gives managers a feel for the morale of their organization, identifies issues employees consider important, and helps tap into employee anxieties. The grapevine also serves employees' needs: small talk creates a sense of closeness and friendship among those who share information, although research suggests it often does so at the expense of those in the "out" group.[23]

Can managers entirely eliminate rumors? No. What they should do, however, is minimize the negative consequences of rumors by limiting their range and impact. Exhibit 11-5 offers a few suggestions.

Electronic Communications

6 Analyze the advantages and challenges of electronic communication.

An indispensable—and in about 71 percent of cases, the primary—medium of communication in today's organizations is electronic. Electronic communications include e-mail, text messaging, networking software, blogs, and video conferencing. Let's discuss each.

E-mail   E-mail uses the Internet to transmit and receive computer-generated text and documents. Its growth has been spectacular, and its use is now so pervasive it's hard to imagine life without it.

E-mail messages can be quickly written, edited, and stored. They can be distributed to one person or thousands with a click of a mouse. Recipients can read them at their own convenience. And the cost of sending formal e-mail messages to employees is a fraction of the cost of printing, duplicating, and distributing a comparable letter or brochure.[24]

E-mail is not without drawbacks. The following are some of the most significant limitations and what organizations should do to reduce or eliminate them:

- *Misinterpreting the message.* It's true we often misinterpret verbal messages, but the potential to misinterpret e-mail is even greater. One research team at New York University found we can accurately decode an e-mail's intent and tone only 50 percent of the time, yet most of us vastly overestimate our ability to send and interpret clear messages. If you're sending an important message, make sure you reread it for clarity.[25]

grapevine *An organization's informal communication network.*

- *Communicating negative messages.* E-mail may not be the best way to communicate negative information. When Radio Shack decided to lay off 400 employees, it drew an avalanche of scorn inside and outside the company by doing it via e-mail. Employees need to be careful communicating negative messages via e-mail, too. Justen Deal, age 22, wrote an e-mail critical of some strategic decisions made by his employer, pharmaceutical giant Kaiser Permanente, and questioning the financing of several information technology projects. Within hours, Deal's computer was seized; he was later fired.[26]
- *Time-consuming nature of e-mail.* An estimated 62 trillion e-mails are sent every year, of which approximately 60 percent, or 36 trillion, are non-spam messages,[27] and someone has to answer all those non-spam messages! A survey of Canadian managers revealed 58 percent spent 2 to 4 hours per day reading and responding to e-mails. The average worker checks his or her e-mail 50 times a day. Some people, such as venture capitalist and Dallas Mavericks owner Mark Cuban, receive more than a thousand messages a day (Cuban says 10 percent are of the "I want" variety). Although you probably don't receive *that* many, most of us have trouble keeping up with all e-mail, especially as we advance in our career. Experts suggest the following strategies:
  - *Don't check e-mail in the morning.* Take care of important tasks before getting ensnared in e-mails. Otherwise, you may never get to those tasks.
  - *Check e-mail in batches.* Don't check e-mail continually throughout the day. Some experts suggest twice a day. "You wouldn't want to do a new load of laundry every time you have a dirty pair of socks," says one expert.
  - *Unsubscribe.* Stop newsletters and other subscriptions you don't really need.
  - *Stop sending e-mail.* The best way to receive lots of e-mail is to send lots of e-mail, so send less. Shorter e-mails garner shorter responses. "A well-written message can and should be as concise as possible," says one expert.
  - *Declare e-mail bankruptcy.* Some people, like recording artist Moby and venture capitalist Fred Wilson, become so overwhelmed by e-mail they declare "e-mail bankruptcy." They wipe out their entire inbox and start over. *Although some of these steps may not work for you, keep in mind that e-mail can be less productive than it seems: We often seem busy but get less accomplished through e-mail than we might think.*[28]
- *E-mail emotions.* We tend to think of e-mail as a sort of sterile, faceless form of communication. Some researchers say the lack of visual and vocal cues means emotionally positive messages, like those including praise, will be seen as more emotionally neutral than the sender intended.[29] But as you no doubt know, e-mails are often highly emotional. One CEO said, "I've seen people not talk to each other, turf wars break out and people quit their jobs as a result of e-mails." E-mail tends to have a disinhibiting effect on people; without the recipient's facial expression to temper their emotional expression, senders write things they'd never be comfortable saying in person. If you find yourself angry or upset as you write an e-mail, save it as a draft, and look at it again once you are on a more even keel. When others send flaming messages, remain calm and try not to respond in kind. And, as hard as it might sometimes be, try to see the flaming message from the other party's point of view. That in itself may calm your nerves.[30]
- *Privacy concerns.* There are two privacy issues with e-mail. First, your e-mails may be, and often are, monitored. You can't always trust the recipient of your e-mail to keep it confidential, either. For these reasons, you shouldn't write anything you wouldn't want made public. Before Walmart fired marketing VP Julie Roehm, its managers examined her e-mails for evidence of an inappropriate romantic relationship. Second, you need to exercise caution in forwarding e-mail from your company's e-mail account to a personal, or

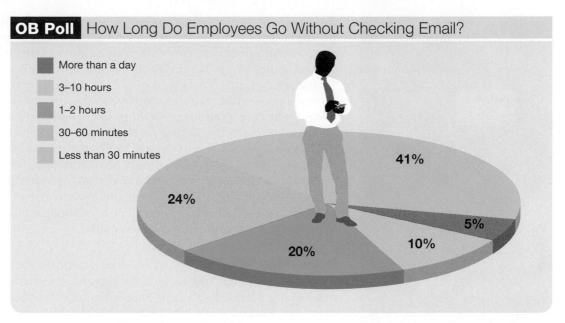

OB Poll   How Long Do Employees Go Without Checking Email?

- More than a day
- 3–10 hours
- 1–2 hours
- 30–60 minutes
- Less than 30 minutes

41%
24%
20%
10%
5%

Source: Based on Studylogic poll for Starwood Hotels and Resorts/Sheraton.

"public" (for example, Gmail, Yahoo!, MSN), e-mail account. These accounts often aren't as secure as corporate accounts, so when you forward a company e-mail to them, you may be violating your organization's policy or unintentionally disclosing confidential data. Many employers hire vendors to sift through e-mails, using software to catch not only the obvious key words ("insider trading") but the vague ("that thing we talked about") or guilt ridden ("regret"). Another survey revealed nearly 40 percent of companies have employees whose only job is to read other employees' e-mail. You are being watched—so be careful what you e-mail![31]

Instant Messaging and Text Messaging   Like e-mail, instant messaging (IM) and text messaging (TM) use electronic media. Unlike e-mail, though, IM and TM either occur in real time (IM) or use portable communication devices (TM). In just a few years, IM and TM have become pervasive. As you no doubt know from experience, IM is usually sent via desktop or laptop computer, whereas TM is transmitted via cellphones or handheld devices such as BlackBerrys.

The growth of TM has been spectacular. In 2001, for instance, just 8 percent of U.S. employees were using it. Now that number is more than 50 percent[32] because IM and TM represent fast and inexpensive means for managers to stay in touch with employees and for employees to stay in touch with each other. In an increasing number of cases, this isn't just a luxury, it's a business imperative. Bill Green, CEO of the consulting firm Accenture, doesn't have a permanent office. Since he's on the road all the time, visiting Accenture's 100 locations scattered across the globe, TM is essential for him to keep in touch. Although there aren't many other examples so dramatic, the great advantage of TM is that it is flexible; with it, you can be reached almost anywhere, anytime.[33]

Despite their advantages, IM and TM aren't going to replace e-mail. E-mail is still probably a better device for conveying long messages that must be saved. IM is preferable for one- or two-line messages that would just clutter up an e-mail inbox. On the downside, some IM and TM users find the technology intrusive and distracting. Their continual presence can make it hard for employees to concentrate and stay focused. A survey of managers revealed that in 86 percent of meetings, at least some participants checked TM, and another survey revealed

The World's 1st Airline SMS Bookin

Malaysia's airline AirAsia is taking advantage of the flexibility of text messaging to make it more convenient for travelers to book flights. AirAsia flight attendants are shown here with a mobile phone billboard during the launch of the world's first airline booking through a short messaging service (SMS) on cell phones. The SMS makes it easier for travelers to book their seats as the service allows them to choose their flights, confirm the booking, and pay for their seats by text messaging from the convenience of their mobile phone wherever they are.

20 percent of managers report having been castigated for using wireless devices during meetings.[34] Finally, because instant messages can be intercepted easily, many organizations are concerned about the security of IM and TM.[35]

One other point: It's important to not let the informality of text messaging ("omg! r u serious? brb") spill over into business e-mails. Many prefer to keep business communication relatively formal. A survey of employers revealed that 58 percent rate grammar, spelling, and punctuation as "very important" in e-mail messages.[36] By making sure your professional communications are, well, professional, you'll show yourself to be mature and serious. Avoid jargon and slang, use formal titles, use formal e-mail addresses for yourself (lose that party-girl@yahoo.com), take care to make your message concise and well written. None of this means, of course, that you have to give up TM or IM; you just need to maintain the boundaries between how you communicate with your friends and how you communicate professionally.

Networking Software   Nowhere has communication been more transformed than in networking. You are doubtless familiar with and perhaps a user of social networking platforms such as Facebook and MySpace. Rather than being one huge site, Facebook, which has 60 million active users, is actually composed of separate networks based on schools, companies, or regions. Individuals over age 25 are now its fastest-growing group of users.

More than 100 million users have created accounts at MySpace. This site averages more than 117 billion hits per month. LinkedIn, XING, and ZoomInfo are all professional Web sites that allow users to set up lists of contacts and do everything from casually "pinging" them with updates to hosting chat rooms for all or some of the users' contacts. Some companies, such as IBM, have their own social networks. IBM is selling its BluePages tool to companies and individual users. Microsoft is doing the same thing with its SharePoint tool.

To get the most out of social networks and avoid irritating your contacts, use them for high-value items only—not as an everyday or even every-week tool. Remember that a prospective employer might check your MySpace or Facebook entry. Some entrepreneurs have developed software that mines such Web sites for companies (or individuals) that want to check up on a job applicant (or potential date). So keep in mind that what you post may be read by people other than your intended contacts.[37]

Blogs   Sun Microsystems CEO Jonathan Schwartz is a big fan of the **blog (Web log)**, Web sites about a single person or company that are usually updated daily. He encourages his employees to have them and has one himself (blogs.sun.com/jonathan). Schwartz's blog averages 400,000 hits per month, and Schwartz, like Apple's managers, allows Sun customers to post comments about the company's products on its Web site.

Obviously, Schwartz is not the only fan of blogs. Experts estimate that more than 112 million blogs and more than 350 million blog entries are now read daily. Millions of U.S. workers have blogs, including thousands of Microsoft employees. And, of course, many organizations and organizational leaders have blogs that speak for the organization.

As a variant of Blogs (which are generally either personal or company-owned), **Twitter** is a service that allows users to post "micro-blog" entries about any topic, including work. Many organizational leaders send Twitter messages ("tweets"), but as the upcoming Ethical Choice notes, they can come from any employee about any work topic, leaving organizations with less control over the communication of important or sensitive information.

So what's the downside? Although some companies have policies in place governing the content of blogs, many don't, and 39 percent of individual bloggers say

Sunita Williams, a NASA astronaut commander and the woman who has spent the longest time in space, used videoconferencing to speak to students and journalists at The American Center in Kolkata, India. The videoconferencing technology allowed the students and journalists to interact with Williams as she discussed her experiences aboard the Space Station *Atlantis.* The interactive meeting gave Williams the opportunity to answer questions about her job as a U.S. Navy experimental test pilot and as a helicopter pilot during the Gulf War.

they have posted comments that could be construed as harmful to their company's reputation. Many bloggers think their personal blogs are outside their employer's purview, but if someone else in a company happens to read a blog entry, there is nothing to keep him or her from sharing that information with others, and the employee could be dismissed as a result. Schwartz says that Sun would not fire an employee over any blog entry short of one that broke the law. "Our blogging policy is 'Be authentic. Period,'" he says. But most organizations are unlikely to be so forgiving of any blog entry that might cast a negative light on them.

When Andrew McDonald landed an internship with Comedy Central, he started a blog his first day at work. His supervisors asked him to change various things about it, essentially removing all specific references to his employer. Kelly Kreth was fired from her job as a marketing director for blogging about her co-workers. So was Jessa Werner, who later said, "I came to the realization that I probably shouldn't have been blogging about work."

One legal expert notes, "Employee bloggers mistakenly believe the First Amendment gives them the right to say whatever they want on their personal blogs. Wrong!" Also, beware of posting personal blog entries from work. More than three-quarters of employers actively monitor employees' Web site connections. In short, if you are going to have a personal blog, maintain a strict work–personal "firewall."[38]

Video Conferencing   *Video conferencing* permits employees in an organization to have meetings with people at different locations. Live audio and video images of members allow them to see, hear, and talk with each other. Video conferencing technology, in effect, allows employees to conduct interactive meetings without the necessity of being physically in the same location.

Peter Quirk, a program manager with EMC Corporation, uses video conferencing to hold monthly meetings of employees at various locations and many other meetings as well. Doing so saves travel expenses and time. However, Quirk notes it's especially important to stimulate questions and involve all participants in order to avoid someone who is linked in but disengaged. Sun Microsystem's Karen Rhode agrees special efforts must be made to engage remote participants, suggesting "You can poll people, people can ask questions, you can do an engaging presentation."[39]

Managing Information

We all have more information at our disposal than ever. It brings us many benefits, but also two important challenges: information overload, and information security. We consider each in turn.

Dealing with Information Overload   Do you find yourself bombarded with information—from e-mail, blogs, Internet surfing, IM's, cellphones, and televisions? You're not alone. Basex, a company that looks at worker efficiency, found the largest part of an average worker's day—43 percent—is spent on matters that are neither important nor urgent, such as responding to non-crucial e-mails and surfing the Web. (In fairness to e-mail, Basex also found 25 percent of an employee's time was spent composing and responding to important e-mail.)

blog (Web log)   *A Web site where entries are written, and generally displayed in reverse chronological order, about news, events, and personal diary entries.*

Twitter   *A free blogging and networking service where users send and read messages known as tweets, many of which concern OB issues.*

Intel designed an 8-month experiment to see how limiting **information overload** might aid productivity. One group of employees was told to limit both digital and in-person contact for 4 hours on Tuesdays, while another group followed its usual routine. The first group was more productive, and 75 percent of its members suggested the program be expanded. "It's huge. We were expecting less," remarked Nathan Zeldes, an Intel engineer who led the experiments. "When people are uninterrupted they can sit back and design chips and really think."

Some of the biggest technologies companies, including Microsoft, Intel, Google, and IBM, are banding together to study the issue more systematically. As one of the team members, IBM's John Tang, noted, "There's a competitive advantage to figuring out how to address this problem."

We have already reviewed some ways of reducing the time sunk into e-mails. More generally, as the Intel study shows, it may make sense to connect to technology less frequently, to, in the words of one article, "avoid letting the drumbeat of digital missives constantly shake up and reorder to-do lists." Lynaia Lutes, an account supervisor for a small Texas company, was able to think much more strategically by taking a break from digital information each day. In the past, she said, "I basically completed an assignment" but didn't approach it strategically. By creating such breaks for yourself, you may be better able to prioritize and think about the big picture and, thereby, be more effective.[40]

Always on Call   As information technology and immediate communication have become a more prevalent component of modern organizational life, more

An Ethical Choice

Managing Your Tweeting and Twittering

Zachary Weiner, CEO of the Chicago-based ad agency Luxuryreach, has decidedly mixed feelings when he reads employees twittering and tweeting about topics such as how demanding a boss he is, how hung over they feel, and how "totally not into" a client they are. On one hand, he finds the messages engrossing. "I can't lie. It's entertaining," he says. On the other hand, he has to wince at some of the sensitive and potentially damaging information that's revealed.

Given the nature of social networking sites such as Twitter and Facebook, it's a concern most employers share. They don't want to suppress or control what many employees believe is free and personal expression. But managers whose job is to look out for the welfare of their organization worry about embarrassing posts, secrets lost to rivals, and loss of goodwill. "You can talk yourself into all sorts of doomsday scenarios," says Intel Chief Information Officer Diane Bryant.

Some of the damage is real. Cisco lawyer Richard Frankel authored a blog in which he mouthed off about a lawsuit in which Cisco was a defendant. After a $15,000 bounty was put up to determine the blogger's identity, Frankel went public, generating another lawsuit against the company and himself.

To balance your desire to network and express yourself with your ethical responsibility to your company, follow the following rules established by IBM:

1. Be personally responsible for any content you publish. Don't write anything you wouldn't be comfortable having your employer read.
2. Keep in mind that what you publish could be public for a long time.
3. If you're writing about your company, be transparent about your role in the organization.
4. Get approval from the organization before posting private or internal conversations.
5. Be up-front about correcting errors and updating previous posts.

Sources: Based on M. Conlin and M. MacMillan, "Managing the Tweets," *Business Week* (June 1, 2009), pp. 20–21; H. Green and R. D. Hof, "Six Million Users: Nothing to Twitter At," *Business Week* (March 16, 2009), pp. 51–52; and A. Hawkins, "Shut Up, Already," *Forbes* (April 7, 2008), p. 44.

employees find they are never able to get offline. The addictive potential of constant communication is so great that some harried managers jokingly refer to their BlackBerrys as "Crackberries."[41] Some business travelers were disappointed when airlines began offering wireless Internet connections in flight because they could no longer use their time in flight as a rare opportunity to relax without a constant barrage of organizational communications. The negative impacts of these communication devices can spill over into employees' personal lives as well. Both workers and their spouses relate the use of electronic communication technologies outside work to higher levels of work–life conflict.[42] Employees must balance the need for constant communication with their own personal need for breaks from work, or they risk burnout from being on call 24 hours a day.

Information Security   Security is a huge concern for nearly all organizations with private or proprietary information about clients, customers, and employees. A Merrill Lynch survey of 50 executives found 52 percent rated leaks of company information as their number-one information security concern, topping viruses and hackers. In response, most companies actively monitor employee Internet use and e-mail records, and some even use video surveillance and record phone conversations. Necessary though they may be, such practices may seem invasive to employees. An organization can buttress employee concerns by involving them in the creation of information-security policies and giving them some control over how their personal information is used.[43]

Choice of Communication Channel

7   Show how channel richness underlies the choice of communication channel.

Neal L. Patterson, CEO at medical software maker Cerner Corp., likes e-mail. Maybe too much so. Upset with his staff's work ethic, he recently sent a seething e-mail to his firm's 400 managers.[44] Here are some of its highlights:

Hell will freeze over before this CEO implements ANOTHER EMPLOYEE benefit in this Culture. . . . We are getting less than 40 hours of work from a large number of our Kansas City-based employees. The parking lot is sparsely used at 8 A.M.; likewise at 5 P.M. As managers—you either do not know what your EMPLOYEES are doing; or YOU do not CARE. . . . You have a problem and you will fix it or I will replace you. . . . What you are doing, as managers, with this company makes me SICK.

Patterson's e-mail suggested managers schedule meetings at 7:00 A.M., 6:00 P.M., and Saturday mornings; promised a staff reduction of 5 percent and institution of a time-clock system; and announced his intention to charge unapproved absences to employees' vacation time.

Within hours, copies of the e-mail had made their way onto a Yahoo! Web site. And within 3 days, Cerner's stock price had plummeted 22 percent. Although we can wonder whether such harsh criticism should be communicated at all, one thing is clear: Patterson erred by selecting the wrong channel for his message. Such an emotional and sensitive message might have been better received in a face-to-face meeting.

information overload   *A condition in which information inflow exceeds an individual's processing capacity.*

Exhibit 11-6   Information Richness of Communication Channels

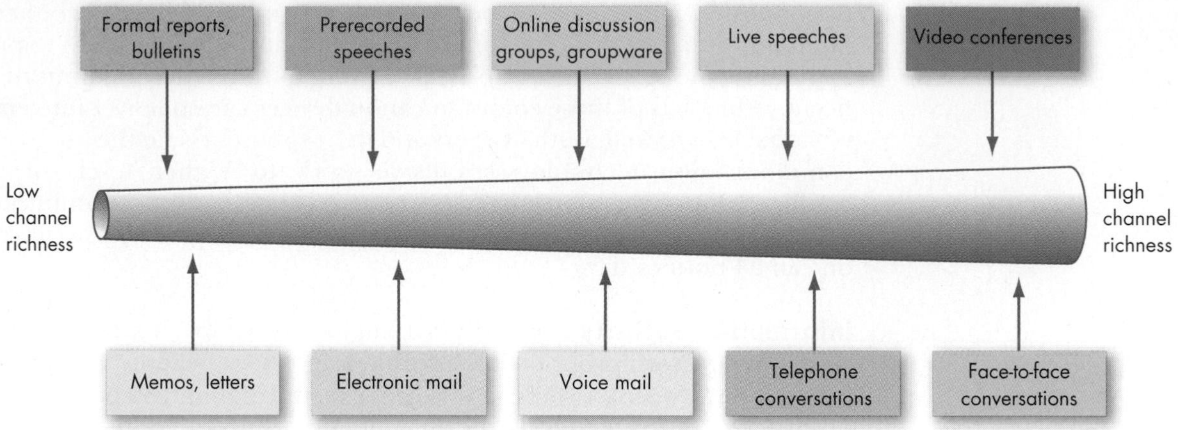

Source: Based on R. H. Lengel and R. L. Daft, "The Selection of Communication Media as an Executive Skill," *Academy of Management Executive,* August 1988, pp. 225–232; and R. L. Daft and R. H. Lengel, "Organizational Information Requirements, Media Richness, and Structural Design," *Managerial Science,* May 1996, pp. 554–572. Reproduced from R. L. Daft and R. A. Noe, *Organizational Behavior* (Fort Worth, TX: Harcourt, 2001), p. 311.

Why do people choose one channel of communication over another—say a phone call instead of a face-to-face talk? A model of media richness helps explain channel selection among managers.[45]

Channels differ in their capacity to convey information. Some are *rich* in that they can (1) handle multiple cues simultaneously, (2) facilitate rapid feedback, and (3) be very personal. Others are *lean* in that they score low on these factors. As Exhibit 11-6 illustrates, face-to-face conversation scores highest in **channel richness** because it transmits the most information per communication episode—multiple information cues (words, postures, facial expressions, gestures, intonations), immediate feedback (both verbal and nonverbal), and the personal touch of being present. Impersonal written media such as formal reports and bulletins rate lowest in richness.

The choice of channel depends on whether the message is routine or nonroutine. Routine messages tend to be straightforward and have minimal ambiguity; channels low in richness can carry them efficiently. Nonroutine communications are likely to be complicated and have the potential for misunderstanding. Managers can communicate them effectively only by selecting rich channels. Recalling Cerner Corp., it appears Neal Patterson used a channel relatively low in richness (e-mail) to convey a message that, because of its nonroutine nature and complexity, should have been conveyed using a rich communication medium.

Evidence indicates high-performing managers tend to be more media sensitive than low-performing managers.[46] They're better able to match appropriate media richness with the ambiguity level in the message.

The past decade has been characterized by facility closings, large layoffs, restructuring, merging, consolidating, and the introduction of new products and services at an accelerated pace—all nonroutine messages high in ambiguity and requiring the use of channels that can convey a large amount of information. It's no coincidence that more senior managers have been using meetings to facilitate communication and regularly leaving their offices to manage by walking around. They are relying on richer channels of communication to transmit the more ambiguous messages they need to convey.

Barriers to Effective Communication

8 Identify common barriers to effective communication.

A number of barriers can retard or distort effective communication. In this section, we highlight the most important of these barriers.

Filtering

Filtering refers to a sender's purposely manipulating information so the receiver will see it more favorably. A manager who tells his boss what he feels the boss wants to hear is filtering information.

The more vertical levels in the organization's hierarchy, the more opportunities there are for filtering. But some filtering will occur wherever there are status differences. Factors such as fear of conveying bad news and the desire to please the boss often lead employees to tell their superiors what they think they want to hear, thus distorting upward communications.

Selective Perception

We have mentioned selective perception before in this book. It appears again here because the receivers in the communication process selectively see and hear based on their needs, motivations, experience, background, and other personal characteristics. Receivers also project their interests and expectations into communications as they decode them. An employment interviewer who expects a female job applicant to put her family ahead of her career is likely to see that in all female applicants, regardless of whether they actually feel that way. As we said in Chapter 6, we don't see reality; we interpret what we see and call it reality.

Information Overload

Individuals have a finite capacity for processing data. When the information we have to work with exceeds our processing capacity, the result is information overload. We've seen that dealing with it has become a huge challenge for individuals and for organizations. It's a barrier to communication that you can manage—to some degree—by following the steps outlined previously in this chapter.

What happens when individuals have more information than they can sort and use? They tend to select, ignore, pass over, or forget information. Or they may put off further processing until the overload situation is over. In any case, the result is lost information and less effective communication. This makes it all the more important to deal with information overload.

Emotions

You may interpret the same message differently when you're angry or distraught than when you're happy. Extreme emotions such as jubilation or depression are most likely to hinder effective communication. In such instances, we are most prone to disregard our rational and objective thinking processes and substitute emotional judgments.

channel richness *The amount of information that can be transmitted during a communication episode.*

filtering *A sender's manipulation of information so that it will be seen more favorably by the receiver.*

Call-center operators at Wipro Spectramind in New Delhi, India, speak English while serving their customers from the United States and the United Kingdom. Even though the operators and customers speak a common language, communication barriers exist because of differences in the countries' cultures and language accents. To overcome these barriers, the operators receive training in American and British pop culture so they can make small talk. They're also taught to speak with Western accents so they can be more easily understood by their calling clients.

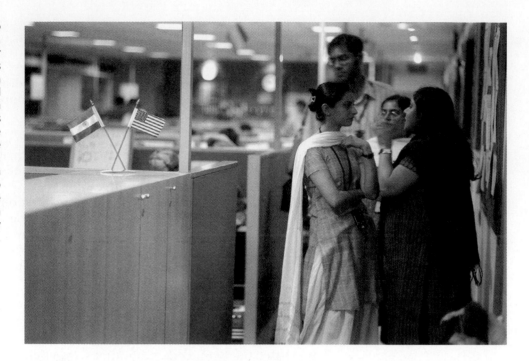

Language

Even when we're communicating in the same language, words mean different things to different people. Age and context are two of the biggest factors that influence such differences.

When Michael Schiller, a business consultant, was talking with his 15-year-old daughter about where she was going with her friends, he told her, "You need to recognize your ARAs and measure against them." Schiller said that in response, his daughter "looked at him like he was from outer space." (For the record, ARA stands for accountability, responsibility, and authority.) Those new to corporate lingo may find acronyms such as *ARA,* words such as *skeds* (schedules), and phrases such as *bake your noodle* (provide a service) bewildering, in the same way parents may be mystified by teen slang.[47]

In short, our use of language is far from uniform. If we knew how each of us modified the language, we could minimize communication difficulties, but we usually don't know. Senders tend to assume the words and terms they use mean the same to the receiver as to them. This assumption is often incorrect.

Silence

It's easy to ignore silence or lack of communication, precisely because it is defined by the absence of information. However, research suggests silence and withholding communication are both common and problematic.[48] One survey found over 85 percent of managers reported remaining silent about at least one issue of significant concern.[49] Employee silence means managers lack information about ongoing operational problems. And silence regarding discrimination, harassment, corruption, and misconduct means top management cannot take action to eliminate this behavior. Finally, employees who are silent about important issues may also experience psychological stress.

Silence is less likely where minority opinions are treated with respect, work-group identification is high, and high procedural justice prevails.[50] Practically, this means managers must make sure they behave in a supportive manner when employees voice divergent opinions or express concerns, and they must take these concerns under advisement. One act of ignoring or belittling an employee for expressing concerns may well lead the employee to withhold important future communication.

Communication Apprehension

An estimated 5 to 20 percent of the population[51] suffers debilitating **communication apprehension**, or social anxiety. These people experience undue tension and anxiety in oral communication, written communication, or both.[52] They may find it extremely difficult to talk with others face to face or may become extremely anxious when they have to use the telephone, relying instead on memos or faxes when a phone call would be faster and more appropriate.

Studies show oral-communication apprehensives avoid situations, such as teaching, for which oral communication is a dominant requirement.[53] But almost all jobs require *some* oral communication. Of greater concern is evidence that high oral-communication apprehensives distort the communication demands of their jobs in order to minimize the need for communication.[54] So be aware some few people severely limit their oral communication and rationalize this practice by telling themselves it isn't necessary for them to do their job effectively.

Gender Differences

Deborah Tannen's research shows men tend to use talk to emphasize status, whereas women tend to use it to create connections. These tendencies, of course, don't apply to *every* man and *every* woman. As Tannen puts it, "a larger percentage of women or men *as a group* talk in a particular way, or individual women and men *are more likely* to talk one way or the other."[55] Women speak and hear a language of connection and intimacy; men speak and hear a language of status, power, and independence. So, for many men, conversations are a means to preserve independence and maintain status in a hierarchical social order. For many women, conversations are negotiations for closeness in which people try to seek and give confirmation and support.

Men frequently complain that women talk on and on about their problems. Women criticize men for not listening. What's happening is that when men hear a problem, they assert their desire for independence and control by offering solutions. Many women, on the other hand, view telling a problem as a means to promote closeness and gain support and connection, not to get advice. Mutual understanding is symmetrical. But giving advice is asymmetrical—it sets up the advice giver as more knowledgeable, more reasonable, and more in control. This contributes to distancing men and women in their efforts to communicate.

"Politically Correct" Communication

A final barrier to effective communication is politically correct communication, which is so concerned with being inoffensive that meaning and simplicity are lost or free expression is hampered.

Plenty of words and phrases invoke neither racial slur nor politically correct language. But our desire to avoid offense can also block communication by keeping us from saying what's really on our mind, or it can alter our communication

communication apprehension
Undue tension and anxiety about oral communication, written communication, or both.

---

by making it unclear. When does being respectful turn into being politically correct? Consider a few examples:[56]

- The *Los Angeles Times* allows its journalists to use the term *old age* but cautions that the onset of old age varies from "person to person," so individuals in a group of 75-year-olds aren't necessarily all old.
- CNN has fined its broadcasters for using the word *foreign* instead of *international.*
- The Little People of America (LPA) association prefers the term *little people* to *dwarfs* or *midgets.*

We must be sensitive about words that do stereotype, intimidate, and insult individuals. But there's a downside to political correctness: it can complicate our vocabulary and make it harder to communicate accurately. You probably know what the following terms mean: *garbage, quotas,* and *women.* But each has been found to offend one or more groups. They've been replaced with terms such as *postconsumer waste materials, educational equity,* and *people of gender,* terms much less likely to convey a uniform message than the words they supplanted and that reduce the likelihood our messages will be received as we intended.

There is no simple solution to this dilemma. However, you should be aware of the trade-offs and the need to find a proper balance.

Global Implications

9 Show how to overcome the potential problems in cross-cultural communication.

Effective communication is difficult under the best of conditions. Cross-cultural factors clearly create the potential for increased communication problems. This is illustrated in Exhibit 11-7. A gesture that is well understood and acceptable in one culture can be meaningless or lewd in another. Only 18 percent of companies have documented strategies for communicating with employees across cultures, and only 31 percent require that corporate messages be customized for consumption in other cultures. Procter & Gamble seems to be an exception; more than half of the company's employees don't speak English as their first language, so the company focuses on simple messages to make sure everyone knows what's important.[57]

Cultural Barriers Researchers have identified a number of problems related to language difficulties in cross-cultural communications.[58]

First are *barriers caused by semantics.* Words mean different things to different people, particularly people from different national cultures. Some words don't translate between cultures. The Finnish word *sisu* means something akin to "guts" or "dogged persistence" but is essentially untranslatable into English. The new capitalists in Russia may have difficulty communicating with British or Canadian counterparts because English terms such as *efficiency, free market,* and *regulation* have no direct Russian equivalents.

Second are *barriers caused by word connotations.* Words imply different things in different languages. Negotiations between U.S. and Japanese executives can be difficult because the Japanese word *hai* translates as "yes," but its connotation is "Yes, I'm listening" rather than "Yes, I agree."

Third are *barriers caused by tone differences.* In some cultures, language is formal; in others, it's informal. In some cultures, the tone changes depending on the context: People speak differently at home, in social situations, and at work. Using a personal, informal style when a more formal style is expected can be embarrassing.

| Exhibit **11-7** | Hand Gestures Mean Different Things in Different Countries |

The A-OK Sign

In the United States, this is just a friendly sign for "All right!" or "Good going." In Australia and Islamic countries, it is equivalent to what generations of high school students know as "flipping the bird."

The "Hook'em Horns" Sign

This sign encourages University of Texas athletes, and it's a good luck gesture in Brazil and Venezuela. In parts of Africa, it is a curse. In Italy, it is signaling to another that "your spouse is being unfaithful."

"V" for Victory Sign

In many parts of the world, this means "victory" or "peace." In England, if the palm and fingers face inward, it means "Up yours!" especially if executed with an upward jerk of the fingers.

Finger-Beckoning Sign

This sign means "come here" in the United States. In Malaysia, it is used only for calling animals. In Indonesia and Australia, it is used for beckoning "ladies of the night."

Source: Hand Gestures Mean Different Things in Different Countries, Roger E. Axtell, *Gestures: The Do's and Taboo's of Body Language Around the World* © 1991, J. Wiley & Sons, Inc. Reprinted by permission.

Fourth are *differences in tolerance for conflict and methods for resolving conflicts.* Individuals from individualist cultures tend to be more comfortable with direct conflicts and will make the source of their disagreements overt. Collectivists are more likely to acknowledge conflict only implicitly and avoid emotionally charged disputes. They may attribute conflicts to the situation more than to the individuals and therefore may not require explicit apologies to repair relationships, whereas individualists prefer explicit statements accepting responsibility for conflicts and public apologies to restore relationships.

Cultural Context   Cultures tend to differ in the degree to which context influences the meaning individuals take from communication.[59] In **high-context cultures** such as China, Korea, Japan, and Vietnam, people rely heavily on nonverbal and subtle situational cues in communicating with others, and a person's official status, place in society, and reputation carry considerable weight. What is *not* said may be more significant than what *is* said. In contrast, people from Europe and North America reflect their **low-context cultures**. They

high-context cultures   *Cultures that rely heavily on nonverbal and subtle situational cues in communication.*

low-context cultures   *Cultures that rely heavily on words to convey meaning in communication.*

International OB

Lost in Translation?

Many U.S. companies have overseas parents, including DaimlerChrysler, Bertelsmann, Diageo, and the Anglo-Dutch company Unilever. Many others have an overseas presence—for example, Ford has manufacturing plants in Belgium, Germany, Spain, Sweden, Turkey, and the United Kingdom. To complicate matters, mergers and acquisitions mean companies are often owned by multiple overseas parents, creating an even greater strain on communication. Although English is the dominant language at many multinational companies, failing to speak a host country's language can make it tougher for managers to do their jobs well. Online communications are even more fraught with potential for misunderstanding because they lack visual and vocal cues that would indicate the sender's emotional meaning. Such communication problems make it tougher to conduct

business effectively and may result in lost opportunities.

To avoid such problems, many companies require their managers to learn the local language and customs. German-based Siemens requires its managers to learn their host country's language. Ernst Behrens, head of China operations, learned to speak Mandarin fluently. Robert Kimmett, a former board member, believes learning a host country's language gives managers "a better grasp of what is going on inside a company . . . not just the facts and figures but also texture and nuance."

However, learning a foreign language can be difficult. Asian languages are particularly challenging for North Americans. To compensate, U.S. managers sometimes rely solely on body language and facial expressions to communicate. But cultural differences in these nonverbal forms of communication may result in serious misunderstandings. Managers

with individualist orientations should be careful about being too direct when communicating with collectivists and work to develop trust. Collectivist managers should be prepared to make more linear, cause-and-effect arguments when communicating with individualists and recognize that direct communication from individualists is not necessarily conveying disapproval or anger.

Sources: Based on K. Kanhold, D. Bilefsky, M. Karnitschnig, and G. Parker, "Lost in Translation? Managers at Multinationals May Miss the Job's Nuances if They Speak Only English," *Wall Street Journal,* May 18, 2004, p. B1; Y. Fujimoto, N. Bahfen, J. Fermelise, and C. E. J. Härtel, "The Global Village: Online Cross-Cultural Communication and HRM," *Cross Cultural Management* 14, no. 1 (2007), pp. 7–22; H. Ren, and B. Gray, "Repairing Relationship Conflict: How Violation Types and Culture Influence the Effectiveness of Restoration Rituals," *Academy of Management Review* 34, no. 1 (2009), pp. 105–126.

Exhibit 11-8

High- versus Low-Context Cultures

High context ▲

Chinese
Korean
Japanese
Vietnamese
Arab
Greek
Spanish
Italian
English
North American
Scandinavian
Swiss
German

Low context ▼

---

rely essentially on spoken and written words to convey meaning; body language and formal titles are secondary (see Exhibit 11-8).

These contextual differences actually mean quite a lot in terms of communication. Communication in high-context cultures implies considerably more trust by both parties. What may appear to be casual and insignificant conversation in fact reflects the desire to build a relationship and create trust. Oral agreements imply strong commitments in high-context cultures. And who you are—your age, seniority, rank in the organization—is highly valued and heavily influences your credibility. But in low-context cultures, enforceable contracts tend to be in writing, precisely worded, and highly legalistic. Similarly, low-context cultures value directness. Managers are expected to be explicit and precise in conveying intended meaning. It's quite different in high-context cultures, in which managers tend to "make suggestions" rather than give orders.

A Cultural Guide   When communicating with people from a different culture, what can you do to reduce misinterpretations? Begin by trying to assess the cultural context. You're likely to have fewer difficulties if it's similar to yours. The following rules can be helpful:[60]

1. **Assume differences until similarity is proven.**   Most of us assume others are more similar to us than they actually are. You are less likely to err if you assume they are different from you until proven otherwise.

2. **Emphasize description rather than interpretation or evaluation.**   Interpreting or evaluating what someone has said or done draws more on your own culture and background than on the observed situation. So delay judgment until you've had sufficient time to observe and interpret the situation from the differing perspectives of all concerned.

3. **Practice empathy.**   Before sending a message, put yourself in the recipient's shoes. What are his or her values, experiences, and frames of reference? What do you know about his or her education, upbringing, and background that can give you added insight? Try to see the other person as he or she really is.

4. **Treat your interpretations as a working hypothesis.**   Once you've developed an explanation for a new situation or think you empathize with someone from a foreign culture, treat your interpretation as a hypothesis that needs further testing rather than as a certainty. Carefully assess the feedback recipients provide you, to see whether it confirms your hypothesis. For important decisions or communiqués, check with other foreign and home-country colleagues to make sure your interpretations are on target.

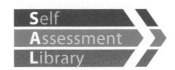

HOW GOOD ARE MY LISTENING SKILLS?

In the Self-Assessment Library (available on CD or online), take assessment II.A.2 (How Good Are My Listening Skills?).

Summary and Implications for Managers

You've probably discovered the link between communication and employee satisfaction in this chapter: the less uncertainty, the greater the satisfaction. Distortions, ambiguities, and incongruities between verbal and nonverbal messages all increase uncertainty and reduce satisfaction.[61]

The less distortion, the more employees will receive goals, feedback, and other management messages as intended.[62] This, in turn, should reduce ambiguities and clarify the group's task. Extensive use of vertical, lateral, and informal channels also increase communication flow, reduce uncertainty, and improve group performance and satisfaction.

Perfect communication is unattainable. Yet a positive relationship exists between effective communication (which includes perceived trust, perceived accuracy, desire for interaction, top-management receptiveness, and upward information requirements) and worker productivity.[63] Choosing the correct channel, being an effective listener, and using feedback can make for more effective communication. But the human factor generates distortions we can never fully eliminate. Whatever the sender's expectations, the message as decoded in the receiver's mind represents his or her reality. And this reality will determine performance, along with the individual's level of motivation and degree of satisfaction.

Despite the great advantages of electronic communication, its pitfalls are also numerous. Because we gather so much meaning from the way a message is communicated (voice tone, facial expressions, body language), the potential for misunderstandings in electronic communication is great. We need to use e-mail, IM, TM, and networking software wisely, or we'll not be as effective as we might.

Finally, by keeping in mind communication barriers such as gender and culture, we can overcome them and increase our communication effectiveness.

POINT ⟷ COUNTERPOINT

Keep It Secret

POINT

We're better off keeping more things to ourselves. Workplace gossip is out of control, and we can't trust most people with secrets. Tell a friend never, ever to tell something to someone else, and you've aroused in them an irresistible desire to share the juicy news. A good rule of thumb is that if you're sure a confidante has told no one else, he or she has probably told only three other people. You might think this reaction is paranoid, but research suggests so-called confidantes rarely keep secrets, even when they swear they will.

Keeping our own secrets is normal, and most children learn to do it at any early age. People survive by protecting themselves, and someone keeping a secret usually has a good reason.

Even when we feel like confiding in someone else, it's prudent to keep confidential information to ourselves. Few are able to keep secrets, and if we fear certain negative consequences of telling our secrets (our confidante will think less of us or tell others), those fears not only don't keep us from blabbing—they are often justified.

It's even more important to keep organizational secrets. Organizations are rumor mills, and we can permanently damage our careers and the organizations for which we work by disclosing confidential information. Improper disclosure of organizational proprietary information is a huge cost and concern for organizations. A recent poll of managers revealed that 84 percent of employees think it's very common for employees to engage in office gossip, while 63 percent of managers think it has a negative effect on the workplace.

COUNTERPOINT

The problem with keeping secrets is that they're expensive to maintain.

One social psychologist found that the more people are instructed to keep something to themselves, the more they see the secret in everything they do. "We don't realize that in keeping it secret we've created an obsession in a jar," he says. So keeping things hidden takes a toll on our psyche—it (usually unnecessarily) adds to the mental burdens we carry with us.

Another psychologist found these costs are real. He discovered that young people who experienced a traumatic experience often had more health problems later in life, and after further research he found out why: Generally, these people concealed the event from others. An experiment showed that when people shared traumatic events they experienced, they had fewer health problems later than people who hadn't. There is no single reason why sharing these traumatic events seems to help people, but the result has been found repeatedly.

There's another positive effect of gossip: The threat of it helps people behave. One study revealed that in a "dictator game," concern about gossip led individuals to share resources more equally. So for our own well-being and that of others, we're better off sharing than keeping secrets.

Sources: Based on A. van Iterson and S. R. Clegg, "The Politics of Gossip and Denial in Interorganizational Relations," *Human Relations* 61, no. 8 (2008), pp. 1117–1137; "Top Managers Don't Appreciate Office Gossip," *USA Today* (December 24, 2008), p. B1; E. Jaffe, "The Science Behind Secrets," *APS Observer,* July 2006, pp. 20–22; and J. Piazza and J. M. Bering, "Concerns about Reputation via Gossip Promote Generous Allocations in an Economic Game," *Evolution and Human Behavior* 29, no. 3 (2008), pp. 172–178.

Questions for Review

1 What are the primary functions of the communication process in organizations?

2 What are the key parts of the communication process, and how do you distinguish formal and informal communication?

3 What are the differences among downward, upward, and lateral communication?

4 What are the unique challenges to oral, written, and nonverbal communication?

5 How are formal communication networks and the grapevine similar and different?

6 What are the main forms of electronic communication? What are their unique benefits and challenges?

7 Why is channel richness fundamental to the choice of communication channels?

8 What are some common barriers to effective communication?

9 What unique problems underlie cross-cultural communication?

Experiential Exercise

AN ABSENCE OF NONVERBAL COMMUNICATION

This exercise will help you to see the value of nonverbal communication to interpersonal relations.

1. The class is to split up into pairs (Party A and Party B).

2. Party A is to select a topic from the following list:
   a. Managing in the Middle East is significantly different from managing in North America.
   b. Employee turnover in an organization can be functional.
   c. Some conflict in an organization is good.
   d. Whistle-blowers do more harm than good for an organization.
   e. An employer has a responsibility to provide every employee with an interesting and challenging job.
   f. Everyone should register to vote.
   g. Organizations should require all employees to undergo regular drug tests.
   h. Individuals who have majored in business or economics make better employees than those who have majored in history or English.
   i. The place where you get your college degree is more important in determining your career success than what you learn while you're there.
   j. It's unethical for a manager to purposely distort communications to get a favorable outcome.

3. Party B is to choose a position on this topic (for example, arguing *against* the view "Some conflict in an organization is good"). Party A now must automatically take the opposite position.

4. The two parties have 10 minutes in which to debate their topic. The catch is that the individuals can only communicate verbally. They may *not* use gestures, facial movements, body movements, or any other nonverbal communication. It may help for each party to sit on their hands to remind them of their restrictions and to maintain an expressionless look.

5. After the debate is over, form groups of six to eight and spend 15 minutes discussing the following:
   a. How effective was communication during these debates?
   b. What barriers to communication existed?
   c. What purposes does nonverbal communication serve?
   d. Relate the lessons learned in this exercise to problems that might occur when communicating on the telephone or through e-mail.

Ethical Dilemma

DEFINING THE BOUNDARIES OF TECHNOLOGY

You work for a company that has no specific policies regarding non–work-related uses of computers and the Internet. It also has no electronic monitoring devices to determine what employees are doing on their computers. Are any of the following actions unethical? Explain your position on each.

1. Using the company's e-mail system for personal reasons during the workday

2. Playing computer games during the workday

3. Using your office computer for personal use (to check ESPN.com, to shop online) during the workday

4. Looking for a mate on an Internet dating service during the workday

5. Visiting "adult" Web sites on your office computer during the workday

6. Using your employer's portable communication device (for example, a BlackBerry) for personal use

7. Conducting any of the preceding activities at work but before or after normal work hours

8. For telecommuters working from home, using a computer and Internet access line paid for by your employer to visit online shopping or dating-service sites during normal working hours

Case Incident 1

DIANNA ABDALA

Consider the case of Dianna Abdala. In 2005, Abdala was a recent graduate of Suffolk University's law school. She passed the bar exam and was offered a job at a law firm started by William Korman, a former state prosecutor.

The following is a summary of their e-mail communications:

- - - - -Original Message- - - - -
From: Dianna Abdala
Sent: Friday, February 03, 2006 9:23 P.M.
To: William A. Korman
Subject: Thank you
Dear Attorney Korman,
At this time, I am writing to inform you that I will not be accepting your offer. After careful consideration, I have come to the conclusion that the pay you are offering would neither fulfill me nor support the lifestyle I am living in light of the work I would be doing for you. I have decided instead to work for myself, and reap 100 percent of the benefits that I sew [sic].
Thank you for the interviews.
Dianna L. Abdala, Esq.

- - - - -Original Message- - - - -
From: William A. Korman
To: Dianna Abdala
Sent: Monday, February 06, 2006 12:15 P.M.
Subject: RE: Thank you
Dianna- -
Given that you had two interviews, were offered and accepted the job (indeed, you had a definite start date), I

am surprised that you chose an e-mail and a 9:30 P.M. voice-mail message to convey this information to me. It smacks of immaturity and is quite unprofessional. Indeed, I did rely upon your acceptance by ordering stationary [sic] and business cards with your name, reformatting a computer, and setting up both internal and external e-mails for you here at the office. While I do not quarrel with your reasoning, I am extremely disappointed in the way this played out. I sincerely wish you the best of luck in your future endeavors.
Will Korman

- - - - -Original Message- - - - -
From: Dianna Abdala
Sent: Monday, February 06, 2006 4:01 P.M.
To: William A. Korman
Subject: Re: Thank you
A real lawyer would have put the contract into writing and not exercised any such reliance until he did so.
Again, thank you.

- - - - -Original Message- - - - -
From: William A. Korman
To: Dianna Abdala
Sent: Monday, February 06, 2006 4:18 P.M.
Subject: RE: Thank you
Thank you for the refresher course on contracts. This is not a bar exam question. You need to realize that this is a very small legal community, especially the criminal defense bar. Do you really want to start pissing off more experienced lawyers at this early stage of your career?

-----Original Message-----
From: Dianna Abdala
To: William A. Korman
Sent: Monday, February 06, 2006 4:28 P.M.
Subject: Re: Thank you
bla bla bla

After this e-mail exchange, Korman forwarded the correspondence to several colleagues, and it quickly spread.

Questions

1. With whom do you side here—Abdala or Korman?

2. What mistakes do you think each party made?

3. Do you think this exchange will damage Abdala's career? Korman's firm?

4. What does this exchange tell you about the limitations of e-mail?

Sources: "Dianna Abdala," *Wikipedia* (en.wikipedia.org/wiki/Dianna_Abdala); and J. Sandberg, "Infamous Email Writers Aren't Always Killing Their Careers After All," *Wall Street Journal* (February 21, 2006), p. B1.

Case Incident 2

SHOULD COMPANIES THAT FIRE SHOOT FIRST?

In the recessions in the early eighties and nineties and after the 2001 terrorist attacks, layoffs were fairly private affairs. To be sure, news would often leak out to local and national media outlets, but companies did their best to keep it as quiet as possible. One consequence of the growth of the Internet in general, and of social networking sites in particular, is that this is no longer possible.

When Starbucks laid off employees in 2008 and 2009, the website StarbucksGossip.com received a barrage of posts from disgruntled employees. One 10-year employee wrote, "This company is going to lose every great partner that it has. I am sick and tired of being blamed for not meeting my budget when the economy is in a recession. I used to be proud of my company . . . now I am embarrassed and feel physically ill every time I have to go to work."

Some companies are taking a more proactive approach. When Tesla Motors laid off employees, its CEO, Elon Musk, posted a blog entry on the topic just before announcing the layoffs to employees. "We had to say something to prevent articles being written that were not accurate," he said.

"Today, whatever you say inside a company will end up in a blog," says Rusy Rueff, a former executive at Pepsico. "So, you have a choice as a company—you can either be proactive and say, 'Here's what's going on,' or you can allow someone else to write the story for you."

Illustrating the perils of *ignoring* the blogosphere, when newspaper giant Gannett announced it was laying off 10 percent of its employees, it posted no blog entries and made no statement. Jim Hopkins, a 20-year veteran who left the company just before the layoffs, writes the unofficial Gannett Blog. "I try to give the unvarnished truth. I don't think the company offers the same level of candor to employees," he said. Gannett spokeswoman Tara Connell replied, "We attempt to make those personal communications happen as quickly as possible."

Says blog expert Andy Sernovitz, "There are hold-out companies that still wish there was traditional P.R. control of the message, but that day is long over."

Questions

1. Do you think Tesla CEO Elon Musk did the right thing when he blogged about impending layoffs just before announcing them to company employees? Why or why not?

2. Do you think employees have a responsibility to be careful about what they blog about their company? Why or why not?

3. Do you think employees who blog about their companies have an ethical responsibility to disclose their identities?

4. How can a company develop a policy for handling communication of sensitive issues inside, and outside, the company?

Sources: Based on C. C. Miller, "In Era of Blog Sniping, Companies Shoot First," *New York Times* (November 5, 2008), pp. B1, B11; M. Allison, "More Layoffs Expected at Starbucks," *Seattle Times* (January 24, 2009), seattletimes.nwsource.com; and C. Hirschman, "Giving Voice to Employee Concerns," *HR Magazine* (August 2008), pp. 51–53.

Endnotes

1. W. D. Cohan, *House of Cards: A Tale of Hubris and Wretched Excess on Wall Street* (New York: Doubleday Books) 2009; L. Thomas, Jr., "2 Face Fraud Charges in Bear Stearns Debacle," *New York Times* (June 20, 2008), pp. A1, A16; H. R. Morley, "Ex-Bear Stearns Manager Cioffi May Face Indictment," *NewJersey.com* (June 18, 2008), www.northjersey.com.

2. See, for example, K. W. Thomas and W. H. Schmidt, "A Survey of Managerial Interests with Respect to Conflict," *Academy of Management Journal*, June 1976, p. 317.

3. "Employers Cite Communication Skills, Honesty/Integrity as Key for Job Candidates," *IPMA-HR Bulletin* (March 23, 2007), p. 1.

4. W. G. Scott and T. R. Mitchell, *Organization Theory: A Structural and Behavioral Analysis* (Homewood, IL: Irwin, 1976).

5. D. K. Berlo, *The Process of Communication* (New York: Holt, Rinehart & Winston, 1960), pp. 30–32.

6. J. Langan-Fox, "Communication in Organizations: Speed, Diversity, Networks, and Influence on Organizational Effectiveness, Human Health, and Relationships," in N. Anderson, D. S. Ones, H. K. Sinangil, and C. Viswesvaran (eds.), *Handbook of Industrial, Work and Organizational Psychology*, vol. 2 (Thousand Oaks, CA: Sage, 2001), p. 190.

7. R. L. Simpson, "Vertical and Horizontal Communication in Formal Organizations," *Administrative Science Quarterly*, September 1959, pp. 188–196; B. Harriman, "Up and Down the Communications Ladder," *Harvard Business Review*, September–October 1974, pp. 143–151; A. G. Walker and J. W. Smither, "A Five-Year Study of Upward Feedback: What Managers Do with Their Results Matter," *Personnel Psychology*, Summer 1999, pp. 393–424; and J. W. Smither and A. G. Walker, "Are the Characteristics of Narrative Comments Related to Improvement in Multirater Feedback Ratings Over Time?" *Journal of Applied Psychology* 89, no. 3 (June 2004), pp. 575–581.

8. P. Dvorak, "How Understanding the 'Why' of Decisions Matters," *Wall Street Journal* (March 19, 2007), p. B3.

9. J. Ewing, "Nokia: Bring on the Employee Rants," *BusinessWeek* (June 22, 2009), p. 50.

10. E. Nichols, "Hyper-Speed Managers," *HRMagazine*, April 2007, pp. 107–110.

11. L. Dulye, "Get Out of Your Office," *HRMagazine*, July 2006, pp. 99–101.

12. L. S. Rashotte, "What Does That Smile Mean? The Meaning of Nonverbal Behaviors in Social Interaction," *Social Psychology Quarterly*, March 2002, pp. 92–102.

13. J. Fast, *Body Language* (Philadelphia: M. Evan, 1970), p. 7.

14. A. Mehrabian, *Nonverbal Communication* (Chicago: Aldine-Atherton, 1972).

15. N. M. Henley, "Body Politics Revisited: What Do We Know Today?" in P. J. Kalbfleisch and M. J. Cody (eds.), *Gender, Power, and Communication in Human Relationships* (Hillsdale, NJ: Lawrence Erlbaum, 1995), pp. 27–61.

16. See, for example, N. B. Kurland and L. H. Pelled, "Passing the Word: Toward a Model of Gossip and Power in the Workplace," *Academy of Management Review*, April 2000, pp. 428–438; and N. Nicholson, "The New Word on Gossip," *Psychology Today*, June 2001, pp. 41–45.

17. Cited in "Heard It Through the Grapevine," *Forbes* (February 10, 1997), p. 22.

18. G. Van Hoye and F. Lievens, "Tapping the Grapevine: A Closer Look at Word-of-Mouth as a Recruitment Source," *Journal of Applied Psychology* 94, no. 2 (2009), pp. 341–352.

19. See, for instance, J. W. Newstrom, R. E. Monczka, and W. E. Reif, "Perceptions of the Grapevine: Its Value and Influence," *Journal of Business Communication*, Spring 1974, pp. 12–20; and S. J. Modic, "Grapevine Rated Most Believable," *IndustryWeek*, May 15, 1989, p. 14.

20. K. Davis, "Management Communication and the Grapevine," *Harvard Business Review*, September–October 1953, pp. 43–49.

21. K. Davis, cited in R. Rowan, "Where Did That Rumor Come From?" *Fortune* (August 13, 1979), p. 134.

22. R. L. Rosnow and G. A. Fine, *Rumor and Gossip: The Social Psychology of Hearsay* (New York: Elsevier, 1976).

23. J. K. Bosson, A. B. Johnson, K. Niederhoffer, and W. B. Swann, Jr., "Interpersonal Chemistry Through Negativity: Bonding by Sharing Negative Attitudes About Others," *Personal Relationships* 13 (2006), pp. 135–150.

24. B. Gates, "How I Work," *Fortune* (April 17, 2006), money .cnn.com.

25. D. Brady, "*!#?@ the E-mail. Can We Talk?" *BusinessWeek* (December 4, 2006), p. 109.

26. E. Binney, "Is E-mail the New Pink Slip?" *HR Magazine*, November 2006, pp. 32–33; and R. L. Rundle, "Critical Case: How an Email Rant Jolted a Big HMO," *Wall Street Journal* (April 24, 2007), pp. A1, A16.

27. S. Hourigan, "62 Trillion Spam Emails Cause Huge Carbon Footprint," *Courier Mail* (April 17, 2009), www.news.com.au/ couriermail.

28. R. Stross, "The Daily Struggle to Avoid Burial by E-Mail," *New York Times* (April 21, 2008), p. BU5; H. Rhodes, "You've Got Mail . . . Again," *Gainesville Sun* (September 29, 2008), pp. 1D,6D.

29. C. Byron, "Carrying Too Heavy a Load? The Communication and Miscommunication of Emotion by Email," *Academy of Management Review* 33, no. 2 (2008), pp. 309–327.

30. D. Goleman, "Flame First, Think Later: New Clues to E-mail Misbehavior," *New York Times* (February 20, 2007), p. D5; and E. Krell, "The Unintended Word," *HRMagazine*, August 2006, pp. 50–54.

31. R. Zeidner, "Keeping E-mail in Check," *HRMagazine*, June 2007, pp. 70–74; "E-mail May Be Hazardous to Your Career," *Fortune* (May 14, 2007), p. 24; J. D. Glater, "Open Secrets," *New York Times* (June 27, 2008), pp. B1, B5.

32. Cited in C. Y. Chen, "The IM Invasion," *Fortune* (May 26, 2003), pp. 135–138.

33. C. Hymowitz, "Have Advice, Will Travel," *Wall Street Journal* (June 5, 2006), pp. B1, B3.

34. A. Williams, "Mind Your BlackBerry or Mind Your Manners," *New York Times* (June 21, 2009), www.nytimes.com.

35. "Survey Finds Mixed Reviews on Checking E-mail During Meetings," *IPMA-HR Bulletin*, April 27, 2007, p. 1.

36. K. Gurchiek, "Shoddy Writing Can Trip Up Employees, Organizations," *SHRM Online*, April 27, 2006, pp. 1–2.

37. D. Lidsky, "It's Not Just Who You Know," *Fast Company*, May 2007, p. 56.

38. A. Bahney, "Interns? No Bloggers Need Apply," *New York Times* (May 25, 2006), pp. 1–2; "Bosses Battle Risk by Firing E-mail,

IM & Blog Violators," *IPMA-HR Bulletin,* January 12, 2007, pp. 1–2; G. Krants, "Blogging with a Vendetta," *Workforce Week* 8, no. 25 (June 10, 2007), www.workforce.com/section/quick_takes/49486_3.html; D. Jones, "Sun CEO Sees Competitive Advantage in Blogging," *USA Today* (June 26, 2006), p. 7B; and B. Leonard, "Blogs Can Present New Challenges to Employers," *SHRM Online,* March 13, 2006, pp. 1–2.

39. E. Agnvall, "Meetings Go Virtual," *HR Magazine* (January 2009), pp. 74–77.

40. M. Richtel, "Lost in E-mail, Tech Firms Face Self-Made Beast," *New York Times* (June 14, 2008), pp. A1, A14; and M. Johnson, "Quelling Distraction," *HR Magazine* (August 2008), pp. 43–46.

41. D. Harris, "Crackberry Addiction: Gadget Users Compared to Drug Users for Excessive Behavior," *ABCNews Online,* August 23, 2006, abcnews.go.com/WNT/Technology/story?id=2348779.

42. W. R. Boswell and J. B. Olson-Buchanan, "The Use of Communication Technologies After Hours: The Role of Work-Attitudes and Work-Life Conflict," *Journal of Management* 33, no. 4 (2007), pp. 592–610.

43. "At Many Companies, Hunt for Leakers Expands Arsenal of Monitoring Tactics," *Wall Street Journal* (September 11, 2006), pp. B1, B3; and B. J. Alge, G. A. Ballinger, S. Tangirala, and J. L. Oakley, "Information Privacy in Organizations: Empowering Creative and Extrarole Performance," *Journal of Applied Psychology* 91, no. 1 (2006), pp. 221–232.

44. T. M. Burton and R. E. Silverman, "Lots of Empty Spaces in Cerner Parking Lot Get CEO Riled Up," *Wall Street Journal* (March 30, 2001), p. B3; and E. Wong, "A Stinging Office Memo Boomerangs," *New York Times* (April 5, 2001), p. C1.

45. See R. L. Daft and R. H. Lengel, "Information Richness: A New Approach to Managerial Behavior and Organization Design," in B. M. Staw and L. L. Cummings (eds.), *Research in Organizational Behavior,* vol. 6 (Greenwich, CT: JAI Press, 1984), pp. 191–233; R. L. Daft and R. H. Lengel, "Organizational Information Requirements, Media Richness, and Structural Design," *Managerial Science,* May 1986, pp. 554–572; R. E. Rice, "Task Analyzability, Use of New Media, and Effectiveness," *Organization Science,* November 1992, pp. 475–500; S. G. Straus and J. E. McGrath, "Does the Medium Matter? The Interaction of Task Type and Technology on Group Performance and Member Reaction," *Journal of Applied Psychology,* February 1994, pp. 87–97; L. K. Trevino, J. Webster, and E. W. Stein, "Making Connections: Complementary Influences on Communication Media Choices, Attitudes, and Use," *Organization Science,* March–April 2000, pp. 163–182; and N. Kock, "The Psychobiological Model: Towards a New Theory of Computer-Mediated Communication Based on Darwinian Evolution," *Organization Science* 15, no. 3 (May–June 2004), pp. 327–348.

46. R. L. Daft, R. H. Lengel, and L. K. Trevino, "Message Equivocality, Media Selection, and Manager Performance: Implications for Information Systems," *MIS Quarterly,* September 1987, pp. 355–368.

47. J. Sandberg, "The Jargon Jumble," *Wall Street Journal* (October 24, 2006), p. B1.

48. E. W. Morrison and F. J. Milliken, "Organizational Silence: A Barrier to Change and Development in a Pluralistic World,"

Academy of Management Review 25, no. 4 (2000), pp. 706–725; and B. E. Ashforth and V. Anand, "The Normalization of Corruption in Organizations," *Research in Organizational Behavior* 25, (2003), pp. 1–52.

49. F. J. Milliken, E. W. Morrison, and P. F. Hewlin, "An Exploratory Study of Employee Silence: Issues That Employees Don't Communicate Upward and Why," *Journal of Management Studies* 40, no. 6 (2003), pp. 1453–1476.

50. S. Tangirala and R. Ramunujam, "Employee Silence on Critical Work Issues: The Cross-Level Effects of Procedural Justice Climate," *Personnel Psychology* 61, no. 1 (2008), pp. 37–68; and F. Bowen and K. Blackmon, "Spirals of Silence: The Dynamic Effects of Diversity on Organizational Voice," *Journal of Management Studies* 40, no. 6 (2003), pp. 1393–1417.

51. B. R. Schlenker and M. R. Leary, "Social Anxiety and Self-Presentation: A Conceptualization and Model," *Psychological Bulletin* 92, (1982), pp. 641–669; and L. A. Withers, and L. L. Vernon, "To Err Is Human: Embarrassment, Attachment, and Communication Apprehension," *Personality and Individual Differences* 40, no. 1 (2006), pp. 99–110.

52. See, for instance, B. H. Spitzberg and M. L. Hecht, "A Competent Model of Relational Competence," *Human Communication Research,* Summer 1984, pp. 575–599; and S. K. Opt and D. A. Loffredo, "Rethinking Communication Apprehension: A Myers-Briggs Perspective," *Journal of Psychology,* September 2000, pp. 556–570.

53. See, for example, L. Stafford and J. A. Daly, "Conversational Memory: The Effects of Instructional Set and Recall Mode on Memory for Natural Conversations," *Human Communication Research,* Spring 1984, pp. 379–402; and T. L. Rodebaugh, "I Might Look OK, But I'm Still Doubtful, Anxious, and Avoidant: The Mixed Effects of Enhanced Video Feedback on Social Anxiety Symptoms," *Behaviour Research & Therapy* 42, no. 12 (December 2004), pp. 1435–1451. Also see J. A. Daly and J. C. McCroskey, "Occupational Desirability and Choice as a Function of Communication Apprehension," *Journal of Counseling Psychology* 22, no. 4 (1975), pp. 309–313.

54. J. A. Daly and M. D. Miller, "The Empirical Development of an Instrument of Writing Apprehension," *Research in the Teaching of English,* Winter 1975, pp. 242–249.

55. D. Tannen, *Talking from 9 to 5: Men and Women at Work* (New York: Harper, 2001), p. 15.

56. Cited in J. Leo, "Falling for Sensitivity," *U.S. News & World Report,* December 13, 1993, p. 27.

57. R. E. Axtell, *Gestures: The Do's and Taboos of Body Language Around the World* (New York: Wiley, 1991); Watson Wyatt Worldwide, "Effective Communication: A Leading Indicator of Financial Performance—2005/2006 Communication ROI Study,"www.watsonwyatt.com/research/resrender.asp?id=w-868; and A. Markels, "Turning the Tide at P&G," *U.S. News & World Report,* October 30, 2006, p. 69.

58. See M. Munter, "Cross-Cultural Communication for Managers," *Business Horizons,* May–June 1993, pp. 75–76; and H. Ren and B. Gray, "Repairing Relationship Conflict: How Violation Types and Culture Influence the Effectiveness of Restoration Rituals," *Academy of Management Review* 34, no. 1 (2009), pp. 105–126.

59. See E. T. Hall, *Beyond Culture* (Garden City, NY: Anchor Press/Doubleday, 1976); E. T. Hall and M. R. Hall,

Understanding Cultural Differences (Yarmouth, ME: Intercultural Press, 1990); W. L. Adair, "Integrative Sequences and Negotiation Outcome in Same- and Mixed-Culture Negotiations," *International Journal of Conflict Management* 14, no. 3–4 (2003), pp. 1359–1392; W. L. Adair and J. M. Brett, "The Negotiation Dance: Time, Culture, and Behavioral Sequences in Negotiation," *Organization Science* 16, no. 1 (2005), pp. 33–51; E. Giebels and P. J. Taylor, "Interaction Patterns in Crisis Negotiations: Persuasive Arguments and Cultural Differences," *Journal of Applied Psychology* 94, no. 1 (2009), pp. 5–19; and Y. Fujimoto, N. Bahfen, J. Fermelise, and C. E. J. Härtel, "The Global Village: Online Cross-Cultural Communication and HRM," *Cross Cultural Management* 14, no. 1 (2007), pp. 7–22.

60. N. Adler, *International Dimensions of Organizational Behavior,* 4th ed. (Cincinnati, OH: South-Western Publishing, 2002), p. 94.

61. See, for example. R. S. Schuler, "A Role Perception Transactional Process Model for Organizational Communication-Outcome Relationships," *Organizational Behavior and Human Performance,* April 1979, pp. 268–291.

62. J. P. Walsh, S. J. Ashford, and T. E. Hill, "Feedback Obstruction: The Influence of the Information Environment on Employee Turnover Intentions," *Human Relations,* January 1985, pp. 23–46.

63. S. A. Hellweg and S. L. Phillips, "Communication and Productivity in Organizations: A State-of-the-Art Review," in *Proceedings of the 40th Annual Academy of Management Conference,* Detroit, 1980, pp. 188–192. See also B. A. Bechky, "Sharing Meaning Across Occupational Communities: The Transformation of Understanding on a Production Floor," *Organization Science* 14, no. 3 (May–June 2003), pp. 312–330.

LEARNING OBJECTIVES

After studying this chapter, you should be able to:

1 Define *leadership* and contrast leadership and management.

2 Summarize the conclusions of trait theories of leadership.

3 Identify the central tenets and main limitations of behavioral theories.

4 Assess contingency theories of leadership by their level of support.

5 Compare and contrast *charismatic* and *transformational leadership*.

6 Define *authentic leadership* and show why effective leaders exemplify ethics and trust.

7 Demonstrate the role mentoring plays in our understanding of leadership.

8 Address challenges to the effectiveness of leadership.

9 Assess whether charismatic and transformational leadership generalize across cultures.

Leadership

12

I am more afraid of an army of 100 sheep led by a lion than an army of 100 lions led by a sheep.

—Talleyrand

PRIVATE EQUITY'S POSTER BOY

If it's true that "Nice guys finish last," there is no better proof than Stephen Schwarzman, chief executive of the Blackstone Group, who says his mission in life is to "inflict pain" and "kill off" his rivals. "I want war," he told the *Wall Street Journal,* "not a series of skirmishes." And win in business he has. In 20 years, he has made Blackstone one of the most profitable—and most feared—investment groups on Wall Street, with assets approaching $200 billion.

Though these are not easy times for any investment bank, Blackstone has largely avoided the pitfalls of subprime mortgages and mortgage-backed securities. Some of this strategy might be considered good fortune—Blackstone invests much more heavily in commercial than in residential real estate. However, some credit is due to Schwarzman's foresight. As he notes, "We were cautious in the so-called golden age. We were the least aggressive of all the big firms in the first half of 2007. We were very concerned about the high prices of deals and the vast amount of liquidity fuelling the boom. . . . Things always come to an end, and when they do they end badly."

Not only is Schwarzman smart and driven; he likes the attention his success has drawn. When he turned 60, his birthday party might have made Caligula blush. The affair was emceed by comedian Martin Short. Rod Stewart performed. Marvin Hamlisch put on a number from *A Chorus Line.* Singer Patti LaBelle led the Abyssinian Baptist Church choir in a song about Schwarzman. Who staged this event? Schwarzman himself! When Blackstone executives prepared a video tribute to him to be played at the event, Schwarzman intervened to squelch any roasting or other jokes played at his expense.

Schwarzman owns residences in Manhattan (a 35-room Park Avenue triplex, for which he paid $37 million), in the Hamptons (a Federal-style house, for which he paid $34 million), in Palm Beach (a 13,000-square-foot mansion, which, at $20.5 million, is the slum of the bunch), in Saint-Tropez, and in Jamaica. "I love houses," Schwarzman says. *The New Yorker* called him "the designated villain of an era . . . of heedless self-indulgence."

As you might imagine, Schwarzman is not the easiest guy to work for. While sunning himself at his Palm Beach estate, he complained that an employee wasn't wearing the proper black shoes with his uniform. On another occasion, he reportedly fired a Blackstone executive for the sound his nose made when he breathed.

Given his success, his lifestyle, and his combative personality, you might imagine Schwarzman is immune to the ridicule, resentment, and criticism he receives. "How does it feel?" he asked, and then answered his own question: "Unattractive. No thinking person wants to be reduced to a caricature."[1]

375

s Blackstone's Stephen Schwarzman shows, leaders often are not like other people. But what makes them so? Intelligence? Drive? Luck? A certain leadership style? These are some of the questions we'll tackle in this chapter. To assess yourself on another set of qualities that we'll discuss shortly, take the following self-assessment.

In this chapter, we look at what makes an effective leader and what differentiates leaders from nonleaders. First, we present trait theories, which dominated the study of leadership up to the late 1940s. Then we discuss behavioral theories, popular until the late 1960s. Next, we introduce contingency and interactive theories. Finally, we discuss the most contemporary approaches: charismatic, transformational, and authentic leadership. But first, let's clarify what we mean by *leadership*.

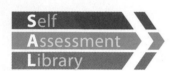

WHAT'S MY LEADERSHIP STYLE?

In the Self-Assessment Library (available on CD and online) take assessment II.B.1 (What's My Leadership Style?) and answer the following questions.

1. *How did you score on the two scales?*
2. *Do you think a leader can be both task oriented and people oriented? Do you think there are situations in which a leader has to make a choice between the two styles?*
3. *Do you think your leadership style will change over time? Why or why not?*

What Is Leadership?

1 Define *leadership* and contrast leadership and management.

Leadership and *management* are often confused. What's the difference? John Kotter of the Harvard Business School argues that management is about coping with complexity.[2] Good management brings about order and consistency by drawing up formal plans, designing rigid organization structures, and monitoring results against the plans. Leadership, in contrast, is about coping with change. Leaders establish direction by developing a vision of the future; then they align people by communicating this vision and inspiring them to overcome hurdles.

Although Kotter provides separate definitions of the two terms, both researchers and practicing managers frequently make no such distinctions. So we need to present leadership in a way that can capture how it is used in theory and practice.

We define **leadership** as the ability to influence a group toward the achievement of a vision or set of goals. The source of this influence may be formal, such as that provided by managerial rank in an organization. But not all leaders are managers, nor, for that matter, are all managers leaders. Just because an organization provides its managers with certain formal rights is no assurance they will lead effectively. Nonsanctioned leadership—the ability to influence that arises outside the formal structure of the organization—is often as important or more important than formal influence. In other words, leaders can emerge from within a group as well as by formal appointment.

Organizations need strong leadership *and* strong management for optimal effectiveness. We need leaders today to challenge the status quo, create visions

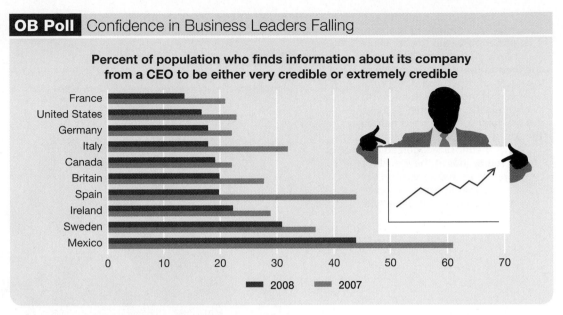

OB Poll Confidence in Business Leaders Falling

Percent of population who finds information about its company from a CEO to be either very credible or extremely credible

Legend: ■ 2008 ■ 2007

Source: Based on Edelman trust Barometer 2008 (http://www.edelman.com/TRUST/2008/TrustBarometer08_Final.pdf)

of the future, and inspire organizational members to want to achieve the visions. We also need managers to formulate detailed plans, create efficient organizational structures, and oversee day-to-day operations.

Trait Theories

2 Summarize the conclusions of trait theories of leadership.

Throughout history, strong leaders—Buddha, Napoleon, Mao, Churchill, Roosevelt, Reagan—have been described in terms of their traits. **Trait theories of leadership** thus focus on personal qualities and characteristics. We recognize leaders like South Africa's Nelson Mandela, Virgin Group CEO Richard Branson, Apple co-founder Steve Jobs, and American Express chairman Ken Chenault as *charismatic, enthusiastic,* and *courageous.* The search for personality, social, physical, or intellectual attributes that differentiate leaders from nonleaders goes back to the earliest stages of leadership research.

Early research efforts at isolating leadership traits resulted in a number of dead ends. A review in the late 1960s of 20 different studies identified nearly 80 leadership traits, but only 5 were common to 4 or more of the investigations.[3] By the 1990s, after numerous studies and analyses, about the best we could say was that most leaders "are not like other people," but the particular traits that characterized them varied a great deal from review to review.[4] It was a pretty confusing state of affairs.

A breakthrough, of sorts, came when researchers began organizing traits around the Big Five personality framework (see Chapter 5).[5] Most of the dozens of traits in various leadership reviews fit under one of the Big Five (ambition and

leadership   *The ability to influence a group toward the achievement of a vision or set of goals.*

trait theories of leadership   *Theories that consider personal qualities and characteristics that differentiate leaders from nonleaders.*

The personal qualities and characteristics of Richard Branson, chairman of Virgin Group, make him a great leader. Branson is described as fun-loving, sensitive to the needs of others, hard working, innovative, charismatic, enthusiastic, energetic, decisive, and risk taking. These traits helped the British entrepreneur build one of the most recognized and respected brands in the world for products and services in the business areas of travel, entertainment, and lifestyle.

energy are part of extraversion, for instance), giving strong support to traits as predictors of leadership.

A comprehensive review of the leadership literature, when organized around the Big Five, has found extraversion to be the most important trait of effective leaders[6] but more strongly related to leader emergence than to leader effectiveness. Sociable and dominant people are more likely to assert themselves in group situations, but leaders need to make sure they're not too assertive—one study found leaders who scored very high on assertiveness were less effective than those who were moderately high.[7]

Unlike agreeableness and emotional stability, conscientiousness and openness to experience also showed strong relationships to leadership, though not quite as strong as extraversion. Overall, the trait approach does have something to offer. Leaders who like being around people and are able to assert themselves (extraverted), disciplined and able to keep commitments they make (conscientious), and creative and flexible (open) do have an apparent advantage when it comes to leadership, suggesting good leaders do have key traits in common.

One reason is that conscientiousness and extraversion are positively related to leaders' self-efficacy, which explained most of the variance in subordinates' ratings of leader performance.[8] People are more likely to follow someone who is confident she's going in the right direction.

Another trait that may indicate effective leadership is emotional intelligence (EI), discussed in Chapter 4. Advocates of EI argue that without it, a person can have outstanding training, a highly analytical mind, a compelling vision, and an endless supply of terrific ideas but still not make a great leader. This may be especially true as individuals move up in an organization.[9] Why is EI so critical to effective leadership? A core component of EI is empathy. Empathetic leaders can sense others' needs, listen to what followers say (and don't say), and read the reactions of others. As one leader noted, "The caring part of empathy, es-

An Ethical Choice

Working for a Toxic Boss

Although we expect much of leaders, rarely do they meet the most basic definitions of effectiveness. A recent Florida State University study of 700 workers revealed that many employees believe their supervisors don't give credit when it's due, gossip about them behind their backs, and don't keep their word. The situation is so bad that for many employees, the study's lead author says, "they don't leave their company, they leave their boss."

Among the findings of the study, the following were reported by participants:

- 39 percent: Their supervisor failed to keep promises.
- 37 percent: Their supervisor failed to give credit when due.
- 31 percent: Their supervisor gave them the "silent treatment" in the past year.
- 27 percent: Their supervisor made negative comments about them to other employees or managers.

- 24 percent: Their supervisor invaded their privacy.
- 23 percent: Their supervisor blames others to cover up mistakes or minimize embarrassment.

Why do companies promote such people into leadership positions? No doubt, there are several answers. However, there are some ways you can deal more effectively with a toxic boss:

1. **Empathize, and don't take it personally.** This is hard to do. It's difficult to understand how someone can be mean spirited, unprofessional, or even abusive. But if you try to understand your boss's perspective it may help you cope with the behavior more effectively. And realize it's not about you—people who are abusive are almost always that way with others, too.
2. **Draw a line.** When a behavior is clearly inappropriate or abusive, stand up for yourself. At some point, no job is worth being

harassed or abused. And you may find standing up does not cost you your job—it has a good chance of ending, or at least reducing, the poor treatment.
3. **Don't sabotage or be vindictive.** If you take revenge, you become part of the problem.
4. **Be patient and take notes.** We're not suggesting a palace coup to unseat your boss—that strategy can go very wrong—but you may find it useful to have notes at your disposal should the boss shine the spotlight on you.

Sources: Based on A. McKee, "Neutralize Your Toxic Boss," *Harvard Business School Conversation Starter* (January 20, 2009), blogs.harvardbusiness.org; "Toxic Bosses: How to Live with the S.O.B." *Business Week* (August 14, 2008), www.businessweek.com; D. Fost, "Survey Finds Many Workers Mistrust Bosses," *San Francisco Chronicle*, January 3, 2007, www.SFGate.com; and T. Weiss, "The Narcissistic CEO," *Forbes* (August 29, 2006); www.forbes.com.

pecially for the people with whom you work, is what inspires people to stay with a leader when the going gets rough. The mere fact that someone cares is more often than not rewarded with loyalty."[10]

The link between EI and leadership effectiveness is still much less investigated than other traits. One reviewer noted, "Speculating about the practical utility of the EI construct might be premature. Despite such warnings, EI is being viewed as a panacea for many organizational malaises with recent suggestions that EI is essential for leadership effectiveness."[11] But until more rigorous evidence accumulates, we can't be confident about the connection.

Based on the latest findings, we offer two conclusions. First, traits can predict leadership. Twenty years ago, the evidence suggested otherwise. But this was probably due to the lack of a valid framework for classifying and organizing traits. The Big Five seem to have rectified that. Second, traits do a better job predicting the emergence of leaders and the appearance of leadership than actually distinguishing between *effective* and *ineffective* leaders.[12] The fact that an individual exhibits the traits and others consider that person to be a leader does not necessarily mean the leader is successful at getting his or her group to achieve its goals.

Behavioral Theories

3 Identify the central tenets and main limitations of behavioral theories.

The failures of early trait studies led researchers in the late 1940s through the 1960s to go in a different direction. They wondered whether there was something unique in the way effective leaders *behave*. Trait research provides a basis for *selecting* the right people for leadership. In contrast, behavioral studies implied we could *train* people to be leaders. Many argued that **behavioral theories of leadership** had advantages over trait theories.

The most comprehensive and replicated behavioral theories resulted from the Ohio State Studies in the late 1940s,[13] which sought to identify independent dimensions of leader behavior. Beginning with more than a thousand dimensions, the studies narrowed the list to two that substantially accounted for most of the leadership behavior described by employees. Researchers called these *initiating structure* and *consideration.*

Initiating structure is the extent to which a leader is likely to define and structure his or her role and those of employees in the search for goal attainment. It includes behavior that attempts to organize work, work relationships, and goals. A leader high in initiating structure is someone who "assigns group members to particular tasks," "expects workers to maintain definite standards of performance," and "emphasizes the meeting of deadlines."

Consideration is the extent to which a person's job relationships are characterized by mutual trust, respect for employees' ideas, and regard for their feelings. A leader high in consideration helps employees with personal problems, is friendly and approachable, treats all employees as equals, and expresses appreciation and support. In a recent survey, when asked to indicate the factors that most motivated them at work, 66 percent of employees mentioned appreciation.[14]

Leadership studies at the University of Michigan's Survey Research Center had similar objectives: to locate behavioral characteristics of leaders that appeared related to performance effectiveness. The Michigan group also came up with two behavioral dimensions: the **employee-oriented leader** emphasized interpersonal relationships by taking a personal interest in the needs of employees and accepting individual differences among them; the **production-oriented leader** emphasized the technical or task aspects of the job—concern focused on accomplishing the group's tasks. These dimensions are closely related to the Ohio State dimensions. Employee-oriented leadership is similar to consideration, and production-oriented leadership is similar to initiating structure. In fact, most leadership researchers use the terms synonymously.[15]

At one time, the results of testing behavioral theories were thought to be disappointing. One 1992 review concluded, "Overall, the research based on a two-factor conceptualization of leadership behavior has added little to our knowledge about effective leadership."[16] However, a more recent review of 160 studies found the followers of leaders high in consideration were more satisfied with their jobs, were more motivated, and had more respect for their leader. Initiating structure was more strongly related to higher levels of group and organization productivity and more positive performance evaluations.

Sally Jewell, chief executive of Recreational Equipment, Inc., is an employee-oriented leader. During her tenure as CEO, Jewell has turned a struggling company into one with record sales. But she credits REI's success to the ideas and work of employees, stating that she doesn't believe in "hero CEOs." Jewell respects each employee's contributions to the company and includes in her leadership team people who are very different from herself. Described as a leader high in consideration, she listens to employees' suggestions and empowers them in performing their jobs.

Summary of Trait Theories and Behavioral Theories

Leaders who have certain traits and who display consideration and structuring behaviors do appear to be more effective. Perhaps you're wondering whether conscientious leaders (trait) are more likely to be structuring (behavior), and extraverted leaders (trait) to be considerate (behavior). Unfortunately, we can't be sure there is a connection. Future research is needed to integrate these approaches.

Some leaders may have the right traits or display the right behaviors and still fail. And many leaders who leave while their organizations are still successful—G.E.'s Jack Welch or Procter & Gamble's A. G. Lafley—have their legacies clouded by events after their departure. As important as traits and behaviors are in identifying effective or ineffective leaders, they do not guarantee success. The context matters, too.

Contingency Theories

4 Assess contingency theories of leadership by their level of support.

Some tough-minded leaders seem to gain a lot of admirers when they take over struggling companies and help lead them out of the doldrums. Home Depot and Chrysler didn't hire former CEO Bob Nardelli for his winning personality. However, such leaders also seem to be quickly dismissed when the situation stabilizes.

The rise and fall of leaders like Bob Nardelli illustrate that predicting leadership success is more complex than isolating a few traits or behaviors. In their cases, what worked in very bad times and in very good times didn't seem to translate into long-term success. The failure by researchers in the mid-twentieth century to obtain consistent results led to a focus on situational influences. The relationship between leadership style and effectiveness suggested that under condition *a*, style *x* would be appropriate, whereas style *y* was more suitable for condition *b*, and style *z* for condition *c*. But what *were* conditions *a*, *b*, *c*? It was one thing to say leadership effectiveness depends on them and another to be able to identify them. We next consider three approaches to isolating situational variables: the Fiedler model, Hersey and Blanchard's situational theory, and path-goal theory.

The Fiedler Model

The first comprehensive contingency model for leadership was developed by Fred Fiedler.[17] The **Fiedler contingency model** proposes that effective group performance depends on the proper match between the leader's style and the degree to which the situation gives the leader control.

Identifying Leadership Style Fiedler believes a key factor in leadership success is the individual's basic leadership style. He created the **least preferred co-worker (LPC) questionnaire** to identify that style by measuring whether a

behavioral theories of leadership *Theories proposing that specific behaviors differentiate leaders from nonleaders.*

initiating structure *The extent to which a leader is likely to define and structure his or her role and those of subordinates in the search for goal attainment.*

consideration *The extent to which a leader is likely to have job relationships characterized by mutual trust, respect for subordinates' ideas, and regard for their feelings.*

employee-oriented leader *A leader who emphasizes interpersonal relations, takes a personal interest in the needs of employees, and accepts individual differences among members.*

production-oriented leader *A leader who emphasizes technical or task aspects of the job.*

Fiedler contingency model *The theory that effective groups depend on a proper match between a leader's style of interacting with subordinates and the degree to which the situation gives control and influence to the leader.*

least preferred co-worker (LPC) questionnaire *An instrument that purports to measure whether a person is task or relationship oriented.*

person is task or relationship oriented. The LPC questionnaire asks respondents to think of all the co-workers they have ever had and describe the one person they *least enjoyed* working with by rating that person on a scale of 1 to 8 for each of 16 sets of contrasting adjectives (such as pleasant–unpleasant, efficient–inefficient, open–guarded, supportive–hostile). If you describe the person you are least able to work with in favorable terms (a high LPC score), Fiedler would label you *relationship oriented*. In contrast, if you see your least-preferred co-worker in relatively unfavorable terms (a low LPC score), you are primarily interested in productivity and are *task oriented*. About 16 percent of respondents score in the middle range[18] and thus fall outside the theory's predictions. The rest of our discussion relates to the 84 percent who score in either the high or low range of the LPC questionnaire.

Fiedler assumes an individual's leadership style is fixed. This means if a situation requires a task-oriented leader and the person in the leadership position is relationship oriented, either the situation has to be modified or the leader has to be replaced to achieve optimal effectiveness.

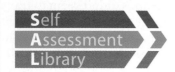

WHAT'S MY LPC SCORE?

In the Self-Assessment Library (available on CD and online) take assessment IV.E.5 (What's My LPC Score?).

Defining the Situation   After assessing an individual's basic leadership style through the LPC questionnaire, we match the leader with the situation. Fiedler has identified three contingency or situational dimensions:

1. **Leader–member relations** is the degree of confidence, trust, and respect members have in their leader.
2. **Task structure** is the degree to which the job assignments are procedurized (that is, structured or unstructured).
3. **Position power** is the degree of influence a leader has over power variables such as hiring, firing, discipline, promotions, and salary increases.

The next step is to evaluate the situation in terms of these three variables. Fiedler states that the better the leader–member relations, the more highly structured the job, and the stronger the position power, the more control the leader has. A very favorable situation (in which the leader has a great deal of control) might include a payroll manager who is well respected and whose employees have confidence in her (good leader–member relations); activities to be done—such as wage computation, check writing, and report filing—that are specific and clear (high task structure); and provision of considerable freedom to reward and punish employees (strong position power). An unfavorable situation might be that of the disliked chairperson of a volunteer United Way fundraising team. In this job, the leader has very little control.

Matching Leaders and Situations   Combining the three contingency dimensions yields eight possible situations in which leaders can find themselves (Exhibit 12-1). The Fiedler model proposes matching an individual's LPC score and these eight situations to achieve maximum leadership effectiveness.[19] Fiedler concluded that task-oriented leaders perform better in situations very favorable to them and very unfavorable. So when faced with a category I, II, III,

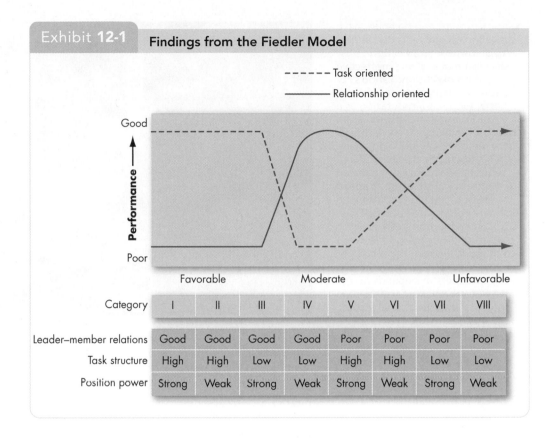

Exhibit **12-1**   **Findings from the Fiedler Model**

Category	I	II	III	IV	V	VI	VII	VIII
Leader–member relations	Good	Good	Good	Good	Poor	Poor	Poor	Poor
Task structure	High	High	Low	Low	High	High	Low	Low
Position power	Strong	Weak	Strong	Weak	Strong	Weak	Strong	Weak

VII, or VIII situation, task-oriented leaders perform better. Relationship-oriented leaders, however, perform better in moderately favorable situations—categories IV through VI. In recent years, Fiedler has condensed these eight situations down to three.[20] He now says task-oriented leaders perform best in situations of high and low control, while relationship-oriented leaders perform best in moderate control situations.

How would you apply Fiedler's findings? You would match leaders—in terms of their LPC scores—with the type of situation—in terms of leader–member relations, task structure, and position power—for which they were best suited. But remember that Fiedler views an individual's leadership style as fixed. Therefore, there are only two ways to improve leader effectiveness.

First, you can change the leader to fit the situation—as a baseball manager puts a right- or left-handed pitcher into the game depending on the hitter. If a group situation rates highly unfavorable but is currently led by a relationship-oriented manager, the group's performance could be improved under a manager who is task oriented. The second alternative is to change the situation to fit the leader, by restructuring tasks or increasing or decreasing the leader's power to control factors such as salary increases, promotions, and disciplinary actions.

leader–member relations   *The degree of confidence, trust, and respect subordinates have in their leader.*

task structure   *The degree to which job assignments are procedurized.*

position power   *Influence derived from one's formal structural position in the organization; includes power to hire, fire, discipline, promote, and give salary increases.*

Yahoo's growth and revenues have slowed in recent years due in part to an unstructured culture, slow decision making, and ineffective decision execution. Yahoo's co-founder Jerry Yang hired Carol Bartz, who has a reputation as a taskmaster and disciplinarian capable of making tough decisions, to get the company growing again. As CEO, Bartz has streamlined and centralized Yahoo's complicated organizational structure to speed decision making and formed a Customer Advocacy Group to listen to and be more responsive to customers. According to Fiedler's contingency model, the success of Bartz in restoring Yahoo's status as a digital superstar depends on the match between her leadership style and situational factors.

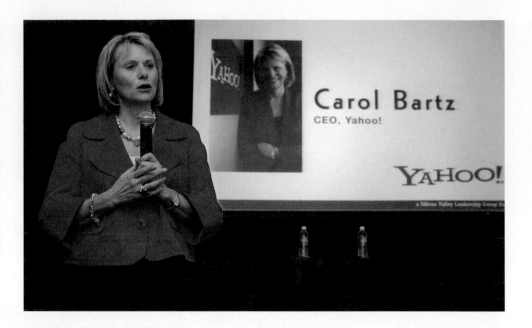

Evaluation   Studies testing the overall validity of the Fiedler model find considerable evidence to support substantial parts of it.[21] If we use only three categories rather than the original eight, there is ample evidence to support Fiedler's conclusions.[22] But the logic underlying the LPC questionnaire is not well understood, and respondents' scores are not stable.[23] The contingency variables are also complex and difficult for practitioners to assess.[24]

Other Contingency Theories

Though LPC theory is the most widely researched contingency theory, three others deserve mention.

Situational Leadership Theory   **Situational leadership theory (SLT)** focuses on the followers. It says successful leadership is achieved by selecting the right leadership style contingent on the followers' *readiness,* or the extent to which they are willing and able to accomplish a specific task. A leader should choose one of four behaviors depending on follower readiness.

If followers are *unable* and *unwilling* to do a task, the leader needs to give clear and specific directions; if they are *unable* and *willing,* the leader needs to display high task orientation to compensate for followers' lack of ability and high relationship orientation to get them to "buy into" the leader's desires. If followers are *able* and *unwilling,* the leader needs to use a supportive and participative style; if they are both *able* and *willing,* the leader doesn't need to do much.

SLT has intuitive appeal. It acknowledges the importance of followers and builds on the logic that leaders can compensate for their limited ability and motivation. Yet research efforts to test and support the theory have generally been disappointing.[25] Why? Possible explanations include internal ambiguities and inconsistencies in the model itself as well as problems with research methodology in tests. So despite its intuitive appeal and wide popularity, any endorsement must be cautious for now.

Path–Goal Theory   Developed by Robert House, **path–goal theory** extracts elements from the Ohio State leadership research on initiating structure and consideration and the expectancy theory of motivation.[26] It says it's the leader's job to provide followers with the information, support, or other resources necessary to achieve their goals. (The term *path-goal* implies effective leaders clarify followers' paths to their work goals and make the journey easier by reducing roadblocks.)

According to path-goal theory, whether a leader should be directive or supportive or should demonstrate some other behavior depends on complex analysis of the situation. It predicts the following:

- Directive leadership yields greater satisfaction when tasks are ambiguous or stressful than when they are highly structured and well laid out.
- Supportive leadership results in high performance and satisfaction when employees are performing structured tasks.
- Directive leadership is likely to be perceived as redundant among employees with high ability or considerable experience.

Testing path-goal theory has not been easy. A review of the evidence suggests mixed support, saying "These results suggest that either effective leadership does not rest in the removal of roadblocks and pitfalls to employee path instrumentalities as path-goal theories propose or that the nature of these hindrances is not in accord with the proposition of the theories." Another review found the lack of support "shocking and disappointing."[27] Others argue that adequate tests of the theory have yet to be conducted.[28] Thus the jury is still out. Because path-goal theory is so complex to test, that may remain the case for some time.

Leader-Participation Model   The final contingency theory we cover argues that *the way* the leader makes decisions is as important as *what* she or he decides. Victor Vroom and Phillip Yetton's **leader-participation model** relates leadership behavior and participation in decision making.[29] Like path-goal theory, it says leader behavior must adjust to reflect the task structure. The model is normative—it provides a decision tree of seven contingencies and five leadership styles for determining the form and amount of participation in decision making.

Research testing both the original and revised leader-participation models has not been encouraging, although the revised model rates higher in effectiveness.[30] Criticism focuses on the model's complexity and the variables it omits.[31] Although Vroom and Jago have developed a computer program to guide managers through all the decision branches in the revised model, it's not very realistic to expect practicing managers to consider 12 contingency variables, eight problem types, and five leadership styles to select the decision process for a problem.

As one leadership scholar noted, "Leaders do not exist in a vacuum"; leadership is a symbiotic relationship between leaders and followers.[32] But the theories we've covered to this point assume leaders use a fairly homogeneous style with everyone in their work unit. Think about your experiences in groups. Did leaders often act very differently toward different people? Our next theory considers differences in the relationships leaders form with different followers.

---

situational leadership theory (SLT) *A contingency theory that focuses on followers' readiness.*

path–goal theory *A theory that states that it is the leader's job to assist followers in attaining their goals and to provide the necessary direction and/or support to ensure that their goals are compatible with the overall objectives of the group or organization.*

leader-participation model *A leadership theory that provides a set of rules to determine the form and amount of participative decision making in different situations.*

Leader–Member Exchange (LMX) Theory

Think of a leader you know. Did this leader have favorites who made up his or her in-group? If you answered "yes," you're acknowledging the foundation of leader–member exchange theory.[33] **Leader–member exchange (LMX) theory** argues that, because of time pressures, leaders establish a special relationship with a small group of their followers. These individuals make up the in-group— they are trusted, get a disproportionate amount of the leader's attention, and are more likely to receive special privileges. Other followers fall into the out-group.

The theory proposes that early in the history of the interaction between a leader and a given follower, the leader implicitly categorizes the follower as an "in" or an "out," and that relationship is relatively stable over time. Leaders induce LMX by rewarding those employees with whom they want a closer linkage and punishing those with whom they do not.[34] But for the LMX relationship to remain intact, the leader and the follower must invest in the relationship.

Just how the leader chooses who falls into each category is unclear, but there is evidence in-group members have demographic, attitude, and personality characteristics similar to those of their leader or a higher level of competence than out-group members[35] (see Exhibit 12-2). Leaders and followers of the same gender tend to have closer (higher LMX) relationships than those of different genders.[36] Even though the leader does the choosing, the follower's characteristics drive the categorizing decision.

Research to test LMX theory has been generally supportive, with substantive evidence that leaders do differentiate among followers; these disparities are far from random; and followers with in-group status will have higher performance ratings, engage in more helping or "citizenship" behaviors at work, and report greater satisfaction with their superior.[37] These positive findings for in-group members shouldn't be surprising, given our knowledge of self-fulfilling prophecy (see Chapter 6). Leaders invest their resources with those they expect to perform best. And believing in-group members are the most competent, leaders treat them as such and unwittingly fulfill their prophecy.[38] These relationships may be stronger when followers have a more active role in shaping their own job performance. Research on 287 software developers and 164 supervisors showed leader–member relationships have a stronger impact on employee performance and attitudes when employees have higher levels of autonomy and a more internal locus of control.[39]

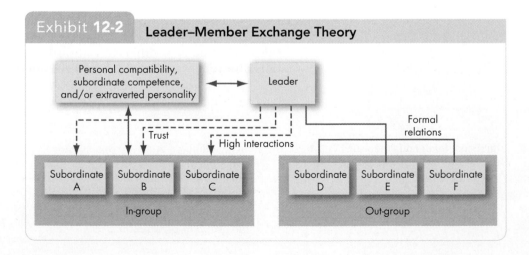

Exhibit **12-2**   Leader–Member Exchange Theory

International OB

Cultivating an International Perspective: A Necessity for Leaders

Accounting and consulting firm PricewaterhouseCoopers (PwC) is serious about expanding the worldview of its up-and-coming leaders. So the company started the Ulysses Program, which sends the company's potential leaders to foreign countries to gain knowledge and experience in cultural diversity.

One group of managers went on an 8-week consulting assignment in the Namibian outback. Their job? To help village leaders deal with the growing AIDS crisis. Without PowerPoint presentations and e-mail, the managers quickly learned to communicate in a more traditional way—face to face.

They were forced to rely less on quick technologies and more on cultivating relationships with diverse clients.

PwC hopes that by experiencing diversity firsthand, its managers will be better equipped to handle issues in any culture and more likely to find creative, unconventional solutions to complex problems. Without access to their usual resources, they can realize what they are able to accomplish. In essence, they are forced to become leaders.

Participants in the Ulysses Program tout its benefits. "I thought my purpose was to give," said Alain Michaud, who spent his time in Paraguay. "I'm

privileged. I live in a good country so why not give to a country in need? But I got more than I gave."

Other companies have taken notice of the Ulysses Program; Johnson & Johnson and Cisco Systems are just two that have adopted similar programs.

Sources: Based on S. Whittaker, "World of Opportunity in Humanitarian Work Abroad," *The StarPhoenix* (December 27, 2008), www2.canada.com; A. Shirreffs, "PricewaterhouseCoopers LLP," *Atlanta Business Chronicle* (September 26, 2008), www.bizjournals.com/atlanta; and J. Hempel and S. Porges, "It Takes a Village—and a Consultant," *BusinessWeek* (September 6, 2004), p. 76.

Charismatic Leadership and Transformational Leadership

5 Compare and contrast *charismatic* and *transformational leadership*.

In this section, we present two contemporary leadership theories—charismatic leadership and transformational leadership—which have a common theme: they view leaders as individuals who inspire followers through their words, ideas, and behaviors.

Charismatic Leadership

John F. Kennedy, Martin Luther King Jr., Ronald Reagan, Bill Clinton, Mary Kay Ash (founder of Mary Kay Cosmetics), and Steve Jobs (co-founder of Apple Computer) are frequently cited as charismatic leaders. What do they have in common?

What Is Charismatic Leadership?   Max Weber, a sociologist, defined *charisma* (from the Greek for "gift") more than a century ago as "a certain quality of an individual personality, by virtue of which he or she is set apart from ordinary people and treated as endowed with supernatural, superhuman, or at least specifically exceptional powers or qualities. These are not accessible to the

leader–member exchange (LMX) theory   *A theory that supports leaders' creation of in-groups and out-groups; subordinates with in-group status will have higher performance ratings, less turnover, and greater job satisfaction.*

| Exhibit 12-3 | Key Characteristics of Charismatic Leaders |

1. *Vision and articulation.* Has a vision—expressed as an idealized goal—that proposes a future better than the status quo; and is able to clarify the importance of the vision in terms that are understandable to others.

2. *Personal risk.* Willing to take on high personal risk, incur high costs, and engage in self-sacrifice to achieve the vision.

3. *Sensitivity to follower needs.* Perceptive of others' abilities and responsive to their needs and feelings.

4. *Unconventional behavior.* Engages in behaviors that are perceived as novel and counter to norms.

Source: Based on J. A. Conger and R. N. Kanungo, *Charismatic Leadership in Organizations* (Thousand Oaks, CA: Sage, 1998), p. 94.

ordinary person and are regarded as of divine origin or as exemplary, and on the basis of them the individual concerned is treated as a leader."[40] Weber argued that charismatic leadership was one of several ideal types of authority.

The first researcher to consider charismatic leadership in terms of OB was Robert House. According to House's **charismatic leadership theory**, followers attribute heroic or extraordinary leadership abilities when they observe certain behaviors.[41] A number of studies have attempted to identify the characteristics of charismatic leaders: they have a vision, they are willing to take personal risks to achieve that vision, they are sensitive to follower needs, and they exhibit extraordinary behaviors[42] (see Exhibit 12-3).

Are Charismatic Leaders Born or Made?   Are charismatic leaders born with their qualities? Or can people actually learn to be charismatic leaders? Yes, and yes.

Individuals *are* born with traits that make them charismatic. In fact, studies of identical twins have found they score similarly on charismatic leadership measures, even if they were raised in different households and had never met. Personality is also related to charismatic leadership; charismatic leaders are likely to be extraverted, self-confident, and achievement oriented.[43] Consider Presidents Barack Obama and Ronald Reagan: Like them or not, they are often compared because both possess the qualities of charismatic leaders.

Although a small minority thinks charisma is inherited and cannot be learned, most experts believe individuals can be trained to exhibit charismatic behaviors.[44] After all, just because we inherit certain tendencies doesn't mean we can't learn to change. One set of authors proposes a three-step process.[45] First, develop an aura of charisma by maintaining an optimistic view; using passion as a catalyst for generating enthusiasm; and communicating with the whole body, not just with words. Second, draw others in by creating a bond that inspires them to follow. Third, bring out the potential in followers by tapping into their emotions.

The approach seems to work, according to researchers who have scripted undergraduate business students to "play" charismatic.[46] The students were taught to articulate an overarching goal, communicate high performance expectations, exhibit confidence in the ability of followers to meet these expectations, and empathize with the needs of their followers; they learned to project a powerful, confident, and dynamic presence; and they practiced using a captivating and engaging voice. They were also trained to evoke charismatic nonverbal characteristics: They alternated between pacing and sitting on the edges of their desks, leaned toward the subjects, maintained direct eye contact, and had relaxed postures and animated facial expressions. Their followers had higher task performance, task adjustment, and adjustment to the leader and the group than did followers of noncharismatic leaders.

How Charismatic Leaders Influence Followers   How do charismatic leaders actually influence followers? Evidence suggests a four-step process.[47] It begins with articulating an appealing **vision**, a long-term strategy for attaining a goal by linking the present with a better future for the organization. Desirable visions fit the times and circumstances and reflect the uniqueness of the organization. Steve Jobs championed the iPod at Apple, noting, "It's as Apple as anything Apple has ever done." People in the organization must also believe the vision is challenging yet attainable. The iPod achieved Apple's goal of offering groundbreaking and easy-to-use-technology.

Second a vision is incomplete without an accompanying **vision statement**, a formal articulation of an organization's vision or mission. Charismatic leaders may use vision statements to imprint on followers an overarching goal and purpose. They then communicate high performance expectations and express confidence that followers can attain them. This enhances follower self-esteem and self-confidence.

Next, through words and actions the leader conveys a new set of values and sets an example for followers to imitate. One study of Israeli bank employees showed charismatic leaders were more effective because their employees personally identified with them. Charismatic leaders also set a tone of cooperation and mutual support. A study of 115 government employees found they had a stronger sense of personal belonging at work when they had charismatic leaders, increasing their willingness to engage in helping and compliance-oriented behavior.[48]

Finally, the charismatic leader engages in emotion-inducing and often unconventional behavior to demonstrate courage and conviction about the vision. Followers "catch" the emotions their leader is conveying.[49]

Does Effective Charismatic Leadership Depend on the Situation?   Research shows impressive correlations between charismatic leadership and high performance and satisfaction among followers.[50] People working for charismatic leaders are motivated to exert extra effort and, because they like and respect their leader, express greater satisfaction. Organizations with charismatic CEOs are also more profitable, and charismatic college professors enjoy higher course evaluations.[51] However, charisma may not always be generalizable; its effectiveness may depend on the situation. Charisma appears most successful when the follower's task has an ideological component or the environment includes a high degree of stress and uncertainty.[52] Even in laboratory studies, when people are psychologically aroused, they are more likely to respond to charismatic leaders.[53] This may explain why, when charismatic leaders surface, it's likely to be in politics or religion, or during wartime or when a business is in its infancy or facing a life-threatening crisis. Franklin D. Roosevelt offered a vision to get the United States out of the Great Depression in the 1930s. In the early 1970s, on the brink of bankruptcy, Chrysler Corporation needed a leader with unconventional ideas to reinvent it, and Lee Iacocca fulfilled that need. In 1997, when Apple Computer was floundering and lacking direction, the board persuaded charismatic co-founder Steve Jobs to return as interim CEO and return the company to its innovative roots.

Another situational factor apparently limiting charisma is level in the organization. Top executives create vision, and charisma probably better explains their successes and failures than those of lower-level managers. It's more difficult to

charismatic leadership theory   *A leadership theory that states that followers make attributions of heroic or extraordinary leadership abilities when they observe certain behaviors.*

vision   *A long-term strategy for attaining a goal or goals.*

vision statement   *A formal articulation of an organization's vision or mission.*

utilize a person's charismatic leadership qualities in lower-level management jobs or to align his or her visions with the larger goals of the organization as a whole.

Finally, people are especially receptive to charismatic leadership when they sense a crisis, when they are under stress, or when they fear for their lives. And some peoples' personalities are especially susceptible to charismatic leadership.[54] Consider self-esteem. An individual who lacks self-esteem and questions his or her self-worth is more likely to absorb a leader's direction rather than establish his or her own way of leading or thinking.

The Dark Side of Charismatic Leadership   Charismatic business leaders like AIG's Hank Greenberg, GE's Jack Welch, Tyco's Dennis Kozlowski, Southwest Airlines' Herb Kelleher, Disney's Michael Eisner, and HP's Carly Fiorina became celebrities on the order of David Beckham and Madonna. Every company wanted a charismatic CEO, and to attract them boards of directors gave them unprecedented autonomy and resources—the use of private jets and multimillion-dollar penthouses, interest-free loans to buy beach homes and artwork, security staffs, and similar benefits befitting royalty. One study showed charismatic CEOs were able to leverage higher salaries even when their performance was mediocre.[55]

Unfortunately, charismatic leaders who are larger than life don't necessarily act in the best interests of their organizations.[56] Many used their power to remake companies in their own image and allowed their own interest and personal goals to override the goals of the organization. The results at companies such as Enron, Tyco, WorldCom, and HealthSouth were leaders who recklessly used organizational resources for their personal benefit, and executives who violated laws and ethical boundaries to inflate stock prices and allow leaders to cash in millions of dollars in stock options.

We don't mean to suggest charismatic leadership isn't effective; overall it is. But a charismatic leader isn't always the answer. Success depends, to some extent, on the situation and on the leader's vision. Some charismatic leaders—Hitler, for example—are all too successful at convincing their followers to pursue a vision that can be disastrous.

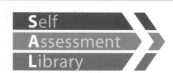

HOW CHARISMATIC AM I?

In the Self-Assessment Library (available on CD and online), take assessment II.B.2 (How Charismatic Am I?).

Transformational Leadership

A stream of research has focused on differentiating transformational from transactional leaders.[57] The Ohio State studies, Fiedler's model, and path-goal theory describe **transactional leaders**, who guide their followers toward established goals by clarifying role and task requirements. **Transformational leaders** inspire followers to transcend their self-interests for the good of the organization and can have an extraordinary effect on their followers. Andrea Jung at Avon, Richard Branson of the Virgin Group, and Jim McNerney of Boeing are all transformational leaders. They pay attention to the concerns and needs of individual followers; they change followers' awareness of issues by helping them look at old problems in new ways; and they excite and inspire followers to put out extra effort to achieve group goals. Exhibit 12-4 briefly identifies and defines the characteristics that differentiate these two types of leaders.

Exhibit 12-4	Characteristics of Transactional and Transformational Leaders

Transactional Leader

Contingent Reward: Contracts exchange of rewards for effort, promises rewards for good performance, recognizes accomplishments.

Management by Exception (active): Watches and searches for deviations from rules and standards, takes correct action.

Management by Exception (passive): Intervenes only if standards are not met.

Laissez-Faire: Abdicates responsibilities, avoids making decisions.

Transformational Leader

Idealized Influence: Provides vision and sense of mission, instills pride, gains respect and trust.

Inspirational Motivation: Communicates high expectations, uses symbols to focus efforts, expresses important purposes in simple ways.

Intellectual Stimulation: Promotes intelligence, rationality, and careful problem solving.

Individualized Consideration: Gives personal attention, treats each employee individually, coaches, advises.

Source: B. M. Bass, "From Transactional to Transformational Leadership: Learning to Share the Vision," *Organizational Dynamics,* Winter 1990, p. 22. Reprinted by permission of the publisher, American Management Association, New York. All rights reserved.

Transactional and transformational leadership aren't opposing approaches to getting things done.[58] They complement each other, though they're not equally important. Transformational leadership *builds on* transactional leadership and produces levels of follower effort and performance beyond what transactional leadership alone can do. But the reverse isn't true. So if you are a good transactional leader but do not have transformational qualities, you'll likely only be a mediocre leader. The best leaders are transactional *and* transformational.

Full Range of Leadership Model Exhibit 12-5 shows the full range of leadership model. Laissez-faire is the most passive and therefore least effective of leader behaviors.[59] Management by exception—active or passive—is slightly better than laissez-faire, but it's still considered ineffective. Management-by-exception leaders tend to be available only when there is a problem, which is often too late. Contingent reward leadership can be an effective style of leadership but will not get employees to go above and beyond the call of duty.

Only with the four remaining styles—all aspects of transformational leadership—are leaders able to motivate followers to perform above expectations and transcend their self-interest for the sake of the organization. Individualized consideration, intellectual stimulation, inspirational motivation, and idealized influence all result in extra effort from workers, higher productivity, higher morale and satisfaction, higher organizational effectiveness, lower turnover, lower absenteeism, and greater organizational adaptability. Based on

transactional leaders *Leaders who guide or motivate their followers in the direction of established goals by clarifying role and task requirements.*

transformational leaders *Leaders who inspire followers to transcend their own self-interests and who are capable of having a profound and extraordinary effect on followers.*

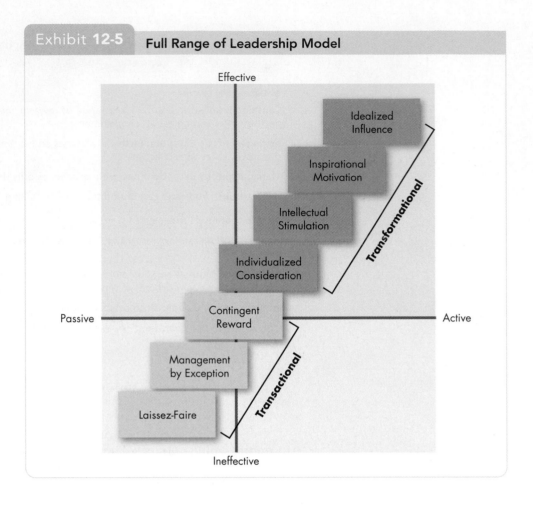

Exhibit 12-5   Full Range of Leadership Model

this model, leaders are generally most effective when they regularly use each of the four transformational behaviors.

How Transformational Leadership Works   Transformational leaders are more effective because they are more creative but also because they encourage those who follow them to be creative, too.[60] In companies with transformational leaders, there is greater decentralization of responsibility, managers have more propensity to take risks, and compensation plans are geared toward long-term results, all of which facilitate corporate entrepreneurship.[61]

Companies with transformational leaders also show greater agreement among top managers about the organization's goals, which yields superior organizational performance.[62] Similar results, showing that transformational leaders improve performance by building consensus among group members, have been demonstrated in the Israeli military.[63] Transformational leaders are able to increase follower self-efficacy, giving the group a "can do" spirit.[64] Followers are more likely to pursue ambitious goals, agree on the strategic goals of the organization, and believe the goals they are pursuing are personally important.[65] VeriSign's CEO, Stratton Sclavos, says, "It comes down to charting a course—having the ability to articulate for your employees where you're headed and how you're going to get there. Even more important is choosing people to work with who have that same level of passion, commitment, fear, and competitiveness to drive toward those same goals."[66]

Sclavos' remark about goals brings up vision. Just as vision helps explain how charismatic leadership works, vision explains part of the effect of transformational leadership. One study found vision was even more important than a charismatic (effusive, dynamic, lively) communication style in explaining the success of entrepreneurial firms.[67] Finally, transformational leadership engenders commitment on the part of followers and instills greater trust in the leader.[68]

Evaluation of Transformational Leadership   Transformational leadership has been impressively supported at various job levels and in disparate occupations (school principals, teachers, marine commanders, ministers, presidents of MBA associations, military cadets, union shop stewards, sales reps). One recent study of R&D firms found teams whose project leaders scored high on transformational leadership produced better-quality products as judged 1 year later and were more profitable 5 years later.[69] A review of 87 studies testing transformational leadership found it was related to the motivation and satisfaction of followers and the higher performance and perceived effectiveness of leaders.[70]

Transformational leadership isn't equally effective in all situations, however. It has a greater impact on the bottom line in smaller, privately held firms than in more complicated organizations.[71] The personal nature of transformational leadership may be most effective when leaders can directly interact with the workforce and make decisions than when they report to an external board of directors or deal with a complex bureaucratic structure. Another study showed transformational leaders were more effective in improving group potency in teams higher in power distance and collectivism.[72] Where group members are highly individualistic and don't readily cede decision-making authority, transformational leadership might not have much impact.

Transformational leadership theory is not perfect. There are concerns about whether contingent reward leadership is strictly a characteristic of transactional leaders only. And contrary to the full range of leadership model, the 4 I's in transformational leadership are not always superior in effectiveness to transactional leadership (contingent reward leadership sometimes works as well as transformational leadership).

In summary, transformational leadership is more strongly correlated than transactional leadership with lower turnover rates, higher productivity, lower employee stress and burnout, and higher employee satisfaction.[73] Like charisma, it can be learned. One study of Canadian bank managers found branches managed by those who underwent transformational leadership training performed significantly better than branches whose managers did not receive training. Other studies show similar results.[74]

Transformational Leadership versus Charismatic Leadership   Are transformational leadership and charismatic leadership the same? Researcher Robert House considers them synonymous, calling the differences "modest" and "minor." However, one researcher who disagrees says, "The purely charismatic [leader] may want followers to adopt the charismatic's world view and go no further; the transformational leader will attempt to instill in followers the ability to question not only established views but eventually those established by the leader."[75] Although many researchers believe transformational is broader than charismatic leadership, a leader who scores high on transformational leadership is also likely to score high on charisma. Therefore, in practice, they may be roughly equivalent.

Authentic Leadership: Ethics and Trust Are the Foundation of Leadership

6 Define *authentic leadership* and show why effective leaders exemplify ethics and trust.

Although theories have increased our understanding of effective leadership, they do not explicitly deal with the role of ethics and trust, which some argue is essential to complete the picture. Here we consider these two concepts under the rubric of authentic leadership.[76]

What Is Authentic Leadership?

Mike Ullman, J. C. Penney CEO, argues that leaders have to be selfless, listen well, and be honest. Campbell Soup's CEO Douglas R. Conant is decidedly understated. When asked to reflect on the strong performance of Campbell Soup, he demurs, "We're hitting our stride a little bit more (than our peers)." He regularly admits mistakes and often says, "I can do better." Ullman and Conant appear to be good exemplars of authentic leadership.[77]

Authentic leaders know who they are, know what they believe in and value, and act on those values and beliefs openly and candidly. Their followers consider them ethical people. The primary quality produced by authentic leadership, therefore, is trust. Authentic leaders share information, encourage open communication, and stick to their ideals. The result: people come to have faith in them.

Because the concept is new, there has been little research on authentic leadership. However, it's a promising way to think about ethics and trust in leadership because it focuses on the moral aspects of being a leader. Transformational or charismatic leaders can have a vision, and communicate it persuasively, but sometimes the vision is wrong (as in the case of Hitler), or the leader is more concerned with his or her own needs or pleasures, as were Dennis Kozlowski (ex-CEO of Tyco) and Jeff Skilling (ex-CEO of Enron).[78]

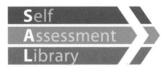

AM I AN ETHICAL LEADER?

In the Self-Assessment Library (available on CD and online), take assessment IV.E.4 (Am I an Ethical Leader?).

Ethics and Leadership

Only recently have researchers begun to consider the ethical implications in leadership.[79] Why now? One reason may be the growing interest in ethics throughout the field of management. Another may be the discovery that many past leaders—such as Martin Luther King Jr., John F. Kennedy, and Thomas Jefferson—suffered ethical shortcomings. Some companies, like Boeing, are tying executive compensation to ethics to reinforce the idea that, in CEO Jim McNerney's words, "there's no compromise between doing things the right way and performance."[80]

Ethics and leadership intersect at a number of junctures. Transformational leaders have been described as fostering moral virtue when they try to change the attitudes and behaviors of followers.[81] Charisma, too, has an ethical component. Unethical leaders use their charisma to enhance *power over* followers, directed toward self-serving ends. Ethical leaders use it in a socially constructive way to serve others.[82] Leaders who treat their followers with fairness, especially by providing honest, frequent, and accurate information, are seen as more effective.[83] Because top executives set the moral tone for an organization, they need to set high ethical standards, demonstrate those standards through their own behavior, and encourage and reward integrity in others while avoiding abuses of power such as giving themselves large raises and bonuses while seeking to cut costs by laying off longtime employees.

Leadership is not value free. In assessing its effectiveness we need to address the *means* a leader uses in trying to achieve goals, as well as the content of those goals. Scholars have tried to integrate ethical and charismatic leadership by advancing the idea of **socialized charismatic leadership**—leadership that conveys other centered (not self centered) values by leaders who model ethical conduct.[84] Socialized charismatic leaders are able to bring employee values in line with their own values through their words and actions.[85]

Trust and Leadership

Trust is a psychological state that exists when you agree to make yourself vulnerable to another because you have positive expectations about how things are going to turn out.[86] Even though you aren't completely in control of the situation, you are willing to take a chance that the other person will come through for you.

Trust is a primary attribute associated with leadership; breaking it can have serious adverse effects on a group's performance.[87] As one author noted, "Part of the leader's task has been, and continues to be, working with people to find and solve problems, but whether leaders gain access to the knowledge and creative thinking they need to solve problems depends on how much people trust them. Trust and trust-worthiness modulate the leader's access to knowledge and cooperation."[88]

Followers who trust a leader are willing to be vulnerable to the leader's actions, confident their rights and interests will not be abused.[89] Transformational leaders create support for their ideas in part by arguing that their direction will be in everyone's best interests. People are unlikely to look up to or follow someone they perceive as dishonest or likely to take advantage of them. "Honesty is absolutely essential to leadership. If people are going to follow someone willingly, whether it be into battle or into the boardroom, they first want to assure themselves that the person is worthy of their trust."[90]

In a simple contractual exchange of goods and services, your employer is legally bound to pay you for fulfilling your job description. But today's rapid reorganizations, diffusion of responsibility, and collaborative team-based work style mean employment relationships are not stable long-term contracts with explicit terms. Rather, they are more fundamentally based on trusting relationships than ever before. You have to trust that if you show your supervisor a creative project you've been working on, she won't steal the credit behind your back. You have to trust that extra work you've been doing will be recognized in your performance appraisal. In contemporary organizations, where less work is closely documented and specified, voluntary employee contribution based on trust is

authentic leaders *Leaders who know who they are, know what they believe in and value, and act on those values and beliefs openly and candidly. Their followers would consider them to be ethical people.*

socialized charismatic leadership *A leadership concept that states that leaders convey values that are other centered versus self centered and who role-model ethical conduct.*

trust *A positive expectation that another will not act opportunistically.*

absolutely necessary. And only a trusted leader will be able to encourage employees to reach beyond themselves to a transformational goal.

How Is Trust Developed?

Trust isn't just about the leader; the characteristics of the followers will also influence the development of trust.

What key characteristics lead us to believe a leader is trustworthy? Evidence has identified three: integrity, benevolence, and ability (see Exhibit 12-6).[91]

Integrity refers to honesty and truthfulness. It seems the most critical of the three in assessing another's trustworthiness.[92] When 570 white-collar employees were recently given a list of 28 attributes related to leadership, they rated honesty the most important by far.[93] Integrity also means having consistency between what you do and say. "Nothing is noticed more quickly . . . than a discrepancy between what executives preach and what they expect their associates to practice."[94]

Benevolence means the trusted person has your interests at heart, even if yours aren't necessarily in line with theirs. Caring and supportive behavior is part of the emotional bond between leaders and followers.

Ability encompasses an individual's technical and interpersonal knowledge and skills. Even a highly principled person with the best intentions in the world won't be trusted to accomplish a positive outcome for you if you don't have faith in his or her ability to get the job done. Does the person know what he or she is talking about? You're unlikely to listen to or depend on someone whose abilities you don't respect.

Trust as a Process

Trust propensity refers to how likely a particular employee is to trust a leader. Some people are simply more likely to believe others can be trusted.[95] Those who carefully document every promise or conversation with their supervisors aren't very high in trust propensity, and they probably aren't going to take a leader's word for anything. Those who think most people are basically honest and forthright will be much more likely to seek out evidence that their leaders have behaved in a trustworthy manner. Trust propensity is closely linked to the personality trait of agreeableness, while people with lower self-esteem are less likely to trust others.[96]

Time is the final ingredient in the recipe for trust. Trust doesn't happen immediately: We come to trust people based on observing their behavior over

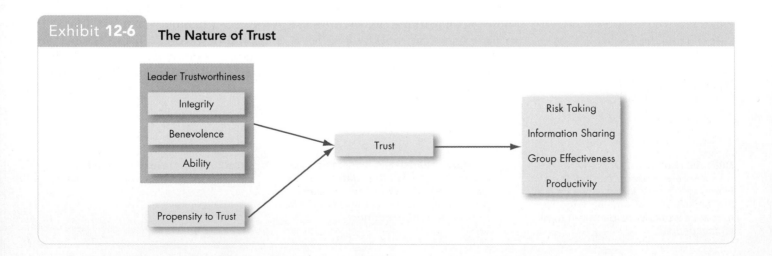

Exhibit **12-6**   **The Nature of Trust**

Leader Trustworthiness
- Integrity
- Benevolence
- Ability

Propensity to Trust

Trust

- Risk Taking
- Information Sharing
- Group Effectiveness
- Productivity

a period of time.[97] Leaders need to demonstrate they have integrity, benevolence, and ability in situations where trust is important, say where they could behave opportunistically or let employees down but don't. Trust can also be won in the ability domain simply by demonstrating competence.

Leaders who break the psychological contract with workers, demonstrating they aren't trustworthy, will find employees are less satisfied and less committed, have higher intentions to turnover, engage in less citizenship behavior, and have lower task performance.[98] Once it is violated, trust can be regained, but only in certain situations that depend on the type of violation.[99] If the cause is lack of ability, it's usually best to apologize and recognize you should have done better. When lack of integrity is the problem, though, apologies don't do much good. Regardless of the violation, simply saying nothing or refusing to confirm or deny guilt is never an effective strategy for regaining trust. Trust can be restored when we observe a consistent pattern of trustworthy behavior by the transgressor. However, if the transgressor used deception, trust never fully returns, not even after apologies, promises, or a consistent pattern of trustworthy actions.[100]

What Are the Consequences of Trust?

Trust between supervisors and employees is related to a number of positive employment outcomes. Here are just a few of the most important that research has shown:

- *Trust encourages taking risks.* Whenever employees decide to deviate from the usual way of doing things, or to take their supervisors' word on a new direction, they are taking a risk. In both cases, a trusting relationship can facilitate that leap.
- *Trust facilitates information sharing.* One big reason employees fail to express concerns at work is that they don't feel psychologically safe revealing their views. When managers demonstrate they will give employees' ideas a fair hearing and show they are concerned enough to actively make changes, employees are more willing to speak out.[101]
- *Trusting groups are more effective.* When a leader sets a trusting tone in a group, members are more willing to help each other and exert extra effort for one another, which further increases trust. Conversely, members of mistrusting groups tend to be suspicious of each other, are constantly on guard against exploitation, and restrict communication with others in the group. These actions tend to undermine and eventually destroy the group.
- *Trust enhances productivity.* The bottom-line interest of companies also appears positively influenced by trust. Employees who trust their supervisors tend to receive higher performance ratings.[102] Mistrust focuses attention on the differences in member interests, making it difficult for people to visualize common goals. People respond by concealing information and secretly pursuing their own interests. A climate of mistrust tends to stimulate dysfunctional forms of conflict and retard cooperation.

Leading for the Future: Mentoring

7 Demonstrate the role mentoring plays in our understanding of leadership.

Leaders often take responsibility for developing future leaders. Their role as mentors helps preserve and develop organizational culture and knowledge over time. Let's consider what makes mentoring valuable as well as its potential pitfalls.

Exhibit 12-7 Career and Psychological Functions of the Mentoring Relationship

Career Functions	Psychosocial Functions
• Lobbying to get the protégé challenging and visible assignments	• Counseling the protégé to bolster his or her self-confidence
• Coaching the protégé to help develop his or her skills and achieve work objectives	• Sharing personal experiences with the protégé
• Providing exposure to influential individuals within the organization	• Providing friendship and acceptance
• Protecting the protégé from possible risks to his or her reputation	• Acting as a role model
• Sponsoring the protégé by nominating him or her for potential advances or promotions	
• Acting as a sounding board for ideas the protégé might be hesitant to share with a direct supervisor	

Mentoring

A **mentor** is a senior employee who sponsors and supports a less-experienced employee, a protégé. Successful mentors are good teachers. They present ideas clearly, listen well, and empathize with protégés' problems. Mentoring relationships serve both career functions and psychosocial functions (see Exhibit 12-7).[103]

Traditional informal mentoring relationships develop when leaders identify a less experienced, lower-level employee who appears to have potential for future development.[104] The protégé will often be tested with a particularly challenging assignment. If he or she performs acceptably, the mentor will develop the relationship, informally showing the protégé how the organization *really* works outside its formal structures and procedures. Protégés can also learn how the mentor has navigated early career issues or led effectively and how to work through problems with minimal stress.

Why would a leader want to be a mentor?[105] Many feel they have something to share with the younger generation and want to provide a legacy. Mentoring also provides unfiltered access to the attitudes of lower-ranking employees, and

Myth or Science?

"Men Make Better Leaders Than Women"

This statement is false. Little evidence supports the belief that men make better leaders than women; indeed, though the differences are small, evidence suggests just the opposite.

The stereotype that men made better leaders assumed they were inherently better skilled for leadership due to having a stronger task focus, lower emotionality, and a greater propensity to be directive. The most recent evidence suggests that while there is a great deal of overlap between males and females in their leadership styles, on average women do have a slight edge over men. A recent review of 45 companies found female leaders were more transformational than males. The authors concluded, "These data attest to the ability of women to perform very well in leadership roles in contemporary organizations."

Men continue to dominate leadership positions; only 2.6 percent of *Fortune 500* CEOs are women. But being chosen as leader is not the same as performing well once selected. Research suggests more individuals prefer male leaders. Given the evidence we've reviewed here, those preferences deserve serious reexamination.[106]

protégés can be an excellent source of early warning signals that identify potential organizational problems.

Are all employees in an organization equally likely to participate in a mentoring relationship? Unfortunately, no.[107] In the United States, upper managers in most organizations have traditionally been white males, and because mentors tend to select protégés similar to themselves in background, education, gender, race, ethnicity, and religion, minorities and women are less likely to be chosen. "People naturally move to mentor and can more easily communicate with those with whom they most closely identify."[108] Senior male managers may also select male protégés to minimize problems such as sexual attraction or gossip.

Many organizations have created formal programs to ensure mentoring relationships are equally available to minorities and women.[109] Although begun with the best intentions, these formal relationships are not as effective as informal ones.[110]

Poor planning and design may often be the reason. Mentor commitment is critical to a program's effectiveness; mentors must see the relationship as beneficial to themselves and the protégé. The protégé, too, must feel he or she has input into the relationship; someone who feels it's foisted on him or her will just go through the motions.[111] Formal mentoring programs are also most likely to succeed if they appropriately match the work style, needs, and skills of protégé and mentor.[112]

You might assume mentoring is valuable for career success, but research suggests the gains are primarily psychological. Benefits to objective outcomes like compensation and job performance are very small. One review concluded, "Though mentoring may not be properly labeled an utterly useless concept to careers, neither can it be argued to be as important as the main effects of other influences on career success such as ability and personality."[113] It may *feel* nice to have a mentor, but it doesn't appear that having a good mentor, or any mentor, is critical to your career. Mentors may be effective not because of the functions they provide but because of the resources they can obtain: A mentor connected to a powerful network can build relationships that will help the protégé advance. Most evidence suggests that network ties, whether built through a mentor or not, are a significant predictor of career success.[114] If a mentor is not well connected or not a very strong performer, the best mentoring advice in the world will not be very beneficial.

When Scott Flanders became CEO of Freedom Communications, he told his managers to *limit* the time they spent mentoring their staffs. Tom Mattia, a manager at Coca-Cola who oversees 90 direct reports, finds he has to practice "mentoring on the go."[115]

Challenges to the Leadership Construct

8 Address challenges to the effectiveness of leadership.

"In the 1500s, people ascribed all events they didn't understand to God. Why did the crops fail? God. Why did someone die? God. Now our all-purpose explanation is leadership."[116] But much of an organization's success or failure is due to factors outside the influence of leadership. Sometimes it's just a matter of being in the right or wrong place at a given time.

mentor *A senior employee who sponsors and supports a less-experienced employee, called a protégé.*

Richard Wagoner was fired as CEO and chairman of General Motors. His leadership was faulted for playing a part in the automaker's bankruptcy, with critics saying that he did not force much-needed radical change in reducing debt, cutting costs, and investing in fuel-efficient cars. Wagoner, however, inherited a messy situation and accomplished much in fixing GM during his 9 years as CEO. He cut GM's U.S. workforce from 177,000 to about 92,000, closed factories, saved billions of dollars by globalizing engineering, manufacturing, and design, and led a resurgence in quality and performance. But the attribution approach to leadership would suggest a reverse causality: that GM's failures caused people to question his leadership, and not the other way around.

In this section, we present two perspectives and one technological change that challenge accepted beliefs about the value of leadership.

Leadership as an Attribution

As you may remember from Chapter 6, attribution theory examines how people try to make sense of cause-and-effect relationships. The **attribution theory of leadership** says leadership is merely an attribution people make about other individuals.[117] Thus we attribute to leaders intelligence, outgoing personality, strong verbal skills, aggressiveness, understanding, and industriousness.[118] At the organizational level, we tend to see leaders, rightly or wrongly, as responsible for extremely negative or extremely positive performance.[119]

One longitudinal study of 128 major U.S. corporations found that, whereas perceptions of CEO charisma did not lead to objective company performance, company performance did lead to perceptions of charisma.[120] Employee perceptions of their leaders' behaviors are significant predictors of leader blame for failure, even after taking leaders' self-assessments into account.[121] A study of over 3,000 employees from Western Europe, the United States, and the Middle East found people who tended to "romanticize" leadership in general were more likely to believe their own leaders were transformational.[122]

When Merrill Lynch began to lose billions in 2008 as a result of its investments in mortgage securities, it wasn't long before CEO Stan O'Neal lost his job. He appeared before the House Oversight and Government Reform Committee of the U.S. Congress for what one committee member termed "a public flogging." CNBC's Jim Cramer called him "Wall Street's Wicked Witch." Others criticized O'Neal's golf handicap, some called him a "criminal," and others suggested Merrill's losses represented "attempted destruction."[123]

Whether O'Neal was responsible for the losses at Merrill or deserved his nine-figure severance package are difficult questions to answer. However, it is not difficult to argue that he probably changed very little between 2004 when *Fortune* described him as a "turnaround genius" and 2009 when he was fired. What did change was the performance of the organization he led. It's not necessarily wrong to terminate a CEO for failing or flagging financial performance. However, O'Neal's story illustrates the power of the attribution approach to leadership: hero and genius when things are going well, villain when they aren't.

We also make demographic assumptions about leaders. Respondents in a study assumed a leader described with no identifying racial information was white at a rate beyond the base rate of white employees in a company. In scenarios where identical leadership situations are described but the leaders' race is manipulated, white leaders are rated as more effective than leaders of other racial groups.[124] Other data suggest women's perceived success as transformational leaders may be based on demographic characteristics. Teams prefer male leaders when aggressively competing against other teams, but they prefer female leaders when the competition is within teams and calls for improving positive relationships within the group.[125]

Attribution theory suggests what's important is projecting the *appearance* of being a leader rather than focusing on *actual accomplishments*. Leader-wannabes who can shape the perception that they're smart, personable, verbally adept, aggressive, hardworking, and consistent in their style can increase the probability their bosses, colleagues, and employees will view them as effective leaders.

Substitutes for and Neutralizers of Leadership

One theory of leadership suggests that in many situations leaders' actions are irrelevant.[126] Experience and training are among the **substitutes** that can replace the need for a leader's support or ability to create structure. Organizational charac-

Exhibit 12-8	Substitutes for and Neutralizers of Leadership	

Defining Characteristics	Relationship-Oriented Leadership	Task-Oriented Leadership
Individual		
Experience/training	No effect on	Substitutes for
Professionalism	Substitutes for	Substitutes for
Indifference to rewards	Neutralizes	Neutralizes
Job		
Highly structured task	No effect on	Substitutes for
Provides its own feedback	No effect on	Substitutes for
Intrinsically satisfying	Substitutes for	No effect on
Organization		
Explicit formalized goals	No effect on	Substitutes for
Rigid rules and procedures	No effect on	Substitutes for
Cohesive work groups	Substitutes for	Substitutes for

Source: Based on S. Kerr and J. M. Jermier, "Substitutes for Leadership: Their Meaning and Measurement," *Organizational Behavior and Human Performance,* December 1978, p. 378.

teristics such as explicit formalized goals, rigid rules and procedures, and cohesive work groups can also replace formal leadership, while indifference to organizational rewards can neutralize its effects. **Neutralizers** make it impossible for leader behavior to make any difference to follower outcomes (see Exhibit 12-8).

This observation shouldn't be too surprising. After all, we've introduced a number of variables—such as attitudes, personality, ability, and group norms—that affect employee performance and satisfaction. It's simplistic to think employees are guided to goal accomplishments solely by the actions of their leader. Leadership is simply another independent variable in our overall OB model.

There are many possible substitutes for and neutralizers of many different types of leader behaviors across many different situations. Moreover, sometimes the difference between substitutes and neutralizers is fuzzy. If I'm working on a task that's intrinsically enjoyable, theory predicts leadership will be less important because the task itself provides enough motivation. But does that mean intrinsically enjoyable tasks neutralize leadership effects, or substitute for them, or both? Another problem is that while substitutes for leadership (such as employee characteristics, the nature of the task, and so forth) matter to performance, that doesn't necessarily mean that leadership doesn't.[127]

Online Leadership

How do you lead people who are physically separated from you and with whom you communicate electronically? This question has so far received minimal attention from OB researchers.[128] But today's managers and their employees are increasingly linked by networks rather than geographic proximity. Obvious examples include managers who regularly use e-mail to communicate with their staff, managers who oversee virtual projects or teams, and managers whose telecommuting employees are linked to the office by an Internet connection.

attribution theory of leadership *A leadership theory that says that leadership is merely an attribution that people make about other individuals.*

substitutes *Attributes, such as experience and training, that can replace the need for a leader's support or ability to create structure.*

neutralizers *Attributes that make it impossible for leader behavior to make any difference to follower outcomes.*

Networked communication is a powerful channel that can build and enhance leadership effectiveness. But when misused, it can undermine much of what a leader has achieved through verbal communication. We propose that online leaders have to think carefully about what actions they want their digital messages to initiate.

Online leaders also confront unique challenges, the greatest of which appears to be developing and maintaining trust. **Identification-based trust**, based on a mutual understanding of each other's intentions and appreciation of the others wants and desires, is particularly difficult to achieve without face-to-face interaction.[129] It's not yet clear whether it's even possible for employees to identify with or trust leaders with whom they communicate only electronically.[130] And online negotiations can also be hindered because parties express lower levels of trust.[131]

This discussion leads us to the tentative conclusion that, for an increasing number of managers, good leadership skills may include the abilities to communicate support, trust, and inspiration through keyboarded words and accurately read emotions in others' messages. In electronic communication, writing skills are likely to become an extension of interpersonal skills.

Finding and Creating Effective Leaders

How can organizations find or create effective leaders? Let's try to answer that question.

Selecting Leaders

The entire process organizations go through to fill management positions is essentially an exercise in trying to identify effective leaders. You might begin by reviewing the knowledge, skills, and abilities needed to do the job effectively. Personality tests can identify traits associated with leadership—extraversion, conscientiousness, and openness to experience. Testing to find a leadership-candidate's score on self-monitoring also makes sense; high self-monitors are better at reading situations and adjusting their behavior accordingly. Given the value of social skills in managerial effectiveness, candidates with high emotional intelligence should have an advantage, especially in situations requiring transformational leadership.[132]

Experience is a poor predictor of leader effectiveness, but situation-specific experience is relevant. You can interview to determine whether a candidate's prior experience fits the situation you're trying to fill and to identify whether he or she has leadership traits, such as extraversion, self-confidence, a vision, the verbal skills to frame issues, or a charismatic physical presence.

Since nothing lasts forever, the most important event an organization needs to plan for is a change in leadership. By his own account, in his last years at GE, Jack Welch spent more time picking his successor than doing anything else. Other organizations seem to spend no time on leadership succession and are surprised when their picks turn out poorly. University of Kentucky chose its men's basketball coach Billy Gillispie within 2 weeks of the departure of Tubby Smith. Yet within 2 years Gillispie had been fired, causing observers to wonder if Kentucky had done its homework in leadership succession.

Training Leaders

Organizations spend billions of dollars on leadership training and development.[133] These efforts take many forms—from $50,000 executive leadership programs offered by universities such as Harvard to sailing experiences offered by the Outward Bound program. Business schools, including some elite programs such as those at Dartmouth, MIT, and Stanford, are placing renewed emphasis on leadership development. Some companies, too, place a lot of emphasis on leadership development. Goldman Sachs is well known for developing leaders; *BusinessWeek* called it the "Leadership Factory."[134]

How can managers get maximum effect from their leadership-training budgets?[135] First, let's recognize the obvious. Leadership training of any kind is likely to be more successful with high self-monitors. Such individuals have the flexibility to change their behavior.

Second, what can organizations teach that might be related to higher leader effectiveness? Probably not "vision creation" but, likely, implementation skills. We can train people to develop "an understanding about content themes critical to effective visions."[136] We can also teach skills such as trust building and mentoring. And leaders can be taught situational-analysis skills. They can learn how to evaluate situations, modify them to better fit their style, and assess which leader behaviors might be most effective in given situations. A number of companies turn to executive coaches to help senior managers improve their leadership skills.[137] Charles Schwab, eBay, Pfizer, Unilever, and American Express have hired coaches to help top executives one on one to improve their interpersonal skills and act less autocratically.[138]

Behavioral training through modeling exercises can increase an individual's ability to exhibit charismatic leadership qualities. Recall the researchers who scripted undergraduate business students to "play" charismatic, which is a case in point.[139] Finally, leaders can be trained in transformational leadership skills that have bottom-line results, whether in the financial performance of Canadian banks or the effectiveness of soldiers in the Israeli Defense Forces.[140]

Global Implications

9 Assess whether charismatic and transformational leadership generalize across cultures.

Most of the research discussed in this chapter was conducted in English-speaking countries. We know very little about how culture might influence the validity of the theories, particularly in Eastern cultures. However, a recent analysis of the Global Leadership and Organizational Behavior Effectiveness (GLOBE) research project (see Chapter 5 for more details) has produced some useful preliminary insights.[141]

The study sought to address how culture might affect a U.S. manager given 2 years to lead a project in four prototypical countries whose cultures diverged in different ways: Brazil, France, Egypt, and China. Let's consider each.

- *Brazil* Based on the values of Brazilian employees, a U.S. manager leading a team in Brazil would need to be team oriented, participative, and humane. Leaders high on consideration who emphasize participative decision making and have high LPC scores would be best suited to managing employees in this culture. As one Brazilian manager said in the study, "We do not prefer leaders who take self-governing decisions and act alone without engaging the group. That's part of who we are."

identification-based trust   *Trust based on a mutual understanding of each other's intentions and appreciation of each other's wants and desires.*

Transformational leadership is also effective in China and other parts of the world. Wang Jianzhou is the CEO of China Mobile, the world's largest cellular service provider with more than 500 million subscribers. With vision and foresight, Jianzhou is expanding mobile service throughout China's vast rural areas and plans to expand in emerging markets such as Africa, Asia, and Latin America. Proactive and positive, Jianzhou's leadership draws from his extensive knowledge of and more than 30 years of experience in the telecommunications industry. He is shown here during the launching ceremony of China Mobile's Ophone operating system platform that the company researched and developed on its own and the Ophone cellphones that compete with Apple's iPhone.

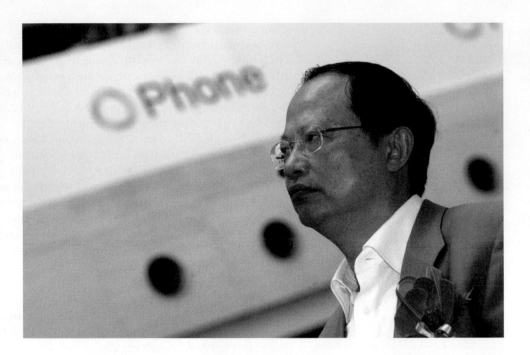

- *France* Compared to U.S. employees, the French have a more bureaucratic view of leaders and are less likely to expect them to be humane and considerate. A leader high on initiating structure (relatively task oriented) will do best and can make decisions in a relatively autocratic manner. A manager who scores high on consideration (people oriented) may find that style backfiring in France.
- *Egypt* Employees in Egypt are more likely to value team-oriented and participative leadership than U.S. employees. However, Egypt is also a relatively high-power-distance culture, meaning status differences between leaders and followers are expected. How would a U.S. manager be participative yet demonstrate his or her high level of status? The leader should ask employees for their opinions, try to minimize conflicts, but not be afraid to take charge and make the final decision (after consulting team members).
- *China* According to the GLOBE study, Chinese culture emphasizes being polite, considerate, and unselfish, but it also has a high performance orientation. These two factors suggest consideration and initiating structure may both be important. Although Chinese culture is relatively participative compared to that of the United States, there are also status differences between leaders and employees. This suggests a moderately participative style may work best.

Though we have little research to confirm these conclusions, and there will always be variation across employees (not every Brazilian is more collective than every U.S. employee), the GLOBE study suggests leaders need to take culture into account whenever managing employees from different cultures.

More generally, the GLOBE study—of 18,000 leaders from 825 organizations in 62 countries—reveals there *are* some universal aspects to leadership. A number of elements making up transformational leadership appear associated with effective leadership, regardless of the country.[142] This conclusion is very important because it disputes the contingency view that leadership style needs to adapt to cultural differences.

What elements of transformational leadership appear universal? Vision, foresight, providing encouragement, trustworthiness, dynamism, positiveness, and proactiveness. Two members of the GLOBE team concluded that "effective business leaders in any country are expected by their subordinates to provide a powerful and proactive vision to guide the company into the future, strong motivational skills to stimulate all employees to fulfill the vision, and excellent planning skills to assist in implementing the vision."[143]

A vision is important in any culture, then, but how it is formed and communicated may still need to vary by culture. A GE executive who used his U.S. leadership style in Japan recalls, "Nothing happened. I quickly realized that I had to adapt my approach, to act more as a consultant to my colleagues and to adopt a team-based motivational decision-making process rather than the more vocal style which tends to be common in the West. In Japan the silence of a leader means far more than a thousand words uttered by somebody else."[144]

Summary and Implications for Managers

Leadership plays a central part in understanding group behavior, for it's the leader who usually directs us toward our goals. Knowing what makes a good leader should thus be valuable in improving group performance.

The early search for a set of universal leadership traits failed. However, recent efforts using the Big Five personality framework have generated much more encouraging results. Extraversion, conscientiousness, and openness to experience show strong and consistent relationships to leadership.

The behavioral approach's major contribution was narrowing leadership into task-oriented (initiating structure) and people-oriented (consideration) styles. By considering the situation in which the leader operates, contingency theories promised to improve on the behavioral approach, but with the exception of LPC theory they have not fared well in leadership research.

Research on charismatic and transformational leadership has made major contributions to our understanding of leadership effectiveness. Organizations are increasingly searching for managers who can exhibit transformational leadership qualities. They want leaders with vision and the charisma to carry out their vision.

Effective managers today must also be authentic and develop trusting relationships with those they seek to lead because, as organizations have become less stable and predictable, strong bonds of trust are replacing bureaucratic rules in defining expectations and relationships. Managers who aren't trusted aren't likely to be effective leaders.

For managers who must fill key positions in their organization with effective leaders, we have shown that tests and interviews help identify people with leadership qualities. Managers should also consider investing in leadership training such as formal courses, workshops, rotating job responsibilities, coaching, and mentoring.

Leaders Are Born, Not Made

In the United States, people are socialized to believe they can be whoever they want to be—and that includes being a leader. While that makes for a nice children's tale (like *The Little Engine That Could*—"I think I can, I think I can"), life is not always wrapped in pretty little packages, and this is one example. Being an effective leader has more to do with what you're born with than what you do with what you have.

That leaders are born, not made, isn't a new idea. The Victorian-era historian Thomas Carlyle wrote, "History is nothing but the biography of a few great men." Although today we should modify this to include women, his point still rings true: Great leaders are what make teams, companies, and even countries great. Can anyone disagree that people like Abraham Lincoln and Franklin Roosevelt were visionary political leaders? Or that Joan of Arc and George Patton were brilliant and courageous military leaders? Or that Henry Ford, Jack Welch, Steve Jobs, and Rupert Murdoch are gifted business leaders? As one reviewer of the literature put it, "Leaders are not like other people." They have the right stuff—stuff the rest of us don't have, or have in lesser quantities.

If you're not yet convinced, a recent study of several hundred identical twins separated at birth found an amazing correlation in their ascendance into leadership roles. These twins were raised in totally different environments—some rich, some poor, some by educated parents, others by relatively uneducated parents, some in cities, others in small towns. But despite their different environments, each pair had striking similarities in terms of whether they became leaders. Other research has found that shared environment—being raised in the same household, for example—has very little influence on leadership emergence.

Despite what we might like to believe, the evidence is clear: A substantial part of leadership is a product of our genes. If we have the right stuff, we're destined to be effective leaders. If we don't, we're unlikely to excel in that role. Leadership cannot be for everyone, and we make a mistake in thinking everyone is equally capable of being a good leader.[145]

Of course, personal qualities and characteristics matter to leadership, as they do to most other behaviors. But the real key is what you do with what you have.

If great leadership were merely the possession of a few key traits—say intelligence and personality—we could simply give people a test and select the most intelligent, extraverted, and conscientious people to be leaders. But that would be a disaster. Leadership is much too complex to be reduced to a simple formula of traits. As smart as Steve Jobs is, there are smarter and more extraverted people out there—thousands of them. That isn't the essence of what makes Jobs, or political or military leaders, great. It is a combination of factors—upbringing, early business experiences, learning from failure, and driving ambition.

Second, great leaders tell us the key to their leadership success is not the characteristics they had at birth but what they learned along the way.

Take Warren Buffett, admired not only for his investing prowess but also as a leader and boss. Being a great leader, according to Buffett, is a matter of acquiring the right habits. "The chains of habit are too light to be noticed until they are too heavy to be broken," he says. Buffett argues that characteristics or habits such as intelligence, trustworthiness, and integrity are the most important to leadership—and at least the latter two can be developed. He says, "You need integrity, intelligence, and energy to succeed. Integrity is totally a matter of choice—and it is habit forming."

Finally, this focus on "great men and great women" is not very productive even if great leaders are born. People need to believe in something, and one of those things is that they can improve themselves. Who would want to think we were only some accumulation of genetic markers and our life just a stage in which our genes played themselves out? People like the optimistic story of *The Little Engine That Could* because we have a choice to think positively (we can become good leaders) or negatively (leaders are predetermined), and it's better to be positive.[146]

Questions for Review

1 Are leadership and management different from one another? If so, how?

2 What is the difference between trait and behavioral theories? Are the theories valid?

3 What is Fiedler's contingency model? Has it been supported in research?

4 How do charismatic and transformational leadership compare and contrast? Are they valid?

5 What is authentic leadership? Why do ethics and trust matter to leadership?

6 How is mentoring valuable to leadership? What are the keys to effective mentoring?

7 Do you agree there are situations in which leadership is not necessary? Why or why not?

8 How can organizations select and develop effective leaders?

9 Do charismatic and transformational leadership generalize across cultures?

Experiential Exercise

WHAT IS A LEADER?

1. Working on your own, write down 12 adjectives that describe an effective business leader.

2. Break into groups of four or five. Appoint a note taker and spokesperson. Compare your lists of adjectives, making a new list of those common across two or more persons' lists. (Count synonyms—steadfast and unwavering, for example—as the same.)

3. Each spokesperson should present the group's list to the class.

4. Are there many similarities among the lists? What does this tell you about the nature of leadership?

Ethical Dilemma

WHOLE FOODS' RAHODEB

Whole Foods, a fast-growing chain of upscale grocery stores, has long been a Wall Street favorite. It regularly appears on *Fortune*'s list of *100 Best Companies to Work For* (it was #22 in 2008) and has spawned its share of competitors, including Fresh Market and Wild Oats.

Given that most industry analysts see a bright future for upscale organic markets like Whole Foods, it's no surprise they have attracted their share of investor blogs. One prominent blogger, "Rahodeb," consistently extolled the virtues of Whole Foods stock and derided Wild Oats. Rahodeb predicted Wild Oats would eventually be forced into bankruptcy and the Whole Foods stock price would grow at an annual rate of 18 percent. Rahodeb's Yahoo! Finance blog entries were widely read because he seemed to have special insights into the industry and into Whole Foods in particular.

Would it surprise you to learn that Rahodeb was exposed in 2007 as Whole Foods co-founder and CEO John

Mackey? ("Rahodeb" is an anagram of "Deborah," the name of Mackey's wife.) What's more, while Rahodeb was talking down Wild Oats stock, Whole Foods was in the process of acquiring Wild Oats, and deriding the target may have made the acquisition easier and cheaper. Because the companies often have stores in the same cities, the Federal Trade Commission (FTC) attempted to block the acquisition and was responsible for "outing" Mackey. In March 2009, Whole Foods agreed to disgorge 31 of the Wild Oats stores it had acquired, drop use of the Wild Oats name, and undertake other actions that nullified the benefits of the acquisition.

Mackey lamented the debacle—not his secret blogging but the Wild Oats acquisition. He said, "We would be better off today if we hadn't done this deal—taking on all this debt right before the economy collapsed." By 2008, Mackey was blogging again, under his real name. His posts are neither as frequent nor as interesting as Rahodeb's.

Do you think it is unethical for a company leader like Mackey to pose as an investor, talking up his or her company's stock price while talking down his competitor's? Would Mackey's behavior affect your willingness to work for or invest in Whole Foods?

Sources: Based on T. W. Martin, "Whole Foods to Sell 31 Stores in FTC Deal," *Wall Street Journal* (March 7, 2009), p. B5; M. Fraser and S. Dutta, "Yes, CEOs Should Facebook And Twitter," *Forbes* (March 11, 2009), www.forbes.com; D. Kesmodel and J. R. Wilke, "Whole Foods Is Hot, Wild Oats a Dud—So Said 'Rahodeb,'" *Wall Street Journal* (July 12, 2007), pp. A1, A10; and G. Farrell and P. Davidson, "Whole Foods' CEO Was Busy Guy Online," *USA Today,* July 13, 2007, p. 4B.

Case Incident 1

THE MAKING OF A GREAT PRESIDENT

What does it take to be a great U.S. president? A C-SPAN survey of 64 U.S. history scholars rated the U.S. presidents from George Washington to George W. Bush. Here are the top ten:

1. Abraham Lincoln
2. George Washington
3. Franklin D. Roosevelt
4. Theodore Roosevelt
5. Harry S. Truman
6. John F. Kennedy
7. Thomas Jefferson
8. Dwight D. Eisenhower
9. Woodrow Wilson
10. Ronald Reagan

Recent presidents didn't fare particularly well in the rankings: George H. W. Bush is #36; Bill Clinton is #15; George W. Bush is #18; and Jimmy Carter is #25.

Questions

1. Do you think leaders in other contexts (business, sports, religion) exhibit the same qualities as great U.S. presidents?
2. How important do you think charisma is to a president's greatness?
3. Do you think being in the right place at the right time could influence presidential greatness?
4. Do you think historians can be biased in evaluating a president's greatness? If so, how?

Source: Based on C-SPAN 2009 Historians Presidential Leadership Survey (www.c-span.org/presidentialsurvey/Overall-Ranking.aspx).

Case Incident 2

LEADERSHIP FACTORIES

Companies differ markedly in their ability to produce future leaders, as several recent analyses of the 1,187 largest publicly traded U.S. companies revealed. Among the CEOs in one study, a remarkable total of 26 once worked at General Electric (GE).

However, as the following table shows, on a per-employee basis that earns GE only tenth place in terms of the likelihood of a current or former employee becoming CEO of a large company. Top on the list is management consulting firm McKinsey & Company. Amazingly, if we extrapolate into the future from the current stock of McKinsey alums who are CEOs, of every 690 McKinsey employees, one will become CEO of a Fortune 1000 company.

Company	Size (employees)	CEOs produced	Odds
McKinsey & Co.	11,000	16	690:1
Deloitte & Touche	17,170	8	2,150:1
Baxter International	48,000	11	4,365:1
PricewaterhouseCoopers	47,750	10	4,775:1
Ernst & Young	103,000	12	8,585:1
Merrill Lynch	62,200	7	8,885:1
Motorola	66,000	7	9,430:1
Intel	88,100	8	11,010:1
Procter & Gamble (P&G)	138,000	12	11,500:1
General Electric (GE)	300,000	26	11,540:1

Some companies did not fare nearly as well, such as Citigroup (odds: 30,180:1), AT&T (odds: 23,220:1) and Johnson & Johnson (odds: 15,275:1).

While some might dismiss the results, not surprisingly, the companies at the top of the list do not. "We are a leadership engine and a talent machine," said retiring P&G CEO A. G. Lafley.

Questions

1. Management consulting firms did very well on a per-employee basis, partly because they are mostly comprised of managers (as opposed to blue-collar or entry-level workers). How big a factor do you think composition of the workforce is in likelihood of producing a CEO?

2. Do you think so-called leadership factories are also better places for non-leaders to work? Why or why not?

3. Assume you had job offers from two companies that differed only in how often they produced CEOs. Would this difference affect your decision?

4. Do these data give any credence to the value of leader selection and leader development? Why or why not?

Sources: Based on D. McCarthy, "The 2008 Best Companies for Leaders," *Great Leadership* (February 17, 2009), http://www.greatleadership bydan.com/2009/02/2008-best-companies-for-leaders.html; F. Hansen, "Building Better Leaders . . . Faster," *Workforce Management* (June 9, 2008), pp. 25–28; and D. Jones, "Some Firms' Fertile Soil Grows Crop of Future CEOs," *USA Today* (January 9, 2008), pp. 1B, 2B.

Endnotes

1. J. B. Stewart, "The Birthday Party," *The New Yorker* (February 18, 2008), pp. 100–113; N. D. Schwartz, "Wall Street's Man of the Moment," *Fortune* (February 21, 2007), money.cnn.com/magazines/fortune/fortune_archive/2007/03/05/8401261; and H. Sender and M. Langley, "How Blackstone's Chief Became $7 Billion Man," *Wall Street Journal* (June 13, 2007), pp. A1, A13.

2. J. P. Kotter, "What Leaders Really Do," *Harvard Business Review*, May–June 1990, pp. 103–111; and J. P. Kotter, *A Force for Change: How Leadership Differs from Management* (New York: The Free Press, 1990).

3. J. G. Geier, "A Trait Approach to the Study of Leadership in Small Groups," *Journal of Communication*, December 1967, pp. 316–323.

4. S. A. Kirkpatrick and E. A. Locke, "Leadership: Do Traits Matter?" *Academy of Management Executive*, May 1991, pp. 48–60; and S. J. Zaccaro, R. J. Foti, and D. A. Kenny, "Self-Monitoring and Trait-Based Variance in Leadership: An Investigation of Leader Flexibility Across Multiple Group Situations," *Journal of Applied Psychology*, April 1991, pp. 308–315.

5. See T. A. Judge, J. E. Bono, R. Ilies, and M. Werner, "Personality and Leadership: A Review," paper presented at the 15th Annual Conference of the Society for Industrial and Organizational Psychology, New Orleans, 2000; and T. A. Judge, J. E. Bono, R. Ilies, and M. W. Gerhardt, "Personality and Leadership: A Qualitative and Quantitative Review," *Journal of Applied Psychology*, August 2002, pp. 765–780.

6. Judge, Bono, Ilies, and Gerhardt, "Personality and Leadership."

7. D. R. Ames and F. J. Flynn, "What Breaks a Leader: The Curvilinear Relation Between Assertiveness and Leadership," *Journal of Personality and Social Psychology* 92, no. 2 (2007), pp. 307–324.

8. K. Ng, S. Ang, and K. Chan, "Personality and Leader Effectiveness: A Moderated Mediation Model of Leadership Self-Efficacy, Job Demands, and Job Autonomy," *Journal of Applied Psychology* 93, no. 4 (2008), pp. 733–743.

9. This section is based on D. Goleman, "What Makes a Leader?" *Harvard Business Review*, November–December 1998, pp. 93–102; J. M. George, "Emotions and Leadership: The Role of Emotional Intelligence," *Human Relations*, August 2000, pp. 1027–1055; C.-S. Wong and K. S. Law, "The Effects of Leader and Follower Emotional Intelligence on Performance and Attitude: An Exploratory Study," *Leadership Quarterly*, June 2002, pp. 243–274; and D. R. Caruso and C. J. Wolfe, "Emotional Intelligence and Leadership Development," in D. David and S. J. Zaccaro (eds.), *Leader Development for Transforming Organizations: Growing Leaders for Tomorrow* (Mahwah, NJ: Lawrence Erlbaum, 2004), pp. 237–263.

10. J. Champy, "The Hidden Qualities of Great Leaders," *Fast Company* 76 (November 2003), p. 135.

11. J. Antonakis, "Why 'Emotional Intelligence' Does Not Predict Leadership Effectiveness: A Comment on Prati, Douglas, Ferris, Ammeter, and Buckley (2003)," *International Journal of Organizational Analysis* 11 (2003), pp. 355–361. See also M. Zeidner, G. Matthews, and R. D. Roberts, "Emotional Intelligence in the Workplace: A Critical Review," *Applied Psychology: An International Review* 53 (2004), pp. 371–399.

12. Ibid., p. 7; R. G. Lord, C. L. DeVader, and G. M. Alliger, "A Meta-analysis of the Relation Between Personality Traits and Leadership Perceptions: An Application of Validity Generalization Procedures," *Journal of Applied Psychology*, August 1986, pp. 402–410; and J. A. Smith and R. J. Foti, "A Pattern Approach to the Study of Leader Emergence," *Leadership Quarterly*, Summer 1998, pp. 147–160.

13. R. M. Stogdill and A. E. Coons (eds.), *Leader Behavior: Its Description and Measurement*, Research Monograph no. 88 (Columbus: Ohio State University, Bureau of Business Research, 1951). This research is updated in C. A. Schriesheim, C. C. Cogliser, and L. L. Neider, "Is It 'Trustworthy'? A Multiple-Levels-of-Analysis Reexamination of an Ohio State Leadership Study, with Implications for Future Research," *Leadership Quarterly*, Summer 1995, pp. 111–145; and T. A. Judge, R. F. Piccolo, and R. Ilies, "The Forgotten Ones? The Validity of Consideration and Initiating Structure in Leadership Research," *Journal of Applied Psychology*, February 2004, pp. 36–51.

14. D. Akst, "The Rewards of Recognizing a Job Well Done," *Wall Street Journal* (January 31, 2007), p. D9.

15. Judge, Piccolo, and Ilies, "The Forgotten Ones?"

16. G. Yukl and D. D. Van Fleet, "Theory and Research on Leadership in Organizations," in M. D. Dunnette and L. M. Hough (eds.), *Handbook of Industrial and Organizational Psychology*, vol. 2 (Palo Alto, CA: Consulting Psychologists Press, 1992), pp. 147–197.

17. F. E. Fiedler, *A Theory of Leadership Effectiveness* (New York: McGraw-Hill, 1967).

18. S. Shiflett, "Is There a Problem with the LPC Score in LEADER MATCH?" *Personnel Psychology*, Winter 1981, pp. 765–769.

19. F. E. Fiedler, M. M. Chemers, and L. Mahar, *Improving Leadership Effectiveness: The Leader Match Concept* (New York: Wiley, 1977).

20. Cited in R. J. House and R. N. Aditya, "The Social Scientific Study of Leadership," p. 422.

21. L. H. Peters, D. D. Hartke, and J. T. Pohlmann, "Fiedler's Contingency Theory of Leadership: An Application of the Meta-analysis Procedures of Schmidt and Hunter," *Psychological Bulletin*, March 1985, pp. 274–285; C. A. Schriesheim, B. J. Tepper, and L. A. Tetrault, "Least Preferred Coworker Score, Situational Control, and Leadership Effectiveness: A Meta-analysis of Contingency Model Performance Predictions," *Journal of Applied Psychology*, August 1994, pp. 561–573; and R. Ayman, M. M. Chemers, and F. Fiedler, "The Contingency Model of Leadership Effectiveness: Its Levels of Analysis," *Leadership Quarterly*, Summer 1995, pp. 147–167.

22. House and Aditya, "The Social Scientific Study of Leadership."

23. See, for instance, R. W. Rice, "Psychometric Properties of the Esteem for the Least Preferred Coworker (LPC) Scale," *Academy of Management Review*, January 1978, pp. 106–118; C. A. Schriesheim, B. D. Bannister, and W. H. Money, "Psychometric Properties of the LPC Scale: An Extension of Rice's Review," *Academy of Management Review*, April 1979,

pp. 287–290; and J. K. Kennedy, J. M. Houston, M. A. Korgaard, and D. D. Gallo, "Construct Space of the Least Preferred Coworker (LPC) Scale," *Educational & Psychological Measurement,* Fall 1987, pp. 807–814.

24. See E. H. Schein, *Organizational Psychology,* 3rd ed. (Upper Saddle River, NJ: Prentice Hall, 1980), pp. 116–117; and B. Kabanoff, "A Critique of Leader Match and Its Implications for Leadership Research," *Personnel Psychology,* Winter 1981, pp. 749–764.

25. See, for instance, Ibid., pp. 67–84; C. L. Graeff, "Evolution of Situational Leadership Theory: A Critical Review," *Leadership Quarterly* 8, no. 2 (1997), pp. 153–170; and R. P. Vecchio and K. J. Boatwright, "Preferences for Idealized Styles of Supervision," *Leadership Quarterly,* August 2002, pp. 327–342.

26. R. J. House, "A Path-Goal Theory of Leader Effectiveness," *Administrative Science Quarterly,* September 1971, pp. 321–338; R. J. House and T. R. Mitchell, "Path-Goal Theory of Leadership," *Journal of Contemporary Business,* Autumn 1974, pp. 81–97; and R. J. House, "Path-Goal Theory of Leadership: Lessons, Legacy, and a Reformulated Theory," *Leadership Quarterly,* Fall 1996, pp. 323–352.

27. J. C. Wofford and L. Z. Liska, "Path-Goal Theories of Leadership: A Meta-analysis," *Journal of Management,* Winter 1993, pp. 857–876; and P. M. Podsakoff, S. B. MacKenzie, and M. Ahearne, "Searching for a Needle in a Haystack: Trying to Identify the Illusive Moderators of Leadership Behaviors," *Journal of Management* 21 (1995), pp. 423–470.

28. J. R. Villa, J. P. Howell, and P. W. Dorfman, "Problems with Detecting Moderators in Leadership Research Using Moderated Multiple Regression," *Leadership Quarterly* 14 (2003), pp. 3–23; C. A. Schriesheim and L. Neider, "Path-Goal Leadership Theory: The Long and Winding Road," *Leadership Quarterly* 7 (1996), pp. 317–321; and M. G. Evans, "R. J. House's 'A Path-Goal Theory of Leader Effectiveness,'" *Leadership Quarterly* 7 (1996), pp. 305–309.

29. See V. H. Vroom and P. W. Yetton, *Leadership and Decision-Making* (Pittsburgh: University of Pittsburgh Press, 1973); and V. H. Vroom and A. G. Jago, "The Role of the Situation in Leadership," *American Psychologist,* January 2007, pp. 17–24.

30. See, for example, R. H. G. Field, "A Test of the Vroom-Yetton Normative Model of Leadership," *Journal of Applied Psychology,* October 1982, pp. 523–532; C. R. Leana, "Power Relinquishment Versus Power Sharing: Theoretical Clarification and Empirical Comparison of Delegation and Participation," *Journal of Applied Psychology,* May 1987, pp. 228–233; J. T. Ettling and A. G. Jago, "Participation Under Conditions of Conflict: More on the Validity of the Vroom-Yetton Model," *Journal of Management Studies,* January 1988, pp. 73–83; R. H. G. Field and R. J. House, "A Test of the Vroom-Yetton Model Using Manager and Subordinate Reports," *Journal of Applied Psychology,* June 1990, pp. 362–366; and R. H. G. Field and J. P. Andrews, "Testing the Incremental Validity of the Vroom-Jago Versus Vroom-Yetton Models of Participation in Decision Making," *Journal of Behavioral Decision Making,* December 1998, pp. 251–261.

31. House and Aditya, "The Social Scientific Study of Leadership," p. 428.

32. W. Bennis, "The Challenges of Leadership in the Modern World," *American Psychologist,* January 2007, pp. 2–5.

33. R. M. Dienesch and R. C. Liden, "Leader–Member Exchange Model of Leadership: A Critique and Further Development," *Academy of Management Review,* July 1986, pp. 618–634; G. B. Graen and M. Uhl-Bien, "Relationship-Based Approach to Leadership: Development of Leader–Member Exchange (LMX) Theory of Leadership Over 25 Years: Applying a Multi-Domain Perspective," *Leadership Quarterly,* Summer 1995, pp. 219–247; R. C. Liden, R. T. Sparrowe, and S. J. Wayne, "Leader–Member Exchange Theory: The Past and Potential for the Future," in G. R. Ferris (ed.), *Research in Personnel and Human Resource Management,* vol. 15 (Greenwich, CT: JAI Press, 1997), pp. 47–119; and C. A. Schriesheim, S. L. Castro, X. Zhou, and F. J. Yammarino, "The Folly of Theorizing 'A' but Testing 'B': A Selective Level-of-Analysis Review of the Field and a Detailed Leader–Member Exchange Illustration," *Leadership Quarterly,* Winter 2001, pp. 515–551.

34. R. Liden and G. Graen, "Generalizability of the Vertical Dyad Linkage Model of Leadership," *Academy of Management Journal,* September 1980, pp. 451–465; R. C. Liden, S. J. Wayne, and D. Stilwell, "A Longitudinal Study of the Early Development of Leader–Member Exchanges," *Journal of Applied Psychology,* August 1993, pp. 662–674; S. J. Wayne, L. M. Shore, W. H. Bommer, and L. E. Tetrick, "The Role of Fair Treatment and Rewards in Perceptions of Organizational Support and Leader–Member Exchange," *Journal of Applied Psychology* 87, no. 3 (June 2002), pp. 590–598; and S. S. Masterson, K. Lewis, and B. M. Goldman, "Integrating Justice and Social Exchange: The Differing Effects of Fair Procedures and Treatment on Work Relationships," *Academy of Management Journal* 43, no. 4 (August 2000), pp. 738–748.

35. D. Duchon, S. G. Green, and T. D. Taber, "Vertical Dyad Linkage: A Longitudinal Assessment of Antecedents, Measures, and Consequences," *Journal of Applied Psychology,* February 1986, pp. 56–60; Liden, Wayne, and Stilwell, "A Longitudinal Study on the Early Development of Leader–Member Exchanges"; and M. Uhl-Bien, "Relationship Development as a Key Ingredient for Leadership Development," in S. E. Murphy and R. E. Riggio (eds.), *Future of Leadership Development* (Mahwah, NJ: Lawrence Erlbaum, 2003) pp. 129–147.

36. R. Vecchio and D. M. Brazil, "Leadership and Sex-Similarity: A Comparison in a Military Setting," *Personnel Psychology* 60 (2007), pp. 303–335.

37. See, for instance, C. R. Gerstner and D. V. Day, "Meta-analytic Review of Leader–Member Exchange Theory: Correlates and Construct Issues," *Journal of Applied Psychology,* December 1997, pp. 827–844; R. Ilies, J. D. Nahrgang, and F. P. Morgeson, "Leader–Member Exchange and Citizenship Behaviors: A Meta-analysis," *Journal of Applied Psychology* 92, no. 1 (2007), pp. 269–277; and Z. Chen, W. Lam, and J. A. Zhong, "Leader–Member Exchange and Member Performance: A New Look at Individual-Level Negative Feedback-Seeking Behavior and Team-Level Empowerment Culture," *Journal of Applied Psychology* 92, no. 1 (2007), pp. 202–212.

38. D. Eden, "Leadership and Expectations: Pygmalion Effects and Other Self-fulfilling Prophecies in Organizations," *Leadership Quarterly,* Winter 1992, pp. 278–279.

39. M. Ozer, "Personal and Task-Related Moderators of Leader-Member Exchange Among Software Developers," *Journal of Applied Psychology* 93, no. 5 (2008), pp. 1174–1182.

40. M. Weber, *The Theory of Social and Economic Organization*, A. M. Henderson and T. Parsons (trans.) (New York: The Free Press, 1947).

41. J. A. Conger and R. N. Kanungo, "Behavioral Dimensions of Charismatic Leadership," in J. A. Conger, R. N. Kanungo, and Associates (eds.), *Charismatic Leadership* (San Francisco: Jossey-Bass, 1988), p. 79.

42. J. A. Conger and R. N. Kanungo, *Charismatic Leadership in Organizations* (Thousand Oaks, CA: Sage, 1998); and R. Awamleh and W. L. Gardner, "Perceptions of Leader Charisma and Effectiveness: The Effects of Vision Content, Delivery, and Organizational Performance," *Leadership Quarterly*, Fall 1999, pp. 345–373.

43. R. J. House and J. M. Howell, "Personality and Charismatic Leadership," *Leadership Quarterly* 3 (1992), pp. 81–108; D. N. Den Hartog and P. L. Koopman, "Leadership in Organizations," in N. Anderson and D. S. Ones (eds.), *Handbook of Industrial, Work and Organizational Psychology*, vol. 2 (Thousand Oaks, CA: Sage, 2002), pp. 166–187.

44. See J. A. Conger and R. N. Kanungo, "Training Charismatic Leadership: A Risky and Critical Task," *Charismatic Leadership* (San Francisco: Jossey-Bass, 1988), pp. 309–323; A. J. Towler, "Effects of Charismatic Influence Training on Attitudes, Behavior, and Performance," *Personnel Psychology*, Summer 2003, pp. 363–381; and M. Frese, S. Beimel, and S. Schoenborn, "Action Training for Charismatic Leadership: Two Evaluations of Studies of a Commercial Training Module on Inspirational Communication of a Vision," *Personnel Psychology*, Autumn 2003, pp. 671–697.

45. R. J. Richardson and S. K. Thayer, *The Charisma Factor: How to Develop Your Natural Leadership Ability* (Upper Saddle River, NJ: Prentice Hall, 1993).

46. J. M. Howell and P. J. Frost, "A Laboratory Study of Charismatic Leadership," *Organizational Behavior and Human Decision Processes*, April 1989, pp. 243–269. See also Frese, Beimel, and Schoenborn, "Action Training for Charismatic Leadership."

47. B. Shamir, R. J. House, and M. B. Arthur, "The Motivational Effects of Charismatic Leadership: A Self-Concept Theory," *Organization Science*, November 1993, pp. 577–594.

48. D. N. Den Hartog, A. H. B. De Hoogh, and A. E. Keegan, "The Interactive Effects of Belongingness and Charisma on Helping and Compliance," *Journal of Applied Psychology* 92, no. 4 (2007), pp. 1131–1139.

49. A. Erez, V. F. Misangyi, D. E. Johnson, M. A. LePine, and K. C. Halverson, "Stirring the Hearts of Followers: Charismatic Leadership as the Transferal of Affect," *Journal of Applied Psychology* 93, no. 3 (2008), pp. 602–615. For reviews on the role of vision in leadership, see S. J. Zaccaro, "Visionary and Inspirational Models of Executive Leadership: Empirical Review and Evaluation," in S. J. Zaccaro (ed.), *The Nature of Executive Leadership: A Conceptual and Empirical Analysis of Success* (Washington, DC: American Psychological Association, 2001), pp. 259–278; and M. Hauser and R. J. House, "Lead Through Vision and Values," in E. A. Locke (ed.), *Handbook of Principles of Organizational Behavior* (Malden, MA: Blackwell, 2004), pp. 257–273.

50. D. A. Waldman, B. M. Bass, and F. J. Yammarino, "Adding to Contingent-Reward Behavior: The Augmenting Effect of Charismatic Leadership," *Group & Organization Studies*, December 1990, pp. 381–394; and S. A. Kirkpatrick and E. A. Locke, "Direct and Indirect Effects of Three Core Charismatic Leadership Components on Performance and Attitudes," *Journal of Applied Psychology*, February 1996, pp. 36–51.

51. A. H. B. de Hoogh, D. N. Den Hartog, P. L. Koopman, H. Thierry, P. T. van den Berg, and J. G. van der Weide, "Charismatic Leadership, Environmental Dynamism, and Performance," *European Journal of Work & Organizational Psychology*, December 2004, pp. 447–471; S. Harvey, M. Martin, and D. Stout, "Instructor's Transformational Leadership: University Student Attitudes and Ratings," *Psychological Reports*, April 2003, pp. 395–402; and D. A. Waldman, M. Javidan, and P. Varella, "Charismatic Leadership at the Strategic Level: A New Application of Upper Echelons Theory," *Leadership Quarterly*, June 2004, pp. 355–380.

52. R. J. House, "A 1976 Theory of Charismatic Leadership," in J. G. Hunt and L. L. Larson (eds.), *Leadership: The Cutting Edge* (Carbondale: Southern Illinois University Press, 1977), pp. 189–207; and Robert J. House and Ram N. Aditya, "The Social Scientific Study of Leadership," *Journal of Management* 23, no. 3 (1997), p. 441.

53. J. C. Pastor, M. Mayo, and B. Shamir, "Adding Fuel to Fire: The Impact of Followers' Arousal on Ratings of Charisma," *Journal of Applied Psychology* 92, no. 6 (2007), pp. 1584–1596.

54. F. Cohen, S. Solomon, M. Maxfield, T. Pyszczynski, and J. Greenberg, "Fatal Attraction: The Effects of Mortality Salience on Evaluations of Charismatic, Task-Oriented, and Relationship-Oriented Leaders," *Psychological Sciences*, December 2004, pp. 846–851; and M. G. Ehrhart and K. J. Klein, "Predicting Followers' Preferences for Charismatic Leadership: The Influence of Follower Values and Personality," *Leadership Quarterly*, Summer 2001, pp. 153–179.

55. H. L. Tosi, V. Misangyi, A. Fanelli, D. A. Waldman, and F. J. Yammarino, "CEO Charisma, Compensation, and Firm Performance," *Leadership Quarterly*, June 2004, pp. 405–420.

56. See, for instance, R. Khurana, *Searching for a Corporate Savior: The Irrational Quest for Charismatic CEOs* (Princeton, NJ: Princeton University Press, 2002); and J. A. Raelin, "The Myth of Charismatic Leaders," *Training & Development*, March 2003, pp. 47–54.

57. See, for instance, B. M. Bass, B. J. Avolio, D. I. Jung, and Y. Berson, "Predicting Unit Performance by Assessing Transformational and Transactional Leadership," *Journal of Applied Psychology*, April 2003, pp. 207–218; and T. A. Judge and R. F. Piccolo, "Transformational and Transactional Leadership: A Meta-analytic Test of Their Relative Validity," *Journal of Applied Psychology*, October 2004, pp. 755–768.

58. B. M. Bass, "Leadership: Good, Better, Best," *Organizational Dynamics*, Winter 1985, pp. 26–40; and J. Seltzer and B. M. Bass, "Transformational Leadership: Beyond Initiation and Consideration," *Journal of Management*, December 1990, pp. 693–703.

59. T. R. Hinkin and C. A. Schriescheim, "An Examination of 'Nonleadership': From Laissez-Faire Leadership to Leader Reward Omission and Punishment Omission," *Journal of Applied Psychology* 93, no. 6 (2008), pp. 1234–1248.

60. S. J. Shin and J. Zhou, "Transformational Leadership, Conservation, and Creativity: Evidence from Korea," *Academy of Management Journal*, December 2003, pp. 703–714; V. J. García-Morales, F. J. Lloréns-Montes, and A. J. Verdú-Jover, "The Effects of Transformational Leadership on Organizational Performance Through Knowledge and Innovation," *British Journal of Management* 19, no. 4 (2008), pp. 299–313; and S. A. Eisenbeiss, D. van Knippenberg, and S. Boerner, "Transformational Leadership and Team Innovation: Integrating Team Climate Principles," *Journal of Applied Psychology* 93, no. 6 (2008), pp. 1438–1446.

61. Y. Ling, Z. Simsek, M. H. Lubatkin, and J. F. Veiga, "Transformational Leadership's Role in Promoting Corporate Entrepreneurship: Examining the CEO-TMT Interface," *Academy of Management Journal* 51, no. 3 (2008), pp. 557–576.

62. A. E. Colbert, A. E. Kristof-Brown, B. H. Bradley, and M. R. Barrick, "CEO Transformational Leadership: The Role of Goal Importance Congruence in Top Management Teams," *Academy of Management Journal* 51, no. 1 (2008), pp. 81–96.

63. D. Zohar and O. Tenne-Gazit, "Transformational Leadership and Group Interaction as Climate Antecedents: A Social Network Analysis," *Journal of Applied Psychology* 93, no. 4 (2008), pp. 744–757.

64. F. O. Walumbwa, B. J. Avolio, and W. Zhu, "How Transformational Leadership Weaves Its Influence on Individual Job Performance: The Role of Identification and Efficacy Beliefs," *Personnel Psychology* 61, no. 4 (2008), pp. 793–825.

65. J. E. Bono and T. A. Judge, "Self-Concordance at Work: Toward Understanding the Motivational Effects of Transformational Leaders," *Academy of Management Journal*, October 2003, pp. 554–571; Y. Berson and B. J. Avolio, "Transformational Leadership and the Dissemination of Organizational Goals: A Case Study of a Telecommunication Firm," *Leadership Quarterly*, October 2004, pp. 625–646; and J. Schaubroeck, S. S. K. Lam, and S. E. Cha, "Embracing Transformational Leadership: Team Values and the Impact of Leader Behavior on Team Performance," *Journal of Applied Psychology* 92, no. 4 (2007), pp. 1020–1030.

66. S. Shinn, "21st-Century Engineer," *BizEd*, January/February, 2005, pp. 18–23.

67. J. R. Baum, E. A. Locke, and S. A. Kirkpatrick, "A Longitudinal Study of the Relation of Vision and Vision Communication to Venture Growth in Entrepreneurial Firms," *Journal of Applied Psychology*, February 2000, pp. 43–54.

68. B. J. Avolio, W. Zhu, W. Koh, and P. Bhatia, "Transformational Leadership and Organizational Commitment: Mediating Role of Psychological Empowerment and Moderating Role of Structural Distance," *Journal of Organizational Behavior*, December 2004, pp. 951–968; and T. Dvir, N. Kass, and B. Shamir, "The Emotional Bond: Vision and Organizational Commitment Among High-Tech Employees," *Journal of Organizational Change Management* 17, no. 2 (2004), pp. 126–143.

69. R. T. Keller, "Transformational Leadership, Initiating Structure, and Substitutes for Leadership: A Longitudinal Study of Research and Development Project Team Performance," *Journal of Applied Psychology* 91, no. 1 (2006), pp. 202–210.

70. Judge and Piccolo, "Transformational and Transactional Leadership."

71. Y. Ling, Z. Simsek, M. H. Lubatkin, and J. F. Veiga, "The Impact of Transformational CEOs on the Performance of Small- to Medium-Sized Firms: Does Organizational Context Matter?" *Journal of Applied Psychology* 93, no. 4 (2008), pp. 923–934.

72. J. Schaubroeck, S. S. K. Lam, and S. E. Cha, "Embracing Transformational Leadership."

73. H. Hetland, G. M. Sandal, and T. B. Johnsen, "Burnout in the Information Technology Sector: Does Leadership Matter?" *European Journal of Work and Organizational Psychology* 16, no. 1 (2007), pp. 58–75; and K. B. Lowe, K. G. Kroeck, and N. Sivasubramaniam, "Effectiveness Correlates of Transformational and Transactional Leadership: A Meta-analytic Review of the MLQ Literature," *Leadership Quarterly*, Fall 1996, pp. 385–425.

74. See, for instance, J. Barling, T. Weber, and E. K. Kelloway, "Effects of Transformational Leadership Training on Attitudinal and Financial Outcomes: A Field Experiment," *Journal of Applied Psychology*, December 1996, pp. 827–832; and T. Dvir, D. Eden, and B. J. Avolio, "Impact of Transformational Leadership on Follower Development and Performance: A Field Experiment," *Academy of Management Journal*, August 2002, pp. 735–744.

75. B. J. Avolio and B. M. Bass, "Transformational Leadership, Charisma and Beyond," working paper, School of Management, State University of New York, Binghamton, 1985, p. 14.

76. See B. J. Avolio, W. L. Gardner, F. O. Walumbwa, F. Luthans, and D. R. May, "Unlocking the Mask: A Look at the Process by Which Authentic Leaders Impact Follower Attitudes and Behaviors," *Leadership Quarterly*, December 2004, pp. 801–823; W. L. Gardner and J. R. Schermerhorn, Jr., "Performance Gains Through Positive Organizational Behavior and Authentic Leadership," *Organizational Dynamics*, August 2004, pp. 270–281; and M. M. Novicevic, M. G. Harvey, M. R. Buckley, J. A. Brown-Radford, and R. Evans, "Authentic Leadership: A Historical Perspective," *Journal of Leadership and Organizational Behavior* 13, no. 1 (2006), pp. 64–76.

77. C. Tan, "CEO Pinching Penney in a Slowing Economy," *Wall Street Journal* (January 31, 2008), pp. 1–2; and A. Carter, "Lighting a Fire Under Campbell," *BusinessWeek* (December 4, 2006), pp. 96–101.

78. R. Ilies, F. P. Morgeson, and J. D. Nahrgang, "Authentic Leadership and Eudaemonic Wellbeing: Understanding Leader-Follower Outcomes," *Leadership Quarterly* 16 (2005), pp. 373–394.

79. This section is based on E. P. Hollander, "Ethical Challenges in the Leader–Follower Relationship," *Business Ethics Quarterly*, January 1995, pp. 55–65; J. C. Rost, "Leadership: A Discussion About Ethics," *Business Ethics Quarterly*, January 1995, pp. 129–142; L. K. Treviño, M. Brown, and L. P. Hartman, "A Qualitative Investigation of Perceived Executive Ethical Leadership: Perceptions from Inside and Outside the Executive Suite," *Human Relations*, January 2003, pp. 5–37; and R. M. Fulmer, "The Challenge of Ethical Leadership," *Organizational Dynamics* 33, no. 3 (2004), pp. 307–317.

80. J. L. Lunsford, "Piloting Boeing's New Course," *Wall Street Journal* (June 13, 2006), pp. B1, B3.

81. J. M. Burns, *Leadership* (New York: Harper & Row, 1978).

82. J. M. Howell and B. J. Avolio, "The Ethics of Charismatic Leadership: Submission or Liberation?" *Academy of Management Executive,* May 1992, pp. 43–55.

83. D. van Knippenberg, D. De Cremer, and B. van Knippenberg, "Leadership and Fairness: The State of the Art," *European Journal of Work and Organizational Psychology* 16, no. 2 (2007), pp. 113–140.

84. M. E. Brown and L. K. Treviño, "Socialized Charismatic Leadership, Values Congruence, and Deviance in Work Groups," *Journal of Applied Psychology* 91, no. 4 (2006), pp. 954–962.

85. M. E. Brown and L. K. Treviño, "Leader-Follower Values Congruence: Are Socialized Charismatic Leaders Better Able to Achieve It?" *Journal of Applied Psychology* 94, no. 2 (2009), pp. 478–490.

86. D. M. Rousseau, S. B. Sitkin, R. S. Burt, and C. Camerer, "Not So Different After All: A Cross-Discipline View of Trust," *Academy of Management Review,* July 1998, pp. 393–404; and J. A. Simpson, "Psychological Foundations of Trust," *Current Directions in Psychological Science* 16, no. 5 (2007), pp. 264–268.

87. See, for instance, K. Dirks and D. Ferrin, "Trust in Leadership: Meta-analytic Findings and Implications for Research and Practice," *Journal of Applied Psychology* 87, no.4, pp. 611–628; D. I. Jung and B. J. Avolio, "Opening the Black Box: An Experimental Investigation of the Mediating Effects of Trust and Value Congruence on Transformational and Transactional Leadership," *Journal of Organizational Behavior,* December 2000, pp. 949–964; and A. Zacharatos, J. Barling, and R. D. Iverson, "High-Performance Work Systems and Occupational Safety," *Journal of Applied Psychology,* January 2005, pp. 77–93.

88. D. E. Zand, *The Leadership Triad: Knowledge, Trust, and Power* (New York: Oxford University Press, 1997), p. 89.

89. Based on L. T. Hosmer, "Trust: The Connecting Link Between Organizational Theory and Philosophical Ethics," *Academy of Management Review,* April 1995, p. 393; R. C. Mayer, J. H. Davis, and F. D. Schoorman, "An Integrative Model of Organizational Trust," *Academy of Management Review,* July 1995, pp. 709–734; and F. D. Schoorman, R. C. Mayer, and J. H. Davis, "An Integrative Model of Organizational Trust: Past, Present, and Future," *Academy of Management Review* 32, no. 2 (2007), pp. 344–354.

90. J. M. Kouzes and B. Z. Posner, *Credibility: How Leaders Gain and Lose It, and Why People Demand It* (San Francisco: Jossey-Bass, 1993), p. 14.

91. R. C. Mayer, J. H. Davis, and F. D. Schoorman, "An Integrative Model of Organizational Trust"; and J. A. Colquitt, B. A. Scott, and J. A. LePine, "Trust, Trustworthiness, and Trust Propensity: A Meta-analytic Test of Their Unique Relationships with Risk Taking and Job Performance," *Journal of Applied Psychology* 92, no. 4 (2007), pp. 909–927.

92. H. H. Tan and C. S. F. Tan, "Toward the Differentiation of Trust in Supervisor and Trust in Organization," *Genetic, Social, and General Psychology Monographs,* May 2000, pp. 241–260.

93. Cited in D. Jones, "Do You Trust Your CEO?" *USA Today* (February 12, 2003), p. 7B.

94. B. Nanus, *The Leader's Edge: The Seven Keys to Leadership in a Turbulent World* (Chicago: Contemporary Books, 1989), p. 102.

95. R. C. Mayer and J. H. Davis, "The Effect of the Performance Appraisal System on Trust for Management: A Quasi-Experiment," *Journal of Applied Psychology* 84, no. 1 (1999), pp. 123–136; and R. C. Mayer and M. B. Gavin, "Trust in Management and Performance: Who Minds the Shop While the Employees Watch the Boss?" *Academy of Management Journal* 38 (2005), pp. 874–888.

96. J. A. Simpson, "Foundations of Interpersonal Trust," in A. W. Kruglanski and E. T. Higgins (eds.), *Social Psychology: Handbook of Basic Principles,* 2nd ed. (New York: Guilford, 2007), pp. 587–607.

97. Ibid.

98. H. Zhao, S. J. Wayne, B. C. Glibkowski, and J. Bravo, "The Impact of Psychological Contract Breach on Work-Related Outcomes: A Meta-analysis," *Personnel Psychology* 60 (2007), pp. 647–680.

99. D. L. Ferrin, P. H. Kim, C. D. Cooper, and K. T. Dirks, "Silence Speaks Volumes: The Effectiveness of Reticence in Comparison to Apology and Denial for Responding to Integrity- and Competence-Based Trust Violations," *Journal of Applied Psychology* 92, no. 4 (2007), pp. 893–908.

100. M. E. Schweitzer, J. C. Hershey, and E. T. Bradlow, "Promises and Lies: Restoring Violated Trust," *Organizational Behavior and Human Decision Processes* 101, no. 1 (2006), pp. 1–19.

101. J. R. Detert and E. R. Burris, "Leadership Behavior and Employee Voice: Is the Door Really Open?" *Academy of Management Journal* 50, no. 4 (2007), pp. 869–884.

102. J. A. Colquitt, B. A. Scott, and J. A. LePine, "Trust, Trustworthiness, and Trust Propensity."

103. See, for example, M. Murray, *Beyond the Myths and Magic of Mentoring: How to Facilitate an Effective Mentoring Process,* rev. ed. (New York: Wiley, 2001); K. E. Kram, "Phases of the Mentor Relationship," *Academy of Management Journal,* December 1983, pp. 608–625; R. A. Noe, "An Investigation of the Determinants of Successful Assigned Mentoring Relationships," *Personnel Psychology,* Fall 1988, pp. 559–580; and L. Eby, M. Butts, and A. Lockwood, "Protégés' Negative Mentoring Experiences: Construct Development and Nomological Validation," *Personnel Psychology,* Summer 2004, pp. 411–447.

104. B. R. Ragins and J. L. Cotton, "Easier Said than Done: Gender Differences in Perceived Barriers to Gaining a Mentor," *Academy of Management Journal* 34, no. 4 (1993), pp. 939–951; C. R. Wanberg, E. T. Welsh, and S. A. Hezlett, "Mentoring Research: A Review and Dynamic Process Model," in G. R. Ferris and J. J. Martocchio (eds.), *Research in Personnel and Human Resources Management,* vol. 22 (Greenwich, CT: Elsevier Science, 2003), pp. 39–124; and T. D. Allen, "Protégé Selection by Mentors: Contributing Individual and Organizational Factors," *Journal of Vocational Behavior* 65, no. 3 (2004), pp. 469–483.

105. T. D. Allen, M. L. Poteet, J. E. A. Russell, and G. H. Dobbins, "A Field Study of Factors Related to Supervisors' Willingness to Mentor Others," *Journal of Vocational Behavior* 50, no. 1 (1997), pp. 1–22; S. Aryee, Y. W. Chay, and J. Chew, "The Motivation to Mentor Among Managerial Employees in the Maintenance Career Stage: An Interactionist Perspective," *Group and Organization Management* 21, no. 3 (1996), pp. 261–277; L. T. Eby, A. L. Lockwood, and M. Butts, "Perceived Support for Mentoring: A Multiple

Perspectives Approach," *Journal of Vocational Behavior* 68, no. 2 (2006), pp. 267–291; and T. D. Allen, E. Lentz, and R. Day, "Career Success Outcomes Associated with Mentoring Others: A Comparison of Mentors and Nonmentors," *Journal of Career Development* 32, no. 3 (2006), pp. 272–285.

106. D. Jones, "Women CEOs Slowly Gain on Corporate America," www.usatoday.com/money/companies/management/2009-01-01-women-ceos-increase_N.htm; A. H. Eagly, "Female Leadership Advantage and Disadvantage: Resolving the Contradictions," *Psychology of Women Quarterly*, March 2007, pp. 1–12; and A. H. Eagly, M. C. Johannesen-Schmidt, and M. L. van Engen, "Transformational, Transactional, and Laissez-Faire Leadership Styles: A Meta-analysis Comparing Women and Men," *Psychological Bulletin*, July 2003, pp. 569–591.

107. See, for example, K. E. Kram and D. T. Hall, "Mentoring in a Context of Diversity and Turbulence," in E. E. Kossek and S. A. Lobel (eds.), *Managing Diversity* (Cambridge, MA: Blackwell, 1996), pp. 108–136; B. R. Ragins and J. L. Cotton, "Mentor Functions and Outcomes: A Comparison of Men and Women in Formal and Informal Mentoring Relationships," *Journal of Applied Psychology*, August 1999, pp. 529–550; and D. B. Turban, T. W. Dougherty, and F. K. Lee, "Gender, Race, and Perceived Similarity Effects in Developmental Relationships: The Moderating Role of Relationship Duration," *Journal of Vocational Behavior*, October 2002, pp. 240–262.

108. J. A. Wilson and N. S. Elman, "Organizational Benefits of Mentoring," *Academy of Management Executive* 4, no. 4, p. 90.

109. See, for instance, K. Houston-Philpot, "Leadership Development Partnerships at Dow Corning Corporation," *Journal of Organizational Excellence*, Winter 2002, pp. 13–27.

110. Ragins and Cotton, "Mentor Functions and Outcomes"; and C. M. Underhill, "The Effectiveness of Mentoring Programs in Corporate Settings: A Meta-analytical Review of the Literature," *Journal of Vocational Behavior* 68, no. 2 (2006), pp. 292–307.

111. T. D. Allen, E. T. Eby, and E. Lentz, "The Relationship Between Formal Mentoring Program Characteristics and Perceived Program Effectiveness," *Personnel Psychology* 59 (2006), pp. 125–153; T. D. Allen, L. T. Eby, and E. Lentz, "Mentorship Behaviors and Mentorship Quality Associated with Formal Mentoring Programs: Closing the Gap Between Research and Practice," *Journal of Applied Psychology* 91, no. 3 (2006), pp. 567–578; and M. R. Parise and M. L. Forret, "Formal Mentoring Programs: The Relationship of Program Design and Support to Mentors' Perceptions of Benefits and Costs," *Journal of Vocational Behavior* 72, no. 2 (2008), pp. 225–240.

112. L. T. Eby and A. Lockwood, "Protégés' and Mentors' Reactions to Participating in Formal Mentoring Programs: A Qualitative Investigation," *Journal of Vocational Behavior* 67, no. 3 (2005), pp. 441–458; G. T. Chao, "Formal Mentoring: Lessons Learned from Past Practice," *Professional Psychology: Research and Practice* 40, no. 3 (2009), pp. 314–320; C. R. Wanberg, J. D. Kammeyer-Mueller, and M. Marchese, "Mentor and Protégé Predictors and Outcomes of Mentoring in a Formal Mentoring Program," *Journal of Vocational Behavior* 69 (2006), pp. 410–423.

113. T. D. Allen, L. T. Eby, M. L. Poteet, E. Lentz, and L. Lima, "Career Benefits Associated with Mentoring for Protégés: A Meta-analysis," *Journal of Applied Psychology*, February 2004, pp. 127–136; and J. D. Kammeyer-Mueller and T. A. Judge, "A Quantitative Review of the Mentoring Literature: Test of a Model," *Journal of Vocational Behavior* 72 (2008), pp. 269–283.

114. M. K. Feeney and B. Bozeman, "Mentoring and Network Ties," *Human Relations* 61, no. 12 (2008), pp. 1651–1676; N. Bozionelos, "Intra-Organizational Network Resources: How They Relate to Career Success and Organizational Commitment," *Personnel Review* 37, no. 3 (2008), pp. 249–263; and S. A. Hezlett and S. K. Gibson, "Linking Mentoring and Social Capital: Implications for Career and Organization Development," *Advances in Developing Human Resources* 9, no. 3 (2007), pp. 384–412.

115. C. Hymowitz, "Today's Bosses Find Mentoring Isn't Worth the Time and Risks," *Wall Street Journal* (March 13, 2006), p. B1.

116. Comment by Jim Collins, cited in J. Useem, "Conquering Vertical Limits," *Fortune* (February 19, 2001), p. 94.

117. See, for instance, J. R. Meindl, "The Romance of Leadership as a Follower-centric Theory: A Social Constructionist Approach," *Leadership Quarterly*, Fall 1995, pp. 329–341; and B. Schyns, J. Felfe, and H. Blank, "Is Charisma Hyper-Romanticism? Empirical Evidence from New Data and a Meta-analysis," *Applied Psychology: An International Review* 56, no. 4 (2007), pp. 505–527.

118. R. G. Lord, C. L. DeVader, and G. M. Alliger, "A Meta-analysis of the Relation Between Personality Traits and Leadership Perceptions: An Application of Validity Generalization Procedures," *Journal of Applied Psychology*, August 1986, pp. 402–410.

119. J. R. Meindl, S. B. Ehrlich, and J. M. Dukerich, "The Romance of Leadership," *Administrative Science Quarterly*, March 1985, pp. 78–102; and M. C. Bligh, J. C. Kohles, C. L. Pearce, J. E. Justin, and J. F. Stovall, "When the Romance Is Over: Follower Perspectives of Aversive Leadership," *Applied Psychology: An International Review* 56, no. 4 (2007), pp. 528–557.

120. B. R. Agle, N. J. Nagarajan, J. A. Sonnenfeld, and D. Srinivasan, "Does CEO Charisma Matter?" *Academy of Management Journal* 49, no. 1 (2006), pp. 161–174.

121. Bligh, Kohles, Pearce, Justin, and Stovall, "When the Romance Is Over."

122. Schyns, Felfe, and Blank, "Is Charisma Hyper-Romanticism?"

123. J. Cassidy, "Subprime Suspect: The Rise and Fall of Wall Street's First Black C.E.O.," *The New Yorker* (March 31, 2008), pp. 78–91.

124. A. S. Rosette, G. J. Leonardelli, and K. W. Phillips, "The White Standard: Racial Bias in Leader Categorization," *Journal of Applied Psychology* 93, no. 4 (2008), pp. 758–777.

125. M. Van Vugt and B. R. Spisak, "Sex Differences in the Emergence of Leadership During Competitions Within and Between Groups," *Psychological Science* 19, no. 9 (2008), pp. 854–858.

126. S. Kerr and J. M. Jermier, "Substitutes for Leadership: Their Meaning and Measurement," *Organizational Behavior and Human Performance*, December 1978, pp. 375–403; J. M. Jermier and S. Kerr, "Substitutes for Leadership: Their Meaning and Measurement—Contextual Recollections

and Current Observations," *Leadership Quarterly* 8, no. 2 (1997), pp. 95–101; and E. de Vries Reinout, R. A. Roe, and T. C. B. Taillieu, "Need for Leadership as a Moderator of the Relationships Between Leadership and Individual Outcomes," *Leadership Quarterly*, April 2002, pp. 121–138.

127. S. D. Dionne, F. J. Yammarino, L. E. Atwater, and L. R. James, "Neutralizing Substitutes for Leadership Theory: Leadership Effects and Common-Source Bias," *Journal of Applied Psychology*, 87 (2002), pp. 454–464; and J. R. Villa, J. P. Howell, P. W. Dorfman, and D. L. Daniel, "Problems with Detecting Moderators in Leadership Research Using Moderated Multiple Regression," *Leadership Quarterly* 14 (2002), pp. 3–23.

128. L. A. Hambley, T. A. O'Neill, and T. J. B. Kline, "Virtual Team Leadership: The Effects of Leadership Style and Communication Medium on Team Interaction Styles and Outcomes," *Organizational Behavior and Human Decision Processes* 103 (2007), pp. 1–20; and B. J. Avolio and S. S. Kahai, "Adding the 'E' to E-Leadership: How It May Impact Your Leadership," *Organizational Dynamics* 31, no. 4 (2003), pp. 325–338.

129. S. J. Zaccaro and P. Bader, "E-Leadership and the Challenges of Leading E-Teams: Minimizing the Bad and Maximizing the Good," *Organizational Dynamics* 31, no. 4 (2003), pp. 381–385.

130. B. Shamir, "Leadership in Boundaryless Organizations: Disposable or Indispensable?" *European Journal of Work and Organizational Psychology* 8, no. 1 (1999), pp. 49–71.

131. C. E. Naquin and G. D. Paulson, "Online Bargaining and Interpersonal Trust," *Journal of Applied Psychology*, February 2003, pp. 113–120.

132. B. M. Bass, "Cognitive, Social, and Emotional Intelligence of Transformational Leaders," in R. E. Riggio, S. E. Murphy, and F. J. Pirozzolo (eds.), *Multiple Intelligences and Leadership* (Mahwah, NJ: Lawrence Erlbaum, 2002), pp. 113–114.

133. See, for instance, P. Dvorak, "M.B.A. Programs Hone 'Soft Skills,'" *Wall Street Journal* (February 12, 2007), p. B3.

134. J. Weber, "The Leadership Factor," *BusinessWeek* (June 12, 2006), pp. 60–64.

135. See, for instance, Barling, Weber, and Kelloway, "Effects of Transformational Leadership Training on Attitudinal and Financial Outcomes"; and D. V. Day, "Leadership Development: A Review in Context," *Leadership Quarterly*, Winter 2000, pp. 581–613.

136. M. Sashkin, "The Visionary Leader," in J. A. Conger, R. N. Kanungo, et al. (eds.), *Charismatic Leadership* (San Francisco: Jossey-Bass, 1988), p. 150.

137. D. V. Day, "Leadership Development: A Review in Context," *Leadership Quarterly*, Winter 2000, pp. 590–593.

138. M. Conlin, "CEO Coaches," *BusinessWeek* (November 11, 2002), pp. 98–104.

139. Howell and Frost, "A Laboratory Study of Charismatic Leadership."

140. Dvir, Eden, and Avolio, "Impact of Transformational Leadership on Follower Development and Performance"; B. J. Avolio and B. M. Bass, *Developing Potential Across a Full Range of Leadership: Cases on Transactional and Transformational Leadership* (Mahwah, NJ: Lawrence Erlbaum, 2002); A. J. Towler, "Effects of Charismatic Influence Training on Attitudes, Behavior, and Performance," *Personnel Psychology*, Summer 2003, pp. 363–381; and Barling, Weber, and Kelloway, "Effects of Transformational Leadership Training on Attitudinal and Financial Outcomes."

141. M. Javidan, P. W. Dorfman, M. S. de Luque, and R. J. House, "In the Eye of the Beholder: Cross Cultural Lessons in Leadership from Project GLOBE," *Academy of Management Perspectives*, February 2006, pp. 67–90.

142. R. J. House, M. Javidan, P. Hanges, and P. Dorfman, "Understanding Cultures and Implicit Leadership Theories Across the Globe: An Introduction to Project GLOBE," *Journal of World Business*, Spring 2002, pp. 3–10.

143. D. E. Carl and M. Javidan, "Universality of Charismatic Leadership: A Multi-Nation Study," paper presented at the National Academy of Management Conference, Washington, DC, August 2001, p. 29.

144. N. Beccalli, "European Business Forum Asks: Do Companies Get the Leaders They Deserve?" *European Business Forum*, 2003, www.pwcglobal.com/extweb/pwcpublications.nsf/DocID/D1EC3380F589844585256D7300346A1B.

145. R. D. Arvey, Z. Zhang, and B. J. Avolio, "Developmental and Genetic Determinants of Leadership Role Occupancy Among Women," *Journal of Applied Psychology*, May 2007, pp. 693–706.

146. M. Pandya, "Warren Buffett on Investing and Leadership: I'm Wired for This Game," *Wharton Leadership Digest* 3, no. 7 (April 1999), leadership.wharton.upenn.edu/digest/04-99.shtml.

LEARNING OBJECTIVES

After studying this chapter, you should be able to:

1 Define *power* and contrast leadership and power.

2 Contrast the five bases of power.

3 Identify nine power or influence tactics and their contingencies.

4 Show the connection between sexual harassment and the abuse of power.

5 Distinguish between legitimate and illegitimate political behavior.

6 Identify the causes and consequences of political behavior.

7 Apply impression management techniques.

8 Determine whether a political action is ethical.

9 Show the influence of culture on the uses and perceptions of politics.

Power and Politics

Power is not revealed by striking hard or often,
but by striking true. —Honoré de Balzac

DOES POWER CORRUPT?

As you might imagine, whether power corrupts is a difficult question to answer, and, even if the answer is *generally* yes, it surely is not *always* so. Some recent research suggests, however, that power may corrupt how we perceive and react toward others.

Individuals who are primed to experience power are less likely to empathize with others. Such high-power people are more likely to rely heavily on their own vantage point in making group decisions, less likely to take others' perspectives into account, and less accurate in judging others' emotions. Other research suggests those who hold power are more likely to objectify others (to see them in instrumental terms), more likely to behave toward others in hostile ways, and less likely to feel the need to deliberate over decisions.

While all this may suggest power is bad, that's not necessarily so. Some research also suggests possible *benefits* to this lack of perspective taking: powerful people may be more creative and less subject to conformity pressures, probably because they feel freer to see and do as they see fit.

One way researchers studied how power affects perspective taking was to examine how subjects drew a capital "E" on their forehead with an erasable marker. Their hypothesis was that self-oriented people would draw the letter with the prongs facing so they them-selves could read it and that other-oriented people would draw the letter so others could read it. Individuals placed in a high-power group were nearly three times as likely to draw the "E" so they, but not others, could read it.

Studies like these are somewhat contrived—for example, students were often placed into high- and low-power groups based on whether they were asked to write a story about a time when they did or didn't have power. One of the researchers, Joe Magee at New York University, decided to study the really powerful. He was able to gain entry to the Time100 Banquet, a dinner at New York's Lincoln Center that featured the city's most powerful people. He repeated his "E" experiment with them, at least those who would agree. (*Saturday Night Live*'s Amy Poehler refused, saying, "Why would I want to do that?") Surprisingly, most did participate and, even more surprising given the earlier findings, most drew other-oriented "E"s, including gossip columnist Liz Smith, New York City police commissioner Ray Kelly, and former World Bank President Paul Wolfowitz. One who drew a self-oriented "E" was Goldman Sachs CEO Lloyd Blankfein. "I have a big platform," he said with a smile, as he smacked the Post-it on the front of his bald head.[1]

I n both research and practice, *power* and *politics* have been described as the last dirty words. It is easier for most of us to talk about sex or money than about power or political behavior. People who have power deny it, people who want it try not to look like they're seeking it, and those who are good at getting it are secretive about how they do so.[2] To see whether you think your work environment is political, take the following self-assessment.

A major theme of this chapter is that power and political behavior are natural processes in any group or organization. Given that, you need to know how power is acquired and exercised if you are to fully understand organizational behavior. Although you may have heard that "Power corrupts, and absolute power corrupts absolutely," power is not always bad. As one author noted, most medicines can kill if taken in the wrong amount, and thousands die each year in automobile accidents, but we don't abandon chemicals or cars because of the dangers associated with them. Rather, we consider danger an incentive to get training and information that will help us to use these forces productively.[3] The same applies to power. It's a reality of organizational life, and it's not going to go away. By learning how power works in organizations, you'll be better able to use your knowledge to become a more effective manager.

IS MY WORKPLACE POLITICAL?

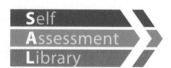

In the Self-Assessment Library (available on CD and online), take assessment IV.F.1 (Is My Workplace Political?). If you don't currently have a job, answer for your most recent job. Then answer the following questions.

1. *How does your score relate to those of your classmates? Do you think your score is accurate? Why or why not?*
2. *Do you think a political workplace is a bad thing? If yes, why? If no, why not?*
3. *What factors cause your workplace to be political?*

A Definition of *Power*

1 Define *power* and contrast leadership and power.

Power refers to a capacity that *A* has to influence the behavior of *B* so *B* acts in accordance with *A*'s wishes.[4]

Someone can thus have power but not use it; it is a capacity or potential. Probably the most important aspect of power is that it is a function of **dependency**. The greater *B*'s dependence on *A*, the greater *A*'s power in the relationship. Dependence, in turn, is based on alternatives that *B* perceives, and the importance *B* places on the alternative(s) *A* controls. A person can have power over you only if he or she controls something you desire. If you want a college degree and have to pass a certain course to get it, and your current instructor is the only faculty member in the college who teaches that course, he or she has power over you. Your alternatives are highly limited, and you place a high degree of importance on obtaining a passing grade. Similarly, if you're attending college on funds totally provided by your parents, you probably recognize the power they hold over you. You're dependent on them for financial support. But once you're out of school, have a job, and are making a good income, your parents' power is reduced significantly. Who among us, though, has not known or heard of a rich relative who is able to control a large number of family members merely through the implicit or explicit threat of "writing them out of the will"?

Contrasting Leadership and Power

A careful comparison of our description of power with our description of leadership in Chapter 12 reveals the concepts are closely intertwined. Leaders use power as a means of attaining group goals.

How are the two terms different? Power does not require goal compatibility, merely dependence. Leadership, on the other hand, requires some congruence between the goals of the leader and those being led. A second difference relates to the direction of influence. Leadership focuses on the downward influence on followers. It minimizes the importance of lateral and upward influence patterns. Power does not. In still another difference, leadership research, for the most part, emphasizes style. It seeks answers to questions such as these: How supportive should a leader be? How much decision making should be shared with followers? In contrast, the research on power focuses on tactics for gaining compliance. It goes beyond the individual as the exerciser of power because groups as well as individuals can use power to control other individuals or groups.

Bases of Power

2 Contrast the five bases of power.

Where does power come from? What gives an individual or a group influence over others? We answer by dividing the bases or sources of power into two general groupings—formal and personal—and then breaking each of these down into more specific categories.[5]

Formal Power

Formal power is based on an individual's position in an organization. It can come from the ability to coerce or reward, or from formal authority.

Coercive Power The **coercive power** base depends on fear of the negative results from failing to comply. It rests on the application, or the threat of application, of physical sanctions such as the infliction of pain, frustration through restriction of movement, or the controlling by force of basic physiological or safety needs.

At the organizational level, *A* has coercive power over *B* if *A* can dismiss, suspend, or demote *B*, assuming *B* values his or her job. If *A* can assign *B* work activities *B* finds unpleasant or treat *B* in a manner *B* finds embarrassing, *A* possesses coercive power over *B*. Coercive power can also come from withholding key information. People in an organization who have data or knowledge others need can make those others dependent on them.

---

power   *A capacity that A has to influence the behavior of B so that B acts in accordance with A's wishes.*

dependency   *B's relationship to A when A possesses something that B requires.*

coercive power   *A power base that is dependent on fear of the negative results from failing to comply.*

Reward Power   The opposite of coercive power is **reward power**, with which people comply because it produces positive benefits; someone who can distribute rewards others view as valuable will have power over them. These rewards can be either financial—such as controlling pay rates, raises, and bonuses—or nonfinancial, including recognition, promotions, interesting work assignments, friendly colleagues, and preferred work shifts or sales territories.[6]

Legitimate Power   In formal groups and organizations, probably the most common access to one or more of the power bases is through **legitimate power**. It represents the formal authority to control and use organizational resources based on structural position in the organization.

Legitimate power is broader than the power to coerce and reward. Specifically, it includes members' acceptance of the authority of a position. We associate power so closely associated with the concept of hierarchy that just drawing longer lines in an organization chart leads people to infer the leaders are especially powerful, and when a powerful executive is described, people tend to put the person at a higher position when drawing an organization chart.[7] When school principals, bank presidents, or army captains speak (assuming their directives are viewed as within the authority of their positions), teachers, tellers, and first lieutenants listen and usually comply.

Personal Power

Many of the most competent and productive chip designers at Intel have power, but they aren't managers and have no formal power. What they have is **personal power**, which comes from an individual's unique characteristics. There are two bases of personal power: expertise and the respect and admiration of others.

Expert Power   **Expert power** is influence wielded as a result of expertise, special skill, or knowledge. As jobs become more specialized, we become increasingly dependent on experts to achieve goals. It is generally acknowledged that physicians have expertise and hence expert power: Most of us follow our doctor's advice. Computer specialists, tax accountants, economists, industrial psychologists, and other specialists wield power as a result of their expertise.

Nike CEO Mark Parker has expert power. Since joining Nike in 1979 as a footwear designer, Parker has been involved in many of Nike's most significant design innovations. His primary responsibilities and leadership positions at Nike have been in product research, design, and development. Nike depends on Parker's expertise in leading the company's innovation initiatives and in setting corporate strategy to achieve the growth of its global business portfolio that includes Converse, Nike Golf, and Cole Haan. Parker is shown here introducing Nike's Considered Design during a news conference about the company's latest products that combine sustainability and innovation.

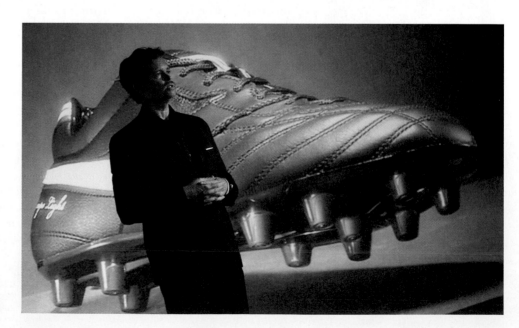

Referent Power   **Referent power** is based on identification with a person who has desirable resources or personal traits. If I like, respect, and admire you, you can exercise power over me because I want to please you.

Referent power develops out of admiration of another and a desire to be like that person. It helps explain, for instance, why celebrities are paid millions of dollars to endorse products in commercials. Marketing research shows people such as LeBron James and Tom Brady have the power to influence your choice of athletic shoes and credit cards. With a little practice, you and I could probably deliver as smooth a sales pitch as these celebrities, but the buying public doesn't identify with you and me. Some people who are not in formal leadership positions nonetheless have referent power and exert influence over others because of their charismatic dynamism, likability, and emotional effects on us.

Which Bases of Power Are Most Effective?

Of the three bases of formal power (coercive, reward, legitimate) and two bases of personal power (expert, referent), which is most important to have? Research suggests pretty clearly that the personal sources of power are most effective. Both expert and referent power are positively related to employees' satisfaction with supervision, their organizational commitment, and their performance, whereas reward and legitimate power seem to be unrelated to these outcomes. One source of formal power—coercive power—actually can backfire in that it is negatively related to employee satisfaction and commitment.[8]

Consider Steve Stoute's company, Translation, which matches pop-star spokespersons with corporations that want to promote their brands. Stoute has paired Gwen Stefani with HP, Justin Timberlake with McDonald's, Beyoncé Knowles with Tommy Hilfiger, and Jay-Z with Reebok. Stoute's business seems to be all about referent power. As one record company executive commented when reflecting on Stoute's successes, "He's the right guy for guiding brands in using the record industry to reach youth culture in a credible way."[9] In other words, people buy products associated with cool figures because they wish to identify with and emulate them.

Dependency: The Key to Power

We have already stated that the most important aspect of power is that it is a function of dependency. In this section, we show how understanding dependency helps us understand power itself.

The General Dependency Postulate

Let's begin with a general postulate: *the greater* B*'s dependency on* A, *the more power* A *has over* B. When you possess anything others require that you alone control, you make them dependent on you, and, therefore, you gain power over them.[10]

---

reward power   *Compliance achieved based on the ability to distribute rewards that others view as valuable.*

legitimate power   *The power a person receives as a result of his or her position in the formal hierarchy of an organization.*

personal power   *Influence derived from an individual's characteristics.*

expert power   *Influence based on special skills or knowledge.*

referent power   *Influence based on identification with a person who has desirable resources or personal traits.*

If something is plentiful, possessing it will not increase your power. But as the old saying goes, "In the land of the blind, the one-eyed man is king!" Conversely, the more you can expand your own options, the less power you place in the hands of others. This explains why most organizations develop multiple suppliers rather than give their business to only one. It also explains why so many aspire to financial independence. It reduces the power others can wield if they can limit our access to opportunities and resources.

What Creates Dependency?

Dependency increases when the resource you control is important, scarce, and nonsubstitutable.[11]

Importance   If nobody wants what you have, it's not going to create dependency. Organizations, for instance, actively seek to avoid uncertainty.[12] We should, therefore, expect that the individuals or groups who can absorb an organization's uncertainty will be perceived as controlling an important resource. A study of industrial organizations found their marketing departments were consistently rated the most powerful.[13] The researcher concluded the most critical uncertainty facing these firms was selling their products, suggesting that engineers, as a group, would be more powerful at technology company Matsushita than at consumer products giant Procter & Gamble. These inferences appear to be generally valid. Matsushita, which is heavily technologically oriented, is highly dependent on its engineers to maintain its products' technical advantages and quality, and so they are a powerful group. At Procter & Gamble, marketing is the name of the game, and marketers are the most powerful occupational group.

Scarcity   Ferruccio Lamborghini, who created the exotic supercars that still carry his name, understood the importance of scarcity and used it to his advantage during World War II. Lamborghini was in Rhodes with the Italian

Because Xerox Corporation has staked its future on development and innovation, Sophie Vandebroek is in a position of power at Xerox. As the company's chief technology officer, she leads the Xerox Innovation Group of 5,000 scientists and engineers who work at the company's global research centers. The group's mission is "to pioneer high-impact technologies that enable us to lead in our core markets and to create future markets for Xerox." The company depends on Vandebroek and her group of scientists and engineers to make that mission a reality.

army. His superiors were impressed with his mechanical skills, as he demonstrated an almost uncanny ability to repair tanks and cars no one else could fix. After the war, he admitted his ability was largely due to his having been the first person on the island to receive the repair manuals, which he memorized and then destroyed so as to become indispensable.[14]

We see the scarcity–dependency relationship in the power of occupational categories. Where the supply of labor is low relative to demand, workers can negotiate compensation and benefits packages far more attractive than can those in occupations with an abundance of candidates. College administrators have no problem today finding English instructors. The market for network systems analysts, in contrast, is extremely tight, with demand high and supply limited. The bargaining power of computer-engineering faculty allows them to negotiate higher salaries, lighter teaching loads, and other benefits.

Nonsubstitutability   The fewer viable substitutes for a resource, the more power control over that resource provides. At universities with strong pressures for the faculty to publish, the more recognition the faculty member receives through publication, the more mobile he or she is, because other universities want faculty who are highly published and visible. Although tenure can alter this relationship by restricting the department head's alternatives, faculty members with few or no publications have the least mobility and are subject to the greatest influence from their superiors.

Power Tactics

3 Identify nine power or influence tactics and their contingencies.

What **power tactics** do people use to translate power bases into specific action? What options do they have for influencing their bosses, co-workers, or employees? In this section, we review popular tactical options and the conditions that may make one more effective than another.

Research has identified nine distinct influence tactics:[15]

- *Legitimacy.* Relying on your authority position or saying a request accords with organizational policies or rules.
- *Rational persuasion.* Presenting logical arguments and factual evidence to demonstrate a request is reasonable.
- *Inspirational appeals.* Developing emotional commitment by appealing to a target's values, needs, hopes, and aspirations.
- *Consultation.* Increasing the target's support by involving him or her in deciding how you will accomplish your plan.
- *Exchange.* Rewarding the target with benefits or favors in exchange for following a request.
- *Personal appeals.* Asking for compliance based on friendship or loyalty.
- *Ingratiation.* Using flattery, praise, or friendly behavior prior to making a request.

power tactics   *Ways in which individuals translate power bases into specific actions.*

Exhibit 13-1	Preferred Power Tactics by Influence Direction	
Upward Influence	**Downward Influence**	**Lateral Influence**
Rational persuasion	Rational persuasion	Rational persuasion
	Inspirational appeals	Consultation
	Pressure	Ingratiation
	Consultation	Exchange
	Ingratiation	Legitimacy
	Exchange	Personal appeals
	Legitimacy	Coalitions

- *Pressure.* Using warnings, repeated demands, and threats.
- *Coalitions.* Enlisting the aid or support of others to persuade the target to agree.

Some tactics are more effective than others. Rational persuasion, inspirational appeals, and consultation tend to be the most effective, especially when the audience is highly interested in the outcomes of a decision process. Pressure tends to backfire and is typically the least effective of the nine tactics.[16] You can also increase your chance of success by using more than one type of tactic at the same time or sequentially, as long as your choices are compatible.[17] Using both ingratiation and legitimacy can lessen the negative reactions from appearing to "dictate" outcomes, but only when the audience does not really care about the outcomes of a decision process or the policy is routine.[18]

Let's consider the most effective way of getting a raise. You can start with rational persuasion. That means doing your homework and carefully thinking through the best way to build your case: figure out how your pay compares to that of peers, or land a competing job offer, or show objective results that testify to your performance. Kitty Dunning, a vice president at Don Jagoda Associates, landed a 16 percent raise when she e-mailed her boss numbers showing she had increased sales.[19] You can also make good use of salary calculators such as Salary.com to compare your pay with comparable others.

But the effectiveness of some influence tactics depends on the direction of influence.[20] As Exhibit 13-1 shows, rational persuasion is the only tactic effective across organizational levels. Inspirational appeals work best as a downward-influencing tactic with subordinates. When pressure works, it's generally downward only. Personal appeals and coalitions are most effective as lateral influence. Other factors that affect the effectiveness of influence include the sequencing of tactics, a person's skill in using the tactic, and the organizational culture.

You're more likely to be effective if you begin with "softer" tactics that rely on personal power, such as personal and inspirational appeals, rational persuasion, and consultation. If these fail, you can move to "harder" tactics, such as exchange, coalitions, and pressure, which emphasize formal power and incur greater costs and risks.[21] Interestingly, a single soft tactic is more effective than a single hard tactic, and combining two soft tactics or a soft tactic and rational persuasion is more effective than any single tactic or combination of hard tactics.[22] The effectiveness of tactics depends on the audience.[23] People especially likely to comply with soft power tactics tend to be more reflective, are intrinsically motivated, have high self-esteem, and have greater desire for control. People especially likely to comply with hard power tactics are more action oriented and extrinsically motivated and are more focused on getting along with others than with getting their own way.

International OB

Influence Tactics in China

Researchers usually examine cross-cultural influences in business by comparing two very different cultures, such as Eastern and Western. However, differences *within* a given culture also matter because they can sometimes be greater than differences between cultures.

China is a big country, housing different cultures and traditions. A recent study examining Mainland Chinese, Taiwanese, and Hong Kong managers explored how the three cultural subgroups differ according to the influence tactics they prefer to use.

Though managers from all three places believe rational persuasion and exchange are the most effective influence tactics, managers in Taiwan tend to use inspirational appeals and ingratiation more than managers from either Mainland China or Hong Kong.

Managers from Hong Kong rate pressure as more effective in influencing others than do managers in Taiwan or Mainland China. Such differences have implications for business relationships. Taiwanese or Mainland Chinese managers may be taken aback by a Hong Kong manager's use of pressure tactics, while managers from Hong Kong may not be persuaded by managers from Taiwan, who tend to use ingratiating tactics. To smooth business transactions, firms should make their managers aware of the differences within cultures.

A study of Swedish, German, Czech, Polish, and Finnish managers found Swedish managers saw mere differences in opinion as conflicts, so they adopted a conflict-avoidant strategy that emphasized more passive forms of persuasion. German man-

agers, on the other hand, saw disagreement as a useful opportunity to gain new knowledge and fostered some rational discussion as an influence technique. Finnish managers preferred discussion-oriented influence tactics as well. Czech and Polish managers believed managers were under pressure to halt conflicts quickly when they arose, since conflict resolution is time consuming. Therefore, the Czech and Polish managers switched to more autocratic, power-oriented influence styles.

Sources: Based on P. P. Fu, T. K. Peng, J. C. Kennedy, and G. Yukl, "A Comparison of Chinese Managers in Hong Kong, Taiwan, and Mainland China," *Organizational Dynamics*, February 2004, pp. 32–46; and E. Szabo, "Meaning and Context of Participation in Five European Countries," *Management Decision* 44, no 2 (2006), pp. 276–289.

People differ in their **political skill**, or their ability to influence others to enhance their own objectives. The politically skilled are more effective users of all of the influence tactics. Political skill also appears more effective when the stakes are high—such as when the individual is accountable for important organizational outcomes. Finally, the politically skilled are able to exert their influence without others detecting it, a key element in being effective (it's damaging to be labeled political).[24]

Finally, we know cultures within organizations differ markedly—some are warm, relaxed, and supportive; others are formal and conservative. The organizational culture in which a person works will have a bearing on which tactics are considered appropriate. Some cultures encourage participation and consultation, some encourage reason, and still others rely on pressure. People who fit the culture of the organization tend to obtain more influence.[25] Specifically, extraverts tend to be more influential in team-oriented organizations, and highly conscientious people are more influential in organizations that value working alone on technical tasks. Part of the reason people who fit the culture are influential is that they are able to perform especially well in the domains deemed

political skill   *The ability to influence others in such a way as to enhance one's objectives.*

most important for success. In other words, they are influential because they are competent. So the organization itself will influence which subset of power tactics is viewed as acceptable for use.

Sexual Harassment: Unequal Power in the Workplace

4 Show the connection between sexual harassment and the abuse of power.

Sexual harassment is wrong. It can also be costly to employers. Just ask executives at Wal-Mart, the World Bank, and the United Nations.[26] Mitsubishi paid $34 million to settle a sexual harassment case. And a former UPS manager won an $80 million suit against UPS on her claims it fostered a hostile work environment when it failed to listen to her complaints of sexual harassment. Of course, it's not only big organizations that run into trouble: A jury awarded Janet Bianco, a nurse at New York's Flushing Hospital, $15 million for harassment she suffered at the hands of Dr. Matthew Miller. After the verdict, Bianco said, "I think that people take it lightly when you say sexual harassment. They don't understand how it affects your life, not only in your job, but in your home, with your friends."[27]

In addition to the legal dangers to sexual harassment, obviously it also can have a negative impact on the work environment, too. Research shows sexual harassment negatively affects job attitudes and leads those who feel harassed to withdraw from the organization. In many cases, reporting sexual harassment doesn't improve the situation because the organization responds in a negative or unhelpful way. When organizational leaders make honest efforts to stop the harassment, the outcomes are much more positive.[28]

Sexual harassment is defined as any unwanted activity of a sexual nature that affects an individual's employment and creates a hostile work environment. The U.S. Supreme Court helped to clarify this definition by adding a key test for determining whether sexual harassment has occurred—when comments or behavior in a work environment "would reasonably be perceived, and [are] perceived, as hostile or abusive."[29] But disagreement continues about what *specifically* constitutes sexual harassment. Organizations have generally made progress in the past decade toward limiting overt forms of sexual harassment. This includes unwanted physical touching, recurring requests for dates when it is made clear the person isn't interested, and coercive threats that a person will lose his or her job for refusing a sexual proposition. Problems today are likely to surface around more subtle forms of sexual harassment—unwanted looks or comments, off-color jokes, sexual artifacts like pinups posted in the workplace, or misinterpretations of where the line between being friendly ends and harassment begins.

A recent review concluded that 58 percent of women report having experienced potentially harassing behaviors, and 24 percent report having experienced sexual harassment at work.[30] One problem with reporting is that sexual harassment is, to some degree, in the eye of the beholder. Women are more likely than men to see a given behavior or set of behaviors as constituting sexual harassment. Men are less likely to see harassment in such behaviors as kissing someone, asking for a date, or making sex-stereotyped jokes. As the authors of this study note, "Although progress has been made at defining sexual harassment, it is still unclear as to whose perspective should be taken."[31] The best approach is to be careful—refrain from any behavior that may be taken as harassing, even if that was not the intent. Realize that what you see as an innocent joke or hug may be seen as harassment by the other party.

This employee was one of 90 workers who filed a sexual harassment lawsuit against Dial Corporation. The female employees alleged that male coworkers and supervisors at a Dial soap factory in Illinois fostered a "permissive culture" that condoned groping, sexual insults, and displays of pornography and that women who reported harassment faced retaliation or inaction by upper management. Although Dial denied wrongdoing, the company agreed to pay $10 million to settle the lawsuit, to revise its harassment policies and procedures, and to comply with federal compliance monitoring at its plant for 2½ years.

Most studies confirm that the concept of power is central to understanding sexual harassment.[32] This seems true whether the harassment comes from a supervisor, a co-worker, or an employee. And sexual harassment is more likely to occur when there are large power differentials. The supervisor–employee dyad best characterizes an unequal power relationship, where formal power gives the supervisor the capacity to reward and coerce. Because employees want favorable performance reviews, salary increases, and the like, supervisors control resources most employees consider important and scarce. Thus sexual harassment by the boss typically creates the greatest difficulty for those being harassed. If there are no witnesses, it is the victim's word against the harasser's. Has this boss harassed others, and, if so, will they come forward or fear retaliation?

Although co-workers don't have legitimate power, they can have influence and use it to sexually harass peers. In fact, although they appear to engage in somewhat less severe forms of harassment than do supervisors, co-workers are the most frequent perpetrators of sexual harassment in organizations. How do co-workers exercise power? Most often it's by providing or withholding information, cooperation, and support. The effective performance of most jobs requires interaction and support from co-workers, especially today because work is often assigned to teams. By threatening to withhold or delay providing information that's necessary for the successful achievement of your work goals, co-workers can exert power over you.

Although it doesn't get nearly as much attention as harassment by a supervisor, as the lawsuit against Philip Morris showed, women in positions of power can be subjected to sexual harassment from males who occupy less powerful positions within the organization. The employee devalues the woman in power by highlighting traditional gender stereotypes that reflect negatively on her (such as helplessness, passivity, or lack of career commitment), usually in an attempt to gain some power over her or minimize power differentials. Increasingly, too, there are cases of women in positions of power harassing male employees.

A recent review of the literature shows the damage caused by sexual harassment. As you would expect, individuals who are sexually harassed report lower job satisfaction and diminished organizational commitment as a result. This review also revealed that sexual harassment undermines the victims' mental and physical health. However, sexual harassment also negatively affects the group in which the victim works, lowering its productivity. The authors of this study conclude that sexual harassment "is significantly and substantively associated with a host of harms."[33]

We have seen how sexual harassment can wreak havoc on an organization, not to mention on the victims themselves. But it can be avoided. A manager's role in preventing sexual harassment is critical. The following are some ways managers can protect themselves and their employees from sexual harassment:

1. Make sure an active policy defines what constitutes sexual harassment, informs employees they can be fired for sexually harassing another employee, and establishes procedures for how complaints can be made.

sexual harassment   *Any unwanted activity of a sexual nature that affects an individual's employment and creates a hostile work environment.*

OB Poll   How Do You Deal with Office Politics?

Participate directly, 20%

Stay out of them completely, 24%

Know what's going on but don't participate, 10%

Don't know, 5%

Source: Based on Accountemps Poll of 522 workers, *USA Today* (November 17, 2008), p. 1B.

2. Ensure employees that they will not encounter retaliation if they issue a complaint.
3. Investigate every complaint and include the legal and human resource departments.
4. Make sure offenders are disciplined or terminated.
5. Set up in-house seminars to raise employee awareness of the issues surrounding sexual harassment.

The bottom line is that managers have a responsibility to protect their employees from a hostile work environment, but they also need to protect themselves. Managers may be unaware that one of their employees is being sexually harassed. But being unaware does not protect them or their organization. If investigators believe a manager could have known about the harassment, both the manager and the company can be held liable.

Politics: Power in Action

5 Distinguish between legitimate and illegitimate political behavior.

When people get together in groups, power will be exerted. People want to carve out a niche from which to exert influence, earn rewards, and advance their careers.[34] When employees in organizations convert their power into action, we describe them as being engaged in politics. Those with good political skills have the ability to use their bases of power effectively.[35]

Definition of *Organizational Politics*

There is no shortage of definitions of *organizational politics*. Essentially they focus on the use of power to affect decision making in an organization or on self-serving and organizationally unsanctioned behaviors.[36] For our purposes, **political behavior** in organizations consists of activities that are not required as part of an individual's formal role but that influence, or attempt to influence, the distribution of advantages and disadvantages within the organization.[37]

This definition encompasses what most people mean when they talk about organizational politics. Political behavior is outside specified job requirements. It requires some attempt to use power bases. It includes efforts to influence the goals, criteria, or processes used for decision making. Our definition is broad enough to include varied political behaviors such as withholding key information from decision makers, joining a coalition, whistle-blowing, spreading rumors, leaking confidential information to the media, exchanging favors with others in the organization for mutual benefit, and lobbying on behalf of or against a particular individual or decision alternative.

Is there a "legitimate" dimension in political behavior?[38] **Legitimate political behavior** refers to normal everyday politics—complaining to your supervisor, bypassing the chain of command, forming coalitions, obstructing organizational policies or decisions through inaction or excessive adherence to rules, and developing contacts outside the organization through professional activities. Different from these is **illegitimate political behavior** that violates the implied rules of the game. Illegitimate activities include sabotage, whistle-blowing, and symbolic protests such as wearing unorthodox dress or protest buttons and calling in sick as a group. Those who pursue such extreme activities are often said to "play hardball."

The vast majority of all organizational political actions are of the legitimate variety. The reasons are pragmatic: extreme forms of illegitimate political behavior pose a very real risk of losing organizational membership or incurring extreme sanctions, particularly if those who use these tactics don't have enough power to ensure they work.

The Reality of Politics

Interviews with experienced managers show that most believe political behavior is a major part of organizational life.[39] Many managers report some use of political behavior is both ethical and necessary, as long as it doesn't directly harm anyone else. They describe politics as a necessary evil and believe someone who *never* uses political behavior will have a hard time getting things done. Most also indicate they had never been trained to use political behavior effectively. But why, you may wonder, must politics exist? Isn't it possible for an organization to be politics free? It's *possible* but unlikely.

Organizations are made up of individuals and groups with different values, goals, and interests.[40] This sets up the potential for conflict over the allocation of limited resources, such as departmental budgets, space, project responsibilities, and salary adjustments.[41] If resources were abundant, then all constituencies within the organization could satisfy their goals. But because they are limited, not everyone's interests can be satisfied. Furthermore, gains by one individual or

political behavior *Activities that are not required as part of a person's formal role in the organization but that influence, or attempt to influence, the distribution of advantages and disadvantages within the organization.*

legitimate political behavior *Normal everyday politics.*

illegitimate political behavior *Extreme political behavior that violates the implied rules of the game.*

group are often *perceived* as coming at the expense of others within the organization (whether they are or not). These forces create real competition among members for the organization's limited resources.

Maybe the most important factor leading to politics within organizations is the realization that most of the "facts" used to allocate the limited resources are open to interpretation. What, for instance, is *good* performance? What's an *adequate* improvement? What constitutes an *unsatisfactory* job? One person's "selfless effort to benefit the organization" is seen by another as a "blatant attempt to further one's interest."[42] The manager of any major league baseball team knows a .400 hitter is a high performer and a .125 hitter is a poor performer. You don't need to be a baseball genius to know you should play your .400 hitter and send the .125 hitter back to the minors. But what if you have to choose between players who hit .280 and .290? Then less objective factors come into play: fielding expertise, attitude, potential, ability to perform in a clutch, loyalty to the team, and so on. More managerial decisions resemble the choice between a .280 and a .290 hitter than between a .125 hitter and a .400 hitter. It is in this large and ambiguous middle ground of organizational life—where the facts *don't* speak for themselves—that politics flourish (see Exhibit 13-2).

Finally, because most decisions have to be made in a climate of ambiguity—where facts are rarely fully objective and thus are open to interpretation—people within organizations will use whatever influence they can to taint the

Exhibit 13-2   Politics Is in the Eye of the Beholder

A behavior one person labels as "organizational politics" is very likely to seem like "effective management" to another. The fact is not that effective management is necessarily political, although in some cases it might be. Rather, a person's reference point determines what he or she classifies as organizational politics. For example, one experimental study showed that power-oriented behavior performed by a permanent, tenured employee is seen as more legitimate and less harsh than the same behavior performed by a temporary employee.[43] Take a look at the following labels used to describe the same phenomenon. These suggest that politics, like beauty, is in the eye of the beholder.

"Political" Label		"Effective Management" Label
1. Blaming others	vs.	Fixing responsibility
2. "Kissing up"	vs.	Developing working relationships
3. Apple polishing	vs.	Demonstrating loyalty
4. Passing the buck	vs.	Delegating authority
5. Covering your rear	vs.	Documenting decisions
6. Creating conflict	vs.	Encouraging change and innovation
7. Forming coalitions	vs.	Facilitating teamwork
8. Whistle-blowing	vs.	Improving efficiency
9. Scheming	vs.	Planning ahead
10. Overachieving	vs.	Competent and capable
11. Ambitious	vs.	Career minded
12. Opportunistic	vs.	Astute
13. Cunning	vs.	Practical minded
14. Arrogant	vs.	Confident
15. Perfectionist	vs.	Attentive to detail

Source: Based on T. C. Krell, M. E. Mendenhall, and J. Sendry, "Doing Research in the Conceptual Morass of Organizational Politics," paper presented at the Western Academy of Management Conference, Hollywood, CA, April 1987.

facts to support their goals and interests. That, of course, creates the activities we call *politicking*.

Therefore, to answer the question of whether it is possible for an organization to be politics free, we can say "yes"—if all members of that organization hold the same goals and interests, if organizational resources are not scarce, and if performance outcomes are completely clear and objective. But that doesn't describe the organizational world in which most of us live.

Causes and Consequences of Political Behavior

Factors Contributing to Political Behavior

Not all groups or organizations are equally political. In some organizations, for instance, politicking is overt and rampant, while in others politics plays a small role in influencing outcomes. Why this variation? Recent research and observation have identified a number of factors that appear to encourage political behavior. Some are individual characteristics, derived from the unique qualities of the people the organization employs; others are a result of the organization's culture or internal environment. Exhibit 13-3 illustrates how both individual and organizational factors can increase political behavior and provide favorable outcomes (increased rewards and averted punishments) for both individuals and groups in the organization.

6 Identify the causes and consequences of political behavior.

Individual Factors At the individual level, researchers have identified certain personality traits, needs, and other factors likely to be related to political behavior. In terms of traits, we find that employees who are high self-monitors, possess an internal locus of control, and have a high need for power are more

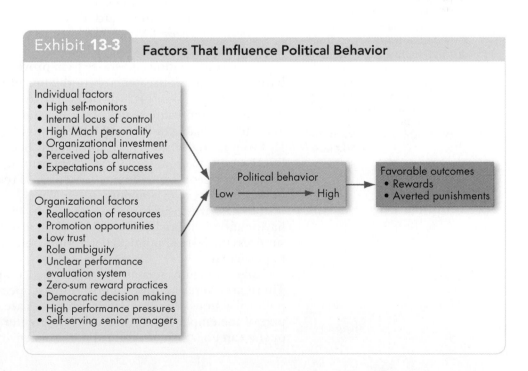

Exhibit 13-3 **Factors That Influence Political Behavior**

Individual factors
- High self-monitors
- Internal locus of control
- High Mach personality
- Organizational investment
- Perceived job alternatives
- Expectations of success

Organizational factors
- Reallocation of resources
- Promotion opportunities
- Low trust
- Role ambiguity
- Unclear performance evaluation system
- Zero-sum reward practices
- Democratic decision making
- High performance pressures
- Self-serving senior managers

Political behavior
Low ——————→ High

Favorable outcomes
- Rewards
- Averted punishments

likely to engage in political behavior.[44] The high self-monitor is more sensitive to social cues, exhibits higher levels of social conformity, and is more likely to be skilled in political behavior than the low self-monitor. Because they believe they can control their environment, individuals with an internal locus of control are more prone to take a proactive stance and attempt to manipulate situations in their favor. Not surprisingly, the Machiavellian personality—characterized by the will to manipulate and the desire for power—is comfortable using politics as a means to further his or her self-interest.

In addition, an individual's investment in the organization, perceived alternatives, and expectations of success influence the degree to which he or she will pursue illegitimate means of political action.[45] The more a person expects increased future benefits from the organization, the more that person has to lose if forced out and the less likely he or she is to use illegitimate means. The more alternative job opportunities an individual has—due to a favorable job market or the possession of scarce skills or knowledge, a prominent reputation, or influential contacts outside the organization—the more likely that individual is to risk illegitimate political actions. Finally, if an individual has a low expectation of success in using illegitimate means, it is unlikely he or she will attempt to do so. High expectations of success in the use of illegitimate means are most likely to be the province of both experienced and powerful individuals with polished political skills and inexperienced and naïve employees who misjudge their chances.

Organizational Factors   Political activity is probably more a function of an organization's characteristics than of individual difference variables. Why? It is so because many organizations have a large number of employees with the individual characteristics we listed, yet the extent of political behavior varies widely.

Although we acknowledge the role individual differences can play in fostering politicking, the evidence more strongly supports the idea that certain situations and cultures promote politics. Specifically, when an organization's resources are declining, when the existing pattern of resources is changing, and when there is opportunity for promotions, politicking is more likely to surface.[46] Cultures characterized by low trust, role ambiguity, unclear performance evaluation systems, zero-sum reward allocation practices, democratic decision making, high pressures for performance, and self-serving senior managers will create breeding grounds for politicking.[47]

When organizations downsize to improve efficiency, reductions in resources have to be made. Threatened with the loss of resources, people may engage in political actions to safeguard what they have. But any changes, especially those that imply significant reallocation of resources within the organization, are likely to stimulate conflict and increase politicking.

Promotion decisions have consistently been found to be one of the most political actions in organizations. The opportunity for promotions or advancement encourages people to compete for a limited resource and to try to positively influence the decision outcome.

The less trust within the organization, the higher the level of political behavior and the more likely it will be of the illegitimate kind. So high trust should suppress the level of political behavior in general and inhibit illegitimate actions in particular.

Role ambiguity means the prescribed employee behaviors are not clear. There are therefore fewer limits to the scope and functions of the employee's political actions. Because political activities are defined as those not required as part of the employee's formal role, the greater the role ambiguity, the more he or she can engage in unnoticed political activity.

After police officer Toshiro Semba (center) blew the whistle on his bosses in the police department, they took his gun away, claiming he was too emotionally unstable to carry a weapon, and reassigned him as a dispatcher. Semba revealed that for decades his superiors wrote false reports to secure public funds and then used the funds for their personal benefit. A district court in Japan ruled that Semba's treatment was retaliation for his exposure of corruption. Traditionally, whistleblowers in Japan have been viewed as traitors, and their exposure of wrongdoing as a betrayal of their superiors. But this perception is changing, as whistleblowers like Semba are being recognized for doing the right thing by exposing illegal, corrupt, or unethical conduct in the workplace.

Myth or Science?

"Power Breeds Contempt"

This statement appears to be true. When people have power bestowed on them, they appear inclined to ignore the perspectives and interests of those without power, says a study completed by a team of researchers from Northwestern, Stanford, and New York University.[48]

In this study, researchers made one group of participants feel powerful by asking them to recall and write about a situation in which they had power over another person. Another group of participants was instructed to recall and write about an incident in which someone had power over them. When the groups were then asked to work together on a problem, participants in the powerful group were much more likely to ignore the perspectives of those in the less powerful group, less able to accurately read their emotional expressions, and less interested in understanding how other individuals see things. The authors of this study conclude that power leads to "the tendency to view other people only in terms of qualities that serve one's personal goals and interests, while failing to consider those features of others that define their humanity."

So, while power has perks, it also appears to have costs—especially in terms of seeing things from the perspective of those with less of it.

Performance evaluation is far from a perfect science. The more organizations use subjective criteria in the appraisal, emphasize a single outcome measure, or allow significant time to pass between the time of an action and its appraisal, the greater the likelihood that an employee can get away with politicking. Subjective performance criteria create ambiguity. The use of a single outcome measure encourages individuals to do whatever is necessary to "look good" on that measure, but that often occurs at the expense of good performance on other important parts of the job that are not being appraised. The time lapse between an action and its appraisal is also a relevant factor. The longer the time, the more unlikely it is that the employee will be held accountable for political behaviors.

Organizations foster politicking when they reduce resources in order to improve performance. As part of a restructuring program, Germany's Allianz AG announced plans to eliminate 5,000 jobs at its German insurance operation and 2,500 jobs at its banking subsidiary. The company stated that the job cuts were necessary to improve efficiency and to increase Allianz's competitiveness and would result in cost savings of between $600 and $750 million. The company's cost-cutting measures stimulated conflict and political activity, as trade union workers joined Allianz employees in staging a token strike to safeguard their jobs.

The more an organization's culture emphasizes the zero-sum or win–lose approach to reward allocations, the more employees will be motivated to engage in politicking. The zero-sum approach treats the reward "pie" as fixed, so any gain one person or group achieves has to come at the expense of another person or group. If I win, you must lose! If $15,000 in annual raises is to be distributed among five employees, any employee who gets more than $3,000 takes money away from one or more of the others. Such a practice encourages making others look bad and increasing the visibility of what you do.

The more pressure employees feel to perform well, the more likely they are to engage in politicking. Being held strictly accountable for outcomes puts great pressure on people to "look good." A person who perceives that his or her entire career is riding on next quarter's sales figures or next month's plant productivity report is motivated to do whatever is necessary to make sure the numbers come out favorably.

Finally, when employees see the people on top engaging in political behavior, especially when they do so successfully and are rewarded for it, a climate is created that supports politicking. Politicking by top management, in a sense, gives permission to those lower in the organization to play politics by implying that such behavior is acceptable.

How Do People Respond to Organizational Politics?

Trish O'Donnell loves her job as a writer on a weekly television comedy series but hates the internal politics. "A couple of the writers here spend more time kissing up to the executive producer than doing any work. And our head writer clearly has his favorites. While they pay me a lot and I get to really use my creativity, I'm sick of having to be on alert for backstabbers and constantly having to self-promote my contributions. I'm tired of doing most of the work and getting little of the credit." Are Trish O'Donnell's comments typical of people who work in highly politicized workplaces? We all know friends or relatives who regularly complain about the politics at their job. But how do people in general react to organizational politics? Let's look at the evidence.

In our previous discussion in this chapter of factors that contribute to political behavior, we focused on the favorable outcomes. But for most people—who have modest political skills or are unwilling to play the politics game—outcomes tend to be predominantly negative. Exhibit 13-4 summarizes the extensive research on the relationship between organizational politics and individual outcomes.[49] Very strong evidence indicates, for instance, that perceptions of organizational politics are negatively related to job satisfaction.[50] The perception of politics also tends to increase job anxiety and stress. This seems due to the perception that, by not engaging in politics, a person may be losing ground to others who are active politickers or, conversely, to the additional pressures felt from having entered into and competing in the political arena.[51] Not surprisingly, when politicking becomes too much to handle, it can lead employees to quit.[52] Finally, preliminary evidence suggests that politics leads to self-reported declines in employee performance, perhaps because employees perceive political environments to be unfair, which demotivates them.[53]

Researchers have also noted several interesting qualifiers. First, the politics–performance relationship appears to be moderated by an individual's understanding of the "hows" and "whys" of organizational politics. "An individual who has a clear understanding of who is responsible for making decisions and why they were selected to be the decision makers would have a better understanding of how and why things happen the way they do than someone who does not understand the decision-making process in the organization."[54] When both politics and understanding are high, performance is likely to increase because the individual will see political actions as an opportunity. This is consistent with

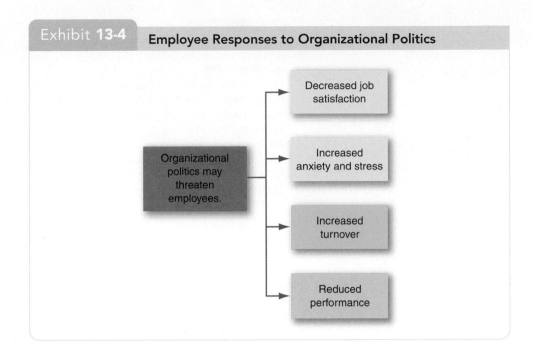

Exhibit 13-4 **Employee Responses to Organizational Politics**

what you might expect among individuals with well-honed political skills. But when understanding is low, individuals are more likely to see politics as a threat, which would have a negative effect on job performance.[55]

Second, when employees see politics as a threat, they often respond with **defensive behaviors**—reactive and protective behaviors to avoid action, blame, or change.[56] (Exhibit 13-5 provides some examples of these behaviors.) And defensive behaviors are often associated with negative feelings toward the job and work environment.[57] In the short run, employees may find that defensiveness protects their self-interest, but in the long run it wears them down. People who consistently rely on defensiveness find that, eventually, it is the only way they know how to behave. At that point, they lose the trust and support of their peers, bosses, employees, and clients.

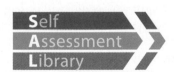

HOW GOOD AM I AT PLAYING POLITICS?

In the Self-Assessment Library (available on CD and online), take assessment II.C.3 (How Good Am I at Playing Politics?).

Impression Management

We know people have an ongoing interest in how others perceive and evaluate them. For example, North Americans spend billions of dollars on diets, health club memberships, cosmetics, and plastic surgery—all intended to make them

defensive behaviors *Reactive and protective behaviors to avoid action, blame, or change.*

Exhibit 13-5   Defensive Behaviors

Avoiding Action

Overconforming. Strictly interpreting your responsibility by saying things like "The rules clearly state . . . " or "This is the way we've always done it."

Buck passing. Transferring responsibility for the execution of a task or decision to someone else.

Playing dumb. Avoiding an unwanted task by falsely pleading ignorance or inability.

Stretching. Prolonging a task so that one person appears to be occupied—for example, turning a two-week task into a 4-month job.

Stalling. Appearing to be more or less supportive publicly while doing little or nothing privately.

Avoiding Blame

Buffing. This is a nice way to refer to "covering your rear." It describes the practice of rigorously documenting activity to project an image of competence and thoroughness.

Playing safe. Evading situations that may reflect unfavorably. It includes taking on only projects with a high probability of success, having risky decisions approved by superiors, qualifying expressions of judgment, and taking neutral positions in conflicts.

Justifying. Developing explanations that lessen one's responsibility for a negative outcome and/or apologizing to demonstrate remorse, or both.

Scapegoating. Placing the blame for a negative outcome on external factors that are not entirely blameworthy.

Misrepresenting. Manipulation of information by distortion, embellishment, deception, selective presentation, or obfuscation.

Avoiding Change

Prevention. Trying to prevent a threatening change from occurring.

Self-protection. Acting in ways to protect one's self-interest during change by guarding information or other resources.

---

7 Apply impression management techniques.

more attractive to others.[58] Being perceived positively by others should have benefits for people in organizations. It might, for instance, help them initially to get the jobs they want in an organization and, once hired, to get favorable evaluations, superior salary increases, and more rapid promotions. In a political context, it might help sway the distribution of advantages in their favor. The process by which individuals attempt to control the impression others form of them is called **impression management (IM)**.[59]

Is everyone concerned with IM? No! Who, then, might we predict will engage in IM? No surprise here. It's our old friend, the high self-monitor.[60] Low self-monitors tend to present images of themselves that are consistent with their personalities, regardless of the beneficial or detrimental effects for them. In contrast, high self-monitors are good at reading situations and molding their appearances and behavior to fit each situation. If you want to control the impression others form of you, what IM techniques can you use? Exhibit 13-6 summarizes some of the most popular and provides an example of each.

Keep in mind that the impressions people use IM to convey are necessarily false (although, of course, they sometimes are true).[61] Excuses, for instance, may be offered with sincerity. Referring to the example in Exhibit 13-6, you can *actually* believe that ads contribute little to sales in your region. But misrepresentation can have a high cost. If you "cry wolf" once too often, no one is likely to believe you when the wolf really comes. So the impression manager must be cautious not to be perceived as insincere or manipulative.[62] As an amusing example of this principle, participants in a study in Switzerland disliked an experimental confederate who claimed to be a personal friend of

Exhibit **13-6**	Impression Management (IM) Techniques

Conformity

Agreeing with someone else's opinion to gain his or her approval is a *form of ingratiation.*

Example: A manager tells his boss, "You're absolutely right on your reorganization plan for the western regional office. I couldn't agree with you more."

Favors

Doing something nice for someone to gain that person's approval is a *form of ingratiation.*

Example: A salesperson says to a prospective client, "I've got two tickets to the theater tonight that I can't use. Take them. Consider it a thank-you for taking the time to talk with me."

Excuses

Explanations of a predicament-creating event aimed at minimizing the apparent severity of the predicament is a *defensive IM technique.*

Example: A sales manager says to her boss, "We failed to get the ad in the paper on time, but no one responds to those ads anyway."

Apologies

Admitting responsibility for an undesirable event and simultaneously seeking to get a pardon for the action is a *defensive IM technique.*

Example: An employee says to his boss, "I'm sorry I made a mistake on the report. Please forgive me."

Self-Promotion

Highlighting one's best qualities, downplaying one's deficits, and calling attention to one's achievements is a *self-focused IM technique.*

Example: A salesperson tells his boss, "Matt worked unsuccessfully for three years to try to get that account. I sewed it up in six weeks. I'm the best closer this company has."

Enhancement

Claiming that something you did is more valuable than most other members of the organizations would think is a *self-focused IM technique.*

Example: A journalist tells his editor, "My work on this celebrity divorce story was really a major boost to our sales" (even though the story only made it to page 3 in the entertainment section).

Flattery

Complimenting others about their virtues in an effort to make oneself appear perceptive and likeable is an *assertive IM technique.*

Example: A new sales trainee says to her peer, "You handled that client's complaint so tactfully! I could never have handled that as well as you did."

Exemplification

Doing more than you need to in an effort to show how dedicated and hard working you are is an *assertive IM technique.*

Example: An employee sends e-mails from his work computer when he works late so that his supervisor will know how long he's been working.

Source: Based on B. R. Schlenker, *Impression Management* (Monterey, CA: Brooks/Cole, 1980); M. C. Bolino, K. M. Kacmar, W. H. Turnley, and J. B. Gilstrap, "A Multi-Level Review of Impression Management Motives and Behaviors," *Journal of Management* 34, no. 6 (2008), pp. 1080–1109; and R. B. Cialdini, "Indirect Tactics of Image Management Beyond Basking," in R. A. Giacalone and P. Rosenfeld (eds.), *Impression Management in the Organization* (Hillsdale, NJ: Lawrence Erlbaum, 1989), pp. 45–71.

impression management (IM) *The process by which individuals attempt to control the impression others form of them.*

the well-liked Swiss tennis star Roger Federer, but they generally liked confederates who just said they were fans.[63] Implausible name-dropping like this can harm people's first impression of you.

Are there *situations* in which individuals are more likely to misrepresent themselves or more likely to get away with it? Yes—situations characterized by high uncertainty or ambiguity provide relatively little information for challenging a fraudulent claim and reduce the risks associated with misrepresentation.[64] The increasing use of telework may be increasing the use of IM. Individuals who work remotely from their supervisors engage in high levels of IM relative to those who work closely with their supervisors.[65]

Most of the studies undertaken to test the effectiveness of IM techniques have related it to two criteria: interview success and performance evaluations. Let's consider each of these.

The evidence indicates most job applicants use IM techniques in interviews[66] and that it works.[67] In one study, for instance, interviewers felt applicants for a position as a customer service representative who used IM techniques performed better in the interview, and they seemed somewhat more inclined to hire these people.[68] Moreover, when the researchers considered applicants' credentials, they concluded it was the IM techniques alone that influenced the interviewers—that is, it didn't seem to matter whether applicants were well or poorly qualified. If they used IM techniques, they did better in the interview.

Some IM techniques work better than others in the interview. Researchers have compared applicants whose IM techniques focused on promoting their accomplishments (called *self-promotion*) to those who focused on complimenting the interviewer and finding areas of agreement (referred to as *ingratiation*). In general, applicants appear to use self-promotion more than ingratiation.[69] What's more, self-promotion tactics may be more important to interviewing success. Applicants who work to create an appearance of competence by enhancing their accomplishments, taking credit for successes, and explaining away failures do better in interviews. These effects reach beyond the interview: Applicants who use more self-promotion tactics also seem to get more follow-up job-site visits, even after adjusting for grade-point average, gender, and job type. Ingratiation also works well in interviews; applicants who compliment the interviewer, agree with his or her opinions, and emphasize areas of fit do better than those who don't.[70]

In terms of performance ratings, the picture is quite different. Ingratiation is positively related to performance ratings, meaning those who ingratiate with their supervisors get higher performance evaluations. However, self-promotion appears to backfire: Those who self-promote actually seem to receive *lower* performance evaluations.[71] There is an important qualifier to this general result. It appears that individuals high in political skill are able to translate IM into higher performance appraisals, whereas those lower in political skill are more likely to be hurt by their IM attempts.[72] Another study of 760 boards of directors found that individuals who ingratiate themselves to current board members (express agreement with the director, point out shared attitudes and opinions, compliment the director) increase their chances of landing on a board.[73]

What explains these results? If you think about them, they make sense. Ingratiating always works because everyone—both interviewers and supervisors—likes to be treated nicely. However, self-promotion may work only in interviews and backfire on the job because, whereas the interviewer has little idea whether you're blowing smoke about your accomplishments, the supervisor knows because it's his or her job to observe you. Thus, if you're going to self-promote, remember that what works in an interview won't always work once you're on the job.

An Ethical Choice

Making Excuses

Excuses are one means of managing impressions so as to avoid negative repercussions of our actions. However, judging from some recent evidence on absenteeism, excuses are also a chance for workers to engage their creative side.

A 2007 survey of nearly 7,000 employees and 3,000 hiring managers revealed some pretty creative excuses for being late for work or absent from work:

"Someone was following me and I drove all around town trying to lose them."

"My girlfriend got mad and destroyed all of my undergarments."

"A skunk got into my house and sprayed all my uniforms."

"My mother-in-law poisoned me."

"My mother-in-law is in jail."

"I blew my nose so hard my back went out."

"I'm too fat to get into my work pants."

Though you have to give the excuse makers high marks for originality, we seriously doubt supervisors bought these excuses. The making of excuses may be one of the few areas in which creativity is bad.

If you're considering making an excuse at work, take the following considerations into account:

1. **Excuses can be effective.** Research indicates that overall excuses do effectively shift blame away from an individual.

2. **Excuses are sometimes ineffective.** Because excuses often work doesn't mean they *always* work. Excuses backfire when they (a) lack believability, (b) rely on conditions that seem likely to recur, and (c) reflect self-absorption—the excuse is all about you. So, if you are going to use an excuse, you should ensure it is believable, it

reflects a one-time event, and it is not self oriented.

3. **Use excuses selectively.** If you use excuses often, you won't be believed even when your excuse is legitimate. Excuses also risk damaging the excuse maker's perceived character. So you have to ask yourself, would you rather shift blame for a negative event or have your character called into question?

Sources: Based on J. M. Tyler and R. S. Feldman, "The Double-Edged Sword of Excuses: When Do They Help, When Do They Hurt," *Journal of Social & Clinical Psychology* 26, no. 6 (2007), pp. 659–688; K. Gurchiek, "'Sorry I'm Late; A Raccoon Stole My Shoe,'" *HRWeek* (May 29, 2007), http://moss07.shrm.org/Publications/HRNews/Pages/CMS_021684.aspx; and K. Gurchiek, "Runaway Horses, Charging Buffalo Kept Workers Home in '06," *HR Week* (December 28, 2006).

The Ethics of Behaving Politically

8 Determine whether a political action is ethical.

Although there are no clear-cut ways to differentiate ethical from unethical politicking, there are some questions you should consider. For example, what is the utility of engaging in politicking? Sometimes we engage in political behavior for little good reason. Major league baseball player Al Martin claimed he played football at USC when in fact he never did. As a baseball player, he had little to gain by pretending to have played football. Outright lies like this may be a rather extreme example of impression management, but many of us have distorted information to make a favorable impression. One thing to keep in mind is whether it's really worth the risk. Another question to ask is this: How does the utility of engaging in the political behavior balance out any harm (or potential harm) it will do to others? Complimenting a supervisor on his or her appearance in order to curry favor is probably much less harmful than grabbing credit for a project that others deserve.

Finally, does the political activity conform to standards of equity and justice? Sometimes it is difficult to weigh the costs and benefits of a political action, but its ethicality is clear. The department head who inflates the performance evaluation of a favored employee and deflates the evaluation of a disfavored employee—and then uses these evaluations to justify giving the former a big raise and nothing to the latter—has treated the disfavored employee unfairly.

Unfortunately, powerful people can become very good at explaining self-serving behaviors in terms of the organization's best interests. They can persuasively argue that unfair actions are really fair and just. Our point is that immoral people can justify almost any behavior. Those who are powerful, articulate, and persuasive are most vulnerable to ethical lapses because they are likely to be able to get away with unethical practices successfully. When faced with an ethical dilemma regarding organizational politics, try to consider whether playing politics is worth the risk and whether others might be harmed in the process. If you have a strong power base, recognize the ability of power to corrupt. Remember that it's a lot easier for the powerless to act ethically, if for no other reason than they typically have very little political discretion to exploit.

Global Implications

9 Show the influence of culture on the uses and perceptions of politics.

Although culture might enter any of the topics we've covered to this point, three questions are particularly important: (1) Does culture influence perceptions of politics? (2) Does culture affect the power of influence tactics people prefer to use? and (3) Does culture influence the effectiveness of different tactics?

Perceptions of Politics

We have already noted that (based on research conducted mostly in the United States) when people see their work environment as political, the effect on their overall work attitudes and behaviors is usually negative. When employees of two agencies in a recent study in Nigeria viewed their work environments as political, they reported higher levels of job distress and were less likely to help their co-workers. Thus, although developing countries such as Nigeria are perhaps more ambiguous and more political environments in which to work, the negative consequences appear to be the same as in the United States.[74]

Preference for Power Tactics

Evidence indicates people in different countries tend to prefer different power tactics.[75] A study comparing managers in the United States and China found that U.S. managers prefer rational appeal, whereas Chinese managers preferred coalition tactics.[76] These differences tend to be consistent with the values in these two countries. Reason is consistent with the U.S. preference for direct confrontation and the use of rational persuasion to influence others and resolve differences. Similarly, coalition tactics are consistent with the Chinese preference for using indirect approaches for difficult or controversial requests. Research also has shown that individuals in Western, individualistic cultures tend to engage in more self-enhancement (such as self-promotion) behaviors than individuals in Eastern, more collectivistic cultures.[77]

Effectiveness of Power Tactics

Are our conclusions about responses to politics globally valid? Should we expect employees in Israel, for instance, to respond the same way to workplace politics that employees in the United States do? Almost all our conclusions on employee reactions to organizational politics are based on studies conducted in North America. The few studies that have included other countries suggest some minor modifications.[78] One study of managers in U.S. culture and three Chinese cultures (People's Republic of China, Hong Kong, Taiwan) found U.S. managers evaluated "gentle persuasion" tactics such as consultation and inspirational appeal as more effective than did their Chinese counterparts.[79] As another example, Israelis and the British seem to generally respond as do North Americans—that is, their perception of organizational politics relates to decreased job satisfaction and increased turnover.[80] But in countries that are more politically unstable, such as Israel, employees seem to demonstrate greater tolerance of intense political processes in the workplace, perhaps because they are used to power struggles and have more experience in coping with them.[81] This suggests that people from politically turbulent countries in the Middle East or Latin America might be more accepting of organizational politics, and even more willing to use aggressive political tactics in the workplace, than people from countries such as Great Britain or Switzerland.

Summary and Implications for Managers

If you want to get things done in a group or an organization, it helps to have power. As a manager who wants to maximize your power, you will want to increase others' dependence on you. You can, for instance, increase your power in relation to your boss by developing knowledge or a skill she needs and for which she perceives no ready substitute. But you will not be alone in attempting to build your power bases. Others, particularly employees and peers, will be seeking to increase your dependence on them, while you are trying to minimize it and increase their dependence on you. The result is a continual battle.

Few employees relish being powerless in their job and organization. It's been argued, for instance, that when people in organizations are difficult, argumentative, and temperamental, it may be that the performance expectations placed on them exceed their resources and capabilities, making them feel powerless.[82]

People respond differently to the various power bases.[83] Expert and referent power are derived from an individual's personal qualities. In contrast, coercion, reward, and legitimate power are essentially organizationally derived. Because people are more likely to enthusiastically accept and commit to an individual whom they admire or whose knowledge they respect (rather than someone who relies on his or her position for influence), the effective use of expert and referent power should lead to higher employee motivation, performance, commitment, and satisfaction.[84] Competence especially appears to offer wide appeal, and its use as a power base results in high performance by group members. The message for managers seems to be "Develop and use your expert power base!"

The power of your boss may also play a role in determining your job satisfaction. "One of the reasons many of us like to work for and with people who are powerful is that they are generally more pleasant—not because it is their native disposition, but because the reputation and reality of being powerful permits them more discretion and more ability to delegate to others."[85]

An effective manager accepts the political nature of organizations. By assessing behavior in a political framework, you can better predict the actions of others and use that information to formulate political strategies that will gain advantages for you and your work unit.

Some people are significantly more politically astute than others, meaning that they are aware of the underlying politics and can manage impressions. Those who are good at playing politics can be expected to get higher performance evaluations and, hence, larger salary increases and more promotions than the politically naïve or inept.[86] The politically astute are also likely to exhibit higher job satisfaction and be better able to neutralize job stressors.[87] Employees who have poor political skills or are unwilling to play the politics game generally relate perceived organizational politics to lower job satisfaction and self-reported performance, increased anxiety, and higher turnover.

Managing Impressions Is Unethical

Managing impressions is wrong for both ethical and practical reasons.

First, managing impressions is just another name for lying. Don't we have a responsibility, both to ourselves and to others, to present ourselves as we really are? The Australian philosopher Tony Coady wrote, "Dishonesty has always been perceived in our culture, and in all cultures but the most bizarre, as a central human vice." Immanuel Kant's categorical imperative asks us to consider the following: If you want to know whether telling a lie on a particular occasion is justifiable, you must try to imagine what would happen if everyone were to lie. Surely you would agree that a world in which no one lies is preferable to one in which lying is common because in such a world we could never trust anyone. Thus, we should try to present the truth as best we can. Impression management goes against this virtue.

Practically speaking, impression management generally backfires in the long run. Remember Sir Walter Scott's quote, "Oh what a tangled web we weave, when first we practice to deceive!" Once we start to distort the facts, where do we stop? Many careers have been undone when discrepancies have been discovered in résumés. J. Terrence Lanni, chairman and CEO of MGM Mirage, was forced out after the *Wall Street Journal* revealed he never obtained the MBA from the University of South Carolina listed on his résumé.[88] At Indiana University's Kelley School of Business, the code of ethics instructs students to provide only truthful information on their résumés and obligates them to be honest in interviews.

People are most satisfied with their jobs when their values match the culture of the organizations. If either side misrepresents itself in the interview process, then odds are people won't fit in the organizations they choose. What's the benefit in this?

This doesn't imply a person shouldn't put his or her best foot forward. But that means exhibiting qualities that are good no matter the context—being friendly, being positive and self-confident, being qualified and competent, while still being honest.

Oh, come on. Get off your high horse. *Everybody* fudges to some degree in the process of applying for a job. If you really told the interviewer what your greatest weakness or worst mistake was, you'd never get hired. What if you answered, "I find it hard to get up in the morning and get to work"?

"White lies" are expected and act as a kind of social lubricant. If we really knew what people were thinking, we'd go crazy. Moreover, you can quote all the philosophy you want, but sometimes it's necessary to lie. Wouldn't you lie to save your family? It's naïve to think we can live in a world without lying.

Sometimes a bit of deception is necessary to get a job. I know a gay applicant who was rejected from a job he really wanted because he told the interviewer he had written two articles for gay magazines. What if he had told the interviewer a little lie? Would harm really have been done? At least he'd have a job.

When an interviewer asks you what you earned on your previous job, that information will be used against you, to pay you a salary lower than you deserve. Is it wrong to boost your salary a bit? Or would it be better to disclose your actual salary and be taken advantage of?

The same goes for complimenting interviewers, agreeing with their opinions, and so forth. If an interviewer tells you, "We believe in community involvement," are you supposed to tell the interviewer you've never volunteered for anything?

Of course you can go too far. We're not advocating that people totally fabricate. What we are talking about here is a reasonable amount of enhancement. If we can help ourselves without doing any real harm, then impression management is not the same as lying and actually is something we should teach others.

Questions for Review

1 How would you define *power?* How is it different from leadership?

2 What are the five bases of power?

3 What are the nine power or influence tactics?

4 In what way is sexual harassment about the abuse of power?

5 What is political behavior, and how would you distinguish between legitimate and illegitimate political behavior?

6 What are the causes and consequences of political behavior?

7 What is impression management, and what are the techniques for managing impressions?

8 How can one determine whether a political action is ethical?

9 How does culture influence perceptions of politics, preferences for different power or influence tactics, and the effectiveness of those tactics?

Experiential Exercise

UNDERSTANDING POWER DYNAMICS

Create Groups

Each student is to turn in a dollar bill (or similar value of currency) to the instructor, and students are then divided into three groups (based on criteria given by the instructor), assigned to their workplaces, and instructed to read the following rules and tasks. The money is divided into thirds, and two-thirds of it is given to the top group, one-third to the middle group, and none to the bottom group.

Conduct Exercise

Groups go to their assigned workplaces and have 30 minutes to complete their tasks.

Rules

Members of the top group are free to enter the space of either of the other groups and to communicate whatever they wish, whenever they wish. Members of the middle group may enter the space of the lower group when they wish but must request permission to enter the top group's space (which the top group can refuse). Members of the lower group may not disturb the top group in any way unless specifically invited by the top. The lower group does have the right to knock on the door of the middle group and request permission to communicate with them (which can also be refused).

The members of the top group have the authority to make any change in the rules that they wish, at any time, with or without notice.

Tasks

- *Top group.* Responsible for the overall effectiveness and learning from the exercise and to decide how to use its money.
- *Middle group.* Assist the top group in providing for the overall welfare of the organization and deciding how to use its money.
- *Bottom group.* Identify the organization's resources and decide how best to provide for learning and the overall effectiveness of the organization.

Debriefing

Each of the three groups chooses two representatives to go to the front of the class and discuss the following:

1. Summarize what occurred within and among the three groups.

2. What are some of the differences between being in the top group and being in the bottom group?

3. What can we learn about power from this experience?

4. How accurate do you think this exercise is in reflecting the reality of resource allocation decisions in large organizations?

Source: Adapted from L. Bolman and T. E. Deal, *Exchange* 3, no. 4 (1979), pp. 38–42. Reprinted by permission of Sage Publications, Inc.

Ethical Dilemma

DOES "APING" OTHERS WORK? IS IT ETHICAL?

You often see children playing the game of mimicking the body movements of others. As it turns out, adults play the game, too, even when they aren't aware of it.

Researchers have been studying the science and art of persuasion for decades, due to its obvious importance. Have you noticed how you click with some people almost immediately, whereas with others you feel ill at ease from the onset? As you might imagine, the "social music" that happens between two people upon meeting has important implications for the future of the social relationship, including whether there is any future to the relationship at all.

One key element to how well two strangers bond is mimicry, or how well one party imitates the verbal and body gestures of another. One study suggested that when a mimic matched subject's body posture (upright, relaxed, or slumped) and position of the arms and legs (legs or arms crossed, hands folded)—in a subtle way, of course—the subject behaved more prosocially toward the mimic (was two to three times more likely to pick up a pen for those who mimicked than for those who did not) and, after the experiment, reported greater liking for the mimic.

In another study, marketing researchers found that if the mimicker matched the body movements of the target person, with a 1- to 2-second delay, the target person was much more inclined to buy the product the mimicker was selling. So if the target person crossed her legs, the mimic waited

1 or 2 seconds and did the same. If she touched her face, the mimic waited again and then did the same. Though none of the target persons picked up on the mimicry, by the end of the short interview they were much more likely to consume a new drink being offered, to predict the drink would be successful, and to indicate they would buy it in the future.

Why does mimicry appear to be so effective? One neuroscientist suggested, "When you're being mimicked in a good way, it communicates a kind of pleasure, a social high you're getting from the other person, and I suspect it activates the areas of the brain involved in sensing reward." Moreover, mirroring another person's movement may, in some unconscious but automatic way, trigger a sense that the person is just like us, and thus deserving of the Golden Rule.

1. Can you recall situations in which mimicry, or the lack of it, affected your bonding with a stranger?

2. If the research findings are true, it suggests that, in cold calls and other first contacts in a business setting, you can achieve an advantage by mimicking the movements of the target person. What do you think of the ethics of doing this? How would you feel if a stranger did it consciously to bond with you?

3. Will the findings presented here affect how you approach your initial contact with strangers? Why or why not?

Sources: Based on M. Iacoboni, "Imitation, Empathy, and Mirror Neurons," *Annual Review of Psychology* 60, no. 1 (2009), pp. 653–670; B. Carey, "You Remind Me of Me," *New York Times* (February 12, 2008), pp. D1, D6; and R. J. Tanner, R. Ferraro, T. L. Chartrand, J. R. Bettman, and R. Van Baaren, "Of Chameleons and Consumption: The Impact of Mimicry on Choice and Preferences," *Journal of Consumer Research* 34, no. 6 (2008), pp. 754–766.

Case Incident 1

DRESSING FOR SUCCESS

Jennifer Cohen thought she had a good grip on her company's dress code. She was wrong.

Cohen works for a marketing firm in Philadelphia. Before a meeting, an older colleague pulled 24-year-old Cohen aside and told her that she was dressing inappropriately by wearing Bermuda shorts and sleeveless tops. Cohen was stunned by the rebuke. "Each generation seems to have a different idea of what is acceptable in the workplace," she said. "In this case, I was highly offended."

What offended Cohen even more was what came next: Cohen wasn't allowed to attend the meeting because her attire was deemed inappropriate.

Cohen's employer is not alone. Although many employers have "casual" days at work, the number of employers who are enforcing more formal dress codes has increased, according to a survey of employers by the Society for Human Resource Management. In 2001, 53 percent of employers allowed casual dress every day. Now that figure is 38 percent. Silicon Valley marketing firm McGrath/Power used to allow casual attire. Now, it enforces a more formal dress code. "The pendulum has swung," says CEO Jonathan Bloom, "We went through a too-casual period. . . . When we were very casual, the quality of the work wasn't as good."

Ironically, as more employers enforce more formal dress codes, other employers known for their formality are going the other way. IBM, which once had a dress code of business suits with white shirts, has thrown out dress codes altogether. IBM researcher Dan Gruhl typically goes to work at IBM's San Jose, California, office in flip-flops and shorts. "Having a relaxed environment encourages you to think more openly," he says. Although not going quite as far as IBM, other traditional employers, such as Ford, General Motors, and Procter & Gamble, have relaxed dress codes.

Still, for every IBM, there are more companies that have tightened the rules. Even the National Basketball Association (NBA) has adopted an off-court dress code for its players. As for Cohen, she still bristles at the dress code. "When you're comfortable, you don't worry," she says. "You focus on your work."

Questions

1. Do you think Cohen had a right to be offended? Why or why not?

2. In explaining why she was offended, Cohen argued, "People my age are taught to express themselves, and saying something negative about someone's fashion is saying something negative about them." Do you agree with Cohen?

3. Does an employer have an unfettered right to set a company's dress code? Why or why not?

4. How far would you go to conform to an organization's dress code? If your boss dressed in a relatively formal manner, would you feel compelled to dress in a like manner to manage impressions?

Sources: Based on S. Armour, "'Business Casual' Causes Confusion," *USA Today* (July 10, 2007), pp. 1B, 2B.

Case Incident 2

THE PERSUASION IMPERATIVE

There may have been a time when a boss gave orders and subordinates followed them. If you've watched the AMC series "Mad Men"—based on Madison Avenue marketing executives in the 1960s—you've seen an image of deference to authority, respectful obedience to those higher up in the hierarchy, and a paternalistic relationship between boss and employee.

With time comes change. Organizations are no longer male dominated as they were in the 1950s. Laws and policies are in place that better protect employees against the sometimes-capricious whims of supervisors.

Another sign of shifting cultural values is the way managers use their power. Commandments are out. Persuasion is in.

When IBM manager Kate Riley Tenant needed to reassign managers and engineers to form a database software team, she had to persuade IBM employees from all corners of the globe, none of whom directly reported to her. According to Tenant, it's a big change from when she started in the field 20 years ago. "You just decided things, and people went off and executed," she said. Now, "not everybody reports to you, and so there's much more negotiation and influence."

John Churchill, a manager with Florida-based Gerdau Ameristeel Corporation, agrees. The question now, he says, is "How do I influence this group and gain credibility?"

At IBM, the challenge of persuading employees across reporting relationships has become so significant that the firm developed a 2-hour online course to help managers persuade other employees to help with projects crucial to is business. IBM's tips for managers include the following:

- Build a shared vision
- Negotiate collaboratively
- Make trade-offs
- Build and maintain your network

Despite meeting initial resistance, after completing the training program, Tenant was able to persuade most IBM managers and engineers to join the team.

This doesn't mean authority has lost all its power. Robert Cialdini, a social psychologist who has studied persuasion for decades, lists authority as one of his keys to influence. Even more important may be the so-called "bandwagon effect" (or what Cialdini called "social proof")—Cialdini and others have found that people are often deeply persuaded by observing what others are doing. From his research, no message more effectively got hotel guests to reuse their towels than citing statistics that others were reusing their towels.

So, if you're a manager who needs to persuade, present the vision behind the request and be collaborative, but it also wouldn't hurt to tell those you're trying to persuade about others who have already agreed to your request.

Questions

1. Are the precepts of the IBM training program consistent with the concepts in this chapter? Why or why not?

2. Again based on the chapter, are there other keys to persuasion and influence that might be added to the IBM program?

3. If you had a manager who wanted you to do something against your initial inclination, which of IBM's elements would work best on you? Why?

4. Drawing from Chapter 5: Personality and Values, do you think generational values explain the changing nature of the employer–employee relationship?

Sources: Based on E. White, "Art of Persuasion Becomes Key," *Wall Street Journal* (May 19, 2008), p. B5; B. Tsui, "Greening with Envy," *The Atlantic* (July/August 2009), www.theatlantic.com; and R. Cialdini, *Influence: The Psychology of Persuasion* (New York: HarperBusiness, 2007).

Endnotes

1. R. Rubin, "The Powers That Be," *USA Today* (March 15, 2008), p. 4D; L. Collins, "The Power Hour," *The New Yorker* (May 26, 2008), pp. 27–28; D. H. Gruenfeld, M. E. Inesi, J. C. Magee, and A. D. Galinsky, "Power and the Objectification of Social Targets," *Journal of Personality and Social Psychology* 95, no. 1 (2008), pp. 111–127. A. D. Galinsky, J. C. Magee, D. H. Gruenfeld, J. A. Whitson, and K. A. Liljenquist, "Power Reduces the Press of the Situation: Implications for Creativity, Conformity, and Dissonance," *Journal of Personality and Social Psychology* 95, no. 6 (2008), pp. 1450–1466; and J. C. Magee and C. A. Langner, "How Personalized and Socialized Power Motivation Facilitate Antisocial and Prosocial Decision-Making," *Journal of Research in Personality* 42, no. 6 (2008), pp. 1547–1559.

2. R. M. Kanter, "Power Failure in Management Circuits," *Harvard Business Review,* July–August 1979, p. 65.

3. J. Pfeffer, "Understanding Power in Organizations," *California Management Review,* Winter 1992, p. 35.

4. Based on B. M. Bass, *Bass & Stogdill's Handbook of Leadership,* 3rd ed. (New York: The Free Press, 1990).

5. J. R. P. French, Jr., and B. Raven, "The Bases of Social Power," in D. Cartwright (ed.), *Studies in Social Power* (Ann Arbor, MI: University of Michigan, Institute for Social Research, 1959), pp. 150–167; B. J. Raven, "The Bases of Power: Origins and Recent Developments," *Journal of Social Issues,* Winter 1993, pp. 227–251; and G. Yukl, "Use Power Effectively," in E. A. Locke (ed.), *Handbook of Principles of Organizational Behavior* (Malden, MA: Blackwell, 2004), pp. 242–247.

6. E. A. Ward, "Social Power Bases of Managers: Emergence of a New Factor," *Journal of Social Psychology,* February 2001, pp. 144–147.

7. S. R. Giessner and T. W. Schubert, "High in the Hierarchy: How Vertical Location and Judgments of Leaders' Power Are Interrelated," *Organizational Behavior and Human Decision Processes* 104, no. 1 (2007), pp. 30–44.

8. P. M. Podsakoff and C. A. Schriesheim, "Field Studies of French and Raven's Bases of Power: Critique, Reanalysis, and Suggestions for Future Research," *Psychological Bulletin,* May 1985, pp. 387–411; T. R. Hinkin and C. A. Schriesheim, "Development and Application of New Scales to Measure the French and Raven (1959) Bases of Social Power," *Journal of Applied Psychology,* August 1989, pp. 561–567; and P. P. Carson, K. D. Carson, and C. W. Roe, "Social Power Bases: A Meta-analytic Examination of Interrelationships and Outcomes," *Journal of Applied Social Psychology* 23, no. 14 (1993), pp. 1150–1169.

9. J. L. Roberts, "Striking a Hot Match," *Newsweek* (January 24, 2005), pp. 54–55.

10. R. E. Emerson, "Power–Dependence Relations," *American Sociological Review,* February 1962, pp. 31–41.

11. H. Mintzberg, *Power In and Around Organizations* (Upper Saddle River, NJ: Prentice Hall, 1983), p. 24.

12. R. M. Cyert and J. G. March, *A Behavioral Theory of the Firm* (Upper Saddle River, NJ: Prentice Hall, 1963).

13. C. Perrow, "Departmental Power and Perspective in Industrial Firms," in M. N. Zald (ed.), *Power in Organizations* (Nashville, TN: Vanderbilt University Press, 1970).

14. N. Foulkes, "Tractor Boy," *High Life,* October 2002, p. 90.

15. See, for example, D. Kipnis and S. M. Schmidt, "Upward-Influence Styles: Relationship with Performance Evaluations, Salary, and Stress," *Administrative Science Quarterly,* December 1988, pp. 528–542; G. Yukl and J. B. Tracey, "Consequences of Influence Tactics Used with Subordinates, Peers, and the Boss," *Journal of Applied Psychology,* August 1992, pp. 525–535; G. Blickle, "Influence Tactics Used by Subordinates: An Empirical Analysis of the Kipnis and Schmidt Subscales," *Psychological Reports,* February 2000, pp. 143–154; and G. Yukl, "Use Power Effectively," pp. 249–252.

16. G. Yukl, *Leadership in Organizations,* 5th ed. (Upper Saddle River, NJ: Prentice Hall, 2002), pp. 141–174; G. R. Ferris, W. A. Hochwarter, C. Douglas, F. R. Blass, R. W. Kolodinksy, and D. C. Treadway, "Social Influence Processes in Organizations and Human Resource Systems," in G. R. Ferris and J. J. Martocchio (eds.), *Research in Personnel and Human Resources Management,* vol. 21 (Oxford, UK: JAI Press/Elsevier, 2003), pp. 65–127; and C. A. Higgins, T. A. Judge, and G. R. Ferris, "Influence Tactics and Work Outcomes: A Meta-analysis," *Journal of Organizational Behavior,* March 2003, pp. 89–106.

17. C. M. Falbe and G. Yukl, "Consequences for Managers of Using Single Influence Tactics and Combinations of Tactics," *Academy of Management Journal,* July 1992, pp. 638–653.

18. R. E. Petty and P. Briñol, "Persuasion: From Single to Multiple to MetaCognitive Processes," *Perspectives on Psychological Science* 3, no. 2 (2008), pp. 137–147.

19. J. Badal, "Getting a Raise from the Boss," *Wall Street Journal* (July 8, 2006), pp. B1, B5.

20. Yukl, *Leadership in Organizations.*

21. Ibid.

22. Falbe and Yukl, "Consequences for Managers of Using Single Influence Tactics and Combinations of Tactics."

23. A. W. Kruglanski, A. Pierro, and E. T. Higgins, "Regulatory Mode and Preferred Leadership Styles: How Fit Increases Job Satisfaction," *Basic and Applied Social Psychology* 29, no. 2 (2007), pp. 137–149; and A. Pierro, L. Cicero, and B. H. Raven, "Motivated Compliance with Bases of Social Power," *Journal of Applied Social Psychology* 38, no. 7 (2008), pp. 1921–1944.

24. G. R. Ferris, D. C. Treadway, P. L. Perrewé, R. L. Brouer, C. Douglas, and S. Lux, "Political Skill in Organizations," *Journal of Management,* June 2007, pp. 290–320; K. J. Harris, K. M. Kacmar, S. Zivnuska, and J. D. Shaw, "The Impact of Political Skill on Impression Management Effectiveness," *Journal of Applied Psychology* 92, no. 1 (2007), pp. 278–285; W. A. Hochwarter, G. R. Ferris, M. B. Gavin, P. L. Perrewé, A. T. Hall, and D. D. Frink," Political Skill as Neutralizer of Felt Accountability–Job Tension Effects on Job Performance Ratings: A Longitudinal Investigation," *Organizational Behavior and Human Decision Processes* 102 (2007), pp. 226–239; and D. C. Treadway, G. R. Ferris, A. B. Duke, G. L. Adams, and J. B. Tatcher, "The Moderating Role of Subordinate Political Skill on Supervisors' Impressions of Subordinate Ingratiation and Ratings of Subordinate Interpersonal Facilitation," *Journal of Applied Psychology* 92, no. 3 (2007), pp. 848–855.

25. C. Anderson, S. E. Spataro, and F. J. Flynn, "Personality and Organizational Culture as Determinants of Influence," *Journal of Applied Psychology* 93, no. 3 (2008), pp. 702–710.

26. S. Stecklow, "Sexual-Harassment Cases Plague U.N.," *Wall Street Journal* (May 21, 2009), p. A1.

27. N. Bode, "Flushing Hospital Nurse Gets $15 Million Award in Sexual Harassment Suit," *New York Daily News* (February 23, 2009), www.nydailynews.com.

28. L. J. Munson, C. Hulin, and F. Drasgow, "Longitudinal Analysis of Dispositional Influences and Sexual Harassment: Effects on Job and Psychological Outcomes," *Personnel Psychology,* Spring 2000, pp. 21–46; T. M. Glomb, L. J. Munson, C. L. Hulin, M. E. Bergman, and F. Drasgow, "Structural Equation Models of Sexual Harassment: Longitudinal Explorations and Cross-Sectional Generalizations," *Journal of Applied Psychology,* February 1999, pp. 14–28; M. E. Bergman, R. D. Langhout, P. A. Palmieri, L. M. Cortina, and L. F. Fitzgerald, "The (Un)reasonableness of Reporting: Antecedents and Consequences of Reporting Sexual Harassment," *Journal of Applied Psychology,* April 2002, pp. 230–242; and L. R. Offermann and A. B. Malamut, "When Leaders Harass: The Impact of Target Perceptions of Organizational Leadership and Climate on Harassment Reporting and Outcomes," *Journal of Applied Psychology,* October 2002, pp. 885–893.

29. S. Silverstein and S. Christian, "Harassment Ruling Raises Free-Speech Issues," *Los Angeles Times,* November 11, 1993, p. D2.

30. R. Ilies, N. Hauserman, S. Schwochau, and J. Stibal, "Reported Incidence Rates of Work-Related Sexual Harassment in the United States: Using Meta-analysis to Explain Reported Rate Disparities," *Personnel Psychology,* Fall 2003, pp. 607–631

31. M. Rotundo, D. Nguyen, and P. R. Sackett, "A Meta-analytic Review of Gender Differences in Perceptions of Sexual Harassment," *Journal of Applied Psychology,* October 2001, pp. 914–922.

32. Ilies, Hauserman, Schwochau, and Stibal, "Reported Incidence Rates of Work-Related Sexual Harassment in the United States; A. B. Malamut and L. R. Offermann, "Coping with Sexual Harassment: Personal, Environmental, and Cognitive Determinants," *Journal of Applied Psychology,* December 2001, pp. 1152–1166; and L. M. Cortina and S. A. Wasti, "Profiles in Coping: Responses to Sexual Harassment Across Persons, Organizations, and Cultures," *Journal of Applied Psychology,* February 2005, pp. 182–192.

33. C. R. Willness, P. Steel, and K. Lee, "A Meta-analysis of the Antecedents and Consequences of Workplace Sexual Harassment," *Personnel Psychology* 60 (2007), pp. 127–162.

34. S. A. Culbert and J. J. McDonough, *The Invisible War: Pursuing Self-Interest at Work* (New York: Wiley, 1980), p. 6.

35. Mintzberg, *Power In and Around Organizations,* p. 26. See also K. M. Kacmar and R. A. Baron, "Organizational Politics: The State of the Field, Links to Related Processes, and an Agenda for Future Research," in G. R. Ferris (ed.), *Research in Personnel and Human Resources Management,* vol. 17 (Greenwich, CT: JAI Press, 1999), pp. 1–39; and G. R. Ferris, D. C. Treadway, R. W. Kolokinsky, W. A. Hochwarter, C. J. Kacmar, and D. D. Frink, "Development and Validation of the Political Skill Inventory," *Journal of Management,* February 2005, pp. 126–152.

36. S. B. Bacharach and E. J. Lawler, "Political Alignments in Organizations," in R. M. Kramer and M. A. Neale (eds.), *Power and Influence in Organizations* (Thousand Oaks, CA: Sage, 1998), pp. 68–69.

37. D. Farrell and J. C. Petersen, "Patterns of Political Behavior in Organizations," *Academy of Management Review,* July 1982, p. 405. For analyses of the controversies underlying the definition of organizational politics, see A. Drory and T. Romm, "The Definition of Organizational Politics: A Review," *Human Relations,* November 1990, pp. 1133–1154; and R. S. Cropanzano, K. M. Kacmar, and D. P. Bozeman, "Organizational Politics, Justice, and Support: Their Differences and Similarities," in R. S. Cropanzano and K. M. Kacmar (eds.), *Organizational Politics, Justice and Support: Managing Social Climate at Work* (Westport, CT: Quorum Books, 1995), pp. 1–18.

38. Farrell and Petersen, "Patterns of Political Behavior in Organizations," pp. 406–407; and A. Drory, "Politics in Organization and Its Perception Within the Organization," *Organization Studies* 9, no. 2 (1988), pp. 165–179.

39. D. A. Buchanan, "You Stab My Back, I'll Stab Yours: Management Experience and Perceptions of Organization Political Behavior," *British Journal of Management* 19, no. 1 (2008), pp. 49–64.

40. J. Pfeffer, *Power in Organizations* (Marshfield, MA: Pitman, 1981).

41. Drory and Romm, "The Definition of Organizational Politics."

42. S. M. Rioux and L. A. Penner, "The Causes of Organizational Citizenship Behavior: A Motivational Analysis," *Journal of Applied Psychology,* December 2001, pp. 1306–1314; and M. A. Finkelstein and L. A. Penner, "Predicting Organizational Citizenship Behavior: Integrating the Functional and Role Identity Approaches," *Social Behavior & Personality* 32, no. 4 (2004), pp. 383–398.

43. J. Schwarzwald, M. Koslowsky, and M. Allouf, "Group Membership, Status, and Social Power Preference," *Journal of Applied Social Psychology* 35, no. 3 (2005), pp. 644–665.

44. See, for example, G. R. Ferris, G. S. Russ, and P. M. Fandt, "Politics in Organizations," in R. A. Giacalone and P. Rosenfeld (eds.), *Impression Management in the Organization*

(Hillsdale, NJ: Lawrence Erlbaum, 1989), pp. 155–156; and W. E. O'Connor and T. G. Morrison, "A Comparison of Situational and Dispositional Predictors of Perceptions of Organizational Politics," *Journal of Psychology*, May 2001, pp. 301–312.

45. Farrell and Petersen, "Patterns of Political Behavior in Organizations," p. 408.

46. G. R. Ferris and K. M. Kacmar, "Perceptions of Organizational Politics," *Journal of Management*, March 1992, pp. 93–116.

47. See, for example, P. M. Fandt and G. R. Ferris, "The Management of Information and Impressions: When Employees Behave Opportunistically," *Organizational Behavior and Human Decision Processes*, February 1990, pp. 140–158; Ferris, Russ, and Fandt, "Politics in Organizations," p. 147; and J. M. L. Poon, "Situational Antecedents and Outcomes of Organizational Politics Perceptions," *Journal of Managerial Psychology* 18, no. 2 (2003), pp. 138–155.

48. A. D. Galinsky, J. C. Magee, M. E. Inesi, and D. H. Gruenfeld, "Power and Perspectives Not Taken," *Psychological Science*, December 2006, pp. 1068–1074.

49. Ferris, Russ, and Fandt, "Politics in Organizations"; and K. M. Kacmar, D. P. Bozeman, D. S. Carlson, and W. P. Anthony, "An Examination of the Perceptions of Organizational Politics Model: Replication and Extension," *Human Relations*, March 1999, pp. 383–416.

50. W. A. Hochwarter, C. Kiewitz, S. L. Castro, P. L. Perrewe, and G. R. Ferris, "Positive Affectivity and Collective Efficacy as Moderators of the Relationship Between Perceived Politics and Job Satisfaction," *Journal of Applied Social Psychology*, May 2003, pp. 1009–1035; and C. C. Rosen, P. E. Levy, and R. J. Hall, "Placing Perceptions of Politics in the Context of Feedback Environment, Employee Attitudes, and Job Performance," *Journal of Applied Psychology* 91, no. 1 (2006), pp. 211–230.

51. G. R. Ferris, D. D. Frink, M. C. Galang, J. Zhou, K. M. Kacmar, and J. L. Howard, "Perceptions of Organizational Politics: Prediction, Stress-Related Implications, and Outcomes," *Human Relations*, February 1996, pp. 233–266; and E. Vigoda, "Stress-Related Aftermaths to Workplace Politics: The Relationships Among Politics, Job Distress, and Aggressive Behavior in Organizations," *Journal of Organizational Behavior*, August 2002, pp. 571–591.

52. C. Kiewitz, W. A. Hochwarter, G. R. Ferris, and S. L. Castro, "The Role of Psychological Climate in Neutralizing the Effects of Organizational Politics on Work Outcomes," *Journal of Applied Social Psychology*, June 2002, pp. 1189–1207; and M. C. Andrews, L. A. Witt, and K. M. Kacmar, "The Interactive Effects of Organizational Politics and Exchange Ideology on Manager Ratings of Retention," *Journal of Vocational Behavior*, April 2003, pp. 357–369.

53. S. Aryee, Z. Chen, and P. S. Budhwar, "Exchange Fairness and Employee Performance: An Examination of the Relationship Between Organizational Politics and Procedural Justice," *Organizational Behavior & Human Decision Processes*, May 2004, pp. 1–14; and Kacmar, Bozeman, Carlson, and Anthony, "An Examination of the Perceptions of Organizational Politics Model."

54. Kacmar, Bozeman, Carlson, and Anthony, "An Examination of the Perceptions of Organizational Politics Model," p. 389.

55. Ibid., p. 409.

56. B. E. Ashforth and R. T. Lee, "Defensive Behavior in Organizations: A Preliminary Model," *Human Relations*, July 1990, pp. 621–648.

57. M. Valle and P. L. Perrewe, "Do Politics Perceptions Relate to Political Behaviors? Tests of an Implicit Assumption and Expanded Model," *Human Relations*, March 2000, pp. 359–386.

58. M. R. Leary and R. M. Kowalski, "Impression Management: A Literature Review and Two-Component Model," *Psychological Bulletin*, January 1990, pp. 34–47.

59. See, for instance, W. L. Gardner and M. J. Martinko, "Impression Management in Organizations," *Journal of Management*, June 1988, pp. 321–338; M. C. Bolino and W. H. Turnley, "More Than One Way to Make an Impression: Exploring Profiles of Impression Management," *Journal of Management* 29, no. 2 (2003), pp. 141–160; S. Zivnuska, K. M. Kacmar, L. A. Witt, D. S. Carlson, and V. K. Bratton, "Interactive Effects of Impression Management and Organizational Politics on Job Performance," *Journal of Organizational Behavior*, August 2004, pp. 627–640; and M. C. Bolino, K. M. Kacmar, W. H. Turnley, and J. B. Gilstrap, "A Multi-Level Review of Impression Management Motives and Behaviors," *Journal of Management* 34, no. 6 (2008), pp. 1080–1109.

60. M. Snyder and J. Copeland, "Self-monitoring Processes in Organizational Settings," in R. A. Giacalone and P. Rosenfeld (eds.), *Impression Management in the Organization* (Hillsdale, NJ: Lawrence Erlbaum, 1989), p. 11; M. C. Bolino and W. H. Turnley, "More than One Way to Make an Impression: Exploring Profiles of Impression Management," *Journal of Management* 29 (2003), pp. 141–160; and W. H. Turnley and M. C. Bolino, "Achieved Desired Images While Avoiding Undesired Images: Exploring the Role of Self-Monitoring in Impression Management," *Journal of Applied Psychology*, April 2001, pp. 351–360.

61. Leary and Kowalski, "Impression Management," p. 40.

62. R. A. Baron, "Impression Management by Applicants During Employment Interviews: The 'Too Much of a Good Thing' Effect," in R. W. Eder and G. R. Ferris (eds.), *The Employment Interview: Theory, Research, and Practice* (Newbury Park, CA: Sage, 1989), pp. 204–215.

63. C. Lebherz, K. Jonas, and B. Tomljenovic, "Are We Known by the Company We Keep? Effects of Name Dropping on First Impressions," *Social Influence* 4, no. 1 (2009), pp. 62–79.

64. Ferris, Russ, and Fandt, "Politics in Organizations."

65. Z. I. Barsness, K. A. Diekmann, and M. L. Seidel, "Motivation and Opportunity: The Role of Remote Work, Demographic Dissimilarity, and Social Network Centrality in Impression Management," *Academy of Management Journal* 48, no. 3 (2005), pp. 401–419.

66. A. P. J. Ellis, B. J. West, A. M. Ryan, and R. P. DeShon, "The Use of Impression Management Tactics in Structural Interviews: A Function of Question Type?" *Journal of Applied Psychology*, December 2002, pp. 1200–1208.

67. C. K. Stevens and A. L. Kristof, "Making the Right Impression: A Field Study of Applicant Impression Management During Job Interviews," *Journal of Applied Psychology* 80 (1995), pp. 587–606; L. A. McFarland, A. M. Ryan, and S. D. Kriska, "Impression Management Use and Effectiveness Across Assessment Methods," *Journal of Management* 29, no. 5 (2003), pp. 641–661; C. A. Higgins and

T. A. Judge, "The Effect of Applicant Influence Tactics on Recruiter Perceptions of Fit and Hiring Recommendations: A Field Study," *Journal of Applied Psychology* 89, no. 4 (2004), pp. 622–632; and W. C. Tsai, C. C. Chen, and S. F. Chiu, "Exploring Boundaries of the Effects of Applicant Impression Management Tactics in Job Interviews," *Journal of Management,* February 2005, pp. 108–125.

68. Gilmore and Ferris, "The Effects of Applicant Impression Management Tactics on Interviewer Judgments."

69. Stevens and Kristof, "Making the Right Impression."

70. C. A. Higgins, T. A. Judge, and G. R. Ferris, "Influence Tactics and Work Outcomes: A Meta-analysis," *Journal of Organizational Behavior,* March 2003, pp. 89–106.

71. Ibid.

72. K. J. Harris, K. M. Kacmar, S. Zivnuska, and J. D. Shaw, "The Impact of Political Skill on Impression Management Effectiveness," *Journal of Applied Psychology* 92, no. 1 (2007), pp. 278–285; and D. C. Treadway, G. R. Ferris, A. B. Duke, G. L. Adams, and J. B. Thatcher, "The Moderating Role of Subordinate Political Skill on Supervisors' Impressions of Subordinate Ingratiation and Ratings of Subordinate Interpersonal Facilitation," *Journal of Applied Psychology* 92, no. 3 (2007), pp. 848–855.

73. J. D. Westphal and I. Stern, "Flattery Will Get You Everywhere (Especially if You Are a Male Caucasian): How Ingratiation, Boardroom Behavior, and Demographic Minority Status Affect Additional Board Appointments of U.S. Companies," *Academy of Management Journal* 50, no. 2 (2007), pp. 267–288.

74. O. J. Labedo, "Perceptions of Organisational Politics: Examination of the Situational Antecedent and Consequences Among Nigeria's Extension Personnel," *Applied Psychology: An International Review* 55, no. 2 (2006), pp. 255–281.

75. P. P. Fu and G. Yukl, "Perceived Effectiveness of Influence Tactics in the United States and China," *Leadership Quarterly,* Summer 2000, pp. 251–266; O. Branzei, "Cultural Explanations of Individual Preferences for Influence Tactics in Cross-Cultural Encounters," *International Journal of Cross Cultural Management,* August 2002, pp. 203–218; G. Yukl, P. P. Fu, and R. McDonald, "Cross-Cultural Differences in Perceived Effectiveness of Influence Tactics for Initiating or Resisting Change," *Applied Psychology: An International Review,* January 2003, pp. 66–82; and P. P. Fu, T. K. Peng, J. C. Kennedy, and G. Yukl, "Examining the Preferences of Influence Tactics in Chinese Societies: A Comparison of Chinese Managers in Hong Kong, Taiwan, and Mainland China," *Organizational Dynamics* 33, no. 1 (2004), pp. 32–46.

76. Fu and Yukl, "Perceived Effectiveness of Influence Tactics in the United States and China."

77. S. J. Heine, "Making Sense of East Asian Self-Enhancement," *Journal of Cross-Cultural Psychology,* September 2003, pp. 596–602.

78. See T. Romm and A. Drory, "Political Behavior in Organizations: A Cross-Cultural Comparison," *International Journal of Value Based Management* 1 (1988), pp. 97–113; and E. Vigoda, "Reactions to Organizational Politics: A Cross-Cultural Examination in Israel and Britain," *Human Relations,* November 2001, pp. 1483–1518.

79. J. L. T. Leong, M. H. Bond, and P. P. Fu, "Perceived Effectiveness of Influence Strategies in the United States and Three Chinese Societies," *International Journal of Cross Cultural Management,* May 2006, pp. 101–120.

80. E. Vigoda, "Reactions to Organizational Politics," p. 1512.

81. Ibid., p. 1510.

82. R. M. Kanter, *Men and Women of the Corporation* (New York: Basic Books, 1977).

83. See, for instance, Falbe and Yukl, "Consequences for Managers of Using Single Influence Tactics and Combinations of Tactics."

84. See M. A. Rahim, "Relationships of Leader Power to Compliance and Satisfaction with Supervision: Evidence from a National Sample of Managers," *Journal of Management,* December 1989, pp. 545–556; P. A. Wilson, "The Effects of Politics and Power on the Organizational Commitment of Federal Executives," *Journal of Management,* Spring 1995, pp. 101–118; and A. R. Elangovan and J. L. Xie, "Effects of Perceived Power of Supervisor on Subordinate Stress and Motivation: The Moderating Role of Subordinate Characteristics," *Journal of Organizational Behavior,* May 1999, pp. 359–373.

85. J. Pfeffer, *Managing with Power: Politics and Influence in Organizations* (Boston: Harvard Business School Press, 1992).

86. G. R. Ferris, P. L. Perrewé, W. P. Anthony, and D. C. Gilmore, "Political Skill at Work," *Organizational Dynamics,* Spring 2000, pp. 25–37; K. K. Ahearn, G. R. Ferris, W. A. Hochwarter, C. Douglas, and A. P. Ammeter, "Leader Political Skill and Team Performance," *Journal of Management* 30, no. 3 (2004), pp. 309–327; and S. E. Seibert, M. L. Kraimer, and J. M. Crant, "What Do Proactive People Do? A Longitudinal Model Linking Proactive Personality and Career Success," *Personnel Psychology,* Winter 2001, pp. 845–874.

87. R. W. Kolodinsky, W. A. Hochwarter, and G. R. Ferris, "Nonlinearity in the Relationship Between Political Skill and Work Outcomes: Convergent Evidence from Three Studies," *Journal of Vocational Behavior,* October 2004, pp. 294–308; W. Hochwarter, "The Interactive Effects of Pro-Political Behavior and Politics Perceptions on Job Satisfaction and Affective Commitment," *Journal of Applied Social Psychology,* July 2003, pp. 1360–1378; and P. L. Perrewé, K. L. Zellars, G. R. Ferris, A. Rossi, C. J. Kacmar, and D. A. Ralston, "Neutralizing Job Stressors: Political Skill as an Antidote to the Dysfunctional Consequences of Role Conflict," *Academy of Management Journal,* February 2004, pp. 141–152.

88. K. J. Winstein and T. Audi, "MGM Mirage CEO to Resign Amid Questions About MBA," *Wall Street Journal* (November 14, 2008), p. B1.

LEARNING OBJECTIVES

After studying this chapter, you should be able to:

1 Define *conflict*.

2 Differentiate between the traditional, interactionist, and managed-conflict views of conflict.

3 Outline the conflict process.

4 Define *negotiation*.

5 Contrast distributive and integrative bargaining.

6 Apply the five steps of the negotiation process.

7 Show how individual differences influence negotiations.

8 Assess the roles and functions of third-party negotiations.

9 Describe cultural differences in negotiations.

Conflict and Negotiation

14

Let us never negotiate out of fear. But let us never fear to negotiate. —John F. Kennedy

KIDNAPPING THE BOSS

Normally you don't think of kidnapping as part of the normal repertoire of hardball negotiation tactics. But it's been used more than once in France. And the outcomes of these kidnappings might surprise you.

In 2009, when Caterpillar announced layoffs at its Grenoble plant as part of a mass layoff of 22,000 employees worldwide, French workers stormed into the office of the plant director and detained him and four other managers. They agreed to release the executives only after the company consented to resume negotiations over the layoffs.

The same year, French workers held hostage plant managers of numerous other companies, including Sony, Gucci, HP, and 3M. Inspired by the "bossnappings" in France, workers have held managers hostage in other countries, including Belgium, Russia, and South Africa.

"Kidnapping the boss is not legal," said one expert, sociologist Jérôme Pélisse. "But it's a way workers have found to make their voices heard." An opinion poll suggested that 56 percent of French blue-collar workers thought the *séquestrations* were acceptable, compared to only 40 percent of white-collar workers. Even

French President Nicolas Sarkozy expressed empathy for the Caterpillar kidnappers and told them, "I will save the site."

German tire maker Continental decided to move its plant closure negotiations from the Clairoix plant to a more secure site to avoid having its managers kidnapped. One French management consultant is even offering a "survival kit" for potential victims; the kit includes a change of clothes and a cell phone preprogrammed with the numbers of family, police, and a psychologist.

How well did the Caterpillar kidnapping work? *Pas très bien,* it seems. Though no employee was charged in the kidnappings, and though the company continued to negotiate with the union, Caterpillar has refused to agree to the union's terms: to reduce the layoffs from 733 to 450 and to increase the amount of the severance package.

Despite the uncertain results, Caterpillar union members believe the kidnapping was justified. "In the U.S., people accept getting fired on the spot, without complaining," said Michel Laboisseret, a union representative who took part in the Caterpillar kidnapping. "We are more willing to pick a fight."[1]

As we see in the Caterpillar example, conflict and negotiation are often complex—and controversial—interpersonal processes. While conflict is generally seen as a negative topic, and negotiation as a positive one, each can generate positive and negative outcomes, and what is deemed positive or negative often depends on one's perspective. Let's first gauge how you handle conflict by taking the following self-assessment.

Self Assessment Library

WHAT'S MY PREFERRED CONFLICT-HANDLING STYLE?

In the Self-Assessment Library (available on CD and online), take assessment II.C.5 (What's My Preferred Conflict-Handling Style?) and answer the following questions.

1. *Judging from your highest score, what's your primary conflict-handling style?*
2. *Do you think your style varies, depending on the situation?*
3. *Would you like to change any aspects of your conflict-handling style?*

A Definition of *Conflict*

1 Define *conflict*.

There has been no shortage of definitions of *conflict*,[2] but common to most is the idea that conflict is a perception. If no one is aware of a conflict, then it is generally agreed no conflict exists. Also needed to begin the conflict process are opposition or incompatibility and some form of interaction.[3]

We can define **conflict**, then, as a process that begins when one party perceives another party has or is about to negatively affect something the first party cares about.[4] This definition is purposely broad. It describes that point in any ongoing activity when an interaction crosses over to become an interparty conflict. It encompasses the wide range of conflicts people experience in organizations: incompatibility of goals, differences over interpretations of facts, disagreements based on behavioral expectations, and the like. Finally, our definition is flexible enough to cover the full range of conflict levels—from overt and violent acts to subtle forms of disagreement.

Transitions in Conflict Thought

2 Differentiate between the traditional, interactionist, and managed-conflict views of conflict.

It is entirely appropriate to say there has been conflict over the role of conflict in groups and organizations. One school of thought has argued that conflict must be avoided—that it indicates a malfunctioning within the group. We call this the *traditional* view. Another perspective proposes not only that conflict can be a positive force in a group but that some conflict is absolutely necessary for a group to perform effectively. We label this the *interactionist* view. Finally, recent research argues that instead of encouraging "good" or discouraging "bad" conflict, it's more important to resolve naturally occurring conflicts productively. This perspective is the *managed conflict* view. Let's take a closer look at each view.

The Traditional View of Conflict

The early approach to conflict assumed all conflict was bad and to be avoided. It was viewed negatively and discussed with such terms as *violence, destruction,* and *irrationality* to reinforce its negative connotation. This **traditional view of conflict** was consistent with attitudes about group behavior that prevailed in the 1930s and 1940s. Conflict was a dysfunctional outcome resulting from poor communication, a lack of openness and trust between people, and the failure of managers to be responsive to the needs and aspirations of their employees.

The view that all conflict is bad certainly offers a simple approach to looking at the behavior of people who create conflict. We need merely direct our attention to the causes of conflict and correct those malfunctions to improve group and organizational performance. This view of conflict fell out of favor for a long time as researchers came to realize that some level of conflict was inevitable.

The Interactionist View of Conflict

The **interactionist view of conflict** encourages conflict on the grounds that a harmonious, peaceful, tranquil, and cooperative group is prone to becoming static, apathetic, and unresponsive to needs for change and innovation.[5] The major contribution of this view is recognizing that a minimal level of conflict can help keep a group viable, self critical, and creative.

The interactionist view does not propose that all conflicts are good. Rather, **functional conflict** supports the goals of the group and improves its performance and is, thus, a constructive form of conflict. A conflict that hinders group performance is a destructive or **dysfunctional conflict**. What differentiates functional from dysfunctional conflict? The evidence indicates we need to look at the *type* of conflict—task, relationship, and process.[6]

Task conflict relates to the content and goals of the work. **Relationship conflict** focuses on interpersonal relationships. **Process conflict** relates to how the work gets done. Studies demonstrate that relationship conflicts are almost always dysfunctional.[7] Why? It appears that the friction and interpersonal hostilities inherent in relationship conflicts increase personality clashes and decrease mutual understanding, which hinders the completion of organizational tasks. Unfortunately, managers spend a lot of effort resolving personality conflicts among staff members; one survey indicated this task consumes 18 percent of their time.[8]

In contrast, low levels of process conflict and low to moderate levels of task conflict can be functional, but only in very specific cases. Recent reviews have shown that task conflicts are usually just as disruptive as relationship conflicts.[9] For process conflict to be productive, it must be kept low. Intense arguments about who should do what become dysfunctional when they create uncertainty about task roles, increase the time to complete tasks, and lead to members working at cross-purposes. Low to moderate levels of task conflict stimulate discussion

---

conflict *A process that begins when one party perceives that another party has negatively affected, or is about to negatively affect, something that the first party cares about.*

traditional view of conflict *The belief that all conflict is harmful and must be avoided.*

interactionist view of conflict *The belief that conflict is not only a positive force in a group but also an absolute necessity for a group to perform effectively.*

functional conflict *Conflict that supports the goals of the group and improves its performance.*

dysfunctional conflict *Conflict that hinders group performance.*

task conflict *Conflict over content and goals of the work.*

relationship conflict *Conflict based on interpersonal relationships.*

process conflict *Conflict over how work gets done.*

Task conflict is often functional, but one of its dangers is that it can escalate and become a battle of wills. As a Target Corporation investor, William Ackman tried, unsuccessfully, for years to convince the company to change its business strategy to improve performance. In 2009 Ackman sought to bring in new board members with a proxy vote. He asked shareholders to elect candidates who Ackman said would bring new ideas to the board, which Ackman claimed was slow in making critical decisions. After a long battle that cost Target $11 million in defending itself, the shareholders voted to keep the current board members. Ackman is shown here meeting with the media after losing the proxy battle in which his candidates received less than 20 percent of the vote.

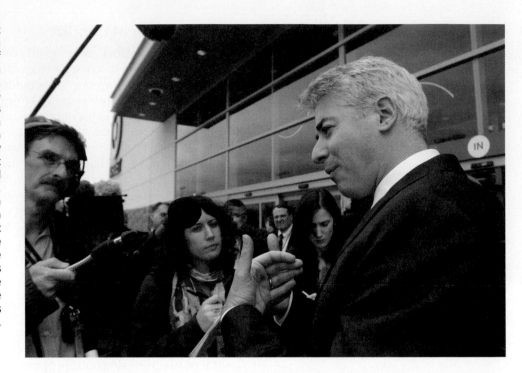

of ideas. This means task conflicts relate positively to creativity and innovation, but they are not related to routine task performance. Groups performing routine tasks that don't require creativity won't benefit from task conflict. Moreover, if the group is already engaged in active discussion of ideas in a nonconfrontational way, adding conflict will not help generate more ideas. Task conflict is also related to these positive outcomes only when all members share the same goals and have high levels of trust.[10]

Resolution Focused View of Conflict

Researchers, including those who had strongly advocated the interactionist view, have begun to recognize some problems with encouraging conflict.[11] As we will see, there are some very specific cases in which conflict can be beneficial. However, workplace conflicts are not productive, they take time away from job tasks or interacting with customers, and hurt feelings and anger often linger after conflicts appear to be over. People seldom can wall off their feelings into neat categories of "task" or "relationship" disagreements, so task conflicts sometimes escalate into relationship conflicts.[12] Conflicts produce stress, which may lead people to become more close minded and adversarial.[13] Studies of conflict in laboratories also fail to take account of the reductions in trust and cooperation that occur even with relationship conflicts. Longer-term studies show that all conflicts reduce trust, respect, and cohesion in groups, which reduces their long-term viability.[14]

In light of these findings, researchers have started to focus more on managing the whole context in which conflicts occur, both before and after the behavioral stage of conflict occurs. A growing body of research, which we review later, suggests we can minimize the negative effects of conflict by focusing on preparing people for conflicts, developing resolution strategies, and facilitating open discussion.

In sum, the traditional view took a shortsighted view in assuming all conflict should be eliminated. The interactionist view that conflict can stimulate active discussion without spilling over into negative, disruptive emotions is incomplete. The managed conflict perspective does recognize that conflict is probably inevitable in most organizations, and it focuses more on productive conflict resolution. The research pendulum has swung from eliminating conflict, to encouraging limited levels of conflict, and now to finding constructive methods for resolving conflicts productively so their disruptive influence can be minimized.

The Conflict Process

3 Outline the conflict process.

The **conflict process** has five stages: potential opposition or incompatibility, cognition and personalization, intentions, behavior, and outcomes. The process is diagrammed in Exhibit 14-1.

Stage I: Potential Opposition or Incompatibility

The first step in the conflict process is the appearance of conditions that create opportunities for conflict to arise. They *need not* lead directly to conflict, but one of these conditions is necessary if conflict is to surface. For simplicity's sake, these conditions (which we can also look at as causes or sources of conflict) have been condensed into three general categories: communication, structure, and personal variables.

Communication Susan had worked in supply-chain management at Bristol-Myers Squibb for 3 years. She enjoyed her work in large part because her boss, Harry Kim, was a great boss. Then Harry got promoted, and Chuck Benson took his place. Six months later Susan says her job is a lot more frustrating. "Harry and I were on the same wavelength. It's not that way with Chuck. He tells me something, and I do it. Then he tells me I did it wrong. I think he means one thing but says something else. It's been like this since the day he arrived. I don't think a day goes by when he isn't yelling at me for something. You know, there are some people you just find it easy to communicate with. Well, Chuck isn't one of those!"

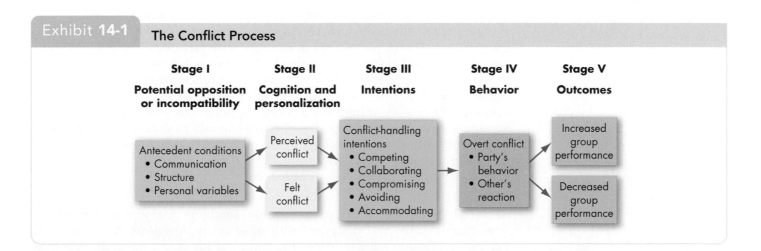

Exhibit 14-1   The Conflict Process

conflict process *A process that has five stages: potential opposition or incompatibility, cognition and personalization, intentions, behavior, and outcomes.*

Susan's comments illustrate that communication can be a source of conflict.[15] They represent the opposing forces that arise from semantic difficulties, misunderstandings, and "noise" in the communication channels. Much of this discussion relates to our comments on communication in Chapter 11.

A review of the research suggests that differing word connotations, jargon, insufficient exchange of information, and noise in the communication channel are all barriers to communication and potential antecedent conditions to conflict. Research has further demonstrated a surprising finding: The potential for conflict increases when either too little or *too much* communication takes place. Apparently, an increase in communication is functional up to a point, after which it is possible to overcommunicate, with a resultant increase in the potential for conflict.

Structure   Charlotte and Mercedes both work at the Portland Furniture Mart—a large discount furniture retailer. Charlotte is a salesperson on the floor, and Mercedes is the company credit manager. The two women have known each other for years and have much in common: They live within two blocks of each other, and their oldest daughters attend the same middle school and are best friends. If Charlotte and Mercedes had different jobs, they might be best friends themselves, but they are constantly fighting battles with each other. Charlotte's job is to sell furniture, and she does it well. But most of her sales are made on credit. Because Mercedes' job is to make sure the company minimizes credit losses, she regularly has to turn down the credit application of a customer with whom Charlotte has just closed a sale. It's nothing personal between the women; the requirements of their jobs just bring them into conflict.

The conflicts between Charlotte and Mercedes are structural in nature. The term *structure* in this context includes variables such as size, degree of specialization in the tasks assigned to group members, jurisdictional clarity, member–goal compatibility, leadership styles, reward systems, and the degree of dependence between groups.

Size and specialization can stimulate conflict. The larger the group and the more specialized its activities, the greater the likelihood of conflict. Tenure and conflict have been found to be inversely related; the potential for conflict is greatest when group members are younger and when turnover is high.

The greater the ambiguity about where responsibility for actions lies, the greater the potential for conflict to emerge. Such jurisdictional ambiguities increase intergroup fighting for control of resources and territory. Diversity of goals among groups is also a major source of conflict. When groups within an organization seek diverse ends, some of which—like sales and credit at Portland Furniture Mart—are inherently at odds, opportunities for conflict increase. Reward systems, too, create conflict when one member's gain comes at another's expense. Finally, if a group is dependent on another group (in contrast to the two being mutually independent), or if interdependence allows one group to gain at another's expense, opposing forces are stimulated.[16]

Personal Variables   Have you ever met someone for whom you felt an immediate dislike? You disagreed with most of the opinions they expressed. Even insignificant characteristics—the sound of his voice, the smirk when he smiled, his personality—annoyed you. We've all met people like that. When you have to work with such individuals, the potential for conflict arises.

Our last category of potential sources of conflict is personal variables, which include personality, emotions, and values. Personality does appear to play a role in the conflict process: some people just tend to get in conflicts a lot. In particular, people high in the personality traits of disagreeableness, neuroticism, or self-monitoring are prone to tangle with other people more often, and to react poorly when conflicts occur.[17] Emotions can also cause conflict. An employee who shows up to work irate from her hectic morning commute may carry that anger with her to her 9:00 A.M. meeting. The problem? Her anger can annoy her colleagues, which can result in a tension-filled meeting.[18]

Stage II: Cognition and Personalization

If the conditions cited in Stage I negatively affect something one party cares about, then the potential for opposition or incompatibility becomes actualized in the second stage.

As we noted in our definition of conflict, one or more of the parties must be aware that antecedent conditions exist. However, because a conflict is a **perceived conflict** does not mean it is personalized. In other words, "*A* may be aware that *B* and *A* are in serious disagreement . . . but it may not make *A* tense or anxious, and it may have no effect whatsoever on *A*'s affection toward *B*."[19] It is at the **felt conflict** level, when individuals become emotionally involved, that parties experience anxiety, tension, frustration, or hostility.

Keep in mind two points. First, Stage II is important because it's where conflict issues tend to be defined. This is the point when the parties decide what the conflict is about.[20] If I define our salary disagreement as a zero-sum situation (if you get the increase in pay you want, there will be just that amount less for me), I am going to be far less willing to compromise than if I frame the conflict as a potential win-win situation (the dollars in the salary pool might be increased so both of us could get the added pay we want). So the definition of a conflict is important because it typically delineates the set of possible settlements.

Our second point is that emotions play a major role in shaping perceptions.[21] Negative emotions allow us to oversimplify issues, lose trust, and put negative interpretations on the other party's behavior.[22] In contrast, positive feelings increase our tendency to see potential relationships among the elements of a problem, to take a broader view of the situation, and to develop more innovative solutions.[23]

Stage III: Intentions

Intentions intervene between people's perceptions and emotions and their overt behavior. They are decisions to act in a given way.[24]

We separate out intentions as a distinct stage because we have to infer the other's intent to know how to respond to his or her behavior. A lot of conflicts are escalated simply because one party attributes the wrong intentions to the other. There is also typically a great deal of slippage between intentions and behavior, so behavior does not always accurately reflect a person's intentions.

Exhibit 14-2 represents one author's effort to identify the primary conflict-handling intentions. Using two dimensions—*cooperativeness* (the degree to which one party attempts to satisfy the other party's concerns) and *assertiveness* (the degree to which one party attempts to satisfy his or her own concerns)—we can identify five conflict-handling intentions: *competing* (assertive and uncooperative), *collaborating* (assertive and cooperative), *avoiding* (unassertive and uncooperative), *accommodating* (unassertive and cooperative), and *compromising* (midrange on both assertiveness and cooperativeness).[25]

---

perceived conflict   *Awareness by one or more parties of the existence of conditions that create opportunities for conflict to arise.*

felt conflict   *Emotional involvement in a conflict that creates anxiety, tenseness, frustration, or hostility.*

intentions   *Decisions to act in a given way.*

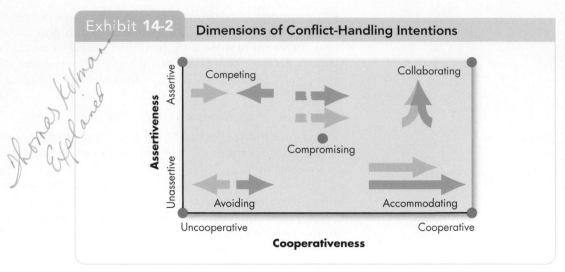

Exhibit **14-2**   **Dimensions of Conflict-Handling Intentions**

Sources: K. Thomas, "Conflict and Negotiation Processes in Organizations," in M. D. Dunnette and L. M. Hough (eds.), *Handbook of Industrial and Organizational Psychology,* 2nd ed., vol. 3 (Palo Alto, CA: Consulting Psychologists Press, 1992), p. 668. Used with permission.

Competing   When one person seeks to satisfy his or her own interests regardless of the impact on the other parties to the conflict, that person is **competing**. You compete when you place a bet that only one person can win, for example.

Collaborating   When parties in conflict each desire to fully satisfy the concerns of all parties, there is cooperation and a search for a mutually beneficial outcome. In **collaborating**, the parties intend to solve a problem by clarifying differences rather than by accommodating various points of view. If you attempt to find a win-win solution that allows both parties' goals to be completely achieved, that's collaborating.

Avoiding   A person may recognize a conflict exists and want to withdraw from or suppress it. Examples of **avoiding** include trying to ignore a conflict and avoiding others with whom you disagree.

Accommodating   A party who seeks to appease an opponent may be willing to place the opponent's interests above his or her own, sacrificing to maintain the relationship. We refer to this intention as **accommodating**. Supporting someone else's opinion despite your reservations about it, for example, is accommodating.

Compromising   In **compromising**, there is no clear winner or loser. Rather, there is a willingness to ration the object of the conflict and accept a solution that provides incomplete satisfaction of both parties' concerns. The distinguishing characteristic of compromising, therefore, is that each party intends to give up something.

Intentions are not always fixed. During the course of a conflict, they might change if the parties are able to see the other's point of view or respond emotionally to the other's behavior. However, research indicates people have preferences among the five conflict-handling intentions we just described.[26] and tend to rely on them quite consistently. We can predict a person's intentions rather well from a combination of intellectual and personality characteristics.

Stage IV: Behavior

When most people think of conflict situations, they tend to focus on Stage IV because this is where conflicts become visible. The behavior stage includes the statements, actions, and reactions made by the conflicting parties, usually as overt attempts to implement their own intentions. As a result of miscalculations or unskilled enactments, overt behaviors sometimes deviate from these original intentions.[27]

It helps to think of Stage IV as a dynamic process of interaction. For example, you make a demand on me, I respond by arguing, you threaten me, I threaten you back, and so on. Exhibit 14-3 provides a way of visualizing conflict behavior. All conflicts exist somewhere along this continuum. At the lower part are conflicts characterized by subtle, indirect, and highly controlled forms of tension, such as a student questioning in class a point the instructor has just made. Conflict intensities escalate as they move upward along the continuum until they become highly destructive. Strikes, riots, and wars clearly fall in this upper range. For the most part, you should assume conflicts that reach the upper ranges of the continuum are almost always dysfunctional. Functional conflicts are typically confined to the lower range of the continuum.

If a conflict is dysfunctional, what can the parties do to de-escalate it? Or, conversely, what options exist if conflict is too low and needs to be increased? This brings us to techniques of **conflict management**. Exhibit 14-4 lists the major resolution and stimulation techniques that allow managers to control conflict levels. We have already described several as conflict-handling intentions. This shouldn't be surprising. Under ideal conditions, a person's intentions should translate into comparable behaviors.

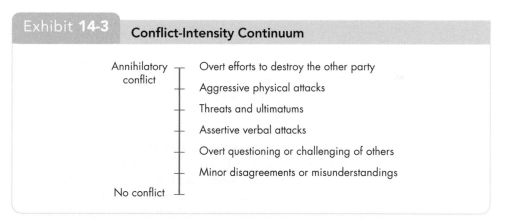

Exhibit 14-3	Conflict-Intensity Continuum

Annihilatory conflict — Overt efforts to destroy the other party

Aggressive physical attacks

Threats and ultimatums

Assertive verbal attacks

Overt questioning or challenging of others

Minor disagreements or misunderstandings

No conflict

Sources: Based on S. P. Robbins, *Managing Organizational Conflict: A Nontraditional Approach* (Upper Saddle River, NJ: Prentice Hall, 1974), pp. 93–97; and F. Glasi, "The Process of Conflict Escalation and the Roles of Third Parties," in G. B. J. Bomers and R. Peterson (eds.), *Conflict Management and Industrial Relations* (Boston: Kluwer-Nijhoff, 1982), pp. 119–140.

competing   *A desire to satisfy one's interests, regardless of the impact on the other party to the conflict.*

collaborating   *A situation in which the parties to a conflict each desire to satisfy fully the concerns of all parties.*

avoiding   *The desire to withdraw from or suppress a conflict.*

accommodating   *The willingness of one party in a conflict to place the opponent's interests above his or her own.*

compromising   *A situation in which each party to a conflict is willing to give up something.*

conflict management   *The use of resolution and stimulation techniques to achieve the desired level of conflict.*

Exhibit 14-4	Conflict-Management Techniques

Conflict-Resolution Techniques

Problem solving	Face-to-face meeting of the conflicting parties for the purpose of identifying the problem and resolving it through open discussion.
Superordinate goals	Creating a shared goal that cannot be attained without the cooperation of each of the conflicting parties.
Expansion of resources	When a conflict is caused by the scarcity of a resource (for example, money, promotion, opportunities, office space), expansion of the resource can create a win-win solution.
Avoidance	Withdrawal from or suppression of the conflict.
Smoothing	Playing down differences while emphasizing common interests between the conflicting parties.
Compromise	Each party to the conflict gives up something of value.
Authoritative command	Management uses its formal authority to resolve the conflict and then communicates its desires to the parties involved.
Altering the human variable	Using behavioral change techniques such as human relations training to alter attitudes and behaviors that cause conflict.
Altering the structural variables	Changing the formal organization structure and the interaction patterns of conflicting parties through job redesign, transfers, creation of coordinating positions, and the like.

Conflict-Stimulation Techniques

Communication	Using ambiguous or threatening messages to increase conflict levels.
Bringing in outsiders	Adding employees to a group whose backgrounds, values, attitudes, or managerial styles differ from those of present members.
Restructuring the organization	Realigning work groups, altering rules and regulations, increasing interdependence, and making similar structural changes to disrupt the status quo.
Appointing a devil's advocate	Designating a critic to purposely argue against the majority positions held by the group.

Source: Based on S. P. Robbins, Managing Organizational Conflict: A Nontraditional Approach (Upper Saddle River, NJ: Prentice Hall, 1974), pp. 59–89.

Stage V: Outcomes

The action–reaction interplay between the conflicting parties results in consequences. As our model demonstrates (see Exhibit 14-1), these outcomes may be functional, if the conflict improves the group's performance, or dysfunctional, if it hinders performance.

Functional Outcomes   How might conflict act as a force to increase group performance? It is hard to visualize a situation in which open or violent aggression could be functional. But it's possible to see how low or moderate levels of conflict could improve the effectiveness of a group. Let's consider some examples and then review the research evidence. Note that all our examples focus on task and process conflicts and exclude the relationship variety.

Conflict is constructive when it improves the quality of decisions, stimulates creativity and innovation, encourages interest and curiosity among group members, provides the medium through which problems can be aired and tensions released, and fosters an environment of self-evaluation and change. The evidence suggests conflict can improve the quality of decision making by allowing all points to be weighed, particularly those that are unusual or held by a minority.[28] Conflict is an antidote for groupthink. It doesn't allow the group to passively rubber-stamp decisions that may be based on weak assumptions, inadequate consideration of relevant alternatives, or other debilities. Conflict challenges the status quo and therefore furthers the creation of new ideas, promotes reassessment of group goals and activities, and increases the probability that the group will respond to change. An open discussion focused on higher-

A lack of functional conflict among General Motors management in past decades resulted in concessions to union demands for generous health benefits and pensions. Burdened by health costs that GM provided to more than one million employees, retirees, and dependents, the automaker was forced into bankruptcy and more mass layoffs even after it closed factories as part of a cost-cutting strategy. The Chevy Blazer SUV shown here was one of the last GM vehicles to roll off the assembly line at a plant in Linden, New Jersey. GM closed the plant after 68 years of operation, which marked the end of automobile manufacturing in a state where the industry once employed thousands of workers and helped fuel the state's economic engine.

order goals can make these functional outcomes more likely. Groups that are extremely polarized do not manage their underlying disagreements effectively and tend to accept suboptimal solutions, or they tend to avoid making decisions altogether rather than working out the conflict.[29]

One company that suffered because it had too little functional conflict was automobile behemoth General Motors.[30] Many of GM's problems, from the late 1960s to the present day, can be traced to a lack of functional conflict. GM hired and promoted individuals who were "yes people," loyal to the point of never questioning company actions. Many, like investor Kirk Kekorian, fault GM management's conflict aversion for its acceding to union demands for generous health care and pension benefits. These costs swelled over time until enormous pension and healthcare obligations weighed the company down. The once-unimaginable bankruptcy of GM in 2009 demonstrates just how damaging a failure to address conflict directly can be.

Research studies in diverse settings confirm the functionality of active discussion. One study found that when groups analyzed decisions made by individual members of the group, the average improvement among groups that discussed differences of opinion frequently was 73 percent higher than in groups characterized by low-conflict conditions.[31] Others have found similar results: Groups whose members have different interests tend to produce higher-quality solutions to a variety of problems than do homogeneous groups.[32] Teams members with greater differences in work styles and experience also tend to share more information with one another.[33]

These observations lead us to predict benefits to organizations from the increasing cultural diversity of the workforce. And that's what the evidence indicates, under most conditions. Heterogeneity among group and organization members can increase creativity, improve the quality of decisions, and facilitate change by enhancing member flexibility.[34] Researchers compared decision-making groups composed of all-Caucasian individuals with groups that also contained members from Asian, Hispanic, and Black ethnic groups. The ethnically diverse groups produced more effective and more feasible ideas, and the unique ideas they generated tended to be of higher quality than the unique ideas produced by the all-Caucasian group.

Dysfunctional Outcomes   The destructive consequences of conflict on the performance of a group or an organization are generally well known: uncontrolled opposition breeds discontent, which acts to dissolve common ties and eventually leads to the destruction of the group. And, of course, a substantial body of literature documents how dysfunctional conflicts can reduce group effectiveness.[35] Among the more undesirable consequences are hampered communication, reductions in group cohesiveness, and subordination of group goals to the primacy of infighting among members. All forms of conflict—even the functional varieties—appear to reduce group member satisfaction and reduce trust.[36] When active discussions turn into open conflicts between members, information sharing between members has been shown to decrease significantly.[37] At the extreme, conflict can bring group functioning to a halt and threaten the group's survival.

We noted that diversity can usually improve group performance and decision making. However, if differences of opinion open up along demographic fault-lines, harmful conflicts result and information sharing decreases.[38] For example, if differences of opinion in a gender-diverse team line up so that men all hold one opinion and women hold another, group members tend to stop listening to one another. They fall into in-group favoritism and won't take the other side's point of view into consideration. Managers in this situation need to pay special attention to these fault lines and emphasize the shared goals of the team.

The demise of an organization as a result of too much conflict isn't as unusual as you might think. One of New York's best-known law firms, Shea & Gould, closed down solely because the 80 partners just couldn't get along.[39] As one legal consultant familiar with the organization said, "This was a firm that had basic and principled differences among the partners that were basically irreconcilable." That same consultant also addressed the partners at their last meeting: "You don't have an economic problem," he said. "You have a personality problem. You hate each other!"

Managing Functional Conflict   If managers recognize that in some situations conflict can be beneficial, what can they do to manage conflict effectively in their organizations?[40]

There seems to be general agreement that managing functional conflict is a tough job, particularly in large U.S. corporations. As one consultant put it, "A high proportion of people who get to the top are conflict avoiders. They don't like hearing negatives; they don't like saying or thinking negative things. They frequently make it up the ladder in part because they don't irritate people on the way up. Another suggests at least 7 of 10 people in U.S. business hush up when their opinions are at odds with those of their superiors, allowing bosses to make mistakes even when they know better.

Such anticonflict cultures may have been tolerable in the past but are not in today's fiercely competitive global economy. Organizations that don't encourage and support dissent may find their survival threatened. Let's look at some approaches organizations are using to encourage their people to challenge the system and develop fresh ideas.

Hewlett-Packard rewards dissenters by recognizing go-against-the-grain types, or people who hold to the ideas they believe in even when management rejects them. Herman Miller Inc., an office furniture manufacturer, has a formal system in which employees evaluate and criticize their bosses. IBM also has a formal system that encourages dissension; employees can question their boss with impunity, and if the disagreement can't be resolved the system provides a third party for counsel. Anheuser-Busch builds devil's advocates into the decision process; when the policy committee considers a major move, such as getting into or out of a business or making a major capital expenditure, it often assigns teams to make the case for each side of the question, and this process frequently results in decisions and alternatives the company hadn't previously considered.

One common ingredient in organizations that successfully manage functional conflict is that they reward dissent and punish conflict avoiders. This is easier said than done. It takes discipline and patience to accept news you don't wish to hear (from dissenters) and to force avoiders to speak up. Former Chrysler CEO Bob Nardelli was famous for subjecting dissenters to tirades and tight-lipped sarcasm, whereas Ford CEO Alan Mulally is noted for his patience in seeking to make Ford's culture more creative, flexible, and less bureaucratic. Often, we perceive that dissenters are slowing progress toward a goal—which may be true, but in so doing they are asking the important question about whether the goal is the right one to pursue.

Groups that resolve conflicts successfully discuss differences of opinion openly and are prepared to manage conflict when it arises.[41] The most disruptive conflicts are those that are never addressed directly. An open discussion makes it much easier to develop a shared perception of the problems at hand; it also allows groups to work toward a mutually acceptable solution. Managers need to emphasize shared interests in resolving conflicts, so groups that disagree with one another don't become too entrenched in their points of view and start to take the conflicts personally. Groups with cooperative conflict styles and a strong underlying identification to the overall group goals are more effective than groups with a more competitive style.[42]

Having considered conflict—its nature, causes, and consequences—we now turn to negotiation, which often resolves conflict.

Negotiation

4 Define *negotiation*.

Negotiation permeates the interactions of almost everyone in groups and organizations. There's the obvious: Labor bargains with management. There's the not-so-obvious: Managers negotiate with employees, peers, and bosses; salespeople negotiate with customers; purchasing agents negotiate with suppliers. And there's the subtle: An employee agrees to cover for a colleague for a few minutes in exchange for some past or future benefit. In today's loosely structured organizations, in which members work with colleagues over whom they have no direct authority and with whom they may not even share a common boss, negotiation skills become critical.

We can define **negotiation** as a process that occurs when two or more parties decide how to allocate scarce resources.[43] Although we commonly think of the outcomes of negotiation in one-shot economic terms, like negotiating over the price of a car, every negotiation in organizations also affects the relationship between the negotiators and the way the negotiators feel about themselves.[44] Depending on how much the parties are going to interact with one another, sometimes maintaining the social relationship and behaving ethically will be just as important as the immediate outcome of each bargain. Note that we use the terms *negotiation* and *bargaining* interchangeably. In this section, we contrast two bargaining strategies, provide a model of the negotiation process, ascertain the

negotiation   *A process in which two or more parties exchange goods or services and attempt to agree on the exchange rate for them.*

OB Poll When to Mention Salary?

When is it appropriate for a job candidate to ask about compensation during the hiring process?

- Other 5%
- Third interview 10%
- At job offer 12%
- Phone interview 17%
- Second interview 26%
- First interview 30%

Source: Based on society for Human Resource Management, *Critical Skills Needs and Resources for the Changing Workforce: Keeping Skills Competitive* (Alexandria, VA: Author), 2008, www.shrm.org/Research/SurveyFindings/Articles/Pages/CriticalSkillsNeeds.aspx.

role of moods and personality traits on bargaining, review gender and cultural differences in negotiation, and take a brief look at third-party negotiations.

Bargaining Strategies

5   Contrast distributive and integrative bargaining.

There are two general approaches to negotiation—*distributive bargaining* and *integrative bargaining*.[45] As Exhibit 14-5 shows, they differ in their goal and motivation, focus, interests, information sharing, and duration of relationship. Let's define each and illustrate the differences.

Distributive Bargaining   You see a used car advertised for sale online. It appears to be just what you've been looking to buy. You go out to see the car. It's

Exhibit 14-5   Distributive Versus Integrative Bargaining

Bargaining Characteristic	Distributive Bargaining	Integrative Bargaining
Goal	Get as much of the pie as possible	Expand the pie so that both parties are satisfied
Motivation	Win-lose	Win-win
Focus	Positions ("I can't go beyond this point on this issue.")	Interests ("Can you explain why this issue is so important to you?")
Interests	Opposed	Congruent
Information sharing	Low (Sharing information will only allow other party to take advantage)	High (Sharing information will allow each party to find ways to satisfy interests of each party)
Duration of relationship	Short term	Long term

great, and you want it. The owner tells you the asking price. You don't want to pay that much. The two of you then negotiate over the price. The negotiating strategy you're engaging in is called **distributive bargaining**. Its most identifying feature is that it operates under zero-sum conditions—that is, any gain I make is at your expense and vice versa. Every dollar you can get the seller to cut from the car's price is a dollar you save, and every dollar more the seller can get from you comes at your expense. So the essence of distributive bargaining is negotiating over who gets what share of a fixed pie. By **fixed pie**, we mean a set amount of goods or services to be divvied up. When the pie is fixed, or parties believe it is, they tend to bargain distributively.

Probably the most widely cited example of distributive bargaining is labor–management negotiations over wages. Typically, labor's representatives come to the bargaining table determined to get as much money as possible out of management. Because every cent labor negotiates increases management's costs, each party bargains aggressively and treats the other as an opponent who must be defeated.

The essence of distributive bargaining is depicted in Exhibit 14-6. Parties *A* and *B* represent two negotiators. Each has a *target point* that defines what he or she would like to achieve. Each also has a *resistance point,* which marks the lowest outcome that is acceptable—the point below which the party would break off negotiations rather than accept a less favorable settlement. The area between these two points makes up each one's aspiration range. As long as there is some overlap between *A*'s and *B*'s aspiration ranges, there exists a settlement range in which each one's aspirations can be met.

When you are engaged in distributive bargaining, research consistently shows one of the best things you can do is make the first offer, and make it an aggressive one. One reason for this is that making the first offer shows power; individuals in power are much more likely to make initial offers, speak first at meetings, and thereby gain the advantage. Another reason, the anchoring bias, was mentioned in Chapter 6. People tend to fixate on initial information. Once that anchoring point is set, they fail to adequately adjust it based on subsequent information. A savvy negotiator sets an anchor with the initial offer, and scores of negotiation studies show that such anchors greatly favor the person who sets it.[46]

Say you have a job offer, and your prospective employer asks you what sort of starting salary you'd be wanting. You've just been given a great gift—you have a chance to set the anchor, meaning you should ask for the highest salary you think the employer could reasonably offer. Asking for a million dollars is only

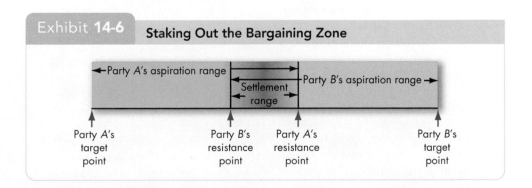

Exhibit 14-6   **Staking Out the Bargaining Zone**

going to make most of us look ridiculous, which is why we suggest being on the high end of what you think is *reasonable*. Too often, we err on the side of caution, afraid of scaring off the employer and thus settling for too little. It *is* possible to scare off an employer, and it's true employers don't like candidates to be assertive in salary negotiations, but liking isn't the same as doing what it takes to hire or retain someone.[47] What happens much more often is that we ask for less than we could have gotten.

Another distributive bargaining tactic is revealing a deadline. Erin is a human resources manager. She is negotiating salary with Ron, who is a highly sought-after new hire. Because Ron knows the company needs him, he decides to play hardball and ask for an extraordinary salary and many benefits. Erin tells Ron the company can't meet his requirements. Ron tells Erin he is going to have to think things over. Worried the company is going to lose Ron to a competitor, Erin decides to tell Ron she is under time pressure and needs to reach an agreement with him immediately, or she will have to offer the job to another candidate. Would you consider Erin to be a savvy negotiator? Well, she is. Why? Negotiators who reveal deadlines speed concessions from their negotiating counterparts, making them reconsider their position. And even though negotiators don't *think* this tactic works, in reality, negotiators who reveal deadlines do better.[48]

Integrative Bargaining   Jake is a 5-year-old Chicago luxury boutique owned by Jim Wetzel and Lance Lawson. In the early days of the business, Wetzel and Lawson had no trouble moving millions of dollars of merchandise from many up-and-coming designers. They developed such a good rapport that many

Myth or Science?

"When Selling in an Auction, Start the Bidding High"

This statement is false. That might surprise you, given that the anchoring bias seems to suggest I should set the initial bid as high as possible. In auctions, however, this would be a mistake. In fact, the opposite strategy is better.

Analyzing auction results on eBay, a group of researchers found that *lower* starting bids generated higher final prices. As just one example, Nikon digital cameras with ridiculously low starting bids (one penny) sold for an average of $312, whereas those with higher starting prices went for an average of $204.

What explains such a counterintuitive result? The researchers found that low starting bids attract more bidders, and this increased traffic generates more competing bidders, so in the end

the price is higher. Although this may seem irrational, negotiation and bidding behavior aren't always rational, and as you've probably experienced firsthand, once you start bidding for something, you want to win, forgetting that for many auctions the one with the highest bid is often the loser (the so-called winner's curse).

If you're thinking of participating in an auction, we have a couple of other myths to dispel here. First, some buyers think sealed-bid auctions—where bidders submit a single bid in a concealed fashion—present an opportunity to get a "steal" because a price war can't develop among bidders. Evidence routinely indicates, however, that sealed-bid auctions are bad for the winning bidder (and thus good for the seller) because the winning bid is

higher than would otherwise be the case. Second, buyers sometimes think jumping bids—placing a bid higher than the auctioneer is asking—is smart strategy because it drives away competing bidders early in the game. Again, this is a myth. Evidence indicates bid jumping is good at causing other bidders to follow suit, thus increasing the value of the winning bid.

Sources: Based on G. Ku, A. D. Galinsky, and J. K. Murnighan, "Starting Low but Ending High: A Reversal of the Anchoring Effect in Auctions," *Journal of Personality and Social Psychology* 90 (June 2006), pp. 975–986; K. Sherstyuk, "A Comparison of First Price Multi-Object Auctions," *Experimental Economics* 12, no. 1 (2009), pp. 42–64; and R. M. Isaac, T. C. Salmon, and A. Zillante, "A Theory of Jump Bidding in Ascending Auctions," *Journal of Economic Behavior & Organization* 62, no. 1 (2007), pp. 144–164.

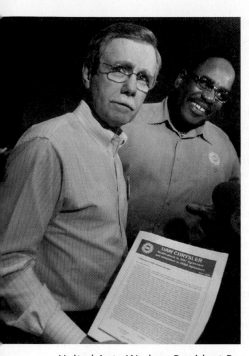

United Auto Workers President Ron Gettelfinger (left) and UAW Vice President General Holiefield and American car companies say they are committed to integrative bargaining in finding mutually acceptable solutions to help boost their competitiveness with foreign automakers. During the economic recession and downturn in auto industry sales, the union and automakers reopened their 4-year contract in 2009 to make changes in the contract that would bring labor costs more in line with those of U.S. competitors. Gettelfinger said the agreements would provide job security for union workers and would help the automakers return to profitability.

designers would send allotments to Jake without requiring advance payment. When the economy soured in 2008, Jake had trouble selling inventory, and the designers found they were not being paid for what they had shipped to the store. Despite the fact that many designers were willing to work with the store on a delayed payment plan, Wetzel and Lawson stopped returning their calls. Lamented one designer, Doo-Ri Chung, "You kind of feel this familiarity with people who supported you for so long. When they have cash-flow issues, you want to make sure you are there for them as well."[49] Ms. Chung's attitude shows the promise of **integrative bargaining**. In contrast to distributive bargaining, integrative bargaining operates under the assumption that one or more settlements can create a win-win solution. Of course, as the Jake example shows and we'll highlight later, integrative bargaining takes "two to tango"—both parties must be engaged for it to work.

In terms of intraorganizational behavior, all things being equal, integrative bargaining is preferable to distributive bargaining because the former builds long-term relationships. Integrative bargaining bonds negotiators and allows them to leave the bargaining table feeling they have achieved a victory. Distributive bargaining, however, leaves one party a loser. It tends to build animosities and deepen divisions when people have to work together on an ongoing basis. Research shows that over repeated bargaining episodes, when the "losing" party feels positive about the negotiation outcome, he is much more likely to bargain cooperatively in subsequent negotiations. This points to an important advantage of integrative negotiations: even when you "win," you want your opponent to feel good about the negotiation.[50]

Why, then, don't we see more integrative bargaining in organizations? The answer lies in the conditions necessary for this type of negotiation to succeed. These include parties who are open with information and candid about their concerns, a sensitivity in both parties to the other's needs and trust, and a willingness by both parties to maintain flexibility.[51] Because these conditions seldom exist in organizations, it isn't surprising that negotiations often take on a win-at-any-cost dynamic.

There are ways to achieve more integrative outcomes. Individuals who bargain in teams reach more integrative agreements than those who bargain individually. This happens because more ideas are generated when more people are at the bargaining table. So try bargaining in teams.[52] Another way to achieve higher joint-gain settlements is to put more issues on the table. The more negotiable issues introduced into a negotiation, the more opportunity for "logrolling," where issues are traded off because people have different preferences. This creates better outcomes for each side than if they negotiated each issue individually.[53]

Finally, you should realize that compromise may be your worst enemy in negotiating a win-win agreement. The reason is that compromising reduces the pressure to bargain integratively. After all, if you or your opponent caves in easily, it doesn't require anyone to be creative to reach a settlement. Thus, people end up settling for less than they could have obtained if they had been forced to consider the other party's interests, trade off issues, and be creative.[54] Think of the classic example in which two sisters are arguing over who gets an orange. Unknown to them, one sister wants the orange to drink the juice, whereas the other wants the orange peel to bake a cake. If one sister simply capitulates and gives the other sister the orange, they will not be forced to

---

integrative bargaining *Negotiation that seeks one or more settlements that can create a win-win solution.*

explore their reasons for wanting the orange, and thus they will never find the win-win solution: They could *each* have the orange because they want different parts of it!

The Negotiation Process

6 Apply the five steps of the negotiation process.

Exhibit 14-7 provides a simplified model of the negotiation process. It views negotiation as made up of five steps: (1) preparation and planning, (2) definition of ground rules, (3) clarification and justification, (4) bargaining and problem solving, and (5) closure and implementation.[55]

Preparation and Planning   Before you start negotiating, you need to do your homework. What's the nature of the conflict? What's the history leading up to this negotiation? Who's involved and what are their perceptions of the conflict? What do you want from the negotiation? What are *your* goals? If you're a supply manager at Dell Computer, for instance, and your goal is to get a significant cost reduction from your supplier of keyboards, make sure this goal stays paramount in your discussions and doesn't get overshadowed by other issues. It often helps to put your goals in writing and develop a range of outcomes—from "most hopeful" to "minimally acceptable"—to keep your attention focused.

You also want to assess what you think are the other party's goals. What are they likely to ask/request? How entrenched is their position likely to be? What intangible or hidden interests may be important to them? On what might they be willing to settle? When you can anticipate your opponent's position, you are better equipped to counter arguments with the facts and figures that support your position.

Relationships will change as a result of a negotiation, so that's another outcome to take into consideration. If you could "win" a negotiation but push the other side into resentment or animosity, it might be wiser to pursue a more compromising style. If preserving the relationship will make you seem weak and easily exploited, you may want to consider a more aggressive style. As an example of how the tone of a relationship set in negotiations matters, consider that people who feel good about the *process* of a job offer negotiation are more satisfied with their jobs and less likely to turn over a year later regardless of their actual *outcomes* from these negotiations.[56] A company that is very successful in negotiating terms of employment that satisfy it but not the new hire pays a price in its long-term relationship with the employee.

Once you've gathered your information, use it to develop a strategy. For example, expert chess players know ahead of time how they will respond to any given situation. As part of your strategy, you should determine your and the other side's **b**est **a**lternative **t**o a **n**egotiated **a**greement (**BATNA**).[57] Your BATNA determines the lowest value acceptable to you for a negotiated agreement. Any offer you receive that is higher than your BATNA is better than an impasse. Conversely, you shouldn't expect success in your negotiation effort unless you're able to make the other side an offer it finds more attractive than its BATNA. If you go into your negotiation having a good idea of what the other party's BATNA is, even if you're not able to meet it you might be able to elicit a change. Think carefully about what the other side is willing to give up. People who underestimate their opponent's willingness to give on key issues before the negotiation even starts end up with lower outcomes from a negotiation.[58]

Definition of Ground Rules   Once you've done your planning and developed a strategy, you're ready to begin defining with the other party the ground rules and procedures of the negotiation itself. Who will do the negotiating? Where will it take place? What time constraints, if any, will apply? To what issues will

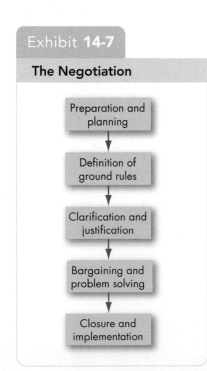

Exhibit 14-7

The Negotiation

Preparation and planning

↓

Definition of ground rules

↓

Clarification and justification

↓

Bargaining and problem solving

↓

Closure and implementation

negotiation be limited? Will you follow a specific procedure if an impasse is reached? During this phase, the parties will also exchange their initial proposals or demands.

Clarification and Justification   When you have exchanged initial positions, both you and the other party will explain, amplify, clarify, bolster, and justify your original demands. This needn't be confrontational. Rather, it's an opportunity for educating and informing each other on the issues, why they are important, and how you arrived at your initial demands. Provide the other party with any documentation that helps support your position.

Bargaining and Problem Solving   The essence of the negotiation process is the actual give-and-take in trying to hash out an agreement. This is where both parties will undoubtedly need to make concessions.

Closure and Implementation   The final step in the negotiation process is formalizing the agreement that has been worked out and developing any procedures necessary for implementation and monitoring. For major negotiations—from labor-management negotiations to bargaining over lease terms to buying a piece of real estate to negotiating a job offer for a senior management position—this requires hammering out the specifics in a formal contract. For most cases, however, closure of the negotiation process is nothing more formal than a handshake.

Individual Differences in Negotiation Effectiveness

7   Show how individual differences influence negotiations.

Are some people better negotiators than others? The answer is more complex than you might think. Three factors influence how effectively individuals negotiate: personality, mood/emotions, and gender.

Personality Traits in Negotiation   Can you predict an opponent's negotiating tactics if you know something about his or her personality? Because personality and negotiation outcomes are related but only weakly, the answer is, at best, "sort of." Negotiators who are agreeable or extraverted are not very successful in distributive bargaining. Why? Because extraverts are outgoing and friendly, they tend to share more information than they should. And agreeable people are more interested in finding ways to cooperate rather than to butt heads. These traits, while slightly helpful in integrative negotiations, are liabilities when interests are opposed. So the best distributive bargainer appears to be a disagreeable introvert—someone more interested in his or her own outcomes than in pleasing the other party and having a pleasant social exchange. People who are highly interested in having positive relationships with other people, and who are not very concerned about their own outcomes, are especially poor negotiators. These people tend to be very anxious about disagreements and plan to give in quickly to avoid unpleasant conflicts even before negotiations start.[59]

Research also suggests intelligence predicts negotiation effectiveness, but, as with personality, the effects aren't especially strong.[60] In a sense, these weak links are good news because they mean you're not severely disadvantaged, even if you're an agreeable extrovert, when it comes time to negotiate. We all can learn to be

BATNA   *The best alternative to a negotiated agreement; the least the individual should accept.*

better negotiators. In fact, people who think so are more likely to do well in negotiations because they persist in their efforts even in the face of temporary setbacks.[61]

Moods/Emotions in Negotiation   Do moods and emotions influence negotiation? They do, but the way they do appears to depend on the type of negotiation. In distributive negotiations, it appears that negotiators in a position of power or equal status who show anger negotiate better outcomes because their anger induces concessions from their opponents. This appears to hold true even when the negotiators are instructed to show anger despite not being truly angry. On the other hand, for those in a less powerful position, displaying anger leads to worse outcomes. So if you're a boss negotiating with a peer or a subordinate, displaying anger may help you, but if you're an employee negotiating with a boss, it might hurt you.

In integrative negotiations, in contrast, positive moods and emotions appear to lead to more integrative agreements (higher levels of joint gain). This may happen because, as we noted in Chapter 4, positive mood is related to creativity.[62]

Gender Differences in Negotiations   Do men and women negotiate differently? And does gender affect negotiation outcomes? The answer to the first question appears to be no.[63] The answer to the second is a qualified yes.[64]

A popular stereotype is that women are more cooperative and pleasant in negotiations than are men. The evidence doesn't support this belief. However, men have been found to negotiate better outcomes than women, although the difference is relatively small. It's been postulated that men and women place divergent values on outcomes. "It is possible that a few hundred dollars more in salary or the corner office is less important to women than forming and maintaining an interpersonal relationship."[65]

The belief that women are "nicer" than men in negotiations is probably due to a confusion between gender and the lower degree of power women typically hold in most large organizations. Because women are expected to be "nice" and men "tough," research shows women are penalized when they ini-

Respected for her intelligence, confident negotiating skills, and successful outcomes, Christine Lagarde was appointed by French President Nicolas Sarkozy to the powerful position of minister for the economy, finance, and employment. As the first female finance minister of a G-8 nation, Lagarde brings to her new post experience as the trade minister of France, where she used her negotiating skills in boosting French exports by 10 percent. Before that, Lagarde was the chairman of the global law firm Baker & McKenzie. Among her tasks, Lagarde is negotiating with France's trade unions to change the country's labor laws, including raising the 35-hour workweek, and is working with other world finance leaders in reforming financial systems on a global scale.

International OB

Negotiating Emotions Across Cultures

As a rule, no one likes to face an angry counterpart in negotiations. However, East Asian negotiators may respond less favorably than people from other cultures.

One article reported that in two separate studies East Asian negotiators were less likely to accept offers from negotiators who displayed anger during negotiations. Another study explicitly compared how U.S. and Chinese negotiators react to an angry counterpart. Chinese negotiators increased their use of distributive negotiating tactics, whereas U.S. negotiators, when confronted with an angry negotiator, decreased their use of these tactics.

Why do East Asian negotiators respond more negatively to angry negotiators? The authors of the first study speculate that the answer may rest in East Asian cultural values. Because their culture emphasizes respect and deference, East Asians may be particularly likely to perceive angry behavior as disrespectful, and thus deserving of uncooperative tactics in response.

Sources: Based on S. Kopelman and A. S. Rosette, "Cultural Variation in Response to Strategic Emotions in Negotiations," *Group Decision and Negotiation* 17, no. 1 (2008), pp. 65–77; and M. Liu, "The Intrapersonal and Interpersonal Effects of Anger on Negotiation Strategies: A Cross-Cultural Investigation," *Human Communication Research* 35, no. 1 (2009), pp. 148–169.

tiate negotiations.[66] What's more, when women and men actually do conform to these stereotypes—women act "nice" and men "tough"—it becomes a self-fulfilling prophecy, reinforcing the stereotypical gender differences between male and female negotiators.[67] Thus, one of the reasons negotiations favor men is that women are "damned if they do, damned if they don't." Negotiate tough and they are penalized for violating a gender stereotype. Negotiate nice and it only reinforces and lets others take advantage of the stereotype.

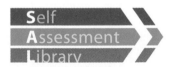

WHAT'S MY NEGOTIATING STYLE?

In the Self-Assessment Library (available on CD and online), take assessment II.C.6 (What's My Negotiating Style?).

Evidence also suggests women's own attitudes and behaviors hurt them in negotiations. Managerial women demonstrate less confidence in anticipation of negotiating and are less satisfied with their performance afterward, even when their performance and the outcomes they achieve are similar to those for men.[68] Women are also less likely than men to see an ambiguous situation as an opportunity for negotiation. It appears that women may unduly penalize themselves by failing to engage in negotiations when such action would be in their best interests.

Third-Party Negotiations

8 Assess the roles and functions of third-party negotiations.

To this point, we've discussed bargaining in terms of direct negotiations. Occasionally, however, individuals or group representatives reach a stalemate and are unable to resolve their differences through direct negotiations. In such cases, they may turn to a third party to help them find a solution. There are four basic third-party roles: mediator, arbitrator, conciliator, and consultant.[69]

How secretive should you be about what you earn? People vary in their responses to this question, and one of the main source of difference tends to be age.

Arielle Green, age 22, doesn't mind discussing her $30,000 annual salary (plus overtime) with friends and colleagues. "There's just more of a feeling of openness in discussing what you make," Green said. According to Green, her parents would never discuss their salary with others. "It's very hush-hush," she noted.

Bill Coleman, chief compensation officer for Salary.com, said, "This is a generation that is much more attuned to teamwork, collaboration, and sharing information. How do you know if $45,000 is a good offer? You go to your friends."

There are both benefits—and risks—in discussing your salary with others. The primary benefit is that you may acquire valuable information about what you should be making, or about what your employer is willing to pay. Two people working in the same job with similar qualifications often do not earn the same salary. So, though asking for more pay simply because a co-worker earns more is likely to be an ineffective negotiating strategy by itself, knowing what co-workers make can help you anchor your pay expectations.

One risk is that you cannot be sure the information you've being given is true. If someone gives you wrong information, you'll be operating from a flawed premise. Another risk is that you might run into an awkward situation. Rebecca Geller, age 29, who works in media relations for a San Francisco company, remembers a brunch at which a school administer wondered whether his aspirations for a $40,000 annual salary were reasonable. He asked, "Why, what do you guys make?" One, a lawyer, sheepishly confessed to a $130,000 annual salary. "There was definitely an awkward silence," Geller said.

Before sharing your salary with others, keep these points in mind:

1. Make sure you are aware of organizational policies, both before and after you join an organization. Many organizations have policies against open disclosure of pay. If you violate such policies, you may risk your job.

2. Realize that sharing, while possibly valuable, can be used against you. Say you are the high earner, and you disclose this information to a co-worker. This co-worker may then demand a higher salary, using your disclosure as justification. While some employers would not hold that against you, others might—including the boss, your colleagues, or even the co-worker to whom you made the disclosure.

3. If you share, it only makes sense to get information in return. More generally, make sure sharing makes sense from your long-term interests. Don't share as a means of appeasing. Giving in once only means you'll be harassed again in the not-too-distant future.

Sources: Based on A. Williams, "Not-So-Personal Finance," *New York Times* (April 27, 2008), pp. S1, S2; R. Zupek, "Things Not to Share with Your Co-workers," Careerbuilder.com (January 3, 2008), msn.careerbuilder.com; and L. Wolgemuth, "Using What You Know About Co-workers' Pay," *U.S. News and World Report* (June 19, 2008), www.usnews.com.

A **mediator** is a neutral third party who facilitates a negotiated solution by using reasoning and persuasion, suggesting alternatives, and the like. Mediators are widely used in labor-management negotiations and in civil court disputes. Their overall effectiveness is fairly impressive. The settlement rate is approximately 60 percent, with negotiator satisfaction at about 75 percent. But the situation is the key to whether mediation will succeed; the conflicting parties must be motivated to bargain and resolve their conflict. In addition, conflict intensity can't be too high; mediation is most effective under moderate levels of conflict. Finally, perceptions of the mediator are important; to be effective, the mediator must be perceived as neutral and noncoercive.

An **arbitrator** is a third party with the authority to dictate an agreement. Arbitration can be voluntary (requested by the parties) or compulsory (forced on the parties by law or contract). The big plus of arbitration over mediation is that it always results in a settlement. Whether or not there is a negative side depends on how heavy handed the arbitrator appears. If one party is left feeling overwhelmingly defeated, that party is certain to be dissatisfied and unlikely to graciously accept the arbitrator's decision. Therefore, the conflict may resurface at a later time.

A **conciliator** is a trusted third party who provides an informal communication link between the negotiator and the opponent. This role was made famous by Robert Duval in the first *Godfather* film. As Don Corleone's adopted son and a lawyer by training, Duval acted as an intermediary between the Corleones and the other Mafioso families. Comparing conciliation to mediation in terms of effectiveness has proven difficult because the two overlap a great deal. In practice, conciliators typically act as more than mere communication conduits. They also engage in fact-finding, interpret messages, and persuade disputants to develop agreements.

A **consultant** is a skilled and impartial third party who attempts to facilitate problem solving through communication and analysis, aided by a knowledge of conflict management. Unlike other third parties, the consultant does not try to settle the issues but rather works to improve relationships between the conflicting parties so they can reach a settlement themselves. Instead of putting forward specific solutions, the consultant tries to help the parties learn to understand and work with each other. This approach has a longer-term focus: to build new and positive perceptions and attitudes between the conflicting parties.

Global Implications

9 Describe cultural differences in negotiations.

Conflict and Culture

Research suggests that differences across countries in conflict resolution strategies may be based on collectivistic tendencies and motives.[70] Collectivist cultures see people as deeply embedded in social situations, whereas individualist cultures see people as autonomous. As a result, collectivists are more likely to seek to preserve relationships and promote the good of the group as a whole than individualists. To preserve peaceful relationships, collectivists will avoid direct expression of conflicts, preferring to use more indirect methods for resolving differences of opinion. Collectivists may also be more interested in demonstrations of concern and working through third parties to resolve disputes, whereas individualists will be more likely to confront differences of opinion directly and openly.

Some research does support this theory. Compared to collectivist Japanese negotiators, their more individualist U.S. counterparts are more likely to see offers from their counterparts as unfair and to reject them. Another study revealed that whereas U.S. managers were more likely to use competing tactics in the face of conflicts, compromising and avoiding are the most preferred methods of conflict management in China.[71] Interview data, however, suggests top management teams in Chinese high-technology firms preferred integration even more than compromising and avoiding.[72]

Cultural Differences in Negotiations

Compared to the research on conflict, there is more research on how negotiating styles vary across national cultures.[73] One study compared U.S. and Japanese

---

mediator *A neutral third party who facilitates a negotiated solution by using reasoning, persuasion, and suggestions for alternatives.*

arbitrator *A third party to a negotiation who has the authority to dictate an agreement.*

conciliator *A trusted third party who provides an informal communication link between the negotiator and the opponent.*

consultant *An impartial third party, skilled in conflict management, who attempts to facilitate creative problem solving through communication and analysis.*

negotiators and found the generally conflict-avoidant Japanese negotiators tended to communicate indirectly and adapt their behaviors to the situation. A follow-up study showed that whereas among U.S. managers making early offers led to the anchoring effect we noted when discussing distributive negotiation, for Japanese negotiators early offers led to more information sharing and better integrative outcomes.[74] In another study, managers with high levels of economic power from Hong Kong, which is a high power-distance country, were more cooperative in negotiations over a shared resource than German and U.S. managers, who were lower in power distance.[75] This suggests that in high power-distance countries, those in positions of power might exercise more restraint.

Another study looked at verbal and nonverbal negotiation tactics exhibited by North Americans, Japanese, and Brazilians during half-hour bargaining sessions.[76] Some of the differences were particularly interesting. The Brazilians on average said "no" 83 times, compared to 5 times for the Japanese and 9 times for the North Americans. The Japanese displayed more than 5 periods of silence lasting longer than 10 seconds during the 30-minute sessions. North Americans averaged 3.5 such periods; the Brazilians had none. The Japanese and North Americans interrupted their opponent about the same number of times, but the Brazilians interrupted 2.5 to 3 times more often than either. Finally, the Japanese and the North Americans had no physical contact with their opponents during negotiations except for handshaking, but the Brazilians touched each other almost 5 times every half hour.

Summary and Implications for Managers

While many people assume conflict lowers group and organizational performance, this assumption is frequently incorrect. Conflict can be either constructive or destructive to the functioning of a group or unit. As shown in Exhibit 14-8, levels of conflict can be either too high or too low. Either extreme hinders performance. An optimal level is one that prevents stagnation, stimulates creativity, allows tensions to be released, and initiates the seeds of change, without being disruptive or preventing coordination of activities.

What advice can we give managers faced with excessive conflict and the need to reduce it? Don't assume one conflict-handling intention will always be best! Select an intention appropriate for the situation. Here are some guidelines:[77]

● Use *competition* when quick, decisive action is vital (in emergencies), on important issues, when unpopular actions need to be implemented (in cost cutting, enforcement of unpopular rules, discipline), on issues vital to the organization's welfare when you know you're right, and against people who take advantage of noncompetitive behavior.
● Use *collaboration* to find an integrative solution when both sets of concerns are too important to be compromised, when your objective is to learn, when you want to merge insights from people with different perspectives or gain commitment by incorporating concerns into a consensus, and when you need to work through feelings that have interfered with a relationship.
● Use *avoidance* when an issue is trivial or symptomatic of other issues, when more important issues are pressing, when you perceive no chance of satisfying your concerns, when potential disruption outweighs the benefits of resolution, to let people cool down and regain perspective, when gathering information supersedes immediate decision, and when others can resolve the conflict more effectively.
● Use *accommodation* when you find you're wrong and to allow a better position to be heard, to learn, to show your reasonableness, when issues are more im-

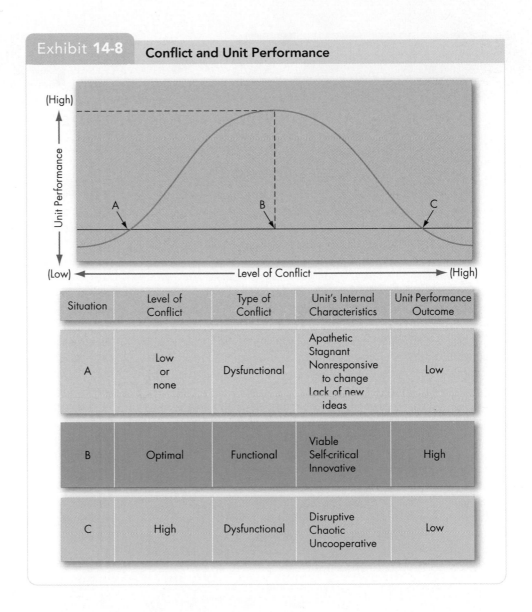

Exhibit 14-8   Conflict and Unit Performance

Situation	Level of Conflict	Type of Conflict	Unit's Internal Characteristics	Unit Performance Outcome
A	Low or none	Dysfunctional	Apathetic Stagnant Nonresponsive to change Lack of new ideas	Low
B	Optimal	Functional	Viable Self-critical Innovative	High
C	High	Dysfunctional	Disruptive Chaotic Uncooperative	Low

portant to others than to yourself and to satisfy others and maintain cooperation, to build social credits for later issues, to minimize loss when you are outmatched and losing, when harmony and stability are especially important, and to allow employees to develop by learning from mistakes.

- Use *compromise* when goals are important but not worth the effort of potential disruption of more assertive approaches, when opponents with equal power are committed to mutually exclusive goals, to achieve temporary settlements to complex issues, to arrive at expedient solutions under time pressure, and as a backup when collaboration or competition is unsuccessful.

Negotiation is an ongoing activity in groups and organizations. Distributive bargaining can resolve disputes, but it often negatively affects the satisfaction of one or more negotiators because it is focused on the short term and because it is confrontational. Integrative bargaining, in contrast, tends to provide outcomes that satisfy all parties and that build lasting relationships. When engaged in negotiation, make sure you set aggressive goals and try to find creative ways to achieve the goals of both parties, especially when you value the long-term relationship with the other party. That doesn't mean sacrificing your self-interest; rather, it means trying to find creative solutions that give both parties what they really want.

Conflict Benefits Organizations

POINT

Let's briefly review how stimulating conflict can provide benefits to the organization:

- **Conflict is a means to solve problems and bring about radical change.** It's an effective device by which management can drastically change the existing power structure, current interaction patterns, and entrenched attitudes. If there is no conflict, it means the real problems aren't being addressed.

- **Conflict facilitates group cohesiveness.** While conflict increases hostility between groups, external threats tend to cause a group to pull together as a unit. Conflict with another group brings together those within each group. Such intragroup cohesion is a critical resource that groups draw on in good and especially in bad times.

- **Conflict improves group and organizational effective-ness.** Groups or organizations devoid of conflict are likely to suffer from apathy, stagnation, groupthink, and other debilitating diseases. In fact, more organizations probably fail because they have *too little* conflict, not because they have too much. Stagnation is the biggest threat to organizations, but since it occurs slowly its ill effects often go unnoticed until it's too late. Conflict can break complacency—though most of us don't like conflict, it often is the last best hope of saving an organization.

COUNTERPOINT

In general, conflicts are dysfunctional, and it is one of management's major responsibilities to keep conflict intensity as low as humanly possible. A few points support this case:

- **The negative consequences from conflict can be devastating.** The list of negatives associated with conflict is awesome. The most obvious are increased turnover, decreased employee satisfaction, inefficiencies between work units, sabotage, and labor grievances and strikes. One study estimated that managing conflict at work costs the average employer nearly 450 days of management time a year.[78]

- **Effective managers build teamwork.** A good manager builds a coordinated team. Conflict works against such an objective. When a team works well, the whole becomes greater than the sum of the parts. Management creates teamwork by minimizing internal conflicts and facilitating internal coordination.

- **Conflict is avoidable.** It may be true that conflict is inevitable when an organization is in a downward spiral, but the goal of good leadership and effective management is to avoid the spiral at the start. You don't see Warren Buffett getting into a lot of conflicts with his board of directors. It's possible they're complacent, but we think it's more likely that Berkshire Hathaway is a well-run company, doing what it should, and avoiding conflict as a result.

Questions for Review

1 What is conflict?

2 What are the differences among the traditional, interactionist, and managed-conflict views of conflict?

3 What are the steps of the conflict process?

4 What is negotiation?

5 What are the differences between distributive and integrative bargaining?

6 What are the five steps in the negotiation process?

7 How do the individual differences of personality and gender influence negotiations?

8 What are the roles and functions of third-party negotiations?

9 How does culture influence negotiations?

Experiential Exercise

A NEGOTIATION ROLE PLAY

This role-play is designed to help you develop your negotiating skills. The class is to break into pairs. One person will play the role of Alex, the department supervisor. The other person will play C. J., Alex's boss. Both participants should read "The Situation," "The Negotiation," and then their role only.

The Situation

Alex and C. J. work for Nike in Beaverton, Oregon. Alex supervises a research laboratory. C. J. is the manager of research and development. Alex and C. J. are former college runners who have worked for Nike for more than 6 years. C. J. has been Alex's boss for 2 years. One of Alex's employees has greatly impressed Alex. This employee is Lisa Roland. Lisa was hired 11 months ago. She is 24 years old and holds a master's degree in mechanical engineering. Her entry-level salary was $47,500 per year. Alex told her that, in accordance with corporation policy, she would receive an initial performance evaluation at 6 months and a comprehensive review after 1 year. Based on her performance record, Lisa was told she could expect a salary adjustment at the time of the 1-year evaluation.

Alex's evaluation of Lisa after 6 months was very positive. Alex commented on the long hours Lisa was putting in, her cooperative spirit, the fact that others in the lab enjoyed working with her, and that she was making an immediate positive impact on the project assigned to her. Now that Lisa's first anniversary is coming up, Alex has again reviewed Lisa's performance. Alex thinks Lisa may be the best new person the R&D group has ever hired. After only a year, Alex has ranked Lisa as the number-3 performer in a department of 11.

Salaries in the department vary greatly. Alex, for instance, has a base salary of $76,000, plus eligibility for a bonus that might add another $7,000 to $12,000 a year.

The salary range of the 11 department members is $38,400 to $66,350. The individual with the lowest salary is a recent hire with a bachelor's degree in physics. The two people whom Alex has rated above Lisa earn base salaries of $59,200 and $66,350. They're both 27 years old and have been at Nike for 3 and 4 years, respectively. The median salary in Alex's department is $54,960.

Alex's Role

You want to give Lisa a big raise. Although she's young, she has proven to be an excellent addition to the department. You don't want to lose her. More importantly, she knows in general what other people in the department are earning, and she thinks she's underpaid. The company typically gives 1-year raises of 5 percent, although 10 percent is not unusual, and 20 to 30 percent increases have been approved on occasion. You'd like to get Lisa as large an increase as C. J. will approve.

C. J.'s Role

All your supervisors typically try to squeeze you for as much money as they can for their people. You understand this because you did the same thing when you were a supervisor, but your boss wants to keep a lid on costs. He wants you to keep raises for recent hires generally in the 5 to 8 percent range. In fact, he's sent a memo to all managers and supervisors saying this. He also said that managers will be evaluated on their ability to maintain budgetary control. However, your boss is also concerned with equity and paying people what they're worth. You feel assured that he will support any salary recommendation you make, as long as it can be justified. Your goal, consistent with cost reduction, is to keep salary increases as low as possible.

The Negotiation

Alex has a meeting scheduled with C. J. to discuss Lisa's performance review and salary adjustment. Take a couple of minutes to think through the facts in this exercise and to prepare a strategy. Then take up to 15 minutes to conduct your negotiation. When your negotiation is complete, the class will compare the various strategies used and pair outcomes.

Ethical Dilemma

IS IT UNETHICAL TO LIE DURING NEGOTIATIONS?

In Chapter 11, we addressed lying in the context of communication. Here we return to the topic of lying but specifically as it relates to negotiation. For many people, there is no such thing as lying when it comes to negotiating.

It's been said that the whole notion of negotiation is built on ethical quicksand: to succeed, you must deceive. Is this true? Apparently, a lot of people think so. One study found 28 percent of negotiators lied about at least one issue during negotiations, while another study found 100 percent either failed to reveal a problem or actively lied about it during negotiations if they were not directly asked about the issue.[79]

On the other hand, truthfulness and openness appear crucial to attaining win-win solutions. After all, any possibility of reaching an integrative negotiation settlement depends on both sides openly disclosing their interests.

Evidence indicates that deception in negotiation can produce short-term advantages (albeit with long-term costs). This, of course, does not mean that what is effective is morally right.

We can probably agree that bald-faced lies during negotiation are wrong. The universal dilemma surrounds the little lies: the omissions, evasions, and concealments that are often necessary to best an opponent.

During negotiations, when is a lie a *lie?* Are exaggerating benefits, downplaying negatives, ignoring flaws, or saying "I don't know," when in reality you do, considered lying? Is declaring "This is my final offer and nonnegotiable" when you're posturing a lie? Is pretending to bend over backward to make meaningful concessions lying? Rather than being considered unethical, these "lies" are considered by many to indicate a negotiator is strong, smart, and savvy.

Or consider the issue of colluding, as when two bidders agree not to bid against one another in a (concealed) effort to keep the bids down. In some cases, such collusion is illegal, but even when it isn't illegal, is it ethical?

Questions

1. When are deception, evasiveness, or collusion out of bounds?

2. Can such tactics be legal and still be unethical?

3. Is it naïve to be completely honest and bare your soul during negotiations?

4. Are the rules of negotiations unique? Is any tactic that will improve your chance of winning acceptable?

Sources: Based on R. Cohen, "Bad Bidness," *New York Times Magazine* (September 2, 2006), p. 22; and M. Olekalns and P. L. Smith, "Loose with the Truth: Predicting Deception in Negotiation," *Journal of Business Ethics* 76, no. 2 (2007), pp. 225–238.

Case Incident 1

DAVID OUT-NEGOTIATING GOLIATH: APOTEX AND BRISTOL-MYERS SQUIBB

Peter Dolan survived many crises in his 5-year tenure as CEO of drug giant Bristol-Myers Squibb, including a corporate accounting scandal, allegations of insider trading, FBI raids of his office, and a stock price that dropped 60 percent during his tenure. But in the end, what may have done Dolan in was his negotiation performance against the head of Apotex, a Canadian drug company founded by Dr. Barry Sherman.

At its peak, Plavix—a drug to prevent heart attacks—was Bristol-Myers' best-selling drug and accounted for a staggering one-third of its profits. So when Apotex developed a generic Plavix knockoff, Dolan sought to negotiate an agreement that would pay Apotex in exchange for a delayed launch of Apotex's generic competitor. Dolan sent one of his closest lieutenants, Andrew Bodnar, to negotiate with Sherman. Bodnar and Sherman developed a good rapport and at several points in their negotiations asked their attorneys to leave them alone. At one key point in the negotiations, Bodnar flew to Toronto alone, without Bristol-Myers' attorneys, as a "gesture of goodwill. The thinking was that the negotiations would be more effective this way."

As Dolan, Bodnar, and Bristol-Myers became increasingly concerned with reaching an agreement with Sherman and Apotex, they developed a blind spot. Privately, Sherman was betting that the Federal Trade Commission (FTC) wouldn't approve the noncompete agreement the two parties were negotiating, and his goal in the negotiation was to extract an agreement from Bristol-Myers that would position Apotex favorably should the FTC reject the deal. Indeed, he nonchalantly inserted a clause in the deal that would require Bristol-Myers to pay Apotex $60 million if the FTC rejected the deal. "I thought the FTC would turn it down, but I didn't let on that I did," Sherman said. "They seemed blind to it."

In the meantime, Apotex covertly began shipping its generic equivalent, and it quickly became the best-selling generic drug ever. Thus, Sherman also managed to launch the generic equivalent without Bristol-Myers even considering the possibility that he would do so while still engaged in negotiations.

"It looks like a much smaller generic private company completely outmaneuvered two of the giants of the pharmaceutical industry," said Gbola Amusa, European pharmaceutical analyst for Sanford C. Bernstein & Company. "It's not clear how or why that happened. The reaction from investors and analysts has ranged from shock to outright anger." Within a few months, Dolan was out at Bristol-Myers.

Questions

1. What principles of distributive negotiation did Sherman use to gain his advantage?

2. Do you think Sherman behaved ethically? Why or why not?

3. What does this incident tell you about the role of deception in negotiation?

Sources: Based on J. Carreyrou and J. S. Lublin, "How Bristol-Myers Fumbled Defense of $4 Billion Drug," *Wall Street Journal* (September 2, 2006), pp. A1, A7; and S. Saul, "Marketers of Plavix Outfoxed on a Deal," *New York Times* (August 9, 2006).

Case Incident 2

MEDIATION: MASTER SOLUTION TO EMPLOYMENT DISPUTES?

We typically think of mediation as the province of marital counselors and labor strife. More organizations use mediation to resolve conflicts than you might think. In fact, in the United States, Canada, Great Britain, Ireland, and India, mediation is growing rapidly as a means to settle employment disputes. We introduced mediation in this chapter; let's look at some examples when it has succeeded and when it has failed.

Mediation has often succeeded:

- When German public-services workers found themselves in a dispute with municipalities over pay and work hours, a strike ensued. The unions were pressing for an 8 percent pay hike, whereas the municipalities proposed a 5 percent pay raise. Two mediators were called in to oversee a mediation process during which strikes were banned. The mediators suggested a 6 percent raise, subsequently accepted by both parties.

- The Equal Employment Opportunity Commission (EEOC), the federal agency that oversees employment discrimination complaints in the United States, uses mediation extensively. Safeway, the third-largest U.S. supermarket chain, uses the EEOC to mediate numerous employment disputes. Says Donna Gwin, Safeway's

Director of Human Resources, "Through mediation, we have had the opportunity to proactively resolve issues and avoid potential charges in the future. We have seen the number of charges filed with EEOC against us actually decline. We believe that our participating in mediation and listening to employees' concerns has contributed to that decline."

However, mediation doesn't always work:

- In 2008, the Screen Actors Guild (SAG) and the Alliance of Motion Picture and Television Producers (AMPTP), representing some 350 studios and production companies, engaged in prolonged negotiations over a new labor agreement. The negotiations failed, and the parties agreed to mediation. However, mediation also failed, and in response SAG asked its members to approve a strike authorization.

- When David Kuchinsky, the former driver for New York Knicks center Eddy Curry, sued Curry for sexual harassment, discrimination, and failure to pay $93,000 in wages and reimbursements, the parties agreed to mediation. However, after the sides failed to reach a settlement during mediation, Kuchinsky reinstated his lawsuit, and Curry filed a $50,000 countersuit.

Questions

1. Drawing from the preceding examples, what factors do you think differentiate occasions when mediation was successful and when it failed?

2. One successful mediator, Boston's Paul Finn, argues that if the disputing parties are seeking justice, "It's best to go somewhere else." Why do you think he says that?

3. Do you think a mediator should find out *why* the parties want what they want? Why or why not?

4. The EEOC reports that whereas 85 percent of employees agree to mediate their charges, employers agree to mediate only 30 percent of the time. Why do you think this disparity exists?

Sources: Based on M. Kapko, "Actors Union Seeks Strike Vote After Federal Mediation Fails," *Forbes* (November 23, 2008), www.forbes.com; K. Tyler, "Mediating a Better Outcome," *HR Magazine* (November 2007), pp. 63–66; A. K. Finkle, "A Mediation Primer," *IPMA Newsletter* (May 2008), pp. 26–38; and K. O'Brien, "The Closer," *Boston Globe* (April 12, 2009), www.boston.com.

Endnotes

1. D. Gauthier-Villars and L. Abboud, "In France, Boss Can Become Hostage," *Wall Street Journal* (April 3, 2009), pp. B1, B5; A. Chrisafis, "Sacked French Sony Workers Release Boss from Captivity," *The Guardian* (March 13, 2009), www.guardian.co.uk; D. Jolly, "Taking the Boss Hostage? In France, It's a Labor Tactic," *New York Times* (April 3, 2009), www.nytimes.com; and "Many French Say Taking Boss Hostage Okay," *Newsmax* (April 7, 2009), moneynews.newsmax.com.

2. See, for instance, L. Pondy, "Reflections on Organizational Conflict," *Journal of Organizational Behavior* 13, no. 3 (1992), pp. 257–261; and D. Tjosvold, "Defining Conflict and Making Choices About Its Management: Lighting the Dark Side of Organizational Life," *International Journal of Conflict Management* 17, no. 2 (2006), pp. 87–95.

3. L. L. Putnam and M. S. Poole, "Conflict and Negotiation," in F. M. Jablin, L. L. Putnam, K. H. Roberts, and L. W. Porter (eds.), *Handbook of Organizational Communication: An Interdisciplinary Perspective* (Newbury Park, CA: Sage, 1987), pp. 549–599.

4. K. W. Thomas, "Conflict and Negotiation Processes in Organizations," in M. D. Dunnette and L. M. Hough (eds.), *Handbook of Industrial and Organizational Psychology*, 2nd ed., vol. 3 (Palo Alto, CA: Consulting Psychologists Press, 1992), pp. 651–717.

5. For a comprehensive review of the interactionist approach, see C. De Dreu and E. Van de Vliert (eds.), *Using Conflict in Organizations* (London: Sage, 1997).

6. See K. A. Jehn, "A Multimethod Examination of the Benefits and Detriments of Intragroup Conflict," *Administrative Science Quarterly,* June 1995, pp. 256–282; K. A. Jehn, "A Qualitative Analysis of Conflict Types and Dimensions in Organizational Groups," *Administrative Science Quarterly,* September 1997, pp. 530–557; K. A. Jehn and E. A. Mannix, "The Dynamic Nature of Conflict: A Longitudinal Study of Intragroup Conflict and Group Performance," *Academy of Management Journal,* April 2001, pp. 238–251; and C. K. W. De Dreu and L. R. Weingart, "Task Versus Relationship Conflict, Team Performance, and Team Member Satisfaction: A Meta-analysis," *Journal of Applied Psychology,* August 2003, pp. 741–749.

7. J. Yang and K. W. Mossholder, "Decoupling Task and Relationship Conflict: The Role of Intragroup Emotional Processing," *Journal of Organizational Behavior* 25, no. 5 (August 2004), pp. 589–605; and N. Gamero, V. González-Romá, and J. M. Peiró, "The Influence of Intra-Team Conflict on Work Teams' Affective Climate: A Longitudinal Study," *Journal of Occupational and Organizational Psychology* 81, no. 1 (2008), pp. 47–69.

8. "Survey Shows Managers Have Their Hands Full Resolving Staff Personality Conflicts," *IPMA-HR Bulletin,* November 3, 2006.

9. C. K. W. De Dreu and L. R. Weingart, "Task Versus Relationship Conflict, Team Performance, and Team Member Satisfaction."

10. C. K.W. De Dreu and M. A. West, "Minority Dissent and Team Innovation: The Importance of Participation in Decision Making," *Journal of Applied Psychology* 86, no. 6 (2001), pp. 1191–1201.

11. C. K. W. De Dreu, "The Virtue and Vice of Workplace Conflict: Food for (Pessimistic) Thought," *Journal of Organizational Behavior* 29, no. 1 (2008), pp. 5–18.

12. R. S. Peterson and K. J. Behfar, "The Dynamic Relationship Between Performance Feedback, Trust, and Conflict in Groups: A Longitudinal Study," *Organizational Behavior and Human Decision Process* 92, no. 1–2 (2003), pp. 102–112.

13. L. M. Penny and P. E. Spector, "Job Stress, Incivility, and Counterproductive Work Behavior: The Moderating Role of Negative Affectivity," *Journal of Organizational Behavior* 26, no. 7 (2005), pp. 777–796.

14. K. A. Jehn, L. Greer, S. Levine, and G. Szulanski, "The Effects of Conflict Types, Dimensions, and Emergent States on Group Outcomes," *Group Decision and Negotiation* 17, no. 6 (2008), pp. 465–495.

15. R. S. Peterson and K. J. Behfar, "The Dynamic Relationship Between Performance Feedback, Trust, and Conflict in Groups: A Longitudinal Study," *Organizational Behavior & Human Decision Processes,* September–November 2003, pp. 102–112.

16. Jehn, "A Multimethod Examination of the Benefits and Detriments of Intragroup Conflict."

17. T. M. Glomb and H. Liao, "Interpersonal Aggression in Work Groups: Social Influence, Reciprocal, and Individual Effects," *Academy of Management Journal* 46, no. 4 (2003), pp. 486–496; and V. Venkataramani and R. S. Dalal, "Who

Helps and Who Harms? Relational Aspects of Interpersonal Helping and Harming in Organizations," *Journal of Applied Psychology* 92, no. 4 (2007), pp. 952–966.

18. R. Friedman, C. Anderson, J. Brett, M. Olekalns, N. Goates, and C. C. Lisco, "The Positive and Negative Effects of Anger on Dispute Resolution: Evidence from Electronically Mediated Disputes," *Journal of Applied Psychology*, April 2004, pp. 369–376.

19. L. R. Pondy, "Organizational Conflict: Concepts and Models," *Administrative Science Quarterly*, September 1967, p. 302.

20. See, for instance, R. L. Pinkley, "Dimensions of Conflict Frame: Disputant Interpretations of Conflict," *Journal of Applied Psychology*, April 1990, pp. 117–126; and R. L. Pinkley and G. B. Northcraft, "Conflict Frames of Reference: Implications for Dispute Processes and Outcomes," *Academy of Management Journal*, February 1994, pp. 193–205.

21. A. M. Isen, A. A. Labroo, and P. Durlach, "An Influence of Product and Brand Name on Positive Affect: Implicit and Explicit Measures," *Motivation & Emotion*, March 2004, pp. 43–63.

22. Ibid.

23. P. J. D. Carnevale and A. M. Isen, "The Influence of Positive Affect and Visual Access on the Discovery of Integrative Solutions in Bilateral Negotiations," *Organizational Behavior and Human Decision Processes*, February 1986, pp. 1–13.

24. Thomas, "Conflict and Negotiation Processes in Organizations."

25. Ibid.

26. See R. A. Baron, "Personality and Organizational Conflict: Effects of the Type A Behavior Pattern and Self-monitoring," *Organizational Behavior and Human Decision Processes*, October 1989, pp. 281–296; R. J. Volkema and T. J. Bergmann, "Conflict Styles as Indicators of Behavioral Patterns in Interpersonal Conflicts," *Journal of Social Psychology*, February 1995, pp. 5–15; and J. A. Rhoades, J. Arnold, and C. Jay, "The Role of Affective Traits and Affective States in Disputants' Motivation and Behavior During Episodes of Organizational Conflict," *Journal of Organizational Behavior*, May 2001, pp. 329–345.

27. Thomas, "Conflict and Negotiation Processes in Organizations."

28. See, for instance, K. A. Jehn, "Enhancing Effectiveness: An Investigation of Advantages and Disadvantages of Value-Based Intragroup Conflict," *International Journal of Conflict Management*, July 1994, pp. 223–238; R. L. Priem, D. A. Harrison, and N. K. Muir, "Structured Conflict and Consensus Outcomes in Group Decision Making," *Journal of Management* 21, no. 4 (1995), pp. 691–710; and K. A. Jehn and E. A. Mannix, "The Dynamic Nature of Conflict: A Longitudinal Study of Intragroup Conflict and Group Performance," *Academy of Management Journal*, April 2001, pp. 238–251.

29. B. A. Nijstad and S. C. Kaps, "Taking the Easy Way Out: Preference Diversity, Decision Strategies, and Decision Refusal in Groups," *Journal of Personality and Social Psychology* 94, no. 5 (2008), pp. 860–870.

30. See, for instance, J. Griffiths, "End of an Era as Lumbering GM Crashes," *Financial Times*, June 1, 2009, p. 24.

31. J. Hall and M. S. Williams, "A Comparison of Decision-Making Performances in Established and Ad-hoc Groups," *Journal of Personality and Social Psychology*, February 1966, p. 217.

32. R. L. Hoffman, "Homogeneity of Member Personality and Its Effect on Group Problem-Solving," *Journal of Abnormal and Social Psychology*, January 1959, pp. 27–32; R. L. Hoffman and N. R. F. Maier, "Quality and Acceptance of Problem Solutions by Members of Homogeneous and Heterogeneous Groups," *Journal of Abnormal and Social Psychology*, March 1961, pp. 401–407; and P. Pitcher and A. D. Smith, "Top Management Team Heterogeneity: Personality, Power, and Proxies," *Organization Science*, January–February 2001, pp. 1–18.

33. M. E. Zellmer-Bruhn, M. M. Maloney, A. D. Bhappu, and R. Salvador, "When and How Do Differences Matter? An Exploration of Perceived Similarity in Teams," *Organizational Behavior and Human Decision Processes* 107, no. 1 (2008), pp. 41–59.

34. See T. H. Cox, S. A. Lobel, and P. L. McLeod, "Effects of Ethnic Group Cultural Differences on Cooperative Behavior on a Group Task," *Academy of Management Journal*, December 1991, pp. 827–847; and D. van Knippenberg, C. K. W. De Dreu, and A. C. Homan, "Work Group Diversity and Group Performance: An Integrative Model and Research Agenda," *Journal of Applied Psychology*, December 2004, pp. 1008–1022.

35. For example, see J. A. Wall, Jr., and R. R. Callister, "Conflict and Its Management," pp. 523–526, for evidence supporting the argument that conflict is almost uniformly dysfunctional. See also P. J. Hinds, and D. E. Bailey, "Out of Sight, Out of Sync: Understanding Conflict in Distributed Teams," *Organization Science*, November–December 2003, pp. 615–632.

36. K. A. Jehn, L. Greer, S. Levine, and G. Szulanski, "The Effects of Conflict Types, Dimensions, and Emergent States on Group Outcomes."

37. Zellmer-Bruhn, Maloney, Bhappu, and Salvador, "When and How Do Differences Matter?"

38. K. B. Dahlin, L. R. Weingart, and P. J. Hinds, "Team Diversity and Information Use," *Academy of Management Journal* 48, no. 6 (2005), pp. 1107–1123; and M. J. Pearsall, A. P. J. Ellis, and J. M. Evans, "Unlocking the Effects of Gender Faultlines on Team Creativity: Is Activation the Key?" *Journal of Applied Psychology* 93, no. 1 (2008), pp. 225–234.

39. M. Geyelin and E. Felsenthal, "Irreconcilable Differences Force Shea & Gould Closure," *Wall Street Journal* (January 31, 1994), p. B1.

40. This section is based on F. Sommerfield, "Paying the Troops to Buck the System," *Business Month*, May 1990, pp. 77–79; W. Kiechel III, "How to Escape the Echo Chamber," *Fortune* (June 18, 1990), pp. 129–130; E. Van de Vliert and C. De Dreu, "Optimizing Performance by Stimulating Conflict," *International Journal of Conflict Management*, July 1994, pp. 211–222; E. Van de Vliert, "Enhancing Performance by Conflict-Stimulating Intervention," in C. De Dreu and E. Van de Vliert (eds.), *Using Conflict in Organizations* (London: Sage, 1997), pp. 208–222; K. M. Eisenhardt, J. L. Kahwajy, and L. J. Bourgeois III, "How Management Teams Can Have a Good Fight," *Harvard Business Review*, July–August 1997, pp. 77–85; S. Wetlaufer, "Common Sense and Conflict," *Harvard Business Review*, January–February 2000, pp. 114–124; and G. A. Okhuysen and K. M. Eisenhardt, "Excel Through Group Process," in E. A. Locke (ed.), *Handbook of Principles of Organizational Behavior* (Malden, MA: Blackwell, 2004), pp. 216–218.

41. K. J. Behfar, R. S. Peterson, E. A. Mannix, and W. M. K. Trochim, "The Critical Role of Conflict Resolution in Teams: A Close Look at the Links Between Conflict Type, Conflict Management Strategies, and Team Outcomes," *Journal of Applied Psychology* 93, no. 1 (2008), pp. 170–188; A. G. Tekleab, N. R. Quigley, and P. E. Tesluk, "A Longitudinal Study of Team Conflict, Conflict Management, Cohesion, and Team Effectiveness," *Group and Organization Management* 34, no. 2 (2009), pp. 170–205; and E. Van de Vliert, M. C. Euwema, and S. E. Huismans, "Managing Conflict with a Subordinate or a Superior: Effectiveness of Conglomerated Behavior," *Journal of Applied Psychology* 80 (1995), pp. 271–281.

42. A. Somech, H. S. Desivilya, and H. Lidogoster, "Team Conflict Management and Team Effectiveness: The Effects of Task Interdependence and Team Identification," *Journal of Organizational Behavior* 30, no. 3 (2009), pp. 359–378.

43. M. H. Bazerman, J. R. Curhan, D. A. Moore, and K. L. Valley, "Negotiation," *Annual Review of Psychology* 51 (2000), pp. 279–314.

44. See, for example, D. R. Ames, "Assertiveness Expectancies: How Hard People Push Depends on the Consequences They Predict," *Journal of Personality and Social Psychology* 95, no. 6 (2008), pp. 1541–1557; and J. R. Curhan, H. A. Elfenbein, and H. Xu, "What Do People Value When They Negotiate? Mapping the Domain of Subjective Value in Negotiation," *Journal of Personality and Social Psychology* 91, no. 3 (2006), pp. 493–512.

45. R. E. Walton and R. B. McKersie, *A Behavioral Theory of Labor Negotiations: An Analysis of a Social Interaction System* (New York: McGraw-Hill, 1965).

46. J. C. Magee, A. D. Galinsky, and D. H. Gruenfeld, "Power, Propensity to Negotiate, and Moving First in Competitive Interactions," *Personality and Social Psychology Bulletin,* February 2007, pp. 200–212.

47. H. R. Bowles, L. Babcock, and L. Lei, "Social Incentives for Gender Differences in the Propensity to Initiative Negotiations: Sometimes It Does Hurt to Ask," *Organizational Behavior and Human Decision Processes* 103 (2007), pp. 84–103.

48. D. A. Moore, "Myopic Prediction, Self-Destructive Secrecy, and the Unexpected Benefits of Revealing Final Deadlines in Negotiation," *Organizational Behavior & Human Decision Processes,* July 2004, pp. 125–139.

49. E. Wilson, "The Trouble with Jake," *New York Times* (July 15, 2009), www.nytimes.com.

50. J. R. Curhan, H. A. Elfenbein, and H. Xu, "What Do People Value When They Negotiate? Mapping the Domain of Subjective Value in Negotiation," *Journal of Personality and Social Psychology* 91, no. 3 (2006), pp. 493–512.

51. Thomas, "Conflict and Negotiation Processes in Organizations."

52. P. M. Morgan and R. S. Tindale, "Group vs. Individual Performance in Mixed-Motive Situations: Exploring an Inconsistency," *Organizational Behavior & Human Decision Processes,* January 2002, pp. 44–65.

53. C. E. Naquin, "The Agony of Opportunity in Negotiation: Number of Negotiable Issues, Counterfactual Thinking, and Feelings of Satisfaction," *Organizational Behavior & Human Decision Processes,* May 2003, pp. 97–107.

54. C. K. W. De Dreu, L. R. Weingart, and S. Kwon, "Influence of Social Motives on Integrative Negotiation: A Meta-analytic Review and Test of Two Theories," *Journal of Personality & Social Psychology,* May 2000, pp. 889–905.

55. This model is based on R. J. Lewicki, "Bargaining and Negotiation," *Exchange: The Organizational Behavior Teaching Journal* 6, no. 2 (1981), pp. 39–40.

56. J. R. Curhan, H. A. Elfenbein, and G. J. Kilduff, "Getting Off on the Right Foot: Subjective Value Versus Economic Value in Predicting Longitudinal Job Outcomes from Job Offer Negotiations," *Journal of Applied Psychology* 94, no. 2 (2009), pp. 524–534.

57. M. H. Bazerman and M. A. Neale, *Negotiating Rationally* (New York: The Free Press, 1992), pp. 67–68.

58. R. P. Larrick and G. Wu, "Claiming a Large Slice of a Small Pie: Asymmetric Disconfirmation in Negotiation," *Journal of Personality and Social Psychology* 93, no. 2 (2007), pp. 212–233.

59. E. T. Amanatullah, M. W. Morris, and J. R. Curhan, "Negotiators Who Give Too Much: Unmitigated Communion, Relational Anxieties, and Economic Costs in Distributive and Integrative Bargaining," *Journal of Personality and Social Psychology* 95, no. 3 (2008), pp. 723–738.

60. B. Barry and R. A. Friedman, "Bargainer Characteristics in Distributive and Integrative Negotiation," *Journal of Personality & Social Psychology,* February 1998, pp. 345–359.

61. L. J. Kray and M. P. Haselhuhn, "Implicit Negotiations Beliefs and Performance: Experimental and Longitudinal Evidence," *Journal of Personality and Social Psychology* 93, no. 1 (2007), pp. 49–64.

62. S. Kopelman, A. S. Rosette, and L. Thompson, "The Three Faces of Eve: Strategic Displays of Positive, Negative, and Neutral Emotions in Negotiations," *Organizational Behavior and Human Decision Processes* 99 (2006), pp. 81–101; G. A. Gan Kleef and S. Côté, "Expressing Anger in Conflict: When It Helps and When It Hurts," *Journal of Applied Psychology* 92, no. 6 (2007), pp. 1157–1569; and J. M. Brett, M. Olekalns, R. Friedman, N. Goates, C. Anderson, C. C. Lisco, "Sticks and Stones: Language, Face, and Online Dispute Resolution," *Academy of Management Journal* 50, no. 1 (2007), pp. 85–99.

63. C. Watson and L. R. Hoffman, "Managers as Negotiators: A Test of Power Versus Gender as Predictors of Feelings, Behavior, and Outcomes," *Leadership Quarterly,* Spring 1996, pp. 63–85.

64. A. E. Walters, A. F. Stuhlmacher, and L. L. Meyer, "Gender and Negotiator Competitiveness: A Meta-analysis," *Organizational Behavior and Human Decision Processes,* October 1998, pp. 1–29; and A. F. Stuhlmacher and A. E. Walters, "Gender Differences in Negotiation Outcome: A Meta-analysis," *Personnel Psychology,* Autumn 1999, pp. 653–677.

65. Stuhlmacher and Walters, "Gender Differences in Negotiation Outcome," p. 655.

66. Bowles, Babcock, and Lei, "Social Incentives for Gender Differences in the Propensity to Initiative Negotiations."

67. L. J. Kray, A. D. Galinsky, and L. Thompson, "Reversing the Gender Gap in Negotiations: An Exploration of Stereotype Regeneration," *Organizational Behavior & Human Decision Processes,* March 2002, pp. 386–409.

68. D. A. Small, M. Gelfand, L. Babcock, and H. Gettman, "Who Goes to the Bargaining Table? The Influence of Gender and Framing on the Initiation of Negotiation," *Journal of Personality and Social Psychology* 93, no. 4, pp. 600–613; and C. K. Stevens, A. G. Bavetta, and M. E. Gist, "Gender

Differences in the Acquisition of Salary Negotiation Skills: The Role of Goals, Self-Efficacy, and Perceived Control," *Journal of Applied Psychology* 78, no. 5 (October 1993), pp. 723–735.

69. Wall and Blum, "Negotiations," pp. 283–287.

70. H. R. Markus and S. Kitayama, "Culture and the Self: Implications for Cognition, Emotion, and Motivation," *Psychological Review* 98, no. 2 (1991), pp. 224–253; and H. Ren and B. Gray, "Repairing Relationship Conflict: How Violation Types and Culture Influence the Effectiveness of Restoration Rituals," *Academy of Management Review* 34, no. 1 (2009), pp. 105–126.

71. M. J. Gelfand, M. Higgins, L. H. Nishii, J. L. Raver, A. Dominguez, F. Murakami, S. Yamaguchi, and M. Toyama, "Culture and Egocentric Perceptions of Fairness in Conflict and Negotiation," *Journal of Applied Psychology*, October 2002, pp. 833–845; and Z. Ma, "Chinese Conflict Management Styles and Negotiation Behaviours: An Empirical Test," *International Journal of Cross Cultural Management*, April 2007, pp. 101–119.

72. P. P. Fu, X. H. Yan, Y. Li, E. Wang, and S. Peng, "Examining Conflict-Handling Approaches by Chinese Top Management Teams in IT Firms," *International Journal of Conflict Management* 19, no. 3 (2008), pp. 188–209.

73. Gelfand et al., "Culture and Egocentric Perceptions of Fairness in Conflict and Negotiation," pp. 833–845; and

X. Lin and S. J. Miller, "Negotiation Approaches: Direct and Indirect Effect of National Culture," *International Marketing Review* 20, no. 3 (2003), pp. 286–303.

74. W. L. Adair, T. Okumura, and J. M. Brett, "Negotiation Behavior When Cultures Collide: The United States and Japan," *Journal of Applied Psychology*, June 2001, pp. 371–385; and W. L. Adair, L. Weingart, and J. Brett, "The Timing and Function of Offers in U.S. and Japanese Negotiations," *Journal of Applied Psychology* 92, no. 4 (2007), pp. 1056–1068.

75. S. Kopelman, "The Effect of Culture and Power on Cooperation in Commons Dilemmas: Implications for Global Resource Management," *Organizational Behavior and Human Decision Processes* 108, no. 1 (2009), pp. 153–163.

76. J. Graham, "The Influence of Culture on Business Negotiations," *Journal of International Business Studies*, Spring 1985, pp. 81–96.

77. K. W. Thomas, "Toward Multidimensional Values in Teaching: The Example of Conflict Behaviors," *Academy of Management Review*, July 1977, p. 487.

78. Q. Reade, "Workplace Conflict Is Time-consuming Problem for Business," *PersonnelToday.com*, September 30, 2004, www .personneltoday.co.uk.

79. K. O'Connor and P. Carnevale, "A Nasty but Effective Negotiation Strategy: Misrepresentation of a Common-Value Issue," *Personality and Social Psychology Bulletin*, May 1997, pp. 504–515.

LEARNING OBJECTIVES

After studying this chapter, you should be able to:

1 Identify the six elements of an organization's structure.

2 Identify the characteristics of a bureaucracy.

3 Describe a matrix organization.

4 Identify the characteristics of a virtual organization.

5 Show why managers want to create boundaryless organizations.

6 Demonstrate how organizational structures differ, and contrast mechanistic and organic structural models.

7 Analyze the behavioral implications of different organizational designs.

8 Show how globalization affects organizational structure.

Foundations of Organization Structure

Every revolution evaporates and leaves behind only the slime of a new bureaucracy. —Franz Kafka

RESTRUCTURING CHRYSLER

Chrysler's economic troubles are well documented. It has struggled financially for the past decade under two owners: first German giant Daimler-Benz, then U.S. private equity firm Cerberus Capital Management. On April 30, 2009, Chrysler simultaneously filed for Chapter 11 bankruptcy protection and announced a plan for its acquisition by Italian automaker Fiat. Fiat holds a 20 percent stake in the new company, with an option to increase this to 35 percent and eventually 51 percent. The deal was finalized on June 10, 2009, at the behest of the Obama administration and with considerable financial support from U.S. taxpayers.

It has not taken Sergio Marchionne, Fiat's CEO since 2004, long to settle into his new job. He seems intent on restructuring Chrysler not only financially but in the way the company operates.

Rather than occupying the top-floor executive tower suite of his predecessor, Bob Nardelli, Marchionne took a fourth-floor office in the adjoining technical center. Those close to him say Marchionne took this office to stay close to the engineers and managers who make day-to-day decisions at the automaker.

More important, immediately after taking over, Marchionne announced a series of changes to Chrysler's organization structure.

First, each of Chrysler's brands—Chrysler, Jeep, Dodge, and Mopar (the parts manufacturer)—will be distinct business units with profit and loss responsibility, and younger, marketing-oriented executives, rather than the more traditional engineers, in charge. "That's a mirror image of what he did at Fiat," says a longtime Fiat executive.

Second, Marchionne has dramatically flattened the managerial ranks to speed decision making and move managers closer to the business of manufacturing and marketing autos. Twenty-three senior managers will report directly to him; his predecessor Nardelli only had a handful of direct reports.

Third, while Marchionne is committed to establishing brand boundaries and responsibilities, he seems equally intent on fusing boundaries between Fiat and Chrysler wherever feasible, including integrating production, research and development, and marketing operations. For example, he intends to install Fiat platforms at Chrysler plants and use Fiat's sales force to sell Jeeps and other Chrysler models worldwide.

In his first memo to Chrysler employees, Marchionne talked about changing Chrysler's structure and compared it to his past restructuring efforts at Fiat: "Five years ago, I stepped into a very similar situation at Fiat. It was perceived by many as a failing, lethargic automaker that produced low-quality cars and was stymied by endless bureaucracies." He pledged to succeed at Chrysler as he has at Fiat. While it's difficult to tell whether he will succeed, most would agree with his statement about the auto industry: "A serious restructuring of the automotive industry is now absolutely necessary if it is to be economically viable."[1]

Structural decisions like Sergio Marchionne's at Chrysler are arguably the most fundamental ones a leader has to make. Before we delve into the elements of an organization's structure and how they can affect behavior, consider how you might react to one type of organizational structure—the bureaucratic structure—by taking the following self-assessment.

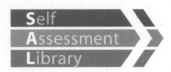

DO I LIKE BUREAUCRACY?

In the Self-Assessment Library (available on CD and online), take assessment IV.F.2 (Do I Like Bureaucracy?) and answer the following questions.

1. *Judging from the results, how willing are you to work in a bureaucratic organization?*
2. *Do you think scores on this measure matter? Why or why not?*
3. *Do you think people who score very low (or even very high) on this measure should try to adjust their preferences based on where they are working?*

What Is Organizational Structure?

1 Identify the six elements of an organization's structure.

An **organizational structure** defines how job tasks are formally divided, grouped, and coordinated. Managers need to address six key elements when they design their organization's structure: work specialization, departmentalization, chain of command, span of control, centralization and decentralization, and formalization.[2] Exhibit 15-1 presents each of these elements as answers to an important structural question, and the following sections describe them.

Work Specialization

Early in the twentieth century, Henry Ford became rich by building automobiles on an assembly line. Every Ford worker was assigned a specific, repetitive task such as putting on the right-front wheel or installing the right-front door. By dividing jobs into small standardized tasks that could be performed over and over, Ford was able to produce a car every 10 seconds, using employees who had relatively limited skills.

Ford demonstrated that work can be performed more efficiently if employees are allowed to specialize. Today we use the term **work specialization**, or *division of labor,* to describe the degree to which activities in the organization are subdivided into separate jobs. The essence of work specialization is to divide a job into a number of steps, each completed by a separate individual. In essence, individuals specialize in doing part of an activity rather than the entirety.

Exhibit 15-1	Key Design Questions and Answers for Designing the Proper Organizational Structure

The Key Question	The Answer Is Provided By
1. To what degree are activities subdivided into separate jobs?	Work specialization
2. On what basis will jobs be grouped together?	Departmentalization
3. To whom do individuals and groups report?	Chain of command
4. How many individuals can a manager efficiently and effectively direct?	Span of control
5. Where does decision-making authority lie?	Centralization and decentralization
6. To what degree will there be rules and regulations to direct employees and managers?	Formalization

By the late 1940s, most manufacturing jobs in industrialized countries featured high work specialization. Because not all employees in an organization have the same skills, management saw specialization as a means of making the most efficient use of its employees' skills and even successfully improving them through repetition. Less time is spent in changing tasks, putting away tools and equipment from a prior step, and getting ready for another. Equally important, it's easier and less costly to find and train workers to do specific and repetitive tasks, especially in highly sophisticated and complex operations. Could Cessna produce one Citation jet a year if one person had to build the entire plane alone? Not likely! Finally, work specialization increases efficiency and productivity by encouraging the creation of special inventions and machinery.

For much of the first half of the twentieth century, managers thus viewed work specialization as an unending source of increased productivity. And they were probably right. When specialization was not widely practiced, its introduction almost always generated higher productivity. But by the 1960s, it increasingly seemed a good thing can be carried too far. Human diseconomies from specialization began to surface as boredom, fatigue, stress, low productivity, poor quality, increased absenteeism, and high turnover, which more than offset the economic advantages (see Exhibit 15-2). Managers could increase productivity now by enlarging, rather than narrowing, the scope of job activities. Giving employees a variety of activities to do, allowing them to do a whole and complete job, and putting them into teams with interchangeable skills often achieved significantly higher output, with increased employee satisfaction.

Most managers today recognize the economies specialization provides in certain jobs and the problems when it's carried too far. High work specialization helps McDonald's make and sell hamburgers and fries efficiently and aids medical specialists in most health maintenance organizations.

organizational structure   *The way in which job tasks are formally divided, grouped, and coordinated.*

work specialization   *The degree to which tasks in an organization are subdivided into separate jobs.*

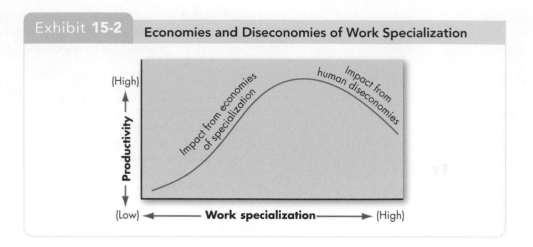

Exhibit 15-2   **Economies and Diseconomies of Work Specialization**

Departmentalization

Once jobs are divided through work specialization, they must be grouped so common tasks can be coordinated. The basis by which jobs are grouped is called **departmentalization**.

One of the most popular ways to group activities is by *functions* performed. A manufacturing manager might organize a plant into engineering, accounting, manufacturing, personnel, and supply specialists departments. A hospital might have departments devoted to research, surgery, intensive care, accounting, and so forth. A professional football franchise might have departments entitled Player Personnel, Ticket Sales, and Travel and Accommodations. The major advantage of this type of functional departmentalization is efficiencies gained from putting like specialists together.

We can also departmentalize jobs by the type of *product* or *service* the organization produces. Procter & Gamble places each major product—such as Tide,

Work is specialized at the Russian factories that manufacture the wooden nesting dolls called matryoshkas. At this factory outside Moscow, individuals specialize in doing part of the doll production, from the craftsmen who carve the dolls to the painters who decorate them. Work specialization brings efficiency to doll production, as some 50 employees can make 100 matryoshkas every two days.

Pampers, Charmin, and Pringles—under an executive who has complete global responsibility for it. The major advantage here is increased accountability for performance, since all activities related to a specific product or service are under the direction of a single manager.

When a firm is departmentalized on the basis of *geography,* or territory, the sales function, for instance, may have western, southern, midwestern, and eastern regions, each, in effect, a department organized around geography. This form is valuable when an organization's customers are scattered over a large geographic area and have similar needs based on their location.

Process departmentalization works for processing customers as well as products. If you've ever been to a state motor vehicle office to get a driver's license, you probably went through several departments before receiving your license. In one typical state, applicants go through three steps, each handled by a separate department: (1) validation by motor vehicles division, (2) processing by the licensing department, and (3) payment collection by the treasury department.

A final category of departmentalization uses the particular type of *customer* the organization seeks to reach. Microsoft, for example, is organized around four customer markets: consumers, large corporations, software developers, and small businesses. Customers in each department have a common set of problems and needs best met by having specialists for each.

Large organizations may use all the forms of departmentalization we've described. A major Japanese electronics firm organizes each of its divisions along functional lines, its manufacturing units around processes, sales around seven geographic regions, and each sales region into four customer groupings. In a strong recent trend among organizations of all sizes, rigid functional departmentalization is increasingly complemented by teams that cross traditional departmental lines. As we described in Chapter 10, as tasks have become more complex and more diverse skills are needed to accomplish them, management has turned to cross-functional teams.

Chain of Command

While the chain of command was once a basic cornerstone in the design of organizations, it has far less importance today.[3] But contemporary managers should still consider its implications. The **chain of command** is an unbroken line of authority that extends from the top of the organization to the lowest echelon and clarifies who reports to whom. It answers questions such as "To whom do I go if I have a problem?" and "To whom am I responsible?"

We can't discuss the chain of command without also discussing *authority* and *unity of command.* **Authority** refers to the rights inherent in a managerial position to give orders and expect them to be obeyed. To facilitate coordination, each managerial position is given a place in the chain of command, and each manager is given a degree of authority in order to meet his or her responsibilities. The principle of **unity of command** helps preserve the concept of an unbroken

departmentalization   *The basis by which jobs in an organization are grouped together.*

chain of command   *The unbroken line of authority that extends from the top of the organization to the lowest echelon and clarifies who reports to whom.*

authority   *The rights inherent in a managerial position to give orders and to expect the orders to be obeyed.*

unity of command   *The idea that a subordinate should have only one superior to whom he or she is directly responsible.*

line of authority. It says a person should have one and only one superior to whom he or she is directly responsible. If the unity of command is broken, an employee might have to cope with conflicting demands or priorities from several superiors.

Times change, and so do the basic tenets of organizational design. A low-level employee today can access information in seconds that was available only to top managers a generation ago. Networked computers allow employees anywhere in an organization to communicate with anyone else without going through formal channels. Operating employees are empowered to make decisions previously reserved for management. Add the popularity of self-managed and cross-functional teams and the creation of new structural designs that include multiple bosses, and you can see why authority and unity of command hold less relevance. Many organizations still find they can be most productive by enforcing the chain of command. There just seem to be fewer of them today.

Span of Control

How many employees can a manager efficiently and effectively direct? This question of **span of control** is important because it largely determines the number of levels and managers an organization has. All things being equal, the wider or larger the span, the more efficient the organization.

Assume two organizations each have about 4,100 operative-level employees. One has a uniform span of four and the other a span of eight. As Exhibit 15-3 illustrates, the wider span will have two fewer levels and approximately 800 fewer managers. If the average manager makes $50,000 a year, the wider span will save $40 million a year in management salaries! Obviously, wider spans are more efficient in terms of cost. However, at some point when supervisors no longer have time to provide the necessary leadership and support, they reduce effectiveness and employee performance suffers.

Narrow or small spans have their advocates. By keeping the span of control to five or six employees, a manager can maintain close control.[4] But narrow spans have three major drawbacks. First, they're expensive because they add levels of management. Second, they make vertical communication in the organization more complex. The added levels of hierarchy slow down decision making

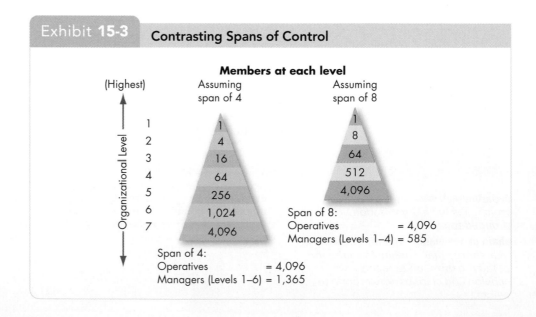

Exhibit 15-3   Contrasting Spans of Control

Members at each level

Organizational level (Highest → arrow)

Assuming span of 4

Level	
1	1
2	4
3	16
4	64
5	256
6	1,024
7	4,096

Span of 4:
Operatives   = 4,096
Managers (Levels 1–6) = 1,365

Assuming span of 8

| 1 |
| 8 |
| 64 |
| 512 |
| 4,096 |

Span of 8:
Operatives   = 4,096
Managers (Levels 1–4) = 585

and tend to isolate upper management. Third, narrow spans encourage overly tight supervision and discourage employee autonomy.

The trend in recent years has been toward wider spans of control.[5] They're consistent with firms' efforts to reduce costs, cut overhead, speed decision making, increase flexibility, get closer to customers, and empower employees. However, to ensure performance doesn't suffer because of these wider spans, organizations have been investing heavily in employee training. Managers recognize they can handle a wider span when employees know their jobs inside and out or can turn to co-workers when they have questions.

Centralization and Decentralization

Centralization refers to the degree to which decision making is concentrated at a single point in the organization. In *centralized* organizations, top managers make all the decisions, and lower-level managers merely carry out their directives. In organizations at the other extreme, *decentralized* decision making is pushed down to the managers closest to the action.

The concept of centralization includes only formal authority—that is, the rights inherent in a position. An organization characterized by centralization is inherently different structurally from one that's decentralized. A decentralized organization can act more quickly to solve problems, more people provide input into decisions, and employees are less likely to feel alienated from those who make decisions that affect their work lives.

Management efforts to make organizations more flexible and responsive have produced a recent trend toward decentralized decision making by lower-level managers, who are closer to the action and typically have more detailed knowledge about problems than top managers. Sears and JCPenney have given their store managers considerably more discretion in choosing what merchandise to stock. This allows those stores to compete more effectively against local merchants.

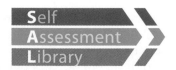

HOW WILLING AM I TO DELEGATE?

In the Self-Assessment Library (available on CD and online), take assessment III.A.2 (How Willing Am I to Delegate?).

Formalization

Formalization refers to the degree to which jobs within the organization are standardized. If a job is highly formalized, the incumbent has a minimum amount of discretion over what, when, and how to do it. Employees can be expected always to handle the same input in exactly the same way, resulting in a consistent and uniform output. There are explicit job descriptions, lots of organizational rules, and clearly defined procedures covering work processes in organizations in which there is high formalization. Where formalization is low, job behaviors are relatively unprogrammed, and employees have a great deal of freedom to exercise discretion in their work. Standardization not only eliminates the

---

span of control   *The number of subordinates a manager can efficiently and effectively direct.*

centralization   *The degree to which decision making is concentrated at a single point in an organization.*

formalization   *The degree to which jobs within an organization are standardized.*

An Ethical Choice

"I Fell into a Big Black Hole"

When Dieter Weidenbrueck sold his business to a much larger company, Parametric Technology, he had trouble adapting to Parametric's organization structure.

It's a familiar situation—not only to entrepreneurs, like Weidenbrueck, but also to employees who once worked for small companies in which structures were loose, latitude was high, the culture informal and close knit. When moving to a company with a larger, more formal structure, employees, like Weidenbrueck, can find the new structure maddeningly bureaucratic. "I fell into a big black hole," said Weidenbrueck.

When Weidenbrueck became frustrated, he turned to Jim Heppelmann, an entrepreneur who had sold his company to Parametric a decade earlier. Heppelmann empathized with Weidenbrueck's frustrations, telling him he too ran into "a fair amount of frustration and complexity." However, Heppelmann also noted that, over time, he saw many opportunities in the size and formality of the new organization's structure.

Here are some suggestions for coping with an organization structure that is not to your liking:

1. Employees often have more control over how their work is structured than they think. If you trust your boss, engage him or her in an honest, open conversation, and suggest some alternative arrangements you think make sense for both you and the organization. Avoid whining, be positive and constructive, and be prepared in case your boss shoots down your ideas. Sometimes things are

as they are for reasons you didn't know or understand.
2. Resist tilting at windmills. Try to proactively and positively change what you can, but avoid attacking a structure you likely cannot change or railing against changes that were made above your pay grade.
3. In the end, if you cannot adapt, then leave, but only after you have quietly explored alternatives. The bureaucratic grass is not always greener on the other side.

Sources: Based on E. White, "Growing Pains: Adapting After a Merger," *Wall Street Journal* (February 26, 2008), p. B6; J. Pourdehnad, "Cutting Through the Red Tape," *Business Week Video Library,* feedroom.businessweek.com/?fr_story= 452e19eb5bbf830baffee6945c3ba01b12fb 4199; and S. Yang, "Bureaucracy versus High Performance: Work Reorganization in the 1990s," *Journal of Socio-Economics* 37, no. 5 (2008), pp. 1825–1845.

possibility of employees engaging in alternative behaviors, but it even removes the need for employees to consider alternatives.

The degree of formalization can vary widely between and within organizations. Certain jobs are well known to have little formalization. Publishing representatives who call on college professors to inform them of their company's new publications have a great deal of freedom in their jobs. They have only a general sales pitch, which they tailor as needed, and rules and procedures governing their behavior may be little more than the requirement to submit a weekly sales report and suggestions on what to emphasize in forthcoming titles. At the other extreme, clerical and editorial employees in the same publishing houses may need to be at their desks by 8:00 A.M. and follow a set of precise procedures dictated by management.

Common Organizational Designs

2 Identify the characteristics of a bureaucracy.

We now turn to three of the more common organizational designs: the *simple structure,* the *bureaucracy,* and the *matrix structure.*

The Simple Structure

What do a small retail store, an electronics firm run by a hard-driving entrepreneur, and an airline's "war room" in the midst of a pilot's strike have in common? They probably all use the **simple structure**.

Exhibit 15-4 A Simple Structure (Jack Gold's Men's Store)

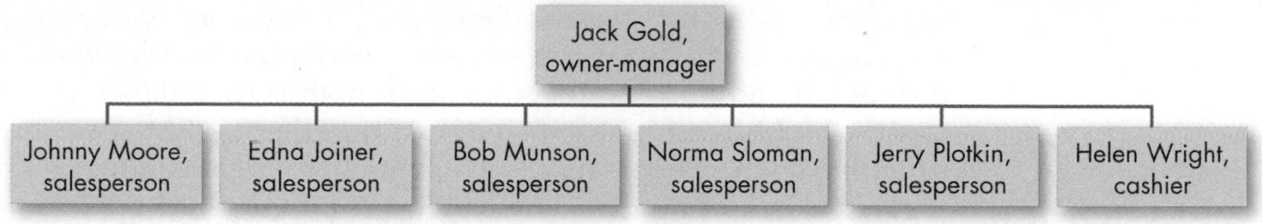
Jack Gold, owner-manager
Johnny Moore, salesperson
Edna Joiner, salesperson
Bob Munson, salesperson
Norma Sloman, salesperson
Jerry Plotkin, salesperson
Helen Wright, cashier

We can think of the simple structure in terms of what it is *not* rather than what it is. The simple structure is not elaborate.[6] It has a low degree of departmentalization, wide spans of control, authority centralized in a single person, and little formalization. It is a "flat" organization; it usually has only two or three vertical levels, a loose body of employees, and one individual in whom the decision-making authority is centralized.

The simple structure is most widely practiced in small businesses in which the manager and owner are one and the same. Exhibit 15-4 is an organization chart for a retail men's store owned and managed by Jack Gold. Although he employs five full-time salespeople, a cashier, and extra personnel for weekends and holidays, Jack "runs the show." Large companies, in times of crisis, often simplify their structures as a means of focusing their resources. When Anne Mulcahy took over Xerox, its product mix and management structure were overly complex. She simplified both, cutting corporate overhead by 26 percent. "It's a case of placing your bets in a few areas" she says[7]

The strength of the simple structure lies in its simplicity. It's fast, flexible, and inexpensive to operate, and accountability is clear. One major weakness is that it's difficult to maintain in anything other than small organizations. It becomes increasingly inadequate as an organization grows because its low formalization and high centralization tend to create information overload at the top. As size increases, decision making typically becomes slower and can eventually come to a standstill as the single executive tries to continue making all the decisions. This proves the undoing of many small businesses. When an organization begins to employ 50 or 100 people, it's very difficult for the owner-manager to make all the choices. If the structure isn't changed and made more elaborate, the firm often loses momentum and can eventually fail. The simple structure's other weakness is that it's risky—everything depends on one person. One illness can literally destroy the organization's information and decision-making center.

The Bureaucracy

Standardization! That's the key concept that underlies all bureaucracies. Consider the bank where you keep your checking account, the department store where you buy clothes, or the government offices that collect your taxes, enforce health regulations, or provide local fire protection. They all rely on standardized work processes for coordination and control.

simple structure *An organization structure characterized by a low degree of departmentalization, wide spans of control, authority centralized in a single person, and little formalization.*

The **bureaucracy** is characterized by highly routine operating tasks achieved through specialization, very formalized rules and regulations, tasks grouped into functional departments, centralized authority, narrow spans of control, and decision making that follows the chain of command. As the opening quote to this chapter attests, *bureaucracy* is a dirty word in many people's minds. However, it does have advantages. Its primary strength is its ability to perform standardized activities in a highly efficient manner. Putting like specialties together in functional departments results in economies of scale, minimum duplication of personnel and equipment, and employees who have the opportunity to talk "the same language" among their peers. Bureaucracies can get by with less talented—and, hence, less costly—middle- and lower-level managers. Rules and regulations substitute for managerial discretion. Standardized operations and high formalization allow decision making to be centralized. There is little need for innovative and experienced decision makers below the level of senior executives.

Listen in on a dialogue among four executives in one company: "You know, nothing happens in this place until we *produce* something," said the production executive. "Wrong," commented the research and development manager. "Nothing happens until we *design* something!" "What are you talking about?" asked the marketing executive. "Nothing happens here until we *sell* something!" The exasperated accounting manager responded, "It doesn't matter what you produce, design, or sell. No one knows what happens until we *tally up the results!*" This conversation highlights that specialization creates subunit conflicts in which functional-unit goals can override the overall goals of the organization.

The other major weakness of a bureaucracy is something we've all witnessed: obsessive concern with following the rules. When cases don't precisely fit the rules, there is no room for modification. The bureaucracy is efficient only as long as employees confront familiar problems with programmed decision rules.

The Matrix Structure

3 Describe a matrix organization.

Another popular organizational design option is the **matrix structure**. You'll find it in advertising agencies, aerospace firms, research and development laboratories, construction companies, hospitals, government

Hospitals benefit from standardized work processes and procedures common to a bureaucratic structure because they help employees perform their jobs efficiently. When faced with financial problems, management at Crouse Hospital in Syracuse, New York, decided that its structure was too bureaucratic and hierarchical. Top managers brought together employees from all levels and areas and asked them to find innovative solutions needed to remake every aspect of the hospital, from creating a new mission statement to designing new work processes. With more employee involvement, Crouse raised its revenues and quality, provided more services to the community, and dramatically improved its relationship with employees, such as the registered nurse shown here.

International OB

Structuring Organizations Across National Borders

Because business, economic, and political conditions facing organizations are constantly shifting, organizations that don't adapt die. Multinational organizations in particular may find their business developing abroad in a way that their current structure doesn't fit.

This situation faced Graham Kill when he decided his company, Irdeto—which develops and markets content-protection software for video and pay TV—could no longer be solely based in its Amsterdam headquarters. Irdeto's sales had been growing fastest in Asia for years and had come to represent 39 percent of Irdeto's $170 million in annual sales. Kill expected that number to be more than 50 percent within five years, so he declared Beijing his company's second headquarters and promptly moved his family there.

Why did Kill make such a radical move? Most of his reasons relate to

the need to connect to employees and customers in markets where the business is happening. European software giant SAP restructured itself, decentralizing operations away from its Walldorf, Germany, headquarters and pushing them out to seven locations around the world, including the United States and India. U.S.-based Tyson Foods also decentralized its structure, giving more autonomy to managers overseeing operations in important developing markets like China.

Such decentralizing efforts are not without their challenges, such as communication. Irdeto found it needed to make a major investment in videoconferencing, and it changed its career management systems so most executives rotate between the Amsterdam and Beijing headquarters. Kill found the OB needs of employees in each location were quite different. Amsterdam employees needed reassurance their jobs

were safe, along with training in how and when to use videoconferencing to keep in touch with Beijing employees (7 hours ahead of Amsterdam). Kill started a training program for Beijing employees during which they learned to make and implement decisions more autonomously than is their custom. Patricia van der Velden, Irdeto's VP of Human Resources, said most employees have embraced Irdeto's dual structure. "We have noticed that employees are motivated by the global career opportunities provided by Irdeto."

Sources: Based on P. Dvorak, "How Irdeto Split Headquarters," *Wall Street Journal* (January 7, 2008), p. B3; L. Cheong, "Q&A: Patricia van der Velden/Irdeto," *Human Resources Online* (September 1, 2008), www.humanresourcesonline.net; and C. Hymowitz, "Executives in China Need Both Autonomy and Fast Access to Boss," *Wall Street Journal* (May 10, 2005), p. B1.

agencies, universities, management consulting firms, and entertainment companies.[8] It combines two forms of departmentalization: functional and product.

The strength of functional departmentalization is putting like specialists together, which minimizes the number necessary while allowing the pooling and sharing of specialized resources across products. Its major disadvantage is the difficulty of coordinating the tasks of diverse functional specialists on time and within budget. Product departmentalization has exactly the opposite benefits and disadvantages. It facilitates coordination among specialties to achieve on-time completion and meet budget targets. It provides clear responsibility for all activities related to a product but with duplication of activities and costs. The matrix attempts to gain the strengths of each, while avoiding their weaknesses.

bureaucracy *An organization structure with highly routine operating tasks achieved through specialization, very formalized rules and regulations, tasks that are grouped into functional departments, centralized authority, narrow spans of control, and decision making that follows the chain of command.*

matrix structure *An organization structure that creates dual lines of authority and combines functional and product departmentalization.*

The most obvious structural characteristic of the matrix is that it breaks the unity-of-command concept. Employees in the matrix have two bosses: their functional department managers and their product managers.

Exhibit 15-5 shows the matrix form in a college of business administration. The academic departments of accounting, decision and information systems, marketing, and so forth are functional units. Overlaid on them are specific programs (that is, products). Thus, members in a matrix structure have a dual chain of command: to their functional department and to their product groups. A professor of accounting teaching an undergraduate course may report to the director of undergraduate programs as well as to the chairperson of the accounting department.

The strength of the matrix is its ability to facilitate coordination when the organization has a number of complex and interdependent activities. Direct and frequent contacts between different specialties in the matrix can let information permeate the organization and more quickly reach the people who need it. The matrix reduces "bureaupathologies"—the dual lines of authority reduce people's tendency to become so busy protecting their little worlds that the organization's goals become secondary. A matrix also achieves economics of scale and facilitates the allocation of specialists by providing both the best resources and an effective way of ensuring their efficient deployment.

The major disadvantages of the matrix lie in the confusion it creates, its propensity to foster power struggles, and the stress it places on individuals.[9] Without the unity-of-command concept, ambiguity about who reports to whom is significantly increased and often leads to conflict. It's not unusual for product managers to fight over getting the best specialists assigned to their products. Bureaucracy reduces the potential for power grabs by defining the rules of the game. When those rules are "up for grabs" in a matrix, power struggles between functional and product managers result. For individuals who desire security and absence from ambiguity, this work climate can be stressful. Reporting to more than one boss introduces role conflict, and unclear expectations introduce role ambiguity. The comfort of bureaucracy's predictability is replaced by insecurity and stress.

Exhibit 15-5   **Matrix Structure for a College of Business Administration**

Programs / Academic Departments	Undergraduate	Master's	Ph.D.	Research	Executive Development	Community Service
Accounting						
Finance						
Decision and Information Systems						
Management						
Marketing						

New Design Options

Senior managers in a number of organizations have been working to develop new structural options that can better help their firms to compete effectively. Many result in fewer layers of hierarchy and more emphasis on opening the boundaries of the organization.[10] In this section, we describe two such structural designs: the *virtual organization* and the *boundaryless organization*. We'll also discuss how efforts to reduce bureaucracy and increase strategic focus have made downsizing routine.

The Virtual Organization

4 Identify the characteristics of a virtual organization.

Why own when you can rent? That question captures the essence of the **virtual organization** (also sometimes called the *network,* or *modular,* organization), typically a small, core organization that outsources major business functions.[11] In structural terms, the virtual organization is highly centralized, with little or no departmentalization.

The prototype of the virtual structure is today's movie-making organization. In Hollywood's golden era, movies were made by huge, vertically integrated corporations. Studios such as MGM, Warner Brothers, and 20th Century Fox owned large movie lots and employed thousands of full-time specialists—set designers, camera people, film editors, directors, and even actors. Today, most movies are made by a collection of individuals and small companies who come together and make films project by project.[12] This structural form allows each project to be staffed with the talent best suited to its demands, rather than just the people employed by the studio. It minimizes bureaucratic overhead because

The Boeing Company outsourced the production of about 70 percent of the components for its new 787 Dreamliner passenger jet aircraft. For example, Alenia Aeronautica of Italy produced the plane's rear fuselage and horizontal stabilizer, and Mitsubishi Motors of Japan created the wings. Although global outsourcing helped Boeing reduce the plane's development and production costs, the extreme complexities of such a structure was also responsible for delay after delay in bringing the cutting-edge aircraft to market. Pictured here is the 787 Dreamliner assembly line surrounded by rows of workers at their computers as the planes are built at Boeing's 42-acre factory in Everett, Washington.

virtual organization *A small, core organization that outsources major business functions.*

there is no lasting organization to maintain. And it lessens long-term risks and their costs because there is no long term—a team is assembled for a finite period and then disbanded.

Ancle Hsu and David Ji run a virtual organization. Their firm, California-based Apex Digital, is one of the world's largest producers of DVD players, yet the company neither owns a factory nor employs an engineer. It contracts out everything to firms in China. With minimal investment, Apex has grown from nothing to annual sales of over $500 million in just 3 years. Similarly, Newman's Own, the food products company founded by Paul Newman, sells over $120 million in food every year yet employs only 19 people. This is possible because it outsources almost everything: manufacturing, procurement, shipping, and quality control.

What's going on here? A quest for maximum flexibility. These virtual organizations have created networks of relationships that allow them to contract out manufacturing, distribution, marketing, or any other business function management feels others can do better or more cheaply. The virtual organization stands in sharp contrast to the typical bureaucracy and concentrates on what it does best. For most U.S. firms, that means design or marketing.

Exhibit 15-6 shows a virtual organization in which management outsources all the primary functions of the business. The core of the organization is a small group of executives whose job is to oversee directly any activities done in house and to coordinate relationships with the other organizations that manufacture, distribute, and perform other crucial functions for the virtual organization. The dotted lines represent the relationships typically maintained under contracts. In essence, managers in virtual structures spend most of their time coordinating and controlling external relations, typically by way of computer-network links.

The major advantage of the virtual organization is its flexibility, which allows individuals with an innovative idea and little money, such as Ancle Hsu and David Ji, to successfully compete against the likes of Sony, Hitachi, and Sharp Electronics.

Virtual organizations' drawbacks have become increasingly clear as their popularity has grown. [13] They are in a state of perpetual flux and reorganization, which means roles, goals, and responsibilities are unclear: This sets the stage for political behavior. Those who work frequently with virtual organizations also note cultural alignment and shared goals can be lost because of the low degree of interaction among members. Team members who are geographically dis-

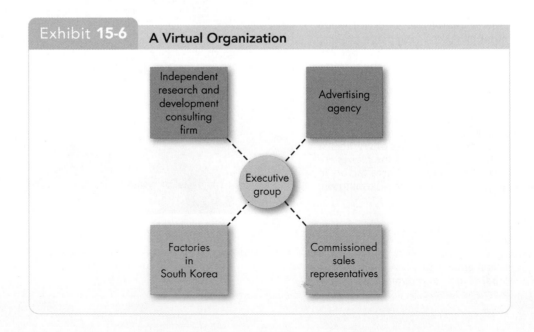

Exhibit 15-6   A Virtual Organization

Independent research and development consulting firm

Advertising agency

Executive group

Factories in South Korea

Commissioned sales representatives

persed and communicate only intermittently find it difficult to share information and knowledge, which can limit innovation and slow response time. Ironically, some virtual organizations are less adaptable and innovative than those with well-established communication and collaboration networks. A leadership presence that reinforces the organization's purpose and facilitates communication is thus especially valuable.

The Boundaryless Organization

5 Show why managers want to create boundaryless organizations.

General Electric's former chairman, Jack Welch, coined the term **boundaryless organization** to describe what he wanted GE to become: a "family grocery store."[14] That is, in spite of GE's monstrous size (2008 revenues were $177 billion), Welch wanted to eliminate *vertical* and *horizontal* boundaries within it and break down *external* barriers between the company and its customers and suppliers. The boundaryless organization seeks to eliminate the chain of command, have limitless spans of control, and replace departments with empowered teams. Although GE has not yet achieved this boundaryless state—and probably never will—it has made significant progress toward that end. So have other companies, such as Hewlett-Packard, AT&T, Motorola, and 3M. Let's see what a boundaryless organization looks like and what some firms are doing to make it a reality.[15]

By removing vertical boundaries, management flattens the hierarchy and minimizes status and rank. Cross-hierarchical teams (which include top executives, middle managers, supervisors, and operative employees), participative decision-making practices, and the use of 360-degree performance appraisals (in which peers and others above and below the employee evaluate performance) are examples of what GE is doing to break down vertical boundaries. At Oticon A/S, a $160-million-per-year Danish hearing aid manufacturer, all traces of hierarchy have disappeared. Everyone works at uniform mobile workstations, and project teams, not functions or departments, coordinate work.

Functional departments create horizontal boundaries that stifle interaction among functions, product lines, and units. The way to reduce them is to replace functional departments with cross-functional teams and organize activities around processes. Xerox now develops new products through multidisciplinary teams that work in a single process instead of around narrow functional tasks. Some AT&T units are now doing annual budgets based not on functions or departments but on processes, such as the maintenance of a worldwide telecommunications network. Another way management can cut through horizontal barriers is to use lateral transfers, rotating people into and out of different functional areas. This approach turns specialists into generalists.

The Leaner Organization: Organization Downsizing

The goal of the new organizational forms we've described is to improve agility by creating a lean, focused, and flexible organization. Companies may need to cut divisions that aren't adding value. Downsizing is a systematic effort to make an organization leaner by selling off business units, closing locations, or reducing staff. It has been very controversial because of its potential negative impacts on employees.

boundaryless organization *An organization that seeks to eliminate the chain of command, have limitless spans of control, and replace departments with empowered teams.*

BMW Group operates as a boundaryless organization in designing, developing, and producing its BMW, Rolls-Royce, and Mini cars. The automaker uses virtual tools such as computer-aided design and simulation models and a flexible production network of 14 plants in 12 countries to respond quickly to fluctuations in the market and individual customer preferences. BMW's boundaryless structure drives innovative ideas by eliminating vertical and horizontal barriers among workers and creating an environment of learning and experimentation. From their first day on the job, employees are encouraged to build a network of relationships from all functional areas and across all divisions to speed innovation and problem-solving.

The radical shrinking of Chrysler and General Motors in recent years was a case of downsizing due to loss of market share and changes in consumer demand. These companies probably needed to downsize just to survive. Others downsize to direct all their efforts toward their core competencies. After a series of costly acquisitions, VeriSign decided to divest itself of most of its business units and return to its original strategic focus on e-commerce security and online identity protection.[16] Some companies focus on lean management techniques to reduce bureaucracy and speed decision making. Park Nicollet Health Services in Minneapolis eliminated fixed budgets and pushed managers to reduce costs as part of a transformation to lean production; it was able to save at least $15 million per year[17] and adapt to changes in the healthcare market much more quickly.

Despite the advantages of being a lean organization, the impact of downsizing on organizational performance has been very controversial.[18] Reducing the size of the workforce has an immediately positive outcome in the huge reduction in wage costs. Companies downsizing to improve strategic focus often see positive effects on stock prices after the announcement. On the other hand, among companies that only cut employees but don't restructure, profits and stock prices usually decline. Part of the problem is the effect of downsizing on employee attitudes. Those who remain often feel worried about future layoffs and may be less committed to the organization.[19] Stress reactions can lead to increased sickness absences, lower concentration on the job, and lower creativity. In companies that don't invest much in their employees, downsizing can also lead to more voluntary turnover so vital human capital is lost. The result is a company that is more anemic than lean.

Companies can reduce negative impacts by preparing for the post-downsizing environment in advance, thus alleviating some employee stress and strengthening support for the new strategic direction.[20] The following are some effective strategies for downsizing and suggestions for implementing them. Most are closely linked to the principles for organizational justice we've discussed previously:

- *Investment.* Companies that downsize to focus on core competencies are more effective when they invest in high-involvement work practices afterward.

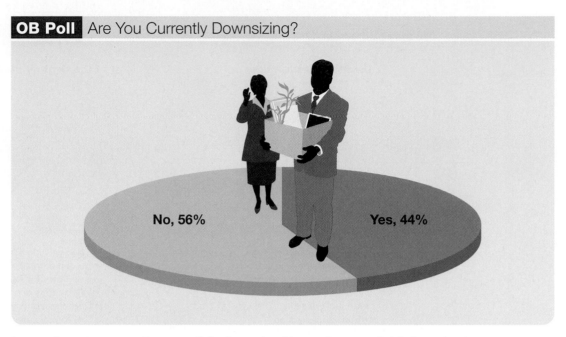

OB Poll Are You Currently Downsizing?

No, 56%

Yes, 44%

Source: Based on *Are You Downsizing?* (an ongoing poll of employer-members of the National Association of Wholesalers-Distributors), www.smartbrief.com/news/NAW/poll_result.jsp?pollName=NAW11192001Layoffs&issueid=73F877E5-E1BE-4301-9B75-9CC69D71A84A.

- *Communication.* When employers make efforts to discuss downsizing with employees early, employees are less worried about the outcomes and feel the company is taking their perspective into account.
- *Participation.* Employees worry less if they can participate in the process in some way. In some companies, voluntary early retirement programs or severance packages can help achieve leanness without layoffs.
- *Assistance.* Providing severance, extended health care benefits, and job search assistance demonstrates a company does really care about its employees and honors their contributions.

Companies that make themselves lean can be more agile, efficient, and productive—but only if they make cuts carefully and help employees through the process.

Why Do Structures Differ?

6 Demonstrate how organizational structures differ, and contrast mechanistic and organic structural models.

We've described organizational designs ranging from the highly structured bureaucracy to the amorphous boundaryless organization. The other designs we discussed exist somewhere between these extremes.

Exhibit 15-7 recaps our discussions by presenting two extreme models of organizational design. One we'll call the **mechanistic model**. It's

mechanistic model *A structure characterized by extensive departmentalization, high formalization, a limited information network, and centralization.*

Exhibit **15-7**   Mechanistic versus Organic Models

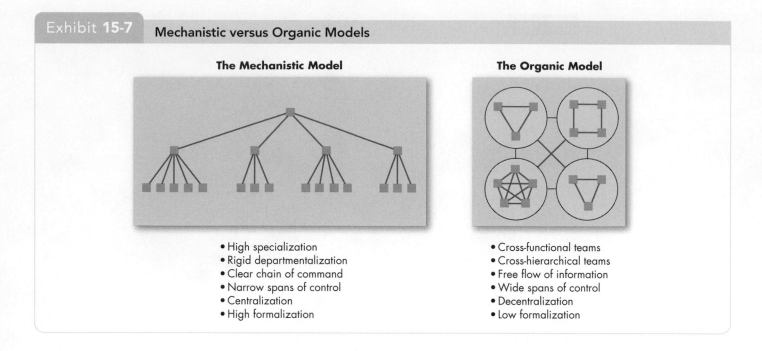

The Mechanistic Model

- High specialization
- Rigid departmentalization
- Clear chain of command
- Narrow spans of control
- Centralization
- High formalization

The Organic Model

- Cross-functional teams
- Cross-hierarchical teams
- Free flow of information
- Wide spans of control
- Decentralization
- Low formalization

generally synonymous with the bureaucracy in that it has highly standardized processes for work, high formalization, and more managerial hierarchy. The other extreme, the **organic model**, looks a lot like the boundaryless organization. It's flat, has fewer formal procedures for making decisions, has multiple decision makers, and favors flexible practices.[21]

With these two models in mind, let's ask a few questions: Why are some organizations structured along more mechanistic lines whereas others follow organic characteristics? What forces influence the choice of design? In this section we present the major causes or determinants of an organization's structure.[22]

Strategy

Because structure is a means to achieve objectives, and objectives derive from the organization's overall strategy, it's only logical that strategy and structure should be closely linked. In fact, structure should follow strategy. If management significantly changes the organization's strategy, the structure must change to accommodate.[23]

Most current strategy frameworks focus on three strategy dimensions—innovation, cost minimization, and imitation—and the structural design that works best with each.[24]

To what degree does an organization introduce major new products or services? An **innovation strategy** strives to achieve meaningful and unique innovations. Obviously, not all firms pursue innovation. Apple and 3M do, but conservative retailer Marks & Spencer doesn't. Innovative firms will use competitive pay and benefits to attract top candidates and motivate employees to take risks. Some degree of mechanistic structure can actually benefit innovation. Well-developed communication channels, policies for enhancing long-term commitment, and clear channels of authority all may make it easier to make rapid changes smoothly.

An organization pursuing a **cost-minimization strategy** tightly controls costs, refrains from incurring unnecessary expenses, and cuts prices in selling a basic product. This describes the strategy pursued by Walmart and the makers of

Exhibit 15-8	The Strategy–Structure Relationship

Strategy	Structural Option
Innovation	**Organic:** A loose structure; low specialization, low formalization, decentralized
Cost minimization	**Mechanistic:** Tight control; extensive work specialization, high formalization, high centralization
Imitation	**Mechanistic and organic:** Mix of loose with tight properties; tight controls over current activities and looser controls for new undertakings

generic or store-label grocery products. Cost-minimizing organizations pursue fewer policies meant to develop commitment among their workforce.

Organizations following an **imitation strategy** try to both minimize risk and maximize opportunity for profit, moving new products or new markets only after innovators have proven their viability. Mass-market fashion manufacturers that copy designer styles follow this strategy, as do firms such as Hewlett-Packard and Caterpillar. They follow smaller and more innovative competitors with superior products, but only after competitors have demonstrated the market is there.

Exhibit 15-8 describes the structural option that best matches each strategy. Innovators need the flexibility of the organic structure, whereas cost minimizers seek the efficiency and stability of the mechanistic structure. Imitators combine the two structures. They use a mechanistic structure to maintain tight controls and low costs in their current activities but create organic subunits in which to pursue new undertakings.

Organization Size

An organization's size significantly affects its structure.[25] Organizations that employ 2,000 or more people tend to have more specialization, more departmentalization, more vertical levels, and more rules and regulations than do small organizations. However, size becomes less important as an organization expands. Why? At around 2,000 employees, an organization is already fairly mechanistic; 500 more employees won't have much impact. But adding 500 employees to an organization of only 300 is likely to significantly shift it toward a more mechanistic structure.

Technology

Technology describes the way an organization transfers inputs into outputs. Every organization has at least one technology for converting financial, human, and physical resources into products or services. Ford Motor Company uses an assembly-line process to make its products. Colleges may use a number of instructional technologies—the ever-popular lecture method, the case-analysis

---

organic model *A structure that is flat, uses cross-hierarchical and cross-functional teams, has low formalization, possesses a comprehensive information network, and relies on participative decision making.*

innovation strategy *A strategy that emphasizes the introduction of major new products and services.*

cost-minimization strategy *A strategy that emphasizes tight cost controls, avoidance of unnecessary innovation or marketing expenses, and price cutting.*

imitation strategy *A strategy that seeks to move into new products or new markets only after their viability has already been proven.*

technology *The way in which an organization transfers its inputs into outputs.*

The degree of routineness differentiates technologies. At Wallstrip.com, nonroutineness characterizes the customized work of employees who create an entertaining daily Web video show and accompanying blog about the stock market. The show relies heavily on the knowledge of specialists such as host Lindsay Campbell and writer/producer Adam Elend, who are shown here in the production studio where they're getting ready to film an episode of their show.

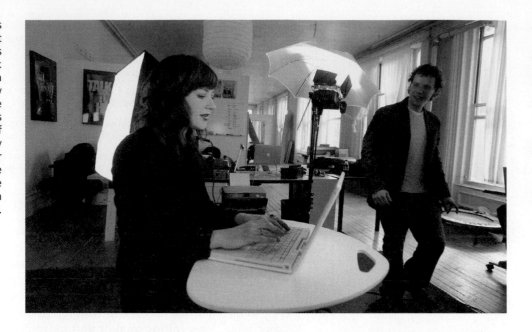

method, the experiential exercise method, the programmed learning method. Regardless, organizational structures adapt to their technology.

Numerous studies have examined the technology–structure relationship.[26] The common theme that differentiates technologies is their *degree of routineness*. Routine activities are characterized by automated and standardized operations. Nonroutine activities are customized. Examples of routine activities are injection-mold production of plastic knobs, automated transaction processing of sales transactions, and printing and binding of this book. Nonroutine activities are customized. They include varied operations such as furniture restoring, custom shoemaking, and genetic research. Nonroutine activities are customized and require frequent revision and updating. Examples of nonroutine activities are furniture restoring, genetic research, and the writing and editing of this book.

Environment

An organization's **environment** includes outside institutions or forces that can affect its performance, such as suppliers, customers, competitors, government regulatory agencies, and public pressure groups. And an organization's structure can be affected by environmental uncertainty. Static environments create significantly less uncertainty for managers than do dynamic ones. And because uncertainty is a threat to an organization's effectiveness, management will try to minimize it through adjustments in the organization's structure. They may, for example, broaden their structure to sense and respond to threats. Most companies, including Pepsi and Southwest Airlines, have added social networking departments to their structure so as to respond to negative information posted on blogs. Or companies may form strategic alliances with other companies, such as when Microsoft and Yahoo joined forces to better compete with Google.[27]

Any organization's environment has three dimensions: capacity, volatility, and complexity.[28] *Capacity* refers to the degree to which the environment can support growth. Rich and growing environments generate excess resources, which can buffer the organization in times of relative scarcity.

Volatility describes the degree of instability in the environment. A dynamic environment with a high degree of unpredictable change makes it difficult for management to make accurate predictions. Because information technology changes at such a rapid place, for instance, more organizations' environments are becoming volatile.

Myth or Science?

"People Are Our Most Important Asset"

Though it's said so often it may generate a cynical reaction, there is evidence that for most companies, people are their most important asset. The knowledge-based view of the firm proposes that companies can create value only when they have the information and know-how to put their intellectual assets to use effectively.

When we separate the U.S. economy into hard or tangible sectors (manufacturing, real estate) and soft or intangible sectors (medical care, communications, education), soft industries provide 79 percent of all jobs and 76 percent of GDP, suggesting so-called knowledge workers are increas-

ingly important to the economy. Yet many organizational structures tend to be based on physical rather than intellectual resources.

U.S. auto manufacturers focus their structure on physical assets—product lines or component systems—and outsource some parts making or assembly. Japanese auto manufacturers such as Toyota or Honda, conversely, focus on developing the intellectual products in house (design and engineering) and outsource some or most manufacturing and assembly to the countries where they sell their products. It has been argued that these structural differences account for the intangible design and engineering advantages Japanese automakers enjoy.

The authors of a recent study note, "While managing professional intellect is clearly the key to value creation and profitability for most companies, few have arrived at systematic structures for developing, focusing, leveraging, and measuring their intellectual capabilities." Database management software may help link employee needs for information with the best internal sources to help develop intellectual resources, but organizations have struggled to make the best use of these tools.

So, even if most organizations argue people are their most important asset, they aren't structured to make maximum use of it.[29]

Finally, *complexity* is the degree of heterogeneity and concentration among environmental elements. Simple environments—like in the tobacco industry—are homogeneous and concentrated. Environments characterized by heterogeneity and dispersion—like the broadband industry—arc complex and diverse, with numerous competitors.

Exhibit 15-9 summarizes our definition of the environment along its three dimensions. The arrows indicate movement toward higher uncertainty. So

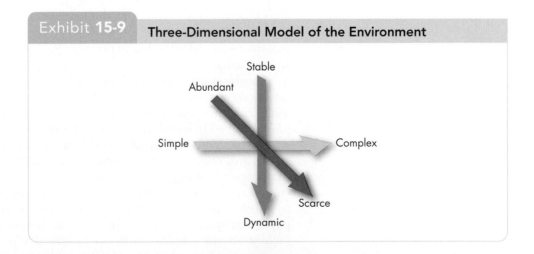

Exhibit **15-9**   Three-Dimensional Model of the Environment

environment *Institutions or forces outside an organization that potentially affect the organization's performance.*

organizations that operate in environments characterized as scarce, dynamic, and complex face the greatest degree of uncertainty because they have high unpredictability, little room for error, and a diverse set of elements in the environment to monitor constantly.

Given this three-dimensional definition of *environment,* we can offer some general conclusions about environmental uncertainty and structural arrangements. The more scarce, dynamic, and complex the environment, the more organic a structure should be. The more abundant, stable, and simple the environment, the more the mechanistic structure will be preferred.

Organizational Designs and Employee Behavior

7   Analyze the behavioral implications of different organizational designs.

We opened this chapter by implying that an organization's structure can have significant effects on its members. What might those effects be?

A review of the evidence leads to a pretty clear conclusion: You can't generalize! Not everyone prefers the freedom and flexibility of organic structures. Different factors stand out in different structures as well. In highly formalized, heavily structured, mechanistic organizations, the level of fairness in formal policies and procedures is a very important predictor of satisfaction. In more personal, individually adaptive organic organizations, employees value interpersonal justice more.[30] Some people are most productive and satisfied when work tasks are standardized and ambiguity minimized—that is, in mechanistic structures. So any discussion of the effect of organizational design on employee behavior has to address individual differences. To do so, let's consider employee preferences for work specialization, span of control, and centralization.[31]

The evidence generally indicates that *work specialization* contributes to higher employee productivity—but at the price of reduced job satisfaction. However, work specialization is not an unending source of higher productivity. Problems start to surface, and productivity begins to suffer, when the human diseconomies of doing repetitive and narrow tasks overtake the economies of specialization. As the workforce has become more highly educated and desirous of jobs that are intrinsically rewarding, we seem to reach the point at which productivity begins to decline more quickly than in the past.

There is still a segment of the workforce that prefers the routine and repetitiveness of highly specialized jobs. Some individuals want work that makes minimal intellectual demands and provides the security of routine; for them, high work specialization is a source of job satisfaction. The question, of course, is whether they represent 2 percent of the workforce or 52 percent. Given that some self-selection operates in the choice of careers, we might conclude that negative behavioral outcomes from high specialization are most likely to surface in professional jobs occupied by individuals with high needs for personal growth and diversity.

It is probably safe to say no evidence supports a relationship between *span of control* and employee performance. Although it is intuitively attractive to argue that large spans might lead to higher employee performance because they provide more distant supervision and more opportunity for personal initiative, the research fails to support this notion. At this point it's impossible to state that any particular span of control is best for producing high performance or high satisfaction among employees. Some people like to be left alone; others prefer the security of a boss who is quickly available at all times. Consistent with several of the contingency theories of leadership discussed in Chapter 12, we would expect factors such as employees' experiences and abilities and the degree of structure in their tasks to explain when wide or narrow spans of control are likely to contribute to their performance and job satisfaction. However, some evidence indicates that a *manager's* job satisfaction increases as the number of employees supervised increases.

We find fairly strong evidence linking *centralization* and job satisfaction. In general, organizations that are less centralized have a greater amount of autonomy. And autonomy appears positively related to job satisfaction. But, again, individual differences surface. While one employee may value freedom, another may find autonomous environments frustratingly ambiguous.

Our conclusion: To maximize employee performance and satisfaction, managers must take individual differences, such as experience, personality, and the work task, into account. Culture should factor in, too.

We can draw one obvious insight: People don't select employers randomly. They are attracted to, are selected by, and stay with organizations that suit their personal characteristics.[32] Job candidates who prefer predictability are likely to seek out and take employment in mechanistic structures, and those who want autonomy are more likely to end up in an organic structure. So the effect of structure on employee behavior is undoubtedly reduced when the selection process facilitates proper matching of individual characteristics with organizational characteristics.

Global Implications

8 Show how globalization affects organizational structure.

When we think about how culture influences how organizations are to be structured, several questions come to mind. First, does culture really matter to organizational structure? Second, do employees in different countries vary in their perceptions of different types of organizational structures? Finally, how do cultural considerations fit with our discussion of the boundaryless organization? Let's tackle each question in turn.

Culture and Organizational Structure   Does culture really affect organizational structure? The answer might seem obvious—yes!—but there are reasons it may not matter as much as you think. The U.S. model of business has been very influential on organizational structures in other countries. Moreover, U.S. structures themselves have been influenced by structures in other countries (especially Japan, Great Britain, and Germany). However, cultural concerns still might be important. Bureaucratic structures still dominate in many parts of Europe and Asia. One management expert argues that U.S. management often places too much emphasis on individual leadership, which may be jarring in countries where decision making is more decentralized.[33]

Culture and Employee Structure Preferences   Although research is slim, it does suggest national culture influences the preference for structure.[34] Organizations that operate with people from high power-distance cultures, such as Greece, France, and most of Latin America, find that their employees are much more accepting of mechanistic structures than are employees from low power-distance countries. So consider cultural differences along with individual differences when predicting how structure will affect employee performance and satisfaction.

Culture and the Boundaryless Organization   When fully operational, the boundaryless organization also breaks down barriers created by geography.

These employees stand in formation to attend a meeting before they start their jobs at a restaurant in Urumqi, China. It's a common practice in China for employers to gather employees before they begin work to give them a pep talk and instructions for their work day. This daily ritual is acceptable to Chinese employees because power distance is high in China and workers are much more accepting of mechanistic structures than those from lower power-distance cultures. Research suggests that a nation's culture and its employees' preference for structure will influence worker performance and satisfaction.

Today most large U.S. companies see themselves as global corporations and may well do as much business overseas as in the United States (as does Coca-Cola, for example). As a result, many companies struggle with the problem of how to incorporate geographic regions into their structure. The boundaryless organization provides one solution because it considers geography more of a tactical, logistical issue than a structural one. In short, the goal of the boundaryless organization is to break down cultural barriers.

One way to do so is through strategic alliances. Firms such as NEC Corporation, Boeing, and Apple each have strategic alliances or joint partnerships with dozens of companies. These alliances blur the distinction between one organization and another as employees work on joint projects. And some companies allow customers to perform functions previously done by management. Some AT&T units receive bonuses based on customer evaluations of the teams that serve them. Finally, telecommuting is blurring organizational boundaries. The security analyst with Merrill Lynch who does his job from his ranch in Montana or the software designer in Boulder, Colorado, who works for a San Francisco firm are just two of the millions of workers doing their jobs outside the physical boundaries of their employers' premises.

Summary and Implications for Managers

The theme of this chapter is that an organization's internal structure contributes to explaining and predicting behavior. That is, in addition to individual and group factors, the structural relationships in which people work has a bearing on employee attitudes and behavior.

What's the basis for this argument? To the degree that an organization's structure reduces ambiguity for employees and clarifies concerns such as "What am I supposed to do?" "How am I supposed to do it?" "To whom do I report?" and "To whom do I go if I have a problem?" it shapes their attitudes and facilitates and motivates them to higher levels of performance.

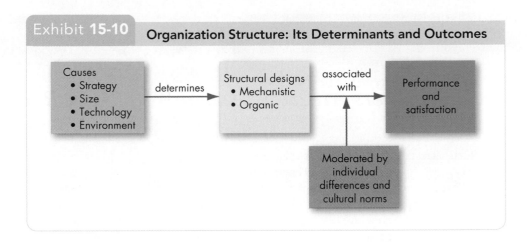

Exhibit 15-10   **Organization Structure: Its Determinants and Outcomes**

Of course, structure also constrains employees to the extent that it limits and controls what they do. Organizations structured around high levels of formalization and specialization, strict adherence to the chain of command, limited delegation of authority, and narrow spans of control give employees little autonomy. Controls in such organizations are tight, and behavior tends to vary within a narrow range. Structures with limited specialization, low formalization, and wide spans of control provide employees greater freedom and thus are characterized by greater behavioral diversity.

Exhibit 15-10 summarizes what we've discussed. Strategy, size, technology, and environment determine the type of structure an organization will have. For simplicity's sake, we can classify structural designs as either mechanistic or organic. The specific effect of structural designs on performance and satisfaction is moderated by employees' individual preferences and cultural norms.

Finally, technology makes some organizational structures increasingly amorphous. This allows a manager the flexibility to take employee preferences, experience, and culture into account and design work systems that truly motivate.

Mergers Are an Excellent Way to Get Rid of Employees

Firms often undertake mergers to eliminate the competition (by acquiring it) or to harvest another organization's assets. While we might argue over the social costs and benefits of these motives, an even darker agenda lies implicit in most mergers: to reduce headcount, a nice way of saying "fire employees."

When mergers or acquisitions take place, almost without exception employees lose their jobs. And those who aren't fired often find their jobs redefined, their responsibilities expanded, and their career prospects thwarted.

Ask Scot Theuer, age 52, a pilot with US Airways for 22 years. "My career advancement has been delayed because of mergers," he says. He's not alone. When Pfizer announced its intention to acquire fellow pharmaceutical company Wyeth, it said it would eliminate 20,000 jobs from the combined company within 3 years. The reality is often far worse than companies acknowledge when mergers are up for regulatory approval. When telecommunications giant Alltel announced it was acquiring a local Nebraska phone company, it claimed there would be few cuts. Of 900 employees before the takeover, 200 are left.

Even US Airways CEO Doug Parker, after experiencing the pain and conflict of merging his firm with America West Airlines, concedes, "Just putting two airlines together doesn't automatically create value."[35]

The business environment is dynamic: Change is the only constant. Markets emerge and die, competitors arise, and unexpected opportunities and threats present themselves. Mergers and acquisitions are one way for businesses to adapt to change and remain both nimble and competitive. That's why nearly all major U.S. companies that were around in the 1970s have merged with other companies—in the United States and abroad.

It's true some job cuts often follow mergers and acquisitions. However, these cuts are often an attempt to restore competitiveness. Competition is fierce, companies are in a constant struggle for survival, and failing to exploit opportunities often proves fatal. A company that fails to merge with other companies faces extinction, which means the loss of *all* its jobs. Downsizing is surely better for employees overall than extinction.

Many successful, if underreported, mergers have benefited employees. When German pharmaceutical Merck KGaA acquired Swiss Serono, many employee groups worried about job losses, reduced pay, and stunted career prospects. The new company—Merck Serono International—committed itself to addressing these concerns. In the words of VP Geoffrey Matthews, the company sought "to take advantage of ways the companies were complimentary, rather than focus on cost reduction." Managers brought employees into decision making about restructuring the company and made sure both companies had equal representation. A Citigroup research analyst said of the merger, "The value of the company improved considerably, and since then it's been throwing off more synergies."

So, to criticize mergers as inherently bad for a few employees is like claiming poor execution makes poor practice.[36]

Questions for Review

1 What are the six key elements that define an organization's structure?

2 What is a bureaucracy, and how does it differ from a simple structure?

3 What is a matrix organization?

4 What are the characteristics of a virtual organization?

5 How can managers create a boundaryless organization?

6 Why do organizational structures differ, and what is the difference between a mechanistic structure and an organic structure?

7 What are the behavioral implications of different organizational designs?

8 How does globalization affect organizational structure?

Experiential Exercise

AUTHORITY FIGURES

Purpose
To learn about one's experiences with and feelings about authority.

Time
Approximately 75 minutes.

Procedure

1. Your instructor will separate class members into groups based on their birth order. Groups are formed consisting of "only children," "eldest," "middle," and "youngest," according to placement in families. Larger groups will be broken into smaller ones, with four or five members, to allow for freer conversation.

2. Each group member should talk about how he or she "typically reacts to the authority of others." Focus should be on specific situations that offer general information about how individuals deal with authority figures (for example, bosses, teachers, parents, or coaches). The group has 25 minutes to develop a written list of how the group generally deals with others' authority. Be sure to separate tendencies that group members share and those they do not.

3. Repeat step 2, except this time discuss how group members "typically are as authority figures." Again make a list of shared characteristics.

4. Each group will share its general conclusions with the entire class.

5. Class discussion will focus on questions such as these:

   a. What patterned differences have surfaced between the groups?

   b. What may account for these differences?

   c. What hypotheses might explain the connection between how individuals react to the authority of others and how they are as authority figures?

Source: This exercise is adapted from W. A. Kahn, "An Exercise of Authority," *Organizational Behavior Teaching Review* 14, no. 2 (1989–1990), pp. 28–42. Reprinted with permission.

Ethical Dilemma

HOW MUCH SHOULD DIRECTORS DIRECT?

One critical structural element of most corporations of any size is the board of directors. And formally at least, chief executives report to the directors. Informally, however, many boards defer to the CEO and *advise* more than *direct*.

Many have placed the blame for the financial meltdown of 2008–2009 on lax boards. Business media have called boards "absolutely useless" and "a sham." A Citibank in-

vestor argued for replacing the bank's board of directors, saying the board "failed to protect shareholders from excessive exposure to credit, market, liquidity, and operational risk." Securities and Exchange Commission Chairman Mary Schapiro launched an investigation into whether boards exercised sufficient control over company leaders. Alistair Darling, Britain's chancellor of the

Exchequer, said of boards, "If there is anyone in this room, or in the industry, who thinks that they can carry on as if nothing has happened, they need to think again."

You might think an active board is always good for an organization. However, like most structural decisions, an activist board has downsides and risks. When directors are empowered, they can become "free agents" who pursue their own agendas, including some that may conflict with the CEO's. Conflict among board members at Hewlett-Packard almost did the company in and ended the careers of two CEOs.

In addition, dissident board members may make statements or disclose information that goes against company interests. When the AFL-CIO union secured a meeting with Home Depot director Bonnie Hill, some company executives were concerned she might disclose private information. Though that didn't appear to happen, we can

imagine some rogue board members undermining a CEO strategy they don't like through such unauthorized communiqués. A final danger is the possibility that board members will micromanage a CEO's strategy. When top management of one company went to the board with a proposal for executive bonuses, the board hired its own pay consultants. Such actions don't go over well with CEOs. As one said, "You don't need someone guiding your hand."

Questions

1. How active do you think boards should be?
2. Should directors mix with employees to obtain company information from the ranks? Why or why not?
3. Where is the line between representing shareholders' interests and micromanaging or second-guessing the CEO?

Sources: Based on L. Moyer, "Citi Circus?" *Forbes* (April 20, 2009), www.forbes.com; M. M. Thomas, "We The Taxpayers," *Forbes* (February 5, 2009), www.forbes.com; J. Werdigier, "British Regulator Criticizes Culture of Bank Boards," *New York Times* (June 17, 2009), www.nytimes.com; K. Whitehouse, "Move Over, CEO: Here Come the Directors," *Wall Street Journal* (October 9, 2006), pp. R1, R4.

Case Incident 1

CAN A STRUCTURE BE *TOO* FLAT?

Steelmaker Nucor likes to think it has management figured out. And with good reason. It is the darling of the business press. Its management practices are often favorably reviewed in management texts. And it's been effective by nearly any business metric.

There's one fundamental management practice that Nucor doesn't appear to have mastered: how to structure itself.

Nucor has always prided itself on having just three levels of management separating the CEO from factory workers. With Nucor's structure, plant managers report directly to CEO Dan DiMicco. As Nucor continues to grow, though, DiMicco is finding it increasingly hard to maintain this simple structure. So, in 2006 DiMicco added another layer of management, creating a new layer of five executive vice presidents. "I needed to be free to make decisions on trade battles," he said.

Still, even with the new layer in its structure, Nucor is remarkably lean and simple. U.S. Steel employs 1,200 people at its corporate headquarters, compared to a scant 66 at

Nucor's. At Nucor, managers still answer their own phone calls and e-mails, and the firm has no corporate jet. Even companies as comparatively lean as Toyota appear fat and complicated compared to Nucor. "You're going to get at least ten layers at Toyota before you get to the president," says a former Toyota engineer.

Questions

1. How does the Nucor case illustrate the limitations of the simple organizational structure?
2. Do you think other organizations should attempt to replicate Nucor's structure? Why or why not?
3. Why do you think other organizations have developed structures much more complex than Nucor's?
4. Generally, organizational structures tend to reflect the views of the CEO. As more and more "new blood" comes into Nucor, do you think the structure will begin to look like that of other organizations?

Source: P. Glader, "It's Not Easy Being Lean," *Wall Street Journal* (June 19, 2006), pp. B1, B3.

Case Incident 2

SIEMENS' SIMPLE STRUCTURE—NOT

There is perhaps no tougher task for an executive than to restructure a European organization. Ask former Siemens CEO Klaus Kleinfeld.

Siemens, with 77 billion euros in revenue in 2008, some 427,000 employees, and branches in 190 countries, is one of the largest electronics companies in the world. Although the company has long been respected for its engineering prowess, it's also derided for its sluggishness and mechanistic structure. So when Kleinfeld took over as CEO, he sought to restructure the company along the lines of what Jack Welch did at General Electric. He has tried to make the structure less bureaucratic so decisions are made more quickly. He spun off underperforming businesses. And he simplified the company's structure.

Kleinfeld's efforts drew angry protests from employee groups, with constant picket lines outside his corporate offices. One of the challenges of transforming European organizations is the customary active participation of employees in executive decisions. Half the seats on the Seimens board of directors are allocated to labor representatives. Not surprisingly, the labor groups did not react positively to Kleinfeld's GE-like restructuring efforts. In his efforts to speed those efforts, labor groups alleged, Kleinfeld secretly bankrolled a business-friendly workers' group to try to undermine Germany's main industrial union.

Due to this and other allegations, Kleinfeld was forced out in June 2007 and replaced by Peter Löscher. Löscher has found the same tensions between inertia and the need for restructuring. Only a month after becoming CEO, Löscher was faced with a decision whether to spin off the firm's underperforming 10 billion-euro auto parts unit, VDO. He had to weigh the forces for stability, which want to protect worker interests, against U.S.-style pressures for financial performance. One of VDO's possible buyers is a U.S. company, TRW, the controlling interest of which is held by Blackstone, a U.S. private equity firm. German labor representatives have derided such private equity firms as "locusts." When Löscher decided to sell VDO to German tire giant Continental Corporation, Continental promptly began to downsize and restructure the unit's operations.

Löscher has continued to restructure Siemens. In mid-2008, he announced elimination of nearly 17,000 jobs worldwide. He also announced plans to consolidate more business units and reorganize the company's operations geographically. "The speed at which business is changing worldwide has increased considerably, and we're orienting Siemens accordingly," Löscher said.

Since the switch from Kleinfeld to Löscher, Siemens has experienced its ups and downs. Since 2008, its stock price has fallen 26 percent on the European stock exchange and is down 31 percent on the New York Stock Exchange. That is better than some competitors, such as France's Alcatel-Lucent (down 83 percent) and General Electric (down 69 percent), and worse than others, such as IBM (up 8 percent) and the Swiss/Swedish conglomerate ABB (down 15 percent).

Though Löscher's restructuring efforts have generated far less controversy than Kleinfeld's, that doesn't mean they went over well with all constituents. Of the 2008 job cuts, Werner Neugebauer, regional director for a union representing many Siemens employees, said, "The planned job cuts are incomprehensible nor acceptable for these reasons, and in this extent, completely exaggerated."

When asked by a reporter whether the cuts would be controversial, Löscher retorted, "I couldn't care less how it's portrayed." He paused a moment, then added, "Maybe that's the wrong term. I do care."

Questions

1. What do Kleinfeld's efforts at Siemens tell you about the difficulties of restructuring organizations?

2. Why do you think Löscher's restructuring decisions have generated less controversy than did Kleinfeld's?

3. Assume a colleague read this case and concluded "This case proves restructuring efforts do not improve a company's financial performance." How would you respond to this statement?

4. Do you think a CEO who decides to restructure or downsize a company takes the well-being of employees into account? Should he or she do so? Why or why not?

Sources: Based on A. Davidson, "Peter Löscher Makes Siemens Less German," *The Sunday Times* (June 29, 2008), business.timesonline.co.uk; G. Frey, "Siemens Cutting 17K Jobs Worldwide to Cut Costs," *Fox News* (July 8, 2008), www.foxnews.com; M. Esterl and D. Crawford, "Siemens CEO Put to Early Test," *Wall Street Journal* (July 23, 2007), p. A8; and J. Ewing, "Siemens' Culture Clash," *BusinessWeek* (January 29, 2007), pp. 42–46.

Endnotes

1. N. E. Boudette, "Fiat CEO Sets New Tone at Chrysler," *Wall Street Journal* (June 19, 2009), p. B1; P. Gumbel, "Chrysler's Sergio Marchionne: The Turnaround Artista," *Time* (June 18, 2009), www.time.com; and "Fiat: Restructuring of Auto Industry Necessary," *Associated Press* (June 18, 2009), www.ap.org.

2. See, for instance, R. L. Daft, *Organization Theory and Design*, 10th ed. (Cincinnati, OH: South-Western Publishing, 2010).

3. C. Hymowitz, "Managers Suddenly Have to Answer to a Crowd of Bosses," *Wall Street Journal* (August 12, 2003), p. B1.

4. See, for instance, J. H. Gittell, "Supervisory Span, Relational Coordination, and Flight Departure Performance: A Reassessment of Postbureaucracy Theory," *Organization Science*, July–August 2001, pp. 468–483.

5. J. Child and R. G. McGrath, "Organizations Unfettered: Organizational Form in an Information-Intensive Economy," *Academy of Management Journal*, December 2001, pp. 1135–1148.

6. H. Mintzberg, *Structure in Fives: Designing Effective Organizations* (Upper Saddle River, NJ: Prentice Hall, 1983), p. 157.

7. W. M. Bulkeley, "Back from the Brink," *Wall Street Journal* (April 24, 2006), pp. B1, B3.

8. L. R. Burns and D. R. Wholey, "Adoption and Abandonment of Matrix Management Programs: Effects of Organizational Characteristics and Interorganizational Networks," *Academy of Management Journal*, February 1993, pp. 106–138.

9. See, for instance, T. Sy and L. S. D'Annunzio, "Challenges and Strategies of Matrix Organizations: Top-Level and Mid-Level Managers' Perspectives," *Human Resource Planning* 28, no. 1 (2005), pp. 39–48; and T. Sy and S. Cote, "Emotional Intelligence: A Key Ability to Succeed in the Matrix Organization," *Journal of Management Development* 23, no. 5 (2004), pp. 437–455.

10. N. Anand and R. L. Daft, "What Is the Right Organization Design?" *Organizational Dynamics* 36, no. 4 (2007), pp. 329–344.

11. See, for instance, R. E. Miles and C. C. Snow, "The New Network Firm: A Spherical Structure Built on Human Investment Philosophy," *Organizational Dynamics*, Spring 1995, pp. 5–18; D. Pescovitz, "The Company Where Everybody's a Temp," *New York Times Magazine* (June 11, 2000), pp. 94–96; B. Hedberg, G. Dahlgren, J. Hansson, and N. Olve, *Virtual Organizations and Beyond* (New York: Wiley, 2001); N. S. Contractor, S. Wasserman, and K. Faust, "Testing Multitheoretical, Multilevel Hypotheses About Organizational Networks: An Analytic Framework and Empirical Example," *Academy of Management Review* 31, no. 3 (2006) pp. 681–703; and Y. Shin, "A Person-Environment Fit Model for Virtual Organizations," *Journal of Management*, October 2004, pp. 725–743.

12. J. Bates, "Making Movies and Moving On," *Los Angeles Times* (January 19, 1998), p. A1.

13. C. B. Gibson and J. L. Gibbs, "Unpacking the Concept of Virtuality: The Effects of Geographic Dispersion, Electronic Dependence, Dynamic Structure, and National Diversity on Team Innovation," *Administrative Science Quarterly* 51, no. 3 (2006), pp. 451–495; and H. M. Latapie and V. N. Tran, "Subculture Formation, Evolution, and Conflict Between Regional Teams in Virtual Organizations," *The Business Review*, Summer 2007, pp. 189–193.

14. "GE: Just Your Average Everyday $60 Billion Family Grocery Store," *IndustryWeek*, May 2, 1994, pp. 13–18.

15. The following is based on D. D. Davis, "Form, Function and Strategy in Boundaryless Organizations," in A. Howard (ed.), *The Changing Nature of Work* (San Francisco: Jossey-Bass, 1995), pp. 112–138; P. Roberts, "We Are One Company, No Matter Where We Are. Time and Space Are Irrelevant," *Fast Company*, April–May 1998, pp. 122–128; R. L. Cross, A. Yan, and M. R. Louis, "Boundary Activities in 'Boundaryless' Organizations: A Case Study of a Transformation to a Team-Based Structure," *Human Relations*, June 2000, pp. 841–868; and R. Ashkenas, D. Ulrich, T. Jick, and S. Kerr, *The Boundaryless Organization: Breaking the Chains of Organizational Structure*, revised and updated (San Francisco: Jossey-Bass, 2002).

16. B. White, "VeriSign to Slim Down, Sharpen Its Focus," *Wall Street Journal* (November 14, 2007), p. A12.

17. S. Player, "Leading the Way to Lean," *Business Finance*, May 2007, pp. 13-16.

18. See J. P. Guthrie and D. K. Datta, "Dumb and Dumber: The Impact of Downsizing on Firm Performance as Moderated by Industry Conditions," *Organization Science* 19, no. 1 (2008), pp. 108–123; W. F. Cascio, C. E. Young, and J. R. Morris, "Financial Consequences of Employment-Change Decisions in Major U.S. Corporations," *Academy of Management Journal* 40 (1997), pp. 1175–1189; and K. P. De Meuse, T. J. Bergmann, P. A. Vanderheiden, and C. E. Roraff, "New Evidence Regarding Organizational Downsizing and a Firm's Financial Performance: A Long-Term Analysis," *Journal of Managerial Issues* 16, no. 2 (2004), pp. 155–177.

19. See, for example, C. O. Trevor and A. J. Nyberg, "Keeping Your Headcount When All About You Are Losing Theirs: Downsizing, Voluntary Turnover Rates, and the Moderating Role of HR Practices," *Academy of Management Journal* 51, no. 2 (2008), pp. 259–276; S. Moore, L. Grunberg, and E. Greenberg, "Surviving Repeated Waves of Organizational Downsizing: The Recency, Duration, and Order Effects Associated with Different Forms of Layoff Contact," *Anxiety, Stress & Coping: An International Journal* 19, no. 3 (2006), pp. 309–329; T. M. Probst, S. M. Stewart, M. L. Gruys, and B. W. Tierney, "Productivity, Counterproductivity and Creativity: The Ups and Downs of Job Insecurity," *Journal of Occupational and Organizational Psychology* 80, no. 3 (2007), pp. 479–497; and J. E. Ferrie, M. J. Shipley, M. G. Marmot, P. Martikainen, S. Stansfeld, and G. D. Smith, "Job Insecurity in White-Collar Workers: Toward an Explanation of Associations with Health," *Journal of Occupational Health Psychology* 6, no. 1 (2001), pp. 26–42.

20. C. D. Zatzick, and R. D. Iverson, "High-Involvement Management and Workforce Reduction: Competitive Advantage or Disadvantage?" *Academy of Management Journal* 49, no. 5 (2006), pp. 999–1015; A. Travaglione, and B. Cross, "Diminishing the Social Network in Organizations: Does There Need to Be Such a Phenomenon as 'Survivor Syndrome' After Downsizing?" *Strategic Change* 15, no. 1 (2006), pp. 1–13; and J. D. Kammeyer-Mueller, H. Liao, and R. D. Arvey, "Downsizing and Organizational Performance: A Review of the Literature from a Stakeholder Perspective," *Research in Personnel and Human Resources Management* 20 (2001), pp. 269–329.

21. T. Burns and G. M. Stalker, *The Management of Innovation* (London: Tavistock, 1961); and J. A. Courtright, G. T. Fairhurst, and L. E. Rogers, "Interaction Patterns in Organic and Mechanistic Systems," *Academy of Management Journal*, December 1989, pp. 773–802.

22. This analysis is referred to as a contingency approach to organization design. See, for instance, J. M. Pennings, "Structural Contingency Theory: A Reappraisal," in B. M. Staw and L. L. Cummings (eds.), *Research in Organizational Behavior*, vol. 14 (Greenwich, CT: JAI Press, 1992), pp. 267–309; J. R. Hollenbeck, H. Moon, A. P. J. Ellis, B. J. West, D. R. Ilgen, L. Sheppard, C. O. L. H. Porter, and J. A. Wagner III, "Structural Contingency Theory and Individual Differences: Examination of External and Internal Person-Team Fit," *Journal of Applied Psychology*, June 2002, pp. 599–606; and A. Drach-Zahavy and A. Freund, "Team Effectiveness Under Stress: A Structural Contingency Approach," *Journal of Organizational Behavior* 28, no. 4 (2007), pp. 423–450.

23. The strategy–structure thesis was originally proposed in A. D. Chandler, Jr., *Strategy and Structure: Chapters in the History of the Industrial Enterprise* (Cambridge, MA: MIT Press, 1962). For an updated analysis, see T. L. Amburgey and T. Dacin, "As the Left Foot Follows the Right? The Dynamics of Strategic and Structural Change," *Academy of Management Journal*, December 1994, pp. 1427–1452.

24. See R. E. Miles and C. C. Snow, *Organizational Strategy, Structure, and Process* (New York: McGraw-Hill, 1978); D. C. Galunic and K. M. Eisenhardt, "Renewing the Strategy–Structure–Performance Paradigm," in B. M. Staw and L. L. Cummings (eds.), *Research in Organizational Behavior*, vol. 16 (Greenwich, CT: JAI Press, 1994), pp. 215–255; and S. M. Toh, F. P. Morgeson, and M. A. Campion, "Human Resource Configurations: Investigating Fit with the Organizational Context," *Journal of Applied Psychology* 93, no. 4 (2008), pp. 864–882.

25. See, for instance, P. M. Blau and R. A. Schoenherr, *The Structure of Organizations* (New York: Basic Books, 1971); D. S. Pugh, "The Aston Program of Research: Retrospect and Prospect," in A. H. Van de Ven and W. F. Joyce (eds.), *Perspectives on Organization Design and Behavior* (New York: Wiley, 1981), pp. 135–166; R. Z. Gooding and J. A. Wagner III, "A Meta-analytic Review of the Relationship Between Size and Performance: The Productivity and Efficiency of Organizations and Their Subunits," *Administrative Science Quarterly*, December 1985, pp. 462–481; and A. C. Bluedorn, "Pilgrim's Progress: Trends and Convergence in Research on Organizational Size and Environments," *Journal of Management,* Summer 1993, pp. 163–192.

26. See C. Perrow, "A Framework for the Comparative Analysis of Organizations," *American Sociological Review*, April 1967, pp. 194–208; J. Hage and M. Aiken, "Routine Technology, Social Structure, and Organizational Goals," *Administrative Science Quarterly*, September 1969, pp. 366–377; C. C. Miller, W. H. Glick, Y. Wang, and G. P. Huber, "Understanding Technology-Structure Relationships: Theory Development and Meta-analytic Theory Testing," *Academy of Management Journal*, June 1991, pp. 370–399; and W. D. Sine, H. Mitsuhashi, and D. A. Kirsch, "Revisiting Burns and Stalker: Formal Structure and New Venture Performance in Emerging Economic Sectors," *Academy of Management Journal* 49, no. 1 (2006), pp. 121–132.

27. See F. E. Emery and E. Trist, "The Causal Texture of Organizational Environments," *Human Relations*, February 1965, pp. 21–32; P. Lawrence and J. W. Lorsch, *Organization and Environment: Managing Differentiation and Integration* (Boston: Harvard Business School, Division of Research, 1967); M. Yasai-Ardekani, "Structural Adaptations to Environments," *Academy of Management Review*, January 1986, pp. 9–21; Bluedorn, "Pilgrim's Progress"; and M. Arndt and B. Bigelow, "Presenting Structural Innovation in an Institutional Environment: Hospitals' Use of Impression Management," *Administrative Science Quarterly*, September 2000, pp. 494–522.

28. G. G. Dess and D. W. Beard, "Dimensions of Organizational Task Environments," *Administrative Science Quarterly*, March 1984, pp. 52–73; E. A. Gerloff, N. K. Muir, and W. D. Bodensteiner, "Three Components of Perceived Environmental Uncertainty: An Exploratory Analysis of the Effects of Aggregation," *Journal of Management,* December 1991, pp. 749–768; and O. Shenkar, N. Aranya, and T. Almor, "Construct Dimensions in the Contingency Model: An Analysis Comparing Metric and Non-metric Multivariate Instruments," *Human Relations,* May 1995, pp. 559–580.

29. J. B. Quinn, P. Anderson, and S. Finkelstein, "Leveraging Intellect," *Academy of Management Executive*, November 2005, pp. 78–94; and T. H. Reus, A. L. Ranft, B. T. Lamont, and G. L. Adams, "An Interpretive Systems View of Knowledge Investments," *Academy of Management Review* 34, no. 3 (2009), pp. 382–400.

30. C. S. Spell and T. J. Arnold, "A Multi-Level Analysis of Organizational Justice and Climate, Structure, and Employee Mental Health," *Journal of Management* 33, no. 5 (2007), pp. 724–751; and M. L. Ambrose and M. Schminke, "Organization Structure as a Moderator of the Relationship Between Procedural Justice, Interactional Justice, Perceived Organizational Support, and Supervisory Trust," *Journal of Applied Psychology* 88, no. 2 (2003), pp. 295–305.

31. See, for instance, L. W. Porter and E. E. Lawler III, "Properties of Organization Structure in Relation to Job Attitudes and Job Behavior," *Psychological Bulletin,* July 1965, pp. 23–51; L. R. James and A. P. Jones, "Organization Structure: A Review of Structural Dimensions and Their Conceptual Relationships with Individual Attitudes and Behavior," *Organizational Behavior and Human Performance*, June 1976, pp. 74–113; C. S. Spell and T. J. Arnold, "A Multi-Level Analysis of Organizational Justice Climate, Structure, and Employee Mental Health," *Journal of Management* 33, no. 5 (2007), pp. 724–751; and J. D. Shaw and N. Gupta, "Job Complexity, Performance, and Well-Being: When Does Supplies-Values Fit Matter? *Personnel Psychology* 57, no. 4, 847–879.

32. See, for instance, B. Schneider, H. W. Goldstein, and D. B. Smith, "The ASA Framework: An Update," *Personnel Psychology* 48, no. 4 (1995), pp. 747–773; and R. E. Ployhart, J. A. Weekley, and K. Baughman, "The Structure and Function of Human Capital Emergence: A Multilevel Examination of the Attraction-Selection-Attrition Model," *Academy of Management Journal* 49, no. 4 (2006), pp. 661–677.

33. P. Dvorak, "Making U.S. Management Ideas Work Elsewhere," *Wall Street Journal* (May 22, 2006), p. B3.

34. See, for example, P. R. Harris and R. T. Moran, *Managing Cultural Differences*, 5th ed. (Houston, TX: Gulf Publishing, 1999).

35. P. McGeehan, "Thousands of Job Cuts Likely After Drug Merger," *New York Times* (January 26, 2009), www.nytimes.com; C. Palmeri, "A Cautionary Tale for Airline Mergers," *BusinessWeek* (March 17, 2008), p. 66; and M. Adams, "Pilots Have Much to Lose During Mergers," *USA Today* (March 10, 2008), p. 3B.

36. N. M. Davis, "Merger Kept 'the Best of Both'," *HR Magazine* (November 2008), pp. 54–56.

LEARNING OBJECTIVES

After studying this chapter, you should be able to:

1 Define *organizational culture* and describe its common characteristics.

2 Compare the functional and dysfunctional effects of organizational culture on people and the organization.

3 Identify the factors that create and sustain an organization's culture.

4 Show how culture is transmitted to employees.

5 Demonstrate how an ethical culture can be created.

6 Describe a positive organizational culture.

7 Identify characteristics of a spiritual culture.

8 Show how national culture may affect the way organizational culture is transported to a different country.

Organizational Culture

16

When I hear the word culture, I reach for my
Browning. —Hanns Johst

IS A 5S CULTURE FOR YOU?

Jay Scovie looked at his work space. He took pride in how nice and tidy he had made it look. As it turns out, his pride was misplaced. Sweeping visible clutter from your work space by packing it into boxes hidden in a closet was not acceptable to his employer, Japanese manufacturer Kyocera. Scovie's habit drew the attention of Dan Brown, Kyocera's newly appointed inspector. "It became a topic of repeated conversation," Scovie said.

Why the obsession with order? Kyocera has joined a growing list of organizations that base their culture on 5S, a concept borrowed from lean manufacturing and based on five phases or principals:

1. **Sorting (Seiri).** Going through all tools, materials, and supplies so as to keep only what is essential.
2. **Straightening (Seiton).** Arranging tools, supplies, equipment, and parts in a manner that promotes maximum efficiency. For every thing there should be a place, and every thing should be in its place.
3. **Shining (Seisō).** Systematic cleaning to make the workplace and work space as clean and neat as possible. At the end of the shift or workday, every thing is left as it was when the workday started.
4. **Standardizing (Seiketsu).** Knowing exactly what your responsibilities are to keep the first three S's.

5. **Sustaining (Shitsuke).** Maintaining and reviewing standards, rigorous review, and inspection to ensure order does not slowly slip back into disorder or chaos.

Other companies are following Kyocera in making 5S an important part of their culture. Lawn mower manufacturer Toro organizes printer output according to 5S principles, and Virginia Mason Hospital in Seattle uses 5S to coordinate office space and arrange the placement of medical equipment, such as stethoscopes. Paul Levy, President and CEO of Beth Israel Deaconess Medical Center in Boston, has used 5S to reduce errors and time lost searching for equipment.

At Kyocera, Brown exercises some discretion—he asked one employee to remove a hook on her door while allowing another to keep a whale figurine on her desk. "You have to figure out how to balance being too picky with upholding the purpose of the program," he said. While Brown was happy with Scovie's desk (if not the closet), he wanted to look inside. Scovie tried to redirect the conversation but relented when Brown pressed. Inside one of Scovie's desk drawers was a box full of CDs, small electronic devices, and items Kyocera no longer makes. "Obviously, we're at the sorting stage here," Scovie told Brown."[1]

A strong organizational culture provides stability to an organization. But as the chapter-opening example shows, it's not for everyone. And for some organizations, it can also be a major barrier to change. In this chapter, we show that every organization has a culture that, depending on its strength, can have a significant influence on the attitudes and behaviors of organization members. First let's figure out what kind of organizational culture you prefer. Take the self-assessment to find out.

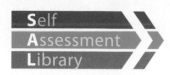

WHAT'S THE RIGHT ORGANIZATIONAL CULTURE FOR ME?

In the Self-Assessment Library (available on CD and online), take assessment III.B.1 (What's the Right Organizational Culture for Me?) and answer the following questions.

1. *Judging from your results, do you fit better in a more formal and structured culture or in a more informal and unstructured culture?*
2. *Did your results surprise you? Why do you think you scored as you did?*
3. *How might your results affect your career path?*

What Is Organizational Culture?

1 Define *organizational culture* and describe its common characteristics.

An executive once was asked what he thought *organizational culture* meant. He gave essentially the same answer a U.S. Supreme Court justice once gave in attempting to define pornography: "I can't define it, but I know it when I see it." We, however, need a basic definition of organizational culture to better understand the phenomenon. In this section we propose one and review several related ideas.

A Definition of *Organizational Culture*

Organizational culture refers to a system of shared meaning held by members that distinguishes the organization from other organizations.[2] Seven primary characteristics seem to capture the essence of an organization's culture:[3]

1. **Innovation and risk taking.**   The degree to which employees are encouraged to be innovative and take risks.
2. **Attention to detail.**   The degree to which employees are expected to exhibit precision, analysis, and attention to detail.
3. **Outcome orientation.**   The degree to which management focuses on results or outcomes rather than on the techniques and processes used to achieve them.
4. **People orientation.**   The degree to which management decisions take into consideration the effect of outcomes on people within the organization.
5. **Team orientation.**   The degree to which work activities are organized around teams rather than individuals.
6. **Aggressiveness.**   The degree to which people are aggressive and competitive rather than easygoing.
7. **Stability.**   The degree to which organizational activities emphasize maintaining the status quo in contrast to growth.

Each of these characteristics exists on a continuum from low to high. Appraising the organization on these seven characteristics, then, gives a compos-

Exhibit **16-1**	Contrasting Organizational Cultures

Organization A

This organization is a manufacturing firm. Managers are expected to fully document all decisions, and "good managers" are those who can provide detailed data to support their recommendations. Creative decisions that incur significant change or risk are not encouraged. Because managers of failed projects are openly criticized and penalized, managers try not to implement ideas that deviate much from the status quo. One lower-level manager quoted an often-used phrase in the company: "If it ain't broke, don't fix it."

There are extensive rules and regulations in this firm that employees are required to follow. Managers supervise employees closely to ensure there are no deviations. Management is concerned with high productivity, regardless of the impact on employee morale or turnover.

Work activities are designed around individuals. There are distinct departments and lines of authority, and employees are expected to minimize formal contact with other employees outside their functional area or line of command. Performance evaluations and rewards emphasize individual effort, although seniority tends to be the primary factor in the determination of pay raises and promotions.

Organization B

This organization is also a manufacturing firm. Here, however, management encourages and rewards risk taking and change. Decisions based on intuition are valued as much as those that are well rationalized. Management prides itself on its history of experimenting with new technologies and its success in regularly introducing innovative products. Managers or employees who have a good idea are encouraged to "run with it." And failures are treated as "learning experiences." The company prides itself on being market driven and rapidly responsive to the changing needs of its customers.

There are few rules and regulations for employees to follow, and supervision is loose because management believes that its employees are hardworking and trustworthy. Management is concerned with high productivity but believes that this comes through treating its people right. The company is proud of its reputation as being a good place to work.

Job activities are designed around work teams, and team members are encouraged to interact with people across functions and authority levels. Employees talk positively about the competition between teams. Individuals and teams have goals, and bonuses are based on achievement of these outcomes. Employees are given considerable autonomy in choosing the means by which the goals are attained.

ite picture of the organization's culture. This picture becomes the basis for feelings of shared understanding members have about the organization, how things are done in it, and the way members are supposed to behave. Exhibit 16-1 demonstrates how these characteristics can be mixed to create highly diverse organizations.

Culture Is a Descriptive Term

Organizational culture is concerned with how employees perceive the characteristics of an organization's culture, not with whether they like them—that is, it's a descriptive term. This is important because it differentiates this concept from job satisfaction.

Research on organizational culture has sought to measure how employees see their organization: Does it encourage teamwork? Does it reward innovation?

organizational culture *A system of shared meaning held by members that distinguishes the organization from other organizations.*

Does it stifle initiative? In contrast, *job satisfaction* seeks to measure how employees feel about the organization's expectations, reward practices, and the like. Although the two terms undoubtedly have overlapping characteristics, keep in mind that *organizational culture* is descriptive, whereas *job satisfaction* is evaluative.

Do Organizations Have Uniform Cultures?

Organizational culture represents a common perception the organization's members hold. We should expect, therefore, that individuals with different backgrounds or at different levels in the organization will tend to describe its culture in similar terms.[4]

That doesn't mean, however, that there are no subcultures within any given culture. Most large organizations have a dominant culture and numerous subcultures.[5] A **dominant culture** expresses the core values shared by a majority of the organization's members. When we talk about an organization's culture, we are referring to its dominant culture, which gives an organization its distinct personality.[6] **Subcultures** tend to develop in large organizations to reflect common problems, situations, or experiences faced by groups of members in the same department or location. The purchasing department can have a subculture that includes the **core values** of the dominant culture plus additional values unique to members of the purchasing department.

If organizations were composed only of numerous subcultures, organizational culture as an independent variable would be significantly less powerful. It is the "shared meaning" aspect of culture that makes it such a potent device for guiding and shaping behavior. That's what allows us to say, for example, that Microsoft's culture values aggressiveness and risk taking[7] and to use that information to better understand the behavior of Microsoft executives and employees. But many organizations also have subcultures that can influence members' behavior.

Strong versus Weak Cultures

It's possible to differentiate between strong and weak cultures.[8] If most employees (responding to management surveys) have the same opinions about the organization's mission and values, the culture is strong; if opinions vary widely, the culture is weak.

In a **strong culture**, the organization's core values are both intensely held and widely shared.[9] The more members who accept the core values and the greater their commitment, the stronger the culture and the greater its influence on member behavior because the high degree of sharedness and intensity creates an internal climate of high behavioral control. Nordstrom employees know in no uncertain terms what is expected of them, and these expectations go a long way in shaping their behavior. In contrast, Nordstrom competitor Macy's, which has struggled through an identity crisis, is working to remake its culture.

A strong culture should reduce employee turnover, because it demonstrates high agreement about what the organization represents. Such unanimity of purpose builds cohesiveness, loyalty, and organizational commitment. These qualities, in turn, lessen employees' propensity to leave.[10]

Culture versus Formalization

We've seen that high formalization creates predictability, orderliness, and consistency. A strong culture achieves the same end without the need for written documentation.[11] Therefore, we should view formalization and culture as two different roads to a common destination. The stronger an organization's culture, the less management need be concerned with developing formal rules and regulations to guide employee behavior. Those guides will be internalized in employees when they accept the organization's culture.

International OB

Managing Across Organizational Boundaries

Another manifestation of culture is as a feature of a nation or group of nations. An obvious question for multinational corporations then is whether it is better to establish a single strong organizational culture across different nations or to adopt different cultural practices in each country. Research suggests the best management practice is to develop a strong unifying mission, while allowing teams to accomplish their work in ways that suit each nation's culture.

In a study of 230 organizations in different industries from regions including North America, Asia, Europe, the Middle East, and Africa, having a strong and positive organizational culture was associated with increased organizational effectiveness. Across countries,

practices such as empowerment, team orientation, establishing a clear strategic direction, and providing a recognized vision were related to greater success in all countries. However, the practices were not equally important. Empowerment appeared more important in individualistic than in collectivistic countries.

Another study of 115 teams in five different multinational corporations found that when companies emphasized a unified global integration of business operations, teams shared less information. The reason might be that home office culture was dictating policies, leading teams to be less proactive about making changes. On the other hand, encouraging local teams to find their own solutions for

their own cultural context resulted in greater learning and performance.

Overall, these studies show a productive organizational culture is associated with increased sales growth, profitability, employee satisfaction, and overall organizational performance. Part of this effective management strategy means empowering managers to take local context into account.

Sources: Based on D. R. Denison, S. Haaland, and P. Goelzer, "Corporate Culture and Organizational Effectiveness: Is Asia Different from the Rest of the World?" *Organizational Dynamics*, February 2004, pp. 98–109; and M. Zellmer-Bruhn and C. Gibson, "Multinational Organizational Context: Implications for Team Learning and Performance," *Academy of Management Journal* 49, no. 3 (2006), pp. 501–518.

What Do Cultures Do?

2 Compare the functional and dysfunctional effects of organizational culture on people and the organization.

Let's more carefully review the role culture performs and whether it can ever be a liability for an organization.

Culture's Functions

First, culture has a boundary-defining role: it creates distinctions between one organization and others. Second, it conveys a sense of identity for organization members. Third, culture facilitates the generation of commitment to something larger than individual self-interest. Fourth, it enhances the stability of the social system. Culture is the social glue that helps hold the organization together by providing appropriate standards for what employees should say and do. Finally, it is a sense-making and control mechanism that

---

dominant culture *A culture that expresses the core values that are shared by a majority of the organization's members.*

subcultures *Minicultures within an organization, typically defined by department designations and geographical separation.*

core values *The primary or dominant values that are accepted throughout the organization.*

strong culture *A culture in which the core values are intensely held and widely shared.*

guides and shapes employees' attitudes and behavior. This last function is of particular interest to us.[12] Culture defines the rules of the game:

> Culture by definition is elusive, intangible, implicit, and taken for granted. But every organization develops a core set of assumptions, understandings, and implicit rules that govern day-to-day behavior in the workplace. . . . Until newcomers learn the rules, they are not accepted as full-fledged members of the organization. Transgressions of the rules on the part of high-level executives or front-line employees result in universal disapproval and powerful penalties. Conformity to the rules becomes the primary basis for reward and upward mobility.[13]

Today's trend toward decentralized organizations makes culture more important than ever, but ironically it also makes establishing a strong culture more difficult. When formal authority and control systems are reduced, culture's *shared meaning* points everyone in the same direction. However, employees organized in teams may show greater allegiance to their team and its values than to the values of the organization as a whole. In virtual organizations, the lack of frequent face-to-face contact makes establishing a common set of norms very difficult. Strong leadership that communicates frequently about common goals and priorities is especially important in innovative organizations.[14]

Individual–organization "fit"—that is, whether the applicant's or employee's attitudes and behavior are compatible with the culture—strongly influences who gets a job offer, a favorable performance review, or a promotion. It's no coincidence that Disney theme park employees appear almost universally attractive, clean, and wholesome with bright smiles. The company selects employees who will maintain that image. On the job, a strong culture, supported by formal rules and regulations, ensures they will act in a relatively uniform and predictable way.

Culture Creates Climate

If you've worked with someone whose positive attitude inspired you to do your best, or with a lackluster team that drained your motivation, you've experienced the effects of climate. **Organizational climate** refers to the shared perceptions organizational members have about their organization and work environment.[15] This aspect of culture is like team spirit at the organizational level. When everyone has the same general feelings about what's important or how well things are working, the effect of these attitudes will be more than the sum of the individual parts. The same appears true for organizations. One meta-analysis found that across dozens of different samples, psychological climate was strongly related to individuals' level of job satisfaction, involvement, commitment, and motivation.[16] A positive overall workplace climate has been linked to higher customer satisfaction and financial performance as well.[17]

Dozens of dimensions of climate have been studied, including safety, justice, diversity, and customer service, to name a few.[18] A person who encounters a positive climate for performance will think about doing a good job more often and will believe others support his or her success. Someone who encounters a positive climate for diversity will feel more comfortable collaborating with coworkers regardless of their demographic background. Climate also influences the habits people adopt. If the climate for safety is positive, everyone wears safety gear and follows safety procedures even if individually they wouldn't normally think very often about being safe.

Culture as a Liability

Culture enhances organizational commitment and increases the consistency of employee behavior. These are clearly benefits to an organization. From an employee's standpoint, culture is valuable because it spells out how things are done

Facebook describes itself as "a cutting-edge technology company, constantly taking on new challenges in the worlds of milliseconds and terabytes." The vast majority of the company's employees are under 40, and enjoy the excitement of working in a fast-paced environment with considerable change and ambiguity. Facebook says it encourages employees to interact in a creative climate that encourages experimentation and tolerates conflict and risk. Facebook fosters a fun-loving, casual, and collegial identity in its employees.

and what's important. But we shouldn't ignore the potentially dysfunctional aspects of culture, especially a strong one, on an organization's effectiveness.

Institutionalization   When an organization undergoes **institutionalization** and becomes *institutionalized*—that is, it is valued for itself and not for the goods or services it produces—it takes on a life of its own, apart from its founders or members.[19] It doesn't go out of business even if its original goals are no longer relevant. Acceptable modes of behavior become largely self evident to members, and although this isn't entirely negative, it does mean behaviors and habits that should be questioned and analyzed become taken for granted, which can stifle innovation and make maintaining the organization's culture an end in itself.

Barriers to Change   Culture is a liability when the shared values are not in agreement with those that further the organization's effectiveness. This is most likely when an organization's environment is undergoing rapid change, and its entrenched culture may no longer be appropriate.[20] Consistency of behavior, an asset in a stable environment, may then burden the organization and make it difficult to respond to changes. This helps explain the challenges executives have recently faced at Citigroup, Eastman Kodak, Yahoo, Airbus, and the U.S. Federal Bureau of Investigation.[21] Strong cultures worked well for them in the past but become barriers to change when "business as usual" is no longer effective.

Barriers to Diversity   Hiring new employees who differ from the majority in race, age, gender, disability, or other characteristics creates a paradox:[22] Management wants to demonstrate support for the differences these employees bring to the workplace, but newcomers who wish to fit in must accept the organization's core cultural values. Because diverse behaviors and unique strengths are likely to diminish as people attempt to assimilate, strong cultures can become liabilities when they effectively eliminate these advantages.

By limiting the range of acceptable values and styles, strong cultures put considerable pressure on employees to conform. In some instances, such as the widely publicized Texaco case in which senior managers made disparaging remarks about minorities (settled on behalf of 1,400 employees for $176 million), a strong culture that condones prejudice can even undermine formal corporate diversity policies.[23] Strong cultures can also be liabilities when they support institutional bias or become insensitive to people who are different.

Barriers to Acquisitions and Mergers   Historically, when management looked at acquisition or merger decisions, the key factors were financial advantage and product synergy. In recent years, cultural compatibility has become the primary concern.[24] All things being equal, whether the acquisition actually works seems to have more to do with how well the two organizations' cultures match up.

A survey by consulting firm A. T. Kearney revealed that 58 percent of mergers failed to reach the value goals set by top managers.[25] The primary cause of failure is conflicting organizational cultures. As one expert commented, "Mergers have an unusually high failure rate, and it's always because of people issues." The

organizational climate   *The shared perceptions organizational members have about their organization and work environment.*

institutionalization   *A condition that occurs when an organization takes on a life of its own, apart from any of its members, and acquires immortality.*

"People Socialize Themselves"

This statement is true to a significant degree. Although we generally think of socialization as the process by which a person is shaped by his or her environment—and indeed that influence is the major focus of socialization research—more evidence is accumulating that many people socialize themselves or at least substantially mold their socialization experiences.

People with a proactive personality are much better at learning the ropes than newcomers. As we noted in Chapter 5, they identify opportunities, show initiative by asking questions and seeking help, and take action—and they learn more because they seek out more information and feedback.

Proactive personality types are also better at networking and achieve a closer fit with the culture of their organization—they build their own "so-cial capital." More effectively socialized into the organization, they like their jobs more, perform them better, and show less propensity to quit. Proactive people, it seems, do a lot to socialize *themselves* into the culture of an organization.

This doesn't mean socialization doesn't matter, but only that people are not passive actors in the process. How well someone is socialized into a new culture may depend more on his or her personality than anything else.[26]

$183 billion merger between America Online (AOL) and Time Warner in 2001 was the largest in U.S. corporate history. It was also a disaster. Only 2 years later, the stock had fallen an astounding 90 percent, and the new company reported what was then the largest financial loss in U.S. history. To this day, Time Warner stock—trading around $25 per share in late 2009—remains at a fraction of its former price (around $200 per share before the merger). Culture clash is commonly argued to be one of the causes of AOL Time Warner's problems. As one expert noted, "In some ways the merger of AOL and Time Warner was like the marriage of a teenager to a middle-aged banker. The cultures were vastly different. There were open collars and jeans at AOL. Time Warner was more buttoned-down." [27]

Creating and Sustaining Culture

3 Identify the factors that create and sustain an organization's culture.

An organization's culture doesn't pop out of thin air, and once established it rarely fades away. What forces influence the creation of a culture? What reinforces and sustains them once they're in place?

How a Culture Begins

An organization's current customs, traditions, and general way of doing things are largely due to what it has done before and how successful it was in doing it. This leads us to the ultimate source of an organization's culture: its founders.[28] Founders traditionally have a major impact on an organization's early culture. Free of previous customs or ideologies, they have a vision of what the organization should be, and its small size makes it easy to impose that vision on all members.

Culture creation occurs in three ways.[29] First, founders hire and keep only employees who think and feel the same way they do. Second, they indoctrinate and socialize these employees to their way of thinking and feeling. And finally, the founders' own behavior encourages employees to identify with them and internalize their beliefs, values, and assumptions. When the organization succeeds, the founders' personality becomes embedded in the culture.

The fierce, competitive style and disciplined, authoritarian nature of Hyundai, the giant Korean conglomerate, are the same characteristics often used to describe founder Chung Ju-Yung. Other founders with immeasurable impact on their organization's culture include Bill Gates at Microsoft, Ingvar Kamprad at IKEA, Herb Kelleher at Southwest Airlines, Fred Smith at FedEx, and Richard Branson at the Virgin Group.

Keeping a Culture Alive

Once a culture is in place, practices within the organization maintain it by giving employees a set of similar experiences.[30] The selection process, performance evaluation criteria, training and development activities, and promotion procedures (all discussed in Chapter 17) ensure those hired fit in with the culture, reward those who support it, and penalize (and even expel) those who challenge it. Three forces play a particularly important part in sustaining a culture: selection practices, the actions of top management, and socialization methods. Let's take a closer look at each.

Tony Hsieh, CEO of Zappos.com, is also the architect of the company's culture. Hsieh invited all employees to participate in creating ten core values that define the culture of Zappos and serve as the framework from which all decisions are made. These core values are: deliver WOW through service; embrace and drive change; create fun and a little weirdness; be adventurous, creative, and open-minded; pursue growth and learning; build open and honest relationships with communication; build a positive team and family spirit; do more with less; be passionate and determined; and be humble. Hsieh builds and maintains its culture through the company's hiring process and training programs to ensure that employees are committed to the core values.

Selection   The explicit goal of the selection process is to identify and hire individuals with the knowledge, skills, and abilities to perform successfully. The final decision, because it's significantly influenced by the decision maker's judgment of how well the candidates will fit into the organization, identifies people whose values are essentially consistent with at least a good portion of the organization's.[31] Selection also provides information to applicants. Those who perceive a conflict between their values and those of the organization can remove themselves from the applicant pool. Selection thus becomes a two-way street, allowing employer or applicant to avoid a mismatch and sustaining an organization's culture by selecting out those who might attack or undermine its core values.

W. L. Gore & Associates, the maker of Gore-Tex fabric used in outerwear, prides itself on its democratic culture and teamwork. There are no job titles at Gore, nor bosses nor chains of command. All work is done in teams. In Gore's selection process, teams of employees put job applicants through extensive interviews to ensure they can deal with the level of uncertainty, flexibility, and teamwork that's normal in Gore plants. Not surprisingly, W. L. Gore appears regularly on *Fortune*'s list of "100 Best Companies to Work For" (#15 in 2009).[32]

Top Management   The actions of top management also have a major impact on the organization's culture.[33] Through words and behavior, senior executives establish norms that filter through the organization about, for instance, whether risk taking is desirable, how much freedom managers should give employees, what is appropriate dress, and what actions pay off in terms of pay raises, promotions, and other rewards.

The culture of supermarket chain Wegmans—which believes driven, happy, and loyal employees are more eager to help one another and provide exemplary customer service—is a direct result of the beliefs of the Wegman family. The chain began in 1930 when brothers John and Walter Wegman opened their first grocery store in Rochester, New York. Its focus on fine foods quickly separated it from other grocers—a focus maintained by the company's employees, many of whom are hired based on their interest in food. In 1950, Walter's son Robert became president and immediately added a generous number of employee benefits such as profit sharing and medical coverage, completely paid for by the company. Now Robert's son Danny is president of the company, and he has continued the Wegmans tradition of taking care of employees. To date, Wegmans has paid more than $54 million in college scholarships for its employees, both full time and part time. Pay is well above the market average, making annual turnover for full-time employees a mere 6 percent, according to the Food Marketing Institute. The industry average is 24 percent. Wegman's regularly appears on *Fortune*'s list as well (#5 in 2009).

Socialization   No matter how good a job the organization does in recruiting and selection, new employees are not fully indoctrinated in the organization's culture and can disrupt beliefs and customs already in place. The process that helps new employees adapt to the prevailing culture is **socialization**.[34]

For example, all Marines must go through boot camp, where they "prove" their commitment. At the same time, the Marine trainers are indoctrinating new recruits in the "Marine way." All new employees at Neumann Homes in Warrenville, Illinois, go through a 40-hour orientation program.[35] They're introduced to the company's values and culture through a variety of activities, including a customer service lunch, an interactive departmental roundtable fair, and presentations about the company's core values that new hires make to the CEO. For incoming employees in the upper ranks, companies often put considerably more time and effort into the socialization process. As an example of the dark side of socialization, German giant Siemens used bribes so widely that a German government official said, "Bribery was Siemens' business model. Siemens had institutionalized corruption." Managers were frequently socialized on how to bribe officials, where to obtain the money (bribes were referred to as "NA" for *nützliche Aufwendungen* or "useful money"), and how to hide it in a sham accounting system. In the end, 2,700 of Siemens' contracts were found to be won through bribes, and when they were discovered, the company and its managers faced myriad penalties.[36]

We can think of socialization as a process with three stages: prearrival, encounter, and metamorphosis.[37] This process, shown in Exhibit 16-2, has an impact on the new employee's work productivity, commitment to the organization's objectives, and eventual decision to stay with the organization.

The **prearrival stage** explicitly recognizes that each individual arrives with a set of values, attitudes, and expectations about both the work to be done and the organization. One major purpose of a business school, for example, is to socialize business students to the attitudes and behaviors business firms want. Newcomers to high-profile organizations with a strong market position will make their own assumptions about what it must be like to work there.[38] Most new recruits will expect Nike to be dynamic and exciting, a prestigious law firm to be high in pressure and rewards, and the Marine Corps to require both discipline and courage. No matter how well managers think they can socialize newcomers, however, the most important predictor of future behavior is past behavior. What people know before they join the organization, and how proactive their personality is, are critical predictors of how well they adjust to a new culture.[39]

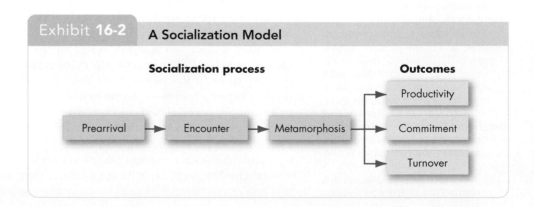

Exhibit 16-2   A Socialization Model

One way to capitalize on the importance of prehire characteristics in socialization is to use the selection process to inform prospective employees about the organization as a whole. We've also seen how the selection process ensures the inclusion of the "right type"—those who will fit in. "Indeed, the ability of the individual to present the appropriate face during the selection process determines his ability to move into the organization in the first place. Thus, success depends on the degree to which the aspiring member has correctly anticipated the expectations and desires of those in the organization in charge of selection."[40]

On entry into the organization, the new member enters the **encounter stage** and confronts the possibility that expectations—about the job, co-workers, the boss, and the organization in general—may differ from reality. If expectations were fairly accurate, the encounter stage merely cements earlier perceptions. However, this is often not the case. At the extreme, a new member may become disillusioned enough with the reality to resign. Proper recruiting and selection should significantly reduce that outcome, along with encouraging friendship ties in the organization—newcomers are more committed when friends and co-workers help them "learn the ropes."[41]

Finally, to work out any problems discovered during the encounter stage, the new member changes or goes through the **metamorphosis stage**. The options presented in Exhibit 16-3 are alternatives designed to bring about the desired

---

Exhibit 16-3   Entry Socialization Options

Formal vs. Informal The more a new employee is segregated from the ongoing work setting and differentiated in some way to make explicit his or her newcomer's role, the more socialization is formal. Specific orientation and training programs are examples. Informal socialization puts the new employee directly into the job, with little or no special attention.

Individual vs. Collective New members can be socialized individually. This describes how it's done in many professional offices. They can also be grouped together and processed through an identical set of experiences, as in military boot camp.

Fixed vs. Variable This refers to the time schedule in which newcomers make the transition from outsider to insider. A fixed schedule establishes standardized stages of transition. This characterizes rotational training programs. It also includes probationary periods, such as the 8- to 10-year "associate" status used by accounting and law firms before deciding on whether or not a candidate is made a partner. Variable schedules give no advance notice of their transition timetable. Variable schedules describe the typical promotion system, in which one is not advanced to the next stage until one is "ready."

Serial vs. Random Serial socialization is characterized by the use of role models who train and encourage the newcomer. Apprenticeship and mentoring programs are examples. In random socialization, role models are deliberately withheld. New employees are left on their own to figure things out.

Investiture vs. Divestiture Investiture socialization assumes that the newcomer's qualities and qualifications are the necessary ingredients for job success, so these qualities and qualifications are confirmed and supported. Divestiture socialization tries to strip away certain characteristics of the recruit. Fraternity and sorority "pledges" go through divestiture socialization to shape them into the proper role.

---

socialization *A process that adapts employees to the organization's culture.*

prearrival stage *The period of learning in the socialization process that occurs before a new employee joins the organization.*

encounter stage *The stage in the socialization process in which a new employee sees what the organization is really like and confronts the possibility that expectations and reality may diverge.*

metamorphosis stage *The stage in the socialization process in which a new employee changes and adjusts to the job, work group, and organization.*

Exhibit 16-4   How Organization Cultures Form

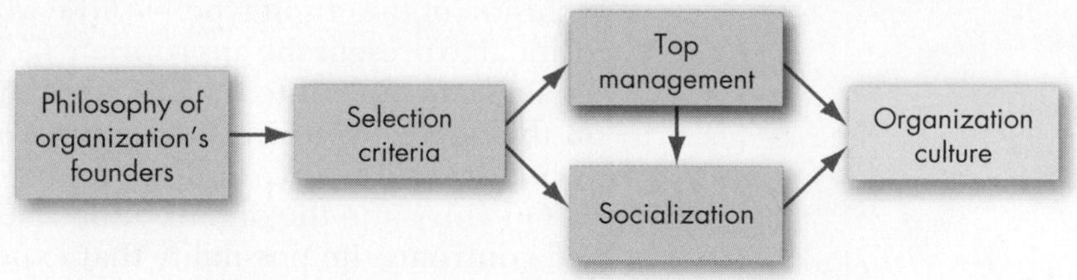

metamorphosis. Most research suggests there are two major "bundles" of socialization practices. The more management relies on formal, collective, sequential, fixed, and serial socialization programs and emphasize divestiture, the more likely newcomers' differences will be stripped away and replaced by standardized predictable behaviors. These *institutional* practices are common in police departments, fire departments, and other organizations that value rule following and order. Programs that are informal, individual, random, variable, and disjunctive and emphasize investiture are more likely to give newcomers an innovative sense of their role and methods of working. Creative fields, such as research and development, advertising, and filmmaking, rely on these *individual* practices. Most research suggests high levels of institutional practices encourage person–organization fit and high levels of commitment, whereas individual practices produce more role innovation.[42]

The three-part entry socialization process is complete when new members have become comfortable with the organization and their job. They have internalized and accepted the norms of the organization and their work group, are confident in their competence, and feel trusted and valued by their peers. They understand the system—not only their own tasks but the rules, procedures, and informally accepted practices as well. Finally, they know what is expected of them and what criteria will be used to measure and evaluate their work. As Exhibit 16-2 showed, successful metamorphosis should have a positive impact on new employees' productivity and their commitment to the organization and reduce their propensity to leave the organization.

Summary: How Cultures Form

Exhibit 16-4 summarizes how an organization's culture is established and sustained. The original culture derives from the founder's philosophy and strongly influences hiring criteria as the firm grows. Top managers' actions set the general climate, including what is acceptable behavior and what is not. The way employees are socialized will depend both on the degree of success achieved in matching new employees' values to those of the organization in the selection process, and on top management's preference for socialization methods.

How Employees Learn Culture

4 Show how culture is transmitted to employees.

Culture is transmitted to employees in a number of forms, the most potent being stories, rituals, material symbols, and language.

Stories

When Henry Ford II was chairman of Ford Motor Company, you would have been hard pressed to find a manager who hadn't heard how he reminded his executives, when they got too arrogant, "It's my name that's on the building." The message was clear: Henry Ford II ran the company.

A number of senior Nike executives spend much of their time serving as corporate storytellers. And the stories they tell are meant to convey what Nike is about.[43] When they tell how co-founder (and Oregon track coach) Bill Bowerman went to his workshop and poured rubber into his wife's waffle iron to create a better running shoe, they're talking about Nike's spirit of innovation. When new hires hear tales of Oregon running star Steve Prefontaine's battles to make running a professional sport and attain better-performance equipment, they learn of Nike's commitment to helping athletes.

Stories such as these circulate through many organizations. They typically contain a narrative of events about the organization's founders, rule breaking, rags-to-riches successes, reductions in the workforce, relocation of employees, reactions to past mistakes, and organizational coping.[44] These stories anchor the present in the past and explain and legitimate current practices.

Rituals

Rituals are repetitive sequences of activities that express and reinforce the key values of the organization—what goals are most important, which people are important, and which people are expendable.[45] One of the better-known is Walmart's company chant. Begun by the company's founder, Sam Walton, as a way to motivate and unite his workforce, "Gimme a W, gimme an A, gimme an L, gimme a squiggle, give me an M, A, R, T!" has become a ritual that bonds workers and reinforces Walton's belief in the value of his employees to the company's success. Similar corporate chants are used by IBM, Ericsson, Novell, Deutsche Bank, and PricewaterhouseCoopers.[46]

Material Symbols

Alcoa headquarters doesn't look like your typical head-office operation. There are few individual offices, even for senior executives. The space is essentially made up of cubicles, common areas, and meeting rooms. This informality conveys to employees that Alcoa values openness, equality, creativity, and flexibility. Some corporations provide their top executives with chauffeur-driven limousines and a corporate jet. Others drive the company car themselves and travel in the economy section.

The layout of corporate headquarters, the types of automobiles top executives are given, and the presence or absence of corporate aircraft are a few examples of **material symbols**. Others include the size of offices, the elegance of furnishings, executive perks, and attire.[47] These convey to employees who is important, the degree of egalitarianism top management desires, and the kinds of behavior that are appropriate, such as risk taking, conservative, authoritarian, participative, individualistic, or social.

rituals   *Repetitive sequences of activities that express and reinforce the key values of the organization, which goals are most important, which people are important, and which are expendable.*

material symbols   *What conveys to employees who is important, the degree of egalitarianism top management desires, and the kinds of behavior that are appropriate.*

At Walmart, culture is transmitted to employees through the daily ritual of the "Walmart cheer," which was written by company founder Sam Walton. In this photo a store manager leads employees in the motivational chant "Give me a W, give me an A" and so on that spells the company name and ends with "Who's number one? The customer! Always!" The cheer helps preserve a small-family spirit and work environment within the world's largest retailer and keeps employees focused on serving the customer.

Language

Many organizations and subunits within them use language to help members identify with the culture, attest to their acceptance of it, and help preserve it. Unique terms describe equipment, officers, key individuals, suppliers, customers, or products that relate to the business. New employees may at first be overwhelmed by acronyms and jargon, that, once assimilated, act as a common denominator to unite members of a given culture or subculture. If you're a new employee at Boeing, you'll find yourself learning a unique vocabulary, including *BOLD* (Boeing online data), *CATIA* (computer-graphics-aided three-dimensional interactive application), *MAIDS* (manufacturing assembly and installation data system), *POP* (purchased outside production), and *SLO* (service-level objectives).[48]

Creating an Ethical Organizational Culture

5 Demonstrate how an ethical culture can be created.

The organizational culture most likely to shape high ethical standards among its members is one that's high in risk tolerance, low to moderate in aggressiveness, and focused on means as well as outcomes.[49] This type of culture also takes a long-term perspective and balances the rights of multiple stakeholders, including the communities in which the business operates, its employees, and its stockholders. Managers are supported for taking risks and innovating, discouraged from engaging in unbridled competition, and guided to pay attention not just to *what* goals are achieved but also to *how*.

If the culture is strong and supports high ethical standards, it should have a very powerful and positive influence on employee behavior. Johnson & Johnson has a strong culture that has long stressed corporate obligations to customers, employees, the community, and shareholders, in that order.

When poisoned bottles of Tylenol (a Johnson & Johnson product) were found in stores some years ago, company employees independently pulled the product from shelves across the United States before management had even issued a statement about the tampering. No one had to tell these individuals what was morally right; they knew what Johnson & Johnson would expect them to do. On the other hand, a strong culture that encourages pushing the limits can be a powerful force in shaping unethical behavior. Enron's aggressive culture, with its unrelenting pressure on executives to rapidly expand earnings, encouraged ethical lapses and eventually contributed to the company's downfall.[50]

What can management do to create a more ethical culture? Research suggests managers can have an effect on the ethical behavior of employees by adhering to the following principles:[51]

- *Be a visible role model.* Employees will look to the actions of top management as a benchmark for appropriate behavior. Senior managers taking the ethical high road send a positive message to all employees.
- *Communicate ethical expectations.* Minimize ethical ambiguities by creating and disseminating an organizational code of ethics. The code should state the organization's primary values and the ethical rules employees are expected to follow.
- *Provide ethical training.* Set up seminars, workshops, and similar ethical training programs. Use these to reinforce the organization's standards of conduct, clarify what practices are and are not permissible, and address potential ethical dilemmas.
- *Visibly reward ethical acts and punish unethical ones.* Include in managers' performance appraisals a point-by-point evaluation of how their decisions measure up against the organization's code of ethics. Review the means taken to achieve goals as well as the ends themselves. Visibly reward those who act ethically. Just as important, unethical acts should be conspicuously punished.
- *Provide protective mechanisms.* Provide formal mechanisms so employees can discuss ethical dilemmas and report unethical behavior without fear of reprimand. These might include ethical counselors, ombudsmen, or ethical officers.

Setting a positive ethical climate has to start at the top of the organization.[52] A study of 195 managers demonstrated that when top management emphasizes strong ethical values, supervisors are more likely to practice ethical leadership. This positive ethical attitude transfers down to line employees, who show lower levels of deviant behavior and higher levels of cooperation and assistance. The general ethical behavior and attitudes of other members of the department matter too for shaping individual ethical behavior. Finally, employees whose ethical values are similar to those of their department are more likely to be promoted, so we can think of ethical culture as flowing from the bottom up as well.[53]

Creating a Positive Organizational Culture

6   Describe a positive organizational culture.

At first blush, creating a positive culture may sound hopelessly naïve or like a Dilbert-style conspiracy. The one thing that makes us believe this trend is here to stay, however, are signs that management practice and OB research are converging.

A **positive organizational culture** emphasizes building on employee strengths, rewards more than it punishes, and emphasizes individual vitality and growth.[54] Let's consider each of these areas.

Building on Employee Strengths   A lot of OB, and of management practice, considers how to fix employee problems. Although a positive organizational culture does not ignore problems, it does emphasize showing workers how they can capitalize on their strengths. As management guru Peter Drucker said, "Most Americans do not know what their strengths are. When you ask them, they look at you with a blank stare, or they respond in terms of subject knowledge, which is the wrong answer." Do you know what your strengths are? Wouldn't it be better to be in an organizational culture that helped you discover them, and learn ways to make the most of them?

Larry Hammond used this approach—finding and exploiting employee strengths—when you'd least expect it: during his firm's darkest days. Hammond is CEO of Auglaize Provico, an agribusiness company based in Ohio. The company was in the midst of its worst financial struggles and had to lay off one-quarter of its workforce. At that nadir, Hammond decided to try a different approach. Rather than dwell on what was wrong, he took advantage of what was right. "If you really want to [excel], you have to know yourself—you have to know what you're good at, and you have to know what you're not so good at," says Hammond. With the help of Gallup consultant Barry Conchie, Hammond focused on discovering and using employee strengths and helped the company turn itself around. "You ask Larry [Hammond] what the difference is, and he'll say that it's individuals using their natural talents," says Conchie.[55] One employee may be strong in ideation (the ability to find connections between seemingly disparate phenomena) and learn to use that strength more often and effectively, while another may discover and develop the skill of consistency (the ability to set clear rules and adhere to them).

Rewarding More Than Punishing   Although most organizations are sufficiently focused on extrinsic rewards such as pay and promotions, they often forget about the power of smaller (and cheaper) rewards such as praise. Part of creating a positive organizational culture is "catching employees doing something right." Another part is articulating praise. Many managers withhold praise either because they're afraid employees will coast or because they think praise is not valued. Because employees generally don't ask for praise, managers usually don't realize the costs of failing to do it. Failing to praise can become a silent killer, like escalating blood pressure.

Consider Elżbieta Górska-Kolodziejczyk, a plant manager for International Paper's facility in Kwidzyn, Poland. The job environment at the plant is bleak and difficult. Employees work in a windowless basement. Staffing is roughly one-third its prior level, while production has tripled. These challenges had done in the previous three managers. So, when Górska-Kolodziejczyk took over, she knew she had her work cut out for her. Although she had many items on her list of ways to transform the organization, at the top were recognition and praise. She initially found it difficult to give praise to those who weren't used to it, especially men. "They were like cement at the beginning," she said. "Like cement." Over time, however, she found they valued and even reciprocated praise. One day a department supervisor pulled her over to tell her she was doing a good job. "This I do remember, yes," she said.[56]

Emphasizing Vitality and Growth   A positive organizational culture emphasizes not only organizational effectiveness but also individuals' growth.

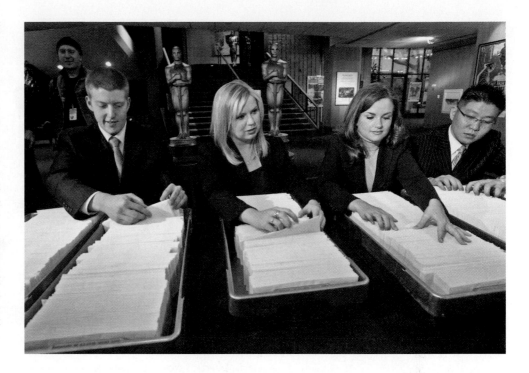

Employees of PricewaterhouseCoopers work within a positive organizational culture that emphasizes individuals' vitality and growth. One of the largest accounting firms in the world, PwC offers employees continual professional and individual learning opportunities on the job, at clients' workplaces, and in formal training programs. PwC's Learning and Education Group provides access to the latest information on industry standards and best practices, and seminars and classes help employees develop their technical skills. PwC has coaches and mentors to help employees design a personalized career path. Shown here is a PwC team counting the Oscars ballots for the Academy of Motion Picture Arts and Sciences, a company client for more than 75 years.

No organization will get the best from employees who see themselves as mere tools or parts of the organization. A positive culture recognizes the difference between a job and a career and supports not only what the employee does to contribute to organizational effectiveness but also what the organization can do to make the employee more effective (personally and professionally).

Although it may take more creativity to encourage employee growth in some types of industries, consider the fast-paced food industry. Philippe Lescornez leads a team of employees at Masterfoods in Belgium. One of his team members is Didier Brynaert, who works in Luxembourg, nearly 150 miles from the Masterfoods Belgian headquarters. Brynaert was considered a good sales promoter who was meeting expectations. Lescornez decided Brynaert's job could be made more important if he were seen less as just another sales promoter and more as an expert on the unique features of the Luxembourg market. So Lescornez asked Brynaert for information he could share with the home office. He hoped that by raising Brynaert's profile in Brussels, he could create in him a greater sense of ownership for his remote sales territory. "I started to communicate much more what he did to other people [within the company], because there's quite some distance between the Brussels office and the section he's working in. So I started to communicate, communicate, communicate. The more I communicated, the more he started to provide material," says Lescornez. As a result, "Now he's recognized as the specialist for Luxembourg—the guy who is able to build a strong relationship with the Luxembourg clients," says Lescornez. What's good for Brynaert is, of course, also good for Lescornez, who gets credit for helping Brynaert grow and develop.[57]

positive organizational culture *A culture that emphasizes building on employee strengths, rewards more than punishes, and emphasizes individual vitality and growth.*

OB Poll Is Your Organization's Culture Religious, Secular, or Somewhere In-Between?

Religious, 10%

Secular, 32%

In-Between, 58%

Source: Based on *Religion and Corporate Culture* (2008 survey of 543 human resource professionals). Alexandria, VA: Society for Human Resource Management.

Limits of Positive Culture Is a positive culture a panacea? Though companies such as GE, Xerox, Boeing, and 3M have embraced aspects of a positive organizational culture, it is a new enough idea for us to be uncertain about how and when it works best.

Not all cultures value being positive as much as U.S. culture does, and, even within U.S. culture, there surely are limits to how far we should go to preserve a positive culture. For example, Admiral, a British insurance company, has established a Ministry of Fun in its call centers to organize such events as poem writings, foosball, conker (a British game involving chestnuts) competitions, and fancy dress days. When does the pursuit of a positive culture start to seem coercive or even Orwellian? As one critic notes, "Promoting a social orthodoxy of positiveness focuses on a particular constellation of desirable states and traits but, in so doing, can stigmatize those who fail to fit the template."[58]

Our point is that there may be benefits to establishing a positive culture, but an organization also needs to be careful to be objective and not pursue it past the point of effectiveness.

Spirituality and Organizational Culture

What do Southwest Airlines, Hewlett-Packard, Ford, The Men's Wearhouse, Tyson Foods, Wetherill Associates, and Tom's of Maine have in common? They're among a growing number of organizations that have embraced workplace spirituality.

What Is Spirituality?

Workplace spirituality is *not* about organized religious practices. It's not about God or theology. **Workplace spirituality** recognizes that people have an inner life that nourishes and is nourished by meaningful work in the context of community.[59] Organizations that promote a spiritual culture recognize that people have both a mind and a spirit, seek to find meaning and purpose in their work, and desire to connect with other human beings and be part of a community. Many of the topics we have discussed—ranging from job design (designing work that is meaningful to employees) to transformational leadership (leadership practices that emphasize a higher-order purpose and self-transcendent goals—are well matched to the concept of organizational spirituality. When a company emphasizes its commitment to paying Third World suppliers a fair (above-market) price for their coffee to facilitate community development—as did Starbucks— or encourages employees to share prayers or inspirational messages through e-mail—as did Interstate Batteries —it is encouraging a more spiritual culture.[60]

Why Spirituality Now?

As we noted in our discussion of emotions in Chapter 4, the myth of rationality assumed the well-run organization eliminated feelings. Concern about an employee's inner life had no role in the perfectly rational model. But just as we've now come to realize that the study of emotions improves our understanding of organizational behavior, an awareness of spirituality can help us better understand employee behavior in the twenty-first century.

Of course, employees have always had an inner life. So why has the search for meaning and purposefulness in work surfaced now? We summarize the reasons in Exhibit 16-5.

Characteristics of a Spiritual Organization

The concept of workplace spirituality draws on our previous discussions of topics such as values, ethics, motivation, leadership, and work–life balance. Spiritual organizations are concerned with helping people develop and reach their full potential. Similarly, organizations concerned with spirituality are more likely to directly address problems created by work–life conflicts. What differentiates spiritual organizations from their nonspiritual counterparts? Although research

Exhibit **16-5**	Reasons for the Growing Interest in Spirituality

- As a counterbalance to the pressures and stress of a turbulent pace of life. Contemporary lifestyles—single-parent families, geographic mobility, the temporary nature of jobs, new technologies that create distance between people—underscore the lack of community many people feel and increase the need for involvement and connection.

- Formalized religion hasn't worked for many people, and they continue to look for anchors to replace lack of faith and to fill a growing feeling of emptiness.

- Job demands have made the workplace dominant in many people's lives, yet they continue to question the meaning of work.

- The desire to integrate personal life values with one's professional life.

- An increasing number of people are finding that the pursuit of more material acquisitions leaves them unfulfilled.

workplace spirituality   *The recognition that people have an inner life that nourishes and is nourished by meaningful work that takes place in the context of community.*

Mark Trang, an employee of Salesforce.com, teaches business basics to fifth-grade students at an elementary school. Salesforce.com encourages every employee to donate 1 percent of his or her working time to the community, which gives employees the chance to integrate personal life values with their professional lives. By volunteering, employees experience the joy and satisfaction that comes from helping others. Employees give to the community by feeding the homeless, tutoring kids, gardening in community parks, lending computer expertise to nonprofit groups, and providing disaster relief.

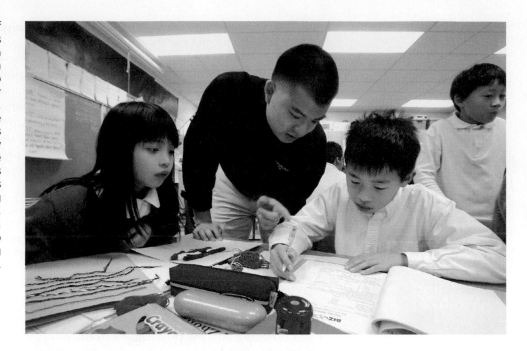

on this question is only preliminary, our review identified four cultural characteristics that tend to be evident in spiritual organizations:[61]

- *Strong sense of purpose.* Spiritual organizations build their cultures around a meaningful purpose. Although profits may be important, they're not the primary values of the organization. People want to be inspired by a purpose they believe is important and worthwhile.

- *Trust and respect.* Spiritual organizations are characterized by mutual trust, honesty, and openness. Managers aren't afraid to admit mistakes. The president of Wetherill Associates, a highly successful auto parts distribution firm, says, "We don't tell lies here, and everyone knows it. We are specific and honest about quality and suitability of the product for our customers' needs, even if we know they might not be able to detect any problem."[62]

- *Humanistic work practices.* These practices embraced by spiritual organizations include flexible work schedules, group- and organization-based rewards, narrowing of pay and status differentials, guarantees of individual worker rights, employee empowerment, and job security. Hewlett-Packard has handled temporary downturns through voluntary attrition and shortened workweeks (shared by all), and it has managed longer-term declines with early retirements and buyouts.

- *Toleration of employee expression.* The final characteristic that differentiates spiritually based organizations is that they don't stifle employee emotions. They allow people to be themselves—to express their moods and feelings without guilt or fear of reprimand. Employees at Southwest Airlines are encouraged to express their sense of humor on the job, to act spontaneously, and to make their work fun.

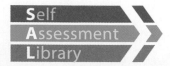

HOW SPIRITUAL AM I?

In the Self-Assessment Library (available on CD and online), take assessment IV.A.4 (How Spiritual Am I?). Note: People's scores on this measure vary from time to time, so take that into account when interpreting the results.

Criticisms of Spirituality

7 Identify characteristics of a spiritual culture.

Critics of the spirituality movement in organizations have focused on three issues. First is the question of scientific foundation. What really is workplace spirituality? Is it just a new management buzzword? Second, are spiritual organizations legitimate? Specifically, do organizations have the right to impose spiritual values on their employees? Third is the question of economics: Are spirituality and profits compatible?

First, as you might imagine, there is very little research on workplace spirituality. We don't know whether the concept will have staying power. Do the cultural characteristics we just identified really separate spiritual organizations? Spirituality has been defined so broadly in some sources that practices from job rotation to corporate retreats at meditation centers have been identified as spiritual practices. Do employees of so-called spiritual organizations perceive that they work in spiritual organizations? Although research suggests support for workplace spirituality, the questions we've posed need to be answered before the concept gains full credibility.

On the second question, an emphasis on spirituality can clearly make some employees uneasy. Critics might argue that secular institutions, especially business firms, have no business imposing spiritual values on employees. This criticism is undoubtedly valid when spirituality is defined as bringing religion and God into the workplace.[63] However, the criticism seems less stinging when the goal is limited to helping employees find meaning in their work lives. If the concerns listed in Exhibit 16-5 truly characterize a growing segment of the workforce, then perhaps the time is right for organizations to help employees find meaning and purpose in their work and to use the workplace as a source of community.

Finally, whether spirituality and profits are compatible objectives is certainly relevant for managers and investors in business. The evidence, although limited, indicates they are. A recent research study by a major consulting firm found companies that introduced spiritually based techniques improved productivity and significantly reduced turnover.[64] Another study found organizations that provided their employees with opportunities for spiritual development outperformed those that didn't.[65] Other studies also report that spirituality in organizations was positively related to creativity, employee satisfaction, job involvement, and organizational commitment.[66] And if you're looking for a single case to make the argument for spirituality, it's hard to beat Southwest Airlines. Southwest has one of the lowest employee turnover rates in the airline industry; it consistently has the lowest labor costs per miles flown of any major airline; it regularly outpaces its competitors for achieving on-time arrivals and fewest customer complaints; and it has proven itself to be the most consistently profitable airline in the United States.[67]

Global Implications

8 Show how national culture may affect the way organizational culture is transported to a different country.

We considered global cultural values (collectivism–individualism, power distance, and so on) in Chapter 5. Here our focus is a bit narrower: How is organizational culture affected by a global context? As the opening vignette suggests, organizational cultures are so powerful they often transcend national boundaries. But that doesn't mean organizations should, or could, be blissfully ignorant of local culture.

Organizational cultures often reflect national culture. The culture at AirAsia, a Malaysian-based airline, emphasizes informal dress so as not to create status differences. The carrier has lots of parties, participative management, and no

An Ethical Choice

Working in a Spiritual Culture

The vast majority of U.S. adults describe themselves as religious—in a 2008 poll 78 percent describe themselves as Christian, and 92 percent describe themselves as spiritual. It is not surprising, therefore, that spirituality often blends into organizational cultures. As we have noted in describing a spiritual culture, it usually accommodates most beliefs. However, some organizational leaders go further. Coca-Cola Bottling Consolidated, the second-largest Coca-Cola bottler with 5,800 employees in 11 states, has a company mission and values statement that places faith front and center. The statement begins with "Our Values Honor God." Austaco Ltd., a Texas-based company with 1,800 employees, calls itself "a Christian company—Christ- or God-centered."

As important as spirituality is to most in the United States, a rising number (though still a small minority) describe themselves as atheists or agnostics, and that is much more the case for Europeans. It's obvious, too, that while most U.S. adults are Christians, millions have other religious beliefs.

What happens if you find yourself working in a company whose prevailing religious culture is at odds with your own? According to Victoria Leyva, then a human resources manager at the University of Chicago Hospital, Joan Shaw, the human resources director, became verbally aggressive when she learned about Leyva's religious views. "I remember being very sad," Leyva said. In Britain, Caroline Petrie, a nurse, was suspended for offering to pray for a patient; Naphtali Chondol, a social worker, was fired for giving a Bible to a client; and Nadia Eweida, a British Airways ticket agent, was prohibited from wearing a cross at work.

Here is some advice if you must navigate an uncomfortable situation due to a mismatch between the culture and your beliefs:

1. Resist creating oppression in your own mind where it doesn't exist. Just because your religious views are at odds with the culture doesn't mean your career is necessarily doomed there. We do business with people of different faiths all the time. Working with a company with a different idea of spirituality works for many.

2. Religious discrimination claims to the Equal Employment Opportunity Commission (EEOC) have grown by 54 percent since 2002. If you think you have been treated negatively because of your religious beliefs, look into the matter further. Also recognize that the EEOC finds in most cases that the person bringing the charge has no standing or merit for his or her claim. To see whether your claim might be meritorious, go to eeoc.gov/policy/docs/qanda_religion.html.

3. Talk with your supervisor or the human resources manager because they are often in the best position to stop religious harassment or accommodate your views.

Sources: Based on C. S. Stewart, "Office Politics and God," *Salon* (June 24, 2009), dir.salon.com; R. J. Grossman, "Religion at Work," *HR Magazine* (December 2008), pp. 27–33; M. Rice-Oxley, "Some British Christians Feel Oppressed in the Public Square," *Christian Science Monitor* (February 26, 2009), www.csmonitor.com.

private offices, reflecting Malaysia's relatively collectivistic culture. However, the culture of US Airways does not reflect the same degree of informality. If US Airways were to set up operations in Malaysia or merge with AirAsia, it would need to take these cultural differences into account. So when an organization opens up operations in another country, it ignores the local culture at its own risk.

One of the primary things U.S. managers can do is to be culturally sensitive. The United States is a dominant force in business and in culture, and with that influence comes a reputation. "We are broadly seen throughout the world as arrogant people, totally self-absorbed and loud," says one U.S. executive. Companies such as American Airlines, Lowe's, Novell, ExxonMobil, and Microsoft have implemented training programs to sensitize their managers to cultural differences. Some ways in which U.S. managers can be culturally sensitive include talking in a low tone of voice, speaking slowly, listening more, and avoiding discussions of religion and politics.

The management of ethical behavior is one area where national culture can rub up against corporate culture.[68] Many strategies for improving ethical behavior are based on the values and beliefs of the host country. U.S. managers endorse the supremacy of anonymous market forces and implicitly or explicitly view profit maximization as a moral obligation for business organizations. This worldview sees bribery, nepotism, and favoring personal contacts as highly unethical. Any action that deviates from profit maximization may indicate that inappropriate or corrupt behavior may be occurring. In contrast, managers in developing economies are more likely to see ethical decisions as embedded in a social environment. That means doing special favors for family and friends is not only appropriate but may even be an ethical responsibility. Managers in many nations also view capitalism skeptically and believe the interests of workers should be put on a par with the interests of shareholders.

U.S. employees are not the only ones who need to be culturally sensitive. Three times a week, employees at the Canadian unit of Japanese video game maker Koei begin the day by standing next to their desks, facing their boss, and saying "Good morning" in unison. Employees then deliver short speeches on topics that range from corporate principles to 3D game engines. Koei also has employees punch a time clock and asks women to serve tea to top executive guests. Although these practices are consistent with Koei's culture, they do not fit Canadian culture very well. "It's kind of like school," says one Canadian employee.[69]

Summary and Implications for Managers

Exhibit 16-6 depicts organizational culture as an intervening variable. Employees form an overall subjective perception of the organization based on factors such as degree of risk tolerance, team emphasis, and support of people. This overall perception becomes, in effect, the organization's culture or personality and affects employee performance and satisfaction, with stronger cultures having greater impact.

Just as people's personalities tend to be stable over time, so too do strong cultures. This makes a strong culture difficult for managers to change if it becomes mismatched to its environment. But as this chapter's Point/Counterpoint demonstrates, changing an organization's culture is a long and difficult process. Thus, at least in the short term, managers should treat their organization's culture as relatively fixed.

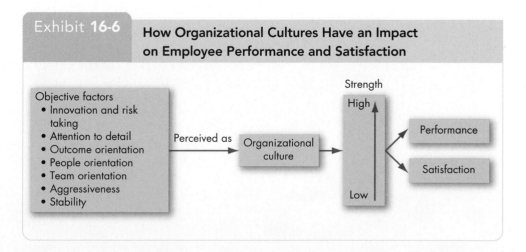

Exhibit 16-6 How Organizational Cultures Have an Impact on Employee Performance and Satisfaction

One of the most important managerial implications of organizational culture relates to selection decisions. Hiring individuals whose values don't align with those of the organization is likely to yield employees who lack motivation and commitment and are dissatisfied with their jobs and the organization.[70] Not surprisingly, employee "misfits" have considerably higher turnover rates.[71]

An employee's performance also depends to a considerable degree on knowing what to do and not do. Understanding the right way to do a job indicates proper socialization.

As a manager, you can shape the culture of your work environment. All managers can especially do their part to create an ethical culture and to consider spirituality and its role in creating a positive organizational culture. Often you can do as much to shape your organizational culture as the culture of the organization shapes you.

Organizational Cultures Can't Be Changed

An organization's culture is made up of relatively stable characteristics. It develops over many years and is rooted in deeply held values to which employees are strongly committed. In addition, a number of forces continually operate to maintain a given culture. These include written statements about the organization's mission and philosophy, the design of physical spaces and buildings, the dominant leadership style, hiring criteria, past promotion practices, entrenched rituals, popular stories about key people and events, the organization's historic performance evaluation criteria, and the organization's formal structure.

Selection and promotion policies are particularly important devices that work against cultural change. Employees choose an organization in part because they perceive their values to be a good fit with it. They become comfortable with that fit and will strongly resist efforts to disturb the equilibrium. Top executives also select senior managers who will sustain the current culture. Organizations such as Ford, VW, and the U.S. Postal Service, all of which historically attracted people looking for stable and highly structured environments, can attest to the difficulty of trying to reshape the culture. Even attempts to change by going outside the organization to hire a new chief executive are unlikely to be effective. The culture is more likely to change the executive than the other way around.

We're not saying culture can *never* be changed. Usually when an organization confronts a crisis that threatens its survival, members do respond to efforts to change the culture. However, anything less than that is unlikely to be effective.

Changing an organization's culture is extremely difficult, but it *can* be done. The evidence suggests that cultural change is most likely to take place when most or all of the following conditions exist:

- **A dramatic crisis.** This is a shock that undermines the status quo and calls into question the relevance of the current culture. Examples are a surprising financial setback, the loss of a major customer, and a dramatic technological breakthrough by a competitor.
- **Turnover in leadership.** New top leadership, which can provide an alternative set of key values, may be perceived as more capable of responding to the crisis (as when Mark Hurd replaced Carly Fiorina at HP).
- **Young and small organizations.** The younger the organization, the less entrenched its culture will be. It's also easier for management to communicate new values when the organization is small.
- **Weak culture.** The more widely held a culture is and the higher the agreement among members on its values, the more difficult it will be to change. Weak cultures are more amenable to change than strong ones.

If all or most of these conditions exist, the following management actions may lead to change: initiating new stories and rituals, selecting and promoting employees who espouse the new values, changing the reward system to support the new values, and undermining current subcultures through transfers, job rotation, and terminations.

Under the best conditions, these actions won't result in an immediate or dramatic shift in the culture. In the final analysis, cultural change is a lengthy process—measured in years rather than in months. But it can happen, as the success of new leadership in turning around the cultures at companies such as IBM, 3M, and GE attests.

Questions for Review

1 What is organizational culture, and what are its common characteristics?

2 What are the functional and dysfunctional effects of organizational culture?

3 What factors create and sustain an organization's culture?

4 How is culture transmitted to employees?

5 How can an ethical culture be created?

6 What is a positive organizational culture?

7 What are the characteristics of a spiritual culture?

8 How does national culture affect how organizational culture is transported to a different country?

Experiential Exercise

RATE YOUR CLASSROOM CULTURE

Listed here are 14 statements. Using the 5-item scale (from Strongly Agree to Strongly Disagree), respond to each statement by circling the number that best represents your opinion.

	Strongly Agree	Agree	Neutral	Disagree	Strongly Disagree
1. I feel comfortable challenging statements made by my instructor.	1	2	3	4	5
2. My instructor heavily penalizes assignments that are not turned in on time.	1	2	3	4	5
3. My instructor believes that "It's final results that count."	1	2	3	4	5
4. My instructor is sensitive to my personal needs and problems.	1	2	3	4	5
5. A large portion of my grade depends on how well I work with others in the class.	1	2	3	4	5
6. I often feel nervous and tense when I come to class.	1	2	3	4	5
7. My instructor seems to prefer stability over change.	1	2	3	4	5
8. My instructor encourages me to develop new and different ideas.	1	2	3	4	5
9. My instructor has little tolerance for sloppy thinking.	1	2	3	4	5
10. My instructor is more concerned with how I came to a conclusion than with the conclusion itself.	1	2	3	4	5
11. My instructor treats all students alike.	1	2	3	4	5
12. My instructor frowns on class members helping each other with assignments.	1	2	3	4	5
13. Aggressive and competitive people have a distinct advantage in this class.	1	2	3	4	5
14. My instructor encourages me to see the world differently.	1	2	3	4	5

Calculate your total score by adding up the numbers you circled. Your score will fall between 14 and 70.

A high score (49 or above) describes an open, risk-taking, supportive, humanistic, team-oriented, easygoing, growth-oriented culture. A low score (35 or below) describes a closed, structured, task-oriented, individualistic, tense, and stability-oriented culture. Note that differences count, so a score of 60 is a more open culture than one that scores 50. Also, realize that one culture isn't preferable over another. The "right" culture depends on you and your preferences for a learning environment.

Form teams of five to seven members each. Compare your scores. How closely do they align? Discuss and resolve any discrepancies. Based on your team's analysis, what type of student do you think would perform best in this class?

Ethical Dilemma

IS THERE ROOM FOR SNOOPING IN AN ORGANIZATION'S CULTURE?

Many companies spy on their employees—sometimes with and sometimes without their knowledge or consent. Organizations differ in their culture of surveillance. Some differences are due to the type of business. A U.S. Department of Defense contractor has more reason—perhaps even an obligation—to spy on its employees than does an orange juice producer.

However, surveillance in most industries is on the upswing. There are several reasons, including the huge growth of two sectors with theft and security problems—services and information technology, respectively—and the increased availability of surveillance technology.

Consider the following surveillance actions, and decide for each whether it would never be ethical (mark N), would sometimes be ethical (mark S), or would always be ethical (mark A). For those you mark S, indicate on what factors your judgment would depend.

1. Sifting through an employee's trash for evidence of wrongdoing
2. Periodically reading e-mail messages for disclosure of confidential information or inappropriate use
3. Conducting video surveillance of work space
4. Monitoring Web sites visited by employees and determining the appropriateness and work relatedness of those visited
5. Taping phone conversations
6. Posing as a job candidate, an investor, a customer, or a colleague (when the real purpose is to solicit information)

Would you be less likely to work for an employer that engaged in some of these methods? Why or why not? Do you think use of surveillance says something about an organization's culture?

Case Incident 1

MERGERS DON'T ALWAYS LEAD TO CULTURE CLASHES

A lot of mergers lead to culture clashes and, ultimately, failure. So in 2005 when banking giant Bank of America (BOA) announced its $35 billion acquisition of credit card giant MBNA, many thought that in a few years this merger would join the heap of those done in by cultural differences.

MBNA's culture was characterized by a free-wheeling, entrepreneurial spirit that was also quite secretive. MBNA employees also were accustomed to the high life. Their corporate headquarters in Wilmington, Delaware, could be described as lavish, and employees throughout the company enjoyed high salaries and generous perks—from the private golf course at its headquarters to its fleet of corporate jets and private yachts.

Bank of America, in contrast, grew by thrift. It was a low-cost, no-nonsense operation. Unlike MBNA, it believed that size and smarts were more important than speed. It was an acquisition machine that some likened to *Star Trek*'s relentless Borg collective.

In short, the cultures in the two companies were very, very different.

Although these cultural differences seemed a recipe for disaster, it appears, judging from the reactions of BOA and MBNA employees, that the merger has worked. How can this be?

BOA had the foresight to know which MBNA practices to attempt to change and which to keep in place. Especially critical was BOA's appreciation and respect for MBNA's culture. "On Day 1, I was directed that this was not like the ones you are used to," said Clifford Skelton, who had helped manage BOA's acquisition of FleetBoston Financial before moving on to MBNA.

To try to manage the cultural transition, executives of both companies began by comparing thousands of practices covering everything from hiring to call-center operations. In many cases, BOA chose to keep MBNA's cultural practices in place. In other cases, BOA did impose its will on MBNA. For example, because MBNA's pay rates were well above market, many MBNA managers were forced to swallow a steep pay cut. Some MBNA employees left, but most remained.

In other cases, the cultures co-adapted. For example, MBNA's dress code was much more formal than BOA's business-casual approach. In the end, a hybrid code was adopted, where business suits were expected in the credit-card division's corporate offices and in front of clients, but business casual was the norm otherwise.

While most believe the merger has been successful, there are tensions. Some BOA managers see MBNA managers as arrogant and autocratic. Some MBNA managers see their BOA counterparts as bureaucratic.

What about those famous MBNA perks? As you might have guessed, most have disappeared. All but one of the corporate jets is gone. The golf course was donated to the state of Delaware. Gone, too, are most of the works of art that hung in MBNA's corporate offices.

Of course, BOA made another, more recent and much larger acquisition: Merrill Lynch. Whether the BOA–Merrill merger proves a success is still too early to tell.

Questions

1. In what ways were the cultures of Bank of America and MBNA incompatible?

2. Why do you think their cultures appeared to mesh rather than clash?

3. Do you think culture is important to the success of a merger/acquisition? Why or why not?

4. How much of the smooth transition, if any, do you think comes from both companies glossing over real differences in an effort to make the merger work?

Sources: Based on E. Dash, "A Clash of Cultures, Averted," *New York Times* (February 20, 2007), pp. B1, B3; L. Moyer, "Bank of America Lewis Must Wait on His Fate," *Forbes* (April 29, 2009), www.forbes.com.

Case Incident 2

GOOGLE AND P&G SWAP EMPLOYEES

The cultures of Google and Procter & Gamble (P&G) could not be more different. P&G is notoriously controlled, disciplined, scalable, and rigid—so much so that employees call themselves "Proctoids." Google is just as famous for its laid-back, unstandardized, free-flowing culture.

So what would cause these two large, successful examples of strong—yet dissimilar—corporate culture decide to socialize one another's employees? One reason clearly is marketing: P&G sees more of its future marketing efforts occurring online, and Google, of course, is an ideal fit for that strategy. Google, for its part, sees P&G as the ultimate "heavy hitter" buyer for its ad space (P&G is the biggest advertiser in the world).

However, it also seems clear this is about more than marketing. After all, P&G and Google do business with plenty of organizations with which they don't swap employees. Both companies believe that by exposing key managers to a culture that emphasizes innovation, but in a wholly different way, they can push their own innovation even further.

Sometimes we learn the most from the ways in which we are different, and that's certainly the case here. In one of the early employee swaps, Denise Chudy, a Google sales-team leader, stunned P&G managers with recent data indicating online search for the word *coupons* was up 50 percent in the past year. P&G staffers see themselves as members of one of the world's most innovative and data-driven organizations, famous for tracking consumer preferences, product use, and buying behavior. They are not easily stunned. To enter Google's own universe was a humbling, and challenging, learning experience.

Google's swapped employees are learning something, too. When poring over decades of marketing materials on P&G's Tide detergent and the firm's allegiance to bright orange packaging, Google employee Jen Bradburn wrote, "It's a help to know not to mess with the orange too much."

Differences, of course, are still apparent. When one P&G manager showed Google employees a 1954 ad for Tide, he proudly noted, "That's when you reached 70 percent to 80 percent of your audience with television." The Google team laughed in astonishment.

Questions

1. Do you think the employee swap between Google and P&G is a good idea for all companies? Why or why not? Why do so few companies do this?

2. One of the reasons P&G and Google agreed to the swap was to transmit the best aspects of the other company's culture to their own. Drawing from this chapter, describe how culture might be transmitted in such swaps.

3. Which culture—Google's or P&G's—do you think would fit you best? Why?

4. Would you enjoy an employee swap with a company with a very different culture? Why or why not?

Sources: Based on E. Byron, "A New Odd Couple: Google, P&G Swap Workers to Spur Innovation," *Wall Street Journal* (November 19, 2008), pp. A1, A18; A. G. Lafley, "P&G's Innovation Culture," *strategy+business (August 28, 2008), pp. 1–7; and "P&G, Google Swap Workers for Research,"* Silicon Valley/San Jose Business Journal *(November 20, 2008), www.bizjournals.com/sanjose.*

Endnotes

1. J. Jargon, "Neatness Counts at Kyocera and Others in the 5S Club," *Wall Street Journal* (October 27, 2008), pp. A1, A15; R. Gapp, R. Fisher, and K. Kobayashi, "Implementing 5S within a Japanese Context: An Integrated Management System," *Management Decision* 46, no. 4 (2008), pp. 565–579; and R. Hough, "5S Implementation Methodology," *Management Services* 52, no. 2 (2008), pp. 44–45.

2. See, for example, H. S. Becker, "Culture: A Sociological View," *Yale Review,* Summer 1982, pp. 513–527; and E. H. Schein, *Organizational Culture and Leadership* (San Francisco: Jossey-Bass, 1985), p. 168.

3. This seven-item description is based on C. A. O'Reilly III, J. Chatman, and D. F. Caldwell, "People and Organizational Culture: A Profile Comparison Approach to Assessing Person-Organization Fit," *Academy of Management Journal,* September 1991, pp. 487–516; and J. A. Chatman and K. A. Jehn, "Assessing the Relationship Between Industry Characteristics and Organizational Culture: How Different Can You Be?" *Academy of Management Journal,* June 1994, pp. 522–553.

4. The view that there will be consistency among perceptions of organizational culture has been called the "integration" perspective. For a review of this perspective and conflicting approaches, see D. Meyerson and J. Martin, "Cultural Change: An Integration of Three Different Views," *Journal of Management Studies,* November 1987, pp. 623–647; and P. J. Frost, L. F. Moore, M. R. Louis, C. C. Lundberg, and J. Martin (eds.), *Reframing Organizational Culture* (Newbury Park, CA: Sage, 1991).

5. See J. M. Jermier, J. W. Slocum, Jr., L. W. Fry, and J. Gaines, "Organizational Subcultures in a Soft Bureaucracy: Resistance Behind the Myth and Facade of an Official Culture," *Organization Science,* May 1991, pp. 170–194; S. A. Sackmann, "Culture and Subcultures: An Analysis of Organizational Knowledge," *Administrative Science Quarterly,* March 1992, pp. 140–161; and G. Hofstede, "Identifying Organizational Subcultures: An Empirical Approach," *Journal of Management Studies,* January 1998, pp. 1–12.

6. D. A. Hoffman and L. M. Jones, "Leadership, Collective Personality, and Performance," *Journal of Applied Psychology* 90, no. 3 (2005), pp. 509–522.

7. S. Hamm, "No Letup—And No Apologies," *BusinessWeek* (October 26, 1998), pp. 58–64; and C. Carlson, "Former Intel Exec Slams Microsoft Culture," *eWEEK.com,* March 26, 2002, www.eweek.com/article2/0,1759,94976,00.asp.

8. See, for example, G. G. Gordon and N. DiTomaso, "Predicting Corporate Performance from Organizational Culture," *Journal of Management Studies,* November 1992, pp. 793–798; J. B. Sorensen, "The Strength of Corporate Culture and the Reliability of Firm Performance," *Administrative Science Quarterly,* March 2002, pp. 70–91; and J. Rosenthal and M. A. Masarech, "High-Performance Cultures: How Values Can Drive Business Results," *Journal of Organizational Excellence,* Spring 2003, pp. 3–18.

9. Y. Wiener, "Forms of Value Systems: A Focus on Organizational Effectiveness and Cultural Change and Maintenance," *Academy of Management Review,* October 1988, p. 536; and B. Schneider, A. N. Salvaggio, and M. Subirats, "Climate Strength: A New Direction for Climate Research," *Journal of Applied Psychology* 87 (2002), pp. 220–229.

10. R. T. Mowday, L. W. Porter, and R. M. Steers, *Employee Linkages: The Psychology of Commitment, Absenteeism, and Turnover* (New York: Academic Press, 1982); C. Vandenberghe, "Organizational Culture, Person-Culture Fit, and Turnover: A Replication in the Health Care Industry," *Journal of Organizational Behavior,* March 1999, pp. 175–184; and M. Schulte, C. Ostroff, S. Shmulyian, and A. Kinicki, "Organizational Climate Configurations: Relationships to Collective Attitudes, Customer Satisfaction, and Financial Performance," *Journal of Applied Psychology* 94, no. 3 (2009), pp. 618–634.

11. S. L. Dolan and S. Garcia, "Managing by Values: Cultural Redesign for Strategic Organizational Change at the Dawn of the Twenty-First Century," *Journal of Management Development* 21, no. 2 (2002), pp. 101–117.

12. See C. A. O'Reilly and J. A. Chatman, "Culture as Social Control: Corporations, Cults, and Commitment," in B. M. Staw and L. L. Cummings (eds.), *Research in Organizational Behavior,* vol. 18 (Greenwich, CT: JAI Press, 1996), pp. 157–200. See also M. Pinae Cunha, "The 'Best Place to Be': Managing Control and Employee Loyalty in a Knowledge-Intensive Company," *Journal of Applied Behavioral Science,* December 2002, pp. 481–495.

13. T. E. Deal and A. A. Kennedy, "Culture: A New Look Through Old Lenses," *Journal of Applied Behavioral Sciences,* November 1983, p. 501.

14. Y. Ling, Z. Simsek, M. H. Lubatkin, and J. F. Veiga, "Transformational Leadership's Role in Promoting Corporate Entrepreneurship: Examining the CEO-TMT Interface," *Academy of Management Journal* 51, no. 3 (2008), pp. 557–576; and A. Malhotra, A. Majchrzak, and B. Rosen, Benson, "Leading virtual teams," *Academy of Management Perspectives* 21, no. 1 (2007), pp. 60–70.

15. D. Denison, "What Is the Difference Between Organizational Culture and Organizational Climate? A Native's Point of View on a Decade of Paradigm Wars," *Academy of Management Review* 21 (1996) pp. 519–654; and L. R. James, C. C. Choi, C. E. Ko, P. K. McNeil, M. K. Minton, M. A. Wright, and K. Kim, "Organizational and Psychological Climate: A Review of Theory and Research," *European Journal of Work and Organizational Psychology* 17, no. 1 (2008), pp. 5–32.

16. J. Z. Carr, A. M. Schmidt, J. K. Ford, and R. P. DeShon, "Climate Perceptions Matter: A Meta-analytic Path Analysis Relating Molar Climate, Cognitive and Affective States, and Individual Level Work Outcomes," *Journal of Applied Psychology* 88, no. (2003), pp. 605–619.

17. M. Schulte, C. Ostroff, S. Shmulyian, and A. Kinicki, "Organizational Climate Configurations: Relationships to Collective Attitudes, Customer Satisfaction, and Financial Performance."

18. See, for example, Z. S. Byrne, J. Stoner, K. R. Thompson, and W. Hochwarter, "The Interactive Effects of Conscientiousness, Work Effort, and Psychological Climate on Job Performance," *Journal of Vocational Behavior* 66, no. 2 (2005), pp. 326–338; D. S. Pugh, J. Dietz, A. P. Brief, and J. W. Wiley, "Looking Inside and Out: The Impact of Employee and Community Demographic Composition on Organizational Diversity Climate," *Journal of Applied Psychology* 93, no. 6 (2008), pp. 1422–1428; and J. C. Wallace, E. Popp, and S. Mondore, "Safety Climate as a Mediator Between Foundation Climates and Occupational Accidents: A Group-Level Investigation," *Journal of Applied Psychology* 91, no. 3 (2006), pp. 681–688.

19. R. L. Jepperson, "Institutions, Institutional Effects, and Institutionalism," in W. W. Powell and P. J. DiMaggio (eds.), *The New Institutionalism in Organizational Analysis* (Chicago: University of Chicago Press, 1991), pp. 143–163; G. F. Lanzara and G. Patriotta, "The Institutionalization of Knowledge in an Automotive Factory: Templates, Inscriptions, and the Problems of Durability," *Organization Studies* 28, no. 5 (2007), pp. 635–660; and T. B. Lawrence, M. K. Mauws, B. Dyck, and R. F. Kleysen, "The Politics of Organizational Learning: Integrating Power into the 4I Framework," *Academy of Management Review,* January 2005, pp. 180–191.

20. Sorensen, "The Strength of Corporate Culture and the Reliability of Firm Performance."

21. See, for instance, P. L. Moore, "She's Here to Fix the Xerox," *BusinessWeek* (August 6, 2001), pp. 47–48; and C. Ragavan, "FBI Inc.," *U.S. News & World Report* (June 18, 2001), pp. 15–21.

22. See T. Cox, Jr., *Cultural Diversity in Organizations: Theory, Research & Practice* (San Francisco: Berrett-Koehler, 1993), pp. 162–170; L. Grensing-Pophal, "Hiring to Fit Your Corporate Culture," *HRMagazine,* August 1999, pp. 50–54; and D. L. Stone, E. F. Stone-Romero, and K. M. Lukaszewski, "The Impact of Cultural Values on the Acceptance and Effectiveness of Human Resource Management Policies and Practices," *Human Resource Management Review* 17, no. 2 (2007), pp. 152–165.

23. K. Labich, "No More Crude at Texaco," *Fortune* (September 6, 1999), pp. 205–212; and "Rooting Out Racism," *BusinessWeek* (January 10, 2000), p. 66.

24. S. Cartwright and C. L. Cooper, "The Role of Culture Compatibility in Successful Organizational Marriages," *Academy of Management Executive,* May 1993, pp. 57–70; R. A. Weber and C. F. Camerer, "Cultural Conflict and Merger Failure: An Experimental Approach," *Management Science,* April 2003, pp. 400–412; and I. H. Gleibs, A. Mummendey, and P. Noack, "Predictors of Change in Postmerger Identification During a Merger Process: A Longitudinal Study," *Journal of Personality and Social Psychology* 95, no. 5 (2008), pp. 1095–1112.

25. P. Gumbel, "Return of the Urge to Merge," *Time Europe Magazine* (July 13, 2003), www.time.com/time/europe/magazine/article/0,13005,901030721-464418,00.html.

26. T. A. Lambert, L. T. Eby, and M. P. Reeves, "Predictors of Networking Intensity and Network Quality Among White-Collar Job Seekers," *Journal of Career Development,* June 2006, pp. 351–365; and J. A. Thompson, "Proactive Personality and Job Performance: A Social Capital Perspective," *Journal of Applied Psychology,* September 2005, pp. 1011–1017.

27. S. F. Gale, "Memo to AOL Time Warner: Why Mergers Fail—Case Studies," *Workforce Management,* February 2003, www.workforce.com; and W. Bock, "Mergers, Bubbles, and Steve Case," *Wally Bock's Monday Memo,* January 20, 2003, www.mondaymemo.net/030120feature.htm.

28. E. H. Schein, "The Role of the Founder in Creating Organizational Culture," *Organizational Dynamics,* Summer 1983, pp. 13–28.

29. E. H. Schein, "Leadership and Organizational Culture," in F. Hesselbein, M. Goldsmith, and R. Beckhard (eds.), *The Leader of the Future* (San Francisco: Jossey-Bass, 1996), pp. 61–62.

30. See, for example, J. R. Harrison and G. R. Carroll, "Keeping the Faith: A Model of Cultural Transmission in Formal Organizations," *Administrative Science Quarterly,* December 1991, pp. 552–582; and D. E. Bowen and C. Ostroff, "The 'Strength' of the HRM System, Organizational Climate Formation, and Firm Performance," *Academy of Management Review* 29 (2004), pp. 203–221.

31. B. Schneider, H. W. Goldstein, and D. B. Smith, "The ASA Framework: An Update," *Personnel Psychology,* Winter 1995, pp. 747–773; D. M. Cable and T. A. Judge, "Interviewers' Perceptions of Person-Organization Fit and Organizational Selection Decisions," *Journal of Applied Psychology,* August 1997, pp. 546–561; M. L. Verquer, T. A. Beehr, and S. H. Wagner, "A Meta-analysis of Relations Between Person-Organization Fit and Work Attitudes," *Journal of Vocational Behavior,* December 2003, pp. 473–489; and W. Li, Y. Wang, P. Taylor, K. Shi, and D. He, "The Influence of Organizational Culture on Work-Related Personality Requirement Ratings: A Multilevel Analysis," *International Journal of Selection and Assessment* 16, no. 4 (2008), pp. 366–384.

32. R. Levering and M. Moskowitz, "And the Winners Are . . . ," *Fortune* (February 2, 2009), pp. 67–78.

33. D. C. Hambrick and P. A. Mason, "Upper Echelons: The Organization as a Reflection of Its Top Managers," *Academy of Management Review,* April 1984, pp. 193–206; B. P. Niehoff, C. A. Enz, and R. A. Grover, "The Impact of Top-Management Actions on Employee Attitudes and Perceptions," *Group & Organization Studies,* September 1990, pp. 337–352; and H. M. Trice and J. M. Beyer, "Cultural Leadership in Organizations," *Organization Science,* May 1991, pp. 149–169.

34. See, for instance, J. P. Wanous, *Organizational Entry,* 2nd ed. (New York: Addison-Wesley, 1992); G. T. Chao, A. M. O'Leary-Kelly, S. Wolf, H. J. Klein, and P. D. Gardner, "Organizational Socialization: Its Content and Consequences," *Journal of Applied Psychology,* October 1994, pp. 730–743; B. E. Ashforth, A. M. Saks, and R. T. Lee, "Socialization and Newcomer Adjustment: The Role of Organizational Context," *Human Relations,* July 1998, pp. 897–926; D. A. Major, "Effective Newcomer Socialization into High-Performance Organizational Cultures," in N. M. Ashkanasy, C. P. M. Wilderom, and M. F. Peterson (eds.), *Handbook of Organizational Culture & Climate,* pp. 355–368; D. M. Cable and C. K. Parsons, "Socialization Tactics and Person-Organization Fit," *Personnel Psychology,* Spring 2001, pp. 1–23; and K. Rollag, "The Impact of Relative Tenure on Newcomer Socialization Dynamics," *Journal of Organizational Behavior,* November 2004, pp. 853–872.

35. S. Schubert and T. C. Miller, "Where Bribery Was Just a Line Item," *New York Times* (December 21, 2008), pp. 1, 6.

36. K. Rhodes, "Breaking in the Top Dogs," *Training,* February 2000, pp. 67–74.

37. J. Van Maanen and E. H. Schein, "Career Development," in J. R. Hackman and J. L. Suttle (eds.), *Improving Life at Work* (Santa Monica, CA: Goodyear, 1977), pp. 58–62; and D. C. Feldman, "The Multiple Socialization of Organization Members," *Academy of Management Review,* April 1981, p. 310.

38. C. J. Collins, "The Interactive Effects of Recruitment Practices and Product Awareness on Job Seekers' Employer Knowledge and Application Behaviors," *Journal of Applied Psychology* 92, no. 1 (2007), pp. 180–190.

39. G. Chen and R. J. Klimoski, "The Impact of Expectations on Newcomer Performance in Teams as Mediated by Work Characteristics, Social Exchanges, and Empowerment," *Academy of Management Journal* 46 (2003), pp. 591–607; C. R. Wanberg and J. D. Kammeyer-Mueller, "Predictors and Outcomes of Proactivity in the Socialization Process," *Journal of Applied Psychology* 85 (2000), pp. 373–385; J. D. Kammeyer-Mueller and C. R. Wanberg, "Unwrapping the Organizational Entry Process: Disentangling Multiple Antecedents and Their Pathways to Adjustment," *Journal of Applied Psychology* 88 (2003), pp. 779–794; and E. W. Morrison, "Longitudinal Study of the Effects of Information Seeking on Newcomer Socialization," *Journal of Applied Psychology* 78 (2003), pp. 173–183.

40. Van Maanen and Schein, "Career Development," p. 59.

41. E. W. Morrison, "Newcomers' Relationships: The Role of Social Network Ties During Socialization," *Academy of Management Journal* 45 (2002), pp. 1149–1160.

42. T. N. Bauer, T. Bodner, B. Erdogan, D. M. Truxillo, and J. S. Tucker, "Newcomer Adjustment During Organizational Socialization: A Meta-analytic Review of Antecedents, Outcomes, and Methods," *Journal of Applied Psychology* 92, no. 3 (2007), pp. 707–721.

43. E. Ransdell, "The Nike Story? Just Tell It!" *Fast Company,* January–February 2000, pp. 44–46.

44. D. M. Boje, "The Storytelling Organization: A Study of Story Performance in an Office-Supply Firm," *Administrative Science Quarterly,* March 1991, pp. 106–126; C. H. Deutsch, "The Parables of Corporate Culture," *New York Times* (October 13, 1991), p. F25; and M. Ricketts and J. G. Seiling, "Language, Metaphors, and Stories: Catalysts for Meaning Making in Organizations," *Organization Development Journal,* Winter 2003, pp. 33–43.

45. See K. Kamoche, "Rhetoric, Ritualism, and Totemism in Human Resource Management," *Human Relations,* April 1995, pp. 367–385.

46. V. Matthews, "Starting Every Day with a Shout and a Song," *Financial Times* (May 2, 2001), p. 11; and M. Gimein, "Sam Walton Made Us a Promise," *Fortune* (March 18, 2002), pp. 121–130.

47. A. Rafaeli and M. G. Pratt, "Tailored Meanings: On the Meaning and Impact of Organizational Dress," *Academy of Management Review,* January 1993, pp. 32–55; and J. M. Higgins and C. McAllaster, "Want Innovation? Then Use Cultural Artifacts That Support It," *Organizational Dynamics,* August 2002, pp. 74–84.

48. *DCAcronyms* (Seattle: Boeing, April 1997).

49. See B. Victor and J. B. Cullen, "The Organizational Bases of Ethical Work Climates," *Administrative Science Quarterly,* March 1988, pp. 101–125; R. L. Dufresne, "An Action Learning Perspective on Effective Implementation of Academic Honor Codes," *Group & Organization Management,* April 2004, pp. 201–218; and A. Ardichvilli, J. A. Mitchell, and D. Jondle, "Characteristics of Ethical Business Cultures," *Journal of Business Ethics* 85, no. 4 (2009), pp. 445–451.

50. J. A. Byrne, "The Environment Was Ripe for Abuse," *BusinessWeek* (February 25, 2002), pp. 118–120; and A. Raghavan, K. Kranhold, and A. Barrionuevo, "How Enron Bosses Created a Culture of Pushing Limits," *Wall Street Journal* (August 26, 2002), p. A1.

51. J. P. Mulki, J. F. Jaramillo, and W. B. Locander, "Critical Role of Leadership on Ethical Climate and Salesperson Behaviors," *Journal of Business Ethics* 86, no. 2 (2009), pp. 125–141; M. Schminke, M. L. Ambrose, and D. O. Neubaum, "The Effect of Leader Moral Development on Ethical Climate and Employee Attitudes," *Organizational Behavior and Human Decision Processes* 97, no. 2 (2005), pp. 135–151; and M. E. Brown, L. K. Treviño, and D. A. Harrison, "Ethical Leadership: A Social Learning Perspective for Construct Development and Testing," *Organizational Behavior and Human Decision Processes* 97, no. 2 (2005), pp. 117–134.

52. D. M. Mayer, M. Kuenzi, R. Greenbaum, M. Bardes, and S. Salvador, "How Low Does Ethical Leadership Flow? Test of a Trickle-Down Model," *Organizational Behavior and Human Decision Processes* 108, no. 1 (2009), pp. 1–13.

53. M. L. Gruys, S. M. Stewart, J. Goodstein, M. N. Bing, and A. C. Wicks, "Values Enactment in Organizations: A Multi-Level Examination," *Journal of Management* 34, no. 4 (2008), pp. 806–843.

54. D. L. Nelson and C. L. Cooper (eds.), *Positive Organizational Behavior* (London: Sage, 2007); K. S. Cameron, J. E. Dutton, and R. E. Quinn (eds.), *Positive Organizational Scholarship: Foundations of a New Discipline* (San Francisco: Berrett-Koehler, 2003); and F. Luthans and C. M. Youssef, "Emerging Positive Organizational Behavior," *Journal of Management,* June 2007, pp. 321–349.

55. J. Robison, "Great Leadership Under Fire," *Gallup Leadership Journal,* March 8, 2007, pp. 1–3.

56. R. Wagner and J. K. Harter, *12: The Elements of Great Managing* (New York: Gallup Press, 2006).

57. R. Wagner and J. K. Harter, "Performance Reviews Without the Anxiety," *Gallup Leadership Journal*, July 12, 2007, pp. 1–4; and Wagner and Harter, *12: The Elements of Great Managing*.

58. S. Fineman, "On Being Positive: Concerns and Counterpoints," *Academy of Management Review* 31, no. 2 (2006), pp. 270–291.

59. D. P. Ashmos and D. Duchon, "Spirituality at Work: A Conceptualization and Measure," *Journal of Management Inquiry*, June 2000, p. 139; and E. Poole, "Organisational Spirituality: A Literature Review," *Journal of Business Ethics* 84, no. 4 (2009), pp. 577–588.

60. L. W. Fry and J. W. Slocum, "Managing the Triple Bottom Line Through Spiritual Leadership," *Organizational Dynamics* 37, no. 1 (2008), pp. 86–96.

61. This section is based on I. A. Mitroff and E. A. Denton, *A Spiritual Audit of Corporate America: A Hard Look at Spirituality, Religion, and Values in the Workplace* (San Francisco: Jossey-Bass, 1999); J. Milliman, J. Ferguson, D. Trickett, and B. Condemi, "Spirit and Community at Southwest Airlines: An Investigation of a Spiritual Values-Based Model," *Journal of Organizational Change Management* 12, no. 3 (1999), pp. 221–233; and E. H. Burack, "Spirituality in the Workplace," *Journal of Organizational Change Management* 12, no. 3 (1999), pp. 280–291.

62. Cited in Wagner-Marsh and Conley, "The Fourth Wave," p. 295.

63. M. Conlin, "Religion in the Workplace: The Growing Presence of Spirituality in Corporate America," *BusinessWeek* (November 1, 1999), pp. 151–158; and P. Paul, "A Holier Holiday Season," *American Demographics*, December 2001, pp. 41–45.

64. Cited in Conlin, "Religion in the Workplace," p. 153.

65. C. P. Neck and J. F. Milliman, "Thought Self-Leadership: Finding Spiritual Fulfillment in Organizational Life," *Journal of Managerial Psychology* 9, no. 8 (1994), p. 9; for a recent review, see J.-C. Garcia-Zamor, "Workplace Spirituality and Organizational Performance," *Public Administration Review*, May–June 2003, pp. 355–363.

66. P. H. Mirvis, "Soul Work in Organizations," *Organization Science* 8, no. 2 (1997), p. 193; A. Rego and M. Pina e Cunha, "Workplace Spirituality and Organizational Commitment: An Empirical Study," *Journal of Organizational Change Management* 21, no. 1 (2008), pp. 53–75; and R. W. Kolodinsky, R. A. Giacalone, and C. L. Jurkiewicz, "Workplace Values and Outcomes: Exploring Personal, Organizational, and Interactive Workplace Spirituality," *Journal of Business Ethics* 81, no. 2 (2008), pp. 465–480.

67. Cited in Milliman et al., "Spirit and Community at Southwest Airlines."

68. D. J. McCarthy and S. M. Puffer, "Interpreting the Ethicality of Corporate Governance Decision in Russia: Utilizing Integrative Social Contracts Theory to Evaluate the Relevance of Agency Theory Norms," *Academy of Management Review* 33, no. 1 (2008), pp. 11–31.

69. P. Dvorak, "A Firm's Culture Can Get Lost in Translation," *Wall Street Journal* (April 3, 2006), pp. B1, B3; K. Kranhold, "The Immelt Era, Five Years Old, Transforms GE," *Wall Street Journal* (September 11, 2006), pp. B1, B3; and S. McCartney, "Teaching Americans How to Behave Abroad," *Wall Street Journal* (April 11, 2006), pp. D1, D4.

70. J. A. Chatman, "Matching People and Organizations: Selection and Socialization in Public Accounting Firms," *Administrative Science Quarterly*, September 1991, pp. 459–484; and A. E. M. Van Vianen, "Person-Organization Fit: The Match Between Newcomers' and Recruiters' Preferences for Organizational Cultures," *Personnel Psychology*, Spring 2000, pp. 113–149.

71. J. E. Sheridan, "Organizational Culture and Employee Retention," *Academy of Management Journal*, December 1992, pp. 1036–1056.

LEARNING OBJECTIVES

After studying this chapter, you should be able to:

1 Define *initial selection*, and identify the most useful methods.

2 Define *substantive selection*, and identify the most useful methods.

3 Define *contingent selection*, and contrast the arguments for and against drug testing.

4 Compare the four main types of training.

5 Contrast formal and informal training methods

6 Contrast on-the-job and off-the-job training.

7 Describe the purposes of performance evaluation and list the methods by which it can be done.

8 Show how managers can improve performance evaluations.

9 Describe how organizations can manage work-family conflicts.

10 Show how a global context affects human resource management.

Human Resource Policies and Practices

To manage people well, companies should . . .
elevate HR to a position of power and primacy
in the organization. —Jack Welch

SMARTS IN THE NFL

Perhaps no aspect of managing human resources is more interesting or surprising than this: A 12-minute paper-and-pencil test is arguably the single best method for selecting employees in most occupations, including, perhaps, National Football League (NFL) quarterbacks.

We're talking about the Wonderlic Personnel Test, one of the most extensively validated tests ever. (We first discussed it in Chapter 2.) The Wonderlic has been used in hundreds of occupations, but nowhere is its use more intriguing than in the NFL combine.

As NFL fans know, prior to the football draft every year, potential draftees go through a "combine" where their skills are tested: They run, they bench press, they scrimmage—and they also take the Wonderlic. Although players and members of the media often express skepticism about the validity of the test, evidence suggests it works.

Scores range from 0 to 50, with the average about 19. The average chemist scores 31, compared to 26 for a journalist, 22 for a bank teller, and 15 for a warehouse worker. Among football players, scores vary by position. Offensive linemen and quarterbacks, on average, have much higher scores than running backs, cornerbacks, or middle linebackers.

Most NFL experts will tell you intelligence is most important for the positions of quarterback and offensive lineman, in large part because of the extensive playbook they have to learn and remember. Here are Wonderlic scores for some quarterbacks who are starting or have recently started in the NFL (the scores of some players—such as Kurt Warner, Jake Delhomme, and Matt Cassel—are unavailable).

Very intelligent (30 or higher). Alex Smith: 40; Eli Manning: 39; Brian Griese: 39; Matthew Stafford: 38; Charlie Frye: 38; Matt Leinart: 35; Kellen Clemens: 35; Aaron Rodgers: 35; Tom Brady: 33; Sage Rosenfels: 32; Matt Ryan: 32; Joey Harrington: 32; Matt Schaub: 31; Trent Edwards: 31; Tony Romo: 30; Philip Rivers: 30; Kerry Collins: 30; Jeff Garcia: 30

Intelligent (25 to 29). Brady Quinn: 29; Matt Hasselbeck: 29; Marc Bulger: 29; Rex Grossman: 29; Mark Sanchez: 28; Drew Brees: 28; Peyton Manning: 28; Joe Flacco: 27; Jason Campbell: 27; Jay Cutler: 26; Kyle Orton: 26; Carson Palmer: 26; Ben Roethlisberger: 25; Byron Leftwich: 25; Shaun Hill: 25; Chad Pennington: 25; Chase Daniel: 25

Average (18 to 24). JaMarcus Russell: 24; Brodie Croyle: 24; David Carr: 24; Brett Favre: 22; Chad Henne: 22; Chris Simms: 22; Tyler Thigpen: 21; Luke McCown: 20; Michael Vick: 20; Tarvaris Jackson: 19; Derek Anderson: 19; Daunte Culpepper: 18

Below average (17 or lower). Vince Young: 15; David Garrard: 14; Donovan McNabb: 14

It's clear that NFL quarterbacks are very smart—they score far above average relative to the U.S. population. Do differences among the quarterbacks predict success? You might have your own opinion, but clearly we aren't talking about a perfect relationship. It appears that a certain level of intellect is required to make it as an NFL quarterback, but after a certain point your arm (and legs) are as important as your brains.

Some complain the Wonderlic gets more weight than it deserves. Things have come a long way since former Harvard player and Rhodes scholar Pat McInally's perfect score cost him in the draft because he was seen as *too* smart. McInally spent 10 years in the NFL and now works for Wonderlic.[1]

The message of this chapter is that human resource (HR) policies and practices—such as employee selection, training, and performance management—influence an organization's effectiveness.[2] However, studies show managers—even HR managers—often don't know which HR practices work and which don't. To see how much you know (before learning the right answers in this chapter), take the self-assessment.

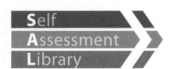

HOW MUCH DO I KNOW ABOUT HUMAN RESOURCE MANAGEMENT (HRM)?

In the Self-Assessment Library (available on CD and online), take assessment IV.G.2 (How Much Do I Know About HRM?) and answer the following questions:

1. *How did you score compared to your classmates'? Did the results surprise you?*
2. *How much of effective HRM is common sense?*
3. *Do you think your score will improve after you read this chapter?*

Selection Practices

It's been said the most important HR decision you can make is deciding whom to hire. That makes sense—if you can figure out who the right people are. The objective of effective selection is to figure out who these right people are, by matching individual characteristics (ability, experience, and so on) with the requirements of the job.[3] When management fails to get a proper match, employee performance and satisfaction both suffer.

How the Selection Process Works

Exhibit 17-1 shows how the selection process works in most organizations. Having decided to apply for a job, applicants go through several stages—three are shown in the exhibit—during which they can be rejected at any time. In practice, some organizations forgo some of these steps in the interests of time. (A meat-packing plant may hire someone who walks in the door, but there is not a long line of people who want to "thread" a pig's intestines for a living.) But most organizations follow a process that looks something like this. Let's go into a bit more detail about each of the stages.

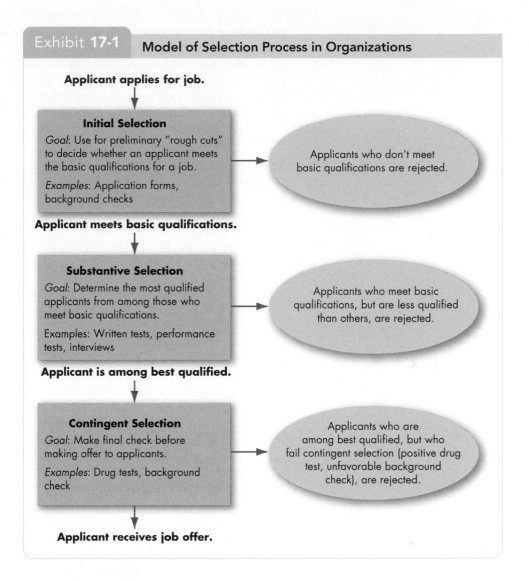

Exhibit 17-1   **Model of Selection Process in Organizations**

Applicant applies for job.

Initial Selection

Goal: Use for preliminary "rough cuts" to decide whether an applicant meets the basic qualifications for a job.

Examples: Application forms, background checks

→ Applicants who don't meet basic qualifications are rejected.

Applicant meets basic qualifications.

Substantive Selection

Goal: Determine the most qualified applicants from among those who meet basic qualifications.

Examples: Written tests, performance tests, interviews

→ Applicants who meet basic qualifications, but are less qualified than others, are rejected.

Applicant is among best qualified.

Contingent Selection

Goal: Make final check before making offer to applicants.

Examples: Drug tests, background check

→ Applicants who are among best qualified, but who fail contingent selection (positive drug test, unfavorable background check), are rejected.

Applicant receives job offer.

Initial Selection

1 Define *initial selection,* and identify the most useful methods.

Initial selection devices are the first information applicants submit and are used for preliminary rough cuts to decide whether the applicant meets the basic qualifications for a job. Application forms (including letters of recommendation) are initial selection devices. We list background checks as either an initial selection device or a contingent selection device, depending on how the organization does it. Some organizations prefer to look into an applicant's background right away. Others wait until the applicant is about ready to be hired, contingent on everything else checking out.

Application Forms   You've no doubt submitted your fair share of applications. By itself, the information submitted on an application form is not a very useful predictor of performance. However, it can be a good initial screen. For example, there's no sense spending time interviewing an applicant for a registered nurse position if he doesn't have the proper credentials (education, certification, experience). Many organizations encourage applicants to apply online. It takes only a few minutes, and the form can be forwarded to the people responsible for making the hiring decision. The Starbucks Web site includes a career center page where prospective employees can search for available positions by location or job type and then apply online.

Managers must be careful about the questions they ask on applications. It's pretty obvious questions about race, gender, and nationality are disallowed. However, it might surprise you that other questions also put companies in legal jeopardy. For example, it generally is not permissible to ask about prior arrest records or even convictions unless the answer is job related.

Background Checks   More than 80 percent of employers conduct reference checks on applicants at some point in the hiring process. The reason is obvious: They want to know how an applicant did in past jobs and whether former employers would recommend hiring the person. The problem is that rarely do former employers provide useful information. In fact, nearly two-thirds of employers refuse to provide detailed reference information on applicants because they are afraid of being sued for saying something bad about a former employee. Although this concern is often unfounded (employers are safe as long as they stick to documented facts), in our litigious society most employers play it safe. The result is a paradox: most employers want reference information, but few will give it out.

Letters of recommendation are another form of background check. These also aren't as useful as they may seem. Applicants select those who will write good things about them, so almost all letters of recommendation are positive. In the end, readers either ignore them or read "between the lines" to try to find hidden meaning there.

Finally, some employers check credit histories or criminal records. A bank hiring tellers, for example, would probably want to know about an applicant's criminal and credit histories. Increasingly, credit checks are being used for non-banking jobs. Kevin Palmer's offer of a job with a property management company evaporated after the company performed a credit check on him (which revealed a bankruptcy in his past).[4] Despite the trend, because of the invasive nature of such checks, employers need to be sure there is a need for them. To further complicate matters, however, *not* checking can carry a legal cost. Manor Park Nursing Home in Texas failed to do a criminal background check of an employee who later sexually assaulted a resident of the home. The jury awarded the plaintiff $1.1 million, concluding the nursing home was negligent for failing to conduct a background check.[5]

Substantive Selection

2 Define *substantive selection,* and identify the most useful methods.

If an applicant passes the initial screens, next are substantive selection methods. These are the heart of the selection process and include written tests, performance tests, and interviews.

Written Tests   Long popular as selection devices, written tests—called "paper-and-pencil" tests, though most are now available online—declined in use between the late 1960s and mid-1980s, especially in the United States. They were frequently characterized as discriminatory, and many organizations had not validated them as job related. The past 20 years, however, have seen a resurgence, and today more than 60 percent of all U.S. organizations and most of the Fortune 1000 use some type of employment test.[6] Managers recognize that valid tests can help predict who will be successful on the job.[7] Applicants, however, tend to view written tests as less valid and fair than interviews or performance tests.[8] Typical written tests include (1) intelligence or cognitive ability tests, (2) personality tests, (3) integrity tests, and (4) interest inventories.

Written tests are the heart of the selection process at Cabela's, a specialty retailer of hunting, fishing, camping, and other outdoor merchandise. Job applicants for Cabela's contact center and retail stores are given a difficult 150-question test that measures the depth of their knowledge of outdoor sports. Cabela's management believes that the tests are helpful in determining who will succeed in providing customers with exceptional service and product knowledge.

Tests of intellectual ability, spatial and mechanical ability, perceptual accuracy, and motor ability have proven valid predictors for many skilled, semi-skilled, and unskilled operative jobs in industrial organizations.[9] Intelligence tests have proven to be particularly good predictors for jobs that include cognitively complex tasks (like learning the ever more complex playbooks in the NFL).[10] Many experts say intelligence tests are the *single best* selection measure across jobs, and that they are at least as valid in the European Union (EU) nations as in the United States.[11]

Personality tests are inexpensive and simple to administer, and in the past decade their use has grown. Japanese automakers staffing U.S. plants have relied heavily on written tests to identify high performers.[12] Getting a job with Toyota can require up to 3 days of testing and interviewing. Organizations use numerous measures of the Big Five traits in selection decisions. The traits that best predict job performance are conscientiousness and positive self-concept.[13] This makes sense in that conscientious people tend to be motivated and dependable, and positive people are "can-do" oriented and persistent.

As ethical problems have increased in organizations, integrity tests have gained popularity. These paper-and-pencil tests measure factors such as dependability, carefulness, responsibility, and honesty; they have proven to be powerful predictors of supervisory ratings of job performance and of theft, discipline problems, and excessive absenteeism.[14]

Performance-Simulation Tests   What better way to find out whether applicants can do a job successfully than by having them do it? That's precisely the logic of performance-simulation tests.

Although they are more complicated to develop and administer than written tests, performance-simulation tests have higher *face validity* (which measures whether applicants perceive the measures to be accurate), and their popularity has increased. The two best-known are work samples and assessment centers.

International OB

Does Personality Testing Work Outside the United States?

Given that early research linking the Big Five personality traits to job performance was conducted in the United States (see Chapter 5), you might wonder whether the traits found useful for selecting employees there—especially conscientiousness—also work in other countries.

Average levels of personality traits do vary across nations: People in East Asian cultures are more introverted and neurotic, individuals in African nations more agreeable, and people in South American countries more open. However, evidence suggests that within each nation, employees who score highest on the traits—especially conscientiousness—also are more effective at work. Conscientiousness predicts job performance of European workers nearly exactly as well as it does that of U.S. workers. Less research exists on how conscientiousness and the other Big Five traits predict job performance elsewhere—particularly Asia—but it does suggest conscientiousness is important to work effectiveness in Asia, too.

Evidence also indicates that core self-evaluations, reflecting the degree to which individuals have a positive view of themselves, also lead to worker effectiveness inside and outside the United States. Studies of core self-evaluations in France, Japan, China, Greece, Britain, Sweden, Germany, and the Netherlands all show that employees with a positive self-concept appear happier and more effective at work. These studies strongly suggest that while values do vary across cultures, organizations can profitably select employees based on personality tests regardless of culture.

Sources: Based on D. P. Schmitt, J. Allik, R. R. McCrae, et al., "The Geographic Distribution of Big Five Personality Traits: Patterns and Profiles of Human Self-Description Across 56 Nations," *Journal of Cross-Cultural Psychology* 38, no. 2 (2007), pp. 173–212; T. A. Judge, "Core Self-Evaluations and Work Success," *Current Directions in Psychological Science* 18, no. 1 (2009), pp. 58–62; and B. S. Connelly and D. S. Ones, "The Personality of Corruption: A National-Level Analysis," *Cross-Cultural Research* 42, no. 4 (2008), pp. 353–385.

Work sample tests are hands-on simulations of part or all of the work that applicants for routine jobs must perform. Each work sample element is matched with a job-performance element to measure applicants' knowledge, skills, and abilities with more validity than written aptitude and personality tests.[15] Work samples are widely used in the hiring of skilled workers, such as welders, machinists, carpenters, and electricians. Job candidates for production jobs at BMW's factory in South Carolina have 90 minutes to perform a variety of typical work tasks on a specially built simulated assembly line.[16]

A more elaborate set of performance-simulation tests, specifically designed to evaluate a candidate's managerial potential, is administered in **assessment centers**. Line executives, supervisors, trained psychologists, or all evaluate candidates as they go through a single to several days of exercises that simulate real problems they would confront on the job.[17] A candidate might be required to play the role of a manager who must decide how to respond to ten memos in an in-basket within a 2-hour period.

To reduce the costs of job simulations, many organizations have started to use situational judgment tests, which ask applicants how they would perform in a variety of job situations and compare their answers to those of high-performing employees.[18] These tests have shown impressive validity and may be more objective than assessment centers.

Interviews   Of all the selection devices organizations around the globe use to differentiate candidates, the interview remains the most common.[19] It also tends to have a disproportionate amount of influence. The candidate who performs poorly in the employment interview is likely to be cut from the applicant pool regardless of experience, test scores, or letters of recommendation. Conversely, "all too often, the person most polished in job-seeking techniques, particularly

Myth or Science?

"It's First Impressions That Count"

This statement is true. When we meet someone for the first time, we notice a number of things including physical characteristics, clothing, firmness of handshake, gestures, and tone of voice. We use our observations to fit the person into ready-made categories, and these first impressions tend to hold greater weight than information we receive later.

The best evidence that first impressions count comes from research on employment interviews. Interviewers often know whether they will hire someone soon after the opening handshake and small talk.[20] It appears a firm handshake really does affect interviewer judgments.

Research on applicant appearance confirms the power of first impressions.[21] Attractive applicants fare better in interviews, and overweight applicants are penalized. People show especially strong preference for attractive opposite-sex applicants, and there was some evidence that female interviewers actually prefer unattractive female applicants over attractive female applicants.

Another study revealed just how superficial interviewer judgments often are. Researchers responded to employment ads in Chicago and Boston with fake résumés of high and low quality and used names that were traditionally African American (Kenya and Hakim) and Caucasian (Allison and Brad). Résumés with Caucasian names received 50 percent more callbacks than those with African American names. While 27 percent of the high-quality résumés with Caucasian names received callbacks, only 8 percent of the high-quality résumés with African American names did.[22]

A final body of confirming research finds interviewers' post-interview evaluations of applicants substantially conform to their pre-interview impressions.[23] That is, first impressions carry considerable weight in shaping final evaluations, assuming the interview elicits no highly negative information.

those used in the interview process, is the one hired, even though he or she may not be the best candidate for the position."[24]

These findings are relevant because of the interview's typical nature.[25] The popular unstructured interview—short, casual, and made up of random questions—is simply not a very effective selection device.[26] The data it gathers are typically biased and often only modestly related to future job performance. Still, managers are reluctant to use *structured interviews* in place of their favorite questions, such as "If you could be any animal, what would you be, and why?"[27]

Without structure, interviewers tend to favor applicants who share their attitudes, give undue weight to negative information, and allow the order in which applicants are interviewed to influence their evaluations.[28] To reduce such bias and improve the validity of interviews, managers should adopt a standardized set of questions, a uniform method of recording information, and standardized ratings of applicants' qualifications. Interview effectiveness also improves when employers use *behavioral structured interviews,* probably because these assessments are less influenced by a variety of interviewer biases.[29] They require applicants to describe how they handled specific problems and situations in previous jobs based on the assumption that past behavior offers the best predictor of future behavior. Panel interviews also minimize the influence of individual biases and have higher validity.

In practice, most organizations use interviews as more than a prediction-of-performance device.[30] Companies as diverse as Southwest Airlines, Disney, Bank

work sample tests *Hands-on simulations of part or all of the work that applicants for routine jobs must perform.*

assessment centers *A set of performance-simulation tests designed to evaluate a candidate's managerial potential.*

of America, Microsoft, Procter & Gamble, and Harrah's Entertainment use them to assess applicant–organization fit. So in addition to evaluating specific, job-related skills, they are looking at personality characteristics and personal values to find individuals who fit the organization's culture and image.

Contingent Selection

3 Define *contingent selection,* and contrast the arguments for and against drug testing.

If applicants pass the substantive selection methods, they are ready to be hired, contingent on a final check. One common contingent method is a drug test. Publix grocery stores make a tentative offer to applicants contingent on their passing such a test and checking out as drug free. For both legal and practical reasons, drug tests typically screen out individuals who have used marijuana but not alcohol—alcohol is legal and leaves the system in 24 hours.

Drug testing is controversial. Many applicants think testing without reasonable suspicion is invasive or unfair and say they should be tested on job-performance factors, not lifestyle choices that may not be relevant. Employers might counter that drug use and abuse are extremely costly, not just in financial terms but also in terms of people's safety. They have the law on their side. The U.S. Supreme Court has concluded that drug tests are "minimally invasive" selection procedures that as a rule do not violate individuals' rights.

Drug tests are not cheap. If the first test result (typically a urine test) is positive, the result is reanalyzed to verify it. Contrary to popular claims, results are generally precise and quite accurate, indicating the specific type of drug in the applicant's system, and not easily faked. Despite the controversy, drug testing is probably here to stay.

Under the Americans with Disabilities Act, firms may not require employees to pass a medical exam before a job offer is made. However, they can conduct medical exams *after* making a contingent offer, to determine whether an applicant is physically or mentally able to do the job. Employers also sometimes use medical exams to find out whether and how they can accommodate employees with disabilities. For jobs requiring exposure to heavy physical or psychological demands, such as air traffic controllers or firefighters, medical exams are obviously an important indicator of ability to perform.

Training and Development Programs

Competent employees don't remain competent forever. Skills deteriorate and can become obsolete, and new skills need to be learned. That's why U.S. corporations with a hundred or more employees spent more than $51 billion on formal training in a recent year.[31] IBM, Accenture, Intel, and Lockheed Martin have each spent over $300 million per year on employee training.[32]

Types of Training

4 Compare the four main types of training.

Training can include everything from teaching employees basic reading skills to conducting advanced courses in executive leadership. Here we discuss four general skill categories—basic literacy, technical skills, interpersonal skills, and problem-solving skills—and ethics training.

Basic Literacy Skills   Statistics show that nearly 40 percent of the U.S. labor force and more than 50 percent of high school graduates don't possess the basic work skills needed to perform in today's workplace.[33] The National Institute of

Learning estimates this literacy problem costs corporate America about $60 billion per year in lost productivity.[34] The challenge isn't unique to the United States. It's a worldwide problem—from the most developed countries to the least.[35] For many undeveloped countries, widespread illiteracy means there is almost no hope of competing in a global economy.

Organizations increasingly have to teach employees basic reading and math skills. A literacy audit showed that employees at gun manufacturer Smith & Wesson needed at least an eighth-grade reading level to do typical workplace tasks.[36] Yet 30 percent of the company's 676 workers with no degree scored below eighth-grade levels in either reading or math. After the first round of basic-skills classes, company paid and on company time, 70 percent of attendees brought their skills up to the target level, allowing them to do a better job. They displayed greater ease in writing and reading charts, graphs, and bulletin boards, increased abilities to use fractions and decimals, better overall communication, and a significant increase in confidence.

Technical Skills   Most training is directed at upgrading and improving an employee's technical skills, increasingly important for two reasons: new technology and new structural designs in the organization.

Many auto repair workers require extensive training to fix and maintain recent models with computer-monitored engines, electronic stabilizing systems, global positioning systems (GPS), keyless remote entry, and other innovations. Such technology has also required production employees to learn a whole new set of skills.[37]

As organizations flatten their structures, expand their use of teams, and break down traditional departmental barriers, employees need mastery of a wider variety of tasks and increased knowledge of how their organization operates. The restructuring of jobs at Miller Brewing around empowered teams has led management to introduce a comprehensive business literacy program to help employees better understand competition, the state of the beer industry, where the company's revenues come from, how costs are calculated, and where employees fit into the company's value chain.[38]

Interpersonal Skills   Almost all employees belong to a work unit, and their work performance depends on their ability to effectively interact with their co-workers and boss. Some employees have excellent interpersonal abilities, but others require training to improve listening, communicating, and team-building skills.

Problem-Solving Skills   Problem-solving training for managers and other employees can include activities to sharpen their logic, reasoning, and problem-defining skills as well as their abilities to assess causation, develop and analyze alternatives, and select solutions. Problem-solving training has become a part of almost every organizational effort to introduce self-managed teams or implement quality-management programs.

What About Ethics Training?   About 75 percent of employees working in the 1,000 largest U.S. corporations receive ethics training[39] either during new-employee orientation, as part of ongoing developmental programs, or as periodic reinforcement of ethical principles.[40] But the jury is still out on whether you can actually teach ethics.[41]

Critics argue that ethics are based on values, and value systems are learned by example at an early age. By the time employees are hired, their ethical values are fixed. Some research does suggest ethics training does not have a significant long-term effect on participants' values, and even that exposure to business and law school programs *decreases* students' level of prosocial ethical values.[42]

There's a heavy focus on teamwork and unit cohesion for this squad of midshipmen during their 18-hour long Sea Trials training at the U.S. Naval Academy. Learning how to become a team player and recognizing the value of teamwork are part of the interpersonal skills training for cadets who are finishing their freshman year at the academy. Working together to complete a challenge, such as transporting the log shown here, is the objective of the training, because the tasks cannot be completed by individuals alone. The training also teaches cadets the skills of encouraging and motivating peers to succeed as part of building unity among squad members.

Supporters of ethics training say values *can* be learned and changed after early childhood. And even if they couldn't, ethics training helps employees recognize ethical dilemmas and become more aware of the ethical issues underlying their actions. It also reaffirms an organization's expectations that members will act ethically. Individuals who have greater exposure to organizational ethics codes and ethics training do tend to be more satisfied and perceive their organizations as more socially responsible, so ethics training does have some positive effects.[43]

Training Methods

5 Contrast formal and informal training methods

Historically, *training* meant "formal training," planned in advance and having a structured format. However, recent evidence indicates 70 percent of workplace learning takes place in *informal training*—unstructured, unplanned, and easily adapted to situations and individuals—for teaching skills and keeping employees current.[44] In reality, most informal training is nothing other than employees helping each other out. They share information and solve work-related problems together. Thus many managers are now supportive of what used to be considered "idle chatter." At a Siemens plant in North Carolina, management recognizes that people needn't be on the production line to be working.[45] Discussions around the water cooler or in the cafeteria weren't, as managers thought, about nonwork topics such as sports or politics. They largely focused on solving work-related problems. So now Siemens' management encourages such casual meetings.

On-the-job training methods include job rotation, apprenticeships, understudy assignments, and formal mentoring programs. But because they often disrupt the workplace, organizations invest in *off-the-job training*. The $51 billion figure we cited for training was largely spent on the formal off-the-job variety, the most popular being live classroom lectures. But it also encompasses videotapes, public seminars, self-study programs, Internet courses, satellite-beamed television classes, and group activities that use role-plays and case studies.

The fastest-growing training medium is probably computer-based training, or e-training.[46] Kinko's has created an internal network that allows its 20,000 employees to take online courses covering everything from products to policies.[47] Cisco Systems provides a curriculum of training courses on its corporate in-

At Ito Yokado, the largest supermarket chain in Japan, week-long training for new employees includes role-playing exercises. The group of young men shown here is learning the proper techniques of guiding blind, disabled, and elderly people. This off-the-job training technique of role-playing is effective because employees become sensitive to the special needs of shoppers who require extra assistance.

tranet, organized by job titles, specific technologies, and products.[48] E-learning systems emphasize learner control over the pace and content of instruction, allow e-learners to interact through online communities, and incorporate other techniques such as simulations and group discussions. Computer-based training that let learners actively participate in exercises and quizzes was more effective than traditional classroom instruction.[49]

On the positive side, e-training increases flexibility because organizations can deliver materials anywhere, anytime. It also seems fast and efficient. On the other hand, it's expensive to design self-paced online materials, employees miss the social interaction of a classroom, online learners are more susceptible to distractions, and "clicking through" training without actually engaging in practice activities provides no assurance employees have actually learned anything.[50]

Individualizing Formal Training to Fit the Employee's Learning Style

6   Contrast on-the-job and off-the-job training.

The way you process, internalize, and remember new and difficult material isn't necessarily the same way others do. To be effective, formal training should be individualized to reflect the predominant learning style of the employee.[51]

Some people absorb information better when they read about it. They can learn to use a new software program by sitting in their study reading the manual. Some people learn best by observation. They can watch someone use the software for a while and then copy what they've done. Listeners rely heavily on their auditory senses to absorb information. They prefer to learn by listening to an audiotape. People who prefer a participating style learn by doing. They want to sit down, launch the software, and gain hands-on experience by practicing.

We can translate these learning styles into teaching methods that maximize learning. Readers should be given books or other reading material to review;

watchers should get the opportunity to observe individuals modeling the new skills either in person or on video; listeners will benefit from hearing lectures or audiotapes; and participants will benefit most from experiential opportunities in which they can simulate and practice the new skills.

Good teachers recognize that students learn differently and use multiple teaching methods: they assign readings before class; give lectures; use visual aids to illustrate concepts; and have students participate in group projects, case analyses, role-plays, and experiential learning exercises. If you know the preferred style of an employee, you can design a formal training program to take advantage of this preference. If you don't have that information, it's probably best to design the program to use a variety of learning styles. Overreliance on a single style places individuals who don't learn well from that style at a disadvantage.

Evaluating Effectiveness

The effectiveness of a training program can refer to the level of student satisfaction, the amount students learn, the extent to which they transfer the material from training to their jobs, or the financial return on investments in training.[52] These results are not always related. Some people who have a positive experience in an upbeat, fun class learn very little; some who learn a great deal have difficulty figuring out how to use their knowledge at work; and changes in employee behavior are often not large enough to justify the expense of training. This means rigorous measurement of multiple training outcomes should be a part of every training effort.

Not all training methods are equally effective. Lecture styles have a poor reputation but are surprisingly effective. On the other hand, conducting a needs assessment prior to training was relatively unimportant in predicting a program's success.[53]

The success of training also depends on the individual. If individuals are unmotivated, they will learn very little. What creates training motivation? Personality is important: Those with an internal locus of control, high conscientiousness, high cognitive ability, and high self-efficacy learn more. The climate also is important: When trainees believe there are opportunities and resources to let them apply their newly learned skills, they are more motivated and do better in training programs.[54] Finally, after-training support from supervisors and co-workers has a strong influence on whether employees transfer their learning into new behavior.[55] An effective training program requires not just teaching the skills but also changing the work environment to support the trainees.

Performance Evaluation

7 Describe the purposes of performance evaluation and list the methods by which it can be done.

Would you study differently or exert a different level of effort for a college course graded on a pass–fail basis than for one that awarded letter grades A to F? Students typically tell us they study harder when letter grades are at stake. When they take a course on a pass–fail basis, they tend to do just enough to ensure a passing grade.

This finding illustrates how performance-evaluation systems influence behavior. Major determinants of your in-class behavior and out-of-class studying effort in college are the criteria and techniques your instructor uses to evaluate your performance. What applies in the college context also applies to employees at work. In this section, we show how the choice of a performance-evaluation system and the way it's administered can be an important force influencing employee behavior.

What Is Performance?

In the past most organizations assessed only how well employees performed the tasks listed on a job description, but today's less hierarchical and more service-oriented organizations require more. Researchers now recognize three major types of behavior that constitute performance at work:

1. **Task performance.**   Performing the duties and responsibilities that contribute to the production of a good or service or to administrative tasks. This includes most of the tasks in a conventional job description.
2. **Citizenship**.   Actions that contribute to the psychological environment of the organization, such as helping others when not required, supporting organizational objectives, treating co-workers with respect, making constructive suggestions, and saying positive things about the workplace.
3. **Counterproductivity.**   Actions that actively damage the organization. These behaviors include stealing, damaging company property, behaving aggressively toward co-workers, and avoidable absences.

Most managers believe good performance means doing well on the first two dimensions and avoiding the third.[56] A person who does core job tasks very well but is rude and aggressive toward co-workers is not going to be considered a good employee in most organizations, and even the most pleasant and upbeat worker who can't do the main job tasks well is not going to be a good employee.

Purposes of Performance Evaluation

Performance evaluation serves a number of purposes.[57] One is to help management make general *human resource decisions* about promotions, transfers, and terminations. Evaluations also *identify training and development needs*. They *pinpoint employee skills and competencies* for which remedial programs can be developed. Finally, they *provide feedback to employees* on how the organization views their performance and are often the *basis for reward allocations* including merit pay increases.

Because our interest is in organizational behavior, here we emphasize performance evaluation as a mechanism for providing feedback and determining reward allocations.

What Do We Evaluate?

The criteria management chooses to evaluate will have a major influence on what employees do. The three most popular sets of criteria are individual task outcomes, behaviors, and traits.

Individual Task Outcomes   If ends count rather than means, management should evaluate an employee's task on outcomes such as quantity produced, scrap generated, and cost per unit of production for a plant manager or on overall sales volume in the territory, dollar increase in sales, and number of new accounts established for a salesperson.

task performance *performing the duties and responsibilities that contribute to the production of a good or service or to administrative tasks*

citizenship *actions that contribute to the psychological environment of the organization, such as helping others when not required*

counterproductivity *actions that actively damage the organization, including stealing, behaving aggressively toward co-workers, or being late or absent*

General Electric Company evaluates the performance of its corporate managers, including the group of GE's top executives in India shown here, on five "growth traits." The traits are inclusiveness, imagination/courage, expertise, external focus, and clear thinking/decisiveness. By evaluating its 5,000 top managers on these traits, GE believes it will generate corporate leaders who will help the company achieve its goal of building the revenue growth of its business units that operate throughout the world.

Behaviors   It's difficult to attribute specific outcomes to the actions of employees in advisory or support positions or employees whose work assignments are part of a group effort. We may readily evaluate the group's performance, but if it is hard to identify the contribution of each group member, management will often evaluate the employee's behavior. A plant manager might be evaluated on promptness in submitting monthly reports or leadership style, and a salesperson on average number of contact calls made per day or sick days used per year.

Measured behaviors needn't be limited to those directly related to individual productivity.[58] As we pointed out in discussing organizational citizenship behavior (see Chapters 1 and 3), helping others, making suggestions for improvements, and volunteering for extra duties make work groups and organizations more effective and often are incorporated into evaluations of employee performance.

Traits   The weakest criteria, because they're farthest removed from actual job performance, are individual traits.[59] Having a good attitude, showing confidence, being dependable, looking busy, or possessing a wealth of experience may or may not be highly correlated with positive task outcomes, but it's naïve to ignore the reality that organizations still use such traits to assess job performance.

Who Should Do the Evaluating?

Who should evaluate an employee's performance? By tradition the task has fallen to managers, because they are held responsible for their employees' performance. But others may do the job better.

With many of today's organizations using self-managed teams, telecommuting, and other organizing devices that distance bosses from employees, the immediate superior may not be the most reliable judge of an employee's performance. Peers and even subordinates are being asked to take part in the process, and employees are participating in their own evaluation. A recent survey found about half of executives and 53 percent of employees now have input into their performance evaluations.[60] As you might expect, self-evaluations often suffer from overinflated

Exhibit **17-2**	**360-Degree Evaluations**

The primary objective of the 360-degree performance evaluation is to pool feedback from all of the employee's customers.

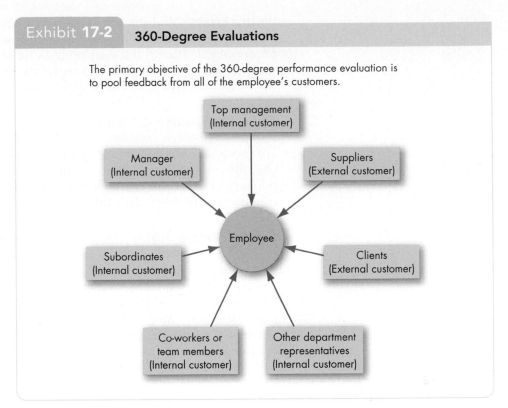

Source: Adapted from *Personnel Journal,* November 1994, p. 100.

assessment and self-serving bias, and they seldom agree with superiors' ratings.[61] They are probably better suited to developmental than evaluative purposes and should be combined with other sources of information to reduce rating errors.

In most situations, in fact, it is highly advisable to use multiple sources of ratings. Any individual performance rating may say as much about the rater as about the person being evaluated. By averaging across raters, we can obtain a more reliable, unbiased, and accurate performance evaluation.

The latest approach to performance evaluation is 360-degree evaluations.[62] These provide performance feedback from the employee's full circle of daily contacts, from mailroom workers to customers to bosses to peers (see Exhibit 17-2). The number of appraisals can be as few as 3 or 4 or as many as 25; most organizations collect 5 to 10 per employee.

Some firms using 360-degree programs are Alcoa, DuPont, Levi Strauss, Honeywell, UPS, Sprint, AT&T, and W. L. Gore & Associates. What's the appeal? By relying on feedback from co-workers, customers, and subordinates, these organizations are hoping to give everyone a sense of participation in the review process and gain more accurate readings on employee performance.

Evidence on the effectiveness of the 360-degree evaluation is mixed.[63] It provides employees with a wider perspective on their performance, but many organizations don't spend the time to train evaluators in giving constructive criticism. Some allow employees to choose the peers and subordinates who evaluate them, which can artificially inflate feedback. It's also difficult to reconcile disagreements between rater groups.

Methods of Performance Evaluation

We've discussed *what* we evaluate and *who* should do the evaluating. Now we ask: *How* do we evaluate an employee's performance? What are the specific techniques for evaluation?

Written Essays   Probably the simplest method is to write a narrative describing an employee's strengths, weaknesses, past performance, potential, and suggestions for improvement. The written essay requires no complex forms or extensive training to complete. But in this method a useful appraisal may be determined as much by the evaluator's writing skill as by the employee's actual level of performance.

Critical Incidents   **Critical incidents** focus the evaluator's attention on the difference between executing a job effectively and executing it ineffectively. The appraiser describes what the employee did in a situation that was especially effective or ineffective, citing only specific behaviors, not vaguely defined personality traits. A list of such critical incidents provides a rich set of examples to show the employee desirable behaviors and those that call for improvement.

Graphic Rating Scales   One of the oldest and most popular methods of evaluation is **graphic rating scales**. The evaluator goes through a set of performance factors, such as quantity and quality of work, depth of knowledge, cooperation, attendance, and initiative, and rates each on incremental scales. The scales may specify, say, five points, so *job knowledge* might be rated 1 ("is poorly informed about work duties") to 5 ("has complete mastery of all phases of the job"). Although they don't provide the depth of information that essays or critical incidents do, graphic rating scales are less time consuming to develop and administer and allow for quantitative analysis and comparison.

Behaviorally Anchored Rating Scales   **Behaviorally anchored rating scales (BARS)** combine major elements from the critical incident and graphic rating scale approaches. The appraiser rates the employees on items along a continuum, but the items are examples of actual behavior on the job rather than general descriptions or traits. Participants first contribute specific illustrations of effective and ineffective behavior, which are translated into a set of performance dimensions with varying levels of quality.

Forced Comparisons   **Forced comparisons** evaluate one individual's performance against the performance of another or others. It is a relative rather than an absolute measuring device. The two most popular comparisons are group order ranking and individual ranking.

   Group order ranking requires the evaluator to place employees into a particular classification, such as top one-fifth or second one-fifth. If a rater has 20 employees, only 4 can be in the top fifth and, of course, 4 must also be relegated to the bottom fifth. This method is often used in recommending students to graduate schools.

   The **individual ranking** approach rank-orders employees from best to worst. If the manager is required to appraise 30 employees, the difference between the 1st and 2nd employee is assumed to be the same as that between the 21st and 22nd. Some employees may be closely grouped, but no ties are permitted. The result is a clear ordering from the highest performer to the lowest.

   One parallel to forced ranking is forced distribution of college grades. Why would universities do this? As shown in Exhibit 17-3, the average GPA of a Princeton University undergraduate has gotten much higher over time.[64]

   It's not just Princeton. The average GPA at Wheaton College was 2.75 in 1962; now it's 3.40. At Pomona College, the average GPA was 3.06 in 1970; now it's 3.43. About half the grades at Duke, Harvard, and Columbia are in the "A" range. At Harvard, 91 percent of seniors graduated with some sort of honors in 2001. These are just randomly selected examples. Almost all universities have seen considerable grade inflation, although, interestingly, it may be more severe at prestigious institutions.

Exhibit 17-3   Grade Inflation at Four Universities: Princeton, UCLA, UW-Milwaukee, and Auburn

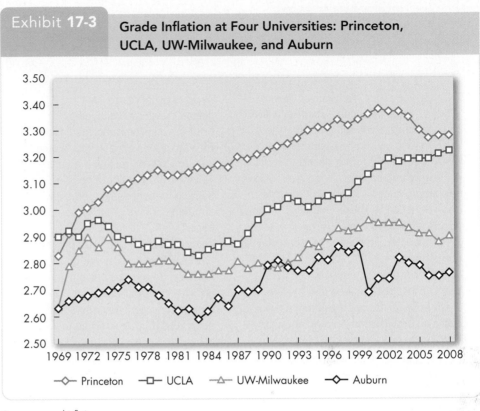

Source: www.gradeinflation.com.

In response to grade inflation, some colleges have instituted forced grade distributions whereby professors must give a certain percentage of A's, B's, and C's. This is exactly what Princeton recently did; each department can now give A's to no more than 35 percent of its students. Natasha Gopaul, a Princeton senior, commented, "You do feel you might be one of the ones they just cut off."

Suggestions for Improving Performance Evaluations

8 Show how managers can improve performance evaluations.

The performance-evaluation process is a potential minefield. Evaluators can unconsciously inflate evaluations (positive leniency), understate performance (negative leniency), or allow the assessment of one characteristic to unduly influence the assessment of others (the halo error). Some appraisers bias their evaluations by unconsciously favoring people who have qualities and traits similar to their own (the similarity error).

---

critical incidents *A way of evaluating the behaviors that are key in making the difference between executing a job effectively and executing it ineffectively.*

graphic rating scales *An evaluation method in which the evaluator rates performance factors on an incremental scale.*

behaviorally anchored rating scales (BARS) *Scales that combine major elements from the critical incident and*

graphic rating scale approaches. The appraiser rates the employees based on items along a continuum, but the points are examples of actual behavior on the given job rather than general descriptions or traits.

forced comparison *Method of performance evaluation where an employee's performance is made in explicit comparison to others (e.g., an employee may rank third out of 10 employees in her work unit.)*

group order ranking *An evaluation method that places employees into a particular classification, such as quartiles.*

individual ranking *An evaluation method that rank-orders employees from best to worst.*

An Ethical Choice

Is Honesty the Best Policy in Getting a Job?

Yes and no. Are you surprised? On one hand, despite what organizations may tell you, there *are* right and wrong answers for nearly every question you are asked in tests or interviews. This suggests you should provide the "socially desirable" answer: to put it more coarsely, "fake good" when you can.

Of course, there are ethical concerns here.

There are also practical considerations. The right answer is not always clear. So in faking good you might, ironically, be providing the wrong answers.

What to do? Here is our best advice:

1. **Put your best foot forward, within reason.** If a test or interviewer question asks about your behavior or attitudes, answer for your best realistic self. This is not a time to be hard on yourself.

2. **Avoid answers you couldn't defend.** Just because you're putting your "best realistic" foot forward doesn't mean you should lose touch with reality. If an interviewer asks you about your biggest weakness, you probably shouldn't answer, "I just work too hard."

3. **Know yourself.** If you are a person who is tough on yourself or modest, then make a special effort to put your best foot forward and describe yourself positively. If you're someone who is bold and confident (think Donald Trump), then you probably shouldn't make such an effort, as you run the risk of coming off as arrogant or brash.

4. **Watch your résumé.** Résumés are a special case—see our discussion in the *Ethical Dilemma* at the end of this chapter.

5. **Match yourself to the organization.** When Rob Sparno found himself unemployed, for each job he sought he spent a great deal of time asking himself "What do they want? What keeps them up at night?" He then thought through how his skills, abilities, and experiences would address those questions. The beauty of this approach is that it is effective, and it doesn't require compromising your values.

Sources: Based on J. L. Yang, "How to Get a Job," *Fortune* (April 13, 2009), pp. 49–56; A. Byrne, "True or False, Both Right," *The Australian* (July 19, 2008), www.theaustralian.news.com.au; and S. Smith, "Jobseekers Put on False Face at Interview," *The Scotsman* (January 14, 2008), news.scotsman.com/uk.

And, of course, some evaluators see the evaluation process as a political opportunity to overtly reward or punish employees they like or dislike. Although no protections *guarantee* accurate performance evaluations, the following suggestions can make the process more objective and fair.

Use Multiple Evaluators   As the number of evaluators increases, the probability of attaining more accurate information increases. We often see multiple evaluators in competitions in such sports as diving and gymnastics. A set of evaluators judges a performance, the highest and lowest scores are dropped, and the final evaluation is made up of those remaining. The logic of multiple evaluators applies to organizations as well. If an employee has had ten supervisors, nine having rated her excellent and one poor, we can safely discount the one poor evaluation. By moving employees around within the organization to gain a number of evaluations, or by using multiple assessors (as in 360-degree appraisals), we increase the probability of achieving more valid and reliable evaluations.

Evaluate Selectively   To increase agreement among them, appraisers should evaluate only where they have some expertise.[65] They should thus be as close as possible, in organizational level, to the individual being evaluated. The more levels that separate them, the less opportunity the evaluator has to observe the individual's behavior and, not surprisingly, the greater the possibility for inaccuracies.

Train Evaluators   If you can't *find* good evaluators, *make* them. Training evaluators can produce more accurate raters.[66] Most rater training courses emphasize changing the raters' frame of reference by teaching them what to look for, so everyone in the organization defines *good performance* in the same way. Another effective training technique is to encourage raters to describe the employee's behavior in as much detail as possible. Providing more detail encourages raters to remember more about the employee's performance, rather than just acting on their feelings about the employee at the moment.

Provide Employees with Due Process   The concept of *due process* can be applied to appraisals to increase the perception that employees are being treated fairly.[67] Three features characterize due process systems: (1) Individuals are provided with adequate notice of what is expected of them; (2) all evidence relevant to a proposed violation is aired in a fair hearing so the individuals affected can respond; and (3) the final decision is based on the evidence and free of bias.

Considerable evidence shows evaluation systems often violate employees' due process by providing infrequent and relatively general performance feedback, allowing them little input into the appraisal process, and knowingly introducing bias. However, when due process has been part of the evaluation system, employees report positive reactions to the appraisal process, perceive it as more accurate, and express increased intent to remain with the organization.

Providing Performance Feedback

Few activities are more unpleasant for many managers than providing performance feedback to employees.[68] In fact, unless pressured by organizational policies and controls, managers are likely to ignore this responsibility.[69]

Why? First, even though almost every employee could stand to improve in some areas, managers fear confrontation when presenting negative feedback. This apprehension apparently applies even when people give negative feedback to a computer! Bill Gates reports that Microsoft conducted a project requiring users to rate their experience with a computer. "When we had the computer the users had worked with ask for an evaluation of its performance, the responses tended to be positive. But when we had a second computer ask the same people to evaluate their encounters with the first machine, the people were significantly more critical. Their reluctance to criticize the first computer 'to its face' suggested that they didn't want to hurt its feelings, even though they knew it was only a machine."[70]

Second, many employees do tend to become defensive when their weaknesses are pointed out. Instead of accepting the feedback as constructive and a basis for improving performance, some criticize the manager or redirect blame to someone else. A survey of 151 area managers in Philadelphia, for instance, found 98 percent encountered some type of aggression after giving employees negative appraisals.[71]

Finally, employees tend to have an inflated assessment of their own performance. Statistically speaking, half of all employees must be below-average performers. But the average employee's estimate of his or her own performance level generally falls around the 75th percentile.[72] So even when managers are providing good news, employees are likely to perceive it as not good enough.

The solution to the problem is not to ignore it but to train managers to conduct constructive feedback sessions. An effective review—in which the employee perceives the appraisal as fair, the manager as sincere, and the climate as constructive—can leave the employee feeling upbeat, informed about areas needing improvement, and determined to correct them.[73] It probably won't surprise you that employees in a bad mood are much less likely to take advice than employees in a good mood.[74] Appraisals should also be as specific as possible. People are most likely to overrate their own performance when asked about overall job performance, but they can be more objective when feedback is about a specific area.[75] It's also hard to figure out how to improve your performance globally—it's much easier to improve in specific areas. In addition, the performance review should be a counseling activity more than a judgment process, best accomplished by allowing it to evolve from the employee's own self-evaluation.

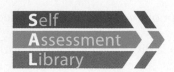

HOW GOOD AM I AT GIVING PERFORMANCE FEEDBACK?

In the Self-Assessment Library (available on CD and online), take assessment III.A.3 (How Good Am I at Giving Performance Feedback?).

Managing Work–Life Conflicts in Organizations

9 Describe how organizations can manage work-family conflicts.

We introduced work–life balance in Chapter 1 and discussed the blurring lines between work life and personal life. Here we specifically focus on what organizations can do to help employees reduce conflicts.

Work–life conflicts grabbed management's attention in the 1980s, largely as a result of the growing number of women, with dependent children, entering the workforce. In response, most major organizations took actions to make their workplaces more family friendly.[76] They introduced on-site child care, summer day camps, flextime, job sharing, leaves for school functions, telecommuting, and part-time employment. But organizations quickly realized work–life conflicts were not limited to female employees with children. Male workers and women without children were also facing this problem. Heavy workloads and increased travel demands, for instance, made it increasingly hard for many employees to meet both work and personal responsibilities. A Harvard study found 82 percent of men between the ages of 20 and 39 said a "family-friendly" schedule was their most important job criterion.[77]

Organizations are modifying their workplaces with scheduling options and benefits to accommodate the varied needs of a diverse workforce. Employees at the corporate office of retailer Eddie Bauer have flexible scheduling, plus a full array of on-site services, including dry cleaning pickup and delivery, an ATM, a gym with personal trainers, flu shots, Weight Watchers classes, and financial seminars.[78] Exhibit 17-4 lists some initiatives to help employees reduce work–life conflicts.

Time pressures aren't the primary problem underlying these conflicts.[79] It's the psychological incursion of work into the family domain and vice versa when people are worrying about personal problems at work and thinking about work problems at home. So dad may make it home in time for dinner, but his mind is elsewhere. This suggests organizations should spend less effort helping employees with time-management issues and more helping them clearly segment their lives. Keeping workloads reasonable, reducing work-related travel, and offering on-site quality child care are examples of practices that can help in this endeavor.

Not surprisingly, people differ in their preference for scheduling options and benefits.[80] Some prefer organizational initiatives that better segment work from their personal lives, as flextime, job sharing, and part-time hours do by allowing employees to schedule work hours less likely to conflict with personal responsibilities. Others prefer ways to integrate work and personal life, such as on-site child care, gym facilities, and company-sponsored family picnics.

Exhibit **17-4**	**Work–Life Initiatives**	

Strategy	Program or Policy	Organizational Example
Time-based strategies Allstate, 75 percent do.	• Flextime	At General Mills, 45 percent of employees use flextime; at
	• Job sharing	Wegmans offers job sharing, compressed workweeks, and telecommuting.
	• Leave for new parents	Ernst & Young provides full-pay maternity leave, and gives new dads up to 6 weeks of leave at full pay.
	• Transportation	Google transports employees to and from work via a bus network the company owns and operates.
	• Telecommuting	At KPMG, 65 percent of staffers use telecommuting, flextime, or compressed workweek.
	• Paid time off for community service	Umpqua Bank provides employees with 40 hours of paid time off per year to devote to community service (in addition to regular vacation time).
Information-based strategies	• Work/life support	UBS' Working Parents Group provides mentoring, and the Career Comeback program offers advice for parents reentering the workforce.
	• Relocation assistance	ADP will help employees sell their old house or will help them find renters (and pay employees the difference between rent and mortgage until the house sells).
	• Eldercare resources	Hallmark provides free consultations and personal family needs assessments from elder-care experts.
	• Counseling services	Campbell Soup offers medical decision support, traveling health station tours, counseling service to help employees and their families balance work–life demands, health risk appraisal, lifestyle management coaching, worksite wellness, smoking cessation, preventive care coverage, nurselines, and disease management.
Money-based strategies	• Insurance subsidies	Ceridian Canada provides subsidies for pet insurance.
	• Flexible benefits	Royal Bank of Scotland (RBS) employees are provided with a cash account (called a Value Account), from which they can purchase the benefits that best suit them.
	• Adoption assistance	Carswell provides $5,000 adoptive assistance per adopted child; Bain & Co. reimburses up to $10,000 per adoptee.
	• Discounts for child-care tuition	AstraZeneca, Booz Allen Hamilton, and PricewaterhouseCoopers provide discounts for child care.
	• Direct financial assistance	Baptist Health South Florida provides $10,000 loan for first-time home buyers.
	• Domestic partner benefits	American Airlines provides same-sex domestic partner benefits and offers equal health coverage and travel privileges to same-sex partners of its employees.
	• Scholarships, tuition reimbursement	HSBC provides tuition reimbursement and scholarships for children of employees.
Direct services	• On-site child care	SAS offers two on-site child care centers at its Cary, NC, headquarters.
	• Fitness center	Raytheon offers full-service, no-cost fitness center and recreation park.
	• Summer child care	IBM staff can send their children to the firm's science/tech summer programs for free.
	• On-site conveniences	Genentech has on-site car wash, dental care, and hair salon.
	• Concierge services	Genentech also provides concierge service.
	• Free or discounted company products	Research in Motion (RIM) gives new employees free BlackBerry and covers usage and service fees; Mars sells its candy bars to employees at cost.

(continued)

Exhibit 17-4	Work–Life Initiatives *continued*	
Strategy	**Program or Policy**	**Organizational Example**
Culture-change strategies	• Establishing work–life balanced culture; training for managers to help employees deal with work/life conflicts	GlaxoSmithKline focuses on concept of "healthy high performance"; Dell survey asks employees to rate their managers on work–life commitment, while two office blogs provide a forum for staff discussions about work–life issues.
	• Tie manager pay to employee satisfaction	Lucent, Marriott, Merck, Pfizer, Prudential, and Xerox, among others, tie manager pay to employee satisfaction.
	• Focus on employees' actual performance, not "face time"	Monsanto and Best Buy encourage employee evaluations to be based on quantifiable goals and results, regardless of where or at what time work is completed.

Sources: Based on I. Chang, I. Cohen, M. Dodd, et al., "2008 100 Best Companies," *Working Mother* (August 12, 2009), www.workingmother.com; "Campbell Recognized by National Business Group on Health as a Leading Employer Promoting Healthy Lifestyles for Its Employees," Fox Business (June 25, 2009), www.foxbusiness.com; C. Said, "Bay Area Scores in Best Firm Rankings," *San Francisco Chronicle* (January 10, 2006), www.sfgate.com; S. Linstedt, "Wegmans Ranked Fifth-Best Place to Work by Fortune Magazine," *Buffalo News* (January 23, 2009), www.buffalonews.com; "Umpqua Bank Employees Contribute More Than 22,000 Community Service Hours in 2007," *Business Wire* (January 09, 2008), www.accessmylibrary.com; L. Palmer, "Are We a Family-Friendly Nation?" *Redbook* (July 29, 2009), www.sfgate.com; and C. A. Thompson, "Managing the Work–Life Balance Act: An Introductory Exercise," *Journal of Management Education*, April 2002, p. 210.

Global Implications

10 Show how a global context affects human resource management.

Many of the human resource policies and practices discussed in this chapter have to be modified to reflect cultural differences.[81] But those like training, participation, and results-oriented appraisals that have been shown to be important predictors of product and financial performance in North America have also been linked to higher performance and lower turnover in east and southeast Asia.[82] To illustrate differences across cultures in the implementation and success of HRM practices, let's briefly look at the universality of selection practices and the importance of performance evaluation in different cultures.

Recruiting and Selection

You might suspect that cultural values lead to different effects for recruiting messages, and research backs up this intuition. One study found that respondents high in power distance viewed organizational reputation as a more important job choice factor than did individuals who were lower in power choice.[83] A recent study of 300 large organizations in 22 countries demonstrated that selection practices differ by nation.[84] The use of educational qualifications in screening candidates seems to be a universal practice, but different countries emphasize different selection techniques. Structured interviews were popular in some countries and nonexistent in others. The study authors suggested that "certain cultures may find structured interviews antithetical to beliefs about how one should conduct an interpersonal interaction or the extent to which one should trust the judgment of the interviewer."[85] Other research shows that across the Netherlands, the United States, France, Spain, Portugal, and Singapore, most applicants prefer interviews and work sample tests and dislike use of personal contacts and integrity tests.[86] There was little variation in preferences across these countries.

These studies, combined with earlier research, tell us there is great variation in recruiting and selection processes across countries but also important commonalities. Global firms that attempt to implement standardized worldwide se-

Executives of ImageNet Company (in red jackets), one of Japan's top Internet clothing retailers, conducted job interviews atop Mount Fuji, Japan's highest mountain. Of the 20 candidates who applied for one of four job openings, 11 succeeded in reaching the summit of the 12,388-foot mountain for the interview. ImageNet staged the unique interview to identify candidates who are highly motivated, determined to succeed, and prepared for unusual challenges. In the United States and most European nations, this type of interview would run afoul of equal employment opportunity laws.

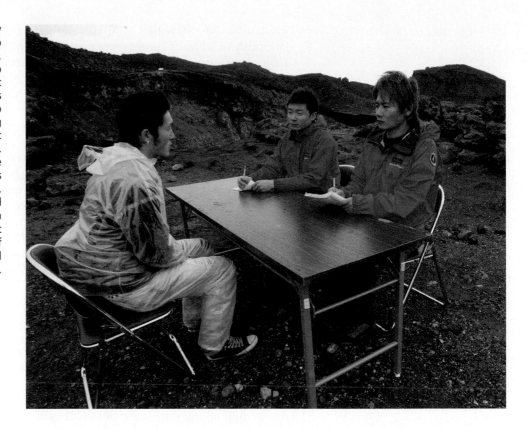

lection practices can expect considerable resistance from local managers. Managers need to modify policies and practices to reflect culture-based norms and social values, as well as legal and economic differences.

Training and Development

To understand how national culture affects training, let's think about how it might influence the way people learn and apply their new skills. A study of 68 organizations in 14 different countries found that in nations high in uncertainty avoidance, safety training had a smaller impact because employees already tend to practice safe behavior without training.[87] They were less likely to apply job safety training in novel situations, however, because they were more prone to follow standard operating procedures. More research on how to provide effective training internationally is needed.

Performance Evaluation

Many cultures are not particularly concerned with performance appraisal or look at it differently than do managers in the United States and Canada.

Let's examine performance evaluation in the context of four cultural dimensions: individualism/collectivism, a person's relationship to the environment, time orientation, and focus of responsibility.

Individual-oriented cultures such as the United States emphasize formal performance-evaluation systems more than informal systems. They advocate written evaluations performed at regular intervals, the results of which managers share with employees and use in the determination of rewards. On the other hand, the collectivist cultures that dominate Asia and much of Latin America are characterized by more informal systems—downplaying formal feedback and disconnecting reward allocations from performance ratings. Some of these differences may be narrowing, however. In Korea, Singapore, and even Japan, the use of performance evaluation has increased dramatically in the past decade, though not always smoothly or without controversy. One survey of Korean employees revealed that a majority questioned the validity of their performance-evaluation results.[88]

U.S. and Canadian organizations hold people responsible for their actions because people in these countries believe they can dominate their environment. In Middle Eastern countries, on the other hand, performance evaluations aren't widely used because managers tend to see people as subject to their environment.

Some countries, such as the United States, have a short-term time orientation. Performance evaluations are likely to be frequent in such a culture—at least once a year. In Japan, however, where people hold a long-term time frame, performance appraisals may occur only every 5 or 10 years.

Israel's culture values group activities much more than does the culture of the United States or Canada. So, whereas North American managers traditionally emphasize the individual in performance evaluations, their counterparts in Israel are more likely to emphasize group contributions and performance.

Summary and Implications for Managers

An organization's human resource policies and practices create important forces that shape employee behavior and attitudes. In this chapter, we specifically discussed the influence of selection practices, training and development programs, and performance-evaluation systems.

Selection Practices   If properly designed, an organization's selection practices will identify competent candidates and accurately match them to the job and the organization.

Although employee selection is far from a science, some organizations fail to design a selection system that can achieve the right person–job fit. When hiring errors are made, the chosen candidate's performance may be less than satisfactory without an investment in training to improve his or her skills. At worst, the new hire will prove unacceptable, and the firm will need to find a replacement. Individuals who are less qualified or who otherwise don't fit the organization are also likely to feel anxious, tense, uncomfortable, and likely dissatisfied with the job.

Training and Development Programs   The most obvious effect of training programs is direct improvement in the skills necessary to successfully complete the job. Increased ability thus improves potential, but whether that potential becomes realized is largely an issue of motivation.

A second benefit of training is that it increases an employee's self-efficacy, a person's expectation that he or she can successfully execute the behaviors required to produce an outcome (see Chapter 7).[89] Employees with high self-efficacy have strong expectations about their abilities to perform in new situations. They're confident and expect to be successful. Training, then, is a means to positively affect self-efficacy because employees may be more willing to undertake job tasks and exert a high level of effort. Or in expectancy terms (see Chapter 7), individuals are more likely to perceive their effort as leading to performance.

Performance Evaluation   A major goal of performance evaluation is to assess an individual's performance accurately as a basis for allocating rewards. If evaluation is inaccurate or emphasizes the wrong criteria, employees will be over- or underrewarded. As demonstrated in Chapter 7, in our discussion of equity theory, evaluations perceived as unfair can result in reduced effort, increases in absenteeism, or a search for alternative job opportunities. The content of the performance evaluation also influences employee performance and satisfaction.[90] Specifically, performance and satisfaction are increased when the evaluation is based on behavioral and results-oriented criteria, when career issues as well as performance issues are discussed, and when the employee has an opportunity to participate in the evaluation.

POINT  COUNTERPOINT

Telecommuting Makes Good Business Sense

In a sense, telecommuting and flexible schedules are old news. Many companies have allowed and encouraged employees to work flexible schedules for years. However, in another sense, the logic and impetus for flexible schedules is stronger than ever.

The first and most obvious reason is changes in how and where work is done. Confining the "workplace" to some arbitrarily chosen office makes less and less sense for more and more organizations. The global consulting firm Accenture is so unwilling to maintain the hoary old "office bunker" mentality that it actually asks its 178,000 worldwide employees to make reservations for office space when they need it. Accenture finds its non-office culture fits the distributed, global nature of its business and better connects employees to clients.

Second, organizations are realizing that offering telecommuting and other flexible schedules allows them to attract and retain the best talent. New entrants into the workforce value autonomy, creativity, and virtual access over routines, structures, and dress codes.

Third, while managers are a main source of opposition to telework, once exposed to it they become much more positive. As a *Wall Street Journal* article noted in describing flexible workers, "Allowed to find their own equilibrium between work and private lives, they tend to put work first." Managers see this through experience. A review of 46 studies on telecommuting revealed positive effects on employee productivity and morale.

There are too many arguments in favor of telecommuting and flexible schedules for organizations to ignore. A recent survey of employers indicated 63 percent offer flexible work schedules; they are ahead of the curve.

Telecommuting and other flexible schedules are among those management fads the business press loves to shower with praise. Like most other fads, however, they don't stand up to close scrutiny and logical analysis.

Managers don't view telecommuters very positively. And if you respond honestly and objectively, you would have a hard time advising employees to indulge in flexible work schedules when doing so hurts their career. A recent study gives some interesting support.

More than two-thirds of employees surveyed (68 percent) thought working at home made them more productive. However, when managers were surveyed, more than one-third (37 percent) thought that if allowed to work at home, staff would use their so-called working hours for personal activities.

Sure, employees want flexible schedules and rationalize their preferences by arguing that it helps them get more done. But a lot of managers know better—while some of "working at home" does include work, another part is spent doing nonwork-related activities such as chores, personal or family activities, and so on. That's exactly why employees want it so much.

If you asked employees "Would you like to get paid the same for working half as many hours?" most employees would probably say "Sure!" But that doesn't mean management should give employees something for nothing. Effective HRM sometimes means not giving employees what they want.

Sources: Based on J. Marquez, "Connecting a Virtual Workforce," *Workforce Management* (September 22, 2008), pp 1–25; D. Pauleen and B. Harmer, "Away from the Desk . . . Always," *Wall Street Journal* (December 15, 2008), p. B8; R. Zeidner, "Telecommuting: The Good, the Bad, and the Unknown," *HR Magazine* (May 2008), p. 10; D. Fost, "They're Working on Their Own, Just Side by Side," *New York Times* (February 20, 2008), p. 5; and R. Scally, "'Working From Home Today'—That's Not What Your Boss Thinks," *Workforce Week,* May 6, 2007, p. 1.

Questions for Review

1 What is initial selection, and what are the most useful initial selection methods?

2 What is substantive selection, and what are the most useful substantive selection methods?

3 What is contingent selection, and what are the arguments for and against drug testing?

4 What are the four main types of training?

5 What are the differences between formal and informal training methods and between on-the-job and off-the-job training?

6 What are the main purposes of performance evaluation?

7 How can organizations improve their performance-evaluation processes?

8 How can organizations help reduce work–family conflicts?

9 How is human resource management affected by a global context?

10 Show how a global context affects human resource management.

Experiential Exercise

EVALUATING PERFORMANCE AND PROVIDING FEEDBACK

Objective
To experience the assessment of performance and observe the provision of performance feedback.

Time
Approximately 30 minutes.

Procedure
Select a class leader—either a volunteer or someone chosen by your instructor. The class leader will preside over the class discussion and perform the role of manager in the evaluation review.

Your instructor will leave the room. The class leader is then to spend up to 15 minutes helping the class to evaluate your instructor. Your instructor understands that this is only a class exercise and is prepared to accept criticism (and, of course, any praise you may want to convey). Your instructor also recognizes that the leader's evaluation is actually a composite of many students' input. So be open and honest in your evaluation and have confidence that your instructor will not be vindictive.

Research has identified seven performance dimensions to the college instructor's job: (1) instructor knowledge,

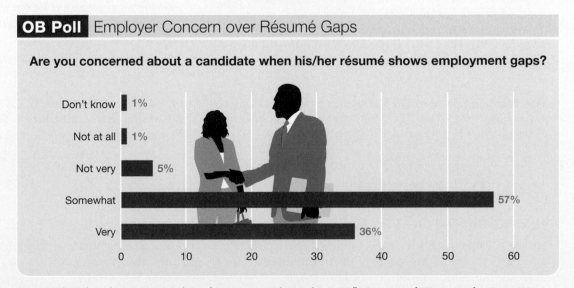

OB Poll Employer Concern over Résumé Gaps

Are you concerned about a candidate when his/her résumé shows employment gaps?

- Don't know 1%
- Not at all 1%
- Not very 5%
- Somewhat 57%
- Very 36%

(axis: 0, 10, 20, 30, 40, 50, 60)

Source: Based on "Closing the Gap: Expert Provides Tips for Overcoming Breaks in Employment," OfficeTeam survey of 150 executives from Fortune 1000 (November 24, 2008), www.officeteam.com/PressRoom?id=2345.

(2) testing procedures, (3) student–teacher relations, (4) organizational skills, (5) communication skills, (6) subject relevance, and (7) utility of assignments. The discussion of your instructor's performance should focus on these seven dimensions. The leader may want to take notes for personal use but will not be required to give your instructor any written documentation.

When the 15-minute class discussion is complete, the leader will invite the instructor back into the room. The performance review will begin as soon as the instructor walks through the door, with the class leader becoming the manager and the instructor playing himself or herself.

When completed, class discussion will focus on performance-evaluation criteria and how well your class leader did in providing performance feedback.

Ethical Dilemma

IS IT UNETHICAL TO "SHAPE" YOUR RÉSUMÉ?

When does putting a positive spin on your accomplishments cross over the line to become misrepresentation or lying? Does a résumé have to be 100 percent truthful? Apparently, a lot of people don't think so. Studies have found that nearly half of all résumés contain at least one lie. Inflated credentials have cost many executives their jobs—some uncovered through the efforts of Barry Minkow, who served prison time for his role in the ZZZZ Best stock swindle and who now investigates corporations and their executives.

To help you clarify your ethical views on this issue, consider the following situations and answer the questions for each.

1. Sean has left a job for which his title was credit clerk. When looking for a new job, he lists his previous title as "credit analyst." He thinks it sounds more impressive. Is this retitling of a former job wrong? Why or why not?

2. About 8 years ago, Michiko took 9 months off between jobs to travel overseas. Afraid that people might consider her unstable or lacking in career motivation, she stated in her résumé that she was engaged in "independent consulting activities" during the period. Was she wrong? How else could she have described this time period on her résumé?

3. David is the 46-year-old CEO of a Fortune 1000 company. He enrolled in Pacific Coast Baptist College 20 years ago but never got a degree. Just 9 months after he was appointed CEO, a local newspaper reported he had lied on his résumé by indicating a bachelor's degree in psychology that he doesn't have. Should he be terminated? If yes, why, and if not, what should his employer do about David's missing credentials? (This scenario is based on a true story; to find out more, enter "David Edmondson" and "résumé" in your favorite search engine.)

4. Kayla sent out 100 applications for an administrative assistant position but received only one callback. Believing her master's degree and past academic teaching experience were getting in the way, she removed them from her résumé. Lauren has 26 years of marketing experience but didn't want to show it, so she made her résumé look less senior by eliminating certain jobs and other experiences. Rashad was laid off from his VP post at Wells Fargo. In searching for middle management jobs, he removed his VP title from his résumé. Did Kayla, Lauren, and Rashad misrepresent themselves?

Sources: Based on J. Porter, "The New Résumé: Dumb and Dumber," *Wall Street Journal* (May 26, 2009), p. D5; J. S. Lublin, "When Big Résumés Chase Small Jobs," *Wall Street Journal* (March 3, 2009), p. D6; K. J. Winstein, "Inflated Credentials Surface in Executive Suite," *Wall Street Journal* (November 13, 2008), pp. B1, B6.

Case Incident 1

PEERING INTO YOUR PAST

In this age of seemingly social and humanitarian values, it's ironic that employers are peering deeper than ever into our backgrounds, often without our knowledge.

In large part, this change is a reflection of our economic times. Though there are skill shortages in some industries, most employers have plenty of applicants from which to

choose, meaning they can afford to carefully check into applicants' backgrounds. And check they have—employment screening is booming.

Background checks are done with the applicant's authorization in most, but not all, cases. One staffing expert said, "I'm shocked how many employers are not getting applicant authorizations." Moreover, when a background check does reveal a problem, most employers don't inform the applicant that this is the reason for their rejection. When Theodore Pendergrass was rejected for a store supervisor job at Walgreens, the company, unlike most, told him the background screening firm ChoicePoint found a past employer had accused him of stealing $7,313 in merchandise. Pendergrass was shocked. "I wanted to cry," he said. Despite proving the charges false, Pendergrass was similarly rejected by other employers that used ChoicePoint, including CVS and Target. Eventually Starbucks, which doesn't use screening firms for entry-level positions, hired him.

This is not to suggest background checks have no merit. Past behavior often forecasts the future, and malfeasance is a huge problem for most companies. Across industries, roughly 10 percent of applicants have criminal records, and more have driving violations (48 percent), employment verification problems on their application or résumé (48 percent), or credit problems (43 percent).

Background checks don't stop with screening firms. A *lot* of companies also mine the Internet—including Twitter, Facebook, MySpace, message boards, and blogs—for information about prospective job candidates. Flight attendant Ellen Simonetti lost her job at Delta after she posted some suggestive pictures of herself in uniform (even though she didn't identify Delta as her employer). She sued Delta and lost. Heather Armstrong wrote about her job in a blog and was fired. She started a Web site (Dooce .com), which spawned a neologism—"Dooced"—to describe workers fired for what they post on the Web.

Questions

1. Do you think employers have a right to investigate applicants by Googling them or exploring sites such as MySpace or Twitter? What about checking out their current employers?

2. When applicants apply for a job, typically they give employers permission to look into their background. Do you agree this absolves employers of moral blame for such "digging"?

3. If you worked for a consumer products company that asked you to develop a background check policy, what would be some central tenets of your recommended program?

4. As we noted in this chapter, if an employer doesn't check the background of an applicant with a criminal history who then harms others at work, the employer can be liable for "negligent hiring." What do you think of such a policy? Does it influence your attitudes toward background checking?

5. Some individuals are turning the tables and checking out prospective employers by posing as customers or clients. Couldn't an applicant argue "What's good for the goose is good for the gander"?

Sources: Based on F. Hansen, "Caution Amid the Credit Crunch," *Workforce Management* (February 16, 2009), pp. 35–39; C. Terhune, "The Trouble with Background Checks," *Business Week* (June 9, 2008), pp. 54–58; J. S. Lublin, "Job Seekers Go Undercover to Check Out Employers," *Wall Street Journal* (November 24, 2008), p. B4; and S. Foss, M. Collin, "You Are What You Post," *Business Week* (March 27, 2006), pp. 52–53.

Case Incident 2

JOB CANDIDATES WITHOUT STRONG SAT SCORES NEED NOT APPLY

Many high school students probably believe that once they get into college, their SAT scores are a thing of the past. However, many job seekers are discovering their would-be employers are asking for their SAT scores as part of the selection process. Donna Chan, a 23-year-old graduate of New York's Wagner College, learned that one of the minimum requirements for many of the entry-level financial services jobs she was seeking was a combined SAT score of 1300. According to the College Board, the organization that administers the exam, the average combined math and verbal score of the freshman class of 2005 (the last class to take the old version of the SAT) was 1028. Donna Chan's score was "in the 1200s"—a good score to be sure but not good enough to obtain any of the positions she was seek-ing, even though she obtained a 3.9 grade-point average in college. "I think it's asking a bit much," says Chan. "That's something high school kids have to worry about. After four years of working hard, I think you've paid your dues, and unless you're applying to *Princeton Review* or some math-related, analytical job, I don't see the relevance."

Apparently, however, some recruiters do. Alan Sage, a vice president at systems-management software company Configuresoft Inc., says SAT scores are a good predictor of success in his company, and he regularly has applicants submit their scores when applying for sales positions. He set the mark at a combined score of 1200—lower than Donna Chan faced but nonetheless well above average. Says Sage, "In my experience, people with high SAT scores tend to do better." Sage himself scored between 1200 and 1300. He adds, however, that "we wouldn't exclude someone from an interview if he or she didn't score high."

Seppy Basilli, vice president of Kaplan Inc., one of several companies that provides instruction on taking the SAT, believes companies are misusing SAT scores. "It's such a maligned instrument," he says. "It's not designed to measure job performance, and the kind of person who performs well on the SATs is not necessarily the kind of person who will perform well sitting at her desk." Morgan Denny, who works as a headhunter in New York, shares a similar opinion. Though his clients typically want to consider only applicants with high SAT scores, Denny often shows his clients applicants he believes are strong candidates for the position despite a lower score. "The SAT is an annoyance for us and an annoyance for our candidates," says Denny.

Some individuals, such as Kristin Carnahan, a spokesperson for the College Board, feel companies should use other measures of cognitive ability, such as college grades, which are also more recent indicators than SAT scores. However, grades aren't standardized across institutions, so they can't be compared like SAT scores can.

Grade inflation (Exhibit 17-3) also may make it more difficult for recruiters to assess an applicant's GPA. Because OB research has shown cognitive ability is a strong predictor of job performance—and the SAT is supposedly a measure of cognitive ability—many companies may continue to use the SAT as a benchmark for job applicants.

Questions

1. Is it fair for organizations to require minimum scores on standardized tests such as the SAT? Why or why not?

2. As a recruiter choosing between two individuals with different SAT scores, would you have difficulty giving the job to the applicant with the lower score? On what additional factors might your choice depend?

3. What other indicators of job performance, besides SAT scores, could you use to screen job applicants? What are the advantages and disadvantages of each?

4. Suppose you worked at a company that used SAT scores for hiring purposes. How would you handle diverse applicants, such as those from a foreign country who may not have taken the SAT?

Sources: Based on S. Foss, "Background Check—Background Search," *American Chronicle,* July 12, 2007; and K. J. Dunham, "Career Journal: More Employers Ask Job Seekers for SAT Scores," *Wall Street Journal* (October 28, 2003), p. B1.

Endnotes

1. M. Mirabile, "NFL Quarterback Wonderlic Scores," MacMirabile.com, June 26, 2009, www.macmirabile.com/Wonderlic.htm; "Georgia's Matthew Stafford Stands Out with NFL Wonderlic Score," *Los Angeles Times* (March 22, 2009), www.latimes.com; and L. Robertson, "Wonderlic Test Just Part of a Thorough NFL Draft Vetting Process," *Miami Herald* (April 24, 2009), www.miamiherald.com.

2. See B. Becker and B. Gerhart, "The Impact of Human Resource Management on Organizational Performance: Progress and Prospects," *Academy of Management Journal,* August 1996, pp. 779–801; M. A. Huselid, S. E. Jackson, and R. S. Schuler, "Technical and Strategic Human Resource Management Effectiveness as Determinants of Firm Performance," *Academy of Management Journal,* February 1997, pp. 171–188; C. J. Collins, and K. D. Clark, "Strategic Human Resource Practices, Top Management Team Social Networks, and Firm Performance: The Role of Human Resource Practices in Creating Organizational Competitive Advantage," *Academy of Management Journal,* December 2003, pp. 740–751; D. E. Bowen and C. Ostroff, "Understanding HRM–Firm Performance Linkages: The Role of the 'Strength' of the HRM System," *Academy of Management Review,* April 2004, pp. 203–221; and K. Birdi, C. Clegg, M. Patterson, A. Robinson, C. B. Stride, T. D. Wall, and S. J. Wood, "The Impact of Human Resource and Operational Management Practices on Company Productivity: A Longitudinal Study," *Personnel Psychology* 61, no. 3 (2008), pp. 467–501.

3. See, for instance, A. L. Kristof-Brown, R. D. Zimmerman, and E. C. Johnson, "Consequences of Individual's Fit at Work: A Meta-analysis of Person-Job, Person-Organization, Person-Group, and Person-Supervisor Fit," *Personnel Psychology* 58, no. 2 (2005), pp. 281–342; and D. S. DeRue and F. P. Morgeson, "Stability and Change in Person-Team and Person-Role Fit over Time: The Effects of Growth Satisfaction, Performance, and General Self-Efficacy," *Journal of Applied Psychology* 92, no. 5 (2007), pp. 1242–1253.

4. J. D. Glater, "Another Hurdle for the Jobless: Credit Inquiries," *New York Times* (August 6, 2009), www.nytimes.com.

5. C. Lachnit, "The Cost of Not Doing Background Checks," *Workforce Management,* www.workforce.com.

6. Cited in J. H. Prager, "Nasty or Nice: 56-Question Quiz," *Wall Street Journal* (February 22, 2000), p. A4; and H. Wessel, "Personality Tests Grow Popular," *Seattle Post–Intelligencer* (August 3, 2003), p. G1.

7. G. Nicholsen, "Screen and Glean: Good Screening and Background Checks Help Make the Right Match for Every Open Position," *Workforce,* October 2000, pp. 70–72.

8. J. P. Hausknecht, D. V. Day, and S. C. Thomas, "Applicant Reactions to Selection Procedures: An Updated Model and Meta-analysis," *Personnel Psychology,* September 2004, pp. 639–683.

9. E. E. Ghiselli, "The Validity of Aptitude Tests in Personnel Selection," *Personnel Psychology,* Winter 1973, p. 475.

10. F. L. Schmidt, and J. Hunter, "General Mental Ability in the World of Work: Occupational Attainment and Job Performance," *Journal of Personality and Social Psychology* 86, no. 1 (2004), pp. 162–173; and F. L. Schmidt, J. A. Shaffer,

and I. Oh, "Increased Accuracy for Range Restriction Corrections: Implications for the Role of Personality and General Mental Ability in Job and Training Performance," *Personnel Psychology* 61, no. 4 (2008), pp. 827–868.

11. J. F. Salgado, N. Anderson, S. Moscoso, C. Bertua, F. de Fruyt, and J. P. Rolland, "A Meta-analytic Study of General Mental Ability Validity for Different Occupations in the European Community," *Journal of Applied Psychology,* December 2003, pp. 1068–1081.

12. J. Flint, "Can You Tell Applesauce from Pickles?" *Forbes* (October 9, 1995), pp. 106–108.

13. M. R. Barrick, M. K. Mount, and T. A. Judge, "Personality and Performance at the Beginning of the New Millennium: What Do We Know and Where Do We Go Next?" *International Journal of Selection & Assessment*, March–June 2001, pp. 9–30; M. R. Barrick, G. L. Stewart, and M. Piotrowski, "Personality and Job Performance: Test of the Mediating Effects of Motivation Among Sales Representatives," *Journal of Applied Psychology*, February 2002, pp. 43–51; and C. J. Thoresen, J. C. Bradley, P. D. Bliese, and J. D. Thoresen, "The Big Five Personality Traits and Individual Job Performance and Growth Trajectories in Maintenance and Transitional Job Stages," *Journal of Applied Psychology,* October 2004, pp. 835–853.

14. D. S. Ones, C. Viswesvaran, and F. L. Schmidt, "Comprehensive Meta-analysis of Integrity Test Validities: Findings and Implications for Personnel Selection and Theories of Job Performance," *Journal of Applied Psychology,* August 1993, pp. 679–703; D. S. Ones, C. Viswesvaran, and F. L. Schmidt, "Personality and Absenteeism: A Meta-analysis of Integrity Tests," *European Journal of Personality,* March–April 2003, Supplement 1, pp. S19–S38; and C. M. Berry, P. R. Sackett, and S. Wiemann, "A Review of Recent Developments in Integrity Test Research," *Personnel Psychology* 60, no. 2 (2007), pp. 271–301.

15. J. J. Asher and J. A. Sciarrino, "Realistic Work Sample Tests: A Review," *Personnel Psychology,* Winter 1974, pp. 519–533; I. T. Robertson and R. S. Kandola, "Work Sample Tests: Validity, Adverse Impact and Applicant Reaction," *Journal of Occupational Psychology,* Spring 1982, pp. 171–182; and M. Callinan and I. T. Robertson, "Work Sample Testing," *International Journal of Selection & Assessment,* December 2000, pp. 248–260.

16. P. Carbonara, "Hire for Attitude, Train for Skill," *Fast Company,* Greatest Hits, vol. 1, 1997, p. 68.

17. See, for instance, A. C. Spychalski, M. A. Quinones, B. B. Gaugler, and K. Pohley, "A Survey of Assessment Center Practices in Organizations in the United States, *Personnel Psychology,* Spring 1997, pp. 71–90; C. Woodruffe, *Development and Assessment Centres: Identifying and Assessing Competence* (London: Institute of Personnel and Development, 2000); and J. Schettler, "Building Bench Strength," *Training,* June 2002, pp. 55–58.

18. F. Lievens, H. Peeters, and E. Schollaert, "Situational Judgment Tests: A Review of Recent Research," *Personnel Review* 37, no. 4 (2008), pp. 426–441.

19. R. A. Posthuma, F. P. Moregeson, and M. A. Campion, "Beyond Employment Interview Validity: A Comprehensive Narrative Review of Recent Research and Trend Over Time," *Personnel Psychology,* Spring 2002, p. 1; and S. L. Wilk and P. Cappelli, "Understanding the Determinants of Employer Use of Selection Methods," *Personnel Psychology,* Spring 2003, p. 111.

20. "Survey Finds Employers Form Opinions of Job Interviewees Within 10 Minutes," *IPMA-HR Bulletin,* April 21, 2007, p. 1; and G. L. Stewart, S. L. Dustin, M. R. Barrick, and T. C. Darnold, "Exploring the Handshake in Employment Interviews," *Journal of Applied Psychology* 93, no. 5 (2008), pp. 1139–1146.

21. N. R. Bardack and F. T. McAndrew, "The Influence of Physical Attractiveness and Manner of Dress on Success in a Simulated Personnel Decision," *Journal of Social Psychology,* August 1985, pp. 777–778; M. Hosoda, E. F. Stone-Romero, and G. Coats, "The Effects of Physical Attractiveness on Job-Related Outcomes: A Meta-analysis of Experimental Studies," *Personnel Psychology* 56, no. 2 (2003), pp. 431–462; and M. F. Luxen and F. J. R. van de Vijver, "Facial Attractiveness, Sexual Selection, and Personnel Selection: When Evolved Preferences Matter," *Journal of Organizational Behavior* 27, no. 2 (2006), pp. 241–255.

22. K. M. Engemann and M. T. Owyang, "What's in a Name?" *The Regional Economist,* January 2006, pp. 10–11.

23. J. F. Salgado and S. Moscoso, "Validity of the Structured Behavioral Interview," *Revista de Psicología del Trabajo y de las Organizaciones* 11 (1995), pp. 9–24. See also S. Moscoso and J. F. Salgado, "Psychometric Properties of a Structured Behavioral Interview to Hire Private Security Personnel," *Journal of Business and Psychology,* Fall 2001, pp. 51–59.

24. T. J. Hanson and J. C. Balestreri-Spero, "An Alternative to Interviews," *Personnel Journal,* June 1985, p. 114. See also T. W. Dougherty, D. B. Turban, and J. C. Callender, "Confirming First Impressions in the Employment Interview: A Field Study of Interviewer Behavior," *Journal of Applied Psychology,* October 1994, pp. 659–665.

25. K. I. van der Zee, A. B. Bakker, and P. Bakker, "Why Are Structured Interviews So Rarely Used in Personnel Selection?" *Journal of Applied Psychology,* February 2002, pp. 176–184.

26. See M. A. McDaniel, D. L. Whetzel, F. L. Schmidt, and S. D. Maurer, "The Validity of Employment Interviews: A Comprehensive Review and Meta-analysis," *Journal of Applied Psychology,* August 1994, pp. 599–616; M. A. Campion, D. K. Palmer, and J. E. Campion, "A Review of Structure in the Selection Interview," *Personnel Psychology,* Autumn 1997, pp. 655–702; and A. I. Huffcutt and D. J. Woehr, "Further Analysis of Employment Interview Validity: A Quantitative Evaluation of Interviewer-Related Structuring Methods," *Journal of Organizational Behavior,* July 1999, pp. 549–560.

27. van der Zee, Bakker, and Bakker, "Why Are Structured Interviews So Rarely Used in Personnel Selection?"

28. R. E. Carlson, "Effect of Interview Information in Altering Valid Impressions," *Journal of Applied Psychology,* February 1971, pp. 66–72; M. London and M. D. Hakel, "Effects of Applicant Stereotypes, Order, and Information on Interview Impressions," *Journal of Applied Psychology,* April 1974, pp. 157–162; E. C. Webster, *The Employment Interview: A Social Judgment Process* (Ontario, Canada: S.I.P., 1982); and T. W. Dougherty, D. B. Turban, and J. C. Callender, "Confirming First Impressions in the Employment Interview: A Field Study of Interviewer Behavior," *Journal of Applied Psychology,* October 1994, pp. 659–665.

29. F. L. Schmidt and R. D. Zimmerman, "A Counterintuitive Hypothesis About Employment Interview Validity and Some Supporting Evidence," *Journal of Applied Psychology* 89, no. 3 (2004), pp. 553–561.

30. See G. A. Adams, T. C. Elacqua, and S. M. Colarelli, "The Employment Interview as a Sociometric Selection Technique," *Journal of Group Psychotherapy,* Fall 1994, pp. 99–113; R. L. Dipboye, "Structured and Unstructured Selection Interviews: Beyond the Job-Fit Model," *Research in Personnel Human Resource Management* 12 (1994), pp. 79–123; B. Schneider, D. B. Smith, S. Taylor, and J. Fleenor, "Personality and Organizations: A Test of the Homogeneity of Personality Hypothesis," *Journal of Applied Psychology,* June 1998, pp. 462–470; and M. Burke, "Funny Business," *Forbes* (June 9, 2003), p. 173.

31. Cited in *Training,* October 2003, p. 21.

32. Cited in *Training,* March 2003, p. 20.

33. "Basic Skills Training Pays Off for Employers," *HRMagazine,* October 1999, p. 32.

34. D. Baynton, "America's $60 Billion Problem," *Training,* May 2001, p. 51.

35. A. Bernstein, "The Time Bomb in the Workforce: Illiteracy," *BusinessWeek* (February 25, 2002), p. 122; and M. Smulian, "England Fails on Numeracy and Literacy," *Public Finance,* February 6, 2009, p. 13.

36. Baynton, "America's $60 Billion Problem," p. 52.

37. C. Ansberry, "A New Blue-Collar World," *Wall Street Journal* (June 30, 2003), p. B1.

38. J. Barbarian, "Mark Spear: Director of Management and Organizational Development, Miller Brewing Co.," *Training,* October 2001, pp. 34–38.

39. G. R. Weaver, L. K. Trevino, and P. L. Cochran, "Corporate Ethics Practices in the Mid-1990's: An Empirical Study of the Fortune 1000," *Journal of Business Ethics,* February 1999, pp. 283–294.

40. M. B. Wood, *Business Ethics in Uncertain Times* (Upper Saddle River, NJ: Prentice Hall, 2004), p. 61.

41. See, for example, D. Seligman, "Oxymoron 101," *Forbes* (October 28, 2002), pp. 160–164; and R. B. Schmitt, "Companies Add Ethics Training; Will It Work?" *Wall Street Journal* (November 4, 2002), p. B1.

42. W. R. Allen, P. Bacdayan, K. B. Kowalski, and M. H. Roy, "Examining the Impact of Ethics Training on Business Student Values," *Education and Training* 47, no. 3 (2005), pp. 170–182; A. Lämsä, M. Vehkaperä, T. Puttonen, and H. Pesonen, "Effect of Business Education on Women and Men Students' Attitudes on Corporate Responsibility in Society," *Journal of Business Ethics* 82, no. 1 (2008), pp. 45–58; and K. M. Sheldon and L. S. Krieger, "Understanding the Negative Effects of Legal Education on Law Students: A Longitudinal Test of Self-Determination Theory," *Personality and Social Psychology Bulletin* 33, no. 6 (2007), pp. 883–897.

43. S. Valentine and G. Fleischman, "Ethics Programs, Perceived Corporate Social Responsibility, and Job Satisfaction," *Journal of Business Ethics* 77, no. 2 (2008), pp. 159–172.

44. K. Dobbs, "The U.S. Department of Labor Estimates That 70 Percent of Workplace Learning Occurs Informally," *Sales & Marketing Management,* November 2000, pp. 94–98.

45. S. J. Wells, "Forget the Formal Training. Try Chatting at the Water Cooler," *New York Times* (May 10, 1998), p. BU-11.

46. See, for instance, K. G. Brown, "Using Computers to Deliver Training: Which Employees Learn and Why?" *Personnel Psychology,* Summer 2001, pp. 271–296; L. K. Long and R. D. Smith, "The Role of Web-Based Distance Learning in HR Development," *Journal of Management Development* 23, no. 3 (2004), pp. 270–284; and R. E. Derouin, B. A. Fritzsche, and E. Salas, "E-Learning in Organizations," *Journal of Management* 31, no. 3 (2005), pp. 920–940.

47. "Web Smart 50: Kinko's," *BusinessWeek* (November 24, 2003), p. 101.

48. A. Muoio, "Cisco's Quick Study," *Fast Company,* October 2000, pp. 287–295.

49. T. Sitzman, K. Kraiger, D. Stewart, and R. Wisher, "The Comparative Effectiveness of Web-Based and Classroom Instruction: A Meta-analysis," *Personnel Psychology* 59, no. 3 (2006), pp. 623–664.

50. E. A. Ensher, T. R. Nielson, and E. Grant-Vallone, "Tales from the Hiring Line: Effects of the Internet and Technology on HR Processes," *Organizational Dynamics* 31, no. 3 (2002), pp. 232–233.

51. D. A. Kolb, "Management and the Learning Process," *California Management Review,* Spring 1976, pp. 21–31; and B. Filipczak, "Different Strokes: Learning Styles in the Classroom," *Training,* March 1995, pp. 43–48.

52. G. M. Alliger, S. I. Tannenbaum, W. Bennett, H. Traver, and A. Shotland, "A Meta-analysis of the Relations Among Training Criteria," *Personnel Psychology* 50, no. 2 (1997), pp. 341–358; and T. Sitzmann, K. G. Brown, W. J. Casper, K. Ely, and R. D. Zimmerman, "A Review and Meta-analysis of the Nomological Network of Trainee Reactions," *Journal of Applied Psychology* 93, no. 2 (2008), pp. 280–295.

53. W. J. Arthur, Jr., W. Bennett, Jr., P. S. Edens, and S. T. Bell, "Effectiveness of Training in Organizations: A Meta-analysis of Design and Evaluation Features," *Journal of Applied Psychology,* April 2003, pp. 234–245.

54. J. A. Colquitt, J. A. LePine, and R. A. Noe, "Toward an Integrative Theory of Training Motivation: A Meta-analytic Path Analysis of 20 Years of Research," *Journal of Applied Psychology,* October 2000, pp. 678–707.

55. See L. A. Burke and H. S. Hutchins, "Training Transfer: An Integrative Literature Review," *Human Resource Development Review* 6 (2007), pp. 263–296; and D. S. Chiaburu and S. V. Marinova, "What Predicts Skill Transfer? An Exploratory Study of Goal Orientation, Training Self-Efficacy, and Organizational Supports," *International Journal of Training and Development* 9, no. 2 (2005); pp. 110–123.

56. M. Rotundo and P. R. Sackett, "The Relative Importance of Task, Citizenship, and Counterproductive Performance to Global Ratings of Job Performance: A Policy Capturing Approach," *Journal of Applied Psychology* 87, no. 1 (2002), pp. 66–80; and S. W. Whiting, P. M. Podsakoff, and J. R. Pierce, "Effects of Task Performance, Helping, Voice, and Organizational Loyalty on Performance Appraisal Ratings," *Journal of Applied Psychology* 93, no. 1 (2008), pp. 125–139.

57. W. F. Cascio, *Applied Psychology in Human Resource Management,* 5th ed. (Upper Saddle River, NJ: Prentice Hall, 1998), p. 59.

58. See W. C. Borman and S. J. Motowidlo, "Expanding the Criterion Domain to Include Elements of Contextual Performance," in N. Schmitt and W. C. Borman (eds.), *Personnel Selection in Organizations* (San Francisco, CA: Jossey-Bass, 1993), pp. 71–98; W. H. Bommer, J. L. Johnson, G. A. Rich, P. M. Podsakoff, and S. B. MacKenzie, "On the Interchangeability of Objective and Subjective Measures of Employee Performance: A Meta-analysis," *Personnel Psychology,*

Autumn 1995, pp. 587–605; and S. E. Scullen, M. K. Mount, and T. A. Judge, "Evidence of the Construct Validity of Developmental Ratings of Managerial Performance," *Journal of Applied Psychology,* February 2003, pp. 50–66.

59. A. H. Locher and K. S. Teel, "Appraisal Trends," *Personnel Journal,* September 1988, pp. 139–145.

60. Cited in S. Armour, "Job Reviews Take on Added Significance in Down Times," *USA Today* (July 23, 2003), p. 4B.

61. D. J. Woehr, M. K. Sheehan, and W. Bennett, "Assessing Measurement Equivalence Across Rating Sources: A Multitrait-Multirater Approach," *Journal of Applied Psychology* 90, no. 3 (2005), pp. 592–600; and H. Heidemeier and K. Moser, "Self–Other Agreement in Job Performance Ratings: A Meta-analytic Test of a Process Model," *Journal of Applied Psychology* 94, no. 2 (March 2009), pp. 353–370.

62. See, for instance, J. D. Facteau and S. B. Craig, "Are Performance Appraisal Ratings from Different Rating Sources Compatible?" *Journal of Applied Psychology,* April 2001, pp. 215–227; J. F. Brett and L. E. Atwater, "360-Degree Feedback: Accuracy, Reactions, and Perceptions of Usefulness," *Journal of Applied Psychology,* October 2001, pp. 930–942; F. Luthans and S. J. Peterson, "360 Degree Feedback with Systematic Coaching: Empirical Analysis Suggests a Winning Combination," *Human Resource Management,* Fall 2003, pp. 243–256; and B. I. J. M. van der Heijden and A. H. J. Nijhof, "The Value of Subjectivity: Problems and Prospects for 360-Degree Appraisal Systems," *International Journal of Human Resource Management,* May 2004, pp. 493–511.

63. Atkins and Wood, "Self Versus Others' Ratings as Predictors of Assessment Center Ratings"; and B. Pfau, I. Kay, K. M. Nowack, and J. Ghorpade, "Does 360-Degree Feedback Negatively Affect Company Performance?" *HRMagazine* 47, no. 6 (June 2002), pp. 54–59.

64. "Princeton Cracks Down on Grade Inflation," *USA Today* (January 22, 2005), www.usatoday.com/news/education/2005-01-22-princeton-grade-inflation_x.htm.

65. See, for instance, J. W. Hedge and W. C. Borman, "Changing Conceptions and Practices in Performance Appraisal," in A. Howard (ed.), *The Changing Nature of Work* (San Francisco, CA: Jossey-Bass, 1995), pp. 453–459.

66. See, for instance, D. J. Woehr, "Understanding Frame-of-Reference Training: The Impact of Training on the Recall of Performance Information," *Journal of Applied Psychology,* August 1994, pp. 525–534; K. L. Uggerslev and L. M. Sulsky, "Using Frame-of-Reference Training to Understand the Implications of Rater Idiosyncrasy for Rating Accuracy," *Journal of Applied Psychology* 93, no. 3 (2008), pp. 711–719; and R. F. Martell and D. P. Evans, "Source-Monitoring Training: Toward Reducing Rater Expectancy Effects in Behavioral Measurement," *Journal of Applied Psychology* 90, no. 5 (2005), pp. 956–963.

67. M. S. Taylor, K. B. Tracy, M. K. Renard, J. K. Harrison, and S. J. Carroll, "Due Process in Performance Appraisal: A Quasi-Experiment in Procedural Justice," *Administrative Science Quarterly,* September 1995, pp. 495–523.

68. J. S. Lublin, "It's Shape-up Time for Performance Reviews," *Wall Street Journal* (October 3, 1994), p. B1.

69. Much of this section is based on H. H. Meyer, "A Solution to the Performance Appraisal Feedback Enigma," *Academy of Management Executive,* February 1991, pp. 68–76.

70. B. Gates, *The Road Ahead* (New York: Viking, 1995), p. 86.

71. T. D. Schelhardt, "It's Time to Evaluate Your Work, and All Involved Are Groaning," *Wall Street Journal* (November 19, 1996), p. A1.

72. R. J. Burke, "Why Performance Appraisal Systems Fail," *Personnel Administration,* June 1972, pp. 32–40.

73. B. D. Cawley, L. M. Keeping, and P. E. Levy, "Participation in the Performance Appraisal Process and Employee Reactions: A Meta-analytic Review of Field Investigations," *Journal of Applied Psychology,* August 1998, pp. 615–633; and P. E. Levy and J. R. Williams, "The Social Context of Performance Appraisal: A Review and Framework for the Future," *Journal of Management* 30, no. 6 (2004), pp. 881–905.

74. F. Gino and M. E. Schweitzer, "Blinded by Anger or Feeling the Love: How Emotions Influence Advice Taking," *Journal of Applied Psychology* 93, no. 3 (5), pp. 1165–1173.

75. H. Heidemeier and K. Moser, "Self–Other Agreement in Job Performance Ratings."

76. See, for instance, *Harvard Business Review on Work and Life Balance* (Boston: Harvard Business School Press, 2000); and R. Rapoport, L. Bailyn, J. K. Fletcher, and B. H. Pruitt, *Beyond Work-Family Balance* (San Francisco: Jossey-Bass, 2002).

77. "On the Daddy Track," *Wall Street Journal* (May 11, 2000), p. A1.

78. K. Weiss, "Eddie Bauer Uses Time as an Employee Benefit," *Journal of Organizational Excellence,* Winter 2002, pp. 67–72.

79. S. D. Friedman and J. H. Greenhaus, *Work and Family—Allies or Enemies?* (New York: Oxford University Press, 2000).

80. J. S. Michel and M. B. Hargis, "Linking Mechanisms of Work-Family Conflict and Segmentation," *Journal of Vocational Behavior* 73, no. 3 (2008), pp. 509–522; G. E. Kreiner, "Consequences of Work-Home Segmentation or Integration: A Person-Environment Fit Perspective," *Journal of Organizational Behavior* 27, no. 4 (2006), pp. 485–507; and C. A. Bulger, R. A. Matthews, and M. E. Hoffman, "Work and Personal Life Boundary Management: Boundary Strength, Work/Personal Life Balance, and the Segmentation-Integration Continuum," *Journal of Occupational Health Psychology* 12, no. 4 (2007), pp. 365–375.

81. See, for instance, C. Fletcher and E. L. Perry, "Performance Appraisal and Feedback: A Consideration of National Culture and a Review of Contemporary Research and Future Trends," in N. Anderson, D. S. Ones, H. K. Sinangil, and C. Viswesvaran (eds.), *Handbook of Industrial, Work, & Organizational Psychology,* vol. 1 (Thousand Oaks, CA: Sage, 2001), pp. 127–144; and D. L. Stone, E. F. Stone-Romero, and K. M. Lukaszewski, "The Impact of Cultural Values on the Acceptance and Effectiveness of Human Resource Management Policies and Practices," *Human Resource Management Review* 17, no. 2 (2007), pp. 152–165.

82. M. K. Miah and A. Bird, "The Impact of Culture on HRM Styles and Firm Performance: Evidence from Japanese Parents, Japanese Subsidiaries/Joint Ventures, and South Asian Local Companies," *International Journal of Human Resource Management* 18, no. 5 (2007), pp. 908–923; S. Akhtar, D. Z. Ding, and G. L. Ge, "Strategic HRM Practice and Their Impact on Company Performance in Chinese Enterprises," *Human Resource Management* 47, no. 1 (2008), pp. 15–32; and Z. Y. Yalabik, S. Chen, J. Lawler, and K. Kim, "High Performance Work System and Organizational Turnover in East and Southeast Asian Countries," *Industrial Relations* 47, no. 1 (2008), pp. 145–152.

83. D. L. Stone, R. D. Johnson, E. F. Stone-Romero, and M. Hartman, "A Comparative Study of Hispanic–American and Anglo–American Cultural Values and Job Choice Preferences," *Management Research* 4, no. 1 (2006), pp. 8–21.

84. A. M. Ryan, L. McFarland, H. Baron, and R. Page, "An International Look at Selection Practices: Nation and Culture as Explanations for Variability in Practice," *Personnel Psychology,* Summer 1999, pp. 359–392.

85. Ibid., p. 386.

86. N. Anderson and C. Witvliet, "Fairness Reactions to Personnel Selection Methods: An International Comparison Between the Netherlands, the United States, France, Spain, Portugal, and Singapore," *International Journal of Selection and Assessment* 16, no. 1 (2008), pp. 1–13.

87. M. J. Burke, S. Chan-Serafin, R. Salvador, A. Smith, and S. A. Sarpy, "The Role of National Culture and Organizational Climate in Safety Training Effectiveness," *European Journal of Work and Organizational Psychology* 17, no. 1 (2008), pp. 133–152.

88. J. Han, "Does Performance-Based Salary System Suit Korea?" *The Korea Times* (January 15, 2008), www.koreatimes.co.kr.

89. P. C. Earley, "Self or Group? Cultural Effects of Training on Self-Efficacy and Performance," *Administrative Science Quarterly,* March 1994, pp. 89–117.

90. B. R. Nathan, A. M. Mohrman, Jr., and J. Milliman, "Interpersonal Relations as a Context for the Effects of Appraisal Interviews on Performance and Satisfaction: A Longitudinal Study," *Academy of Management Journal* 34, no. 2 (June 1991), pp. 352–369; and Cawley, Keeping, and Levy, "Participation in the Performance Appraisal Process and Employee Reactions."

LEARNING OBJECTIVES

After studying this chapter, you should be able to:

1 Identify forces that act as stimulants to change and contrast planned and unplanned change.

2 List the sources for resistance to change.

3 Compare the four main approaches to managing organizational change.

4 Demonstrate two ways of creating a culture for change.

5 Define *stress* and identify its potential sources.

6 Identify the consequences of stress.

7 Contrast the individual and organizational approaches to managing stress.

8 Explain global differences in organizational change and work stress.

Organizational Change and Stress Management

It is not the strongest of the species that survives, nor the most intelligent, but the one most responsive to change. —Charles Darwin

CHANGE OR DIE, OR CHANGE AND DIE?

As we noted in Chapter 6, hindsight bias is a huge problem in understanding human and organizational behavior. Everything is all too clear with the benefit of hindsight. Take the example of one recent organizational failure: Circuit City.

Not long ago, it was heady times at Circuit City. Though the 60-year-old company long trailed its upstart rival Best Buy, in 2001 it began to close the gap. Indeed, Circuit City's stock gained more in 2004, 2005, and 2006 than Best Buy's or Radio Shack's. By 2009, however, it was trading at $0.20 per share, and cash flow had disappeared. After failing to find a buyer, Circuit City shuttered its 567 stores in the United States and 765 stores in Canada. Its 34,000 employees were jobless, and the second-largest U.S. consumer electronics chain was gone.

What went wrong? Experts point to two attempts to transformation that backfired. First, Circuit City made a strategic decision to locate its stores in areas where real estate was cheap. Second, in 2007 it laid off 3,400 of its most experienced sales staff to control costs. In both cases the company saved money, but it paid a heavy price in customer traffic and employee morale. Circuit City also made another major change.

Following the practice of its faster-growing rival and believing consumers tired of the "hard sell," in 2003 the firm eliminated its sales commission structure. While most customers probably don't like pushy salespeople, Circuit City's move also meant some of its most knowledgeable salespeople went elsewhere.

Though Circuit City might fairly be faulted for making changes that turned out badly, two contributing factors were hardly unique to its fall. First, and most obvious of course, was the economy. Signs of the looming recession, all too obvious in hindsight, were not much heeded in 2007.

Second, of all the sectors that struggled in the global recession, none did so more than retailing. In 2008–2009 alone, a whole host of retailers either shut down or declared bankruptcy, including Eddie Bauer, Sharper Image, Linens 'n Things, and Goody's. Other retailers such as Sears and K-Mart continue to struggle mightily.

It's often said that firms must "change or die," and one postmortem proclaimed, "Circuit City became complacent—a fatal mistake." But was Circuit City undone by changes it didn't make, or by the ones it did?[1]

This chapter is about change and stress. We describe environmental forces that require firms to change, why people and organizations often resist change, and how this resistance can be overcome. We review processes for managing organizational change. Then we move to the topic of stress and its sources and consequences. In closing we discuss what individuals and organizations can do to better manage stress levels.

First, see how well you handle change by taking the following self-assessment.

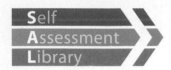

HOW WELL DO I RESPOND TO TURBULENT CHANGE?

In the Self-Assessment Library (available on CD and online), take assessment III.C.1 (How Well Do I Respond to Turbulent Change?) and answer the following questions.

1. *How did you score? Are you surprised by your score?*
2. *During what time of your life have you experienced the most change? How did you deal with it? Would you handle these changes in the same way today? Why or why not?*
3. *Are there ways you might reduce your resistance to change?*

Forces for Change

1 Identify forces that act as stimulants to change and contrast planned and unplanned change.

No company today is in a particularly stable environment. Even those with dominant market share must change, sometimes radically. While Microsoft has struggled with its controversial operating system Vista, it has also been trying to outflank rivals such as Google and smaller companies offering free, Web-based software. How well Microsoft performs is a function not of managing one change but of weathering both short- and long-term changes.

Thus, "Change or die!" is the rallying cry among today's managers worldwide. Exhibit 18-1 summarizes six specific forces stimulating change.

In a number of places in this book, we've discussed the *changing nature of the workforce.* Almost every organization must adjust to a multicultural environment, demographic changes, immigration, and outsourcing. *Technology* is continually changing jobs and organizations. It is not hard to imagine the very idea of an office becoming an antiquated concept in the near future.

The housing and financial sectors recently have experienced extraordinary *economic shocks,* leading to the elimination, bankruptcy, or acquisition of some of the best-known U.S. companies, including Bear Stearns, Merrill Lynch, Lehman Brothers, Countrywide Financial, Washington Mutual, and Ameriquest. Tens of thousands of jobs were lost and may never return. After years of declining bankruptcies, the global recession caused the bankruptcy of auto manufacturers General Motors and Chrysler, retailers Circuit City and Eddie Bauer, and myriad other organizations.

Competition is changing. Competitors are as likely to come from across the ocean as from across town. Successful organizations will be fast on their feet, capable of developing new products rapidly and getting them to market quickly. In other words, they'll be flexible and will require an equally flexible and responsive workforce. Increasingly, in the United States and Europe, the govern-

| Exhibit 18-1 | Forces for Change |

Force	Examples
Nature of the workforce	More cultural diversity
	Aging population
	Increased immigration and outsourcing
Technology	Faster, cheaper, and more mobile computers and handheld devices
	Emergence and growth of social networking sites
	Deciphering of the human genetic code
Economic shocks	Rise and fall of global housing market
	Financial sector collapse
	Global recession
Competition	Global competitors
	Mergers and consolidations
	Increased government regulation of commerce
Social trends	Increased environmental awareness
	Liberalization of attitudes toward gay, lesbian, and transgender employees
	More multitasking and connectivity
World politics	Rising health care costs
	Negative social attitudes toward business and executives
	Opening of markets in China

ment regulates business practices, including executive pay. Employment rights have been extended to gay, lesbian, and transgender employees.

Social trends don't remain static. Consumers now meet and share information in chat rooms and blogs. Companies must continually adjust product and marketing strategies to be sensitive to changing social trends, as Liz Claiborne did when it sold off brands (such as Ellen Tracy), de-emphasized large vendors such as Macy's, and streamlined operations and cut staff. Consumers, employees, and organizational leaders are more sensitive to environmental concerns. "Green" practices are quickly becoming expected rather than optional.

Not even globalization's strongest proponents could have imagined how *world politics* would change in recent years. We've seen the breakup of the Soviet Union, the opening of China and Southeast Asia, and the rise of Muslim fundamentalism. Through the industrialized world, businesses—particularly in the banking and financial sectors—have come under new scrutiny.

Planned Change

A group of housekeeping employees who work for a small hotel confronted the owner: "It's very hard for most of us to maintain rigid 7-to-4 work hours," said their spokeswoman. "Each of us has significant family and personal responsibilities. And rigid hours don't work for us. We're going to begin looking for someplace else to work if you don't set up flexible work hours." The owner listened thoughtfully to the group's ultimatum and agreed to its request. The next day, the owner introduced a flextime plan for these employees.

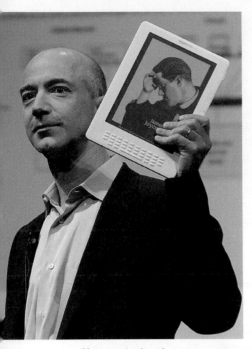

Jeff Bezos is the change agent at Amazon.com. He founded the company as an online bookstore in 1994 and then built it into the largest retailer on the Web that sells everything from groceries to electronics. Amazon.com changed from a seller of electronics to also become a product developer when it created the Kindle reading device and the Kindle service for downloading books in less than 60 seconds. In his drive for change at Amazon, Bezos combines a long-term orientation with identifying a customer need. Bezos is shown here unveiling the Kindle DX, the large-screen version of the original Kindle designed for reading newspapers, magazines, and textbooks.

A major automobile manufacturer spent several billion dollars to install state-of-the-art robotics. One area that would receive the new equipment was quality control, where sophisticated computers would significantly improve the company's ability to find and correct defects. Because the new equipment would dramatically change the jobs in the quality-control area, and because management anticipated considerable employee resistance to it, executives were developing a program to help people become familiar with it and deal with any anxieties they might be feeling.

Both these scenarios are examples of **change**, or making things different. However, only the second scenario describes a **planned change**. Many changes are like the one that occurred at the hotel: They just happen. Some organizations treat all change as an accidental occurrence. In this chapter, we address change as an intentional, goal-oriented activity.

What are the goals of planned change? First, it seeks to improve the ability of the organization to adapt to changes in its environment. Second, it seeks to change employee behavior.

Who in organizations is responsible for managing change activities? The answer is **change agents**.[2] They see a future for the organization that others have not identified, and they are able to motivate, invent, and implement this vision. Change agents can be managers or nonmanagers, current or new employees, or outside consultants. When he accepted the presidency of Harvard University in 2001, Lawrence Summers aggressively sought to shake up the complacent institution by, among other things, reshaping the undergraduate curriculum, more directly engaging the university with problems in education and public health, and reorganizing to consolidate more power in the president's office.[3] His change efforts generated tremendous resistance, particularly among faculty. Finally, in 2006, when Summers suggested women were less able to excel in science than men, the faculty revolted, and in a few weeks Summers was forced to resign. Despite Summers' support among students, his efforts at change (and the brusque way in which he implemented them) had ruffled too many feathers. In 2007, he was replaced with Drew Gilpin Faust, Harvard's first female president, who promised to be less aggressive in instituting changes.[4]

Many change agents fail because organizational members resist change. In the next section, we discuss this resistance to change and what managers can do about it.

Resistance to Change

2 List the sources for resistance to change.

Our egos are fragile, and we often see change as threatening. One recent study showed that even when employees are shown data that suggest they need to change, they latch onto whatever data they can find that suggests they are okay and don't need to change.[5] Employees who have negative feelings about a change cope by not thinking about it, increasing their use of sick time, and quitting. All these reactions can sap the organization of vital energy when it is most needed.[6]

Resistance to change can be positive if it leads to open discussion and debate.[7] These responses are usually preferable to apathy or silence and can indicate that members of the organization are engaged in the process, providing change agents an opportunity to explain the change effort. Change agents can also use resistance to modify the change to fit the preferences of other members of the organization. When they treat resistance only as a threat, rather than a point of view to be discussed, they may increase dysfunctional conflict.

Resistance doesn't necessarily surface in standardized ways. It can be overt, implicit, immediate, or deferred. It's easiest for management to deal with overt and immediate resistance, such as complaints, a work slowdown, or a strike threat. The greater challenge is managing resistance that is implicit or deferred. These responses—loss of loyalty or motivation, increased errors or absenteeism—are more subtle and more difficult to recognize for what they are. Deferred actions also cloud the link between the change and the reaction to it and may surface weeks, months, or even years later. Or a single change of little inherent impact may be the straw that breaks the camel's back because resistance to earlier changes has been deferred and stockpiled.

Exhibit 18-2 summarizes major forces for resistance to change, categorized by their sources. Individual sources reside in human characteristics such as perceptions, personalities, and needs. Organizational sources reside in the structural makeup of organizations themselves.

Exhibit 18-2   **Sources of Resistance to Change**

Individual Sources

Habit—To cope with life's complexities, we rely on habits or programmed responses. But when confronted with change, this tendency to respond in our accustomed ways becomes a source of resistance.

Security—People with a high need for security are likely to resist change because it threatens their feelings of safety.

Economic factors—Changes in job tasks or established work routines can arouse economic fears if people are concerned that they won't be able to perform the new tasks or routines to their previous standards, especially when pay is closely tied to productivity.

Fear of the unknown—Change substitutes ambiguity and uncertainty for the unknown.

Selective information processing—Individuals are guilty of selectively processing information in order to keep their perceptions intact. They hear what they want to hear, and they ignore information that challenges the world they've created.

Organizational Sources

Structural inertia—Organizations have built-in mechanisms—such as their selection processes and formalized regulations—to produce stability. When an organization is confronted with change, this structural inertia acts as a counterbalance to sustain stability.

Limited focus of change—Organizations consist of a number of interdependent subsystems. One can't be changed without affecting the others. So limited changes in subsystems tend to be nullified by the larger system.

Group inertia—Even if individuals want to change their behavior, group norms may act as a constraint.

Threat to expertise—Changes in organizational patterns may threaten the expertise of specialized groups.

Threat to established power relationships—Any redistribution of decision-making authority can threaten long-established power relationships within the organization.

---

change *Making things different.*
planned change *Change activities that are intentional and goal oriented.*

change agents *Persons who act as catalysts and assume the responsibility for managing change activities.*

It's worth noting that not all change is good. Speed can lead to bad decisions, and sometimes those initiating change fail to realize the full magnitude of the effects or their true costs. Rapid, transformational change is risky, and some organizations, such as Baring Brothers Bank in the United Kingdom, have collapsed for this reason.[8] Change agents need to carefully think through the full implications.

Overcoming Resistance to Change

Seven tactics can help change agents deal with resistance to change.[9] Let's review them briefly.

Education and Communication   Communicating the logic of a change can reduce employee resistance on two levels. First, it fights the effects of misinformation and poor communication: If employees receive the full facts and clear up misunderstandings, resistance should subside. Second, communication can help "sell" the need for change by packaging it properly.[10] A study of German companies revealed changes are most effective when a company communicates a rationale that balances the interests of various stakeholders (shareholders, employees, community, customers) rather than those of shareholders only.[11]

Participation   It's difficult to resist a change decision in which we've participated. Assuming participants have the expertise to make a meaningful contribution, their involvement can reduce resistance, obtain commitment, and increase the quality of the change decision. However, against these advantages are the negatives: potential for a poor solution and great consumption of time.

Building Support and Commitment   When employees' fear and anxiety are high, counseling and therapy, new-skills training, or a short paid leave of absence may facilitate adjustment. When managers or employees have low emotional commitment to change, they favor the status quo and resist it.[12] So firing up employees can also help them emotionally commit to the change rather than embrace the status quo.

Develop Positive Relationships   People are more willing to accept changes if they trust the managers implementing them.[13] One study surveyed 235 employees from a large housing corporation in the Netherlands that was experiencing a merger. Those who had a more positive relationship with their supervisors, and who felt that the work environment supported development, were much more positive about the change process.[14]

Implementing Changes Fairly   One way organizations can minimize negative impact is to make sure change is implemented fairly. As we saw in Chapter 7, procedural fairness is especially important when employees perceive an outcome as negative, so it's crucial that employees see the reason for the change and perceive its implementation as consistent and fair.[15]

Manipulation and Cooptation   *Manipulation* refers to covert influence attempts. Twisting facts to make them more attractive, withholding information, and creating false rumors to get employees to accept change are all examples of manipulation. If management threatens to close a manufacturing plant whose employees are resisting an across-the-board pay cut, and if the threat is actually untrue, management is using manipulation. *Cooptation,* on the other hand, combines manipulation and participation. It seeks to "buy off" the leaders of a resistance group by giving them a key role, seeking their advice not to find a better solution but to get their endorsement. Both manipulation and cooptation are relatively inexpensive ways to gain the support of adversaries, but they can backfire if the targets become aware they are being tricked or used. Once that's discovered, the change agent's credibility may drop to zero.

Selecting People Who Accept Change   Research suggests the ability to easily accept and adapt to *change* is related to personality—some people simply have more positive attitudes about change than others.[16] Such individuals are open to experience, take a positive attitude toward change, are willing to take risks, and are flexible in their behavior. One study of managers in the United States, Europe, and Asia found those with a positive self-concept and high risk tolerance coped better with organizational change. A study of 258 police officers found those higher in growth-needs strength, internal locus of control, and internal work motivation had more positive attitudes about organizational change efforts.[17] Another study found that selecting people based on a resistance-to-change scale worked well in winnowing out those who tended to be rigid or react emotionally to change.[18] Individuals higher in general mental ability are also better able to learn and adapt to changes in the workplace.[19] In sum, an impressive body of evidence shows organizations can facilitate change by selecting people predisposed to accept it.

Coercion   Last on the list of tactics is *coercion,* the application of direct threats or force on the resisters. If management really is determined to close a manufacturing plant whose employees don't acquiesce to a pay cut, the company is using coercion. Other examples are threats of transfer, loss of promotions, negative performance evaluations, and a poor letter of recommendation. The advantages and drawbacks of coercion are approximately the same as for manipulation and cooptation.

The Politics of Change

No discussion of resistance would be complete without a brief mention of the politics of change. Because change invariably threatens the status quo, it inherently implies political activity.[20]

Politics suggests the impetus for change is more likely to come from outside change agents, employees new to the organization (who have less invested in the status quo), or managers slightly removed from the main power structure. Managers who have spent their entire careers with a single organization and achieved a senior position in the hierarchy are often major impediments to change. It is a very real threat to their status and position. Yet they may be expected to implement changes to demonstrate they're not merely caretakers. By acting as change agents, they can convey to stockholders, suppliers, employees, and customers that they are addressing problems and adapting to a dynamic environment. Of course, as you might guess, when forced to introduce change, these longtime power holders tend to implement incremental changes. Radical change is too threatening. This explains why boards of directors that recognize the imperative for rapid and radical change frequently turn to outside candidates for new leadership.[21]

Approaches to Managing Organizational Change

3 Compare the four main approaches to managing organizational change.

Now we turn to several approaches to managing change: Lewin's classic three-step model of the change process, Kotter's eight-step plan, action research, and organizational development.

Lewin's Three-Step Model

Kurt Lewin argued that successful change in organizations should follow three steps: **unfreezing** the status quo, **movement** to a desired end state, and **refreezing** the new change to make it permanent.[22] (See Exhibit 18-3.)

Consider a large oil company with three divisional marketing offices in Seattle, San Francisco, and Los Angeles that it decided to consolidate into a single regional San Francisco office. The decision was made in New York and the people affected had no say whatsoever in the choice. The reorganization meant transferring more than 150 employees, eliminating some duplicate managerial positions, and instituting a new hierarchy of command.

This status quo is an equilibrium state. To move from equilibrium—to overcome the pressures of both individual resistance and group conformity—unfreezing must happen in one of three ways. (See Exhibit 18-4.) The **driving forces**, which direct behavior away from the status quo, can be increased. The **restraining forces**, which hinder movement away from equilibrium, can be decreased. A third alternative is to combine the first two approaches. Companies that have been successful in the past are likely to encounter restraining forces because people question the need for change.[23] Similarly, research shows that companies with strong cultures excel at incremental change but are overcome by restraining forces against radical change.[24]

The oil company's management could expect employee resistance to the consolidation. Those in Seattle or Los Angeles may not want to transfer to another city, pull youngsters out of school, make new friends, adapt to new co-workers, or undergo the reassignment of responsibilities. Positive incentives such as pay increases, liberal moving expenses, and low-cost mortgage funds for new homes in San Francisco might encourage employees to accept the change. Management might also unfreeze acceptance of the status quo by removing restraining forces. It could counsel employees individually, hearing and clarifying each employee's specific concerns and apprehensions. Assuming most are unjustified, the counselor could assure employees there was nothing to fear and offer tangible evidence that restraining forces are unwarranted. If resistance is extremely high, management may have to resort to both reducing resistance and increasing the attractiveness of the alternative if the unfreezing is to be successful.

Research on organizational change has shown that, to be effective, change has to happen quickly.[25] Organizations that build up to change do less well than those that get to and through the movement stage quickly.

Once change has been implemented, to be successful the new situation must be refrozen so it can be sustained over time. Without this last step, change will likely be short lived and employees will attempt to revert to the previous equilibrium state. The objective of refreezing, then, is to stabilize the new situation by balancing the driving and restraining forces.

Exhibit 18-3   **Lewin's Three-Step Change Model**

Unfreezing → Movement → Refreezing

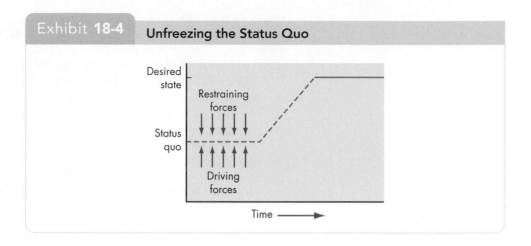

Exhibit **18-4**   Unfreezing the Status Quo

How could the oil company's management refreeze its consolidation change? By systematically replacing temporary forces with permanent ones. Management might impose a permanent upward adjustment of salaries. The formal rules and regulations governing behavior of those affected by the change should also be revised to reinforce the new situation. Over time, of course, the work group's own norms will evolve to sustain the new equilibrium. But until that point is reached, management will have to rely on more formal mechanisms.

Kotter's Eight-Step Plan for Implementing Change

John Kotter of the Harvard Business School built on Lewin's three-step model to create a more detailed approach for implementing change.[26] Kotter began by listing common mistakes managers make when trying to initiate change. They may fail to create a sense of urgency about the need for change, to create a coalition for managing the change process, to have a vision for change and effectively communicate it, to remove obstacles that could impede the vision's achievement, to provide short-term and achievable goals, and to anchor the changes into the organization's culture. They may also declare victory too soon.

Kotter then established eight sequential steps to overcome these problems. They're listed in Exhibit 18-5.

Notice how Kotter's first four steps essentially extrapolate Lewin's "unfreezing" stage. Steps 5 through 7 represent "movement," and the final step works on "refreezing." So Kotter's contribution lies in providing managers and change agents with a more detailed guide for successfully implementing change.

Action Research

Action research is a change process based on the systematic collection of data and selection of a change action based on what the analyzed data indicate.[27] Its value is in providing a scientific methodology for managing planned change.

---

unfreezing *Changing to overcome the pressures of both individual resistance and group conformity.*

movement *A change process that transforms the organization from the status quo to a desired end state.*

refreezing *Stabilizing a change intervention by balancing driving and restraining forces.*

driving forces *Forces that direct behavior away from the status quo.*

restraining forces *Forces that hinder movement from the existing equilibrium.*

action research *A change process based on systematic collection of data and then selection of a change action based on what the analyzed data indicate.*

Exhibit 18-5	Kotter's Eight-Step Plan for Implementing Change

1. Establish a sense of urgency by creating a compelling reason for why change is needed.
2. Form a coalition with enough power to lead the change.
3. Create a new vision to direct the change and strategies for achieving the vision.
4. Communicate the vision throughout the organization.
5. Empower others to act on the vision by removing barriers to change and encouraging risk taking and creative problem solving.
6. Plan for, create, and reward short-term "wins" that move the organization toward the new vision.
7. Consolidate improvements, reassess changes, and make necessary adjustments in the new programs.
8. Reinforce the changes by demonstrating the relationship between new behaviors and organizational success.

Source: Based on J. P. Kotter, *Leading Change* (Boston: Harvard Business School Press, 1996).

Action research consists of five steps (note how they closely parallel the scientific method): diagnosis, analysis, feedback, action, and evaluation.

The change agent, often an outside consultant in action research, begins by gathering information about problems, concerns, and needed changes from members of the organization. This *diagnosis* is analogous to the physician's search to find specifically what ails a patient. In action research, the change agent asks questions, reviews records, and interviews employees and listens to their concerns.

Diagnosis is followed by *analysis.* What problems do people key in on? What patterns do these problems seem to take? The change agent synthesizes this information into primary concerns, problem areas, and possible actions.

Action research requires the people who will participate in any change program to help identify the problem and determine the solution. So the third step—*feedback*—requires sharing with employees what has been found from the first and second steps. The employees, with the help of the change agent, develop action plans for bringing about any needed change.

Now the *action* part of action research is set in motion. The employees and the change agent carry out the specific actions they have identified to correct the problem.

The final step, consistent with the scientific underpinnings of action research, is *evaluation* of the action plan's effectiveness, using the initial data gathered as a benchmark.

Action research provides at least two specific benefits. First, it's problem focused. The change agent objectively looks for problems, and the type of problem determines the type of change action. Although this may seem intuitively obvious, a lot of change activities aren't done this way. Rather, they're solution centered. The change agent has a favorite solution—for example, implementing flextime, teams, or a process reengineering program—and then seeks out problems that the solution fits.

Second, because action research engages employees so thoroughly in the process, it reduces resistance to change. Once employees have actively participated in the feedback stage, the change process typically takes on a momentum of its own under their sustained pressure to bring it about.

Organizational Development

Organizational development (OD) is a collection of change methods that try to improve organizational effectiveness and employee well-being.[28]

These retirement center employees participate in a simulated training program to help them understand the diminishing abilities of the older population that is growing in developing nations worldwide. While wearing glasses that blurred their vision, they collaborated in devising a driving route. The exercise was part of a training program called Xtreme Aging that is designed to simulate the diminished abilities associated with old age. The training has become a regular part of many nursing and medical school curricula and corporate training programs to help participants grow in their understanding of and sensitivity to the needs of their older customers and fellow workers.

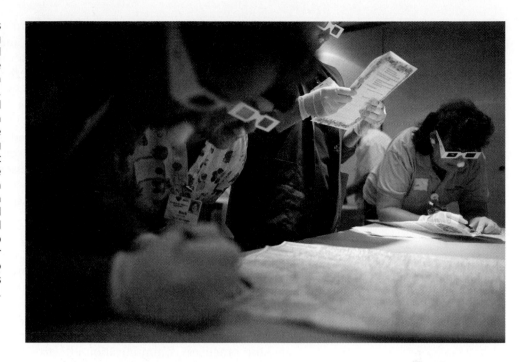

OD methods value human and organizational growth, collaborative and participative processes, and a spirit of inquiry.[29] Contemporary OD borrows heavily from postmodern philosophy in placing heavy emphasis on the subjective ways in which people see their environment. The focus is on how individuals make sense of their work environment. The change agent may take the lead in OD, but there is a strong emphasis on collaboration. These are the underlying values in most OD efforts:

1. **Respect for people.**   Individuals are perceived as responsible, conscientious, and caring. They should be treated with dignity and respect.
2. **Trust and support.**   An effective and healthy organization is characterized by trust, authenticity, openness, and a supportive climate.
3. **Power equalization.**   Effective organizations deemphasize hierarchical authority and control.
4. **Confrontation.**   Problems should be openly confronted, not swept under the rug.
5. **Participation.**   The more engaged in the decisions they are, the more people affected by a change will be committed to implementing them.

What are some OD techniques or interventions for bringing about change? Here are six.

Sensitivity Training   A variety of names—**sensitivity training**, laboratory training, encounter groups, or T-groups (training groups)—all refer to an early

organizational development (OD) *A collection of planned change interventions, built on humanistic–democratic values, that seeks to improve organizational effectiveness and employee well-being.*

sensitivity training *Training groups that seek to change behavior through unstructured group interaction.*

method of changing behavior through unstructured group interaction.[30] Members were brought together in a free and open environment in which participants discuss themselves and their interactive processes, loosely directed by a professional behavioral scientist who created the opportunity to express ideas, beliefs, and attitudes without taking any leadership role. The group was process oriented, which means individuals learned through observing and participating rather than being told.

Many participants found these unstructured groups intimidating, chaotic, and damaging to work relationships. Although extremely popular in the 1960s, they diminished in use during the 1970s and have essentially disappeared. However, organizational interventions such as diversity training, executive coaching, and team-building exercises are descendants of this early OD intervention technique.

Survey Feedback   One tool for assessing attitudes held by organizational members, identifying discrepancies among member perceptions, and solving these differences is the **survey feedback** approach.[31]

Everyone in an organization can participate in survey feedback, but of key importance is the organizational "family"—the manager of any given unit and the employees who report directly to him or her. All usually complete a questionnaire about their perceptions and attitudes on a range of topics, including decision-making practices; communication effectiveness; coordination among units; and satisfaction with the organization, job, peers, and immediate supervisor.

Data from this questionnaire are tabulated with data pertaining to an individual's specific "family" and to the entire organization and then distributed to employees. These data become the springboard for identifying problems and clarifying issues that may be creating difficulties for people. Particular attention is given to encouraging discussion and ensuring it focuses on issues and ideas and not on attacking individuals. For instance, are people listening? Are new ideas being generated? Can decision making, interpersonal relations, or job assignments be improved? Answers should lead the group to commit to various remedies for the problems identified.

Process Consultation   Managers often sense their unit's performance can be improved but are unable to identify what to improve and how. The purpose of **process consultation (PC)** is for an outside consultant to assist a client, usually a manager, "to perceive, understand, and act upon process events" with which the manager must deal.[32] These events might include work flow, informal relationships among unit members, and formal communication channels.

PC is similar to sensitivity training in assuming we can improve organizational effectiveness by dealing with interpersonal problems and in emphasizing involvement. But PC is more task directed, and consultants are there to "give the client 'insight' into what is going on around him, within him, and between him and other people."[33] They do not solve the organization's problems but rather guide or coach the client to solve his or her own problems after *jointly* diagnosing what needs improvement. The client develops the skill to analyze processes within his or her unit and can continue to call on it long after the consultant is gone. Because the client actively participates in both the diagnosis and the development of alternatives, he or she arrives at greater understanding of the process and the remedy and is less resistant to the action plan chosen.

Team Building   We've noted throughout this book that organizations increasingly rely on teams to accomplish work tasks. **Team building** uses high-interaction group activities to increase trust and openness among team members, improve coordinative efforts, and increase team performance.[34] Here

To increase trust and openness between management and union employees, American Airlines CEO Gerard Arpey (right in photo) formed problem-solving teams that worked on finding ways to improve efficiency and service. A joint leadership team of senior managers and union officials meets monthly to discuss strategy and finances, another team communicates with employees through American's and union Web sites, and other teams of flight attendants and airport workers are trying to improve customer service. To resolve the problem of funding pensions, Arpey is shown here joining pilots and flight attendants in lobbying Congress for support of pension reform legislation.

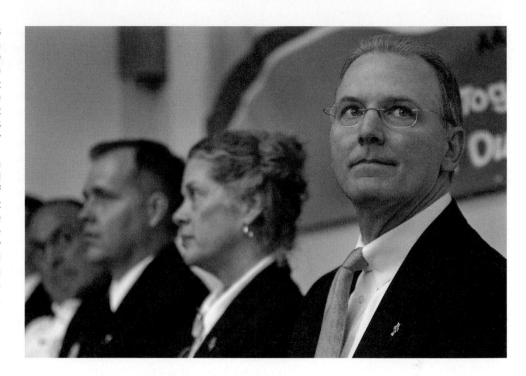

we emphasize the intragroup level, meaning organizational families (command groups) as well as committees, project teams, self-managed teams, and task groups.

Team building typically includes goal setting, development of interpersonal relations among team members, role analysis to clarify each member's role and responsibilities, and team process analysis. It may emphasize or exclude certain activities, depending on the purpose of the development effort and the specific problems with which the team is confronted. Basically, however, team building uses high interaction among members to increase trust and openness.

Intergroup Development   A major area of concern in OD is dysfunctional conflict between groups. **Intergroup development** seeks to change groups' attitudes, stereotypes, and perceptions about each other. Here training sessions closely resemble diversity training (in fact, diversity training largely evolved from intergroup development in OD), except rather than focusing on demographic differences, they focus on differences among occupations, departments, or divisions within an organization.

In one company, the engineers saw the accounting department as composed of shy and conservative types, and the human resources department as having a

survey feedback   *The use of questionnaires to identify discrepancies among member perceptions; discussion follows, and remedies are suggested.*

process consultation (PC)   *A meeting in which a consultant assists a client in understanding process events with which he or she must deal and identifying processes that need improvement.*

team building   *High interaction among team members to increase trust and openness.*

intergroup development   *OD efforts to change the attitudes, stereotypes, and perceptions that groups have of each other.*

bunch of "ultra-liberals more concerned that some protected group of employees might get their feelings hurt than with the company making a profit." Such stereotypes can have an obvious negative impact on coordination efforts among departments.

Among several approaches for improving intergroup relations,[35] a popular one emphasizes problem solving.[36] Each group meets independently to list its perceptions of itself and of the other group, and how it believes the other group perceives it. The groups share their lists, discuss similarities and differences, and look for the causes of disparities. Are the groups' goals at odds? Were perceptions distorted? On what basis were stereotypes formulated? Have some differences been caused by misunderstanding of intentions? Have words and concepts been defined differently by each group? Answers to questions like these clarify the exact nature of the conflict.

Once they have identified the causes of the difficulty, the groups move to the integration phase—developing solutions to improve relations between them. Subgroups can be formed of members from each of the conflicting groups to conduct further diagnosis and formulate alternative solutions.

Appreciative Inquiry   Most OD approaches are problem centered. They identify a problem or set of problems, then look for a solution. **Appreciative inquiry (AI)** instead accentuates the positive.[37] Rather than looking for problems to fix, it seeks to identify the unique qualities and special strengths of an organization, which members can build on to improve performance. That is, AI focuses on an organization's successes rather than its problems.

The AI process consists of four steps—discovery, dreaming, design, and discovery—often played out in a large-group meeting over a 2- or 3-day time period and overseen by a trained change agent. *Discovery* sets out to identify what people think are the organization's strengths. Employees recount times they felt the organization worked best or when they specifically felt most satisfied with their jobs. In *dreaming,* employees use information from the discovery phase to speculate on possible futures, such as what the organization will be like in 5 years. In *design,* participants find a common vision of how the organization will look in the future and agree on its unique qualities. For the fourth step, participants seek to define the organization's *destiny* or how to fulfill their dream, and they typically write action plans and develop implementation strategies.

AI has proven an effective change strategy in organizations such as GTE, Roadway Express, and the U.S. Navy. American Express used AI to revitalize its culture during a lean economy. In workshops employees described how they already felt proud of working at American Express and were encouraged to create a change vision by describing how it could be better in the future. The efforts led to some very concrete improvements. Senior managers were able to use employees' information to better their methods of making financial forecasts, improve IT investments, and create new performance-management tools for managers. The end result was a renewed culture focused on winning attitudes and behaviors.[38]

Creating a Culture for Change

4   Demonstrate two ways of creating a culture for change.

We've considered how organizations can *adapt* to change. But recently, some OB scholars have focused on a more proactive approach—how organizations can *embrace* change by transforming their cultures. In this section we review two such approaches: stimulating an innovative culture and creating a learning organization.

Stimulating a Culture of Innovation

How can an organization become more innovative? An excellent model is W. L. Gore, the $1.4-billion-per-year company best known as the maker of Gore-Tex fabric.[39] Gore has developed a reputation as one of the most innovative U.S. companies by developing a stream of diverse products—including guitar strings, dental floss, medical devices, and fuel cells.

What's the secret of Gore's success? What can other organizations do to duplicate its track record for innovation? Although there is no guaranteed formula, certain characteristics surface repeatedly when researchers study innovative organizations. We've grouped them into structural, cultural, and human resource categories. Change agents should consider introducing these characteristics into their organization to create an innovative climate. Before we look at these characteristics, however, let's clarify what we mean by innovation.

Definition of *Innovation* We said change refers to making things different. **Innovation**, a more specialized kind of change, is a new idea applied to initiating or improving a product, process, or service.[40] So all innovations imply change, but not all changes necessarily introduce new ideas or lead to significant improvements. Innovations can range from small incremental improvements, such as netbook computers, to radical breakthroughs, such as Toyota's battery-powered Prius.

Innovation is a specialized kind of change whereby a new idea is applied to initiating or improving a product, process, or service. Twitter, for example, is an innovation in the distribution of information. Twitter's founders Evan Williams (left) and Biz Stone shown in this photo and Jack Dorsey launched their new communication tool for sending 140-character messages, or tweets, from a computer or mobile device. As a social network, Twitter allows users to have live digital conversations. By using Twitter's search feature, users can have a real-time view into other people's conversations.

appreciative inquiry (AI) *An approach that seeks to identify the unique qualities and special strengths of an organization, which can then be built on to improve performance.*

innovation *A new idea applied to initiating or improving a product, process, or service.*

Sources of Innovation *Structural variables* have been the most studied potential source of innovation.[41] A comprehensive review of the structure–innovation relationship leads to the following conclusions.[42] First, organic structures positively influence innovation. Because they're lower in vertical differentiation, formalization, and centralization, organic organizations facilitate the flexibility, adaptation, and cross-fertilization that make the adoption of innovations easier. Second, long tenure in management is associated with innovation. Managerial tenure apparently provides legitimacy and knowledge of how to accomplish tasks and obtain desired outcomes. Third, innovation is nurtured when there are slack resources. Having an abundance of resources allows an organization to afford to purchase innovations, bear the cost of instituting them, and absorb failures. Finally, interunit communication is high in innovative organizations.[43] These organizations are high users of committees, task forces, cross-functional teams, and other mechanisms that facilitate interaction across departmental lines.

Innovative organizations tend to have similar *cultures*. They encourage experimentation. They reward both successes and failures. They celebrate mistakes. Unfortunately, in too many organizations, people are rewarded for the absence of failures rather than for the presence of successes. Such cultures extinguish risk taking and innovation. People will suggest and try new ideas only when they feel such behaviors exact no penalties. Managers in innovative organizations recognize that failures are a natural by-product of venturing into the unknown. Alex Rodriguez is one of baseball's best players still playing, yet in his career he has more strikeouts (1,702) than home runs (574) or runs batted in (1,669). And he is remembered (and paid $27.5 million per year) for the latter two, not the former one (though, sadly, he'll also be remembered for his admitted steroid use).

Within the *human resources* category, innovative organizations actively promote the training and development of their members so they keep current, offer high job security so employees don't fear getting fired for making mistakes, and encourage individuals to become champions of change. Once a new idea is developed, **idea champions** actively and enthusiastically promote it, build support, overcome resistance, and ensure it's implemented.[44] Champions have common personality characteristics: extremely high self-confidence, persistence, energy, and a tendency to take risks. They also display characteristics associated with transformational leadership—they inspire and energize others with their vision of an innovation's potential and their strong personal conviction about their mission. They are also good at gaining the commitment of others. Idea champions have jobs that provide considerable decision-making discretion; this autonomy helps them introduce and implement innovations.[45]

Creating a Learning Organization

Another way an organization can proactively manage change is to make continuous growth part of its culture—to become a learning organization.[46] In this section, we describe what a learning organization looks like and methods for managing learning.

What's a Learning Organization?   Just as individuals learn, so too do organizations. A **learning organization** has developed the continuous capacity to adapt and change. "All organizations learn, whether they consciously choose to or not—it is a fundamental requirement for their sustained existence."[47] Some organizations just do it better than others.

Most organizations engage in **single-loop learning**.[48] When they detect errors, their correction process relies on past routines and present policies. In con-

Exhibit 18-6	Characteristics of a Learning Organization

1. There exists a shared vision that everyone agrees on.
2. People discard their old ways of thinking and the standard routines they use for solving problems or doing their jobs.
3. Members think of all organizational processes, activities, functions, and interactions with the environment as part of a system of interrelationships.
4. People openly communicate with each other (across vertical and horizontal boundaries) without fear of criticism or punishment.
5. People sublimate their personal self-interest and fragmented departmental interests to work together to achieve the organization's shared vision.

Source: Based on P. M. Senge, *The Fifth Discipline* (New York: Doubleday, 1990).

trast, learning organizations use **double-loop learning**. They correct errors by *modifying* objectives, policies, and standard routines. Double-loop learning challenges deeply rooted assumptions and norms. It provides opportunities for radically different solutions to problems and dramatic jumps in improvement.

Exhibit 18-6 summarizes the five basic characteristics of a learning organization. It's one in which people put aside their old ways of thinking, learn to be open with each other, understand how their organization really works, form a plan or vision everyone can agree on, and work together to achieve that vision.[49]

Proponents of the learning organization envision it as a remedy for three fundamental problems of traditional organizations: fragmentation, competition, and reactiveness.[50] First, *fragmentation* based on specialization creates "walls" and "chimneys" that separate different functions into independent and often warring fiefdoms. Second, an overemphasis on *competition* often undermines collaboration. Managers compete to show who is right, who knows more, or who is more persuasive. Divisions compete when they ought to cooperate and share knowledge. Team leaders compete to show who the best manager is. And third, *reactiveness* misdirects management's attention to problem solving rather than creation. The problem solver tries to make something go away, while a creator tries to bring something new into being. An emphasis on reactiveness pushes out innovation and continuous improvement and, in its place, encourages people to run around "putting out fires."

Managing Learning   What can managers do to make their firms learning organizations? Here are some suggestions:

- *Establish a strategy.* Management needs to make explicit its commitment to change, innovation, and continuous improvement.
- *Redesign the organization's structure.* The formal structure can be a serious impediment to learning. Flattening the structure, eliminating or combining departments, and increasing the use of cross-functional teams, reinforces interdependence and reduces boundaries.

idea champions *Individuals who take an innovation and actively and enthusiastically promote the idea, build support, overcome resistance, and ensure that the idea is implemented.*

learning organization *An organization that has developed the continuous capacity to adapt and change.*

single-loop learning *A process of correcting errors using past routines and present policies.*

double-loop learning *A process of correcting errors by modifying the organization's objectives, policies, and standard routines.*

● *Reshape the organization's culture.* To become a learning organization, managers must demonstrate by their actions that taking risks and admitting failures are desirable. That means rewarding people who take chances and make mistakes. And management needs to encourage functional conflict. "The key to unlocking real openness at work," says one expert on learning organizations, "is to teach people to give up having to be in agreement. We think agreement is so important. Who cares? You have to bring paradoxes, conflicts, and dilemmas out in the open, so collectively we can be more intelligent than we can be individually."[51]

An excellent illustration of creating a learning organization is CEO Richard Clark's efforts at Merck. In addition to changing Merck's structure to allow innovation to flow from patients and doctors, Clark is trying to reward researchers for taking risks, even if their risky ideas end in failure. Merck's transformed strategy, structure, and culture may or may not succeed, but that's part of the risk of stimulating change through creating a learning organization.

Work Stress and Its Management

5 Define *stress* and identify its potential sources.

Friends say they're stressed from greater workloads and longer hours because of downsizing at their companies. Parents worry about the lack of job stability and reminisce about a time when a job with a large company implied lifetime security. We read surveys in which employees complain about the stress of trying to balance work and family responsibilities.[52] Indeed, as Exhibit 18-7 shows, work is, for most people, the most important source of stress in life. What are the causes and consequences of stress, and what can individuals and organizations do to reduce it?

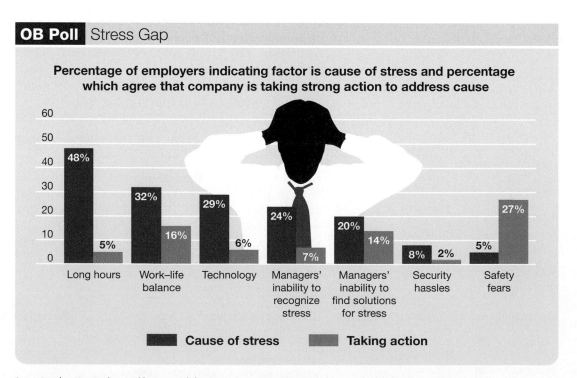

OB Poll Stress Gap

Percentage of employers indicating factor is cause of stress and percentage which agree that company is taking strong action to address cause

■ **Cause of stress**   ■ **Taking action**

Source: Based on "Few Employers Addressing Workplace Stress, Watson Wyatt Surveys Find," press release (February 14, 2008), www.watsonwyatt.com/news/press.asp?ID=18643.

Exhibit **18-7**	Work Is the Biggest Source of Stress for Most

"What area of your life causes you the most stress on a regular basis?"

Area	Causes most stress
My job	26%
My finances	20%
My relationships	21%
My children	10%
School	8%
Fear of a disaster/terror attack	3%
Other	8%

Source: 2009 Stress Management poll of 7,807 individuals
(stress.about.com/gi/pages/poll.htm?linkback=&poll_id=2213421040&poll1=1&poll3=1&submit1=Submit+Vote).

What Is Stress?

Stress is a dynamic condition in which an individual is confronted with an opportunity, demand, or resource related to what the individual desires and for which the outcome is perceived to be both uncertain and important.[53] This is a complicated definition. Let's look at its components more closely.

Although stress is typically discussed in a negative context, it is not necessarily bad in and of itself; it also has a positive value.[54] It's an opportunity when it offers potential gain. Consider, for example, the superior performance an athlete or stage performer gives in a "clutch" situation. Such individuals often use stress positively to rise to the occasion and perform at their maximum. Similarly, many professionals see the pressures of heavy workloads and deadlines as positive challenges that enhance the quality of their work and the satisfaction they get from their job.

Recently, researchers have argued that **challenge stressors**—or stressors associated with workload, pressure to complete tasks, and time urgency—operate quite differently from **hindrance stressors**—or stressors that keep you from reaching your goals (for example, red tape, office politics, confusion over job responsibilities). Although research is just starting to accumulate, early evidence suggests challenge stressors produce less strain than hindrance stressors.[55] A meta-analysis of responses from more than 35,000 individuals showed role ambiguity, role conflict, role overload, job insecurity, environmental uncertainty, and situational constraints were all consistently negatively related to job performance.[56] There is also evidence that challenge stress improves job performance in a supportive work environment, whereas hindrance stress reduces job performance in all work environments.[57]

Researchers have sought to clarify the conditions under which each type of stress exists. It appears that employees who have a stronger affective commitment

stress *A dynamic condition in which an individual is confronted with an opportunity, a demand, or a resource related to what the individual desires and for which the outcome is perceived to be both uncertain and important.*

challenge stressors *Stressors associated with workload, pressure to complete tasks, and time urgency.*

hindrance stressors *Stressors that keep you from reaching your goals (for example, red tape, office politics, confusion over job responsibilities).*

to their organization can transfer psychological stress into greater focus and higher sales performance, whereas employees with low levels of commitment perform worse under stress.[58] And when challenge stress increases, those with high levels of organizational support have higher role-based performance, but those with low levels of organizational support do not.[59]

More typically, stress is associated with **demands** and **resources**. Demands are responsibilities, pressures, obligations, and uncertainties individuals face in the workplace. Resources are things within an individual's control that he or she can use to resolve the demands. Let's discuss what this demands–resources model means.[60]

When you take a test at school or you undergo your annual performance review at work, you feel stress because you confront opportunities and performance pressures. A good performance review may lead to a promotion, greater responsibilities, and a higher salary. A poor review may prevent you from getting a promotion. An extremely poor review might even result in your being fired. To the extent you can apply resources to the demands on you—such as being prepared, placing the exam or review in perspective, or obtaining social support—you will feel less stress.

Research suggests adequate resources help reduce the stressful nature of demands when demands and resources match. If emotional demands are stressing you, having emotional resources in the form of social support is especially important. If the demands are cognitive—say, information overload—then job resources in the form of computer support or information are more important. Thus, under the demands–resources perspective, having resources to cope with stress is just as important in offsetting it as demands are in increasing it.[61]

Potential Sources of Stress

What causes stress? As the model in Exhibit 18-8 shows, there are three categories of potential stressors: environmental, organizational, and personal. Let's take a look at each.[62]

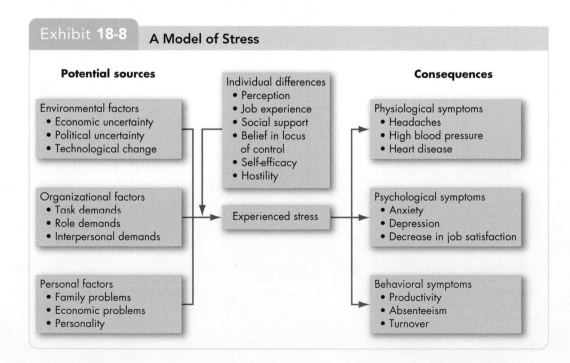

Exhibit 18-8   A Model of Stress

Potential sources

Environmental factors
• Economic uncertainty
• Political uncertainty
• Technological change

Organizational factors
• Task demands
• Role demands
• Interpersonal demands

Personal factors
• Family problems
• Economic problems
• Personality

Individual differences
• Perception
• Job experience
• Social support
• Belief in locus of control
• Self-efficacy
• Hostility

Experienced stress

Consequences

Physiological symptoms
• Headaches
• High blood pressure
• Heart disease

Psychological symptoms
• Anxiety
• Depression
• Decrease in job satisfaction

Behavioral symptoms
• Productivity
• Absenteeism
• Turnover

Myth or Science?

"Job Stress Can Kill You"

This statement appears to be true. Self-reports of job stress are negatively correlated with all sorts of indicators of physical and mental health. A problem with many of these studies, however, is that causality is a bit hard to establish: Does job stress cause poor health, or does poor health increase the stress of the job? It's also possible a third variable causes both: neurotic individuals report both more stress and poorer health, which might call into question the causal link from job stress to health.

A recent study, though, suggests job stress may indeed lead to poor health. In this study, 972 participants, ages 35 to 59, returned to work after experiencing a heart attack. The researchers followed them for 6 years. Those who returned to high-stress jobs were 2.2 times more likely to suffer another heart attack (or be hospitalized for a heart condition) than those in low-stress jobs. One of the researchers deemed the effect "very important" and concluded the risk factor was roughly the same as that of smoking or high blood pressure.

Another recent study with a strong design—an eight-year study of 7,810 Finnish forestry workers—found those who suffered severe levels of job stress, in the form of high psychological burnout, were 3.8 times more likely to suffer from disability at a later date. Yet another long-term study of 3,190 Japanese men revealed that working in a high-stress job roughly doubled the odds of suffering a later stroke.

Thus, it appears the implications of working in a high-stress job can be very severe—and life threatening.

Sources: Based on A. Tsutsumi, K. Kayaba, K. Kario, and S. Ishikawa, "Prospective Study on Occupational Stress and Risk of Stroke," *Archives of Internal Medicine* 169, no. 1 (2009), pp. 56–61; K. Ahola, S. Toppinen-Tanner, P. Huuhtanen, A. Koskinen, A. Väänänen, "Occupational Burnout and Chronic Work Disability: An Eight-year Cohort Study on Pensioning Among Finnish Forest Industry Workers," *Journal of Affective Disorders* 115, no. 1–2 (2009), pp. 150–159; C. Aboa-Eboulé, C. Brisson, E. Maunsell, B. Mâsse, R. Bourbonnais, M. Vézina, et al., "Job Strain and Risk of Acute Recurrent Coronary Heart Disease Events," *Journal of the American Medical Association (JAMA)* 298, no. 14 (2007), pp. 1652–1660.

Environmental Factors   Just as environmental uncertainty influences the design of an organization's structure, it also influences stress levels among employees in that organization. Indeed, uncertainty is the biggest reason people have trouble coping with organizational changes.[63] There are three main types of environmental uncertainty: economic, political, and technological.

Changes in the business cycle create *economic uncertainties*. When the economy is contracting, for example, people become increasingly anxious about their job security. *Political uncertainties* don't tend to create stress among North Americans as they do for employees in countries such as Haiti or Venezuela. The obvious reason is that the United States and Canada have stable political systems, in which change is typically implemented in an orderly manner. Yet political threats and changes, even in countries such as the United States and Canada, can induce stress. Threats by Quebec to separate from Canada, or the difficulties of East Germany reintegrating with West Germany, lead to political uncertainty that becomes stressful to people in these countries.[64] Because innovations can make an employee's skills and experience obsolete in a very short time, computers, robotics, automation, and similar forms of *technological change* are a threat to many people and cause them stress.

Organizational Factors   There is no shortage of factors within an organization that can cause stress. Pressures to avoid errors or complete tasks in a limited time,

---

demands   *Responsibilities, pressures, obligations, and even uncertainties that individuals face in the workplace.*

resources   *Things within an individual's control that can be used to resolve demands.*

Task demands are organizational factors that can cause stress. These call center employees of Encore Capital Group in Gurgaon, India, have the difficult job of collecting mostly credit card and auto debts of Americans. The nature of their job can cause stress, as the people they call may be abusive, emotional, frustrated, sad, or angry. Encore strives to reduce the on-the-job stress of its call center workers by teaching them how to empathize with the delinquent borrowers and how to handle verbal abuse. Collectors learn that the debtors respond to them when they are very polite and respectful and never raise their voice.

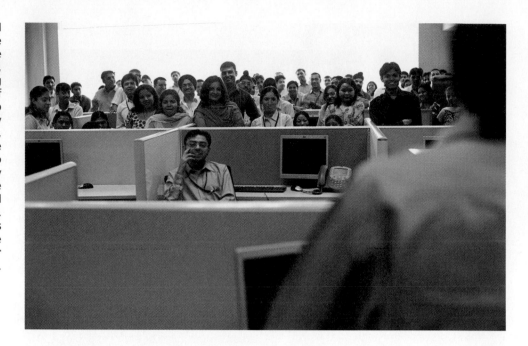

work overload, a demanding and insensitive boss, and unpleasant co-workers are a few examples. We've categorized these factors around task, role, and interpersonal demands.[65]

Task demands relate to a person's job. They include the design of the job (its degrees of autonomy, task variety, degree of automation), working conditions, and the physical work layout. Assembly lines can put pressure on people when they perceive the line's speed to be excessive. Working in an overcrowded room or a visible location where noise and interruptions are constant can increase anxiety and stress.[66] As customer service grows ever more important, emotional labor becomes a source of stress.[67] Imagine being a flight attendant for Southwest Airlines or a cashier at Starbucks. Do you think you could put on a happy face when you're having a bad day?

Role demands relate to pressures placed on a person as a function of the particular role he or she plays in the organization. Role conflicts create expectations that may be hard to reconcile or satisfy. Role overload occurs when the employee is expected to do more than time permits. Role ambiguity means role expectations are not clearly understood and the employee is not sure what to do. Individuals who face high situational constraints (such as fixed work hours or demanding job responsibilities) are also less able to engage in the proactive coping behaviors that reduce stress levels.[68] When faced with hassles at work they will not only have higher levels of distress at the time, but they'll also be less likely to take steps to eliminate stressors in the future.

Interpersonal demands are pressures created by other employees. Lack of social support from colleagues and poor interpersonal relationships can cause stress, especially among employees with a high social need. A rapidly growing body of research has also shown that negative co-worker and supervisor behaviors, including fights, bullying, incivility, racial harassment, and sexual harassment, are especially strongly related to stress at work.[69]

Personal Factors   The typical individual works about 40 to 50 hours a week. But the experiences and problems people encounter in the other 120-plus can spill over to the job. Our final category, then, is factors in the employee's personal life: family issues, personal economic problems, and inherent personality characteristics.

National surveys consistently show people hold *family* and personal relationships dear. Marital difficulties, the breaking of a close relationship, and discipline troubles with children create stresses employees often can't leave at the front door when they arrive at work.[70]

Regardless of income level—people who make $80,000 per year seem to have as much trouble handling their finances as those who earn $18,000—some people are poor money managers or have wants that exceed their earning capacity. The *economic* problems of overextended financial resources create stress and siphon attention away from work.

Studies in three diverse organizations found that participants who reported stress symptoms before beginning a job accounted for most of the variance in stress symptoms reported nine months later.[71] The researchers concluded that some people may have an inherent tendency to accentuate negative aspects of the world. If this is true, then a significant individual factor that influences stress is a person's basic disposition. That is, stress symptoms expressed on the job may actually originate in the person's *personality*.

Stressors Are Additive   When we review stressors individually, it's easy to overlook that stress is an additive phenomenon—it builds up.[72] Each new and persistent stressor adds to an individual's stress level. So a single stressor may be relatively unimportant in and of itself, but if it's added to an already high level of stress, it can be the straw that breaks the camel's back. To appraise the total amount of stress an individual is under, we have to sum up his or her opportunity stresses, constraint stresses, and demand stresses.

Individual Differences

Some people thrive on stressful situations, while others are overwhelmed by them. What differentiates people in terms of their ability to handle stress? What individual difference variables moderate the relationship between *potential* stressors and *experienced* stress? At least four variables—perception, job experience, social support, and personality—are relevant.

In Chapter 6, we demonstrated that employees react in response to their perception of reality, rather than to reality itself. *Perception*, therefore, will moderate the relationship between a potential stress condition and an employee's reaction to it. Layoffs may cause one person to fear losing his job, while another sees an opportunity to get a large severance allowance and start her own business. So stress potential doesn't lie in objective conditions; rather, it lies in an employee's interpretation of those conditions.

Experience on the job tends to be negatively related to work stress. Why? Two explanations have been offered.[73] First is selective withdrawal. Voluntary turnover is more probable among people who experience more stress. Therefore, people who remain with an organization longer are those with more stress-resistant traits or those more resistant to the stress characteristics of their organization. Second, people eventually develop coping mechanisms to deal with stress. Because this takes time, senior members of the organization are more likely to be fully adapted and should experience less stress.

Social support—collegial relationships with co-workers or supervisors—can buffer the impact of stress.[74] It acts as a palliative, mitigating the negative effects of even high-strain jobs.

Perhaps the most widely studied *personality* trait in stress is Type A personality, discussed in Chapter 5. Type A—particularly the aspect that manifests itself in hostility and anger—is associated with increased levels of stress and risk for heart disease.[75] People who are quick to anger, maintain a persistently hostile outlook, and project a cynical mistrust of others are at increased risk of experiencing stress in situations.

Workaholism is another personal characteristic related to stress levels. Workaholics are people obsessed with their work; they put in an enormous number of hours, think about work even when not working, and create additional work responsibilities to satisfy an inner compulsion to work more. In some ways, they might seem like ideal employees. That's probably why when most people are asked in interviews what their greatest weakness is, they reflexively say "I just work too hard." However, there is a difference between working hard and working compulsively. Workaholics are not necessarily more productive than other employees, despite their extreme efforts. The strain of putting in such a high level of work effort eventually begins to wear on the workaholic, leading to higher levels of work–life conflict and psychological burnout.[76]

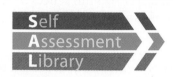

HOW STRESSFUL IS MY LIFE?

In the Self-Assessment Library (available on CD and online), take assessment III.C.2 (How Stressful Is My Life?).

Consequences of Stress

6   Identify the consequences of stress.

Stress shows itself in a number of ways, such as high blood pressure, ulcers, irritability, difficulty making routine decisions, loss of appetite, accident proneness, and the like. These symptoms fit under three general categories: physiological, psychological, and behavioral symptoms.[77]

Physiological Symptoms Most early concern with stress was directed at physiological symptoms because most researchers were specialists in the health and medical sciences. Their work led to the conclusion that stress could create changes in metabolism, increase heart and breathing rates and blood pressure, bring on headaches, and induce heart attacks.

Because symptoms are complex and difficult to measure objectively, the link between stress and particular physiological effects is not clear. Traditionally, researchers concluded there were few, if any, consistent relationships.[78] More recently, some evidence suggests stress may have harmful physiological effects. One study linked stressful job demands increase susceptibility to upper respiratory illnesses and poor immune system functioning, especially for individuals with low self-efficacy.[79]

Psychological Symptoms Job dissatisfaction is "the simplest and most obvious psychological effect" of stress.[80] But stress shows itself in other psychological states—for instance, tension, anxiety, irritability, boredom, and procrastination.

Jobs that make multiple and conflicting demands or that lack clarity about the incumbent's duties, authority, and responsibilities increase both stress and dissatisfaction.[81] Similarly, the less control people have over the pace of their work, the greater the stress and dissatisfaction. Although more research is needed to clarify the relationship, jobs that provide a low level of variety, significance, autonomy, feedback, and identity appear to create stress and reduce satisfaction and involvement in the job.[82] Not everyone reacts to autonomy in the same way, however. For those who have an external locus of control, increased job control increases the tendency to experience stress and exhaustion.[83]

An Ethical Choice

Your Responsibility to Your Stress

You are likely to have substantial control over the types of work you pursue once you've completed your education. Although your choice does not necessarily have ethical implications for others, it does have ethical implications for you, if you believe you have a duty to manage your own well-being. Here's what you can do:

1. Avoid high-stress jobs. According to the U.S. Centers for Disease Control and Prevention (CDC), some jobs—such as stockbroker, customer service/complaint worker, police officer, waiter, medical intern, secretary, and air

traffic controller—are known to be stressful for most people. Unless you're confident in your ability to handle stress in these jobs, avoid them.
2. If you do experience stress at work, try to find a job that has plenty of control (so you can decide how to perform your work) and supportive co-workers. Control and social support each have moderating effects on the experience of stress.
3. Don't assume this exercise rules out a financially rewarding career: Money is the top stressor

reported by people under age 30. So by all means, pursue a career that pays you well. But also realize there *are* jobs that don't have a high degree of stress but still pay competitively.

Sources: Based on S. Martin, "Money Is the Stressor for Americans," *Monitor on Psychology* (December 2008), pp. 28–29; *Helicobacter pylori and Peptic Ulcer Disease,* Centers for Disease Control and Prevention, U.S. Department of Health and Human Services, www.cdc.gov/ulcer; and M. Maynard, "Maybe the Toughest Job Aloft," *New York Times,* August 15, 2006, pp. C1, C6.

Behavioral Symptoms   Behavior-related stress symptoms include changes in productivity, absence, and turnover, as well as changes in eating habits, increased smoking or consumption of alcohol, rapid speech, fidgeting, and sleep disorders.[84]

A significant amount of research has investigated the stress–performance relationship. The most widely studied pattern of this relationship is the inverted U shown in Exhibit 18-9.[85]

The logic underlying the inverted U is that low to moderate levels of stress stimulate the body and increase its ability to react. Individuals then often perform their tasks better, more intensely, or more rapidly. But too much stress places unattainable demands on a person, which result in lower performance.

Exhibit 18-9	The Proposed Inverted-U Relationship Between Stress and Job Performance

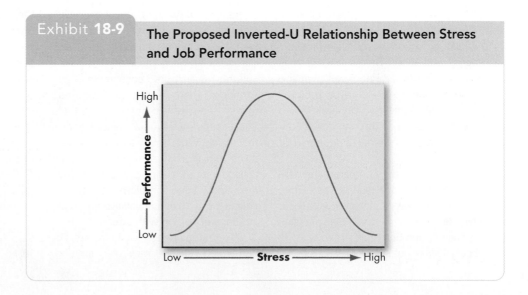

The inverted U may also describe our reaction to stress over time as well as to changes in stress intensity. That is, even moderate levels of stress can have a negative influence on performance over the long term as the continued intensity of the stress wears down the individual and saps energy resources. An athlete may be able to use the positive effects of stress to obtain higher performance during every Saturday game in the fall season, or a sales executive may be able to psych herself up for her presentation at the annual national meeting. But moderate levels of stress experienced continually over long periods, such as by the emergency-room staff in a large urban hospital, can result in lower performance. This may explain why emergency room staff are frequently rotated, and why it is unusual for individuals to spend the bulk of their career in such an environment, exposed to the risk of "career burnout."

In spite of the popularity and intuitive appeal of the inverted-U model, it doesn't get a lot of empirical support.[86] We should be careful of assuming it accurately depicts the stress–performance relationship.

Managing Stress

7   Contrast the individual and organizational approaches to managing stress.

Because low to moderate levels of stress can be functional and lead to higher performance, management may not be concerned when employees experience them. Employees, however, are likely to perceive even low levels of stress as undesirable. It's not unlikely, therefore, for employees and management to have different notions of what constitutes an acceptable level of stress on the job. What management may consider to be "a positive stimulus that keeps the adrenaline running" is very likely to be seen as "excessive pressure" by the employee. Keep this in mind as we discuss individual and organizational approaches toward managing stress.[87]

Individual Approaches   An employee can take personal responsibility for reducing stress levels. Individual strategies that have proven effective include

---

International OB

Coping with Stress: East and West

In several places in this chapter, we've noted that social support can play an important role in effectively coping with stress. Stress, of course, is a human universal: People all over the world experience it. However, the way they deal with it generally—and whether they do so through social support specifically—seems to depend a lot on culture.

A recent review compared the tendency to seek social support to relieve stress among Asians (Koreans, Japanese, Chinese, and Vietnamese), Asian Americans, and European Americans. Its conclusions might surprise you.

Asians and Asian Americans are significantly less likely to cope with stress by seeking social support than are European Americans. Given that Asian cultures are more collectivist than American and European cultures, that's somewhat counterintuitive. Social support, after all, would seem the collectivistic thing to do. The authors explain, however, that because collectivists strive for group harmony, they may keep problems to themselves rather than use social support as a means of coping with stress.

What's the upshot? Collectivists experiencing stress may be limiting themselves in terms of coping mechanisms and may need to find other means of coping with work-related stress.

Sources: Based on H. S. Kim, D. K. Sherman, and S. E. Taylor, "Culture and Social Support," *American Psychologist* 63, no. 6 (2008), pp. 518–526; S. Taylor, D. K. Sherman, H. S. Kim, J. Jarcho, K. Takagi, and M. Dunagan, "Culture and Social Support: Who Seeks It and Why?" *Journal of Personality and Social Psychology,* September 2004, pp. 354–362; and S. E. Taylor, W. Welch, H. S. Kim, and D. K. Sherman, "Cultural Differences in the Impact of Social Support on Psychological and Biological Stress Responses," *Psychological Science* 18, no. 9 (2007), pp. 831–837.

This group of Chinese working women participate in a yoga class in Beijing as a way to deal with excessive stress levels caused by long working hours and trying to achieve a work/life balance. Working women in China have high levels of stress because in Chinese culture women are expected to take more responsibility for family matters than in other cultures. As an individual approach to managing stress, yoga is a noncompetitive physical exercise that combines stretching, mental imagery, breathing control, physical postures, and meditation. Yoga reduces stress, anxiety, and muscle tension, provides a mental diversion from work pressures, and promotes physical well-being by lowering blood pressure and heart rate.

time-management techniques, increased physical exercise, relaxation training, and expanded social support networks.

Many people manage their time poorly. The well-organized employee, like the well-organized student, can often accomplish twice as much as the person who is poorly organized. So an understanding and utilization of basic time-management principles can help individuals better cope with tensions created by job demands.[88] A few of the best-known time-management principles are (1) making daily lists of activities to be accomplished, (2) prioritizing activities by importance and urgency, (3) scheduling activities according to the priorities set, and (4) knowing your daily cycle and handling the most demanding parts of your job when you are most alert and productive.[89]

Physicians have recommended noncompetitive physical exercise, such as aerobics, walking, jogging, swimming, and riding a bicycle, as a way to deal with excessive stress levels. These forms of *physical exercise* increase heart capacity, lower the at-rest heart rate, provide a mental diversion from work pressures, and even slow the physical and mental effects of aging.[90]

Individuals can teach themselves to reduce tension through *relaxation techniques* such as meditation, hypnosis, and biofeedback. The objective is to reach a state of deep physical relaxation, in which you feel somewhat detached from the immediate environment and from body sensations.[91] Deep relaxation for 15 or 20 minutes a day releases tension and provides a pronounced sense of peacefulness, as well as significant changes in heart rate, blood pressure, and other physiological factors.

As we have noted, friends, family, or work colleagues talk to provide an outlet when stress levels become excessive. Expanding your *social support network* provides someone to hear your problems and offer a more objective perspective on the situation than your own.

Organizational Approaches   Several factors that cause stress—particularly task and role demands—are controlled by management and thus can be modified or changed. Strategies to consider include improved personnel selection and job placement, training, realistic goal setting, redesign of jobs, increased employee involvement, improved organizational communication, employee sabbaticals, and corporate wellness programs.

Certain jobs are more stressful than others but, as already noted, individuals differ in their response to stressful situations. We know individuals with little experience or an external locus of control tend to be more prone to stress. *Selection and placement* decisions should take these facts into consideration. Obviously, management shouldn't restrict hiring to only experienced individuals with an internal locus, but such individuals may adapt better to high-stress jobs and perform those jobs more effectively. Similarly, *training* can increase an individual's self-efficacy and thus lessen job strain.

We discussed *goal setting* in Chapter 7. Individuals perform better when they have specific and challenging goals and receive feedback on their progress toward these goals. Goals can reduce stress as well as provide motivation.[92] Employees who are highly committed to their goals and see purpose in their jobs experience less stress because they are more likely to perceive stressors as challenges rather than hindrances. Specific goals perceived as attainable clarify performance expectations. In addition, goal feedback reduces uncertainties about actual job performance. The result is less employee frustration, role ambiguity, and stress.

Redesigning jobs to give employees more responsibility, more meaningful work, more autonomy, and increased feedback can reduce stress because these factors give employees greater control over work activities and lessen dependence on others. But as we noted in our discussion of work design, not all employees want enriched jobs. The right redesign for employees with a low need for growth might be less responsibility and increased specialization. If individuals prefer structure and routine, reducing skill variety should also reduce uncertainties and stress levels.

Role stress is detrimental to a large extent because employees feel uncertain about goals, expectations, how they'll be evaluated, and the like. By giving these employees a voice in the decisions that directly affect their job performance, management can increase employee control and reduce role stress. So managers should consider *increasing employee involvement* in decision making.[93]

Increasing formal *organizational communication* with employees reduces uncertainty by lessening role ambiguity and role conflict. Given the importance that perceptions play in moderating the stress–response relationship, management can also use effective communications as a means to shape employee perceptions. Remember that what employees categorize as demands, threats, or opportunities is an interpretation, and that interpretation can be affected by the symbols and actions communicated by management.

Some employees need an occasional escape from the frenetic pace of their work. Companies including Charles Schwab, DuPont, L.L. Bean, Nike, and 3Com have begun to provide extended voluntary leaves.[94] These *sabbaticals*—ranging in length from a few weeks to several months—allow employees to travel, relax, or pursue personal projects that consume time beyond normal vacations. Proponents say they can revive and rejuvenate workers who might be headed for burnout.

Our final suggestion is organizationally supported **wellness programs**. These typically provide workshops to help people quit smoking, control alcohol use, lose weight, eat better, and develop a regular exercise program; they focus on the employee's total physical and mental condition.[95] Some help employees improve their psychological health as well. A meta-analysis of 36 programs designed to reduce stress (including wellness programs) showed that interventions to help employees reframe stressful situations and use active coping strategies led to an appreciable reduction in stress levels.[96] Most wellness programs assume employees need to take personal responsibility for their physical and mental health and that the organization is merely a means to that end.

Cindy Russell poses with her assembled gear in preparation for a one-month sabbatical to go fly fishing in the South Pacific. Russell is a paralegal with the law firm Alters, Boldt, Brown, Rash, and Culmo in Miami. Like many small companies, the law firm does not have a formal sabbatical program. But Russell approached her boss with the idea, saying that she worked long hours in preparing for trials and desired a longer time away from work than her vacation time allowed. She explained how the fishing trip would help her to decompress and return to work energized and refreshed. Russell was granted the leave, some of it unpaid, after convincing her boss how it would benefit both her and the firm.

Most firms that have introduced wellness programs have found significant benefits. A study of eight Canadian organizations found that every dollar spent on their comprehensive wellness programs generated a return of $1.64, and for high-risk employees, such as smokers, the return was nearly $4.00.[97]

Global Implications

8 Explain global differences in organizational change and work stress.

Organizational Change   A number of change issues we've discussed in this chapter are culture bound. To illustrate, let's briefly look at five questions: (1) Do people believe change is possible? (2) If it's possible, how long will it take to bring it about? (3) Is resistance to change greater in some cultures than in others? (4) Does culture influence how change efforts will be implemented? (5) Do successful idea champions do things differently in different cultures?

Do people believe change is possible? Remember that cultures vary in terms of beliefs about their ability to control their environment. In cultures in which people believe that they can dominate their environment, individuals will take a proactive view of change. This, for example, would describe the United States and Canada. In many other countries, such as Iran and Saudi Arabia, people see themselves as subjugated to their environment and thus will tend to take a passive approach toward change.

If change is possible, how long will it take to bring it about? A culture's time orientation can help us answer this question. Societies that focus on the long

wellness programs   *Organizationally supported programs that focus on the employee's total physical and mental condition.*

term, such as Japan, will demonstrate considerable patience while waiting for positive outcomes from change efforts. In societies with a short-term focus, such as the United States and Canada, people expect quick improvements and will seek change programs that promise fast results.

Is resistance to change greater in some cultures than in others? Resistance to change will be influenced by a society's reliance on tradition. Italians, as an example, focus on the past, whereas U.S. adults emphasize the present. Italians, therefore, should generally be more resistant to change efforts than their U.S. counterparts.

Does culture influence how change efforts will be implemented? Power distance can help with this issue. In high–power distance cultures, such as Spain or Thailand, change efforts will tend to be autocratically implemented by top management. In contrast, low–power distance cultures value democratic methods. We'd predict, therefore, a greater use of participation in countries such as Denmark and the Netherlands.

Finally, do successful idea champions do things differently in different cultures? Yes.[98] People in collectivist cultures prefer appeals for cross-functional support for innovation efforts; people in high–power distance cultures prefer champions to work closely with those in authority to approve innovative activities before work is begun; and the higher the uncertainty avoidance of a society, the more champions should work within the organization's rules and procedures to develop the innovation. These findings suggest that effective managers will alter their organization's championing strategies to reflect cultural values. So, for instance, although idea champions in Russia might succeed by ignoring budgetary limitations and working around confining procedures, champions in Austria, Denmark, Germany, or other cultures high in uncertainty avoidance will be more effective by closely following budgets and procedures.

Stress   In considering global differences in stress, there are three questions to answer: (1) Do the causes of stress vary across countries? (2) Do the outcomes of stress vary across cultures? and (3) Do the factors that lessen the effects of stress vary by culture? Let's deal with each of these questions in turn.

First, research suggests the job conditions that cause stress show some differences across cultures. One study of U.S. and Chinese employees revealed that whereas U.S. employees were stressed by a lack of control, Chinese employees were stressed by job evaluations and lack of training. While the job conditions that lead to stress may differ across countries, it doesn't appear that personality effects on stress are different across cultures. One study of employees in Hungary, Italy, the United Kingdom, Israel, and the United States found Type A personality traits (see Chapter 5) predicted stress equally well across countries.[99] A study of 5,270 managers from 20 countries found individuals from individualistic countries such as the United States, Canada, and the United Kingdom experienced higher levels of stress due to work interfering with family than did individuals from collectivist countries in Asia and Latin America.[100] The authors proposed that this may occur because in collectivist cultures working extra hours is seen as a sacrifice to help the family, whereas in individualistic cultures work is seen as a means to personal achievement that takes away from the family.

Second, evidence tends to suggest that stressors are associated with perceived stress and strains among employees in different countries. In other words, stress is equally bad for employees of all cultures.[101]

Third, although not all factors that reduce stress have been compared across cultures, research does suggest that, whereas the demand to work long hours leads to stress, this stress can be reduced by such resources of social support as having friends or family with whom to talk. A recent study found this to be true of workers in a diverse set of countries (Australia, Canada, England, New Zealand, the United States, China, Taiwan, Argentina, Brazil, Colombia, Ecuador, Mexico, Peru, and Uruguay).[102]

Summary and Implications for Managers

The need for change has been implied throughout this text. "A casual reflection on change should indicate that it encompasses almost all of our concepts in the organizational behavior literature."[103] For instance, think about attitudes, motivation, work teams, communication, leadership, organizational structures, human resource practices, and organizational cultures. Change was an integral part in our discussion of each.

If environments were perfectly static, if employees' skills and abilities were always up to date and incapable of deteriorating, and if tomorrow were always exactly the same as today, organizational change would have little or no relevance to managers. But the real world is turbulent, requiring organizations and their members to undergo dynamic change if they are to perform at competitive levels.

Managers are the primary change agents in most organizations. By the decisions they make and their role-modeling behaviors, they shape the organization's change culture. Management decisions related to structural design, cultural factors, and human resource policies largely determine the level of innovation within the organization. Management policies and practices will determine the degree to which the organization learns and adapts to changing environmental factors.

We found that the existence of work stress, in and of itself, need not imply lower performance. The evidence indicates that stress can be either a positive or a negative influence on employee performance. Low to moderate amounts of stress enable many people to perform their jobs better by increasing their work intensity, alertness, and ability to react. However, a high level of stress, or even a moderate amount sustained over a long period, eventually takes its toll, and performance declines. The impact of stress on satisfaction is far more straightforward. Job-related tension tends to decrease general job satisfaction.[104] Even though low to moderate levels of stress may improve job performance, employees find stress dissatisfying.

POINT   COUNTERPOINT

Managing Change Is an Episodic Activity

POINT

Organizational change is an episodic activity. That is, it starts at some point, proceeds through a series of steps, and culminates in some outcome that participants hope is an improvement over the starting point. It has a beginning, a middle, and an end.

Lewin's three-step model represents a classic illustration of this perspective. Change is seen as a break in the organization's equilibrium. The status quo has been disturbed, and change is necessary to establish a new equilibrium state. The objective of refreezing is to stabilize the new situation by balancing the driving and restraining forces.

Some experts have argued that organizational change should be thought of as balancing a system of five interacting variables within the organization—people, tasks, technology, structure, and strategy. A change in any one variable has repercussions on one or more of the others. This perspective is episodic in that it treats organizational change as essentially an effort to sustain equilibrium. A change in one variable begins a chain of events that, if properly managed, requires adjustments in the other variables to achieve a new state of equilibrium.

Another way to conceptualize the episodic view of looking at change is to think of managing change as analogous to captaining a ship. The organization is like a large ship traveling across the calm Mediterranean Sea to a specific port. The ship's captain has made this exact trip hundreds of times before with the same crew. Every once in a while, however, a storm will appear, and the crew has to respond. The captain will make the appropriate adjustments—that is, will implement changes—and, having maneuvered through the storm, will return the ship to calm waters. Like this ship's voyage, managing an organization is a journey with a beginning and an end, and implementing change as a response to a break in the status quo is needed only occasionally.

COUNTERPOINT

The episodic approach for handling organizational change has become obsolete. Developed in the 1950s and 1960s, it reflects the environment of those times by treating change as the occasional disturbance in an otherwise peaceful and predictable world. However, it bears little resemblance to today's environment of constant and chaotic change.[105]

If you want to understand what it's like to manage change in today's organizations, think of it as equivalent to permanent white-water rafting.[106] The organization is not a large ship but, rather, more like a 40-foot raft. Rather than sailing a calm sea, this raft must traverse a raging river that is an uninterrupted flow of white-water rapids. To make things worse, the raft is manned by 10 people who have never worked together or traveled the river before, much of the trip takes place in the dark, the river is dotted by unexpected turns and obstacles, the exact destination is not clear, and at irregular intervals the raft needs to pull to shore, where some new crew members are added and others leave. Change is a natural state, and managing it is a continual process—that is, managers never experience the luxury of escaping the white-water rapids.

The stability and predictability characterized by the episodic perspective no longer captures the world we live in. Disruptions in the status quo are not occasional, temporary, and followed by a return to an equilibrium state. There is, in fact, no equilibrium state. Managers today face constant change, bordering on chaos. They're being forced to play a game they've never played before, governed by rules that are created as the game progresses.

Questions for Review

1 What forces act as stimulants to change, and what is the difference between planned and unplanned change?

2 What forces act as sources of resistance to change?

3 What are the four main approaches to managing organizational change?

4 How can managers create a culture for change?

5 What is stress, and what are the possible sources of stress?

6 What are the consequences of stress?

7 What are the individual and organizational approaches to managing stress?

8 What does research tell us about global differences in organizational change and work stress?

Experiential Exercise

POWER AND THE CHANGING ENVIRONMENT

Objectives

1. To describe the forces for change influencing power differentials in organizational and interpersonal relationships.

2. To understand the effect of technological, legal/political, economic, and social changes on the power of individuals within an organization.

The Situation

Your organization manufactures golf carts and sells them to country clubs, golf courses, and consumers. Your team is faced with the task of assessing how environmental changes will affect individuals' organizational power. Read each of the five scenarios and then, for each, identify the five members in the organization whose power will increase most in light of the environmental condition(s). (*Note:* m = male, (f) = female.)

Accountant-CPA (m)

Advertising expert (m)

Chemist (m)

Chief financial officer (f)

Computer programmer (f)

Corporate trainer (m)

General manager (m)

Human resource manager (f)

Industrial engineer (m)

In-house counsel (m)

Marketing manager (f)

Operations manager (f)

Product designer (m)

Public relations expert (m)

Securities analyst (m)

1. New computer-aided manufacturing technologies are being introduced in the workplace during the next 2 to 18 months.

2. New federal emission standards are being legislated by the government that will essentially make gas-powered golf carts (40 percent of your current business) obsolete.

3. Sales are way down for two reasons: (a) a decline in the number of individuals playing golf and (b) your competitor was faster to embrace lithium batteries, which allow golf carts to run longer without another charge.

4. Given the growth of golf courses in other places (especially India, China, and Southeast Asia), the company is planning to go international in the next 12 to 18 months.

5. The U.S. Equal Employment Opportunity Commission is applying pressure to balance the male–female population in the organization's upper hierarchy by threatening to publicize the predominance of men in upper management.

The Procedure

1. Divide the class into teams of three to four students each.

2. Teams should read each scenario and identify the five members whose power will increase most in light of the external environmental conditions described.

3. Teams should then address this question: Assuming that the five environmental changes are taking place at once, which five members of the organization will now have the most power?

4. After 20 to 30 minutes, representatives of each team will be selected to present and justify their conclusions to the entire class. Discussion will begin with scenario 1 and proceed through scenario 5 and the "all at once" scenario.

Source: Adapted from J. E. Barbuto, Jr., "Power and the Changing Environment," *Journal of Management Education,* April 2000, pp. 288–296.

Ethical Dilemma

STRESSING OUT EMPLOYEES IS YOUR JOB

Some of the most admired business leaders argue that the only way to get the most out of people is to stretch them. Both business anecdotes and research evidence seem to back this view. "If you do know how to get there, it's not a stretch target," former GE CEO Jack Welch has said. "We have found that by reaching for what appears to be the impossible, we often actually do the impossible; and even when we don't quite make it, we inevitably wind up doing much better than we would have done."[107]

As for the research evidence, we noted in Chapter 7 that goal-setting theory—whereby managers set the most difficult goals to which employees will commit—is perhaps the best-supported theory of motivation. The implication is that to be the most effective manager you need to push, push, and push more.

But does this pose an ethical dilemma for managers? What if you learned that pushing employees to the brink came at the expense of their health or their family life? While it seems true that managers get the performance they expect, it also seems likely that some people push themselves too hard. When Kathie Nunley, who travels more than 100 days each year, had to miss the occasion when her son won an art competition, the only person she could share her news with was the Delta ticket agent. "It hit me how sad it was that I was sharing this moment with an airline agent rather than my son," she said.

On the one hand, you may argue that employees should be responsible for their own welfare, and that it would be paternalistic, and encourage mediocrity, for organizations to "care for" employees. On the other hand, if your stretch goals mean your best employees are those who give it all for the organization—even putting aside their own personal or family interests—is that what you wish your results as a manager to be?

Questions

1. Do you think there is a trade-off between the positive (higher performance) and negative (increased stress) effects of stretch goals?

2. Do you think a manager should consider stress when setting stretch goals for employees? If you answered no, what should a manager do if a valued employee complains of too much stress? If you answered yes, how might you consider stress in setting goals?

3. How do you think you would respond to stretch goals? Would they increase your performance? Would they stress you?

Case Incident 1

INNOVATION—AND CONTINUITY—AT TOYOTA

If you ask experts in organizational innovation about Toyota, you'll often see a bemused expression on their faces. Toyota is a bit hard to figure, innovation wise.

On the one hand, the company has been one of the most successful corporations in the world for a generation. It is now the world's largest car company and shows no signs of giving up that title anytime soon. It must be doing *something* innovative to continue to thrive when business conditions, consumer preferences, government regulation, and global competition continue to change, sometimes rather dramatically.

Toyota also produced the first, and to date the only, successful mass-produced hybrid car, the Prius. Other companies have attempted to follow suit, only to find their entries coming up short in expert ratings, new car sales, and resale value.

On the other hand, Toyota's products are widely thought to be more "liked than loved," and its cars are often criticized for being imitations rather than innovations. The company is notorious for its "stodgy and bureaucratic" structure, for the fact that all its senior executives are Japanese males, and for its worshipping of the past (a bust of the company's founder, Kiichiro Toyoda, appears in the lobby, and in its 74-year history only three individuals outside the Toyoda family have led it). These hardly seem the hallmarks of an innovative, transformational organization.

So is Toyota an innovative company, or not?

The answer depends on how you define innovation. Judged by the innovations in its products, notwithstanding the Prius (which, despite its success, still amounts to a small percentage of Toyota's sales), we would not deem it a particularly innovative organization. However, when we defined an innovative culture elsewhere in this text, we emphasized two points. First, it is not judged only by an organization's products. Production, service, marketing, and other business processes are less observable to the outsider but are arguably more important to sustained success. Second, innovation can be incremental. Is a company that loudly reinvents itself every 10 years really more innovative than one that makes steady, incremental changes more or less continuously?

It's clear that on both these points—innovation as process as well as product, and lasting incremental innovation—Toyota excels. Toyota has made numerous workplace innovations, including the *andon* cord—whereby any worker can halt the production line when he or she sees a problem—and its focus on lean and nimble manufacturing processes that allow it to switch the vehicle being manufactured in nearly every plant within days. On the second point, *kaizen* manufacturing—a method of continuous improvement—is nearly synonymous with Toyota. As one expert commented, "Instead of trying to throw long touchdown passes, Toyota moves down the field by means of short and steady gains."

Studies consistently show that most efforts at organizational transformation fail and are abandoned. Perhaps if more companies thought about innovation the Toyota way—in terms of process rather than product and of slow and continuous improvement rather than radical change—they'd be more likely to realize the innovations, and organizational success, they wish to achieve.

Questions

1. Would you consider Toyota to be an innovative organization? Why or why not?

2. Do you think Toyota's potentially inbred leadership hinders, or explains, its successes?

3. In 2009, Toyota reported a loss for the first time in its history. Do you think that given its culture it will have more problems dealing with the loss than other automakers?

4. The new president of Toyota, Akio Toyoda (grandson of the founder), has said, "Everyone says Toyota is the best company in the world, but the consumer doesn't care about the world. They care if we are the best in town." What do you think he means by that?

Source: Based on M. Graban, "Toyota Leaders Get a Lecture from a Toyoda," *Manufacturing Business Technology* (June 28, 2009), www .mbtmag.com; M. Maynard, "At Toyota, a Giant Strives to Show Agility," *New York Times* (February 22, 2008), pp. B1, C4; and J. Surowiecki, "The Open Secret of Success," *The New Yorker* (May 12, 2008), p. 48.

Case Incident 2

THE RISE OF EXTREME JOBS

Before Barbara Agoglia left her job at American Express, she was spending 13 hours a day working and commuting. She also had to be available via cell phone 24/7. The last straw came when she didn't have time to wait with her school-age son at his bus stop. Carolyn Buck also has an extreme job. She usually works more than 60 hours a week for Ernst & Young and often has to travel to India and China.

Agoglia and Buck are not alone. Most U.S. adults are working more hours than ever, but one group in particular stands out: those with extreme jobs—people who spend more than half their time working and commuting to and from work. More than 1.7 million people consider their jobs *too* extreme, according to a recent study.

What accounts for the rise in extreme jobs? It's not entirely clear, but the usual suspects of globalization, technology, and competitiveness are high on everyone's lists.

As extreme as Agoglia and Buck's jobs may seem, U.S. workers may have it comparatively easy. Most surveys indicate extreme jobs are worse in developing counties. A 2006 *Harvard Business Review* study of managers in 33 global companies indicated that, compared to U.S. managers, managers in developing countries were more than twice as likely to have extreme jobs.

For those who hold extreme jobs, personal life often takes a back seat. Forty-four percent take fewer than 10 vacation days per year. Many individuals with extreme jobs see society changing into a "winner takes all" mode, where those who are willing to go the extra mile will reap a disproportionate share of the intrinsic and extrinsic rewards.

Why do people take extreme jobs (or allow their jobs to become extreme)? A 2006 study suggested that, for both men and women, the number 1 reason for working long, stressful hours is not pay. Rather, it's the rush they get from doing stimulating or challenging work. As one Asian manager said, "Building this business in markets where no one has done anything like this before is enormously exciting. And important. We've built distribution centers that are vital to China's growth—they contribute to the overall prospects of our economy."

Although this sounds all good, the situation is more complicated when you ask holders of extreme jobs about what their jobs cost them. Among them, 66 percent of men and 77 percent of women say their job interferes with their ability to maintain a home. For those with extreme jobs who have children, 65 percent of men and 33 percent of women say it keeps them from having a relationship with their children. And 46 percent of male and female extreme job holders say their jobs interfere with having a strong relationship with their spouse. About half the members of each group say it interferes with their sex life. "I can't even fathom having a boyfriend," says one extreme job holder. Another, Chris Cicchinelli, was so concerned about being out of touch with work during his honeymoon that he got a satellite phone. Even that didn't help. He ended up cutting his 10-day honeymoon to 5 days. "I had major anxiety," he said.

Questions

1. Do you think you will ever have an extreme job? Are you sure? Explain.

2. Why do you think the number of extreme jobs has risen?

3. Do you think organizations should encourage extreme jobs, discourage them, or completely leave them to an employee's discretion?

4. Why do you think people take extreme jobs in the first place?

Sources: Based on T. Weiss, "How Extreme Is Your Job?" *Forbes* (February 1, 2007), p. 1; S. A. Hewlett and C. B. Luce, "Extreme Jobs," *Harvard Business Review,* December 2006, pp. 49–58; and S. Armour, "Hi, I'm Joan, and I'm a Workaholic," *USA Today,* May 23, 2007, pp. 1B, 2B.

Endnotes

1. Based on S. Rosenbloom, "Circuit City to Shut Down," *New York Times* (January 16, 2009), www.nytimes.com; M. Bustillo, "Retailer Circuit City to Liquidate," *Wall Street Journal* (January 17, 2009), p. B1; and A. Hamilton, "Why Circuit City Busted, While Best Buy Boomed," *Time* (November, 11, 2008).

2. See, for instance, J. Birkinshaw, G. Hamel, and M. J. Mol, "Management Innovation," *Academy of Management Review* 33, no. 4 (2008), pp. 825–845; and J. Welch and S. Welch, "What Change Agents Are Made Of," *Business Week* (October 20, 2008), p. 96.

3. J. Taub, "Harvard Radical," *New York Times Magazine* (August 24, 2003), pp. 28–45.

4. A. Finder, P. D. Healy, and K. Zernike, "President of Harvard Resigns, Ending Stormy 5-Year Tenure," *New York Times* (February 22, 2006), pp. A1, A19.

5. P. G. Audia and S. Brion, "Reluctant to Change: Self-Enhancing Responses to Diverging Performance Measures," *Organizational Behavior and Human Decision Processes* 102 (2007), pp. 255–269.

6. M. Fugate, A. J. Kinicki, and G. E. Prussia, "Employee Coping with Organizational Change: An Examination of Alternative Theoretical Perspectives and Models," *Personnel Psychology* 61, no. 1 (2008), pp. 1–36.

7. J. D. Ford, L. W. Ford, and A. D'Amelio, "Resistance to Change: The Rest of the Story," *Academy of Management Review* 33, no. 2 (2008), pp. 362–377.

8. M. T. Hannan, L. Pólos, and G. R. Carroll, "The Fog of Change: Opacity and Asperity in Organizations," *Administrative Science Quarterly,* September 2003. pp. 399–432.

9. J. P. Kotter and L. A. Schlesinger, "Choosing Strategies for Change," *Harvard Business Review,* March–April 1979, pp. 106–114.

10. J. E. Dutton, S. J. Ashford, R. M. O'Neill, and K. A. Lawrence, "Moves That Matter: Issue Selling and Organizational Change," *Academy of Management Journal,* August 2001, pp. 716–736.

11. P. C. Fiss and E. J. Zajac, "The Symbolic Management of Strategic Change: Sensegiving via Framing and Decoupling," *Academy of Management Journal* 49, no. 6 (2006), pp. 1173–1193.

12. Q. N. Huy, "Emotional Balancing of Organizational Continuity and Radical Change: The Contribution of Middle Managers," *Administrative Science Quarterly,* March 2002, pp. 31–69; D. M. Herold, D. B. Fedor, and S. D. Caldwell, "Beyond Change Management: A Multilevel Investigation of Contextual and Personal Influences on Employees' Commitment to Change," *Journal of Applied Psychology* 92, no. 4 (2007), pp. 942–951; and G. B. Cunningham, "The Relationships Among Commitment to Change, Coping with Change, and Turnover Intentions," *European Journal of Work and Organizational Psychology* 15, no. 1 (2006), pp. 29–45.

13. J. P. Kotter, "Leading Change: Why Transformational Efforts Fail," *Harvard Business Review* 85, January 2007, p. 96–103.

14. K. van Dam, S. Oreg, and B. Schyns, "Daily Work Contexts and Resistance to Organisational Change: The Role of Leader-Member Exchange, Development Climate, and Change Process Characteristics," *Applied Psychology: An International Review* 57, no. 2 (2008), pp. 313–334.

15. D. B. Fedor, S. Caldwell, and D. M. Herold, "The Effects of Organizational Changes on Employee Commitment: A Multilevel Investigation," *Personnel Psychology* 59 (2006), pp. 1–29.

16. S. Oreg, "Personality, Context, and Resistance to Organizational Change," *European Journal of Work and Organizational Psychology* 15, no. 1 (2006), pp. 73–101.

17. S. M. Elias, "Employee Commitment in Times of Change: Assessing the Importance of Attitudes Toward Organizational Change," *Journal of Management* 35, no. 1 (2009), pp. 37–55.

18. J. A. LePine, J. A. Colquitt, and A. Erez, "Adaptability to Changing Task Contexts: Effects of General Cognitive Ability, Conscientiousness, and Openness to Experience," *Personnel Psychology,* Fall, 2000, pp. 563–593; T. A. Judge, C. J. Thoresen, V. Pucik, and T. M. Welbourne, "Managerial Coping with Organizational Change: A Dispositional Perspective," *Journal of Applied Psychology,* February 1999, pp. 107–122; and S. Oreg, "Resistance to Change: Developing an Individual Differences Measure," *Journal of Applied Psychology,* August 2003, pp. 680–693.

19. J. W. B. Lang and P. D. Bliese, "General Mental Ability and Two Types of Adaptation to Unforeseen Change: Applying Discontinuous Growth Models to the Task-Change Paradigm," *Journal of Applied Psychology* 94, no. 2 (2009), pp. 411–428.

20. See J. Pfeffer, *Managing with Power: Politics and Influence in Organizations* (Boston: Harvard Business School Press, 1992), pp. 7, and 318–320.

21. See, for instance, A. Karaevli, "Performance Consequences for New CEO 'Outsiderness': Moderating Effects of Pre- and

Post-Succession Contexts," *Strategic Management Journal* 28, no. 7 (2007), pp. 681–706.

22. K. Lewin, *Field Theory in Social Science* (New York: Harper & Row, 1951).

23. P. G. Audia, E. A. Locke, and K. G. Smith, "The Paradox of Success: An Archival and a Laboratory Study of Strategic Persistence Following Radical Environmental Change," *Academy of Management Journal,* October 2000, pp. 837–853; and P. G. Audia and S. Brion, "Reluctant to Change: Self-Enhancing Responses to Diverging Performance Measures," *Organizational Behavior and Human Decision Processes* 102, no. 2 (2007), pp. 255–269.

24. J. B. Sorensen, "The Strength of Corporate Culture and the Reliability of Firm Performance," *Administrative Science Quarterly,* March 2002, pp. 70–91.

25. J. Amis, T. Slack, and C. R. Hinings, "The Pace, Sequence, and Linearity of Radical Change," *Academy of Management Journal,* February 2004, pp. 15–39; and E. Autio, H. J. Sapienza, and J. G. Almeida, "Effects of Age at Entry, Knowledge Intensity, and Imitability on International Growth," *Academy of Management Journal,* October 2000, pp. 909–924.

26. J. P. Kotter, "Leading Changes: Why Transformation Efforts Fail," *Harvard Business Review,* March–April 1995, pp. 59–67; and J. P. Kotter, *Leading Change* (Harvard Business School Press, 1996).

27. See, for example, C. Eden and C. Huxham, "Action Research for the Study of Organizations," in S. R. Clegg, C. Hardy, and W. R. Nord (eds.), *Handbook of Organization Studies* (London: Sage, 1996); and L. S. Lüscher and M. W. Lewis, "Organizational Change and Managerial Sensemaking: Working Through Paradox," *Academy of Management Journal* 51, no. 2 (2008), pp. 221–240.

28. For a sampling of various OD definitions, see H. K. Sinangil and F. Avallone, "Organizational Development and Change," in N. Anderson, D. S. Ones, H. K. Sinangil, and C. Viswesvaran (eds.), *Handbook of Industrial, Work and Organizational Psychology,* vol. 2 (Thousand Oaks, CA: Sage, 2001), pp. 332–335; and R. J. Marshak and D. Grant, "Organizational Discourse and New Organization Development Practices," *British Journal of Management* 19, no. 1 (2008), pp. S7–S19.

29. See, for instance, R. Lines, "Influence of Participation in Strategic Change: Resistance, Organizational Commitment and Change Goal Achievement," *Journal of Change Management,* September 2004, pp. 193–215.

30. S. Highhouse, "A History of the T-Group and Its Early Application in Management Development," *Group Dynamics: Theory, Research, & Practice,* December 2002, pp. 277–290.

31. J. E. Edwards and M. D. Thomas, "The Organizational Survey Process: General Steps and Practical Considerations," in P. Rosenfeld, J. E. Edwards, and M. D. Thomas (eds.), *Improving Organizational Surveys: New Directions, Methods, and Applications* (Newbury Park, CA: Sage, 1993), pp. 3–28.

32. E. H. Schein, *Process Consultation: Its Role in Organizational Development,* 2nd ed. (Reading, MA: Addison-Wesley, 1988), p. 9. See also E. H. Schein, *Process Consultation Revisited: Building Helpful Relationships* (Reading, MA: Addison-Wesley, 1999).

33. Schein, *Process Consultation.*

34. W. Dyer, *Team Building: Issues and Alternatives* (Reading, MA: Addison-Wesley, 1994).

35. See, for example, E. H. Neilsen, "Understanding and Managing Intergroup Conflict," in J. W. Lorsch and P. R. Lawrence (eds.), *Managing Group and Intergroup Relations* (Homewood, IL: Irwin-Dorsey, 1972), pp. 329–343.

36. R. R. Blake, J. S. Mouton, and R. L. Sloma, "The Union–Management Intergroup Laboratory: Strategy for Resolving Intergroup Conflict," *Journal of Applied Behavioral Science,* no. 1 (1965), pp. 25–57.

37. See, for example, R. Fry, F. Barrett, J. Seiling, and D. Whitney (eds.), A*ppreciative Inquiry & Organizational Transformation: Reports From the Field* (Westport, CT: Quorum, 2002); J. K. Barge and C. Oliver, "Working with Appreciation in Managerial Practice," *Academy of Management Review,* January 2003, pp. 124–142; and D. van der Haar and D. M. Hosking, "Evaluating Appreciative Inquiry: A Relational Constructionist Perspective," *Human Relations,* August 2004, pp. 1017–1036.

38. G. Giglio, S. Michalcova, and C. Yates, "Instilling a Culture of Winning at American Express," *Organization Development Journal* 25, no. 4 (2007), pp. P33–P37.

39. D. Anfuso, "Core Values Shape W. L. Gore's Innovative Culture," *Workforce,* March 1999, pp. 48–51; and A. Harrington, "Who's Afraid of a New Product?" *Fortune* (November 10, 2003), pp. 189–192.

40. See, for instance, R. M. Kanter, "When a Thousand Flowers Bloom: Structural, Collective and Social Conditions for Innovation in Organizations," in B. M. Staw and L. L. Cummings (eds.), *Research in Organizational Behavior,* vol. 10 (Greenwich, CT: JAI Press, 1988), pp. 169–211.

41. F. Damanpour, "Organizational Innovation: A Meta-analysis of Effects of Determinants and Moderators," *Academy of Management Journal,* September 1991, p. 557.

42. Ibid., pp. 555–590.

43. See P. R. Monge, M. D. Cozzens, and N. S. Contractor, "Communication and Motivational Predictors of the Dynamics of Organizational Innovation," *Organization Science,* May 1992, pp. 250–274.

44. J. M. Howell and C. A. Higgins, "Champions of Change," *Business Quarterly,* Spring 1990, pp. 31–32; and D. L. Day, "Raising Radicals: Different Processes for Championing Innovative Corporate Ventures," *Organization Science,* May 1994, pp. 148–172.

45. Howell and Higgins, "Champions of Change."

46. Scc, for example, T. B. Lawrence, M. K. Mauws, B. Dyck, and R. F. Kleysen, "The Politics of Organizational Learning: Integrating Power into the 4I Framework," *Academy of Management Review,* January 2005, pp. 180–191.

47. D. H. Kim, "The Link Between Individual and Organizational Learning," *Sloan Management Review,* Fall 1993, p. 37.

48. C. Argyris and D. A. Schon, *Organizational Learning* (Reading, MA: Addison-Wesley, 1978).

49. B. Dumaine, "Mr. Learning Organization," *Fortune* (October 17, 1994), p. 148.

50. F. Kofman and P. M. Senge, "Communities of Commitment: The Heart of Learning Organizations," *Organizational Dynamics,* Autumn 1993, pp. 5–23.

51. Dumaine, "Mr. Learning Organization," p. 154.

52. See, for instance, S. Armour, "Rising Job Stress Could Affect Bottom Line," *USA Today* (July 29, 2003), p. 1B; J. Schramm, "Work/Life On Hold," *HRMagazine* 53, October 2008, p. 120.

53. Adapted from R. S. Schuler, "Definition and Conceptualization of Stress in Organizations," *Organizational Behavior and Human Performance,* April 1980, p. 189. For an updated review of definitions, see C. L. Cooper, P. J. Dewe, and M. P. O'Driscoll, *Organizational Stress: A Review and Critique of Theory, Research, and Applications* (Thousand Oaks, CA: Sage, 2002).

54. See, for instance, M. A. Cavanaugh, W. R. Boswell, M. V. Roehling, and J. W. Boudreau, "An Empirical Examination of Self-Reported Work Stress Among U.S. Managers," *Journal of Applied Psychology,* February 2000, pp. 65–74.

55. N. P. Podsakoff, J. A. LePine, and M. A. LePine, "Differential Challenge-Hindrance Stressor Relationships with Job Attitudes, Turnover Intentions, Turnover, and Withdrawal Behavior: A Meta-analysis," *Journal of Applied Psychology* 92, no. 2 (2007), pp. 438–454; and J. A. LePine, M. A. LePine, and C. L. Jackson, "Challenge and Hindrance Stress: Relationships with Exhaustion, Motivation to Learn, and Learning Performance," *Journal of Applied Psychology,* October 2004, pp. 883–891.

56. S. Gilboa, A. Shirom, Y. Fried, and C. Cooper, "A Meta-analysis of Work Demand Stressors and Job Performance: Examining Main and Moderating Effects," *Personnel Psychology* 61, no. 2 (2008), pp. 227–271.

57. J. C. Wallace, B. D. Edwards, T. Arnold, M. L. Frazier, and D. M. Finch, "Work Stressors, Role-Based Performance, and the Moderating Influence of Organizational Support," *Journal of Applied Psychology* 94, no. 1 (2009), pp. 254–262.

58. L. W. Hunter and S. M. B. Thatcher, "Feeling the Heat: Effects of Stress, Commitment, and Job Experience on Job Performance," *Academy of Management Journal* 50, no. 4 (2007), pp. 953–968.

59. J. C. Wallace, B. D. Edwards, T. Arnold, M. L. Frazier, and D. M. Finch, "Work Stressors, Role-Based Performance, and the Moderating Influence of Organizational Support," *Journal of Applied Psychology* 94, no. 1 (2009), pp. 254–262.

60. N. W. Van Yperen and O. Janssen, "Fatigued and Dissatisfied or Fatigued but Satisfied? Goal Orientations and Responses to High Job Demands," *Academy of Management Journal,* December 2002, pp. 1161–1171; and N. W. Van Yperen and M. Hagedoorn, "Do High Job Demands Increase Intrinsic Motivation or Fatigue or Both? The Role of Job Control and Job Social Support," *Academy of Management Journal,* June 2003, pp. 339–348.

61. J. de Jonge and C. Dormann, "Stressors, Resources, and Strain at Work: A Longitudinal Test of the Triple-Match Principle," *Journal of Applied Psychology* 91, no. 5 (2006), pp. 1359–1374.

62. This section is adapted from C. L. Cooper and R. Payne, *Stress at Work* (London: Wiley, 1978); S. Parasuraman and J. A. Alutto, "Sources and Outcomes of Stress in Organizational Settings: Toward the Development of a Structural Model," *Academy of Management Journal* 27, no. 2 (June 1984), pp. 330–350; and P. M. Hart and C. L. Cooper, "Occupational Stress: Toward a More Integrated Framework," in N. Anderson, D. S. Ones, H. K. Sinangil, and C. Viswesvaran (eds.), *Handbook of Industrial, Work and Organizational Psychology,* vol. 2 (London: Sage, 2001), pp. 93–114.

63. A. E. Rafferty and M. A. Griffin, "Perceptions of Organizational Change: A Stress and Coping Perspective," *Journal of Applied Psychology* 71, no. 5 (2007), pp. 1154–1162.

64. H. Garst, M. Frese, and P. C. M. Molenaar, "The Temporal Factor of Change in Stressor-Strain Relationships: A Growth Curve Model on a Longitudinal Study in East Germany," *Journal of Applied Psychology,* June 2000, pp. 417–438.

65. See, for example, M. L. Fox, D. J. Dwyer, and D. C. Ganster, "Effects of Stressful Job Demands and Control of Physiological and Attitudinal Outcomes in a Hospital Setting," *Academy of Management Journal,* April 1993, pp. 289–318.

66. G. W. Evans and D. Johnson, "Stress and Open-Office Noise," *Journal of Applied Psychology,* October 2000, pp. 779–783.

67. T. M. Glomb, J. D. Kammeyer-Mueller, and M. Rotundo, "Emotional Labor Demands and Compensating Wage Differentials," *Journal of Applied Psychology,* August 2004, pp. 700–714; and A. A. Grandey, "When 'The Show Must Go On': Surface Acting and Deep Acting as Determinants of Emotional Exhaustion and Peer-Rated Service Delivery," *Academy of Management Journal,* February 2003, pp. 86–96.

68. C. Fritz and S. Sonnentag, "Antecedents of Day-Level Proactive Behavior: A Look at Job Stressors and Positive Affect During the Workday," *Journal of Management* 35, no. 1 (2009), pp. 94–111.

69. S. Lim, L. M. Cortina, and V. J. Magley, "Personal and Workgroup Incivility: Impact on Work and Health Outcomes," *Journal of Applied Psychology* 93, no. 1 (2008), pp. 95–107; N. T. Buchanan, and L. F. Fitzgerald, "Effects of Racial and Sexual Harassment on Work and the Psychological Well-Being of African American Women," *Journal of Occupational Health Psychology* 13, no. 2 (2008), pp. 137–151; C. R. Willness, P. Steel, and K. Lee, "A Meta-analysis of the Antecedents and Consequences of Workplace Sexual Harassment," *Personnel Psychology* 60, no. 1 (2007), pp. 127–162; and B. Moreno-Jiménez, A. Rodríguez-Muñoz, J. C. Pastor, A. I. Sanz-Vergel, and E. Garrosa, "The Moderating Effects of Psychological Detachment and Thoughts of Revenge in Workplace Bullying," *Personality and Individual Differences* 46, no. 3 (2009), pp. 359–364.

70. V. S. Major, K. J. Klein, and M. G. Ehrhart, "Work Time, Work Interference with Family, and Psychological Distress," *Journal of Applied Psychology,* June 2002, pp. 427–436. See also P. E. Spector, C. L. Cooper, S. Poelmans, T. D. Allen, M. O'Driscoll, J. I. Sanchez, et al., "A Cross-National Comparative Study of Work-Family Stressors, Working Hours, and Well-Being: China and Latin America Versus the Anglo World," *Personnel Psychology,* Spring 2004, pp. 119–142.

71. D. L. Nelson and C. Sutton, "Chronic Work Stress and Coping: A Longitudinal Study and Suggested New Directions," *Academy of Management Journal,* December 1990, pp. 859–869.

72. H. Selye, *The Stress of Life,* rev. ed. (New York: McGraw-Hill, 1956).

73. S. J. Motowidlo, J. S. Packard, and M. R. Manning, "Occupational Stress: Its Causes and Consequences for Job Performance," *Journal of Applied Psychology,* November 1987, pp. 619–620.

74. See J. B. Halbesleben, "Sources of Social Support and Burnout: A Meta-analytic Test of the Conservation of Resources Model," *Journal of Applied Psychology* 91, no. 5 (2006), pp. 1134–1145; N. Bolger and D. Amarel, "Effects of Social Support Visibility on Adjustment to Stress: Experimental Evidence," *Journal of Applied Psychology* 92, no. 3

(2007), pp. 458–475; and N. A. Bowling, T. A. Beehr, and W. M. Swader, "Giving and Receiving Social Support at Work: The Roles of Personality and Reciprocity," *Journal of Vocational Behavior* 67 (2005), pp. 476–489.

75. R. Williams, *The Trusting Heart: Great News About Type A Behavior* (New York: Times Books, 1989).

76. R. J. Burke, A. M. Richardson, and M. Mortinussen, "Workaholism Among Norwegian Managers: Work and Well-Being Outcomes," *Journal of Organizational Change Management* 7 (2004), pp. 459-470; and W. B. Schaufeli, T. W. Taris, and W. van Rhenen, "Workaholism, Burnout, and Work Engagement: Three of a Kind or Three Different Kinds of Employee Well-Being," *Applied Psychology: An International Review* 57, no. 2 (2008), pp. 173–203.

77. Schuler, "Definition and Conceptualization of Stress," pp. 200–205; and R. L. Kahn and M. Byosiere, "Stress in Organizations," in M. D. Dunnette and L. M. Hough (eds.), *Handbook of Industrial and Organizational Psychology,* 2nd ed., vol. 3 (Palo Alto, CA: Consulting sychologists Press, 1992), pp. 604–610.

78. See T. A. Beehr and J. E. Newman, "Job Stress, Employee Health, and Organizational Effectiveness: A Facet Analysis, Model, and Literature Review," *Personnel Psychology,* Winter 1978, pp. 665–699; and B. D. Steffy and J. W. Jones, "Workplace Stress and Indicators of Coronary-Disease Risk," *Academy of Management Journal,* September 1988, pp. 686–698.

79. J. Schaubroeck, J. R. Jones, and J. L. Xie, "Individual Differences in Utilizing Control to Cope with Job Demands: Effects on Susceptibility to Infectious Disease," *Journal of Applied Psychology,* April 2001, pp. 265–278.

80. Steffy and Jones, "Workplace Stress and Indicators of Coronary-Disease Risk," p. 687.

81. C. L. Cooper and J. Marshall, "Occupational Sources of Stress: A Review of the Literature Relating to Coronary Heart Disease and Mental Ill Health," *Journal of Occupational Psychology* 49, no. 1 (1976), pp. 11–28.

82. J. R. Hackman and G. R. Oldham, "Development of the Job Diagnostic Survey," *Journal of Applied Psychology,* April 1975, pp. 159–170.

83. L. L. Meier, N. K. Semmer, A. Elfering, and N. Jacobshagen, "The Double Meaning of Control: Three-Way Interactions Between Internal Resources, Job Control, and Stressors at Work," *Journal of Occupational Health Psychology* 13, no. 3 (2008), pp. 244–258.

84. E. M. de Croon, J. K. Sluiter, R. W. B. Blonk, J. P. J. Broersen, and M. H. W. Frings-Dresen, "Stressful Work, Psychological Job Strain, and Turnover: A 2-Year Prospective Cohort Study of Truck Drivers," *Journal of Applied Psychology,* June 2004, pp. 442–454; and R. Cropanzano, D. E. Rupp, and Z. S. Byrne, "The Relationship of Emotional Exhaustion to Work Attitudes, Job Performance, and Organizational Citizenship Behaviors," *Journal of Applied Psychology,* February 2003. pp. 160–169.

85. See, for instance, S. Zivnuska, C. Kiewitz, W. A. Hochwarter, P. L. Perrewe, and K. L. Zellars, "What Is Too Much or Too Little? The Curvilinear Effects of Job Tension on Turnover Intent, Value Attainment, and Job Satisfaction," *Journal of Applied Social Psychology,* July 2002, pp. 1344–1360.

86. L. A. Muse, S. G. Harris, and H. S. Field, "Has the Inverted-U Theory of Stress and Job Performance Had a Fair Test?" *Human Performance* 16, no. 4 (2003), pp. 349–364.

87. The following discussion has been influenced by J. E. Newman and T. A. Beehr, "Personal and Organizational Strategies for Handling Job Stress," *Personnel Psychology,* Spring 1979, pp. 1–38; J. M. Ivancevich and M. T. Matteson, "Organizational Level Stress Management Interventions: A Review and Recommendations," *Journal of Organizational Behavior Management,* Fall–Winter 1986, pp. 229–248; M. T. Matteson and J. M. Ivancevich, "Individual Stress Management Interventions: Evaluation of Techniques," *Journal of Management Psychology,* January 1987, pp. 24–30; J. M. Ivancevich, M. T. Matteson, S. M. Freedman, and J. S. Phillips, "Worksite Stress Management Interventions," *American Psychologist,* February 1990, pp. 252–261; and R. Schwarzer, "Manage Stress at Work Through Preventive and Proactive Coping," in E. A. Locke (ed.), *Handbook of Principles of Organizational Behavior* (Malden, MA: Blackwell, 2004), pp. 342–355.

88. T. H. Macan, "Time Management: Test of a Process Model," *Journal of Applied Psychology,* June 1994, pp. 381–391; and B. J. C. Claessens, W. Van Eerde, C. G. Rutte, and R. A. Roe, "Planning Behavior and Perceived Control of Time at Work," *Journal of Organizational Behavior,* December 2004, pp. 937–950.

89. See, for example, G. Lawrence-Ell, *The Invisible Clock: A Practical Revolution in Finding Time for Everyone and Everything* (Seaside Park, NJ: Kingsland Hall, 2002); and B. Tracy, *Time Power* (New York: AMACOM, 2004).

90. S. A. Devi, "Aging Brain: Prevention of Oxidative Stress by Vitamin E and Exercise," *ScientificWorldJournal* 9 (2009), pp. 366–372. See also J. Kiely and G. Hodgson, "Stress in the Prison Service: The Benefits of Exercise Programs," *Human Relations,* June 1990, pp. 551–572.

91. E. J. Forbes and R. J. Pekala, "Psychophysiological Effects of Several Stress Management Techniques," *Psychological Reports,* February 1993, pp. 19–27; and M. Der Hovanesian, "Zen and the Art of Corporate Productivity," *BusinessWeek* (July 28, 2003), p. 56.

92. E. R. Greenglass and L. Fiksenbaum, "Proactive Coping, Positive Affect, and Well-Being: Testing for Mediation Using Path Analysis," *European Psychologist* 14, no. 1 (2009), pp. 29–39; and P. Miquelon and R. J. Vallerand, "Goal Motives, Well-Being, and Physical Health: Happiness and Self-Realization as Psychological Resources under Challenge," *Motivation and Emotion* 30, no. 4 (2006), pp. 259–272.

93. S. E. Jackson, "Participation in Decision Making as a Strategy for Reducing Job-Related Strain," *Journal of Applied Psychology,* February 1983, pp. 3–19.

94. S. Greengard, "It's About Time," *Industry Week,* February 7, 2000, pp. 47–50; S. Nayyar, "Gimme a Break," *American Demographics,* June 2002, p. 6; S. Greengard, "It's About Time," *IndustryWeek,* February 7, 2000, pp. 47–50; and S. Nayyar, "Gimme a Break," *American Demographics,* June 2002, p. 6.

95. See, for instance, B. Leonard, "Health Care Costs Increase Interest in Wellness Programs," *HRMagazine,* September 2001, pp. 35–36; and "Healthy, Happy and Productive," *Training,* February 2003, p. 16.

96. K. M. Richardson and H. R. Rothstein, "Effects of Occupational Stress Management Intervention Programs: A Meta-analysis," *Journal of Occupational Health Psychology* 13, no. 1 (2008), pp. 69–93.

97. D. Brown, "Wellness Programs Bring Healthy Bottom Line," *Canadian HR Reporter,* December 17, 2001, pp. 1 and ff.

98. See S. Shane, S. Venkataraman, and I. MacMillan, "Cultural Differences in Innovation Championing Strategies," *Journal of Management* 21, no. 5 (1995), pp. 931–952.

99. J. Chen, C. Silverthorne, and J. Hung, "Organization Communication, Job Stress, Organizational Commitment, and Job Performance of Accounting Professionals in Taiwan and America," *Leadership & Organization Development Journal* 27, no. 4 (2006), pp. 242–249; C. Liu, P. E. Spector, and L. Shi, "Cross-National Job Stress: A Quantitative and Qualitative Study," *Journal of Organizational Behavior,* February 2007, pp. 209–239.

100. P. E. Spector, T. D. Allen, S. A. Y. Poelmans, L. M. Lapierre, C. L. Cooper, M. O'Driscoll, et al., "Cross National Differences in Relationships of Work Demands, Job Satisfaction, and Turnover Intention with Work-Family Conflict," *Personnel Psychology* 60, no. 4 (2007), pp. 805–835.

101. H. M. Addae and X. Wang, "Stress at Work: Linear and Curvilinear Effects of Psychological-, Job-, and Organization-Related Factors: An Exploratory Study of Trinidad and Tobago," *International Journal of Stress Management,* November 2006, pp. 476–493.

102. P. E. Spector et al., "A Cross-National Comparative Study of Work-Family Stressors, Working Hours, and Well-Being: China and Latin America Versus the Anglo World," *Personnel Psychology,* Spring 2004, pp. 119–142.

103. P. S. Goodman and L. B. Kurke, "Studies of Change in Organizations: A Status Report," in P. S. Goodman (ed.), *Change in Organizations* (San Francisco: Jossey-Bass, 1982), p. 1.

104. Kahn and Byosiere, "Stress in Organizations," pp. 605–608.

105. For contrasting views on episodic and continuous change, see K. E. Weick and R. E. Quinn, "Organizational Change and Development," in J. T. Spence, J. M. Darley, and D. J. Foss (eds.), *Annual Review of Psychology,* vol. 50 (Palo Alto, CA: Annual Reviews, 1999), pp. 361–386.

106. This perspective is based on P. B. Vaill, *Managing as a Performing Art: New Ideas for a World of Chaotic Change* (San Francisco: Jossey-Bass, 1989).

107. J. D. Breul, "Setting Stretch Goals Helps Agencies Exceed Their Reach," *Government Leader 1,* no. 9 (September/October 2006), www.governmentleader.com/issues/1_9/commentary/205-1.html); G. Stoller, "Frequent Business Travelers Pack Guilt, *USA Today* (June 22, 2006), www.usatoday.com/money/biztravel/2006-06-21-road-warriors-usat_x.htm.

Appendix A Research in Organizational Behavior

> For every complex problem, there is a solution that is simple, neat, and wrong.
> —H.L. Mencken

A number of years ago, a friend of mine was excited because he had read about the findings from a research study that finally, once and for all, resolved the question of what it takes to make it to the top in a large corporation. I doubted there was any simple answer to this question but, not wanting to dampen his enthusiasm, I asked him to tell me of what he had read. The answer, according to my friend, was *participation in college athletics*. To say I was skeptical of his claim is a gross understatement, so I asked him to tell me more.

The study encompassed 1,700 successful senior executives at the 500 largest U.S. corporations. The researchers found that half of these executives had played varsity-level college sports.[1] My friend, who happens to be good with statistics, informed me that since fewer than 2 percent of all college students participate in intercollegiate athletics, the probability of this finding occurring by mere chance is less than 1 in 10 million! He concluded his analysis by telling me that, based on this research, I should encourage my management students to get into shape and to make one of the varsity teams.

My friend was somewhat perturbed when I suggested that his conclusions were likely to be flawed. These executives were all males who attended college in the 1940s and 1950s. Would his advice be meaningful to females in the twenty-first century? These executives also weren't your typical college students. For the most part, they had attended elite private colleges such as Princeton and Amherst, where a large proportion of the student body participates in intercollegiate sports. And these "jocks" hadn't necessarily played football or basketball; many had participated in golf, tennis, baseball, cross-country running, crew, rugby, and similar minor sports. Moreover, maybe the researchers had confused the direction of causality. That is, maybe individuals with the motivation and ability to make it to the top of a large corporation are drawn to competitive activities like college athletics.

My friend was guilty of misusing research data. Of course, he is not alone. We are all continually bombarded with reports of experiments that link certain substances to cancer in mice and surveys that show changing attitudes toward sex among college students, for example. Many of these studies are carefully designed, with great caution taken to note the implications and limitations of the findings. But some studies are poorly designed, making their conclusions at best suspect, and at worst meaningless.

Rather than attempting to make you a researcher, the purpose of this appendix is to increase your awareness as a consumer of behavioral research. A knowledge of research methods will allow you to appreciate more fully the care in data collection that underlies the information and conclusions presented in this text. Moreover, an understanding of research methods will make you a more skilled evaluator of the OB studies you will encounter in business and professional journals. So an appreciation of behavioral research is important because (1) it's the foundation on which the theories in this text are built, and (2) it will benefit you in future years when you read reports of research and attempt to assess their value.

Purposes of Research

Research is concerned with the systematic gathering of information. Its purpose is to help us in our search for the truth. Although we will never find ultimate truth—in our case, that would be to know precisely how any person or group would behave in any organizational context—ongoing research adds to our body of OB knowledge by supporting some theories, contradicting others, and suggesting new theories to replace those that fail to gain support.

Research Terminology

Researchers have their own vocabulary for communicating among themselves and with outsiders. The following briefly defines some of the more popular terms you're likely to encounter in behavioral science studies.[2]

Variable

A *variable* is any general characteristic that can be measured and that changes in amplitude, intensity, or both. Some examples of OB variables found in this textbook are job satisfaction, employee productivity, work stress, ability, personality, and group norms.

Hypothesis

A tentative explanation of the relationship between two or more variables is called a *hypothesis*. My friend's statement that participation in college athletics leads to a top executive position in a large corporation is an example of a hypothesis. Until confirmed by empirical research, a hypothcsis remains only a tentative explanation.

Dependent Variable

A *dependent variable* is a response that is affected by an independent variable. In terms of the hypothesis, it is the variable that the researcher is interested in explaining. Referring back to our opening example, the dependent variable in my friend's hypothesis was executive succession. In organizational behavior research, the most popular dependent variables are productivity, absenteeism, turnover, job satisfaction, and organizational commitment.[3]

Independent Variable

An *independent variable* is the presumed cause of some change in the dependent variable. Participating in varsity athletics was the independent variable in my friend's hypothesis. Popular independent variables studied by OB researchers include intelligence, personality, job satisfaction, experience, motivation, reinforcement patterns, leadership style, reward allocations, selection methods, and organization design.

You may have noticed we said that job satisfaction is frequently used by OB researchers as both a dependent and an independent variable. This is not an error. It merely reflects that the label given to a variable depends on its place in the hypothesis. In the statement "Increases in job satisfaction lead to reduced turnover," job satisfaction is an independent variable. However, in the statement "Increases in money lead to higher job satisfaction," job satisfaction becomes a dependent variable.

Moderating Variable

A *moderating variable* abates the effect of the independent variable on the dependent variable. It might also be thought of as the contingency variable: If X (independent variable), then Y (dependent variable) will occur, but only under conditions Z (moderating variable). To translate this into a real-life example, we might say that if we increase the amount of direct supervision in the work area (X), then there will be a change in worker productivity (Y), but this effect will be moderated by the complexity of the tasks being performed (Z).

Causality

A hypothesis, by definition, implies a relationship. That is, it implies a presumed cause and effect. This direction of cause and effect is called *causality*. Changes in the independent variable are assumed to cause changes in the dependent variable. However, in behavioral research, it's possible to make an incorrect assumption of causality when relationships are found. For example, early behavioral scientists found a relationship between employee satisfaction and productivity. They concluded that a happy worker was a productive worker. Follow-up research has supported the relationship, but disconfirmed the direction of the arrow. The evidence more correctly suggests that high productivity leads to satisfaction rather than the other way around.

Correlation Coefficient

It's one thing to know that there is a relationship between two or more variables. It's another to know the *strength* of that relationship. The term *correlation coefficient* is used to indicate that strength, and is expressed as a number between –1.00 (a perfect negative relationship) and +1.00 (a perfect positive correlation).

When two variables vary directly with one another, the correlation will be expressed as a positive number. When they vary inversely—that is, one increases as the other decreases—the correlation will be expressed as a negative number. If the two variables vary independently of each other, we say that the correlation between them is zero.

For example, a researcher might survey a group of employees to determine the satisfaction of each with his or her job. Then, using company absenteeism reports, the researcher could correlate the job satisfaction scores against individual attendance records to determine whether employees who are more satisfied with their jobs have better attendance records than their counterparts who indicated lower job satisfaction. Let's suppose the researcher found a correlation coefficient of +0.50 between satisfaction and attendance. Would that be a strong association? There is, unfortunately, no precise numerical cutoff separating strong and weak relationships. A standard statistical test would need to be applied to determine whether the relationship was a significant one.

A final point needs to be made before we move on: A correlation coefficient measures only the strength of association between two variables. A high value does *not* imply causality. The length of women's skirts and stock market prices, for instance, have long been noted to be highly correlated, but one should be careful not to infer that a causal relationship between the two exists. In this instance, the high correlation is more happenstance than predictive.

Theory

The final term we introduce in this section is *theory*. Theory describes a set of systematically interrelated concepts or hypotheses that purports to explain and predict phenomena. In OB, theories are also frequently referred to as *models*. We use the two terms interchangeably.

There are no shortages of theories in OB. For instance, we have theories to describe what motivates people, the most effective leadership styles, the best way to resolve conflicts, and how people acquire power. In some cases, we have half a dozen or more separate theories that purport to explain and predict a given phenomenon. In such cases, is one right and the others wrong? No! They tend to reflect science at work—researchers testing previous theories, modifying them, and, when appropriate, proposing new models that may prove to have higher explanatory and predictive powers. Multiple theories attempting to explain common phenomena merely attest that OB is an active discipline, still growing and evolving.

Evaluating Research

As a potential consumer of behavioral research, you should follow the dictum of *caveat emptor*—let the buyer beware! In evaluating any research study, you need to ask three questions.[4]

Is it valid? Is the study actually measuring what it claims to be measuring? A number of psychological tests have been discarded by employers in recent years because they have not been found to be valid measures of the applicants' ability to do a given job successfully. But the validity issue is relevant to all research studies. So, if you find a study that links cohesive work teams with higher productivity, you want to know how each of these variables was measured and whether it is actually measuring what it is supposed to be measuring.

Is it reliable? Reliability refers to consistency of measurement. If you were to have your height measured every day with a wooden yardstick, you'd get highly reliable results. On the other hand, if you were measured each day by an elastic tape measure, there would probably be considerable disparity between your height measurements from one day to the next. Your height, of course, doesn't change from day to day. The variability is due to the unreliability of the measuring device. So if a company asked a group of its employees to complete a reliable job satisfaction questionnaire, and then repeat the questionnaire six months later, we'd expect the results to be very similar—provided nothing changed in the interim that might significantly affect employee satisfaction.

Is it generalizable? Are the results of the research study generalizable to groups of individuals other than those who participated in the original study? Be aware, for example, of the limitations that might exist in research that uses college students as subjects. Are the findings in such studies generalizable to full-time employees in real jobs? Similarly, how generalizable to the overall work population are the results from a study that assesses job stress among 10 nuclear power plant engineers in the hamlet of Mahone Bay, Nova Scotia?

Research Design

Doing research is an exercise in trade-offs. Richness of information typically comes with reduced generalizability. The more a researcher seeks to control for confounding variables, the less realistic his or her results are likely to be. High precision, generalizability, and control almost always translate into higher costs. When researchers make choices about whom they'll study, where their research will be done, the methods they'll use to collect data, and so on, they must make some concessions. Good research designs are not perfect, but they do carefully reflect the questions being addressed. Keep these facts in mind as we review the strengths and weaknesses of five popular research designs: case studies, field surveys, laboratory experiments, field experiments, and aggregate quantitative reviews.

Case Study

You pick up a copy of Soichiro Honda's autobiography. In it he describes his impoverished childhood; his decisions to open a small garage, assemble motorcycles, and eventually build automobiles; and how this led to the creation of one of the largest and most successful corporations in the world. Or you're in a business class and the instructor distributes a 50-page handout covering two companies: Wal-Mart and Kmart. The handout details the two firms' histories; describes their corporate strategies, management philosophies, and merchandising plans; and includes copies of their recent balance sheets and income statements. The instructor asks the class members to read the handout, analyze the data, and determine why Wal-Mart has been so much more successful than Kmart in recent years.

Soichiro Honda's autobiography and the Wal-Mart and Kmart handouts are case studies. Drawn from real-life situations, case studies present an in-depth analysis of one setting. They are thorough descriptions, rich in details about an individual, a group, or an organization. The primary source of information in case studies is obtained through observation, occasionally backed up by interviews and a review of records and documents.

Case studies have their drawbacks. They're open to the perceptual bias and subjective interpretations of the observer. The reader of a case is captive to what the observer/case writer chooses to include and exclude. Cases also trade off generalizability for depth of information and richness of detail. Because it's always dangerous to generalize from a sample of one, case studies make it difficult to prove or reject a hypothesis. On the other hand, you can't ignore the in-depth analysis that cases often provide. They are an excellent device for initial exploratory research and for evaluating real-life problems in organizations.

Field Survey

A lengthy questionnaire was created to assess the use of ethics policies, formal ethics structures, formalized activities such as ethics training, and executive involvement in ethics programs among billion-dollar corporations. The public affairs or corporate communications office of all *Fortune* 500 industrial firms and 500 service corporations were contacted to get the name and address of the "officer most responsible for dealing with ethics and conduct issues" in each firm. The questionnaire, with a cover letter explaining the nature of the study, was mailed to these 1,000 officers. Of the total, 254 returned a completed questionnaire, for a response rate just above 25 percent. The results of the survey found, among other things, that 77 percent had formal codes of ethics and 54 percent had a single officer specifically assigned to deal with ethics and conduct issues.[5]

The preceding study illustrates a typical field survey. A sample of respondents (in this case, 1,000 corporate officers in the largest U.S. publicly held corporations) was selected to represent a larger group that was under examination (billion-dollar U.S. business firms). The respondents were then surveyed using a questionnaire or interviewed to collect data on particular characteristics (the content and structure of ethics programs and practices) of interest to the researchers. The standardization of response items allows for data to be easily quantified, analyzed, and summarized, and for the researchers to make inferences from the representative sample about the larger population.

The field survey provides economies for doing research. It's less costly to sample a population than to obtain data from every member of that population. (There are, for instance, more than 5,000 U.S. business firms with sales in excess of a billion dollars; and since some of these are privately held and don't release financial data to the public, they are excluded from the *Fortune* list). Moreover, as the ethics study illustrates, field surveys provide an efficient way to find out how people feel about issues or how they say they behave. These data can then be easily quantified.

But the field survey has a number of potential weaknesses. First, mailed questionnaires rarely obtain 100 percent returns. Low response rates call into question whether conclusions based on respondents' answers are generalizable to nonrespondents. Second, the format is better at tapping respondents' attitudes and perceptions than behaviors. Third, responses can suffer from social desirability; that is, people saying what they think the researcher wants to hear. Fourth, since field surveys are designed to focus on specific issues, they're a relatively poor means of acquiring depth of information. Finally, the quality of the generalizations is largely a factor of the population chosen. Responses from executives at *Fortune* 500 firms, for instance, tell us nothing about small- or medium-sized firms or not-for-profit organizations. In summary, even a well-designed field survey trades off depth of information for breadth, generalizability, and economic efficiencies.

Laboratory Experiment

The following study is a classic example of the laboratory experiment. A researcher, Stanley Milgram, wondered how far individuals would go in following commands. If subjects were placed in the role of a teacher in a learning experiment and told by an experimenter to administer a shock to a learner each time that learner made a mistake, would the subjects follow the commands of the experimenter? Would their willingness to comply decrease as the intensity of the shock was increased?

To test these hypotheses, Milgram hired a set of subjects. Each was led to believe that the experiment was to investigate the effect of punishment on memory. Their job was to act as teachers and administer punishment whenever the learner made a mistake on the learning test.

Punishment was administered by an electric shock. The subject sat in front of a shock generator with 30 levels of shock—beginning at zero and progressing in 15-volt increments to a high of 450 volts. The demarcations of these positions ranged from "Slight Shock" at 15 volts to "Danger: Severe Shock" at 450 volts. To increase the realism of the experiment, the subjects received a sample shock of 45 volts and saw the learner—a pleasant, mild-mannered man about 50 years old—strapped into an "electric chair" in an adjacent room. Of course, the learner was an actor, and the electric shocks were phony, but the subjects didn't know this.

Taking his seat in front of the shock generator, the subject was directed to begin at the lowest shock level and to increase the shock intensity to the next level each time the learner made a mistake or failed to respond.

When the test began, the shock intensity rose rapidly because the learner made many errors. The subject got verbal feedback from the learner: At 75 volts, the learner began to grunt and moan; at 150 volts, he demanded to be released from the experiment; at 180 volts, he cried out that he could no longer stand the pain; and at 300 volts, he insisted that he be let out, yelled about his heart condition, screamed, and then failed to respond to further questions.

Most subjects protested and, fearful they might kill the learner if the increased shocks were to bring on a heart attack, insisted they could not go on with their job. Hesitations or protests by the subject were met by the experimenter's statement, "You have no choice, you must go on! Your job is to punish the learner's mistakes." Of course, the subjects did have a choice. All they had to do was stand up and walk out.

The majority of the subjects dissented. But dissension isn't synonymous with disobedience. Sixty-two percent of the subjects increased the shock level to the maximum of 450 volts. The average level of shock administered by the remaining 38 percent was nearly 370 volts.[6]

In a laboratory experiment such as that conducted by Milgram, an artificial environment is created by the researcher. Then the researcher manipulates an independent variable under controlled conditions. Finally, since all other things are held equal, the researcher is able to conclude that any change in the dependent variable is due to the manipulation or change imposed on the independent variable. Note that, because of the controlled conditions, the researcher is able to imply causation between the independent and dependent variables.

The laboratory experiment trades off realism and generalizability for precision and control. It provides a high degree of control over variables and precise measurement of those variables. But findings from laboratory studies are often difficult to generalize to the real world of work. This is because the artificial laboratory rarely duplicates the intricacies and nuances of real organizations. In addition, many laboratory experiments deal with phenomena that cannot be reproduced or applied to real-life situations.

Field Experiment

The following is an example of a field experiment. The management of a large company is interested in determining the impact that a four-day workweek would have on employee absenteeism. To be more specific, management wants to know if employees working four 10-hour days have lower absence rates than similar employees working the traditional five-day week of 8 hours each day. Because the company is large, it has a number of manufacturing plants that employ essentially similar workforces. Two of these are chosen for the experiment, both located in the greater Cleveland area. Obviously, it would not be appropriate to compare two similar-sized plants if one is in rural Mississippi and the other is in urban Copenhagen because factors such as national culture, transportation, and weather might be more likely to explain any differences found than changes in the number of days worked per week.

In one plant, the experiment was put into place—workers began the four-day week. At the other plant, which became the control group, no changes were made in the employees' five-day week. Absence data were gathered from the company's records at both locations for a period of 18 months. This extended time period lessened the possibility that any results would be distorted by the mere novelty of changes being implemented in the experimental plant. After 18 months, management found that absenteeism had dropped by 40 percent at the experimental plant, and by only 6 percent in the control plant. Because of the design of this study, management believed that the larger drop in absences at the experimental plant was due to the introduction of the compressed workweek.

The field experiment is similar to the laboratory experiment, except it is conducted in a real organization. The natural setting is more realistic than the laboratory setting, and this enhances validity but hinders control. In addition, unless control groups are maintained, there can be a loss of control if extraneous forces intervene—for example, an employee strike, a major layoff, or a corporate restructuring. Maybe the greatest concern with field studies has to do with organizational selection bias. Not all organizations are going to allow outside researchers to come in and study their employees and operations. This is especially true of organizations that have serious problems. Therefore, since most published studies in OB are done by outside researchers, the selection bias might work toward the publication of studies conducted almost exclusively at successful and well-managed organizations.

Our general conclusion is that, of the four research designs we've discussed to this point, the field experiment typically provides the most valid and generalizable findings and, except for its high cost, trades off the least to get the most.[7]

Aggregate Quantitative Reviews

What's the overall effect of organizational behavior modification (OB Mod) on task performance? There have been a number of field experiments that have sought to throw light on this question. Unfortunately, the wide range of effects from these various studies makes it hard to generalize.

To try to reconcile these diverse findings, two researchers reviewed all the empirical studies they could find on the impact of OB Mod on task performance over a 20-year period.[8] After discarding reports that had inadequate information, had nonquantitative data, or didn't meet all conditions associated with principles of behavioral modification, the researchers narrowed their set to 19 studies that included data on 2,818 individuals. Using an aggregating technique called *meta-analysis,* the researchers were able to synthesize the studies quantitatively and to conclude that the average person's task performance will rise from the 50th percentile to the 67th percentile after an OB Mod intervention.

The OB Mod–task performance review done by these researchers illustrates the use of meta-analysis, a quantitative form of literature review that enables researchers to look at validity findings from a comprehensive set of individual studies, and then apply a formula to them to determine if they consistently produced similar results.[9] If results prove to be consistent, it allows researchers to conclude more confidently that validity is generalizable. Meta-analysis is a means for overcoming the potentially imprecise interpretations of qualitative reviews and to synthesize variations in quantitative studies. In addition, the technique enables researchers to identify potential moderating variables between an independent and a dependent variable.

In the past 25 years, there's been a surge in the popularity of this research method. Why? It appears to offer a more objective means for doing traditional literature reviews. Although the use of meta-analysis requires researchers to make a number of judgment calls, which can introduce a considerable amount of subjectivity into the process, there is no arguing that meta-analysis reviews have now become widespread in the OB literature.

Ethics in Research

Researchers are not always tactful or candid with subjects when they do their studies. For instance, questions in field surveys may be perceived as embarrassing by respondents or as an invasion of privacy. Also, researchers in laboratory studies have been known to deceive participants about the true purpose of their experiment "because they felt deception was necessary to get honest responses."[10]

The "learning experiments" conducted by Stanley Milgram, which were conducted more than 30 years ago, have been widely criticized by psychologists on ethical grounds. He lied to subjects, telling them his study was investigating learning, when, in fact, he was concerned with obedience. The shock machine he used was a fake. Even the "learner" was an accomplice of Milgram's who had been trained to act as if he were hurt and in pain. Yet ethical lapses continue. For instance, in 2001, a professor of organizational behavior at Columbia University sent out a common letter on university letterhead to 240 New York City restaurants in which he detailed how he had eaten at this restaurant with his wife in celebration of their wedding anniversary, how he had gotten food poisoning, and that he had spent the night in his bathroom throwing up.[11] The letter closed with: "Although it is not my intention to file any reports with the Better Business Bureau or the Department of Health, I want you to understand what I went through in anticipation that you will respond accordingly. I await your response." The fictitious letter was part of the professor's study to determine how restaurants responded to complaints. But it created culinary chaos among many of the restaurant owners, managers, and chefs as they reviewed menus and produce deliveries for possibly spoiled food, and questioned kitchen workers about possible lapses. A follow-up letter of apology from the university for "an egregious error in judgment by a junior faculty member" did little to offset the distress it created for those affected.

Professional associations like the American Psychological Association, the American Sociological Association, and the Academy of Management have published formal guidelines for the conduct of research. Yet the ethical debate continues. On one side are those who argue that strict ethical controls can damage the scientific validity of an experiment and cripple future research. Deception, for example, is often necessary to avoid contaminating results. Moreover, proponents of minimizing ethical controls note that few subjects have been appreciably harmed by deceptive experiments. Even in Milgram's highly manipulative experiment, only 1.3 percent of the subjects reported negative feelings about their experience. The other side of this debate focuses on the rights of participants. Those favoring strict ethical controls argue that no procedure should ever be emotionally or physically distressing to subjects, and that, as professionals, researchers are obliged to be completely honest with their subjects and to protect the subjects' privacy at all costs.

Summary

The subject of organizational behavior is composed of a large number of theories that are research based. Research studies, when cumulatively integrated, become theories, and theories are proposed and followed by research studies designed to validate them. The concepts that make up OB, therefore, are only as valid as the research that supports them.

The topics and issues in this book are for the most part research-derived. They represent the result of systematic information gathering rather than merely hunch, intuition, or opinion. This doesn't mean, of course, that we have all the answers to OB issues. Many require far more corroborating evidence. The generalizability of others is limited by the research methods used. But new information is being created and published at an accelerated rate. To keep up with the latest findings, we strongly encourage you to regularly review the latest research in organizational behavior. The more academic work can be found in journals such as the *Academy of Management Journal, Academy of Management Review, Administrative Science Quarterly, Human Relations, Journal of Applied Psychology, Journal of Management, Journal of Organizational Behavior,* and *Leadership Quarterly.* For more practical interpretations of OB research findings, you may want to read the *Academy of Management Execuive, California Management Review, Harvard Business Review, Organizational Dynamics,* and the *Sloan Management Review.*

Endnotes

1. J. A. Byrne, "Executive Sweat," *Forbes,* May 20, 1985, pp. 198–200.

2. See D. P. Schwab, *Research Methods for Organizational Behavior* (Mahwah, NJ: Lawrence Erlbaum Associates, 1999); and S. G. Rogelberg (ed.), *Blackwell Handbook of Research Methods in Industrial and Organizational Psychology* (Malden, MA: Blackwell, 2002).

3. B. M. Staw and G. R. Oldham, "Reconsidering Our Dependent Variables: A Critique and Empirical Study," *Academy of Management Journal,* December 1978, pp. 539–559; and B. M. Staw, "Organizational Behavior: A Review and Reformulation of the Field's Outcome Variables," in M. R. Rosenzweig and L. W. Porter (eds.), *Annual Review of Psychology,* vol. 35 (Palo Alto, CA: Annual Reviews, 1984), pp. 627–666.

4. R. S. Blackburn, "Experimental Design in Organizational Settings," in J. W. Lorsch (ed.), *Handbook of Organizational Behavior* (Upper Saddle River, NJ: Prentice Hall, 1987), pp. 127–128; and F. L. Schmidt, C. Viswesvaran, D. S. Ones, "Reliability Is Not Validity and Validity Is Not Reliability," *Personnel Psychology,* Winter 2000, pp. 901–912.

5. G. R. Weaver, L. K. Trevino, and P. L. Cochran, "Corporate Ethics Practices in the Mid-1990's: An Empirical Study of the Fortune 1000," *Journal of Business Ethics,* February 1999, pp. 283–294.

6. S. Milgram, *Obedience to Authority* (New York: Harper & Row, 1974). For a critique of this research, see T. Blass, "Understanding Behavior in the Milgram Obedience Experiment: The Role of Personality, Situations, and Their Interactions," *Journal of Personality and Social Psychology,* March 1991, pp. 398–413.

7. See, for example, W. N. Kaghan, A. L. Strauss, S. R. Barley, M. Y. Brannen, and R. J. Thomas, "The Practice and Uses of Field Research in the 21st Century Organization," *Journal of Management Inquiry,* March 1999, pp. 67–81.

8. A. D. Stajkovic and F. Luthans, "A Meta-Analysis of the Effects of Organizational Behavior Modification on Task Performance, 1975–1995," *Academy of Management Journal,* October 1997, pp. 1122–1149.

9. See, for example, K. Zakzanis, "The Reliability of Meta Analytic Review," *Psychological Reports,* August 1998, pp. 215–222; C. Ostroff and D. A. Harrison, "Meta-Analysis, Level of Analysis, and Best Estimates of Population Correlations: Cautions for Interpreting Meta-Analytic Results in Organizational Behavior," *Journal of Applied Psychology,* April 1999, pp. 260–270; R. Rosenthal and M. R. DiMatteo, "Meta-Analysis: Recent Developments in Quantitative Methods for Literature Reviews," in S. T. Fiske, D. L. Schacter, and C. Zahn-Wacher (eds.), *Annual Review of Psychology,* vol. 52 (Palo Alto, CA: Annual Reviews, 2001), pp. 59–82; and F. L. Schmidt and J. E. Hunter, "Meta-Analysis," in N. Anderson, D. S. Ones, H. K. Sinangil, and C. Viswesvaran (eds.), *Handbook of Industrial, Work & Organizational Psychology,* vol. 1 (Thousand Oaks, CA: Sage, 2001), pp. 51–70.

10. For more on ethical issues in research, see T. L. Beauchamp, R. R. Faden, R. J. Wallace, Jr., and L. Walters (eds.), *Ethical Issues in Social Science Research* (Baltimore, MD: Johns Hopkins University Press, 1982); and J. G. Adair, "Ethics of Psychological Research: New Policies, Continuing Issues, New Concerns," *Canadian Psychology,* February 2001, pp. 25–37.

11. J. Kifner, "Scholar Sets Off Gastronomic False Alarm," *New York Times,* September 8, 2001, p. A1.

Comprehensive Cases

Managing Motivation in a Difficult Economy

Learning Goals

In this case, you'll have an opportunity to assess a motivational program designed to re-energize a troubled company's workforce. Acting on behalf of the company's executive board, you'll evaluate the board's current strategy based on survey data. You'll also advise board members about improving the effectiveness of this program based on what you've learned about goal setting and motivation in organizations.

Major Topic Areas

- Changing nature of work
- Diversity and age
- Goal setting
- Organizational downsizing
- Organizational justice

The Scenario

Morgan-Moe's drug stores are in trouble. A major regional player in the retail industry, the company has hundreds of stores in the upper Midwest. Unfortunately, a sharp decline in the region's manufacturing economy has put management in a serious financial bind. Revenues have been consistently dwindling. Customers spend less, and the stores have had to switch their focus to very low-margin commodities, such as milk and generic drugs, rather than the high-margin impulse-buy items that used to be the company's bread and butter. The firm has had to close quite a few locations, reversing its expansion plans for the first time since it incorporated.

Being that this is uncharted territory for the company, Jim Claussen, vice president for human relations, had been struggling with how to address the issue with employees. As the company's fortunes worsened, he could see that employees were becoming more and more disaffected. Their insecurity about their jobs was taking a toll on attitudes. The company's downsizing was big news, and the employees didn't like what they were hearing.

Media reports of Morgan-Moe's store closings have focused on the lack of advance notice or communication from the company's corporate offices, as well as the lack of severance payments for departing employees. In the absence of official information, rumors and gossip have spread like wildfire among remaining employees. A few angry blogs developed by laid-off employees, like IHateMorganMoe.blogspot.com, have made the morale and public relations picture even worse.

Morgan-Moe is changing in other ways as well. The average age of its workforce is increasing rapidly. A couple of factors have contributed to this shift. First, fewer qualified young people are around because many families have moved south to find jobs. Second, stores have been actively encouraged to hire older workers, such as retirees looking for some supplemental income. Managers are very receptive to these older workers because they are more mature, miss fewer days of work, and do not have child-care responsibilities. They are also often more qualified than younger workers because they have more experience, sometimes in the managerial or executive ranks.

These older workers have been a great asset to the company in troubled times, but they are especially likely to leave if things get bad. If these older workers start to leave the company, taking their hard-earned experience with them, it seems likely that Morgan-Moe will sink deeper toward bankruptcy.

The System

Claussen wasn't quite sure how to respond to employees' sense of hopelessness and fear until a friend gave him a book entitled *Man's Search for Meaning*. The book was written by a psychologist named Victor Frankl who survived the concentration camps at Auschwitz. Frankl found that those who had a clear sense of purpose, a reason to live, were more likely to persevere in the face of nearly unspeakable suffering. Something about this book, and its advocacy of finding meaning and direction as a way to triumph over adversity, really stuck with Claussen. He thought he might be able to apply its lessons to his workforce. He proposed the idea of a new direction for management to the company's executive committee, and they reluctantly agreed to try his suggestions.

Over the last 6 months, stores throughout the company have used a performance management system that, as Claussen says, "gets people to buy into the idea of performing so that they can see some real results in their stores. It's all about seeing that your work serves a broader purpose. I read about how some companies have been sharing store performance information with employees to get them to understand what their jobs really mean and participate in making changes, and I thought that was something we'd be able to do."

The HR team came up with five options for the management system. Corporate allowed individual managers to choose the option they thought would work best with their employees so that managers wouldn't feel too much like a rapid change was being forced on them. Program I is opting out of the new idea, continuing to stay the course and providing employees with little to no information or opportunities for participation. Program II tracks employee absence and sick leave and shares that information with individual employees, giving them feedback about things they can control. Management takes no further action. Program III tracks sales and inventory replacement rates across shifts. As in Program II, information is shared with employees, but without providing employee feedback about absence and sick leave. Program IV, the most comprehensive, tracks the same information as Programs II and III. Managers communicate it in weekly brainstorming sessions, during which employees try to determine what they can do better in the future and make suggestions for improving store performance. Program V keeps the idea of brainstorming but doesn't provide employees with information about their behavior or company profits.

Since implementing the system, Claussen has spoken with several managers about what motivated them to choose the program they did. Artie Washington, who chose Program IV, said, "I want to have my employees' input on how to keep the store running smoothly. Everybody worries about their job security in this economy. Letting them know what's going on and giving them ways to change things keeps them involved."

Betty Alvarez couldn't disagree more. She selected Program I. "I would rather have my employees doing their jobs than going to meetings to talk about doing their jobs. That's what management is for." Michael

Ostremski, another proponent of Program I, added, "It's okay for the employees to feel a little uncertain—if they think we're in the clear, they'll slack off. If they think we're in trouble, they'll give up."

Cal Martins also questions the need to provide information to the whole team, but he chose Program II. "A person should know where he or she stands in the job, but they don't have to know about everyone else. It creates unnecessary tension."

This is somewhat similar to Cindy Ang's reason for picking Program V. "When we have our brainstorming meetings, I learn what they [the employees] think is most pressing, not what some spreadsheet says. It gives me a better feel for what's going on in my store. Numbers count, of course, but they don't tell you everything. I was also a little worried that employees would be upset if they saw that we aren't performing well."

Results to Date

Claussen is convinced the most elaborate procedure (Program IV) is the most effective, but not everyone in the executive committee is won over by his advocacy. Although they have supported the test implementation of the system because it appears to have relatively low costs, others on the committee want to see results. CEO Jean Masterson has asked for a complete breakdown of the performance of the various stores over the past 4 years. She's especially interested in seeing how sales figures and turnover rates have been affected by the new program.

The company has been collecting data in spreadsheets on sales and turnover rates, and it prepared the following report, which also estimates the dollar cost of staff time taken up in each method. These costs are based on the number of hours employees spend working on the program multiplied by their wage rate. Estimates of turnover, profit, and staff time are collected per store. Profit and turnover data include means and standard deviations across locations; profit is net of the monthly time cost. Turnover information refers to the percentage of employees who either quit or are terminated in a month.

To see if any patterns emerged in managers' selection of programs, the company calculated relationships between program selection and various attributes of the stores. Program I was selected most frequently by the oldest stores and those in the most economically distressed areas. Programs II and III were selected most frequently by stores in urban areas and in areas where the workforce was younger on average. Programs IV and V were selected most frequently in stores in rural areas, and especially where the workforce is older on average.

Program	Methods	# of Stores	Average Turnover	Weekly Profit per Month	Monthly Staff Time Cost
Program I	Traditional management	83	Mean = 30% SD = 10%	Mean = $5,700 SD = $3,000	None
Program II	Share absence and sick leave	27	Mean = 23% SD = 14%	Mean = $7,000 SD = $5,800	$1,960
Program III	Share sales and inventory	35	Mean = 37% SD = 20%	Mean = $11,000 SD = $2,700	$2,440
Program IV	Share information and brainstorm	67	Mean = 17% SD = 20%	Mean = $13,000 SD = $3,400	$3,420
Program V	Brainstorm without sharing information	87	Mean = 21% SD = 12%	Mean = $14,000 SD = $2,400	$2,750

Your Assignment

Your task is to prepare a report for the company's executive committee on the effectiveness of these programs. Make certain it is in the form of a professional business document. Your audience won't necessarily know about the organizational principles you're describing, so make sure you provide detailed explanations that someone in a real business can understand.

When you write, make sure you touch on the following points:

1. Consider the five management systems as variables in an experiment. Identify the independent and dependent variables and explain how they are related to one another.
2. Based on the discussion of independent and dependent variables in the textbook, is there anything else you'd like to measure as an outcome?
3. Look over the data and decide which method of management appears most effective in generating revenues and reducing turnover, and why. Which methods appear least effective, and why?
4. Are there any concerns you have about this data?
   a. Does a comparison of the number of stores using each method influence your conclusions at all?
   b. Does the fact that managers are selecting the specific program to use (including Program I, which

continues the status quo) affect the inferences you can draw about program success?
   c. What are the advantages of randomly assigning different conditions to the stores instead of using this self-selection process?
5. How does the changing nature of the workforce and the economy, described in your textbook and in the case, affect your conclusions about how to manage retail employees? Does the participation of a more experienced workforce help or hurt these programs? Why might these programs work differently in an economy that isn't doing so poorly?
6. Claussen essentially designed the program on his own, with very little research into goal setting and motivation. Based on your textbook, how well has he done? Which parts of the program appear to fit well with research evidence on goal setting? What parts would you change to get more substantial improvements in employee motivation?
7. Describe the feelings employees might have when these systems are implemented that could help or hinder the program's success. What advice would you give managers about how to implement the programs so they match the principles of organizational justice described in your textbook?

CASE 2

Repairing Jobs That Fail to Satisfy

Learning Goals

Companies often divide up work as a way to improve efficiency, but specialization can lead to negative consequences. DrainFlow is a company that has effectively used specialization to reduce costs relative to its competitors' costs for years, but rising customer complaints suggest the firm's strong position may be slipping. After reading the case, you will suggest some ways it can create more interesting work for employees. You'll also tackle the problem of finding people qualified and ready to perform the multiple responsibilities required in these jobs.

Major Topic Areas

- Job design
- Job satisfaction
- Personality
- Emotional labor

The Scenario

DrainFlow is a large residential and commercial plumbing maintenance firm that operates around the United States. It has been a major player in residential plumbing for decades, and its familiar rhyming motto, "When Your Drain Won't Go, Call DrainFlow," has been plastered on billboards since the 1960s.

Lee Reynaldo has been a regional manager at DrainFlow for about 2 years. She used to work for a newer competing chain, Lightning Plumber, that has been drawing more and more customers from DrainFlow. Although her job at DrainFlow pays more, Lee isn't happy with the way things are going. She's noticed the work environment just isn't as vital or energetic as the environment she saw at Lightning.

Lee thinks the problem is that employees aren't motivated to provide the type of customer service Lightning Plumber employees offer. She recently sent surveys to customers to collect information about performance, and the data confirmed her fears. Although 60 percent of respondents said they were satisfied with their experience and would use DrainFlow again, 40 percent felt their experience was not good, and 30 percent said they

would use a competitor the next time they had a plumbing problem.

Lee is wondering whether DrainFlow's job design might be contributing to its problems in retaining customers. DrainFlow has about 2,000 employees in four basic job categories: plumbers, plumber's assistants, order processors, and billing representatives. This structure is designed to keep costs as low as possible. Plumbers make very high wages, whereas plumber's assistants make about one-quarter of what a licensed plumber makes. Using plumber's assistants is therefore a very cost-effective strategy that has enabled DrainFlow to easily undercut the competition when it comes to price. Order processors make even less than assistants but about the same as billing processors. All work is very specialized, but employees are often dependent on another job category to perform at their most efficient level.

Like most plumbing companies, DrainFlow gets business mostly from the Yellow Pages and the Internet. Customers either call in to describe a plumbing problem or submit an online request for plumbing services, receiving a return call with information within 24 hours. In either case, DrainFlow's order processors listen to the customer's description of the problem to determine whether a plumber or a plumber's assistant should make the service call. The job is then assigned accordingly, and a service provider goes to the location. When the job has been completed, via cell phone a billing representative relays the fee to the service rep, who presents a bill to the customer for payment. Billing representatives can take customers' credit card payments by phone or e-mail an invoice for online payment.

The Problem

Although specialization does cut costs significantly, Lee is worried about customer dissatisfaction. According to her survey, about 25 percent of customer contacts ended in no service call because customers were confused by the diagnostic questions the order processors asked and because the order processors did not have sufficient knowledge or skill to explain the situation. That means fully one in four people who call DrainFlow to hire a plumber are worse than dissatisfied: they aren't customers at all! The remaining 75 percent of calls that did end in a customer service encounter resulted in other problems.

The most frequent complaints Lee found in the customer surveys were about response time and cost, especially when the wrong person was sent to a job. A plumber's assistant cannot complete a more technically complicated job. The appointment has to be rescheduled, and the customer's time and the staff's time have been wasted. The resulting delay often caused customers in these situations to decline further contact with DrainFlow—many of them decided to go with Lightning Plumber.

"When I arrive at a job I can't take care of," says plumber's assistant Jim Larson, "the customer gets ticked off. They thought they were getting a licensed plumber, since they were calling for a plumber. Telling them they have to have someone else come out doesn't go over well."

On the other hand, when a plumber responds to a job easily handled by a plumber's assistant, the customer is still charged at the plumber's higher pay rate. Licensed plumber Luis Berger also does not like being in the position of giving customers bad news. "If I get called out to do something like snake a drain, the customer isn't expecting a hefty bill. I'm caught between a rock and a hard place—I don't set the rates or make the appointments, but I'm the one who gets it from the customer." Plumbers also resent being sent to do such simple work.

Susie McCarty is one of DrainFlow's order processors. She's frustrated too when the wrong person is sent to a job but feels she and the other order processors are doing the best they can. "We have a survey we're supposed to follow with the calls to find out what the problem is and who needs to take the job," she explains. "The customers don't know that we have a standard form, so

they think we can answer all their questions. Most of us don't know any more about plumbing than the caller. If they don't use the terms on the survey, we don't understand what they're talking about. A plumber would, but we're not plumbers; we just take the calls."

Customer service issues also involve the billing representatives. They are the ones who have to keep contacting customers about payment. "It's not my fault the wrong guy was sent," says Elizabeth Monty. "If two guys went out, that's two trips. If a plumber did the work, you pay plumber rates. Some of these customers don't get that I didn't take their first call, and so I get yelled at." The billing representatives also complain that they see only the tail end of the process, so they don't know what the original call entailed. The job is fairly impersonal, and much of the work is recording customer complaints. Remember—40 percent of customers aren't satisfied, and it's the billing representatives who take the brunt of their negative reactions on the phone.

As you can probably tell, all employees have to engage in emotional labor, as described in your textbook, and many lack the skills or personality traits to complete the customer interaction component of their jobs. They aren't trained to provide customer service, and they see their work mostly in technical, or mechanical, terms. Quite a few are actually anxious about speaking directly with customers. The office staff (order processors and billing representatives) realize customer service is part of their job, but they also find dealing with negative feedback from customers and co-workers taxing.

A couple of years ago a management consulting company was hired to survey DrainFlow worker attitudes. The results showed they were less satisfied than workers in other comparable jobs. The following table provides a breakdown of respondent satisfaction levels across a number of categories:

	DrainFlow Plumbers	DrainFlow Plumber Assistants	DrainFlow Office Workers	Average Plumber	Average Office Workers
I am satisfied with the work I am asked to do.	3.7	2.5	2.5	4.3	3.5
I am satisfied with my working conditions.	3.8	2.4	3.7	4.1	4.2
I am satisfied with my interactions with co-workers.	3.5	3.2	2.7	3.8	3.9
I am satisfied with my interactions with my supervisor.	2.5	2.3	2.2	3.5	3.4

The information about average plumbers and average office workers is taken from the management consulting company's records of other companies. They aren't exactly surprising, given some of the complaints DrainFlow employees have made. Top management is worried about these results, but they haven't been able to formulate a solution. The traditional DrainFlow culture has been focused on cost containment, and the "soft stuff" like employee satisfaction hasn't been a major issue.

The Proposed Solution

The company is in trouble, and as revenues shrink and the cost savings that were supposed to be achieved by dividing up work fail to materialize, a change seems to be in order.

Lee is proposing using cash rewards to improve performance among employees. She thinks if employees were paid based on work outcomes, they'd work harder to satisfy customers. Because it's not easy to measure how satisfied people are with the initial call-in, Lee would like to give the order processors a small reward for every 20 calls successfully completed. For the hands-on work, she'd like to have each billing representative collect information about customer satisfaction for each completed call. If no complaints are made and the job is handled promptly, a moderate cash reward would be given to the plumber or plumber's assistant. If the customer indicates real satisfaction with the service, a larger cash reward would be provided.

Lee also wants to find people who are a better fit with the company's new goals. Current hiring procedure relies on unstructured interviews with each location's general manager, and little consistency is found in the way these managers choose employees. Most lack training in customer service and organizational behavior. Lee thinks it would be better if hiring methods were standardized across all branches in her region to help managers identify recruits who can actually succeed in the job.

Your Assignment

Your task is to prepare a report for Lee on the potential effectiveness of her cash reward and structured-interview programs. Make certain it is in the form of a professional business document that you'd actually give to an experienced manager at this level of a fairly large corporation. Lee is very smart when it comes to managing finances and running a plumbing business, but she won't necessarily know about the organizational behavior principles you're describing. Because any new proposals must be passed through top management, you should also address their concerns about cost containment. You'll need to make a strong evidence-based financial case that changing the management style will benefit the company.

When you write, make sure you touch on the following points:

1. Although it's clear employees are not especially satisfied with their work, do you think this is a reason for concern? Does research suggest satisfied workers are actually better at their jobs? Are any other behavioral outcomes associated with job satisfaction?

2. Using job characteristics theory, explain why the present system of job design may be contributing to employee dissatisfaction. Describe some ways you could help employees feel more satisfied with their work by redesigning their jobs.

3. Lee has a somewhat vague idea about how to implement the cash rewards system. Describe some of the specific ways you would make the reward system work better, based on the case.

4. Explain the advantages and disadvantages of using financial incentives in a program of this nature. What, if any, potential problems might arise if people are given money for achieving customer satisfaction goals? What other types of incentives might be considered?

5. Create a specific plan to assess whether the reward system is working. What are the dependent variables that should change if the system works? How will you go about measuring success?

6. What types of hiring recommendations would you make to find people better suited for these jobs? Which Big Five personality traits would be useful for the customer service responsibilities and emotional labor?

Building a Coalition

Learning Goals

Many of the most important organizational behavior challenges require coordinating plans and goals among groups. This case describes a multiorganizational effort, but the same principles of accommodation and compromise also apply when trying to work with multiple divisions within a single organization. You'll create a blueprint for managing a complex development team's progress, steering team members away from negative conflicts and toward productive discussion. You'll also be asked to help create a new message for executives so they can lead effectively.

Major Topic Areas

- Group dynamics
- Maximizing team performance
- Organizational culture
- Integrative bargaining

The Scenario

The Woodson Foundation, a large nonprofit social service agency, is teaming up with the public school system in Washington, D.C. to improve student outcomes. There's ample room for improvement. The schools have problems with truancy, low student performance, and crime. New staff quickly burn out as their initial enthusiasm for helping students is blunted by the harsh realities they encounter in the classroom. Turnover among new teachers is very high, and many of the best and brightest are the most likely to leave for schools that aren't as troubled.

The plan is to create an experimental after-school program that will combine the Woodson Foundation's skill in raising private money and coordinating community leaders with the educational expertise of school staff. Ideally, the system will be financially self-sufficient, which is important because less money is available for schools than in the past. After several months of negotiation, the leaders of the Woodson Foundation and the school system have agreed that the best course is to develop a new agency that will draw on resources from both organizations. The Woodson foundation will provide logistical support and program development and measurement staff; the school system will provide classrooms and teaching staff.

The first stage in bringing this new plan to fruition is the formation of an executive development team. This team will span multiple functional areas and establish the operating plan for improving school performance. Its cross-organizational nature means representatives from both the Woodson Foundation and the school district must participate. The National Coalition for Parental Involvement in Education (NCPIE) is also going to be a major partner in the program, acting as a representative for parents on behalf of the PTA.

Conflict and Agreement in the Development Team

While it would be perfect if all the groups could work together easily to improve student outcomes, there is little doubt some substantive conflicts will arise. Each group has its own interests, and in some cases these are directly opposed to one another.

School district representatives want to ensure the new jobs will be unionized and will operate in a way consistent with current school board policies. They are very concerned that if Woodson assumes too dominant a role, the school board won't be able to control the operations of the new system. The complexity of the school system has led to the development of a highly complex bureaucratic structure over time, and administrators want to make sure their policies and procedures will still hold for teachers in these programs even outside the regular school day. They also worry that jobs going into the new system will take funding from other school district jobs.

Woodson, founded by entrepreneur Theodore Woodson around 1910, still bears the hallmarks of its founder's way of doing business. Woodson emphasized efficiency and experimentation in everything he did. Many of the foundation's charities have won awards for minimizing costs while still providing excellent services. Their focus on using hard data to measure performance for all their initiatives is not consistent with the school district culture.

Finally, the NCPIE is driven by a mission to increase parental control. The organization believes that when communities are able to drive their own educational methods, students and parents are better able to achieve success together. The organization is strongly committed to celebrating diversity along racial, gender, ethnic, and disability status categories. Its members are most interested in the process by which changes are made, ensuring everyone has the ability to weigh in.

Some demographic diversity issues complicate the team's situation. Most of the students served by the Washington, D.C., school district are African American, along with large populations of Caucasians and Hispanics. The NCPIE makeup generally matches the demographic diversity of the areas served by the public schools. The Woodson foundation, based in northern Virginia, is predominantly staffed by Caucasian professionals. There is some concern with the idea that a new group that does not understand the demographic concerns of the community will be so involved in a major change in educational administration. The leadership of the new program will have to be able to present an effective message for generating enthusiasm for the program across diverse stakeholder groups.

Although the groups differ in important ways, it's also worth considering what they have in common. All are interested in meeting the needs of students. All would like to increase student learning. The school system does benefit from anything that increases student test scores. And the Woodson Foundation and NCPIE are united in their desire to see more parents engaged in the system.

Candidates for the Development Team

The development team will consist of three individuals—HR representatives from the Woodson Foundation, the schools, and the NCPIE—who have prepared the following list of potential candidates for consideration.

Victoria Adams is the superintendent of schools for Washington, D.C. She spearheaded the initial communication with the Woodson Foundation and has been building support among teachers and principals. She thinks the schools and the foundation need to have larger roles than the parents and communities. "Of course we want their involvement and support, but as the professionals, we should have more say when it comes to making decisions and implementing programs. We don't want to shut anyone out, but we have to be realistic about what the parents can do."

Duane Hardy has been a principal in the Washington area for over 15 years. He also thinks the schools should have the most power. "We're the ones who work with these kids every day. I've watched class sizes get bigger, and scores and graduation rates go down. Yes, we need to fix this, but these outside groups can't understand the limitations we're dealing with. We have the community, the politicians, the taxpayers—everyone watching what we're doing, everyone thinking they know what's best. The parents, at least, have more of a stake in this."

"The most important thing is the kids," says second-year teacher Ari Kaufman. He is well liked by his students but doesn't get along well with other faculty members. He's seen as a "squeaky wheel." "The schools need change so badly. And how did they get this way? From too little outside involvement."

Community organizer Mason Dupree doesn't like the level of bureaucracy either. He worries that the school's answer to its problems is to throw more money at them. "I know these kids. I grew up in these neighborhoods. My parents knew every single teacher I had. The schools wanted our involvement then. Now all they want is our money. And I wouldn't mind giving it to them if I thought it would be used responsibly, not spent on raises for people who haven't shown they can get the job done."

Meredith Watson, with the Woodson Foundation, agrees the schools have become less focused on the families. A former teacher, she left the field of education after being in the classroom for 6 years. "There is so much waste in the system," she complains. "Jobs are unnecessarily duplicated, change processes are needlessly convoluted. Unless you're an insider already, you can't get anything done. These parents want to be involved. They know their kids best."

Unlike her NCPIE colleagues, Candace Sharpe thinks the schools are doing the best they can. She is a county social worker, relatively new to the D.C. area. "Parents say they want to be involved but then don't follow through. *We* need to step it up, *we* need to lead the way. Lasting change doesn't come from the outside, it comes from the home."

Victor Martinez has been at the Woodson Foundation for 10 years, starting as an intern straight out of college. "It's sometimes hard to see a situation when you're in the thick of it," he explains. "Nobody likes to be told they're doing something wrong, but sometimes it has to be said. We all know there are flaws in the system. We can't keep the status quo. It just isn't cutting it."

Strategies for the Program Team

Once the basic membership and principles for the development team have been established, the program team would also like to develop a handbook for those who will be running the new program. Ideally, this set of principles can help train new leaders to create an inspirational message that will facilitate success. The actual content of the program and the nature of the message will be hammered out by the development team, but it is still possible to generate some overriding principles for the program team in advance of these decisions.

Your Assignment

The Woodson Foundation, the NCPIE, and the schools have asked you to provide some information about how to form teams effectively. They would like your response to explain what should be done at each step of the way, from the selection of appropriate team members to setting group priorities and goals, setting deadlines, and describing effective methods for resolving conflicts that arise. After this, they'd like you to prepare a brief set of principles for leaders of the newly established program. That means you will have two audiences: the development team, which will receive one report on how it can effectively design the program, and the program team, which will receive one report on how it can effectively lead the new program.

The following points should help you form a comprehensive message for the development team:

1. The development team will be more effective if members have some idea about how groups and teams typically operate. Review the dominant perspectives on team formation and performance from the chapters in the book for the committee so it can know what to expect.
2. Given the profiles of candidates for the development team, provide suggestions for who would likely be a good group member and who might be less effective in this situation. Be sure you are using

the research on groups and teams in the textbook to defend your choices.

3. Using principles from the chapters on groups and teams, describe how you will advise the team to manage conflict effectively.
4. Describe how integrative negotiation strategies might achieve joint goals for the development team.

The following points should help you form a message for the program team:

1. Leaders of the new combined organization should have a good idea of the culture of the school district, the NCPIE, and the Woodson Foundation because they will need to manage relationships with all three groups on an ongoing basis. How would you describe the culture of these various stakeholder organizations? Use concepts from the chapter on organizational culture to describe how they differ and how they are similar.
2. Consider how leaders of the new program can generate a transformational message and encourage employee and parent trust. Using material from the chapter on leadership, describe how you would advise leaders to accomplish these ends.
3. Given the potential for demographic fault lines in negotiating these changes, what would you advise as a strategy for managing diversity issues for program leaders?

4 Boundaryless Organizations

Learning Goals

The multinational organization is an increasingly common and important part of the economy. This case takes you into the world of a cutting-edge music software business seeking success across three very different national and organizational cultures. Its managers need to make important decisions about how to structure work processes so employees can be satisfied and productive doing very different tasks.

Major Topic Areas

- Organizational structure and boundaryless organizations

- Organizational culture
- Human resources
- Organizational socialization

The Scenario

Newskool Grooves is a transnational company developing music software. The software is used to compose music, play recordings in clubs, and produce albums. Founder and CEO Gerd Finger is, understandably, the company's biggest fan. "I started this company from nothing, from just me, my ideas, and my computer. I love music—love playing music, love writing programs for making music, love listening to music—and the money is nice, too." Gerd says he never wanted to work for someone else, to give away his ideas and let someone else profit from them. He wanted to keep control over them, and their image. "Newskool Grooves is always ahead of the pack. In this business, if you can't keep up, you're out. And we are the company everyone else must keep up with. Everyone knows when they get something from us, they're getting only the best and the newest."

The company headquarters are in Berlin, the nerve center for the organization, where new products are developed and the organizational strategy is established. Newskool outsources a great deal of its coding work to programmers in Kiev, Ukraine. Its marketing efforts are increasingly based in its Los Angeles offices. This division of labor is at least partially based on technical expertise and cost issues. The German team excels at design and production tasks. Because most of Newskool's customers are English speakers, the Los Angeles office has been the best group to write ads and market products. The Kiev offices are filled with outstanding programmers who don't require the very high rates of compensation you'd find in German or U.S. offices. The combination of high-tech software, rapid reorganization, and outsourcing makes Newskool the very definition of a boundaryless organization.

Gerd also makes the final decision on hiring every employee for the company and places a heavy emphasis on independent work styles. "Why would I want to put my company in the hands of people I can't count on?" he asks with a laugh. "They have to believe in what we're doing here, really understand our direction and be able to go with it. I'm not the babysitter, I'm not the school master handing out homework. School time is over. This is the real world."

The Work Culture

Employees want to work at this company because it's cutting edge. Newskool's software is used by a number of dance musicians and DJs, who have been the firm's core market, seeing it as a relatively expensive but very high-quality and innovative brand. Whenever the rest of the market for music software goes in one direction, it seems like Newskool heads in a completely different direction in an effort to keep itself separate from the pack. This strategy has tended to pay off. While competitors develop similar products and therefore need to continually lower their prices to compete with one another, Newskool has kept revenues high by creating completely new types of products that don't face this type of price competition.

Unfortunately, computer piracy has eroded Newskool's ability to make money with just software-based music tools, and it has had to move into the pro-

duction of hardware, such as drum machines and amplifiers that incorporate its computer technology. Making this massive market change might be challenging for some companies, but for an organization that reinvents itself every 2 or 3 years like Newskool does, the bigger fight is a constant war against stagnation and rigidity.

The organization has a very decentralized culture. With only 115 employees, the original management philosophy of allowing all employees to participate in decision making and innovation is still the lifeblood of the company's culture. One developer notes, "At Newskool, they want you to be part of the process. If you are a person who wants to do what you're told at work, you're in trouble. Most times, they can't tell you what they want you to do next—they don't even know what comes next! That's why they hire employees who are creative, people who can try to make the next thing happen. It's challenging, but a lot of us think it's very much an exciting environment."

The Boundaryless Environment

Because so much of the work can be performed on computers, Gerd decided early to allow employees to work outside the office. The senior management in Berlin and Los Angeles are both quite happy with this arrangement. Because some marketing work does require face-to-face contact, the Los Angeles office has weekly in-person meetings. Employees who like Newskool are happiest when they can work through the night and sleep most of the day, firing up their computers to get work done at the drop of a hat. Project discussions often happen via social networking on the company's intranet.

The Kiev offices have been less eager to work with the boundaryless model. Managers say their computer programmers find working with so little structure rather uncomfortable. They are more used to the idea of a strong leadership structure and well-defined work processes.

"When I started," says one manager, "Gerd said getting in touch with him would be no problem, getting in touch with L.A. would be no problem. We're small, we're family, he said. Well, it is a problem. When I call L.A., they say to wait until their meeting day. I can't always wait until they decide to get together. I call Gerd—he says, 'Figure it out.' Then when I do, he says it isn't right and we have to start again. If he just told me in the first place, we would have done it."

Some recent events have also shaken up the company's usual way of doing business. Developers in the corporate offices had a major communications breakdown about their hardware DJ controller, which required many hours of discussion to resolve. It seems that people who seldom met face to face had all made progress—but had moved in opposite directions! To test and design the company's hardware products, employees apparently need to do more than send each other code; sometimes they need to collaborate face to face. Some spirited disagreements have been voiced within the organization about how to move forward in this new environment.

The offices are experiencing additional difficulties. Since the shift to newer products, Sandra Pelham in the Los Angeles office has been more critical of the company. "With the software, we were more limited in the kinds of advertising media we could access. So now, with the hardware—real instruments—we finally thought, 'All right, this is something we can work with!' We had a whole slate of musicians and DJs and producers to contact for endorsements, but Gerd said, 'No way.' He didn't want customers who only cared that a celebrity liked us. He scrapped the whole campaign. He says we're all about creativity and doing our own thing—until we don't want to do things his way."

Although the organization is not without problems, there is little question Newskool has been a standout success in the computer music software industry. While many are shuttering their operations, Newskool is using its market power to push forward the next generation of electronic music-making tools. As Gerd Finger puts it, "Once the rest of the industry has gotten together and figured out how they're all going to cope with change, they'll look around and see that we're already three miles ahead of them down the road to the future."

Your Assignment

Gerd has asked for your advice on how to keep his organization successful. He wants to have some sort of benchmark for how other boundaryless organizations in the tech sector stay competitive despite the challenges of so many workers heading in so many different directions. You will need to prepare a report for the company's executive committee. Your report should read like a proposal to a corporate executive who has a great deal of knowledge about the technical aspects of his company but might not have much knowledge of organizational behavior.

When you write, make sure you touch on the following points:

1. Identify some of the problems likely to occur in a boundaryless organization like Newskool Grooves. What are the advantages of boundaryless organizations?
2. Consider some of the cultural issues that will affect a company operating in such different parts of the world and whose employees may not be representative of the national cultures of each country. Are the conflicts you observe a function of the different types of work people have to perform?
3. Based on what you know about motivation and personality, what types of people are likely to be satisfied in each area of the company? Use concepts from job characteristics theory and the emerging social relationships perspective on work to describe what might need to change to increase employee satisfaction in all areas.
4. What types of human resources practices need to be implemented in this sort of organization? What principles of selection and hiring are likely to be effective? Which Big Five traits and abilities might Newskool supervisors want to use for selection?
5. What kind of performance measures might you want to see for each office?
6. How can the company establish a socialization program that will maximize employee creativity and independence? Do employees in all its locations need equal levels of creativity?

The Stress of Caring

Learning Goals

One of the most consistent changes in the structure of work over the past few decades has been a shift from a manufacturing economy to a service economy. More workers are now engaged in jobs that include providing care and assistance, especially in education and medicine. This work is satisfying for some people, but it can also be highly stressful. In the following scenario, consider how a company in the nursing care industry is responding to the challenges of the new environment.

Major Topic Areas

- Stress
- Organizational change
- Emotions
- Leadership

The Scenario

Parkway Nursing Care is an organization facing a massive change. The company was founded in 1972 with just two nursing homes in Phoenix, Arizona. The company was very successful, and throughout the 1980s it continued to turn a consistent profit while slowly acquiring or building 30 more units. This low-profile approach changed forever in 1993 when venture capitalist Robert Quine decided to make a major investment in expanding Parkway in return for a portion of its profits over the coming years. The number of nursing homes exploded, and Parkway was operating 180 homes by the year 2000.

The company now has 220 facilities in the southwestern United States, with an average of 115 beds per facility and a total of nearly 30,000 employees. In addition to health care facilities, it also provides skilled in-home nursing care. Parkway is seen as one of the best care facilities in the region, and it has won numerous awards for its achievements in the field.

As members of the baby boom generation become senior citizens, the need for skilled care will only increase. Parkway wants to make sure it is in a good position to meet this growing need. This means the company must continue expanding rapidly.

The pressure for growth is one significant challenge, but it's not the only one. The nursing home industry has come under increasing government scrutiny following investigations that turned up widespread patient abuse and billing fraud. Parkway has always had outstanding patient care, and no substantiated claim of abuse or neglect in any of its homes has ever been made, but the need for increased documentation will still affect the company. As the federal government tries to trim Medicare expenses, Parkway may face a reduction in funding.

The Problem

As growth has continued, Parkway has remained committed to providing dignity and health to all residents in its facilities. The board of directors wants to see renewed commitment to the firm's mission and core values, not a diffusion of its culture. Its members are worried there might be problems to address. Interviews with employees suggest there's plenty to worry about.

Shift leader Maxine Vernon has been with Parkway for 15 years. "Now that the government keeps a closer eye on our staffing levels, I've seen management do what it can to keep positions filled, and I don't always agree with who is hired. Some of the basic job skills can be taught, sure, but how to *care* for our patients—a lot of these new kids just don't pick up on that."

"The problem isn't with staff—it's with Parkway's focus on filling the beds," says nurse's aide Bobby Reed. "When I started here, Parkway's reputation was still about the service. Now it's about numbers. No one is intentionally negligent—there just are too many patients to see."

A recent college graduate with a B.A. in psychology, Dalton Manetti is more stressed than he expected he would be. "These aren't the sweet grannies you see in the movies. Our patients are demanding. They complain about everything, even about being called patients, probably because most of them think they shouldn't be here in the first place. A lot of times, their gripes amount to nothing, but we have to log them in anyway."

Carmen Frank has been with Parkway almost a year and is already considering finding a new job. "I knew there were going to be physical parts to this job, and I thought I'd be able to handle that. It's not like I was looking for a desk job, you know? I go home after every shift with aches all over—my back, my arms, my legs. I've never had to take so much time off from a job because I hurt. And then when I come back, I feel like the rest of the staff thinks I'm weak."

"I started working here right out of high school because it was the best-paid of the jobs I could get," says Niecey Wilson. "I had no idea what I was getting myself into. Now I really like my job. Next year I'm going to start taking some night classes so I can move into another position. But some of the staff just think of this as any other job. They don't see the patients as people, more like inventory. If they want to work with inventory, they should get a job in retail."

Last month, the company's human resources department pulled the following information from its records at the request of the board of directors. The numbers provide some quantitative support for the concerns voiced by staff.

Injuries to staff occur mostly because of back strain from lifting patients. Patient incidents reflect injuries due to slips, falls, medication errors, or other accidents. Certified absences are days off from work due to medically verified illnesses or injuries. Other absences are days missed that are not due to injuries or illnesses; these are excused absences (unexcused absences are grounds for immediate firing).

Year	Patients	Injuries Per Staff Member	Incidents per Patient	Certified Absences per Staff	Other Absence per Staff	Turnover Rate
2000	21,200	3.32	4.98	4.55	3.14	0.31
2001	22,300	3.97	5.37	5.09	3.31	0.29
2002	22,600	4.87	5.92	4.71	3.47	0.28
2003	23,100	4.10	6.36	5.11	3.61	0.35
2004	23,300	4.21	6.87	5.66	4.03	0.31
2005	23,450	5.03	7.36	5.33	3.45	0.28
2006	23,600	5.84	7.88	5.28	4.24	0.36
2007	24,500	5.62	8.35	5.86	4.06	0.33
2008	24,100	7.12	8.84	5.63	3.89	0.35
2009	25,300	6.95	9.34	6.11	4.28	0.35

Using Organizational Development to Combat Stress and Improve Performance

The company wants to use such organizational development methods as appreciative inquiry (AI) to create change and re-energize its sense of mission. As the chapter on organizational change explains, AI procedures systematically collect employee input and then use this information to create a change message everyone can support. The human resources department conducted focus groups, asking employees to describe some of their concerns and suggestions for the future. The focus groups highlighted a number of suggestions, although they don't all suggest movement in the same direction.

Many suggestions concerned schedule flexibility. One representative comment was this: "Most of the stress on this job comes because we can't take time off when we need it. The LPNs [licensed practical nurses, who do much of the care] and orderlies can't take time off when they need to, but a lot of them are single parents or primary caregivers for their own children. When they have to leave for child care responsibilities, the work suffers and there's no contingency plan to help smooth things over. Then everyone who is left has to work extra hard. The person who takes time off feels guilty, and there can be fights over taking time off. If we had some way of covering these emergency absences, we'd all be a lot happier, and I think the care would be a lot better."

Other suggestions proposed a better method for communicating information across shifts. Most of the documentation for shift work is done in large spiral notebooks. When a new shift begins, staff members say they don't have much time to check on what happened in the previous shift. Some younger caregivers would like to have a method that lets them document patient outcomes electronically because they type faster than they can write. The older caregivers are more committed to the paper-based process, in part because they think switching systems would require a lot of work. (Government regulations on health care reporting require that any documentation be made in a form that cannot be altered after the fact, to prevent covering up abuse, so specialized software systems must be used for electronic documentation.)

Finally, the nursing care staff believes its perspectives on patient care are seldom given an appropriate hearing. "We're the ones who are with the patients most of the time, but when it comes to doing this the right way, our point of view gets lost. We really could save a lot of money by eliminating some of these unnecessary routines and programs, but it's something management always just says it will consider." Staff members seem to want some way to provide suggestions for improvement, but it isn't clear what method they would prefer.

Your Assignment

Parkway has taken some initial steps toward a new direction, but clearly it has a lot of work left to do. You've been brought in as a change management consultant to help the company change its culture and respond to the stress that employees experience. Remember to create your report as if for the leadership of a major corporation.

When you write your recommendations, make sure you touch on the following points:

1. What do the data on employee injuries, incidents, absences, and turnover suggest to you? Is there reason for concern about the company's direction?

2. The company is going to be making some significant changes based on the AI process, and most change efforts are associated with resistance. What are the most common forms of resistance, and which would you expect to see at Parkway?

3. Given the board of directors' desire to re-energize the workforce, what advice would you provide for creating a leadership strategy? What leader behaviors should nursing home directors and nurse supervisors demonstrate?

4. What are the major sources of job stress at Parkway? What does the research on employee stress suggest you should do to help minimize the experience of psychological strain for employees? Create a plan for how to reduce stress among employees.

5. Based on the information collected in the focus groups, design a survey to hand out to employees. What sort of data should the survey gather? What types of data analysis methods would you like to employ for these data?

Credits

Indexes

651

Organization Index

*References followed by b indicate boxes;
e, exhibits; f, figure; n, notes*

Glindex A Combined Glossary/Subject Index

in communication, 344
and goal setting, 215
in performance evaluation, 571–572, 579–580
Feeling types, 137
Felt conflict, *Emotional involvement in a conflict that creates anxiety, tenseness, frustration, or hostility,* 459
Felt emotions, *An individual's actual emotions,* 110
Femininity, *A national culture attribute that indicates little differentiation between male and female roles; a high rating indicates that women are treated as the equals of men in all aspects of the society,* 153. *See also* Women
Fiedler contingency model, *The theory that effective groups depend on a proper match between a leader's style of interacting with subordinates and the degree to which the situation gives control and influence to the leader,* 381–384
Figurehead role, 6
Filtering, *A sender's manipulation of information so that it will be seen more favorably by the receiver,* 359
First impressions, 559b
Fish!, 31
Five-stage group-development model, *The five distinct stages groups go through: forming, storming, norming, performing, and adjourning,* 279–281
Fixed pie, *The belief that there is only a set amount of goods or services to be divvied up between the parties,* 467
Flattery, and political behavior, 439e
Flexible benefits, *A benefits plan that allows each employee to put together a benefit package individually tailored to his or her own needs and situation,* 259–260, 261, 263–264
Flexible spending plans, 261
Flextime, *Flexible work hours,* 247–249
Flynn Effect, 63–64
Formal channels, *Communication channels established by an organization to transmit messages related to the professional activities of members,* 344, 345
Formal group, *A designated work group defined by an organization's structure,* 276, 277
Formalization, *The degree to which jobs within an organization are standardized,* 493–494
Formal regulations, 185
Formal small-group networks, 349–350
Forming stage, *The first stage in group development, characterized by much uncertainty,* 279–280
France, 404
Friendship group, *People brought together because they share one or more common characteristics,* 277
Functional conflict, *Conflict that supports the goals of the group and improves its performance,* 455, 463, 464–465
Functions, of managers, 5–6
Fundamental attribution error, *The tendency to underestimate the influence of external factors and overestimate the influence of internal factors when making judgments about the behavior of others,* 171

G
Gainsharing, *A formula-based group incentive plan,* 258, 259
Galatea effect, 218–219
Gender
  and communication, 361
  and education bias, 46b
  as emotion source, 108
  identity, 51
  influence on decision making, 184–185
  and leadership, 398b
  in negotiation, 472–473
  same-sex comparison, 222
  of team members, 323–324
  in the workforce, 45–46
  See also Women
General dependency postulate, 423–424
General mental ability (GMA), *An overall factor of intelligence, as suggested by the positive correlations among specific intellectual ability dimensions,* 52, 54
Generation Nexters, 149
Generation Xers, 148–149
Generation Yers, 149
Globalization
  and communication, 343f, 364b
  and perceptual differences, 172b
  response to, 16–17
  variations in OB, 30
  and workforce diversity, 58–59
Global Leadership and Organizational Behavior Effectiveness (GLOBE), 156, 403–405
Goals, of effective teams, 327
Goal-setting theory, 228, 229, 230, 232
Goal-setting theory, *A theory that says that specific and difficult goals, with feedback, lead to higher performance,* 214–217
and accomplishment, 229
directing behavior, 228
exercise for, 232
for managers, 230
Gossip, 366
Grapevine, *An organization's informal communication network,* 350–351
Graphic rating scales, *An evaluation method in which the evaluator rates performance factors on an incremental scale,* 568, 569
Gratitude, and job satisfaction, 92–93
Group-level variables, 28, 29e
Group order ranking, *An evaluation method that places employees into a particular classification, such as quartiles,* 568, 569
Group polarization, 298
Group(s), *Two or more individuals, interacting and interdependent, who have come together to achieve particular objectives,* 276–277
cohesiveness in, 293–294
decision making in, 298–300
defining, classifying, 276–277
diversity in, 56

effectiveness of, 299–300
effects of processes on, 326e
exercises on, 304–307
forming, 277–279
vs. individuals, 295
and job design, 303
norms of, 285–290
roles of, 282–285
size of, 292–293
stages of development in, 279–281
vs. teams, 315–316
See also Teams
Groupshift, *A change in decision risk between a group's decision and an individual decision that a member within the group would make; the shift can be toward either conservatism or greater risk,* 296, 297, 298
Groupthink, *A phenomenon in which the norm for consensus overrides the realistic appraisal of alternative courses of action,* 296–298, 462

H
Halo effect, *The tendency to draw a general impression about an individual on the basis of a single characteristic,* 173
Hand gestures, 363e
Harmonic Wealth, 3
Hawthorne studies, 286–287
Heredity, *Factors determined at conception; one's biological, physiological, and inherent psychological makeup,* 135–136
Hierarchy of needs, *Abraham Maslow's hierarchy of five needs—physiological, safety, social, esteem, and self-actualization—in which, as each need is substantially satisfied, the next need becomes dominant,* 205–206, 229, 230
High-ability teams, 322
High-context cultures, *Cultures that rely heavily on nonverbal and subtle situational cues in communication,* 363–364
Higher-order needs, *Needs that are satisfied internally, such as social, esteem, and self-actualization needs,* 206, 207
High Machs, 141–142
Hindrance stressors, *Stressors that keep you from reaching your goals (for example, red tape, office politics, confusion over job responsibilities),* 607
Hindsight bias, *The tendency to believe falsely, after an outcome of an event is actually known, that one would have accurately predicted that outcome,* 182–183, 184
Hispanic workers, 17, 39, 55–56
Historical precedent, and decision making, 186
Hofstede's framework, for assessing culture, 153–156
Honesty, in jobseeking, 570b
Human resource management, 8
Human resource policies, practices
  global implications of, 574–576
  performance evaluation, 564–572
  selection practices of, 554–560